Manchester *The Greatest* CITY

M.C.F.C.
Superbia In Proelio
TM

THE COMPLETE HISTORY OF MANCHESTER CITY FOOTBALL CLUB

Gary James

POLAR PUBLISHING

DEDICATION: To Michael & Anna (the next generation of Blues), and to Heidi for all your support.

First published in Great Britain 1997 by Polar Group Ltd., 9-17 Tuxford Road, Leicester LE4 9WE, England
This revised and updated edition published 2002 by Polar Group Ltd.

ISBN 1 899538 22 4

British Library Cataloguing in Publication Data. A catalogue record for this book is available from the British Library.

Edited by Julian Baskcomb; Assistant Editor Julia Byrne

Designed by Trevor Hartley

Printed by Polar Print Group Ltd., 9-17 Tuxford Road, Leicester LE4 9WE. Tel: (0116) 274 4700

Contents

Introduction

When the original version of ***Manchester - The Greatest City*** was released in 1997 City were struggling at the foot of Division One and heading for relegation. Despite the pain and despair of that period it was a huge success, and received universal praise. Some claimed it was the finest football history book ever produced, while others bombarded the publishers with requests for an update the moment the first version sold out. To say we were all amazed with the response is an understatement.

Since 1997 City have embarked on an incredible journey with visits to Division Two, Wembley, the Premier League, and finally the period ended with the Blues winning the League Championship. As a result of this incredible story it became essential to update The Greatest City to take account of these five rollercoaster years.

The actual decision to update the book occurred during the first few weeks of the 2001-02 season when City's fate was far from clear. Since then I have been busy working with the publishers to finalise content. We felt it important to review the entire story and see how the book could be improved. In a few places we have corrected mistakes and omissions from the first version. A great deal of information was provided in the original version on City's great 1930s star Peter Doherty, however I felt we needed to provide a bit more focus to his career by creating a profile of him on page 160. Naturally, most of the other changes concern the final few seasons and the profiles of those recently connected with the club.

The history of this book needs some explanation. As a supporter of the Blues since birth, it used to disappoint me during the mid 1980s that there were very few books on the history of this great club. There seemed to be shelf upon shelf of books on Manchester United, Liverpool, and even Everton around at this time, and I felt Manchester's Blues deserved more.

In 1987 I wrote to a company based in Nottingham with an idea to write a complete history of the Maine Road stadium. Although they liked that idea they felt something focused directly on the club would be a better start. ***"From Maine Men To Banana Citizens"***, was published in April 1989. Sadly, the book was not of the right quality and its production had suffered with a number of problems, in particular the death of my co-author Keith Mellor. It did not fill the gap in the way I'd anticipated. Nevertheless, my collection of photographs, drawings and memorabilia livened up that book and it quickly sold out.

From that moment on I was driven to write more about my favourite club and its personalities, and reconsidered my original idea of a book on Maine Road. I decided the time still wasn't right for a book on the stadium (incidentally, this will finally be published following City's move from Maine Road in 2003), and joined up with a United fan to write a history of the Manchester derby. ***The Pride of Manchester*** was published in July 1991, by which time I had already started writing my third book.

While applying the finishing touches to "The Pride", I started researching Joe Mercer's life and career. I had decided to write about his entire life, not simply the 'easy option' of his City period, and I spent considerable time travelling all over the UK interviewing and researching for the book I felt had to be written.

"Football With A Smile" was published in December 1993, during City's take-over battle, and had sold out within a year proving that football followers were seriously interested in Joe. A paperback version followed and, if I have my way, one day I would still like to turn the entire story into either a play or a video. I believe Joe deserves that.

After Joe's story was published I was quite despondent. My other ideas were not taking off, and few publishers were prepared to gamble on producing quality publications connected with the Blues. I spoke with Julian Baskcomb at Polar. He was convinced supporters would be interested in any book on City providing it was of the highest quality, and suggested writing a full history of the club. Julian rekindled my enthusiasm and this book started to develop the moment I put the 'phone down.

The original version came out in 1997, and during the following five years I made my notes, ready for any potential update. Many other City works have been published since the first version came out, and both the publishers and I have considered whether the City market was becoming saturated. We thought long and hard about issuing an updated version, but the requests from supporters and booksellers became so great that we just had to release this version. "Back by popular demand" is an over-used phrase, but for this book it's a genuine statement.

Throughout the planning, research and the writing of ***"Manchester - The Greatest City"*** I tried to ensure I captured the mood of the time by including comments from supporters, players, managers, administrators and, occasionally, opponents. I felt this approach was important as it allowed me, as author, to write my story based on informed comment. Much of my writing assesses what has been said and tries to provide an objective view, however the quotes I have included bring the entire story to life.

There are also eye-witness reports on games and incidents from the 1880s through to the modern era.

As a supporter I have always felt that the views of the ordinary fan need to be recorded and understood. In recent years books like Nick Hornby's "Fever Pitch" have allowed fans to speak out and express their feelings and, although this is a history of Manchester City F.C., I have tried to ensure this book provides a taste of the strength of feeling we all have for our club. It would have been easy for me to write a dry, rather formulaic club history, but it would not have appealed to the people I want to reach. A living 'biography of the Blues' is what I have aimed for; something that appeals to fans of every age; something that doesn't merely record the main events of the club, but brings to life the emotion and love we all feel.

Incidentally, an editorial in the *Times* following City's promotion in 2002 claimed "Fever Pitch" could not convey the true spirit of football as it was based around Arsenal and not Manchester City. The editorial added: "Hornby is expecting the reader to accept that he has lived a life in which he was never relegated and always played the offside trap just so. Brilliant though Hornby, and indeed the Gunners are, the fact is that the true drama of human life cannot be played out against a background of Arsenal." City fans know those experiences well.

Hopefully, ***Manchester: The Greatest City*** combines the supporter-focused view as experienced by all Blues, with the actual story of the club as seen through the eyes of City officials and the media. It's a mix rarely included in any book and, at times, it has proven extremely difficult to ensure the right balance. Overall, I feel the mix is just about right. I hope you agree.

Although this book has taken up too much of my free time, I am delighted with the result. I hope you enjoy it and feel enthused by its content. No doubt every reader will be keen to relive certain events, and I hope you all feel satisfied with the details of your particular favourite period. I also believe you will be entertained by those periods that on the surface seem less inspiring.

To end, allow me to make a final plea. Although I have tried to ensure I cover every period in the way it deserves to be covered both in terms of text and illustrations, there are certain periods in the club's history where little is known, or few photographs exist. In terms of illustrations, I have spent years searching for early City photographs, and have included in this book all the photographs I have discovered on Hyde Road. As far as I'm aware these are the only known surviving photograph of games at the old ground. I know for certain hundreds of photographs were taken during the period 1905 to 1923 at City's home games, yet only a handful still exist. If you know of any additional photographs or can provide additional comment about that ground, or indeed on Maine Road, then please contact me care of the publishers.

I hope you enjoy this book as much as I have enjoyed researching and writing about the Blues over the years.

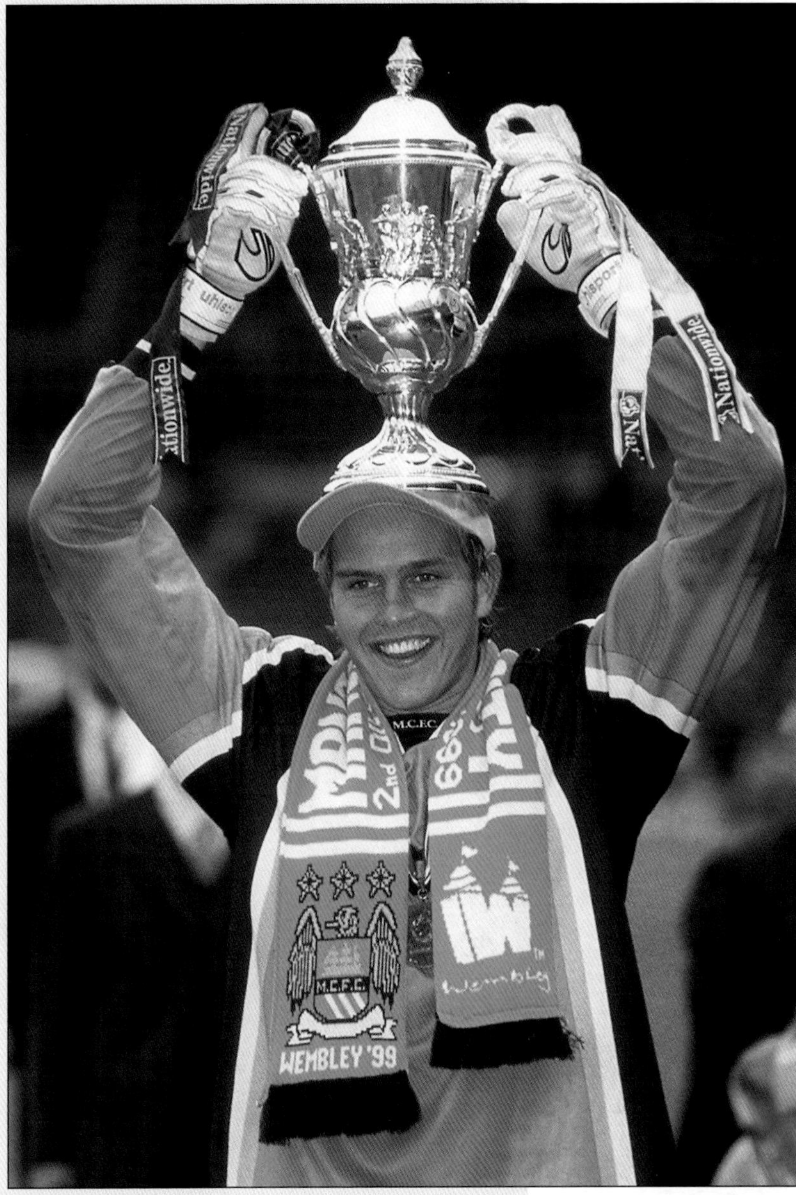

Gary James
West Yorkshire
www.footballhistorian.co.uk
31st August 2002

Acknowledgements

PICTURE ACKNOWLEDGEMENTS & ARCHIVE SOURCES

Most of the photographs and newspaper cuttings in this publication have come from the author's personal collection. Other articles, interviews and photographs have been taken from or supplied by the following:

Manchester City F.C., Action Images, Colorsport, Empics, Paul Marriott Photography, Sporting Pictures, Allsport, Professional Sport International, David Munden Photography, John Peters, The Hulton-Getty Collection, The Manchester Evening News & Guardian, The Manchester Chronicle, Athletic News, Umpire News, The Weekly News, The Daily Mail, The Daily Express, The Daily Mirror, The Independent, The Sun, The Observer, The Times, The Telegraph, The British Film Institute, The North West Film Archive at Manchester Metropolitan University, The Illustrated London News, The British Library, the BBC, Granada Media, Sky TV, GMR, and Piccadilly.

Others who have supplied illustrations include: Stewart Beckett, Frank Borson, Barbara Clarke, Phil Crossley, Kevin Cummins, Phil Gatenby, Garth Dykes, Josh Langton, Paul Leach, the Mercer family, Phil Noble, Ray Shepley, Crosland & Cros Ward and Steve Worthington.

There are a number of other photographs included in this book, the source of which we have been unable to trace. The owners are cordially invited to contact the publishers in writing providing proof of copyright.

As always I am grateful to many, many people. It still amazes me when other historical books are produced with few, if any, acknowledgements as no book on any club or personality can ever be described as being solely one person's work. I have been very fortunate over the years so many people have been interested enough to help me in my research, and I would like to take this opportunity of thanking you all.

Clearly I must thank Manchester City F.C. for allowing me to tell the tale. As with the first edition, I have been allowed a free hand and, as you will see from the text, have been able to tell the story as it deserves to be told. I am happy with the freedom allowed me by David Bernstein and Chris Bird. Thanks also to the other club personnel who have helped me over the years, in particular Dennis Tueart and Bernard Halford.

There have been many others who have provided much assistance with this version. They include Andy Noise - who came in towards the end and offered support when needed most - Noel Bayley, Dennis Chapman, the late John Maddocks and David Scally.

Others who have provided assistance include Malcolm Allison, Ron Atkinson, Carol Barber, Colin Bell, Ashley Birch, W. Birtles, Alan Blackburn, John Bond, Tony Book, Peter Brophy, Mark Brown, John Bullock, Pete Bulmer, David Butler, Sean Cable, Dave Cash, Paul & Barry Chuckle, Roy Clarke, Simon Clegg, Johnny Crossan, Phil Crossley, Willie Donachie, Geoff Donkin, John Edminson, Sir Tom Finney, Ernest France, Ray Goble, Bob Goodwin, George Graham, the late Tony Heap, Bryan Horsnell, Greg Hughes, the late Harry Hughes, Simon Inglis, Geoffrey Ireland, Paul James, Paul Joannou, Graham Kelly, Mike Kelly, George Kirby, Paul Leach, Francis Lee, Paul MacNamara, Norah & David Mercer, Janice Monk, Phil Noble, Paul Oldfield, Glyn Pardoe, Ian Penney, Heidi Pickup, Stuart Renshaw, David Ricketts, Joe Royle, Maynard Scott, Ray Shepley, Ken Smallwood, Paul Taylor, David Ticehurst, Dave & Sue Wallace, Andy Ward, David Whalley, Chris Williams, Cyril Williams, Peter Williams, Arthur Wood, Steve Worthington and Bob Young. Another footballing man to whom I must pay special tribute is the late Peter Swales.

There have also been a number of people who have assisted via the supporters' internet news service, MCIVTA. Some of these have been acknowledged above, however I would also like to publicly thank all of the other MCIVTA correspondents who have offered advice, suggestions and support since the original version of this book was published in 1997. I would also like to thank all those supporters quoted in the main text of this book.

In addition I have been assisted by various members of the Association of Football Statisticians, and the Society of Authors. I am a member of both organisations and would like to record here my thanks for all their help.

Thanks also to library staff throughout Britain, especially those at Manchester Central Library.

As always, I have received assistance from various members of the media. They include: Mike Barnett (who performed the best review of the initial version of this book), the late Bryan Brett, Richard Burgess, Ian Cheeseman, Bob Greaves, Paul Hince, Alistair Mann, Carl Morris, John Motson, Jimmy Wagg and Richard Whitehead. Thanks also to James H. Reeve who assisted me enormously with my earlier works, and has always given my writing a few decent plugs. Thanks.

Julian Baskcomb, Julia Byrne and their colleagues at Polar have once again performed magnificently. For well over a decade now we have worked well together. They are renowned for producing quality publications. Additionally, I am grateful for the tremendous design and layout of Trevor Hartley. He has made this a beautiful publication once again. Thanks.

Thanks once again to my family - Heidi, Michael and Anna. You've provided me with terrific support once more. Also, thanks to the other members of the James and Ward families who have supported me throughout.

As with any publication, I am certain there are many other people who have helped along the way. If I have overlooked your contribution please don't feel slighted in any way. It's simply that the last few years have been exceptionally busy ones and it has not always been possible to record or remember every name. Sorry. Undoubtedly, there will also be a number of people who assist me in one form or another the moment this page is printed. Again, if you fall into this category thank you.

I hope you enjoy this version of *"Manchester - The Greatest City"*, and that it gives you all you expect. I know it is inevitable some mistakes will have crept in, but I sincerely hope there are not too many. If you do find any then please write to me via the publishers. In addition, if you have information that you feel may help my understanding of City's grounds, or of any other period of Blue history, then again please write, or email **mainerd@polargroup.co.uk**

Thanks,

GARY JAMES

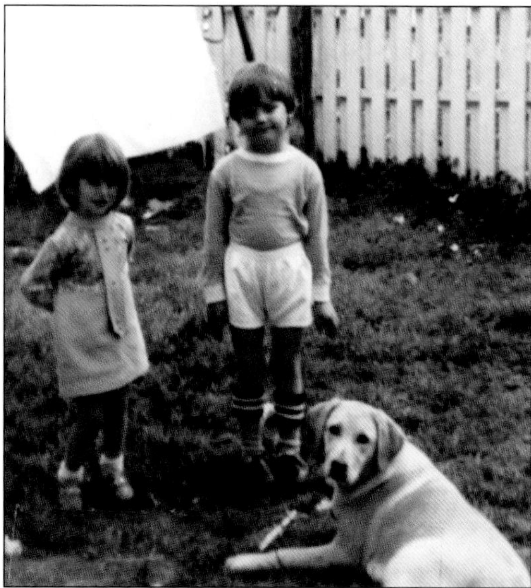

The author, aged 6, wearing his first City kit. Photographed with him are sister Tracey and dog Kim.

I'm City 'til I Die!

The role of City's supporters is a very important one and has always clearly been a major reason for the club's success. For this reason, this section appears at the beginning of City's history, and everyone connected with the club should realise that supporters' views must always be at the forefront of any thinking.

Ever since the earliest years of Ardwick AFC Blues supporters have been incredibly loyal and given the club magnificent support. The transformation from Ardwick to City would never have occurred had it not been for the determination of so many East Manchester based Blues. They raised funds, canvassed opinion and took part in various meetings at Manchester's first Blue pub - The now demolished Hyde Road Hotel. Their interest quickly established City as Manchester's most popular club.

One of City's first backers was supporter Bob Roden. For the club's first forty years Roden was recognised as City's first historian. In 1928 he looked back on some of the earliest methods Ardwick used to pay its way: "I remember how, one Saturday, we got Liverpool to come to Hyde Road under a guarantee of £25. And it rained heavens hard that day. Instead of the bumper gate expected we took about four pounds. I was in the Hyde Road Hotel after the game. Jos Parlby, our secretary, was there too, for all the business of the club was contracted in the hotel. In came the Liverpool secretary for his cheque. Jos gave him one for the agreed £25, and we hadn't got a ha'penny in the bank!"

"But Jos wasn't so rash as he seemed. The next day was Sunday, and the day after New Year's Day - which meant that the bank wouldn't be open. We played Rotherham on New Year's Day, took a gate, and Jos was sitting on the doorstep of the bank when they opened their doors on Tuesday morning to pay in the £25."

City was very much a club for the people of Ardwick and Gorton in those days and the club developed, in much the same way as a modern Sunday league side, with supporters and players organising raffles and the like. Though Joshua Parlby was officially the secretary he himself was a supporter of the club in the truest sense of the word. He was not a football man who happened to join the Blues, he was a football fan who chose to help Ardwick.

Roden remembers Parlby's financial wizardry working again during the 1893-4 season - Ardwick's last: "The financial bogey popped up his head again. We had to play Woolwich Arsenal away. Now this was a difficulty, for we were so hard up we hadn't enough money to pay train fares to the Arsenal ground, and we knew that if we didn't complete the programme our chances of election would be prejudiced."

"The resourceful Jos Parlby found a solution. He embarked on the train with his team, though none of them had tickets. They kept the door shut, and the railway people didn't discover their stoniness until they were at London. I don't know what story Jos told, but he got away with it and was allowed to pay the fares after he'd taken our share of the gate at the Woolwich game."

Once the rather small time Ardwick reformed as City, the club was put on a much stronger footing thanks to the generosity of many supporters who helped invest in the new limited company.

In 1904 supporters turned out in force to welcome their heroes back from Manchester's first

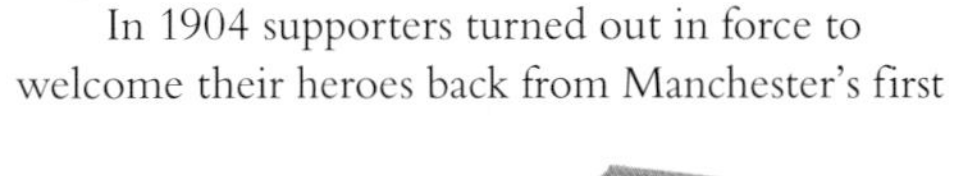

major trophy success, despite a desire by the local government and police force to quell any celebrations. A couple of years later those same supporters organised petitions in an attempt to persuade the F.A. to rescind their diabolical ban of so many important players and directors. That bid failed, and the years that followed really proved the value of City's fanatical support as the Hyde Road club recovered from the greatest loss of players endured by any English side regardless of tragedy or punishment.

In those days the atmosphere at home games was something special. As early as the 1890s supporters had worn fancy dress, and brought musical instruments to matches. Uniquely, this feeling of fun has continued right through to the modern era.

Throughout history City has been one of the best supported clubs in Britain. The move to Maine Road allowed the Blues to capitalise on its popularity - as will the move to the City of Manchester Stadium - and for a while in the 1920s the team was the best supported of all League clubs. Since 1910 the average attendance has only dropped below 20,000 on three occasions (18,201 in 1963-4, 14,753 in 1964-5, and 19,471 in 1987-8), and even then the Blues average has been closer to 35,000 than 20,000 for most of the other seasons. Since the Hillsborough disaster in 1989, Maine Road's capacity has been significantly reduced from over 52,500 to a final capacity of around 35,000, achieved via temporary seating filling almost every gap imaginable. This is clearly insufficient for City's fanatical fans.

Regardless of the stadium size, supporters have always tried to enjoy themselves. The 1980s proved to the whole world the spirit of the Blues when fans took to carrying inflatable bananas to matches. The Stoke match on Boxing Day 1988 saw over 12,000 Blues travelling to the Potteries carrying inflatables, and mainly in fancy dress. It was a marvellous sight, although regrettably the majority of the media failed to even mention the event let alone show the magnitude of it. Somehow news did spread as far as the States. Oasis' Noel Gallagher often told a story of his trip in a New York cab: "The cabbie asked where in England I was from, so I told him, then he asked 'do you like soccer?' I said 'yeah' and then he went on about the Reds, so I stopped him and said it was City. He thought for a minute and then said 'Ah, City... Are they the guys who carry inflatable fruit?' I replied, 'yeah, that's City... we carry inflatable fruit!' It summed it up really!"

At the time of the banana craze City had little to celebrate apart from occasional victories and promotion in 1989. Throughout the 80s and 90s fans had been promised success, but frequently endured abysmal failure, yet the loyalty of City's support rarely wavered. Average attendances remained high.

Supporters were unhappy with the club's direction, but they were not deserting the club. Newcastle United and Leeds United are just two clubs often complimented for the loyalty of their support, yet both have attracted significantly lower average attendances than City overall during the last thirty years or so. Neither of those clubs has quite endured the depths the Blues have and, significantly, neither side is forced to share its city with another major club, let alone co-exist with a corporation as enormous as Manchester United PLC.

During the 1980s struggles the fanzine culture developed and, as with all clubs in a similar situation, the supporters developed their own. First was the now defunct 'Blueprint' (created by Mike Kelly), followed by Dave Wallace's 'King of the Kippax', and then Noel Bayley's 'Electric Blue'. This last fanzine was later renamed 'Bert Trautmann's Helmet' (after the infamous Stan Boardman joke) when an adult publication of the same name threatened legal action. Interestingly, both Bayley and Wallace were involved with Blueprint for a while but, as City fans had more to say than most other club's supporters, it was important to establish different voices and approaches. Several other fanzines have since been developed, though none seem to have the staying power of the Wallace and Bayley publications, although Bayley regularly comments on pulling the plug on his excellent publication once City move to the new stadium - an action supporters hope he fails to carry out.

Eventually, the supporters, the fanzines and various pressure groups helped to remove Peter Swales from power, and for a while it seemed the club belonged to the fans, especially when new Chairman Francis Lee promised a 'Fan on the Board'. This concept worked for a while, but many felt it wasn't thought out properly, nor given a chance to succeed. Those circumstances led to criticism from a number of fans, and the scheme was replaced by a fans' committee with representatives from supporters' groups and the fanzines. This has also received criticism from time to time, however it clearly demonstrates the need for the club to listen to its supporters, and for fans to provide as much feedback as possible. Despite the apparent close relationship with the club, supporters retained their independence and continued to make their feelings known to the management and board, particularly during the Alan Ball and Frank Clark periods.

Looking to the future, the move to the new 48,000-seater stadium is likely to test the resolve of some supporters, however the overwhelming majority of fans see the move as being vital to re-establish the club as a European power. City fans have the chance to make the City of Manchester Stadium a fortress by demonstrating their passion and loyalty.

City fans are THE MOST important part of this great club. They have saved City in the past and now deserve the success. As history proves, Maine Road has not been big enough for the Blues since the late eighties. The move will help the club leap forward, just as the move to Maine Road helped City springboard forward eighty years earlier.

Chapter One

INDUSTRIAL MANCHESTER

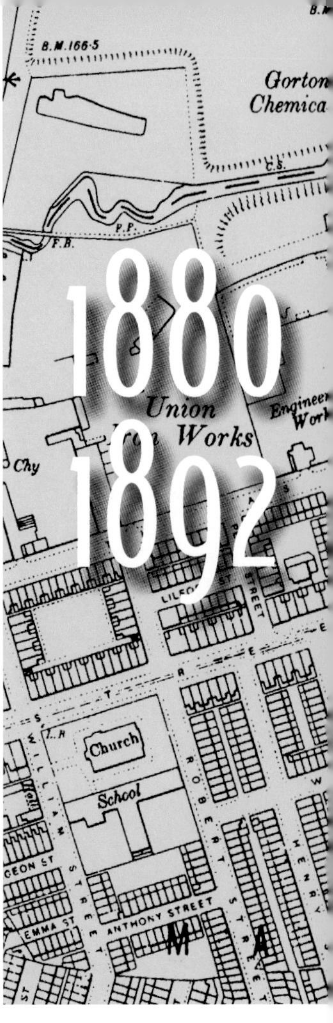

THE early history of Manchester City must be seen in context with the history of Manchester itself, indeed the whole history of the club is closely linked with the development of the world's first industrial city. During the period 1800 to 1851 the population of the Manchester area trebled to 1,063,000, within another fifty years it had reached 2,149,000. Immigrants came from rural England, Ireland, and continental Europe, especially Germany. They were attracted by the cotton industry and by the opportunities being created by industrial prosperity.

To cope with this influx, large numbers of 'Coronation Street' style terraced houses - and worse - were built on the rural land surrounding the city centre. Areas such as Ardwick Green, Bradford, Rusholme, and Gorton became densely populated suburbs of the growing city. With the growth of urban Manchester came religion and, not surprisingly, alcohol. On what seemed like every corner of the city's biggest streets, public houses were developed to give the men a break from the pressures of their grim industrial lives.

Hyde Road, the main thoroughfare from Manchester to the Cheshire town of Hyde, some eight miles away, was one of the city's busiest roads, and a prime example of how Manchester had developed. Industry, terraced housing, churches and plenty of 'pubs' could be found along its route.

Along the Hyde Road, a short distance from the city centre, was Gorton. Officially a town in its own right at the time - it remained an independent urban district until 1890, when it was absorbed into the city. Gorton had developed throughout the 1800s, and by 1880 was an established residential and industrial area. During the 1860s West Gorton was still developing, although as one correspondent wrote in January 1870:

"The first noticeable peculiarity which will strike the visitor is mud, the presence of which can easily be accounted for by the fact that West Gorton possesses one and a half properly laid out streets."

On 30th November 1865 religion entered the lives of the people of West Gorton when St. Mark's Church, Clowes Street was consecrated by the Bishop of Manchester. A few days later, on 5th December, the Reverend Arthur Connell was inducted. Maybe the church was built to provide hope for the area, maybe it was needed as a release from the pressures of day to day life. Who knows? What is known, however, is that the building of this church eventually led to the founding of Manchester City Football Club.

In the late 1870s Miss G. Connell, the daughter of the Reverend, suggested forming a working men's club to look after the well being of the male half of the congregation. Perhaps she had realised that too much time was being spent in the pubs of Gorton, or even worse, perhaps the younger menfolk were engaging in the terrifying local pastime of 'Scuttling'. Scuttling was the local expression for fighting, and throughout the 1870s and 1880s the Manchester districts of Gorton, Openshaw, and Bradford were exposed to regular outbreaks. One report from this period appeared in the *Ashton Reporter* under the title 'Openshaw V. Gorton'. The following extract describes the scenes close to Clowes St:

"According to one of the witnesses the bother commenced soon after breakfast and was on more or less all day. When Constable Wilson arrived on the scene, a little before seven o'clock in the evening, he found gathered on one side of Gorton Brook some lads and lasses from Openshaw and on the opposite side of the brook a similar gang of lads and lasses belonging to Gorton. They were engaged in the delightful occupation of storming each other."

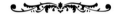

In the late 1870s Miss G. Connell, the daughter of the Reverend, suggested forming a working men's club to look after the well being of the male half of the congregation

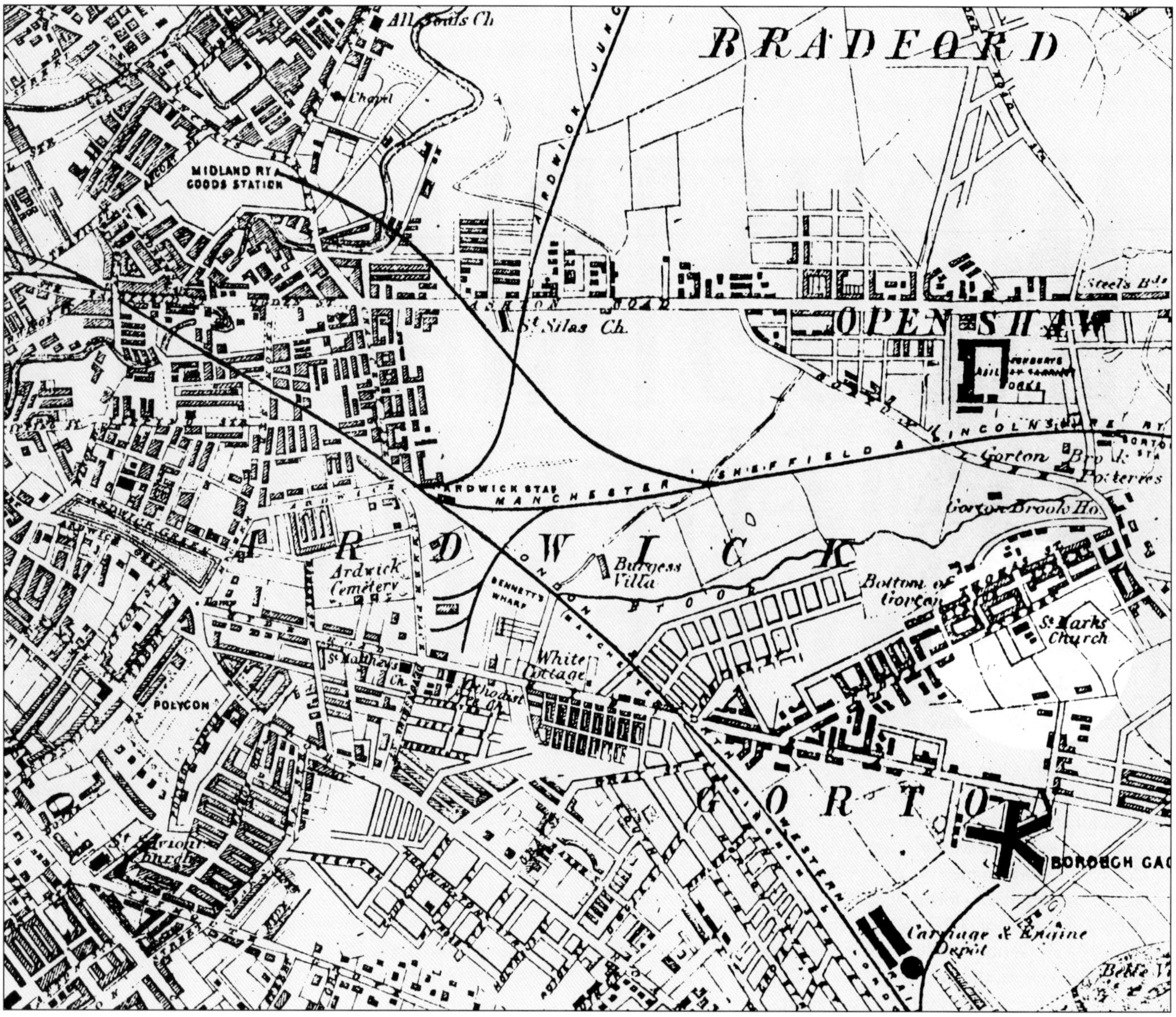

Bradshaw's Plan of Manchester c.1870 shows the recently constructed St. Mark's Church on Clowes Street. The area close to Thomas Street marked 'Bottom of Gorton' may well have been the first football pitch used by St. Mark's, although years of investigation have failed to prove conclusively the exact location of the pitch. Some City historians have suggested the pitch was somewhere on Clowes Street, however this area was so built up by the early 1880s it seems unlikely. Note also the building marked as White Cottage on Hyde Road is on the site where the Hyde Road Hotel was later built.

Slightly north of this map is the area of land where the City Of Manchester Stadium was erected in 2002.

St. Mark's Church

"Some of them, said the officer, had their belts off, but they were not sufficiently close to be able to use them. This is bad, but the state of terrorism excited by the scuttlers' conduct is worse. In explanation of the fact that rowdyism was allowed to go on for so long a time, it was stated that the people living in the vicinity were afraid to inform the police, as they knew that the result would be that their windows would be broken."

"This will give to those people who happily live in districts where scuttling is unknown some idea of what it means."

Perhaps Miss G. Connell wanted to provide activities to release aggression in a more productive manner than the Scuttles, or maybe she simply felt that organised male activities would help develop a healthier community identity, the Scuttles having encouraged something of a decline. In 1877, a women's group had been established with much success, and a year later the Parish of St. Mark's opened a newly built church hall at the corner of Hyde Road and Ashmore Street to provide the community with a decent meeting place. In 1879, Miss Connell set about the idea of the Working Men's club, unfortunately the men were a little reticent with only a handful turning up at the first few Tuesday night sessions. She persevered and gradually, after several attempts, the working men's meetings became

St. Mark's Church shortly before demolition in the mid 1970s.

popular, especially when the committee decided to form a cricket team and a lending library.

Two of St. Mark's Church wardens, Messrs Beastow and Goodyeare were given the job of developing the working men's club. Indeed it was William Beastow's idea to form the cricket side. In 1880, the following year, a football club was founded - St. Mark's (West Gorton). William Beastow was a Company Secretary at the local Union Iron Works, and soon found his positions at both the church, where he chaired the Tuesday night meetings, and the iron works, helped attract the right sort of players. During the development of the football side he managed to recruit respectable, hardworking players, including his two sons, Charles and John. In actual fact, most of the football contingent were simply the cricketers looking for sporting activity all year round.

St. Mark's was very much a local side for local people, similar in many ways to a present day pub team. The idea of the club was to bring together the local menfolk, and perhaps use football as a release from the pressures of the world's first industrial city. Games were actually played on a rough piece of ground close to the church on Clowes Street. Looking back to this time it is extremely difficult to locate the exact site of this pitch. According to the *Book Of Football* published in 1905 the land had been developed between 1881 and 1905 into the Brooks & Doxey's Union Iron Works - the company William Beastow worked for. Their factory was actually on Thomas Street, the next street to Clowes Street, and maps from the late 1880s do show sufficient land next to the original factory for a football pitch while also showing that the whole of Clowes Street had been built on. The land at Brooks & Doxey's is more or less in a straight line north of St. Mark's Church, and so could easily be their first pitch. Unfortunately, many years of investigation have yet to prove conclusively exactly where this first pitch was.

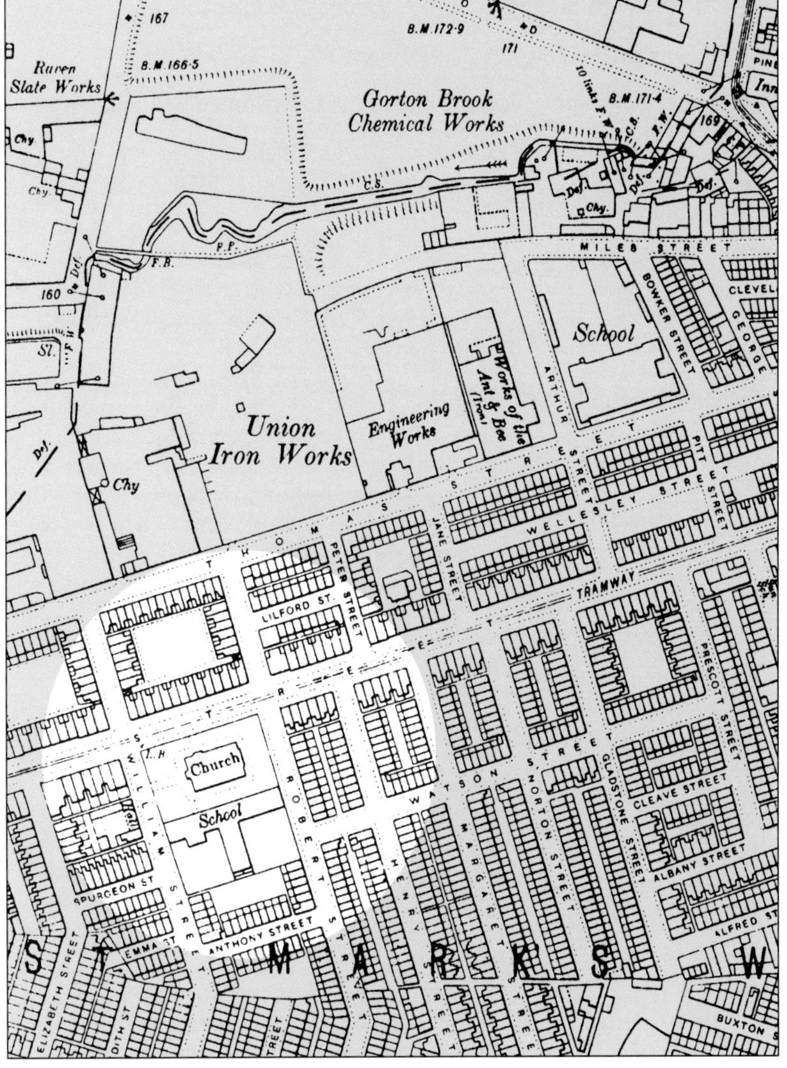

St. Mark's Church on Clowes Street during the 1880s. The Union Iron Works on Thomas Street employed William Beastow, and the original pitch may have been close by.

It seems reasonable to assume the Brooks & Doxey's land was the club's first pitch, and that William Beastow perhaps noticed the land's potential from his office window. If this was not the pitch, then it really is difficult to pinpoint where else in the Clowes Street area could have been free for football at this time.

Wherever the pitch was, it must be remembered that in 1880 it was nothing more than wasteland. Beastow and Goodyeare believed it was good enough for their purpose however, and the fledgling club played its first reported game there on 13th November 1880, with the first opponents being another church based outfit from Macclesfield:

The fledgling club played its first reported game on 13th November 1880

"A match was played between the Baptist Church (Macclesfield) and St. Mark's (West Gorton) on Saturday on the ground of the latter, and resulted as follows: Baptist 2 goals, St. Mark's 1 goal."

Both teams fielded twelve players which was not unknown at the time. Often teams would play with anything from eight to thirteen or even more. The numbers were not important, the game was, and although St. Mark's lost this particular fixture the match is one of the most important milestones in the club's history. For the record, the first 'lucky' twelve players with a suggestion of the positions they played were:

Charles Beastow

W. Sumner (Capt) **Frederick Hopkinson**

Walter Chew **H. Heggs** **W. Downing**

Richard Hopkinson **Edward Kitchen** **A. McDonald** **J. Pilkington**

John Beastow **J. Collinge**

Without that game, and the dedication of locals like Beastow and Goodyeare, Manchester City F.C. would never have existed.

The second known game took place two weeks later, with St. Mark's managing to achieve a goalless draw with a team called Arcadians from Harpurhey. Newspaper reports exist for a further five matches that season, with the last game taking place at Stalybridge on 19th March 1881. This was actually the club's first victory, but was perhaps not unexpected as the home side, Stalybridge Clarence, could only find eight of their regular players. Three volunteers from the crowd filled the positions and at half time the makeshift Clarence side were leading by a single goal. Richard Hopkinson, who is believed to have been a teacher at St.Mark's School, turned the game round for the Gortonians with a couple of quick goals - the first after a neat dribble along the right wing, the second direct from a corner. J. Collinge scored a third for St. Mark's, while the match report credited the captain Sumner and goalkeeper Kitchen as the side's 'men of the match'. St. Mark's won the game by three goals to one.

The following season saw the club develop further. A decision was taken to move to a more professional playing surface, and they chose the Kirkmanshulme Cricket Club ground, a five acre site on Redgate Lane, close to the large Belle Vue Zoological Gardens. Apart from a pavilion in one corner of the ground, there were no facilities for spectators. This was still better than the club's first pitch though, and in any case the playing surface would have been far superior, at least until the footballers started to use it. In one of St. Mark's games during the first season, the *Reporter* newspaper quoted that the ground was 'in a very sloppy state, and consequently the falls were very numerous.' That game ended with the club's heaviest defeat - a 7-0 drubbing by Hurst from Ashton-Under-Lyne - and probably the most embarrassing day for the embryonic club. If St. Mark's aimed to achieve a solid image, the players could not afford to be humiliated either on the pitch or because it.

At the cricket ground, the club managed to attract players from outside the St. Mark's parish, and so in November 1881 the church understandably removed its patronage. The side became known as West Gorton (St. Mark's) and during the 1881/2 season are known to have played a total of twelve games. The first game after the name change was the club's initial meeting with Newton Heath on 12th November 1881, which attracted an attendance of around 3,000. The 'Heathens', who went on to become Manchester United in 1902, defeated West Gorton by three goals to nil in what was described as a 'pleasant game'. What might the reporter make of derby matches today! Two goals were scored in the first half, one an own goal by one of West Gorton's 'backs'. It is not reported who scored the goal, all the *Ashton Reporter* wording says is that the player was "attempting to stop a shot by Thomas".

The following week West Gorton achieved their first victory of the season with St. Mark's parishioner J. Pilkington providing the only goal in the away game with Arcadians, although it must be made clear that Arcadians were continually having to defend as the St. Mark's men put in their best attacking display so far. They even had a goal disallowed: "the ball striking the cross-bar, and fell in a slanting position, which the goalkeeper then knocked back into play. The West Gorton appeal for a goal was, however, disallowed by the Arcadians' umpire."

The year ended with a 3-0 defeat at Broadbottom on New Year's Eve. The fact that Gorton only managed to field nine players appears to be the reason why the match was so one sided especially as, only two months later, the home fixture between the two clubs ended 3-0 in West Gorton's favour. Although it is fair to say that the St. Mark's men were rather inconsistent.

On 14th January they defeated Haughton Dale 8-1, with J. Collinge scoring a remarkable five goals, yet two weeks later were embarrassed by a 6-0 defeat at Hurst. It has to be said that the side was still coming to terms with football. Many of the players had only played the occasional game and some were merely St. Mark's parishioners who, to be frank, should never have walked onto a football pitch. These pioneers, though, were the life of the club. They raised funds and performed many of the supportive tasks, organising away games for example, and therefore had a right to participate in the games. Without them West Gorton (St. Mark's) would have died.

The only other game worth noting in the club's second season was the return match with Newton

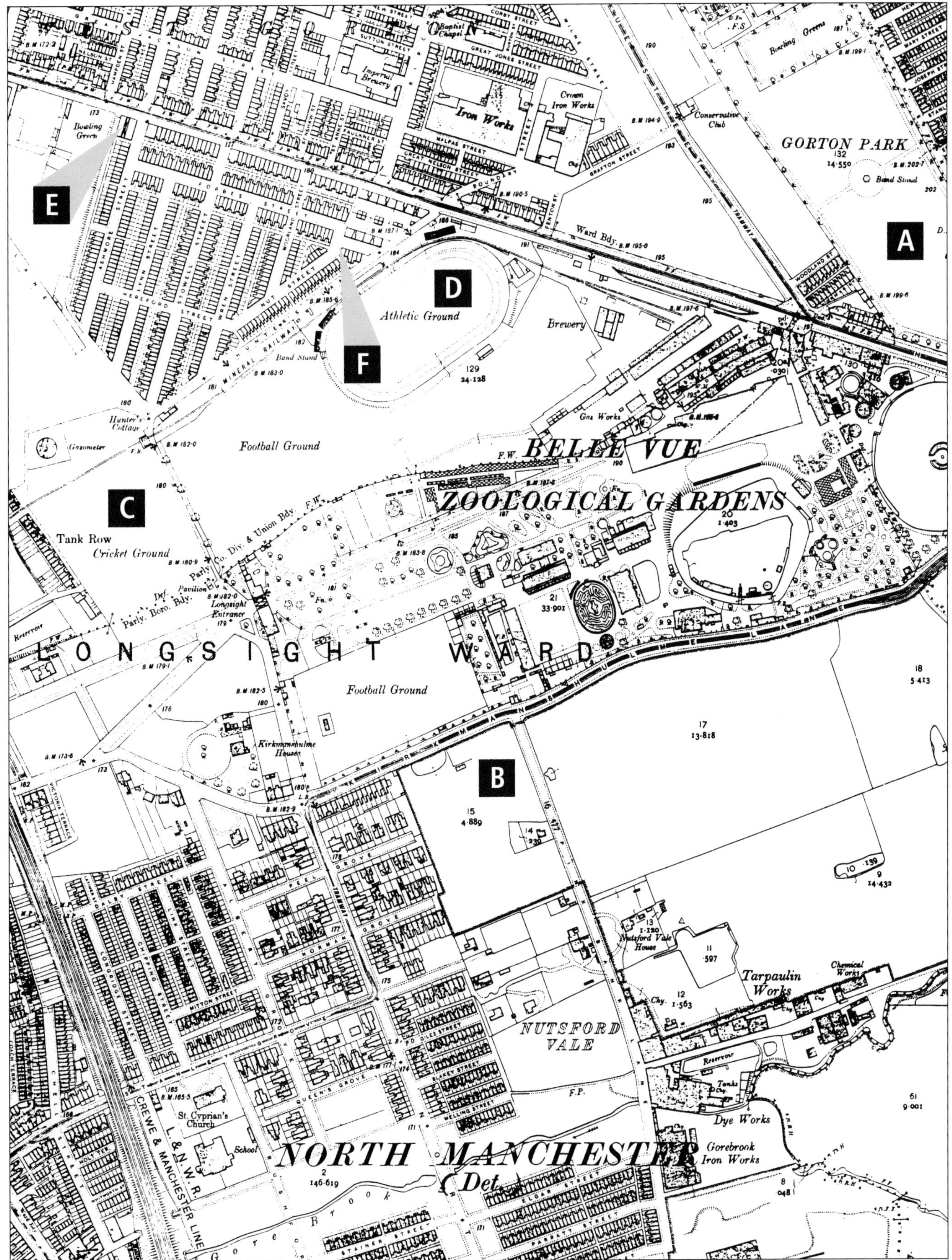

A 1905 map of the Belle Vue area showing significant locations from early years, including 3 possible grounds.

A = Clemington Park/Queen's Road

B = Pink Bank Lane

C = Kirkmanshulme Cricket Club

D = Belle Vue Ground. The 1889 Floodlit game to raise money for the Hyde miners was played here.

E = St. Mark's Church Hall. The meeting to form a football team was held here.

F = Nut Street - where Billy Meredith lived for a while.

J. Collinge obtained possession in front of the Gorton goal then proceeded to run the full length of the pitch, before sending the ball flying between the Heathens' posts amid loud cheering.

Heath at the Kirkmanshulme Cricket ground. Gorton gained revenge for the 3-0 defeat in their first encounter, as they overturned Newton Heath 2-1. Gorton had managed to take the lead as early as the eighth minute, and then had to hold off the Heathens who had been awarded a couple of consecutive corners. The second actually lead to Gorton's second goal. J. Collinge obtained possession in front of the Gorton goal then proceeded to run the full length of the pitch, before sending the ball flying between the Heathens' posts amid loud cheering. The score remained 2-0 until late in the game when, according to reports, the Heathens baffled the home 'keeper Kitchen by performing several good passes before the ball entered the goal. Exactly how baffled Kitchen was we don't know, but we do know the game was well attended.

The crowd that day was reported as 'around 5,000', although it would be unfair and ridiculous to suggest that this was the actual attendance. It seems incredible that somewhere in the region of a sixth of Gorton's population would have been able to attend a game which, at that point, was not regarded as a 'derby' or an important fixture whatsoever. Nevertheless, it does provide an indication as to how popular West Gorton (St. Mark's) were becoming.

At the end of the season the Kirkmanshulme C.C. asked the footballers to find another ground as their playing surface had been badly damaged, or at least they felt that it was no longer the perfect pitch one would expect for a gentlemanly game of cricket. Maybe the damage had been caused by the large attendance at the Newton Heath game, West Gorton's last at the Cricket ground, or perhaps it was simply down to general wear and tear on the pitch. West Gorton (St. Mark's) were now desperate for a new ground - any ground!

The whole of Gorton was still expanding rapidly. New streets were being established all the time, while various factories and industry to support the railways were providing employment for the increasing population. In fact the only area of Gorton not growing was the amount of land available for recreational activities, thus making it exceptionally difficult for West Gorton (St. Mark's) to find the perfect venue.

It is at this point where the history of the club seems to have become confused over the years. The facts appear to be that the club moved to land off Queen's Road, approximately three quarters of a mile east of Clowes Street, along the Hyde Road. Here, at a venue reported as 'Clemington Park' in the local *Reporter* newspaper, the club played a total of eight home games during the 1882-3 and 1883-4 seasons. In addition, they are known to have played only another nine away games during those seasons.

Incredibly, a total of 26 players - including ten St. Mark's originals from the 1880-1 season - featured in the nine known games from 1882-3. What is more remarkable, considering the number of players available, was that in only three of these games did West Gorton have a full complement of eleven players. Even when playing at home, Gorton struggled to find enough players. Why so many 'squad' players? And why so much difficulty in raising a side?

The large pool of players may be accounted for by comment in David Williams' *Famous Football Clubs - Manchester City* booklet published in the 1940s. According to Williams: "A West Gorton club, playing in scarlet and black, had got going in Queen's Road, West Gorton, however, and the pitchless St. Mark's men threw in their lot there. In later years this ground developed into a park, but it looked more 'parky' than anything else in those days."

Williams' comments would account for the influx of players, and potentially could account for other difficulties during the season. Maybe the merger caused friction between members of the two former clubs' committees, and thus made team selection extremely difficult. Looking back it is almost impossible to say with any certainty how the club was structured during this period. We do know that prior to the move to Queen's Road the committee was made up of loyal St. Mark's men, and that afterwards the key positions were taken up by members of the original club. We do not know, however, the names of those officially responsible for the running of the club between 1882 and 1884.

Another puzzle is the number of games played during these years. Again Williams' booklet quotes that West Gorton played a total of twenty games, losing only four, during the 1883-4 season, whereas all other sources claim the club played only eight games during that season. Although it is impossible to say where Williams obtained his information - potentially there could have been players from this period still alive when Williams performed his research - it seems more credible that West Gorton did feature in around twenty games, and that the side were beginning to achieve better results.

Interestingly the improved results perhaps came about because of a further change in the structure of the club. Another local side, Gorton Athletic, found themselves groundless and so, with a little give and take on both sides, the two Gortonian teams merged. The merger was fraught with difficulty and lasted for one season only.

Match reports that exist for games during this season tend to suggest that for the first time in their history West Gorton, incorporating the Gorton Athletic players, were playing as a team. Four successive games in March 1884 all ended in victory: Bentfield (3-0), Broadbottom (0-5), Greenheys (1-5), and the local derby with Gorton Villa (7-0). The game against Bentfield was interesting as it was the first defeat suffered by that club in two years, while the Gorton Villa meeting seems to support the theory that West Gorton played more than the reported eight games. It took place with potentially at least one month of the season remaining and is the last reported game that season. It also appears to be the only meeting between the two clubs. No doubt two progressive sides from the same district would have met again that season, unfortunately no evidence exists to suggest this.

Attendances for the merged side were impressive. None reached the heights of two seasons earlier, but the 1-0 victory at home to Furness Vale was witnessed by a crowd of around 1,000. Considering the Queen's Road venue was nothing more than an open field, that attendance was quite remarkable.

The summer of 1884 was not a pleasant one as the Gorton Athletic contingent seemed to be continually at odds with those from West Gorton. Eventually, Walter Chew and Edward Kitchen, two of the St. Mark's men driving forward the West

Gortonians, decided to leave the Athletic contingent behind and reform under the new title of Gorton Association Football Club.

Over the next couple of years the men left at Queen's Road renamed the club West Gorton Athletic, with the emphasis firmly on the athletic, and moved to land close to the Gorton Brook Hotel at the top of Clowes Street. Eventually the club faded into the mists of time.

The newly formed Gorton A.F.C. struggled to find a new ground and at one point were in serious danger of going out of business altogether. The season had already started when on 25th October 1884 a notice appeared in the *Gorton Advertiser* outlining the club's new name and that 'a suitable ground has been secured near Belle Vue Station. Mr. E. Kitchen, Railway Cottages, Longsight, has been appointed Secretary.'

The new location was yet another piece of local wasteland, this time off Pink Bank Lane on the southern side of the Belle Vue Gardens. It was not too far from the Kirkmanshulme C.C. ground, and had been suggested by a young forward named Lawrence Furniss. Over the next fifty years, Furniss was to become one of the most influential men in driving the club forward. Indeed, by the time City won the League Championship for the first time in 1937 Furniss was club President. With Furniss's knowledge of the land, and a few negotiations with the landlord, the Gorton club were able to make progress. An annual rent of £6 was set and Edward Kitchen was free to organise fixtures.

Around this time Gorton took the first step towards organised football by applying to join the Manchester & District F.A. The moment they were accepted Gorton knew they were on their way. A little careful planning over the next few years would help put Gorton at the forefront of Manchester football.

Although few match reports exist for the 1884-5 season, the Annual Dinner was reported in the *Gorton Advertiser* and provides an interesting insight into the success of the team during that first season:

Virtually all the names mentioned in that article had links with the club's earliest formation at St. Mark's, and it's interesting that Frederick Hopkinson chose to sing 'The Old Brigade'. Was there a feeling that the club - which was made up of mostly St. Mark's parishioners - was now back on course after a couple of years struggling to survive. Interestingly, the senior committee men and driving force behind the club were James Moores and William Beastow. Moores was the senior church warden at St. Mark's and a member of the Union Iron Works Board of Directors, while Beastow also maintained influential positions at both organisations. Both the welfare of the community and the leisure pursuits available were important in helping to establish a satisfied workforce.

Beastow himself had tried to provide identity for the Gorton team in October 1884 by presenting them with a complete set of black jerseys emblazoned with a white cross. The cross was significant as it signalled that the St. Mark's connection was still there, while at the same time the Gorton name emphasised that the side aimed to represent the whole of the district. Local MP Richard Peacock backed the club by providing a donation of five pounds - this was a substantial sum especially when all the club's expenses totalled nine pounds and sixpence. Without that support Gorton could easily have gone out of business. Instead the club was once again able to move forward.

Lawrence Furniss (above) devoted his life to the Blues. He was involved with the club from the 1880s and held almost every role possible - player, secretary, director, chairman and president.

GORTON ASSOCIATION FOOTBALL CLUB

The first Annual Dinner in connection with the above club was held on Monday evening, 20th April 1885, at the Justice Birch Hotel, Hyde Road, where there was a good attendance. Mr. and Mrs. Pitt served an excellent dinner, and it was thoroughly enjoyed. Afterwards, Mr. James Moores presided, and Mr. W.H. Beastow was vice-chairman. The loyal toasts were honoured, interspersed with the songs 'Hearts Of Oak' by Mr. Chew, and 'The Old Brigade' by Mr. F. Hopkinson. The toast, 'The Manchester & District Association', was heartily received and acknowledged by Mr. Colbert, the President of the Manchester & District F.A., who was in attendance as the guest-of-honour.

Mr. F. Hopkinson read the Annual Report, which stated that the club, though only formed in October last, had made considerable progress. It has a membership of about twenty-five active members, with a promise of a good increase next season. The first team last season played 16 matches, 7 of which were won, 7 lost, and 2 drawn; number of goals scored 31, as against 21 scored by their opponents.

In conclusion, the Report said that, financially, there was a balance on the right side, and all that was required for the success of the club was a good ground. Other toasts then followed, and songs were given by Messrs. F. Hopkinson, Furniss, Barber and others, the evening being very agreeably spent. Mr. R. Hopkinson ably officiated as Pianist.

During the summer of 1885 it is believed Gorton were able to move away from the rough and ready Pink Bank Lane, to land owned by the Bull's Head Hotel on Reddish Lane on the very eastern side of Gorton, approximately three miles from the club's birth place. The landlord of the Bull's Head charged the footballers £6 per annum to use the pitch and change in the public house. At last Gorton were able to announce where they played with some degree of pride.

Gorton's general performance was improving at this time although their position in the overall Manchester footballing fraternity was not particularly good. Local rivals Gorton Villa were by far the more superior, and further afield the names of Newton Heath, West Manchester, and Gorton's old adversaries Hurst were the ones the general public were becoming accustomed to hearing. Indeed Hurst were the first winners of the Manchester District Cup in 1885 while Gorton lost in the first round. The following year they again fell at the first hurdle losing 2-1 away to Pendleton Olympic. Gorton still had a long way to go, but with the enthusiasm of forward thinking men like Lawrence Furniss, who had been forced to retire through injury, the club was able to progress.

During 1886-7 Gorton did progress and in the first round of the Manchester Cup they defeated arch-rivals and former bedfellows West Gorton Athletic 5-1 at the Bull's Head ground, with two of the goals being scored by Jack Hodgetts, a new recruit who would later become the first professional with the club. The second round pitted Gorton away to Newton Heath - a team that had featured in every Manchester Cup final so far - and although the Gortonians were determined to win they were, quite simply, overpowered with the Heathens winning an easy tie 11-1. Nevertheless, the Manchester Cup of 1886-7 is important as it shows the increase in Gorton's stature. On the one hand they were easily beaten by the Heathens, on the other they proved they were a cut above some of their traditional rivals. Reports also show that the Gorton players were far from happy at succumbing to Newton Heath. They took defeat badly, so badly that the *Reporter* newspaper tried to cheer the Gortonians up by looking into the future: "Perhaps in another season or two Gorton will be able to avenge itself. It is as yet but a young club, and there is plenty of time to show of what stuff its members are made."

Ashton Cup 1886-7

Gorton reached the semi-final of this competition without winning a game. The first round ended in a 3-1 home defeat by Gorton Villa, but the Gorton committee somehow managed to get Villa expelled, leaving the home side free to contemplate the next round. Sadly, there is no trace of any second round Gorton match taking place, but there is an article that appeared in the Gorton Reporter which suggests that Gorton's secretary, Walter Chew, was acting as some form of detective, uncovering wrong doing: "Hurst look fair set to receive Denton as their opponents in the final tie for the Ashton Charity Cup - that is, if a certain party by the name of Chew - who, I hear, is again on the warpath - does not upset the Denton men's calculations. Mr. Chew is a treasure to Gorton A.F.C By the aid of his amateur detective abilities, the Gorton team have reached the semi-final, although they have not yet won a match in this competition. It therefore behoves Denton to 'mind their P's and Q's'." Gorton lost the semi-final in controversial circumstances, after walking off the field following Denton's sixth goal. The game continued with Denton scoring a seventh before the referee abandoned the match.

By the summer of 1887 Gorton were faced with a rent increase at the Bull's Head, although it is not known exactly how much was demanded, nor if the Gorton committee seriously considered staying. The land they had used was not in an ideal location - it was closer to the rather less developed Reddish than Gorton centre - and even though it was probably Gorton's best venue, it was far from perfect. If the club had any kind of ambition it needed to search for a better site in a densely populated district. Its roots were in West Gorton and many felt the club should return home.

Club Captain K. McKenzie solved the problem when he realised that some wasteland close to his house could be converted into the perfect home. McKenzie lived in Bennett Street, Ardwick, and every lunchtime he would take a short cut from Bennett's Timber Yard, off Hyde Road, through the L&NWR railway arches, and across the wasteland to Bennett Street. He believed the land could become Gorton's ground and spoke to the committee, who quickly visited the site. At first they must have been appalled by what they saw - an uneven surface, little if any grass, immense puddles (pond is too grand a word for these dirty, polluted, water-filled holes) - but with a little imagination they began to see what could be achieved.

With this site Gorton would be able to develop the club's first all enclosed ground. True, it would take a considerable amount of effort but, after seven years of relative struggle, the Gortonians were prepared to do whatever was necessary to find their own enclosure.

The young Lawrence Furniss searched to find the owners of the land and, after a little investigation, discovered it belonged to the Manchester, Sheffield and Lincolnshire Railway Company. After an initial letter from Walter Chew to Edwin Barker, the company's estate agent, negotiations began. Eventually, Furniss and Chew managed to agree seven months' rental for the sum of £10, and the Gortonians spent considerable time and effort in turning this barren patch of land into a pitch fit for football. By the end of August 1887 it was ready. It may not have been the ideal playing surface, after all for most of the summer the club had been levelling the surface, but it was now home.

Around this time discussions took place as to the name of the club. It was felt that a new home deserved a new beginning and, in any case, the club was no longer within the Gorton boundary. Instead of trying to retain the Gorton moniker, the club members decided to adopt the name of the district they had now moved to, and so during the summer of 1887 Gorton A.F.C. became Ardwick A.F.C.

Many football historians have, over the years, believed the club had moved entirely away from its roots by this point, and that the new 'Hyde Road Ground', as it was to become known, was several miles from the club's origins. This is simply not true. The Hyde Road Ground was several miles from the Bull's Head pitch, but it was actually closer to Clowes Street and St. Mark's Church than any of the other grounds apart from perhaps the first two pitches (the land near Clowes St. and Kirkmanshulme C.C.). In a sense the club came home. Although it was within another district it was merely a third of a mile from the St. Mark's Church itself.

Despite this close proximity to the church, the club decided to make a large public house, the Hyde

ARDWICK v. HYDE.—(Ardwick District Charity Cup, second round).—At Ardwick. Hyde kicked off. Ardwick scored first from the toe of Drinkwater, and from the kick off they took it down and scored again. Then Parker scored for Ardwick, and all the first half Ardwick pressed. On change of ends, with wind in their favour, it was thought that Hyde would press, but it was not so. Parker, Hodgetts, and Callagan scored, and from Manning, at half back, Callagan scored. Then Hyde scored one. McKenzie afterwards scored the eighth for Ardwick, the result being :—

ARDWICK .... 8 goals.
HYDE .... 1 „

A match report of the controversial Ardwick victory over Hyde. The away side complained bitterly that the ground had been unfit and the game was replayed at Hyde.

Road Hotel, its headquarters. With the agreement of the licensee, Richard Stephenson, all the important meetings of the period were held there and, on match days, the hotel would serve as Ardwick's changing rooms - and scene of celebrations (or commiserations) afterwards. With Stephenson's support the club decided to promote itself and raise awareness by inviting any interested party to the club's inaugural meeting. A circular was handed out in the Ardwick and Gorton area to publicise the event.

With this kind of formal notification the local population could not fail to understand the ambition of the club. Local councillor, and member of the influential local brewing family, Stephen Chesters-Thompson was invited to become Honorary President of the club. Over the course of the next thirty years Chesters Brewery would play a major role in the establishment of the club, while also gaining considerable revenue from first, Ardwick's use of the Hyde Road Hotel, then exclusive rights to supply all the bars within the ground.

Another move made during this period was into the world of professional football. Any club with ambition had to attract the best players, and so Ardwick decided to turn professional. In actual fact they chose to pay existing first team player Jack Hodgetts five shillings a week to play for the club, rather than seek other more famous players. Nevertheless it is an important move in the history of the club, and clearly shows how far they had progressed since formation a mere seven years earlier.

Hodgetts, although glad of the money, was a little perturbed by the treatment he received from the other players. Some cold-shouldered him and believed he felt above them. It was really nothing to do with Hodgetts as an individual, more the principle involved. It wasn't long however before the club committee realised the situation would have to change for the good of the club. They reached a decision to allow the rest of the first team players to claim expenses and, to keep the peace, these totalled a maximum figure of five shillings per man. They were officially able to retain their amateur status, whilst enjoying the luxury of expenses. Everybody was happy.

With the club brim full of ambition, a grand opening fixture was arranged for 10th September 1887. Ardwick's first opponents were to be Salford A.F.C. yet for some unknown reason they failed to arrive at the Hyde Road ground. A band had been hired and a crowd of over five hundred had turned up, only to discover Ardwick's birth to be a farce. Over eighty years later, Francis Lee made a famous quote about the possibility of the club winning 'Cups for cock-ups'. He was talking about the club's 1970s ability to make the easy difficult, but he could have been referring to almost any period in the club's chequered past. It seems this 'grand opening' was the first, but by no means the last, 'own-goal' in the club's professional history.

The following week the ground did stage a match - this time Hooley Hill from Denton defeated Ardwick 4-2 in a game played in 'delightful weather' according to the newspaper report. Even so, the quality of the Hyde Road playing surface was quite poor - one of Ardwick's goals was scored from the midst of a puddle, despite the fact that it had not rained at all. Later in the season Ardwick's 8-1 demolition of Hyde in the Ashton & District Cup had to be replayed due to complaints from the Hydonians that the ground was unfit for football. The replay took place at Hyde with Ardwick dominating the game so much that the home side continually hoofed the ball as far away as possible. The match report commented on the amount of times the ball had to be retrieved from the field next to the Hyde ground. Not surprisingly Ardwick easily beat the home side 3-1.

Gradually Ardwick - who were nicknamed the Brewerymen because of their connections with Chesters Brewery - gained passionate support. Perhaps a little too passionate at times. On 26th November 1887, at the end of a 1-0 defeat by

A circular handed out in Gorton and Ardwick to invite all interested parties to Ardwick's first meeting at the Hyde Road Hotel on 30th August 1887.

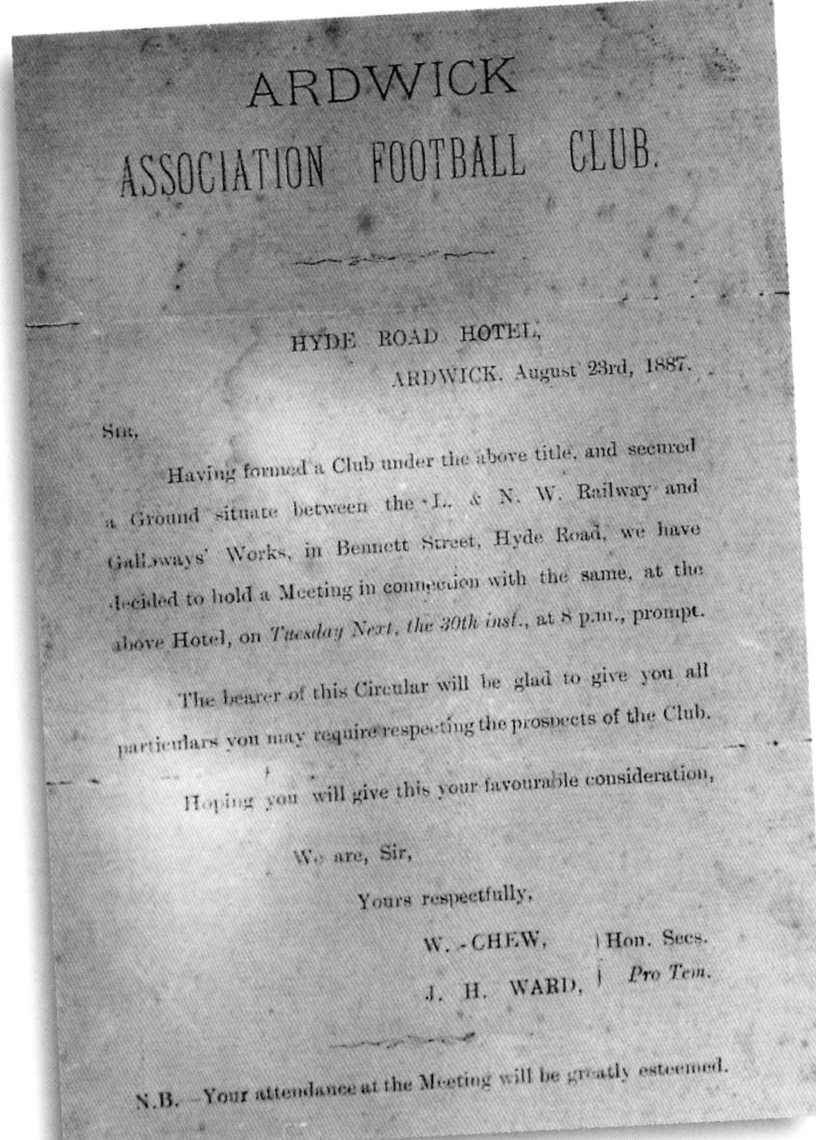

ARDWICK

ASSOCIATION FOOTBALL CLUB.

HYDE ROAD HOTEL,
ARDWICK, August 23rd, 1887.

SIR,

Having formed a Club under the above title, and secured a Ground situate between the L. & N. W. Railway and Galloways' Works, in Bennett Street, Hyde Road, we have decided to hold a Meeting in connection with the same, at the above Hotel, on *Tuesday Next, the 30th inst.*, at 8 p.m., prompt.

The bearer of this Circular will be glad to give you all particulars you may require respecting the prospects of the Club.

Hoping you will give this your favourable consideration,

We are, Sir,

Yours respectfully,

W. CHEW, } Hon. Secs.
J. H. WARD, } *Pro Tem.*

N.B.—Your attendance at the Meeting will be greatly esteemed.

The Hyde Road Hotel

The Hyde Road Hotel - a prominent landmark for over 100 years.

For 36 years the Hyde Road Hotel played a leading role in the life of Manchester City. The first meeting of Ardwick AFC was held there on 30th August 1887 and, seven years later, decisions to re-form as Manchester City were taken in that building. The team often changed into their strip there, and many supporters used it as a meeting place.

For a while a sign on the building proudly proclaimed: "The Headquarters of Manchester City Football Club", and the large public house provided a prestigious facade to what was, for much of the time, a cramped, drab football ground.

After City moved to Maine Road in 1923 the importance of the Hyde Road Hotel diminished and, as industry and the population of the area declined, so did the public house. In 1983 the building was given a new lease of life when it was renamed "The City Gates" under landlord and former Blues player George Heslop *(see page 355)*, however it closed for the last time in 1988 and swiftly deteriorated. Vandalism wrecked much of the building, leaving it in a precarious state by the mid 1990s.

When the first version of this book was published in 1997, it was clear the life of the Hyde Road Hotel depended on the slim hope of an individual or group coming forward with serious ideas on how to save it. The book helped raise awareness of the building's plight and, as a direct response to what he read, young supporter David Scally went to great lengths to try and save the pub. He sent circulars, created a Hyde Road Hotel website and held meetings with various interested

Edenfield, the Hyde Road crowd were reported to have 'stoned the visitors off the field'. Secretary Walter Chew sent a letter to the *Gorton Reporter* denying the incident, nevertheless the local 'paper stood by their report. Interestingly, Jack Hodgetts, who passed away in 1922, was famous for telling his friends about games like this where supporters stoned the away side, although in Hodgetts' version it was always the Ardwick team that were on the receiving end of the supporters' wrath!

Ardwick's passionate supporters followed them to many away games during this first season, most noticeably the Manchester Cup first round tie at Lower Hurst (Ashton-Under-Lyne). Despite losing 3-2 the Ardwick fanatics gave their side great encouragement and continually shouted "Play Up, Ardwick!" - could this have been the club's first chant?

All in all the first season was not a great success. Off the field the club lost £13 despite gate receipts of £47 9s 9d. On it Ardwick achieved a few notable results, but also struggled against, in many cases, weak sides (Astley Bank defeated Ardwick 13-0!). Also, the Hyde Road pitch had not stood up to the rigours of a football season. Nevertheless it still had better prospects than any of the other venues used in the 1880s, and with the right financial backing Ardwick knew they could develop the ground as and when required.

Over the course of the next twelve months significant progress was made. With the help of Chesters, Ardwick built a grandstand capable of holding 1,000 spectators, and for the sum of £5 15s the club's first pay box - turnstile was not an appropriate name - was erected. With the new pay box the club raised £213 gate money, income exceeding expenditure by roughly £39. Amazingly only 5 shillings had been spent on medical requirements. Perhaps a pint of Chesters was the Ardwick team's cure-all!

In addition the club attracted a number of wealthy backers to complement the Chesters' money. John Allison was one of Ardwick's benefactors during this period. In September 1888 he refused to accept any change from the half crown he tendered as he entered via the club's new pay box. Officials from the club made contact with him to explain that he had overpaid, yet he still insisted on the club keeping the extra cash. Quickly Ardwick established links with Allison, who became famous for developing various methods of pain relief and ways of achieving fitness using water treatment and technology, and asked him to become a director of the club. The Brewerymen needed all the support they could muster although, with Lawrence Furniss as the new secretary, the club was in safe hands.

On 26th February 1889 Ardwick featured in a friendly floodlit match against Newton Heath at Belle Vue, close to Hyde Road. The game was a charity match in aid of the Hyde Colliery disaster and raised

parties. Sadly he did not receive enough support to make real progress. It seems few were interested enough to help preserve this important part of City's history.

In March 2001 *The Times* featured the building as one of their first 'Football Blue Plaque' sites. Their view was the building was a vital piece of football history and should be preserved. Whether the article had any bearing on what followed is unclear, but what is known however is that a month later scaffolding mysteriously appeared around the club's former HQ.

By 19th May 2001 the building had vanished completely. City's first match following its demolition ended in a 1-2 defeat by Chelsea on the last day of the 2000-01 relegation season and little attention was given to the building's final days. In fact many supporters were unaware of its demise for some time.

Regrettably, the Hyde Road Hotel has now joined Manchester's list of demolished former sporting landmarks: White City, Belle Vue, The Imperial Hotel, Manchester Racecourse - the list is endless. In a city proud of its sporting heritage it's a travesty nothing has been done to save so many of these sites.

The Hyde Road Hotel pictured in a dilapidated state in February 1996 (above) and shrouded in scaffolding (left) in April 2001, prior to demolition.

£140 with an attendance of around 12,000. The result was a 3-2 defeat even though the Ardwick side was strengthened by the inclusion of players from other local sides. Nevertheless it perhaps proved that the gulf between the Heathens and Ardwick was narrowing.

With the Football League now in operation teams like Ardwick realised how far they could go and, although most of Ardwick's fixtures remained friendlies, the club was adopting a more professional approach. In May 1890 Furniss and Allison decided the time was right to look beyond the confines of Manchester, and head off in search of quality professionals. They journeyed to Scotland where, in next to no time, they signed the brilliant Dundee based goalkeeper Douglas. They had to rely on the services of an agent, P. Allen, who received £10 commission, but nevertheless had finally signed a player of genuine quality.

While in Scotland they raided the Ayr squad, signing Robson, Campbell and McWhinnie, and also Young from Glasgow Northern. Back in England, they obtained the services of several Bolton Wanderers players - 'Wally' Rushton, Milne, McWhirter,

NEWTON HEATH v. ARDWICK DISTRICT

This match was played at Belle Vue Gardens last night before a tremendous crowd, the "gate" being for the benefit of the Hyde Explosion Fund. There were twenty of the Wells's lights round the ground, but still there seemed to be some difficulty in seeing the ball at times, especially when it was off the ground. It was stated that there had been quite 6,000 tickets sold, and the gates were crowded for over two hours before the time for starting, so that there would be quite 10,000 people present, and it ought to result in a considerable addition to the fund. Mr. Charles Jennison kicked off, and R. G. Barlow was referee. The game was not a success as an exhibition of football, but still at times there was some good bits of play, which were applauded by the spectators, who seemed to be quite enthusiastic. The chief feature of the match was the cheering when the ball was kicked either over the bar or outside, as most of the spectators were sure it went through. The scoring done was four goals by Newton Heath and one by the District, but, unfortunately for the former, one of theirs was put through his own goal by Powell. Score:—Newton Heath, three goals; Ardwick and District, two goals.

In January 1889 an explosion at the Hyde coal mine, some five miles from Ardwick, resulted in the death of 23 miners. Ardwick and Newton Heath agreed to play a friendly under floodlights in aid of the disaster fund.

A preview of the 1890-91 season which highlights Ardwick's desire to become Manchester's dominant club.

OTHER LANCASHIRE CLUBS.

The Ardwick Club have a thoroughly good working committee, who, besides retaining the whole of last season's players, have enlisted a regular cohort of powerful players, all of good standing. The team now on the spot is made up from the following:—

Douglas (Dundee Our Boys), Leather, and Warman, goal; Robson (Ayr), Haydock (Bolton Wanderers), Bennett, Heard, backs; Milne, McWhirter, Whittle, Pearson (Bolton Wanderers), Watmough, "Jones," half-backs; David Weir (captain), Rushton (Bolton Wanderers), Campbell (Ayr), McWhinnie (Ayr Athletic), McColl (Burnley), Haworth, Hodgetts, O'Brian, forwards.

There will also be three new players from Scotland, all of whom have signed the professional form. McColl, who had signed for Burnley, it will be noticed, has been released by them. The ground has been re-turfed, drained, and otherwise improved to the tune of over £600, and its central situation, surrounded by railways and trams, warrants the outlay. The public of Manchester have been judiciously catered for by the arrangement of a very strong list of home fixtures, and many more of the Ardwick big gates are looked forward to. In view of Ardwick's bold bid for the supremacy of Manchester, the three matches with Newton Heath and the two against West Manchester will be very instructive. Matches with the Bolton Wanderers, Blackburn Rovers, West Bromwich Albion, Derby County, and Accrington are already on the list, while the executive expect other League clubs at Ardwick during the season.

Ardwick v Witton September 1890

Ardwick v. Witton.—On the ground of the former, before 3000 spectators. Weir started the ball for the home team, and play was very even for a time. The home forwards, however, soon began to take the lead, Weir and McColl playing a grand game. The visitors' backs and goalkeeper defended well, and it was some time before M'Whinnie opened the scoring. Weir and Rushton also added goals, and at half-time the home team were leading by 3 goals to nil. From the re-start the home team had matters pretty much their own way, but Forrest kept goal admirably and saved a number of shots from a good corner by M'Whirton. One of the backs put the ball through his own goal, and Weir, Rushton, and Young each scored. Ardwick won easily by 8 goals to nil.

Ardwick v Heywood Central September 1890

Ardwick v. Heywood Central.—At Ardwick, before 5000 spectators. Weir started for the home team, and they were not long before they began to take the upper hand. One of the visitors' backs deliberately fisted the ball, and from the free kick McWhinnie scored; the visitors then gained two fruitless corners; the central forwards continued to press, but Douglas and Robson defended well. The home forwards then broke away, McColl being prominent: Rushton shooting through. The home team were now having most of the play, and Weir added 2 goals before half-time. The home forwards went away from the start and Weir shot over. The game then became very even, the home half-backs showing up well. McWhinnie then got one through and Weir followed with a sixth after the goalkeeper had twice saved. McColl soon after put in a long shot which McWhinnie headed through. McColl had then to leave the ground through receiving a nasty knock in the face. The home team, however, continued to press, Jarrett putting in some good work, Ardwick eventually winning by 7 goals to nil.

Ardwick's Friendlies 1887-1891

For some reason the majority of these matches were played at home. Either the Ardwick management were unable to pay travel expenses, or the opposition were not keen to reimburse the club. In 1890-91 Ardwick played 42 friendlies, but only five were played away from home. In addition, the month of April 1891 saw Ardwick play on the 4th, 6th, 11th, 13th, 15th, 20th, 25th, 27th and 29th with only two of those games away from home. Perhaps the teams that complained of fixture pile-ups during the 1996-7 season should have tried Ardwick's demanding schedule.

Haydock, Whittle and Pearson. They were also fortunate to sign the English International, Davie Weir, from the Trotters.

All this activity did help the club progress, but it also created a certain amount of controversy for a team that many regarded as 'young upstarts'. When Ardwick signed Walker of Burnley they immediately found themselves on the Football League's blacklist. Apparently Ardwick had poached the player. In those days transfer agreements between Football League clubs and those still on the outside were not in existence, making it possible for teams like Ardwick to attempt to sign whoever they wanted, whenever they wanted. In December 1890, the Football League tried to counter this by introducing a rule that forbade League clubs from organising fixtures against clubs found guilty of poaching. Ardwick, found guilty, were prohibited from arranging lucrative fixtures against any League club - a move guaranteed to penalise any ambitious club.

The 'Brewery Men' had even paid Walker £5 to travel to Manchester in an attempt to sign him. League clubs were told not to do business with the 'upstarts' from Manchester and those that did - such as Preston who arranged a fixture with Ardwick - were officially censured.

After two months of struggle, Ardwick apologised and offered Walker back to Burnley. Interestingly, there is no trace of Walker ever actually turning out for Ardwick's first team. Ardwick were removed from the blacklist and allowed to continue their quest for big time fixtures. They desired a place in football's hierarchy and in 1890-91 entered the F.A. Cup for the first time. In a qualifying match they defeated Liverpool Stanley 12-0 with the impressive Davie Weir scoring a hat trick yet, for some unknown reason, their next game in the competition did not take place. They were due to face Halliwell, a team from Bolton, away from home but no record exists to show the match actually took place. Perhaps Ardwick managed to arrange a more lucrative fixture at Hyde Road. Whatever occurred, Halliwell did go through to the next round.

The early 1890s really saw the club take off. Attendances were increasing - reaching 5,000 for several games - the squad was strengthened, and the ground improved. In the summer of 1890, Ardwick spent over £600 returfing and draining the playing surface, while also improving access by agreeing with Chesters to open up an additional entrance by the path at the side of the Hyde Road Hotel. Chesters also increased the number of bars within the ground. Looking back it is relatively easy to understand the reasoning behind Chesters involvement in the club - any venue where 5,000 men regularly congregate must stand a decent chance of selling large quantities of alcohol - yet it is also essential that the Ardwick view is considered. Without the close partnership with Chesters the club could easily have gone under. They would certainly not have been able to develop the ground in the fashion they had. It was a mutually beneficial partnership for both organisations.

In April 1891 a major landmark in the history of the club was reached when the Brewerymen overcame Newton Heath 1-0 in the Manchester Cup final. The influential Ardwick captain Davie Weir scored in the seventh minute to give the unfancied Ardwickites the trophy. According to match reports the game was rather even, although Ardwick did actually have another goal disallowed. Nevertheless, the victory finally made the footballing fraternity sit up and notice the Cambridge Blues. Newton Heath had featured in every Manchester Cup final since inception, and were clearly one of the biggest Manchester sides, whereas Ardwick had struggled to shake off the image of a small time club. By winning the Manchester Cup Ardwick were able to declare 'We've arrived!'

Success in the trophy perhaps went a little to their heads when at the 1891 Football League AGM Ardwick - along with Darwen, Newton Heath, Nottingham Forest, Stoke, and Sunderland Albion - applied for the first time to join the 'big boys' when the League was expanding from 12 to 14 clubs. All the applicants, with the exception of Ardwick, were members of the Football Alliance - a league originally set up to rival the Football League. Not surprisingly, Ardwick failed to gain admittance, as did their Manchester rivals Newton Heath. The two new places were filled by Stoke, who had won the Alliance, and Darwen.

Although attempts to join the Football League ended in failure, Ardwick did find themselves accepted into the Alliance for the start of the 1891-2 season. Apart from local knock-out competitions and the occasional appearance in qualifying rounds of the F.A. Cup, this was Ardwick's first attempt at organised football. It was their chance to move away from the image of a team fit for nothing but friendlies into a world where they could achieve their many aims.

Newton Heath were the only other Manchester side in the Alliance, and so it was quite a feat for the Brewerymen to enter the league. During the pre-season they had developed the ground further - the club boasted that it had 'stand accommodation for 3,000 spectators', and had strengthened the side with Archie Ferguson from Heart of Midlothian, Hugh Morris from Chirk, with Bob Milarvie transferring from Newton Heath. In addition they played two pre-season friendlies at Hyde Road, the first a 2-2 draw with West Manchester, the second a 2-1 win over Gainsborough Trinity. Ardwick believed they were ready for the Alliance.

The season started at home to Bootle with a crowd of approximately 6,000. Although Ardwick went in at half time only one goal up, they had dominated the first half with Whittle providing the goal, Weir having one disallowed for offside, and McWhinnie heading over.

The second half was more of a mixed game with Bootle equalising early on, quickly followed by a second while Ardwick's Robson lay injured - *The Umpire* newspaper described him as being "badly kicked". Ardwick were determined to put in a good performance in front of the Hyde Road crowd and, after much pressure, Davies equalised. More Ardwick pressure followed and in the final quarter McWhinnie provided an excellent pass to Morris who sent the ball through for the home side's third goal.

Ardwick, in typical Blues style, then allowed Bootle to score straight from the kick off. Apparently, Bootle charged down the pitch and provided Grierson with the opportunity of scoring from a low shot, and so a game Ardwick badly wanted to win ended in an exciting 3-3 draw. Nevertheless it was an indication that perhaps Ardwick were ready for this kind of organised approach to football.

MANCHESTER SENIOR CUP.—Semi-final

West Manchester v. Ardwick.—On the ground of the Manchester Athletic Club at Old Trafford. Lambie kicked off for Ardwick, and West soon pressed, but only for a time, as Ardwick took the ball down and Milne scored. Siddeley had hard lines in not scoring, Douglas saving clumsily. Ardwick again pressed, McWhinnie and Weir scoring. West played up and had hard lines, the ball striking the crossbar. Half-time: Ardwick, 3 goals; West, nil. On resuming play was even, Siddeley putting in some good shots. Allison centred skilfully, and Shaw gained a goal. Weir soon after scored for Ardwick. Final:

ARDWICK ....4 goals.
WEST MANCHESTER ....1 „

West Manchester v Ardwick (Manchester Cup semi-final) March 1891

LANCASHIRE JUNIOR CUP.—Final

Ardwick v. Blackpool.—Played at Preston, before 6000 spectators. Ardwick kicked off with the wind, and had the best of the opening exchanges, but Blackpool scored in three minutes. The Mancestrians, by dint of good forward work, equalised from the foot of Lambie, this goal being most cleverly obtained. Davidson showed up with some fine kicking. The game was very fast, and each goal in turn was rapidly visited. Blackpool scored twice, and led at half-time by 3 goals to 1. On resuming the game was most evenly and hotly contested, though the Blackpudlians were most persistent in their endeavours to score. Robson and Milarvie defended gallantly, and were undoubtedly the means of saving a more severe defeat. The Fylde men were much quicker and smarter on the ball, though each side strove their utmost. There was no further score, and Blackpool again won the Cup by 3 goals to 1.

Ardwick v Blackpool Lancashire Junior Cup Final March 1891

Ardwick v. Celtic.—At Ardwick, before 8000 spectators. The visitors brought a splendid team, and a good game was witnessed. The visitors pressed a little, but the home team retaliated. The Celts came again, and Dowds registered their first point. This was followed by another, and then McWhirter, from a splendid pass from Milne, scored the first for the home team. Just before the interval Campbell scored for the Celts. Half-time: Celtic 3 goals; Ardwick, 1 goal. The visitors played by far the better game in the second half, goals being scored for them by Dowds, Campbell, and MacMahon. Lambie obtained the second point for Ardwick. Result:—

CELTIC .... 7 goals
ARDWICK .... 2 „

Ardwick v Celtic March 1891

THE ALLIANCE.

Results up to date:—

	Pld	Won	Lst	Drn	Goals For	Goals Agst	Pts
Notts Forest	3	3	0	0	15	2	6
Small Heath	2	1	0	1	6	2	3
Birmingh'm St. George's	2	1	0	1	5	3	3
Burton Swifts	3	1	2	0	4	10	2
Ardwick	1	0	0	1	3	3	1
Bootle	2	0	1	1	4	7	1
Crewe Alexandra	—	—	—	—	—	—	—
Grimsby Town	—	—	—	—	—	—	—
Lincoln City	—	—	—	—	—	—	—
Newton Heath	1	0	1	0	2	3	0
Sheffield Wednesday	—	—	—	—	—	—	—
Walsall Town Swifts	2	0	2	0	2	8	0

Ardwick v. Bootle.—At Ardwick, before quite 6000 spectators, Mecnie started the game for the visitors and play was even for some time. Weir shot the ball through, but offside was given, and the Bootle left wing was prominent, but Whittle relieved. The home team had considerably the best of matters, and Whittle scored and Dunning conceded a corner from a hot shot by Davies, and McWhinnie headed over from a good pass by Milarvie. Half-time, Ardwick 1; Bootle 0. Weir restarted the game, and the visitors ran down, Davies shooting outside, and Montgomery shot over the bar. The visitors had the best of matters and Montgomery scored with a good shot. The home team pressed, and McWhinnie headed outside. Robson was badly kicked, and whilst he was on the ground the visitors scored. The home team now played up, and after some good passing, Davies sent the ball through, and the score was again even. From a splendid run by the home forwards M'Whinnie put in a fast shot, but Dunning saved. The home team pressed, and from a good pass by M'Whinnie, Morris sent the ball through. From the kick-off the visitors ran down, and Grierson scored with a low shot, an exciting game ending in a draw. Final:—

ARDWICK .... 3 goals.
BOOTLE .... 3 „

Ardwick v Bootle September 1891 First game in the Alliance

SATURDAY'S FOOTBALL.

THE ASSOCIATION GAME.

ENGLISH CUP.

QUALIFYING STAGE.—FIRST ROUND.

Newton Heath v. Ardwick.—At Newton Heath, 10,000 being present. The game was started by M'Whinnie, and Newton Heath were the first to attack, Farman and Edge getting well down, and the former got in a grand shot, which Douglas saved. The game was not a quiet affair, and several free kicks were soon given. Milarvie and Dewar were next to the front with a good run, but the former was stopped by Roger Doughty, a foul being given against him. Bob M'Farlane was cheered for a couple of grand saves. Edge then spoiled a chance by selfish play. A free kick was nicely placed by Clements, and it was very luckily got away. Newton Heath were having a shade the best of it, but were weak in front of goal. Edge put in a grand centre, and Stewart shot in, but Douglas just cleared, falling full length in doing so. Newton Heath made a determined attack, and their opponents had a lively time, but they at last got the ball away. It did not stop long, as Stewart was instrumental in getting it away. R Doughty retired for a short time, being injured. A penalty kick was given to Ardwick, but was got rid of by Slater. The Ardwick goalkeeper was repeatedly cheered for grand play. The whole of the home forwards were playing grandly, and were attacking severely for a long time, and at last Sneddon got in a low shot, which bumped and deceived Douglas, and before he could recover Sharp was on him. This success was greeted with cheers. Soon after half-time was called. A rather long interval was taken, but Newton Heath attacked first, and Dobson had to give a corner. Farman put it behind. The Ardwick right next got away, but were easily beaten. The home team came again with a big rush, and another corner had to be conceded, nothing being done again. Ardwick next had a short turn at their opponents' end, but M'Farlane got rid of the attack by a fine kick. Stewart had a chance, but he shot out. Morris and Davies made a good run, but Clements kicked out. Sharp got down and shot, Douglas only just putting it round the post. From this point of the game the "Heathens" had all their own way, Farman and Doughty putting the ball through. Ardwick now got away with a nice run, and from a free kick Pearson scored the first for the visitors. Newton Heath again attacked, and Farman put the ball past Douglas for the fourth time, and Edge shortly afterwards put on the fifth, "time" being called with the score:—

NEWTON HEATH .... 5 GOALS
ARDWICK .... 1 GOAL

A match report from the Newton Heath-Ardwick FA Cup match of 1891.

18/04/91

Manchester Cup Final

City's first appearance in the final of this competition brought receipts of £216 and an attendance of 10,000, and was played at the ground of West Manchester

Overall in the League that season, Ardwick achieved a great deal. Although they only finished seventh out of twelve clubs, they did manage a few interesting results. They defeated Walsall Town Swifts 6-0 at Hyde Road, and drew the home derby game with Newton Heath 2-2. In fact 1891-2 was probably the first real season of rivalry between the two Manchester clubs. Prior to the Alliance, Ardwick's main 'derby' rivals were all minor clubs from the Gorton area - indeed they continued to play friendlies against Gorton Villa up until 1893 - however, once the two sides met in the Manchester Cup final of 1891, and then faced each other in the Alliance, they were meeting as equals. Their first season as opponents in the Alliance allowed the large Manchester population to have a choice - Newton Heath or Ardwick. Although Newton Heath had been the more successful club so far, Ardwick were perhaps seen as being more progressive and were already the better supported of the two. The Hyde Road derby attracted a crowd of over 10,000, whereas the Heathens home game at North Road was watched by around 4,000. Even the Hyde Road derby attendance was bettered by Ardwick on two other occasions in the Alliance that season. Support wasn't Ardwick's problem though, results against the Heathens were. The first meeting of the season between the two clubs was actually in the F.A. Cup when Newton Heath ran out easy winners 5-1 on 3rd October. Seven days later the two Manchester sides met again, this time Ardwick managed to keep the score down to 3-1. If Ardwick wanted to be Manchester's dominant side, then they had to beat the Heathens on a regular basis.

Apart from the games with Newton Heath, Ardwick did manage to prove their pedigree and position as one of the strongest clubs in the Manchester area when they won the Manchester Cup for the second year running. This time the Brewerymen convincingly defeated Football League side Bolton Wanderers 4-1, although the game itself had to be delayed. Two minutes before the scheduled start the two sides entered the Newton Heath pitch at North Road, only to discover they were both wearing white shirts and dark blue shorts. A quick search around the ground failed to find an alternative strip, and so a man was sent in a hansom cab to fetch different colours. He returned thirty minutes later with a set of red and black shirts.

The game eventually kicked off at 4:05, with Ardwick having most of the play throughout the first half. However, 'just as the whistle was about to be blown', according to a contemporary match report, Munro scored for Bolton. Within a minute Hugh Morris made it 1-1. Not long after the interval captain Davie Weir, a former Bolton player who had been dropped then reinstated for fear that he would not try against his old club, dribbled from the half way line, before firing a shot past the Bolton goalkeeper. From a Weir free-kick, John Milne scored Ardwick's third, and then a few minutes later Bob Milarvie sent the ball goalwards for what seemed like a certain goal, only to see Davie Weir poach the fourth Ardwick goal - who was it said the captain wouldn't try against his old club?

Ardwick had now reached a point in their history where they could look back with pride. The Blues no longer had to worry about finding a ground, or a game for that matter. They were on the up and up.

Ardwick v. Internationals (D Weir's Benefit).—At Ardwick, before 4000 spectators, Coleman started on behalf of Ardwick, who at once took the ball up the field, sending in shot after shot, all of which proved abortive. A corner to Ardwick was kept out by Stones. After this the Internationals began to play up, and Weir sent in a shot which Douglas saved at the expense of a corner. A nice run by the Ardwick forwards enabled Milarvie to secure the first point amidst cheers. On restarting the Internationals were not long before they equalised. Even play followed until the Ardwickites made a grand run, and Milarvie sent in a grand shot, which caused Stones to handle. At this point Ardwick were having the best of matters. When half-time arrived the score stood 1 goal each. On changing ends Ardwick went away with a rush, and sent in a good number of shots, but could not score. After this Ardwick had one disallowed for off-side. The Internationals now made their way to the Ardwick goal, and, through some nice passing among the forwards, Edge gave them the lead. A couple of corners fell to Ardwick, both of which proved fruitless. Ardwick pressed, and with a long, swift shot Milarvie made the score even just before time. Result:—

ARDWICK .... 2 goals.
INTERNATIONALS .... 2 „

Ardwick v Internationals, Davie Weir's benefit match 9th April 1892. The game ended 2-2.

MANCHESTER SENIOR CUP.

(FINAL TIE.)

BOLTON WANDERERS v. ARDWICK.

The above competition reached the final stages when Ardwick (holders) met Bolton Wanderers, on the Newton Heath ground at North-road. This is the first time the Wanderers have appeared in the final for this cup, as they only entered at the beginning of this season. In former years the result of the competition was practically a foregone conclusion, as Newton Heath won the cup year after year; but the rapid strides made by Ardwick put more interest into the affair, and last year they managed to beat the "Heathens" by 1 goal to nothing. This is the first time since the competition was started that Newton Heath have not appeared in the final. In the preliminary encounters Ardwick had to meet Heywood Central and Fairfield, whilst the Wanderers have beaten Stockport County and Newton Heath. Both teams put forth their best eleven for the match under notice, and it was not surprising that a fast game was witnessed. The Ardwick committee have had their team training at Matlock, whilst the "Trotters" have done what they required at home. The game was not started until 4.5. There would be about 8000 spectators present, when Cassidy started the ball for the Wanderers against a stiff wind. Ardwick at once took up the running, but Milarvie when hard pressed put the leather into touch. The ball was then worked down, but Robson took care of Bentley, and his final went wide by several yards. The goal-kick afforded some relief, and Sutcliffe had to use his hands to a capital shot from Milne. The ball still hovered in close proximity to the Bolton goal, but Davies at length put the ball wide of the uprights. The Bolton forwards by some nice passing got the leather away, but Middleton intervened, and Sutcliffe had to save a slow shot from Milarvie. The Ardwickites, assisted by the wind, were playing a good game, and Jones was compelled to give a corner. The ball was well placed, but Paley came to the rescue, and Cassidy missed the mark by the nearest possible margin. The Wanderers then assailed, and Douglas, in saving a shot from Bentley, was compelled to give a corner, but nothing resulted. Munro now had a capital chance, but instead of rushing away he sent the ball to the centre. Milne here got the leather, and the Ardwick forwards rushed away, but Sutcliffe by some splendid play prevented them from scoring. A free kick to Ardwick followed, but Gardiner was successful, and with a tall kick transferred the ball to the opposite end, but the Ardwick backs were in excellent trim, and cleared time after time. The Ardwickites got away again, and Sutcliffe only just saved a shot from Milne by giving another corner, but the kick did not result in anything. Just as the whistle was about to be blown Munro scored through a miskick by Robson. The Ardwick forwards at the restart rushed up, and Morris made the score 1 each, which was the score at half-time. After the interval, Milne restarted the ball for Ardwick, and Bentley immediately shot into touch. The play, on the restart, was again in favour of the Wanderers; but the defence of the Alliance team was grand. Robson, with a beautiful kick, got the leather away. Weir, getting the ball at the centre, evaded all his opponents, and beat Sutcliffe with a beautiful shot, which was greeted with loud and prolonged cheering. This reverse put the League team on their mettle, and Douglas had to be on the alert to keep his goal intact, and after several attempts, Bentley put the ball high over the bar. Ardwick then broke away and gained a free kick close to the Bolton goal. Weir took it, and Milne tipped the ball past Sutcliffe. On restarting, the Boltonites went at it more determined than ever, but Ardwick were not to be beaten, and kept them well in hand. The Alliance team again went away, and Milarvie putting the ball across, Weir notched the fourth. The Wanderers now played like a beaten team, allowing their opponents to run round them. Ardwick, though, had certainly the best of matters during this half, playing against the wind with surprising energy. Cassidy now forced his way through several opponents, but Robson intervened and cleared. Time was at length called, Ardwick gaining a decisive victory. Final:—

ARDWICK .... 4 goals
BOLTON WANDERERS .... 1 „

An Umpire newspaper report of Ardwick's success in the Manchester Cup for the second year running.

Chapter Two

PROMOTING MANCHESTER

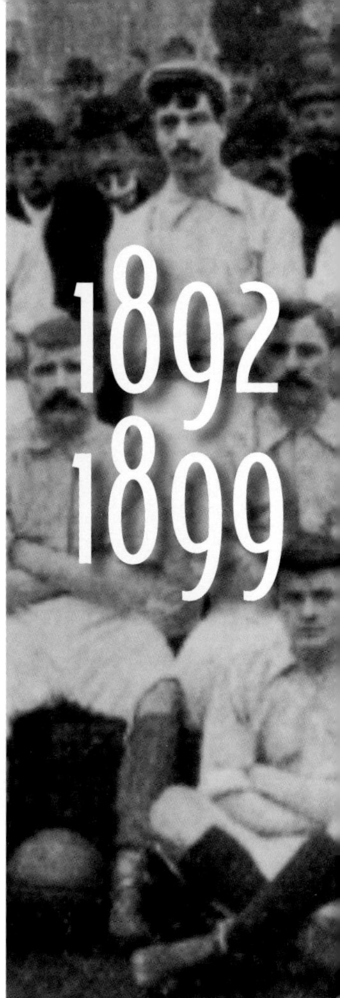

IN 1892 Ardwick Association Football Club made a significant move towards the ultimate goal of being one of the country's elite teams. The Football League had been in existence for four years without a representative from Manchester - the city was not unique - but by 1892 every ambitious club in the country realised the League offered potential.

Ardwick's application a year earlier was rejected mainly because the Brewerymen lacked experience. The other applicants had all been members of the Alliance, including arch-rivals Newton Heath. Like Ardwick, Newton Heath failed, although as already noted Ardwick's reputation at this time was minor compared with the Heathens.

The League in its infancy was very much like a 'gentleman's club'. Ardwick, not being members, were often seen as being working class upstarts with few rights. Ardwick wanted the best and were not afraid to bend the rules to achieve their aims. For instance, they tried to sign the best players and felt financial inducements were an acceptable means of business. The Football League disagreed. They had already put into force maximum signing-on fees and had made poaching illegal. None of this seemed to concern Ardwick even after they had been blacklisted during the 1890-91 season for poaching a player. In 1892 Wolverhampton Wanderers supplied the League with strong evidence proving that Ardwick had tried to poach a Wolves player. Fortunately, Ardwick were not alone. Many clubs outside of the League took similar steps to recruit the best.

Nevertheless, it wasn't long before the Brewerymen were in with a chance of achieving their aim of joining the Football League. A decision had been taken in April 1892 to form a second division of twelve clubs and expand the First Division to sixteen. The additional clubs would mainly come from the Alliance - a league which had realistically been the Second Division in any case - with Nottingham Forest, Wednesday, and Newton Heath all applying and being accepted into the enlarged First Division. Ardwick joined Darwen, Burton Swifts, Grimsby Town, Bootle, Walsall Town Swifts, Small Heath Alliance, Crewe Alexandra, Lincoln City, Burslem Port Vale, Sheffield United, and Northwich Victoria in the new division.

Interestingly, other applicants to join the League included the newly formed Liverpool, who were rejected before the vote was made, Newcastle East End (later Newcastle United), Middlesbrough and Middlesbrough Ironopolis.

So Ardwick had at last made it into football's elite, although it must be said that many Ardwickites must have felt a little envious of Manchester rivals Newton Heath who had been allowed straight into the First Division. Ardwick were by this time the better supported of the two clubs, and seemed to offer more potential, even if Newton Heath had performed better in the Alliance. It was only natural they received their chance with the 'big boys', and just a pity that Ardwick couldn't be given that opportunity also.

As with Ardwick's first game in the Alliance, the Brewerymen made their debut in the Football League at home to Bootle in a game that perhaps helped to set the typical Manchester image for any newcomer. Not only was the Hyde Road ground surrounded by industry, railways, and row after row of terraced housing, but the day itself was particularly grey with heavy rain throughout the match. The poor conditions helped push the attendance down to around 4,000, but those brave souls that stood and

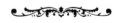

On 9th April 1892 an Ardwick side played a team made up of international players at Hyde Road in a benefit match for captain Davie Weir. Bob Milarvie scored twice for Ardwick and the game ended in a draw before a 4,000 crowd. (see cutting on facing page)

AAFC

1892 - 93.

Ardwick Association Football Club

SEASON 1892-93.

Available to

UNCOVERED STANDS (BOYS)

No. 50

Name John Bickett

Address 9 [illegible] Ardwick

Sec.'s Signature [illegible]

NOT TRANSFERABLE, and if found to be used by anyone other than the person whose name it bears, the ticket will be withheld.

Shottin & Co., Printers, 67, London Road, Manchester.

A boy's season ticket for the 1892-93 season, Ardwick's first in the Football League. This actual ticket was stored in Manchester Central Library until December 1996, when it was stolen. The library are naturally keen to discover its whereabouts.

cheered their heroes on were rewarded with an excellent Ardwick goal feast.

The final result was a 7-0 victory, putting the Mancunians at the top of the very first Second Division table on 3rd September 1892, although the following day's *Umpire* newspaper mistakenly placed the club second behind Small Heath (later Birmingham City) who had won their game 4-1. Amongst the goalscorers were Joe Davies, who scored the first Ardwick League hat-trick, and Hugh Morris, who scored the club's first goal in the League. Interestingly, the Brewerymen were also awarded their first League penalty when Hutchison was adjudged to have fouled J. Angus, who had joined the club from Third Lanark only two weeks earlier. Ardwick's new captain Dave Russell, a former member of the Preston side which achieved the double in 1888-9, sent the penalty straight into McLaughlin's hands.

Apart from Angus and Russell, most of the Ardwick squad had featured for the club in the previous campaign; even former captain Davie Weir had chosen to stay despite a few disagreements with the club prior to the 1892 Manchester Cup Final. Weir had refused to go to Matlock with the team for their build up to the final after it was suggested he would not want to see his old side Bolton lose to Ardwick. The issue was resolved at the time, but during the summer the news broke that Weir had signed for Bolton. A short while later he changed his mind, and returned to Ardwick. Nevertheless, it must have been obvious to his many admirers in both Manchester and Bolton that Weir's heart didn't really lie at Hyde Road. It was no surprise when, in the following January, he returned to the Wanderers.

The fact that the gifted Weir was left out of Bolton's first ever F.A. Cup final appearance in 1894 because of what has been described as his 'individualistic temperament that caused arguments with other members of the team', may provide an indication to the type of player Weir was. He had the skill, and it appears he had the fight, but he was not the perfect team player, despite being Ardwick captain for two seasons.

With or without Weir, Ardwick did make progress during this season. They remained undefeated in the first six games - a feat that saw them head the table - and right up until Christmas looked capable of winning the Division. Sadly, the New Year saw the club's fortunes dip as defeat followed defeat. In fact only two further games were won all season. Despite the loss of form Ardwick still managed to end the season in fifth place.

If the club had managed to maintain its early season form, or simply finish in the top three, they would have entered the end of season Test Matches to determine promotion and relegation. As it was Ardwick could only sit back and ponder what might have been as Hyde Road played host to the play off game that saw Second Division Darwen overcome Notts County from the First.

As the life of Ardwick, and subsequently Manchester City, always seems to be linked with that of Manchester United it's worth making a comparison of the two clubs' first season in the League. Overall, Ardwick had acquitted themselves well whereas Newton Heath, who had been elected straight into the First Division had performed abysmally. They finished last out of sixteen clubs, five points below nearest rivals Accrington who themselves had struggled to raise a team on occasions (they resigned at the end of the season).

In the Test Matches they faced Second Division champions Small Heath, and scraped a 1-1 draw at Stoke. The Heathens finally got their act together in the replay at Bramall Lane, where they achieved a decisive 5-2 victory. Nevertheless, the gap between the two Manchester clubs was not significant. Ardwick may have been officially a division lower, but in reality it was Ardwick who were winning the plaudits. The general Manchester public were interested in winners and at the time Ardwick appealed to an ever growing population.

In May 1893, the League's first officially titled Management Committee was elected with an Ardwick man, Joshua Parlby, becoming one of the two Second Division representatives. Parlby was an interesting, 'larger than life' character. His beard, size, and rather loud manner earned him the apt nickname 'Falstaff'. He was quite a clever character who knew how to achieve what he wanted. In later years the great Billy Meredith described his persuasive skills: "There are some men whose silver tongues are said to have the power of charming song-birds from the trees, and I believe Josh Parlby was one of them."

Parlby had moved to Manchester in 1892 as licensee of the Wellington Hotel on Stockport Road, and quickly established links with the Hyde Road club. Some historians claim that earlier in life he had played for Stoke, and also became a member of their committee, and his knowledge of the game helped him influence matters at Hyde Road.

So much so, that within twelve months of joining the club he replaced Lawrence Furniss as Ardwick's secretary. Furniss remained at the club, after all he was still an important member and could use his own experience to push the club further, however it was felt that the smooth talking newcomer might be able to get a little more out of the team, and provide a strong voice in the League's hierarchy. Parlby became Ardwick's first paid secretary, earning a weekly wage of fifty shillings.

Ardwick believed Parlby was the man to push them forward. Unfortunately his first season as secretary coincided with a series of amazing failures both on and off the pitch. The campaign started brightly with a 6-1 victory over Middlesbrough Ironopolis in Ardwick's second game, but apart from that and the 8-1 thrashing of Burslem Port Vale in October, there were few opportunities to cheer for the Ardwick faithful. New League arrivals Newcastle United, Liverpool and Royal Arsenal all did the double over a Manchester side that was clearly losing the momentum of the previous four or five seasons.

The lowest moment on the pitch came when Small Heath defeated the Brewerymen 10-2 in Birmingham. Even though Ardwick's goalkeeper, Harry Stones, had to leave the field injured for a while, this was still a major blow to morale. It had all felt so different in August when *The Umpire* newspaper claimed Ardwick were 'making satisfactory progress, and altogether the prospects of the club are brighter than for some time past'.

As early as October, the Ardwick committee were concerned with matters on the pitch and the financial position of the club. They called a meeting of season ticket holders to discuss the situation, with the result being that everyone agreed the club must carry on until the end of the season when, it was felt, it should be allowed to die. From then until the end of March the committee chose not to hold any official meetings, and Josh Parlby was given the unenviable task of smooth talking his way past the club's many creditors. There was also the small matter of completing the League programme, not a simple task at a club forced to sell many of its better players to stay alive.

In January 1894 goalkeeper William Douglas, who had been one of the real Ardwick stars since signing in May 1890, was transferred to First Division strugglers Newton Heath, thus becoming the first player to move from the Blues to the Heathens. In the same month full back David Robson, another who had been with the club since May 1890, moved to Wolverhampton Wanderers. Earlier Ardwick had lost the services of Hugh Morris, Joe Davies and J Yates to Sheffield United, leaving the squad seriously weak. These were suddenly desperate times.

A total of thirty-six players featured in the club's 28 League games that season, with the team altered for almost every game. For one match, a 1-1 draw away to Crewe Alexandra, Ardwick were forced to field only ten men when Daniel Whittle and a reserve missed the train. Such was the state of confusion surrounding the club at the time.

At one point the club were close to losing their Hyde Road ground when the landlords, the Manchester, Sheffield and Lincolnshire Railway Company, gave notice to Chesters Brewery that they wished to close the entrance adjacent to the Hyde Road Hotel. It seems that the railway company had plans to recover the ground from the club for breaching the agreement - presumably Ardwick were behind in their rent.

By this time Chesters had spent over £2,500 repairing the ground, and investing in the bars, and were not prepared to lose that investment, nor the potential beer sales a popular football club would create. The brewery persuaded the railway company to keep the entrance open for the rest of the season, and at the same time lease the ground to them instead of Ardwick. Chesters would pay the rates and bear the expense of keeping the ground in a fit state for football. On 25th March 1894 they also agreed and signed a document to underlet the ground to the football club.

Two weeks later, on the 8th April, with still one game to go and Ardwick trapped in the re-election zone, the *The Umpire* reported on the ongoing

Joshua Parlby, a larger than life figure who did much to further the status of Manchester football. He was a member of the League's management committee from 1893 to 1899.

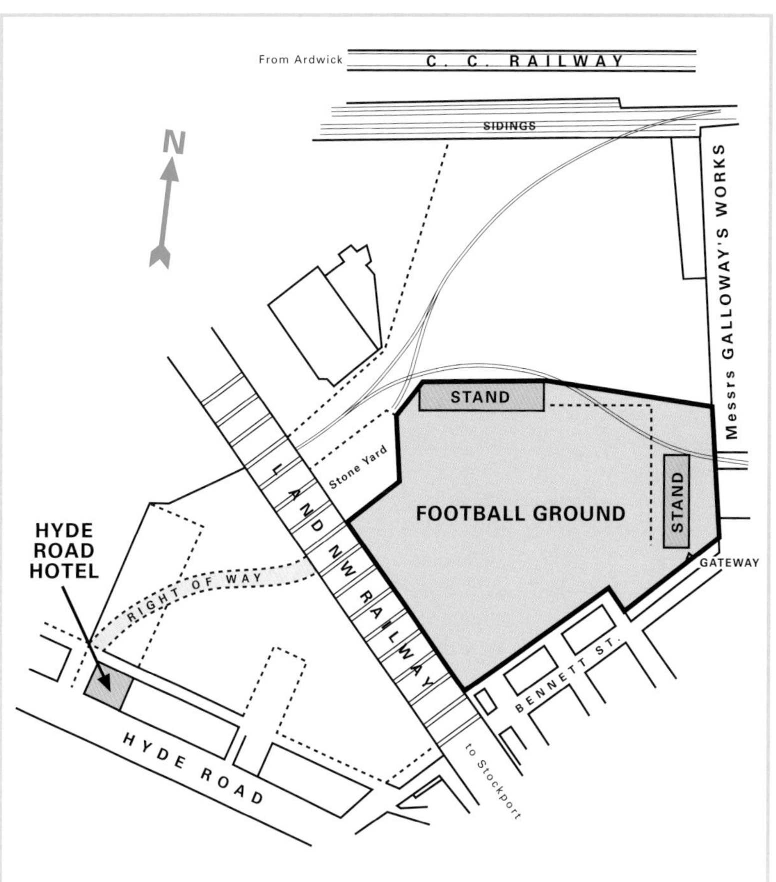

Map from 1894 showing the layout of the Hyde Road ground. The stand at the top is the 1887 Grand Stand paid for by Chesters' Brewery. The entrance from the Hyde Road Hotel was along the 'right of way'.

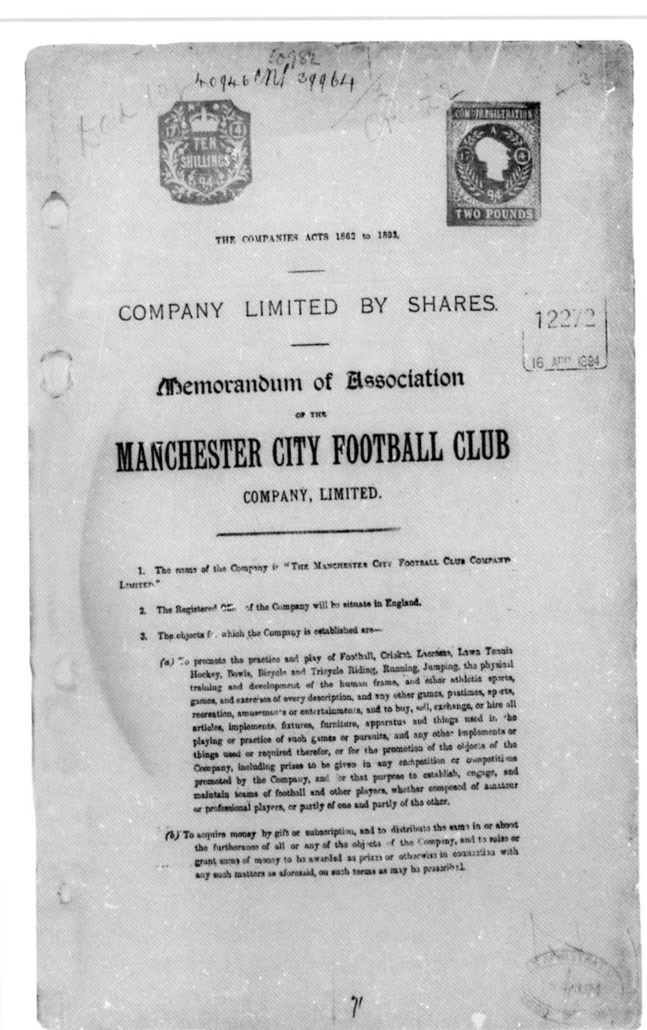
THE COMPANIES ACTS 1862 to 1893.

COMPANY LIMITED BY SHARES.

12272

16 APR 1894

Memorandum of Association

OF THE

MANCHESTER CITY FOOTBALL CLUB

COMPANY, LIMITED.

1. The name of the Company is "THE MANCHESTER CITY FOOTBALL CLUB COMPANY LIMITED."

2. The Registered Office of the Company will be situate in England.

3. The objects for which the Company is established are—

(a) To promote the practice and play of Football, Cricket, Lacrosse, Lawn Tennis Hockey, Bowls, Bicycle and Tricycle Riding, Running, Jumping, the physical training and development of the human frame, and other athletic sports, games, and exercises of every description, and any other games, pastimes, sports, recreation, amusements or entertainments, and to buy, sell, exchange, or hire all articles, implements, fixtures, furniture, apparatus and things used in the playing or practice of such games or pursuits, and any other implements or things used or required therefor, or for the promotion of the objects of the Company, including prizes to be given in any competition or competitions promoted by the Company, and for that purpose to establish, engage, and maintain teams of football and other players, whether composed of amateur or professional players, or partly of one and partly of the other.

(b) To acquire money by gift or subscription, and to distribute the same in or about the furtherance of all or any of the objects of the Company, and to raise or grant sums of money to be awarded as prizes or otherwise in connection with any such matters as aforesaid, on such terms as may be prescribed.

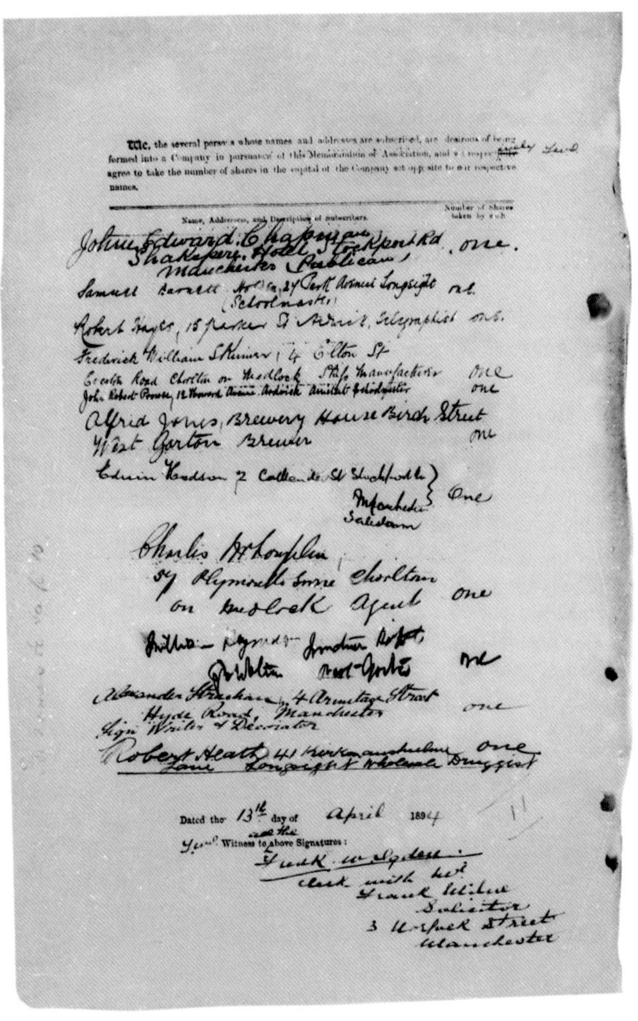
We, the several persons whose names and addresses are subscribed, are desirous of being formed into a Company in pursuance of this Memorandum of Association, and we respectively agree to take the number of shares in the capital of the Company set opposite to our respective names.

Name, Addresses, and Description of subscribers.	Number of Shares taken by each
John Edward Chapman, Shakespeare Hotel, Stockport Rd, Manchester, Publican	one
Samuel Barrett, 24 Park Avenue Longsight (Schoolmaster)	one
Robert Hayes, Telegraphist	one
Frederick William Skinner	one
John Robert Powell	one
Alfred Jones, Brewery House Birch Street, West Gorton, Brewer	one
Edwin Hodson	one
Charles McLoughlin, Chorlton on Medlock, Agent	one
Alexander Strachan, Hyde Road, Manchester, Sign Writer & Decorator	one
Robert Heath, Longsight, Wholesale Druggist	one

Dated the 13th day of April 1894

Witness to the above Signatures:

Frank ... Clerk with ... Solicitor, Manchester

Two pages of the Memorandum of Association which registered City as a limited company in April 1894. The first page lists the main rules of the company, the other lists all of the original shareholders including chairman John Edward Chapman.
Note Rule 3(a)...
'The objects for which the Company is established are:- To promote the practice and play of Football, Cricket, Lacrosse, Lawn Tennis, Hockey, Bowls, Bicycle and Tricycle Riding, Running, Jumping, the physical training and development of the human frame, and other athletic sports, games and excercises of every description...'

confusion surrounding the finances and future of the club. The article outlined plans by some season ticket holders to form a new club called Manchester City Football Club. It seems that on Wednesday 4th April 1894 Manchester City F.C. applied for affiliation to the Lancashire F.A. The Lancashire F.A. stated that it would accept City's application providing the club could produce an agreement proving it had a ground to play on. City immediately stated they would be using the Ardwick Hyde Road ground and would reach an agreement with the landlords within a week.

However, John Allison felt strongly that Ardwick should still carry on, despite what was agreed at the October meeting, and that the Brewerymen would continue to use Hyde Road. The club now appeared to be split in two with Allison finding support to play on from the bulk of the Ardwick committee, while Joshua Parlby charmed the season ticket holders to back his bold plan for a new 'Manchester' club.

Parlby's enthusiasm persuaded many of the ordinary supporters that the time was right to lay the name Ardwick to rest, and move forward with a more ambitious title. He wanted a club to match the pride that the whole of Manchester was feeling in 1894. The world's first industrial city was still growing at an incredible rate with many ambitious developments taking place. In fact on New Year's Day 1894 Queen Victoria opened the Manchester Ship Canal - a sign that the city's growth would continue for some time as the canal offered Manchester terrific development possibilities as an inland seaport. There was still great suffering and discomfort in the area - any city developing at the speed Manchester did in the latter half of the nineteenth century would have experienced this - however it was compensated for by the enormous pride the population felt in the city's many achievements. Now Parlby, and his supporters, wanted a football team to represent the whole of Manchester - a team everybody could feel equally proud of.

The Umpire reported that many Mancunians who had not previously supported Ardwick were sending applications to purchase shares in the new club. Parlby appeared to be achieving part of his aim, but now needed to secure the ground and use his skills of persuasion to bring John Allison and the others round to his way of thinking.

Parlby succeeded and on Thursday 12th April at a rather crowded meeting of the Manchester City supporters, it was announced that opposition to the new club had been abandoned, and everyone was now pulling behind the new 'City' club. A couple of days later Ardwick played their last game - a 5-2 defeat away to Walsall Town Swifts - finishing the season thirteenth out of fifteen.

The following Monday, 16th April, Manchester City Football Club Limited became a registered company, with its registered address being given as 31 Halsbury Street, Stockport Road, Manchester. Making reference to the end of Ardwick A.F.C. the club's new motto was 'Even in our own ashes live our wonted fires'. The new club wanted to be an outfit far superior to Ardwick, and with Joshua Parlby driving the club forward no one could doubt that the City men would achieve their aims. Already Chesters had agreed to provide finance to support the new club.

Parlby's first task after the formation of City was to somehow get the club accepted into the Football League. The League officials had known about Ardwick's plight all season and must have viewed the new club suspiciously. Was Manchester City simply Ardwick in disguise?

At the League AGM Parlby spoke convincingly of the ambition, finances and strength of the new club. It seems he used all his persuasive powers to impress the League committee, while gaining City enough votes to tie with Leicester Fosse and so force their way into the Second Division. As Ardwick had finished in the bottom four they would have had to apply for re-election in any case, however it is extremely doubtful Ardwick would have received the twenty votes City did, even with Parlby's eloquence.

Once again, Parlby headed the poll for a place on the League Management Committee. In an article published some fifty years later Joshua Parlby's stirring speech at the meeting was remembered as one of the most impressive of all time and one which older supporters still talkedof. Whether tales of the speech were handed down and embellished by each story-teller is not known, but it is true to say that Parlby's remarkable role in gaining acceptance of a club with no players and little finance was one of, if not the, most important moments in the history of the club. Without Parlby's persuasion, and some would say behind the scenes conniving, the club would probably have never arisen from the ashes of Ardwick.

With City's acceptance into the League came the requirement to find top quality replacements for the players that Ardwick had been forced to sell. In June 1894 the *The Umpire* reported on Joshua Parlby's transfer activity:

> The Manchester City Football Club have this week secured M. Calvey, the centre forward of Blackburn Rovers. He played for them in about half the League Matches and all through the cup ties. He is a fine young fellow, who learned his football in the army. He has weight and youth on his side, and should make a big name for himself.
> R. Jones, the centre half of the Everton Combination team, has also been engaged. He has often taken the place of Holt in League matches. He is a finished player, placing the ball with great judgement, and is a very hard worker.
> H. Smith, the right full back of Blackpool, has recently thrown in his lot with the new "City" club, and comes with a big reputation well earned. From the foregoing it will be seen that Mr. Parlby and his colleagues are doing their utmost to secure a strong team.

The report actually got one of the details wrong. H. E. Smith joined City from Blackburn Rovers not Blackpool - perhaps the reporter was looking forward to his own holiday at Manchester's favourite destination!

Calvey, Jones and Smith all featured in City's first League game, alongside a further seven debutants. The only player in this opening fixture to have played for Ardwick was full back Fred Dyer, proving that this club was not simply Ardwick in disguise. The ground, supporters, and bulk of the committee may have been the same, but the playing squad was entirely different.

Of the new players in this opening fixture away to Bury on 1st September mention must be made of twenty year old Charlie Williams. Williams was a rather unorthodox goalkeeper - the Bruce Grobbelaar of his day - and had joined City from Arsenal, with whom he had featured in over eighty first team games including the club's first ever League fixture (a 2-2 draw with fellow newcomers Newcastle on 2nd September 1893). Williams was to play for City for a total of eight years, winning many admirers with his often eccentric displays.

Others appearing in this first City game included the half backs George Mann and Joe Nash, who had been signed from Blackburn and Nelson respectively. Also, playing his first game for the club was Pat Finnerhan, who had been spotted by City director Lawrence Furniss when he refereed a game involving Finnerhan's club, Northwich Victoria, . The former Northwich player was a tricky inside right who always seemed able to retain the ball until the absolute perfect moment to dispatch it to a team mate on his way to goal. In his first two seasons with City he was ever present in the League.

Despite the huge influx of players - or indeed because of the creation of a new side - City lost their opening fixture 4-2. The club fared a little better in their second game, a 1-1 draw at home to Burton

Alfred Jones, one of the original City directors. Born in Wiltshire in 1850, he moved to Manchester at the age of 20 where he progressed from being a labourer to running a brewery inside ten years. He is pictured below, three years before his death in 1943, with daughter Annie Louisa Potts, grandaughter Emmy Williams, and great grandson Peter Williams. Records of his early shareholding were lost in the City fire of 1920. He probably gave his shares to his son-in-law Robert Potts, who was recorded as a shareholder in the 1920s and '30s. There is no record of these shares being sold and copies of the annual accounts were sent to Robert Potts until the late 1940s.

John Edward Chapman was one of the founding members of Manchester City, and was for eight consecutive years the club's Chairman. He pushed the club forward, alongside the likes of Parlby and Furniss.

Wanderers, but the first taste of success for the new side came on 8th September at Hyde Road when a crowd of around 4,000 saw City defeat Burslem Port Vale 4-1, the goals provided by Calvey (2), Mann, and Finnerhan. A 2-1 away victory the following week against Walsall Town Swifts helped the club move up the table but, unfortunately, this was to be their last victory until the return match with Walsall (who eventually ended the season third from bottom). Jim Sharples notched the first 'Manchester City' league hat trick to help the Blues win that game 6-1 on 6th October.

Within two weeks City made one of their most important signings of all time when the Welsh wizard Billy Meredith was brought to Manchester from Chirk. City had been playing Sandy Rowan out of position on the right wing and some of the players were clearly unhappy with the situation, including one suspects Rowan himself. Pat Finnerhan urged the club to approach his former colleague Meredith. Finnerhan's views led the Blues to seriously consider Meredith whom Lawrence Furniss had spotted in the first place playing alongside Finnerhan for Northwich. Indeed Meredith had actually played at Hyde Road against Ardwick in January 1894.

Something else that forced the club to look to strengthen the side was the departure of four players to Baltimore in the New York Soccer League during October. An American football agent had spent considerable effort illegally persuading members of the City squad that their lives would be much better if they moved away from the grime of Manchester to the land of opportunity. Four players - Wallace, Little, Ferguson, and Calvey - believed the agent and left the Blues for the States, forcing secretary Joshua Parlby to strengthen the side.

According to legend, Parlby and Chairman John Chapman, the City representatives who journeyed to Chirk, North Wales to sign Meredith, were chased around the village, forced to disguise themselves and had to stand Meredith's mining colleagues drinks in the local pub before being allowed to talk to the gifted Welsh international. It is also said that the City men were ducked in the village pond and given a very rough time by the locals. Eventually Meredith signed amateur forms with the club after insisting he be allowed to continue to live and work in Wales. His plan was to work in the mine all week, and then travel to Manchester at weekends. City arranged lodging for him in a house on Clowes Street, close to St. Mark's Church, and provided a £5 signing-on fee.

Meredith's first game for the club was an exciting 5-4 defeat away to Newcastle United on 27th October. Seven days later he changed with his new team mates in the Hyde Road Hotel and then made his home debut in the game that all Mancunians had been looking forward to - the first league meeting between City and Newton Heath. The Heathens had been relegated to Division Two at the end of 1893-4 via a defeat in the Test Matches to Second Division Champions Liverpool. While the new City club were trying to build for the future, Newton Heath were able to adjust to life in the Second rather easily. Prior to the derby they had lost only once in seven games. City on the other hand had played eleven games winning four and drawing one. In spite of City's mixed form they were becoming known for excitement as during the course of those eleven games they had both scored and conceded thirty goals.

Although City were hopeful, it was no real surprise when the Heathens defeated the Blues 5-2. By this time games between City and Newton Heath were clearly derby matches using the term as we know it today. The largest Hyde Road crowd of the season - somewhere in the region of 14,000 - viewed the match as the 'Championship of Cottonopolis' and already both sides had their favourite players. City supporters were thrilled to see the young Billy Meredith make a name for himself by scoring both City's goals in this first league derby. Alongside Meredith, Pat Finnerhan was fast becoming a City favourite, while the Blues supporters also had time for their opponent's goalkeeper William Douglas. Former Ardwickite Douglas was greeted with loud cheers by the Hyde Road regulars - perhaps in the end they regretted giving him such a warm welcome!

The first line-up as Manchester City, 1894-95.

Back (left to right): Mr J.R.Prowse, R.Milarvie, D.Robson, C.Williams, F.Dyer, J.Broad (Trainer).

Middle: J.McBride, W.Bowman, T.Chapman, H.Clifford, G.E.Mann.

Front: T.Little, J.Sharples, W.McReddie, A.Rowan, P.Finnerhan, W.Meredith.

Billy Meredith, with toothpick in his mouth, quickly established himself at Hyde Road

Some time later Meredith wrote about his first derby: "....I got a little cheer to myself as I trotted off and I had the satisfaction of knowing that I had made a good start in my first home match."

By the time of the next derby meeting City were putting together a few decent results, although Boxing Day must have been a particularly bad day for the Blues as Burton Wanderers defeated them 8-0. This was the first game of the season when they failed to score, despite fielding their regular squad. Nevertheless City were making progress.

The game on 5th January at Newton Heath ended in a 4-1 defeat and, although the scoreline makes the game appear one sided, *The Umpire* match report actually says that the Heathens owed their victory to luck and brilliant 'keeping by Douglas. At one point in the first half City were awarded several free kicks but somehow Douglas kept all their goal attempts out. In the second period the home side were forced to play defensively for a large portion of the half. Nevertheless it was the Heathens who achieved the first League double. No matter how City played, or how successful the club was becoming in terms of attracting the best players and bigger support, Newton Heath still appeared to be the more successful of the two.

By March City had moved further up the table and, on 23rd, achieved their best result of the season when they defeated Lincoln City 11-3. This remains City's record scoreline to this day. For the record the City goalscorers were Pat Finnerhan (2), Billy Meredith (2), Sandy Rowan (2), Bob Milarvie and four from William McReddie, a forward who signed from Stoke in October. Incredibly, one of Lincoln's goals was an own goal by a Manchester player.

With City's improved form during the second half of the season the Blues eventually ended the season in a creditable ninth place out of sixteen. Their Manchester rivals finished third, missing promotion by losing their Test Match 3-0 to Stoke. City may not have reached the heights touched by the Heathens but were certainly in a position to build.

1895-6 saw City develop further, with Finnerhan, Meredith, and Rowan in outstanding goal scoring form, and ever present Charlie Williams keeping the debits down. The derby matches with Newton Heath perhaps indicate how the side was progressing. In October at North Road, Sandy Rowan provided City's equaliser after the Blues had gone behind through 'a somewhat lucky goal' as *The Umpire* report stated. Two months later, League leaders City defeated their Manchester rivals for the first time in the League. The biggest derby attendance up to that point - somewhere in the region of 20,000 - watched as Robert Hill, the Blues new signing from Sheffield United, scored a beauty in the fourth minute. The Hyde Road crowd had plenty to cheer about as City seemed to have the initiative. They pushed forward in numbers, with Meredith and Rowan supplying most of the Blues' chances. However, the Heathens were better on the break and it was actually from a City attack that the away side found the equaliser. City half-back Thomas Chapman twice found himself able to send in a shot to test the Heathens' 'keeper Douglas, only to see the ball break kindly to the feet of his opponents' defence. Quickly, on the second such attempt, the Heathens moved the ball up field to Joe Cassidy - who four years later would sign for the Blues - who proceeded to fire in a fine shot to level the score.

After the Newton Heath equaliser, City continued to dominate the match, playing in fine passing style, and it was no surprise when they regained the lead. This is how *The Umpire* newspaper reported the goal and the final stages of the match:

"The crowd cheered Meredith for dodging Cartwright, and working round Erentz, he beat Douglas with a magnificent shot, the uproar being tremendous. Still keen but fair football continued to be the order, and Williams put out three or four times in quick succession. Though a corner was awarded to Newton Heath in the last minute, it proved ineffectual, and City won a good game, in which much better football was shown than is usual in local contests. That the City won on their merits will be the verdict of fair-minded observers. They combined better, and were quicker on the ball than their rivals, their passing being of a very high order. The coffers of both organisations will benefit largely. The takings amounting to £410."

After the match City remained at the top of the Division with 24 points, with Burton Wanderers one point behind in second place; Liverpool after playing an extra two games were third with the same number of points as Burton. Newton Heath were fourth, seven points behind City. The big test would come in City's two games with promotion hopefuls Liverpool. On New Year's Day the Blues travelled to Anfield aiming to bring some meaning to the table. Due to mixed conditions between the Manchester derby and the Liverpool match City hadn't played a game, while both Liverpool and Burton Wanderers had won both the games they played. City had dropped to third place, three points behind both rivals, but with four games in hand over Liverpool and two over Burton. Unfortunately on the day, City were unable to put Liverpool under the kind of pressure they required.

Alf Edge, a forward born in Stoke circa 1865, joined Ardwick on 15th January 1894 from Northwich Victoria and made his debut 12 days later against his former club. The game ended 4-2 to Ardwick at Hyde Road and became Edge's only appearance for the Blues. Earlier in his career he had been with Manchester rivals Newton Heath and co-incidentally had made his debut against Ardwick in the 1891 F.A. Cup match between the two sides. It was a successful game for the forward as he scored one of the Heathens' five goals. In 1892 he also found the net at Hyde Road while playing for a team of internationals against Ardwick in a benefit match for Davie Weir.

THE UMPIRE

"WITHOUT FEAR OR FAVOUR."

SUNDAY, FEBRUARY 9, 1896.

SPORTING FANCIES.

FEW people will regret that Blackburn Rovers succeeded in pulling-off their Lancashire Cup-tie at Hyde-road yesterday. A Lancashire or English Cup Competition without the Rovers loses half its interest for the general public, and the feeling of regret was pretty general when the West Bromwich Albion knocked them out of the National Competition a week ago. For yesterday's match the Rovers' team had undergone considerable alterations and repairs, and evidently with good effect, for they gave the 20,000 people who visited the Manchester City ground an excellent taste of their staying qualities.

But the City were by no means disgraced. For two hours the struggle lasted, and during all that time it cannot be said that either team showed form superior to the other. After half-an-hour's play the Rovers scored, and Hill equalised in the second half. When the regulation time was up the score was still one each, so the clubs decided to go on for the extra half hour. It was during this period that Blackburn scored the winning goal, the ball being scrimmaged through from a corner. The play at times was rough, and one player was ordered off the field, but as this matter will probably occupy the attention of the Lancashire Association the least said under that head the better. The "gate" was a magnificent one, the sum of £804 being realised. Half of this handsome amount will act as a salve to the wounded feelings of the City executive.

Comments on the Lancashire Cup tie with Blackburn. City may have lost, but as can clearly be seen from this article, they were becoming a team capable of challenging football's elite.

The end result was that the Blues went down 3-1 before an Anfield crowd of around 15,000.

In the return fixture on 3rd April, Good Friday, a massive 30,000 Hyde Road crowd saw the two sides fight out a 1-1 draw in what was in effect the Championship decider. City needed to win this game to stand any chance of taking the title as prior to the game Liverpool were four points clear of the Blues, with a far superior goal average. This was the Anfield club's last game of the season whereas City still had fixtures against Leicester and Notts County to complete. In the end the draw was not good enough for the Blues, but it did mean that if they won their last two fixtures they would end the season in second place and feature in the Test Match play offs.

Within the next five days City despatched Leicester (2-1) and Notts County (2-0) and ended the season level with Liverpool on 46 points, while Grimsby and Burton Wanderers were four points behind in third and fourth spot respectively. All City needed to do was play with the same conviction through the Test Matches and they would be in the First Division, alongside the then Lancashire giants Preston, Bolton, Blackburn, Burnley, Bury and Everton.

In 1896 the Test Matches were to be played on a mini-league basis with Liverpool and City each facing the two bottom clubs in Division One - Small Heath (later Birmingham City), and West Bromwich Albion - home and away. The same points system would operate as in the League (2 for a win, 1 for a draw), and the two teams at the top of the table would play the following season in Division One, the others would be in the Second Division.

City's first Test Match fixture was at home to the First Division's bottom club, West Bromwich Albion, on 18th April, and was billed as 'the most important Manchester City fixture so far'. The directors raised admission prices from sixpence to a shilling believing the Manchester public would pay for the chance to help City into the 'top league'. Despite fantastic weather conditions the increased admission kept the attendance down to 8,000 according to *The Umpire* newspaper, and 6,000 according to other sources, with gate receipts of £298. It seems many supporters boycotted the game to demonstrate to the management of the club their anger at the unnecessary price increase. The directors must have been concerned that their plan backfired totally. As can be seen, the gate receipts were considerably smaller than the December derby game even though the Test Match was much more important, and of a higher profile. Not only did the low attendance affect the club's balance sheet, it also affected support inside the ground.

By this point City supporters were famous for creating a carnival-like atmosphere at big games, something City fans repeated ninety years later with the inflatable banana craze. Regularly during the 1890s supporters played bugles and drums when the Blues attacked and would, occasionally, wear fancy dress. For the right reasons match reports of the period often quoted the fans behaviour as much as the incidents on the pitch. This carnival spirit helped lift many a game for the Blues and the noise and fervour all added to the experience of being a Blue. Without this atmosphere, even on the brightest of days, Hyde Road must have provided a very real picture of gloomy, grimy, industrial Manchester; a tightly packed ground, surrounded by terraced streets, factories, and railway viaducts. Typical Manchester, many would say, but then it has always been the people, and in particular the City supporters, who have brightened this part of the industrial city.

Without the great noisy crowd City went a goal down in only the third minute, apparently City's great extrovert 'keeper, Charlie Williams was 'all at sea' as Albion's Perry sent his shot over the heads of City's defence. The ball hit the cross bar and rebounded in. The sizeable Albion support in the crowd made all the noise and, at times, it must have seemed as if the game was being played in the Midlands not Manchester. Nevertheless, City fought back and for much of the game they piled on the pressure. Both Rowan and Finnerhan had shots saved, before Finnerhan scored through a 'capital shot'. In the second half the pace of the game slowed as the heat started to affect the players. Both sides attacked, but neither could find the goal until virtually the last minute when an Albion forward put the ball in the net only for it to be disallowed. The game ended 1-1. Not a bad result, but not good enough for a home side aiming to achieve promotion.

At Anfield on the same day, Liverpool performed to the level City required when they defeated Small Heath 4-0.

Two days later in the return fixture, at Stoney Lane, West Bromwich, City suffered a heavy 6-1 defeat. Even with this result all was not lost as Small Heath held Liverpool to a no score draw. If the Blues could win their two games against Small Heath and other results went their way, City could still take one of the two Division One places.

On April 25th at Hyde Road the Blues faced Small Heath in a game they had to win and they managed it in some style. It was a match the Blues dominated from start to finish and, by the time the final whistle was blown, City were the victors by three goals to nil. At Anfield, Liverpool defeated Albion 2-0. The future looked bright again, especially as the City directors had returned admission prices to their normal Hyde Road level. City still had to win the return fixture with Small Heath and hope that

MANCHESTER CITY v. WEST BROMWICH ALBION.

Probably this—the first test match—can be noted as the most important match Manchester City have so far contested in their brief history, and in opening the final short tournament before their own supporters, the Hyde-roaders were distinctly favoured. Adverse comment was general as to the advance in the prices of admission, which appeared to have materially affected the attendance, for despite the superb character of the weather, only about 8000 persons viewed the game. Great care and attention had evidently been bestowed upon the playing portion, and everything seemed to point to a scientific display. The Mancunians only changed Davies for Gillies, but consequent upon Bassett's absence the visitors' front rank underwent a complete change. Teams:—

MANCHESTER CITY.—Williams, goal; Ditchfield and Robson, backs; Mann, Chapman, and M'Bride, half-backs; Meredith, Finnerhan, Rowan, Gillies, and Morris, forwards.

WEST BROMWICH ALBION.—Reader, goal; Horton and Williams, backs; T Perry, Higgins, and Taggart, half-backs; M'Leod, Hutchinson, Hewitt, W Richards, and J Richards, forwards.

Referee: Mr J West.

The home skipper won the toss and took advantage of the powerful sun. Hewitt started, and twice in as many minutes the visitors got down, but were repulsed on each occasion. After a break-away by the Mancunians, the Albion again got going, and a free kick was given in their favour. The ball was well placed, and Perry meeting the ball lifted it over the heads of several opponents, and striking the crossbar the ball rebounded through, Williams being at sea. Three minutes having only elapsed and the Albion being a goal in front, their supporters were naturally in high glee. On restarting the home forwards forged ahead and Horton had to use his head from a shot by Chapman. However, the visitors were not long in again working their way into the home half. Hutchinson put in a capital shot, and W Richards put the ball through, but was given off-side. The home left were next prominent, but Morris finished with a miserable shot. Higgins was the means of sending play to the opposite end, but Ditchfield, with a capital kick, removed the danger. A free kick in favour of the Blue and Whites put the Albion goal in danger, but after a brisk attack Williams punted away. The visitors playing strongly again invaded home half, McLeod landed wide. A nice piece of work by Rowan enabled the City left to go away, and a corner fell to them, but it was smartly got rid of. The Mancunians, however, were straining every nerve to get on a level footing, and Williams saved a capital shot from Finnerhan. The ball went to Meredith, and Reader had to use his hands to a high shot from the Welsh International. A free kick was given to the local team, but the ball was sent round the post. Some good work by the Albion again caused the home team to act on the defensive, Robson having to give a corner, but the ball dropped behind. Another flag-kick came to the visitors, and then W Richards left the field for a few minutes. The Mancunians pressed and Rowan had a capital chance to equalise, but he missed it. Horton and his partner were called upon, and then Finnerhan with a capital shot succeeded in drawing level. The visitors were getting dangerous, when they were penalised, and from the free kick Manchester should have obtained the lead, but two or three of the forwards dallied, and Perry rushed the ball away. The Albion were pressed again, and had to clear by giving a corner, when after a warm struggle the ball was rushed away. Half-time:—Manchester City, 1 goal; West Bromwich, 1 goal. Rowan restarted, and from a free kick Reader was immediately called upon. Another shot he got rid of by giving a corner, and from this Taggart gave his forwards an opportunity, which they quickly took advantage of. The ball was, however, sent into touch. Then the game was stopped a few seconds owing to Mann and Ditchfield being injured. They did not leave the field, however, and after a brief delay the game was resumed. Some smart work by the City halves was deservedly applauded, but the ball again found a resting-place in touch. Keeping play in the Albion half, both Williams and Reader had to clear. Directly afterwards Meredith had the goal at his mercy, but he made a most miserable attempt to score. A visit was paid to the home end, but Robson lifted the ball away, and then Morris shot, but Reader carried the sphere round the post. From the flag kick, McLeod got away, but the attack was smartly got rid of. Williams cleared another attack by the home forwards, and then Hewitt tested the abilities of Williams, who was somewhat lucky in giving a corner, which, however, proved of little service. A free kick close to the Albion goal threatened danger, but Gillies just missed, the ball striking the outside of the netting. Williams, the West Bromwich back, played a great game, and repeatedly checked the efforts of the Mancunians. The game was anything but exciting, and it was evident that the heat was telling upon the players. Meredith darted away, but Williams stopped him, and then the visitors' left went away. At this point Ditchfield was hurt and had to be assisted from the field. The game had scarcely been restarted when Hutchinson was hurt, causing another stoppage. Ditchfield reappeared, and then Reader was troubled. A lively attack was made on the visitors' goal, and a corner came, but without result. Near the close the visitors' centre put in the net, but the point was disallowed. Final:—

MANCHESTER CITY............	1 GOAL
WEST BROMWICH ALBION......	1 GOAL

Manchester City v. Small Heath.—The opening games in the trial-by-merit competition have so far gone against these antagonists, who made their appearance on the Hyde-road ground, before a much better crowd than patronised the Albion match, this undoubtedly being due to the wiser policy which prevailed in charging popular prices. There would probably be about 8000 persons present when the teams entered the enclosure. Small Heath won the toss, and took advantage of the slight wind, and the sun was also in their favour. Rowan started, and McBride had to stop Hands. Then a free kick was given against the Heathens, but Morris shot wide of the mark. The play was quickly taken towards the City goal, but Ditchfield cleared in fine style. Leak returned the leather, and after some smart passing by Robertson and Jones, the Manchester back put in a feeble shot, and a corner was the only result. This was followed by a smart piece of work by the whole of the Manchester forwards, but Lester just got his hand to the ball in time. Rowan, after a smart cross shot from Meredith, missed a grand chance by shooting wide. Another attack was made on the Heathens' goal, and Davies shot. Lester tried to kick the ball, but missed it. He turned round at the leather a second time and kicked it through his own goal. The restart saw the home forwards again on the attack, but Meredith, with a capital shot, just missed the post. The Heathens had an innings, but the Manchester defenders, playing a strong game, gave them very few opportunities. The ball went away on the left, and Morris, with a capital long shot, sent the ball flying past the Heathens' goal. A break-away by the visitors resulted in Hallam shooting wide. Some more pretty work by the home forwards again put the visitors on the defensive, Meredith striking the post. The play ruled rather in favour of the Mancunians, who were putting in a great amount of work. Oliver just got his toe to another capital centre, but the relief was only of short duration, Miller causing the backs to look alive. However, the Heathens' goal escaped. The play was transferred to the other end, and a long shot by Jones went into touch. The visitors again got going, and Robson, in giving a corner, nearly put the ball through his own goal. The ball was well placed, but Miller worked it away, and then after a smart run Rowan had to send dead. A free kick helped the Heathens to invade the home quarters, but the defence proved strong enough to check the attack, to the delight of their followers. The Mancunians again got the ball down, but Oliver was instrumental in clearing. Farnell stopped another run by the home left pair, and then Robertson shot wide of the posts. The visitors' halves played a capital game and repeatedly checked the home forwards. The Heathens' forwards played a very poor game, and their shooting was very erratic. Oliver cleared again, and Robson being called upon, he responded in very poor style. The whistle then blew for half-time, with Manchester City leading by 1 goal to nil. On the game being resumed, the Manchester men almost got in through a couple of blunders, but the Small Heath goal just escaped. After some mid-field play, the visitors went down in determined fashion, and Robson was beaten, but McBride rushed in and cleared. The Heathens tried hard to draw level, and Williams was lucky in getting rid of a shot from Wheldon. The game was much slower than in the initial period, several of the players appearing to hang out signals of distress. Rowan headed a run into the Heathens' half, but Oliver cleared and Hands twice got away, but on each occasion put in a long shot, which was easily cleared. Miller sent the ball forward, and a warm attack was made on the visitors' goal, a flag-kick having to be given. The Small Heath goal was kept intact, however, and then Farnell tried a long one, from which Ditchfield gave a corner. From this Williams had to clear, and then Morris raced away. Lester went to meet him but missed the ball, and it looked like a second point being added to the home total. However, the home right were set up, and Leak dashed in and cleared. Shortly afterwards this player was injured, and the game was stopped for a few minutes. On resuming, the visitors made tracks for the home goal, but off-side drove them back. This enabled the home right pair to get away, and a corner had to be given. The ball dropped right in front, but Morris made a poor attempt to score. Rowan next sent the ball on the wing, but Morris dropped it just over the bar and Finnerhan, a moment later, steered the ball round the post. Afterwards Oliver had to clear a long shot from Mann, after which, at the opposite end, Robertson shot dead. Hallam shot, and the ball struck the crossbar and dropped into play, Ditchfield clearing from almost under the bar. A corner in favour of Morris was well beaten away by Oliver, and McBride earned the round of applause which followed some clever work. Towards the end Morris, with a [illegible], fast shot increased the City's lead, whilst Davies scored the third from a free kick. Final:—

MANCHESTER CITY............	3 GOALS
SMALL HEATH................	NIL

Match reports from City's disappointing 1-1 draw with West Bromwich Albion in the first Test Match and the 3-0 defeat of Small Heath on 25th April 1896.

Liverpool either drew or beat Albion to be certain of promotion. If both Albion and City were to win their final fixtures then goal average would determine the team second to Liverpool. All the ifs and maybes were written about in the local papers, and discussed in the pubs of Manchester leading up to the game. City's attempts to reach the 'top league' was the talking point in the city. Nothing else mattered.

In the end all the permutations were unimportant as City were completely humiliated by Small Heath at Coventry Road, Birmingham. The Blues went down to an 8-0 thrashing and were left to spend the next season in the Second Division. In the other fixture, Liverpool lost 2-0 to Albion, thus ensuring both those sides met again in the First Division. The Blues were devastated, and it could not have made it any easier knowing that Small Heath would be relegated to the Second Division to face them again. If only City had spent more time planning for their opening fixture against Albion. With normal admission prices, and a City victory, it might have been all so different.

Despite the feeling of failure at the season's end, it had been quite a successful period for the 'Cambridge Blues'. They had achieved their highest position so far, and had made quite a large profit. In the close season they used some of this cash to build dressing rooms, sharing the cost with Chesters' Brewery, who must have been pleased with the profits being generated by the usually large Hyde Road crowds.

City used to hold a regular public practice match between the first team and reserves prior to the start of the season. As this article suggests these games were popular with supporters

The opening of the football season would appear to be anxiously awaited in the country, for reports come to hand of large crowds witnessing the practice games all over the country. There was a splendid attendance the other night to see Manchester City's team put through their paces; and at Anfield on Thursday evening no fewer than 15,000 spectators turned up to see the Liverpool club's first practice game. Equally large crowds witness the Everton men getting themselves into form. With two teams in the League, lovers of football in Liverpool can have the pleasure of seeing a high class game every Saturday during the season, the fixtures having been so arranged as to allow of this. When will Manchester have two teams in the First League?

The following season was perhaps a transitional one. The Blues were still suffering from their 'knock-back' in the Test Matches when the season opened. Only two of their opening ten fixtures ended in victory, and a depressing, drizzly, Hyde Road derby ended goalless. City needed reshaping and secretary Sam Ormerod, who had replaced Josh Parlby some twelve months earlier, decided to bring in some new blood while keeping Pat Finnerhan, George Mann, Billy Meredith, and goalkeeper Charlie Williams as the nucleus of the side.

Full back Dick Ray was signed in May 1896 after playing for Burslem Port Vale, half back Charlie Bannister arrived from Newtown, and forward William Townley arrived from Darwen. Townley was quite a famous player who had scored a hat trick for Blackburn Rovers in the 1890 F.A. Cup Final. Other players to make their debuts for City during the season were William 'Doc' Holmes, a Matlock born centre-half who had been bought from Chesterfield in the close season, and centre forward Billy Gillespie signed from Lincoln City in January 1897. Gillespie was the brother of Newton Heath's Matthew, and was one of City's first target men. He was the kind of player who always seemed to appear in the penalty box ready to latch onto a Meredith cross, and more often than not would find the target. Strong and fearless, in the 1930s he was remembered in the *Manchester Football News* by J.C. Clegg: "The way he would dive in to head the ball at the risk of maiming himself was enough to make the spectators shudder. At times he would literally hurl himself at the ball and not infrequently did he follow it into the net." No doubt he also forced the opposing goalkeeper into the net!

Gillespie seems to have been quite a character. Apart from his skills on the football field he became infamous for off the field activities. The big city life, in particular the brewing industry that seemed so closely linked with everybody at Hyde Road, caused Gillespie one or two problems. According to tales handed down through the generations, Gillespie liked his drink so much that he was frequently dropped for failing to be sober for matches. Other stories say he actually played while he was drunk. When looking at his career as a whole it can be seen that in his later years at City he did miss the occasional game for reasons that it seems hard to determine, however from the moment he signed in January 1897 through to September 1898 he featured in 44 consecutive League games.

Other problems affecting Gillespie appear to be money related. City's great winger Billy Meredith took Gillespie in hand and would regularly take him

The City team line-up prior to the League match with Newcastle on 17th October 1896 at Hyde Road.

Back (left to right): Mr S.Ormerod, Ditchfield, Bannister, Williams, Ray, Broad.

Middle: Meredith, Finnerhan, Lewis, Hill, Robinson.

Front: Mann and McBride.

Billy Gillespie's bustling style worried most opposition goalkeepers. His technique usually forced the 'keeper into the net with the ball!

training or fishing to keep him from the city's distractions. The Welshman would also keep hold of his colleague's money for him, making sure he banked a little each week. Meredith would more or less provide Gillespie with pocket money as and when required to save the centre forward from blowing it all in one go.

In spite of all these potential problems, Billy Gillespie was a tremendous buy for the club. He scored on his debut - a 3-1 defeat at Darwen - and provided a further three goals in the ten matches that followed. Unfortunately, his goals and the signing of the other players were not enough to see City achieve the Test Matches as the Blues ended the season in sixth place, seven points behind second placed Newton Heath. Nevertheless there was hope that the next season could provide the Blues with a real promotion chance. The new players had bedded down and by the end of the 1896-7 season had started to play as a team. Incidentally, Manchester rivals Newton Heath found success eluded them, as it had City, in the Test Matches

During the close season City again strengthened the squad; this time they signed two players by the name William Smith. Fortunately, in those days the chant of 'There's only one William Smith' had not been devised, nevertheless to avoid confusion between the two players a decision was taken to provide both Smiths with nicknames after the towns they arrived from. The right-half had signed from Buxton on 24th April 1897, while the inside-right was given the name Stockport after signing from County. Both 'Buxton' and 'Stockport' Smith made their debuts in City's 3-0 Hyde Road victory over Gainsborough Trinity. Billy Meredith, Billy Gillespie, and Fred Williams provided the goals.

City's only point dropped in their first nine games was in the 1-1 draw with Newton Heath at Clayton. The Blues had been behind for much of the game through a Matt Gillespie goal - perhaps brother Billy should have had a quiet word with him. Then, in the last minute Dick Ray scored 'a clever goal with a high cross'. According to the *The Umpire* report of the game the City faithful cheered loudly and the excitement was intense. It seems this was a typical derby match for tension, atmosphere and excitement. The 20,000 crowd was also the largest Newton Heath home attendance up to this point.

As the season progressed City's form seemed to falter rather too frequently for a side determined to move out of the division. The Blues finished the season in third place - a point above Newton Heath - but missed the Test Match play offs by six points. They had let themselves down rather too often in the final analysis.

In the close season, City and Chesters combined

Billy 'Doc' Holmes joined City in July 1896 and scored the first of his four goals for City during the 4-0 defeat of Leicester Fosse on 13/3/1897.

City 1897-98.

Back (left to right): J.Broad (Trainer), M.J.Chapman (Director), 'Bert' Read, C.Williams, B.Smith, W.Holmes, 'Dick' Ray, Mr S.Ormerod (Secretray).

Middle: W.Meredith, J.Whiteside, W.Gillespie, S.Smith.

Front: R.Moffatt, F.Williams.

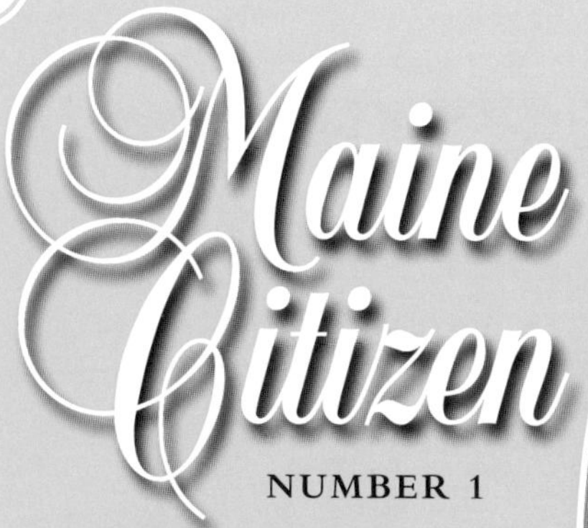

NUMBER 1

JIMMY ROSS

Throughout the history of Manchester City there are good examples of how the arrival of a particular type of experienced player would help the team combine as a unit. Tommy Hutchison and Gerry Gow are perhaps the most famous examples, but the trend itself probably started in 1899 with the arrival of one of the nineteenth century's greatest footballers Jimmy Ross.

Ross had been an outstanding forward with Preston North End throughout the 1880s. In fact, had it not been for the fact that his best goalscoring achievements took place prior to the formation of the Football League, it is possible that even today he would hold Preston's goalscoring record. Between 1884 and 1888 he scored over 250 goals in only 220 games as Preston's team of 'Invincibles' dominated football.

While at Deepdale he also played a leading role in the 26-0 destruction of Ardwick's near neighbours Hyde, scoring 7 (sometimes quoted as 8) in this famous 1887 cup match. He also scored a further 6 during Preston's 18-0 destruction of Reading in an 1894 cup tie. It was no wonder he was given the nickname the "Little Demon" as he terrorised defences.

After eleven years at Preston he moved on to Liverpool where he made a total of 85 appearances, scoring 40 goals. He was also Liverpool's top scorer during the 1895-6 season. The move to Anfield was a controversial one as Ross had been forced to promise his elder brother Nick, on his deathbed, that he would never leave Deepdale and, when the time came, the Liverpool management insisted that he sign after they had made a £75 down payment. Ross, possibly feeling unable to break the agreement, went on to become one of Liverpool's greatest players of the period.

After moving to Burnley in 1897, he joined City in February 1899 and immediately used his vast experience to ensure the Blues won promotion from the Second Division. He replaced "Stockport" Smith in attack and in only 9 appearances scored 7 goals. Not one of those final 9 games ended in defeat as Ross and Meredith combined perfectly.

Meredith always maintained that he was taught a great deal about the game by Ross and admitted that his experienced colleague was something of a hero to the young Welshman. During the First Division seasons that followed, many journalists presented a view that Meredith only performed well when Ross himself was on form. This wasn't entirely true, but it is a fact that Meredith gained more from Ross at this time than any other player.

During 1901-02 Ross only managed a handful of games and passed away during 1902 after playing in every season of the Football League, mostly in the top division. His life in football had seen many achievements although there was one honour he clearly deserved but never attained - an international cap. He was born in Glasgow and would undoubtedly have been a regular for Scotland had he played north of the border. Unfortunately, at this time, Scotland would only select players actually based with Scottish clubs. Ross had settled in Lancashire and clearly enjoyed his pivotal role in English football. Nevertheless he still deserved international recognition.

Ross arrived at City as an experienced, highly successful player. His knowledge and guidance proved vital in helping the Blues become the first team to gain automatic promotion. His career at Hyde Road was fairly brief, but his impact paved the way for Cup glory in 1904. Meredith was always grateful to the wise Scotsman. Modern day Mancunians should also recognise his contribution.

ROSS' PLAYING RECORD

	LEAGUE		FA CUP		TOTAL	
	App	Gls	App	Gls	App	Gls
1898-99	9	7	0	0	9	7
1899-1900	26	10	1	1	27	11
1900-01	25	3	1	0	26	3
1901-02	7	1	1*	0	8	1
TOTAL	67	21	3	1	70	22

* = Abandoned

Gillespie opens the scoring for Manchester City

1897-98 was particularly good for Billy Gillespie who ended the season as top scorer with 18 goals from 30 games. He was also one of three 'everpresents'.

to form a 'Grand Stand Syndicate' to raise funds to erect a new covered stand. Chesters took 250 £1 shares and advanced more money at a low rate of interest. They also negotiated with the Railway Company to keep the ground rental at the same level for the following five years. Together the Blues and the brewery tried to raise £1,500 for a stand from the Fulham Pageant, transport it to Manchester, and re-erect it on the 'sixpence' side at Hyde Road. Hyde Road was now a ground fit for top class football. It had attracted a few large crowds - regularly achieving 20,000 for derby matches, and the exceedingly large 30,000 for the Good Friday 1896 meeting with Liverpool - and provided decent accommodation. However, it was still not good enough for the large City crowds, even though it had played host to a representative game when, on 6th November 1897, the Football League defeated the Irish League 8-1. The Football League side that day included two City players - goalkeeper Charlie Williams, and half-back William 'Doc' Holmes.

The 1898-9 season was to be the first with automatic promotion and relegation. The Test Matches were discontinued after a suspiciously convenient no score draw allowed both Burnley and Stoke to play in the First Division. City were keen to grasp this opportunity to move out of the Second Division once and for all.

They started the season in style defeating Grimsby 7-2 with hat tricks from Meredith and Gillespie. In fact goal scoring was something City seemed particularly good at as only two games ended without the Blues scoring, while they hit three or more in sixteen League matches. The highlight of the season must have been the 10-0 thrashing of Darwen at Hyde Road. Meredith scored his third hat trick of the season that day but even he was outshone by Fred Williams who scored five.

The Athletic News, taking a swipe at the so called aristocratic teams like Aston Villa and Stoke, described City's win: "After such a victorious issue you would expect to hear of clock-work movements from wing to wing and all the rest of the Aston-cum-Stokey-Villa class jargon. Such was far from being the case. Gillespie's, Dougal's and Meredith's goals were superb individual efforts - 'aid' in each of which would have been a misfortune."

THE OFFICIAL PROGRAMME

The ONLY OFFICIAL ORGAN OF Manchester City, Newton Heath, Broughton Rangers, & Salford Clubs

No. 2. SATURDAY, SEPTEMBER 10th. ONE PENNY.

ENTERED AT STATIONERS HALL.

TO FOOTBALL PATRONS!

The Official Football Programme is the ONLY list allowed to be sold on the grounds of the MANCHESTER CITY, NEWTON HEATH, SALFORD and BROUGHTON RANGERS,

The "PROGRAMME" is also sold in the approaches to the Grounds, and can be had from all Newsagents.

Be sure and ask for the Official Programme.

Amusements.

COMEDY THEATRE—To-Night. THE PRIVATE SECRETARY. Popular prices: 2s. 6d., 1s., 9d., and 6d. Monday, Sept. 12th, The Moody-Manners Opera Company.

THEATRE ROYAL. TO-NIGHT at 7-30. TWO LITTLE VAGABONDS.

PRINCE'S THEATRE. TO-NIGHT at 7-30. A GREEK SLAVE, by Mr. GEO. EDWARDS' CO.

FREE TRADE HALL. 2-30 and 7-30. HAMILTON'S HISPANO-AMERICAN WAR EXCURSIONS and GREAT VARIETY TROUPE.

ZOOLOGICAL GARDENS, BELLE VUE. Open every day from 10 a.m. The Grand Spectacle of the STORMING OF DARGAI. Admission: Firework Days until 4 p.m., 6d. each; after 4 p.m. 1s. each.

NEW BRIGHTON TOWER,
(The Highest Structure in England)
GRAND THEATRE OF VARIETIES.
Admission Free. Seats Extra. Four Permanent Bands. 30 Acres of Gardens. Old English Fair. Ascents to Top of Tower, 6d.
ILLUMINATIONS. Eleven Thousand Electric Lamps.
MAGNIFICENT BALL ROOM.
Ferry Steamers and Mersey Tunnel Railway provide quick and constant service from Liverpool. Entrance to Gardens, 6d.

Bedford Park Athletic Grounds
ROCK FERRY,
Adjoining L. & N. W., G. W., and Mersey Tunnel Joint Station.
These Grounds are available for all classes of
SPORTS—CYCLING, RUNNING, COURSING, PIGEON SHOOTING, TRAINING, &c.
Also the grounds of the
ROCK FERRY FOOTBALL CLUB.
For terms apply—
Mr. LUKE LEES, Proprietor,
Bedford Hotel, Rock Ferry.

THE CINDERELLA FUND CONTINUES TO-DAY, GIVE WHAT YOU CAN. 3

H. HIBBARD, Athletic Outfitter
Purveyor to the Everton & Liverpool Football Clubs.
THE BOSS BALL Used by the Everton and Liverpool league teams acknowled'd to keep its shape and wear the longest of any ball made.
Shirts any Colour in Stock, Knickers, Boots, Shinguards, &c.
H. HIBBARD, Richmond Street, LIVERPOOL.

"PALMER TYRES."

BROUGHTON RANGERS v. OLDHAM.

BROUGHTON RANGERS.

Back.
Hacking 1

Three-Quarters.
Jackson 2, Chapman 3, Barratt 4, G. Lewis 5

Half-Backs.
Messenger 6, Nelson 7

Forwards.
Deakin 8, Steel 9, Blacklock 10, Mumberson 11
Lazonby 12, Thompson 13, Lamb 14, Stickney 15

Forwards.
Broome 16, J. Davies 17, Merrill 18, J. Lees 19
Edwards 20, Moffatt 21, Fraser 22, Bonsor 23

Half-Backs.
Lawton 24, A. Lees 25

Three-Quarters.
Williams 26, S. Lees 27, T. Davies 28, Martin 29

Back.
Thomas 30

Kick-off 3-0. OLDHAM.

NOTE.—In case of any Final Alteration in the Teams as given above, a notice will be sent round the Enclosure giving the name of the substituted player, and the number of the position in which he will play.

The shareholders have been lucky in obtaining the services of those two old friends of the Club, Messrs. W. Crompton and Harry Smith, and it will be no fault of the gentlemen mentioned if there is not a big improvement before long. Their abilities are well-known, and they should do the Club a lot of good.

* * *

NEWTON RESERVE v. LEYLAND.

The following players will represent Newton Reserve in their match at Leyland, to-day:—Caine, Whitney, J.Turner, Simpson, Brooks, R. Turner, Ratcliffe, Arnold, Lee, Harrison and Roberts.

* * *

On returning from the match, at Newton Heath, last Saturday, our representative called at the "Holt Town Tavern," in Mitchell Street, to have a chat with mine host (Alec. Peak), and was pleased to sample some of his fine Ales and Cigars, which proved to be of excellent quality. Patrons are also treated to a first-rate concert on Monday, Friday and Saturday nights.

Manchester City Fixtures.

Date.	Club.	For	Agt	Date.	Club.	For	Agt
Sept. 1–				Jan. 2–h	Glossop North End		
" 3–h	Grimsby Town	7	2	" 7–h	Newton Heath		
" 10–a	Newton Heath	0	3	" 14–a	New Brighton		
" 17–h	New Brighton	1	1	" 21–h	Lincoln City		
" 24–a	Lincoln City	1	3	" 28–	E.C. 1st r'nd proper.		
Oct. 1–h	Woolwich	3	1	Feb. 4–h	Luton Town		
" 8–a	Luton Town	3	0	" 11–a	Leicester (L.C.)		
" 15–h	Leicestor Fosse	3	1	" 14.–	Shrove Tuesday		
" 22–a	Darwen	2	0	" 18–h	Darwen		
" 29–a		2	1	" 25–a	Gainsborough		
Nov. 5–a	Barnsley	1	1	Mar. 4–h	Barnsley (L.C.)		
" 12–a	Glossop North End	2	1	" 11–	Manchester Cup		
" 19–h	Walsall	2	0	" 18–a	Walsall		
" 26–a	Burton Swifts	3	3	" 25–h	Burton Swifts		
Dec. 3–h	Burslem Port Vale	3	1	" 31–h	Gainsborough		
" 10–	Loughborough	3	1	April 1–a	Burslem Port Vale		
" 17–h	Loughborough	5	0	" 3–a	Woolwich		
" 19–h	Fleetwood Rangers	6	1	" 8–h	Small Heath		
" 24–a	Blackpool	4	2	" 15–			
" 26–h	Newton Heath	4	0	" 22–h	Blackpool		
" 27–a	Small Heath	1	4	" 29–			
" 31–a	Grimsby Town						

G. SUMNER, (LATE CLUBBIE)
Running Pump Maker,
490 OLDHAM ROAD, MANCHESTER.

Manchester City Notes.

The Xmas Eve and Boxing Day of 1898, will be green spots in the memory of the thousands who interest themselves in the well-being of the City Club, because the Xmastide was in all respects a merry one in the most respectable interpretation of the word. It brought four points and 8 goals to 2, and considerable joy, which would have carried it almost to the point of frenzy if success had attended the efforts at Small Heath, on Tuesday. But let that pass. The Blackpool match on Saturday was a foregone conclusion, and it may be dismissed with the observation that the City players did not find so very much difficulty in finishing on the right side, their shooting being as deadly as it has so frequently been recently.

Monday was the great day, and the "Citizens" can congratulate themselves upon a magnificent display, and a thoroughly merited victory. Although it is to the interests of both Clubs that they should do as much as possible to assist each other to the first division, sentiment was not permitted to intervene, as the City directorate reccgnised that the Club had to make their bow to opponents on foreign ground, which has already been trodden by the "Heathens," therefore, it was not advisable to lose the chance of any points. It was borne in mind that Newton Heath had been to Woolwich, Leicester, New Brighton, and Small Heath, places which were strange to City up to that point of the season.

It is not putting a too formidable construction upon the facts to say that Newton Heath were almost completely overwhelmed, and while there was much to praise with the combination, fineness of attack, and dash of the City, it must be conceded that their opponents helped them more than a little. "Di" Jones practice of going close to his half-backs came off for once in a way, but that was through the other half-backs not tumbling to his presence. Meredith played a grand game up to the time he was hurt, but it says a great deal for the other forwards, that two goals were scored after he was rendered nearly helpless. Every man did himself credit, and the play of the City was worthy of such a great occasion. Four to none was a great blow to the "Heathens," but they courted it, and have themselves greatly to blame for it.

The Cinderella Fund continues to-day, look out for the boxes.

This is the first official programme for a Manchester derby. At that time the programme was a joint publication, with equal space allotted to each club. The City Notes on page 3 make interesting reading.

1898-99 DIVISION TWO CHAMPIONSHIP DETAILS

RESULTS	HOME	AWAY
Grimsby Town	W 7-2	W 2-1
Newton Heath	W 4-0	L 0-3
New Brighton	D 1-1	W 1-0
Lincoln City	W 3-1	L 1-3
Woolwich Arsenal	W 3-1	W 1-0
Luton Town	W 2-0	W 3-0
Leicester Fosse	W 3-1	D 1-1
Darwen	W 10-0	W 2-0
Barnsley	W 5-0	D 1-1
Glossop North End	L 0-2	W 2-1
Walsall	W 2-0	D 1-1
Burton Swifts	W 6-0	D 3-3
Burslem Port Vale	W 3-1	D 1-1
Loughborough Town	W 5-0	W 3-1
Blackpool	W 4-1	W 4-2
Small Heath	W 2-0	L 1-4
Gainsborough Trinity	W 4-0	L 1-3

REGULAR SIDE:
Williams (C)
Ray
Jones
Moffatt
Smith (Buxton)
Holmes
Meredith
Smith (Stockport)
Gillespie
Williams (F)
Dougal

MANAGER:
Sam Ormerod

LARGEST VICTORY: 10-0 v Darwen (H) 18/2/99

HEAVIEST DEFEAT: 1-4 v Small Heath (A) 27/12/98

AVERAGE HOME ATTENDANCE: c.9,200

HIGHEST HOME ATTENDANCE: c.20,000 v Newton Heath 26/12/98, v Small Heath 8/4/99

HIGHEST AWAY ATTENDANCE: c.15,000 v Newton Heath 10/9/98

LEAGUE APPEARANCES: 34 Moffatt, Smith (Buxton), 33 Williams (C), Meredith, 31 Dougal, 30 Gillespie, 27 Jones, 25 Smith (Stockport), Williams (F), 24 Ray, Holmes, 20 Read, 11 Cowie, 9 Ross, 6 Munn, 4 Whitehead, 3 Bowman, 1 Chappell

LEAGUE GOALS: 29 Meredith, 17 Gillespie, 11 Williams (F), 8 Smith (Stockport), 7 Dougal, Ross, 4 Moffatt, 3 Cowie, 2 Whitehead, 1 Read, Ray, Jones, Smith (Buxton)

Eighteen-year-old outside left Fred Threlfall signed from Preston on 23rd June 1898 but didn't make it into City's first team until the 1899-1900 season. He weighed 11st and his height was 5'10".

The newspaper went on to describe individual players with the most interesting comment proving that City's Gillespie was quite a mean player: "His tendency to push the goalkeeper through with the ball was in evidence throughout the game and often he missed the mark and had to find his way out of the network." There's no doubt that Gillespie intimidated more opponents than anyone else on the City side. Although, in the latter half of the twentieth century he would be severely dealt with, during the 1890s he was encouraged to play like this. At least it added grit, determination and excitement.

Gillespie's barging technique had also been seen in another significant game during the season - the Hyde Road derby. In the Boxing Day game the Heathens 'keeper Frank Barrett clearly had the ball in his hands when Gillespie provided his usual party piece by pushing both Barrett and the ball into the net for City's third goal. The Blues eventually defeated the Heathens 4-0 and even had a George Dougal effort disallowed for off side.

City's fine form continued and about a month before the end of the season they were certainties for the Second Division title. In their last game of the campaign they defeated Blackpool 4-1. Gillespie provided the first goal - 'a terrific shot' according to the *The Umpire* - but was later penalised for charging the Blackpool 'keeper who was trying to make a save from Buxton Smith. Perhaps Gillespie was now a

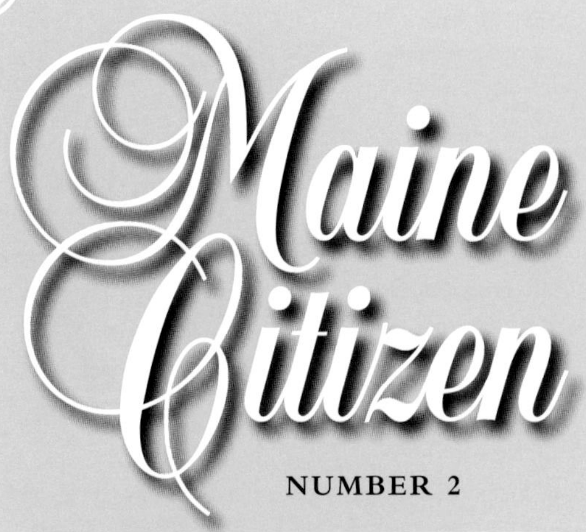

NUMBER 2

BILLY MEREDITH

Billy Meredith is without doubt the greatest player ever to have played for both Manchester clubs. His Manchester playing career lasted from 1894 until 1924 and saw him become the most talked about famous footballer of his generation. He is certainly the most renowned and written about of all pre-World War II Manchester based players, and without doubt helped shape Manchester's knowledge and love of the game. There is little new that can be said about the player.

He joined City during the club's inaugural season after the collapse of Ardwick, and immediately impressed by netting twice in the first ever Manchester League derby. This was his opening home game for City, and had followed his debut a week earlier at Newcastle. Co-incidentally, thirty years later his career ended in an F.A. Cup semi-final against the Geordies.

Meredith's achievements are many and cannot possibly be given justice here, but put simply he was a regular Welsh international, Cup Final goal scorer and captain, twice F.A. Cup winner, twice League Championship medal winner, film and theatre star, one of the creators of the Players' Union, and co-founder of the city's 'third team' Manchester Central.

Playing at Belle Vue, Manchester Central was a side created during the late 1920s to fill the void left by City's move to Maine Road. Meredith and his colleagues aimed to turn the club into a League side first, then hoped it could challenge United to become the area's second side. Ultimately, they dreamed, Central would match the achievements and pulling power of City. The experiment failed as the club were unable to gain admittance into the League, but it reinforces that Meredith's leading role in Manchester football was not simply on the pitch.

His exploits on film and in the theatre helped maintain his high profile, while regular newspaper articles made him the first footballing star. Not until the 1950s, possibly the 60s, would a player receive quite so much media attention.

At Hyde Road he enjoyed captaining a side managed by the wise Tom Maley, and the two of them must be held chiefly responsible for bringing the F.A. Cup to Manchester for the first time in 1904. That success should have been the start of many, especially as the Blues narrowly missed out on the Championship two years running. Sadly, the possibility of further glory collapsed when City were investigated by the F.A. - Meredith again playing a central role as he was accused of trying to bribe Aston Villa's Alec Leake. Meredith claimed he was innocent at first and started to brief the media about all kinds of illegal activity by club officials. He believed he was being made the scapegoat, and for a while his actions and determination to blame the club's management brought much shame on the Blues.

The supporters never held this against him, even when the F.A. punishments almost killed the club they loved, and during the First World War he returned to Hyde Road to help train the players and to guest in 114 matches.

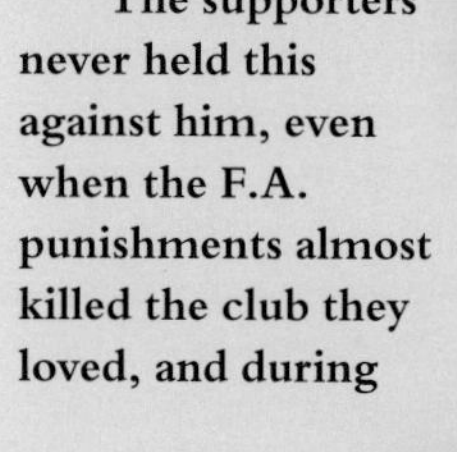

After the war a dispute with United led to Meredith returning on a permanent basis to City. In 1923 the club moved to Maine Road and on 1st March of the following year he played his first senior match at the new stadium. A week later a then record crowd of 76,166 came mainly to see Meredith as City drew 0-0 with Cardiff in the Cup. The news that he was still playing in the first team during his fiftieth year astounded many, but it merely demonstrated Meredith's love of the game.

Supporters who saw him play remain convinced he was one of the best players of all time. They also firmly believe that even at the age of 49 he was determined to put in a good performance. Comparisons with Stanley Matthews are perhaps a little unfair and notoriously difficult to justify, but fans who saw both perform claim the 49 year old Meredith actually played, whereas the 50 year old Matthews merely 'appeared'. There is a subtle difference.

In April 1958 Meredith died at the age of 83 and was buried at Southern Cemetery. 1950s City player and Welshman Roy Clarke attended the funeral. Proving that interest in the player has not waned, in 1997 a television documentary about his life was broadcast on BBC 2 Wales. It deserved a viewing in Manchester.

Meredith helped create both City and United's trophy winning heritage, and as such deserves to be recognised as one of Manchester's Maine Citizens.

MEREDITH'S PLAYING RECORD

	LEAGUE		FA CUP		TEST M		TOTAL	
	App	Gls	App	Gls	App	Gls	App	Gls
1894-95	18	12	0	0	-	-	18	12
1895-1896	29	12	0	0	4	1	33	13
1896-97	27	10	1	0	-	-	28	10
1897-98	30	12	2	0	-	-	32	12
1898-99	33	29	1	1	-	-	34	30
1899-1900	33	14	2	0	-	-	35	14
1900-01	34	7	1	0	-	-	35	7
1901-02	33	8	4	0	-	-	37	8
1902-03	34	22	1	0	-	-	35	22
1903-04	34	11	6	1	-	-	40	12
1904-05	33	8	2	1	-	-	35	9
1921-22	25	0	0	0	-	-	25	0
1922-23	1	0	0	0	-	-	1	0
1923-24	2	0	4	1	-	-	6	1
TOTAL	366	145	24	4	4	1	394	151

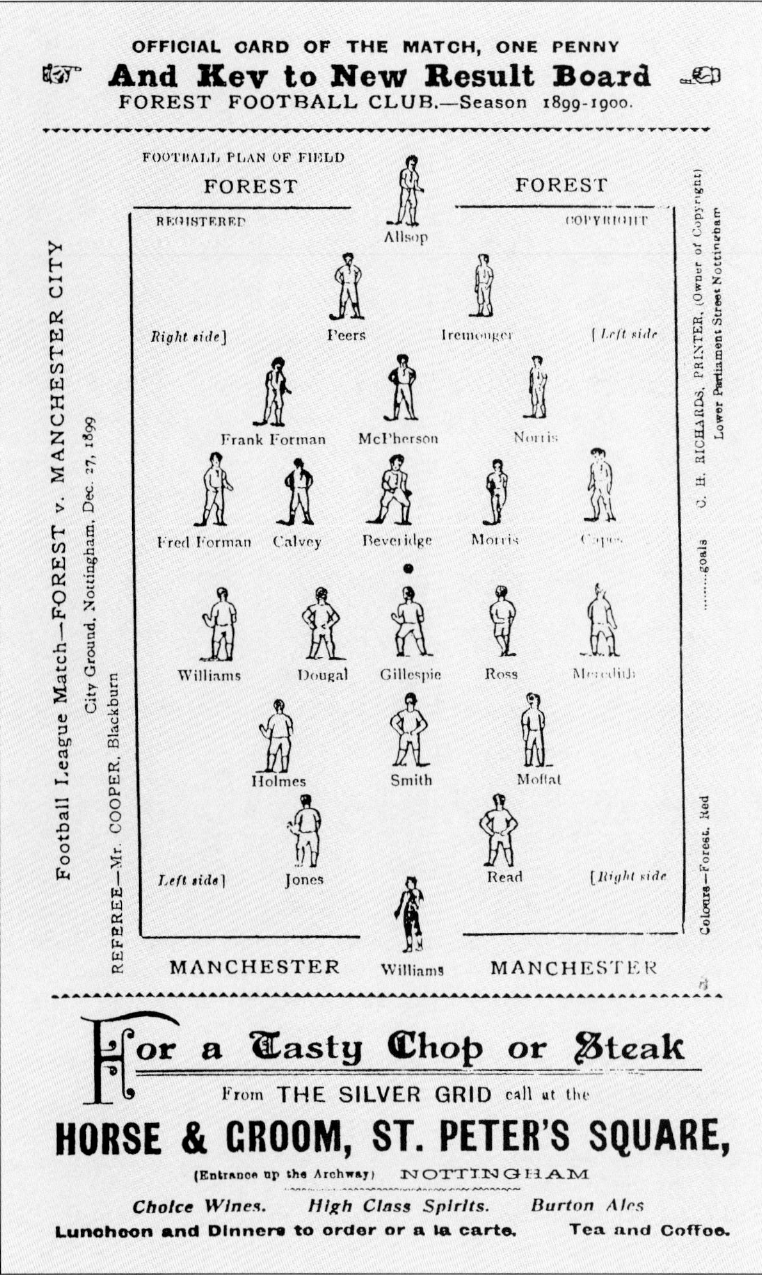

OFFICIAL CARD OF THE MATCH, ONE PENNY

And Key to New Result Board

FOREST FOOTBALL CLUB.—Season 1899-1900.

Football League Match—FOREST v. MANCHESTER CITY

City Ground, Nottingham, Dec. 27, 1899

REFEREE—Mr. COOPER, Blackburn

FOOTBALL PLAN OF FIELD

FOREST FOREST

REGISTERED COPYRIGHT

Allsop

Right side] Peers Iremonger [Left side

Frank Forman McPherson Norris

Fred Forman Calvey Beveridge Morris Capes

Williams Dougal Gillespie Ross Meredith

Holmes Smith Moffat

Left side] Jones Read [Right side

Williams

MANCHESTER MANCHESTER

.......goals

Colours—Forest, Red

C. H. RICHARDS, PRINTER, (Owner of Copyright) Lower Parliament Street Nottingham

The official Nottingham Forest programme for their 2-0 victory over City on 27th December 1899. This was City's last away game of the 19th Century.

marked man, or perhaps he'd used the technique once too often. New recruit Jimmy Ross provided the second goal with a 'curling shot', while City's third came from Meredith - although the referee had to consult both linesmen before allowing this one to stand. Blackpool soon pulled one back, but late in the game Meredith scored his second with a 'high shot'. And so the Blues ended the season as Champions, six points above their nearest rivals Glossop (who had only been elected to the League that season). To celebrate their promotion and provide the players with financial reward, both sides played each other home and away. The proceeds from these games were given to the players.

City's high scoring had been the decisive factor; their 92 goals being far superior to the tally for any other club in either division that season. The Welsh winger Billy Meredith - by this point football's first true 'star' - provided 29 goals, the bustling Billy Gillespie 17, and Fred Williams 11.

Jimmy Ross, who had played in only nine games had scored seven. Ross, who signed from Burnley for a reported £50, was one of the League's earliest and most influential players. He had been a member of the famous Preston North End 'Invincibles', and had scored an incredible seven goals when Preston beat Hyde 26-0 in the record breaking F.A. Cup tie of 15th October 1887 - a game in which the referee is reputed to have lost his watch and allowed play to last two hours. In addition, he was the Football League's top scorer in 1890 (24 goals), and was quite a character.

Years later Billy Meredith, looking back on his City days, remembered Ross with great affection: "I must confess that Ross will always be my favourite hero. He was good at everything he put his hand to and what he didn't know about football wasn't worth knowing. At billiards and card games he was an expert. Though he must have been thirty-four at least when he joined us, he was able to win seventy yard handicaps with ease and did so. He could talk like a lawyer and on and off the pitch his comic sayings had us in stitches." It seems the introduction of the experienced Ross at a crucial stage in the season was what City needed to guarantee success.

Although everything was bright on the pitch, there were still a few concerns off it. There was a belief that Hyde Road was not good enough for First Division football. No matter what the club did to improve the facilities, it would always be a cramped ground. Access was restricted to two sides, and the shape of the enclosure made the erection of huge stands almost impossible. Because of potential problems with the large crowds City expected in the First Division, the club management looked at what was available further down Hyde Road at Belle Vue.

Belle Vue was a huge pleasure gardens and entertainment centre. Like City, it offered Mancunians a release from the daily grind - and was hugely popular. Alongside the pleasure gardens was the Belle Vue Athletics track which had played host to the floodlit friendly between Ardwick and Newton Heath in 1889. This ground offered potential. Already it was a popular sporting venue, was relatively close to City's Hyde Road ground, and was only yards away from the St. Mark's Church Hall where City were founded. It had perfect access, was capable of holding between forty and fifty thousand and seemed to offer everything that Hyde Road did not. However, for some unknown reason it was decided to stay at Hyde Road and erect the Fulham Pageant stand. Perhaps Chesters were keen to keep their investment in Ardwick. The Belle Vue venue may not have offered the brewery as many money making opportunities, or maybe everyone associated with the club simply felt Hyde Road was home, and that it should be given at least one more season. After all, both the club and brewery knew the ground rental could not increase for another four years thanks to the agreement struck the previous year, and that Hyde Road had become an established football ground.

Whatever the reason, City decided to refurbish Hyde Road ready for top flight soccer. They wanted to be a real credit to Manchester and, although Newton Heath had featured in the First Division in 1892 to 1894, City were proud of the fact they were the first of the two Manchester sides to reach Division One on merit. All they needed to do now was prove how a successful Manchester side could benefit football.

Chapter Three

MEREDITH THE FIRST STAR

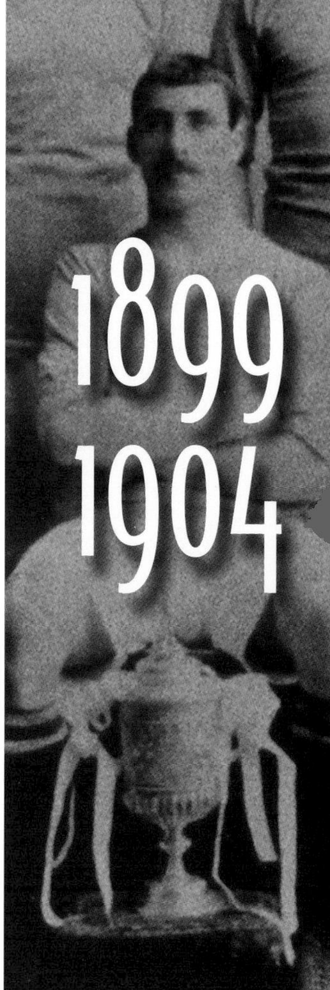

WITH City's promotion came major interest in Manchester's ability to sustain a top flight club. Newton Heath had spent two seasons in the First Division but had never actually achieved a great deal, while City had not yet featured in this class of football. Even in the club's developing years, prior to joining the League, the Blues' friendlies with the major sides of the day - Preston, Celtic, Blackburn etc., almost always ended with City on the losing side. Occasional victories, such as the 1892 Manchester Cup success against Bolton, brought th Blues to the public's notice but these games were simply one-offs. City's arrival in the First Division would test the club's strengths.

In addition to the strength of the playing side, Hyde Road itself would be tested. Following the decision to remain at the ground, improvements had been made. The 1887 stand, paid for by Chesters, had been replaced by the new 75 yard long stand which, according to *The Umpire* newspaper, could accommodate 4,000 spectators under cover and would help the ground provide a decent view for over 28,000. Over the course of the next year or so other improvements were added, including better access to the ground via new turnstiles installed on Bennett Street and behind the Hyde Road Hotel. The dressing rooms now had Russian and Turkish plunge baths and the secretary, Sam Ormerod, even had his own office and telephone. The club was moving in the right direction.

The opening fixture in the First Division was away to Blackburn Rovers. Blackburn had finished the previous season in sixth place, and had only lost two games at home all season. The game was not going to be an easy one, but then no match in the First could be classed as easy for the Blues.

A crowd of around 10,000, many travelling from Manchester, saw the Blues lose an exciting match by the odd goal in seven. City's scorers that day were Billy Meredith, Jimmy Ross, and Fred Williams. The Blues may not have won the game but their performance satisfied all Mancunians in the crowd. They had put on a fine show and could only have been looking forward to their next game - the first Division One match at Hyde Road. City's opponents on 9th September 1899 for this milestone of a match were the previous season's F.A. Cup finalists Derby County, captained by legendary England international goalscorer Steve Bloomer.

A 22,000 attendance provided a good atmosphere for the game. When the players entered the field the noise from the City supporters was described as being 'electrifying', and certainly did a great deal to lift the players on what could have been a tense occasion.

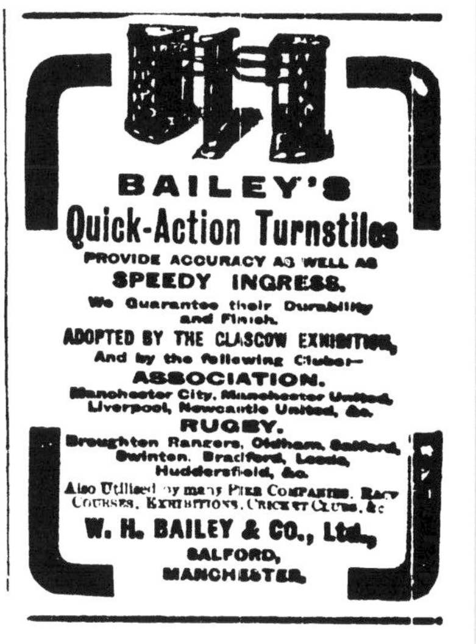

Adverts for turnstiles in the Athletic News, listing City as customers.

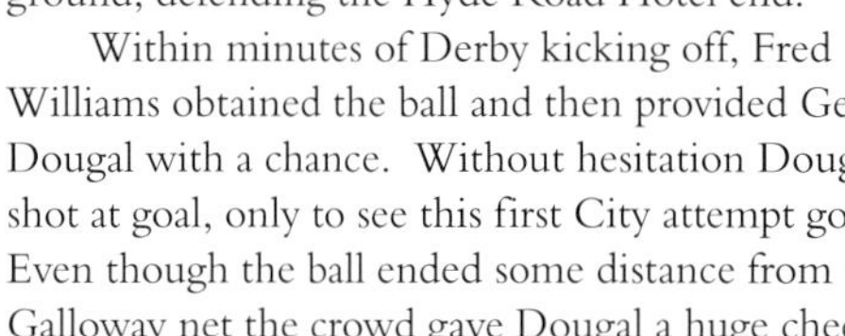

City captain Billy Meredith won the toss and elected to play towards the Galloway Works end of the ground, defending the Hyde Road Hotel end.

Within minutes of Derby kicking off, Fred Williams obtained the ball and then provided George Dougal with a chance. Without hesitation Dougal shot at goal, only to see this first City attempt go wide. Even though the ball ended some distance from the Galloway net the crowd gave Dougal a huge cheer and a good round of applause.

According to reports, City dominated play with the visitor's defence having "a particularly warm time". Billy Gillespie forced Derby's Fryer to make a great save from the City forward's header. Perhaps luckily for Fryer, Gillespie was not close enough to force both the ball and the player over the line! It seems that City really did pile on the pressure for much of the first half, although Derby did make the occasional surge forward. Interestingly, goal expert Steve Bloomer was unable to get so much as a look in as the Blues defence managed to curtail any advance he tried to make.

The oldest known action photo from a match at Hyde Road. Di Jones is the City player closest to the camera, slightly forward of the goal. The terracing in the background is City's Popular stand. Taken during the 1900-01 season.

Then, after a short spell of pressure from Derby the first goal came in the twenty-fifth minute.

Appropriately it was the home side who took the lead with *The Umpire* newspaper describing what was a controversial goal as follows: "Play, however, was again in favour of the City men before very long, and F. Williams and Dougal bustling Methven, the former shot in goal. Fryer saved, but the home forwards coming in a body pushed the ball through. There was apparently a doubt in the mind of the referee as to the legitimacy of the point for, on Derby protesting, he had to consult both linesmen before giving his decision in favour of the home side; and on his pointing to the centre the crowd sent a mighty roar."

The goal was credited to, who else but Billy Gillespie. The old trick had worked again.

A few minutes later veteran Jimmy Ross scored City's second. *The Athletic News*, talking about City's right wing players, stressed the importance of Jimmy Ross and his partner the great Billy Meredith: "For real brilliance the right wing took the biscuit....In fact, there are few, if any, better men at outside right (Meredith). His partner, the veteran Ross, of whom it is predicted every season that he has had his day, is in reality taking a second lease of footballing life, despite the paucity of head-covering, and as a wing the two will cause some trouble".

The Blues were still leading 2-0 when the second half commenced. Almost immediately the ageless Ross and dribbling wizard Meredith combined to put Derby under more pressure, but an ankle injury to Ross limited City's chances for a short while. When the former Preston man returned a few minutes later, the Blues resumed the attack.

It wasn't long before City increased their lead, this time through Meredith, although there is some doubt over whether the 26 year old Meredith actually scored or merely claimed the goal. It seems that Billy Gillespie may have had the final decisive touch but Meredith bagged it. In the *Topical Times* some twenty years later Meredith provided his view of why the goal was actually his: "From the corner flag I kicked at goal and the ball curled under the bar but, striking the upright, bounced back. To save disputes Gillespie promptly headed it into the net but it was agreed that I had scored the goal all right, and at that time I was supposed to have taken out a patent for goals of this kind."

According to *The Umpire* match report the goal came not from a corner, but via a magnificent run by Meredith, and that Gillespie provided the finishing touch as Derby's Fryer was about to save Meredith's shot. Nevertheless, the newspaper did stress Meredith's involvement claiming: "credit must be awarded to the City captain for the achievement."

A short while later Meredith increased City's lead to four by a rather magnificent solo effort. The following is Meredith's own view of the goal which, unlike his first effort, seems to match almost word for word *The Umpire* description: "A free-kick had been given against us and I was quite near my own goal when I fastened on to the ball. Carrying it at my toes I galloped down the field, the whole of the Derby team hot upon my heels. Keeping the lead the whole length of the field, I found myself with only Fryer to beat. Giving a mighty kick, I let fly at the goal and the keeper only just managed to touch the ball before it curled itself into the corner of the net, the force sufficient to send Fryer spinning. I rather liked that goal, thinking it above the average, and I can remember the chase I led the field that day."

City's trainer Jimmy Broad was so impressed with Meredith's solo effort he raced up and down the touch line celebrating, and the club was so pleased with their first home appearance in Division One that they allowed Meredith to claim the match ball. The Blues had not only arrived in the First Division, but they were also providing much excitement. In their following game, City won 4-1 at their Lancashire rivals Bury, with both Meredith and Ross finding the net once again.

Ross followed that by providing two goals in City's 5-1 victory over Notts County at Hyde Road seven days later. By this time secretary Sam Ormerod was delighted with the club's progress. Sixteen goals and three victories in the club's opening four fixtures signified that the Blues were more than a match for the big boys of the First Division and, being a big city club, they were able to draw decent sized crowds. Ormerod, pleased by the popularity of his side, told the *Athletic News*: "I really do wish they would stop coming, or else we shall have to make more extensive alterations to the ground. We have taken £350 in season ticket money alone thus far. Our accountant is taxed to the limit and we are contemplating another huge stand to take up the space at the Hyde Road entrance from the railway arch."

Although City's attendances were constant - a regular 20,000 plus - their success did not last. A series of ten games from December to March without victory saw the Blues slip down the table and, for the first time, the press started to point an accusing finger at Meredith and Ross. One article claimed that Meredith was absolutely brilliant when he was being well served by his colleagues but when the going got tough, Meredith disappeared. It seems that at this stage in the Welshman's career he needed the experienced Jimmy Ross more than Ross needed him.

City's trainer Jimmy Broad was so impressed with Meredith's solo effort he raced up and down the touch line celebrating, and the club was so pleased with their first home appearance in Division One that they allowed Meredith to claim the match ball.

One article claimed that Meredith: "doesn't like donkey-work and if his partner is off, Meredith is off too. The worst of it is that, with Meredith off colour, there doesn't seem to be much stuffing left in the City attack - not even when Ross is playing."

Even with this concern over Meredith's playing ability, he still managed to end the season as City's top scorer with fourteen goals in the thirty-three League games he played. The next season, however, saw the player really struggle to find the net as he only managed seven goals from thirty-four games. That may have been fine for most players but not for City's star man. By this time Meredith was hugely popular with the general public. Even in those days of limited media coverage, you didn't need to come from Manchester or understand football to know who Meredith was. Newspapers provided pen-pictures of the stars with cartoonists depicting the face and features for all to see. Unfortunately, Meredith also found that fame could lead to ridicule as cartoonists begun to make fun of the lean spell he was having. In one cartoon marked 'Run Dry', Meredith has placed a bucket marked 'goals' under a pump with the comment: "It's very funny. I can't get anything at all now - look you!"

With the latter half of the 1899-1900 season and 1900-01 seeing Meredith struggle for goals it's no wonder the Blues themselves could not maintain the form they had enjoyed in September 1899. An off form Meredith, regardless of the strength of the rest of the side, was not going to help the Blues. Nor could they drop the clean living Welshman as he, above everybody else, was City's star and the man many supporters had come to watch. Jimmy Ross may have been a fine player, but in his City days he did not have the wherewithal to attract large support, and Billy Gillespie, City's other key goalscorer, was perhaps a little too keen to 'bend the rules' for most supporters liking - from a fans perspective he would probably have been the perfect player one hundred years later, however.

Even with the emerging concerns at the start of the new century, City did manage to end their first Division One season in a satisfying seventh place. The most pleasing part was probably the fact that the Blues finished above all their Lancastrian rivals - teams such as Preston, Bury, and Blackburn who had dominated football in the north-west.

Although much was made of the role of players such as Ross and Meredith, City's position was achieved through the hard work of the whole team. Players like the eccentric goalkeeper Charlie Williams, who not only kept the opposition at bay but also ended up on the score sheet in one match, although many historians firmly believe this was actually an own goal by the opposition 'keeper. The game was the return match with Sunderland on 14th April 1900 at Roker Park, played in windy conditions. City full back, Bert Read, who always had to concentrate when close to Williams because it was often difficult to predict what the goalkeeper would do next, had a perfect view of how the goal was scored. He often recounted the following version of events: "I picked up the ball, placed it, and then just lifted it with my toe into Charlie Williams' hands. He drove it plumb down the centre of the field. It bounced, each time, so it seemed, gaining speed. Porteous and Gow, the Sunderland backs, were taken by surprise. They got in each other's way and the ball sailed towards Doig, the famous Scottish international goalkeeper. He seemed to have it covered, but a sudden gust of wind swung the ball off his fingertips into the net."

Williams was one of the key City players at this time, and many believed that only his unorthodox goalkeeping style prevented him from playing for England. Another important player during the Blues' first Division One season was the experienced Welsh international full back David Jones. 'Di', as he was known to City supporters, signed for the Blues at the end of September 1898, and made his debut in the 3-0 victory over Luton on 8th October 1898, early in City's promotion season. Although he played a defensive role, he did make it onto City's scoresheet a mere six weeks into his Hyde Road career when he combined with Billy Gillespie to give the Blues a 2-0 victory at home to Walsall.

Prior to City, Jones had given Bolton ten years service, captaining the Trotters' 1894 F.A. Cup Final side. He had also, on several occasions, tried to persuade his former Chirk team mate, Billy Meredith, to sign for Bolton. Fortunately for City he failed in his attempts. It was possibly the opportunity of playing with Meredith once more that attracted him to the progressive Hyde Road club in 1898, although he was probably aware of the potential for a successful Manchester side when, over ten years earlier, he featured in a few games for Newton Heath.

During the 1899-1900 season Jones was ever-present in City's thirty-four League games and two F.A. Cup matches. Charlie Williams, centre-half 'Buxton' Smith, and wing-half 'Doc' Holmes also appeared in every game, helping to provide a little consistency in defence during the club's inaugural Division One season.

As the Blues adjusted to life in the top flight, Sam Ormerod frequently tried to strengthen the squad.

Charlie Williams - the often eccentric goalkeeper was a key City player at this time.

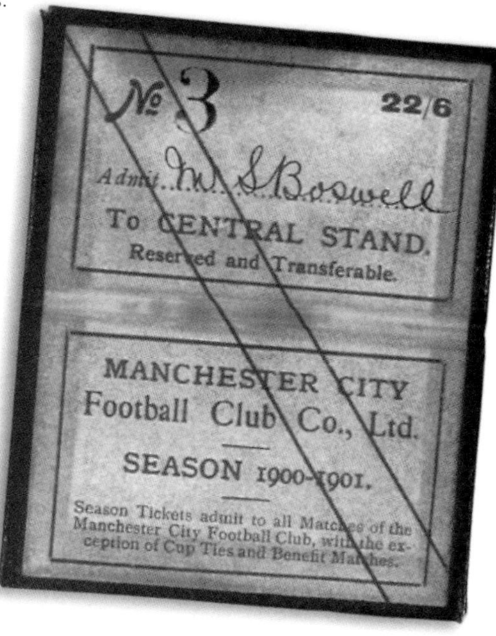

Both sides of a Season Ticket for Hyde Road in season 1900-01.

Future Prime Minister AJ Balfour visited Hyde Road in September 1900 for the 2-0 victory over Stoke. He and his daughter were welcomed by City chairman John Chapman and (bottom) then inspected one of Chesters' refreshment bars in the main stand.

One player he succeeded in bringing to the club was the well known Joe Cassidy from neighbours Newton Heath. Cassidy was a 'strong and burly' forward who was 27 by the time he signed for the Blues. For Newton Heath, he had provided much needed fire power during the 1893 Test Matches, helping to prolong the club's First Division status for one further season, and over the course of the next six years he scored four goals for the Heathens in derby matches against City. The Blues knew only too well what kind of danger he posed in front of goal.

When he moved to City for a weekly wage of £4, the Newton Heath directors admitted Cassidy was the best forward they had ever had, and it was only because the club was in such dire financial straits that they were prepared to let him go. According to the Heathens they sold Cassidy to the Blues for £250 to ease their debts.

Cassidy made his debut in the final game of 1899-1900, but it was the following season when he was really able to prove his worth as he ended top scorer with fourteen goals. His opening goal came in City's third game of the season - a 1-0 victory at home to Nottingham Forest.

The Blues' next home game was quite a newsworthy event as local M.P. and future Prime Minister A.J. Balfour attended Hyde Road for the visit of Stoke. Naturally, all the newspapers of the day provided reports on his visit, while the *Illustrated London News* went one stage further and sent a photographer. Balfour, accompanied by City Chairman John Chapman, was introduced to the captains and, after City had won the toss to select ends, was given the task of starting the game for the visitors. Mr. Balfour took a short run before sending the ball some thirty yards towards the City goal. According to reports of the period he quickly left the field as play was going on around him. Whether activity on the pitch was as frenzied as usual at the start of the match isn't known, although the thought of the local M.P. rushing off the pitch as the likes of Meredith and Jones charged around paints an interesting picture. Fortunately, Billy Gillespie was missing from the line-up that day, thus preventing the embarrassing situation of having a City forward 'charging' the future Prime Minister!

Mr. Balfour did actually leave the pitch safely, even though the Blues were quick to obtain the loose ball and attack the Stoke goal. Within the first five minutes both Fred Williams and Joe Cassidy forced Wilkes, the Stoke goalkeeper, to make daring saves, proving that City were keen to win in front of their distinguished visitor.

A mere ten minutes into the game, the Blues rather expectedly took the lead through a Joe Davies effort. According to match reports, the early stages of the game were totally one sided. The *Manchester Evening News* outlined City's domination by describing the action after the opening goal had been scored: "The home players continued to have all the best of the play, Meredith in particular distinguishing himself. With the exception of the occasional breakaway, Stoke were continually on the defensive, and it was not long before a second goal was scored as the result of a fine centre by Meredith. There was no doubt about the way in which the other City forwards were taking their captain's centre. With a lead of two goals the City men still played with dash and vigour. The effective play was not always on the right wing, Dougal and Williams combining in a way which raised the enthusiasm of the spectators very considerably".

As the game progressed Stoke did get their act together a little, and in the latter stages of the first half they managed to test Charlie Williams a little. City's extrovert 'keeper performed well enough to keep the score at 2-0 into the half-time interval.

The second half was nowhere near as exciting as the first - the *Manchester Evening News* suggested this may have been because A.J. Balfour had quietly departed from the ground a few moments prior to the interval, although the truth of the matter was that City felt they had done enough. Later in the half the visitors did put the Blues under pressure, although when the Stoke forward, Benbow, was forced to leave the pitch through injury, their chances became limited. Benbow was off the pitch for approximately ten minutes before coming back on, and although he was clearly suffering from the injury and shock he "pluckily played outside left" according to the report, before retiring three minutes later.

With Stoke down to ten men, City should have increased their lead, however Stoke defended brilliantly to ensure the score remained at 2-0.

The 1900-01 season was perhaps one of consolidation. It was only the Blues' second campaign in the First Division, and the club were still finding their feet against some of their more illustrious rivals - a fact proved by City's disappointing 7-1 defeat on 1st December at Aston Villa. A number of players had been brought into the club since promotion and City secretary/manager Sam Ormerod was still trying to mould a team that could live comfortably in the division. Although the likes of Villa were able to embarrass the Blues, it is worth noting that City were certainly better than the Second Division sides they had left behind. In the Manchester Cup final City defeated arch rivals Newton Heath 4-0 in a competition which at this point in football history was much more important to Mancunians than the F.A. Cup.

Nevertheless, victory over Newton Heath was easy and certainly expected. For Sam Ormerod to build a team that would be remembered nationally he needed full co-operation from the directors and committee of the ever-growing Manchester City.

Ormerod was perhaps handicapped by the fact that City were still a young club, and many of the directors and business people connected with the side were from the club's humble origins. Although support and performance on the pitch had improved over the years, there were question marks over the general direction of the club. Joshua Parlby was still involved, contributing his views whenever they were needed, and often when they were not. While other committee men chipped in with their own perceptions of how the team were performing. Some comments were accurate and relevant, while others merely caused confusion, and possibly bitterness. The quiet Ormerod was rarely able to have the final say over team selection as he formed part of a three man committee, nor could he buy or sell players without reaching full agreement with the committee.

Joe Cassidy was one player affected by this approach when, after scoring fourteen goals in only thirty-one League games the committee - not Ormerod - decided he was not worth his £4 a week salary. He was sold to Middlesbrough in May 1901 for the ridiculously low figure of £75, thereby creating a loss of £175 on the deal. At Middlesbrough he became a hero when he scored the first ever League

AJ Balfour meets City captain Billy Meredith in September 1900 (top) and then starts the game, against Stoke, by kicking towards the Stone Yard End.

Team photo of 1901/02 season, taken in front of the Hyde Road Main Stand.

Back (left to right): Cleveland (Asst. Sec.), Jones, Smith, Dartnell, Holmes, Read, Orr, McIntyre, Moffatt, R.Jones, Hosie.

Front: L.Ormerod (Secretary), Hunter, Frost, Bevan, Morgan, Meredith, Gillespie, Threlfall, Hurst, J.Broad (Trainer).

goal at Ayresome Park. Sadly, in April 1916 the *Manchester Football News* reported: "Joe Cassidy, whose connection with Manchester football extended over such a long period, has had a mental breakdown."

In addition to their involvement in the buying and selling of players, the City directors would have conversations with their own particular favourites, and if a player expressed concern at his role or involvement within the team the directors would act. Likewise, if a director was particularly pleased with the performance of 'his' player, he would pay him a bonus. All of this meddling by the directors and committee caused the knowledgeable and experienced Ormerod many problems. While the team performed well everybody was happy, but when results started to go against the Blues it was Ormerod who would be held accountable.

And so 1900-01 may not have been a successful season but, when the general direction of the club is taken into consideration, it must clearly be seen as a satisfactory one. Unfortunately the next twelve months would see the club suffer as the 'committee approach' seriously affected Ormerod's plans.

The 1901-02 campaign opened with two consecutive away games. The first at Everton ended in a 3-1 defeat - Billy Meredith, who had married Ellen Negus, his childhood sweetheart at City's church, St. Mark's, earlier in the year, scored the City consolation goal. The second game also ended in defeat, this time Sunderland were the victors by 1-0. A week later Hyde Road witnessed a heavy 4-1 defeat by Small Heath. Ormerod was under intense pressure yet, for the fourth game in a row, significant changes were made for the trip to Derby on 21st September.

A 2-0 defeat at Derby seemed to be the catalyst for widespread criticism of Ormerod. Critics accused him of chopping and changing the team - a point illustrated by the fact he had already used nineteen players in four games, with only four ever-presents even at this early stage.

Before City's next game on 5th October at Notts County, the *Athletic News*' journalist 'Harricus' tried to discover why the Blues were failing: "I had a chat with Sam Ormerod on Friday afternoon; the City secretary is one of the old originals of Lancashire football and a capital referee in his time. Manchester's lowly position formed, of course, the chosen topic for conversation. The genial Sam thinks his club is the victim of circumstance inasmuch as four of the five matches have been played away from home and, being thus handicapped as no other club is, he could hardly be sanguine of success at Nottingham but he thinks City's time will come. When I took him to task on the week to week chopping and changing of the team he said that personally he wasn't in favour of it, but what with letter writers and others, the lot of the directors wasn't a happy one, and no-one was more anxious than they were that City should rank with the best."

Although 'Harricus' mistakenly stated that City had played one more fixture than they actually had, his comments and those of Ormerod, do provide an indication of how Ormerod was not free to pull all the strings. Not only did the directors contribute to team selection, but it seems the general public, could also influence team affairs. Even at this early stage in the season it seemed that Ormerod was powerless, and that First Division survival was not within his control.

Results improved over the next month - City somehow achieved two Hyde Road victories and an away draw - but it was not enough to silence the critics. 'Harricus', whose initial comments could have been used to describe City's inconsistency by many journalists over the years, accused Ormerod of inactivity: "A greater monument to folly and incapacity than the figure of Manchester City this season we have rarely seen. There was a time when we thought the shafts of satire and ridicule would rouse the club to action. But they have availed not. It is quite time the shareholders held a mass meeting and particularly invited the directors and officials. What is Mr. Ormerod doing? IS ANYBODY DOING ANYTHING?"

Three successive defeats - including a 5-0 hammering by Sheffield United - and further team changes throughout November caused 'Harricus' to go on the attack again: "We neither see nor hear of displays of acumen, enterprise and business activity by the directorate and their servants. Two men are badly needed at Hyde Road - one shrewd and commanding personality with the ability to put the finances on the sound basis they ought to be, and to see that affairs are conducted in a business-like manner, and another is a shrewd and sound judge of a player and especially a budding player."

City were a club in rapid decline. The final comment by 'Harricus' was a deliberate attack on Ormerod who, at this stage in his City career, seemed to be struggling to direct the club forward. Any team which still included the veteran Jimmy Ross could hardly have been one for the future, despite the player's track record.

Ross had been playing in the League since its formation in 1888, and had also been a regular in the Preston side for the four years prior to the League's formation. He was without doubt a veteran, and was an obvious example of City's problems. Ormerod needed to develop the side, but didn't seem capable of creating a situation whereby the older players could move to one side as the newer players fitted in. Under Ormerod there seemed no chance of building the foundations for the future, especially with the directors still meddling in team affairs.

While results went against City on the pitch, off it the likes of John Allison were working hard to put overall control of the club into the hands of one or two powerful men. Allison had been involved with City since the Ardwick days - in fact it was Allison who, for a while in 1894, believed the club should continue as Ardwick A.F.C. Now, after a period off the City board, Allison was convinced he could help create the right environment for a successful City. His contacts included the wealthy newspaper baron Edward Hulton who was easily persuaded to help the club.

One of Hulton's newspapers was the *Athletic News*, and looking back one wonders whether the newspaper's attacks on Ormerod and the City directorate had anything to do with this fact. Probably not, but it was quite obvious that once Hulton became involved in the club, Ormerod's days were numbered, especially with Allison's close involvement. Allison had many ideas of how the City side should be shaped and, with results continuing to go against Ormerod during the first weeks of 1902, Allison acted.

Although still at the club, Ormerod's power was effectively taken from him in February, while John Allison sought to strengthen the side. Allison had connections with Celtic in Glasgow, and was able to use these links to bolster the City side immediately. Allegedly, he used Billy Meredith as bait to tempt the great Celtic manager Willie Maley, but the Welshman remained at City with an improved wage - it's worth noting that Meredith was already earning substantially more than the £4 a week maximum wage, and that ultimately City's wage structure would cause the club a great deal of problems.

Negotiations between Allison and Celtic resulted in City signing Willie McOustra, an inside-forward, and Jimmy Drummond, a twenty year old inside-left. Interestingly, Celtic's Tom Hynds had already signed for the Blues on 27th September 1901, again proving the strong links between the two sides.

According to Celtic, the club were offered a transfer fee they simply could not refuse for McOustra and Drummond - approximately £600 - and so reluctantly they allowed the two men to go south. The previous season McOustra had hit the headlines and gained a few admirers by scoring the only goal of an 'Auld Firm' derby match described as 'The Cup-tie of the Century', while Drummond had been described as having 'passing ability above the average'. It is fair to say though, that neither player was vital to Celtic at the time. Drummond had suffered with a number of injuries over the season and after a Celtic game with Hearts on 2nd November had been described as 'painfully unfit", nevertheless Allison was right to bring the talent in.

Another arrival around this time was the sizeable goalkeeper Jack Hillman. Hillman, 6 ft tall and weighing 16 stone, came with a reputation for being a little eccentric, and made his debut for City in the 1-0 home victory over Notts County on 1st February. He had been signed from Burnley as a replacement for the equally eccentric Charlie Williams, who remained at the club until the close season, then moved to Tottenham Hotspur where he became understudy to George Clawley, before moving on to Southampton.

Edward Hulton was backing John Allison all the way by promising to pay for any player Allison needed to strengthen the Blues. This kind of benefactor was extremely useful to the club. It enabled them to compete for almost anyone and, if City had been better placed in the League, may have helped the club avoid relegation. As it was City's results did improve enough to give the club a normally safe 28 points from 34 games; unfortunately in 1902 it wasn't quite enough and the Blues returned to the

Thomas Hynds joined City on 27th September 1901 from Celtic and by the time of his suspension in 1906 had established himself as probably the best City half-back up until the First World War.

John Allison at work in his Matlock House Hydro attempting to cure a Stoke player's injured arm by using heat treatment. Allison was a leading figure in the early history of City.

Second Division to meet their old adversaries Newton Heath.

Relegation provided Allison and Hulton with the perfect opportunity to find a little breathing space to rebuild the team and take stock of the club's overall situation. At City's Annual General Meeting in June, the directors revealed the club had taken approximately £8,000 in gate receipts - a tremendous figure - but even this wasn't enough to put the club into profit. When the balance sheet was revealed, the Blues proved to be nearly £1,000 in debt. General criticism was made of the way the directors had wildly spent money on travelling expenses and on the players' bonuses and wages.

Sammy Frost throws himself in front of yet another opponent and comes away with the ball.

Again, the warning signs were evident that the club were overly keen to pay the players more than was absolutely necessary, although it seems that many other big city clubs were equally profligate in this area.

Sam Ormerod was also on the receiving end of much criticism; understandably he resigned. It is obvious that team selection and motivation was not all it should have been during the season, but whether this was entirely Ormerod's fault is not clear. Certainly he was the man officially in charge of the playing side, but 'selection committee' pressure had caused him to alter his side willy-nilly. His first seasons in charge proved most productive but, in reality, it seems the club had indeed lost direction. It was time for a change and Allison knew who he wanted to bring in.

Not surprisingly, Allison returned to his old friends at Celtic and invited 37 year old Tom Maley, a Celtic director and brother of Celtic Manager Willie, to be the new City Secretary. Tom Maley was a Celtic man through and through and had been involved with the club since formation in 1888. First as a player (inside-left), then as a director and committee man driving the club forward. During the latter half of the 1901-2 season he travelled to Hyde Road on a couple of occasions, prompting early City historians to suggest that Allison had already made a move for Maley before Ormerod resigned.

The Maley family were major influences in the early years of Scottish football, and back in 1890 their connection with Manchester started when Willie Maley guested with Ardwick over Easter. Six years later he returned to Hyde Road again as a guest, playing in City's 5-1 victory over Loughborough in the Second Division. These guest outings coincided with similar appearances for Everton causing one to suspect that Maley enjoyed some kind of busman's holiday. During one of Willie's trips to Manchester he would almost certainly have spent time at John Allison's 'Matlock House Hydro' on Hyde Road, where players were provided with the latest treatments for football injuries. Maybe this is where Allison's connections with Celtic stemmed from.

Now with a new manager, and fresh direction, the Blues prepared for their return to the Second Division, although news of the deaths of two of Hyde Road's greatest players rocked the club's preparations. First, veteran Jimmy Ross died on 12th June, a mere four and a half months after making his last first team appearance. This last showing was, appropriately, against Preston North End in the First Round of the F.A. Cup, although it must have been an unusual final game for the former 'Preston Invincible' as it was abandoned in extra-time with the score standing at 1-1.

The second death was Welsh international Di Jones who fell and gashed his knee during the annual public practice match in August. The club's doctor treated Di's injuries and sent him home. A week later he was dead. The wound had turned septic because it had not been treated properly.

These deaths deeply affected everybody at the club, and Tom Maley did all he could to lift the gloom. He also looked to strengthen the side. He signed inside-forward Sandy Turnbull from Hurlford (Scotland) in July, full-back Bob Davidson from Celtic (to replace Jones), and outside-left Frank Booth from Stockport County. He also provided Sammy Frost with the opportunity to establish himself in the City first team. Brought to City in May 1901 as an inside-right, Frost had been found wanting and made only two League appearances for City during Ormerod's 'season of changes'. Under Maley, Frost was tried at right-half, and quickly made a name for himself.

One journalist of the period enthused about Frost's unorthodox style: "Frost at half-back is unique. As a tackler he is a positive 'original'. Along comes the opponent with the ball. Does Frost put out a boot on either side? Not he. His modus operandi is far more certain and far reaching. The ex-Millwallian simply throws himself across and in front of his opponent. 'You can go along as far as you like' quoth Frost, 'but you will have to take me with you'. Small wonder that some people assert that Frost will get himself killed someday."

Maley also allowed another half-back, Tom Hynds, to express himself in the side. Hynds had played in 29 League games the previous season, and so could be regarded as one of Ormerod's regulars, but under Maley he really did prove his ability, establishing himself as probably the best half-back in City's history up until that time. Maley may have been encouraged by the fact that Hynds was an ex-Celtic player despite his being with City since 27th September 1901.

Under the new secretary City progressed. Maley was keen on seeing more of the Scottish passing game as opposed to traditional English kick and rush, and with his signings, and of course the likes of Meredith, Maley was determined to mould City into a stylish outfit. He was a great tactician, and clearly chose players who fitted his plan rather than great individuals. Maley's team attacked the Second Division with panache. Only five games ended in defeat, unfortunately one of these was the Hyde Road derby with neighbours Manchester United.

During City's period in the First Division their rivals, Newton Heath had struggled to keep alive. City were supported by average crowds of around 17,000 while the Heathens had been watched by approximately 6,000. In 1901-2 they finished the season in their lowest position since formation, and off the pitch the club was in dire financial straits. The only remedy was a relaunch, and by 28th April the club re-emerged under a new title, Manchester United. For the start of the 1902-3 season United chose to adopt new club colours of red shirts and white shorts. The first derby match of the season, Christmas Day 1902, was therefore the first League meeting of the 'Reds' and the 'Blues' of Manchester. That game, which all reports describe as being dominated by the Blues, ended 1-1 at Clayton.

Making his debut in this match was full-back Johnny McMahon, who had been signed from Preston on 17th December. Another new player around this time was Leyland-born Jimmy Bannister who was signed from Chorley during the close-season, but only made his debut on 6th December. Eventually, Bannister was to become the perfect inside-forward foil to Billy Meredith who described the Lancastrian as "the best partner I ever had. No one fed me better than Jimmy...he was equal to any inside-right playing in League football. I shall always think of him as one of the cleverest and most unselfish partners I have ever been blessed with."

Apart from the five League defeats, City's season was a successful one. They won 25 of their 34 League games and scored 95 goals. Many of these came during the latter part of the season when table-toppers City achieved crushing victories over Burnley (6-0), Burslem Port Vale (7-1), and Gainsborough Trinity (9-0).

With the score at 5-0 at half time in the home game against Port Vale, the referee is reported to have gone into the Vale dressing room to drag out the reluctant players, while the Gainsborough game had somehow remained goalless for the first twenty-five minutes. Top scorer during this season was ace goal poacher Billy Gillespie with 30 goals from 32 appearances. Sadly, it's not known exactly how many of these were the result of Gillespie's infamous 'barging' technique.

With the right results, tactical direction, talented players, and financial investment, City were once again promoted into the First Division. Manchester needed a top class club and with Edward Hulton's backing the Blues were taking shape. They also received good coverage in the main sporting newspapers of the day. Surely it was no co-incidence that City's main backer was also the proprietor of several popular 'papers.

Livingstone and Meredith soon became the perfect partnership.

1902-03 DIVISION TWO CHAMPIONSHIP DETAILS

RESULTS	HOME	AWAY
Lincoln City	W 3-1	L 0-1
Small Heath	W 4-0	L 0-4
Leicester Fosse	W 3-1	D 1-1
Chesterfield	W 4-2	W 1-0
Burnley	W 6-0	D 1-1
Preston North End	W 1-0	W 2-0
Burslem Port Vale	W 7-1	W 4-1
Gainsborough Trinity	W 9-0	W 3-0
Woolwich Arsenal	W 4-1	L 0-1
Burton United	W 2-0	W 5-0
Bristol City	D 2-2	L 2-3
Glossop North End	W 5-2	W 1-0
Barnsley	W 3-2	W 3-0
Stockport County	W 5-0	W 2-0
Blackpool	W 2-0	W 3-0
Manchester United	L 0-2	D 1-1
Doncaster Rovers	W 4-1	W 2-1

REGULAR SIDE:
Hillman
McMahon
Davidson
Frost
Hynds
McOustra
Meredith
Bannister
Gillespie
Turnbull
Threlfall

MANAGER:
Tom Maley

LARGEST VICTORY: 9-0 V Gainsborough Trinity (H) 28/2/03

HEAVIEST DEFEAT: 0-4 V Small Heath (A) 13/9/02

AVERAGE HOME ATTENDANCE: c.16,000

HIGHEST HOME ATTENDANCE: c.30,000 V Manchester United 10/4/03

HIGHEST AWAY ATTENDANCE: c.40,000 V Manchester United 25/12/02

LEAGUE APPEARANCES: 34 Meredith, 32 McOustra, Gillespie, 31 Hillman, Hynds, 30 Frost, 26 Davidson, 25 Threlfall, 22 Turnbull, 21 Bannister, 17 McMahon, 14 Drummond, 13 Orr, 11 Holmes, 9 Booth, 8 Miller, 6 Bevan, 3 Dearden, Edmondsen, Hosie, 2 Slater, 1 Moffatt

LEAGUE GOALS: 30 Gillespie, 22 Meredith, 13 Bannister, 12 Turnbull, 5 Threlfall, 4 McOustra, 3 Drummond, 2 Miller, 1 Hynds, Bevan

Promotion gave the Blues added impetus, and was to spark the first great era for football in Manchester. Tom Maley, recognising not all his signings had worked out for the best, made a few adjustments. The former Celtic inside-left, Jimmy Drummond, failed to impress and, after being described as "awkward and slow", was first dropped into the reserves, then in October 1903 was transferred to Partick Thistle. The player signed alongside him, Willie McOustra, had also struggled to make the right impression mainly due to injury, although he remained at the club and was to play an important role two years later.

Players brought in included the amateur half-back, Sam Ashworth, as replacement for McOustra, left-back Herbert Burgess, and inside-forward George Livingstone. Burgess was an Openshaw born player who had made his Football League debut at the age of 18 for Glossop against Liverpool. His original 'trial' game for Glossop was actually a reserve match against City at Hyde Road, but it wasn't until he was 21 that the Blues spotted his real potential. City paid a fee of around £250 for the 5ft 5 inch 'Mighty Atom' who, while with the Blues, became the smallest full-back ever to play for England.

George Livingstone, or 'Geordie' as he was known to the players, must be unique in that, during a career spanning three decades, he appeared for both Manchester clubs and both Celtic and Rangers.

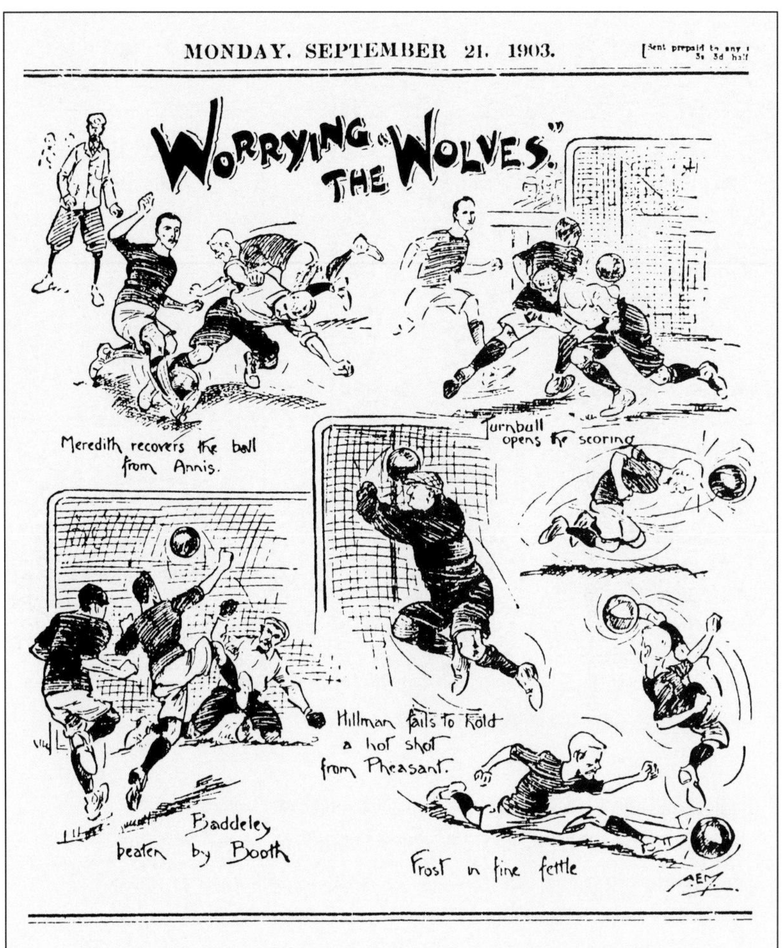

MONDAY. SEPTEMBER 21. 1903.
"WORRYING THE WOLVES."
Meredith recovers the ball from Annis.
Turnbull opens the scoring
Hillman fails to hold a hot shot from Pheasant.
Baddeley beaten by Booth
Frost in fine fettle

City's 4-1 win over Wolves at Hyde Road on 19th September 1903 clearly highlights the role of 'man of the match' Sammy Frost, in what was an important victory for Maley's side.

He also had a spell with Liverpool, but never quite made it to Everton to complete the treble. It was actually from Liverpool that he was signed for City in May 1903, although Tom Maley had secured his signature when they met one day in Greenock. Geordie joined the Blues after building a bit of a reputation as a physical player. This started in his days at Celtic where he often found himself involved in 'rough' activity. Nevertheless, it was this kind of forward that would add a bit more steel to Maley's side. Quickly he established himself, prompting the *Athletic News* to comment: "George Livingstone disdains style. He is all utility and a resolute thrusting forward who not only creates openings for Meredith but opens out the game by playing passes to the other wing in the style I used to admire when J. Devey was commander-in-chief of Aston Villa. He makes himself the hub of the game when he is on the ball."

And so, with a strengthened side, 1903-4 unfolded into the greatest season Manchester had known up to that time. The opening four games in the First Division were all won, with the best result coming in City's 4-1 victory over Wolves at Hyde Road, while new boy Livingstone provided one of the goals that helped City to 2-1 victory in their opening fixture at Stoke.

In the 3-1 win at Bury on 7th November, Livingstone again proved his worth when he and Meredith combined perfectly. Another of Maley's buys, Herbert Burgess, illustrated that it wasn't simply the Scotsman who was value for money as he gave a quite brilliant display.

With such fine performances in the League Maley's side really developed as a unit. Until the secretary's arrival the Blues had bought and discovered some great players but had never created a great side. Too often they had relied on the likes of Meredith, Gillespie, or Ross to find a goal from somewhere... anywhere! Now with the right direction and an increased tactical awareness they had become a team in the truest sense. The side were determined to achieve something and team spirit was never higher. In at least one newspaper article City's 'grit' had been described as the main reason for the team's rapid rise up the League. The article went on to state that the team 'grafted' for one another and that no matter what the obstacle, the Blues would overcome it.

By the time the F.A. Cup First Round was played on 6th February 1904, City were well placed for an assault on the League Championship, something that only a few months earlier had seemed so far away most Mancunians daren't even dream about it. After all, City were hardly regarded as one of the famous Lancastrian clubs, let alone one of football's elite. But Maley believed in his players, and with internationals like Meredith and Burgess in the side he had every right to feel the Blues could do it.

The First Round of the F.A. Cup may have come

RICHARDS FINDS A TOUGH HANDFUL IN LYONS
BURGESS GIVES A BRILLIANT DISPLAY

Scenes from the 3-1 defeat of Bury on 7th November 1903.

along at the right moment for Maley. It allowed him to divert attention from the League for a short while. With City's fine performances to date, it also meant that for the first real occasion in the Cup the Blues could put out a side capable of success. Up until this point City had never really achieved much in the Cup; their best seasons had only seen them reach the Second Round (1897-98 and 1901-02).

For the first tie of the 1903-04 season City were at home to Sunderland who over the previous four seasons had consistently finished in the top three. This year was not quite as successful, but they had still performed well and experienced some exciting victories. In their two previous games they had defeated Bury 6-0 and Blackburn Rovers 3-1, while the December meeting of City and Sunderland gave little indication of how the cup meeting might go as it ended in a 1-1 draw.

And so on 6th February a crowd of approximately 23,000, the largest Hyde Road F.A. Cup attendance so far, looked forward to a great City performance. They were not disappointed as City defeated Sunderland by three goals to two with Billy Meredith in outstanding form, setting up the first two goals. For the first Billy Gillespie sent Meredith forward 'like a greyhound from the leash' according to one scribe. The Welshman crossed to Livingstone who forced a corner. From the kick, taken by captain Meredith of course, Gillespie headed past the Sunderland 'keeper Doig.

For City's second goal, the Welsh wizard showcased his skills by dribbling past several players before crossing to Sandy Turnbull, whose header 'fairly bamboozled Doig', according to the *Athletic News*. Turnbull added City's third later in the game when he and Doig both attempted to gain control of a loose ball. With the goalkeeper scrambling on the floor, the City man took the ball out of Doig's reach and forced it goalwards.

Following a hectic game, City received glowing reports in the sporting press over the course of the next three days. Turnbull was praised for two crucial goals, while Meredith once again stole the headlines with his overall performance. According to the *Athletic News*: "The City captain was the raider-in-chief and undoubtedly the most dazzling forward on the field. Assiduously supplied, the famous Welshman hardly ever failed to respond to the calls made upon him. His command of the ball as he threaded his way through the maze of his adversaries commanded admiration. Against a team of such class Meredith has not often given a more dazzling display. R.J. Jackson, hard worker as he is, was quite unable to hold him in check and Rhodes, who has probably not seen Meredith before and knows not his wary antagonist, was altogether floundering about like an inexperienced schoolboy. I have no wish to be guilty of exaggeration, but Meredith was the King of the Realm."

The draw for the second round pitted City away to Second Division Woolwich Arsenal, who had defeated Fulham 1-0 in the previous round. The Blues defeated the Gunners 2-0 with goals from Sandy Turnbull and Frank Booth, prompting the *Manchester Evening News* to print a cartoon of Billy Meredith leapfrogging over the Gunners while Tom Maley, dressed in kilt, watches.

Frank Booth, one of the scorers and City's

City photographed with the Manchester Cup and the Second Division Championship shield at Hyde Road during 1903.

Back: G.Livingstone, Drummond, Hynds, Davidson, Hillman, Holmes, J.Edmundson, Moffat.

Middle: W.Meredith, Graigie, L.Jones, H.Burgess, S.Frost, W.Bannister, Pearson, F.Threlfall, R.Moffat (Assistant Trainer).

Front: (left to right): J.Broad (Trainer), P.Slater, Dearden, W.Gillespie, Lyon, A.Turnbull, McOustra, Booth, Forman.

Circled: J.McMahon, T.E.Maley (Secretary).

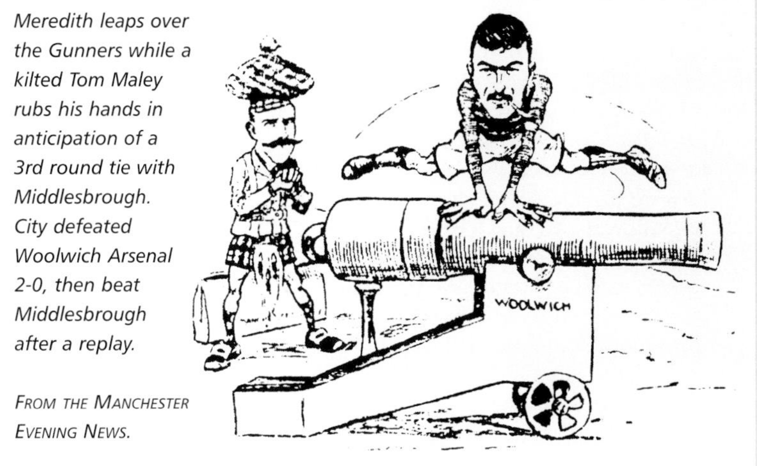

Meredith leaps over the Gunners while a kilted Tom Maley rubs his hands in anticipation of a 3rd round tie with Middlesbrough. City defeated Woolwich Arsenal 2-0, then beat Middlesbrough after a replay.

FROM THE MANCHESTER EVENING NEWS.

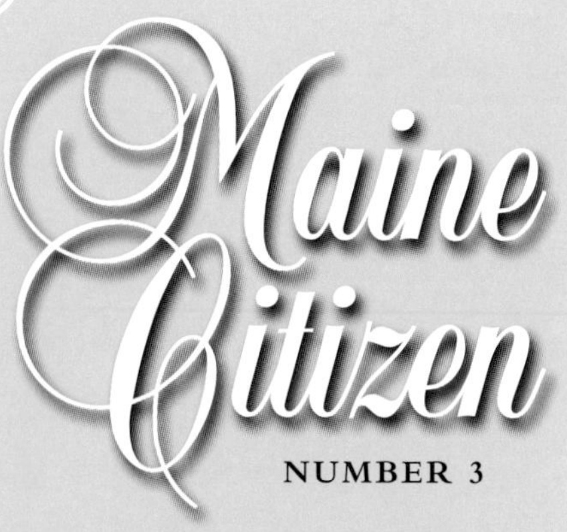

NUMBER 3

BILLY GILLESPIE

Opponents would probably describe Billy Gillespie as a 'dirty' player, whilst also secretly wishing the entertaining forward could play for their side. He had a trademark habit of forcing the ball - and often the goalkeeper - over the line and into the net. City fans loved it and for most of his time at Hyde Road Gillespie was idolised.

There were times, however, when his bohemian approach to life caused a few problems. He found it difficult to control his spending and was fortunate to be looked after by City's great captain Billy Meredith. The Welshman encouraged him to control his excesses, helping him open a bank account and put some money away each week. Often the two of them would go on fishing trips, away from the clubs and pubs of Manchester.

Meredith's assistance didn't always work - stories related by supporters of the period suggest Gillespie liked his alcohol so much that he was frequently dropped for being drunk. Some fans claim he was actually drunk during certain games at Hyde Road. Despite these negative aspects, Gillespie proved to be one of City's most consistent performers at a time when the club was rapidly improving its status in football. For four of his nine seasons he was City's top goal scorer.

He scored on his debut, and provided a total of 126 goals in 218 League appearances. As a centre forward he enjoyed playing with Meredith, Booth, and Threlfall - each of whom provided him with terrific service - and ensured that he was always in the right place at the right time for any chance, or half chance that came his way. He delighted in attacking the opposition and didn't care who tried to get in his way. His broad, bustling manner ensured no defender would stand in his path for too long.

If he had been a player a century later he would have been regarded as a loveable rogue. The kind of player who cared little about reputations, and would probably have felt more at home standing on the terraces cheering his side on, than sitting in the directors' box pontificating.

Gillespie was unfortunate that he was unable to add a League Championship medal to his 1904 Cup medal. He played a leading role in the side that should have been allowed to develop at Hyde Road, and saw his hopes for League success fail as the F.A. started its investigations into the club. Unlike his colleagues, he felt the time had come to give up on English football when the authorities seemed intent on destroying his club. According to some reports he married and emigrated to Canada, others say he travelled to Cape Town to prospect for diamonds. He was disgusted with his treatment and, although he would certainly have interested Manchester United, felt he could no longer play in a country where some clubs were treated differently to others.

As a protest, he never paid the £50 fine imposed as a result of the investigations. This final act of defiance was typical of the man and did much to reinforce his image with City's loyal supporters. For years afterwards 'stories' kept appearing in the local 'papers of his antics overseas that helped to fuel the legend and maintain his special place in the hearts of Manchester's fans.

After finding a new career as an electrician in Montreal, in 1934 he travelled back to Manchester for a holiday with his wife, and met up with his mentor Billy Meredith and the aged trainer Jimmy Broad. His return brought much interest from the local media with the *Daily Mirror's* sports editor, Stacey Lintott, interviewing the goal scoring legend.

Although he could hardly be described as an articulate footballer, it is obvious his contribution to the Blue cause helped City attain true success. Some may feel he was the wild man of Hyde Road, but he was simply the type of player to benefit from the skills of others. Without him even Meredith and City may have struggled to find real success.

GILLESPIE'S PLAYING RECORD

	LEAGUE		FA CUP		TOTAL	
	App	Gls	App	Gls	App	Gls
1896-97	11	4	0	0	11	4
1897-98	30	18	2	1	32	19
1898-99	30	17	1	1	31	18
1899-1900	28	8	2	0	30	8
1900-01	23	9	0	0	23	9
1901-02	24	15	0	0	24	15
1902-03	32	30	1	0	33	30
1903-04	24	18	6	3	30	21
1904-05	16	7	1	1	17	8
TOTAL	218	126	13	6	231	132

outside-left, had joined City in April 1902 making his first appearance for the club in a friendly with Celtic on 1st September 1902. That friendly outing brought a little bad luck as fairly early on in the match he accidentally collided with Celtic's right-back Hugh Watson and was forced to leave the field for twenty minutes or so. When he returned however he seemed more determined than ever to prove his capabilities and when a chance came along he scored what was described as a 'very fine' goal to give City a 1-0 victory.

Throughout Booth's career prior to the Arsenal game he had been rather unlucky with injuries and, at times, must have seriously considered concentrating on a life outside of the sport. He was a hatter by trade, coming from the local millinery areas surrounding the towns of Hyde and Denton, and had only completed his apprenticeship in 1903. Nevertheless a career in football had to be more appealing than life in one of the large hat factories of East Manchester.

After the tie with Arsenal at Plumstead, George Robey, a famous northern music hall comedian with a love of football, took the City team to visit the capital's top music halls. Such light relief was needed in the City camp as realisation was now dawning that the Blues might seriously be contenders for the League and Cup double which, at this point in history, had only been achieved by Preston (1889) and Aston Villa (1897). For a side whose only national success so far had been to win the Second Division, this must have seemed an impossible dream but, as the season progressed it became increasingly likely.

In the Third Round - the quarter-final - City were drawn at home to First Division Middlesbrough. A record 30,022 paid £1,150 to see how far Maley's determined team could go; unfortunately they went home a little disappointed as the game ended goalless. A few days later the replay at Middlesbrough saw the Blues face a side backed by a fanatical crowd.
It seemed the whole of Middlesbrough packed inside the ground as a partisan crowd of 33,000 supported their heroes. Local schools and factories closed early to allow fans to attend, and all the local dignitaries were in evidence. This replay was Middlesbrough's chance of glory, unfortunately for them it was also City's.

In the end the Blues won the game 3-1 with goals from Livingstone, Gillespie, and Turnbull. For the first time ever a Manchester side had reached the semi-final of football's most famous competition.

The draw for the semi brought City and their rivals for the League title, Sheffield Wednesday, together while the other tie was to be competed between Bolton and Derby County. Wednesday were reigning League Champions and were defensively strong. Would they be too tough for the Blues powerful attack?

A crowd of 53,000 attended a wet Goodison Park for the 'clash of the styles'. At this time Goodison was by far the best stadium in the Football League and a fitting venue; Maley was determined his tactics and style of play would overcome Wednesday's defence. From the whistle City attacked, completely overpowering a Wednesday side captained by the English international half-back, Tom Crawshaw.

After only twenty-one minutes the Blues took the lead. A Meredith shot hit the crossbar and rebounded to Gillespie who bundled the ball over the line. A cartoon of the game in the *Athletic News* gives the impression that Jack Lyall, the Wednesday 'keeper who later transferred to City, moved out of the way. Possibly he had already experienced Gillespie's method of 'bundling' the ball into the net, and was keen to avoid it at all costs!

By half-time City's domination was rewarded with a second goal, as Sandy Turnbull hooked in a Meredith cross. In the second half, Turnbull provided a third to guarantee a City victory. This goal was simply a superb effort and was described by the *Athletic News* as the goal of the season: "Livingstone, by really clever dribbling near the centre line, was able to make a very clever pass to Meredith, who spread all sail and steered straight ahead, with Burton hanging on to his left shoulder all the way. But Meredith kept possession, and, although only about a foot in front of his antagonist, he made a marvellous right foot back centre, the ball whizzing past Burton. This was done at a most difficult angle, and Turnbull, who had followed up, volleyed with his instep, and like a flash of lightning, the ball was in the net."

Like the rest of the people in Goodison Park that day, Billy Meredith remembered it as a fantastic goal: "I never saw anything like it. I had centred square and Sandy took the ball first time when it was well off the ground and drove it into the net with marvellous

The realisation was now dawning that the Blues might seriously be contenders for the League and Cup double which, at this point in history, had only been achieved by Preston (1889) and Aston Villa (1897).

A cartoon from the Athletic News depicting City's 3-0 semi-final win over Sheffield Wednesday at Goodison Park.

force. The amazing thing was that the ball kept low all the way. You will understand the pace of the shot when I say the ball hit the net at Goodison Park and came out while the goalkeeper was still tumbling!"

The game ended with a fine 3-0 victory for Maley's City, and put a Manchester side into the F.A. Cup Final for the first time. Mancunians were ecstatic. It is extremely difficult to explain now exactly how strong that feeling of success was without it sounding over the top, but it is important to record that this moment was seen as one of Manchester's greatest achievements. Until this time the city of Manchester had been famous for the Ship Canal and industry, and was seen as a grim, sprawling, northern city with little to recommend it to non-Mancunians. Its people were proud of their city and its achievements, but they had not found it possible to demonstrate their city was better, more successful, than anywhere else. Sport, and in particular football, now allowed them to prove that Manchester really was a leading city. If Manchester's football team could succeed then Manchester really was an important place to be.

'Sandy' Turnbull's volley against Sheffield Wednesday in the semi-final was described by the Athletic News as the 'goal of the season'.

Mancunians united to support the Blues - even United fans wanted 'big brother' City to succeed - and the general feeling was one of working together. Tom Maley's 'team' approach was working and long serving trainer Jimmy Broad enjoyed the atmosphere: "It was a real pleasure to train that team. They were all as keen as mustard and always to be found together...Tom Maley, who understands the players perfectly, was always on the best of terms with his team and joined in any fun that was going on. At our sing-songs, Tom usually contributed a recitation and he did very well too. Turnbull, I think, was our best vocalist but McOustra and Burgess ran him pretty close for that honour. Jack Hillman was past master at making 'stump' speeches. When asked to do something serious he invariably settled back in his chair, lit his pipe and rolled out the tale of 'Young Lochinvar'. Billy Meredith spent most of his leisure-time enjoying the efforts of others. Bill was always very quiet when the others were giving an impromptu concert, but Bill relished it all the same."

With the Cup semi-final over the Blues could concentrate on the League for the following month or so. A couple of days after the semi, City emphasised they were one of the most powerful teams of the period, stretching their unbeaten run by defeating Wolves 6-1 on 21st March. City had not lost a game since December and were hitting the headlines regularly. Most journalists praised their style, confidence, and team play: "They move with a smartness and precision which could not fail to evoke admiration, the forwards sweeping along like one man brooking no resistance.......backs and half-backs never knew what was going to happen next; now a feint, now a pass, now a short dribble, maybe a shot or a wide pass to the wings, to be followed by a true, insidious centre - all these moves were executed with a perfect understanding and with clockwork precision."

It was incredible the Blues had managed to keep up the pressure at the top of the League for so long. Not only was this their first season back in the Division, but the cup run had created a fixture pile-up. In March alone City played three cup games and three League games in the space of twenty-one days. This may seem normal for a successful Premier League side in the 1990s, but in 1904 with an eighteen club division and only one cup competition, this was daunting. Nevertheless, the Blues not only survived but for a period they thrived.

On March 26th, however, the pressure increased as they faced semi-final opponents, Wednesday, away in the League. Unlike the cup match seven days earlier, City were not able to break down the strong Wednesday defence, and when Harry Chapman gave Wednesday the lead, the Blues were unable to fight back. The game ended 1-0, giving Wednesday a four point advantage over City. Close behind the Blues were Aston Villa and Newcastle, whom City were to face in their next League game.

On April Fool's Day against Newcastle, City disappointed again as they suffered a 3-1 defeat at Hyde Road. Was the pressure getting to them? Tom Maley must have been worried that City's troubles had arrived at a time when the Blues needed to be at their best. They certainly needed to keep calm. The day after the Newcastle defeat, City faced Sunderland at Hyde Road. With a few team changes, the Blues won 2-1 with both goals coming from the in-form Sandy Turnbull. Maley was a happy man, especially when he heard Notts County had beaten Wednesday, and that Villa had lost to Bury. The gap between City and Wednesday was now back to two points, but Villa were close behind and Newcastle had moved above the Blues after victory over Blackburn. Maley knew he somehow had to keep City's team spirit and attitude right.

On 4th April more good news came the Blues way as they discovered Wednesday had lost to Everton, thereby presenting City with a game in hand. The last few weeks of the season would really test City's nerve, especially as Maley was forced to make team changes. A combination of injuries and loss of form forced Maley into the transfer market and on 7th April he purchased Irvine Thornley from Glossop. This was a transfer that less than two years later would help create City's shock downfall, but back in April 1904 it helped keep City on course for the League and Cup double. Thornley's debut was the away game to West Bromwich Albion on 9th April. Unfortunately, this resulted in a disappointing 2-1 defeat while Wednesday achieved victory in the Sheffield derby on the same day. The Blues were once again four points

behind Wednesday, while Newcastle with only one game to go were a point ahead of City.

Between April 9th and 16th City played four matches to catch up with Wednesday on the number of games played. With more necessary team changes it was difficult for Maley to find the right level of balance, but somehow he did as the Blues gained points. Frank Norgrove, another player from Glossop whose transfer later caused City much heartache, signed on 15th April and made his debut next day, while other squad players, such as the long serving William 'Doc' Holmes, filled in when required.

By the end of a 4-0 victory over Small Heath, City were on 44 points with one game - away at Everton - to go, while their main championship rivals, Wednesday, were one point behind with two games to go. Newcastle's season was already over - they finished on 42 points - and Aston Villa were now unable to catch the Blues. City were convinced they could still pull off the double, although they had to ensure they defeated Everton in the last game and hope Wednesday failed to pick up maximum points.

Before the League programme could reach its conclusion City had the small matter of the F.A. Cup Final to consider, as this was scheduled for Saturday 23rd April - the day Wednesday would face Aston Villa in the crucial League game.

City's 1904 Cup Final side deserve to be recognised as one of the all-time great teams regardless of how the Final or the League programme ended. The side had developed from virtually nothing into one capable of true talent and performance. The people of Manchester deserved a little pleasure after the years of struggle while supporting both City and United and, with a trip to London available, all Mancunians decided to celebrate. Most of the pubs and working men's clubs in the Ardwick area and in the city, organised excursions to the capital. Many set off early on Friday morning determined to make a holiday of it, and reporters from all the North's leading newspapers journeyed with them.

With City's final opponents being Bolton Wanderers, the whole affair became known as 'The Lancastrian Invasion', and many Londoners must have been surprised at what for many would have been their first sight of 'Northerners'. The now defunct, 'Blue-biased', *Manchester Evening Chronicle* carried a report on the situation in London: "The true character of the London invasion could not be gleaned until midnight and during the early hours of Saturday morning. At Euston, St. Pancras, King's Cross and Marylebone, the trains, heavy laden, steamed in continuously. 'What a cheer!' I heard a jovial porter say, shortly after midnight. 'This is great, ain't it? Blimey! Did you ever see so many pubs in bottles? What, oh! Don't they grub?' And truly, the trippers upheld the tradition of the North. Each little party seemed to have brought their own stack of provisions for the weekend. Nine gallon barrels of beer, stone jars of whisky and big baskets filled with 'baggins' were almost as plentiful as blackberries in Autumn, while there could never have been as many toastmasters on Euston station before, 'Good Health!' rang perpetually in one's ears. 'Hooray!', 'Play up, City!'

For many Londoners, the excited City supporters must have re-enforced their stereotypical view of the North, but who cared? At least they added colour to a rain soaked London morning. For many Blues this would have been their first, and possibly their only, trip to the capital, and no doubt they wanted to take in a few of the sights. Unfortunately, the morning was so miserable that most Mancunians remained at the stations. St. Pancras is reported to have had more people packed on to its platforms that morning than at any other time, while at least sixteen thousand people arrived at Euston during the night with nowhere else to go.

By about seven o'clock some of the more enthusiastic supporters ventured out of the stations to explore the capital. It must have seemed like young birds leaving their nests for the first time as the Blues fans were eager to leave, but uncertain what they would find. Gradually, as more left the security of the station others plucked up the courage. By ten o'clock the sun was shining and most Blues had taken flight. Only the late arrivals remained.

For the directors of Manchester City the journey to London was also a great adventure. They obtained a horse-drawn carriage and, with eleven or twelve on the roof, and around six inside, they travelled south. Every one of the directors must have been proud, but could any of them have been as chuffed as Lawrence Furniss who had been connected with the club since the early 1880s, and secretary/manager when the club first entered the League? Travelling with Furniss were the club's two other former secretaries - Josh Parlby and Sam Ormerod. Parlby was, of course, still an important member of the City directorate, whereas Ormerod was actually Stockport County's secretary/manager. By involving Ormerod in City's moment of glory, the Blues signalled they did not hold Ormerod personally to blame for City's relegation two years earlier, and in some small way the former manager was being thanked for the work he had put in during his time at Hyde Road.

Another man travelling with the directors was J.J. Bentley, the President of the Football League and former Bolton Secretary/manager. Bentley was also a leading journalist for the Hulton owned *Umpire* newspaper who, only the night before, had made comments about City making the headlines too often.

It's worth considering exactly what Tom Maley had achieved with City so far. He had built a team in the truest sense of the word, he had pushed that side to promotion, and then seen his players dominate most First Division and Cup games since. His team had hit the headlines on several occasions and many of his players had become household names. J.J. Bentley commented on City's headline grabbing ability in his article in The Umpire newspaper on the eve of the Final: "Since the City have become famous and especially as the Cup Finalists, it has been considered the proper thing to give every detail of their doings and I'm quite expecting to read that, while shaving, Meredith accidentally came across a little wart and the great international actually lost ten drops of his precious blood..."

Skipper Billy Meredith leads his team to the Final.

FA Cup Winners 1904

The Cup Final was, for the tenth consecutive year, to be played at Crystal Palace, at the time a huge pleasure gardens and leisure complex. Although the venue was enormous - over 114,000 attended the 1901 Final - not everybody was guaranteed a good view. Many spectators sought whatever vantage point they could, with the many trees surrounding the ground packed with supporters. Even the journalists searched for the best spots. The *Athletic News* created quite a spectacle by obtaining a gas-filled balloon for the day. They had the intention of providing a bird's eye view of events for their readers.

A NORTHERN IMPORTATION
COLOURED UMBRELLAS USED AS PARTY BADGES

As the crowd gathered at the Palace ground, Tom Maley chose his team for what was hoped to be the first leg of the double. The team selected was a powerful one: Hillman, McMahon, Burgess, Frost, Hynds, Ashworth, Meredith, Livingstone, Gillespie, Turnbull, and Booth. There was no place for the long-serving 'Doc' Holmes, who had played in the quarter and semi-finals. Holmes was bitterly disappointed on hearing the news, and immediately took hold of his boots and threw them out of the dressing room window. Maley had replaced him with the amateur Sam Ashworth and, when considering the cold facts, it's easy to understand why. Holmes was very much a fringe player in Maley's City whereas the hardworking Ashworth was a key member of the team. Nevertheless, Holmes was a City man through and through. He had helped the club move away from its Second Division roots and now wanted to play a major part in bringing the Cup to Manchester for the first time.

Uncovered Stand DD, CRYSTAL PALACE.
Uncovered Stand DD, 5/-

The Football Association Challenge Cup.
FINAL TIE,
Saturday, April 23rd, 1904.
Kick Off at 3.30 p.m.
The Holder of this Ticket is requested to occupy the Seat by 3.15 p.m.
No. 989 This Ticket does NOT admit to the Palace.

A 1904 FA Cup Final ticket. Original cost five shillings. If a similar ticket from this match was auctioned today who knows what price it would fetch?

While Maley was attempting to calm the dressing room atmosphere, the *Manchester Evening Chronicle* reporters surveyed the scene prior to the big game: "It was an animated throng, one in which the spirit of partisanship was appreciably more lively than was the case among southern people. The rink was fringed with thousands of ardent Lancastrians, every man a connoisseur. Nearly everyone was willing to back his fancy, win or lose; the dark and the light-blue favours were strongly reminiscent of the University Boat Race. Manchester City seemed the favourites as was only to be expected, but the average Bolton supporter had almost an adoring faith in the potential of the 'Trotters'."

The article went on to describe that there were a large number of ladies present in the crowd and that the majority of these supported City. It seems that the reporter was quite surprised to find that the female members of the crowd were shouting and making as much noise as the men. Later, he described the now dry conditions and state of the ground: "The ground looked in beautiful condition after the rainfall of the previous day and there was no great amount of wind to make its presence felt on the course of the flying ball.

"Of course, there was the usual crowd wandering on the fringes of the field of play and the tedium of waiting was relieved by the Crystal Palace band, but away on the far terraces, behind the southern goal, the famous Boys Band of St. Joseph's were cheering on their supporters with spirited strains. As the time approached, the policemen in their usual persuasive manner, expeditiously cleared the precincts of the pavilion so that the teams could make their way on to the ground. Several enthusiastic Boltonians were to be noticed with bright parasols and white sleeved hats ornamented with trotters."

The *Daily Graphic's* report of the moments leading up to the game concentrated on the size of the crowd. The actual attendance was a disappointing 61,374, with receipts totalling £3,000. The early morning rain had put off those within a morning's travel of the Palace and, to be honest, many Lancastrians simply could not afford the expense of journeying to London and all that entailed.

The Cup Final referee Mr A.J. Barker of Hanley.

Nevertheless, it did compare with the attendance for the previous year's final (Bury v Derby County) and the finals pre-1901. In the end, any attendance of over sixty thousand for an all-Lancastrian final played in London before the days of comfortable wages and multi transport systems has to be significant. The *Daily Graphic* reporter acknowledged the large Lancastrian support: "None of the ordinary incidents of such a day were wanting. It would scarcely seem like a Cup tie day now if half the people there were not speaking in a provincial dialect. On Saturday it seemed as though three-fourths of the people were speaking in it, and the remaining fourth were ineffectually trying to imitate them.

Then there were the usual crowded trains, the rush for good standing places, the struggles for the refreshment tables, the usual notices imploring you not to climb up into the trees in order to get a view of the match - and the usual number of people who disregarded such notices, and came to no harm for their lawlessness. The only thing wanting was about another fifty thousand people to make the place uncomfortable for everyone.

"Ticket holders were asked to be in their places by a quarter past three, and among the eleven thousand odd people who obeyed this injunction were the Prime-Minister, the Colonial Secretary and Mrs. Lyttleton, the Hon. R. Lyttleton, and Lord Stanley. Mr. Balfour and Mr. Lyttleton were soon recognised by the crowd, and heartily cheered."

Prime-Minister Balfour was, of course, the man who almost four years earlier had visited Hyde Road after being persuaded by Stephen Chester Thompson to become a patron of the club. Was Balfour the first Prime-Minister to be a Blue? Or, like many other politicians, was the link with City a convenient way to gain votes? Most likely the latter!

Other celebrities to attend City's first final included the music hall stars George Robey and Harry Lauder, and cricketers C.B Fry, Wilfred Rhodes, Gilbert Jessop, and the larger than life W.G. Grace. The Cup Final was, by this time, established as one of the most important sporting occasions.

The Fruit of
That Forbidden
Tree
(Milton)

In preparation for the 3.30 pm kick off, the teams entered the field. Meredith was the first man out, leading the Sky Blues as captain. Bolton, dressed in white shirts, followed. Meredith won the toss and elected to play towards the southern goal where the Boys' Band of St. Joseph's entertained the City followers. The band had followed City to most of the key games that season, bringing a little extra atmosphere to the terraces. No big game was complete without St. Joseph's musical accompaniment.

Once the match kicked off the Palace's slippery pitch helped Bolton keep apace with City. The two sides seemed well matched for a while, with Bolton testing Hillman on a couple of occasions early on. Bolton were playing with much hustle and bustle, while the Blues were trying to play with style. It only seemed a matter of time before Maley's men took control: "As the game proceeded the Bolton Wanderers seemed to be getting a little loose in their play, while their opponents were improving. Several times the Manchester forwards quite outplayed the Wanderers, and, passing very neatly, with a great deal of head work, nearly scored. They tried again and again, and anyone could see that if a goal was to be scored, Meredith, the Manchester City captain, was the man to kick it. The game was getting uncomfortably warm for the Wanderers when Davies, their goalkeeper, was charged over [by Gillespie, no doubt!], and the free kick put matters right for a time. Manchester returned to the attack, and Davies had a good deal of work to do. Eventually Meredith seized the opportunity he had been working for and shot the ball crosswise into the Bolton goal. From the seats occupied by representatives of the *Daily Graphic* Meredith appeared to be off-side when he scored, and one is inclined to think that Davies was of the same opinion, for he but simply held his arms out. However, the goal was not questioned and, to the accompaniment of loud cheers and the waving of hats and sticks, play began again. The crowds were delighted at the prospect of seeing the match definitely decided, and one of Manchester's supporters was so enthusiastic in his praise of Meredith that he left his seat and attempted to walk out to the field, apparently with the intention of embracing the Manchester captain. Two policemen reasoned with him, but he insisted on going, and at length five policemen escorted him away for a time."

The debate about whether the goal was offside or not raged on for years. Bolton supporters firmly believed the goal should not have been counted while Meredith, throughout his life, was adamant it was legitimate. In 1904 the off-side rule stated that at least

The prize... the old trophy.

1904 FA CUP RUN

R1	Sunderland	H	W 3-2
R2	Woolwich Arsenal	A	W 2-0
R3	Middlesbrough	H	D 0-0
	Middlesbrough	A	W 3-1
SF	Sheffield Wednesday	N*	W 3-0
F	Bolton Wanderers	N**	W 1-0

* = Goodison Park
** = Crystal Palace Ground

FACTS & FIGURES

	P	W	D	L	F	A
HOME	2	1	1	0	3	2
AWAY	4	4	0	0	9	1
TOTAL	6	5	1	0	12	3

CUP FINAL DETAILS

23 April 1904 at The Crystal Palace
MANCHESTER CITY 1
BOLTON WANDERERS 0

CITY: Hillman, McMahon, Burgess, Frost, Hynds, Ashworth, Meredith, Livingstone, Gillespie, Turnbull, Booth
BOLTON: Davies, Brown, Struthers, Clifford, Greenhalgh, Freebairn, Stokes, Marsh, Yenson, White, Taylor
GOAL: Meredith

ATTENDANCE: 61,372
REFEREE: A J Barker (Hanley)
GUEST OF HONOUR: Lord Alfred Lyttleton
MANAGER: Tom Maley
CAPTAIN: Billy Meredith

How the artist from 'The Illustrated Sporting & Dramatic News' saw the Cup-winning goal, from the right boot of Billy Meredith.

three opponents must be goalside of the attacker when the ball was played. According to many journalists at the game that had not been the case. J.J. Bentley who, it must be remembered, was the former Bolton secretary, firmly believed that Meredith was a couple of yards offside. This seemed a bit presumptious, especially as his place in the pavilion was at an awkward angle, and gave a far from perfect view.

Interestingly, the players themselves did not appeal at the time, leading to suspicions that the goal only became controversial as the game progressed and Bolton's chances diminished. According to all reports City certainly deserved their lead and comfortably kept Bolton at a safe distance. In the second half the Blues seemed to relax a little, while still retaining overall control. Some believed the Blues were saving themselves for the important League game against Everton the following Monday. A fact perhaps borne out by Meredith's deliberate attempts at time wasting by moving in to offside positions.

City's relaxed approach did provide Bolton with a few chances, but there was never really any danger, and the Blues won a Final they dominated, by Meredith's controversial goal. As the match ended thousands swarmed onto the pitch in front of the pavilion to see the Colonial Secretary, Alfred Lyttleton, present the Cup to Maley's City. The *Daily Graphic* reported on the moment and the speeches made: "Mr. Lyttleton, who was loudly cheered, said that in presenting the Cup he was sure Manchester City would not object to his first word being to Bolton. They had played a losing game well, under desperate conditions, and had a given a fine exhibition of pluck, energy and endurance. As one who had taken part in the game of Association Football, he congratulated Manchester City on their well deserved and splendid victory. He had hardly seen such a good match since he played for England against Scotland six and twenty years ago. It was true that England lost that match, but he would ask the Prime Minister to look up the records and see who it was that scored England's one goal."

Meredith attacks Bolton's goal.

The cup presentation by Lord Alfred Lyttleton to City captain and goalscorer Billy Meredith.

"Mr. Balfour, in calling upon the crowd to thank Mr. Lyttleton for coming to present the Cup, said that Mr. Lyttleton had spoken to them as an expert, while he could only speak as an admiring ignoramus. He was glad the tie had been fought out between two Lancastrian teams, and he was sure they would pardon his satisfaction at the success of Manchester City"

On receiving the Cup Meredith is reported to have said, "I'm sure it has given me great pleasure to win the Cup", although he later denied making those comments as they appeared so amusing to him when he saw them in print. Regardless of the actual words spoken, it must have been an otherwise memorable day for Meredith and everyone connected with City. At Hyde Road a crowd of 8,000 attending a reserve game, gave a tremendous roar of delight when the score was chalked on to a scoreboard in the stand. Elsewhere in Manchester the news soon spread and the whole city started to celebrate, and prepare for the return of its heroes.

Although most Mancunians were keen to see the conquering City side bring home the Cup, the civic leaders and police rather surprisingly refused to support any plans for celebration. When a civic reception was suggested Manchester's leaders gave a response along the lines of 'Manchester is an industrial city and has no time for merriment'. When asked about a special home-coming, the Chief Constable retorted, "I am not interested!"

It was all quite sad but, perhaps they simply did not know what positive role football could have in the lives of Mancunians. Maybe they were concerned that too much time had already been spent organising the trips to London and so on. Unfortunately for the Police Chief, the people of Manchester were very much interested in welcoming back their heroes and, on the Sunday, huge crowds took to the streets of Britain's first industrial city to see its first trophy winners. The *Athletic News*, as always, followed the triumphal procession: "As soon as they caught sight of

"Got It."
The English Cup.
OXO is repeating the successes of last season, when no fewer than 215 walkers trained and won on OXO.
In addition to carrying the 1st, 2nd, and 3rd men home to victory at the 50 miles' Lancashire walk on Saturday, the 15th April, 1904, the very latest triumph for OXO is the winning of the English Association Football Cup. The following letter speaks for itself:—
Manchester, 7th April, 1904.
"I have much pleasure in testifying to the sustaining properties of OXO, the 'City' team having used it regularly during the Season."
(Signed) THOS. E. MALEY,
Secretary and Manager,
MANCHESTER CITY FOOTBALL CLUB.
OXO

MANCHESTER CITY SECURE THE CUP.

YE OLDE TROTTER

Trotters supporters.

Meredith puts through the cup-winner.

Taylor makes good use of White's clever pass

Brown disturbs the City attack.

The Premier greets "W.G."

Hillman collars the ball at the finish

George Livingstone's 1904 Cup Winner's medal, auctioned at Christies many years later.

the trophy trimmed with blue and white ribbons which Meredith now and then raised above his head, they gave vent to prodigious cheering. Most of the windows of the upper stories were packed with people whose plaudits, added to by the blowing of a bugle here and there and the music of the band, made a deafening sound.

"To the accompaniment of incessant cheering, the procession made its way at walking pace down Dale Street where what might be called the welcome of the middle-classes was exchanged for that of the proletariat. It came from rough working men and larrikins and beshawled women and children in arms and hand, and was hearty if not heartier than had gone before."

For the first time, regardless of class, Manchester's people felt they had achieved something. They were united in their support of the Cup winners and after tasting success for the first time, they were keen to see City find further glory.

The only black moment that weekend came when Manchester heard the news that as the Blues defeated Bolton, their League rivals, Sheffield Wednesday, had gained a further two points by beating Aston Villa 4-2. This meant Wednesday were a point ahead of City with both teams due to play one more game. Both matches were to be played away from home with Wednesday at fourteenth-placed Derby County on the 30th, while City would face fourth-placed Everton on Monday 25th. The Sky Blues knew they had to win and hope Wednesday lost to stand any chance of lifting their first title, and of course the coveted double.

Unfortunately, the exertions of Cup Final weekend had affected the players, and City's match with Everton became a bit of an anti-climax. The same eleven players who had performed so well at the Palace went down to a single goal from Taylor. Wednesday, without playing, were Champions for the second year running, and the Blues were left to rue what might have been. Sheffield Wednesday, incidentally, went on to beat Derby 2-0 and so end the season three points above Maley's City.

Regardless of how the League programme ended, City were the team of the season. The team had won many admirers with their stylish approach, and had dominated the headlines in the popular sporting press. Tom Maley deserved the plaudits after turning City from a team of individuals going nowhere, into a star-studded side in the truest sense of the phrase.

1903-4 was the season when Manchester City proved what a successful Manchester club could achieve. Not only had the Blues found success, they had also become one of the wealthiest clubs in England. Their strong financial position meant they could tempt almost anyone to join the club, and they had the financial clout to look after those already there. Unfortunately, City's generosity would ultimately cause their downfall.

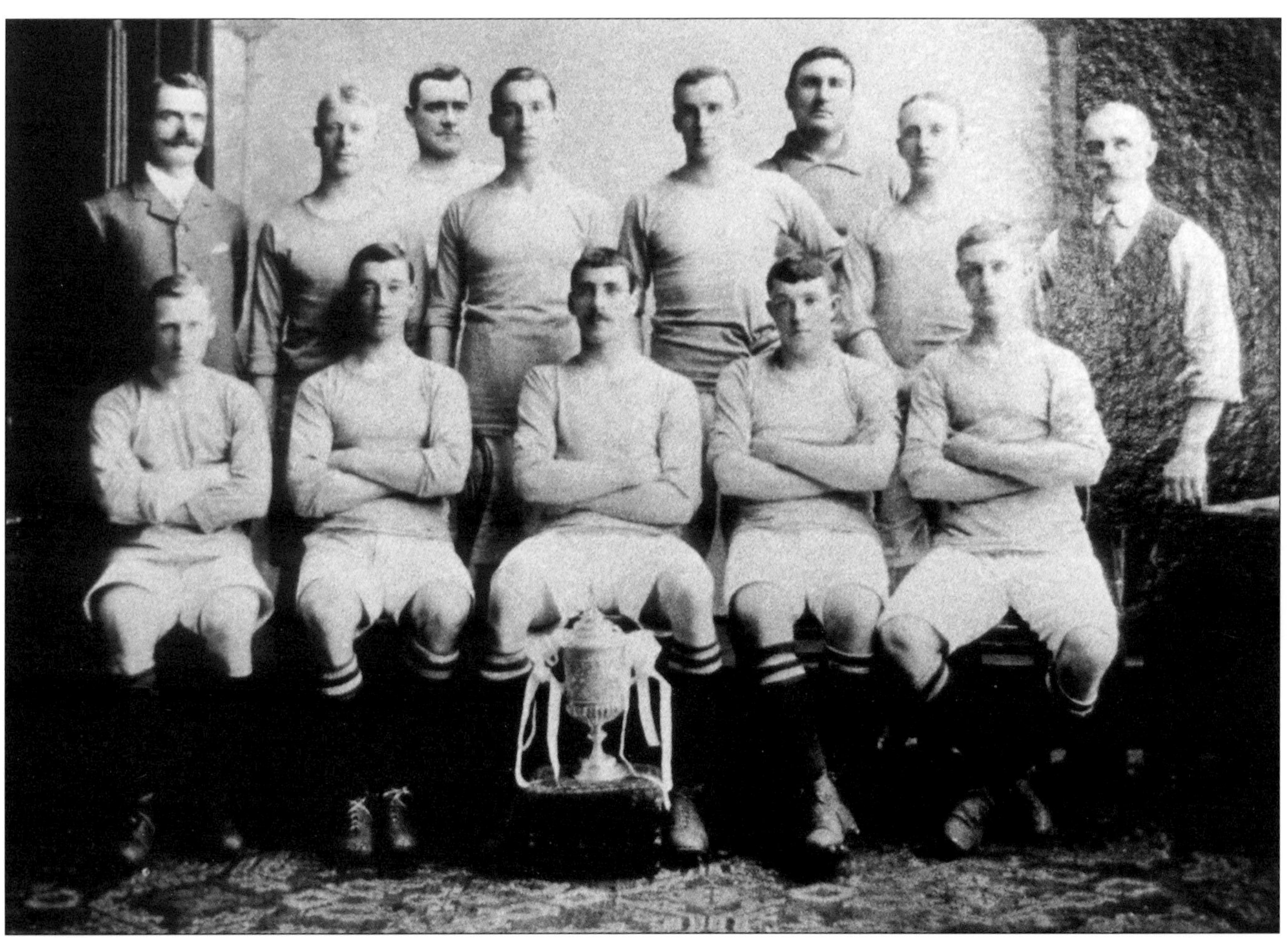

Manchester City 1903-04 - English Cup Winners, First Divison Runners-up and Joint Holders of the Manchester Cup.
Back (left to right): T.E.Maley (Secretary & Manager), S.Frost, W.J.Gillespie, J.McMahon, T.Hynds, J.Hillman, S.B.Ashworth, J.Broad (Trainer).
Front: H.Burgess, G.T.Livingstone, W.Meredith, A.Turnbull, F.Booth.

Chapter Four

SCANDAL & STRUGGLE

THE Cup success and runners up in the League fired City with greater ambition. The club, under the direction of Edward Hulton and John Allison, was aiming for the top. City's success showed what was possible and, with increased revenue from the 1903-4 season, the Blues were able to enlarge the Hyde Road stands. Over £2,000 worth of improvements helped increase capacity by around 10,000 with the Blues' management confident the fans would flock to see Manchester's top club.

Unfortunately for the Blues, others were increasingly showing the wrong sort of interest in the Club. The Football Association, 'a southern body dominated by amateurs' according to many northerners at the time, were unhappy with City's success. According to John Harding's excellent biography of Billy Meredith, *Football Wizard*, the F.A. believed clubs such as City were too professional and there was a real danger of football's amateur, sporting, nature disappearing forever. Before football was lost completely to the northern professionals, the F.A. decided to teach the main culprits a lesson.

Within two weeks of City's triumphal procession through Manchester, the F.A. secretary, F.J. Wall, and a member of the F.A. General Council, J. Lewis, arrived at Hyde Road demanding to see the club's books. They spent the whole close season examining City's accounts determined to find proof of illegal wages and bonuses, yet found nothing tangible. Then they discovered discrepancies in the transfers of Frank Norgrove and Irvine Thornley from Glossop. Apparently, the F.A. had also been investigating Glossop, another northern 'professional' outfit, when they uncovered suspicious information and discrepancies between that and City's books. In City's accounts were forged receipts for unusual payments that coincided with the players' transfers. The F.A. determined that these were actually signing on fees far in excess of the £10 maximum then allowed.

To preserve its amateur image, the F.A. had insisted on maximum signing on fees in addition to the £4 maximum wage rule. Most First Division clubs broke the rules but some were simply more adept at balancing the books and not bringing undue attention to themselves. As Meredith once said: "Of course clubs are not punished for breaking laws. They are punished for being found out."

Meredith's view was accurate - City were a club unable to keep their activities quiet. Dating back to Ardwick days they had been in trouble with the F.A. for poaching players, and by 1904 were viewed as a nouveau riche club determined to buy success. The establishment, in the form of the F.A., were out to get the Blues.

In October 1904, as a result of the investigations, City were fined £250, Irvine Thornley was suspended for the rest of the season, and Hyde Road was ordered to be closed for two games. In addition, directors Joshua Parlby, John Chapman, and Lawrence Furniss were banned for three years, while the Finance Director, G. Madders, was suspended for life. This was a major blow for the club and for the men involved, especially Parlby, Chapman, and Furniss.

Furniss's and Parlby's places in City's history have always been clear - both managed the club and both had helped create Manchester City as we know it today - but what is rarely documented is the role John Chapman played. Chapman had also been involved with the club since the Ardwick days and, together with Parlby, had signed Meredith. He had also been

John Lewis, a member of the F.A. General Council, arrived at Hyde Road to examine City's books more-or-less as soon as the Cup had been won. Did the F.A. have it in for the young upstarts?

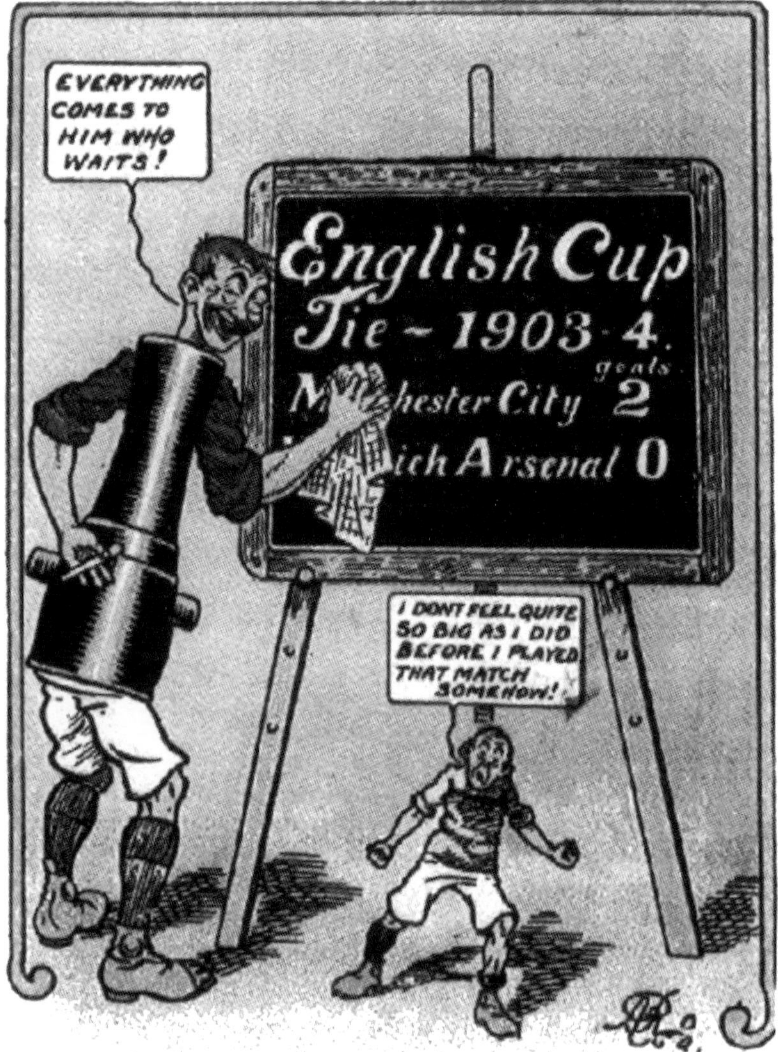

A postcard produced celebrating Arsenal's revenge over City. They defeated the Blues 1-0 on the 10th December 1904, ten months after City's 2-0 victory in the F.A. Cup.

A watch presented to secretary/manager Tom Maley to commemorate City's success in the 1904 F.A. Cup. Now a much sought-after collector's piece.

extremely generous financially, and had helped the club sign many other players. He was a well known figure in the city and, a few days after the Cup success, *The Umpire* newspaper honoured him by featuring him as an 'Umpire Favourite'.

'Umpire Favourite's' were typically players who had made the news for one reason or another - Billy Meredith, Tom Hynds, and Frank Booth had all featured - John Chapman was the first non-player to be chosen. *The Umpire* stressed his importance to Manchester: "Ever since that time [1894] Mr. Chapman has been a member of the Board, and for eight unbroken years he was the Chairman. The name of John Chapman is known to most of the many thousands who claim to be numbered among the supporters of Manchester City, but it may safely be said that comparatively few are aware to what extent they are indebted to the gentleman who for so long presided over the destinies of the club. Though now a prosperous organisation, Manchester City has not always been in that happy position, and in the early years of its existence, when an effort was being made to get together a team worthy of representing a city like Manchester - a costly business - the subject of this sketch was always ready to furnish the sinews of war whenever necessary. In this and in other ways, such, for instance, as visiting different places for the purpose of watching men who had been 'spotted' as likely to prove of service to the club, Mr. Chapman has always been ready to render assistance."

Irvine Thornley, who had only been with the club since April, was already popular with the supporters and it was a tremendous disappointment that he was to miss the bulk of the 1904-5 season, especially as he had already scored the only two City goals in the four games he had participated in. Fortunately for Thornley, his enforced absence probably prevented him from getting involved in the bigger scandal that was about to engulf the club and cause the *Athletic News* journalist James Catton, who used the pen name Tityrus, to state that City are: "like the poor. We always have them with us. It seems we cannot escape from them."

Before further investigations, City were able to play a little football. Although the opening five fixtures only resulted in one win and two draws, Maley's outfit still had the look of Championship contenders. From 8th October they put together a run of four games without defeat and scored a total of thirteen goals. The bustling Gillespie, who rejoined the side after Thornley's ban, contributed three of those goals and had already rediscovered his touch.

As the year progressed, convincing victories over Wolves (5-1), Sunderland (5-2), and Derby County (6-0) established the Blues in the top half of the table, while the New Year brought official recognition to all the players for the part they had played in the Cup success. At a special commemorative dinner held at the Grand Hotel on Aytoun Street on 9th January, the players, trainer Jimmy Broad, and Secretary/Manager Tom Maley were presented with commemorative gold watches paid for by collections amongst City's large following.

What made the presentation more special was the knowledge that many Mancunians were suffering great hardship at the time, both financially and health wise. The winter of 1904-5 had been particularly harsh with many locals dying of cold and malnutrition. Unemployment was high and a relief fund was set up. To boost funds music hall entertainer and supporter of City at the final, George Robey, brought a 'Team of Internationals' to Hyde Road on 23rd January to raise money. At that game, and others at Hyde Road, blankets were carried around the pitch for people to throw coins into. Although City were a wealthy and successful club, many of the club's supporters had little else to cheer. Maybe this is why City mattered so much to Mancunians. It gave them a successful escape from the grim reality of life in Edwardian Manchester.

From the turn of the year through to mid-March City were undefeated in eight League games, taking the Blues back to the top of the League. With Bolton gaining revenge in the second round of the F.A. Cup - they defeated City 2-1 at Hyde Road - Maley was determined to see his side capture the title. By mid April with only four games to go City, Newcastle, and Everton challenged for top spot, although it was apparent that City had the harder run in.

On the 15th Everton faced Small Heath, a team on the fringe of the title race, at Goodison Park, while City met reigning champions Sheffield Wednesday at Hyde Road. Newcastle, like City the year before, had the small matter of facing Aston Villa in the 1905 F.A. Cup Final to overcome before turning their attentions back to the League.

At Goodison, Everton defeated Stoke 2-1 to increase their points tally to 45 while City struggled to match Wednesday. After being a goal behind for much of the game, Billy Meredith found City's equaliser in the last ten minutes. Maley's City had lost their rhythm, but were not out of the race yet. With three games to go they were three points behind Everton and equal with Newcastle, although the Cup finalists had one game in hand and, significantly, had failed in their bid to capture the F.A. Cup. It was now a question of nerve. Could Everton hold on to their lead? Would Newcastle be more determined? Could Maley rekindle his team spirit of twelve months earlier?

The 21st April was perhaps the most significant date. Newcastle faced Stoke in their first League game since the final while City and Everton met at Hyde Road. A crowd of over 40,000 packed into the ground and, although it is difficult to prove, many believe the attendance that day was the largest at the ground so far and potentially the largest ever at Hyde Road. Another 40,000 game some fifteen years later against Burnley is more likely to be the highest actual attendance however, although the abandoned Cup match v. Sunderland in 1913 had an official crowd of 41,709.

The game was an ill tempered one and, although City won 2-0 with goals from Tom Hynds and George Livingstone, an off the ball incident made the game noteworthy. Everton's Tom Booth, who had only played an handful of games all season, brutally 'flattened' City's Frank Booth. Both players were cautioned - inevitably City had retaliated - and Hyde Road became a ground of hate. The police had to escort the players from the pitch and it was perhaps only the fact City had defeated the League leaders that stopped incidents occurring off the pitch.

In Liverpool the feeling was that City's Booth had provoked his namesake, and that the Everton man was justified in his action. Mancunians on the other hand believed no amount of provocation could justify the type of brutal attack that had occurred.

With the game ending in controversy, much of the post match comment concerned the physical side of the contest and ignored the fact that the Blues were only one point behind Everton with two games remaining. Unfortunately, Newcastle had levelled with City and had a game in hand - a north-east derby the following day against Sunderland. City needed the Geordies to fail.

By the end of play on the 22nd April, City's position had improved even though they had not played. Newcastle were defeated 3-1 and Everton, who remained a point in front of the two challengers, lost 2-1 at Arsenal. Two days later it was the turn of Newcastle to rest as City and Everton played crucial games away from home - Wolves v. City, and Nottingham Forest v. Everton. Both sides achieved convincing victories, with City winning 3-0, to keep up the pressure. On the 26th Newcastle levelled with City after a 3-1 victory over Sheffield Wednesday, making the final day of the season a tense affair. With the two sides level, a mere one point behind Everton who had already completed their League programme, the title race was wide open. City knew they had to win and hope that Newcastle failed as the Blues' goal average was inferior to the Geordies.

The final fixtures saw Newcastle away at near neighbours Middlesbrough, while the Blues travelled to Villa Park to face the Cup winners. Billy Meredith later recalled the City attitude: "Aston Villa had no

The WEST END CLOTHIERS' COMPANY, LTD.,
For HIGH-CLASS TAILORING at POPULAR PRICES. 41, HIGH STREET, SHEFFIELD.

Sheffield Wednesday v. Manchester City.

VOL. 5 Played at Owlerton, Sheffield, November 26th, 1904. No. 13

Wednesday.

Right Wing. Left Wing.

1 Lyall

BACKS:

2 Slavin 3 Burton

HALF-BACKS:

4 Ferrier 5 Crawshaw 6 Ruddlesdin

FORWARDS:

7 Davis 8 V. S. Simpson 9 Wilson 10 Malloch 11 Simpson

Referee: Mr. J. Adams, Birmingham.

Should any Alteration be made, a notice will be sent round giving the name of the substituted player, and the number of the position in which he will play.

Published by J. WHITHAM, 19, Vincent Road, Sheffield.

Linesmen: Messrs. Wright and James.

FORWARDS:

12 Booth 13 Turnbull 14 Gillespie 15 Livingstone 16 Meredith

HALF-BACKS:

17 Moffat 18 Hynds 19 Frost

BACKS:

20 Burgess 21 McMahon

22 Hillman

Left Wing. Right Wing.

Manchester City.

The WEST END CLOTHIERS' COMPANY, Ltd., TROUSERS from 10/6 Per Pair, TO MEASURE.

The WEST END CLOTHIERS' COMPANY, Ltd., REAL INDIGO DYED SERGE SUITS, from 37/6 TO MEASURE.

The WEST END CLOTHIERS' COMPANY, LTD.,
For HIGH-CLASS TAILORING at POPULAR PRICES,
41, HIGH STREET, SHEFFIELD

The team sheet from City's visit to Sheffield Wednesday on the 26th November 1904.

Turnbull heads through number Two.

Sandy Turnbull hit four of City's six goals against Derby.

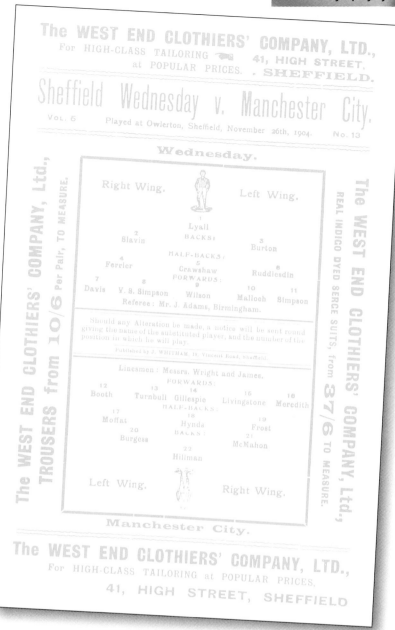

The 1905 F.A. Cup semi-final between Newcastle United and Sheffield Wednesday was staged at Hyde Road in front of a 40,000 crowd. In the top picture is the Main Stand, in the bottom picture is the Popular Side. Note the many supporters seated on the touchline.

chance of taking the honour. Our officials were very keen on us finishing with level points and we were offered a good bonus if we managed to do this. Our blood was up and the game wasn't the pleasantest."

As Meredith stated the game did not demonstrate the gentlemanly side of football, if anything it showed how physical football could become with numerous off the ball incidents and dangerous tackles. It seems that Villa, who had never really liked playing either Manchester club, wanted to finish the season in the style they had shown at the Palace the week before. They did not want the 'ungentlemanly professionals' from Manchester to achieve further success, especially as they were still regarded as young upstarts with no tradition. Looking back it is difficult to understand exactly how the Blues were viewed, but as an analogy with the 1980s and 1990s it is safe to say Villa were the early century's equivalent of Manchester United in terms of F.A. support and media interest, whereas City were similar to Wimbledon. In the eyes of many, they had appeared from nowhere to challenge the establishment. Sadly, the establishment, especially in the early 1900s, would always win.

With Villa determined to put City in their place, the Blues resorted to the tactics many suspected came naturally. Maley's City let themselves down, and conceded goals to Villa's Garraty, Hampton, and Hall. The pressure was on. Two second half goals from George Livingstone, and Sandy Turnbull brought the Blues back into it but it wasn't enough. During the final thirty minutes the game became progressively more violent with Sandy Turnbull seemingly involved in every incident. The *Bolton Football Field* reporter outlined his view: "Turnbull was in his dourest dribbling mood, dashing about the ball with his whole heart set on victory. Leake found him a real hard opponent and, becoming annoyed at the rough impact, gathered up a handful of dirt and hurled it at the City man. Turnbull was not hurt and responded with an acknowledgement favoured by the bourgeoisie - thrusting two fingers in a figurative manner at the Villa man. He then says that Leake appeared to look towards the referee as though appealing, and not catching his eye, 'gave Turnbull a backhander'. The latter immediately responded with his fists and Leake was restrained by his fellow players from retaliating further."

Although Turnbull had developed a reputation for a rough style of play it appears that he was not the guilty one this time. Unfortunately, Leake was viewed as a gentleman and many were convinced that he would only react, not provoke. The Villa biased

Sports Argus tried to convince its readership that Leake was entirely innocent and that he had merely enquired what Turnbull was doing rather than throw dirt at him and give him a 'backhander'. It also stated that the City man had hit Leake at least twice.

The game continued but frequent fights broke out, spoiling any chance City had of equalising. Despite the result and the realisation that City had lost out in the title race, it was a relief when the final whistle went. However, the controversy did not end there as the *Bolton Football Field* reported: "Turnbull was coming off the ground (I think he was almost the first of the City players) and was going down the covered passage to the visitors' dressing room when someone, not a player, sprang out from the urinal and grabbed Turnbull, pulled him inside the Villa dressing room and the door was shut behind him. I thought the whole thing was in fun until, within a few seconds, the door was opened and Turnbull was pitched out heavily, by whom I could not see. He was yelling with pain and fright, and he had obviously been badly handled for his right cheek was grazed with a black mark or dirt (something like a cyclist describes as a cinder rash) and he had a mark on his ribs where he had been kicked."

Nobody disputed that Turnbull had been the victim of a deliberate attack by Villa men, but incredibly the Birmingham *Sports Argus* tried to justify it, thus causing further insults to fly from Manchester to Birmingham and vice versa. Significantly, it wasn't merely the Villa players and employees who were attacking the City men as police had to be called into the ground to protect the Manchester players. Leaving Villa Park was also a nightmare as an angry mob stoned the City party. A season that had promised so much ended in disgraceful scenes.

The F.A. had to act, especially as City's game against Everton had also been viewed as a battle. They set up a special committee to meet in Derby to consider the events at both matches, but it quickly became apparent that the investigations were not merely about the violence. Meeting behind closed doors, the committee took considerable steps to understand everything that surrounded the two games and, as the summer progressed, they interviewed player after player in their quest for the full facts. This all seemed overly suspicious, especially to the northern newspapers who were now convinced that the committee were fishing for a bigger catch than merely a disrepute charge against one or two players. With the F.A. meeting in secret rumour spread throughout football, with most northerners convinced the 'southern' F.A. would make City the scapegoats.

Eventually on 4th August 1905, a month before the new season started, the F.A. committee produced their surprising findings. Firstly, they suspended J.T. Howcroft and R. T. Johns - the referees of the games at Goodison and Villa respectively - for a month each for failing to control the games. Howcroft in particular was criticised for 'extraordinary feebleness in a critical match'. Then they announced that Tom Booth of Everton and City's Sandy Turnbull were to be suspended for one month, yet no mention was made of Villa's Leake. Also, that Booth's sentence would be suspended because of: "previous good conduct and the provocation received." And finally, the most shocking news of the whole affair: "The Commissioners also reported on statements brought to their notice with regard to W. Meredith of Manchester having offered a sum of money to a player of Aston Villa to let Manchester City win the match. W. Meredith is suspended from football from 4th August until April 1906."

The people of Manchester - and Wales - were outraged that football's greatest player could be found guilty of bribery. Meredith, staying in Chirk during the close season, spoke to the press: "I am entirely innocent and am suffering for others. Such an allegation as that of bribery is preposterous! I could never risk my reputation and future by such an action and I repeat that I never made such an offer. It is totally unjustifiable and grossly unfair. This sort of thing will demoralise Association Football. Manchester has not many friends among the Association officials and I doubt if the decision will be reversed or the suspension lessened if the whole case is reopened and enquired into." He added that Aston Villa had too much influence within the F.A. and that, "Manchester City is becoming too popular to suit some other clubs."

The general feeling was that Manchester City had suffered because, as Meredith had stated, City were simply too popular. In Simon Inglis' review of football's major scandals, *Soccer in The Dock*, that theory is followed in more detail: "Alec Leake was not even mentioned, even though it had been plainly stated that Turnbull had been assaulted by Villa players after the game. Small wonder therefore that in the eyes of many neutrals the F.A. appeared to bear a grudge against Manchester City, a nouveau riche club with no traditions. Villa, in contrast, were solidly reliable, brimming with honours and very much part of the football establishment. Some commentators noted caustically that Leake was an England international while the other players were not. Meredith meanwhile complained, 'Had I been anyone but a Welshman I should have been better dealt with.' But Harricus of *Athletic News* said the F.A.'s methods had seemed 'un-English, most autocratic and arbitrary.'"

It certainly does appear that the Blues had suffered merely because of who they were and not through the actual actions, nevertheless the F.A. must have had some evidence to suggest that Meredith was guilty. As the weeks passed, further details emerged. It seemed that Leake had laughed off Meredith's bribery attempt at the time, thinking it to be very much a joke, but as the F.A. commission investigated the Villa-City match a 'responsible gentleman from Birmingham' came forward to state that he had overheard the conversation. Leake was interrogated further and was apparently forced to admit that Meredith had attempted to bribe him. Meredith claimed that he had not attempted to bribe the player but did admit to having a conversation with him. Instead of offering him £10, he claimed to have offered his congratulations to Leake for lifting the F.A. Cup.

The matter did not end there, however. City's complaints and the anti-F.A. comments that appeared in the mainly northern sporting press upset the councillors of the F.A. They felt their actions were right and, if anything, became more interested in the affairs of City because of the proclamation of innocence. They appointed an auditor, Tom Hindle,

The people of Manchester and Wales were outraged that football's greatest player could be found guilty of bribery.

Alec Leake, the Aston Villa player who claimed Billy Meredith had attempted to bribe him to throw the Villa-City game on 29th April 1905. He was also said to have thrown dirt at City's Turnbull who retaliated by sticking two fingers up to the Villa man.

Suspended from English football sine die

Manager Tom Maley and former Chairman W. Forrest

Suspended for seven months

Directors Allison and Davies

SEVENTEEN players suspended and fined

Meredith
Livingstone
Hynds
McMahon
Hillman
Turnbull
Booth
Burgess
Frost
Bannister
Dearden
Gillespie
Holmes
Edmundson
Davidson
Lyon
Ashworth

to keep a close watch on the club and report anything out of the ordinary. Because of the state of most leading clubs at the time, not only City, it was not long before Hindle became suspicious.

Meredith, while banned from all football activity, still appeared at Hyde Road asking for his wages and generally expecting the Blues to look after him: "Though the F.A. suspended me, I felt strongly that my club would see that I was not the loser financially. At the beginning of the trouble it looked as if the club was going to recognise this, but later I found them shilly-shallying and putting me off until I got tired."

Understandably, for a man who had dedicated over ten years to the club he expected that club to care for him, especially when on the first day of the ban (4th August 1905) Tom Maley sent him a letter suggesting that he would always be a member of the City, but would have to 'lie low' until Hindle had gone away. The fact was that the Blues were not allowed to support him - the F.A. had made it quite clear that the player and the club were not to support each other.

Because of this, every visit or demand by Meredith caused the club tremendous embarrassment. There is no doubt the club wanted to look after him, after all they needed him to return once his suspension ended, however they were forbidden from doing so. Meredith could not accept this and regularly arrived at the ground only to be told he was not welcome. Arguments were witnessed by Tom Hindle, the F.A. auditor, and the club were in real danger of being investigated once again. Hindle persuaded Maley to report Meredith to avoid an F.A. investigation.

Maley's letter presented an unpleasant picture of City's relationship with their first truly great captain: "I am instructed by my directors to bring to the notice of your Association the conduct of William Meredith, a player of this club at present under suspension. This player has been in attendance at almost all the principal matches at our ground and invariably frequented the dressing room and offices despite requests not to do so." The letter sent on 14th February 1906 went on to say that Meredith had periodically approached the board for his wages, and when his requests were turned down the player made threats. Basically, the letter gave the impression Meredith was a parasite. This was something neither Maley nor the City Board believed, however it seemed the only way to avoid further investigation. Unfortunately, it failed.

Meredith was so appalled by the club's actions he started to speak out about the incident with Leake. The F.A. immediately set up a new commission and started to interview the City players and management not only about the bribe, but also about illegal payments to players. Meredith now claimed that he had offered Leake £10, but told the commission this was at Tom Maley's suggestion with full approval from the rest of the City team. City were no longer a united team, and with their former captain's revelations that he was not the only member involved in the attempted bribe, the rest of the squad were to be interrogated. Any unified front and spirit that existed prior to the Villa game must surely have disappeared by this point.

Tom Maley, when questioned, was adamant he did not have anything to do with the attempted bribery. He was aware three players had talked about the idea but that one of them clearly stated that he would not stoop so low. He did not reveal who the players were, but it is apparent that Meredith was one of the party. The other issue being pursued by the commission was the question of illegal payments. Maley did not deny that payments had been made to players in excess of the maximum, but claimed this seemed common business practice in England and that he only continued to follow the club's standard practices. He stated that if all First Division clubs were investigated, not four would come out 'scatheless'.

City were certainly guilty of paying above the maximum but if the F.A. had carried out a similar investigation at all the leading clubs they would have found the same situation.

Unfortunately, City were the team under the spotlight and, as they and their friends in the media had already criticised the F.A., they were to be the ones taught a lesson. The Edward Hulton-owned *Athletic News* not only blamed the F.A. it also pointed the finger at Meredith: "The famous footballer determined not only to admit that he had made an offer to Alec Leake - an offence which ought to have ended his football career - not only that he had been most lavishly and generously paid by the club which ran dreadful risks to give him all they had except the goalposts, but dragged everyone else he could into the same mess.

No sense of gratitude for all the managers who, over the years, remunerated him so that he became comparatively rich, no ideals of friendship for the men who, admitting his enviable playing skills, had done everything they could for him, and no feeling of loyalty for the comrades who had fought side by side with him in many a scrap of hard games restrained this man from divulging the secrets of his masters and colleagues.

It would have been honourable to confess his own deeds, to express his sorrow and promise an amendment that he promised to fulfil but he took a course that amounted to revenge after he had been simply killed by kindness by the club whose colours he wore."

On Thursday 31st May 1906 commissioners J.C. Clegg, Charles Crump, and D. B. Woolfall reported on what they had discovered. They were of the opinion that City had been overpaying for years and that the players had actually gained the power and had demanded illegal payments. With the maximum wage at £4, it was revealed that Meredith had been earning £6 and that Livingstone had demanded and received £6 10s. Even the amateur Sam Ashworth had received £50 on top of £25 expenses, and was subsequently declared a professional by the commission.

If all of this wasn't bad enough then came the real shock. A total of seventeen current and former players were to be suspended until 1st January 1907. Maley and former Chairman W. Forrest were to be suspended from English football sine die, while directors Allison and Davies were to be suspended for seven months. City were fined £250 and the suspended players had to pay a total of £900 in fines: Meredith (£100), Livingstone (£100), Hynds (£75), McMahon (£75), Hillman, Turnbull, Booth, Burgess, Frost, Bannister, Dearden, Gillespie, and Holmes (all £50), Edmundson, Davidson, Lyon, and Ashworth (all £25).

The club was virtually dead. No club in the history of football has ever suffered to such an extent, regardless of tragedy or bans. No matter what irregularities there were, did City really deserve to be treated so harshly? What makes the matter so incredible is that the club were no worse than most of their big name rivals, any of whom could have been investigated and banned to the same extent.

City's first golden period ended in shame. The 1905-6 season, which had seen the Meredith-less club challenge for the title once again, ended with the Blues in fifth place. Not surprisingly, a loss of form had coincided with the F.A. investigation. Although it is impossible to say what the Maley inspired City side may have achieved, it still angers many associated with the Blues that the club were so cruelly attacked at a time when they should have been dominating football. If the side had remained together, would they have won the League? Would the Cup have resided at Hyde Road again? An indication of what City should have achieved appears in the history of Manchester United from 1907 to 1911. Suffice it to say that the Blues presented Manchester United with their first opportunity to be successful.

One point worth making is that City were not the only side to suffer as a result of the suspensions. Four of the players were already with other clubs - Ashworth with Everton, Lyon with Preston, Holmes at Clapton Orient, and Davidson at Airdrie. Those clubs felt they should not be penalised for another team's errors, although it was only Airdrie who had the opportunity to defy the ban. They persuaded the Scottish F.A. to ignore their English equivalent body and managed to play Davidson whenever necessary.

Three players still left at Hyde Road appealed as they had been reserve players during 1904-5 and, even after bonuses were included, had not received the maximum £208. Their appeal failed, as did a petition signed by 4,128 City supporters against all the suspensions.

With all these players banned from playing for City, the Blues had to find replacements. They also had the small matter of finding a manager and directors to fill the void created by the bans. The Derby County secretary-manager Harry Newbould was approached and accepted the offer of taking over

An Athletic News cartoon of City's 3-1 win over Bolton before a 38,000 crowd at Hyde Road shows Frank Booth netting for the Blues.

from Tom Maley. In his younger days, Newbould had made a name for himself as a sprinter, before joining Derby St Luke's as an outside right. In 1896 he joined Derby County as assistant secretary and four years later became the club's first official secretary-manager. When City approached him about the Hyde Road vacancy they knew he was already becoming disenchanted with the Rams, as he had been forced to sell star player Steve Bloomer to Middlesbrough. The football world were surprised when he took up the Hyde Road offer but, perhaps, he still felt the club had great potential. He was aware of the crowd pulling potential of the Blues, and would almost certainly have been aware of how Mancunians had greeted City's 1904 Cup victory, the year after Newbould's Derby had lost 6-0 to Bury at the same stage.

Another reason why Newbould would be made welcome at Hyde Road was that he was actually a qualified accountant. City needed to make sure they would be whiter than white, even if the rest of the First Division was made up of teams bending the rules as and when they saw fit. From the moment the bans were first discussed, Billy Meredith was fully aware of the 'do as I say, not as I do' approach: "The League met and representatives of each club voted in favour of the punishment meted out to us being enforced. And while their representatives were passing this pious resolution most of them had other representatives busy trying to persuade the 'villains whose punishment had been so well deserved' to sign for them under conditions very much better in most cases than the ones we had been ruled by at Hyde Road."

A City side missing the banned Billy Meredith defeated Bury 4-2 at Gigg Lane on 23rd September 1905. Here an Athletic News illustration shows Willie McOustra heading clear in that game.

Regardless of the approaches going on in the background, City still held the banned players' registrations and would do so until the end of December. In the meantime, Newbould tried to find players - any players! - to take City forward. With the club all but destroyed, his task was an enormous one. To understand how major the task was, imagine the same events occurring in 1991 to Alex Ferguson's Manchester United a mere year after winning the F.A. Cup, thus becoming his first successful side. Immediately, United would have lost the bulk of Ferguson's first team squad, they would have lost a potentially great manager, and several influential members of the Board would have been removed. Knowing what United have since achieved, would the same have happened to City? Could United expect to recover? This example is only quoted to give an indication of the task facing Newbould, and the loss that the Blues endured. No one will ever know what the side would have achieved, but neutral observers have always believed that City were treated abysmally. Because of this, avoiding relegation in 1906-7 had to be Newbould's target. Anything more than that would simply be a bonus.

When Newbould joined City in July 1906, there were only eleven players available. The northern based Football League tried to encourage clubs to help the Blues, but recruiting players was not an easy task. Newbould approached almost every club, and was regularly confronted with demands for large transfer fees. Walter Smith, the Leicester Fosse goalkeeper, was signed for the relatively high fee of £600 from the

1906/07 City team group, photographed outside the dressing rooms at Hyde Road.

Back (left to right): H.J.Newbould, R.Chatt, J.Buchan, J.Christie, W.Smith, F.Davies, W.McOustra, F.Farrell, J.Young.

Middle: T.Kelso, R.Grieve, A.Steel, G.Dorsett, W.L.Jones, J.Whittaker.

Front: W.Banks, A.Fisher, J.Conlin.

Second Division club, while several other players were simply too expensive. Newbould's job was extremely difficult, although he did find an ally in the former Bolton secretary, J.J. Bentley. Bentley, in addition to being President of the League, was Manchester United's chairman and, with one eye on the banned City players who would be available from the end of the year, he offered to help the Blues through the difficult close season. At one point he even directed a Brighton forward called Fisher who was due to sign for United to Hyde Road.

Other players to arrive at Hyde Road included the goalscoring Robert Grieve and the giant Bill Eadie both from Greenock Morton. In addition, Bradford City's England international Jimmy Conlin arrived to take over the outside left position from the suspended Frank Booth, and full-back Tommy Kelso arrived from Third Lanark. Other positions were filled by players who had been signed towards the end of the previous season, such as half-back Alex Steel from Ayr United, and Scottish international George Stewart from Hibernian.

Jimmy Conlin made his debut in the heatwave game of 1st September 1906 against Woolwich Arsenal at Hyde Road. City were defeated 4-1 and ended the match with only SIX players!

As can clearly be seen, the Blues relied heavily on Scottish imports. Maybe their English counterparts were not keen to join a club that was simply no longer able to make the illegal payments that were part and parcel of the English game. Newbould's first League game in charge was the opening fixture at home to Arsenal on 1st September 1906 refereed by the same man who officiated the 1904 Cup Final, A.J. Barker. City's team, including five debutants, was Davies, Christie, Kelso, Steel, Buchan, Dorsett, Stewart, Thornley, Grieve, Jones, and Conlin. In extreme heat, the Blues took the field before a low Hyde Road crowd of around 18,000. The weather - it was ninety degrees in the shade - had a tremendous impact on the game as the players found it difficult to cope, although for some unknown reason the City men suffered more than their opponents.

After thirty minutes Arsenal took the lead as City's large number of debutants ran into difficulties. A couple of minutes later Irvine Thornley fell "prostrate and very ill" according to one report and was taken from the field. For the rest of the match he lay flat on his back trying to recover from sunstroke and dehydration. A few moments after Arsenal found the net for the second time, Jimmy Conlin collapsed. He had adopted the fashionable Blackpool beach method of sun protection, playing with a knotted handkerchief on his head, but even that hadn't been able to save him.

At half time City lost another man when Robert Grieve failed to reappear. Down to eight men, with three forwards missing, the Blues stood no chance of matching the Gunners, but referee Barker refused to abandon the game. Bravely the Blues fought on, and for a while Newbould pushed one of his defenders up front to compensate for the three missing men. This gave the Blues a formation made up of three attackers, three half-backs, one full-back and a goalkeeper. Five minutes into the half, winger Jimmy Conlin bravely returned to the pitch to give City a little more hope.

After a short spell of City pressure, George Dorsett scored for the Blues to make it 2-1, but the effort was perhaps a little too much for the former West Bromwich player as he collapsed with exhaustion a few moments later. Any hope of equalising disappeared with Dorsett as Arsenal now dominated the match completely. Bravely City played on, but it wasn't long before the Gunners provided a couple of goals to take the score up to 4-1. Shortly afterwards City lost Tommy Kelso, then Jimmy Buchan, leaving only six City players on the pitch, three of whom - including goalkeeper Davies - were making their debuts.

Somehow the six Blues held out until the final whistle, in a game that provided new secretary-manager Newbould with yet more problems. Two days later the new look City travelled to Everton with remarkably only two changes - Fisher replaced Thornley and Kelso made way for Norgrove. Unfortunately, any hope that this game would see the Blues fortunes change were quickly dashed as City suffered their heaviest defeat of all time as Everton annihilated Newbould's side 9-1. Debutant Fisher provided the consolation goal - at least J.J. Bentley was able to say his 'diversion' technique had saved the Blues from a more humiliating scoreline.

The next game, away to Sheffield Wednesday, saw the Blues suffer further with a 3-1 defeat, but the first real moment of joy for Newbould came in City's next home game on 15th September. With goals from Jones and Thornley City gained a 2-2 draw with Bury before a crowd of approximately 20,000. It may have only been a point but the Blues deserved to celebrate. The point was a vital morale booster and gave City hope. After another 2-2 draw, this time away to Newbould's old side Derby, the Blues snatched two points with a 3-2 victory at Middlesbrough. Slowly but surely the team appeared to be getting their act together, although Newbould was still finding it difficult to determine his preferred side as he had already used a total of seventeen players in a mere six games. Consistency, something City have never excelled at, was a long way off.

The most satisfying moment of the opening dozen fixtures came on 20th October when City entertained Aston Villa. A crowd of over thirty thousand attended Hyde Road for a game many spectators saw as a grudge match. The Blues felt they needed to defeat Villa to gain revenge for the problems of the past year or so. The bribery and illegal payments investigations all stemmed from the infamous match at Villa Park and many felt Villa deserved to be taught a lesson on the pitch. Of the players who faced Villa on that fateful day in 1905, only Norgrove and Jones would play in the grudge match.

Thanks to two goals from Thornley, and a goal apiece from Stewart and Conlin City ended the game 4-2 winners. Many felt some justice had been done, although one game could in no way compensate for the suffering the Blues had endured. Nevertheless, the Blues felt it was a positive step forward; unfortunately they were wrong as results over the next six weeks left them struggling.

The grudge match between City and Aston Villa at Hyde Road ended with City winning 4-2 on 20th October 1906.

On 1st December the Blues faced newly promoted Manchester United in the first derby match for over three years. Sadly both sides had found the First Division a struggle so far that season with United on fourteen points and City on nine from the same number of games. The first Division One derby was eagerly awaited: "Football fever raged in Manchester this afternoon. I never saw such unbounded enthusiasm in the City. Starting at Cromwell's monument there was a continuous stream of vehicles right away to Hyde Road and pedestrians in similar processions. Five in a hansom cab was no uncommon sight."

With the backing of a noisy 40,000 crowd, providing receipts of £1,100, at Hyde Road, City wanted to prove that even without Meredith and Co. they were still the dominant Manchester side. According to the *Manchester Guardian*, when the Blues entered the field "a roar rose that will ring in sensitive ears for a week".

In an exciting match, the Blues satisfied all their fans with a convincing 3-0 victory. The City stars that day included Billy Lot Jones, who scored a stylish goal after twenty minutes; George Stewart, who had an

The senes at Hyde Road for the first Manchester derby in Division One, 1st December 1906. The official attendance was 40,000 - City won 3-0.

The Athletic News cartoon of the game shows Bill Eadie and Walter Smith in fine form.

Manchester City's Victory.

A centre by Wall off Hill's head.

Bonthron scored for his opponents.

Charlie Roberts was the mainstay of United.

Eadie was here, there, and everywhere

Jones converted a centre from Thornley.

Smith, the new idol at Ardwick.

effort deflected in for City's second goal and scored the third; goalkeeper Walter Smith, who was chaired from the field, and the lanky Bill Eadie. According to the *Athletic News* cartoon of the game Eadie was 'here, there, and everywhere' - maybe this was an early form of the crude modern day chant.

The game proved City were still the dominant force. Writing in the *Daily Dispatch*, the 'Veteran' believed City were in total control: "The great match is over! City proved themselves to be on the day's play a far superior side; in fact, so far superior that the form can hardly really be true."

Despite the great victory the most noteworthy event of the day actually took place in the Hyde Road offices after the game, when bargaining for the banned players commenced in earnest. The players' bans were due to be lifted on 1st January, but as there were so many involved, and the purchasing clubs keen to see the players take the field immediately into the New Year, the transfer deals had to be completed quickly. In reality the bargaining had been going on for some time, especially for the international players, but the F.A. agreed that deals could be struck in December. For the City management the sooner the event was over the better. It was already twenty months since the infamous game with Villa and the Blues were simply unable to move forward, especially as much needed capital would be gained by the Hyde Road sales. It's worth noting the main business was carried out at the ground, although some activity did take place subsequently at the Queen's Hotel in the city centre. Some footballing historians have mistakenly located the whole sale at the Queen's Hotel.

According to reports there were representatives from at least eight clubs at Hyde Road, with the majority interested in the tough England left-back Herbert Burgess, known by City fans as the Mighty Atom. Rumours circulated the north-west that Burgess had signed for Celtic for a sum of around £1,000, but it simply was not true. Whether City spread the rumours on purpose to increase the price is not known, but interestingly there were rumours about virtually every player.

Eventually, on 5th December, Burgess signed for Manchester United for the sum of £750, much to the disgust of both Celtic and Everton. Everton were so incensed City had transferred Burgess to their friends at United they complained to the League, causing City further heartache. It seems the Blues of Manchester and Liverpool had made an agreement whereby Burgess would join Everton with a player arriving at Hyde Road in return. Realising they would not receive the cash value, City broke the agreement and made a quick sale instead. Under the heading 'More rumours and a few facts', the *Daily Dispatch* broke the news to Manchester on 6th December, and added: "The inexorable laws of the Football Association have decreed that he shall not play again for City, and therefore it is only fitting that he should go to Clayton. I think the supporters of the City club will be pleased that the matter is definitely settled, for I am sure they would prefer that Burgess remained in Manchester."

In addition to Burgess, United's first great manager, Ernest Mangnall, signed Sandy Turnbull, Jimmy Bannister, and the man who was such a hero to the Mancunian masses Billy Meredith. Each of these signings is officially recorded as 5th December, although there is no doubt Meredith had signed for the Reds some months earlier on a free transfer. The fact City received nothing for their brilliant captain angered many. For a time the Blues had tried to sell him but Meredith, totally bemused by events at Hyde Road, produced an agreement between him and the club stating that he would be entitled to a benefit match and a minimum sum of £600. This was the main reason he had pursued the club throughout his suspension.

The F.A. again became involved and declared they could force the Blues to honour the agreement. Meredith was adamant the Blues should not receive a penny for his transfer: "The City club put a transfer of £600 on my head. And United were prepared to pay it. But I refused to let them pay a halfpenny. I had cost no fee and I was determined that I would have no fee placed on my head .... I was prepared to fight the matter. The City club were not. I was given a free transfer and, as a result, I got £500 from a gentleman to sign for Manchester United and he also paid the £100 fine to the F.A."

In effect Meredith had come out of the whole affair a real winner. With City battle-weary he was able to obtain the terms he wanted and had actually

Three of the City players expected to sign for Manchester United. Burgess and Bannister did move to Clayton, but Edmondson joined Bolton instead.

managed to pocket the equivalent of well over two years official wages - a vast amount - plus managed to avoid the fine. He was also guaranteed a warm welcome at United because, no matter what had occurred at City, Meredith was still loved by all Mancunians. There was no real animosity between the public and Meredith, nor was there a loathing of United by City fans. In fact, as suggested by the *Daily Dispatch* article, the majority of Blues were delighted that the bulk of their banned side was to remain in Manchester. If nothing else, it gave City's 'poor relations' a chance to match the exploits of the Hyde Road club.

In addition to the transfers to United, it's worth detailing what occurred to a few of the other Hyde Road favourites. Johnny McMahon and Frank Booth signed for Bury for a total of around £750. Tom Hynds moved to Arsenal. Former Celtic man George Livingstone returned to Glasgow with Rangers, although two years later he would travel back to Manchester to join Meredith and Co. at United.

Sammy Frost and goalkeeper Jack Hillman signed for Southern League Millwall, although it was not a particularly good move for the 35 year old 'keeper as, a short while later, an elbow injury ended his career and left one arm permanently crooked. For Frost the move was perfect as it enabled a return to the successful chain of sweet shops he had been forced to leave behind when he signed for City in 1901.

Another player worth mentioning is the bustling Billy Gillespie. The controversial player was so disgusted with how he and his colleagues had been treated that he emigrated, although the country he moved to varies depending on which account is read. One version, from the summer of 1905, stated he "has taken unto himself a wife and left the football field for the diamond fields of South Africa", another claimed he had moved to the States without paying his fine and taken his boots with him. According to John Harding's biography of Meredith, '*Football Wizard*', details of Gillespie's exploits in America and Canada kept English soccer fans entertained for years after his ban.

With the transfers more or less completed, the City management were able to move away from the politics and the wrangling and concentrate on the League and Cup. Unfortunately City were dogged by inconsistency in the League, and in the Cup the Blues suffered defeat by a single goal in the first round replay at home to Blackburn. The game at Ewood Park had ended 2-2.

Action from City's 2-1 defeat at Arsenal on 21st September 1907. The City scorer was Irvine Thornley.

Action from the Fulham-City F.A.Cup tie, 26th February 1908. Fulham won 3-1 in front of a crowd of 37,000.

In February, using proceeds from the transfers of the banned players, City bought Dave Ross, a forward from Norwich. In a complicated deal, they paid the East Anglian club £1,000 with a further £200 going to his former club Bury. The Blues also agreed to play Norwich in a friendly during April. Ross was an eleven stone 22 year old, and it was hoped would help give City's attack a little consistency. According to a 1907 'Football Who's Who', Ross was born in Darwen and lived in Bury, while away from football his life revolved around the relatively new and expensive hobby of photography. Robert Grieve, a partner of Ross's in the attack was recorded as being a Goss China collector, while William Hall, City's 'keeper for a while late in 1906 was a steeplejack by profession. The Blues certainly had a surprising cross-section of talent.

City's inconsistency remained until the end of the season with the only real newsworthy game the derby match at Clayton. For the first time the Blues faced Burgess, Meredith, and Turnbull and the new-look United in a game many believed would show United now possessed all the talent. The first half saw City take the initiative and with a strong wind behind they pushed forward. After approximately ten minutes Burgess, the former City man, raised his hand to block a centre from George Dorsett. The referee immediately awarded a penalty, which Dorsett converted, and City seemed on course to embarrass their former stars.

Early in the second half the roving Bill Eadie was hurt in a collision with Billy Meredith and forced to leave the field. Down to ten men the Blues still retained control for a while, but gradually United gained the upper hand and with fifteen minutes to go Charlie Roberts equalised. Walter Smith, in the City goal, was described by the *Athletic News* as being 'shocked' that United had actually scored. Whether this was an indication City had dominated the game, or simply the fact Smith found it hard to accept that he could concede a goal isn't known! Nevertheless, the ten man City side battled on and a few minutes later Jimmy Conlin put the ball into the United net. Unfortunately the goal was ruled out for offside, although the *Athletic News* reporter was not certain whether it should have been awarded or not: "My view was obscured by a hat fitted on the head of a lady who stood in front of me, and also by one of the thick posts which support the stand. I have by the way a bone to pick with the United club. I arrived an hour and a quarter before the time of starting and was informed that there was no accommodation in the Pressroom, which was largely occupied by people whose business it would be interesting to know." The reporter went on to complain about the poor press facilities and accused United of disrespect towards a reporter from "the recognised national football 'paper'."

The game ended level, although ten man City must have gained a moral victory after their fine performance. Nevertheless they also secured a much needed point and followed it up seven days later with another draw. This time the Hyde Road return with Stoke ended 2-2 with goals from George Stewart and Billy Lot Jones. Unfortunately, the final two games of the season - away to Blackburn, and home to Sunderland - ended in defeat leaving the Blues in 17th position on 32 points - five above the relegation zone. All connected with the club, especially Manager Newbould, must have been relieved that a difficult season had ended in safety. Back in August anything but relegation would have been viewed as success.

After the inconsistency of 1906-7, Newbould was determined his side would find some stability. In his

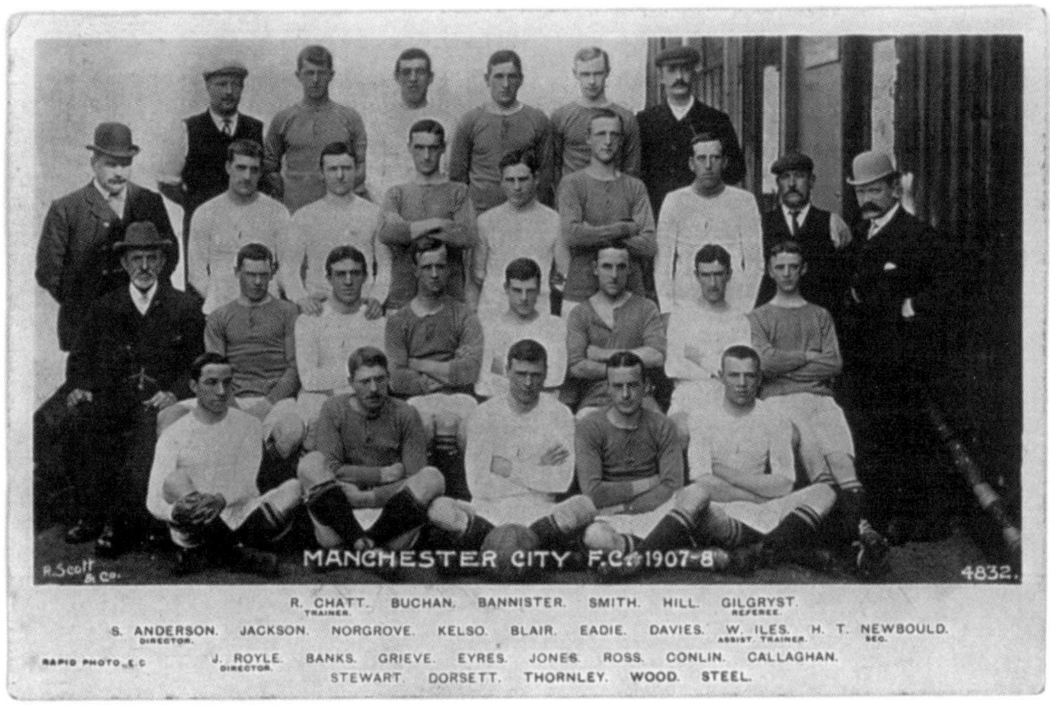

A postcard of City's 1907/08 side. The photograph was taken prior to the Annual practice match and even includes the referee.

first season in charge he had regularly been forced to change his side and, because of the problems off the pitch, had been introducing players throughout the season. He had also experimented with some positional changes.

For example, Jimmy Blair was signed from Arsenal in November as a forward, played in the attack during the December derby, but by the time of the April game with United, Newbould was operating him as a left half-back in place of Willie McOustra. That change was a great success, as was Newbould's purchase of Walter Smith.

Prior to Smith's arrival, City had used four different goalkeepers within the space of a year. Once Newbould bought Smith, he was convinced he could build a consistent side. In 1907-8 Smith became the club's first ever-present since Meredith in 1903-4, but even then Smith played in 44 League and Cup games as opposed to Meredith's 40.

With City's goal safe, and a general feeling of satisfaction within the club, the season started without any major signings. A 5-2 opening day victory at Sunderland, with Robert Grieve scoring an hat-trick, provided hope and, although results were mixed throughout the opening five months, the Blues picked up enough points to maintain a healthy position.

In December the music hall comedian George Robey reassembled the 1904 Cup winning team to face the present day side in a charity match at Hyde Road. City supporters were delighted to see the triumphal old boys back in town. The only player missing was the robust Billy Gillespie who was still enjoying life abroad. His place was taken on the day by George Robey himself, who even managed to score a goal for the old boys. Whether the goal was anything like one of Gillespie's 'push the goalie into the net' specials wasn't recorded by the press of the day, but we can be certain Robey would have tried to provide a comic touch to the affair.

The charity game ended 4-3 to the City new boys which, if nothing else, would have allowed Newbould the satisfaction of saying his side were still making gradual progress forwards.

By the start of April the Blues had performed well enough to retain an outside chance of winning the title, but they were nine points behind eventual champions Manchester United. United, with Meredith & Co., had really combined as a team and City supporters, though delighted the Championship had arrived in Manchester for the first time, must have wondered what Maley's City side might have achieved if the illegal payments scandal had never erupted. If nothing else, it had pushed City back several years and by default given United their first taste of glory. Regardless of the 'what ifs', City had recovered well enough to challenge in 1907-8 and, by the time of the Hyde Road derby match on 18th April, they were keen to finish runners up to the Reds. Regrettably, the game was not the exciting match most expected and, with the few chances that came City's way going wide, the game ended goalless. Nevertheless it gave City a vital point to lift their total to 41 with two games left, while Newcastle had 42 points with one game remaining. Aston Villa and Sheffield Wednesday were also close behind, but the Blues felt neither side would pose a real threat, especially Villa who had to face United at Clayton in one of their two final fixtures.

In typical City style, the Blues missed out on second place largely due to their own failings as games against Bristol City and Blackburn Rovers both ended goalless while Aston Villa defeated United 2-1, and Chelsea 3-1 to take second place on goal average. Newcastle lost their last game away to Middlesbrough, thereby giving the Blues third spot.

Although this was a creditable feat, the popular opinion was Manchester should have filled the two leading positions to provide much-needed civic pride on both sides. It took another sixty years before Manchester was able to boast its clubs were officially the top two in the League. Then of course it was City who celebrated the Championship.

With City finishing so close to the top of the table, optimism filled Hyde Road and its environs. There was a belief City could match United's achievement and once again challenge for the title.

Jimmy Blair (above) and Walter Smith (below) - two successful signings by Harry Newbould.

Unfortunately, the inconsistency of Newbould's first season in charge returned with City putting in some fine performances - a 5-1 victory against the season's Cup finalists Bristol City is a good example - yet in other games the Blues simply conceded too many goals. Prime examples include a 6-3 defeat at Everton, 5-1 at Notts County, and 4-0 at Sheffield United.

A complimentary City season ticket for the 1908/09 season.

On 16th January, City faced Tottenham in the F.A. Cup first round at Hyde Road. Incredibly, Newbould dropped two of his star players Irvine Thornley and Jimmy Blair. Both were perfectly fit, yet newspaper reports suggested the two star players had made excessive bonus demands. The club denied this, but even so concern was raised.

The Cup-tie crowd of around 20,000 expected a great City victory as the Blues took a two goal lead through the experienced Tom Holford, but it wasn't to be. Tottenham fought their way back into the game and quickly levelled the scores. Then fortune shone City's way as the Blues were awarded a penalty. George Dorsett, playing instead of Jimmy Blair, stepped up to take the kick, but somehow managed to miss the target. After two further goals - one for Spurs and another by Holford for City - Bill Eadie tripped Bert Middlemiss in the area, giving Tottenham the perfect chance to take the lead. The game ended 4-3 to Second Division Spurs and manager Newbould was left to consider where the Blues had failed. Not for the first time in their history, City desperately needed to find consistency.

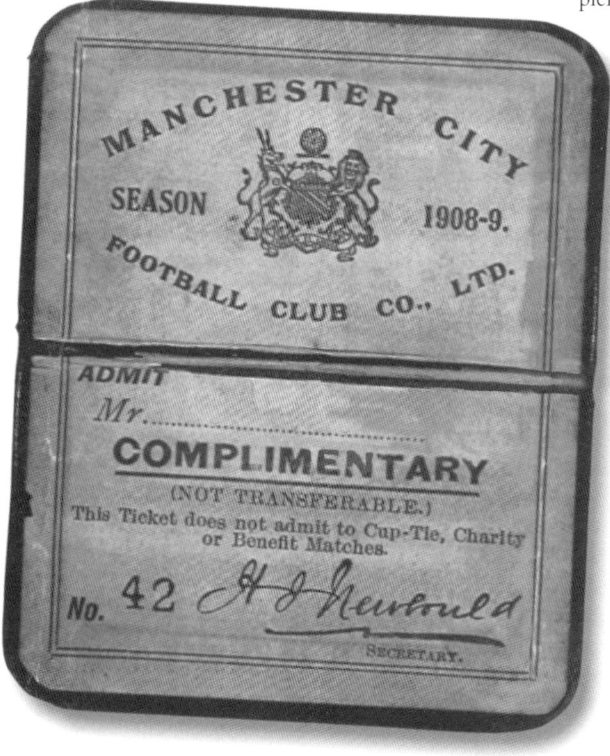

There were also reminders of what might have been across at Clayton where former Blue George Livingstone joined Meredith and Co. in the red of United. His debut was the eighteenth League Manchester derby on 23rd January 1909. A particularly bad day for City fans as Livingstone scored twice in United's 3-1 home victory. The *Athletic News* made much of the fact that Livingstone was yet another former Blue: "It is a singular coincidence that he should make his debut against his old club, and, by the way, no fewer than three of the famous City forwards were in the United forward line, while another, Booth, was playing the part of a spectator, and I have no doubt that the fifth man, William Gillespie, was anxiously awaiting the result across the Atlantic." No doubt, if he did manage to hear the score, Gillespie would have been as disappointed as all true Blues.

By 9th April City were perilously close to relegation, although with six games to go and 32 points in the bag the future was totally in their own hands. Leicester Fosse were bottom on 21 points with seven games left to play, Bradford City were three points ahead of Leicester with the same number of games, while Bury were on 29 points with only four games to go, although one of these was at home to City. Below City there was also Nottingham Forest (30 points), and Liverpool (31 points). There were plenty of other teams within reach, including Manchester United who were a mere point above the Blues.

Clearly, City felt safe. A few victories or even a few draws should have been enough, however, City being City, it wasn't that easy. A poor Easter, saw the Blues lose to Sunderland on Good Friday and to relegation favourites Bury the following day, before managing a 2-1 win over fellow strugglers Nottingham Forest on Tuesday 13th April. City were putting themselves in danger and, as only one of their remaining three fixtures was at Hyde Road, needed to perform at their best, especially as Bury and Bradford were picking up more points.

At Hyde Road on 17th April Irvine Thornley provided his 18th League goal of the season, but it wasn't enough as visitors Sheffield United won 3-1 with two goals from Kitchen and another from Batty. With two games remaining the Blues were in trouble but still remained in control especially as both Bury and Notts County had already completed their campaigns, both ending on 36 points, two more than City. Liverpool were level with the Blues but only had one game to play, Notts County had 35 points (one match remaining), while Bradford City were by this time a mere two points behind City. Bradford perhaps offered City the most comfort as they had to face Manchester United, who were now safe on 37 points, in their one remaining game.

City's match at Aston Villa on Saturday 26th April was a tense affair, played in a strong wind: "science was thrown to the winds which blew so gustily, and the players went at it hammer and tongs." Significantly, when the first couple of goals arrived they came by means of penalties with Wallace converting for Villa, and James Buchan scoring for the Blues. The tension remained throughout the match when, in the final five minutes, a foul by Bill Eadie gave Villa a free kick. Walters' shot seemed to remain in the air for an eternity before it dropped a fraction under the bar to give Villa the points. City's final game on Wednesday 28th at Bristol City was vital, especially as both Bradford City and Liverpool had the advantage of playing their final matches after the City game finished, on Thursday 29th and Friday 30th respectively.

As City took to the field at Bristol they knew a point would see them clear. They defended well and as the game progressed into the final ten minutes seemed content to let the game end in a no score draw. It would certainly have given them safety but, as City have discovered on other similar occasions - 1983 being a prime example - the Blues should always expect the unexpected. With only two minutes remaining a Bristol effort was diverted past Walter Smith into the City net. Some reports say the increasingly unlucky Bill Eadie deflected the ball, other sources suggest Tommy Kelso was the guilty party. It was immaterial really, what mattered was the fact that the Blues had fallen from a position of relative safety to near relegation. They had to cross their fingers and hope either Bradford, against United, or Liverpool, away to Champions Newcastle, would fail to win.

At Manningham Lane, Bradford, the Cup winners United were keen to help their Mancunian rivals. Regretfully, Bradford City took overall control of the game, and it was no surprise when O'Rourke provided Bradford with the only goal of the match. The following day at Newcastle, Liverpool won by the same scoreline. City were down.

The final table put City in nineteenth place on 34 points, nine more than bottom club Leicester, but the same as Bradford in the 'safe' eighteenth position. From a position of relative safety the Blues had created themselves a relegation nightmare. Their goal average was inferior to Bradford City and, quite simply, they had let themselves down during the last month of the season. One more point was all that was needed.

City needed the summer break to take stock of the situation. There would be no panic removal of the manager though. Despite relegation, Newbould had achieved a great deal during his two years at Hyde Road.

Manchester City 1908/09.

Back row (left to right): R.Grieve, J.Blair, W.Smith.

Fourth row: W.Iles (Asst. Trainer), F.Davies, A.Winterburn, W.Bottomley, J.Wilkinson, D.Coupe, E.Henderson, R.Harrison.

Third row: F.Norgrove, G.Dorsett, B.Jackson, J.Buchan, W.Eadie, T.Kelso, C.Webb, H.Hancock, Bannister, R.Chatt (Trainer).

Second row: H.J.Newbould (Secretary), J.Wood, G.Stewart, C.Broomfield, W.Jones, T.Holford, D.Ross, C.Burgess, J.Conlin, F.McCartan (Asst. Secretary).

Front: F.Buckley, A.Powell, I.Thornley, P.Hill.

Two photos taken during City's 2-1 win over Middlesbrough on 14th April, 1911. The top picture shows spectators standing in the Main Stand paddock - all wearing hats! - the picture below shows the Popular side.

Action photographs from games at Hyde Road are exceptionally rare. No other City publication has ever shown action pictures from Hyde Road, and those included in this book are the only known surviving examples.

Chapter Five

PROMOTION AND WAR

AFTER a five year period when City's fortunes always seemed to be determined by others, mainly the F.A., it was hoped the next decade would bring the club a little stability and success. Before the Blues could achieve these aims they somehow had to gain promotion.

Relegation at a time when Manchester United were enjoying their first golden era was difficult to accept, especially as the Reds success largely came as a result of the Blues illegal payments scandal. Nevertheless, under City's fifth secretary-manager Harry Newbould, the Blues were not too distraught and quickly set about returning to the First Division. He believed his side to be good enough for promotion, all they lacked was consistency. If the Blues had found that during the previous year, relegation would never have been an issue.

The only significant signing of 1909 was in April when George Wynn, a former Welsh cup winner, was signed from Wrexham. Despite being purchased before the end of City's relegation season, inside-forward Wynn did not make his debut until Christmas Day away to Bradford. Before this moment he remained patiently in the reserves, and watched City's opening games. The initial fixture was a disappointing 2-1 defeat at home to Blackpool - Irvine Thornley provided the Blue goal. If Newbould had thought promotion would be a simple affair then that game convinced him otherwise.

Two days later, however, with four team changes, including the return of Bert Jackson and Tom Holford, City looked a much improved side as they defeated Leicester Fosse 3-1. Further joy followed a week later as Lincoln were trounced 6-2. By the time of Wynn's Christmas debut, the Blues were beginning to look more than capable of promotion and had won ten and drawn four of their seventeen games. Captain Irvine Thornley had been the star man, scoring twelve goals in those seventeen matches. Unfortunately, his appearances for the rest of the season would be limited through injury. Billy Lot Jones relished the chance of replacing Thornley as captain and in many games throughout the season proved his leadership qualities.

Although Wynn's debut was a disappointing 2-0 defeat, he was quickly able to demonstrate his influence as he scored a total of six goals in the same number of matches. In fact, by the end of the season he had totalled ten goals in twenty games and seen the Blues undefeated in every game in which he scored.

In addition to Wynn, another man instrumental in City's climb up the table was new goalkeeper Jack Lyall, signed from Sheffield Wednesday in September. Lyall had taken over the number one spot from Walter Smith, although this was far from the end of Smith's Hyde Road career as the following seasons proved.

With Lyall performing well and the whole team playing consistently - something so many City teams over the years have struggled to do - Newbould must have been content with the way the Blues were progressing, and it was not only in the League. In the F.A. Cup they defeated Workington 2-1, Southampton 5-0, and old adversaries Aston Villa 2-1 - all away from home. As March approached Blues fans started to believe this could be their year for the double of Second Division title and the F.A. Cup. Unfortunately, as is often the case with Manchester City, the world fell apart during a three week spell in March.

On the fifth, Swindon Town beat City 2-0 in the Cup, before a then record crowd of 14,429 for the Wiltshire club. Up to that point, this was by far the biggest moment in the club's history and caused much

Scottish international Jack Lyall signed on 15th September 1909 and made his debut in a goalless draw with Blackpool ten days later. He went on to make 44 League & Cup appearances in two seasons with the Blues.

1909-10 DIVISION TWO CHAMPIONSHIP DETAILS

RESULTS	HOME	AWAY
Blackpool	L 1-2	D 0-0
Leicester Fosse	W 2-0	W 3-1
Lincoln City	W 6-2	W 2-0
Clapton Orient	W 2-1	L 2-3
Hull City	W 3-0	W 2-1
Derby County	W 2-1	L 1-3
Stockport County	W 2-1	W 2-1
Glossop North End	D 3-3	W 3-0
Gainsborough Trinity	W 3-1	W 3-1
Birmingham City	W 3-0	D 1-1
West Bromwich Albion	W 3-2	D 0-0
Oldham Athletic	L 0-2	L 0-1
Fulham	W 3-1	D 1-1
Burnley	W 4-0	D 3-3
Leeds City	W 3-0	W 3-1
Wolverhampton W	W 6-0	L 2-3
Bradford (PA)	W 3-1	L 0-2
Grimsby Town	W 2-0	W 1-0
Barnsley	D 0-0	D 1-1

REGULAR SIDE:

Lyall
Kelso
Jackson
Buchan/Bottomley
Eadie
Dorsett
Stewart
Wynn
Holford
Jones
Conlin

MANAGER:

Harry Newbould

LARGEST VICTORY: 6-0 v Wolverhampton Wanderers (H) 18/12/09

HEAVIEST DEFEAT: 1-3 v Derby County (A) 16/3/10

AVERAGE HOME ATTENDANCE: c.18,400

HIGHEST HOME ATTENDANCE: c.40,000 v Oldham Athletic 26/3/10

HIGHEST AWAY ATTENDANCE: 19,536 v Oldham Athletic 13/11/09

LEAGUE APPEARANCES: 38 Dorsett, 37 Jones, 35 Jackson, Conlin, 33 Lyall, 30 Holford, 28 Kelso, 23 Eadie, Thornley, 22 Stewart, 20 Buchan, Wynn, 14 Bottomley, 11 Ross, 9 Wilkinson, 8 Norgrove, 7 Chapelow, 6 Gould, 4 Burgess, 3 Furr, Smith, 2 Blair, Brown, James, 1 Coupe, Davies, Swann

LEAGUE GOALS: 13 Dorsett, 12 Holford, Thornley, Jones, 11 Conlin, 10 Wynn, 6 Ross, 2 Eadie, Gould, 1 Stewart

embarrassment for City. Four days later, the Blues could only manage a midweek no score draw at home to Barnsley, before a 3-0 victory over Birmingham on the 12th provided a little relief. It did not last for long though, and on the following Wednesday a real 'four pointer' with Derby ended in defeat. With both sides heading for promotion, the Blues had once again let themselves down at a crucial stage.

A no score draw away to West Bromwich Albion provided more concern, but then on Good Friday 25th March captain Billy Lot Jones rekindled City's drive by scoring the only goal of the match at Grimsby.

On Easter Saturday a crowd of over 40,000 - the highest Hyde Road attendance of the season - turned out for the visit of promotion hopefuls Oldham Athletic. Irvine Thornley had selected this as his benefit game and could not have picked one better in terms of money raised. According to reports of the period he collected around £1,000 although the directors' report stated:

"The amount cannot be now stated with exactitude owing to the fact that there has to be deducted the expenses of the day, in addition to certain sums already paid and yet to be paid as compensation for accidents which occurred on the day of the match."

It appears the rather dilapidated Hyde Road ground should not have held such a large attendance and this contributed towards a few injuries to spectators. In 1910, as with most periods in football history, spectator comfort was not really seen as an issue. It would take minor accidents (including one at Maine Road sixteen years later), and several major disasters, before the authorities looked seriously into the problems. The idea for many years was to 'pack 'em in', especially for a derby match with promotion rivals Oldham.

Although the attendance provided Thornley with much satisfaction, the result did not as City went down 2-0. Again, they had failed to win a crucial 'four pointer'. Newbould and the City team did learn their lesson however, and on Easter Monday rediscovered their winning ways as Gainsborough were defeated 3-1. From then until the last Saturday of the season the Blues were undefeated, scoring a total of fifteen goals in six games. Billy Lot Jones, in Thornley's absence, had successfully steered the Blues back into Division One.

The final game of the season saw City beaten 3-2 at Wolverhampton, but it hardly mattered as, over the course of the previous few weeks, promotion rivals Derby and Hull wilted under the pressure, allowing City to end the season as Champions, one point ahead of second placed Oldham. This was the Blues third Second Division title since 1899, and followed a season of relative consistency - relative to the rest of City's history that is - with 23 victories, eight draws and only seven defeats.

Training 1910 style - a rather suspicious group of City players enjoy a spot of light training in Southport prior to one of the 1909/10 season Cup ties.

Dorsett's finish to a fine run.

George Dorsett ended the 1909-10 season as top scorer with 13 goals from 38 games. He'd signed for the Blues in December 1904 for £450. After 193 League appearances with City he was forced to retire through injury.

Joe Dorsett joined his brother George at City in August 1910, and made his debut in the 1-1 draw with Preston on 3rd September.

During the close season, the club went on a European tour, defeating sides from Hamburg and Gothenburg (twice), while also achieving a victory in one of two games against a Danish XI. This rather successful trip appears to have been City's first venture outside of the British Isles, at a time when few travelled abroad in any case.

While City were overseas, Hyde Road was given a much-needed facelift. A 1908 Ordnance Survey map provides a good impression of how primitive Hyde Road was at this point in its history. Only the four thousand seater Main Stand, erected eleven years earlier, provided cover from Manchester's notorious rain, while the terracing behind each goal was in irregular sections. Even the popular side reduced in size from an extremely large bank at one end, to virtually nothing at the other. To appreciate the problem, imagine the unusually shaped terracing which occupied the space behind the goal at Southampton's Dell ground for many years. Although a similarly awkward shape, the Hyde Road terracing was much larger.

The 1910 close season saw City spend somewhere in the region of £3,000 on three roofs and other improvements to the ground. Apart from the fact Hyde Road was in poor condition, another reason for the sudden outlay may have been the opening of Manchester United's new Old Trafford ground on 19th February 1910. This move by the Reds provided them with the opportunity of pulling in larger crowds than City. To counteract this, City boasted the newly-refurbished Hyde Road would hold over 35,000 under cover. Old Trafford could only manage about a quarter of that. It's not known whether City's plans were made before Old Trafford opened but, whatever City's reasons, covered accommodation on all four sides of a ground for such a large figure was exceptional in those days. In fact, it was not until the 1970s that Old Trafford, and indeed Maine Road, could claim roofing on all sides.

Each of the three roofs erected by City were multi-spans, although a great deal of mystery surrounds the roof at the Galloway end of the ground, to the left of the Main Stand. The only photographs that survive show all the metalwork for a multi-span roof but there appears to be no actual cover. Whether this was an accident that occurred later in City's history isn't known.

Behind the opposite goal another multi-span was erected, which had five spans and six front and six back stanchions, and was merely placed over the irregular sectioned terracing. The same occurred, with a similar roof on the Popular Side, opposite the Main Stand. Here a roof with much larger individual spans was erected.

Multi-span roofs were unusual, even in 1910, but were essential at Hyde Road as they allowed spans of different lengths and depths to be developed if necessary, whereas a traditional single span roof - something like the old Kippax roof - would only really be able to cover a regular shaped area of terracing.

The company contracted to erect these roofs is believed to be 'Humphreys Ltd' of Knightsbridge who worked on Old Trafford and, three years later, Arsenal's new stadium at Highbury. At both these grounds, and at others across the country, they built multi-span roofs, but Hyde Road is probably the only ground in the world which featured three

The front cover of an itinerary for what is believed to have been City's first continental tour.

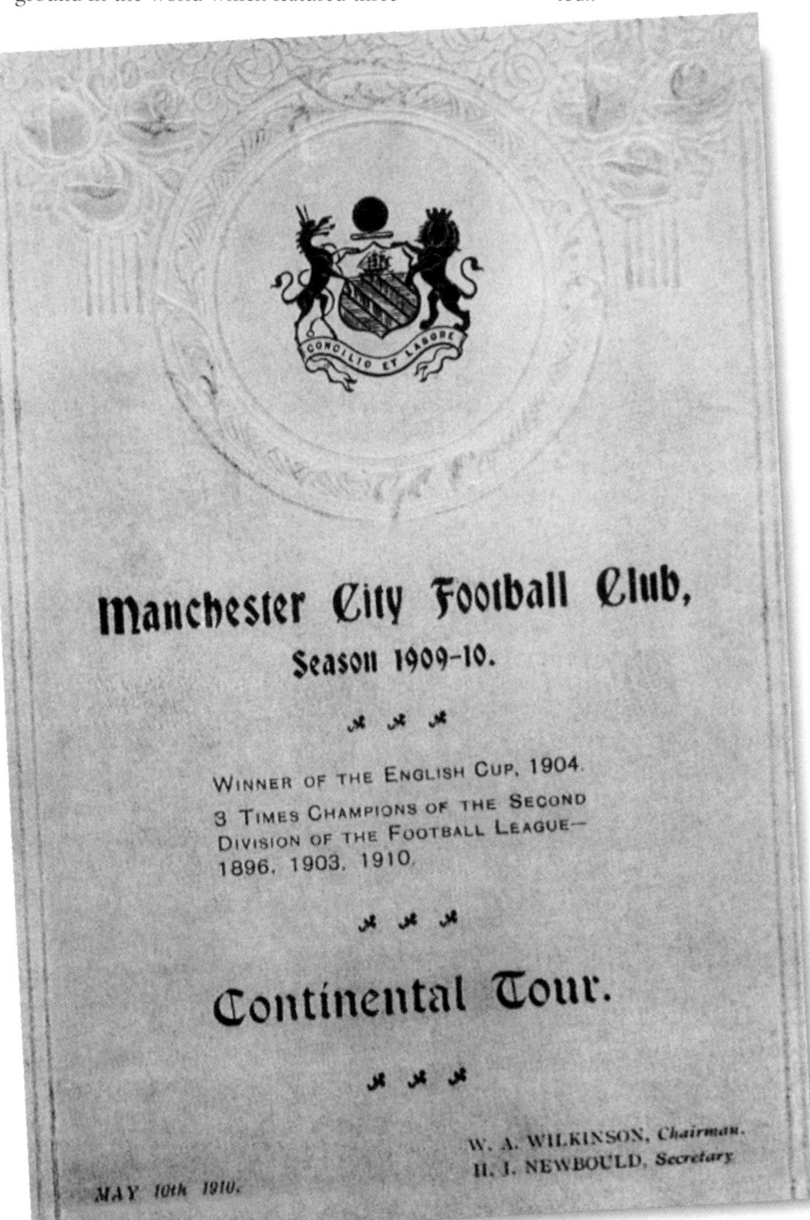

CONCILIO ET LABORE
Manchester City Football Club,
Season 1909-10.
Winner of the English Cup, 1904.
3 Times Champions of the Second Division of the Football League—
1896. 1903. 1910.
Continental Tour.
May 10th 1910.
W. A. WILKINSON, Chairman.
H. J. NEWBOULD, Secretary.

An advertisement for Humphreys Ltd., a company which specialised in erecting multi span roofs and were probably the builders of City's three roofs during the 1910 close season.

FOOTBALL CLUB STANDS, BANKS, TERRACING, AND COMPLETE INSTALLATION,

BY

HUMPHREYS, Ltd., KNIGHTSBRIDGE, LONDON, S.W.

Contractors for the
MANCHESTER UNITED F.C.
MANCHESTER CITY F.C.
BARNSLEY F.C.
MILLWALL F.C.
TOTTENHAM HOTSPUR F.C
COVENTRY CITY F.C., &c.

SPECIAL TERMS.

large roofs of this style. Their only problem, as the Blues would later discover, was that this type of roof was relatively expensive to maintain. Nevertheless in 1910 City were justifiably proud of their refurbished home.

The 'new' Hyde Road's first League fixture saw one of the previous season's stars, George Wynn, hit the headlines with a hat-trick in his First Division debut game. The Blues swamped Bury 5-1 on 1st September 1910 with goalkeeper Jack Lyall in excellent form. He had been awarded the captaincy for the day and, according to the *Daily Dispatch*, fulfilled the role superbly. His performance was one that inspired the others and brought widespread delight: "Seasoned fighter though he is Jack Lyall, the City custodian, will doubtless regard the occasion as one of the happiest in his career."

Despite the excellent start, City's form deteriorated over the course of the next few games as first they drew 1-1 at Preston, then suffered consecutive losses against Notts County, Manchester United (the first derby at Old Trafford), and Liverpool. Following the home defeat by the Merseysiders, the Blues travelled to Bury hoping to repeat their opening day form, but despite goals from Wynn and George Dorsett City suffered a 5-2 upset.

City's poor showing continued and by New Year's Day they were bottom of the table after taking a mere fourteen points from twenty-one games. The New Year however, did bring about a change in fortune. The brilliant, but erratic, Walter Smith was back in goal and the defence further strengthened by the purchase of full back John Chaplin from Dundee in November. On 3rd January David Ross and Billy Lot Jones scored City's goals in a vital 2-1 home win over Tottenham, and four days later, Ross again put his name on the scoresheet when he volleyed home a centre from Joe Dorsett. Dorsett, who had joined his brother George in August, had actually sprinted half the length of the field before crossing to Ross. He also had a hand in City's next game - the Hyde Road derby.

In the first half Dorsett put the Reds under great pressure and, according to *The Umpire* newspaper, there was one shot in particular which "nine times out of ten would have scored". Unfortunately, prior to the interval he had to leave the field injured. It is not recorded how he received the injury, but it was a devastating blow as the Blues not only lost their most influential player in the match, but were also without him for the next six league games.

Even so, City were already a goal in front, thanks to Billy Lot Jones, when Dorsett left the field: "Stewart took the ball along, and, instead of centre-ing, as the defenders anticipated, he merely tapped it to Ross, who skilfully drew out the defence, crossing with the result that two City forwards had an open goal and Jones took the opportunity of giving his side the lead in a very clever manner."

Manchester City 1910/11

Back row (left to right): W.A.Smith, W.Bottomley, R.Humphries, G.Dorsett, R.Codling.

Third row: R.Iles (Asst. Trainer), F.Norgrove, J.Wilkinson, F.Kelso, J.Lyall, H.Jackson, C.Burgess, W.P.Eadie, R.Chatt (Trainer).

Second row: J.Buchan, H.Bentley, G.Stewart, W.C.Humphries, H.J.Newbould (Secretary), W.Gould, W.L.Jones, J.W.Smith, T.Holford, H.Carlton.

Front row: G.Wynn, D.Ross, J.Conlin.

"THE GLORIOUS FIRST": SCENES AT CITY AND BURY MATCH.

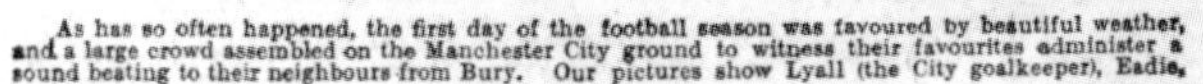
As has so often happened, the first day of the football season was favoured by beautiful weather, and a large crowd assembled on the Manchester City ground to witness their favourites administer a sound beating to their neighbours from Bury. Our pictures show Lyall (the City goalkeeper), Eadie, and Hibbert racing for possession; Kay robbing the City back of the ball; and Eadie, the favourite City centre-half, in one of his characteristic attitudes.

"Daily Dispatch" photograph.

Captains Montgomery (Notts County) and Lyall (City) together with referee Mr. Kirkham before City's 1-0 home defeat on 10th September 1910.

Manchester City, Bristol City, Woolwich Arsenal:—"If YOU please, we want some more"

City struggling in the League and desperate for points are seen here with fellow strugglers Arsenal and Bristol City begging for more to avoid relegation.

Down to ten men throughout the second half, City - in particular Tom Holford and Walter Smith - held United at bay. Inevitably, though, City's old partners in crime Billy Meredith and Sandy Turnbull combined to provide United with the equaliser. With the game ending level, *The Umpire* gave City most of the credit, in particular the play anywhere Holford and the brilliant Smith: "There were none of the United side to compare with Holford and Dorsett. Holford, who seems to have no settled position, faced the most dangerous outside-right in the country with a calmness which did him credit. Other players were indulging in horseplay, but Holford, who used to enjoy a rough and tumble affair, played the game and practically held Meredith in check in the first half, even if the old City player was more frisky afterwards."

"But W. Smith was the man above all others on the City side. His goalkeeping in the first half was wonderful, and to his good work, more than anyone else's, is due the fact that City got a point."

Despite the result, City had to be content they had managed to take a point from a team destined to be champions at the season's end. The directors would also have been pleased that the forty thousand crowd paid impressive receipts of £1,052. Perhaps the refurbished Hyde Road was already playing its part, although it was not all good news as, on the Popular Side, a great deal of crushing occurred with several spectators ferried away from the ground by ambulance.

During 1911 City played a leading role in the formation of the Central League with City director W.A. Wilkinson chairing many of the meetings which led to the League's creation. Another man responsible - some would say the founder of the competition - was Ernest Mangnall, City manager from 1912 to 1924. He performed much of the groundwork, canvassing clubs to gain approval, and played an active role in the League until his death in 1932.

A run of three further draws followed the derby, keeping the Blues in trouble. On April Fool's Day, centre-forward John Smith, who had made his debut in December and had been the only City player criticised by *The Umpire* after the derby with United, proved he was of use by scoring a vital goal in the last minute against Oldham to level the scores. The point gave City hope, and the following week, at home to Everton, goals from Wynn and Thornley gave the Blues two further points while Tom Holford entertained the crowd with all kinds of gymnastic feats including a handspring. Perhaps a relative of Peter Beagrie's was in the crowd that day and passed down the story for the 1990's Everton and City player to follow!

That victory against Everton was backed by another fine win - 2-1 against Middlesbrough before a 35,000 Hyde Road crowd. Two defeats and a draw followed, but they hardly mattered as, at the end of the season, City finished in seventeenth place, six points above Nottingham Forest in twentieth position, and four more than nineteenth placed Bristol City. The Blues would live to fight another day thanks to heroes Smith, Holford, and top scorer Wynn. But would 1911-12 be any different?

Eli Fletcher joined City in May 1911 from Crewe and went on to become one of the club's longest serving players, leaving in June 1926 to become Watford player-manager.

The answer was, not really, as another season of struggle saw the Blues fighting to avoid relegation, despite a few new signings. Forward Sid Hoad came from Blackpool, full-back Eli Fletcher from Crewe, and in November another full-back William Henry arrived from Leicester Fosse, while the attack was further strengthened by the addition of Sandy Young from Tottenham.

Thirty-one-year-old Sandy Young was an interesting purchase for the Blues. He was a muscular, imposing forward who had enjoyed a successful career with Everton - scoring the only goal of the 1906 Cup Final - and had played international football for Scotland, before moving to Tottenham prior to the 1911-12 season. At Spurs he scored three goals in only five appearances but was then left out of the side, and immediately demanded a transfer. City decided to take a gamble on the player, who was later described as having fits of 'temporary insanity'. His time at Hyde Road was not particularly enjoyable, and in the close season he moved back to Merseyside, this time with Liverpool.

Frank Booth returned to City in July 1911 after serving his illegal payments ban. He only made a further four appearances before being forced into retirement. His last game was against Bolton in February 1912. Sadly, he died in June 1919 aged 37.

In 1914 he emigrated to Australia, and the following year was charged with murdering his brother. In June 1916 he was found guilty of manslaughter and sentenced to three years imprisonment, after which he was kept inside for a while longer due to mental instability. Eventually he returned to Scotland, where he died in 1959 at the age of 79. City supporters were already aware of how dangerous Young could be. In 1906 he had managed to score four of Everton's goals in their 9-1 thrashing of City (the Blues heaviest defeat). It was this goal scoring side of Young's makeup that convinced Newbould to sign the player.

The opening day fixture, played in extreme heat before 35,000 at Hyde Road, was the twenty-first League Manchester derby. Once again 27 year old Walter Smith played heroically as the Blues managed to match the champions throughout. The game ended goalless, but at least the Blues had obtained a point. By the time the two sides met again, at the end of December, the Blues had managed only fifteen points from nineteen games.

City had improved after the introduction of Young and Henry on 25th November, but their points total was simply not enough. The first couple of months of 1912 gave Newbould little comfort either, as the Blues lost six of their seven games with only a 1-1 draw - thanks to a last minute goal from George Wynn - against Newcastle bringing any joy. Even that game provided grave concerns as the Blues were awarded three penalties and somehow missed all three, although Wynn's goal did come from the rebound of the last one. The first two penalties were both taken by the normally reliable Eli Fletcher. The first was saved, with the rebound providing Sid Hoad with an opportunity which was also turned away. The second went several yards wide of the left post, and when the third was awarded Fletcher decided enough was enough and allowed Irvine Thornley to try his luck. Again, goalkeeper Blake saved the effort before Wynn raced in to equalise in the last minute.

City's fortunes did change in March, though, when on 16th against Young's former club Everton, Tom Holford was moved out of defence to play the role of centre-forward, due to injuries to Thornley and a ban following his sending off against Villa on 20th January. Holford had played the role before and, as often quoted in the press of the period, was easily able to adapt to any position. But surely no one could have predicted the dramatic nature of his impact as he tore into Everton and scored all of City's goals in their 4-0 Hyde Road victory. No one could believe it, yet twelve days later he helped the Blues achieve another 4-0 home win. This time he netted twice against Bradford City and, looking back with hindsight, it appears obvious now that his efforts helped kick-start City's season.

Less than a month later, a hat-trick from Wynn against Sheffield Wednesday and another brace against basement club Bury lifted the Blues out of the bottom two for the first time. With a fine 2-0 victory on the last day of the season at home to Middlesbrough, the Blues finished fifteenth on thirty-five points - a mere two behind championship favourites United. Fourteen points had been gained in the last eight games to save the Blues with most of the plaudits going to Holford and, once again, Wynn - who scored seventeen goals in thirty-one games.

The star of the previous season, goalkeeper Walter Smith, had only managed twelve appearances. He had suffered with fluid on the knee and on 13th January, minutes before the start of City's cup-tie at Preston, he was unable to continue. Jack Lyall had already moved to Dundee, and so December signing Jim Goodchild hurriedly had to strip and change. The rest of the side were kitted out by the time Goodchild was told he was playing and so, in a rush, he made his way onto the field.

During the game he saved a penalty and managed to keep the Preston forwards at bay. His debut ended with Wynn scoring the only goal in the 88th minute to give City victory. Despite a 1-0 defeat in the second round - at home to Oldham - Goodchild proved he was a good replacement for Smith throughout the last months of the season. The following season saw him start as first choice, although the debate as to who was the better 'keeper would rumble on for the following four years. Fortunately, for the struggling Blues they had two valuable 'keepers.

With so much struggle over the previous couple of years it was no surprise when, early in the 1912-13 season the Blues announced they had a new manager. Newbould's tenure was over. His difficult first few seasons had seen him replace the 1904 Cup side with a team almost as good. Unfortunately he never really developed this to the level required at an enormous city club and, with arch-rivals United now gaining praise, success, and support enough was enough. Early into the new season announcements appeared in the *Athletic News* and the *Daily Dispatch* stating that Ernest Mangnall - the man who had achieved so much success with United - was to leave Old Trafford and take over from Newbould. This was an enormous surprise to Mancunians and, indeed, the whole of football, and would be on a par with Alex Ferguson walking out of Old Trafford in the mid-1990s to join the Blues.

At United, Mangnall had achieved a great deal and, even today, is clearly one of the most important men ever to be associated with the Reds. It was he who purchased Meredith and the other banned City players, and was wholly responsible for turning United from a struggling Second Division side into double League Champions, and Cup winners. In 1910 it was mainly due to his ambition and drive that the Reds left the confines of Clayton for the new 70,000 capacity Old Trafford.

For City to convince him to leave United was some feat, but what was even more remarkable was he still had to take charge of the Reds in one further derby match prior to moving to Hyde Road. The meeting was to be City's second game of the season - five days earlier they would travel to Nottingham to face Notts County. On derby day morning the *Daily Dispatch* columnist 'The Observer' outlined a pessimistic forecast of City's 1912-13 season: "In Manchester we are chiefly interested, perhaps, in wondering what kind of a season City are going to have. To be perfectly candid, because I do not wish to be told afterwards that I waited the course of events, I do not consider the present team good enough to place City in a good position in the table, unless G.W. Webb makes more difference than one is reasonably entitled to expect.

"All the same, I am hoping that when Mr. J.E. Mangnall takes charge an effort will be made to really strengthen the side, because I am forced to believe there is room for it. By the way, I may mention that it is definitely decided Mr. Mangnall will take up his responsibilities at Hyde-road a week today, and, as a matter of fact, he will be with the team at Nottingham today."

Considering the fact Mangnall was at Nottingham, not in London where United faced Arsenal, it must be obvious he did actually play a role in City's opening fixture - not officially of course, but he must have offered some advice. At Meadow Lane, William Henry scored his one and only League goal when he provided the Blues with a forty yard match winner against County. Had he and the others been inspired by the rather negative prospetcs in the *Daily Dispatch*?

The following game was officially Mangnall's last in charge of United, but there has got to be doubt over who decided the tactics to be employed by both sides. It seems crazy to believe that the United players would have listened to future Blue Mangnall, likewise could City afford to take the chance of seeing Mangnall's

Jim 'Naughty Boy' Goodchild joined City in December 1911 after being discarded by Southampton earlier in his career. He stayed with City until August 1927, earning a Cup medal in 1926. He was a firm favourite with the fans.

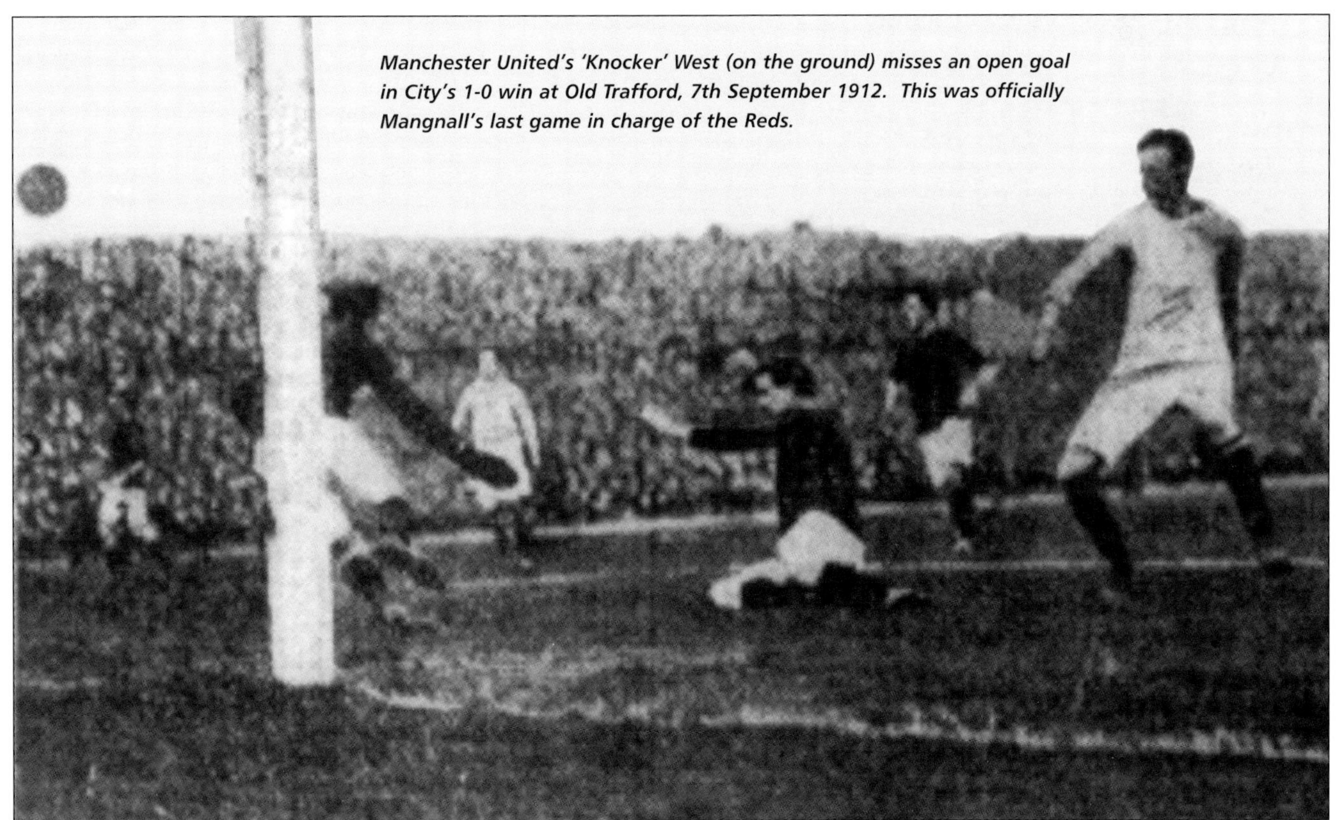

Manchester United's 'Knocker' West (on the ground) misses an open goal in City's 1-0 win at Old Trafford, 7th September 1912. This was officially Mangnall's last game in charge of the Reds.

Old Trafford reign end in victory? As far as the public were concerned, the biggest talking point was not the transfer of Mangnall - that was old hat by this point - it was news the game was to be classed as a testimonial for everybody's hero Billy Meredith.

The game itself was not a classic, but a forty thousand crowd satisfied Meredith's bank balance, and a goal by George Wynn satisfied the Blues. Ernest Mangnall must have had mixed feelings about the result but nevertheless *The Umpire* newspaper reporter summed it up nicely: "United speeded their manager rejoicing with two points to his new club."

Two days later Mangnall took charge at Hyde Road. His first task was to check the state of recent signing George Webb. A strict amateur, Webb arrived at Hyde Road from West Ham in July. As the *Daily Dispatch* recorded he made his debut at Notts County and kept his place at centre-forward for the trip to Old Trafford. Sadly, he was injured rather early in the game and left the field in the first half.

Some weeks later, by the time he was fully recovered from the injury, he discovered money had changed hands between City and the Hammers and, because of his strict amateur beliefs, he was horrified and refused to play for the club again. In November his retirement was confirmed and new manager Mangnall had to remove him from his long term plans. Sadly, the player died of consumption in 1915 at the age of twenty-eight.

Webb's replacement for Mangnall's first game in charge was another recent arrival, Harry Taylor - signed in June from Huddersfield Town. Apart from that essential change, Mangnall selected the same players who had featured at Old Trafford and Meadow Lane for the first home game of the campaign. Aston Villa were the visitors as George Wynn, once again, provided a surprisingly consistent City with the only goal of the game. A 2-1 victory followed against Liverpool prompting the *Daily Dispatch's* 'Observer' to question the sudden transformation: "The City deserve credit for all they have accomplished, but one would have more confidence in them carrying on the good work had they, with practically the same team, not made such an inglorious display last season. Either there was a screw very severely loose in 1911-12, or the present form is too good to last. Which is it?"

On the same day as the article Bolton visited Hyde Road to test City further. In a game watched by a crowd of 33,871 City defeated the Trotters 2-0. Did 'The Observer' have his answer? The rather more upbeat *Athletic News* believed Mangnall and the Blues had made it. Under the heading "Manchester's New Wonder" City's position was outlined: "Manchester City stand out boldly as the only first class team in the two divisions of the league, the Southern and the Scottish Leagues, with the highest possible points to their credit.

RAILWAYS.

GREAT CENTRAL.

FOOTBALL MATCH,
MANCHESTER CITY v. SHEFFIELD WEDNESDAY,
SATURDAY, Dec 7, Dean & Dawson's
HALF-DAY
THROUGH EXPRESS EXCURSION
WILL BE RUN TO
WADSLEY BRIDGE
AND
SHEFFIELD
Leaving MANCHESTER (London Road) [illegible] p.m.
With Three Days' Bookings.
Note.—Wadsley Bridge is the nearest station to the Football Ground.
Tickets in advance at the station, Dean and Dawson, Piccadilly, Manchester, and usual agents.
London. SA.' FAY, General Manager.

An advert for a football special to Wadsley Bridge for City's clash with Sheffield Wednesday on 7th December 1912. Any day trippers who travelled would have been disappointed with the result - a 1-0 defeat.

"The Citizens of Manchester have earned every point in September. Other clubs have remained undefeated, but they have not annexed the maximum marks. Nine years have passed since Manchester City commenced a campaign in this stimulating style."

The article went on to compare previous seasons, quoting 1903-4 as the closest when the Blues opening four games were won, although 1897-8 was actually better with seven straight victories but that was in Division Two.

The *Athletic News*, in a paragraph that could equally apply to the 1980s or mid 1990s, then paid tribute to City's vast army of loyal supporters: "Such a transformation in their fortunes after nine years will be very welcome and comforting to supporters whose loyalty has often been tested but has never failed.

"Manchester City are probably the only club which can draw huge gates when they are a losing team. Their financial possibilities as a winning team cannot be underestimated, as their gate receipts against Aston Villa were £1009 13s. 3d., representing 32,848 persons, and against Bolton Wanderers £1,131 1s. 6d. paid by 33,871 spectators. Manchester City have had a magnificent Autumn tonic."

On 5th October, after a few poor performances, centre-forward Harry Taylor was dropped for the game against Sheffield United. The feeling amongst City's directors was that he was not quite ready for first team football. In his place, Mangnall brought in William Kelly, the former Newcastle player, who had made seven appearances for the Blues the previous season. The change was not successful as the game ended 1-1. Co-incidentally, it was Sheffield United who had ended City's run in 1903. Was this some kind of omen? Would the 1912-13 season be an echo of 1903-4? All City fans hoped so, despite the Sheffield result. Certainly challenging for the League and reaching the Cup Final would be a great tonic for City's large following.

For the following match, Kelly was dropped as was another forward William Wallace. Joe Dorsett, who had missed the two previous games, returned and Tom Holford was moved up front. Leonard Wall, signed from Glossop in October 1910, filled the vacant centre-half position. Although the changes appeared fine on paper, they backfired as City succumbed to a 1-0 defeat at home to Newcastle. Mangnall now decided to recall Taylor, the player the *Daily Dispatch* claimed the directors did not want, in addition to outside-left Wallace. To make way for these changes he dropped Wall and Hoad, pushed Holford back, and moved Joe Dorsett from the left into Hoad's outside right position.

Despite a goal from Wynn, the Blues were beaten 2-1 by Oldham. Mangnall's side had clearly yet to recover from the folly of changing a winning team at the whim of the directors. For the next game, at home to Chelsea, Mangnall dropped Wallace and brought back Sid Hoad. At last, Mangnall got it right as the Blues achieved a 2-0 victory. Interestingly, Harry Taylor scored one of the goals. Had the directors now changed their minds? Although it's not known whether they made any further comment to Mangnall, it is known the forward scored twice in the next game - a 4-0 victory at Arsenal - and kept his place for the following twelve League games.

With their form rediscovered, the Blues continued to mount a challenge for the title until

December when a total of only three points from a possible twelve caused some concern. After an embarrassing 2-0 Hyde Road derby defeat, Mangnall dropped goalkeeper Jim Goodchild and brought back former derby king Walter Smith. His first League game for a year ended in a 4-0 victory over Notts County on 2nd January, with George Wynn, once again, proving to be one of football's finest strikers as he netted twice.

January also saw the start of what supporters hoped would be a terrific cup run. On 11th City easily overcame Birmingham 4-0 at Hyde Road with goals from Sid Hoad, Harry Taylor, and another brace from George Wynn. In the next round the Blues again received a home-tie, this time the opponents were Sunderland and it was a game, it seems, everybody wanted to watch.

Early in the day it was obvious to anyone close to Hyde Road that the crowd was going to be huge as Bennett Street, and other streets in the vicinity, were extremely busy. Indeed by 2pm the City management took the decision to close the gates - even though many ticket-holders remained outside. Naturally, many supporters still tried to gain entry by whatever means possible and by kick-off it was believed there were over fifty thousand in the ground, although the official attendance was recorded as 41,709 (receipts of £1,545). Even that figure was probably too many - when it is recalled only two years earlier crushed supporters had been taken away from the ground in ambulances.

In addition to the numbers inside, the streets close to the entrances were packed with an estimated fifteen thousand. The Hyde Road ground and its environs simply could not cope. Nevertheless, in scenes repeated at several venues over the years - including Wembley in 1923 - the game kicked off with far too many people in the ground.

Sunderland player, and later founder of *Football Monthly*, Charles Buchan, believed the game should not have begun when it did. According to him: "No sooner had the game started than the crowd began to encroach on the field. Before half-time they were three or four yards inside the touchlines."

A Sunderland player consults a couple of officials prior to the F.A. Cup match of February 1913 at Hyde Road being abandoned. The ground simply could not cope with a crowd believed to number over 50,000.

Somehow the game continued with Eli Fletcher and Tom Holford the only City players to make an impression. Indeed, the press claimed Holford played perhaps his best game ever. Nevertheless, five minutes into the second half, Buchan provided the first goal of the game. Despite people on the pitch, play resumed immediately. According to 'The Veteran', writing in the following Monday's *Daily Dispatch*, it was Sunderland's second goal, in the fifty-eighth minute that prompted more supporters to enter the pitch: "Eight minutes later Buchan went through in fine style, and Richardson headed from his centre. It was then the crowd started to encroach again on the Stand

The Popular Side at Hyde Road photographed during City's 2-0 win over Oldham on 12th March 1913. Latics' 'keeper Howard Matthews gathers the ball.

side, and the touch judge complained he could not see the touchline.

"The referee stopped the game, and I thought seemed to be ordering the lines to be re-marked, but then the crowd broke in more, and with the City players obviously appealing for an abandonment this was eventually done."

The report went on to consider the actions of the crowd, the players, and the referee, Mr. Adams, who had already suffered a similar incident at Leeds in the previous season's semi-final. According to the 'Veteran': "he showed commendable patience, but it was not possible for him to atone for the lack of police."

Much of Monday's press detailed the dramatic events surrounding the game with the 'Veteran' perhaps in the best position of all, for he was caught in part of the crush: "The crush amongst the thousand odd ticket holders was terrific - I am able to judge, for I was wedged in it for an hour - and the results might have been serious, while hundreds of ticket-holders never got in at all!"

Naturally, as time moved on, the journalists started to consider who was responsible for the near disaster. The two obvious candidates were the City management and the local police: "Assuming that he had charge of the arrangements, I am rather surprised at Mr. Mangnall being caught napping, but it may be that he has been away with the team and had had little to do with the home management. The chief fault was that the ground was never properly policed to start with, for on big occasions like this there should always be mounted police ready on the ground to assist in clearing the playing piece.

"The crowd certainly broke down some of the gates, and the probabilities are that some five or six thousand people got in that way, but it is doubtful if that would have happened if there had been mounted police to guard the gates in the manner that is done at Liverpool."

Most disagreed with the 'Veteran's view that mounted police should be on the scene 'just in case', but few could disagree with the view that a stronger police presence had been required. In the end the whole question of crowd control should have been debated throughout football but, as with so many other times, the F.A. chose to consider the Hyde Road invasion in isolation. On Monday 3rd February, without performing any form of detailed investigation, the F.A. Council met. Unfortunately for City, J. Lewis, a member of the Council and one of the F.A. men who first investigated City's illegal payment scandal seven years earlier, had been present at Hyde Road for the game. He provided the 'official' view of events.

Tommy Browell scored a goal on his debut against Sheffield Wednesday on 8th November 1913, and went on to total 139 goals in 247 games for the Blues. Sadly, his best years were probably lost to the first World War.

The result of the meeting, which lasted a little over an hour, was that the Blues were to be fined a record £500 - £350 to go to Manchester charities, the rest to the F.A.'s benevolent fund. They were also ordered to replay the game at Sunderland, much to the disgust of Sunderland's supporters who believed they should have been given the game. Despite being two goals down after about fifty-eight minutes, the Blues still had a chance of progression. If they were to overcome Sunderland, their opponents would be Swindon Town at Hyde Road.

The replay took place on Wednesday 5th when an improved City performance still could not prevent the Blues from exiting the competition. Co-incidentally Sunderland won 2-0, after Walter Smith had saved a penalty.

In the League, following the cup defeat, City's form was a little mixed with four losses in March causing a serious dent in City's bid for the title, and with four successive draws in the final weeks of the season the Blues fell to sixth place on forty-four points - ten behind champions Sunderland. Still a creditable position after a few years of struggle, but not nearly as good as their early season form had suggested. Despite his initial predictions, the *Daily Dispatch's* 'Observer' chose not to gloat . After all the Blues, with their ever loyal support, had challenged for most of the season and showed signs of promise and hope for the following campaign.

George Wynn was once again top scorer, this time with fourteen goals from thirty-one games, while Walkden born centre-forward Fred Howard ended the season on eleven goals from a mere sixteen games. He had even managed to score four on his debut on 18th January against Liverpool. Another player making his debut for City that day was Welsh international Edwin Hughes who was signed from Wrexham in December.

The 1913-14 season commenced with a couple of 1-1 draws, followed by a 3-1 victory over Sheffield United. These results, though not perfect by any means, did offer hope. Unfortunately the following nine games saw City move closer and closer to danger as only three points were gained during this period. Any dream Mangnall may have had of the Blues challenging for the title quickly disappeared as the nightmare of yet another relegation battle loomed.

With a total of only four victories by New Year, City needed a dramatic turnaround in their fortunes. Fortunately, an impressive spell during January helped lift the Blues in the League and progress in the Cup. Impressive Cup victories over Fulham, Tottenham, and Blackburn put the Blues into the quarter finals to face Sheffield United at Hyde Road. That game and the subsequent replay ended goalless with a third game, played at Villa Park, finishing 1-0 to Sheffield. For City it was yet another case of what might have been.

The League programme continued to frustrate although there were some interesting results. Derby County were defeated 4-2 with a hat trick from Fred Howard, and Manchester United were vanquished by a single goal at Old Trafford. Interestingly, United were also not having the best of seasons and for this game, which was also classed as a testimonial for United's Sandy Turnbull and George Stacey, *The Umpire* made much of the fact City remained the more popular side:

"From the point of view of attendance, Stacey and Turnbull's benefit match at Old Trafford proved an unqualified success, for the attendance must have exceeded 40,000, but the fact that the United were again beaten, and, worst of all, by their City rivals, should be distinctly unpalatable to themselves and their well-wishers. It was easily to be observed which was the most popular team when the men entered the arena, for the cheer which greeted United was faint as

City 2 Tottenham 1, 24th January 1914. The stand in the background is the Hyde Road Main Stand. This is the only known photo of this stand taken during a City game. Built c.1899, destroyed by fire in 1920.

compared with that which heralded the appearance of the City."

The victory over the Reds and a further three points in their remaining three fixtures gave City a total of 36 points and thirteenth position in the table, one place above United. It was not good enough for Mangnall, nor City's supporters but, once again, there had been a few encouraging signs. Not least the purchases Mangnall made during the season. Half-back Ted Hanney arrived from Reading in November 1913 for £1,200, and forward Tommy Browell made the move from Goodison Park for the considerable sum of £1,780. Browell, in particular, made a tremendous impression, scoring thirteen League goals following his November debut, to become the club's leading League marksman.

For George Wynn, the 1913-14 season had not been a good one. He had struggled with injury for much of the season and only managed to appear in twelve games, scoring three goals. The days of Wynn's reign as City's biggest and best goalscorer were over. Although he would remain on City's books until late 1919, he was never again a regular fixture in the side.

If that season ended with City looking to the future with new players Browell and Hanney, the one that followed closed in confusion. Throughout the early part of 1914 events in Europe suggested football was to take a less important role in the lives of all Europeans as it was obvious to all that the major European powers had begun an arms race. By the time City played their opening fixture, on 1st September, Britain was at war.

On 4th August, following Germany's invasion of Belgium, Britain had declared war on Germany. The general optimism was the war would be over by Christmas and that life should continue as normal, wherever possible. Naturally, vast numbers of men volunteered immediately for the armed forces with everybody expected to do their bit for King and Country but, as far as football was concerned, the game had to continue.

City opened with a fine 4-1 victory over Bradford City at Hyde Road but, because of the situation on the Continent, the crowd was significantly less than for the corresponding fixture the year before. Did football really matter when so many others were already dying? Four days later the Old Trafford derby ended goalless before 20,000. Football, as the F.A. often stated, would continue, although each club was expected to encourage its own players and supporters to volunteer for the forces. City appear to have taken the lead in the north-west with articles appearing in various newspapers. One, entitled "Manchester City's offer", appeared in *The Umpire* stating the City management would help any player, or his dependents, if that player joined the armed forces, so long as the Blues were allowed to take attendance money. The players and officials also agreed to give 5% of their wages to the Prince of Wales' Fund.

By Christmas, of course, the Great War, as it was to become known, was not over. Instead, there was deadlock in the despicable, muddy trenches that stretched from the North Sea to Switzerland. Yet in Manchester at times the suffering could be forgotten temporarily as City enjoyed one of their best seasons in years. Walter Smith was back to his best in goal, and with the support of William Henry, Eli Fletcher, Edwin Hughes, and of course Ted Hanney at centre half, the Blues were defensively strong.

In attack Fred Howard, Harry Taylor, and Tommy Browell were joined by Derby County's star forward Horace

Horace Barnes joined City in May 1914 from Derby. He scored twice during the King's visit to Hyde Road in 1920.

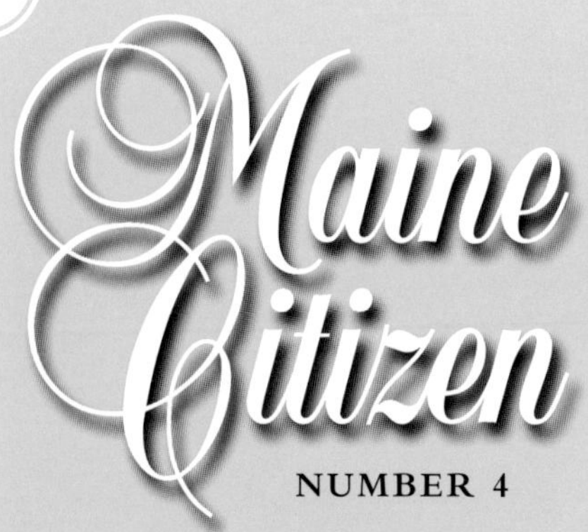

NUMBER 4

TOMMY BROWELL

Tommy Browell remains City's sixth highest League goalscorer with 122 goals from 222 games. This is a notable achievement, especially as the player lost four prime seasons to the Great War. Post-war Browell formed a superb attacking partnership with Horace Barnes, and the pair gained many headlines with City fans arguing for years about which player was the more accomplished.

Browell joined the Blues from Everton in 1913 for a fee of £1,780. It was a large sum for the period, but was one that proved Manager Mangnall's intent to bring quality to Hyde Road. The investment was a shrewd move as the player scored 13 goals in only 27 appearances to become that season's top scorer. This was something he achieved on a further four occasions. His best goal tally came in 1921 when he netted 31 goals to help the Blues finish runners up to Burnley. This was an important season for City fans and one when the popularity of the club proved simply too much for the cramped Hyde Road ground to cope with. Browell, with his great partner Barnes, was a true hero as games regularly became 40,000 sell-outs.

During 1921-2 the Browell-Barnes partnership netted City a total of 41 goals with Barnes unselfishly providing his colleague with the opportunity to finish one goal ahead of him, as he set up the winner for Browell in the final match of the season at home to Newcastle. The following season promised much more for Browell, but a serious ankle injury in September, after only five games and two goals, reduced his appearances. He did manage to play a further ten matches that

Barnes for a record equalling £2,500. This impressive forward line helped the Blues challenge all season long. In fact on 5th April, the largest Hyde Road crowd of the season, attended a game many believed would determine the Championship. Near neighbours Oldham Athletic were the visitors and despite a great deal of pressure at both ends the game between the top two sides ended goalless. For City, on 42 points, the point loss was significant as the Latics were now only two points behind with two games in hand. The pressure was on.

The next game, away to Bradford City, saw them drop another point, and so with only three games left City had virtually conceded the championship. Oldham had defeated Manchester United to put themselves within a point of the Blues but their two games in hand easily gave them the advantage. Also, City's next opponents Everton had started to climb the table and, although it was not obvious at the time, they were the team that really had to be watched.

Against Everton at Hyde Road City conceded a first half goal and, in effect, the title. Within seven days further defeats at Villa and Bradford (Park Avenue), left the Blues to finish in fifth place. Everton, with their impressive late surge, stole the title from Oldham Athletic who have never been that close since. City's final points tally of 43 was only three points less than Everton and was equalled by Blackburn in third place, and Burnley in fourth.

With the situation in Europe worsening it became obvious that City would have to wait some time before they next had the chance of taking the title.

At the end of the 1914-15 season the Football League was suspended and, in its place, regional leagues were created with City forming part of the Lancashire section. That group was exceptionally strong, especially as the top five placed clubs in the Football League all formed part of the new fourteen club league. For the Blues it was a successful period and prompted many to ponder what the club might have achieved had the Football League continued. It always seems petty when references are made to 'what ifs' and 'maybes' but it is a fact that City's first golden era ended prematurely, via the payments scandal, and that City's next big push for the title was also cut short. Nevertheless, the Blues could still feel proud of all they achieved in season 1915-16.

The Lancashire section commenced with a 3-1 victory over Stockport County at Hyde Road. Although the result is interesting in itself, one story connected with the game illustrates how everyone had to do their bit for King and Country. Record signing Horace Barnes had been given employment in a munitions factory and, on the day of the Stockport match, found the only way to guarantee he could play in the game was to be absent from work. He played the match, scored a goal, but then found he had to season, but it was a struggle. He managed to make one less League appearance the following season, but he did feature in the F.A. Cup run of 1924, scoring four goals in five matches.

For some spectators it appeared as if Browell's career with the Blues was nearing its end, but the player's determination and ability proved his critics wrong as he went on to demonstrate his worth during the 1925-6 season. He scored an incredible five goals during an 8-3 demolition of Burnley on 24th October, and had earlier netted all City's goals in an amazing 4-4 draw against Everton.

In the 1926 F.A. Cup run he was on target seven times in five matches. His final game for City was the 3-2 defeat at Newcastle on the last day of that season. Naturally, he scored one of City's consolation goals but even he was unable to prevent the Blues from being relegated.

In September 1926 he moved to Blackpool where he continued to play until he was 39. Afterwards he stayed in the area, becoming a player-coach with Lytham, then Morecambe (Dec 1933-4), before he became a tram driver for Lytham St. Annes Corporation. He died on 5th October 1955, 14 days before his 63rd birthday.

His career at first Hyde Road then Maine Road only yielded one medal as an F.A. Cup Finalist, but Browell's energy helped generate much excitement. He deserved more honours, and would possibly have won a Cup Winner's medal had Bolton's Dick Pym not performed a miraculous save to stop Browell from netting. At the time the City man was amazed and told reporters: "He must have left his fingernails uncut for six months to make that save!"

Browell should be remembered as a City hero who helped prolong the club's life in Division One, while bringing excitement via many fine goal scoring feats. He was a great hero to the Blue masses and it must be more than sheer coincidence that City's popularity increased at a time when he was in such outstanding form. Browell is a true Blue legend.

BROWELL'S PLAYING RECORD

	LEAGUE		FA CUP		TOTAL	
	App	Gls	App	Gls	App	Gls
1913-14	27	13	6	1	33	14
1914-15	10	1	2	0	12	1
1919-20	30	22	2	0	32	22
1920-21	42	31	1	0	43	31
1921-22	38	21	3	5	41	26
1922-23	15	3	0	0	15	3
1923-24	14	4	5	4	19	8
1924-25	14	6	1	0	15	6
1925-26	32	21	5	7	37	28
TOTAL	222	122	25	17	247	139

face the local magistrates who imposed a fine. Naturally, any work connected with the war effort was viewed a little more importantly than helping City defeat Stockport.

Somehow, Barnes managed to play in every one of City's first twelve games, scoring a total of fifteen goals. In addition to his munitions work, he was also performing the vital task of boosting morale - for all Blues at any rate!

On the final day of the Lancashire section league programme City defeated Preston 8-0 to carry off the title by two points from Burnley. Man of the match was undoubtedly Albert Fairclough, who scored five in his first game since 16th October. The other scorers were Joe Cartwright and Horace Barnes, who scored twice to bring his total to 26 from the 24 games he played. Interestingly the Preston side include two Bury players who happened to be at the station when the Preston men arrived. Bury's game had been called off and, as Preston only had nine men, the two Bury boys quickly accepted Preston's offer to play. Many such incidents occurred throughout football during the First World War.

Action from the City v Preston F.A. Cup 1st Round replay at Hyde Road in January 1915. City won 3-0. The pictures show Preston goalkeeper Jones flinging himself at a Howard shot (top) and (bottom) City causing more panic in the visitors area.

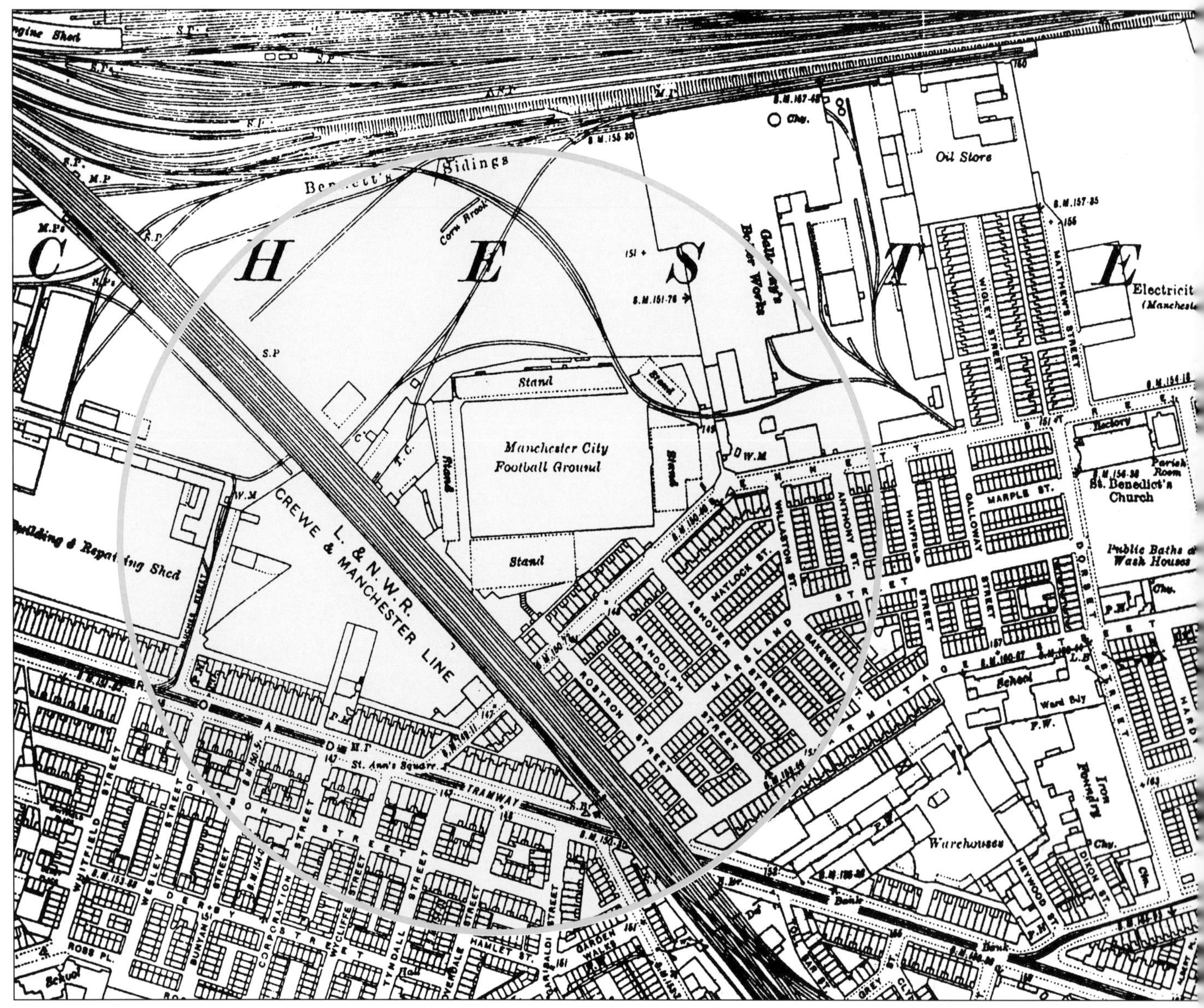

The Hyde Road ground c.1915. Note the railway line cutting into the top right hand corner of the ground. Also the ground's close proximity to City's birthplace at St. Mark's church (circled on the right of the map).

The stands depicted are (clockwise from top): The Main Stand, erected 1899, destroyed by fire 1920; The Boys' Corner; The Galloway End (roofed during the 1910 close season); The Popular Side, roofed in 1910, capacity believed to be c17,000; The Stone Yard Stand also known as the Hyde Road Stand or West Stand.

For the rest of the traditional football season a subsidiary tournament, split into two sections, was organised with City, United, Oldham, Everton, Liverpool, and Stockport County forming the Southern Division. Despite losing their first game 2-0 at Stockport on 4th March, the Blues quickly showed they were a class above the rest. This tournament ended with City as champions, although the previous season's League Champions matched them for points. Mangnall's men could claim they were the most consistent Lancastrian side over the full traditional season. Interestingly, City amassed a total of 48 points from 36 games during the season, compared with Everton's 46 from 38 the previous year.

The first true season of wartime football also saw the return of Billy Meredith to City. On 11th March for the visit of Liverpool, Meredith became a Blue again: "After an absence of close on eleven years, Meredith reappeared in the colours of Manchester City and though it was his first game of the season he could safely take credit to himself that he was unsurpassed by any other forward on the field. Naturally his pace has slackened and he didn't centre with the same facility as of yore. He couldn't lift the somewhat heavy ball, but his feet have not yet lost their cunning and there was none that can backheel with such certainty as he."

Meredith's return to the Blues had been caused through much argument between United and the player, and the prospect of returning to City where Mangnall was now the manager, with Lawrence Furniss back on the Board, did appeal. For the 1916-17 season he became more or less an ever-present, missing only the first three games of the season. After a particularly impressive 4-0 victory over Blackpool, the *Athletic News* remembered Meredith's partnership with Sandy Turnbull:

> **"There is a particular spot on the Hyde Road ground which deserves to be known as 'Meredith's patch'. It is the place from where the famous Welshman has made history, and from where on Saturday in the match with Blackpool, he added to the long and glorious line of successes which he inaugurated twenty-two years ago. The master knows to an inch, almost to the blade of grass, and the manner in which he crossed the ball from the old familiar spot and gave Barnes and Brennan the chances from which they won the match vividly recollects the halcyon days of his wonderful association with 'Sandy' Turnbull. That profitable relationship has**

been broken, never, I fear, to be resumed, but Meredith goes on and on, playing though he was when the majority of his colleagues were at school. Not one amongst them had a greater part in the City's opening victory of the season than the still useful 'Wizard of Wales'."

The 1916-17 season saw City finish fourth in the Lancashire Section, which now included Stoke and Port Vale. In the Subsidiary Tournament City faced both the Potteries clubs and Manchester United home and away, with the results being transferred onto a league table that included all the other clubs in the Lancashire Section. This gave City a position of thirteenth overall out of sixteen clubs.

Sadly in May 1917 the news that Meredith's former partner, Sandy Turnbull had been killed while serving with the Manchester Regiment in the trenches at Arras cast an air of sadness of Manchester. For many others the enjoyment of playing or watching football would also be lost forever.

For the next couple of seasons City performed reasonably well, finishing fourth in the main tournament and achieving an overall position of third in the Subsidiary Tournament in 1918. The following season they ended the main competition in fifth place, while the Subsidiary Section was reorganised to provide section winners - City winning their section - who would then compete on a knockout basis for the Lancashire Cup. City were defeated 1-0 by Oldham, after a 1-1 draw at Hyde Road.

Wartime football was far from perfect, but for City the period was relatively successful, especially as it had helped bring Meredith back to Hyde Road. He was still officially a Manchester United player and, once the war ended and the Football League returned he was expected back at Old Trafford. Naturally, Mangnall and the City faithful wanted their hero to remain but, unfortunately, it was not to be.

At Hyde Road, following the ending of the war on 11th November, City's thoughts had to move towards the future. Was the wartime squad strong enough? Would all the players return? Was Hyde Road still appropriate for staging First Division matches? A lot of these issues required consideration, especially the future of the ground.

At times during the war Hyde Road had been used to stable horses and the venue was far from perfect. Prior to 1914 there had been plenty of problems with crowd control but now, after four years

BILLY MEREDITH
A Blue again

Hyde Road was used for stabling at times during World War One. Here horses line up in front of the Popular Side terracing.

of little maintenance, the stands were not in the best of shape. Even so, in 1917 City pledged their future to their cramped home by taking over the ground lease from Chester's Brewery. It was a significant moment in the history of the club because it more or less ended the link with the brewery which stretched right back to 1887 with the formation of Ardwick. It was also a sign that the successful, rich football club planned to be in total control of their destiny. The annual rent of £500 was insignificant compared with the profits possible from a successful City.

Even so, Hyde Road needed improving. In the mid-1970s one supporter born around the time of City's 1904 Cup win remembered an unusual situation which occurred as a result of a railway line which actually ran through the ground, in front of one stand: "One of my memories of City's Hyde Road days was a unique happening during the 1914-18 War and no other club in the history of soccer can equal this one. Behind the 'Lads-only' stand was Galloway Boiler Works and to reach the railway close by, a loop line ran from the sidings into the ground passing in front of the boys stand, and then into the works. Inch-thick ten foot long iron bars kept us back off the pitch."

"During the interval at one game a huge boiler was being brought from the works when the whole contraption stuck on the sharp curved line, blocking the view for everyone in the stand. Considering the howls of protest that went up from all the lads during the twenty minutes it took to get it moving, it's a wonder the boiler didn't burst!"

For City, the immediate post war period required careful planning if the Blues were to remain Manchester's top club.

Chapter Six

NEW HOME, NEW BEGINNING & AN OLD FAVOURITE

1919 1924

AFTER four seasons of relatively successful regional football, the Blues were ready for the return of national competition. Many of the old familiar faces remained but Ernest Mangnall believed the introduction of a few younger imports might help City achieve the success for which many felt they were poised four years earlier. Although, as events of 1919-20 season would show, Mangnall was a little uncertain of the worth of some of the players, especially as the club had a total of 31 professionals and 55 amateurs on its books at the start of the season.

The team for the opening fixture at home to Sheffield United was in the main a familiar one. The only player not to have played pre-war was Stalybridge born Tommy Broad, a signing from Bristol City in March 1915. Walter Smith was once again the club's number one 'keeper, although Jim Goodchild was determined to regain the green shirt, and Barnes, Browell and Cartwright were there to aid the attack. Even pre-war favourite George Wynn put on the Blue shirt for the Football League's return.

The game ended in a 3-3 draw with Horace Barnes scoring a brace, while Tommy Browell slotted home a late penalty. The next match saw Browell score twice and Cartwright once to defeat Oldham 3-1 at Boundary Park. Five days later George Wynn found the net for the last time in his City career as the Blues were defeated 3-1 by Sheffield United in the return match. Wynn did make one further appearance - another 3-1 against Oldham on 8th September - but his Hyde Road career was over. In November he moved to Coventry City for £300, played in their first season in the League then, after scoring twice in 27 League and Cup appearances, became a bit of a nomad, moving from club to club. He had spells with Llandudno Town, Mansfield and Halifax where, coincidentally he made an appearance during the Shaymen's inaugural season in the League.

One player who made his debut after Wynn departed was William 'Spud' Murphy who replaced Joe Cartwright on the left wing for the bulk of the season. Murphy was an extremely fast player with terrific stamina - a point proved during the war when he took up cross-country running. In February 1918 he joined the Blues, turning professional in May 1919 at the age of twenty-four. His debut was a 4-1 defeat at home to Bolton on 13th September. Seven days later the return game ended 6-2 - this was not a happy period for Walter Smith.

This first season after the war saw many unusual results as teams met the same opponents on consecutive Saturdays, creating an odd feeling of familiarity between sides. Often high scoring victories were followed by heavy defeats - City's games with Notts County were perfect examples. The first ended 4-1 to City at Hyde Road, yet in the return the score was reversed. For a team with a growing tradition for inconsistency this season could easily have been disastrous but fortunately enough points were picked up to ease the situation.

In October, the first post war League Manchester derby was a real thriller, with United taking the lead three times before the Blues levelled at 3-3. This was actually the last appearance of Walter Smith who, it must be said, left Hyde Road after an absolutely appalling game. For much of his City career Smith had saved the Blues with a consistently high standard of goalkeeping, especially in derby games, but in this match he could do nothing right. He was heavily criticised for two of United's goals - for one he hesitated, for another he was dispossessed while bouncing the ball in his area oblivious to the presence

NEWSPAPER.] MONDAY, DECEMBER 29, 1919. TWOPENCE.

SNAPSHOTS IN THE SUNDERLAND MATCH AT MANCHESTER.

A cutting from the Athletic News of City's 1-0 victory over Sunderland at Hyde Road on 27th December 1919. The scorer was City's star player 'Spud' Murphy.

of United's goal-poaching star of the period, Joe Spence. One newspaper report mentioned his name three times - twice for the goals and then once in the final summary: "The City played a greatly improved game all round, and apart from Smith's mistakes, the defence was most faultless".

Smith left Hyde Road for Port Vale where his nightmare in the Manchester derby was rapidly eclipsed by accusations of assault on the morning of his debut. It seems he was falsely accused of assaulting a hotel chambermaid at South Shields prior to his first game for Vale. He was bailed in time to play, but completed the match knowing he was constantly under the watchful eye of a police detective. Fortunately, it was all a mistake and Smith remained with Vale until 1922. At Hyde Road the enduring memories of Smith were his outstanding early derby appearances and his Football League appearance against the Scots in 1915. Like all 'keepers he was a little eccentric - the *Athletic News* once called him: "the only first class goalkeeper in the Country who disdains training" - but he had been a superb player for the Blues.

In addition to the transfer of Smith, the derby also saw the end of Ted Hanney's career. He was transferred to Coventry for an incredible £2,000. Like Smith, Hanney's derby had not been a particularly pleasurable experience - he broke his nose in a collision during the second half - although match reports stated he played well during his spells on the pitch.

The season progressed and Browell and Barnes provided most of City's fire power, causing many to wonder what the two players might have achieved together had the war not ended national competition. They each scored 22 League goals - a tally that made them City's highest scorers since Gillespie's 28 in 1902-3.

These goals, plus the form of Goodchild in goal, helped City reach a respectable seventh place, but the most newsworthy moment of the season came on 27th March 1920 when King George V attended Hyde Road for City's match against Liverpool. The King was on a tour of the North-West when City received the ultimate honour. According to some reports the Hyde Road attendance that day easily exceeded 40,000 with the gates closed around 2.30pm. The Royal Standard was raised from a hastily erected flag pole on the stand at the Galloway End, and the King was introduced to the players and management, including trainer Jimmy Broad who had been at Hyde Road since the beginning.

He took his seat in the old wooden grandstand, which by this time was more than a little decrepit, and watched the game. Horace Barnes scored two late goals to give the Blues a 2-1 victory, and the King much enjoyment - if Manchester based newspapers are to be believed.

It was a tremendous honour for the Blues and confirmed they were one of the most important and famous clubs in Britain, even though Hyde Road was not the grandest of venues. Lifelong City supporter Harry Hughes, born in August 1902, remembers visiting the ground for the first time during this period:

"I thought I must go down and see these wonderful creatures called 'City', and made my way to the ground off Bennett Street. When I arrived I was mystified as to what to do; there were narrow holes for turnstiles and I didn't know what they were at all. Anyway I eventually paid my shilling and staggered into this vast multitude of people. There must have been 30,000 or more. I could hear the voices - a lovely rustling sound like wheat in the wind. The match was against Bolton Wanderers I think, they were a real force in the land of course.

"The ground had metal stanchions - the lattice type - holding up the roofs and much of the ground looked similar. There were houses overlooking the ground, cutting into the Popular Side terracing, and for years I used to ask my mother if we could flit and move into one of those so we could see the ground. During the games you could always see fellas hanging out of their windows, smoking and drinking pints of beer - a sort of executive box of the day.

"My mother used to say 'if you're going to the football make sure you don't come home injured' and I used to reply 'I'm only watching, I'm not playing' because you didn't think you could get injured

Sam Cookson was City's regular choice at full-back from his debut on 1st January 1920 through to 1927. After 306 first team appearances he joined Bradford in September 1928. He died in 1955 at the age of 55.

watching. Occasionally you'd get crushed a little, but there was never really any trouble.

"The funny part of all these games around this time was the Beswick Prize Band. It was nice to hear the crowd whistling the tunes - 'Oh, Comrades' and tunes like that. There was an old fella there - Patsy Hagan I believe his name was. He wore a great hat and carried a huge beagle stick, marching along, moving his stick, beating time. The band were all right - they played all the tunes and the crowd listened and whistled. Can you imagine the whole crowd whistling more or less all in tune? It was great, but this Patsy Hagan looked to be a staunch teetotaller, very serious. When he marched into the corners with his serious face, he'd wave his stick and turn around, and the crowd would point at him and laugh. It was very funny.

"Another funny thing used to occur with the lads selling 'Batty's Football Tablets'. That was a do in itself! The tablets were sold in little pokey bags - a penny a packet, and I remember that at my first game a fella right at the back threw a penny down and the Batty lad caught it. They used to do it all the time. Anyway, the Batty lad threw the packet back up, right to the man who wanted them! Occasionally, the packets would only go halfway up the terracing and the bag would be knocked to the buyer by the others in the crowd - each one knocking it on. Sometimes the bags would burst and we'd all get a tablet! That was part of the fun. Every home game you had to buy Batty's tablets.

MANCHESTER CITY FOOTBALL CLUB, Ltd.

GROUND: HYDE ROAD, MANCHESTER.

Chairman - [illegible] E. CHAPMAN.
Secretary-Manager - - J. E. MANGNALL.

The King's Visit,

Saturday, March 27th, 1920.

Manchester City v. Liverpool,

Kick-off at 3-15 p.m.

The visit of King George V on 27th March 1920. City beat Liverpool 2-1 and the King applauded vigorously according to one newspaper.

"I remember that the Hyde Road crowd were always in good humour and, after that first game, I walked home - I don't think I touched the floor until I got home, I was full of it. I said 'that's for me, I'm going there again'. I loved it and couldn't wait for the next game. I dreamt about it all fortnight."

Certainly the atmosphere at Hyde Road was special, even if the venue was inadequate. Already the City management were aware the time was fast approaching when the club would have to move if it was to achieve its full potential. Even in the early 1920s it was obvious City's policy of make do and mend could not last and a new venue had to be found as Hyde Road offered little scope for improvement. Bennett Street prevented the popular side from being extended - the stand roof only reached a little over half way because of its irregular shape and the proximity of the houses - while Galloway's Works prevented improvements at that end of the ground. The two other sides could not be enlarged because of railway lines and sidings, and a stone yard. Even access was a problem as two sides offered no opportunity for turnstiles or exit points.

With all this in mind the directors and Ernest Mangnall, the manager, considered other sites. The most obvious was Belle Vue, a huge pleasure gardens and zoo a short distance away, close to St. Mark's early venues at Pink Bank Lane, Kirkmanshulme Cricket Club, and Clemington/ Gorton Park. Ardwick had played a floodlit friendly at the Athletic Ground against Newton Heath in 1889, and Billy Meredith had lived adjacent to the running track using it to train on during his first City period. It seemed to offer great potential, yet the City management were not convinced. They had discussed a move to Belle Vue since the turn of the century but Hyde Road always seemed to offer more in terms of familiarity and atmosphere. Hyde Road was home and as the 1920-21 season commenced the 40,000 capacity venue was deemed suitable for another few years at least.

Max Woosnam was a tremendous all round amateur sportsman and popular captain of City. He made his debut against Bradford City on New Year's Day 1920 and captained the Blues at the official opening of Maine Road.

Early season capacity crowds caused more headaches for the management - and uncomfortable crushing for a number of supporters. Across the city United, with their 70,000 stadium, felt they could help and John Davies, United's Chairman, offered the use of Old Trafford. The Blues politely turned him down, but by early November drastic events would alter City's view.

On the night of Saturday 6th November, the main stand was destroyed by fire.
The cause was eventually announced as being a stray cigarette end, not the result of some 'Bonfire Night' prank, but the damage was tremendous. The *Daily Dispatch* were quickly on the scene to uncover the facts and mingle with the large crowd of onlookers: "Shortly after 11 pm it was discovered that flames were issuing from the buildings underneath the Hyde-road end of the Grand Stand. An alarm was raised, but the outbreak spread with such great rapidity that though the City Fire Brigade answered the call very promptly, the stand and adjacent buildings of the club were almost entirely involved before their arrival.

"The structure, which was built of wood, included the dressing-rooms, offices, baths, and the attendants' rooms. In just over an hour the whole building, which was valued at several thousands of pounds, was razed to the ground.

"The flames could be seen for miles around, and thousands of people were attracted to the ground.
A strong body of police was drafted to the scene, but great numbers of people by that time had flocked on to the other stands and made themselves comfortable to watch the rapid progress of the flames. It was an excited crowd, especially when the supports of the roof collapsed. The leaping flames revealed many hundreds of people sitting packed together as on the occasion of some big match.

"The stand was capable of seating about 3,000 people, and in view of the club's difficulties with regard to accommodation the loss is a very serious one."

Over the course of the next few days the *Daily Dispatch* reported City's attempts to recover from the loss and find a suitable venue for the following Saturday's return match with Huddersfield. By Wednesday, it was revealed City had tried to negotiate for the use of Old Trafford but United's terms had become prohibitive. Apparently the Reds wanted a guaranteed income and to keep all receipts in excess of the corresponding fixtures from the previous season. They did state they would pay City if the receipts did not match those of twelve months previous, but the chances of that actually happening were minimal. Many of City's games had been sell-outs and the Blues felt that, with a bigger venue, the crowds would have been higher. 'It wasn't the ground that attracted the supporters it was the team' was City's main argument.

With the two sides failing to reach agreement, and the Blues determined not to cancel the Huddersfield fixture, City took the only option available - they decided to patch up Hyde Road and with typical City spirit 'put on the show'. The *Daily Dispatch* reported the stand would be replaced by an enclosure with an entrance charge of 1s 9d and that the 'Stoneyard Stand', part of the roofed area behind the Hyde Road goal, would be made available for season ticket holders, officials, and the press. The seated area available was not huge, in fact there could only have been approximately 2,000 seats in the stand, but it was the best the club could provide.

With the players changing at Galloways, and a little discomfort in the press and officials section, the game against Huddersfield went ahead as planned. A crowd of 35,000, according to the *Daily Dispatch*, watched a 3-2 City victory and most Mancunians were pleased with what the club had managed to achieve in the time, but the real moment of pride came on the 27th when United were the visitors. Harry Hughes remembers the period well: "United in their benign way offered the use of Old Trafford but City politely refused saying 'Don't worry we'll have a grandstand!' and y'know we did! We had one built by the time we played United. It was made of tongue and groove and varnished. In fact you could still smell the varnish all over the ground. It was pretty rough, but it served its purpose, and as it was all new wood it must have been ten times stronger than the old stand.

"As usual the band came out, formed a circle on the pitch and played all the popular songs of the day. Then they started playing 'I wouldn't leave my little wooden hut for you' and the crowd wasn't slow to notice that, and we all started laughing. Then the referee came on, blew his whistle at the band and told them to get off! So as they marched off they played 'Home Sweet Home' - very apt, very witty!"

If United were still in any doubt that City were at home at Hyde Road by the end of the game they must have realised who the masters were, as the Blues trounced them 3-0. Interestingly, even though the crowd reached 40,000 there was still room on the new terracing. The fire had actually provided the Blues with greater opportunity to satisfy their large support.

The star of the derby match was City's amateur centre-half Max Woosnam, who had made his debut the previous March. He was an all round sportsman, famous for tennis - winning an Olympic Gold at the 1920 Games in Antwerp, football, cricket, and golf. Although United were keen to sign him, he joined City following a recommendation by United player Billy Meredith. Meredith was having a number of problems at United and felt the Blues would treat Woosnam properly.

He was employed at Crossley's - an engine manufacturer - and had to work a five and half day week, which presented serious problems when the Blues were playing some distance away from Manchester. Dutifully he continued to work all morning on the day of a Cup tie at Leicester in March 1920, and was unable to play. When his employers discovered his loyalty to them they insisted that, in future, if City needed him he would play, no matter how early he had to leave work. Basically he was told "play for City or else....".

According to early club histories Woosnam was a fair, clean player, although he was also an "advocate of the healthy shoulder charge."

Other players to arrive around the same time as Woosnam were Sam Cookson, later described as the best uncapped full back of the period, Fred 'Tiny' Fayers, a half-back from Stockport County, and former United player Mick Hamill, signed from Belfast Celtic although City had to pay £1,000 to the Reds as they still held his English registration.

These players, together with fine goalkeeping from Goodchild, and the power of Browell, Barnes, and Murphy enabled the Blues to maintain a strong challenge for the title. Tremendous interest was shown in the club - 40,000 crowds were the norm - while the Irish F.A. showed more interest in one of the season's star players - 'Spud' Murphy. They wrote asking if he had been born in Ireland to which Mangnall replied "He comes from St. Helens, where the pills come from".

City's excellent season continued into 1921 and in March they faced fellow challengers Burnley in a game that would severely test the Hyde Road enclosure. Harry Hughes remembers how the crowd for this match was huge, probably the largest Hyde Road attendance ever, and that as a young man it seemed incredible so many people could pack into the ground: "I managed to get near the front. They had little wooden railings around the pitch to keep the crowd off the turf, but there was never any real danger in those days. Soon the ground became packed beyond ordinary comfort - and we didn't ask for a lot in comfort in those days! Some 'strong arms' lifted me up and put me over the railings onto the turf itself - the holy of holies!

Mick Hamill made his debut in October 1920 and stayed with the Blues for four seasons. He died in July 1943 in tragic and mysterious circumstances - his body was found in a river.

Crowd control failed abysmally at City's 3-0 win over Burnley on 26th March 1921, when probably the largest crowd ever at Hyde Road attended a crucial League match. Notice the large number of spectators on top of the Popular Side roof in the picture below. Fans also clung onto the girders underneath.

City 1 Bradford Park Avenue 0, April 1921.

Tommy Browell scored a penalty after a retake to send Bradford down into the Second Division.

The pictures show goalkeeper Scattergood under pressure from Browell and Warner and (right) Browell doing a flying act.

Anyway, behind me, right at the back there was a huge wooden door with a padlock on - it would have been one of the large exit gates. While I was safely on the pitch, I heard a tremendous noise and turned to see the gate broken down, all splintered, and the crowd surging in. As I was on the pitch I just missed being involved, just missed being crushed. I was lucky, others were injured."

Some fifty-five years after the event another spectator that day, Joe Carley of Heaton Mersey, provided his memory of how others gained free entry: "I was present perched high up in the Boys' Corner, and from my vantage point I could see the upper portion of certain houses in Bennett Street. To my amazement I noticed an open window from where a rope - evidently secured to a bed or other heavy object - crossed the street and was just as securely fastened to a girder supporting the roof over the popular side.

"From the window emerged a youth who swung himself, hand over hand, across Bennett Street and into the ground. Whereupon the rope was quickly untied, or cut, withdrawn into the house and the window slammed shut!

"It was a dangerous procedure which the harassed police had much difficulty in stopping, as they were so busy attending to the jostling, angry and disappointed crowds in the street below."

The *Daily Dispatch* reported the amazing scenes in full - including details of a stand fire that was quickly dealt with and the fact many supporters took up positions on the roof itself. As with the Sunderland game nine years earlier, the extraordinary scenes proved Hyde Road simply was not good enough or large enough for City. The Blues were immensely popular with an average attendance of over 31,000 - the largest up until that point - and Hyde Road was hindering the club's growth. There was also much cause for concern from a health and safety angle, although at this point few seemed bothered if a handful of supporters received minor injuries.

On the day itself, the Blues were simply concerned with winning and ending Burnley's tremendous run of thirty games without defeat. Horace Barnes scored twice - one from a free kick forty yards out - and Tommy Johnson provided another to give the Blues an impressive 3-0 win, but within a week hopes of achieving the title reduced as both Burnley and Middlesbrough defeated City in their return matches. A fine sequence of five victories and a draw followed but by the final day of the season City had no chance of catching Burnley and, after a 1-1 draw at Newcastle, City ended the season in second place five points behind their Lancastrian rivals. Even with Burnley clearly head and shoulders above the rest, it was still regarded as a terrific season for the popular Blues.

In addition to their title challenge, City also played an important part in Bradford Park Avenue's relegation battle. The Yorkshire club visited Hyde Road on 23rd April needing victory to stand any real chance of avoiding the drop, but fate was not on their side as City were awarded a penalty fifteen minutes from the end. It seems Spud Murphy was tackled, rather innocuously, a fraction inside the box. Harry Hughes remembers Tommy Browell taking the kick: "Bradford's goalkeeper was called Scattergood - I remember the name because it was so unusual - he was leaping about trying to put Browell off his shot and when the player shot, the ball went yards wide of the mark. Scattergood had succeeded and the Bradford people cheered, but the referee ordered it to be retaken. Browell scored with the second shot and some cruel man in the crowd shouted 'how's it going to be in the Second Division next season then?' and Scattergood looked around at the supporter, picked up the ball out of the net and threw it right at this fella's face! The crowd went wild and the players dragged Scattergood away, else he'd have been murdered. That goal basically put Bradford down."

In addition to the Scattergood affair, Harry Hughes clearly recalls the following home game - a 3-1 victory over Newcastle - not for the game itself but for the fact it was nominated as Jim Goodchild's benefit match: "When it was a player's benefit they'd plaster posters on all the walls in the area. Well, for this one all the posters said 'CITY versus NEWCASTLE UNITED - GOODCHILD'S BENEFIT' and so we all went along because he was a

The first post war season saw a dramatic turnover in the playing staff of the club. At the start of the season the Blues had 31 professionals and 55 amateurs on their books. Understandably, they asked the Football League for permission to release 33 of these amateurs on 29th September 1919. During the season, however, 23 new amateurs signed along with ten new professionals.
During the following close season eight more professionals and 12 amateurs arrived, while another amateur turned professional. All of this activity was required as the City management came to understand the real effects on the players of the First World War.

bit of a character. At half time they had about six men carrying this huge sheet around the ground and we all threw some coins in. It must have got very heavy, of course, but they managed to hold it. They went off at the end of the interval and before the end of the game they had counted it all, and sent a lad around with a sign saying 'thank you for £750 15s and 4d ha'penny ' or something like that and the crowd all cheered.

"We called him 'naughty boy Goodchild' because of a cartoon that appeared in the 'paper with that caption after some misdemeanour or other."

In the 1970s another City supporter, Mr. B.J. Hill of Hulme, remembered 'naughty boy' Goodchild for another reason: "Jimmy always wore a flat cloth cap when he was playing. Well, in one game, the visitors won a corner, over came the ball, up jumped Jimmy to gather it, and off flew his cap. I can see him now on his hands and knees frantically searching for that cap among the lethal thrashing feet trying to get at the fallen ball.

"The ball was forgotten as far as Jimmy was concerned and he hastily retrieved his cap. But poor Jimmy's secret was out....he was as bald as a billiard ball. You can imagine the reaction of the fans witnessing this amazing episode!"

During the close season the major story in Manchester was not the fact Goodchild was bald, it was the rather more incredible news that Billy Meredith, at the age of 47, was leaving United to return to the Blues in a player-coach capacity. Because of his age and the strength of the City side, few believed he would actually ever play for the Blues, even though he had made a number of appearances for the Reds during 1920-21, but when he was named in the starting line-up for the opening game of the season most Mancunians looked forward to enjoying a glimpse of his old right-wing magic.

A crowd of approximately 35,000 paid to see their hero's return and, after a fine 2-1 victory over Aston Villa, they went home happy, especially as the Blues were now unbeaten in 34 consecutive League games at Hyde Road. This was an astonishing run and one which had made City into the kind of consistent team others desperately wanted to beat. The first club to finally achieve victory over City at Hyde Road was Bolton Wanderers who, in a rather scrappy match, ran out winners by the odd goal in five on 3rd December, by which time City's run had been extended to 41 games.

During the course of the run Tommy Browell and Horace Barnes had been in fine form with the two men somewhat overshadowing the exploits of Meredith. For Barnes, City's 4-1 victory in the Hyde Road derby of 22nd October was particularly sweet as he became only the second man in history to score a hat-trick in a derby game. In addition to the performance of Barnes, the game was noteworthy as it was the last derby to be played at Hyde Road, although no one realised this at the time, and the last 'home' derby to feature Billy Meredith. The reason for this was United were relegated at the end of the season and by the time they returned to Division One, in 1925, the Blues had moved to the rather more palatial Maine Road stadium.

Harry Hughes remembers how, on the eve of the game, a United prankster tried to give the Reds the appearance of home advantage: "The City groundsman arrived very early, about 7am. I don't know why, perhaps like the rest of us the prospect of certain victory over United excited him. It was fortunate that he did arrive because all the railings that went around the pitch used to be blue and white, but on this day some United fan had broken in and painted them all red and white - imagine that at City's ground! It seems that he'd got in in the middle of the night. Well, City weren't having that and by the time of kick off the club had painted them all blue and white again!

"It caused a great deal of merriment in the crowd. The rivalry was friendly then, but we were still rivals! Arguments used to happen of course, occasionally a scuffle, but that was it. You'd certainly never get a player going into the crowd attacking them of course."

Jim Goodchild
According to supporters of the period, that large cloth cap hid a head that was 'as bald as a billiard ball!'

City's line-up for 1921-22 Back (left to right - players only): Cookson, Blair, Fletcher, Hamill. Front: Meredith, either Warner or Woodcock, Browell, Woosnam, Barnes, Murphy, Fayers.

Another match, a 6-1 victory over West Bromwich Albion, during this early part of the season saw Max Woosnam score his first for the club. A story circulating around Manchester at the time suggested Woosnam had promised he would take the entire team for a meal at the upmarket Midland Hotel if he ever scored for the club. According to eye witnesses, the moment club captain Woosnam scored, City's Scottish 'keeper, Tom Blair, threw his gloves into the back of his net and ran the full length of the pitch to congratulate him. Members of the crowd were heard to mutter "he's only interested in that dinner at the Midland". Whether Woosnam paid for the whole team is not known but, being a respectable amateur, no doubt he stood by his word. Within days of the goal one City fan was even moved to write a poem about Woosnam's effort.

By the end of another exciting Hyde Road season the Blues found themselves in tenth position. Not as good as the previous years but there had still been a few high spots, especially with Browell and Barnes netting 41 League goals between them. There were also a couple of black moments; one came in the very last game of the season when Max Woosnam was 'accidentally kicked' according to the *Daily Dispatch*. The player needed an X-ray to determine that the leg was broken, yet remained as positive as ever and refused to blame anyone else: "I went out to tackle Lowe, the Newcastle winger, pushed the ball into touch and got it just below the knee - as I deserved to do. Entirely my own fault."

In effect the injury would cost Woosnam the rest of his City career, although he did manage to make a further five appearances over the following three years. In his boyhood diary, City supporter Joe Carley wrote about the events that followed that match: "After the game, I made my usual trip to the players' entrance for autographs, and stood amongst a silent crowd of sympathisers as Max, still smiling cheerfully, was carried to the ambulance on a stretcher. A small boy detached himself from the onlookers and calmly asked the injured player to sign his book. Before any of the amazed spectators could shoo the boy away, Max asked the stretcher bearers to stop for a moment so he could sign the book."

Visions of the archetypal English gentleman pausing for a moment, thinking nothing of his own predicament, bring this story to life.

On 9th May 1922, three days after the Newcastle game, the local newspapers revealed a story that was to change the direction of the club completely - City were to move away from the Gorton/Ardwick area to the border of Rusholme and Moss Side. For years it had been known the Blues were keen to leave Hyde Road, especially after the fire, but many assumed they would stay within a short distance of their birthplace at Clowes Street.

Belle Vue, the large zoo and pleasure gardens, seemed the obvious location, especially as there was already a sports ground there. The City management did actively consider the site for some two years but eventually rejected it on the grounds that it was too small (roughly around 8 acres), and only a fifty year lease could be obtained from the Jennison family who owned Belle Vue.

Eventually this ground became a major speedway venue - home to the Belle Vue Aces - but, although it lasted longer than the rest of the former pleasure gardens, the ground did not survive into the 1990s, and was demolished in 1987. Its destruction was a sad

City's Managers - The First Nine

At this stage in City's history it's worth pausing to consider the club's first nine managers and their achievements between the 1880s and the Second World War. For most of this time the role of manager was combined with that of club secretary, and it can be difficult determining what responsibility each secretary-manager held. However, the following section attempts to identify the involvement each man had, and provides a general view of their success. In many ways, the men detailed in this section, particularly the first six, made City the giant club it is today.

LAWRENCE FURNISS
1889-1893

As the first real direction-setter, Furniss is without doubt one of the most influential figures in the history of Manchester City. He first became involved with the club as a player with Gorton in the early 1880s and remained involved at various levels for the following 50 years or so.

His playing career came to an end following a serious knee injury and the young Gortonian moved into the administrative side of the club. During the 1880s he was one of their unsung heroes as he took on a considerable number of tasks to ensure the side would grow. He helped the club become more focused and was also responsible for locating at least one of Gorton's grounds. It was inevitable he would become Ardwick's first secretary-manager when the side adopted a more professional outlook and aimed for League football.

Between 1889 and 1893 under Furniss's guidance Ardwick gained admittance to the Football Alliance - a league that included other progressive clubs such as Nottingham Forest, Small Heath (Birmingham City), Newton Heath (Manchester United) and Sheffield Wednesday - and then, after only one season in the Alliance, they became one of the twelve founder members of the Second Division.

He had also brought some exceptional players to the young club, including Bolton's famous England international Davie Weir - a major coup at the time. A Topical Times article from April 1928 outlined some of the key players brought to the club and developed under Furniss. It also reminded its readers of a floodlit match against Preston (probably during 1889) which, no doubt, Furniss had organised: "Douglas, the goalkeeper, was a most worthy one; Robson, a back; McWhirter; McWhinnie, a cherubic little fellow; Campbell, a centre-forward, happened at Hyde Road. But the greatest prize of all was David Weir, who was with Bolton Wanderers. He was the brains of the combination.

"It was a regular cosmopolitan crew that was got together, but it sufficed. It was a great occasion when almost immediately after the launching of the ship, North End, with all their giants, including Nick Ross, came one night to Hyde Road to play in artificial light; but whether the novelty served to raise the wind to any appreciable extent I don't know: I am free to doubt it. Such as Mr. Lawrence Furniss is better able to tell the inner story of the trials and tribulations of those early and ambitious days; but I know enough to be sure that the pioneers of Manchester City, as the club now is, came near to performing the miracle of making silk purses out of a sow's ears."

At the end of Ardwick's first League season they finished fifth, having won nine and drawn three of their 22 fixtures. Furniss had taken the club perhaps further than anyone could

JOSHUA PARLBY
1893-1895

It is believed Joshua Parlby was a Stoke player and committee man prior to arriving in Manchester to take over a public house. He soon became involved with Ardwick and was one of the more vocal committee members. He had already started to play a part in team selection prior to taking over the role of secretary from Furniss in 1893. Parlby was Ardwick's first paid secretary, earning 50 shillings a week.

His time in charge was a traumatic one and he was forced to 'wrangle' his way out of various financial problems that beset the club. Fare-dodging on the railways; careful manipulation of the Ardwick cheque book; and many other scams managed to keep the club in existence for a while, but for much of 1893-4 Parlby did all he could to gain support for a new beginning. The final season of Ardwick saw Parlby's side finish 13th out of 15 clubs, but the club secretary had already sought League approval for the admittance of "Manchester City" to replace Ardwick in the Second Division.

In the late 1920s Billy Meredith recalled Parlby's role in gaining a League place for the newly-formed club and his attempts at player motivation: "If it hadn't been for Jos there would probably have been no Manchester City. He, it was, who practically alone secured their inclusion in the League in 1894. He it was, too, who after we had joined the League gave us 5 shillings bonus if we won, and proceeded to take it from us again if we lost the following week. I can appreciate the humour of that better now than I did then!"

Parlby became secretary of the new club and the opening game for City ended with defeat. Nevertheless, the 1894-5 season saw the Blues finish ninth out of 16 clubs and Parlby had fulfilled his desire. He stood down in the close season due to commitments outside of football - he'd taken over a public house in Bolton - but remained an influential committee man. In fact the reign of his successor, Sam Ormerod, was noted for its constant involvement of Parlby and others. It seems Parlby continued to exert much influence over the players and fellow committee men during the period 1895 to 1905.

As with Furniss, Parlby was a board member until, in 1905, the over-zealous F.A. forced him out of Hyde Road, while almost killing the club. In 1909 he rejoined the board and stayed with the Blues until 1912 when he moved away from the area.

In addition to his active involvement with Ardwick and City, he was also an influential member of the League Management committee for a period in the 1890s. He was City's first truly charismatic manager.

realistically expect and understandably he moved aside for the rather more vocal Joshua Parlby.

Furniss remained an active club man in the following years, and was delighted with the 1904 Cup success. He was a board member between 1903 and the investigations into the alleged bribe scandal, then rejoined the board a decade later, serving as chairman from 1921 to 1928. Some football historians believe he was secretary of Chesterfield (1906-7) during his enforced absence from Hyde Road. By the time of City's 1930s Wembley appearances he was club president and was no doubt proud of how far his side had come since his first involvement on a rather rough park pitch in the early 1880s.

SAM ORMEROD
1895-1902

With both Furniss and Parlby still on the club committee, Sam Ormerod found it exceptionally difficult at times to have the final say over team selection, despite being the most experienced of the three men as a player. Nevertheless, Ormerod managed to achieve a great deal and his first season ended with the Blues reaching the Test Matches (equivalent of the modern day Play Offs) after finishing second. A major administrative cock-up - City angered supporters by raising admission prices to an extortionate level and many fans were simply priced out - gave their opponents the advantage and the Blues failed.

In the seasons that followed Ormerod's City finished sixth, third and, in 1899, Division Two Champions. This was the first season of automatic promotion and City, along

with local rivals Glossop, were promoted into Division One for the first time. Life in the top division wasn't easy and at times the Blues struggled to keep up with the likes of Everton, Sunderland and Aston Villa.

During the 1901-02 campaign Ormerod received more than his fair share of criticism, with the Edward Hulton-owned Athletic News attacking the secretary on a regular basis. Hulton, it must be noted, was becoming involved with the club and it appears that he, together with influential committee-member John Allison, was keen to bring in a vastly more experienced football leader.

After a board restructure and a stormy AGM, Ormerod officially resigned. He later managed Stockport County and Clapton Orient - his best signing was former Blue, Billy 'Doc' Holmes. Ormerod died shortly afterwards during 1906.

Ormerod, who lived at 5 Park Avenue, Longsight, received a great deal of criticism at the time but was actually hampered by the club's committee, not by his own failings. He was undoubtedly a skilled football man and had achieved a great deal in his first few seasons. It was a shame he was rarely given a free hand to pursue his own team selection and tactical plans.

TOM MALEY
1902-1906

The first truly great Manchester manager.

According to a 1920s journalist, Maley was the man who brought great footballing knowledge and success to Manchester: "It was when Tom Maley came to Hyde Road that Manchester City may be said to have entered fully into their kingdom. Under his management, he built a team for the club that was comparable with the mightiest sides in the country."

"I never happened a greater enthusiast than Maley, nor yet a better informed man. If Maley had had average luck he would have gone down in history as one of the most successful managers the game has known. It was to me, at all events, a thousand pities when the powers that be came down with the hammer and imposed wholesale suspensions. Into the rights or wrongs of that most unfortunate happening I do not propose to enter. It is enough to say that so long as Maley was at the helm, the family at Hyde Road was a particularly happy one."

Maley suffered more than most from the unfortunate events of 1905/6, and his role in football history has been tainted forever by the harsh treatment of City by the F.A. However, in the eyes of thousands of City fans he is remembered as the man who brought exciting football and the F.A. Cup to Manchester for the first time. Without his period at Hyde Road, the city may never have found real football success. Many of his players were forced to join United after the scandal of 1905, and went on to bring the Reds their first trophy success only a few years later. Had Maley been allowed to develop his 1904 Cup-winning side further, who knows what success may have come City's way?

He arrived at Hyde Road following relegation in 1902 and immediately encouraged the Blues to play stylish football. His view was that playing in the Scottish passing style would bring the club success and would excite the fans. He was right, but then he was a very knowledgeable football man. He had gained a great deal from his time at Celtic where, together with his famous brother Willie, he enjoyed enormous success. Another brother, Alex, managed Crystal Palace in the 1920s.

Tom Maley's time at Celtic was spent mainly as an administrator and as such he is recorded by Celtic historians as one of the club's most important early figures. Despite being a proud Scotsman, he was born in Portsmouth on 8th November 1864.

At Hyde Road he managed to attract great players and City's popularity increased as a result. After the bribe scandal, he was banned from football sine die, but in July 1910 the F.A. lifted the suspension and the following February he became Bradford Park Avenue's manager. The Yorkshire club gave him full control of team affairs - something unusual at the time - and he remained there until March 1924. During his reign they achieved their highest position (ninth in Division One, 1914-15), and for a period sported his beloved green and white hoops. During the First World War he is said to have acted like an "amateur recruiting sergeant" and was famous for his entertaining lectures.

After Bradford, he is said by some football historians, to have managed Southport between May and October 1925, and then in 1931 he temporarily took over as Celtic manager from his brother during a trip to the USA. It was his first trip to the States.

He died on 24th August 1935 at the age of 70. Had his time at City not ended prematurely, it's possible he would be remembered today as one of football's most successful managers. As it is, he should be remembered as one of Manchester's greatest leaders.

ERNEST MANGNALL 1912-1924

Ernest Mangnall is unique. He is the only man to have managed both Manchester clubs, and it can also be recorded he was mainly responsible for United's move to Old Trafford and City's to Maine Road.

Prior to joining the Blues he had been secretary with Burnley (1900-1903), and then United (September 1903 - August 1912). At United he managed to obtain the services of Billy Meredith and many of the other banned City stars for relatively small sums of money, and with them he brought United two League Championships and the F.A. Cup. Without Mangnall's recruitment of these players it is highly unlikely United would have achieved any form of success during this period. United fans should remember Mangnall as one of their greatest managers, especially as he transformed the club following their collapse in 1902.

In 1912 City stunned the football world when they lured Mangnall from the Reds. Never in the history of football had a manager left a major club for its biggest rivals after so much success. What made the story more of a sensation was the fact Mangnall actually remained in charge of United for the Manchester derby of 7th September 1912. Naturally City defeated the Reds 1-0 at the palatial Old Trafford on the Saturday, and the following Monday

Mangnall moved into his office at the more homely, if cramped, Hyde Road.

At City, he developed a decent-looking side by the time of the First World War, the Blues finishing fifth in Division One at the end of the 1914-5 season. During hostilities he kept the club alive and even brought some trophy success in the first wartime season.

Post-war he developed a very popular side as games at Hyde Road regularly became sell-outs. In 1921 the Blues finished second and Mangnall worked hard to seek a new venue for the increasingly popular club. The 1920-1 season had seen many crowds of over 40,000 - the official limit - and Mangnall as secretary-manager received a great deal of criticism from the press who held him responsible for crowd control. Today it seems crazy that the man responsible for team matters should also be in control of general ground and club matters, but up until the 1940s, later at many clubs (Joe Mercer was one of the main driving forces behind a new stand at Villa Park during the late 50s/early 60s), this was the case.

In 1923 Mangnall helped City move to Maine Road, and in his final season (1923-4) he almost brought them an appearance in the F.A. Cup Final. With the 49-year-old Meredith in the side, Mangnall's men were defeated by Newcastle.

The following May the directors, surprisingly, decided not to renew his contract. He died in 1932 after becoming a director of his home-town team, Bolton. In addition to his roles at Burnley, United, City and Bolton, he was also responsible for founding the Central League and the Football Managers' Association.

He remains one of the most influential football administrators of all time.

HARRY NEWBOULD 1906-1912

Newbould arrived at Hyde Road in the wake of the bribes scandal after surprising the football world by walking out on Derby County. At County he had been a popular figure, never afraid to take whatever action necessary to help the club both on the pitch and financially. One of his boldest moves was to sell the highly successful - and popular - Steve Bloomer to Middlesbrough.

At City, he quickly set about finding players - any players - to fill the gaps left

by the banned Meredith & Co. Inevitably some failed, but many of Newbould's first signings became familiar names to Mancunians for many years - Eadie, Grieve, Blair, Conlin and Smith.

As expected, his first season was one of struggle - City finished 17th out of 20 in Division One - but in 1907-8 he managed to steer City to third place. Sadly, the Blues lacked consistency in 1908-9 and Newbould's side were relegated in 19th place. They immediately bounced back the following season as Champions, and Newbould managed - only just - to keep City in the First Division for the next two terms.

In July 1912 he left City and assisted Academicals (Copenhagen) for a while the following August. He also played a major role with the Manchester-based Players' Union, becoming secretary. He died in 1929.

Overall his time at Hyde Road does not appear to have been that successful, however it must be stated that Newbould was the man who managed to keep the club alive following the events of 1905-6. He was responsible for bringing in some good players and, apart from one season, had managed to prolong City's life in Division One.

DAVID ASHWORTH 1924-1926

David Ashworth joined City from Oldham Athletic in July 1924, after only a year with the Boundary Park club. He had amazed everyone by walking out on Liverpool to take on the Oldham job in February 1923 after bringing the Merseysiders the League Championship the previous season.

At Maine Road, his first season saw City score 68 goals (equal top scorers), but finish tenth out of 22 clubs. During the close season he purchased left

back Phil McCloy from Ayr United for £3,000, and McCloy's debut ended in a 3-2 victory over Cardiff. Sadly, the Blues struggled after this, gaining only two further victories in September and October. One of these - an 8-3 defeat of Burnley - should have brought much confidence to Ashworth's side but the following match two days later ended in an embarrassing 8-3 defeat at Sheffield United.

In November 1925, with the pressure mounting, Ashworth

resigned, although it seems likely he was 'pushed'.

After City he managed Walsall, Caernarfon, and Llanelli then moved to Blackpool shortly before the war. From January 1938 he scouted for Blackpool until his death at the town's Victoria Hospital on 23rd March 1947. He was 79.

Ashworth's was probably the first City appointment to actually fail. Each of his predecessors at Maine Road and Hyde Road had achieved some form of success and had managed to last at least two seasons. Ashworth was only in charge for around 16 months. This may seem a long time in comparison with City's 1990s managers, but was extremely short for this point in football history.

The 1925-6 season saw the Blues reach Wembley, but Ashworth had departed months before the first cup game and could not take credit for City's cup run. Relegation also occurred that season. Indeed, it must be recorded Ashworth should not ultimately be blamed for that, after all the City directorate did not appoint a manager until the very last weeks of the campaign. Had they found a replacement in November it's possible City would have survived. As it was the directors chose to 'do the job' themselves.

Despite the disappointments of Ashworth's reign, it's worth remembering he secured the services of a few excellent players during his brief tenure at Maine Road - the most notable must be Sam Cowan, who was purchased from Doncaster in December 1924.

PETER HODGE
1926-1932

Peter Hodge joined the Blues shortly before relegation in 1926, although he arrived far too late to have any major impact. He came to Maine Road from Leicester City and, as with many of City's earlier appointments, his departure from Filbert Street shocked football, especially as he had guided The Foxes to promotion to the First Division.

At Maine Road he spent the close season of 1926 planning for an immediate return to the top flight, and his side came near, only missing promotion by the tightest goal average margin in history. Their 8-0 victory over Bradford City on the final day of the season was one goal less than the required number, although this wasn't known at the final whistle when the supporters and players celebrated 'getting back'. When announcements were made that Portsmouth had sneaked ahead of the Blues, leaving City third, it was a huge disappointment.

In 1927-8 Hodge fulfilled his dream, however, by seeing City promoted as Champions with 59 points (five more than the previous term). He continued to develop the side, helping Tommy Johnson become a fine centre-forward, and many of his team became household names - Brook, Toseland, Tilson, Busby and Marshall. Others were not so fortunate: goalkeeper Lewis Barber, still on crutches after two operations on a knee, was told his services were no longer required and left to face a grim future as a tradeless cripple. Only players who could offer immediate benefit to Hodge's side were retained.

In 1929-30 Hodge guided the Blues to third place in Division One, but they were still some 13 points behind champions Sheffield Wednesday. Nevertheless, the manager had taken a team that seemed destined to struggle and turned it into a side heading for glory. The two League campaigns that followed were not particularly successful - the Blues finished eighth and 14th - yet progress was being made in the F.A. Cup although City lost 1-0 to Arsenal in the 1932 semi-final.

In March of that year Hodge walked out on Manchester and returned to Leicester City, where he had been promised a five-year contract and a salary increase. On 30th July 1934 he was admitted to Perth Infirmary and died a few days later while still manager of Leicester.

WILF WILD
1932-1946

In terms of trophy success Wilf Wild is City's most successful manager of the pre-Mercer period. He is also the longest serving, leading the side from 1932 until the end of the war. In addition he served the Blues well for a total of 30 years from 1920 until his death in December 1950.

He arrived at Maine Road as assistant secretary to Ernest Mangnall in 1920, and four years later took on the greater share of secretarial duties, the general administration being gradually taken away from the secretary manager. In fact it was Wild who pushed hard to divide the role of secretary manager as he felt administration frequently got in the way of team affairs. However, in 1932 when Hodge returned to Filbert Street, it was Wild who was left with the responsibility for both areas.

Wild performed exceptionally well in both roles. In 1933 and 1934 he guided the Blues to the F.A. Cup Final, with success arriving on the second occasion, and off the field he found himself responsible for the organisation of the highest-attended game at Maine Road - 84,569 v Stoke on 3rd March 1934. The pressure on him during 1933-4 must have been immense, however he not only survived but seemed to thrive.

In 1936-7 he managed City to their first League Championship after selecting players of the calibre of Alec Herd, Sam Barkas, Matt Busby, Peter Doherty - some say the greatest Irish player of all time - and Frank Swift. Despite the success Wild was also a victim of City's peculiarly unpredictable streak when, the following year, the Blues were relegated. Although it wasn't known at the time, it was a particularly bad period to enter the Second Division as war in 1939 ensured the Blues remained out of the top flight until 1947. By that time Wild had reverted back to secretarial duties alone.

He had guided City through the difficulties of war and had managed right up until November 1946 - by which time City were already proving capable of promotion. The pressure of the war years and that first post-war season were too much and he stood down for his former captain, Sam Cowan. Wild remained as secretary until his death four years later. His wife Betty was a popular and familiar presence at the club through to her retirement in the 1960s.

Wild may not be the first name most think of when they talk about great City managers, but he is second only to Joe Mercer in terms of the success he brought the club.

moment for Manchester sport; remember it had staged the 1889 floodlit friendly, and in 1929 Billy Meredith helped to launch a football club called Manchester Central there.

With Belle Vue rejected, City's choice had to offer something special and the press concentrated on the ambitious plans for a new ground. Incredibly, the sixteen and a quarter acre site was to have an eventual covered capacity of 120,000 developed in two phases. The first phase, to be opened in time for the 1923-4 season, would see the Blues build a grandstand seating somewhere in the region of 15,000 and terracing for 55,000. The plan was based on Hampden Park which, in these pre-Wembley days, was the most famous and respected British venue. Once that phase was completed, said the report, City would extend the terracing and erect a roof around the three sides to form a sort of 'C' around the grandstand, thereby reaching the desired 120,000.

Outside the stadium, a 500 space car park was planned and, in front of the grand stand, a forecourt that would allow at least twenty thousand to gather. It would also be possible to allow ingress and egress on all four sides and it seems that City had asked their architects to design the venue so that 120,000 people could evacuate within a 'very few minutes'.

The land, adjacent to the then unknown minor street of Maine Road, cost £5,500 and had been considered two years earlier but was discounted as part of it was covered by a tip and the rest was a clay pit, excavated for brick making. The Blues called in soil experts, and the builders Robert McAlpine, to survey the site before making their announcement.

The news both surprised and excited the Manchester public, and for those brought up on football the Hyde Road way it seemed incredible to think such a venue could be built in Manchester. Ernest Mangnall, on the other hand, knew what was possible. He had been instrumental in United's move to Old Trafford and was now confident that the ever popular City could achieve more and, although plans were scaled down a little over the following months, Mangnall helped the Blues develop a stadium that wasn't simply the best in Manchester, it was the biggest and best club ground in England.

Beneath a feature on the new stadium, the *Manchester Guardian* carried a story that goalkeeper Tom Blair, who had made 38 League appearances during the 1921-2 season was to give up English football and settle with his relatives at Edmonton, Canada, where he played for Bethlehem Steel. Later he joined two clubs in the USA - Fall River and New Brighton. Although City still had Goodchild on their books, the 30 year old was nearing the end of his Hyde Road career and it was felt another 'keeper had to be found. Eventually the Blues signed the amateur Jim Mitchell, who had played for Preston in the 1922 Cup final. True to the traditions of eccentric 'keepers Mitchell had hit the headlines for frantically jumping about in goal trying to put Huddersfield's Willy Smith off as he took the Yorkshire club's penalty in the final.

In another game for Preston, Mitchell mistakenly thought a supporter's whistle was the referee's signal for time, and started to walk off the pitch as the other side were attacking. As he strolled away, the ball was quickly sent goalward and entered the net as the 'keeper realised his mistake. He threw his cap down in disgust and a short while later chose to leave Preston, convinced they would never forgive him.

In addition to these exploits, Mitchell was also remarkable for the fact he wore spectacles during games. Despite the possibility of injury from broken glass, he still bravely coped with the powerful marauding forwards of the day.

Mitchell's debut wasn't until the fifth game of the season - a disappointing 1-0 defeat by Birmingham. The scoreline was bad enough, but even worse was the fact both Eli Fletcher and Tommy Browell were injured and would be out of action for some time. For Fletcher, who would miss the rest of the season, a cartilage operation was required, while Browell had badly strained ankle tendons and would be out until mid-December.

For the next game Tommy Johnson returned to the side in place of Browell, and immediately impressed, providing the only goal of the return match with Birmingham on 16th September. One week later he scored twice while Horace Barnes, who had

MANCHESTER CITY
FOOTBALL SURPRISE.

New Ground Not To Be At Belle Vue.

SITE NEAR MOSS SIDE PURCHASED.

Proposal to Provide Covered Stand Accommodation for 120,000 People.

PLAN OF THE SITE.

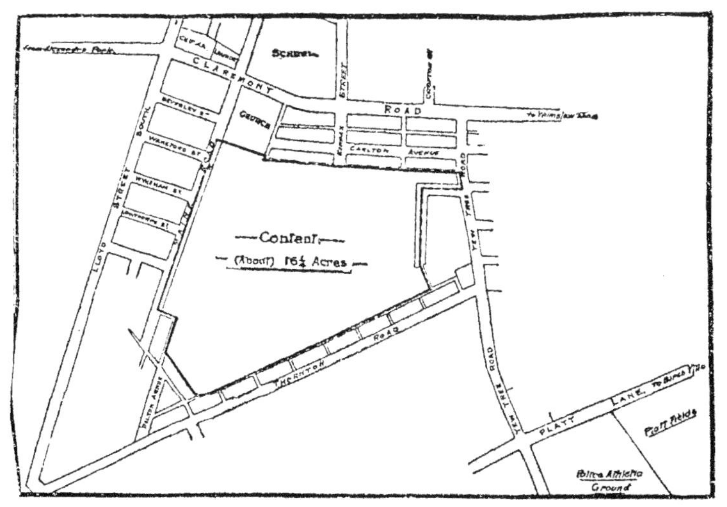

Though the site is on the Withington side of the Moss Side border line, it is, from the point of view of accessibility, most conveniently situated.

The Greenheys terminus of the Manchester tramways is at the corner of the next street, on the north-westerly side—Lloyd-street—200 yards away from the plot.

Wilmslow Road, whence Rusholme, Fallowfield, Palatine Road, and Chorlton circular route cars pass to and from the city, is near to the easterly side of the plot.

The circular route trams from Cheetham Hill via Belle Vue, Dickenson Road and Great Western street, pass the northerly side, along the latter named street 300 yards away, and on the return journey via Moss Lane East the distance is 400 yards from the nearest point.

The Tramways Committee are at present contemplating opening up another route along Claremont Road, thereby getting a connection with Wilmslow Road on the eastern side, and Alexandra Park and Brooks's Bar on the westerly side.

The tramways depot and terminus of the Princess Road route, whence cars run alternatively to Piccadilly and Albert Square, is situate on Princess Road, about 500 yards to the west.

City's plans to move to a new ground are outlined in the Manchester Evening News.

Frank Roberts, a £4,000 signing from Bolton, made his debut in the 2-0 victory over Preston on 21st October 1922.

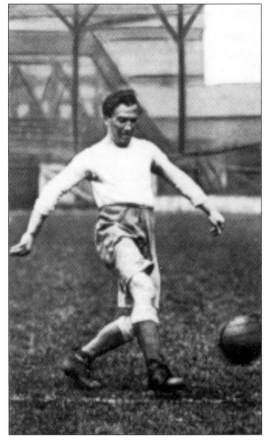

not been on his best form, provided a third in the Hyde Road victory over Huddersfield.

Between them Barnes and Johnson went on to supply a total of 35 League goals that campaign - not quite as good as the Barnes-Browell partnership, but still acceptable, especially for Barnes who provided 21 of them. To aid the cause Mangnall had purchased Bolton Wanderers forward Frank Roberts for a club record fee of around £4,000 in October, and he scored a total of ten League goals.

The Blues ended the season - the last at Hyde Road - in eighth place. It had been a strange campaign following the injuries, with only one player, Charlie Pringle, ever-present. Half-back Pringle had signed in June from St. Mirren and, together with new captain Mick Hamill in the centre half position, helped to give the Blues a little more consistency. Irish international Hamill was a good all round footballer who could play in a number of positions - he'd been an inside forward at United - although his critics felt he lacked that little extra which makes great players.

Interestingly, there were five who only managed single appearances including Meredith, Fred 'Tiny' Fayers (who had been injured in the close season), and Pat Kelly - an October 1920 signing from Belfast Celtic who had struggled to regain fitness following an incident the previous year when he collided with the Chelsea 'keeper and broke his tibia and fibula.

A serious injury to Pat Kelly at Chelsea in March 1922 more or less ended his career. He made a further appearance the following season but was transferred to West Ham in July 1923.

The final League game at Hyde Road was a no score draw with Newcastle on 28th April before a crowd of around 20,000. On the same date Wembley Stadium hosted its first F.A. Cup final and, because of the extraordinary scenes, very little space was given over to the City game in the local 'papers. Instead they concentrated on Bolton's performance and the exploits of Billy, the white horse, in clearing the Wembley pitch.

Three months after the final Hyde Road League match, on 18th August, the last ever game, a practice match, was staged on the pitch. Afterwards the goal posts and a few turnstiles were taken from the old ground and erected at Maine Road.

One of the stands, believed to be the Galloway End, was dismantled and sold to Halifax Town, although its appearance was altered when erected at the Shay.

At Halifax, the stand was no longer a multi-span roof, instead it was erected in a more traditional manner with five stanchions at the front. An inspection of the roof in 1999 proved the metalwork is both the same size and style construction as that favoured by the City management in 1910. However, the section of the stand which matches Hyde Road was erected at the Shay in 1921. Could one of Hyde

Charlie Pringle (right) made his debut on the opening day of the 1922-23 season. He later captained the Blues.

The Skircoat Road Stand at the Shay in 1988. The section of the stand to the left of this photo (the first five stanchions) was once erected at Hyde Road. During the 1990s the roof was reclad, and by the turn of the century plans had been made to replace the stand in its entirety, although this depends on the fortunes of the ground's tenants Halifax Town and Halifax Blue Sox.

Road's stands have been dismantled and sold to Halifax Town a season before City's old ground closed?

The stand at the Shay was extended at some point during its early history, and the roof has since been reclad. There are plans to redevelop the stand – each of the Shay's other sides has been rebuilt between the late 1990s and 2002 – and so the stand may not last for much longer. While it still exists City followers can view a piece of Hyde Road history.

While Hyde Road was dismantled, Maine Road had its finishing touches applied. The original scheme claimed the new venue would be 'The English Hampden', however by the time the stadium opened more comparisons were made with the recently opened Wembley stadium. Many City historians have fallen into the trap of claiming that Maine Road was designed as the Wembley of the north. This may not be true as the City plans had been approved before Wembley was completed, and certainly a long time before the London stadium gained any positive press coverage. However, it is true that the Blues' ambitions were to develop the best stadium in England, and comparisons with Wembley became inevitable.

As many Blues suspected at the time, the original plans were a little over ambitious. It is probable that the claims Hampden would be matched were pure hype, and the club simply knew how to gain positive publicity. By the time the stadium opened the development had been amended a little. Instead of one 'grandstand' seating around 15,000, City's Main Stand would hold 10,000, while the terracing looping around the pitch would hold somewhere in the region of 75,000 spectators - some 20,000 more than the original plan - thereby giving a capacity of between eighty and ninety thousand. This was a phenomenal figure for a team used to playing in a cramped, dilapidated, 40,000 capacity venue.

The possibility of extending Maine Road to cater for the desired capacity of 120,000 probably did not exist, although it is true that with so much land available behind the popular side, later named the Kippax, and a little space behind both ends, the capacity could have increased significantly. However, the effort and cost to extend each section of terracing for a capacity that would never be tested seemed a pointless exercise.

The Scoreboard End, latter day North Stand, being constructed at City's new Maine Road stadium. Note the church behind on the site of the present day City Store.

The Main Stand nearing completion. At its opening day it held 10,000 seated mainly on benches.

An aerial view of Maine Road as it looked at its opening in August 1923. Notice the original Main Stand roof had a semi-circular gable in its centre.

Lawrence Furniss was involved with City from the 1880s. In fact he'd been a player with Gorton and served the club at almost every level.

In almost every respect Maine Road was significantly better than Hyde Road, or indeed the majority of British grounds, although one disappointing aspect must have been the provision of cover. Hyde Road had, at one time, boasted covered accommodation for 35,000, all the new ground could offer was shelter for 10,000. This, though, was still more than many other venues.

On the Friday before the season began, most newspapers carried stories of how the grand opening would overshadow all other football that day, including the Birmingham-Aston Villa derby match. The *Manchester Evening News* seemed particularly proud of the stadium's development: "That this vast stadium should have been practically completed between April 24 and August 24 of this year is the subject for wonder and admiration. It unquestionably creates a record in building construction, and it is a splendid testimonial to the organising powers of the contractors, Sir Robert McAlpine and Sons.

"Most people were freely sceptical as to whether the enclosure would be ready for tomorrow. A month ago it did not seem possible that it could be, but by the employment of hundreds of skilled workmen all but the internal work on the huge stand has been completed, and even the remaining task will not occupy more than a fortnight. As already stated the enclosure will accommodate well over 80,000 spectators.

"Sheer curiosity will attract many hundreds of people to this magnificent new ground in Maine Road, Moss Side, but the bulk of the club's supporters will be keen on participating in what is an historic event in local football activities because of the re-appearance of Max Woosnam, whose career as captain of the team was so unluckily suspended for a whole season owing to the fracture of his leg."

Woosnam's return as captain was a fitting tribute to the all-round sportsman. His injury was the result of an unfortunate accident and had not only deprived him of a year in football, but also prevented him from defending his Wimbledon Doubles title won with Lycett in 1921. He must have been immensely proud to lead the first City side into the brand new stadium.

On the day of the match the *Manchester Evening News* boasted the day would be a proud moment in 'the history of the City's premier football club', although not all Mancunians were convinced the move would be beneficial. For many, the 36-year-old Hyde Road was the only venue for the Blues. Some doubted the unique City atmosphere would survive the transfer away from the club's birthplace, while others thought the ground was too far away. Harry Hughes was one such sceptic who, although realising the densely populated Moss Side/Rusholme area offered potential, felt many Gortonians and Ardwickites would desert the club: "When they moved to Maine Road I thought it wouldn't be popular. None of us did! But we had to accept it. We were all so sad about it at the time, even though Maine Road was the last word in ground design. Hyde Road was home - it was City's ground and had grown with the club - and we loved it despite its appearance. United fans used to say that Old Trafford was better than Hyde Road. They'd say 'you can see at Old Trafford!' and we'd respond 'well there's not many people in your way'. They didn't get big crowds then.

"But Maine Road seemed so far away. It wasn't,

but sometimes I couldn't afford the fare, even though it was only a penny from Belle Vue to Claremont Road. Sometimes I would get a tram - the little single deckers with seats outside - but when I could afford the fare they always seemed too busy, so I'd give up and walk to the new ground. Even though it wasn't our real home the atmosphere was there and we quickly turned it into City's home. Hyde Road became a thing of the past, never forgotten, but rarely missed."

Maine Road's opening game was covered extensively in the local press with the main reports featuring descriptions of the stadium, not the football. In an otherwise excellent piece, the *Manchester Guardian* covered the entire match in one simple passage and failed to mention any of the goalscorers, such was their reporter's lack of interest in the playing side of the day's events. In actual fact the City marksmen were Horace Barnes, who scored the first goal at the ground after about 68 minutes, and Tommy Johnson. In addition Frank Roberts made history as the first player to miss a penalty at the new ground when his shot went straight to the 'keeper. Sheffield United pulled a goal back two minutes from time, but the Blues finished with a 2-1 win before a City record crowd of 56,993.

Despite the excitement of the first game, the Blues found the League programme offered little in terms of enjoyment. A run in October brought four consecutive victories, but apart from that the majority of games up until the New Year ended in defeat, or disappointing 1-1 draws. Many blamed the new pitch which, in parts, became very muddy following a rather wet autumn, although only one home game had ended in defeat up to Christmas. There had also been four drawn matches. The stadium was an easy target and architect Charles Swain, by this time a member of City's Board, received much criticism.

If the development of the stadium grabbed all the headlines - positive and negative - during the first period of the season, the second half concentrated on the incredible news that Billy Meredith was back in the side. At the age of 49, the man who had played in Manchester City's first season, was set to appear at City's new venue. Few could believe it but, in February, it became reality when he took the field for a third round F.A. Cup game at Brighton.

The cup run had started with a 2-1 victory at home to Nottingham Forest. In the second round two draws with Halifax Town forced the sides to play a third game at neutral Old Trafford. This time City, thanks to goals from Roberts (2) and Browell, easily overcame the Shaymen.

It was in the aftermath of this game that the rumours of Meredith's return started to spread. On the eve of the Brighton match the newspapers, both local and national, were full of Meredith stories. Some seemed to ignore the facts, concentrating on the 'human angle' and writing features on this 'greying man in his fiftieth year'. Ignoring his time at United, one report stated that he'd played for the same club - Manchester City - for thirty years. Perhaps to the general public Manchester only had one newsworthy side!

Deservedly, the story was big news though. Especially as many supporters, and journalists for that matter, had not been alive when he first appeared for the club. The *Manchester Evening News* reporter,

A proud day for City as Lawrence Furniss and Max Woosnam introduce Councillor Cundiff, the Lord Mayor of Manchester, to the players prior to Maine Road's opening match on 25th August 1923. Below, the team lists from that day's official programme.

8 BLUE AND WHITE.

Buy The

FOOTBALL CHRONICLE

It contains the CORRECT RESULTS of all the matches—gives interesting and DETAILED ACCOUNTS and COMMENTS of all the principal games.

EVERY SATURDAY FIRST AND CORRECT *TWOPENCE*

Saturday, August 25th, 1923

MANCHESTER CITY

1 **J. F. MITCHELL** Goal

2 **COOKSON** Right Back — 3 **FLETCHER** Left Back

4 **HAMILL** Right Half-Back — 5 **M. WOOSNAM** Centre Half-Back — 6 **PRINGLE** Left Half-Back

7 **DONALDSON** Outside Right — 8 **ROBERTS** Inside Right — 9 **JOHNSON** Centre — 10 **BARNES** Inside Left — 11 **MURPHY** Outside Left

Referee—J. T. HOWCROFT, BOLTON

Kick-off, 3-0 p.m.

12 **TUNSTALL** Outside Left — 13 **GILLESPIE** Inside Left — 14 **JOHNSON** Centre — 15 **SAMPY** Inside Right — 16 **MERCER** Outside Right

17 **GREEN** Left Half-Back — 18 **WAUGH** Centre Half-Back — 19 **PANTLING** Right Half-Back

20 **MILTON** Left Back — 21 **COOK** Right Back

22 **GOUGH** Goal

SHEFFIELD UNITED

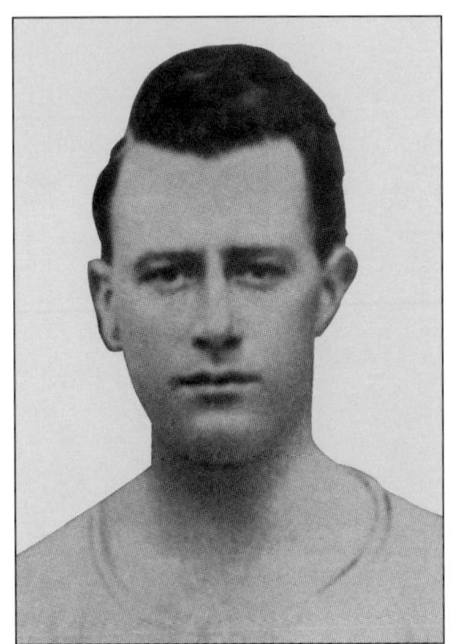

Mick Hamill scored his one and only goal for City in September 1923, during the 4-1 win over Sunderland at the newly opened Maine Road.

although excited by the prospect of a Meredith winner, viewed the shock news as a last desperate act: "Not until last evening did the Manchester City directors decide upon the team they would like to put in the field against Brighton and Hove Albion. In the end they have sprung a surprise upon the public, inasmuch as they have elected to rely upon the services of a player who has, literally, grown grey in the service of the club - Meredith.

"He is, in the opinion of many good judges of the game, the best outside right the club have at their disposal. This may be true. It may also be the mere fact that the officials have had to fall back upon a player of his age casts a reflection upon the club management.

"To all intents and purposes, Meredith ceased to be an active member of the first team two seasons ago. Two things have combined to bring him within range of the rather sensational choice now made - sentiment and his own indomitable will to fret his hold on the football stage a little longer. Though he has not been included in the League team so far this season, he has appeared in Lancashire Cup ties, and, as late as Wednesday week last, with the Central League team. His form has been much to be said in favour of the bold experiment now made.

"The chief argument in his favour is that from one of his classic centres any match might be won, just as it was when he scored the goal that served to bring the English Cup to Hyde Road twenty years ago next month."

According to contemporary reports a record crowd of 24,734 packed into the Goldstone Ground to see City trounce the home side 5-1. The inclusion of Meredith seemed to inspire the rest of the team, and in the second half he even supplied one of the goals, described here in John Harding's *Football Wizard*: "In the second half he had taken on Brighton's left-back, darted past him and then lifted a centre into the goalmouth which the goalkeeper had fumbled and somehow palmed into the net."

Meredith himself was generally pleased with his performance and felt the pace of the game was not too much for him. The following week he played his first League game at Maine Road - a 3-2 defeat of

The legendary Billy Meredith in action at the age of 49 during City's 5-1 FA Cup win at Brighton in February 1924.

Middlesbrough. This meant during his extraordinary career the Welshman had played home games at the four major Manchester venues - Hyde Road, Maine Road, Clayton, and Old Trafford. No one else could ever match that feat. The next game was a quarter-final tie at home to First Division high flyers Cardiff City. The prospect of the match excited everyone. Cardiff 'The Pride Of Wales' against Meredith 'The Footballing Prince Of Wales' was how one journalist described it. Thousands of Welshmen, paying a rail fare of 21s 2d day return from the valleys, made their way to Maine Road for a game that was expected to test the capacity of the new venue. Some had travelled through the night, with a long wait at Shrewsbury, while others had stayed at Manchester's best hotels. According to one report a few Cardiff supporters had booked rooms at the Midland, the Queen's, and at least fifty rooms at the Grand Hotel.

FIVE-HOUR QUEUES AT MAINE ROAD.

Manchester Sprinkled With Cup-Tie Colours.

WHOLE CITY AGOG.

Football Ousts Wireless and Golf.

Many of these Welsh fans arrived at Maine Road and started queuing a full five hours before kick-off. By 12.30 the club decided to open the turnstiles thirty minutes earlier than normal to avoid crowd control problems later. There were also around 150 policemen in the ground, persuading supporters to move from the most congested areas of the popular side. One report concentrated on the size of the crowd and the prospect of whether capacity would be reached. It stated that early indications suggested the crowd would be huge, but Maine Road would not be full. Its reporter also witnessed an activity that many people say occurred at many grounds, but few can prove: "Room was made for the foolish late-comers, and in a little while the congestion was so great that boys were extricated from the mass and rolled over the heads of the spectators in order that they might find sanctuary inside the concrete wall."

The official attendance was in fact 76,166, with receipts of £4,909, more than justifying the value of City's new stadium. For a few moments architect Charles Swain must have paused to consider getting out his old plans to increase the capacity, although even with this huge crowd the terracing still had space for a few thousand more.

The game ended goalless - despite City's superstitious wearing of scarlet as at Brighton - with Meredith unable to keep up with the speed of the game at times. Even so, he was still one of the better players on the pitch and his tactical awareness was much needed.

The replay four days later proved to be just as popular, with a large crowd of around fifty thousand. For this match, Cardiff believed they could contain City by marking Meredith out of the game. They failed. The skilful Meredith may not have been the most pacey player on the pitch, but he was the most knowledgeable and in the second half, with the game still goalless, put together the move that sent City into the semi-finals. The *Topical Times* reporter recorded the event: "Keeping the ball at the end of his toes as surely as though he had it on a piece of string, the veteran glanced in his bird-like fashion to his left, as though he meant to pass in that direction. Blair saw this, and kept his position accordingly; but like a flash the forward darted ahead and leaving the back standing, as it were, he was able to go on and put in a centre which left the Cardiff goal at the mercy of Browell.

"Browell so soon as he had pushed the ball into the net rushed to Meredith to offer his praises; this and that Manchester player surrounded the grand old man for the goal which was designed to take their team to the last round but one of the competition was really his."

The semi-final draw sent City to St. Andrew's, Birmingham to face Newcastle United. The Geordies were not quite the force they had been before the war and City were expected to easily defeat them, especially if they kept faith with their 'lucky' scarlet jerseys. The week before the semi, Meredith played his second League game of the season - a 2-2 home draw with Preston - and prepared to help his side reach Wembley. The media naturally loved the prospect of football's grand old man playing at the relatively new national stadium, and newspaper column after column concentrated on the nostalgic possibility.

The fairytale wasn't to last, however, as City suffered disappointment. Newcastle were a better organised outfit and managed to contain them well. City, and in particular Meredith, barely touched the ball. One reporter summed it up perfectly: "The forwards were never a combined force and, although Roberts made one long dribble, they were not impressive individually. Many of the intended passes sent the ball to opponents. Meredith had many idle moments, although he clapped his hands to tell his colleagues that he was still on the field."

TRAINING FOR THE CUP SEMI-FINAL: W. MEREDITH, OF MANCHESTER CITY.

The veteran Billy Meredith, who is still a power in the Manchester City forward line, is shown training for their semi-final Cup-tie with Newcastle United. Wonderful ball-control has always been a feature of Meredith's play, and much of his time is spent in practising it.

Billy Meredith in training for the FA Cup semi-final with Newcastle - it was to be his last game.

Back in Manchester, many City supporters attending a reserve game against Wolves waited eagerly for the latest score to be carried around the ground. Frank Brown was one such supporter who, during the mid-70s, related the tension of the day: "At the reserve match us eagle-eyed youngsters could tell from the slump, or otherwise, of the boardman's shoulders how the big match was going as soon as he took the first steps from the tunnel. Facing the tunnel we saw

Above: Rival captains Mick Hamill (right) and Frank Hudspeth shake hands prior to the 1924 FA Cup semi-final at St. Andrew's, Birmingham.

Below: City 'keeper Mitchell is unable to stop Newcastle's second goal in the 2-0 defeat.

him. And we knew! A sigh from the spectators nearest the players' tunnel confirmed our fears. By the time he reached our part of the ground we knew the worst - City were a goal down. But plenty of time to go, all was by no means lost.

"Then again the figure started his death march down the tunnel, slower than ever this time. A groan, not a sigh, greeted him as chalked on his board appeared the never to be forgotten figures of: Newcastle 2 City 0. That's how it had finished. Goodbye Wembley."

A 2-0 defeat not only ended the prospect of a Wembley final, it also brought to an end thirty years of League and Cup football for Meredith. It was a sad moment, but it was still a fine achievement for the 49 year old who remains the oldest player to have appeared in the F.A. Cup's senior rounds.

In May, after the Blues finished eleventh in the League, the seven man board of directors decided to end Ernest Mangnall's period of management. His contract was up and the directors felt a change was necessary. In July 1924, he returned to Bolton, his birthplace, to become a director of Wanderers. For twenty-one years he had been manager of one or other of the Manchester clubs, bringing much joy to both the Reds and the Blues. He was one of the driving forces behind United's move to Old Trafford and City's to Maine Road and, like Tom Maley before him, should be remembered for helping to establish Manchester's trophy winning heritage.

Mangnall's successor was Oldham Athletic's David Ashworth, who had a 'get out' clause in his Boundary Park contract which allowed him to leave if 'a better post' became available. This clause worked to City's advantage at the time, but sixty-six years later a similar clause went against the Blues.

Ashworth, known as 'Little Dave' because of his height of only 5ft, was well known throughout football for his bowler hat and waxed moustache. As Liverpool manager he brought the Merseysiders the League title in 1922, yet in January 1923 mysteriously walked out of Anfield to return to Oldham at a time when the Reds were well on their way to winning the championship again. At Maine Road, the prospect of being able to challenge for the title once more encouraged the directors to give 'Little Dave' the job.

As Ashworth's reign began the Blues needed to find the success that their ever loyal supporters and luxurious new stadium deserved.

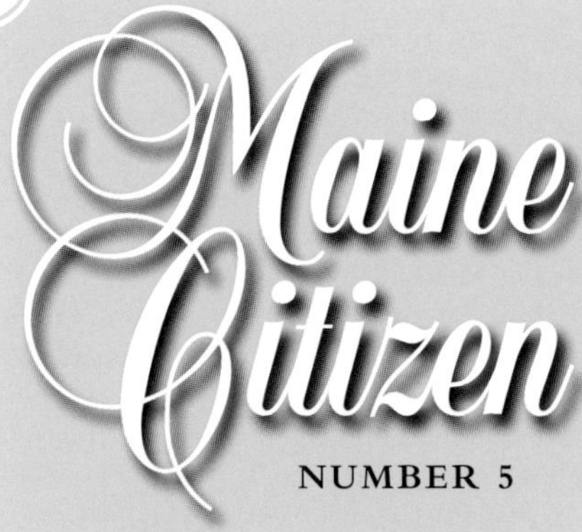

NUMBER 5

HORACE BARNES

Horace Barnes in a 1923-24 City line-up.
Back (left to right): Pringle, Donaldson, Mitchell, Cookson, Fletcher.
Front: Sharp, Roberts, Johnson, Hamill, Barnes, Murphy.

Barnes had an incredible goalscoring record for the Blues and combined perfectly with Tommy Browell throughout the immediate post war period, earning him, quite rightly, much praise from City's supporters and the press of the day. His role in City's history is a significant one, despite the fact the Blues failed to win a trophy during his period. Nevertheless, Barnes holds a very special record - he was the first City goalscorer at Maine Road. He also scored both goals three years earlier when the King attended Hyde Road for the match against Liverpool.

His most famous attribute was a powerful shot, a talent supporters who were fortunate to have seen him play in the 1920s still remember vividly to this day.

According to legend he once hit a 35 yard free kick with such force the ball broke both wrists of the opposing goalkeeper who, rather foolishly it seems, tried to punch it clear. Whether that is true or not is open to debate, but it is certain he possessed one of the most powerful shots in football, and opposition goalkeepers did not enjoy facing a 'Barnes special'.

Born at Wadsley Bridge, near Hillsborough, Horace first made a name for himself at Derby County. Once the Rams were relegated in 1914, they took the decision to sell their prize asset to raise much needed funds.

Both City and Manchester United were keen on the player, but the Reds pulled out of the negotiations when they discovered Derby were demanding a record fee in excess of £2,000. The Old Trafford side could not afford such an outlay, leaving the way clear for the Blues who paid £2,500 at what amounted to an auction attended by similarly wealthy clubs.

Barnes felt the move to Manchester was ideal, especially when he told club officials he was engaged to a Manchester girl. In his first season he scored 12 goals in 25 League games. The war interrupted his League career, although he still managed to make appearances throughout, scoring 73 goals in as many games. During the conflict he worked in a munitions factory and went to France with the R.A.F.

Unlike his colleague Tommy Browell, Barnes did manage to gain international recognition when he played for England against Wales in a Victory International. He also represented the Football League twice.

His scoring record was phenomenal with 120 goals in 217 League games, and on three occasions (once jointly with Browell) Barnes finished the season as City's top scorer. The last occasion was 1923-4. Sadly, the following November the Barnes-Browell partnership was brought to an end when he transferred to Preston. It is no co-incidence that the club's fortunes began to fade once he'd left Maine Road.

After a year at Preston he moved to Oldham, then joined Cheshire League club Ashton National where, in 1928-9 he netted 80 goals! His scoring exploits continued in a "Rest Of Cheshire" game against Port Vale when he managed six in the first half hour. In addition to his footballing skills, he was also a good cricketer.

Once he was unable to earn enough money from football, he took a job as a packer at Mather & Platt in Newton Heath. With the determination and endeavour he always managed to show at Hyde Road and Maine Road he continued working until he was 70. Sadly, he died aged 71 at his home in John Heywood St., Clayton on 12th September 1961.

Apart from the obvious first goal at Maine Road, Barnes will always be remembered by supporters for the attacking spirit, and killer shot that livened up many a match. He was a prolific scorer, and helped City to runners up spot during 1921. In a different era, he would undoubtedly have won many awards with the club.

BARNES' PLAYING RECORD

	LEAGUE		FA CUP		TOTAL	
	App	Gls	App	Gls	App	Gls
1914-15	25	12	4	2	29	12
1919-20	39	22	2	1	41	23
1920-21	41	17	1	0	42	17
1921-22	37	20	3	0	40	20
1922-23	38	21	1	0	39	21
1923-24	23	20	7	2	30	22
1924-25	14	8	0	0	14	8
TOTAL	217	120	18	5	235	125

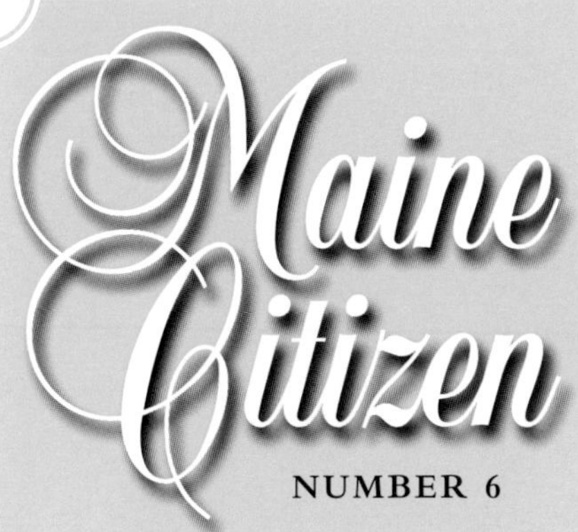

NUMBER 6

TOMMY JOHNSON

Second only to Eric Brook in the list of overall City goalscorers, Tommy Johnson was the Blues best scorer of the 1920s. During the 1928-9 First Division season alone he netted a total of 38 League goals in 39 games to take the club's record of most goals in a season. Even then his total is a substantial seven clear of nearest rival Frank Roberts.

He was a player idolised by the City faithful, so much so that in March 1930 when he left Maine Road to join Everton for £6,000 the majority of supporters voiced their feelings, while others boycotted the club. Three years later, the directors had cause to regret the transfer further when Johnson helped Everton defeat City 3-0 in the F.A. Cup Final. He also collected Second Division and League Championship medals while at Goodison Park.

Johnson was born on 19th August 1901, joined City in February 1919 from his home town team, Dalton Casuals, and scored in his first senior appearance when Blackburn were defeated 5-1 in the Lancashire section of the wartime league. Two weeks later he netted his first hat-trick for the Blues as Port Vale were swept aside 6-1, and immediately became an accepted attacking force in a team full of impressive forwards.

It took the youngster a little while before he was accepted into City's Football League side, once the competition resumed after the war, but after his League debut in February 1920 he managed five goals in ten appearances. He had a similar record the following season, and by the mid 1920s was a vital member of the first team.

In 1926 he appeared in City's F.A. Cup final defeat by Bolton, after scoring a hat-trick in the 6-1 demolition of Clapton Orient, then the following season topped City's goalscoring charts for the first time, netting 25 goals including three in the final game of the season against Bradford. His 19 goal contribution in 1927-8 helped City to promotion, but was one short of top scorer Frank Roberts.

His record breaking 1928-9 season occurred at a time when Johnson was alternating from his customary inside left position to centre forward, and this change in emphasis seemed to help the player, especially in his fifth game of the season when he scored five during a 6-2 victory at Everton. City had arrived late for the match, were subsequently fined, went a goal down early on, and then fought back to win by a four goal margin. It was an amazing match, and one which probably first brought Johnson to the attention of the Merseyside club. His final season at Maine Road brought 11 goals from 30 League games, and helped the management feel justified in selling the fans' favourite.

Throughout his time with City, Johnson had excited the crowd and proved extremely popular, especially with the inhabitants of the Gorton area of Manchester where he lived for a while. He was a prolific goalscorer and was once described as: "an inside forward with a left foot few players have equalled and a penchant for the telling cross field pass."

His impressive form deservedly brought him international honours while in City's colours, and also saw him play for the Football League and the FA XI. Later at Everton, while in his thirties, he made a further three appearances for England.

After great success at Goodison, he moved across Stanley Park and joined Liverpool where he scored 8 goals in 35 League appearances. He ended his career with Darwen.

During the late 1960s he enjoyed City's successes under Joe Mercer, who was a youngster at Goodison during Johnson's time at the club, and attended a few matches with his Everton striking partner Dixie Dean.

On 28th January 1973 Johnson died in Monsall hospital aged 71. He is remembered to this day in Manchester and Liverpool for his contribution to the successes of City and Everton.

He won every honour available to him during his career and contributed greatly to City's exciting 1920s. His 38 goals during 1928-9 will always keep him in City's record books, but he deserves a special place in the history of the club for everything else he achieved during his eleven years in Manchester.

	LEAGUE		FA CUP		TOTAL	
	App	Gls	App	Gls	App	Gls
1919-20	10	5	0	0	10	5
1920-21	12	5	0	0	12	5
1921-22	20	5	3	0	23	5
1922-23	35	14	1	1	36	15
1923-24	30	9	5	0	35	9
1924-25	41	12	1	0	42	12
1925-26	38	15	7	5	45	20
1926-27	38	25	1	0	39	25
1927-28	35	19	3	1	38	20
1928-29	39	38	1	0	40	38
1929-30	30	11	4	1	34	12
TOTAL	328	158	26	8	354	166

Chapter Seven

INCONSISTENT BLUES

DESPITE the appointment of Little Dave Ashworth, the 1924-5 season was barely an improvement on the previous one as the Blues struggled to come to terms with the Maine Road mud. Architect Charles Swain was adamant the drainage was right, but many still criticised his designs. A new groundsman was eventually appointed, but results remained mixed. City ended the season in tenth place on 43 points, with Frank Roberts top scorer with 31 goals. Another fans' favourite, Horace Barnes, moved to Preston during the season after 235 League and Cup appearances and 125 goals for the Blues.

Other changes included the arrival of centre-half Sam Cowan, signed from Doncaster Rovers, and two new wingers Austin and Hicks. Billy Austin cost City £2,000, while Salford born George Hicks arrived from Droylsden. All three men quickly made an impression during Ashworth's first season.

On 29th April 1925 Maine Road hosted a benefit match for living legend Billy Meredith, who by this point had retired from first class football. The teams were a Meredith XI, including City's Charlie Pringle and Frank Roberts, and a Rangers & Celtic XI. Johnny McMahon, one of the banned 1906 Cup winning City players, was one of the linesmen for the day. As in any benefit or testimonial game, players do not always perform to their full ability, yet with Meredith everybody expected him still to be able to perform all his old tricks and enliven the game. Sadly, his fans were disappointed. In a match comparable to many played by the similarly aged Stanley Matthews at the end of his career, most opposition players allowed the grand old man to dribble his way around them. Few tried to stop him, and for the seventeen year old City supporter Joe Carley it was simply a sad exhibition:

"Meredith, at the age of 51, and in spite of his successful comeback in the cup ties of the previous season, played a deplorable game, although given many chances by his opponents, who evidently did not relish tackling an 'old man'. It is never a pleasant sight watching the sporting stars of other days making futile efforts to retain their share of the limelight. Meredith was exceptional in even attempting to play first class football at 51, but over this, his final game, it is best to draw a veil."

George Hicks (right) signed from Droylsden in November 1923 and made two appearances during that season. His first game during 1924-25 came in November, after which he began to establish himself in the side.

The 1925-6 season was expected to see City return to the top of the table and challenge for the game's major honours. Sadly, the season developed into one of City's 'inconsistent specials'. The Blues did manage to reach Wembley for the 1926 Cup Final, but they also struggled appallingly in the League.

The season started well enough with a 3-2 Maine Road victory over Cardiff City, but two successive away defeats quickly followed, causing Ashworth a little concern. Then on 12th September the first derby match at Maine Road provided the Blues with a chance of to prove they were still the dominant force in local football.

According to legend, Sam Cowan did not kick a football until he took part in a local park game wearing only one borrowed boot, at the age of 17. Six years later he was making his debut for City.

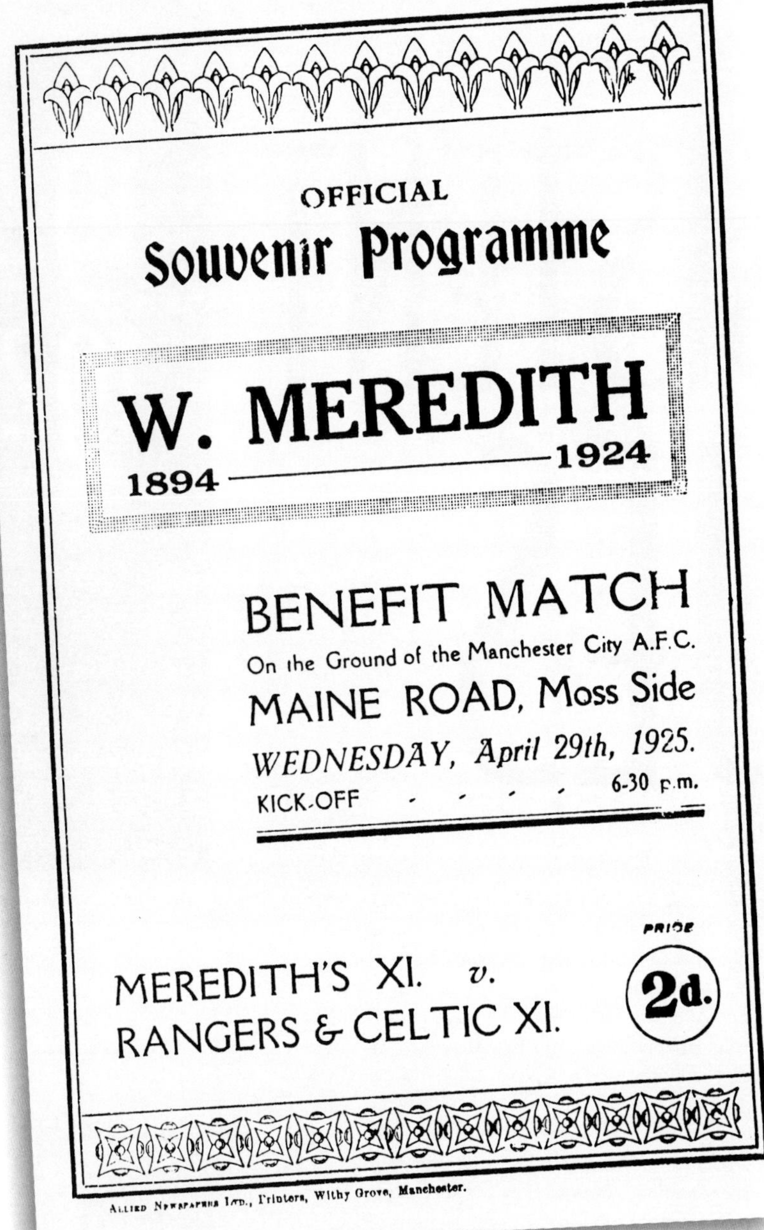

OFFICIAL
Souvenir Programme
W. MEREDITH
1894 1924
BENEFIT MATCH
On the Ground of the Manchester City A.F.C.
MAINE ROAD, Moss Side
WEDNESDAY, April 29th, 1925.
KICK-OFF - - - - 6-30 p.m.
PRICE
2d.
MEREDITH'S XI. v.
RANGERS & CELTIC XI.
Allied Newspapers Ltd., Printers, Withy Grove, Manchester.

Charlie Pringle played in Billy Meredith's final match. It was perhaps a unique situation as Meredith was Pringle's 49-year-old father-in-law!

The *Athletic News* reported that a crowd of 66,000 - the largest derby crowd and record City League attendance at that time - eagerly looked forward to the first clash for four years. Unfortunately, United took the lead first despite much pressure from City.

As the game progressed City increasingly dominated the game and via a Sam Cowan header from a tight angle, the Blues scored a thoroughly deserved equaliser. The *Athletic News* felt Cowan's display was the best by far: "Cowan's headwork was a feature of the match. More, he tackled with grim determination and effectiveness, and distributed the ball with discrimination and accuracy.

"Cowan promises to be all that the City club expected when they brought him from Doncaster Rovers last season. He has all the physical requirements for a centre half-back, and, judging by his display in this match, he has the temperament for the big event. His equalising goal was a masterpiece in headwork and judgement".

The following week the Blues achieved another draw, this time an amazing 4-4 at home to Everton with Tommy 'Boy' Browell scoring all four for City. He had been known as 'Boy' Browell ever since a 1910 match when, at the age of 19, he scored three for Hull City and a report stated: "Ten men and a boy beat Stockport". A little over a month after the draw with Everton Browell notched five of City's eight as they thrashed Burnley 8-3. Together with Frank Roberts, he would end the season on 21 League goals - a welcome return to the form of the three seasons that followed the war.

Two days after this incredible victory City's great unpredictable streak really displayed itself as that same 8-3 scoreline was repeated. Unfortunately, this time it was City on the losing side as Sheffield United humiliated Manchester's top club. Further defeats followed then, in November, with the pressure mounting Ashworth resigned. Indications are he was 'pushed' rather than walked away by choice, but the fact remains his year at Maine Road had not been a good one. The Blues were now totally unpredictable, with fine performances one week and abysmal humiliations the next. Ashworth's appointment was the first to have really failed. Every one of his predecessors enjoyed a little success - the Cup win, runners up in the League, and promotion - and at least a couple of seasons. Before Ashworth's year, Joshua Parlby had managed the club for the shortest period, although his two years in charge had seen the transformation from Ardwick to City and, to be fair, he also played a role throughout Sam Ormerod's time in charge.

The main problem was the Blues looked destined to struggle. Ashworth's only major signing, £3,000 left back Phil McCloy in the close season, had been brought to England from Ayr United and not only had to adapt to English football, but also to the new offside law, which had helped create these frequent high scoring games. During 1928 McCloy, incidentally, helped the young Matt Busby settle in Manchester at a time when the future United manager was feeling particularly homesick.

With Ashworth now gone the directors considered the options, looked around for a manager, and then thought, "we'll do the job ourselves!" It was something Francis Lee joked was an option 70 years later, as he searched for a replacement for first Alan Ball then Steve Coppell during 1996.

The leading voice was Chairman Albert Alexander senior, who took on the larger share of managerial responsibility. League form improved a little during December - two wins, a draw, and two defeats - but consistency remained hard to fathom.

At least in January minds were diverted from the struggle and turned towards the F.A. Cup. The Cup run began with a third round visit to the former Cup Final venue, Crystal Palace, to face the famous amateur side Corinthians. A couple of years earlier Corinthians had knocked Blackburn out of the competition and, with City's patchy form, it appeared the Blues might head the same way, especially as they were losing 3-2 with only three minutes to go. Luck was on City's side however, as the Corinthians' keeper caught a centre, but ran into his full-back, and ended up taking more than four steps without bouncing the ball. The referee penalised the 'keeper and awarded City an indirect free-kick a mere six yards from goal.

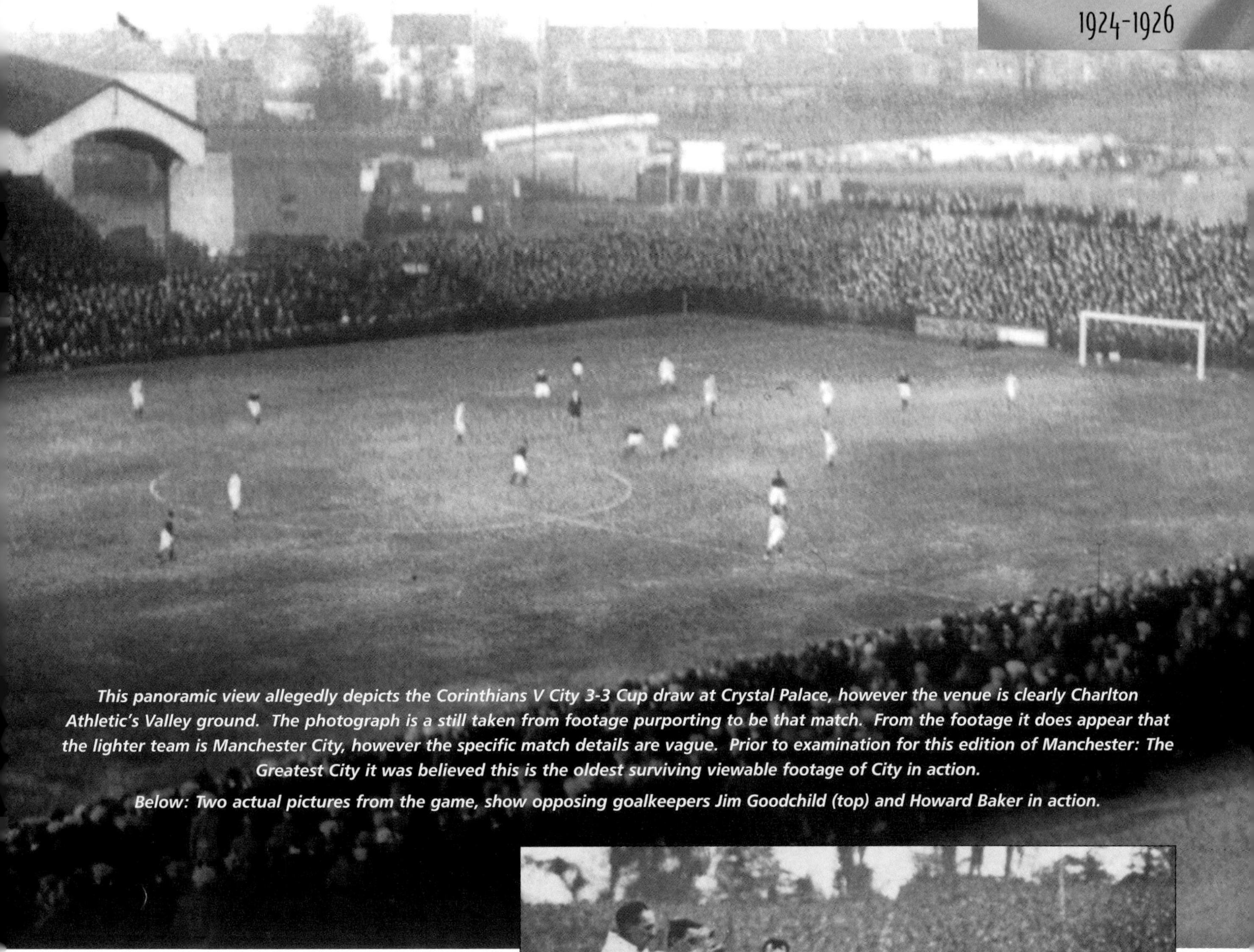

This panoramic view allegedly depicts the Corinthians V City 3-3 Cup draw at Crystal Palace, however the venue is clearly Charlton Athletic's Valley ground. The photograph is a still taken from footage purporting to be that match. From the footage it does appear that the lighter team is Manchester City, however the specific match details are vague. Prior to examination for this edition of Manchester: The Greatest City it was believed this is the oldest surviving viewable footage of City in action.

Below: Two actual pictures from the game, show opposing goalkeepers Jim Goodchild (top) and Howard Baker in action.

The kick was taken, quickly followed by a mad scramble from both sides. Somehow the ball landed at Frank Roberts' feet and the player stabbed home the equaliser.

In the Maine Road replay four days later, the Blues took control and ran out easy 4-0 winners thanks to goals from Billy Austin (two), Tommy Johnson, and George Hicks. The scoreline was repeated in the next round when the Blues faced high flying Huddersfield Town at Maine Road. The Yorkshire club were enjoying the greatest period in their history as Herbert Chapman led them to three successive League titles, and they should have easily defeated the managerless Blues but, again demonstrating City's unpredictability, the home side stood firm and goals from Hicks (two), Browell, and Roberts satisfied the 74,789 crowd.

It wasn't all joy for City's spectators though, as late in the game, a crush barrier collapsed causing many injuries with a number of spectators carried away by stretcher. Even at Britain's newest stadia crowd control was far from perfect.

The fifth round tie brought Crystal Palace to Maine Road for, what turned out to be, a fifteen goal thriller. By half-time the score was 7-0 to the Blues, but Palace would not give up and quickly pulled back four goals. City were knocked out of a period of complacency and soon found their goalscoring touch again. By the end it was 11-4 to City and, according to a number of spectators present on the day, Manchester fans rushed on at the final whistle and

Albert Alexander Senior was Chairman and leading team selector during City's managerless period in the 1925-26 season.

carried off the Palace 'keeper shoulder high. Apparently he had played extremely well and, somehow, managed to keep the score down, although one cannot help wondering if he'd have been given such a reception had the scores been reversed!

Frank Roberts was the City star for this particular game, scoring a remarkable five, while Tommy Browell also earned a few plaudits for his hat-trick.

With no management and such miserable form in the League, no one could believe how City had been able to maintain such strong cup performances. The quarter-final draw sent the Blues down to London for a second time, to face Second Division Clapton Orient on 6th March.

Tommy Johnson provided a hat-trick as City defeated Orient 6-1 to put the Blues into the semi-finals for the second time in three seasons - rather disappointingly City had lost to Preston in the first round in 1925.

The four semi-final teams included two other Lancastrian teams - Bolton and Manchester United - while Swansea Town seemed to offer the easiest route to the final.

When the draw was made Manchester could not believe it as relegation possibles City and newly promoted United were to face each other. It was the draw neither side really wanted. Losing in a semi-final is bad enough, but losing to your closest rivals is simply unbearable.

By the time of the semi, both League derbies had been played. In addition to the 1-1 Maine Road draw in September, the Old Trafford derby had been played in January. Amazingly City's unpredictability gave United the biggest derby shock ever as the Blues, playing skilful, attacking football, totally humiliated United. Justifiably, the Blues took the lead after eighteen minutes when Roberts headed in Austin's corner.

By half-time it was 3-0 with Austin and Roberts combining again for a goal apiece. Johnson added a fourth thirty minutes into the second half, and a little while later Austin added a fifth.

In the last five minutes Hicks scored a sixth from close range. With the score at 6-0 and two minutes remaining the Blues could be forgiven for easing off a little, and allowing Clat Rennox to provide the Reds with a consolation from a goalmouth scramble. The game ended 6-1. The biggest derby victory ever, and the most embarrassing home mauling either side has endured in the history of the fixture. This result was even more remarkable when it is considered United ended the season in ninth place, whereas City struggled.

For the semi-final City prayed for a repeat of their performance two months earlier, although many believed simply gaining victory over the Reds, even by a one goal margin, would suffice. City needed to become the first of the sides to reach Wembley to ensure they remained Manchester's number one club. Their fans certainly deserved it.

With only two first class venues in the Manchester area, the sides had to travel to Bramall Lane, Sheffield, for the game. Naturally, City wore their first choice strip of sky blue, while United were still trying to find the right club colours for their club. In 1902 they had abandoned the green and gold of Newton Heath for red shirts, but by the early twenties

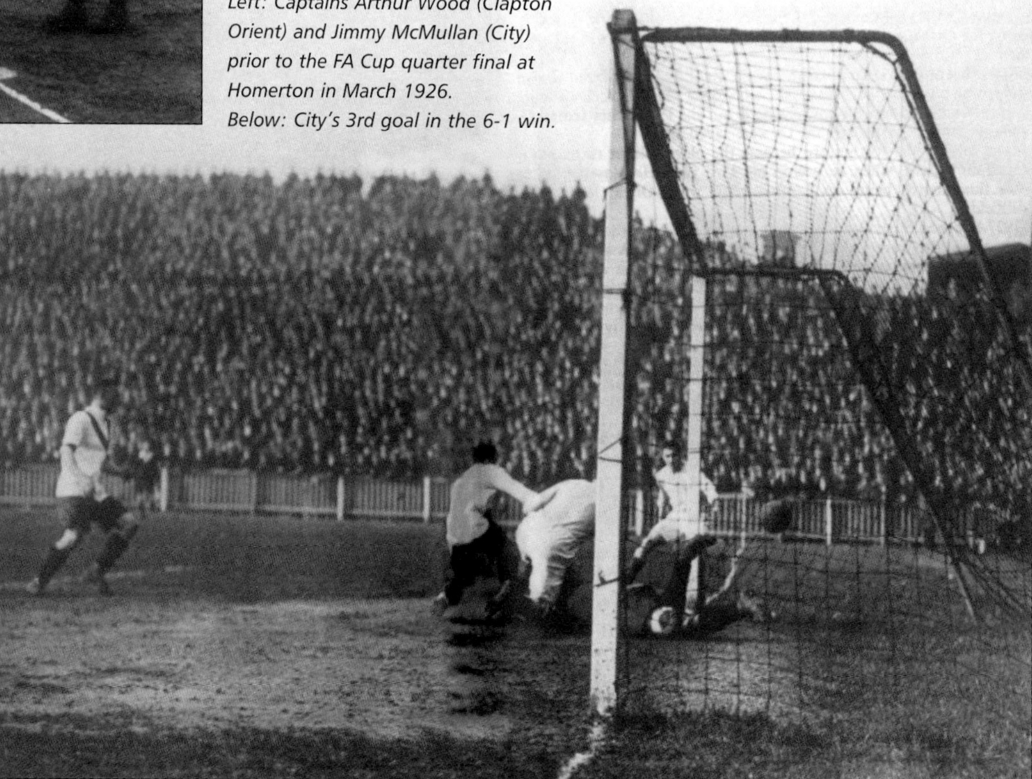

Left: Captains Arthur Wood (Clapton Orient) and Jimmy McMullan (City) prior to the FA Cup quarter final at Homerton in March 1926.
Below: City's 3rd goal in the 6-1 win.

A 1926 cigarette card shows City's Sam Cookson under pressure from an Orient player.

Clapton Orient goalkeeper Arthur Wood is left lying on the floor as a City attacker - believed to be Johnson, closest to the goal - increases the lead.

felt that red was not appropriate as their main colour, and so adopted white shirts with a red V - the same shirts as City's quarter-final opponents Clapton Orient who, co-incidentally, had been defeated 6-1. Right through into the late 1930s United adopted a number of different strips in an attempt to find their most appropriate kit.

City's side for the semi included goalkeeper Jim Goodchild, who was only a week away from celebrating his thirty-fourth birthday. He had been with the Blues since October 1911 and was now in the twilight of his career. Since 1921 he had really been City's second choice 'keeper, although he did manage to make a few appearances each season. The rest of the team was: Cookson, McCloy, Pringle, Cowan, McMullan, Austin, Browell, Roberts, Johnson, and Hicks.

When the game kicked off it was City who looked the more settled side with United, perhaps mindful of what had occurred at Old Trafford, rather nervous. They made plenty of mistakes, misplaced passes, hasty shots, and badly timed tackles. City, on the other hand, were composed, with Sam Cowan putting in a fine display.

In the fourteenth minute the Blues took the lead through a controversial goal. City won a corner kick and, as Hicks curled the ball into the box, Browell jumped above the United defence and headed firmly past goalkeeper Alf Steward. The ball was hooked clear, but the referee immediately signalled for a goal as the ball had clearly crossed the line. In addition to their complaints about the ball not crossing the line, United also claimed Browell had pushed to gain an advantage. The referee would have none of it, however, and the Blues deservedly had the lead.

United's attitude seemed to worsen with petty fouls dominating their play. Frank Barson, United's captain and an extremely tough defender, soon showed what he thought of both the goal and City's dominance by cynically flattening the outstanding Cowan. If that wasn't enough the United man then feigned injury, provoking the crowd further. The referee marched over to him and, after a lengthy lecture, United's captain was allowed to stay on the field, although he was rather more subdued for the rest of the match.

By half-time, despite constant pressure, the Blues remained in the lead with a solitary goal. City's attack was rather unlucky on several occasions in both halves as shots from Austin, Johnson, and Browell all either hit the woodwork, a divot, or were scooped away at the last minute by the United 'keeper.

With only fifteen minutes remaining City increased their lead. Hicks sent a though ball to Browell, who struck it cleanly first time past Steward into the net. Two minutes later, Roberts broke free down the middle, but his miss-hit shot from fifteen yards did not appear dangerous until Steward, who attempted to turn the ball around the post, diverted it into the net.

As stated in the reports of the day, City thoroughly deserved the 3-0 victory and their continued dominance of Manchester football. With much pride the Blues prepared for their first visit to Wembley stadium. Their opponents were Bolton,

United 1 City 6 - the largest victory in the Manchester derby was achieved by the Blues at Old Trafford on 23rd January 1926.

Below: Reds' goalkeeper Steward clears a corner.

Frank Roberts scored twice in the 6-1 humiliation of Manchester United at Old Trafford in the 36th Manchester League derby in January 1926.

who destroyed Swansea in their semi at Tottenham, for what was to be a re-run of the 1904 final.

As with 1904, the final was still played before the League programme was completed so City went into the game haunted by the knowledge they could still be relegated. Winning the cup was something everybody wanted, but by this time in football history, relegation was something to be avoided at all costs. City were well aware how United had struggled to gain promotion for four years, and that a prolonged spell in the Second Division could seriously affect the future of the club, especially with United now back in the First. City needed to remain Manchester's dominant club and simply could not afford relegation. Victory at Wembley would also bring much needed cheer to Manchester's loyal supporters, especially as many were about to enter a period of struggle forced on by the General Strike.

A cigarette card showing United's Alf Steward gathering a shot from City's George Hicks during the 1926 FA Cup semi-final at Bramall Lane.

In the run up, and on the morning of the final everything seemed to go Bolton's way. Firstly, Wanderers had already succeeded at Wembley three years earlier. Secondly, their League form was better - they would eventually finish eighth. Thirdly, the press made them favourites following a cup run that had seen them take part in three replays against lower opposition.

According to the 'papers, the team that struggles most to reach the final usually wins it!

Fourthly, Bolton were able to field ten of the players who had won the Cup in 1923. And finally, The Trotters won the toss for choice of dressing room and elected to use room number 11 - the 'lucky' room. According to the 'papers of the day dressing room 11 had been used by all the teams that had won the Cup at Wembley.

Because of all this hype, City probably felt they stood little chance anyway. Perhaps they should have stayed at home.

WHY CITY WON.

WideSwingingPassesNonplus the United.

WINNERS OF THE FINAL?

AT BRAMALL-LANE, SHEFFIELD.
1s. Admission.
Attendance, 46,450. Receipts, £4,448.

By CHARLIE ROBERTS.

I thought Steward, the Manchester United goalkeeper, might have saved the third goal scored against him at Bramall-lane. Even so, that would have made no difference to City's right to go to Wembley.

The fact of the matter is that United were outplayed by a side who were all enterprise and dash, and never gave their rivals a moment to consider the next move.

But it was dash without slap-dash. Long swinging passes were made swiftly and accurately, and the nearest way was always their route to goal.

It was a very hard, and, in my opinion, a very good game, especially in the second half, when, however, the City adopted better tactics by swinging the ball about. The United's forwards were very poor indeed, and having regard to their limitations they played much too close.

Goodchild's Great Save.

They would have done much better had they taken a leaf from the book of the City. Up to the interval there was not a great deal in it, and one incident, which in my opinion had a big reflection on the result was a save by Goodchild from M'Pherson. At the same time I think the City were deserving of their lead.

It was scored at the end of fourteen minutes' play. Johnson whipped the ball out to Hicks, and he shot for the near corner of the goal. Steward saved, but Roberts dashed into him, and the ball went over the line for a corner.

This Hicks placed nicely, and in the melee Browell headed through. The finishing of the United forwards was very poor indeed, though Goodchild had to save more than once, and he dropped the ball on several occasions, probably due to excitement, which all the players suffered from.

The City played better in the second half, and how Browell missed scoring from close in I am at a loss to know, for he had the goal at his mercy and yet completely missed the ball. However, he made atonement after the first half-hour's play, when Hicks put across a glorious low centre, and Browell coming up crashed the ball into the net.

Roberts's Third Goal.

This settled the issue, but the City were not satisfied, and three minutes later Roberts put on a third goal with a long shot which Steward seemed to have well covered, but he, however, fumbled the ball and it passed off him into the net. The United defence began to tire after this, and they were completely overrun.

The forwards made further raids, but they never looked like scoring. As I have said they played very poorly. Rennox was weak in the extreme, and the only man who did anything at all was Thomas, and that was very little. Up to the interval the half-backs played very well, but they fell away afterwards, especially M'Crae.

Beyond one little lapse I think Barson played very well, and the backs were exceptionally good until the strain told upon them near the end. Steward, too, made some very fine saves, but he ought to have prevented the third goal.

City's Final Prospects.

The City played a fine Cup-tie game, and I cannot see them being beaten in the final. Their forwards were clever, and the half-backs tackled like terriers. The backs were heroic in their resistance, and especially Cookson. I liked him immensely, and I liked the sturdy play of M'Cloy, who gave the best display that ever I have seen from him before. Goodchild was a little nervous at times, but he kept a fine goal.

I cannot discriminate between the half-backs, for they all played so well, but I must commend M'Mullan on his plucky display, for he received a nasty gash above the right eye, which had to be stitched at the end of the game. I thought the sharp dashes of Roberts a very potent factor in the victory, for they were so disconcerting to the opposition.

Next to him I should place Johnson, who was "heady" as well as being one of the most industrious players on the field.

Browell was very quick and good with his head, even if he had missed chances, and I think the two wing men did their work very well, though in my opinion Austin would have done better had he centred a little more instead of shooting at different angles.

Hicks did not come prominently into the picture until the second half, but then he did some splendid work, and especially in nipping in and driving across the goal glorious, low centres.

It was a game that will be remembered, and as I have said for a semi-final I thought the football was above the average.

Manchester City.—Goodchild; Cookson, M'Cloy; Pringle, Cowan, M'Mullan; Austin, Browell, Roberts, Johnson, Hicks.

Manchester United.—Steward; Moore, Silcock; M'Crae, Barson, Mann; Spence, Smith, M'Pherson, Rennox, Thomas.

THE MANCHESTER EVENING NEWS, SATURDAY, APRIL 24, 1926.—3

6 a.m. Queues at Wembley.

ALL LANCASHIRE CUP FINAL.

Great Pilgrimage That Began Before Dawn.

"ARENA NEVER BETTER."

Stadium Bedecked for the King's Visit.

THOUGH followers of football descended upon London to-day from many other parts it was the land of the red and white roses which furnished the most impressive part of the invasion.

It was an all-Lancashire contest for Soccer's premier trophy, and Lancashire men—and women, too—soon infected the capital with their inimitable gaiety and good fellowship.

Here are some glimpses of what to many will remain a memorable day:

3 a.m.—Crowds, wearing their favours, emerge from the main terminal stations.

6 a.m.—Queues, the majority formed by Lancastrians, outside the Stadium gates.

8 a.m.—Enthusiasts who had spent the night in some of the new houses being erected in Wembley's new suburb take up positions in the queues.

An early inspection of the playing pitch at Wembley showed it to be in magnificent condition. "Never better in the history of the Stadium" was the report.

The King's decision to see the Cup Final was not officially announced until this morning. The Stadium was early decorated in honour of His Majesty's visit.

CITY'S TEAM.

Half-back Line Chosen This Morning.

GOOD WISHES!

Salford Lads' Message to Hicks.

The directors of Manchester City decided upon the half-back line in the team to meet Bolton Wanderers. The directors selected:—

Pringle, Cowan, and McMullan.

The team, therefore, is the same as at Sheffield, and comprised:—

Goodchild; Cookson and McCloy; Pringle, Cowan, and McMullan; Austin, Browell, Roberts, Johnson, and Hicks.

Hicks this morning received a telegram from the Salford Lads' Club, for which he played for several seasons. The message ran:—

George Hicks, Manchester City Football Team, Stadium, Wembley.

Best wishes for success from your old club.

CLIFF, Salford Lads' Club.

GAY STADIUM.

Best Turf that Has Ever Known a Final.

(From Our Own Correspondent).

Wembley, Saturday.

The condition of the playing pitch at Wembley is magnificent. It is beautiful. [illegible] has never been better in the history of the Stadium. The rain of the last few days has brought it along wonderfully. It has done it a world of good, as we were [illegible] in getting the turf down. Our inspection of the pitch this morning has more than satisfied us.

This was the statement made to me to-day at the Stadium at Wembley by [illegible]

GRIEVANCES OF THE TICKETLESS.

CROWD ROUGHLY HANDLES PROFITEERS.

COLOURS DILEMMA.

The Londoner who Knew Where He Was.

(From Our Own Correspondent).

Wembley, Saturday.

SHORTLY after eleven the gates were opened to ticket-holders, but many hundreds of people without tickets were assembled outside the main gates.

There were some arguments between officials and people without tickets, and on one occasion a burly Lancashire man endeavoured to hold up a police car while he registered his protests against the method of tickets being allocated to people who had no direct interest in the Final itself.

Traffickers in tickets were roughly handled by some of the crowd whenever they attempted to charge extortionate prices.

An ugly temper was manifested among hundreds who are excluded from the grounds because they had no tickets and a strong force of police was massed in the immediate vicinity of the main gates.

THE GATES OPENED.

The time for opening the turnstiles at Wembley was [illegible] eleven and when that hour arrived crowds of people were [illegible] to the grounds.

[illegible] the Stadium [illegible] warm with spectators, but it [illegible] from being full.

[illegible] gathered in the stand cheered the arrival of celebrities.

There was a cheer for the Lord Mayor of Manchester and for Mr. J. C. Clegg, the President of the F.A.

The favours of the two clubs were every where to be seen and there [illegible]

DETECTIVE'S CHASE.

Roused from Bed by Girl's Screams.

PURSUIT IN NIGHT.

Young Man Sentenced for Assault on Telephone Operator.

How a policeman was roused from his bed by the shrieks of a young girl was described when a young lighterman named Clark was sentenced at Brentford to-day to two months' hard labour for assaulting a telephone operator in a lonely lane at Isleworth.

Clark was caught by Detective Wright, who was in bed at the time but was roused by hearing shrieks from the direction of the lane.

He ran out, half dressed, and saw a man running away, whom he chased for about half a mile.

When he was taking the man to the station they met the girl, who at once identified the accused as having assaulted her.

Clark was given an excellent character by his employer and others, but the Chairman of the Bench said they must protect the public.

The Bench complimented Detective Wright on his conduct of the case.

ROOF-TOP THRILLS.

Alleged Housebreakers Captured after Police Chase.

An excited police chase over the roof tops of a number of shops in Brixton Road (London) led to the appearance of three men at the Lambeth Police Court to-day, charged with breaking and entering, with intent to steal.

They were also charged with being in possession of housebreaking implements by night.

The men were Edwin Charles Failes (27), hawker, of Camberwell; William Frederick Mudge (27), hawker, of Kennington; and Harry Alfred Cattell [illegible] of no fixed abode. They were remanded, bail being refused.

KING OF CLUBS AGAIN.

VICTORY IN NORTH YORKS HANDICAP.

DROPITIN SECOND.

Palomides Wins Opening Event.

1 45—BISHOPTON (S) PLATE. 1 mile. [illegible]

2 15—WESTON [illegible] 6 furlongs. [illegible]

2 45—NORTH YORKSHIRE H'CAP. 1 mile. KING OF CLUBS [illegible] DROPITIN [illegible] PREFECT [illegible]

3 15—CARLTON 2-Y.O. (S) Plate. 5 furlongs. [illegible]

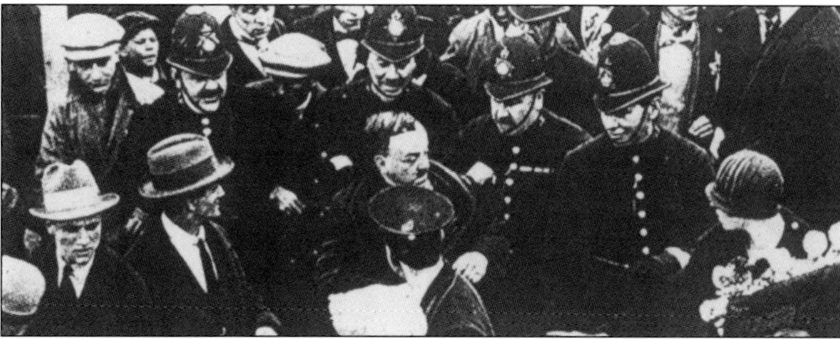

FA Cup Finalists 1926

On the morning of the game the thousands of Lancastrians who arrived at the stadium without tickets were shocked to discover they could only buy them from touts. Ever since that first Wembley final three years earlier, the Cup Final had been an all-ticket affair to ease crowd control. Unfortunately, this allowed the touts to gain a grip. For this final, two shilling tickets were on sale at 15shillings, and occasionally £1, while £10 was demanded for seat tickets. This was an incredible mark-up and angered the many ticketless supporters. According to the *Daily Mail* the fans sought retribution: "As though at a command, they descended on the speculators and in many cases chased them out. For nearly an hour the approaches to the field were the scenes of noisy free-fights, and it was the intervention of the police that saved some of the touts from serious injury."

The *Athletic News* believed the final would be

Ticket touts have always cashed in on the popularity of the Cup Final. The pictures above and left show the touts being protected from angry crowds by the police.

A view of a controversial goalmouth incident as Bolton attack the City goal at Wembley.

Bolton goalkeeper Dick Pym punches clear as City attack.

the last at Wembley as a result of ticket chaos and the F.A.'s general expenditure to stage the fixture there. The report suggested moving back to the old Crystal Palace ground, or potentially to move the final around the country. Proposals which, even now seventy years later, seem a little too radical for the game's governing body.

City's captain was Jimmy McMullan, who had signed the preceding February for £4,700 from Partick Thistle. He was a Scottish international left-half and had already made a name for himself with the Blues after a few good performances. In the final itself, he seemed the most determined of all the City players and at times appeared to pop up anywhere and everywhere on the pitch.

Bolton dominated the opening minutes, while City seemed a little nervous. Within the first twenty minutes, the Wanderers had seen three decent chances go astray as the Blues stood back and watched. The *Athletic News* stated Bolton had obviously planned well, whereas City were "a set of stragglers - earnest but incoherent."

After about twenty-five minutes the Blues began to get into the game: "As soon as the City began to disremember that they had shaken hands with the King and that this was the Cup Final, the fact became apparent to all that there were flaws in the Bolton defence.

"The City did not come to cohesion. They did not take up position so intelligently as the forwards of Bolton. But they were able, by fast, go-ahead methods to bother the backs."

A couple of chances came City's way, but the game remained goalless at half-time. In the second half, Bolton's Dick Pym made a couple of fine saves, especially as the Blues seemed to have the initiative: "For 25 minutes they fought for the decisive goal. Haworth, Greenhalgh, Jennings all wavered. Manchester City sought desperately to deliver the vital blow - a goal would have been sufficient. But it would not come. Hicks shot just over the corner of the goal, Pym had a rare struggle to clear from Hicks' corner-kick, Roberts sent Browell through and, though he overran the ball when gloriously placed, I did not agree with the referee's decision in ruling the inside right out of bounds.

"And just as Bolton were beginning to fight back, in this match of fluctuations, Pym, in their goal, came to the rescue with a match-winning save. There is no exaggeration. When McMullan once again plied Hicks with masterly touch the outside left sustained the high standard of all his previous play by placing the ball precisely in the mouth of goal. Browell's head shot out, and it seemed a score at last.

"As it was very obvious by this stage that a goal would settle all, it is abundantly clear that Pym saved his side when he flung himself full length along the goal-line and turned the ball aside."

Pym received tremendous applause from the Wembley crowd for his fine vital save, but for City this was perhaps the last great chance. The game now swung back to Bolton, and with twelve minutes remaining the deadlock was broken. The ball, with Bolton seemingly going nowhere in midfield. was sent to Butler on the right wing. He immediately darted forward down the touchline followed by McMullan, according to the *Athletic News*: "The little Scotsman was unable to get to grips. He was never sufficiently close to make the tackle. But he hung on, and his object clearly was to force his opponent into such a position that he would find it extremely difficult to deliver a centre that would endanger the goal. At the same time, McMullan sought to get into a position that would render it imperative that the ball, from Butler's centre, would strike his body and so be kept within the front of goal."

Unfortunately, McMullan failed in his mission as Butler somehow managed to send the ball to Vizard on the opposite wing, who in turn weighed up the situation and centred the ball to David Jack, who stood unmarked, right in the centre

1926 FA CUP RUN

R3	Corinthians	A	D 3-3
	Corinthians	H	W 4-0
R4	Huddersfield Town	H	W 4-0
R5	Crystal Palace	H	W 11-4
R6	Clapton Orient	A	W 6-1
SF	Manchester United	N*	W 3-0
F	Bolton Wanderers	N**	L 0-1

* = Bramall Lane
** = Wembley Stadium

FACTS & FIGURES

	P	W	D	L	F	A
HOME	3	3	0	0	19	4
AWAY	4	2	1	1	12	5
TOTAL	7	5	1	1	31	9

CUP FINAL DETAILS

24 April 1926 at Wembley Stadium
MANCHESTER CITY 0
BOLTON WANDERERS 1

CITY: Goodchild, Cookson, McCloy, Pringle, Cowan, McMullan, Austin, Browell, Roberts, Johnson, Hicks
BOLTON: Pym, Haworth, Greenhalgh, Nuttall, Seddon, Jennings, Butler, Jack, Smith (JR), Smith (J), Vizard
GOAL: Jack

ATTENDANCE: 91,547
REFEREE: J. Baker (Crewe)
GUEST OF HONOUR: King George V
MANAGER: Directors' committee, mainly Chairman Albert Alexander
CAPTAIN: Jimmy McMullan

The only goal of the final was scored by an unmarked David Jack (on one knee).

Above: Tommy Browell holds off a challenge, but what are the Bolton players appealing for?

Right: Browell again, beating centre-half Seddon in a duel.

Below: Both finalists gave their name to an OXO advert, just as City had done after the 1904 FA Cup success.

of the City goal. All Jack had to do was bang the ball into the net, leaving Goodchild with no chance to save.

The final few minutes saw plenty of further action as the Blues tried to force an equaliser, but it was not to be. With the final kick of the game, Billy Austin passed the ball to another forward when everybody else expected him to have one final shot. That moment seemed to typify City's season of unpredictability. Nevertheless, the Blues left Wembley a proud side. They had come close to defeating one of the period's leading sides, and had managed a few memorable moments.

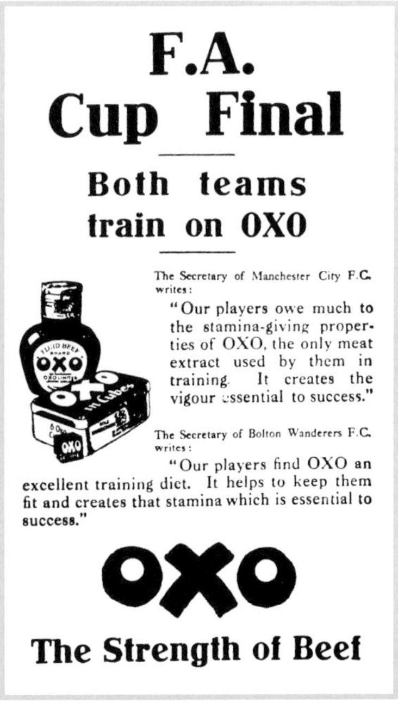

F.A. Cup Final

Both teams train on OXO

The Secretary of Manchester City F.C. writes:

"Our players owe much to the stamina-giving properties of OXO, the only meat extract used by them in training. It creates the vigour essential to success."

The Secretary of Bolton Wanderers F.C. writes:

"Our players find OXO an excellent training diet. It helps to keep them fit and creates that stamina which is essential to success."

The Strength of Beef

City's man of the match was undoubtedly McMullan. The *Daily Mail* paid him tribute: "McMullan was the greatest hearted man of the 22. He was half-back, full-back and forward, all combined in one. His attack was as good as his defence, and it was certainly not his fault that his team were beaten."

The result was a fair one, although everybody associated with the Blues found it difficult to accept. Back in Manchester, in Platt Fields close to Maine Road, large crowds had gathered to listen for news of the final. Loudspeakers had been erected in trees around the park and City fans had listened carefully to an intermittent and rather poor quality commentary. After struggling to listen throughout the game, when the news came through of the goal the fans could not take anymore, and many left immediately for home.

The following Monday's newspapers were full of Bolton's success although, as a sign of the times, both the *Athletic News* and the *Daily Mail* at times seemed more interested in what the King thought of the game. Under the banner headline "The Cup Final That Impressed The King" the *Athletic News* stressed how much he'd enjoyed the game, which seemed remarkably similar to comments made after his visit to Hyde Road in 1920, while the *Daily Mail* commented on the singing of the National Anthem. It stated that 'God Save The King' had never been sung with "such fervour, with such grandeur, with such noble, breath-catching feeling." The 'paper stated this was a demonstration of affection and loyalty to the King, but perhaps the Blues in the crowd sung more enthusiastically believing they had a royal supporter - after all he had attended a City home game - or maybe the Lancastrians were just glad to be there.

MONDAY, APRIL 26. 1926.

Cup Final That Impressed The King.

£12,000 WEMBLEY BILL.

LTON'S MANY HONOURS AT COSTLY STADIUM GROUND.

is generally agreed that there is small chance of another F.A. Cup Final being played at Wembley Stadium, d in that event Bolton Wanderers, by their victory of turday over Manchester City, will hold the honour of

Manchester City, however, were unable to seize the opportunity thus presented. Their forwards have scored with reasonable freedom in the season's ties, yet the inside men failed to snatch the chance.

One reason was that Seddon, though not at his best, for the reason that his constructive play was less successful than usual, continually interrupted their attacks. A tall centre half-back can make himself a general nuisance to the other fellows. Seddon did all that, and it was largely because of his ceaseless intervention with head and foot that the City attacks went

would have been here easy to extol the winners, sportsmen who come to those who lose." His sym out to the losers because very easily have been win had lost with honour.

The King Greatly Imp

At the winners' banq over by Mr. W. Hamer, th chairman— Mr. A. Kin treasurer, and Mr. F. J. W responded to the toast of Association. In his re referred to the trouble th

12 ATHLETIC NEWS, MONDAY APRIL 26, 1926.

A Save, A Centre and Bolton Win

A GOAL DECIDES.

STORY OF FINALS SUSTAINED IN FLUCTUATING FIGHT: By IVAN SHARPE.

BOLTON WANDERERS......1 MANCHESTER CITY......0
(At Wembley Stadium.)

THE Cup Final of 1926 was a story of ebb and flow, of periodical turns of supremacy, of the rise and fall of hopes, until at the end of it all the tale was just the same—a goal decides.

I was writing of the trend of the Cup Final, during a dozen years, a week ago and pointing out how in eight of eleven seasons the issue had turned on the only goal of the game and that, quite often, a streaky sort of goal.

There was little new, then, in the second success of Bolton Wanderers in four games. The battle swayed, the goal was missed by a narrow margin, the decisive stroke turned on an unexpected incident of the game. So it will always be while players are human and the electric atmosphere of the Final causes the coolest man to quiver.

This Final was like the rest of recent

the run—until they got to goal. From Vizard's free-kick, Jack saw the ball pass his toe when only a yard from the goal-line; then John Smith and Butler were left with shooting chances—half-chances are welcome on Cup-day—but drove high and wide.

All Bolton it was for fifteen minutes, and the story was the same until half

their chance. The first half hour of the second half brought no improvement. The snap had departed from the Bolton forwards and, though Seddon was a tireless breaker-up, the defence was decidedly streaky.

This was Manchester City's chance. Could they seize it? For 25 minutes they fought for the decisive goal. Haworth, Greenhalgh, Jennings all wavered. Manchester City sought desperately to deliver the vital blow—a goal would have been sufficient. But it would not come. Hicks shot just over the corner of the goal, Pym had a rare struggle to clear from Hicks' corner-kick, Roberts sent Browell through and, though he overran the ball when gloriously placed, I did not agree with the referee's decision in ruling the inside right out of bounds.

And just as Bolton were beginning to fight back, in this match of fluctuations, Pym, in their goal, came to the rescue with a match-winning save. There is no exaggeration. When M'Mullan once again plied Hicks with masterly touch the outside left sustained the high standard of all his previous play by placing the ball precisely in the mouth of goal. Browell's head shot out, and it seemed a score at last.

As it was very obvious by this stage that a goal would settle all, it is

often brightened the game. Th spasmodic, and it would not to say that they conserved th for the sudden descent or Wanderers' captain often fel in the Joe Smith way, wor will from start to finish. Be wings, however, John Smith happy day. Now and again ball nicely to the wings, and position well for the throu pass that helped Bolton, qui advance. But there was l little leadership or real a reliability in his work.

SEDDON'S VITAL P

Still, I counted the forwa the better section of the te defence was distinctly sh caused his friends to quak then made amends by tha dive for the ball. But what with the backs? Neither Haworth failing to sustain fo pair could easily have be They were uncertain under p that fact must be borne in assessing the work of Pym a backs.

Consequently, I count Se the saviours of his side. finished than usual in his wo never really polished, the tall back was a potent factor in

After the final, City had to pick themselves up for a difficult week in the League. On the Tuesday they faced fellow strugglers Leeds United at Maine Road. It was a tense affair, but goals from Austin and Johnson helped the Blues to a much needed 2-1 victory. It put them a point above Leeds and Burnley. City did have the better goal average, but two points from their final game at Newcastle would guarantee survival.

Sadly, within a minute of the start of the Newcastle match, Hughie Gallacher scored for the home side. Before half-time Frank Roberts equalised, but in the fiftieth minute Gallacher gave Newcastle the lead once more. A little while later, City's chance came again as the Blues were awarded a penalty. Billy Austin took the kick, but sent the ball straight at 'keeper Wilson. It was a bitter blow.

After an hour's play Gallacher notched his hat-trick with a superb header to really end City's chances. Tommy Browell did provide a second three minutes from time, but the damage had already been done. With the game ending 3-2 the Blues still felt they were in with a chance of staying up, after all they had the point advantage and were fourth from bottom, with only two clubs relegated. As they made their way into the dressing room, news came through that both Leeds and Burnley had won their home games by 4-1. The Blues were down.

For the second week running a few blamed Austin, but there had been plenty of mistakes during City's great unpredictable, inconsistent season. Perhaps the biggest mistake of all was not having a manager. The directors may have known about football, but a club of City's size and stature needed a true professional in charge. By the season's end, Albert Alexander senior had appointed a new man, Peter Hodge, but his arrival a few days before the last game could hardly have helped matters.

At least with Hodge at the helm, the Blues could now look towards the future with a little hope. Promotion had to be achieved at the earliest opportunity to ensure City remained the major Manchester force. More than a couple of seasons apart could affect the club forever.

Billy Austin's penalty miss during a crucial Division One game with Newcastle on 1st May 1926 caused many to blame the City outside right. The truth was the side had made too many mistakes in an inconsistent season.

Chapter Eight

RETURN TO WEMBLEY

WITH the appointment of Peter Hodge, City had found a manager who was capable of building a side. At his previous club, Leicester City, he constructed a team that won the Second Division in 1925 - two points ahead of second placed Manchester United - and then managed to consolidate during 1925-6. He had been with Leicester since 1919, after managerial spells with Raith Rovers and Stoke, whom he guided to the Southern League title in 1915. At Leicester he is remembered as the club's first great manager, and the first to have real control over team selection, recruitment, and tactics. It came as a shock to the Midlands club when the approach came from Manchester, especially as Leicester were comfortable in the First, while City were heading for Division Two.

Immediately following the end of the 1925-6 season, it was difficult for City supporters to look forward to the future. True, the appointment of Peter Hodge seemed the right one, but with City in the Second Division and United in the First few could feel much enthusiasm.

The General Strike hardly helped. It started at midnight on Monday 3rd May, just two days after City's last game, and caused much tension, friction, and hardship throughout the country until it ended about ten days later. Some disputes continued throughout the Summer, most notably in the coal mining industry, but gradually life returned to normal.

On 31st July, Hodge made his first major signing when he brought forward Matthew Barrass to City from Sheffield Wednesday.

Exactly one week earlier Mancunians had been excited by another sporting first for the city when the country's first greyhound racing track opened at Belle Vue. The Belle Vue stadium was built on a site many believed to have been considered, in addition to the Belle Vue Athletics ground, by the City management when they were planning to relocate from Hyde Road. It remains in use today for greyhound racing and since the late 1980s for speedway, and is the only surviving part of the original Belle Vue pleasure gardens.

In addition to the Barrass transfer, Hodge did change his personnel further. Stalwart 36 year old Eli Fletcher joined Watford in June as player-manager after 15 years with the Blues, while it was obvious Hodge believed Tommy 'Boy' Browell's time at Maine Road had now come to an end. At the age of 34 Browell was no longer a lad and, despite an excellent effort during the Cup final, it was felt he was no longer the deadly attacking player required.

Browell was left out of the team when the new season opened on 28th August - three days before Lancashire C.C.C won the County Championship for the first time since 1904 - with the visit of Fulham. Barrass started his City career perfectly with a goal on his debut while Austin, Roberts, and Hicks raised the score to 4-2 before a reported 40,000 crowd. City remained undefeated for the next four games before a 1-0 defeat at Reading on 18th September caused a little panic.

Three days before the Reading fixture, Tommy Browell was transferred to Blackpool for £1,500, where he continued to play until 1930.

After the Reading defeat, a few high scoring victories and draws followed as the Blues began to challenge for promotion. As with the previous season, City were scoring plenty of goals as 35 came in their first 13 matches. They were also well supported and continued to attract significantly bigger crowds than Manchester United in the First Division.

Opposite:
Jimmy McMullan leads City out to face Fulham at Maine Road on 28th August 1926 - City's first game back in Division Two. A 40,000 crowd saw the Blues win 4-2 with goals from Austin, Barrass, Roberts and Hicks.

In January 1999, 80-year-old Canadian based City supporter John Berridge contacted Gary James after seeing this photo. According to John the small child leaning over the right wall of the tunnel wearing a woollen hat is he, and his parents are the couple stood fractionally behind and to the right of the child. By chance John's daughter purchased a copy of the first edition of this book on a rare visit to Manchester, and gave it to her father for Christmas 1998.

A BRILLIANT FAILURE.

Wonderful Football and an Amazing Crop of Goals That Was Just One Short: By THE PILGRIM.

WONDERFUL and tragic. Those are the only words that can adequately describe the thrilling finale at Maine-road. It was a game that will never be forgotten.

I have been watching football for many years, but I can recall nothing to equal it. The atmosphere was electric. There were over 50,000 spectators present, and the one concern was how many goals Manchester City would get.

There was never any questioning their ability to win.

EARLY THRILLS

*Manchester City..8 Bradford City......0

Everyone by now had made certain that the City were "in," but still the crowd clamoured for goals, and the players continued to respond. Boot performed wonders, and Roberts, Broadhurst and Johnson must have marvelled at his skill, but for a seventh time he was beaten from a penalty kick after Broadhurst had been tripped up as he was dashing through, and with the last kick of the match the young centre-

Joy was turned to a disappointment that could be felt, but everyone's sympathy was extended to the players and the club. Never has there been such a cruel blow of fate in the history of the League.

More than once has goal average decided the promotion race, but never has there been a finer fight than this, and never has a club had such a distressing experience as the City. To lose their position in the First Division by their failure to convert a penalty kick in their concluding match one season,

Headlines from the tightest promotion race ever. Despite scoring eight, City missed out on promotion by a goal on 7th May 1927. City's goal average was 1.7705, Portsmouth's was 1.7755.

At Christmas the Blues faced promotion challengers Middlesbrough home and away on consecutive days. On Christmas Day they suffered a 5-3 Maine Road defeat, with George Camsell scoring all the visitors goals, while on Boxing Day Frank Roberts supplied a consolation as City went down 2-1. These were significant results as Middlesbrough were in outstanding form and eventually became deserved champions. If City had been able to upset them at Christmas the two sides fortunes may have changed. As it was City needed to achieve some decent results throughout the early part of 1927 to maintain a challenge for second spot.

The following game, a New Year's day 2-1 defeat at Portsmouth, was also significant as Pompey were another side destined to play a part in the promotion race. It was also significant as it was the last match to feature Jim Goodchild. Although he remained with the club until August, he was never likely to appear again once City bought Oldham's Welsh international Bert Gray for £2,250. In August, at the age of 35, Goodchild moved back to the Southampton area to become licensee of the Royal Albert Hotel. He also played a couple of seasons for Guildford City. In 1941 he took over the Cricketers Arms in Eastleigh, before passing away in October 1950 at the age of 58. Though his City career was lengthy, he never quite obtained the honours he deserved. His F.A. Cup finalists' medal should have been accompanied by rather more.

As the season progressed City notched up several high scores, with Bert Gray attempting to keep down the number conceded. The best result had to be the 7-0 thrashing of strugglers Darlington on 18th April. A crowd of around forty thousand watched that game as the Blues nudged closer to promotion. Sadly, Portsmouth also kept up the chase and by the last Saturday of the season both sides were level on 52 points, while Middlesbrough were already certain of the title. Importantly, Portsmouth had the better goal average (82 for and 48 against, with an average of 1.708 as opposed to City's 100 for, 61 against at an average of 1.639).

City's final game was at home to bottom club Bradford City, while Preston travelled to Portsmouth. On a beautiful, warm Manchester day City seemed easily capable of destroying Bradford and within six minutes, backed by a noisy 50,000 crowd, the Blues took the lead through Bell. Ten minutes later Johnson provided a second. By this time the crowd were noisier than ever as news filtered through of the Portsmouth-Preston game which kicked off fifteen minutes later.

Before City could score again, the *Athletic News* noted that tremendous cheering came from City's vast terracing. On investigation, their reporter discovered that Preston had taken the lead at Portsmouth. Then with thirty minutes gone Hicks 'coolly and deliberately' placed the ball into the net for the Blues' third.

The atmosphere was incredible, yet somehow the players remained cool. Seven minutes into the second half Broadhurst provided the fourth via a fine long range shot. A further six minutes later Roberts made it five, then in the 66th minute it was six thanks to Johnson. Everyone now believed City were home and dry, although there appeared to be confused messages coming from the south coast.

In the 81st minute Johnson completed his hat-trick with a penalty, awarded after Broadhurst was tripped as he dashed into the box, and in the final minute of the match Broadhurst made the total eight. Seconds later the whistle sounded and supporters surged onto the pitch to greet their City heroes. The police helped make a path for the players back to the dressing room as fans congratulated them on "getting back", as the *Athletic News* put it.

As the celebrations continued - the band started playing 'Auld Lang Syne' - news came through that Portsmouth were winning, although nobody seemed to know by how much. To be honest few really cared because, unless you were a skilled mathematician, you were unlikely to work out the goal average and, in any case, surely 8-0 gave City a superb chance, didn't it? The answer was that Portsmouth now needed to win their game 5-1, and with those vital fifteen minutes play they had the opportunity to control their own destiny, especially as they were now leading 4-1.

In the 78th minute City's joy turned to sadness as Willie Haines scored his fourth and Portsmouth's fifth. Twelve minutes later the directors were informed via ticker-tape that it was all over. Portsmouth were promoted by the narrowest goal average margin in history. Their average equalled 1.7755, while City's was 1.7705. One more City goal would have given the Blues that vital second promotion spot. Bradford's 'keeper Boot was acclaimed the star of the Maine Road match after pulling off a string of saves, any one of which could have provided City with the goal they had so desperately needed.

Everybody at Maine Road was disappointed. It was a terrible blow. The *Athletic News* felt City had suffered more than most: "Joy was turned to a disappointment that could be felt, but everyone's sympathy was extended to the players and the club. Never has there been such a cruel blow of fate in the history of the League.

"More than once has goal average decided the promotion race, but never has there been a finer fight than this, and never has a club had such a distressing experience as the City. To lose their position in the First Division by their failure to convert a penalty kick in their concluding match one season, and miss promotion by such a slender margin the next, after running up such a score, is without parallel. Another goal would have done it."

Although it's irrelevant now, it's worth noting that had goal difference, rather than average, been the deciding factor then City would have been promoted as their difference was significantly better than Portsmouth's. As it was, the Blues had to pick themselves up and look forward to the next season.

They started the 1927-8 season in determined mood. The annual public practice match on 20th August ended with the first XI defeating the reserves 9-2. Roberts scored five, Broadhurst three and Johnson netted the other. They followed this up with only one defeat in their opening nine League matches, as they endeavoured to ensure promotion. Both games against fellow challengers Leeds ended in Blue victory, while a good away performance against challengers Chelsea, in March, helped City keep control. City lost the services of Bert Gray for a little while in January and February following the third round cup tie with Leeds. Gray had broken a cheek bone after about thirty minutes and was replaced by winger Billy Austin, who managed to keep Leeds from scoring on a few occasions as the Blues won 1-0. In the next round they overcame Sunderland 2-1, but Stoke surprised City 1-0 in the fifth round.

While still scoring plenty of goals, Hodge decided to increase his firepower further by signing two Barnsley forwards, Eric Brook and Fred Tilson for a combined fee of £6,000. Brook was a roaming, unorthodox outside left who was able to play virtually anywhere, and combined perfectly with Tilson. The two men made their debuts, alongside another newcomer - right winger Alf Horne - in a 2-0 win against Grimsby Town on 17th March. Another newcomer to the line-up was Bobby Marshall, who had made his debut two games earlier after signing from Sunderland in March 1928. Marshall started his City career as an inside forward, but a few years later would forge effectively another career at centre-half.

A City team line-up from the 1927-28 season - interestingly this eleven never appeared together in the League or the Cup, although they did all make at least five appearances in the League. Back (left to right): Pringle, Bennett, Cookson, Gray, McCloy, A Bell (Trainer), Broadhurst. Front: P Bell, Roberts, McMullan, Johnson, Hicks, Cowan.

He possessed brilliant ball control, and in his inaugural season scored a total of seven goals in only fourteen appearances.

Brook, Tilson and Marshall would help form the successful City side that would dominate Manchester football for the next decade.

With considerable firepower the Blues once again scored a century of goals, although this time they managed to keep the number conceded down to 59. Not a great deal less than the previous year, but their points tally had increased by five. For the fourth time in their history City achieved promotion as champions. They deserved it, as did City's loyal support which had reached an average of around 38,000. An incredible figure at this point in football's history, and one which gave the Blues the largest following in the League. Not bad for a Second Division side.

Eric Brook (above), Fred Tilson (below) and Bobby Marshall (bottom) - three important signings.

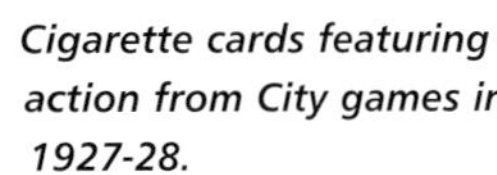

Cigarette cards featuring action from City games in 1927-28.

Left: Swansea Town's Deacon is seen dribbling past Cookson and McCloy in a Maine Road fixture which finished 7-4 in City's favour.

Below: City 'keeper Barber punches clear in the Lancashire Senior Cup Final against Bury at Old Trafford.

1927-28 DIVISION TWO CHAMPIONSHIP DETAILS

RESULTS	HOME	AWAY
Wolverhampton W	W 3-0	D 2-2
Swansea Town	W 7-4	L 3-5
Port Vale	W 1-0	W 2-1
South Shields	W 3-0	W 1-0
Leeds United	W 2-1	W 1-0
Nottingham Forest	D 3-3	W 5-4
Oldham Athletic	W 3-1	L 2-3
Hull City	W 2-1	D 0-0
Preston North End	D 2-2	L 0-1
Blackpool	W 4-1	D 2-2
Reading	W 4-1	D 1-1
Grimsby Town	W 2-0	L 1-4
Chelsea	L 0-1	W 1-0
Clapton Orient	W 5-3	W 2-0
Stoke City	W 4-0	L 0-2
Bristol City	W 4-2	L 0-2
West Bromwich Albion	W 3-1	D 1-1
Southampton	W 6-1	D 1-1
Notts County	W 3-1	L 1-2
Barnsley	W 7-3	W 3-0
Fulham	W 2-1	D 1-1

REGULAR SIDE:

Gray
Ridley
McCloy
Pringle
Cowan
McMullan
Austin or Bell
Roberts or Barrass
Broadhurst
Johnson
Hicks

MANAGER:

Peter Hodge

Phil McCloy (right) made 38 appearances for the Champions.

LARGEST VICTORY: 7-3 V Barnsley (H) 2/1/28

LARGEST WINNING MARGIN: 6-1 V Southampton (H) 28/4/28

HEAVIEST DEFEAT: 1-4 V Grimsby Town (A) 5/11/27

AVERAGE HOME ATTENDANCE: c.37,300

HIGHEST HOME ATTENDANCE: c.60,000 V Preston North End 25/2/28, V Fulham 6/4/28

HIGHEST AWAY ATTENDANCE: 51,813 V Chelsea 24/3/28

LEAGUE APPEARANCES: 38 McCloy, McMullan, 35 Johnson, 32 Gray, 30 Ridley, 28 Cowan, Barrass, Hicks, 26 Roberts, 22 Pringle, 21 Broadhurst, 18 Austin, 16 Bell, 14 Marshall, 12 Brook, 11 Sharp, Cookson, 10 Barber, 7 Horne, Tait, 6 Allen, Tilson, 5 Bennett, 4 Gibbons, 3 Foster, 2 Smelt, Robertson, 1 Appleton, Gorringe

LEAGUE GOALS: 20 Roberts, 19 Johnson, 14 Broadhurst, 10 Hicks, 9 Austin, 7 Marshall, 4 McMullan, Tait, 3 Bell, 2 Barrass, Brook, Horne, Gorringe, 1 Allen, Smelt.

Jimmy McMullan was probably the greatest Scottish half-back of his era and captained his national side to a famous 5-1 victory over England at Wembley in 1928.

JAMES McMULLAN
MANCHESTER CITY

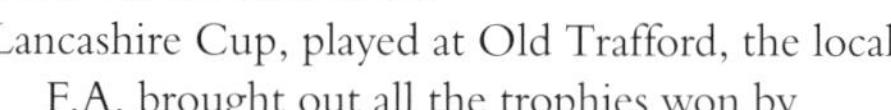

1927-8 was also a successful season in other competitions as the Blues defeated Bury 3-1 in the Lancashire Cup Final, and United 4-2 in the Manchester Cup Final. At the final of the Lancashire Cup, played at Old Trafford, the local F.A. brought out all the trophies won by Lancastrian clubs that season. There was the F.A. Cup (Blackburn Rovers), the League Championship (Everton), the Second Division Championship Shield (City), and the Lancashire Cup itself. City Chairman Lawrence Furniss, associated with the club since the early 1880s, proudly posed for photographs with the trophies and directors of the other clubs.

Before the end of the Lancashire Cup Final, City supporters in the crowd of 23,460 moved around Old Trafford and headed for the area closest to the players tunnel to see the trophy presented. Even with the game still in progress, some supporters ran across the pitch to find the perfect spot. When the referee ended the game, hundreds more invaded the pitch forcing the players to push their way through the dense crowd. Once the team were all safely off the pitch the presentation was made. The gate receipts for the final amounted to £1,365 10s. Not quite as large as when City defeated Bolton in 1921 (£1,640 11s), but it was the second highest figure at the time. The competition, considering the strength of Lancashire football at the time, was an important one.

City chairman Lawrence Furniss (centre) stands proudly behind the Second Division Shield at the 1928 Lancashire Cup Final in which City beat Bury 3-1 at Old Trafford. The Lancashire F.A. showed off all of the major trophies won by its clubs during the season, with the League Championship trophy (Everton) and FA Cup (Blackburn) to the left of City's prize and the Lancashire Cup to the right.

A crowd of over 61,000 watched the first derby since City's 6-1 thrashing of the Reds in 1926. Above: Steward punches clear while Tommy Johnson applies the pressure.

Below: The cover of City's 'Blue and White' programme for the 4-1 victory over Arsenal in September 1928.

THE BIG JUMBO
BREWED FROM THE FINEST MALT —AND CHOICEST HOPS ONLY—
7d. Per Bottle
Obtainable from all the Licensed Houses of
THE PALATINE BOTTLING COMPANY LIMITED
ROYAL BREWERY, MOSS SIDE, MANCHESTER.

MANCHESTER CITY F.C. LTD.
BLUE AND WHITE
OFFICIAL PROGRAMME
Vol 23. No. 5. SEPTEMBER 22nd, 1928. (Entered at Stationers' Hall) TWOPENCE

MANCHESTER AND SALFORD
SAVINGS BANK.
(ESTABLISHED JANUARY 1818) (CERTIFIED UNDER THE ACT OF 1863)
ABSOLUTE SECURITY STRICT SECRECY.
BE THRIFTY
SAVE IN SAFETY
[illegible]
Over 180,700 Depositors with Funds Exceeding £10,000,000
SUMS OF ONE SHILLING AND UPWARDS RECEIVED.
RATE OF INTEREST ALLOWED £2 : 10 : 0 AND £4 : 0 : 0 per cent.
HEAD OFFICE:
BOOTH STREET AND KENNEDY STREET, (with 15 Branches in Manchester and District.)
The nearest Branches to this Ground:—
74, ALEXANDRA ROAD, MOSS SIDE; 25, WILMSLOW ROAD, RUSHOLME.
BANK HOURS, 10 to 3. SATURDAYS, 10 to 12.30.
MONDAY Evenings, 6 to 8. FRIDAY Evenings, 6 to 8.

Despite the success of the previous season, 1928-9 was always going to be a testing one for Peter Hodge. He had introduced a number of players towards the end of the previous campaign and was still, very much, trying to build a side for the future. The opening game - a 4-1 defeat at Birmingham - gave Hodge a few headaches. For the following encounter, the Maine Road derby, Hodge made only one change to his line-up, selecting Frank Roberts instead of centre-forward Tommy Tait, signed the previous March.

Roberts put City ahead with a subtle but swift shot, in a game where United still seemed unable to come to terms with the relatively new offside law. Nevertheless, United did manage to gain the lead by half-time. Such a turnaround surprised many as City seemed to have most of the play, but their firepower was seriously lacking. In the second half, Tommy Johnson provided City's equalising goal, before a crowd of 61,007.

A run of good results throughout September gave City fans much to cheer - especially the 6-2 defeat of reigning champions Everton at Goodison. Tommy Johnson scored five that day. A feat the Everton directors would remember when the time came to look for a player to support 'Dixie' Dean.

Johnson was idolised by the supporters. Harry Hughes, who lived near Johnson in Gorton, remembers that although he was often seen in the Gorton area, he wasn't one for talking about his football: "He lived in Park Avenue, the first house on the right, near Sunny Brow Park. I used to see him quite regularly pushing a pram and, if they'd be playing on the Saturday, he'd be pushing the pram in the morning all around the neighbourhood. You'd all go 'Hello, Tom', and he'd nod his head, and you'd then tell everyone that Tom speaks to you, y'know. Anyway, he was very dignified and always wore a big brimmed trilby - it quickly became very fashionable then! And he always walked with a very deliberate stride, pushing the pram. There was a billiard hall on Hyde Road and he used to go in there and get involved with the wrong set - bookies and the like - but it never really affected him. Never dishonest or anything like that. But they were a real rum lot these 'Smiths' I think they were called. Every time he went into the billiard hall they'd give him the best table out of the 30 odd there, and we used to go in after work just to watch. Learn a few shots and that.

"Then he'd go in the Plough Hotel on Hyde Road, which I also patronised at times. But unlike me, he never had to buy his own beer. All the toadies would buy it, they'd ask him what he was having and he always replied 'I'll have a draught Bass - a pint'. It was the best, most expensive beer in the house! They would ask him his prediction for the City game, and he always said 'I think we'll lose!' That was his stock answer, as if to say 'shut up, I don't want to talk about football'.

"I never ever mentioned football to him. I'd speak with him occasionally. Usually I'd chat with him at the bank - I was always drawing out, he was always paying in!"

With Johnson in fine scoring form, despite his regular pints of draught Bass, the Blues continued to win more than they lost, but the season was never going to see the club challenge. In the Cup City were defeated 3-1 in the third round at Birmingham,

A 1928-29 Season Ticket for the Maine Road Grand Stand (latter day Main Stand) - for 'Ladies or Boys'!

Right: Ernie Toseland, a debutant in the 2-1 defeat of Bury on 20th April 1929. He made a total of 409 first team appearances with the Blues over a 10 year period.

Cartoon (right): Jackie Bray, who made his debut in the 40th Manchester League derby, played on 8th February 1930.

thereby ending any chance of glory in that competition.

At the season's end City finished in a creditable eighth place after an unbeaten run in their final eight games. They had also won the Manchester Cup again, this time defeating Bolton 2-0. Hodge had changed the side a few times during the season, with Bert Gray replaced in goal by Lewis Barber, signed from Halifax Town on 6th June 1927. New signings Billy Felton, a full back from Sheffield Wednesday, and Ernie Toseland, a winger from Coventry, were both regulars by the season's close.

Tommy Johnson's record of 38 League goals that season remains the highest from any City player in a single campaign. During the early part of the 1929-30 season, Johnson again shone. Especially in the annual defeat of United at Old Trafford where he scored the first and should have scored the fourth had the referee not blown for time a second before the ball crossed the line. Nevertheless City's 3-1 October victory again proved who were quite clearly the dominant side as City climbed up the table.

A few weeks after the derby a young Scottish player named Matt Busby made his debut. Busby was about to emigrate with his mother to the USA when Peter Hodge persuaded him to sign for the Blues in February 1928. His debut, against Middlesbrough, was the first of eleven appearances that season. Signed as an inside forward, over the course of the next couple of years City would convert him to a stylish half-back.

Fine results followed the October derby, with City moving gradually up the table. They also progressed to the fifth round of the cup after victories over Tottenham (4-1), and Swindon (10-1). Both games had followed drawn matches. The week before the fifth round tie with Hull, the Blues suffered their first defeat in the Manchester derby since October 1921 after an absolutely dire performance. City's captain Jimmy McMullan had been boasting for some time that the moment was right for the Blues to win the double, but with an embarrassing 1-0 defeat to lowly United the *Athletic News*' Ivan Sharpe laughed off all talk of the double. He did not believe City good enough for the title, nor did he expect the Blues to overcome Hull if they played at the miserable level of the derby game.

The comments hurt, but sadly they were true. In the game with Second Division strugglers Hull, City failed to perform and paid the price with a 2-1 home defeat before a loyal crowd of 61,574. City needed to pick themselves up if they had any ambition of challenging for the title.

In March, a few days after his appearance against Liverpool, Tommy Johnson was sold by Peter Hodge to Everton for £6,000. The move shocked and angered most supporters. Johnson had been the star for a decade and had broken all City's goalscoring records. Not only had he scored more goals in a season than any other player, he was also the club's highest overall goalscorer with 166 goals until Eric Brook surpassed him. Hodge tried to placate the fans by pointing out how Tommy Tait was in fine form, but they would have none of it.

Without Johnson, the Blues did achieve a few decent results in March and April, but really the damage had been done in February. City ended the season in third place, 13 points behind champions Sheffield Wednesday. That would normally have been satisfactory, but after the transfer of Johnson and the Cup failure supporters were disappointed.

The 1930-31 season did little to convince them that Hodge's transfer of Johnson had been sound, especially as Tait left for Bolton in November. Another forward, Fred Tilson, struggled with injury, and City failed to score the goals they were used to. In fact the final tally of 75 helped fuel criticism. Eric Brook, on the wing was the season's top scorer with sixteen, while David Halliday, a November signing from Arsenal, was second after scoring fourteen.

The high points of the campaign came in the two games with lowly United, when the Blues achieved a 4-1 victory at Maine Road and a 3-1 win at Old Trafford.

City's Late Late Show

On 15th September 1928 City arrived late at Goodison Park for the fifth match of the season. The train from Manchester Central station had been delayed by nine minutes, and further problems during the journey resulted in the train arriving 30 minutes late at Liverpool. According to the Athletic News the players made arrangements to change while on the train, then piled into taxis and made their way to Goodison. City's problems didn't end there as the taxis found it difficult getting through the crowd. Eventually, the Blues made it and the game kicked off four minutes late.

In the first minute Everton took the lead then, before half time City equalised. In the second half, an amazing goal avalanche resulted in City winning 6-2 with Johnson scoring five. Understandably, the F.A. investigated City's reasons for being late and insisted the Blues pay a fine. Nevertheless, it had been a remarkable day for Manchester.

Matt Busby made his debut in the 3-1 defeat of Middlesbrough on 2nd November 1929. Around this time a council official found it difficult understanding the Scotsman's accent and recorded his occupation as 'Fruit Boiler' instead of footballer!

United were eventually relegated, but that was only part of the problem as their financial situation was dire, prompting many to suggest the February derby match might be the last ever as United were to go out of business in the summer. Crowds were down to pitiful levels with games against Leicester and Middlesbrough attracting less than four thousand. City supporters felt genuinely sorry for their poor

New Year's Day 1930... The greatest football match ever?

City supporter Joe Carley wrote a diary throughout his life and always maintained the City v Sheffield Wednesday meeting, watched by 54,516 at Maine Road on New Year's Day 1930, was the greatest match ever. Obviously, there are many other contenders but to understand why, his diary entry, reproduced from "Old Friends, Old Times", is included here.

I remember telling my father after the game that I had never seen a better one, and I don't believe I ever shall. Years later, Ernie Blenkinsop, famous Wednesday full-back, wrote his life story in 'Topical Times' and mentioned this particular game as the finest he had ever been in.

The pitch was ankle deep in thick mud and, as I watched cameramen gingerly picking their way across it prior to the players' entry, I guessed we would see a real mud-larking match. All the players were roughly at the peak of their careers. CITY: Barber; Ridley and Felton; Barrass, Cowan and McMullan; Toseland, Marshall, Tait, Johnson and Brook. WEDNESDAY: Brown; Walker and Blenkinsop; Strange, Leach and Marsden; Hooper, Seed, Allen, Burgess and Rimmer.

The game was played at a great pace, but there was only one foul, committed by Seed on McMullan. The players shook hands self-consciously, and no more was the referee worried by 'dirty' play. The players waded through that mud with good open play, switching the point of their attacks about with great ingenuity and bringing their wing-men continually into action. Thrust and counter-thrust. Skill versus skill. I'm sure many of the spectators must have been quite hoarse before one quarter of the match had run its course.

The speed with which the moves were made on that churned-up mud heap was amazing. Wednesday were the first to draw blood, Allen galloping through to score with a great drive taken on the run. Then came the incident which caused much controversy at the time. McMullan had run through in his own inimitable fashion, shaped to pass out to Brook, and as Walker swerved to intercept the 'pass', Jimmy calmly flicked the ball inwards for Tait to race through and smash into the net as Brown came out and flung himself at the centre-forward's feet. "GOAL!" The crowd's yell was changed to one of indignation as the referee disallowed it on the grounds of offside against Tait.

Brown was still lying face downwards after his vain attempt to prevent Tait from shooting, and when the players picked him up his face was a mass of blood where Tait's boot had evidently caught the goalkeeper's head as the ball was driven home. A stretcher was summoned, a bandage tied round the unconscious goalkeeper's forehead, and Blenkinsop went into goal. As the stretcher party approached the stand, Brown recovered, looked feebly around, sat up, slipped off the stretcher, and before anyone could stop him he was ambling back to his goal. He staggered like a drunken man, obviously hurt and weak, but he insisted on playing, and certainly helped to provide some further thrills in that hectic afternoon by his daring and clever goalkeeping.

Shortly before half time, Mark Hooper crossed a high ball for Rimmer to head over Ridley and past Barber into the far corner of the net. City's fans were dismayed, and in spite of the interesting, clever game, a little glum. Twenty minutes after the interval they were even more despondent, for Seed headed another great Hooper centre into the net from close range. 3-0! So the score stood when only 15 minutes of play remained. Then Bobby Marshall wiped off one of the arrears. Five minutes later, with about 8 Wednesday men crowded into their own penalty area, Walker handled the ball. Penalty! Eric Brook, the young City winger drove a powerful shot past Brown. 3-2. How the crowd yelled!

McMullan had the ball 18 yards from goal and at a bad angle; there was no City player suitably placed. In front of him half a dozen Wednesday players, almost shoulder to shoulder, barred the way. The wily Jimmy put his toe under the heavy, mud-laden ball and calmly lobbed it high over the heads of the astounded defenders to drop into the net by the far post! 3-3.

The roar when City equalised was great enough to waken my father from his afternoon nap at South Street! Not yet satisfied, City again swept down on the Wednesday defence while the referee looked meaningfully at his watch. Matt Barrass fired in a tremendous drive from 35 yards, knocking the bandaged Brown into the back of the net, but not before the goalkeeper managed to divert the ball over the crossbar. "Corner!" yelled the frenzied crowd. The corner kick was never taken; a long blast on the referee's whistle signalled the end of the game.

PROFIT AND LOSS ACCOUNT, Year ended 11th May, 1929.

	£ s. d.	£ s. d.
1929		
May 11 To Balance down		42548 18 5
		£42548 18 5

	£ s. d.	£ s
1928		
May 13 By Balance		41377 17 1
1929		
May 11 .. Cottage Rents	91 0 0	
.. Profit as per Revenue A/c.	1080 0 6	
		1171 0
		£42548 18
1929		
May 12 By Balance		£42548 18

BALANCE SHEET, 11th May, 1929.

LIABILITIES	£ s. d.	£ s. d.
Nominal Capital, 2,000 Shares £1 each	2000 0 0	
Subscribed Capital, 1,216 Shares £1 each fully paid	1216 0 0	
		1216 0 0
Forfeited Shares	23 2 6	
Unclaimed Dividends	58 2 8	
		81 5 2
Mortgages	75221 0 8	
		75221 0 8
Sundry Creditors and Income Tax Reserve	3236 5 10	
Bank Overdraft	2367 18 8	
		5604 4 6
Profit and Loss Account	42548 18 5	
		42548 18 5
		£124671 8 9

A. H. HUGHES, ROBT. SMITH } Directors

ASSETS	£ s d	£ s.
Stands, Fixtures, Ground Equipment, and Cottages as at 13th May, 1928	125612 17 9	
Addition	294 8 0	
	125907 5 9	
Less Depreciation	1500 0 0	
		124407 5
Stock, Players' Outfits, etc.	60 0 0	
Sundry Debtors	104 9 0	
Deposit Accounts, Telephone and Gas	23 0 0	
		187 9
Cash at Bank, Dividend Account	58 2 8	
Cash in hand	18 11 4	
		76 14
		£124671 8

Billy Dale made his debut on Boxing Day 1931 after joining City from United.

relations, but perhaps relegation would give United a new lease of life, as it had City.

Harry Hughes remembers the state of United at the time: "I worked in Trafford Park then, and all the locals were United fans. I was working nights and when Saturday morning arrived a couple of them asked 'are you going to see the Rags today?' I didn't know what they meant, and then they explained that United fans had started to call the team the 'Rags' because they were so poor that their kit looked like rags. So after that I knew who they meant, but when I mentioned the Rags, they'd go, 'who the Hell are you talking about?' They didn't like the opposition saying it."

City ended that season in eighth place. Although supporters may not have appreciated it at the time, Peter Hodge was actually taking the club in the right direction. The 1931-32 League programme was not an improvement on the last, but Hodge had been able to field a consistent eleven for much of the season. Len Langford, signed from Nottingham Forest in June 1930, was first choice 'keeper. Toseland, Marshall, Halliday, Tilson, and Brook provided the attack, while the young Matt Busby was now playing wing-half. A year earlier, United had tried to sign Busby. Peter Hodge is alleged to have told them 'Give me £150 and he's yours', but the reply came back that United didn't even have 150 pennies, never mind pounds, and so Busby continued to make a name for himself at Maine Road.

The Blues ended the League campaign in fourteenth position, but it was in the Cup where City's real hopes lay. In the third round at Millwall City, wearing scarlet shirts, conceded a first minute goal. Then two goals from David Halliday gave them the lead, but it wasn't to last as Millwall were awarded a rather dubious penalty. Naturally, they levelled and then in the dying seconds Ernie Toseland provided a vital last minute winner.

Brentford were the visitors in the fourth round when Fred Tilson scored a hat-trick in City's 6-1 demolition before 56,190. The Blues certainly knew how to pull in the crowds. In the next round Derby County arrived at Maine Road very confident, but were sent home smarting after suffering a 3-0 defeat at

Right: City 'keeper Langford is unable to prevent this goal at Bury in the FA Cup 6th Round in 1932. The Blues went on to win 4-3 and set up a semi-final meeting with Arsenal.

Sam Cowan (left) watches anxiously as Arsenal's David Jack challenges Langford in the FA Cup semi-final at Villa Park in 1932. Under the title of "A Golden Goal By Bastin" Pathe News filmed this match. This is believed to be the oldest City-Arsenal fixture on film. Arsenal won 1-0 with a last minute goal from Cliff Bastin.

the hands of Marshall (2) and Brook. Again the crowd was huge - 62,641 - as City maintained their reputation as one of England's best supported clubs.

The quarter-finals produced an all Lancashire tie with City forced to travel to Bury. The first half belonged to the Blues as the goals piled in, but shortly after half-time with the score 4-0, Bury fought back. Somehow City managed to hang on as Bury hauled the score to 4-3 and continued to pressure the City defence. Fortunately, the Blues survived and entered the semi-finals for the third time in eight years.

Their semi-final opponents were to be the mighty Arsenal at Villa Park. It was a game City dominated, yet failed to find the net. The Blues frequently surged forward but they just could not score, while Alex James provided Arsenal with their first chance of the game when his shot was cleared off the line by City defender Billy Felton. Sadly, Felton had a part to play in The Gunners' only other chance of the game when, in the last minute, their centre-forward Lambert took the ball from his feet and sent it across the goal.

The *Manchester Guardian* described what happened next: "Bastin shot, Langford fisted at the ball, it went straight up into the air, hit the cross-bar, dropped back on the line, bounced against the post - and even the spin was in Arsenal's favour, for it broke into instead of away from the net...Lambert and Bastin hugged each other like a family reunion...McMullan stood dumbfounded like some great engineer whose life's masterpiece had been demolished by a paroxysm of nature."

McMullan wasn't the only one left dumbfounded as the whole of the City team, and the supporters who had journeyed to Birmingham, were left shocked by what had occurred. Arsenal had been lucky - a tag that seemed to stick with the London club for most of the next three decades - and had not deserved their place at Wembley. Nevertheless City only had themselves to blame. Felton should not have allowed the ball to be taken from him so easily, while the forwards should have converted at least one of the many chances that came their way.

Unfortunately, after three years with the Blues, Felton was made the scapegoat and was transferred to Tottenham immediately, making his debut the following Saturday away at Swansea Town. After two years with Spurs he moved again to Altrincham, and died in the Manchester area on 22nd April 1977 at the age of 76.

Another man to leave around this time was Peter Hodge, who was tempted back to his old club Leicester City. Leicester were perilously close to relegation and offered Hodge a five year contract and an improved salary. Wilf Wild, the assistant at Maine Road since 1920, reluctantly took full control of team matters. He was an advocate of splitting the role into two - one purely secretarial/administration duties, the other team management. Though he never quite succeeded in dividing the role during his time in charge at Maine Road, he did move some of the administration away.

The 1932-3 season was expected to be a difficult one for Wild. Although the League programme continued much as the previous one had left off, with City as inconsistent as ever, the Cup was a different matter. Wild had worked closely with Hodge throughout the previous six years and knew what Hodge had been planning for the future. Many of Wild's early moves seemed to match those of his predecessor, and there was no serious rebuilding done immediately. However, Wild was his own man, and managed to work with the players to achieve a fine first season.

Eric Brook appeared for the Football League on seven occasions between 1929 and 1937.

City finished sixteenth in the League, but for the second year running it was the Cup that brought most joy to Manchester. In the third round away at Gateshead, City survived the mud to end the game 1-1 thanks to Toseland. The replay, the following Wednesday, banished all thoughts of failure as the Blues swept aside Gateshead 9-0. They'd been leading 8-0 after 63 minutes but, despite calls from the crowd for more, seemed happy to settle for single figures.

Round four brought Walsall to Maine Road to endure a 2-0 defeat thanks to Eric Brook, before 52,085 spectators. Then the fifth round draw sent City to old cup adversaries Bolton. A Burnden Park crowd of 69,920 witnessed a Brook hat-trick and a fourth from Tilson as the Blues overcame the Wanderers 4-2.

New signing Alec Herd, from Hamilton Academicals, was now appearing as an inside-forward. His arrival gave Wild several key players to select from and guaranteed competition for places.

The quarter-final draw sent the Blues on another trip across Lancashire, this time to Burnley where a single goal from Fred Tilson was enough to put City into the semi-final again. This time their opponents were hot favourites Derby County at Leeds Road before a crowd of almost 52,000. The first period was extremely difficult for City as Derby missed a couple of easy chances, while the Blues tried to find their feet.

After this City had the edge in a closely fought game. Eric Brook was the main architect providing the opportunity for the game's first two goals. He centred to right winger Toseland for the first and, in the second half, lobbed beautifully for Tilson to charge between two Derby defenders and head the second. Captain Jimmy McMullan, playing at inside-left to retain his place, provided the third by wriggling past two defenders and the 'keeper before shooting into the net in the 70th minute.

Within a minute Derby had caught Langford off his line, and pulled a goal back. The Rams now had the initiative and with three minutes remaining scored a second. City managed to hang on though, and the game ended 3-2, sending the Blues to Wembley for the second time in seven years.

Sam Cowan shakes hands with his Derby counterpart prior to the 1933 FA Cup semi-final at Leeds Road, Huddersfield. City won 3-2 with goals from McMullan, Tilson and Toseland.

An article highlighting the story that fans rushed to adopt City's Cup Final colours of red and white!

"RED AND WHITE" TRAIN

City Supporters in Good Form

EVERYTHING was red and white and nobody was blue on the 8.40 special from Manchester to Wembley.

Even the railway company had fallen for the prevailing fashion note, and labels each bearing a letter of the alphabet gummed to the windows of the saloon coaches to guide passengers to their reserved seats were—red and white.

One almost expected the guard to start the train with a red and white flag. There were rosettes by the hundred, the idea evidently being the bigger the rosette the better the cup final.

The trains was so long that its coaches reached far beyond the limits of number three platform at London Road.

The "seats reserved" labels on the coach windows told their own story of desks deserted in Manchester to-day.

MANY PARTIES

There were parties from many well-known city firms, parties organised by doctors, club secretaries, hotel landlords, departmental managers and there were even policemen who had a day off in hand.

The most picturesque figures on the train were a man arrayed in a red and white kimono and his followers all of whom wore grosteque bowler hats.

In the centre of the train was a kitchen car where an army of chefs and stewards was hard at work.

"Eat," said one of the stewards in reply to the *Manchester Evening News* query. "Most of them will order grub,

Full story of the game up to the time of going to press on Back Page.

but no one will eat much, I'm afraid. They're all too excited."

When at last the guard blew his whistle there was a tremendous scramble to get aboard.

On the way down the train stopped at Stockport and Wilmslow where further beribboned contingents of finalists were picked up amid much shouting and excitement.

Even Manchester Town Hall felt the lure of the Cup Final.

The Lord Mayor (Alderman Walker) had gone to Wembley by special invitation and there were significantly empty chairs in other departments.

Corridors told their own story and attendants tactfully whispered to inquirers that many councillors were in London.

City's opponents would be Everton, who overcame West Ham 2-1 at Molineux. The Blues were determined to bring the cup back to Manchester but everybody knew it was going to be a tough task, especially as Everton had a number of famous, star players - Sagar, Cresswell, Britton, Geldard, Dean, and of course the former City hero Tommy Johnson. Still, City were capable of good performances and at Wembley the two sides would start as equals for the first ever cup tie between them.

Before the final the question of team colours had to be addressed as both sides traditionally wore blue. In the end both sides changed - Everton wore white while City chose maroon. City's choice of colour seemed to encourage their supporters who donned red and white hats and scarves. In fact one newspaper commented on the dominance of the colour on the railway specials heading off to Wembley. Ever since the cup run of 1924, and potentially before that, City seemed to adopt maroon or scarlet as their change strip - a tradition that has continued, in the main, through to the end of the millennium. Unlike United, who in the early to mid-thirties experimented with a home kit of cherry and white hoops, City have been fairly consistent with both their home and away kit choices. The home shirt has been sky blue since the early 1890s, possibly earlier. In the sixties City adopted red and black stripes away for a while, and in the '70s various strips were tried, but overall maroon has dominated City's second choice.

FA Cup Finalists 1933

On the morning of the final Wilf Wild, after consultation with Chairman Albert Hughes and Dr. Holmes, shocked supporters and the media by announcing Fred Tilson was to be dropped from the side. Tilson had been suffering from a mysterious injury to a leg nerve and, although he passed a fitness test, the doctor noticed him wince when his leg was touched in a certain place. Much to the annoyance of the other players, Wild decided he could not risk the centre-forward and so brought Bobby Marshall in at inside-right and moved Herd into the centre.

From a spectators point of view, one spot of good cheer came when the morning's papers announced that the Wembley caterers had altered their menu to take account of the fact there would be so many Lancastrians in attendance. A spokesman stated that people from the south of England prefer sandwiches, while those from the north prefer meat pies, therefore Wembley had increased their order of pies from 14,000 to 17,000, while the number of sandwiches had been reduced in proportion. With meat pies in their hands, both sets of supporters eagerly awaited the arrival of the two teams.

City captain Sam Cowan led out his side alongside Dixie Dean of Everton and, together with Jimmy McMullan, spent much of his time trying to calm the nerves of the other City men. The sides were lined up and

Left: All roads lead south as City and Everton fans head for Wembley.

Above: The Lancastrian visitors to London flock to watch the Changing of the Guard on Cup Final morning.

Below: Hundreds of neatly parked cars and coaches outside the great stadium.

presented to the Duke of York, who was deputising for his ill father. Interestingly, accompanying the Duke for her first final was his wife, Elizabeth, mother of Queen Elizabeth II, who also attended the 1981 Cup Final.

Within fifteen seconds of the start, City made the first assault as a high centre was caught by the Everton 'keeper Ted Sagar. The save seemed to settle Everton while City seemed to suffer stage fright just as they had in the opening period seven years earlier. Cowan and McMullan tried to steady things, but it was difficult, especially as Cowan began to take on too much. The *Daily Mail* noted that: "He was torn between a determination not to leave Dean and a desire to help his forwards. He broke down between the two."

Langford, in the City goal, was also struggling - first with nerves, then with the strong sunlight. Every time a high ball came across he appeared blinded by the sun. Corner-kicks brought most concern, especially when Everton realised his predicament. After forty minutes a long centre from Britton forced Langford to look skyward. With Dean close in attendance the City 'keeper tried to keep one eye on the ball and one on the bustling forward. Langford missed the ball, as Dean threatened to charge, and the ball landed at Stein's feet. The Everton man simply tapped it in.

Seven minutes after the interval, a similar move caught Langford out again. Britton lobbed the ball

Above: Shirt numbers were worn at a Cup Final for the very first time in 1933 and City players were allocated 12 to 22. Langford, the City 'keeper, is wearing 22.

Right: Matt Busby is introduced to the Duke of York before the game.

Below: Wembley from the air on Cup Final day in 1933 as the teams line up for the pre-match formalities.

into the centre, Langford again considered Dean and the ball. As he tried to catch it below the crossbar, Dean barged into him and both players and the ball ended up in the net. Everton were 2-0 up, and City seemed totally out of it.

Ten minutes from time Everton's Geldard placed a corner kick perfectly for Dunn to head a spectacular third goal.

City did have a few exciting moments of their own, but in reality were never really in the game. Langford made a few saves - it could easily have been four or more - while City's defence failed to help their under pressure 'keeper. The *Daily Mail* gave a truthful assessment of half the City side: "Cann's efforts were of a negative kind, his kicking a matter of wild conjecture. Dale was more timely in his tackles, but he and his partner had no understanding, and their work was flurried and hesitating.

"Busby made a man's job of it at right half. Cowan was too ambitious and attempted too much. Toseland clung to the idea of following the touchline and the cool and calculating Cresswell was never at a loss in dealing with him. Brook strove in spasms - very good work in making ground, unaccountable lapses in finishing."

And so it was Dixie Dean who went up to receive the Cup from the Duke of York, while the optimistic Sam Cowan started telling anybody who cared to listen that City would be back the following year to win the Cup. He had to tell the players and management something as the whole squad was devastated by what had occurred. *The Daily Mail* reporter noticed: "As Dean triumphantly held the Cup aloft for all to see, a little knot of men moved slowly, almost disconsolately, across the turf not fifty yards away from the celebrations. They were the Manchester players.

Above: Rival captains Sam Cowan (left) and Dixie Dean shake hands before the 1933 Cup Final.

Left: City goalkeeper Langford defends a first-half Everton corner at Wembley. McMullan (13) and Cowan are the other visible City players in the foreground.

Below: Billy Dale's FA Cup runners-up medal.

1933 FA CUP RUN

R3	Gateshead	A	D	1-1
	Gateshead	H	W	9-0
R4	Walsall	H	W	2-0
R5	Bolton Wanderers	A	W	4-2
R6	Burnley	A	W	1-0
SF	Derby County	N*	W	3-2
F	Everton	N**	L	0-3

* = Leeds Road, Huddersfield
** = Wembley Stadium

FACTS & FIGURES

	P	W	D	L	F	A
HOME	2	2	0	0	11	0
AWAY	5	3	1	1	9	8
TOTAL	7	5	1	1	20	8

CUP FINAL DETAILS

29 April 1933 at Wembley Stadium
EVERTON 3 MANCHESTER CITY 0

CITY: Langford, Cann, Dale, Busby, Cowan, Bray, Toseland, Marshall, Herd, McMullan, Brook
EVERTON: Sagar, Cook, Cresswell, Britton, White, Thomson, Geldard, Dunn, Dean, Johnson, Stein
GOALS: Stein, Dean, Dunn

ATTENDANCE: 92,950
REFEREE: E. Wood (Sheffield)
GUEST OF HONOUR: The Duke of York
MANAGER: Wilf Wild
CAPTAIN: Sam Cowan

"Not for them the cheers and fetings and a line writ large in the record books. Only the torturing thoughts of the Might-Have Been. Watching them, it was impossible to avoid asking two questions: What was the cause of Manchester's complete inability to reproduce more than a shadow of the form that had earned them the right to play at Wembley? When are we to see real football in a Cup Final?

"The answer to the first question is Nerves. Wembley gripped and shook Manchester City - as it has done other teams - and reduced them to impotence. Only when - and if - these Cup Final Nerves can be eradicated can there be a hope of playing real football at Wembley."

Sam Cowan's thoughts had already moved forward a year, and the time was now right for all connected with City to learn from their mistakes. If they could find a way of overcoming their nerves, then maybe the *Daily Mail* would see real football played by a classy team. City wanted another chance.

Everton's Ted Sagar punches clear as Alec Herd attacks.

Right: Len Langford, blinded by the sun, misjudges the ball under pressure from Dixie Dean, allowing Jack Stein (out of picture) to tap into an empty net and give Everton the lead.

Below: Dixie Dean scores Everton's second after knocking both the ball and Langford to the ground.

Chapter Nine

THE CHAMPIONSHIP ARRIVES

1933 1937

SAM COWAN's remarks that City would be back to win the Cup seemed to give the club a little lift in the months following Wembley. Probably exactly what he intended, but it is doubtful whether he really expected the 1933-4 season to be significantly better than the last. In the League, City achieved fifth place, while the Cup run not only took them to Wembley, but saw the club break many attendance records.

The League programme commenced with a disappointing 3-2 defeat at home to Sheffield Wednesday. Although still with the club, full back Syd Cann had been replaced by Laurie Barnett, who had made infrequent appearances since Wild took control of the team. Matt Busby's uncle, Jimmy McMullan, had taken the opportunity to move to Oldham as player-manager following the 1933 Cup Final. He had been in tears at the final whistle, realising that after over seven years with the Blues, his City career would end as it began with a loser's medal at Wembley. Immediately on moving to Oldham he signed goalkeeper Fred Swift, elder brother of a young man called Frank waiting for his chance at Maine Road.

Eighteen year old Frank Swift's City chance came at Christmas, following a rather surprising 8-0 thrashing at Wolves. Wilf Wild telephoned him on Christmas Eve and told the young 'keeper he was to keep goal away to Derby the following day. Amazingly, Swift was not even a regular in the reserves at this point, spending most of his time as City's A team 'keeper. The result of his debut game was not a great deal better than the Wolves match - the Blues went down 4-1 - but he did enough to retain his place, despite admitting he was to blame for two of the goals. The following day he celebrated his nineteenth birthday with a 2-0 victory in the Derby return match at Maine Road.

On New Year's Day City suffered another large defeat. The Blues had been leading 2-0 at home to West Bromwich Albion when wing-half Jackie Bray was stretchered off. The rain started coming down in torrents, and City quickly lost their way. Albion went on a goalscoring spree, winning 7-2 by the close. Young Swift was convinced he had blown his chance of becoming City's permanent 'keeper. He went home miserable and spent the evening and most of the night going through every one of the goals, looking for mistakes, with his brother Fred. Fortunately for

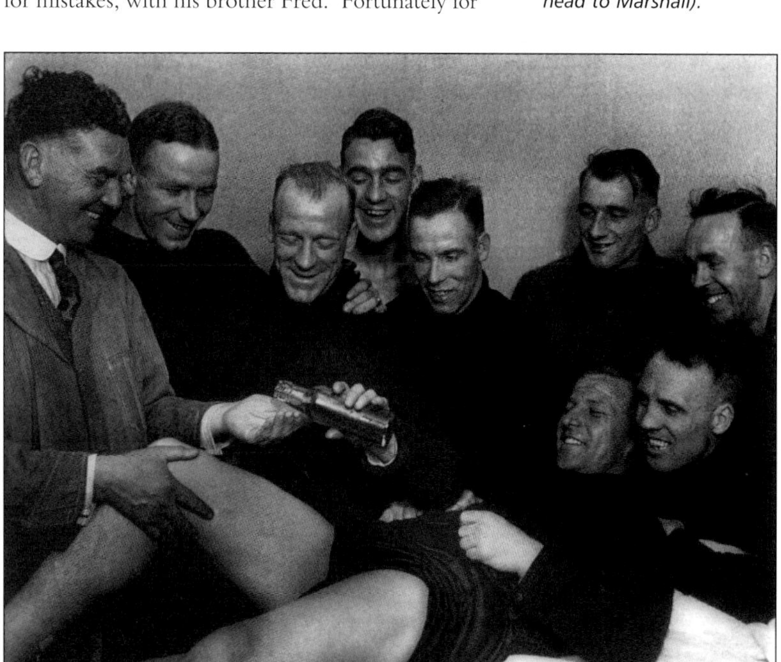

City player Bobby Marshall receives treatment from trainer Alec Bell and players Busby, Brook, Swift, Toseland, Herd, Barnett and Dale (closest head to Marshall).

Swift, Len Langford the regular 'keeper remained out of action with a knee injury, and the only other player available, Nicholls, had been the man who'd conceded eight against Wolves. Swift retained his place.

A 1-1 draw with Leicester followed before the F.A. Cup run commenced with a home tie against Blackburn. The first fifteen minutes of the game saw all the action take place in midfield, then a Blackburn forward broke through City's defence and made his way to goal. Swift, a little nervous, dived too soon but incredibly the ball seemed to be attracted to his right hand, like a nail towards a magnet, and the 'keeper managed to gather the ball. The crowd believed it was an amazing reaction, but Swift rather innocently admitted he'd made a mistake and the save owed much to good fortune.

Regardless of what had occurred, it clearly instilled the young man with a lot of confidence, and from that moment on he stopped more or less everything that came his way. The game ended 3-1 thanks to goals from Toseland (2) and Brook, to send City into the fourth round.

The 1934 City team struggle to hear the Cup draw. Eric Brook (leaning on radio) looks particularly dissatisfied, perhaps he wanted to listen to a different station.

For the second time in five years the Blues were drawn against Hull City; this time Manchester's men were determined to get it right. With goals from Herd and Brook the Blues felt comfortable, especially with the score 2-1 with five minutes to go, but incredibly confusion between Swift and Dale allowed a Hull player to tap in an equaliser. City could not believe it, but at least they had survived and were now able to bring Hull back to Maine Road for what everybody felt would be a massacre.

In the replay the Blues defeated Hull 4-1, and looked forward to their next tie away to Sheffield Wednesday on 17th February.

City's huge pulling power at this time guaranteed enormous attendances wherever they played and the fifth round tie at Hillsborough was no exception as City helped set the ground's attendance record. 72,841 (receipts £5,566) crammed into Wednesday's ground to see what promised to be a tremendous match, although the attendance was perhaps excessive for the venue.

City fan Joe Carley entered his version of the day's events in his diary, starting with his arrival at

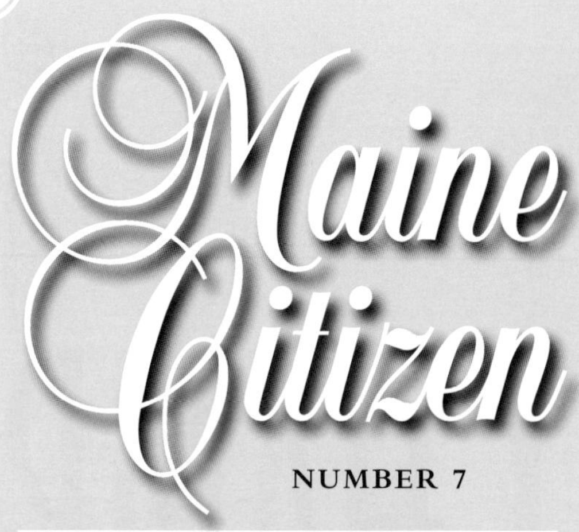

NUMBER 7

ERIC BROOK

Eric Brook is City's record goalscorer and fourth in the list of most appearances, but he very nearly became a hero at rivals Manchester United before joining the Blues. Louis Rocca, United's former chief scout, had been watching Eric play for Wath Athletic as an amateur and was so impressed that he decided to keep a close watch on the player when he moved to Barnsley. Rocca quickly noticed another fine Barnsley player - and future Blue - Fred Tilson and kept in close contact with Barnsley manager Jimmy Commins - a good friend of the United scout.

After a few months Commins met Rocca in Manchester and told him United could sign both players for a combined fee of £5,000. He also warned Rocca: "If you don't take them, they are going to City."

United were still a relatively poor side at this time and, despite considerable effort on Rocca's part, the two men joined City in March 1928. Brook made his debut in the 2-0 victory over Grimsby Town on 17th March before almost 50,000 at Maine Road and went on to appear in 450 League games for the Blues plus the three matches in August and September 1939 which were expunged from the records. He also scored a magnificent 158 League goals (plus one against Leicester in August 1939) which leaves him at the top of the Blues' all-time goalscorers table.

Probably his most impressive goal came in the 1934 Cup match with Stoke. Watched by a record crowd if 84,569, Brook fired home a swirling left foot shot from a spot on the left wing midway between the corner flag at the Platt Lane end and the Kippax tunnel (close to the 1980s segregation fence). Stoke's Welsh international 'keeper, Roy John, stretched to reach the ball but was helpless as it entered the top corner just beyond the reach of his left arm. It was an incredible goal and was variously described as a fluke, a freak shot, or a well placed, well

thought out attempt. Whatever it was, it guaranteed a return to Wembley for Brook who had received a runners' up medal the previous April.

At Wembley in 1934 Brook was delighted when his good friend and team mate Fred Tilson scored twice to bring the Cup home to Manchester.

In addition to F.A. Cup medals, Brook was also an important member of the City side that won the League Championship for the first time in 1937. He was an ever-present that year and also contributed twenty goals to the Blue cause. In 1931 and 1936 he was the club's top scorer and, during his time at Maine Road, he made 18 international appearances. He also played against Wales in a wartime international on 18th November 1939, alongside Frank Swift, Bert Sproston, and Joe Mercer. Sadly, it was his journey to another wartime international that brought a premature end to his football career. After missing the train at Leeds, he and Sam Barkas were travelling by car to Newcastle for a game against Scotland when they were involved in a crash near Ripon. The 32 year old Brook suffered a fractured skull and was told he would never be able to head a ball again.

Undaunted by the accident, he later took a job as a coach driver in his native Mexborough, then for two years became the landlord of the Albion Inn, Halifax. Afterwards he returned to Manchester as a crane driver at Metrovicks. He died at home in Minsterley Parade, Wythenshawe in March 1965 at a time when City were enduring one of their worst ever periods. He was only 57.

Eric Brook will always be remembered as a true Blue hero who, over 30 years after his death, remains the highest City goalscorer of all time.

BROOK'S PLAYING RECORD

	LEAGUE		FA CUP		TOTAL	
	App	Gls	App	Gls	App	Gls
1927-28	12	2	0	0	12	2
1928-29	42	14	1	0	43	14
1929-30	40	16	5	1	45	17
1930-31	42	16	1	0	43	16
1931-32	42	10	5	3	47	1
1932-33	42	15	7	6	49	2
1933-34	38	8	8	3	46	11
1934-35	40	17	1	0	41	17
1935-36	40	13	3	3	43	16
1936-37	42	20	4	2	46	22
1937-38	36	16	4	1	40	17
1938-39	34	11	2	0	36	11
1939-40*	3	1	0	0	3	1
TOTAL	453	159	41	19	494	178

* = League campaign abandoned, then expunged from records due to World War II
These matches are not usually included in official records; they're mentioned here in an attempt to provide a complete picture of Brook's career.

Eric Brook was the only City player United fans would admit to admiring during the mid 1930s.

Page 2. SUNDAY GRAPHIC and SUNDAY NEWS. March 4, 1934.

CUP FANS "TRAPPED" IN AMAZING CROWD

Got In, But Couldn't Get Out

84,569 CRUSH

Whew!

"Record" is too mild—this crowd was not only a record—several records in fact—it was a problem.

84,569.

That is the figure. And they all came to see Manchester City and Stoke City battle out a Cup-tie at Maine-road, Manchester, yesterday.

Oh, yes, it was a record all right. A record for Maine-road and a record for any match (London and its teeming millions included) outside a Cup Final or International match, in this country.

The £5,426 receipts were also well ahead of Maine-road's best.

And many of that 84,569 must have thought of the old coon song, "I'd rather be on the outside a-lookin' in than on the inside a-lookin' out."

That was the problem.

Having got in, hundreds wandered about looking at a solid array of backs—spectators', not players'—and then tried to get out. But they were trapped—until a turnstile was opened to let them out. Some youths scaled a 12ft. wall to get out.

These unfortunate people did not even get a good look at the field, let alone the game.

Besides this huge total London's crowd of 67,000 seems moderate.

Thousands came from Stoke and the Potteries, and last night about half Manchester's population seemed to be wearing the red-and-white colours of Stoke.

Ambulance men were kept busy, and treated about 100 people for crushing and abrasions. Three were taken to Manchester Royal Infirmary.

The Preston crowd was not a record, but the receipts of £3,406 were Deepdale's best.

The attendance at the four Cup-ties was nearly 243,000, and more than one-third of these were at the Manchester game.

Lancashire had three of the ties, but only one Lancashire team survives.

A party of Aston Villa supporters flew to London in five 'planes and circled over Arsenal ground before the match.

MASSES AND MONEY-BAGS

	Attendance	Receipts
Manchester C. v. Stoke C.	84,569	£5,426
Arsenal v. Aston Villa	67,366	£6,366
Bolton W. v. Portsmouth	52,181	£3,778
Preston v. Leicester	38,605	£3,406

City's crowd of 84,569 for the 6th Round FA Cup tie with Stoke in 1934 still stands as a record for any club fixture in England, but many fans struggled to see while others were unable to cope.

The cartoon tries to make light of the 'Fluke from Brook' incident, which brought City's winner, by making references to other fish.

London Road Railway Station: "I fought my way into a carriage as the train drew in. I say 'fought' because of the crowds that struggled to board the train. I secured a seat in a corridor coach, but the crowds still streamed through the door and overflowed into the passage, which soon became jammed. It was a most unpleasant journey. All I could see was the navy-blue waistcoat of some fellow pushed in front of me, and who leaned on the luggage rack above my head throughout the journey. Just after we started another standing passenger made an effort to divest himself of his overcoat in order to make a little more room, but so tightly packed was the crowd that he only managed to get it off half-way, and had to travel to Sheffield in that condition, being unable to get it either on or off.

"At the ground I joined the queue at one of the two shilling turnstiles (the popular side being almost completely filled), and rumours were rife that the gates were being closed. I pushed in with the crowd, paid my two bob, one other person was allowed in after me and then, no more!

"Things were not very comfortable in some parts of the ground and ambulancemen were kept busy. Just before the teams came out a stretcher party passed bearing the blanketed figure of a man killed in the crush."

As with the games at Hyde Road in the early 1920s, nobody seemed concerned about safety. Hundreds were injured and as he waited to take his place on the field, the distressed Frank Swift witnessed much of what Joe Carley had seen: "After we had changed, and were ready for the field, we found that the narrow tunnel from the dressing room to the pitch was blocked by ambulance men tending groaning casualties. After forcing my way through with the other players, I had to stand aside to let pass a stretcher bearing a man crushed to death against the railings on the Spion Kop."

It took football another sixty years and a much greater tragedy at Hillsborough to learn from such basic mistakes. All that mattered was the game itself.

Understandably, the early play was scrappy. Both sets of players made mistakes, but for City a simple

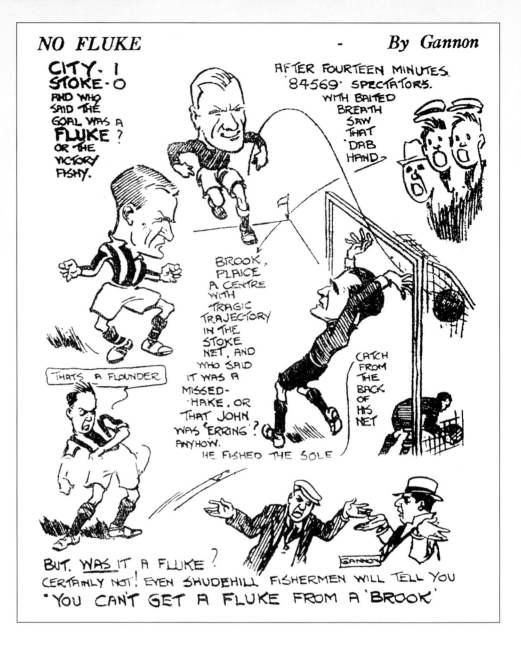

THE BEST GUIDE TO RACING:
Empire News
RACING HANDBOOK
(1934 Edition)
On Sale Everywhere—Price 2d.

Daily Dispatch

THE NATIONAL NEWSPAPER OF THE NORTH.
MONDAY, MARCH 5, 1934

Meet Spring in Radiant Healt
1,000
MEDICAL HINT
On Sale Everywhere

THE WAY TO WEMBLEY
BROOK'S AMAZING SHOT BEAT STOKE

STOP PRESS NEWS

VARIOUSLY CALLED "A FLUKE," "A FREAK," AND "AN AMAZING SHOT."—Brook's long-range effort which brought victory to Manchester City in their Cup-tie against Stoke City at Maine-road, which was watched by a record crowd on Saturday. (Brook is seen second from right in the distance. While the winners' goal might have been a lucky one, Stoke were certainly out of luck when,

miskick by Cowan allowed Wednesday's Dewar to nip in and pass the ball for Rimmer to score. Midway through the half City fought back. Alec Herd received a short pass from a McLuckie free kick, dribbled a considerable length upfield, confusing the Wednesday defence as he went. Then, about twenty-five yards out, he had a crack at goal and scored the equaliser.

Early in the second half Dewar gave Wednesday the lead, but it wasn't to last as, twenty-five minutes from time, Alec Herd scored his second of the match and set up a replay for the following Wednesday afternoon.

As thousands took the afternoon off work, City attracted an incredible attendance of 68,614. Those Mancunians who risked their jobs to attend the game cannot have left disappointed as City won the match 2-0 with a pair of long range efforts. For the first Fred Tilson waited for the ball to bounce in front of Wednesday's centre-half Millership, then nipped round the player with the ball and sent a fine effort crashing into the net. The second came from Bobby Marshall who headed in a forty yard free kick launched by Dale.

City were in the quarter-finals again. This time they faced Stoke City - with a young Stanley Matthews in the side - at Maine Road in a game everybody wanted to see. Harry Hughes recalled leaving work early to find a space on the vast terracing: "We went straight from work. There was a gang of us, and I had a cap on. We probably all did. Anyway, I stood with my back to a barrier and I thought I'd be alright. I knew it would be a good crowd but as it filled up I was moved around and couldn't control where I was going. I soon realised that I was behind a barrier with my chest being pushed in - not the best place to be in a huge crowd. So I decided to duck down under the barrier and come up the other side. As I rose I discovered that I'd come up between a man and his wife or girlfriend and he looked at me in wonderment. Totally astonished that I should have appeared as if by magic between him and his wife. I managed to drop my cap over my eyes and move off before I got myself into trouble!"

The official attendance was 84,569 - the largest ever crowd in the provinces and to this day the record for any club fixture. Many supporters had travelled from Stoke and they mingled with City's support on the Kippax side of the ground. Again, the huge crowd brought a few hazards. At least one barrier collapsed and a few supporters were injured, but in the main the worst problem seemed to be actually seeing the action. For much of the match supporters jostled for position, causing many to complain the attendance was simply too large, but the City management claimed it could have been even greater, after being forced by the police to close the gates some twenty minutes before the game was due to begin.

City had a difficult start as Stoke kept them under pressure for most of the first half. It wasn't to be the visitors' day, however, as Eric Brook received a wide pass way out on the wing and raced for the corner flag. He then slung over a speculative lob from the flank which seemed to change direction in mid-flight. The Stoke 'keeper Roy John appeared to have it covered, jumped up but somehow missed it as it curled past the 'keeper and into the net for the only goal of the match.

In the last minute Stoke were awarded a

A rare picture of the famous 'fluke from Brook' goal against Stoke, before a record crowd. Eric Brook is closest to the packed Kippax.

City's Gate Record of 84,000

GATE CLOSED BEFORE START

BIGGEST CROWD EVER IN PROVINCES

The official gate at Maine Road was 84,569.

This is a record for the provinces.

FOR the first time in the history of Maine Road the gates were closed to-day before Manchester City's sixth round Cup-tie with Stoke. The gates were closed 20 minutes before the start of the match.

SIX "PASS-OUTS" - - - By Gannon
MANCHESTER CITY :- SIX GOALS AND TICKETS TO WEMBLEY. ASTON VILLA. ONE GOAL & PASS OUT CHECKS. AND AFTER THAT FIRST EMBARRASSING MINUTE WHEN SWIFT REFUSED TO RECEIVE A VILLA DEPUTATION.
IT WAS ALL CITY WITH TOSELAND SETTING A "SILVER BULLET" PACE.
AND GOALIE MORTON'S ONLY HOPE WAS TO HAVE PLUCKED UP THE GOALPOST AND PLAYED A STRAIGHT BAT
WITH SAMMY COWAN PLAYING GHOST TO ASTLEY, VILLA'S ATTACKING SHORTCOMINGS WERE GHASTLEY
HE MIGHT HAVE STOPPED TILSON'S HAT-TRICK
SUMMING UP, VILLA SEEMED TO HAVE TRAINED ON "BLIND MAN'S BUFF"
AND BROOKS' HULA-HULA PANTS WERE THE ONLY RAGGED PARTS OF CITY'S DISPLAY.
THE VILLA ARE NOW SLIGHTLY MORE THAN SEMI-DETACHED

City defeated Aston Villa 6-1 in the FA Cup semi-final at Huddersfield on 17th March 1934.

Below: The 1934 Cup Final squad line up for a pre-Wembley photo. Left to right: Brook, Toseland, McLuckie, Herd, Tilson, Bray, Dale, Barnett, Busby, Marshall, Cowan and Swift.

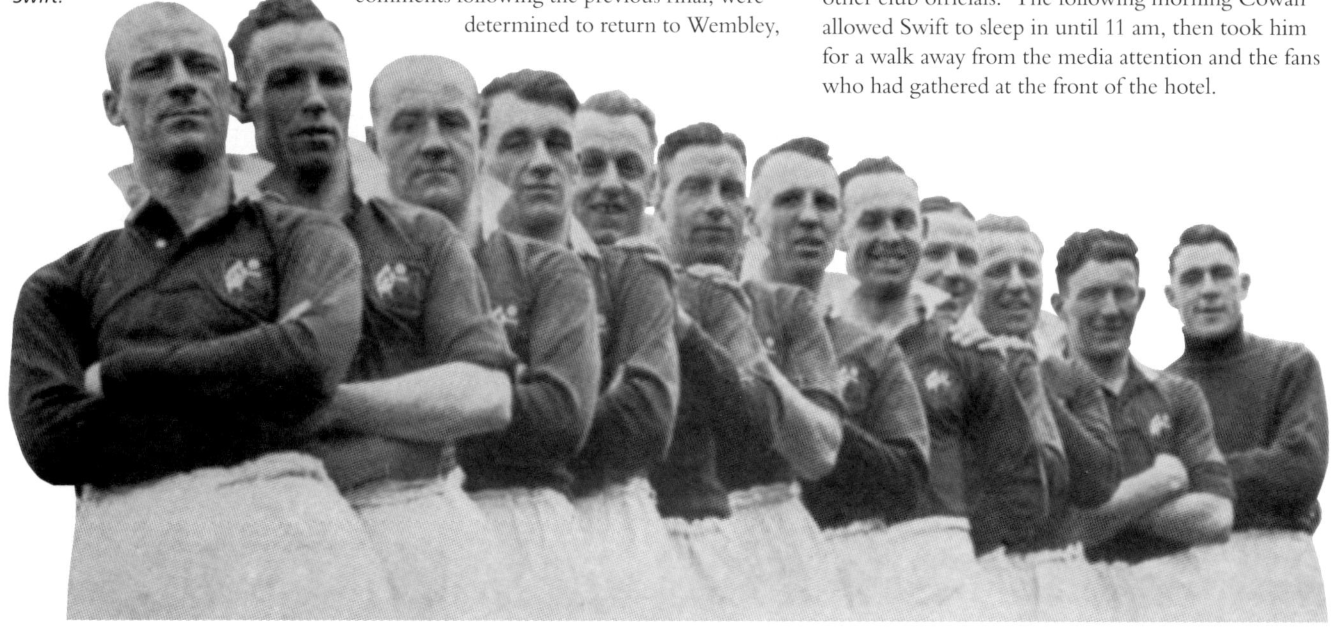

corner and, with everybody bar the 'keeper upfield, the Blues really felt the pressure. Swift's vision was blocked for a while as everybody jumped up. Arthur Turner, Stoke's centre-half, was the one to make contact, but fortunately he headed the ball a fraction over the bar. A few seconds later the whistle went and City were into the semi-final for the third consecutive season.

The semi-final saw the Blues at Leeds Road, Huddersfield, again - this time for a meeting with Aston Villa on a wet and windy afternoon. Villa were favourites for the cup but City, mindful of Cowan's comments following the previous final, were determined to return to Wembley, and quickly set about attacking the Villa goal. Toseland was the first to score for the Blues with a terrific shot past Villa's Morton. Frank Swift in City's net found life a little difficult as The Villans immediately tried to bounce back, but after 34 minutes Fred Tilson fired in City's second despite the close attention of a Villa defender.

Within a minute Alec Herd added a third, and then almost immediately Tilson banged in City's fourth. Three goals in five minutes had really killed off any hopes Villa had of reaching Wembley while Sam Cowan was able to enjoy the half-time break safe in the knowledge that, barring a major upset, his prediction was to come true.

Midway through the second half Fred Tilson added a couple more. Four minutes from time Astley provided Villa with a consolation, although one report suggested the City defenders were too bored to tackle him. The game ended 6-1 - a semi-final record - and the Blues had made it comfortably into their second consecutive Wembley final. This time they faced Portsmouth - the team that had caused so much promotion heartache in 1927.

In preparation for Wembley, City spent a week at the Palace Hotel, Birkdale, Southport. By remarkable co-incidence Portsmouth had pre-booked the same hotel prior to the semi-final. On hearing that City had no intention of moving elsewhere, the Portsmouth directors chose to cancel their Southport break and look elsewhere. The first battle had been won.

In addition to the first eleven, City took a number of reserves to Southport, including Len Langford. At first this troubled Swift who was convinced Langford's experience the previous year would give him the edge. Fortunately for the young 'keeper there was no question of him being displaced and Langford went to Southport with the sole intention of helping his talented colleague prepare.

Another man determined to calm the young Swift was captain Sam Cowan. On the eve of the Cup Final, at their hotel on the edge of Epping Forest, the two men shared a room and Cowan did all he could to keep Swift's mind off the final. They talked for hours about everything but football, while Cowan bathed a septic toe he had kept secret from Wilf Wild and the other club officials. The following morning Cowan allowed Swift to sleep in until 11 am, then took him for a walk away from the media attention and the fans who had gathered at the front of the hotel.

FA Cup Winners 1934

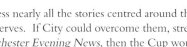

Below: Sam Cowan leads his side out at Wembley followed by Eric Brook and 19-year-old Frank Swift.

Bottom: Billy Dale is introduced to King George V prior to the 1934 Final.

In the press nearly all the stories centred around the players' nerves. If City could overcome them, stressed the *Manchester Evening News*, then the Cup would come to Manchester. As with the 1926 final, many supporters arrived without tickets and, once again, challenged the detestable ticket touts who were selling stand tickets for three times their face value. A few scuffles broke out but the *Evening News* claimed even so it was all fairly good natured.

There were a few incidents that brought sadness to the final, however. A number of coaches had arrived at Leicester Square fairly early in the morning to allow the City fans to spend a morning sight seeing before the final. One supporter, Joseph McGuinness from Simpson Street off Rochdale Road, Manchester, had left his coach to have a look around when another, arriving from Manchester, hit and killed him. On another journey Mr. John Crossen, a director of Glentoran F.C., had a seizure on the train and died before reaching the capital.

Apart from those sad moments, generally the City followers were in good spirit. They kidnapped a sailor

Referee Stanley Rous watches as the two captains wish each other well.

in Trafalgar Square, believing him to be a Portsmouth follower, and made him climb onto the plinth of Nelson's Column. Once up there he defiantly stated 'Pompey will win', before jumping down and disappearing in the crowd.

Other interesting snippets from the newspapers centred around the opening of a new Royal Box, closer to the pitch, and the negotiations between the F.A. and the film companies. The F.A. demanded £700 for the rights to film the game while the newsreel companies claimed this was excessive. On the morning of the match, newsreel officials were caught trying to hide cameras in the most unlikely places. One intended arriving at Wembley with a camera inside a dummy figure of a sailor, pretending it was a Portsmouth mascot. The game was eventually filmed, but there is uncertainty what agreement was reached with the F.A.

In the dressing room, Cowan tried to sooth everybody's nerves. By request Eric Brook sang his favourite song, while Alec Herd sat quietly in a corner reading an Edgar Wallace thriller. Frank Swift began to feel the pressure and so trainer Alec Bell dragged him into the washroom, slapped his face and gave him a glass of whisky. In the Portsmouth dressing room, comedian Bud Flanagan entertained City's opponents.

When the time came, City made their way into the tunnel. Once there, one of the players noticed Alec Herd was missing. Alec Bell re-entered the dressing room to find his namesake still reading his thriller, totally at ease.

Wearing maroon, City took the field to a deafening roar. The teams lined up in front of the new Royal Box and, following the National Anthem, King George V was introduced first to Portsmouth in white shirts, then City.

After the introductions and the kickabout referee Stanley Rous, who had been a linesman for the 1926 final, took the captains to the centre for the toss. Portsmouth won and selected ends, then Tilson kicked off. Immediately he sent the ball to Toseland and the Blues mounted their first attack, although it never really came to anything. Some mixed play followed with Portsmouth's first dangerous move bringing an early test for the youthful Swift. Portsmouth were awarded a free kick a yard outside the box after Bray had brought down Worrall. Nicholl took the kick, but fired straight at Swift. Coolly the 'keeper collected under the bar and then proceeded to hoist a long kick upfield.

City failed to keep the ball and Portsmouth were quickly back hammering at the City goal. Busby handled to give Portsmouth another free kick close to the box. Again this was cleared, but the pressure continued.

Gradually City found their own routes to goal and performed a couple of interesting moves before Alec Herd was cynically bowled over by a Portsmouth defender. City fans and neutrals immediately started booing, something so uncommon at the time the press made comment in most 'papers. Herd was stretchered off, clutching his right leg. A minute later the jeers returned as Toseland was fouled.

Busby took the free kick, but fired over the bar. Just then Herd returned to the field to a fantastic reception, causing the *Manchester Evening News* reporter to state how the City support easily outnumbered that of Portsmouth. Perhaps the two fouls had persuaded neutrals to back the team in maroon.

In the fourteenth minute Brook missed a superb chance to put City in front. He held on just too long and allowed a Portsmouth defender, William Smith, to block his shot.

Nineteen year old Frank Swift, though somewhat nervous, was enjoying himself. A little rain in the opening fifteen minutes had caused him some

Just half-a-crown for a Cup Final ticket, that's just 13p in today's money!

EAST STANDING ENCLOSURE

ENTER AT TURNSTILES **B**
(See Plan on back)

ENTRANCE **19**

EMPIRE STADIUM, WEMBLEY

The Football Association Cup Competition

FINAL TIE

SATURDAY, APRIL 28th, 1934
(Kick-off 3 p.m.)

Price 2/6
(Including Tax)

A. J. Elvin
MANAGING DIRECTOR, Wembley Stadium Limited.

THIS PORTION TO BE RETAINED
(See Conditions on back)

Left: Alec Herd watches as his header goes wide.

Below and inset: Frank Swift keeps the Portsmouth forwards out. City's 19-year-old goalkeeper had a fine game but the tension ultimately shattered him at the final whistle when he fainted. He quickly recovered however to collect his winners medal from the King.

THE ILLUSTRATED LONDON NEWS

SATURDAY, MAY 5, 1934.

THE KING AT THE CUP FINAL: HIS MAJESTY PRESENTING THE CUP TO COWAN, CAPTAIN OF THE WINNING MANCHESTER CITY TEAM, WITH SIR FREDERICK WALL, BARE-HEADED, IN THE BACKGROUND.

His Majesty honoured with his presence the F.A. Cup Final at Wembley Stadium on April 28; and a crowd of more than 93,000 enthusiasts, many of whom had come up from Lancashire and other parts of the country, had the additional opportunity of welcoming the Australian cricket team and of acclaiming Sir Frederick Wall, who is retiring from the secretaryship of the Football Association, having held the post since 1895. A match of unusual interest and excitement ended in a win for Manchester City over Portsmouth by two goals to one. With seventeen minutes to go, Portsmouth were leading by one goal to nothing, but Manchester then scored twice, their second goal coming amid intense excitement only three minutes from the end. Eight of the Manchester team had played in the Cup Final last year, when Manchester lost to Everton, and six of the Portsmouth team had been on the losing side in the Final of 1929.

concern, but in the main he was content. Because of the drizzle he contemplated putting on his gloves but, as he was still learning about first team football, he couldn't make up his mind. He looked down field to his more experienced opposite number, Gilfillan, who had remained gloveless and so the young City man decided to wait. Swift thought: "If Gilfillan puts his gloves on then so will I."

After almost thirty minutes the first goal arrived. Portsmouth's centre-forward Weddle had lobbed the ball over Sam Cowan to outside left Rutherford. He moved towards goal, reached about fifteen yards out, noticed Billy Dale moving towards him, moved the ball from his left foot to his right, then shot towards goal. Swift dived and managed to get his fingers to it, but it was no good, the ball entered the net. Swift believed he knew what was to blame. He told himself he would have saved the goal if only he'd ignored Gilfillan and put on his gloves!

At half-time, Swift remained upset by the incident. Fred Tilson went up to him and, trying to console the 'keeper, said, "Tha doesn't need to worry. I'll plonk two in the next half."

City, unfortunate to be a goal down, returned to the field determined to win the game. The only player who seemed to be lacking the spirit required was Herd, who still appeared shaken following his early injury. He wasn't the only player injured though, as midway through the second half Portsmouth's Worrall and Allen went down. Worrall was attended by the City trainer and made a quick recovery while Allen had to be taken off the field for a while. This gave City a little more space, and they used it to their advantage.

First Herd saw a fine effort hit the bar and go out of play, then Brook and Tilson combined to bring City the equaliser. Brook took the ball into the middle of the field then crossed to Tilson, who had strengthened the left wing the moment Brook moved infield. Tilson, heavily marked, had one chance to score. Mackie came in to tackle and as the two men made contact and Tilson was falling, the City man shot with his left foot past Gilfillan. City were level.

Allen then returned to the field, but it was too late as City now had the initiative. Although it didn't all go City's way as frequent Manchester attacks were broken up by Portsmouth defenders who then quickly sent the ball upfield. At one point almost everybody in the stadium was convinced that Portsmouth were about to take the lead as Worrall sent a powerful header goalward. Swift dived and with his fists made the save of the game.

With tension mounting, the match entered the final five minutes with either team capable of snatching victory. Frantically, both sides applied the pressure, but it was City who gained the decisive advantage when Toseland sent a crossfield pass to Tilson who moved towards the Portsmouth goal. The defenders tried to reach him, but it was to no avail as the City man backed up his half time pledge and fired in his second of the match. Wembley erupted again.

As the final minutes ticked

Left: Samuel Frederick Tilson, known as 'Freddie' to his team mates. He scored both City goals in the 1934 F.A. Cup Final.

1934 FA CUP RUN

R3	Blackburn Rovers	H	W 3-1
R4	Hull City	A	D 2-2
	Hull City	H	W 4-1
R5	Sheffield Wednesday	A	D 2-2
	Sheffield Wednesday	H	W 2-0
R6	Stoke City	H	W 1-0
SF	Aston Villa	N*	W 6-1
F	Portsmouth	N**	W 2-1

* = Leeds Road, Huddersfield
** = Wembley Stadium

FACTS & FIGURES

	P	W	D	L	F	A
HOME	4	4	0	0	10	2
AWAY	4	2	2	0	12	6
TOTAL	8	6	2	0	22	8

CUP FINAL DETAILS

28 April 1934 at Wembley Stadium
CITY 2 PORTSMOUTH 1

CITY: Swift, Barnett, Dale, Busby, Cowan, Bray, Toseland, Marshall, Tilson, Herd, Brook

PORTSMOUTH: Gilfillan, Mackie, Smith (W), Nichol, Allen, Thackeray, Worrall, Smith (JW), Weddle, Easson, Rutherford

GOALS: Tilson (2), Rutherford

ATTENDANCE: 93, 258
REFEREE: S F Rous (Herts)
GUEST OF HONOUR: King George V
MANAGER: Wilf Wild
CAPTAIN: Sam Cowan

Above: City's Cup Final shirt bearing the City of Manchester crest.

Right: The winning smile - Sam Cowan is clearly delighted he kept his promise to return as Cup winners.

City bring the Cup home to Manchester.

Above: Billy Dale's 1934 FA Cup winners medal.

MANCHESTER CITY BRING HOME THE CUP

by, Frank Swift felt the tension. The photographers behind his goal kept shouting the time to him until finally the whistle went. He turned to collect his gloves and fainted. Sam Cowan and Alec Bell rushed over to him, with the trainer immediately pouring cold water on Swift's face. They managed to bring him round but he was still a little dazed as he made his way, with the rest of the team, up to the Royal Box. Fourth in the line up behind Cowan, Brook and Marshall, Swift struggled up the Wembley steps and along to the table set up with the medals. The King enquired how he was feeling and then that was it. Time to celebrate.

City had won the Cup for the second time in their history, and deservedly took time out to celebrate. The team were given a fantastic homecoming with what seemed like the whole of Manchester lining the city's streets. Various speeches were made into a microphone set up on the Town Hall steps, and the players and officials were given a civic reception. It all seemed so different to thirty years earlier when the city's officials found it hard to accept the tonic that football could bring to a grim, industrial city. The Cup win helped to take minds off the growing problems in Europe where fascism was on the increase, and author H.G. Wells had predicted war by 1940. Mancunians enjoyed the success and wanted more.

The 1933-4 League programme still had two games left for the Blues. On 2nd May they suffered a 3-2 defeat at Liverpool, but then on the 5th demolished Wolves 4-0 at Maine Road. Before the kick-off City staff, assisted by a couple of police officers, carried the trophy around the ground on some kind of wooden board. The fans were delighted.

Playing in those final two games was left back Sam Barkas, who joined the Blues from Bradford City on 20th April for a £5,000 fee.

During the week of celebrations an illuminated bus journeyed around the city covered in City's colours. On the front above the bus number, 'City 2 1', was the Manchester coat of arms. On the side the message 'Welcome to the victors' proudly illuminated next to a picture of the F.A. Cup and a drawing of Sam Cowan. Manchester was proud of its team.

At the beginning of the following season the *Topical Times Sporting Annual* announced its six sportsmen of the year. The leading footballer was Matt Busby, who had performed exceptionally well in the Cup Final. The annual believed he was the best right half back in Britain whose ball control was wonderful. The article went on to stress his strengths and reminded its readers that Busby was at long last winning the kind of international recognition he deserved after appearing for Scotland against Wales during the season.

The *Topical Times* also raved about another City player Frank Swift, who they rated, alongside Stanley Matthews, as one of the best discoveries of the season. The Swift article concentrated on the player's tremendous rise in only four months, stressing that he seemed to improve with every game. Accurately, they predicted a glowing future for the lad from Fleetwood.

After all the success of 1933-4, the following season was always going to be difficult. Expectations were high, especially as the Blues had proved to be good cup fighters for three seasons running. The League programme commenced with a 1-1 draw at West Bromwich, where Sam Barkas provided the City goal. Barkas was now a regular, with Wild selecting him ahead of Barnett. The rest of the cup final side remained in the team however.

The next couple of games, both at home, ended in City victory with both Liverpool (3-1) and Sheffield Wednesday finding it difficult to come to terms with a bubbling City. In the match with Wednesday City's outside right Ernie Toseland found himself up against the international, Nibloe. Every time Toseland had the ball he seemed to ease past his opponent, prompting the *Manchester Evening News* to report: "Toseland passed Nibloe with the ease of a crack express train passing a stationary object."

City's fine form continued, although injury forced Wild to make a few changes from time to time. Jimmy Heale, signed from Bristol City in January, frequently replaced Marshall. In fact the newcomer finished the season making 27 League appearances - eight more than Marshall.

As usual City were watched by some enormous crowds. Wednesday, Leeds, Stoke and Derby each attracted around 50,000, while the game with first placed Arsenal on 23rd February attracted 79,491. City, in third place, were only a point behind the Gunners when the two teams met. A packed crowd witnessed a tense 1-1 draw with Ted Drake scoring for the visitors and Eric Brook for the Blues, but it wasn't enough. City needed the victory, especially when a few weeks later they failed at Blackburn and Huddersfield.

Nevertheless, the Blues did manage to achieve a respectable fourth place. One position higher than the previous season. The Cup

Another of Billy Dale's medals - this one from the Charity Shield in which City were beaten 4-0 by Arsenal at Highbury in November 1934.

In May 1934 City embarked on a continental tour. They defeated Racing Club de Paris 3-1, and then drew 3-3 with Fiorentina. On 20th May they travelled to Nice where they lost 5-0 to AC Milan, then defeated Admira Wien 5-3 at the same venue the following day. The final game of the tour was a 4-4 draw with Marseilles Olympique on 27th May.

Above: A tour medal presented to Billy Dale.

Below: The front cover of the Fiorentina-City programme.

A crowd of 79,491 (City's highest in the League) watch a 1-1 draw with Arsenal on 23rd February 1935. Here Ted Drake beats Frank Swift for Arsenal's goal. The Kippax is in the background.

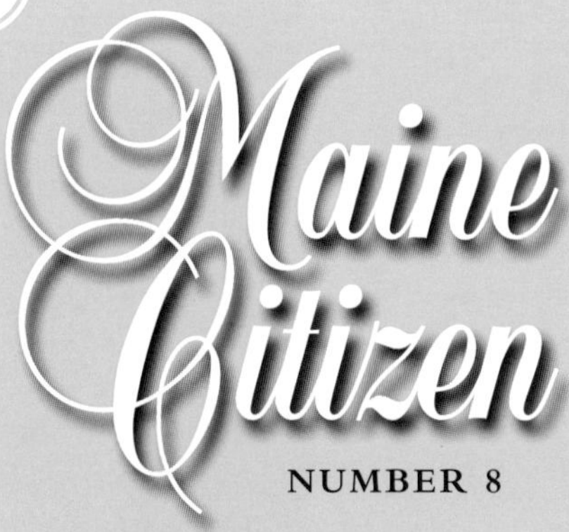

NUMBER 8

SAM COWAN

Sam Cowan holds a unique place in City's history for he is the only player to have appeared in three F.A. Cup finals for the Blues - 1926, 1933, and 1934. The last two appearances were as captain.

He arrived at Maine Road in December 1924 from Doncaster Rovers and made his debut in the 2-2 draw with Birmingham City on 20th of that month. Quickly he established a reputation for his heading ability, with one of his most famous headers coming nine months later to give City an equaliser against United in the first Manchester derby match to take place at Maine Road. Matt Busby, who played with Cowan throughout the early 1930s, remembered: "He could head a ball as far as most of us could kick it." The legendary Dixie Dean, who many would argue was the greatest header of the ball of all time, was also a great fan and aerial duels between City and Everton always became Cowan v Dean. Sadly, the 1933 Wembley confrontation ended in defeat. Nevertheless, Cowan vowed City would be back.

Understandably, his proudest moment came when he succeeded in guiding the Blues to Wembley in 1934 and on to Cup victory over Portsmouth. It was no surprise when his memorable winning smile appeared in almost ever newspaper the following day. The victory was thoroughly deserved and had been made possible by Cowan's dedication. During the Wembley preparations Cowan spent considerable time trying to calm the nerves of his colleagues - in particular the young 'keeper Frank Swift. At this time in football history the captain often performed many of the duties that would later be taken on by managers and coaches, and there is no doubt that Cowan excelled as a man-manager, or motivator. Tilson may have scored the two City goals, but Cowan had coaxed his side to victory.

In addition to the three Wembley appearances, Cowan won a Second Division Championship medal, and earned three English international appearances (France, Belgium, and Austria) between 1926 and 1931. He also appeared for the Football League and in an England trial match (The Rest v England 1931).

After a total of 407 League and Cup matches and 24 goals, he was transferred to Bradford City for a fee of £2,000 (Bradford's second highest at that time). It was a move that angered some supporters, especially when his replacement, £6,000 Robert Donnelly from Partick Thistle, failed to excite.

Sam leads City out at Wembley in 1934.

was a disappointment however, as a third round away tie at Tottenham ended in a 1-0 defeat.

The 1935-6 season commenced without Sam Cowan in the opening day line up. He was replaced by Robert Donnelly, a summer signing from Partick Thistle, although the former captain managed to stay with the Blues until October when he transferred to Bradford City.

During the season other important changes were made, the most notable being the transfer of the highly rated Busby to Liverpool, and the arrival of £10,000 man Peter Doherty. City had converted Busby into a top class wing half and felt unable to turn down Liverpool when the Merseysiders put in an offer of £8,000. Doherty on the other hand was a man City desperately wanted and, at his debut on 22nd February against Preston, a crowd of 39,364 couldn't wait to see what the expensive new player could do.

Doherty, in his autobiography, remembered the problems he encountered in his debut match: "It was an uninspiring debut. Preston, giving a wonderful exhibition of football, beat us 3-1, and Bill Shankly, at right-half, blotted me completely out. Bill has always been a wily tactician, but that day he excelled himself. He dogged my footsteps all afternoon, muttering,

Robert Donnelly joined City in June 1935 as a replacement for the popular Sam Cowan.

After playing for Mossley and becoming Brighton's trainer, he accepted the City manager's job on 3rd December 1946 after Wilf Wild returned to purely secretarial duties. Despite his many strengths, the appointment was not a long one. He guided the Blues to promotion, but found it difficult to concentrate at Maine Road. He wanted to continue his life in Brighton and, after a debate about where his loyalties lay - Brighton or Manchester - he resigned (25th June 1947). He then set up a lucrative physiotherapy business in Hove and worked with Sussex C.C.C. and Brighton Ice Hockey Club. Later he became masseur to the M.C.C. for their 1962 Australian tour.

Interestingly, he also helped Brighton based Newcastle United prepare during the week prior to the 1955 final. He was still a City fanatic nonetheless.

Cowan's exploits as captain brought City success and helped attract huge crowds to Maine Road, while his brief period as manager further proved the importance of his motivational qualities. Sam Barkas, who was captain under Cowan, always remembered his manager's strengths: "We never had a manager until Sam Cowan arrived. Wilfred Wild held the title but he was the secretary and never got involved with team tactics. We were professional enough to know what was needed to keep fit and we worked hard in training without supervision. But Sam was a wonderful motivator."

Roy Clarke was signed by Cowan: "Sam signed me from Cardiff City on 28th May 1947, and coming to the big city for the first time was something of an ordeal. I was overwhelmed with the red carpet treatment. He met me at the station and took me to Maine Road to show me how the big clubs did things."

Clarke remembers Sam's unique team talks: "As the new boy I stood in a corner nervously eyeing seasoned pros like the great Sam Barkas, Frank Swift, and Bert Sproston, wondering what words of wisdom would follow. Then Sam delivered his team talk, all ten words of it. 'You know what to do. Get bloody well stuck in'."

Cowan's main strength was that he was a great motivator. He knew how to get the players to work and used this to drive City to Wembley success as captain, and to the Second Division Championship as manager. He collapsed on 5th October 1964 while refereeing a charity match in aid of Sussex wicketkeeper Jim Parks. It was a big showbiz affair with celebrities such as Tommy Steele taking part. Cowan, aged 62, died in the dressing room.

COWAN'S PLAYING RECORD

	LEAGUE		FA CUP		TOTAL	
	App	Gls	App	Gls	App	Gls
1924-25	21	1	0	0	21	1
1925-26	38	2	7	0	45	2
1926-27	27	2	0	0	27	2
1927-28	28	0	2	0	30	0
1928-29	38	1	1	0	39	1
1929-30	40	1	5	2	45	3
1930-31	40	2	1	0	41	2
1931-32	31	3	5	1	36	4
1932-33	32	4	7	2	39	6
1933-34	32	3	8	0	40	3
1934-35	42	0	1	0	43	0
TOTAL	369	19	37	5	406	24

Billy Dale, who missed just one League game in the 1935-36 season, the 1-0 home defeat by Sunderland in January.

'Great wee team, North End; a great wee team,' and subduing me so effectively that I must have been a grave disappointment to the thousands of City fans who had come along to see the club's expensive capture. During a quiet spell, I heard one of them voice his disapproval very clearly, 'Ten thousand pounds?' he shouted scornfully. 'You mean ten thousand cigarette cards!'"

City ended the season in a rather uninspiring ninth position. It wasn't good enough. In the Cup they had reached the fifth round, but even that seemed rather disappointing after the success of two years earlier. The run started with Portsmouth in the third round. A crowd of 53,340 came to see City defeat their old cup rivals again. This time the score was 3-1 thanks to an Eric Brook hat-trick. In the fourth round another large Maine Road crowd, 65,978, witnessed a 2-1 victory over plucky Third Division side Luton Town - The Hatters' first defeat since 28th September.

The run ended on 15th February before a record Grimsby crowd of around 28,000. Grimsby defeated City 3-2. Two days before the game the rather sad news that twenties' right back Sammy Sharp had died shocked a number of Mancunians.

If reaching the fifth round and finishing ninth was regarded as failure then the 1936-7 season must have brought a little satisfaction to City's large, loyal support. Sam Barkas was now the club's established captain, and with Doherty adding some firepower up front, the season became a successful one, although it hardly seemed possible during the difficult early months of September and October.

Despite exciting victories over Leeds (4-0) and West Bromwich Albion (6-2), an opening day defeat at Middlesbrough and another at Old Trafford in the first derby since February 1931 caused concern amongst City's support. The United defeat was particularly upsetting as the Reds were a side clearly lacking, and destined for an immediate return to the Second Division. Further failures occurred, including a 2-1 defeat at Wolverhampton. Wolves were in the process of rebuilding and had angered many supporters by selling so-called star players. On their approach to Molineux the City players couldn't help noticing some graffiti chalked on a wall, "The turf at the ground is now for sale!". Nevertheless, Wolves outplayed the Blues.

A few exciting victories followed in November and December, including 3-1 at Arsenal and 4-1 against Preston, but the real turnaround came at Christmas with a 2-1 victory over Middlesbrough at Maine Road.

A couple of draws against Grimsby and West Bromwich followed before the return derby match. A Maine Road crowd of 64,862 watched a rather dull, but nonetheless most important, game as City defeated United thanks to a solitary goal from Alec Herd.

In the following League game Toseland, Herd, and Brook each scored as Portsmouth were beaten 3-1 at Maine Road. This had followed City's third round tie away to Wrexham - an easy 3-1 win. In the fourth round City disposed of Accrington Stanley 2-0, before 39,135 at Maine Road, to earn a visit to old F.A. Cup rivals Bolton Wanderers in the next round.

Eric Brook scored a hat-trick as City again knocked Portsmouth out of the FA Cup in 1936.

Frank Swift reads out that City have drawn Accrington Stanley at home in the fourth round of the FA Cup in 1937. Surely even Swift didn't like this many people reading over his shoulder!

Left: *Some of the City fans who travelled to London in large numbers and good spirits for the FA Cup 6th round tie with Millwall in March 1937. They were in for a shock, however, as Millwall won 2-0 to become the first Third Division side to reach the semi-finals.*

Above: *Frank Swift is beaten by a header from Mangnall for the Londoners first goal.*

The Bolton game was an ill tempered affair. City eventually won the match 5-0 but at one point, a moment after Herd had scored the Blues' second goal, it looked as if the match might not continue. Bolton vigorously appealed against Herd's goal, and when play recommenced one of their players, Anderson, was sent off. There were further protests and the whole team considered marching off together, but eventually they were persuaded to stay on to finish a rather tension wracked affair.

The draw for the quarter-finals gave City what appeared an easy route into the semi-finals. The Blues were to travel to Millwall, a Third Division South club. City's thoughts started to turn towards the prospect of a League and Cup Double, although the weaker of the two trophy opportunities seemed to be in the League. A simple victory over Millwall looked most likely, despite the club beating Chelsea and Derby in earlier rounds. It wasn't to be however, as Millwall forced the pace right from the beginning. Dave Mangnall put City under immense pressure and by the 51st minute had scored twice for the home club.

At full time, thousands of Millwall fans invaded the pitch to celebrate their 2-0 giant-killing victory, and the club's entry into the record books as the first Third Division side to enter the semi-finals. It was a devastating blow for City, but with time-honoured football logic it at least allowed them to concentrate on the League.

The return game with Wolves showed how the Blues had improved during the season as a crowd of over 40,000 witnessed Tilson's second hat-trick in two games help to bring a 4-1 victory. Three days earlier he'd scored three against Derby - a big improvement on the October defeat. On 13th March, in City's next League game, two goals from Doherty helped the Blues to a 3-0 win over Huddersfield. A disappointing 1-1 draw at Everton was followed by an excellent Good Friday when City visited Liverpool again. This time they thrilled all City fans as they defeated the Reds 5-0 with goals from Brook (three), Doherty and Herd.

Three days later the return match saw the Blues go goal crazy again as they netted another five, including a seven minute spell during the second half when they scored four. Liverpool did pull a goal back, but the 10-1 aggregate score was a complete humiliation for the Merseyside club. Almost sixty years later Liverpool inflicted an equally humiliating 10-0 aggregate score over the Blues within a similar time frame.

Away at Brentford on 3rd April, City again found the goalscoring touch. Shortly after half-time the Blues were leading 3-0, but then, with the game seemingly won, City sat back and in no time at all, Brentford had pulled the score back to 3-2. At a stage when many teams would have panicked, City regained control and by full-time increased their lead to 6-2. Four days later, the Maine Road return ended in a 2-1 win, thereby placing City second in the League behind Arsenal, who were due to play the Blues three days later on Saturday 10th April.

Games between City and Arsenal during the 1930s always attracted high attendances,

Peter Doherty of City and Ireland - he joined Blues in February 1936 and was a crucial member of the side that won the championship a year later.

A 76,000 crowd watched a 2-0 defeat of Arsenal in at Maine Road on 10th April 1937. Above: Doherty, closely marked by Hapgood, hooks the ball over Gunners' 'keeper Boulton to give City a 35th minute lead. Below: A Daily Dispatch cartoon of the game.*

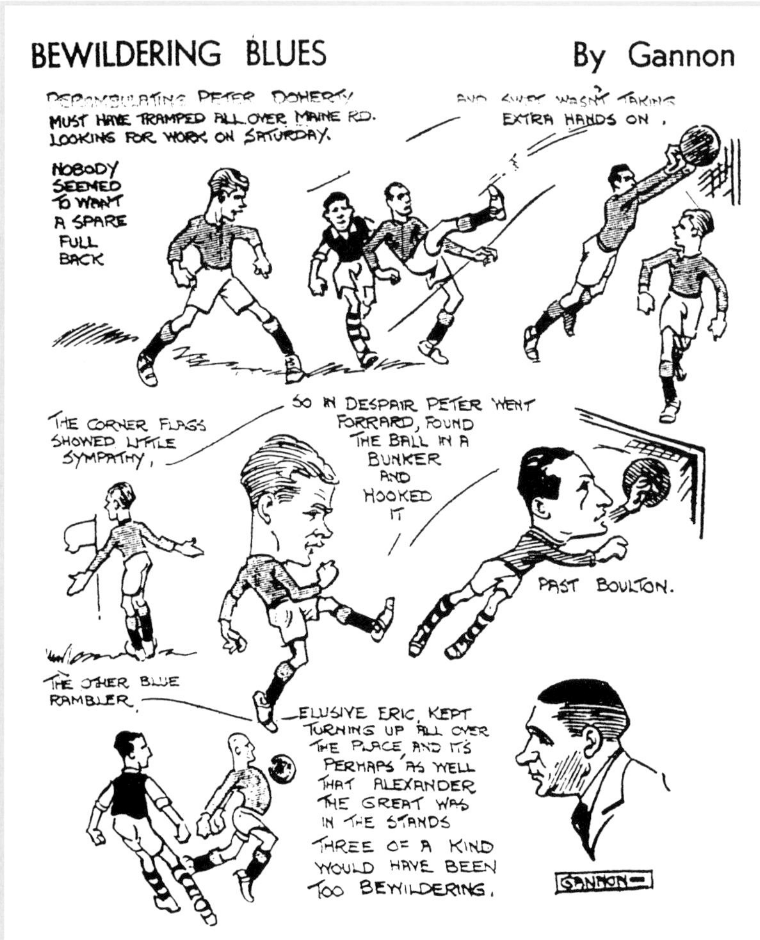

and with both teams occupying the top two places in the league there was no doubt what the match of the day - possibly the season - was going to be. The attendance for this game was quoted at the time as 76,000 - some 13,000 more than the Maine Road derby match - and potentially there were significantly more inside the fourteen year old stadium. As with many other popular matches of the period, City officials helped some supporters - most notably young boys - onto the running track around the pitch. Photos clearly show groups of supporters seated in front of City's white perimeter wall, eager to get a good view of the game.

For the early part of the match City were easily outplayed by the Gunners, but as the game progressed the Blues gradually gained control. In the 35th minute City, now matching Arsenal move for move, seized the initiative. Arsenal's Bernard Joy sliced a clearance straight to Fred Tilson on the left wing. Immediately Tilson steered a long pass to Peter Doherty, who was being closely marked by England captain Eddie Hapgood. With Arsenal's 'keeper Boulton only a yard away and with a very narrow angle, close to the goal line, Doherty somehow hooked the ball into the roof of the net.

Toseland scored a second for the Blues later in the match to give City victory and top spot in the table. With four games left City were confident the title was at long last on its way to Maine Road.

In mid-week they defeated Sunderland 3-1, despite being a goal down as late as the 67th minute, and then on 17th April the Blues played a memorable game at Preston. Both sides were missing players on international duty - City were without Sam Barkas and Jackie Bray - and the conditions were poor to say the least. The pitch was an absolute disgrace, following heavy rain, and the Blues found it difficult to cope with the mud. After 12 minutes they were two goals down and later in the half City's left-back, Robert Donnelly, was injured. With an obvious limp he moved into the outside-left position, while Eric Brook dropped back into defence.

Doherty and Herd kept switching positions hoping to fool Preston's Milne and Shankly, but the ploy was ineffective and abandoned prior to half-time. Early in the second half, with City very much under pressure, the tactic was tried again. This time it worked and Doherty pulled one back for the Blues. A minute later he scored again, and then Alec Herd cracked in City's third from a Toseland centre. Within three minutes the game had turned upside down. The Blues had surprised themselves by taking the lead.

City were now the masters and turned on the kind of football that had deservedly taken them to the top of the table. In another attack, Doherty headed City's fourth goal of the game and 100th League goal of the season and, to make Preston's misery complete, a little before the end the limping Donnelly made it 5-2. With two games left, the Blues simply needed two points to win the title.

At home to Sheffield Wednesday on 24th April, a crowd of 55,000 cheered City on to victory. As with most games that season, the Blues allowed the visitors to dominate the early moves. Gradually, City gained the upper hand and it wasn't long before Eric Brook put them into the lead with a fast, furious drive. Later, Brook told the press, and his City team mates, that he hadn't hit a shot like that for years - if ever! Within minutes Tilson made it 2-0, then a little while later, Frank Swift provided one of his famous 'lofty' clearances. Doherty gained possession in midfield and he and Tilson charged through the Wednesday defence with a rapid interchange of passes. They travelled well over 40 yards, and into the Wednesday penalty area. Tilson made one final pass before Doherty whipped the ball into the net. The Maine Road crowd loved it, and one report described it as 'one of the finest goals scored on any ground'.

At half-time the crowd gave the team, in particular Tilson and Doherty, a tremendous ovation. They desperately wanted the title, and as the game progressed they saw a side whose style of play thoroughly deserved the trophy.

In the second half, Wednesday fought back and managed to retrieve a goal, but City were simply too good for the Yorkshiremen. In the final minutes of the game Eric Brook finished what he had started and scored City's fourth. At the whistle, thousands rushed onto the pitch in celebration. The crowd sang, shouted, and cheered, until captain Sam Barkas, manager Wilf Wild, and Chairman Bob Smith appeared.

The Chairman paid tribute to the team: "It has been a fine achievement, especially as they have not been beaten since last Christmas. On behalf of myself and my fellow directors, I take this opportunity of thanking the players. We are tremendously proud of them."

Sam Barkas stressed City's teamwork: "We have all pulled together. We have been a happy family, and that is one of the secrets of our success."

Like Barkas and Smith, Wilf Wild was a very happy and proud man. Already during his five years in charge he had seen his team win the League and Cup, and feature in another Cup Final. This made him City's most successful manager, which he remained until the arrival of Joe Mercer, although Tom Maley's early reign had perhaps been destined to achieve a deal more until the scandal.

1936-37 FOOTBALL LEAGUE CHAMPIONSHIP DETAILS

RESULTS	HOME	AWAY
Middlesbrough	W 2-1	L 0-2
Leeds United	W 4-0	D 1-1
West Bromwich Albion	W 6-2	D 2-2
Manchester United	W 1-0	L 2-3
Birmingham City	D 1-1	D 2-2
Portsmouth	W 3-1	L 1-2
Chelsea	D 0-0	D 4-4
Stoke City	W 2-1	D 2-2
Charlton Athletic	D 1-1	D 1-1
Derby County	W 3-2	W 5-0
Wolverhampton W	W 4-1	L 1-2
Sunderland	L 2-4	W 3-1
Huddersfield Town	W 3-0	D 1-1
Everton	W 4-1	D 1-1
Bolton Wanderers	D 2-2	W 2-0
Arsenal	W 2-0	W 3-1
Preston North End	W 4-1	W 5-2
Sheffield Wednesday	W 4-1	L 1-5
Grimsby Town	D 1-1	L 3-5
Liverpool	W 5-1	W 5-0
Brentford	W 2-1	W 6-2

REGULAR SIDE:
Swift
Dale
Barkas
Percival
Marshall
Bray
Toseland
Herd
Tilson
Doherty
Brook

MANAGER:
Wilf Wild

LARGEST VICTORY: 6-2 v West Bromwich Albion (H) 5/9/36, Brentford (A) 3/4/37

LARGEST WINNING MARGIN: 5-0 v Derby County (A) 24/2/37, v Liverpool (A) 26/3/37

HEAVIEST DEFEAT: 1-5 v Sheffield Wednesday (A) 19/12/36

AVERAGE HOME ATTENDANCE: c.33,900

HIGHEST HOME ATTENDANCE: c.76,000 v Arsenal 10/4/37

HIGHEST AWAY ATTENDANCE: 68,796 v Manchester United 12/9/36

LEAGUE APPEARANCES: 42 Swift, Percival, Toseland, Brook, 41 Doherty, 40 Bray, 38 Marshall, 36 Dale, 32 Herd, 30 Barkas, 23 Tilson, 13 Clark, 10 Heale, 9 Rodger, 7 Donnelly, 4 Regan, 3 McLeod, 2 McCullough, Neilson, Rogers, 1 Cassidy, Freeman

LEAGUE GOALS: 30 Doherty, 20 Brook, 15 Herd, Tilson, 7 Toseland, Rodger, 6 Heale, 2 Bray, McLeod, 1 Percival, Donnelly, Neilson.

The final game of the season was away to Birmingham City, and the Blues were determined to increase their unbeaten League run to 22 games. With City losing 2-1 inside the last couple of minutes it seemed as if the amazing run would end but then came probably the most unusual goal of the season. Peter Doherty, in his autobiography, recalled the lengths he went to to ensure City's record remained: "A high ball was lobbed down the middle, and Harry Hibbs, the Birmingham 'keeper, and myself raced for it. We collided heavily, and at the moment of impact, I fisted the ball through. To my complete surprise, a goal was signalled, and there wasn't even a murmur of protest. Nobody had seen the infringement. I was credited with a perfectly good goal, and our record was intact!"

Worthy Champions deserve such luck!

Jack Percival, one of four ever-presents during City's Championship-winning season.

Manchester City - 1936-37 League Champions.
Back (left to right): Bray, Percival, Barkas, Swift, Donnelly, Marshall and Dale.
Front: Toseland, Herd, Tilson, Doherty and Brook.

While City were celebrating, across Manchester, United fans were suffering. The 1930s, so far, had seen City enjoy tremendous success. Although Arsenal were perhaps the club of the period, City were their closest rivals - not quite as successful, but better than the rest. Since the mid twenties, the Blues had also been one of the best - occasionally the best - supported clubs of the period while United struggled. The Reds had spent much of the period in the Second Division; had suffered organised boycotts, flirted with many different strips in the hope that they would find a 'lucky' kit and been very much the underdogs to City. At the end of the Blues' Championship season, the Reds were relegated.

When, in 1996, the roles were reversed, relegation was seen as the ultimate humiliation. In 1937 humiliation didn't come into it as City supporters genuinely had sympathy for United, and wanted their friends to quickly return to the top flight.

While City dominated, United came perilously close to extinction. Nobody found joy in that. Manchester needed two top clubs, preferably in the same division.

During the summer both sides prepared for the 1937-8 season. The Champions would open their First Division campaign away to Wolves, while United's opening Second Division game would be at home to Newcastle. Both sides hoped for a memorable season.

MANCHESTER CITY.

CORONATION YEAR CHAMPIONS, 1937

FIRST and foremost in Football fame,
Is Manchester City, who "play the game,"
Right from the start without much luck,
Showing opponents their determined pluck,
They're now "on top" and safely stuck.

DOHERTY, the star, who we praise so loud
In the net placed three against Preston Proud
Valuable points which were 2 of the best,
Inspired his team mates—put Arsenal at rest
Swift in goal, 3 seasons without fail
Is strongly supported by Barkas & Dale,
Our half-backs, Percival, Marshall & Bray,
Noteworthy players, who have won the day.

CENTURY of goals, 'put that in your book'
Helped by Toseland, Herd, Tilson & Brook,
Arsenal of North, our neighbours in distress,
Manchester United have failed to impress,
Perhaps some day they'll have an Eleven,
In Nineteen Hundred and Ninety Seven?
Our Manager & trainer took part in the fight,
No wonder was Wilfred Wild with delight,
Sunderland! Arsenal! Preston!-what a sight!

Fletcher & Son, 41. Tib Street, M/c., 4. (Copyright)

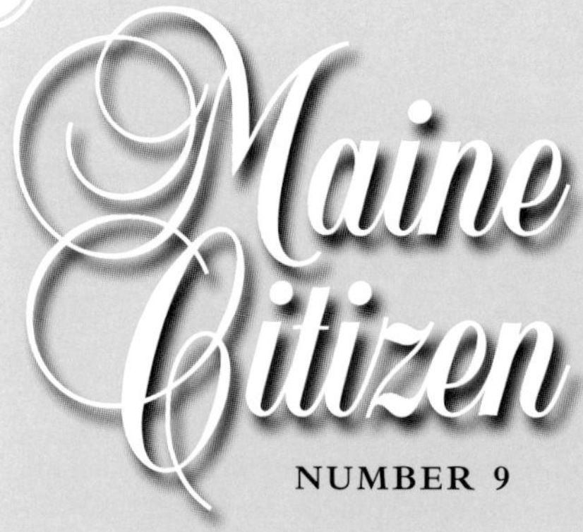

NUMBER 9

FRED TILSON

The 1934 F.A. Cup Final was perhaps the highlight of Fred Tilson's long association with the Blues. He scored both City's goals to ensure victory against Portsmouth at Wembley, bringing great delight to the thousands of Mancunians who had journeyed south - and to young goalkeeper Frank Swift who had felt responsible for allowing Portsmouth to take the lead in the first half..

Tilson was quite a character and, with his broad Yorkshire accent, helped to lighten the mood in the City dressing room on many occasions. It was a characteristic that was to help him through some difficult moments during his career. Through injury he had missed the 1933 final and, prior to that, most of the 1929-30 season, and a few international appearances for England. In fact he had been so unlucky that when Sam Cowan introduced him to King George V in 1934 the captain said: "This is Tilson, your Majesty. He's playing today with two broken legs."

With his strong Yorkshire accent Tilson responded: "Nah, he's nowt but kiddin' thee, your Majesty." Tilson wondered later if the King knew what 'kiddin' meant!

Tilson joined the Blues from Barnsley in March 1928, two days before his colleague Eric Brook. Both signings helped drive City forward. Promotion was achieved at the end of Tilson's first season, although he had only managed to make six appearances, whereas Brook appeared in 14 matches. The following season proved his worth though with 12 goals coming in 22 games. It wasn't until the thirties however that Tilson established himself, especially during the three great Cup runs of 1932-34. In '32 his hat-trick against Brentford in the fourth round and general play in the following matches helped City reach the semi-final. In 1933 he scored six in six games as the Blues marched to Wembley. If he'd been able to play against Everton, it's possible his influence would have made the final a more even contest.

During the 1933-4 Cup run he scored nine in eight games, including four against Aston Villa in the semi-final. That summer he won the first of his England caps, and kept his goalscoring touch with six goals in only four international appearances. As with Colin Bell over 30 years later, both City and England suffered through his injuries.

Deservedly, he won a League Championship medal in 1937 after 15 goals in 23 games, and continued to be viewed as one of City's greatest players. In November 1938, at the age of 35 Wilf Wild understandably believed it was time to cash in on the player and build a side for the future. In a complicated transfer, Wild brought Maurice Dunkley to Maine Road from Northampton Town in exchange for Tilson and two others. To City supporters at the time it seemed Tilson was sold rather cheaply, regardless of his age, and local reporters seemed equally mystified. Others looked back on Tilson's contribution to City's glory years. The *News Chronicle* described him as: "a bundle of pluck and enthusiasm with energy and skill far above the average. His thoughtful and well-timed passes and never-ending foraging not only put Eric Brook on the way to stardom but played a big part in City's rise."

Another newspaper simply stated: "Tilson, in his prime, was the 'Artful Dodger' - a goal snatcher above all else."

He did actually make one further first team appearance for the Blues when, on 30th March 1940 he guested at centre forward in City's 1-1 wartime draw at Stockport County. Later he returned to Maine Road on a permanent basis becoming coach, assistant manager, and then Chief Scout. He remained at City into the Mercer-Allison period, before retiring in 1967. He died in November 1972, aged 69, after a short illness.

Tilson helped bring City great success and scored many important goals. Who knows what else he may have achieved had serious injuries - in particular a bad knock in the October 1929 Manchester derby - not occurred at crucial moments in his career. Tilson was undoubtedly one of the driving forces behind City's great 1930s decade.

TILSON'S PLAYING RECORD

	LEAGUE		FA CUP		TOTAL	
	App	Gls	App	Gls	App	Gls
1927-28	6	0	0	0	6	0
1928-29	22	12	0	0	22	12
1929-30	11	7	1	0	12	7
1930-31	17	4	1	0	18	4
1931-32	37	13	5	3	42	16
1932-33	29	17	6	6	35	23
1933-34	21	12	8	9	29	21
1934-35	34	18	1	0	35	18
1935-36	32	11	2	1	34	12
1936-37	23	15	4	3	27	18
1937-38	13	1	0	0	13	1
TOTAL	245	110	28	22	273	132

City's Greatest Player?

PETER DOHERTY

The question of who is City's greatest-ever player is never going to produce a definitive answer. Each era produces its own heroes. Many of these are acclaimed as the best ever - for example Billy Meredith at the turn of the century, Bert Trautmann in the forties and fifties, Colin Bell in the sixties and seventies, and Georgi Kinkladze in the 1990s. But the real test of how great a player truly is comes many years after that man has stopped playing. When considering the greatest it's vital to predict how the individual will be viewed thirty or even fifty years after he has stopped playing.

Colin Bell is regarded by many as the greatest ever, but an earlier generation remembers another. A man whose status and position in football history has remained high for over fifty years - Peter Doherty. Anyone who saw him play will say he truly was the greatest of all City players.

Doherty was a complete footballer, idolised by City fans for many breathtaking performances. As an inside-forward he seemed perfect - he created chances, continually challenged the opposition, and scored with regularity- but Doherty was more than that. He enthralled supporters with his artistry and was often described as the linchpin of City's 1936-7 Championship winning side. He possessed a great tactical brain and was clearly more gifted than most of his contemporaries.

Bill Shankly once named Doherty as his most difficult opponent, while over twenty years after Doherty had stopped playing, City's great manager Joe Mercer described the player as the greatest ever produced by Ireland. Mercer knew what he was saying. He'd played against Doherty on many occasions, and had also appeared alongside him during wartime matches. He also knew his comment would raise a few eyebrows in the media as another Irishman, George Best, was already being talked of as a

great player. Interestingly, no one appeared to disagree with Mercer's comments at the time and, even today, Doherty is still discussed as an outstanding footballer.

Back in 1974 - a period when George Best had already achieved most, if not all, of his best playing performances - the Rothmans Football Yearbook recorded that Doherty was "regarded by many judges as the greatest player Ireland has ever produced."

According to another author, Dave Bowler, Doherty was: "a truly great player, one who ranks with the likes of George Best as the very finest Northern Ireland has ever produced. For the youngsters of Belfast dreaming of football glory, Doherty was the man to emulate. Belfast's youth could have had no better role model."

One such fan was Danny Blanchflower, captain of Tottenham's 1961 double-winning side. He once admitted: "As a small boy I cherished the name of Manchester City ... my dreams each night were full of the sky blue shirts. I waved the flag for no better reason than that Peter Doherty played for them."

As far as Doherty's playing career is concerned, he joined the Blues for a club record £10,000 in February 1936, making his debut in the 3-1 defeat by Preston on 22nd. Within a year he was the club's top scorer as the Blues won the League Championship for the first time.

The war interrupted his career. It also strained his relationship with the club as his availability for other clubs as a guest player led to petty disputes between the City management and the player. Inevitably he moved on once the war was over and FA Cup success at Derby in 1946 was followed by spells at Huddersfield and Doncaster.

He moved into management at Doncaster and went on to guide Northern Ireland to the 1958 World Cup quarter-finals. It's a little known fact that during the mid-sixties Doherty very nearly became City's manager. The Blues were struggling in Division Two and the City directors had compiled a short-list of candidates. One of those was Peter Doherty while another was Bill Shankly. The man who eventually took the job - and guided City to phenomenal success - was Joe Mercer, but it was very nearly Doherty's role.

Links with City continued throughout Doherty's life. His son Paul was Programme Editor at Maine Road for many years and also became Head of Sport at Granada TV. In addition, Peter Doherty was the man responsible for recommending Kevin Keegan to Liverpool in 1971, so it could be argued he even had an indirect impact on City's promotion during 2002.

In April 1990 Doherty died after a lifetime of sporting achievement. Appropriately, he will always be known as one of City's greatest players. Many would argue he will always remain the greatest.

Chapter Ten

LIVING WITH THE ENEMY

AS champions the Blues were expected to be the team to watch. They were the ones who would supposedly set the football world alight. Sadly, City made the headlines through failure rather than success.

City's dismal season began on 28th August 1937 with a 3-1 defeat at Wolverhampton. A few exciting victories followed, including the 6-1 thrashing of Derby County, but by Christmas it was obvious the Blues were struggling. They continued to score plenty of goals, however, and were expected to finish in safety, well away from danger. It wasn't to be.

An appalling February followed by an equally disastrous March placed City in severe difficulty and caused Manager Wild to enter the transfer market. He purchased wing-half Les McDowall from Sunderland for a little over £7,000, despite the 6ft player only making 13 appearances in his five years at Roker Park. McDowall made his debut on 16th March in City's 1-1 draw at West Bromwich. Around the same time long serving Tilson moved to Northampton Town, as did McCullough and Rodger.

With new blood, City made a little progress in April with nine points and twenty-two goals from eight games. On 2nd April the Blues defeated Chelsea 1-0 at Maine Road to lift them to 18th position, then four days later beat Charlton 5-3 in a game the *Daily Dispatch* described as 'crazy'. Charlton took the lead as early as the third minute, then a minute later Milsom, who'd signed from Bolton in February, equalised. In the 17th minute he nodded in his second and then five minutes later Bray made it 3-1. It remained so to the interval then two minutes into the second half Frank Swift was forced to run some distance from his line to save from Charlton's Tadman. Another Charlton man, Robinson, gained control of the rebound and fired past the City 'keeper, who was desperately trying to scramble his way back, to make it 3-2. Four minutes later the Addicks equalised.

In the 65th minute Pritchard regained the lead for City with a left foot shot from Brook's corner, and 18 minutes from time Milsom scored his hat-trick with a clever run, followed by a shot that went a fraction wide of goalkeeper Bartram's left hand.

Despite Milsom's hat trick, the best City goalscorers of the period were undoubtedly Eric Brook and Peter Doherty. Brook netted four in the 7-1 return with West Bromwich, while Doherty scored a hat-trick as the Blues defeated Leeds 6-2 in their penultimate game.

City were a shade fortunate in their high scoring defeat of West Bromwich as the visitors' goalkeeper, Little, badly bruised his shoulder in the 22nd minute and was forced to leave the field for a spell. When he returned he was unable to move his right arm from his side. Another player, Finch,

Jack Milsom scored 5 goals in 13 games after signing from Bolton in February 1938.

Frank Swift in goal at Molineux during City's opening match of the 1937-38 season.

West Bromwich's full back, also went off with a gashed head following a collision with Eric Brook. On his return he joined Little out on the wing.

By the time of Little's injury the Blues were already two goals up - a Brook penalty in the second minute and a Doherty header twenty minutes later - but once he'd left the field City could not be stopped.

Despite these victories, the Blues were deep in relegation trouble by 23rd April. With three games left, City lay in 21st position on 33 points, although the four clubs above them were only one point better off. Even Blackpool in 12th place could still be relegated. To boost City's attack following a disappointing 2-1 defeat at Bolton, Wilf Wild decided to drop Milsom for the first time since his transfer from Bolton, and replace him with Jimmy Heale for the return match at Charlton. The game ended goalless despite considerable City pressure, while Heale performed well enough to retain his place for the home game with Leeds on 30th April.

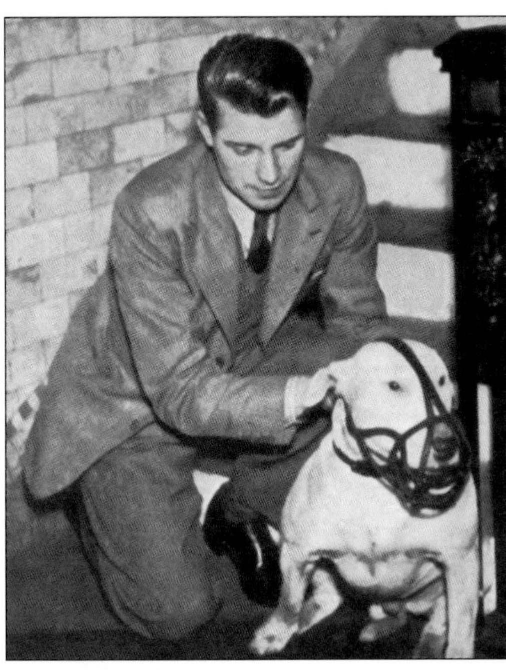

Peter Doherty with a rather fierce looking City mascot.

City won that one 6-2, but remained in danger. The final match was away to Huddersfield, who were also struggling. On the final day of the season seven sides teetered on the brink of the dreaded drop, with both City and Huddersfield only needing a point to survive. A draw seemed the perfect result, but for Huddersfield there was much more at stake. Only a week earlier, the Yorkshiremen had been defeated by Preston in the F.A. Cup final. The game had been a dramatic one, with Huddersfield losing to a goal scored from a penalty awarded twenty seconds from the end of extra time.

Huddersfield were still smarting and needed a morale-boosting victory. A draw would not be god enough, City realised this and went all out for a goal. Despite piling on the pressure luck was not on their side as, in the second half, a magnificent 35 yard drive from Alec Herd proved. The shot hit the cross bar and came down again. The referee waved play on but Peter Doherty, who was fairly close at the time, claimed the ball had entered the net: "In my opinion the ball struck an iron stay at the back of the net and rebounded into play. I could have sworn it was a goal."

In the 78th minute City's luck really did fail when Huddersfield took the lead through a scrappy goal. City continued to push forward but it was no good. As the whistle went the Huddersfield players and supporters celebrated while City had to wait. Memories of the 1927 promotion race came flooding back as the Blues waited to hear how the other results had gone. Eventually the players in the dressing room were given the news that fellow strugglers Grimsby, Portsmouth, Birmingham, and Stoke had all won.

If any one of those sides had been defeated City would have been safe on goal average. As it was the Blues ended the season in 21st place despite scoring more goals than any other team in the division.

City's agony was compounded by further news relayed to the players and supporters - Manchester United had been promoted on goal average. Although it wasn't known at the time, this reversal in Manchester football - during the City of Manchester's centenary year - would affect sport in the city for a number of years, right through to the late 1960s.

In May 1938 Billy Dale (right) moved to Ipswich Town in a complicated deal after making 269 first team appearances.

Some would argue that the repercussions have affected Manchester football right through to the new millennium.

Despite relegation it wasn't all doom and gloom for the Blues. On 4th November City had set Maine Road alight with a 2-0 defeat of Sunderland to win the Charity Shield for the first time in their history, and also reached the sixth round of the F.A. Cup. They lost a thrilling game 3-2 before a then Villa Park record crowd of 75,540. One other cup result worth mentioning was the 3-1 defeat of Millwall in the third round replay, which gained revenge for the previous season's disaster.

1938-9 would place the two sides in the same division for the first time in history following Millwall's promotion from the Third Division South. Their first League meeting on 17th September proved Blues boss Wilf Wild needed to act quickly if he was to fulfil City's dream of an immediate return, as Millwall easily achieved a 6-1 Maine Road victory. For that game Wild had dropped goalkeeper Frank Swift, after three successive defeats. The story was turned into a major news item with journalists from both Manchester evening 'papers, the *News* and the *Chronicle*, and some of the dailies turning up at Swift's house for his view of the affair. Naturally, Swift was far from happy but, with his typical good natured and humorous approach, he laughed at suggestions he was unhappy.

Also missing by this time was Peter Doherty who had damaged ligaments in his right knee during the third game of the season - a 4-2 defeat at Bradford Park Avenue - and his absence created an obvious gap in City's attack. When Alec Herd also went down injured in the 3-3 draw at Blackburn on 24th September Wilf Wild could feel the pressure mounting.

By the end of September the Blues were really struggling after amassing a mere five points from nine games. This put City in the bottom four of the Second Division, and caused some supporters to attack the direction of the club. According to Peter Doherty's autobiography letters arrived at Maine Road addressed to 'The Blind Asylum' and opened with the line 'Dear Blunderers'. Something had to be done.

There was a slight upturn in form during the latter weeks of October, when the Blues achieved a no score draw at Plymouth and a 3-2 Maine Road victory over Sheffield United. Defeat at West Bromwich followed but on 5th November a new look City was ready to face Tottenham at Maine Road.

Full back Eric Westwood, who had signed from United in November 1937, was set to make his debut along with a new signing from Spurs, Bert Sproston. Sproston had actually been selected by Tottenham to play against City, but the player had been struggling to settle in the capital after signing for the London club only four months earlier. City negotiated with Tottenham to bring the Sandbach-born England international back to the north west, and the day before the game signed him for £9,500 - the same sum Spurs had paid Leeds in June. Unusually Sproston made his debut against his former club.

In addition, Peter Doherty returned to the side, although he was far from fully fit. Wild was determined to gain victory and build a promotion-seeking side, no matter what the cost. The Doherty gamble paid off as the Blues won the game 2-0 with the Irishman supplying one of the goals himself. It was also the kick-start City needed as they embarked on a seven game unbeaten run.

From that point on City climbed up the table but were never really able to challenge for promotion - the bad spell during September and early October and injuries throughout the season had seen to that. Even new signing Sproston had to miss seven games during the crucial spring period, after sustaining an injury in the Spurs return game. This was an incredible match for the former Tottenham man as, after his injury, he was moved to outside left with Eric Brook dropping back to defend. While playing as a forward Sproston managed to score to level the game at 2-2 and then, with only a couple of minutes to go, headed in a centre from Maurice Dunkley to give City victory.

The season ended with City in fifth position, five points behind second placed Sheffield United. Considering the start this was a respectable position. It was also true that the Blues remained one of the most prolific sides of the period as City's total of 96 League goals was more than any other club in the League.

With City remaining in Division Two the close season discussions still considered how the Blues could

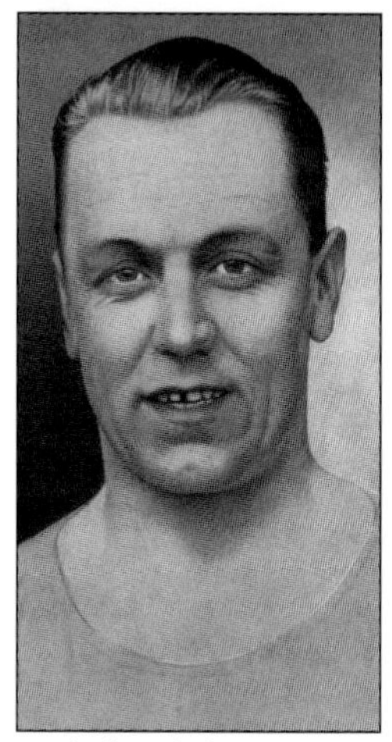

Fred Tilson left City in November 1938 after a total of 273 first team games and 132 goals.

Bert Sproston (below left) joined Peter Doherty at Maine Road for the last season prior to the War.

return to the First. Little did anyone realise their chances of doing this would be delayed for at least another seven years as war was about to sweep Europe.

Throughout the summer months, as the prospect of war increased, many players had enlisted in the Territorial Army or other such national service organisations.

Liverpool went one stage further than most when they became the first team to join the Territorial Army as a club. West Ham and Bolton followed their example and volunteered en masse, while the directors of Manchester United took a less patriotic view: "It is a matter for the individual to decide".

Amid growing uncertainty the 1939-40 season opened with City away to Leicester. The line-up was a familiar one: Swift, Sproston, Westwood, McDowall, Cardwell, Bray, Dunkley, Herd, Heale, Doherty, and Brook. For the unpredictable Sky Blues, the result was a disappointing one as City crashed 4-3 at Filbert Street on Saturday 26th August.

Four days later, as 'The Wizard Of Oz' was making it's way around American cinemas for the first time, City entertained Bury in a 1-1 draw at Maine Road. Understandably, the crowd was a rather subdued 20,000. The following day the evacuation of children from British cities began and within a week over a million children were moved into the country. But, for the time being, football was to continue despite the increasing threat of war.

MILSOM'S TWO GOALS IN BRILLIANT COME-BACK

Manchester City 2, Chesterfield 0

MANCHESTER CITY'S first triumph of the season was the result of an all-round clever display. The whole side worked like a well-oiled machine and had they seized the majority of chances presented to them, they would have won by a much more handsome margin (writes Roamer).

Brook failed with a penalty kick after 10 minutes, when Herd was brought down, but Milsom, restored to centre-forward, gave an I'll-show-em display. He scored two goals, the first after 36 minutes and the second after 56 minutes, and might have accomplished the hat-trick.

Middleton gave a great display in the Chesterfield goal, but after the interval Manchester City simply toyed with the opposition. McDowall and Bray were excellent wing-halves, and the defence of Swift, Sproston, Westwood and Cardwell was more solid than in the first two matches of the season.

Cardwell held a tight grip on Milligan, the visitors' real danger men being Miller, Lyon and Sinclair.

ANOTHER APPEAL IGNORED
AW, ADOLF, BLOW YOUR "SIXTEEN POINTS" WHAT ABOUT MY SIX ?
2 POINTS
2 POINTS
2 POINTS
ACCRINGTON STANLEY
NO MORE HOARDING

'Another Appeal Ignored' Accrington Stanley were the only League side with maximum points after three games. The cancellation of the League programme was a major blow to the club. Their 'A' team didn't mind though .... City defeated them 6-1 in the Lancashire League.

On Saturday 2nd September, the day after the Germans commenced their invasion of Poland, the Blues welcomed Chesterfield while Wilf Wild made one alteration to his line-up, replacing Jimmy Heale with Jack Milsom. The change seemed perfect when the former Bolton forward netted twice to give City a 2-0 victory before 15,000 - this despite Brook missing a penalty in the tenth minute.

In the Central League the Blues defeated Chesterfield 3-0 while City's 'A' team defeated Accrington Stanley 'A' 6-1 in the Lancashire League. Incidentally, Accrington Stanley's first team, playing in the Third Division (North) were the only team in the four divisions with maximum points from three games.

Later in the day news came through that 21 people had died as the result of an air-raid on Warsaw. At noon the following day, as supporters were reading the Sunday reports, Prime Minister Neville Chamberlain announced: "This Country is now at war with Germany. We are ready."

A ban was immediately placed on the assembly of large crowds. One wag joked that the still relatively poorly supported Old Trafford club would have nothing to worry about. Then the announcement was made that the League programme should be cancelled and all players' contracts suspended. City's chance of promotion had gone.

By the end of September, The FA had relaxed their rules and given permission for the organisation of mini-leagues or competitions consisting of teams within straightforward travelling distance. One proviso was that games could only be played on either Saturdays or Bank Holidays, and the attendance had to be less than 8,000 or half the capacity of the ground, whichever was the lower figure. Later this was relaxed a little, providing the match was all ticket. In the *Daily Dispatch* for 20th September news appeared that John Maxwell, the Chief Constable of Manchester, had given approval for crowds of between ten and fifteen thousand. He went on to lay down a number of conditions: "Mr. Maxwell explained that the police were anxious not to be unduly restrictive on the management of the public, but that there must be a safety margin to allow dispersal in case of air raid warning. Among the conditions imposed by the police are:-

"Gas masks must be carried by spectators, a look out must be posted outside the ground to listen for sirens or other warnings, loud-speaker equipment must be installed, and a competent speaker appointed to advise the crowd regarding dispersal and the nearest shelter in case of emergency.

"The Manchester United ground, being outside the city boundary, comes under the authority of

Frank Swift with brother Fred (Bolton Wanderers' goalkeeper), on board their boat close to their family home in Blackpool. Both men were regular fishermen during the summer.

Lancashire County Constabulary, whose decision regarding play is expected today."

In addition to this news players were told by the F.A. they were allowed to receive a wage of 30 shillings a week, with no bonuses, while they played for a club.

During this time of confusion, most of the players who hadn't previously enlisted now joined the forces or obtained work in war-supportive industry, although this often caused friction between club and player. Peter Doherty was offered work in Greenock, Scotland, and immediately City Chairman Robert Smith told the player he would not be allowed to play in Scotland. Discussions took place for some time before Doherty felt forced to turn down the Scottish job and remain in Manchester. Another director found him work in Manchester for a time, then he joined a few Blackpool players at the ordnance factory at Risley. Early in 1940 he decided to volunteer for the R.A.F. At one point he joined City team mate Jackie Bray training as a PT instructor at Uxbridge.

Frank Swift became a special police constable when war broke out but, according to Swift's biography, he became so confused when directing traffic he felt it better to walk away and let the vehicles sort themselves out! Another player, Les McDowall, returned to Scotland and played for St. Mirren for virtually the whole of the hostilities.

By mid-October plans for the new mini-leagues had been formed. City were to play alongside First Division sides United, Everton, Liverpool, Stoke, and the Third Division's Chester, Crewe, New Brighton, Port Vale, Stockport, Tranmere, and Wrexham in the Western League.

The opening fixture on 21st October was a Manchester derby at Old Trafford before a restricted crowd of 7,000. Regardless of the state of the nation, or the size of crowd, the City players saw this match as the perfect opportunity to show City were still equal to the Reds despite the official League placings. With goals from Brook, Doherty, Heale, and Herd the Blues defeated United 4-0. The week after 4,000 watched Wrexham beaten 6-1 at Maine Road. Results didn't always go that well for the Blues - a 7-3 Maine Road trouncing at the hands of Liverpool in January proves this point - but it was a rather successful season considering the situation in the world at large.

Football was a powerful motivator during these early months of the war and in an extremely minor way helped ease the situation. The 22 game league programme ended with City placed fifth on equal

Jimmy Heale was beginning to establish himself in the City side when war broke out. By the time League football returned he had retired.

MANCHESTER CITY

F. CHAPPELL
Goal

2
CLARK
Right Back

3
BRAY
Left Back

4
WALSH
Right Half-Back

5
EASTWOOD
Centre Half Back

6
L. BARDSLEY
Left Half Back

7
KING
Outside Right

8
K. CHISHOLM
Inside Right

9
F. LEECH
Centre

10
DOHERTY
Inside Left

11
C. BARCLAY
Outside Left

Referee:
J. WILLIAMS, Bolton.
Kick-off 3 p.m.

Linesmen:
J. WARD (Red Flag)
J. SPENCER (Blue Flag)

11
WHEELER
Outside Left

10
PATERSON
Inside Left

9
GLIDDEN
Centre

8
SPENCER
Inside Right

7
JONES
Outside Right

6
ANDERSON
Left Half-Back

5
HUGHES
Centre Half Back

4
HILL
Right Half Back

3
KIERAN
Left Back

2
DENNETT
Right Back

BIRKETT
Goal

TRANMERE ROVERS

ONE PENNY

MANCHESTER CITY F. C. Ltd.
OFFICIAL PROGRAMME
BLUE AND WHITE

(Entered at Stationers' Hall.)

Vol. 38. No. 7 SATURDAY, DECEMBER 4th, 1943

JIMMY HEALE IS READY!

CONSIDERING that the Manchester City team has been so unsettled this season, it is very gratifying to see them occupying a good position in the League. The club, owing to war-time conditions, has already called on 33 players for the 14 games of the present campaign. On only one occasion this season have the City been able to play the same team in successive games. These were last October 2 and 9 against Bolton Wanderers and Wrexham respectively.

Still, the City, despite all their difficulties — and they have been as badly hit as any other club—have managed to get a team together week by week, and that is their chief consideration. In the process they have given the younger end every chance of proving themselves, and this policy, though enforced on most occasions, is yielding results. They can point to interesting discoveries. I mention their young goalkeepers, Scales and Chappell; to full-back Jackson; and to Barclay, Dodd, Bardsley, Leech and Worrall.

Here are eight junior players who have been "graded" long before they would have been in normal times, and it is to the credit of every one of them that they have not let the team down. In fact, I will go so far as to say that certain of them would not disgrace any side in the country, and that is a fine tribute to their abilities.

READY FOR THE CALL

MEANWHILE, perhaps one of the most interesting items of news in the City camp is that Jimmy Heale may be seen in the side very soon. I was only able briefly to mention the possibility in last week's programme, because the information did not reach me until the issue was going to press, but I was delighted to see Heale at the City ground last week.

He is in the Manchester City Police Force, and permission has been given for him to turn out again in the City side, although it will be as an amateur, of course. At the moment certain negotiations are taking place

NEXT MATCH HERE
UNITED v. WREXHAM
AT MAINE ROAD KICK-OFF 3 p.m
SATURDAY, DECEMBER 11th, 1943

Printed by Withy Grove Press Limited, Manchester 4.

The front and back cover of City's programme for the 2-2 draw with Tranmere Rovers on 4th December 1943, watched by a crowd of 3,500. A week later City won the return game 6-0.

points with United (fourth) and Everton (third). The Western champions were Stoke, with Liverpool second.

City also played a total of 15 first team friendlies - winning 10, drawing 3 and losing 2. The biggest victories during this sequence both came against Stockport with City winning 5-0 away and 7-2 at home - Jimmy Heale scored four in this match. There was also a War Cup; the first round was to be played over two legs and the draw was regionalised. City drew United and in the first leg defeated the Reds 1-0 at Old Trafford. Unfortunately, City lost the return 2-0 before over 21,000 spectators.

Already teams were having to make use of visiting players, with City giving games to ten different guests. Preston's James McIntosh played his one and only league game for City in the February 1940 Manchester derby, while Fred Tilson and Ernie Toseland both returned for single appearances.

International football also continued throughout the War, although caps were not awarded for these matches. For the Wales v England match on 18th November 1939 Swift, Sproston, and Brook helped England to a 3-2 victory. Two weeks later Sam Barkas and Eric Brook were travelling to Newcastle for a clash with Scotland when they were involved in a car crash. Neither was able to make the game so England fielded a couple of Newcastle men instead. One of them, Tommy Pearson, was actually Scottish. This was typical of the abnormal nature of wartime sport.

As for the two City players involved in the crash, Sam Barkas did not manage to play again for City until February, while Brook badly fractured his skull and was never able to play for the Blues again. It was a tragic end to a wonderful City and England career.

For 1940-41 the leagues were developed further. There would only be two regional leagues with City playing in the Northern section, but for the first time there would be no points awarded at all. Instead the league would be decided on goal average as clubs would be playing an unequal number of matches. Clubs were expected to organise their own fixtures, but each First and Second Division club were asked to play at least two Third Division teams. They were also expected to play over twenty games.

With this rather strange approach to football, where goals were all that mattered, the regularly high scoring Blues were expected to do well. In fact City applied to the F.A. to allow league games to be played on Sundays. Whether this was to squeeze more fixtures in, or simply the hope that Sundays would allow greater attendances isn't known. What is fact is that City played a total of 35 league games, winning 18 and drawing 10. But the important figures were the goals scored and conceded with City finding the net an incredible 104 times - more than any other team in the Northern and Southern sections.

55 goals were conceded giving City an average of 1.89, placing them third behind Preston and Chesterfield. Had the table been decided on goal difference, the high-scoring Blues would have been clear winners.

In the War Cup City progressed past Blackpool, Blackburn, and Everton to face Preston in the fourth round - the northern semi-final. Preston were, without doubt, the real team of the season as they defeated City in the first leg 2-1 and 3-0 in the return and went on to defeat Arsenal in the national final.

One guest player appearing for the Blues in the Preston games, and for much of the season, was United man Harry McShane, the father of actor Ian McShane who years later would also appear in front of City's supporters during filming of football scenes for the film 'Yesterday's Hero'.

Other guest players included another Red, the future United captain and Player of the Year Johnny Carey. Both Carey and McShane found the net at City, with Carey scoring in the 6-4 victory over Bolton while McShane scored twice - once in a 2-2 draw at Burnley on Christmas Day 1940 and once in City's 2-0 defeat of United on 5th October at Old Trafford. During the seven wartime seasons a total of 82 players guested for the Blues.

As war progressed the regional football programme became more complicated; the league schedule was split into two with some games counting as War Cup or Lancashire Cup games. In 1941 the Northern League ended on Christmas Day. Each club played against nine others, home and away, for points rather than goal average. The results for all 38 northern clubs were then compiled into one enormous table. City finished 17th, ten points behind champions Blackpool.

The second half of the season allowed clubs to play as many games as they wished, with the proviso that a minimum of 18 games should be included in the final table. City only managed 17 as Blackpool, who eventually finished runners up in the table, withdrew from two fixtures. The Blues again reached the quarter-final of the War Cup.

The same format existed until 1945 with City finishing 30th out of 48 in the pre-Christmas 1942 league, and 3rd in the post-Christmas championship that followed. 1943-44 saw City finish 17th, then 19th, and reach the semi-final of the northern section of the War Cup. The following season a pre-Christmas City reached the improved position of 10th and then struggled in the New Year, eventually reaching 47th out of 60 clubs.

During the summer of 1945, with peace restored across Europe, the FA and the League made plans to bring football back to normality. It was too late to return to a full pre-war programme and so for the last time football was to be divided on a regional basis with all First and Second Division clubs in the North playing each other home and away. The old Third Division North and South were to be recreated as far as possible to play their own competition. City ended a fairly satisfactory season in tenth place but in the F.A. Cup, which had been reinstated at the request of the clubs, City crashed out in the fourth round to Bradford.

The competition largely followed the style of the War Cup with rounds played on a two legged basis. In the third round City defeated Barrow 8-4 on aggregate, and had managed to defeat Bradford 3-1 at Park Avenue, but in the return City were trounced 8-2 - their record home defeat.

The Blues played a total of 42 first team fixtures, plus the F.A. Cup. In addition, there was the Lancashire Senior Cup and a total of 40 Central League games, while the A team were also back in action playing at Droylsden - one game ended in a 9-3 victory away at Manchester United.

And so, with the ending of hostilities football was able to return to normal, with City back in the Second Division for the start of the 1946-7 season. Although the war rightly overshadowed everything else that occurred during the period it's worth considering a few other moments that affected or involved City and Mancunian football. Firstly, the bombing of Old Trafford's multi-span Main Stand on 11th March 1941 saw the compassionate side of football; City offered to let United use Maine Road for an annual rent of around £5,000 plus a share of gate receipts whilst they were allowed to use United's Cliff ground for reserve fixtures. Older supporters will remember the prospect of ground-sharing during the 1920s which eventually came to nothing.

George Smith scored all four goals in a 4-1 win against United in a War League game in April 1946.

The Reds were also now managed by former City cup winner Matt Busby.

In addition to United using Maine Road, City's stadium hosted the October 1943 Scotland v England international. It was an incredible 8-0 English victory, often regarded as the best national performance of all time. Naturally, Frank Swift was the England 'keeper and future City manager Joe Mercer claimed it was the greatest game he had ever appeared in. The crowd was an impressive wartime figure of 60,000.

In 1946, the FA Cup semi-final replay between Birmingham and Derby was also played at Maine Road. An enormous 80,480 people attended the game, which remains the record attendance for a midweek game between two Football League clubs outside Wembley.

The return of the full League programme for 1946-47 was eagerly awaited. For City a return to the First Division was vital and, from the moment the season opened on 31st August with a 3-0 victory at

Frank Swift makes a daring save during England's 3-0 defeat of Wales at Maine Road on 14th November 1946.

1946-47 DIVISION TWO CHAMPIONSHIP DETAILS

RESULTS	HOME	AWAY
Leicester City	W 1-0	W 3-0
Bury	W 3-1	D 2-2
Chesterfield	D 0-0	W 1-0
Millwall	W 1-0	W 3-1
Bradford (Park Avenue)	W 7-2	D 1-1
Tottenham Hotspur	W 1-0	D 0-0
West Ham United	W 2-0	L 0-1
Sheffield Wednesday	W 2-1	L 0-1
Swansea Town	D 1-1	W 2-1
Newcastle United	L 0-2	L 2-3
West Bromwich Albion	W 5-0	L 1-3
Birmingham City	W 1-0	L 1-3
Coventry City	W 1-0	D 1-1
Nottingham Forest	W 2-1	W 1-0
Southampton	D 1-1	W 1-0
Newport County	W 5-1	W 3-0
Barnsley	W 5-1	W 2-0
Burnley	W 1-0	D 0-0
Plymouth Argyle	W 4-3	W 3-2
Fulham	W 4-0	D 2-2
Luton Town	W 2-0	D 0-0

REGULAR SIDE:

Swift
Sproston
Barkas
Fagan
McDowall
Emptage
Dunkley
Herd
Black
Smith
Westwood

MANAGER:

Wilf Wild then
Sam Cowan from
3rd December

LARGEST VICTORY: 7-2 v Bradford (Park Avenue) (H) 21/9/46

LARGEST WINNING MARGIN: 5 goals - 7-2 v Bradford (Park Avenue) (H) 21/9/46, 5-0 V West Bromwich Albion (H) 2/11/46

HEAVIEST DEFEAT: 1-3 v Birmingham City (A) 9/11/46, West Bromwich Albion (A) 31/5/47

AVERAGE HOME ATTENDANCE: c.37,695

HIGHEST HOME ATTENDANCE: 67,672 v Burnley 10/5/47

HIGHEST AWAY ATTENDANCE: 65,798 v Newcastle United 26/10/46

LEAGUE APPEARANCES: 38 Sproston, Smith, 35 Swift, McDowall, 34 Black, 33 Barkas, 32 Dunkley, 29 Emptage, 28 Herd, Westwood, 20 Fagan, 18 Constantine, 16 Percival, 13 Walsh, 9 Woodroffe, Eastwood, 7 Jackson, Williams, Hope, 6 Thurlow, 5 Capel, 3 Wharton, 2 Rudd, Cardwell, 1 Clarke, Hodgson, Murray, Oakes, Robinson (J), Robinson (P), Rigby, McCormack

LEAGUE GOALS: 23 Smith, 13 Black, 12 Constantine, 11 Herd, 4 Dunkley, 3 McDowall, 2 Sproston, Westwood, Jackson, 1 Walsh, Woodroffe, Capel, Wharton.

Action from the Burnden Park Disaster Fund match at Maine Road, 26th August 1946. Frank Swift, seen here taking the ball off the head of Scotland's Thornton, captained England to a 2-2 draw.

Leicester, the Blues entertained their fans. The team was, in the main, a familiar one with the likes of Swift, Sproston, Barkas, McDowall, Herd, and Westwood appearing, but the great Peter Doherty was no longer at Maine Road. Throughout the war the player and club were at loggerheads with City's directors often refusing to let their valuable asset guest for other clubs. They were angry that he'd been unable to play in a few crucial fixtures - it had been impossible for him to get back to Manchester - and so they forbade him to guest for Derby County. Instead they stated he could play for Manchester United, but as United were playing at Maine Road this seemed to imply that any attempt to turn out for the Reds would bring him into further trouble. Surely he couldn't play for United on City's ground?

In the end the situation became so difficult that Doherty - many claim the greatest League player of all time - asked to be transfer listed. In December 1945 he moved on to Derby County for £7,000. It was a sad loss.

Throughout 1946-47 City, frequently watched by large crowds, challenged for promotion. In November 1946, the no doubt exhausted Wilf Wild ended his fourteen year reign as manager to return to purely secretarial duties. His period in charge had been largely a successful one, with more trophies won under him than any predecessor. He remained in office through to his death in December 1950. Keeping City going throughout the war must have taken its toll.

Wild's replacement was former captain Sam Cowan who accepted the position on 3rd December 1946. The only problem was Cowan had set up a rather successful physiotherapy practice in Brighton and felt he could not move away. Much to the directors' annoyance he commuted to Manchester throughout the season.

On New Year's Day a 4-0 victory over Fulham sent City to the top of the table in style. It also saw the debut of future Liverpool manager Joe Fagan. The Blues were playing like champions but, more importantly, looked ready for the First Division. The only problem was the weather. Postponements dragged the season through to mid June, by which time City started to drop a few points but it hardly mattered. The Blues won the title with 62 points - four more than second placed Burnley. Popular City were back in the First Division.

The 1946-7 promotion season ended on 14th June 1947 - the latest finish ever experienced by the Blues. The final match was a strange one for two reasons. First George Smith scored all City's goals in a 5-1 defeat of Newport to equal Tommy Johnson's record of most goals in a single match. Secondly, Roy Clarke made his debut and was in the middle of achieving the unusual feat of playing consecutive games in three different divisions. His previous game had been for Cardiff in the Third Division South, his debut was in the Second Division, and his next match was in the First Division.

Some of the players who helped City win the Second Division championship in 1946-47.

Back row (left to right): Sproston, Smith, W.Walsh, Black, Cardwell.
Front row: Dunkley, McDowall, Swift, Jackson, Rudd, Barkas.

The Football League
Second Division Championship 1946-47

★ ★

Celebration
Dinner and Dance
of the
Manchester City Football Club Ltd.

★ ★

Grand Hotel
Manchester
12th August, 1947

Left: The cover of a menu for the special banquet held at Manchester's Grand Hotel to celebrate City's return to the top division.

Below: Johnny Hart's invitation to the event.

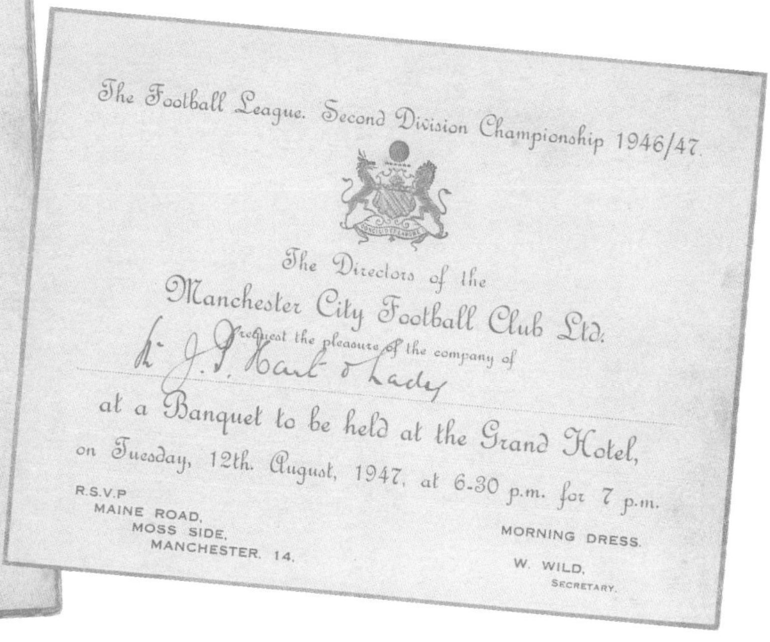

The Football League. Second Division Championship 1946/47.

The Directors of the
Manchester City Football Club Ltd.
request the pleasure of the company of
Mr J. F. Hart & Lady
at a Banquet to be held at the Grand Hotel,
on Tuesday, 12th. August, 1947, at 6-30 p.m. for 7 p.m.

R.S.V.P
MAINE ROAD,
MOSS SIDE,
MANCHESTER. 14.

MORNING DRESS.
W. WILD,
SECRETARY.

Eddie McMorran scored on his debut for City, a 4-3 victory over Wolves on 23rd August 1947.

Despite promotion Sam Cowan was unable to continue as manager. The directors were far from happy with his commuting and so, reluctantly, his brief managerial period was at an end. Cowan's replacement was the former Everton wing-half Jock Thomson - who, incidentally, pre-war had lost his place to Joe Mercer at Everton. At Maine Road Thomson found it difficult to compete with United.

This was a significant period in the history of Manchester football as City, throughout the pre-war era, had been Manchester's best supported and popular club. The war changed all that. With United in the First Division playing at Maine Road many of City's traditional supporters returning from the war chose to watch both clubs. Those who found it difficult to pay for a game every week drifted towards fixtures with the biggest stars - obviously United's games in Division One.

* * *

PROMPT work by the ground staff and everybody else available prevented more serious consequences when fire broke out in the drying room at Maine-road on Wednesday afternoon.

Three sets of playing gear and most of the training gear went up in smoke, and an SOS had to be sent out before a new set of kit was obtained for the match with Derby.

A nasty blow with coupons as they are, and City would be grateful if some of you local teams could come along with some spare training gear.

We can't have our lads doing their practice in boiler suits—or "birthday suits"!

* * *

A snippet from the programme produced for the September 1947 'derby' match.

For many Blues the fact United were now playing good football and challenging for the League, as they did in 1946-47, was good news. City fans had always seen them as the poor relations - remember the Reds had been close to relegation to the Third Division and near extinction during the 30s - and were genuinely pleased for the club. Many saw any success for United as being good for the whole city, especially as a former Blue was helping restore pride to the club. There was only friendly rivalry between the two outfits.

With hindsight, United's stay at Maine Road was bad news for the Blues. Although attendances were generally impressive throughout football, City's crowds were not as great as perhaps they should have been. Remember City had broken many attendance records pre-war. It was now United who had gained the upper hand and were quickly becoming the better supported club. During the early 1980s City's popular chief scout, Harry Godwin, recalled the turning point: "United played at Maine Road just after the war, and because they were a better team than City took over a lot of the support of the men whose loyalty had strayed while they were away in the services, and of those youngsters who were just getting interested. United were looking like a team, and they won the Cup in 1948."

Winning the Cup and finishing as runners up to Arsenal in the League gave the Reds an edge. The United-Arsenal game on 17th January was the first League crowd above 80,000. City's best crowd during 1947-48 was the 78,000 who attended a goalless derby match in September. Apart from that, the best City League crowd was a little over 56,000. Even the normally popular City-Arsenal fixture could only attract 20,782.

A comparison made in 'The Pride Of Manchester' derby book highlighted how United were averaging almost 55,000 for their first nineteen home games of the season, while City were a little short of 42,000 - still impressive but significantly less than United's for the first time in history.

For the Reds, the stay at Maine Road had been a financial bonanza. A *Manchester Evening News* article in October 1949 highlighted the huge increase in United's takings while playing at the higher capacity Maine Road. It revealed United were poised to announce an aggregate profit over the three Maine Road League seasons of £75,000 - easily an all time record. The report noted that the 1949-50 season might not be quite as profitable: "Attendances at remodelled Old Trafford are limited to 60,000 and, therefore, United may not be able to show such handsome dividends at the end of the current season."

United's use of Maine Road contrasted substantially with City's use of Old Trafford for reserve games. At one fixture the gate receipts were £4 15s. As the *Evening News* put it this was barely enough to cover the transport of the playing kit from Maine Road!

City ended their first season back in Division One in tenth position. Sam Barkas, at the age of 38, had left the Blues at the end of the previous term while newcomers Roy Clarke and Eddie McMorran were now regulars. Centre-forward McMorran had signed from Belfast Celtic while Clarke had joined

Johnny Hancocks scores for Wolves at Maine Road in August 1947, with the Platt Lane Stand in the background. The attendance was 67,800.

City in May 1947 and in the process created something of an unusual record by playing in three different divisions of the Football League in three consecutive games. He joined City from Third Division champions Cardiff in time to make his debut in the Blues' last Second Division game, then made his second appearance against Wolves in Division One.

Another player regularly performing well for the Blues was Scottish international Andy Black, who had joined City in June 1946 from Heart of Midlothian. During 1947-48 Black was City's top scorer with 16 goals, three more than George Smith who had made his debut for the Blues during the war. Smith actually signed for City in 1938, but was unable to make his League debut until 1946, by which time a gunshot wound sustained in South Africa had forced an amputation on one arm from the wrist down. He scored all five against Newport on the last day of the 1946-47 season.

In 1948-49 Thomson's City made an uncertain start to the season. Three victories, two draws (including the first derby of the season), and three defeats in their first eight games. There had been no major signings, and Frank Swift's announcement this would be his last season caused a little panic. Swift, who had captained England to an exciting 4-0 defeat of Italy in Turin, wanted to go out at the top. Most agreed with his decision but could not see an obvious replacement at the club.

Perhaps Swift's thoughts had been hastened as a result of the first seven seconds of the opening game at Maine Road when Preston kicked off, worked the ball swiftly to left winger Bobby Langton who ran a few yards and quickly shot. Somehow the ball sneaked in at the near post while Frank was still throwing his cap into the net. The goal equalled the record for the quickest scored in the League. Even so City won the game 3-2.

As the season progressed Alec Thurlow replaced Swift in goal on occasion, but never managed to appear for more than two consecutive games. The Blues were always going to find it difficult to replace the world class Swift. Somebody else whose City playing career was to end during this campaign was Les McDowall, who moved to Wrexham as player-manager. McDowall had captained City for a while pre-war, and was keen to make use of his tactical brain by moving into management.

In December 1948, perhaps aware of the effect United were having on City's gates, the Blues gave their rivals notice to quit. Later that season at Maine Road, United attracted 82,771 for the visit of Bradford Park Avenue, then 81,565 for Yeovil. Still not the record for the stadium but a sure fire warning to the City management that the days of total Blue dominance were over. Manchester City were now the ones who needed a lift.

With the Blues ending the season in a creditable seventh place, Frank Swift did retire at the age of 34. Unfortunately, his intended replacement Alec Thurlow was taken seriously ill with tuberculosis and had gone to Norfolk to convalesce. Sadly, Thurlow was to die in 1956 at the early age of 34. City were desperate. They were caught without a 'keeper and in consternation spent a considerable amount of time persuading Swift to reverse his decision and come out of retirement. The experienced goalkeeper eventually agreed on condition the comeback would only last until the club found a suitable replacement.

Roy Clarke signing for City in May 1947. He has the unusual record of playing three successive games in three different divisions!

Alec Herd left City on a free transfer in March 1948 after making his debut some 15 years earlier. At Stockport in 1951 he played alongside his son, David (later a United star).

Old-timers would writhe at this

By CRAWFORD WHITE

Aston Villa 1, Manchester City 0

MANCHESTER CITY WELL BEATEN

Chelsea 3, Manchester City 0

In pleasant autumn sunshine at Stamford Bridge, forty-five thousand people watched Chelsea win their first Saturday home match of the season.

MANCHESTER CITY FAIL AGAIN

Arsenal 4, Manchester City 1

Association Football

MANCHESTER CITY ERRORS

Manchester City 2, Derby County 2

All too familiar headlines for City fans, these from the 1949-50 season.

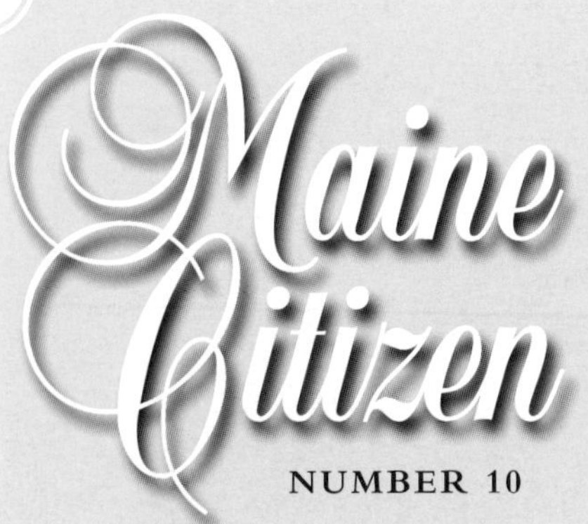

NUMBER 10

FRANK SWIFT

It was no coincidence that Frank Swift's arrival in the City side came at a time when the Blues were poised for great success. He made his debut away at Derby County on Christmas Day 1933 - the day before his 19th birthday - and, despite a disappointing result, kept his place for the remainder of the season. In fact he didn't miss a single League or Cup game until 17th September 1938 (a 6-1 Maine Road defeat by Millwall), and even that was the only match he absented prior to the outbreak of war. During those six seasons he managed to keep 51 clean sheets in 231 League appearances.

Many supporters believe Swift to be the greatest English 'keeper of all time - a belief backed up by his international record. In a fraction over two and a half years Swift made 19 international appearances - keeping nine clean sheets - and became the first goalkeeper to captain England during the twentieth century. He led the side on two occasions, naturally without conceding a goal, and made 14 wartime international appearances. It was one of these wartime matches that Swift contested was the greatest game in which he'd ever played. It took place on 16th October 1943 at Swift's home, Maine Road, and resulted in an 8-0 thrashing of Scotland. Swift: "It was sheer delight to be the goalkeeper in this great side. For long periods I was able to watch the machine swing into action, to note the brilliant half-back play of the three musketeers - Britton, Cullis, Mercer - the terrific shooting of Lawton, the methodical destruction of the Scottish defensive plan by Carter and Hagan, and the sheer wizardry of Stanley Matthews."

On the few occasions the Scots broke through the English defence, they still had to face one of the world's greatest 'keepers. Swift was forced to make a few daring saves, including an incredible swallow-dive stop in the second half. It was no wonder the Scots failed that day.

The 1934 Cup final first brought the 19 year old 'keeper to the attention of the general public. The emotion of the final minutes of the game took its toll, and Swift fainted. Immediately, the press had found an appropriately sensational story to sell the following day's 'papers. Twelve months earlier Frank had paid 2s 6d to watch the Blues face Everton. It was a true footballing fairy tale.

Later in his career he would try to relieve the big match tension for himself and the others by singing, fooling around and by performing many impressions. Apparently, one of his most famous performances was an impression of a lady getting into a very hot bath! It certainly brightened up dull days in Manchester (not that there were many of those during the 1930s!).

On the pitch Swift was the first goalkeeper to use the long, accurate throw to set up an attack. Often, he would pick up the ball one-handed and hurl it effortlessly to a City player's feet, usually beyond the half-way line. People today talk about the great overseas 'keepers and what quality they continue to bring to the English game, but during the 1930s it was Frank Swift who set the pace for others to follow.

In total Swift made 372 first team appearances for the Blues, including Cup games and the three games expunged at the outbreak of war. The years when he would have been in his prime (late twenties/early thirties) were lost to the war.

Who knows what he might have

SWIFT'S PLAYING RECORD

	LEAGUE		FA CUP		TOTAL	
	App	Gls	App	Gls	App	Gls
1933-34	22	0	8	0	30	0
1934-35	42	0	1	0	43	0
1935-36	42	0	3	0	45	0
1936-37	42	0	4	0	46	0
1937-38	42	0	5	0	47	0
1938-39	41	0	2	0	43	0
1939-40*	3	0	0	0	3	0
1946-47	35	0	4	0	39	0
1947-48	33	0	3	0	36	0
1948-49	35	0	1	0	36	0
1949-50	4	0	0	0	4	0
TOTAL	341	0	31	0	372	0

* = League campaign abandoned, then expunged from records due to World War II

achieved if his career had not been interrupted?

It says much about the quality and ability of this giant player that when he announced his retirement City went to extraordinary lengths to persuade him to play on. Also, once his Maine Road career had come to an end, former team mate Matt Busby tried to tempt him to Old Trafford. Swift wisely stuck to his guns and was able to look back on a career that had seen him win both the League and the Cup, captain his country, and finish at the top.

During the fifties Swift continued to follow the fortunes of the Blues, and of his friend Matt Busby at Old Trafford, and was a regular at both venues. He was also a well-loved and respected journalist for the News of the World. His tragic death came prematurely in February 1958 when he travelled with United in his capacity as a journalist for the Reds' European Cup semi-final game in Belgrade. Everyone in Manchester - and in the general football world - suffered as a result of the Munich Air Disaster.

Prior to the flight the 43 year old Swift admitted he was a little scared of flying. No doubt he bravely tried to lift his own spirits with his unique brand of humour and exuberance. He remains the greatest goalkeeper of his generation and, considering his international appearances and years lost to the war, is arguably the greatest City 'keeper of all time. His City replacement, Bert Trautmann, is arguably the greatest overseas 'keeper to have played in the Football League, but whether he was better than Swift is open to debate. Supporters have been making comparisons ever since the 1950s, and no doubt the arguments will rage on forever.

Frank Swift.

Beattie Thomlinson of the Brooks' Bar Supporters' Club, presents Roy Paul with a radio to be used on away trips in 1949.

Swift appeared in the opening game of the 1949-50 season - a 3-3 draw with Aston Villa.

Ronnie Powell replaced him for the second and third games but neither were won, and Swift returned. Finally on 7th September Swift kept a clean sheet with his last League performance - a no score draw at home to Everton. Powell then regained his place but it wasn't to last as City were about to set the football world talking by giving a chance to a former German paratrooper by the name of Bernhard Trautmann.

As soon as City started giving trials to the St. Helen's goalkeeper the protests started. The media loved it. Letters were published from writers claiming to be representatives of various ex-servicemen's organisations and Jewish groups. The newspapers even called for a boycott of the club if Trautmann was named to play.

At Maine Road, Chairman Robert Smith tried to calm the situation: "There is no doubt that many people will be upset by our signing of a German, but I feel we must take the broad view. City need a goalkeeper and we have excellent reports of this man, both as a goalkeeper and an individual."

City captain Eric Westwood, who fought at Normandy, also tried to diffuse the situation. He told Trautmann, "There's no war in this dressing room. We welcome you as any other member of the staff. Just make yourself at home - and good luck."

On 17th October the *Manchester Evening News* believed the German gave a satisfactory display for the reserves at Barnsley, despite suffering from boils and a swollen hand.

Throughout October the newspaper gave simple one or two line comments on Trautmann's performance, although the 'paper seemed to be confused as to what his first name was.

They tried a couple of different spellings before settling for 'Berg'. Perhaps they knew that Berg was

BERG TRAUTMANN

FORWARD SWITCH AND EMPTAGE GOES IN CITY TEAM PURGE

Trautmann in goal and six other changes

BY ERIC THORNTON

MANCHESTER CITY have made seven changes, remodelling their attack and half-back line and giving Berg Trautmann, their German ex-P.O.W. goalkeeper, his first chance in the Football League.

Tommy Powell, the young Welsh goalkeeper, and Albert Emptage, the wing-half from Lincolnshire, go out for the match with Bolton Wanderers at Burnden Park on Saturday.

Only Turnbull retains his posi-

OUR READERS WRITE...

AS a member of that sorely tried and, I fear, diminishing body of Manchester City supporters I read with interest criticisms and suggested

convinced that Clarke is better at inside-left than winger.

Your remarks re the half-back line are my sentiments exactly. We are deplorably weak here, and could City obtain Leuty I suggest:

The wheel full ci

WHEN Stockp the Central Cricket League in of their mains Stanley Smith, a spinner, whom I seeing demonstra and spin to his when they were knickerbocker sta

Beware of

The Manchester Evening News reports the news that Bert Trautmann is to make his debut. Note the miss-spelling of his christian name - Berg is German for mountain! Above: Trautmann with Frank Swift, the goalkeeper who offered plenty of advice during his early days, and (below) signing autographs outside Maine Road.

German for mountain and believed Trautmann was to be City's defensive rock.

Before Trautmann's debut City struggled on, with struggle the operative word. On 18th October the *Evening News* provided the distressing information that City's injury list was the longest ever experienced at the club. Manager Jock Thomson was quoted as saying: "It's so bad that we have never been able to field our strongest team in any game this season. Thank goodness Westwood, Fagan, and Walsh have kept clear of injury."

The saddest injury tale during this period had to be that of Archie Aikman. Aikman was signed from Falkirk for £8,000 during the close season and, before he was even able to appear for the Blues, damaged his breast bone in a car accident. The crash took place on 5th August and for the next three months 5ft 10in Aikman visited Manchester Royal Infirmary four days a week for remedial exercises. The centre-forward, who was desperately needed in City's attack, was keen to regain fitness: "I am fed up being out of the game so long. The doctor says that if I were an ordinary workman I could be back on the job, but my chest is not yet sufficiently sound to take a shoulder charge.

"I've thought sometimes that people might think I wasn't bothering about getting fit, but I am. You want to see the way they've kept me fit at the

infirmary, skipping and bending this way and that. I ache to get into action when I'm watching games, but sometimes I still get a slight clicking in the chest."

Sadly, Aikman never managed to make his League debut for City. He had shown promise when he played in five close season games in Denmark during May 1949, scoring in all but one match, but never made it into the first team. The Blues held his registration until 19th January 1952, after which he returned to Scotland and somehow recovered enough to play in the Scottish League.

With such a large injury list in 1949, City simply had to strengthen the squad but Don Revie, the one player manager Thomson was set on, did not want to come to Maine Road.

Thomson had been chasing the Leicester man since early season and offered £20,000 in October. He was not alone however, as interest in the 22 year old inside forward increased almost daily. By the end of October Arsenal, Hull, Fulham and City were all said to be prepared to spend in excess of £20,000 and possibly provide a player in exchange. Jock Thomson told the *Evening News* City had a house lined up for Revie and in talks the player had seemed very keen on a transfer to Manchester. Arsenal were second favourites to land him.

The chase for Revie's signature dragged on into November with reports suggesting it would take a new transfer record of around £26,000 to bring the player to Maine Road. Eventually, City lost interest and Revie transferred to Hull - said to be the least likely of all the clubs to sign him - for the original sum of £20,000.

On 14th November Eric Thornton, writing in the *Evening News*, shocked the City management by openly stating the Blues would go down if they made no new signings. In a stinging article, the regular City reporter attacked the players he believed were the weak links, and outlined what he thought should be done to bring respectability back to the Blues. Two days later the newspaper published readers' responses to the article. Most were in agreement with Thornton and the overwhelming theme was that the management simply did not know who to buy, or who to play. There was widespread concern over the transfer stories, in particular the attempted signing of Revie, which supporters believed 'put off' the younger players. It was also felt Revie's move to Hull indicated there was something wrong with the atmosphere or the management at Maine Road.

In addition to all this negativity, the news appeared that Trautmann was to make his debut. Considering all the earlier anti-German feeling it must have been rather surprising to read comments from supporters suggesting the German be 'given a go' in the first team, and that Thornton saw his selection as an extremely wise decision.

Trautmann's debut was not quite the success everyone hoped as the game ended in a 3-0 defeat at Bolton. He'd kept a clean sheet through the first half but was unable to stop two attempts and a penalty in the second.

The German was far from happy until he met Frank Swift in the dressing room. Swift had watched the game and felt it only fair to welcome his replacement. He told Trautmann he'd put in a decent performance. Perhaps the former 'keeper had been dreading the game for fear that the new man might not be of the right calibre - remember Swift was still officially a City player, but he had no intention of playing again.

Actually, it was around this time that United tried to lure Swift to Old Trafford. The Reds were struggling to find a replacement for long-serving Jack Crompton, and Matt Busby tried to poach his former Blue team mate. With the initial hostility towards Trautmann and the possibility of boycotts, City could certainly not afford to allow one of their popular all-time greats to move to Old Trafford. Not after everything that had happened since 1937.

Fortunately Swift himself turned Busby down, and the Reds' search continued.

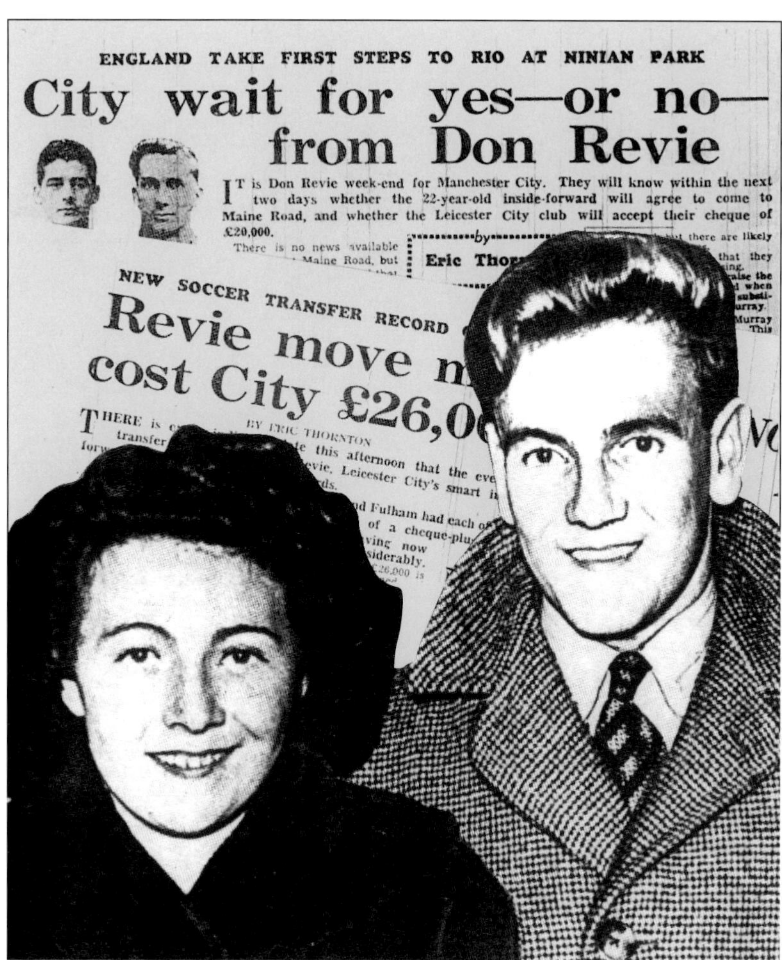

Don Revie travelled to Manchester, with his wife Elsie, to decide his future.

At Maine Road, Trautmann prepared for his home debut. The 'papers called for a boycott. In the end a crowd of 30,501 watched the new man keep a clean sheet while, at the other end, two goals apiece from Andy Black and Roy Clarke gave City victory. Boycotts were forgotten. Who cared what nationality the goalkeeper was so long as he wore the green shirt with pride.

Unfortunately, the next game was different. In dreadful, muddy conditions, Derby County defeated City 7-0 at the Baseball Ground. The Derby fans enjoyed laughing at the City 'keeper. They also took the opportunity to remind Trautmann about the war. It was not a good day. Afterwards Swift reassured Trautmann by pointing out that his own second-ever reserve game over 16 years earlier had ended in a 6-1 crushing at home to Blackburn. The occasional humiliating episode helped develop his character, and he felt certain the new 'keeper would learn from the Derby encounter.

Despite the setbacks - and there were plenty that season! - Trautmann won over the Manchester press and, more importantly, the local population. The Rabbi of Manchester, Alexander Altman did much to ease the situation: "Despite the terrible cruelties we suffered at the hands of the Germans, we would not try to punish an individual German, who is unconnected with these crimes, out of hatred. If this footballer is a decent fellow, I would say there is no harm in it. Each case must be judged on its merits."

Johnny Williamson (above) made his debut on April Fool's Day, 1950.

Les McDowall (below) signed from Sunderland in March 1938, and some 12 years later became the Blues' manager.

London was different, though. During the 1990s City historian, David Whalley, uncovered the story behind City's match at Fulham on 14th January - Trautmann's first in the capital. Whalley believes this was a turning point in the German's relationship with the media in general. Despite the scoreline - City lost 1-0 - Trautmann did much to impress the public and press. Earlier though, he had suffered much abuse. Shouts of 'Kraut' and 'Nazi' rang out. Instead of upsetting the 'keeper, this abuse made the German more determined. Unfortunately, the same would happen with United's Frenchman Eric Cantona every time he faced City during the 1990s.

Trautmann's performance that day was brilliant and earned him a standing ovation. All thoughts of him being a 'Nazi' had gone by full time. One young Fulham fan in the crowd that day, Jim Sims, remembers the game well: "The effect on us at the Cottage was magnetic. We were watching a supreme professional at the top of his trade - a real flesh and blood hero. I am absolutely certain his appearance in the First Division just four years after ceasing hostilities had a major effect on boosting and repairing our relationship with the Germans. He'd been a prisoner of war as a paratrooper, and married an English girl, which all helped. But he gave you that warm glow before the game and you knew you were in for something special. After the game, we all clapped like mad as they made the corridor for him. It was unique. It was as though we were trying to wash away the sins of the world and was pretty emotional."

Trautmann had won over the London press and the public and was now able to enjoy his football. Naturally, the player's attitude had helped. He did little to upset the public, and tried to ensure he appeared human - something few Britons at the time believed was possible.

As the season progressed, despite the performances of the agile German, City struggled. The Blues were heading for relegation and the situation looked desperate. On April Fool's Day, City returned to London for yet another memorable match for City's German 'keeper. It was the return with Arsenal, but it was also two days after Trautmann had married Margaret Friar, the daughter of the St. Helen's secretary Jack Friar. City officials allowed the new Mrs. Trautmann to travel with the party to London as a sort of honeymoon. For the groom it was a far from happy occasion as he was beaten four times. Perhaps he had other things on his mind!

One week later City defeated Burnley 1-0 - the first win since Christmas Eve - and followed up with a 2-1 victory over Wolves. There was still hope, but worries resurfaced with a 3-0 defeat by the same club the next day.

The following game, away at League leaders Sunderland, was an interesting one. City were winning 2-0 when the referee awarded the home side a penalty. Trautmann was unable to stop the shot and Sunderland were back in the match. Later another penalty was awarded against the Blues. This time Trautmann saved it, but the referee ordered it to be retaken. The German was far from happy and booted the ball into the crowd. When it was eventually retrieved and the penalty retaken, Trautmann saved again. This time even the home fans cheered. City centre-forward Dennis Westcott rushed up to the referee and joked: "How did you like that save, ref? Better than the first, wasn't it!"

A couple of draws followed, then City lost their final match at Everton 3-1. They were three points behind Charlton, who were safe in 20th place, but the Blues were relegated despite the consolation of finding an excellent replacement for Swift.

Jock Thomson's rather uninspiring period in charge was now over, and the Blues directors looked for a man who could encourage and lift the players in the way Busby had at Old Trafford. It was not going to be easy to find a man like that. There were few of them in football. If a Busby couldn't be found then what about a man known to the City faithful? Someone tactically aware?

The man chosen was former half-back Les McDowall who had been Wrexham's manager since leaving City only a year or so earlier.

The period 1937 to 1950 had been a difficult one for the Blues. It had started with City by far the most popular and strongest of the Manchester sides and ended with relegation. In 1937 United had been the underdogs, now they had the upper hand. Rather than being Manchester's 'other' club, they began to be seen as adversaries. The Blues had to live with that.

Perversely, Bert Trautmann had been perceived by many as the enemy but was now a hero. For Mancunians, football had changed most dramatically during this difficult period of history.

Chapter Eleven

WEMBLEY DOUBLE

1950 1956

Roy Paul, one of football's greatest captains, made his debut at the start of the 1950-51 season. His arrival helped galvanise new manager McDowall's City team ready for success.

THE Second Division was not the place for one of England's biggest clubs, but it was the appropriate division for a side struggling to come to terms with post war football. Manchester City needed a quick return. Everyone connected with the club hoped new manager Les McDowall would be able to deliver promotion at the first attempt.

During the close season McDowall entered the transfer market and purchased a player destined to be a City legend - wing-half Roy Paul. Paul had impressed greatly with Swansea and was first noticed by Arsenal when the two sides met in the fourth round of the 1949-50 FA Cup. Immediately after the game Arsenal manager Tom Whittaker put in a bid for the Welshman, but the Swansea directors refused to sell. It was bad enough losing the tie to 'Lucky Arsenal' never mind their best player.

Somehow, the following July, McDowall persuaded Swansea to sell for £25,000. Joe Mercer, who captained the Arsenal side that beat Swansea always had a high regard for Paul: "Roy Paul was one of the best players I've ever seen. He gave us a hell of a fright when Swansea came to Arsenal in 1950."

Paul made his debut in City's opening fixture - a 4-2 victory at Preston - and managed to appear in all but one of the League games that season. The one he missed? City's 3-2 away win over his old side Swansea on 21st October, and that because he was playing for Wales. Roy Clarke was also on international duty.

In the second and third games of the season, both played at Maine Road, City defeated Cardiff 2-1 and Bury 5-1, prompting optimistic talk about a swift return to the First Division. For those regulars at City games promotion still seemed a long way off. This report succinctly summed it up: "To the man who relies on figures Manchester City's 5-1 win over Bury at Maine Road on Saturday promises only a short stay in the Second Division, and in terms of plain arithmetic six points from three games confirms this view, but the spectator, who relies on facts rather than figures, is sceptical. He has every reason to be, for Manchester City have not yet shown real strength."

The star of the Bury match was Dennis Westcott who capped his best performance since joining the Blues with a hat-trick. He also had a hand in the fourth goal, providing a centre for Johnny Hart.

Two weeks later the Blues achieved another 5-1 Maine Road victory, this time against Chesterfield. A crowd of 43,485 basked in the autumnal sunshine as City tore into their visitors.

The reporter 'Old International', writing in the *Manchester Guardian* pointed out a few areas of concern. He believed City were a little hesitant in defence and at times it seemed Bert Trautmann and his fellow defenders were struggling to understand each other. He counted three occasions when the Chesterfield forwards had an open goal to shoot at, and claimed they had only missed because they were so surprised at the gaps. Nevertheless, the game gave City another two points and placed them second on 12 points to Birmingham who had a superior goal average.

By 30th September City headed the table. A 1-0 victory against Coventry that day strengthened their lead and set the 'Old International' purring with delight at the way the Blues were now pulling

The City eleven who opened the season at Preston on 19th August 1950. City won 4-2 with goals from Smith (2), Westcott and Clarke.

Back row (left to right): Paul, Rigby, Trautmann, Westwood, Spurdle, Phillips.

Front: Oakes, Hart, Westcott, Smith, Clarke.

together and performing as a team. His concern about City's defence was rapidly disappearing: "The goal was a triumph of observation and judgement, and set the seal on Spurdle's claims to be rated as a player of the first rank.

"Paul, too, played beautifully, and with that air of authority one is entitled to expect from a City captain. Behind him, Westwood lent valuable support in a timely return to form. Here was a glimpse of the old campaigner again - speedy, quick-witted, resolute, with a flair for swift attacking moves on his own. If Westwood's recovery can be maintained, the prospects for City are bright indeed.

"As a result this vied with many a good cup-tie played at Moss Side. For those who like hard shooting, fine goalkeeping, brusque tackling, and 'hair-breadth 'scapes i'th imminent deadly breach' it was ideal. Trautmann, possibly, would win the prize for a flawless performance - his every move is made with such consummate ease and grace - but justice would require a consolation prize for Wood, if only for gallantry under pressure."

The Blues remained unbeaten until 7th October - a run of ten games - when Doncaster staged a remarkable recovery. City were winning 3-0 at half-time, but four second half goals for Doncaster gave the Yorkshire club victory. Two City wins followed but postponements and a few poor results from November through to January hampered progress.

Ken Branagan (right) made his City debut in the 5-3 defeat of Sheffield United on 9th December 1950, after signing in November 1948. In between these dates he had to do 18 months National Service in the army.

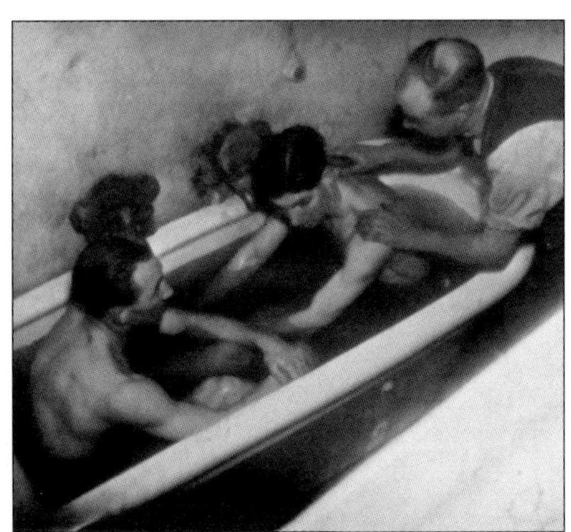

Maine Road always housed the best facilities - ask Roy Clarke!

On 18th November a 4-1 defeat at Blackburn prompted one newspaper to headline the City report with "Bert still disposing the bombs". The German had been released from bomb disposal duties only a few days before, and the report went on to imply he'd been under much more pressure in this game than with his duties. One of Blackburn's goals - scored from a penalty - was struck so ferociously it actually sailed past Trautmann and went through the net itself. The goalkeeper probably felt as if war had been declared once again!

On 2nd December a 1-1 draw at Barnsley kept City in top spot with 26 points from 19 games. Second were Blackburn on the same number of points but they had played one game more. As the season moved into January the Blues started to lose their way a little, but found themselves attacking promotion from a 'games in hand' position. They need not have worried unduly as the months of March and April kept them in contention.

A 4-1 victory at Leeds on 24th March boosted morale and then, two days later, 31,948 watched the City-Notts County fixture end goalless. The game was played in appalling conditions witnessed by the 'Old International': "On a fine stretch of water, lashed by incessant rain, Manchester City and Notts County rewarded all who were inquisitive enough to come and watch it by playing, with great heartiness and much good humour, a novel form of aquatic sports which one heard variously described as 'Splash-ball' and 'Foot-polo'. No goals were scored; and fortunately, no lives were lost through drowning."

The draw placed City fourth on 41 points after 34 games. The division leaders were Preston with 52 points from 36 games. At the start of December they had been 8th on 21 points, but a magnificent run had seen them bypass the opposition. Cardiff were eight points behind in second place. City could still achieve promotion, but it now appeared Preston could not be caught.

A 6-0 thrashing of Barnsley on 21st April was watched by City's third highest crowd of the season - 42,741. The biggest had been 45,693 for the no score draw with Hull on 28th October. With only three games left City's destiny was more or less in their own hands, especially when a point was gained away at Sheffield United. That meant only Cardiff, who were on 49 points from 41 games, could overtake fifty points City. Preston were already certain of the Second Division championship.

On 30th April another point was gained in a goalless draw at Notts County, and then on 5th May City's final game of the season saw the Blues make a 2-2 draw at home to Grimsby, who would be relegated to the Third Division (North) that day. Despite the standing of the two clubs it was Grimsby who were the more impressive on the day. The visitors had taken the lead twice, only to see the Blues fight back for the point. The Blues could have changed the game completely, possibly gaining victory, had Roy Paul managed to score from a penalty before the City fightback got fully underway.

1950-51 DIVISION TWO PROMOTION DETAILS

RESULTS	HOME	AWAY
Preston North End	L 0-3	W 4-2
Cardiff City	W 2-1	D 1-1
Bury	W 5-1	L 0-2
Queens Park Rangers	W 5-2	W 2-1
Grimsby Town	D 2-2	D 4-4
Chesterfield	W 5-1	W 2-1
Leicester City	D 1-1	W 2-1
Luton Town	D 1-1	D 2-2
Coventry City	W 1-0	W 2-0
Doncaster Rovers	D 3-3	L 3-4
Brentford	W 4-0	L 0-2
Swansea Town	L 1-2	W 3-2
Hull City	D 0-0	D 3-3
Leeds United	W 4-1	D 1-1
West Ham United	W 2-0	W 4-2
Blackburn Rovers	W 1-0	L 1-4
Southampton	L 2-3	L 1-2
Barnsley	W 6-0	D 1-1
Sheffield United	W 5-3	D 0-0
Birmingham City	W 3-1	L 0-1
Notts County	D 0-0	D 0-0

REGULAR SIDE:

Trautmann
Phillips
Westwood
Spurdle
Rigby
Paul
Oakes
Hart
Westcott
Smith
Clarke

MANAGER:

Les McDowall

LARGEST VICTORY: 6-0 v Barnsley (H) 21/4/51

LARGEST WINNING MARGIN: 6 goals - 6-0 v Barnsley (H) 21/4/51

HEAVIEST DEFEAT: 1-4 v Blackburn Rovers (A) 18/11/50

AVERAGE HOME ATTENDANCE: c.34,905

HIGHEST HOME ATTENDANCE: 45,693 v Hull City 28/10/50

HIGHEST AWAY ATTENDANCE: 37,400 v Blackburn Rovers 18/11/50

LEAGUE APPEARANCES: 42 Trautmann, 41 Paul, 40 Westcott, 39 Smith, Clarke, 37 Phillips, Westwood, Rigby, 31 Spurdle, 27 Hart, 21 Oakes, 16 McCourt, 11 Meadows, 10 Branagan, 9 Alison, 6 Haddington, Williamson, 5 Fagan, 4 Gunning, 2 Cunliffe, 1 Turnbull, Emptage

LEAGUE GOALS: 25 Westcott, 21 Smith, 14 Hart, 9 Clarke, 4 Spurdle, Haddington, 3 Paul, Oakes, 2 Meadows, Cunliffe

Despite the result, City were back up once again - Cardiff had only managed a point from their last game.

McDowall's first season in charge had been a success. To achieve promotion though he had been forced to bring in more new faces. Left-half Frank McCourt was signed from Bristol Rovers after writing to the club for a trial. He had been keen to move north and fancied his chances at Maine Road. McDowall liked what he saw and gave the player his debut in the first team on 3rd February.

Other newcomers included Ray Haddington - an £8,000 signing from Oldham - and Jimmy Meadows. Haddington was a firm favourite with the Boundary Park support and it must be said his move to City was a curious one. While at Maine Road he featured in only six games, scoring four goals, but at the end of the season was transferred to Stockport County. What had gone wrong?

The Meadows transfer was different. He was signed from Southport and made his debut on 17th March. From that moment until 5th January he was an ever-present.

Jimmy Meadows arrived from Southport in March 1951. His career was cruelly cut short by an injury he received in the 1955 Cup Final.

Jack Oakes (left) made 77 League appearances during his City career.

At last Don Revie signs for the Blues, witnessed by City manager Les McDowall, Mrs Elsie Revie, City director Walter Smith and Hull City chief scout Jack Hill.

The 1951-52 season was always going to be a difficult one for the Blues, especially after some of the performances towards the end of the previous campaign, and to the great tactical brain of manager McDowall it was probably always viewed as a season of consolidation. City fans wanted more, especially as the Reds seemed to be challenging for the title every year, but survival had to be the first priority.

The first ten games only brought seven points and the Blues were struggling, but a fine run from 6th October until mid-November gave them hope. During this period City signed Ivor Broadis and Don Revie. Broadis, a skilful inside forward, moved for a club record £25,000 from Sunderland. Earlier in his career he had played wartime football for Tottenham, amongst others, and benefited from an early exposure to top class colleagues and opponents. In 1946, at the age of 23, he became player-manager of Carlisle, then in February 1949 created history by transferring himself to Sunderland. His arrival at Maine Road coincided with his first real taste of international football when he made his England debut against Austria in November.

Don Revie was already a familiar name to City supporters when he signed from Hull on 18th October. Again, the fee was a reported £25,000 and almost immediately the player was asked why his on off transfer to the Blues in 1949 never occurred and why it took so long to reach a decision: "No player likes a long drawn out transfer serial. Nor for that matter does a football club. It is better for both sides if the parting is swift and sweet. In my case I came in for a lot of unpleasant publicity. It was difficult to make people realise that, although I was determined to leave Leicester, I was not going to do anything rash. I wanted to make sure it was a progressive step."

Revie admitted that at the time a number of clubs were interested in him, with Arsenal the one he would most liked to have played for. However, he felt he wasn't quite ready for the bright lights of London and so considered the rather less exciting north, with City and Hull the teams to choose from: '"I went over to Manchester with my wife, Elsie, to meet Jock Thomson, the City manager at that time. It was raining when we arrived! Somehow we did not seem to fit the place. However, as we were to discover later, those first impressions that Manchester is a gloomy place were to be proved quite wrong."

With Revie and now Broadis, McDowall was convinced City could be a force, but a dreadful run came in the new year when the Blues failed to win for over three months. During this sequence the Blues did draw eight games, but McDowall had to contend with the possibility City could actually be relegated - especially as the first three games in April were all lost - while the Reds challenged for the title.

A City line-up from September 1951.

Back row (left to right): Ernie Phillips, John Rigby, Roy Paul, Bert Trautmann, Frank McCourt, Jack Hannaway, Billy Spurdle.

Front: Jimmy Meadows, Johnny Hart, Johnny Williamson, Roy Clarke.

It was never actually that bad as the ever-impressive Trautmann kept City's goals against figure respectable, and there were enough teams worse than City, but it was not the season expected after the two expensive signings. In the end the Blues finished 15th on 39 points - 11 more than the relegation zone - and the original aim of consolidation was met.

During the season Bert Trautmann missed his first League game since his November 1949 debut. Seventeen year old Derek Williams found himself trying to fill Bert's jersey for the meeting with Blackpool. A Maine Road crowd of 47,437 watched a match that ended goalless. For the young 'keeper it was his one and only City outing before a transfer to Wrexham in 1954.

The 1952-53 season began with two successive defeats (Stoke and Tottenham) before the real test - a Manchester derby with reigning champions United. For this game McDowall called up reserve centre-forward Billy Sowden for what turned into a promising debut. The player gave United's experienced Allenby Chilton an extremely uncomfortable afternoon and, together with Broadis, Clarke and Ewing, put goalkeeper Jack Crompton under a lot of pressure. The youngster was also at the centre of a dispute over a possible City penalty after being brought down in the box.

Ivor Broadis was the star man as he, firstly, split the United defence wide open with a delightful through-ball which left Roy Clarke with only the goalkeeper to beat - which he duly did. Then, in a crowded goal mouth, Broadis trapped a loose ball and smashed an unstoppable half volley past the startled Crompton.

At 2-0 the Maine Road faithful loved every minute but, as the game wore on the Reds threw all they could at City. In the final quarter United pulled one back, but in the end it was not enough. City had defeated their rivals in League football for the first time since January 1937 and the 'Old International' writing in the *Manchester Guardian* seemed to enjoy every minute: "Manchester City gave their loyal and long suffering supporters that experience for which they have watched and prayed these last five years, namely, the right to do honour to a well merited and clear cut victory over their redoubtable neighbours."

After reporting the major incidents of the game, he suggested what the debate in the bars around the city would be over the course of the coming weeks: "This was a game which will be played over and over again in Manchester club circles for many weeks to come and among the main topics for argument might be these - (1) How do United account for their surprising fall from grace? (2) Why have City kept their real form in hiding for so long? (3) Can anyone deny that Spurdle is City's best left half-back, or that Meadows is wasted at outside right? The question as to whether Crompton did - or did not - grasp Sowden by the ankle and pull him down might be kept in reserve as an enlivener should conversation flag. To City supporters it was as clear as a man pulling rhubarb!"

Despite the derby victory, and a 3-3 draw at Tottenham in the next game, City struggled through the Autumn and Winter of 1952. Typical was a 5-4 September defeat at Middlesbrough where both defences seemed particularly porous. One report claimed they were 'badly at sea': "Full-backs lacking

Johnny Hart scored one of City's two goals in the 5-2 defeat by Sunderland on 1st November 1952.

in flexibility, centre-halves who were by no means so commanding as usual, and goalkeepers whose jumpiness belied their reputations, were continually extending handsome invitation to the attacks to go in with confidence and have a good time. The invitation was accepted cheerfully.

"It is a long time since any game at Middlesbrough was so full of incident and, although football crowds certainly like goals, neither club is likely to be content with things as they were on Saturday.

"Four men - one wing half and three forwards - were outstanding on each side and equally deserving, though victory was the reward of one set and defeat of the other. City's four were Paul, Meadows, Revie, and Broadis."

On 20th December City faced Stoke at home. The sides held the bottom two positions in the division and the game was viewed as a real four point fixture. Falling on the last Saturday before Christmas, it was never going to be a popular game, but as the 'Old International' reported the attendance was extremely low: "On Saturday, before depressingly broad stretches of unoccupied terracing - for only 13,000 loyalists had braved the elements and the almost certain prospect of a dreary bout of relegation football - Manchester City and Stoke City met to decide which of them should face the strain of a heavy Christmas programme as wooden spoonists. After a close struggle, marred by a serious accident to Robertson, the Stoke City goalkeeper, and yet ennobled to some extent by the gallant bearing of his ten remaining colleagues, Manchester City won 2-1 and so left their friends from the Potteries reluctantly and undeservedly holding the spoon."

John Rigby made 38 League appearances during 1951-52, his best total while with City.

Bert Trautmann the hero of first away win

Liverpool 0, Manchester City 1

OFFICIALLY, Johnny Hart gave bottom-of-the-table Manchester City their first away victory of the season with a 72nd-minute goal at Liverpool, but most of the **credit** belongs to blond goalkeeper Bert Trautmann.

The next game, played on Boxing Day, saw City defeated 6-2 at Preston. Not the perfect result to prepare for the following week's derby match at Old Trafford! At United, McDowall gave a derby day debut to a raw-boned centre-half called Dave Ewing who had signed for City from Luncarty Juniors in 1949. Incidentally, his reserve team debut had also been against United His first team bow was impressive, even though the match itself was rather drab and colourless. The game ended 1-1 with City gaining more praise in the media than United. This seemed to give the Blues a lift, and seven days later they defeated Swindon Town 7-0 in the F.A. Cup with Johnny Hart scoring four and Roy Little making his debut. They exited in the next round 5-1 in a replay with Luton, but the point was that the derby draw and cup game gave City positives for the rest of the League programme.

On 17th January City travelled to Liverpool for the first League game since the derby. It was a memorable day as - thanks to a goal from Johnny Hart - City defeated Liverpool 1-0 to achieve their first away win since the same fixture in April of the previous year. Although Hart scored, it was Trautmann who was the real hero. He made many brilliant saves, especially in the final minutes when Liverpool sent everyone but the goalkeeper forward for three successive corners. For once Trautmann's efforts had not been in vain. On too many occasions during this season, and indeed the previous one, the German had played superbly only to see silly mistakes by others cost the Blues the game. Deservedly, at Anfield Trautmann gained all the headlines.

Big Dave Ewing made his debut in a 1-1 draw at Manchester United on 3rd January 1953 and quickly established a reputation as a tough centre-half. His vocal encouragement livened up any game!

In the same 'derby' as Ewing made his debut, Eric Westwood (right) played his last game for the Blues, against his old team.

City's next fixture was a 5-1 home win over Middlesbrough, but the Blues' away form was still a worry, especially when a trip to Cardiff ended in a 6-0 defeat on 21st February (two players - Eric Webster and Phil Woosnam - both made their only City appearances in this game). To bolster the attack, McDowall purchased Ken Whitfield from Wolves in time to make his debut in a Maine Road win over of Portsmouth on the last day of the month. A couple of weeks later new winger Harry Anders made his home debut against Aston Villa. Anders, signed from Preston on 6th March, had an impressive game: "New signing Harry Anders, playing in his first home game for Manchester City, delighted the fans with his speed and trickery against Aston Villa, topping the day with a goal a few minutes before the end.

"Broadis again was in brilliant form, while Spurdle celebrated his return to the side with a splendid hat-trick and an all-round display which augurs well for the future."

The game ended 4-1 with City relaxing in the final ten minutes, allowing Villa the chance to pull a goal back. City had not been defeated at Maine Road since 1st November - the problem was away form. If the Blues could get their act together out of Manchester then there was a chance they might climb clear of the relegation zone.

At Sunderland in the next match the Blues were deservedly leading 3-2 as the game entered the final twenty-five minutes when Sunderland laid siege to Trautmann. The City 'keeper was on the receiving end of several successive charges, causing the referee to admonish a number of home players. In the final minute, the pressure was simply too much and Sunderland snatched an equaliser. Despite the scoreline, the game had been exciting for the many City supporters who travelled to Roker Park: "Even a score of 3-3 gives little indication of the number of thrills in this hard, keenly-fought game, and City had good reason to feel aggrieved at being robbed of their second away win of the season. Ivor Broadis, captain for the day against his old club, scored two beauties with his left foot in the 22nd and 32nd minutes."

City's home form continued to impress and then, on 4th April, the Blues achieved their second away win of the season when they saw off championship challengers Charlton 2-1. Charlton had missed a penalty, and put Bert Trautmann under constant pressure, nevertheless the Blues managed to hold on to gain an important victory. Two days later a 1-1 draw at Sheffield brought another vital point, but this was followed by the first Maine Road defeat for five months when eventual champions Arsenal crushed City 4-2. The Blues were close to avoiding relegation - it was all in their own hands.

Sadly, as so often with the Blues, what seemed a relatively simple task became unnecessarily frustrating. The next game was even more depressing than the Arsenal defeat as City's away form failed again. This time another struggling side, Derby, gained a 5-0 victory - it could easily have been

Roy Little made his League debut in the 1-0 win at Anfield on 17th January 1953, the first of 186 League and Cup appearances for City.

On 29th August a trip to Sunderland brought two valuable points in an extraordinary game as the Wearsiders were defeated 5-4. However, the next at home brought City back down to earth.
A disappointing crowd of 24,918 found little to excite them. The *Manchester Guardian* reporter 'Old International' knew the Maine Road club well: "Was it scepticism, or empty stomachs, that quelled the high spirits? Those who had built their hopes on a repeat performance in Saturday's vein were sadly disappointed. Villa beat City by the only goal scored. Or would it be true to say that City beat themselves?

"How appropriate it would have been for those whose earnest hope it was that City's sensational win at Sunderland was no mere flash in the pan, if either of the two fierce shots by Spurdle and Clarke in the first phase of the game had been slightly better placed. But Spurdle's hammer blow, delivered after picking up a foolish back pass by Blanchflower, buried itself into somebody's ribs and when Spurdle rolled the rebound deftly in Clarke's direction, Clarke tore in with his head tucked low between his knees, as his manner is, and shot tantalisingly wide of the far post. The only other incidents of note in the next ten minutes or so were two glorious saves by Trautmann: the real hero more - reliving nightmares of the 7-0 thrashing in December 1949. Both Ewing and Hart were injured during the game, with Hart limping through much of the action. Sadly, the injury prevented him from playing in the vital games which followed. Ivor Broadis had missed the Derby game as he was on international duty, scoring a couple of goals for England. These were the days when England games clashed with the League programme and the clubs with most internationals lost their best players. There was no question of club versus country - country won on every occasion, to the detriment of the League campaign.

Without Hart, but with Broadis back, City were defeated 2-0 at home to Preston causing mutterings on the Maine Road terraces. Fortunately, the next game ended in a 5-0 Maine Road victory over cup finalists Blackpool. Four days later a 3-1 defeat at fellow strugglers Chelsea hardly mattered as City avoided relegation by a point. Stoke and Derby were relegated, with Chelsea's victory lifting them above City on goal average.

Thanks mainly to Bert Trautmann's heroics throughout the season, McDowall's Blues had survived for another year. For the City faithful, the prospect of another relegation struggle was not enticing.

Despite making significant profits in most of the post-war seasons the City directorate did not seem keen to spend cash on expensive new signings for the 1953-4 campaign, even though another difficult season looked likely. As early as the opening game City fans saw little had altered during the summer break as Wednesday beat the Blues 2-0 at Sheffield. Reporters stressed how 'shaky' City's defence looked and how the Blues' play never reached a 'high standard'. Three days later a 4-0 home defeat by Wolves caused season ticket holders to consider the wisdom of their investment.

And then there was light!

A page from the programme for Maine Road's first floodlit game, a friendly with Hearts on 14th October 1953, which City won 6-3. The total cost per game of using the lights was estimated at just £3.

President: Mr. A. ALEXANDER, J.P.
Directors: Mr. R. SMITH (Chairman)
Messrs. A. DOUGLAS, E. GILL, F. R. JOLLY, W. SMITH

Secretary-Manager: Mr. LESLIE J. McDOWALL
'Phone: MOSs Side 1191

THIS THROWS NEW LIGHT ON CITY

By THE EDITOR

ANOTHER milestone in the long history of Manchester City is passed this evening when Maine Road stages its first floodlit match. And we welcome famous Heart of Midlothian as visitors on this historic occasion.

Floodlit football, as most people know, is no novelty in this country, and records show it was tried—in modified form—in the 1880's. On the continent, this type of football has proved highly successful, and although floodlighting in the British Isles is a modern concession to progress, more and more clubs are realising its possibilities, and City readily fell into line. Indeed, Maine Road officials were so determined City should have nothing but the best, they spared no expense getting the finest possible equipment and leading experts to instal it, so their claim to have the finest floodlighting system in the country is well founded.

I daresay many of you will be "new" to floodlit football so you may be interested in some of the background of the Maine Road system. The pitch is illuminated by one hundred 1,000-watt projector lamps operated in three batteries of 24 and one of 18 on the top of the towers at each corner of the ground. There are ten more as ancillary lighting on the stand. The towers, by the way, rise 90 feet above the surface of the playing pitch. Apart from the floodlighting, many smaller lamps have been installed for the benefit of those leaving and entering the ground, and in case you are wondering what will happen if there's a "fuse," an automatic emergency system will cover every contingency. Individual or complete control thus can be made at any point and at any time.

All For £3

For the technically-minded, the system is controlled by a 200-amp main breaker, and each of the four batteries of lights has its own switch control in a cubicle at the base of its tower. Total load for the floodlighting and amenity lighting is 150 kilowatts, and approximate cost of current consumed in say two hours before, during and after the game is £3.

It is a remarkable project reflecting credit on all concerned, especially the firms responsible for the supply, erection and installation of the various equipment—Messrs. Robert Springer Ltd., Philips Electrical Ltd., and Robert Watson and Co. Ltd. (Bolton).

ROLL CALL

DIVISION I

Appearances: Trautmann, Branagan, Ewing, Revie, 13; Paul, Hart, 12; Anders, Spurdle, Little, 11; Clarke, 10; Whitfield, Broadis, 7; Williamson, 6; Hannaway, 2; Davidson, Cunliffe, 1.

Scorers: Hart, 5; Revie, 4; Anders, Whitfield, Spurdle, Clarke, Little, Montgomery (Cardiff o.g.) 1—15.

Joe Hayes was only 17 when he made his debut on 24th October 1953. Over the course of the following 12 seasons he made a total of 363 first team appearances and scored 152 goals.

of the Sunderland battle: and a goalkeeper who can emulate the swift diving grace of a swallow."

The report went on to stress the strength of Trautmann, who by this point in his career was often described as one of, if not the, world's greatest 'keeper. He was also compared to the famous Frank Swift, with supporters often debating the strengths and weaknesses (if any) of the two City match winners. With City's disappointing early 50s form, Trautmann was at least able to show his strengths. In every game he seemed forced to perform some last ditch miraculous save to keep the Blues in the game. Without the impressive German the Blues would not have survived in 1952-3 and by the next season it seemed the 'keeper was expected to save the Blues all over again.

Apart from Trautmann, City did have a few impressive players - Revie, Paul, Spurdle, Anders, and Clarke - but in general the team did not combine well. The 'Old International' often commented on this, with the Villa game particularly worrying: "There was little method or discernible pattern of play observable: just a formless scramble: and one felt grateful for that fine display of marching and counter-marching by the New Zealand Band at half-time which did remind us that there are still such things in the world as order and precision. But for the time being they seem to be eluding City."

Despite the lack of cohesion, City defeated Manchester United 2-0 three days later. This result was achieved without Ivor Broadis who had sensationally been put on the transfer list by Les McDowall, who told reporters, "Following a heart to heart talk between the player and myself, it will be in the best interests of the club and player to part." Broadis moved on to Newcastle at the end of October for around £18,000.

A couple of 1-1 draws followed then a 1-0 defeat at home to Huddersfield, described by one reporter as 'another unbelievably poor display' by the Blues. The struggle continued.

On 24th October Ivor Broadis played his last game for the club, while young Joe Hayes made his debut after being spotted playing Sunday League football in Bolton. Both were commented on in match reports, with Broadis receiving acclaim for having 'intelligent foresight', while Hayes made an impressive debut with two good goalscoring chances.

Despite the positive play of Broadis and Hayes, City lost 3-0. A 3-2 victory over Burnley came next but the all too familiar City season of struggle was unfolding. Improvement came over the Christmas period, and speedy centre-forward Billy McAdams, signed from Distillery on 6th December, made his 2nd January debut a memorable one by scoring a 49th minute equaliser against Sunderland at Maine Road. The game was played in poor, foggy conditions and when Revie hit a winner 11 minutes from time, few knew exactly what had happened.

One reporter, Eric Dunster, had problems with another incident, brought to his attention by the groans and cheers of the crowd at the Platt Lane end of the stadium. It seems the supporters behind the goal were the only ones able to see the action as Sunderland put the ball into the back of the net. Trautmann lay prostrate, the crowd were groaning, and Sunderland players were celebrating, but within moments City supporters began cheering, signalling the goal had been disallowed. Dunster later discovered the goal had been ruled out for offside. In his report he questioned whether the game should have been played at all. City fans didn't care. They might not have seen much of the match, but at least it was a home win.

A week after the Sunderland game, McAdams made quite a name for himself with a hat-trick in City's 5-2 Cup win at Bradford. He followed up with an equaliser in the 56th League derby at Old Trafford. His instant goalscoring streak brought encouragement to the Blues, although typically City's form was not all it should be. In the Cup they were beaten by Spurs in the fourth round when they conceded a most embarrassing goal, and in the League convincing victories against Bolton and Tottenham were peppered by heavy defeats. Consistency has never been City's strongest suit.

On 10th April City faced Middlesbrough at Maine Road and, for once, played perfectly well as a team: "Nothing wrong with City. For once every man made an equal contribution. Their three man success formula of Trautmann, Paul, and Revie which the crowds have come to expect was not needed this time. In fact, Clarke, Meadows, and Spurdle stole the show - Spurdle for brilliant runs and centres, and Clarke and Meadows for two goals each. From the moment Revie began the goalscoring at 14 minutes, relegation anxious Middlesbrough got worse. Clarke made it 2-0. And after McPherson and Lawrie missed good heading chances, there was no escape for Borough. They hardly deserved their two goals."

The result and a 1-0 victory over Chelsea six days later more or less ensured safety. Defeat at West Bromwich on 17th April hardly mattered as it was followed by a 1-1 draw at home to Chelsea and a Maine Road 3-0 victory over Charlton in the last game of the season. The Blues finished the campaign in 17th place, seven points above the relegation zone. It had been another season of under-achievement but Eric Dunster's report offered hope for the future: "City did enough to suggest they may be more successful next season. McTavish has come on splendidly in recent weeks and Spurdle with his keen anticipation and fine turn of speed looks like making the right wing position his own. Hayes, a terrier for work, will be more than a useful stand by for either inside forward position."

For Les McDowall, the 1954-5 season was to be one of experimentation. He brought the players back two weeks earlier than normal, and gave them fairly tough training; 1930s full-back Laurie Barnett pushed them to the limit as McDowall strived to develop a successful side.

For several seasons City had struggled in the League, but McDowall had fresh plans. He had been watching and listening to reports coming from the reserves of a new tactical ploy which seemed to be working. Johnny Williamson, playing at centre-forward in the Central League, dropped back behind the other four forwards in one particular game. The plan was based on the one used so successfully by the Hungarians, who had humbled England twice during the early fifties, and proved totally confusing to the opposition. It also encouraged trainer Fred Tilson. Tilson, of course, was City's thrilling centre-forward during the 1934 Cup run and, although it went against the traditional type of play he enjoyed, he

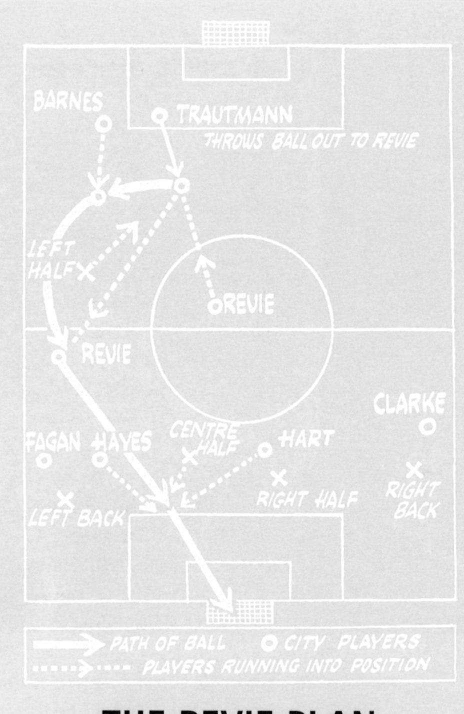

THE REVIE PLAN

These two diagrams show how the Revie Plan operated. In the first diagram a throw out by Trautmann sees Revie and Barnes combine to set up an opportunity for either Hayes or Hart. In the second diagram, a triangular linkup between Revie, Barnes, and Hart confuses the opposition and allows Revie to send the ball to Hayes, who is running into space close to goal.

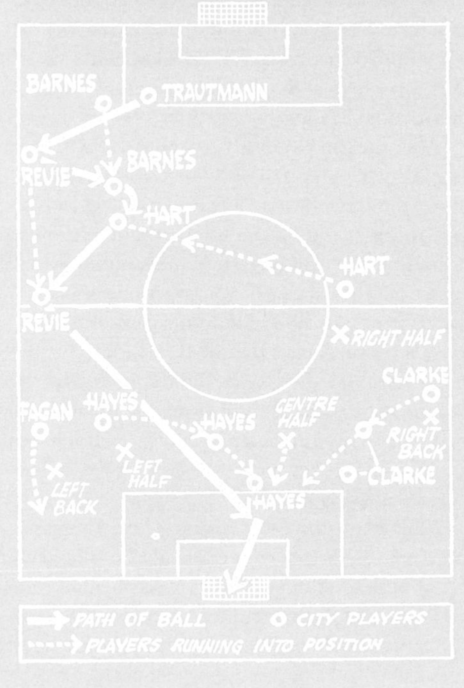

recognised the possibilities. After speaking with McDowall, the reserves tried out the technique during the 1953-4 season.

Johnny Williamson was also enthusiastic. He told Don Revie, in the first team: "It's the answer to all our problems. You just can't stop it when it gets going. This style is ready made for you, Don."

Revie wasn't convinced at this point, but results in the Central League suggested Williamson was right. McDowall also believed the moment had arrived. He called the players together and told them: "We are going to play football this season. By football I mean football. Keep the ball down; no big kicking; no wild clearances from the defence. We want to aim for a smooth link-up from defence to attack, letting the ball do the work, and not leaving chaps to chase a long ball when a short and more accurate pass would suit the situation better."

McDowall took Revie to one side and explained he wanted the player to move into the centre-forward position: "I want you to play there this season. Only you won't be playing an orthodox centre-forward game. You're always saying you like the short square pass with the ball pushed straight to your feet. We're going to give you that chance. I want you to play deep, and I want the other lads to play to you in the open spaces.... It's going to need a lot of stamina on your part to chase about all over the field, but the other lads will have to do just as much running about, too. I want a man as midfield schemer who is prepared to wander about all over the field....and I think you are the man who can do it!"

Don Revie and Ken Barnes worked perfectly together.

The plan came into force on Saturday 21st August 1954 at Preston. City were thrashed 5-0 and Trautmann played brilliantly to keep the score down. Despite heavy criticism from some of the players - Revie in particular - McDowall adamantly refused to change the City plan. Instead he told the players he would give the scheme a full month regardless of results. He also made it clear Preston would have destroyed City no matter which formation had been adopted as they were simply outstanding that day.

The next game saw Sheffield United - a team that had narrowly avoided relegation the previous season - arrive at Maine Road.

They left smarting after a thrilling 5-2 City win. The difference was the addition of Ken Barnes to the side. Barnes had never until then been able to command a regular first team place since signing in 1950, but had been selected by McDowall to play as an attacking wing-half. With Revie operating as a deep-lying centre-forward, Barnes was used to attack, distribute, and link up with Revie. The two worked together perfectly.

The plan did not simply involve one or two players, it was a real team strategy. Even Bert Trautmann was expected to play his part by making long, accurate throws to Revie, who would quickly provide a short pass to Barnes. Revie would move forward, with Barnes holding on to the ball while his

FA Cup 3rd Round
8th January 1955
Derby 1 City 3

Bert Trautmann keeps hold of the ball.

colleague got into position, then Barnes would push the ball down the touchline for Revie to latch onto. By this point the opposition would already be confused, Revie unmarked, and the centre-forward would be able to head for goal in relative freedom. It sounds incredibly simple, yet it worked.

The deep-lying role - eventually dubbed the Revie Plan - really did baffle the opposition. Few knew how to handle it. Players were instructed to mark by numbers, but with a deep number nine confusion reigned.

After the Sheffield United game, City moved upwards, briefly heading the table in September. The Revie Plan kindled much excitement and interest in the Blues, and for the first time since the war City really had the look of a top First Division side. Even United, who were gaining headlines for their crop of brilliant young players, found it difficult to cope with an upturn in City's fortunes. In the Maine Road derby on 25th September the Busby Babes, including the likes of Roger Byrne, Tommy Taylor, and Duncan Edwards, were beaten 3-2. The 'Old International' enjoyed the clash and believed City's new plan had brought the Blues back on a level footing with the Reds. While United were a side full of exciting individuals, he preferred City's team approach:
"It is a strategy which shows off to perfection the strength and maturity of Paul among his younger defenders, and which gives full scope to the inspired wanderings of Revie. City have staked their all on pure football and they are proving that football pays. What is more, by one of those delicious strokes of irony which play round the uncertainties of sport, the City's forwards helped themselves to three goals, and narrowly missed scoring as many more - without taking into account hot claims for an odd penalty or so - against a defence the three least masterful members of which were to be chosen later in the day as England's bulwark against Ireland."

City fans were ecstatic to see the Plan work to such effect against their Manchester rivals. City's methods were now bringing out the best in their players. Johnny Hart, for example, was able to use Revie's roaming to his advantage, as he also started to find space. He delighted in confusing the opposition and always seemed to turn up in the right place at the right time. City's team approach worked wonders.

In January City met United in the fourth round of the F.A. Cup and, again, the Babes were defeated by the City men. Even though United's Allenby Chilton was sent off it was still a great 2-0 victory, thanks to Hayes and Revie. But the biggest humiliation of the season for the Reds was to come only two weeks later (12th February 1955) at Old Trafford when the Revie Plan once again rattled them. By this stage the Busby Babes were acclaimed the best side in Britain, yet they could not defeat City. At Old Trafford City tore into them and, with goals from Johnny Hart, Fionan 'Paddy' Fagan (2), and Joe Hayes (2), won 5-0 to equal the margin of City's emphatic Old Trafford win back in 1926.

After the game, United captain Allenby Chilton was asked what preparations United had made to counter the Revie Plan: "We decided to ignore it. Revie roams so much from midfield and wing to wing that putting one man on him to mark him only results in upsetting the balance of your own side. So we decided to play an all-out attacking game ourselves and by sheer pressure offset the Revie Plan."

Chilton ended by saying the Reds would continue not to change their formation to tackle the Revie Plan. City fans agreed United's tactics were just about perfect - conceding ten goals in three derbies seemed absolutely right!

After a few seasons of despair, City's League programme continued to excite with the Blues ending the season in seventh place, two points behind runners up Wolves, and their best finish since the 1937 Championship. In addition, for the first time since the war City had a higher average attendance than Manchester United. The Blues were re-establishing themselves as one of England's leading clubs.

In the League alone it had been a successful season, but it was in the Cup that City achieved a great deal more.

The Cup run commenced on 8th January with a 3-1 victory at Derby County, then the 2-0 humiliation of United before 74,723 at Maine Road. In blizzard conditions, City travelled to Luton in round five. There Roy Clarke gave City the lead after half an hour, following a centre from Paddy Fagan, and fifteen minutes into the second half the Blues continued to defy the poor conditions as Clarke scored his second. Following the 2-0 victory, City had to travel to Birmingham City for the sixth round. There, an extremely tough tie was settled with a City goal late in the game. The Blues were awarded a free-kick outside the Birmingham penalty area. A fierce low shot by Clarke somehow found Hart who fired the ball into the net while Merrick, the Birmingham 'keeper, dived in vain.

The semi-final draw paired City against Sunderland at Villa Park. Sadly Johnny Hart, who had been such a vital member of City's attack, broke his leg in a League game at Huddersfield the week before the semi-final. This was a tremendous blow, and upset City's rhythm. Nevertheless, the Blues were strong enough to overcome the Wearsiders.

They already had a replacement for Hart - Bobby Johnstone. Johnstone had signed for City from Hibernian at the start of March, prompting many to wonder who would be left out to make way for the exciting Scot. Hart's injury solved McDowall's selection worries, although it remained a major blow.

In the 56th minute of the semi-final Roy Clarke threw himself at a curling cross from Joe Hayes and headed the only goal of the game. It had been another team victory with Roy Little and Dave Ewing performing extremely well in difficult conditions to hold City's defence together.

Sadly, City's injury jinx struck again when, with about three minutes left, Roy Clarke injured a knee and was forced to leave the field. It was another set-back for the Blues and terribly upsetting for a player who had done so much to get City to Wembley.

FA Cup 4th Round
29th January 1955
City 2 United 0

Left: The Sunday Dispatch illustrates a goal line clearance by United's Byrne from Joe Hayes.

Below: Hayes drills the ball past Ray Wood to put the Blues one up.

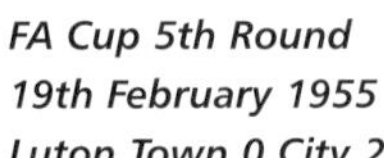

FA Cup 5th Round
19th February 1955
Luton Town 0 City 2

In blizzard conditions Luton's Baynham tries to keep hold of the ball as Roy Clarke and Joe Hayes (no.8) look on.

FA Cup 6th Round
12th March 1955
Birmingham 0 City 1

Right: Birmingham's Gil Merrick is unable to prevent Johnny Hart from scoring the only goal at St. Andrews.

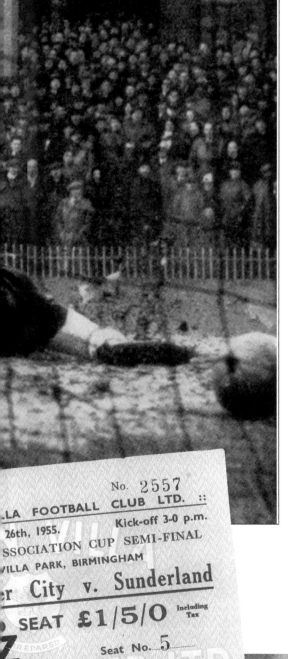

In the final weeks of the season Clarke returned to the City side, but another knock to the knee in the last league game of the season forced him to miss the final.

City's Cup Final opponents were Newcastle United who were recognised as a truly successful cup side after defeating Blackpool in 1951 and Arsenal - captained by Joe Mercer - in 1952. They had beaten minnows York City 2-0 in a semi-final replay.

In the week prior to the final, City stayed in Eastbourne while Clarke went to see specialists in Manchester.

Injury worries continued to plague the Blues; Dave Ewing twisted an ankle in training, Ken Barnes had what was described as 'violent toothache', and Bert Trautmann suffered from fibrositis and seemed unlikely to make the final. It was not a good week on the south coast, although it did bring a high point for one player; on the Thursday before the final, Don Revie travelled to London to receive the Football Writers' Footballer Of The Year award. He was the first City player to receive the honour and told the press that night the award was really one for the whole of Manchester City. The Revie Plan worked because of the entire team, not one man.

For the rest of the players, moving to Weybridge on the eve of the final lightened the atmosphere. They took part in a TV show with Leslie Welsh, the well known memory man, and the Millwall squad. Newcastle should have taken part but felt it would not aid their preparations for the final. City felt the opposite was true and some light-hearted entertainment did much for morale.

After the show - in which little Joe Hayes played a starring role - the players returned to the hotel and prepared for City's first final since 1934. During the night Jimmy Meadows took ill, developing a temperature which seemed destined to become a cold. McDowall must have wondered what misfortune would strike next.

Fortunately, Meadows managed to fight his temperature and, despite advice from a local district nurse for him not to play unless it was absolutely necessary, was determined to take part.

FA Cup semi-final
26th March 1955
City 1 Sunderland 0

Left: Roy Clarke heads City's Villa Park winner. Sadly Clarke was to miss the final through an injury picked up in this game. The same goal pictured from the stand emphasises the muddy conditions in the goalmouth.

No. 2557
LA FOOTBALL CLUB LTD.
26th, 1955. Kick-off 3-0 p.m.
SSOCIATION CUP SEMI-FINAL
VILLA PARK, BIRMINGHAM
r City v. Sunderland
SEAT £1/5/0 Including Tax
Seat No. 5
CE DOOR

FA Cup Finalists 1955

Billy Spurdle became the first Channel Islander to play in an FA Cup Final when he came in for the injured Roy Clarke.

Below: Prince Philip is introduced to the City team by captain Roy Paul.

At the stadium, captain Roy Paul went around the team saying: "Nothing to beat lads. If we just go out there and play the usual accurate passing game we'll run Jimmy Scoular, Jackie Milburn and the others into the ground." He was nervous himself but played a perfect captain's role.

When the time came to leave the dressing room and head up the tunnel, City were warned by Walter Winterbottom, the England manager, that Prince Philip was the guest of honour and: "He doesn't mind players showing natural excitement if they score... but he doesn't want to see any of the players kissing one another after they've scored!" The City players laughed, with Roy Paul shouting that if City scored first he would probably kiss the nearest person - "even if it's the bloody referee!"

Winterbottom left and City trooped out. The Blues were making history that year - the team included the first German to play in a Wembley Cup Final (Trautmann), and the first Channel Islander (Spurdle), also they were the first finalists to enter the field wearing tracksuits. The brilliant blue tracksuits were very grand for the period, but Eric Brook, City's 1930s star, was not impressed. Afterwards in his broad

Yorkshire accent he told Roy Paul: "Tha looked nowt more than pansies in pantaloons."

When the game kicked off, Newcastle raced towards the City goal. Milburn forced a corner off Ewing and from the kick White placed the ball perfectly for Milburn who headed powerfully in off the cross bar. Incredibly, City were a goal down after only 45 seconds. This remained the fastest goal in a

Jackie Milburn's header after just 45 seconds goes in off the underside of the crossbar and Newcastle are one up.

Wembley F.A. Cup Final until Di Matteo netted for Chelsea after 42 seconds in 1997.

Worse was to follow for City in the 19th minute when Jimmy Meadows was injured. His view the day after: "When Bobby Mitchell beat me and pulled the ball back, I was ready, and turned with him. I went to push off with my right foot, and my studs caught in the grass. In effect, the top half of my leg moved forward and the rest stayed put. The pain was indescribable.

"This morning I went to hospital and a specialist told me I had badly strained the knee ligaments and possibly suffered cartilage trouble. The whole of my right leg is in a plaster cast. I have strained ligaments before, but it's never been so painful as this. I'm going to see the club's specialist when I return to Manchester."

The *Daily Mail* revealed Meadows had torn his cruciate ligaments, and the player spent the next few years in a long painful battle to regain fitness and his place in the City team. The tragic story was similar to that Paul Lake suffered in the 1990s.

Ironically, the injury to Meadows happened at more or less the same spot and at the same stage of the game as a similar injury to Walley Barnes of Arsenal in the 1952 final, also against Newcastle. At the time many footballers blamed the lush state of the Wembley pitch for the injuries – the argument was footballers normally experienced heavy, bare pitches by the end of the season and Wembley provided conditions few were used to.

Whatever the cause of the injury, it was a huge blow to the Blues and meant they faced playing the remaining seventy minutes with only ten men. Already a goal down, it was always going to be tough, but Roy Paul tried to pull his team together, just as Joe Mercer had done three years earlier with Arsenal.

For a while the tactic worked.

Bobby Johnstone's header beats Ronnie Simpson to send the sides in level at half-time.

1955 FA CUP RUN

R3	Derby County	A	W	3-1
R4	Manchester United	H	W	2-0
R5	Luton Town	A	W	2-0
R6	Birmingham City	A	W	1-0
SF	Sunderland	N*	W	1-0
F	Newcastle United	N**	L	1-3

* = Villa Park, Birmingham
** = Wembley Stadium

FACTS & FIGURES

	P	W	D	L	F	A
HOME	1	1	0	0	2	0
AWAY	5	4	0	1	8	4
TOTAL	6	5	0	1	10	4

CUP FINAL DETAILS

7 May 1955 at Wembley Stadium

NEWCASTLE UNITED 3
MANCHESTER CITY 1

CITY: Trautmann, Meadows, Little, Barnes, Ewing, Paul, Spurdle, Hayes, Revie, Johnstone, Fagan
NEWCASTLE UNITED: Simpson, Cowell, Batty, Scoular, Stokoe, Casey, White, Milburn, Keeble, Hannah, Mitchell
GOALS: Milburn, Mitchell, Hannah; Johnstone

ATTENDANCE: 100,000
REFEREE: R J Leafe (Nottingham)
GUEST OF HONOUR: Queen Elizabeth II
MANAGER: Les McDowall
CAPTAIN: Roy Paul

Bert Trautmann takes the ball in full flight and (below) times his challenge perfectly to gather the ball at the feet of Newcastle centre-forward Vic Keeble.

A sad sight as Jimmy Meadows is helped from the field after injury brought a premature end to his Cup Final appearance. His studs caught in the lush Wembley turf resulting in torn cruciate ligaments. Already a goal down the Blues had to play the remaining 70 minutes a man short.

City had a twenty minute spell of vintage football and, thanks to a wonderful header from Bobby Johnstone, went into the interval on level terms. The Blues had tried to make the Revie Plan work, but in the second half the odds were very much against McDowall's side. Eight minutes into the second half Bobby Mitchell gave Newcastle the lead. Bert Trautmann felt responsible: "Mitchell had no chance to score from the narrowest possible angle I could cut him down to, so I dived to catch his centre. As I did, he drove the ball straight into the net through the space I had left."

In the 59th minute another Mitchell shot was parried by Trautmann, but George Hannah followed up to score. He told the press: "I just hit it as hard as I could."

City had no way back. The game ended 3-1 with the Blues suffering through injuries to key players throughout the later weeks of the season, not simply on Cup Final day itself. Roy Paul was bitterly disappointed. At the City banquet that evening he almost refused to give a speech, feeling speeches shouldn't be made about losing, but eventually he was persuaded to talk. He stood up, looked around the room at the faces from City's past and present, smiled and boasted: "We'll be back again next year to win it. Sam Cowan knows how I feel. He captained Manchester City's Cup Final team in 1933 and returned a year later to collect the Cup..."

Few at the time believed it, but Paul was determined to be proved right.

Cup Final Memorabilia

A ticket for the 1955 Wembley final and (below) the cover of a menu produced for City's Cup Final Banquet at Manchester Town Hall, autographed by Les McDowall and most of the players.

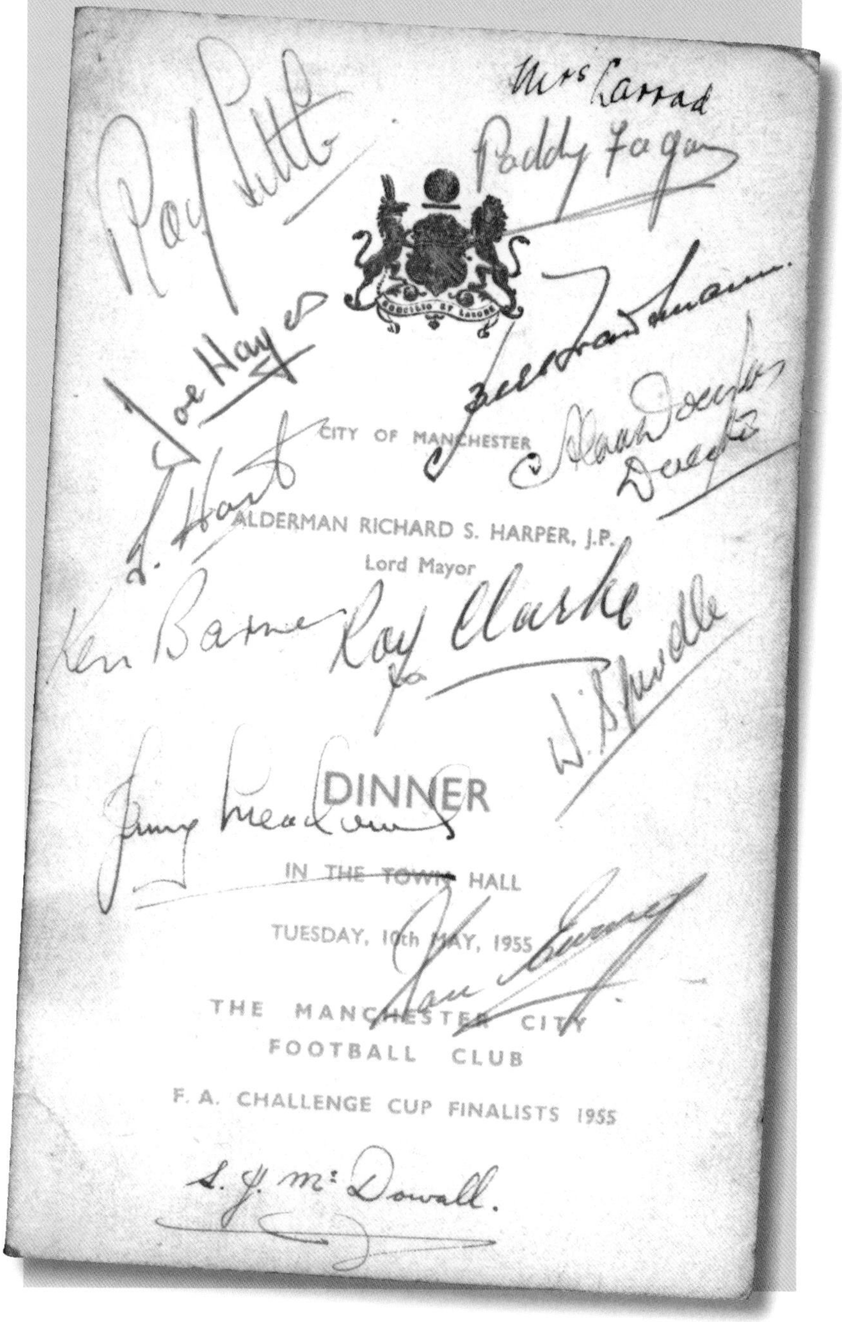

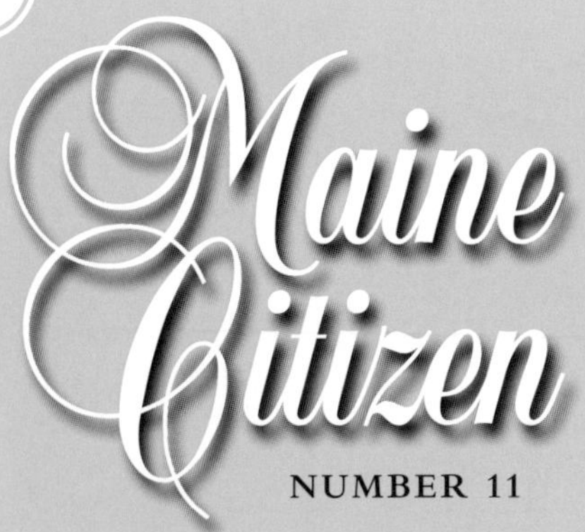

NUMBER 11

ROY CLARKE

Roy Clarke arrived in Manchester uncertain what to expect from a large industrial city. Would the city be as cold as he'd been told? Would Mancunians welcome him? Any concerns he had were quickly dispelled: "I was pretty impressed with Manchester, and once I got to Maine Road I knew I'd made the right move. I found the Mancunians very similar to the Welsh - everywhere you went at Maine Road there would be a cup of tea waiting for you. At first I was frightened to death to go into the dressing room because it was full of all these famous football stars, but I soon got into the swing of things."

Clarke liked it so much that he spent the following fifty years or so with City. First as a player, then assistant coach, followed by pools promoter, then Social Club manager, and later still one of the founders and leading organisers of the ex-players association. Even today in his 70s he still spends a considerable amount of time at Maine Road.

His arrival at Maine Road followed several scouting trips to Cardiff where the City management seemed more interested in inside-forward Billy Rees (who later played for Tottenham). After a number of visits the decision was taken to sign outside-left Clarke instead. It proved to be a wise choice. Over the course of the following decade the young Welshman was to help City reach Wembley twice.

Before he was even into his twenties he had been told his knees were so badly damaged he would never play football again, and when he first arrived at City many claimed he was too frail to make the top grade. Some questioned what he was even doing at the club. They quickly realised though, that appearances can be deceptive as Clarke, often with his head down, would charge forward, looking up at the crucial moment, before body-swerving an opponent and then producing a perfect centre. Eric Todd of the Guardian once said that Clarke was "built for speed rather than comfort". That speed helped bring the glory years back to Maine Road.

The 1955 Cup semi-final should have been one of his most enjoyable games as he scored a marvellous header in the Villa Park mud to give City a place at Wembley for the first time since 1934. However, he was later injured and forced to leave the field. In his third comeback game, co-incidentally at Villa Park, his injury

CLARKE'S PLAYING RECORD

	LEAGUE		FA CUP		TOTAL	
	App	Gls	App	Gls	App	Gls
1946-47	1	0	0	0	1	0
1947-48	36	5	0	0	36	5
1948-49	34	6	1	0	35	6
1949-50	37	9	1	1	38	10
1950-51	39	9	0	0	39	9
1951-52	41	9	2	1	43	10
1952-53	22	3	0	0	22	3
1953-54	35	7	2	1	37	8
1954-55	33	7	5	3	38	10
1955-56	25	6	6	0	31	6
1956-57	40	11	2	0	42	11
1957-58	6	1	1	0	7	1
TOTAL	349	73	20	6	369	79

Don Revie was suspended for 14 days after a fall-out with Les McDowall at the start of season 1955-56.

By the time the 1955-6 season started there appeared to be a major fall-out between Don Revie and Les McDowall. McDowall suspended the player for fourteen days, but Revie still played deep for the opening game of the season at home to Aston Villa. The game ended 2-2 with Revie's name on the scoresheet with a penalty. The following week he scored another penalty, but this time City suffered a shock 7-2 defeat by Wolves. Another 2-2 followed at home to Arsenal then came the Maine Road derby with United. Had the Busby Babes changed their plan after the previous season's defeats?

The game was closer than usual, but it still ended in a Blue victory thanks to a solitary goal from Joe

was aggravated further and he was unable to play in the following week's final. A fit Clarke may well have helped City achieve a little more respectability against the great cup fighters Newcastle.

The following year Clarke was a valuable member of the side that deservedly defeated Birmingham 3-1.

During the 1957-8 season he realised he was nearing the end of his City career and started to take an interest in coaching. For a while he acted as an assistant coach but realised his team mate Jimmy Meadows, whose career had ended as a result of injury in the 1955 final, was also keen on pursuing a coaching role at Maine Road. Generously Clarke stood aside and in September 1958 moved to Stockport County.

During 1966 Roy put considerable time and effort into opening the new City Social Club and remained as manager for almost 25 years, helping bring success of a different kind to the Blues. Today Roy Clarke is rightly remembered for the enjoyment he gave on the pitch, and for the enormous efforts he made off it to turn City into one of the friendliest, most approachable clubs in the world. Arthur Hopcraft's "The Football Man" - one of football's most important literary works - paid Clarke a telling tribute by devoting a great deal of space to the importance of the City Social Club which, during the 1960s, was the first of its kind. Clarke was responsible for making it a huge success for almost a quarter of a century.

At international level, he made 22 appearances for Wales and also won recognition for a different sport when, in 1939, he was a Welsh Schools' Baseball International.

Roy Clarke has been actively involved with City longer than any other former professional player. His contribution has helped the Blues achieve success in many areas, and his loyalty to the Blue cause has guaranteed him a significant place in the history of this great club.

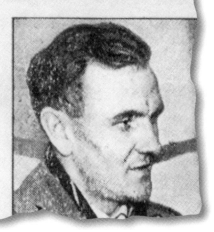

The Daily Mail report that Don Revie has been dropped.

REVIE Dropped–
plan goes
with Joh

MANCHESTER CITY have dropped Revie out of the Revie Plan. The Plan goes on against Everton at Goodison Park today with Scottish international Bobby Johnstone as deep centre forward.

As the club wanted Revie to play at right half, and he preferred to play at centre forward in the reserve side, these rumours of a first-class row spread like the city's fog :—

1. Revie would be asking for a transfer ;
2. Ill-feeling existed between Revie and Johnstone ;

Hayes. In addition to Hayes, Bobby Johnstone was fast becoming a star player, gaining many headlines for his outstanding play. Unfortunately, Johnstone's rise to fame seemed to upset the previous season's hero Don Revie. Newspapers were full of the conflict between the two, although everybody attached to the club played down the story. For a team hoping to improve on their League position, and reach Wembley again it was far from ideal. Nevertheless, the story rumbled on.

On Saturday 19th November 1955 the *Daily Mail* broke the news that Revie had been dropped by McDowall for the game at Everton, and Bobby Johnstone would play the deep lying centre-forward role. Without Revie, City managed a 1-1 draw. The previous two games had ended in defeat - some justification for McDowall's decision.

Apart from a defeat in the next match, at home to Newcastle, City's form improved with an unbeaten run of six games throughout December. To bolster City's attack, McDowall had brought in the multi-talented Jack Dyson. In addition to taking over from Bobby Johnstone in the number ten shirt, Dyson was an excellent cricketer who spent the summer months playing at Old Trafford for Lancashire C.C.C. Over the course of the League programme, Dyson scored 13 goals in 25 appearances to help City climb the table.

The Blues ended the season in fourth place on 46 points - the same total as the previous year's - but again it was the Cup run that set Manchester talking. In the third round City were drawn against Blackpool at Maine Road. Despite poor conditions the game kicked off, and within ten seconds the seasiders were a goal up thanks to Ernie Taylor. Jack Dyson scored an equaliser, but the conditions deteriorated. After a brief stoppage, play resumed but in the 56th minute the match was finally abandoned as fog enveloped the ground.

Four days later, a crowd of over 42,617 - 10,000 more than the original fixture - were present for a 2.15pm Wednesday kick off. The pitch was still in a poor state, but was judged good enough for action. For Blackpool's goalscorer Ernie Taylor, the pitch was not satisfactory, however, and he asked not to play. Without Taylor, Blackpool lost 2-1, with all the goals coming in a thrilling eight minute spell early in the second half. Before the tie City captain Roy Paul said the ground was playable; after the result he admitted it had not been good for the likes of Blackpool's Stanley Matthews, who had been marooned on the touchlines for

Below: Revie trains alone in Withington during his August 1955 suspension.

Joe Hayes heads City's equaliser against Everton in the 1956 FA Cup quarter-final at a packed Maine Road.

much of the match. The sticky conditions suited the Blues, in particular Jack Dyson who ploughed through the mud and puddles to score one of the goals. Bobby Johnstone got the other.

In the fourth round City were drawn away to Southend. It was the first time the two sides had met in a major competition - 41 years later they faced each other in the League for the first time - and a giant-killing act looked possible, especially when the City players saw the state of the pitch. To aid drainage the Southend management had put sand and shells into the turf, causing most players to leave the field with skinned knees.

Despite the conditions City won 1-0 - Joe Hayes' shot only just crept over the muddied goal-line - but the star man was Bert Trautmann. The German had made a number of fine saves. At one point Southend seemed close to being awarded a penalty but one of their forwards admitted later: "I didn't bother appealing, that fellow Trautmann would have stopped anything."

The fifth round brought Liverpool to Maine Road. It also brought Revie back into City's attack. McDowall had played him in the two preceding League games, and now felt Revie could again add something to the Blues' forward play. Roy Clarke was the unfortunate player left out as City again tackled difficult conditions. Watched by over 70,000 fans, neither side could break the deadlock as the icy surface prevented either side performing to their full potential.

For the replay four days later, the weather had not relented. This time, with snow on the ground, and Revie replaced by Clarke, City defeated Liverpool 2-1 after falling a goal behind. The game wasn't without controversy though. When referee Mervyn Griffiths blew his whistle to end the game few actually heard it. The players that did were leaving the field, but Liverpool's Billy Liddell continued to play. So did Trautmann and Ewing, and when the Liverpool man sent a shot past the two City players all three believed the Reds had equalised. The Kop were also convinced, and it took a brave referee to stand up to a number of irate players, supporters, and local journalists after the match.

City travelled back to Manchester delighted and cheerfully anticipated the sixth round visit of Everton to Maine Road. A crowd of 76,129 packed in for a game between two exciting attacking sides. The Merseysiders spent the first 45 minutes stretching City in style. Trautmann was kept on his toes, until beaten by an angled drive from Jimmy Harris. One goal was not a lot to show for all the pressure exerted, and in the second half Everton found it difficult to maintain momentum.

Roy Paul recognised this, and in the 68th minute took a free-kick a little outside the penalty area. He chipped the ball to Joe Hayes, who proceeded to dart forward and nod the ball into the net. Around eight minutes later Johnstone scored the City winner when he threw himself at a Clarke centre. It was a good victory, but for a number of supporters on the vast open popular side terracing the game had not been a comfortable one. Supporter John Lynch: "I remember this match because it was absolutely cram packed. The Kippax was mixed with both City and Everton fans. It was so crowded, you couldn't get out to go to the toilet! Fans were urinating into bottles and passing them down and placing them on the other side of the wall at the front. The police never even batted an eye-lid at this. All I could see was the goal in front of what is now the North Stand. City were 1-0 down at half-time and won 2-1, but I somehow missed all three goals!"

City had made it to the semi-finals again, even if many Blues didn't see the goals! City's opponents at Villa Park were the struggling Tottenham Hotspur. Despite Spurs' lowly position in the League it was the one team the City players were not too keen to face as they played a similar style to City, with talented attacking wing-half Danny Blanchflower usually the root cause of the danger.

The players had no need to worry however as Blanchflower tactically played himself out of the game. He tried to keep close to Bobby Johnstone, who in turn stayed well back behind the other forwards. This upset the Spurs' plan and forced the London club to adapt their attacking policy. In the 40th minute, Roy Clarke received a pass almost at the very spot where his injury had come the year before. This time the Welshman held the ball, drew the Spurs full-back towards him, and then centred for Bobby Johnstone to head home.

Tottenham were unable to come back, although in the final minute they threw everything they had at goal and were almost awarded a penalty. The incident became a major talking point over the weeks that followed, but City 'keeper Trautmann remained adamant he had done nothing wrong: "Tottenham were attacking desperately and there were three men almost on top of me when the ball came over from the right and reached the Spurs left-winger, George Robb. I managed to divert it with the side of my hand, and then fell headlong. I hadn't the slightest idea where the ball was then, and as I lay on the ground, I groped round frantically with outstretched arms, and Robb seemingly tripped over them. There were frantic appeals for a penalty, but they were unsuccessful and when the final whistle went shortly afterwards, I flung my arms round Bill Leiver's neck and kissed him to his evident embarrassment."

The incident brought out all the old prejudices and prompted a large postbag of abusive letters to Maine Road from North London addresses. All the anti-German feeling was resurrected eleven years after the war had ended. Trautmann was most upset and when City played at White Hart Lane a week after the semi-final, he dreaded playing in front of an abusive crowd. It didn't help that Spurs were desperate to avoid relegation.

The German took to the field, greeted by jeers from one particular section of the crowd. They met every fumble, every mistake with laughter, cheering, and yet more abuse. Understandably, Trautmann did not have

Action from the Villa Park semi-final with Tottenham in 1956. Bert Trautmann and Bill Leivers combine to divert a Spurs effort over the bar (above) and Trautmann watches as Leivers prepares to clear further danger (below).

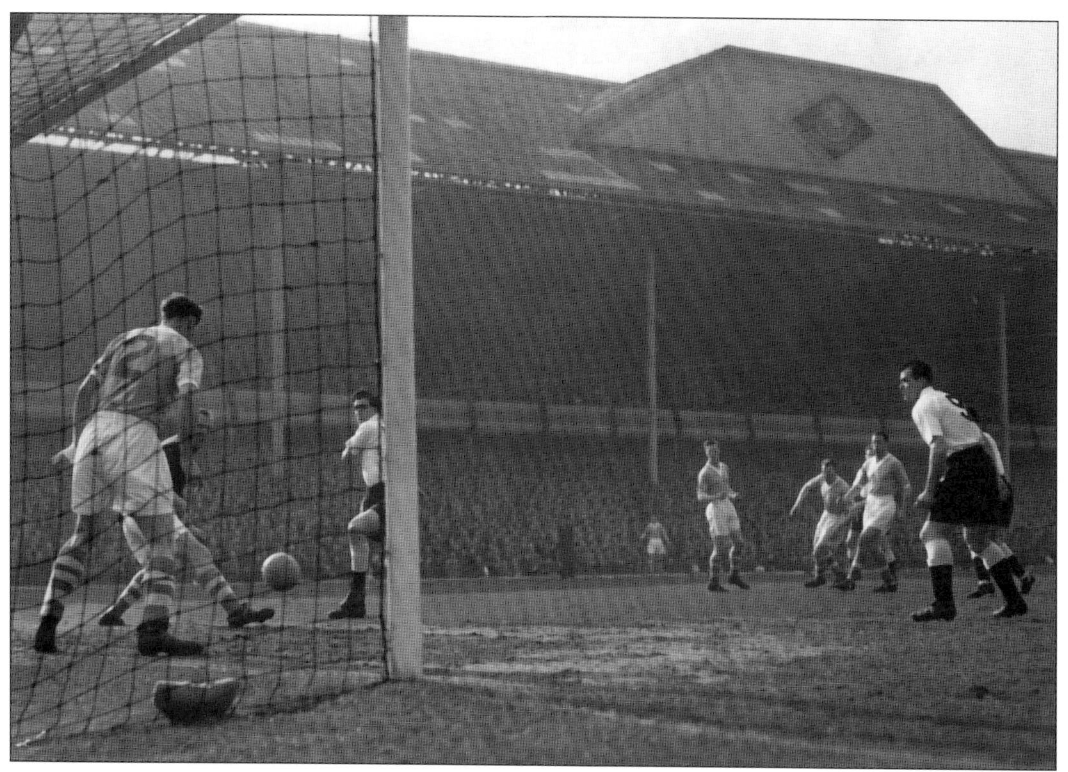

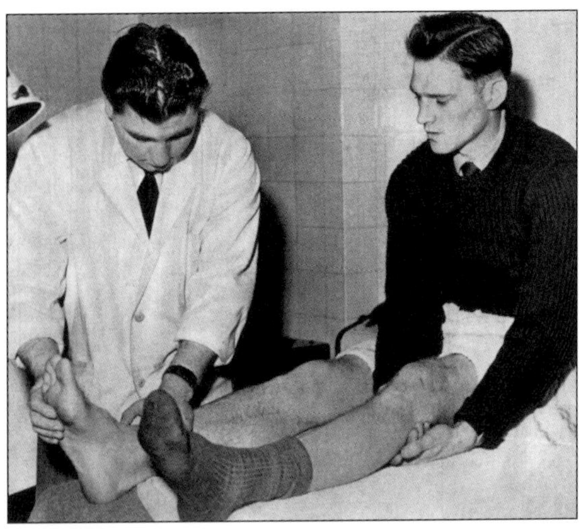

Bill Leivers receives treatment for his injured ankle. There were fears he might miss the final.

the game of his life, and the Blues lost 2-1. The majority of Tottenham fans treated Trautmann as any visiting player can reasonably expect to be treated, but one abusive section disgusted the rest.

After the League game the press got hold of the story and articles appeared across Britain, describing the content of the abusive letters. This prompted more correspondence, although this time Trautmann received over 500 letters of support from all over the country - including London. Shortly afterwards readers of the *Manchester Evening Chronicle* voted him their 'Player of the Year', then the news came through that he was also to be awarded the Football Writers' Player of The Year title.

The City 'keeper was overwhelmed by both the awards, and at the Football Writers' ceremony he thanked the press: "I am deeply moved and sincerely grateful - you have made me a proud and very happy man. I hope I can prove myself worthy of the honour."

The build up to the Cup Final meeting with Birmingham City was full of secrecy and rumour. The secrecy came from Les McDowall who did not tell his players what the final line-up would be until four hours before kick-off. This naturally prompted various rumours - many in print - about who would be left out, and who might play. Much speculation surrounded Don Revie - the forgotten man of football. Bobby Johnstone had been struggling with a nagging calf injury, prompting the press to proclaim 'REVIE MUST PLAY'.

Many supporters were against the thought of including a man who had hardly played a part in getting the Blues to Wembley. Interestingly, inside-right Johnny Hart was now back in contention. After breaking his leg 13 months earlier, he was in full training and had even played and scored in the final League game of the season.

City spent Cup Final week at Eastbourne again and, despite the selection rumours and doubt, kept their spirits up. There was no animosity between the players, after all it was the manager who picked the side. He would be the one responsible.

Twenty-four hours before the game McDowall was presented with another conundrum when Bill Spurdle developed a number of boils. On the Saturday morning Spurdle returned from the doctor with the disappointing news it would be impossible to lance them, therefore the Channel Islander could not possibly play. A short while later McDowall announced his team:

Trautmann, Leivers, Little, Barnes, Ewing, Paul, Johnstone, Hayes, Revie, Dyson and Clarke.

The forgotten man, Revie, was back. It was an important decision and one which would ultimately lead to a City victory.

City fans at Wembley in 1956. It's worth noting City fans appear to have taken inflatable bananas to the match (see bottom right) 30 years before the craze caught on!

FA Cup Winners 1956

In the dressing room before the game, captain Roy Paul kept a close watch on his men. He was determined nerves would not prevent City from performing and checked every player. Trautmann was as cool as ever, while Barnes and Little kept everybody amused with Roy Little impersonating Harry Secombe's Goon Show characters. Jack Dyson looked pale, but Paul knew it was normal for him to suffer some before an important game. Then the captain looked at Don Revie who was engrossed in fiddling around with two bits of old wood. He watched in astonishment as Revie placed the pieces in his jacket pocket. Paul had to find out what was happening and listened as Revie explained how an old gypsy woman had given him the wood, saying that it would bring him luck. She had told him his life was about to undergo a drastic change and that he would meet with success in his job, fulfilling a lifetime's ambition. Paul laughed, but Revie held on to his superstition.

When the time came City, wearing maroon shirts with thin white stripes, entered the field. At the opposite end to the players' tunnel thousands of blue balloons soared into the sky from the Manchester supporters. Immediately the stadium erupted with cheering and then the players started to hear the City fans singing 'She's a Lassie from Lancashire'. This had been City's Cup anthem that year with Manchester supporters singing it regularly. Another popular song from City fans around this period was an adaptation of 'Bless 'em all':

Bless 'em all, Bless 'em all,
Bert Trautmann, Dave Ewing and Paul,
Bless Roy Little who blocks out the wing,
Bless Jack Dyson the penalty king,
And with Leivers and Spurdle so tall,
And Johnstone, the Prince of them all,
Come on the light Blues,
It's always the right blue,
So cheer up me lads,
Bless 'em all

Once again the players were introduced to Prince Philip, then after the toss, Revie kicked off towards the Manchester supporters. Roy Paul watched as City's first move developed. Bill Leivers delicately passed to Revie standing in midfield, who then carried the ball a couple of yards forward, before crossing to Roy Clarke. Revie then sprinted towards the penalty area as Clarke held on to the ball. The Welshman then drew the Birmingham full back out, allowing him to slip the ball to Revie. Revie allowed the ball to run between his legs then flicked it with his right foot.

Joe Hayes had seen the build up and was ready as the ball came towards him. He put in a left foot shot and City took the lead after two minutes and 47 seconds. The goal rocked nervous Birmingham, just as Newcastle's had affected City the year before. Eric Thornton of the *Manchester Evening News* started to believe City would have everything their own way: "Manchester City established themselves as one of the best combinations of soccer artists even that famous Wembley turf has been graced with in post-war years. The million dollar opening which provided Joe Hayes with the leading goal he will never forget spun us into thoughts of a record runaway victory. For it was a magnificent team, finding the right touch at the start and moving beautifully forward."

NORTH TERRACE SEAT (Uncovered)
ENTER AT TURNSTILES (See plan & conditions on back) D
ENTRANCE (LEFT) 3
Row 3 Seat 274
EMPIRE STADIUM, WEMBLEY
The Football Association Cup Competition
FINAL TIE
SATURDAY, MAY 5th, 1956
KICK-OFF 3 p.m.
Price 10/6 (Including Tax)
Chairman & Managing Director Wembley Stadium Limited
THIS PORTION TO BE RETAINED
This Ticket is issued on the condition that it is not re-sold for more than its face value

Despite the early City dominance - Four corners in ten minutes and Joe Hayes forced goalkeeper Merrick to make a fine save in another move - Birmingham equalised in the fourteenth minute. It was against the run of play, especially as Don Revie seemed to dominate the game, but it was vital City kept their heads. Bill Leivers, Dave Ewing, and Roy Little helped keep Birmingham out with Ewing cheekily singing 'Keep Right on to the End of the Road' throughout. The song had been adopted by Birmingham fans throughout the Cup run and Ewing

Above: City huddle together in the players' tunnel while Les McDowall gives a last minute talk to Roy Paul, Don Revie, Bill Leivers and Bert Trautmann.

Left: Ken Barnes is introduced to The Duke of Edinburgh.

Wembley '56
The goals...

3 minutes
City 1 Birmingham 0
Joe Hayes with a left foot drive

14 minutes
City 1 Birmingham 1
Noel Kinsey equalises for the pre-match favourites.

65 minutes
City 2 Birmingham 1
Ken Barnes, Don Revie and Bobby Johnstone are involved in the build-up, Jack Dyson applies the finishing touch.

67 minutes
City 3 Birmingham 1
Bobby Johnstone wriggles past two defenders before hitting a right foot shot past Gil Merrick. In doing so he becomes the first player ever to score in successive finals.

The collision with Birmingham's Peter Murphy which caused Bert Trautmann's neck injury.

used it to wind up his opponents. The score remained 1-1 until half-time, prompting many to suggest the second half would be dominated by Cup favourites Birmingham. Roy Paul refused to accept that. He believed Birmingham were now in the same position as City the previous year, and thought a concerted effort in the second half would kill them off. He felt many of their players were tired. McDowall held the same view and urged his players to keep the ball on the ground.

Twenty minutes into the second half City regained the lead. A throw-in from Barnes reached Revie who played the ball to Johnstone. The ball was moved between Johnstone, Barnes and Dyson, before Dyson tore through to slot it past the advancing Merrick. The City players went crazy, before Paul brought a little calm back to the affair.

Within a minute Trautmann was forced to dive at the feet of a Birmingham forward then, with the ball safely gathered, he produced a long kick to Dyson. The cricketer flicked the ball to Johnstone, who wriggled past two defenders before planting it into the net to become the first player to score in consecutive finals. City were leading 3-1 with around 67 minutes gone. The Cup was coming home.

Birmingham still attacked, but there was no way back for them. Then, fourteen minutes from the end, Birmingham's Murphy charged forward. Bravely Trautmann threw himself at Murphy's feet and grabbed the ball but the collision knocked him out. When he was brought round he clutched his neck. It looked serious, but nobody realised how serious until sometime after. Trautmann and his colleagues believed he had displaced a disc. It was sometime after the final that X-rays taken at Manchester Royal Infirmary revealed he had in fact broken his neck.

For a moment Roy Paul and Les McDowall considered what should be done. Should Roy Little go in goal, or should the big German continue? Trautmann told Paul he wanted to play on. A few minutes after play resumed the German came out to catch a high ball, he collided with Ewing and was knocked out again. Trainer Laurie Barnett, who had played in City's last Cup success when Swift collapsed towards the end of the game, had positioned himself behind the goal ready to help the 'keeper.

For the last ten minutes Dave Ewing did all he could to prevent the Birmingham forwards from getting close to Trautmann's goal. He was magnificent as was captain Roy Paul, who many believed had his finest game that day.

The match ended with City victorious. Roy Paul walked up the famous Wembley steps to take the trophy from the Queen. He thoroughly deserved it. Often his leadership qualities had pushed City forward, through the various rounds of the Cup, and on to Wembley. His confidence had inspired others, but it was the injury to Trautmann and the reappearance of Revie that made the headlines. The *Daily Mail*, under the headline 'Triumph for Revie', stressed Revie's role: "It was Revie, Revie all the way in the F.A. Cup Final. Within three minutes of the start there could be no doubt he was the man for the job. On the sunlit green carpet of Wembley, Birmingham toiled in his shadow. They could never match the brilliant ball play of the smooth Don."

Left: Trautmann makes another daring dive.

1956 FA CUP RUN

R3	Blackpool	H	A# 1-1
	Blackpool	H	W 2-1
R4	Southend United	A	W 1-0
R5	Liverpool	H	D 0-0
	Liverpool	A	W 2-1
R6	Everton	H	W 2-1
SF	Tottenham Hotspur	N*	W 1-0
F	Birmingham City	N**	W 3-1

A# = abandoned
* = Villa Park, Birmingham
** = Wembley Stadium

FACTS & FIGURES

	P	W	D	L	F	A
HOME	3#	2	1#	0	4	2
AWAY	4	4	0	0	7	2
TOTAL	7#	6	1	0	11	4

\# plus 1 abandoned match

CUP FINAL DETAILS

5 May 1956 at Wembley Stadium
MANCHESTER CITY 3
BIRMINGHAM CITY 1

CITY: Trautmann, Leivers, Little, Barnes, Ewing, Paul, Johnstone, Hayes, Revie, Dyson, Clarke
BIRMINGHAM CITY: Merrick, Hall, Green, Newman, Smith, Boyd, Astall, Kinsey, Brown, Murphy, Govan
GOALS: Hayes, Dyson, Johnstone; Kinsey

ATTENDANCE: 100,000
REFEREE: A Bond (Fulham)
GUEST OF HONOUR: Queen Elizabeth II
MANAGER: Les McDowall
CAPTAIN: Roy Paul

Injured Bert Trautmann is congratulated by his opposite number Gil Merrick, and helped from the field by teammates Dave Ewing and Bill Leivers.

Roy Paul receives the FA Cup from the Queen.

Revie himself believed Bill Leivers was the star man: "He had two pain killing injections on his sprained ankle, yet he played the game of his life. Many of our attacking moves stemmed from his intelligent passing which switched defence on to attack."

Every one of the City players deserved credit for the success, and the whole of Manchester was able to celebrate as rivals United had managed to win the League. The *Manchester Evening News* brought out a special edition to celebrate the Manchester League and Cup double. Under the headline "City - We're proud of you!" the newspaper boasted about Manchester being 'King Soccer City of Britain'.

The Monday after the final Manchester prepared for City's homecoming. Every player was touched by the welcome. Trautmann couldn't believe it: "It seemed the whole of Lancashire let alone Manchester had turned out to cheer us as we drove from London Road station to the Town Hall for the civic reception. There was not a spare yard of room to move on the pavements, and even the heftiest policemen had a full time job keeping the milling thousands in check."

City's homecoming was the first outside broadcast by Granada TV. The TV station began broadcasting a few days earlier and decided to test out their equipment with a live 15-minute transmission of City's arrival in Albert Square. However, it didn't go exactly to plan as the team were delayed at the train station, and so experienced radio broadcaster Gerry Loftus was left to fill in time in his first TV presentation. He described the scene outside the Town Hall for nearly 30 minutes before the team bus finally appeared. The entire transmission lasted for 45 minutes and, according to David Lowe – an American TV advisor helping Granada TV in its first few weeks – it was: "the most exciting outside broadcast I have ever seen here or in the States."

For Mancunians everywhere these were very exciting times. Manchester's successful City side were back.

1956 VOUCHER SCHEME

Following the 1955 Cup Final, City became the first side to introduce a voucher system to help determine ticket distribution. Supporters had to collect a specified number of vouchers printed in home programmes, or provide programmes from away matches, to qualify for tickets to the final. There was a great deal of criticism at the start, but it seems the idea was more successful than its predecessors and the club kept faith with the system until the early 1990s.

Ken Barnes takes a celebratory drink from the famous trophy, fag in hand!

Maine Citizen

NUMBER 12

ROY PAUL

Roy Paul was born on 18th April 1920 in South Wales and, like Billy Meredith before him, spent some time as a coal miner before making his mark in football. Incredibly, as a boy he wasn't considered good enough for his school team. Perhaps that helped spur him on and gave him the fearless, determined streak that City fans loved and often still talk about. In his autobiography he commented on his disappointment: "I had three trials in the playground at the little school of Bronllwyn in my native village of Gelli Pentre. Each time I failed."

"Nothing I have ever suffered since - not even that Cup final defeat in 1955 - was ever quite as bad as the bitter disappointments I had at school. After these three trials, the schoolmaster sadly took me to one side and said, 'You are not big enough Paul. Not quick enough and not strong enough... Just keep on trying!'."

He first made his mark professionally playing League football with Swansea, and in 1950 was a star player in the Welsh club's fourth round cup-tie with 'Lucky Arsenal'. The general public felt that Arsenal had been winning games they didn't deserve to and the Swansea match was no exception. With terrific play by Paul, Swansea forsook defence for attack, and the Welshmen came close to a major cup upset. Afterwards the Gunners' manager Tom Whittaker made an offer for the tough wing half Paul, which the Swansea board turned down flat. Whittaker continued to chase the player without success. Then, after a brief spell in South America, the Swansea board realised it was time to cash in on their star player and Paul made the journey north to Manchester.

His first season immediately brought promotion to Division One, but it wasn't until 1955 that City made an impression on the League and Cup. With Paul as captain the Blues finished seventh and reached the Cup final with their determined leader guiding the side forward.

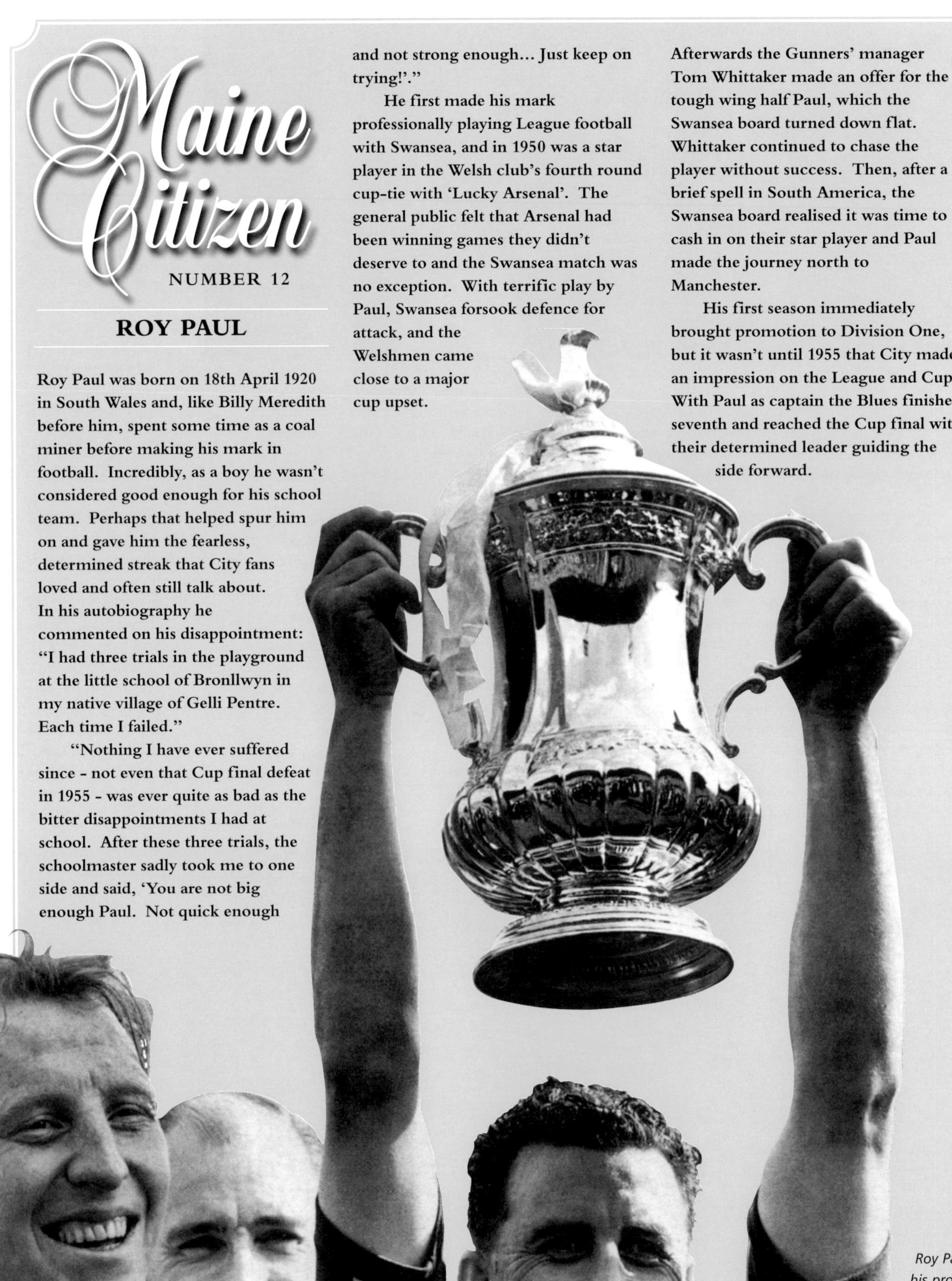

Roy Paul kept his promise by leading City to FA Cup success in 1956, a year after losing out to Newcastle in the final.

The '55 final was probably lost within the first minute when the fastest Wembley final goal until 1997 rocked the Blues after 45 seconds. Paul tried to motivate his players but it was a futile exercise as Newcastle were simply unstoppable - especially when injury to Meadows left City with only ten men.

Defeat was unacceptable to the defiant Welshman and he immediately vowed to lead the Blues back for success the following year. City fans were delighted the following May when Paul's outstanding contribution brought a convincing victory against Birmingham City. Some stories say the City captain actually threatened the rest of the team to play well or else they'd have him to deal with! Wisely, the players gave everything to lift the trophy.

Around this time Paul received much acclaim from other great players of the period. John Charles once admitted that Paul: "was my idol - my ideal when I was a boy". While Newcastle's early 50s Cup winning captain Joe Harvey said: "When I want to show a youngster how a wing half should play I take him to see Roy Paul. He is the complete wing half."

Joe Mercer forever commented on Paul's ability following the Swansea-Arsenal cup tie and admitted he would have enjoyed playing alongside the great Welshman. He also pushed Arsenal's Tom Whittaker to continue to approach Swansea, believing Paul's fighting spirit would help the Gunners achieve more success, even though Paul would have competed with Mercer for the role of captain.

In June 1957, at the age of 37, Paul's time at Maine Road came to an end, although some felt he might have gone on for another year or so. As it was he left just as the great 50s side was breaking up, and the struggles of the late 50s/early 60s were beginning. It would not have been a good time for Paul to stay, and would perhaps have made him a part of City's decline rather than the glory he is deservedly so associated with.

He moved to Worcester on a free transfer, became their player-manager, and later joined Brecon Corinthians and Garw Athletic. He also worked as a lorry driver back in South Wales for a time.

Overall, Paul's time at Maine Road was highly successful, not so much for trophies won, although two Wembley finals was extremely impressive for the period, but for the enjoyment he brought to so many fans. His tough, determined, fearless approach provided City with the fighting spirit they needed and helped restore much pride to the club and its supporters.

Roy Paul is one of the most important City players ever. He was also a great international gaining 24 of his 33 Welsh appearances while with the Blues. Every City side needs a Roy Paul, and every aspiring young player should understand how sheer determination to succeed can often prove the teachers wrong. Roy passed away on 21st May 2002, aged 82.

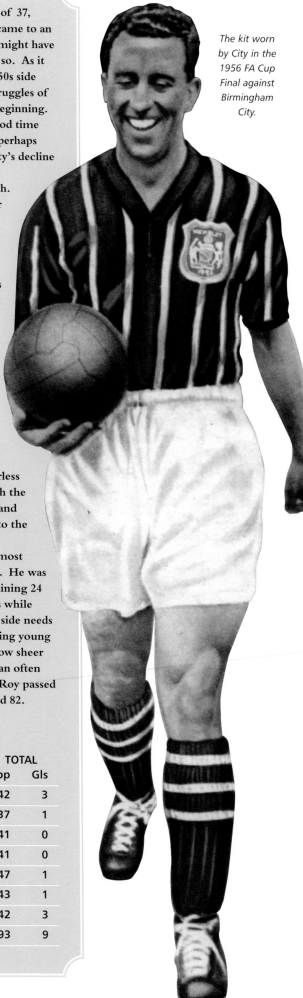

The kit worn by City in the 1956 FA Cup Final against Birmingham City.

ROY PAUL'S PLAYING RECORD

	LEAGUE		FA CUP		TOTAL	
	App	Gls	App	Gls	App	Gls
1950-51	41	3	1	0	42	3
1951-52	35	1	2	0	37	1
1952-53	38	0	3	0	41	0
1953-54	39	0	2	0	41	0
1954-55	41	1	6	0	47	1
1955-56	36	1	7	0	43	1
1956-57	40	3	2	0	42	3
TOTAL	270	9	23	0	293	9

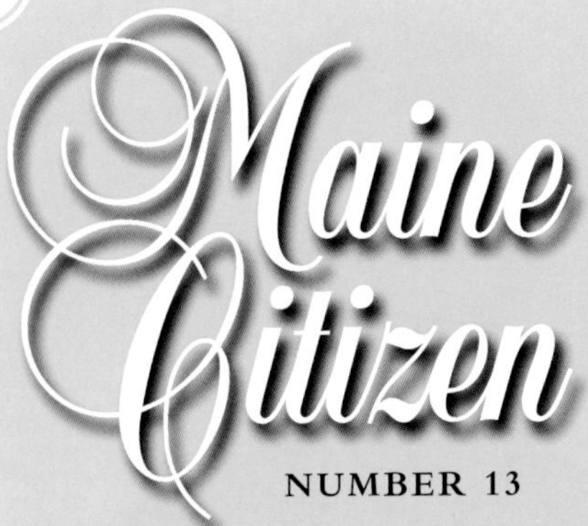

NUMBER 13

JOE HAYES

Joe Hayes' City career began in August 1953 while he worked at a cotton mill. The story goes he arrived for a trial carrying his boots in a brown paper parcel under his arm, scored four early goals, and at the end of the match said in a broad Boltonian accent: "Ta very much for t'game. Can I 'ave me bus fare back 'ome, please?"

Before the end of the month Blues manager Les McDowall not only paid his bus fare home, but also signed up the young player. Less than two months later - on 24th October 1953 - he made his debut at the age of 17 in City's 3-0 defeat at Tottenham. Not the greatest start, but Hayes did to retain his place for the following match - a 3-2 Maine Road defeat of Burnley.

By the end of that first season, the teenager had made 11 appearances, although he was then left out of the side for the opening months of the 1954-5 season. By the time of the 1955 final, however, he had not only made 20 League appearances, but had performed well enough to convince McDowall to give him his chance at Wembley. It wasn't really a gamble as Hayes had played in every round and had even scored in round three at Derby and round four against Manchester United (his first derby match). In fact Hayes enjoyed scoring against the Reds; in 17 League and Cup derbies he netted a total of 10 goals making him joint highest derby goalscorer with Francis Lee. Even then, the 5ft 8in forward deserves further acclaim as he also scored in the abandoned derby of 1960.

Hayes' first Wembley appearance ended in disappointment, but twelve months later it was the Kearsley born player who set the '56 final alight by scoring within three minutes of the start. It was a crucial goal and one which set City up for an exciting 3-1 victory. That season he was also the club's leading League scorer with 23 goals from 42 appearances.

The 1957-8 season was another which saw Hayes making a name for himself as he netted 25 times in the League from only 40 appearances, to help the Blues achieve fifth place. Around the same time he also appeared for the England Under 23 side and for an FA XI.

Sadly, the years that followed were not particularly successful for the Blues as many of the great players from the mid-fifties moved on. Hayes, however, stayed at the club and continued to perform well, despite City's frustrating tactics of the late fifties/early sixties. During season 1961-2 he netted 16 goals in 39 games to maintain his fine strike rate but the following season began to drift in and out of the side, only managing 21 appearances.

The 1963-4 campaign was even more disappointing with a serious knee injury at Bury on 28th September more or less ending his City career. During 1964-5 he bravely made two further appearances (at Huddersfield on 27th February, and at home to Crystal Palace on 19th April), but was never quite the same player again and was transferred to Barnsley during the close season. He was only 29. Had the injury not occurred it's possible he may have played a part in City's rehabilitation under Mercer and Allison.

After 25 appearances with Barnsley he moved on to Wigan and then became Lancaster City's player-manager.

In total Hayes made 363 first team appearances and scored 152 League and Cup goals. He is third behind Eric Brook and Tommy Johnson in the table of overall highest goalscorers and fourth in the list of League goalscorers. Considering the period in which he played, and the fact he appeared in over 130 games less than Brook, for Hayes to be so high up both these lists is a remarkable achievement.

Joe's is not usually one of the first names recalled when supporters talk about great players, but his achievements certainly rank with the best. He was a shade unfortunate after the promise of his first couple of seasons that City appeared to stop developing as a team and never really allowed him to build on his F.A. Cup Winner's medal. Nevertheless his career deserves to be remembered for the excitement and success he helped bring during the great mid-fifties. Joe Hayes was one of City's leading players throughout that period and beyond. He died in 1999.

HAYES' PLAYING RECORD

	LEAGUE		FA CUP		FL CUP		TOTAL	
	App	Gls	App	Gls	App	Gls	App	Gls
1953-54	11	0	0	0	-	-	11	0
1954-55	20	13	6	2	-	-	26	15
1955-56	42	23	7	4	-	-	49	27
1956-57	34	14	0	0	-	-	34	14
1957-58	40	25	1	1	-	-	41	26
1958-59	40	16	2	1	-	-	42	17
1959-60	41	13	1	0	-	-	42	13
1960-61	38	18	4	1	2	1	44	20
1961-62	39	16	2	0	1	0	42	16
1962-63	21	4	1	0	4	0	26	4
1963-64	3	0	0	0	1	0	4	0
1964-65	2	0	0	0	0	0	2	0
TOTAL	331	142	24	9	8	1	363	152

Chapter Twelve

LOSING SUPREMACY

THE months that followed the 1956 F.A. Cup Final were not happy ones for many connected with the Manchester Blues. Bert Trautmann in particular had every reason to feel a little aggrieved. His collision in the final had resulted in a broken neck and the German 'keeper was forced to convalesce, missing the first four months of the season.

Another unhappy player was the unsettled Don Revie. The cunning centre-forward had been disappointed with his treatment at Maine Road for some time and had considered moving on for at least a season. His Cup Final appearance possibly caused a brief change of heart, but in reality he was never going to settle down to life under Les McDowall. By the end of October he told Eric Thompson of the *Daily Mail* he wanted to move on, and had no intention of coming off the transfer list.

On 3rd November he played his last game for the Blues - a 1-1 draw thanks to a goal from City's Jack Dyson - and by 8th November Sunderland put in a bid of £20,000. The 29 year old decided to grasp the opportunity of resurrecting his career and officially signed for the Roker Park club two days later for a fee of £24,000. It was a sad but inevitable loss. Later in his career Revie found lasting fame for his highly successful managerial period at Elland Road, when he resurrected a football club - taking Leeds United from Second Division football to European competition. He followed that with a brief stint as England manager, before deserting the country for a more lucrative position in the United Arab Emirates.

Revie always tried to find security for himself and his family, hence so many transfer requests throughout his playing career. But his clandestine England departure was highly criticised and made the man unpopular at many grounds throughout the country.

By the time of Revie's transfer, the Blues were not enjoying the best of seasons. On the opening day they were trounced 5-1 at Wolves, and it wasn't until the sixth game that City were victorious. A run of six defeats in September and October saw them slip down

Bill Leivers in action against Wolves on the opening day of the 1956-57 season.

George Thompson (above) and John Savage (below) kept goal in Bert Trautmann's absence.

the table. One of the causes was clearly the absence of Trautmann.

Throughout the fifties City felt safe knowing Trautmann always seemed to produce a miraculous save to prevent defeat, but with the German absent the Blues had to find an alternative. Firstly, the former Preston 'keeper George Thompson was tried, but an injury in only his second game forced another change. For the third game of the season City turned to 6ft 4in Jack Savage, who had been signed from Halifax in November 1953. He had performed well in a couple of games - notably the September Old Trafford derby - but the Blues still suffered. Only a fully fit Trautmann could save the Blues' skins.

Although he was far from fit, the popular German returned to the side on 15th December 1956 after playing two reserve games. The result, a 3-2 defeat by high-flying Wolves, saw manager Les McDowall heavily criticised in the media for bringing the player back too soon. Nevertheless, the 'keeper kept his place and gradually his fitness and mobility improved. He remained City's first choice for the rest of the campaign.

City ended the season in a miserable 18th

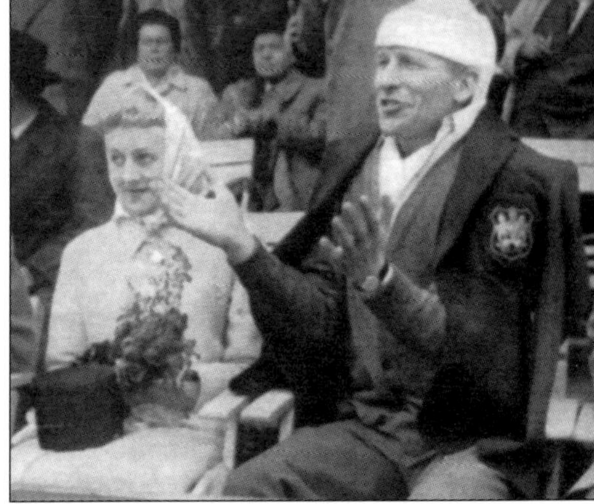

Bert Trautmann, with his neck and head in plaster, was guest of honour at a match in Berlin while recovering from his broken neck.

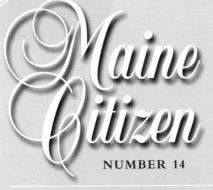

Maine Citizen

NUMBER 14

DON REVIE

History will always remember Don Revie more for his controversial resignation from the England manager's job than his highly successful near 20-year playing career. That is a shame, but is understandable. Even the great Joe Mercer felt let down by Revie; after all it was Mercer's recommendation that more or less guaranteed Revie would follow Mercer's enjoyable period as England caretaker manager.

Whatever the truths about Revie's England experience the fact is he was a skilful, innovative footballer who entertained the public. His early career saw him overcome much scepticism from the Leicester City supporters who at first failed to appreciate his thoughtful approach play. They simply expected the ball to be quickly delivered into the box, whereas Revie preferred to take his time, consider all the options, and then make his move. The famous Leicester Cup run of 1949 finally won over any Filbert Street doubters, but it was at a cost to both the club and the player. Firstly, broken blood vessels in his nose cost him a Wembley appearance and almost his life, while his fine form brought much interest from other clubs, including several calls from Manchester.

For what seemed an eternity City, Hull, Arsenal and a whole host of other clubs chased Revie. The player even arrived in Manchester with his wife Elsie, the niece of Leicester manager John Duncan. They viewed a club house, saw the sights, sheltered from the rain, and then returned to Leicester believing Manchester was a dull, gloomy, miserable place. He later signed for Hull but two years later changed his mind about Manchester, and decided to give the Blues a chance.

City manager Les McDowall was keen to build a good side and hoped that a stylish inside forward of Revie's calibre would help the Blues progress. Sadly, his first three seasons saw City struggle and, according to several friends, Revie felt he had made the wrong decision. He believed he was being moved from wing half to inside forward and back again without much thought, and detested the perennial relegation battles that plagued City in the early 50s. He decided the 1954-5 season was to be his make-or-break year.

He soon discovered Manager Les McDowall also realised it was time for City to start achieving. McDowall had worked with the rest of his staff to perfect a new tactic of playing a deep lying centre forward based on the Hungarian approach. The plan seemed to work in the reserves so McDowall asked Revie to take on the centre forward's role in the first team and gave him the opportunity try it out. Despite a couple of early failures, it was a revelation and quickly became known as the Revie Plan, although Revie was the first to admit it had not been his idea.

With the plan the Blues reached Wembley and Revie became the first

position and avoided relegation by six points. In the F.A. Cup, their third round tie at struggling Newcastle was billed as the 'game of the year'. A crowd of 58,000 were entertained by a performance from both sides that had many pondering why the League was such a struggle. The game ended 1-1 at a rain soaked St. James Park, although Bill McAdams, hampered by the poor conditions, missed a relatively simple chance towards the end.

The following Wednesday a crowd of almost 47,000 saw a match that really deserved its tag as 'game of the year'. Played again in heavy conditions, City were determined to get revenge over Newcastle for the 1955 Final defeat. Within 30 minutes City led 3-0, thanks to a Bob Stokoe own goal, an excellent header from the reliable Bobby Johnstone, and a minute later a Paddy Fagan effort from a fine through pass by McAdams. Newcastle appeared dead and buried, but the game was far from over.

Three minutes into the second half the Magpies fought back with a penalty from Tommy Casey. Sixteen minutes from time Alex Tait brought Newcastle's tally to two, then with the pressure on City's goal mounting the Geordies looked set to find an equaliser. Sure enough, with only five minutes remaining, Newcastle levelled via a Bill Curry header.

November 1956. Don and Elsie Revie read the news they'd been waiting for, that 29-year-old Don was to join Sunderland and leave the City struggles behind.

City player to win the Player of the Year award. He had, at long last, achieved the kind of fame and glory he thirsted. Twelve months later, after several disputes with McDowall, the football world was surprised when Revie was re-introduced to the side in time for the 1956 Cup success. In November 1956 he moved to Sunderland and later became player-manager of Leeds.

At Elland Road Revie put into practice many of the ideas he had developed during his playing career and tried to add a great team spirit. As a player he had been appalled by the treatment he and others received and found it difficult accepting the views of managers who locked themselves away.

He vowed to work closely with his players and made it his business to understand the personal circumstances of all his stars. He also was determined to guarantee the security of his own family and, understandably, sought the best deal possible for himself.

Strangely, considering his own playing style, as a manager his teams seemed to adopt a more physical style of play. His side's uncompromising approach proved effective however, as Leeds rose from the lower reaches of Division Two to glory in Europe.

Sadly, after his England managerial career ended in disgrace Revie became public enemy number one in many people's eyes, and was probably the first England manager who really suffered at the hands of the British press.

Unlike his peers - Busby, Shankly, and Mercer - he was unable to enjoy a period of 'elder statesmanship'. He was never sought by the media for his views on 1980s football, or of the leading personalities. Instead any mention of Revie was in connection with Leeds' negativity of the 70s.

The late 1980s saw him suffer with motor neurone disease, and Revie died in Edinburgh on 26th May 1989. He was only 61. Over a year earlier on 26th September 1987 at Elland Road he was guest of honour for the Leeds versus City Second Division match, and was introduced to the crowd before kick-off.

The loyal Leeds fans gave him a good reception; the City following, however, were uncertain how to treat him. Some cheered, perhaps recalling his role in the mid-fifties, others booed remembering the England fiasco. In some ways it summed up the media's perception that Revie was an enigma.

When considering Revie's life, it's worth remembering how his time at City was successful and that he was one of the key figures during the Blues' mid-50s glory years.

He was an extremely intelligent, skilful footballer who brought honour to the club. He was without doubt, one of City's greatest players and deserves to be remembered for the joy he brought to thousands of Mancunians.

REVIE'S PLAYING RECORD

	LEAGUE		FA CUP		TOTAL	
	App	Gls	App	Gls	App	Gls
1951-52	26	5	2	1	28	6
1952-53	32	6	3	0	35	6
1953-54	37	12	2	1	39	13
1954-55	32	8	6	2	38	10
1955-56	21	4	2	0	23	4
1956-57	14	2	0	0	14	2
TOTAL	162	37	15	4	177	41

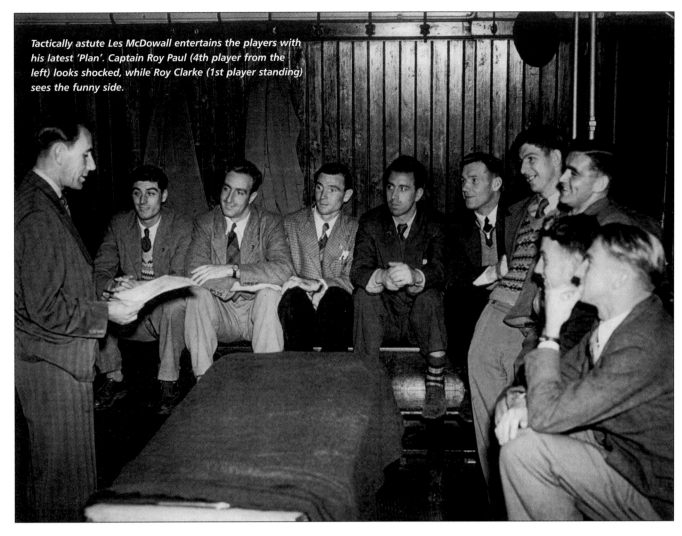

Tactically astute Les McDowall entertains the players with his latest 'Plan'. Captain Roy Paul (4th player from the left) looks shocked, while Roy Clarke (1st player standing) sees the funny side.

According to Newcastle based reporters even the City fans applauded!

City had now lost the initiative. The match went into extra time and the Newcastle supporters began singing the 'Blaydon Races'. The game appeared to be Newcastle's, but with typical City unpredictability the Blues took the lead again. Bobby Johnstone netting his second of the game and third of the tie.

Despite the goal, Newcastle took control and Len White scored twice to end City's hopes of a decent cup run. The game was a typical City spectacle.

Bobby Johnstone scores City's second goal in the amazing Cup match with Newcastle in January 1957. City were leading 3-0 yet lost 5-4.

Blues supporters always know to 'expect the unexpected'. For Newcastle this has been recorded as "arguably the club's most thrilling encounter", and one City supporters have been reminded about on many occasions. If nothing else, it allowed City to feature prominently in all the sporting annuals of the period. *The Big Book Of Football Champions* even claimed this "stirring battle of the giants" ensured the F.A. Cup remained "the greatest sporting competition in the world".

The 1957-8 season followed a similar vein to the Newcastle game with City supporters witnessing an incredible number of goals. In total 204 goals were scored during City's 42 game League programme - an average of 4.86 per match - with the Blues becoming the first side to score and concede 100 goals or more during a season. It was a strange period for the club with changes occurring both on the pitch and behind the scenes. In November George Poyser joined City from Notts County as Assistant Manager, with a brief to improve the club's scouting system. After a playing career that had taken him around the country - Plymouth, Brentford, and Wolves were three of the clubs he moved to - he began coaching at Wolves before taking the manager's position at Meadow Lane.

On the playing side the club lost one of its most influential captains, and gained a couple of bright hopes for the future. After seven eventful seasons Roy Paul decided it was time to move on, joining Worcester on a free transfer as player-manager, while youngsters Colin Barlow and Cliff Sear became established in the side.

Barlow joined City as an amateur in December 1956 and scored on his first team debut at Chelsea on the opening day of the 1957-8 season. He had been recommended to the Blues by former player Billy Walsh who spotted him while coaching at Xaverian College. Barlow played for the 'A' team while on leave from the Royal Dragoon Guards in Germany and was quick to make an impression, especially when he appeared in the first team - a large number of female supporters were delighted every time he ran close to them! During his debut season he scored 17 goals in 39 games despite playing mainly on the right wing.

Full back Cliff Sear was another to make an impression after signing professional forms in January 1957, although he very nearly missed being a City player: "I had previously been a part-timer with the club. In those days I was a 16 year old who worked down the mines at Bershaw Colliery, near my native Wrexham, travelling over to Manchester at weekends to play for the 'B' team at Crown Point. I played regularly enough, but no one said much to me or gave advice and I didn't think I was making much progress. So I left and linked up with Oswestry Town who were then in the Cheshire League. While playing for them, City manager Les McDowall spotted me and a fee of £1,500 was agreed. Oswestry's manager in those days was Alan Ball senior and he used to bring his son with him to watch us play! Shows how time flies."

One game early in the season which both Barlow and Sear were fortunate to miss however was the visit to West Bromwich Albion on 21st September. After an hour of the game City were losing 3-2 but were still in contention, yet the following thirty minutes saw Albion completely overwhelm the Blues 9-2 to register their record win of the century. It was a total humiliation, made even worse in January when Albion also recorded a 5-1 win in the F.A. Cup.

Manager Les McDowall, ever the tactician, had been devising another new plan throughout the early months of the season whereby Keith Marsden, wearing the number ten shirt, would drop back alongside big Dave Ewing to form part of the 'back four' as it became known. Playing with two centre-halfs became commonplace over the years but in the late 1950s it was still an innovation. It confused many, including perhaps even the City players as, after the defeat at Albion, McDowall abandoned it. The unfortunate Marsden broke a leg shortly afterwards and was never destined to make a name for himself as a key City player in the way that Revie had.

Seven days after the League defeat both Barlow and Sear returned to the side. Years later Sear recalled this game and believed it to be one of the club's greatest team performances: "The game was against Tottenham at Maine Road and on an afternoon of torrential rain we ran out winners by 5-1. It was about my third game in the first team and I got my chance because the regular choice, Roy Little, had been left out. On the right, Ken Branagan was also a last minute choice. In fact, he was in the team so late he had to be pulled off the reserve team coach that was going to West Bromwich for a Central League game.

"Bobby Johnstone scored a couple for us. So did Joe Hayes, with Colin Barlow getting the other. I can even recall who got the Spurs goal... It was Ken Branagan who turned the ball past John Savage! It was a tremendous all round team performance by City and

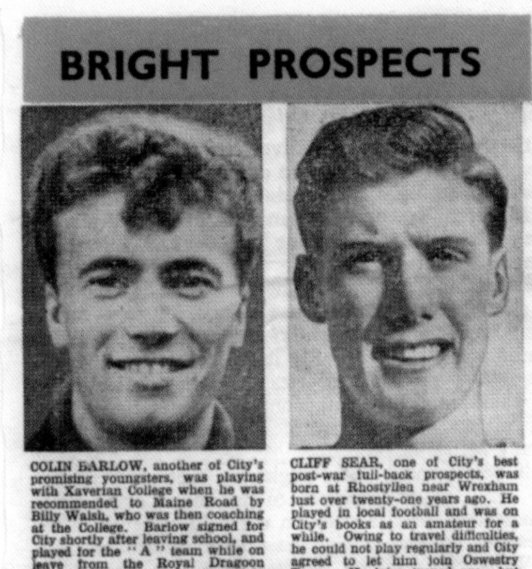

BRIGHT PROSPECTS

COLIN BARLOW, another of City's promising youngsters, was playing with Xaverian College when he was recommended to Maine Road by Billy Walsh, who was then coaching at the College. Barlow signed for City shortly after leaving school, and played for the "A" team while on leave from the Royal Dragoon Guards in Germany. He figured in every forward position except outside left, and when he has allied experience to his speed and enthusiasm, he should make the top grade.

CLIFF SEAR, one of City's best post-war full-back prospects, was born at Rhostyllen near Wrexham just over twenty-one years ago. He played in local football and was on City's books as an amateur for a while. Owing to travel difficulties, he could not play regularly and City agreed to let him join Oswestry Town. He later turned pro., but City were glad to pay Oswestry a nominal fee when they signed him in January. He made his debut at St. Andrew's last season.

The City programme in October 1957 picked out Colin Barlow and Cliff Sear as 'bright prospects'. Both became regular members of the first team during that season; Barlow played 39 games and scored 17 goals, Sear made 29 appearances as full-back.

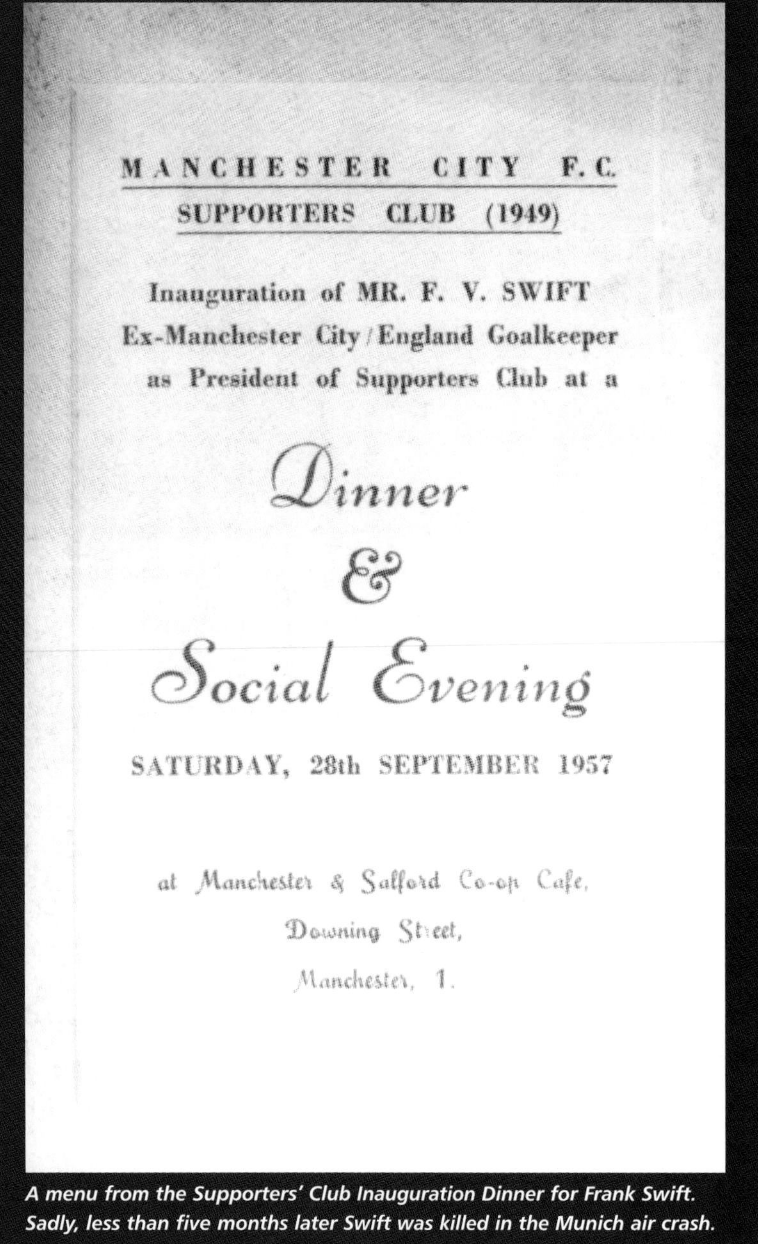

MANCHESTER CITY F.C.
SUPPORTERS CLUB (1949)

Inauguration of MR. F. V. SWIFT
Ex-Manchester City / England Goalkeeper
as President of Supporters Club at a

Dinner
&
Social Evening

SATURDAY, 28th SEPTEMBER 1957

at Manchester & Salford Co-op Cafe,
Downing Street,
Manchester, 1.

A menu from the Supporters' Club Inauguration Dinner for Frank Swift. Sadly, less than five months later Swift was killed in the Munich air crash.

A City line-up from the 1957-58 season.

Back row (left to right): Ewing, Leivers, Barnes, Trautmann, Sear, Warhurst.

Front: Barlow, Hayes, Johnstone, McAdams, Fagan.

11 in 10

Billy McAdams scored in ten consecutive League games between October 9th and December 7th 1957. During that period he actually scored a total of eleven League goals with two coming in the 6-2 annihilation of Everton at the end of that sequence. He also scored a goal in a friendly match during the period.

a good one for me, too, despite a bit of a struggle I had in the first ten minutes or so."

City's crazy season continued, even if the Marsden plan did not. On 7th December Ken Barnes became only the third person to successfully convert three penalties in a Division One game, as City defeated Everton 6-2. Albert Dunlop, who later became a City scout working for Barnes, was the Everton 'keeper that day and Barnes remembers facing Dunlop for each attempt: "I stuck one to the left, one to the right and he was so confused by the time the third award arrived that I could have back-heeled it in!"

In February revenge over West Brom was gained with a 4-1 victory, then seven days later the Blues were defeated 5-1 at Tottenham, although the whole of Manchester was by this time mourning the losses at Munich. Seven United players died in the crash on 6th February, with Duncan Edwards succumbing 15 days later, while other casualties included members of United's backroom staff and a number of journalists. The journalists included many names familiar to City supporters - Don Davies (arguably the finest football writer of the period), Eric Thompson, and Alf Clarke. Sadly, the most famous of all the journalists was former City 'keeper Frank Swift.

Cliff Sear made 279 first team appearances in 11 seasons with City.

Swift had been following United's exploits in the European Cup for the *News Of The World* despite his often quoted fear of flying. His death affected many associated with the Blues and football in general. The *News Of The World* received telegrams, letters, and tributes from readers nationwide who had been touched by the Big Fella's love of life and football. The Munich disaster was a devastating blow for the whole country.

At the game with Tottenham on 8th February, the Blues wore black armbands and a minute's silence was held. City's first home game after the disaster was scheduled for 15th February against Birmingham City, although the match had to be abandoned with the score at 1-1 around half time. The programme for this game was not a typical issue as it featured tribute after tribute. Chairman Alan Douglas offered his condolences and support: "For many, many years there has existed a keen rivalry between the two clubs, but just as we at Maine Road have rejoiced in United's many triumphs, so now we share their sorrow. I would assure Mr. Harold Hardman, the Chairman, his directors, and all associated with Manchester United, that while the blow they have received is a cruel one, it is not a knock-out, and we of Manchester City are convinced United will recover, and eventually return to their exalted place in the world of football. And if we can do anything to help them in any way, however small, to achieve that objective, we shall regard it as a privilege to do it."

Despite the sadness, football had to continue and for City the months that followed were quite entertaining as the Blues moved up the table. The occasional defeat occurred of course - such as an 8-4 at Leicester which ironically followed Trautmann's pre-match comment that he had never had more than seven put past him - but in the main City found a little consistency, with the period between 22nd March and 14th April seeing the Blues pick up nine out of ten points. A 2-1 defeat on the last day of the season against Aston Villa meant City finished in fifth position, although victory could have placed them third, subject to goal average.

Throughout the season they had once again been well supported with the highest League attendance 70,493. Interestingly, the ground now boasted covered accommodation for 50,000 after the Popular Side, or Kippax Street Stand as it now became, was roofed during the 1957 close season. This took Maine Road's covered capacity significantly higher than Old Trafford's and was around 15,000 more than the old covered capacity of Hyde Road. At last the Manchester footballing public had sufficient shelter, although the noisier element of the City crowd preferred to stand on the still open Scoreboard End (later North Stand). It took a few years for the Kippax to gain its fine reputation for atmosphere.

If 1957-8 was a season of high scoring inconsistency, then 1958-9 was one of dismal uniformity. Throughout the club's existence City have strived for consistency. When it arrived in 1958 it saw the Blues plummet down the table rather than challenge for the game's highest honours. 'Consistent mediocrity' was how journalist Arthur Walmsley of the *Manchester Evening Chronicle* described it.

At the start of the season all looked well. The opening game - a 4-3 victory at Burnley after being three down at half time - seemed to indicate the season would follow the pattern of the previous campaign rather than one of failure. After the opening match, City captain Ken Barnes wrote in one newspaper about his displeasure at seeing City pigeon-holed once again: "The old, old game has started. We extracted ourselves from a nasty half-time predicament at Turf Moor last Saturday, went on to win, and found that besides collecting two points we had picked up the old tag 'The Unpredictables' after only one match!"

Although City scored in each of the opening eleven games they simply did not score enough, despite the fact the great Bobby Johnstone was still leading City's attack. Roy Warhurst, the City half-back signed from Birmingham during the 1957 close season, believed the Scotsman was the finest player he ever saw: "Johnstone was the greatest footballer I ever played with or against. I was 29 when I came to City and I'd seen all Britain's best. But there was nobody to compare with Bobby, when he felt like turning it on. Not even Carter, Doherty, Finney, Billy Steele or Matthews. They couldn't touch him.

"My first game for City was a tour game in Holland. Bobby was brilliant. As the locals cheered him off the park I kept thinking 'this is some great outfit I've joined'. It was the greatest display I've seen from any player that night."

During September City purchased George Hannah, a skilful hardworking inside forward from Lincoln City for £20,000. Hannah believed his chances of returning to First Division football had long since vanished, but when the Blues showed interest the Liverpool born player couldn't wait to restart his career. His first City goal came in a 4-1 defeat at his former club Newcastle on 25th October, by which time City were struggling at the foot of the table.

Undoubtedly, 1958-9 was a time of transition, highlighted by the number of new players tried, then discarded. One such was 19 year old Bert Lister who made his debut wearing the number 10 shirt in the 2-0 defeat at Wolves in October. His second appearance came on 31st March at West Bromwich Albion when City succumbed 3-0, but then the youngster was cast aside until transferred to Oldham in September 1960. Although neither game ended successfully, it would seem Lister had done enough during his debut to warrant a decent run. According to one report: "Bert has built his reputation on his ability to grab goals, but though he didn't get one at Molineux, he did quite enough to show

FRANK SWIFT: The Man We'll Miss But Not Forget

The Football Writer.

The Goalkeeper.

By THE SPORTS EDITOR

THE Munich plane disaster touched us all. And to-day I have a melancholy duty. Our sports pages carry no feature article by Frank Swift. Instead, I have to write of Frank Swift, the man we knew.

A melancholy duty it is, yet I am grateful that I can at least pay a tribute from the News of the World to a wonderful personality who gave so much to the soccer public, spectators and readers.

Swifty collected countless friends everywhere in his playing days and then with his writings. He was that sort of man. You liked him and you respected him. His make-up was reflected in what he wrote for us and for you, bright, genial, easy to get along with and without an atom of malice or resentment.

The News of the World and its readers will miss him—but they won't forget him.

For the past two days telegrams, letters, messages and tributes have poured into our offices—from individuals, from organisations, from overseas and from all parts of Great Britain.

"Frank Swift, the goalkeeper and newspaper man, was a man loved by everyone," says secretary Alan Hardaker, in a message on behalf of the Football League.

This so well sums up the feelings of all those who wanted to pay their tribute, from Senor Bernabeau, president of Real Madrid, to the two anonymous girls—"just two football fans"—who called with a bunch of daffodils to place on Frank's grave.

In the News of the World it was John Hepburn of our Northern sports staff who was most closely associated with Frank Swift. So let John Hepburn speak for us all:—

GENIAL JESTER

BIG SWIFTY is no more. The empty seat across the desk keeps staring at me, forcing me out of the numbed disbelief of the past two days. The unopened fan-mail adds stark emphasis.

I mourn a close personal friend and respected colleague. But my loss is unimportant. Football has lost one of the all-time greats—a showman who put back into the game far more than he ever got out of it.

To me, Frank Swift will be remembered not so much as the greatest goalkeeper I ever saw, but as the big genial jester whose ready wit and pleasant personality were loved by millions.

Though he had hung up his boots nine years before, he was still escorted to his car every Saturday after the match he saw by dozens of young autograph-hunters, some of them too young ever to have seen him play.

"I'll worry when they don't ask me," he would say after signing the lot.

I shall never forget the day at Windsor Park, Belfast, last season when Frank was being pressed for his signature in the midst of more than 50 Irish schoolboys after the Ireland-England match. Twenty yards away the England *players* were allowed to file into their bus unmolested—and unnoticed!

Another unforgettable incident at Madrid last year showed that our leading footballers were Swift fans, too. Frank and I were watching Manchester United training for their European Cup match at the Real Madrid stadium when he was dragged out on to the field by Bobby Charlton, Dennis Viollet and Bill Whelan so that they could be photographed with the "Big Fella" as his great friend, Matt Busby, always called him.

Officialdom gave Frank the same royal welcome in board rooms all over the country—and confided in him most of soccer's secrets. The confidence was not misplaced.

Frank Swift hated flying. He often confessed his fears when we were airborne. But he would not let his apprehensions interfere with his desire to follow the fortunes of Manchester United, whom he was convinced would win the European Cup.

It won't be the same without Big Swifty.

An obituary from the News of the World following Frank Swift's death in the Munich Air Disaster. Frank had been following United in Europe for the Sunday newspaper.

George Hannah made 131 first team appearances (16 goals) in a six season Maine Road career. In 1955 he netted for Newcastle against City at Wembley.

that he will play a big part in City's future fortunes."

Another player given an opportunity then discarded was outside left Dennis Fidler, who made one appearance during 1957-8 then four the following season, scoring his solitary goal for the club in a 4-0 victory at Leeds on 21st February 1959. Fidler was a twenty year old inside forward who had once been a junior with United, but found that with so many similar forwards at Maine Road his opportunities were limited. In June 1960 he moved on to Port Vale.

The victory at Leeds helped boost confidence within the club, even though the Blues remained in the lower reaches of the First Division. After 29 games City were 18th on 23 points after winning eight, drawing seven and losing 14. Below were Tottenham (22 points), Leicester (21), Aston Villa (20) and Portsmouth (19). The heroes of the Leeds game included Bert Trautmann, who once again was saving City virtually weekly, and defender Ron Phoenix whose skill in breaking up the Leeds attacks excited City fans. His fine positioning and well-judged tackling kept Leeds at bay and prompted a section of the Elland Road crowd to call out: "give us a chance red head!".

Victories over Portsmouth and Newcastle followed during March, however City's mediocrity reappeared from mid-March onwards. By the time of the last match of the season City were in dire straits. Portsmouth were already down, but the remaining relegation place would go to either Aston Villa or City.

Both sides were on 29 points but Villa had a marginally better goal average (City 0.648, Villa 0.662). It was always going to be a tense occasion, but was made a little more bearable by the news the Blues would kick off at 7.30pm, whereas Villa's visit to fourth placed West Bromwich Albion would commence fifteen minutes earlier. Put simply, City would be aware of Villa's result and still have some time to improve their own situation.

April 25th 1959. Colin Barlow shoots a fraction wide during City's grim 0-0 relegation battle with Joe Mercer's Aston Villa. The result meant either club could still be relegated with one game each left to play.

City's opponents were Leicester City, who had also been struggling but were now three points above City and Villa. The Maine Road match kicked off with Leicester looking the more impressive side. Indeed the Filbert Street men took the lead in the ninth minute. It wasn't long, however, before Bobby Johnstone took control and after a further sixteen minutes lobbed the ball up for the diminutive Joe Hayes to head home.

Early in the second half the Blues took the lead with an effort from Ray Sambrook, after significant skills from Johnstone. Then Bill McAdams forced in a third. There was bad news coming from the Midlands, though. Aston Villa were leading 1-0 from a 66th minute Gerry Hitchens goal and if the two scores remained Villa, not City, would be safe thanks to a superior goal average.

The Aston Villa manager Joe Mercer felt confident his side would survive, and left the Hawthorns a short while before the end as he had a banquet to attend in Wolverhampton in celebration of Billy Wright's 100th cap. In the 88th minute of the Villa game Ronnie Allen scored an equaliser for West Bromwich Albion condemning Mercer's Villa to the Second Division. The goal was greeted with a great roar at Maine Road where, with seventeen minutes left to play, City were able to relax a little.

At full time the celebrations really began. Bert Trautmann had once again performed heroically for much of the season, saving City on many occasions, and the likes of Colin Barlow and Joe Hayes, both aged 23, were the source of a great deal of optimism. Barlow was the season's highest scorer with 17 goals, while Hayes had one less.

There were indications however that 29 year old Bobby Johnstone was nearing the end of his Maine Road career. He had made only 18 League appearances, scoring four goals, during the 1958-9 season and, although he was vital in a number of games, City began to look to a future without him. Les McDowall had already viewed a nineteen year old striker playing for Huddersfield. He appeared to offer a great deal, but the problem was price. City knew they would have to pay a considerable sum to sign the young, exciting forward. His name? Denis Law.

It would take McDowall quite a while to land the youngster, but as the close season began he considered City's strengths and weaknesses. They remained in a period of transition. Old campaigners like Johnstone were on their way out. Indeed, he would leave the club for £7,000 in September 1959, moving to Hibernian. Another of the 1956 Cup Final stars Roy Little, who had been with the club since 1949, had already been transferred – to Brighton in October 1958.

In addition Roy Warhurst, who had only been at Maine Road since June 1957 making 40 appearances, moved on. He felt there was too much unhappiness, and a lack of spirit within the club. He accused the backroom staff of unsettling him and the other players and was desperate to leave: "There was too much back-biting and not enough spirit. I love Manchester but I'd have gone anywhere just to get out of Maine Road. Things just didn't work out." He actually went to Crewe, where he made 51 appearances, before moving again seventeen months later to Oldham.

McDowall had already brought in a couple of new faces when the 1959-60 season began, wingers Clive Colbridge and Andy Kerr. Colbridge had signed from Crewe for £10,000 while Kerr arrived from Partick Thistle. Both started the season but by Christmas Kerr had returned to Scotland, signing for Kilmarnock. Colbridge fared considerably better, however, missing only two League games all season.

In October the Blues defeated United 3-0 in their first League derby victory since September 1955. Joe Hayes, who always maintained a top strike rate against the Reds, was in fine form, scoring twice, with George Hannah providing the other. The match gave the Blues a real boost and the following four games all ended in victory, with Bill McAdams proving a prolific marksman. In only eleven appearances he scored twelve goals. His fine run wasn't to last however as injury forced too many absences. In fact McAdams was an unlucky player, suffering more than most with injuries throughout his career.

He was unable to hold down a place in time to appear in either of the mid-fifties finals and, although he made a total of fifteen international appearances for Northern Ireland, his international career inevitably suffered.

Another whose international appearances were affected because of injury was cricketer/footballer Jack Dyson. He was on the verge of an England call up when, in 1957, he broke a leg in a City pre-season trial match, then late the following March broke his leg again in a comeback game in the Lancashire Cup. For the following couple of years he endeavoured to return to first team action and, on 14th November, he was in the team for the visit of Chelsea. The game ended 1-1 with Dyson securing his successful comeback with a goal.

That game was noteworthy as it also saw the debut of 17 year old Alan Oakes, the man ultimately destined to hold the record for most League appearances with the Blues. In 1959 that figure stood at 450 League games, plus three expunged at the outbreak of war, and was held by thirties star Eric Brook, but Bert Trautmann was second, making his 400th League appearance on 9th March 1960. Trautmann would end his career on 508 League appearances four years later, while Oakes would finish on an incredible 561 League games plus three appearances as substitute. Although the two men would always be bracketed together at the top of the League appearances table there is another reason to link the players at this stage, for in Oakes' debut match the youngster conceded a penalty but was fortunate enough to see the experienced Trautmann pull off one of his now familiar saves.

The week after Trautmann's 400th League appearance, Manager McDowall finally got his man, signing the Scottish striker Denis Law for a British record fee of £55,000 the day before the transfer deadline. It had been a tense negotiation. Law wanted to join Arsenal to link up with his Scottish colleague Tommy Docherty, however, Huddersfield were adamant they would not sell Law for anything less than £55,000.

It all to came to a head at Leeds Road where Arsenal had sent coach Ron Greenwood to negotiate a good deal. At the same time City, represented by Les McDowall and Chairman Alan Douglas, were keen to sign the 20 year old Scotsman. The Gunners had only given Greenwood power to offer £25,000 plus David Herd, making a total of £50,000, whereas McDowall

Clive Colbridge joined City from Crewe in May 1959, and made his debut against Nottingham Forest on the opening day of the 1959-60 season.

In September 1959 Bobby Johnstone moved to Hibernian after playing 138 first team games for the Blues. He was a tremendous player for City throughout the mid '50s and became a hero for thousands of fans - especially after netting in successive Wembley finals.

Billy McAdams was City's top scorer in 1959-60 with 21 league goals.

and Douglas were able to discuss the pros and cons of offering more.

The discussions and negotiations went on while Law played table tennis in the games room. When the young player was summoned he quickly realised his preferred move to Arsenal was off but, after less than ten minutes, he agreed to join the Blues at a price said at the time to be three times his weight in gold.

Law made his debut a memorable one by scoring in City's 4-3 defeat at Leeds on 19th March 1960. Eleven days later he scored again as City beat West Ham United 3-1. He made one other appearance, away at Chelsea, before the player became the subject of his first controversy at the club. Law was selected to play for Scotland at Hampden Park on 9th April - the date of City's vital home game with West Bromwich Albion - and the City management took the view that playing for your country was more important than playing for your club. This upset many supporters, who realised a Law-less City would struggle and that relegation was still a strong possibility. City were only two points above the drop zone.

The controversy heightened when other clubs took a different stance and refused to release players. The City Board then felt justified in asking the League for a postponement, but they refused. In the programme for the game, the Board outlined their views and explained how the circumstance had occurred. The article ended by stressing that the

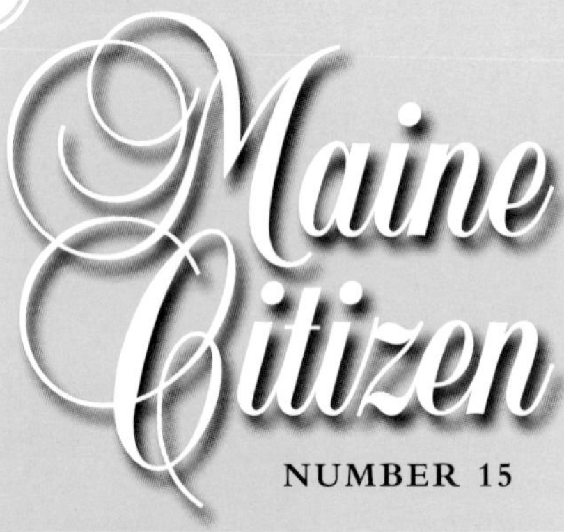

NUMBER 15

BERT TRAUTMANN

Bremen born Bernhard Carl Trautmann is probably the most written about of all Manchester City players - two quality biographies, hundreds, if not thousands, of articles, various profiles, and much more. Even in the 1990s when Uwe Rösler was first making his name with City, several features appeared in England and Germany about the first German to play for the Blues.

It is somewhat difficult because of this to sum up his life, career and the feeling of supporters towards him. The following comments, understandably, only provide a limited view of the great man's importance in the history of the club.

As a boy Trautmann was a decent centre forward and good athlete - he had to be, he was once shot at by a farmer for stealing apples! At 14 he became an apprentice motor mechanic, but the following year war was declared. After completing his trade he joined the Luftwaffe in 1941 as a wireless operator, serving in Poland and Russia. Later he became a paratrooper, winning five medals for bravery. He was captured by both the Russians and the French Resistance, but managed to escape on both occasions. In 1945 he was captured by the Americans, who allowed him to walk free. Bert arrived at a British camp where he was once again made captive.

While at a prisoner of war camp in Ashton-in-Makerfield Bert played football as a centre-half, and in one game injured a knee and pleaded with the goalkeeper to switch places so he could continue. From then on he became the prison's number one. He joined Liverpool Combination club, St.Helens and stayed in England working on a farm and then took part in bomb disposal work in the Liverpool area.

In 1949 he joined City and, despite threats in the press and abusive letters, was generally made welcome. A fantastic game at Fulham helped win over much of the London public, and Trautmann quickly established himself as a true hero. From then until his testimonial game in 1964 he often single-handedly helped City to victory, or saved them from embarrassing defeat. Quite simply, much of City's 50s success is down to Trautmann.

Jock Thomson signs a flu-stricken Trautmann at his bedside.

In 1956, he took over from Don Revie as the Football Writers' Footballer of the Year. Interestingly, this was awarded before he made the headlines for courageously playing on with a broken neck in the 1956 final, proving the honour was thoroughly deserved for all his exploits throughout the season.

Despite his ability, Bert never played for his country. It seems the German authorities had no intention of selecting a man earning fame and fortune in England so soon after the war. Naturally, many German clubs were keen to sign the goalkeeper, including Schalke, but on each occasion Trautmann was persuaded to stay in England. To test Trautmann's skills Don Revie told him he would give away a penalty during a tour match in Germany so Trautmann could save it. The two men laughed about the prospect, but then Revie did give the opposition a spot-kick forcing the 'keeper to really show his mettle. Without any real problem, Trautmann saved the penalty and won yet more admirers.

To compensate for his lack of

situation of club versus country could not be allowed to continue.

As expected, without Law City were defeated 1-0. The return of the Scotsman lifted the Blues and helped them achieve successive 1-0 victories over Bolton Wanderers and Tottenham Hotspur, although controversy surrounded the game at White Hart Lane.

Spurs were awarded a penalty on the stroke of the half-time interval but winger Cliff Jones' kick was brilliantly saved by Bert Trautmann. Jones followed up by slotting the rebound into the net only to find the referee had blown for half time the

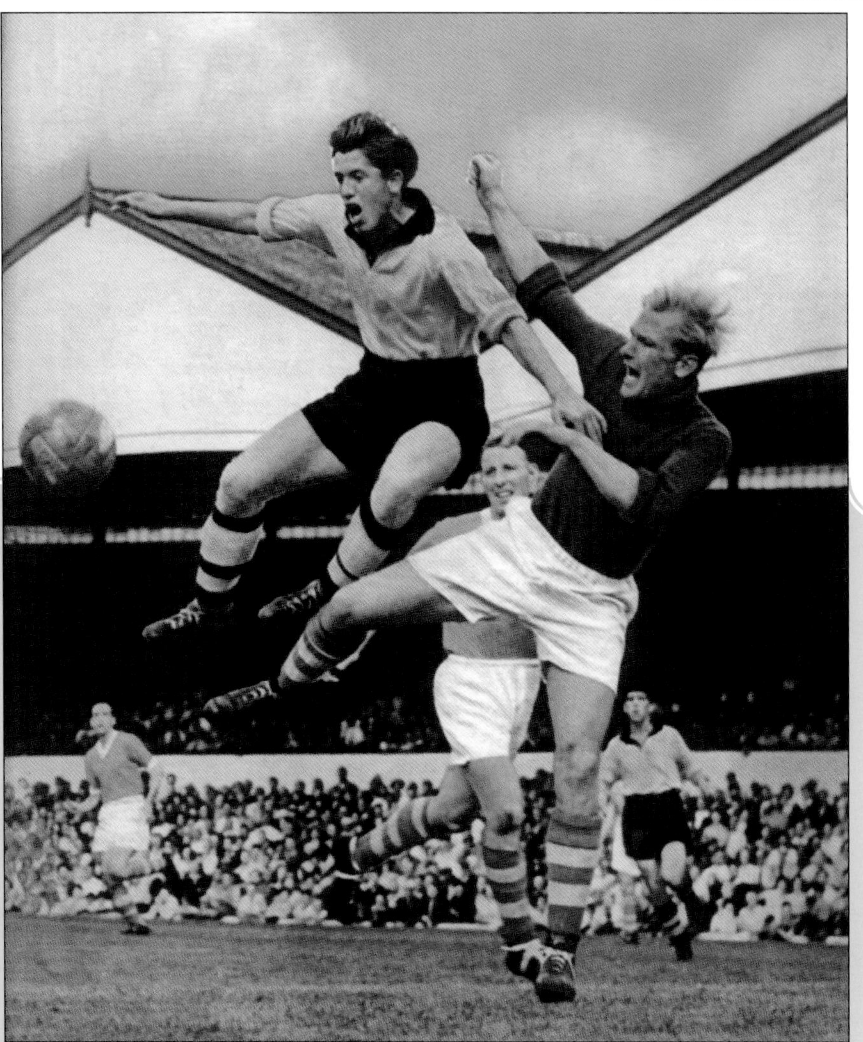

Trautmann keeps Wolves' Peter Broadbent at bay during the 4-2 defeat at Molineux in January 1960.

international football, the League authorities asked Trautmann to captain the Football League against the Irish League at Blackpool on 12th October 1960. The game ended in a 5-2 victory and included another non-English City player, Denis Law. Both men also played against the Italian League.

In 1964 at the age of 40, Trautmann's testimonial was watched by an official crowd of 48,000. Thousands more were locked out of Maine Road, while others managed to find a way in without paying. It seemed as if the whole world wanted to pay their respects to one of the world's greatest players.

Ten years later, Blues fans had a chance to see him play again when he replaced Joe Corrigan in goal for a spell during a testimonial for Johnny Hart. There was an incredible reception that night as some supporters who weren't even born when he last played at Maine Road, were at least able to say they saw one of the greatest 'keepers ever in action. Throughout Trautmann's time in goal Corrigan crouched close by watching, perhaps learning a tip or two.

Despite living overseas during the 1980s and 1990s, Trautmann has regularly returned to England to meet up with his former colleagues, and to watch the occasional game. In 1995 he came back to officially open the stadium's new Kippax Stand. It was a move much appreciated by the supporters.

Throughout his life and footballing career Bert Trautmann epitomised everything people expect of a brilliant player. He was skilful, sporting, brave, courageous and quite simply a great player. It shouldn't be forgotten he also overcame bitter hostility and suffered much hardship. He was, and still is, a remarkable man.

TRAUTMANN'S PLAYING RECORD

	LEAGUE		FA CUP		FL CUP		TOTAL	
	App	Gls	App	Gls	App	Gls	App	Gls
1949-50	26	0	0	0	-	-	26	0
1950-51	42	0	1	0	-	-	43	0
1951-52	41	0	2	0	-	-	43	0
1952-53	42	0	3	0	-	-	45	0
1953-54	42	0	2	0	-	-	44	0
1954-55	40	0	6	0	-	-	46	0
1955-56	40	0	7	0	-	-	47	0
1956-57	21	0	2	0	-	-	23	0
1957-58	34	0	1	0	-	-	35	0
1958-59	41	0	2	0	-	-	43	0
1959-60	41	0	1	0	-	-	42	0
1960-61	40	0	4	0	2	0	46	0
1961-62	40	0	2	0	1	0	43	0
1962-63	15	0	0	0	1	0	16	0
1963-64	3	0	0	0	0	0	3	0
TOTAL	508	0	33	0	4	0	545	0

Ken Barnes welcomes Denis Law to Maine Road in March 1960.

Law takes to the field during his first season with City.

Denis delivers a debut goal in the 4-3 defeat at Leeds.

moment Trautmann saved. To this day Tottenham supporters believe the decision cost their club the Championship as, they argue, Spurs would have won the game and the title would have been clinched on goal average.

What made the decision even worse for Tottenham fans was that City lost 2-1 to Burnley on the last day of the season, thereby guaranteeing the title for the Lancastrian club. By this time, of course, City had reached safety. That was achieved in their fortieth match - a 2-1 win at home to Preston - with Colin Barlow scoring the vital goal a few minutes from the final whistle.

City ended the 1959-60 season in 16th position, missing 15th place by a marginally worse goal average than Everton. It had been an improvement on the previous term, and with record signing Denis Law in their line-up the Blues eagerly anticipated the 1960-61 season. McDowall had made a couple of close season signings, bringing full back Barrie Betts and centre-half Jackie Plenderleith to Maine Road.

Betts had more or less given up all hope of playing in the First Division when a serious spinal injury threatened his career. At the time he was with home town team, Second Division Barnsley, but once his fitness returned a move to Stockport County seemed the only possible way of continuing in the game.

In June 1960, after 112 appearances with County Les McDowall took a gamble on the 28 year old, paying a bargain price of around £8,000. Many questioned the move but Betts quickly established himself, and became the club's first ever-present for four years. He enjoyed the experience: "I had four seasons at Maine Road - they were the best years of my playing life. I only wish that I'd found my way to City ten years earlier than I did."

Although remaining adamant he enjoyed his time at City, the other signing Plenderleith also accepts his move was not entirely successful: "I earned my only Scottish cap with City. I signed from Hibs in July 1960 for £16,500 and by November had won my first cap against Northern Ireland. We won 5-2 but I was dropped. I didn't get picked again simply because I'd lost my place in City's first team.

"Things started to go wrong for me at Maine Road during my second season. I'd asked for a transfer because I thought I was being made a scapegoat and finally it ended with me going back to Scotland to Queen of the South on a free transfer in

The 'no goal' that sparked a protest from championship seeking Tottenham.

September 1963. Despite the fact I had my share of reserve team football and also the fact that the first team seemed to be perpetually struggling I really enjoyed life at Maine Road."

Another player to arrive during 1960 was Gerry Baker, who was signed from St. Mirren on 2nd November, and made his debut three days later in a 3-1 defeat at Bolton. Co-incidentally 16 year old Francis Lee made his Bolton debut in the same game, and a name for himself by both scoring and being booked. Baker joined a City side that had only lost three out of 14 League games, however City's declining results following his arrival caused many to criticise McDowall's decision to bring the 22 year old into the side so soon.

The Blues lost eight of Baker's opening nine League games. Fortunately he provided two goals in the other match, at home to Fulham, to help City to a 3-2 victory. The other goal came from Clive Colbridge.

The mid season slump in 1960-1 seriously affected City's chance of a top ten place and actually placed the club in serious danger of relegation. On 25th March a goalless draw with Bolton which dropped the Blues into 18th position, prompted City fans to express their dissatisfaction. Defeats against Preston and Wolves followed, leaving the Blues on equal points with the bottom club.

A little relief came on 8th April when Denis Law helped City to a 2-1 win - only their third victory of 1961 - over Chelsea. Both Law and Colin Barlow had missed the two previous games and their return helped motivate the side. Two 1-1 draws followed, before City demolished Joe Mercer's Aston Villa 4-1 with goals from Law (2), Barlow and Hayes. The game saved the Blues from the dreaded drop and helped make amends for an earlier 5-1 defeat at Villa Park in December.

City ended the campaign in 13th position, five points above the relegation zone, and City fans pondered another season of 'what might have been'. Apart from the League programme, City fans had good cause to wonder about the Blues' exploits in both the F.A. Cup and the newly formed League Cup. In the new competition City defeated Stockport 3-0 then suffered a 2-0 embarrassment at Second Division Portsmouth, while the F.A. Cup was little better.

It took three games and 390 minutes for City to overcome fellow First Division strugglers Cardiff City, then in the fourth round the Blues were away to Second Division Luton Town.

It was a wet and windy day with the playing surface totally sodden, yet the game still went ahead. Luton's Alec Ashworth was first to take advantage of the conditions with two goals in the opening 18 minutes. By half-time, however, City had fought back with Denis Law scoring a hat-trick.

By the 67th minute Law had increased his tally to six, although his fifth goal had initially been credited to Joe Hayes. It was an amazing feat but as the conditions were

Colin Barlow nets the late winner against Preston in April 1960. It was the goal which saved the Blues from relegation.

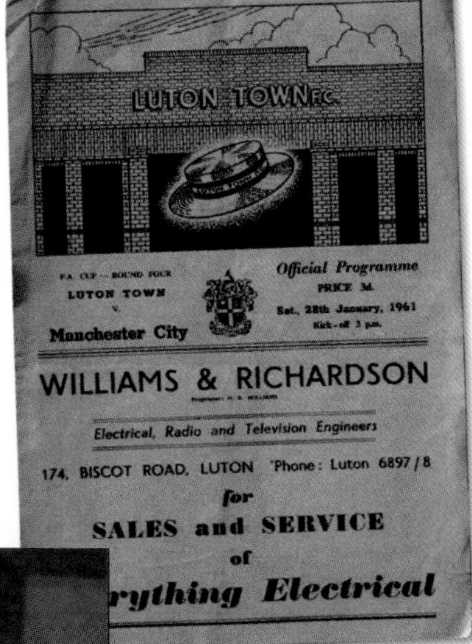

The cover of Luton's programme issued for the abandoned FA Cup meeting with City when Denis Law scored six.

A 1960-61 City line-up.

Back row (left to right): Sear, Plenderleith, Trautmann, Betts, Oakes.

Front row: Barlow, Hannah, Law, Barnes, Hayes, Wagstaffe.

Ken Barnes left the Blues in May 1961 to become player-manager at Wrexham.

Jackie Plenderleith joined City in July 1960. He won his only Scotland cap whilst with the Blues.

Right: Gerry Baker prepares for his debut at Bolton in November 1960.

worsening - according to referee K.R. Tuck and the Luton players - the game was abandoned only two minutes later. Les McDowall was furious, as were many of the City team and the supporters who had travelled from Manchester, but the referee would have none of it.

Four days later the game was replayed. Denis Law remembers the poor playing conditions: "The pitch was terrible because it was raining all the time. But the annoying part of it was that it was even worse when the game was replayed! We had a feeling that we would lose the replay - and we did, 3-1. And I scored the one!"

The Luton F.A. Cup tie was the last Law would play with City for 23 years. During the summer of 1961 he moved to Italy, signing for Torino for a huge fee of £110,000. The money, plus the opportunity to follow the likes of John Charles appealed: "Don't forget that in those days in England the maximum wage was only £20 per week. And when the Italians came over and dangled so many carrots in front of me, big money, wine, food, sunshine, it was too good to turn down.

"John Charles had been out there for a few years and now they were chasing lads like myself and Jimmy Greaves. As it turned out, it wasn't as marvellous as we thought it would be. But if I hadn't gone, I might have regretted it for the rest of my life."

By the time of Law's departure, Les McDowall's City were a rather tired, ordinary side, in dire need of new direction. Crowds had started to diminish - the average dipping below 30,000 for the first time since the 1930s. McDowall was still trying out new ideas and new blood, but the time had come for change. Unlike the 1980s and 1990s it was unusual for a team to sack a manager as soon as any struggles began; instead the view was often taken that "he got us in this mess, he can get us out!"

Despite four or five seasons of struggle, McDowall's job was safe, even though some new direction was necessitated The belief within the club was it was the players who were letting the club down not the manager of eleven years.

With no pressure to quit, McDowall prepared for the 1961-2 season. He spent the money received from Law's transfer on England Under-23 goalscorer Peter Dobing from Blackburn, and the powerful Bobby Kennedy from Kilmarnock. Both made their debuts in a 3-1 Maine Road victory over Leicester on 19th August, with Kennedy grabbing one of the goals.

The team that day was a mix of the old and new and lined up as follows: Trautmann, Betts, Leivers, Cheetham, Ewing, Kennedy, Barlow, Dobing, Baker, Hayes, and Wagstaffe. Ken Barnes had gone in May 1961 to become player-manager of Wrexham after over 250 League appearances for the Blues, leaving only four survivors from the 1956 Cup winning team.

Barrie Betts was now club captain and under his stewardship six of the opening eight games brought victory, but City's change of fortune was not to last and by New Year's Day the Blues had slipped alarmingly after gaining only seven points from sixteen games. That was relegation form.

As results worsened, McDowall once again shuffled the pack, bringing in more new players. One of them, 17 year old Neil Young, turned out to be the find of the season. Young had signed professional forms in February 1961 and made his League debut in

City's 2-1 defeat at Aston Villa. Although he failed to score on that occasion, the youngster remained in the side for the rest of the season, finding the net ten times in only 24 games - a figure that ultimately helped save the club from relegation.

Others tried included wing half and future manager John Benson, forward Paul Aimson, and goalkeeper Harry Dowd. Dowd was probably the most unfortunate of the new boys at this time as there was never any real possibility of him replacing living-legend Bert Trautmann. Dowd was always going to find it difficult during this period at Maine Road, and the two games he did play in hardly helped him take the Number One spot off the heroic German. The first ended in a 4-1 defeat at Blackburn, while his second saw the Blues lose 6-3 at Burnley.

It was no wonder the 23 year old 'keeper continued to seek a trade outside of football before making his debut: "I played for City as an amateur for a number of years because I was studying for my City and Guilds to qualify as a plumber. It wasn't so much that I was particularly desperate to become a plumber. They still had conscription in those days, and if I hadn't been learning a trade, I would have been called up.

"My great pleasure in life was playing football. Simple as that! I got knocked about a bit more in goal, but it was all part of the game."

Another brought into the side was 15 year old Glyn Pardoe - the youngest player ever to appear in City's first team. Pardoe's first game saw him wear the number nine shirt in a 4-1 defeat at home to Birmingham City on 11th April. It was a quiet debut, with the youngster prevented from showing his ability by the overall poor form of the entire City team. He rarely received the ball and couldn't be expected to turn the game around. His second match, however, was entirely different.

City faced Joe Mercer's youthful Aston Villa side at Maine Road before a pitiful crowd of 18,564. Despite early pressure from Villa, City ran out winners thanks to a solitary Neil Young goal. The press the following day were full of praise for the youngsters of both sides, with one report revealing the Villa manager had wandered around the City boardroom after the game with a big, beaming smile. The reporter's view was Mercer was convinced his youthful side would be world beaters within a couple of years and the genial manager was full of optimism. City supporters may like to believe Mercer was so impressed with the likes of Young and Pardoe he thought 'this is the club for me!'

Regardless of Mercer's view, the press also detailed the exploits of the young Pardoe: "I must save the last tribute for 15 year old Glyn Pardoe who made two astonishing runs, had two headers and a shot that almost scored and even now is remarkably hard to shift off the ball. Women or no women, soccer is safe for ever in the hands of our young Pardoes."

The City programme was equal in its praise: "The experiment of giving 15 year old Glyn Pardoe an extended trial was also justified in the Villa game. After his quiet debut game against Birmingham, he was seen to much better effect against Villa and if he didn't set Maine Road alight he surely gave promise that he is going to be a menace to opposing defences in the years to come.

"Certainly these end of season games are invaluable in giving young Pardoe the experience of first team football and although there is no intention of rushing him the experience he is gaining now could well see his development stepped up and his challenge for a regular first team place coming sooner or later."

With four games left to play, the Villa result lifted City to 13th position on 37 points - ten above the relegation zone. Although 21st placed Cardiff City still had five games remaining, the Blues were in effect safe. Pardoe played in two further games - a 3-1 win against Sheffield Wednesday and a 3-1 defeat at Blackpool - but missed the last couple of matches. A 3-1 victory on the final day of the season against Blackburn saw City finish in 12th spot, a marvellous effort considering their abysmal record from September to January.

In the League Cup City were defeated 4-2 at Ipswich and in the F.A. Cup the Blues beat Notts County 1-0 before succumbing to Everton 2-0 at Goodison Park.

The feeling amongst many supporters was City remained a considerable distance from glory in any competition, despite the emergence of the likes of Young and Pardoe. Sooner or later personnel had to change at the top.

Barrie Betts took over the captaincy in 1961-62.

On the day he signed for City young Glyn Pardoe was accompanied by his parents, manager Les McDowall and assistant manager George Poyser on a tour of Maine Road.

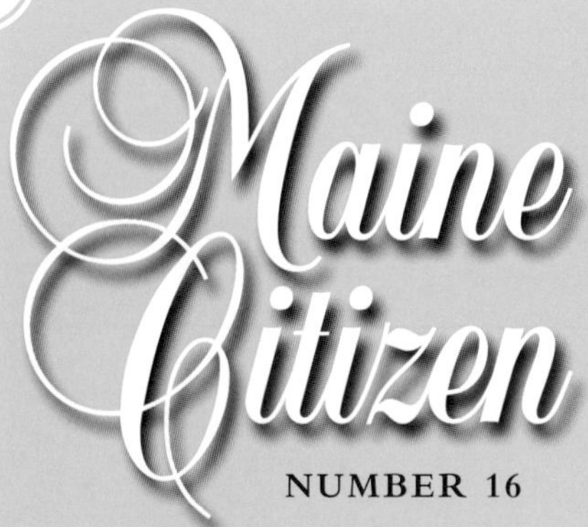

NUMBER 16

DENIS LAW

City fans usually remember Denis Law more for one particular goal than for any other moment in his City career. That cheeky back-heel in 1974 was widely held responsible at the time for 'sending Manchester United into the Second Division'. In actual fact, the goal was irrelevant as United would have gone down in any case, but it became a landmark and inevitably keeps the name of Law in the minds of Blues fans everywhere. Law's City career deserves to be remembered for much more.

He was signed in March 1960 from Huddersfield Town for a record figure of £55,000 - £10,000 more than the previous British transfer record. It was a bold move by Les McDowall and clear proof City were still a force to be reckoned with, particularly as they had managed to fight off the likes of Arsenal to sign the exciting 20 year old.

Law was a lethal finisher, and a genuine crowd-pleaser. His first goal for the Blues came during his debut match at Leeds United on 19th March 1960, although City were defeated by the odd goal in seven. His second League game brought another as West Ham were overcome 3-1 at Maine Road on 30th March. He ended the season with seven appearances.

The following campaign he was top scorer with 19 League strikes - one more than Joe Hayes - and again made the headlines with an amazing feat in an abandoned cup tie. On 28th January City were beating Luton 6-2 with Law netting all City's goals, when the match was abandoned. In the replay, Law again scored but this time the Blues lost 3-1 in conditions which Law believes were even worse than the original game.

In addition to his performances for City, Law made a name for himself with his country. He made five international appearances during his first two seasons at Maine Road, and was an obvious choice for his beloved Scotland.

All the media interest which understandably focused on Law helped to make him known throughout the footballing world and, with City still struggling to find consistency during the early sixties, it was perhaps inevitable he would move on. In the end he was transferred to Italian side Torino for another record. This time he became Britain's first £100,000 footballer when the Italians paid City £110,000 for his signature in July 1961.

After a little over a year in Italy, Law returned to Manchester, this time to join United. In his first season there he helped the Reds avoid relegation, but regrettably City suffered as a consequence. While at Old Trafford, Law found all the success that had not seemed possible at Maine Road.

In July 1973 after becoming a legend with the Reds he was given a free transfer. City manager Johnny Hart quickly made arrangements to sign the player, and on his second City debut he again scored (twice) as Birmingham were defeated 3-1. Of the City side he joined in 1973 only Alan Oakes remained from Law's final game in 1961, and the Blues were in an entirely different position.

The late sixties and early seventies had seen City achieve phenomenal success so this time, instead of joining a poor, struggling City side, Law was part of a band of entertainers capable of tremendous success. He had also joined a team renowned for its unpredictability!

Johnny Hart was replaced by disciplinarian Ron Saunders as manager, and the entire mood of the club changed. Saunders seemed at odds with many of the more senior professionals and his handling of the stars was often attacked. For a while there were rumours of player power, especially when City started plummeting down the table. Inevitably, Saunders was sacked and his replacement, Tony Book, thankfully changed the whole approach. On the final day of the season, it was as a member of Book's side that Law scored his last - and most memorable - goal.

It was also his last kick in League football, and he has often said it was the worst he ever felt after scoring a goal.

Less than two months earlier he made his farewell appearance at Wembley as a member of City's League Cup final team. That game ended in a 2-1 defeat, but then it did take place during Ron Saunders' period as manager. Had the atmosphere of the club altered prior to Wembley then it's possible Law's illustrious career would have ended with a League Cup winners' medal.

Denis Law only managed three seasons with City in total, but in each of those he did enough to make headlines and become a member of City's hall of fame.

During the mid 1970s The King's Head pub at Crown Point, Denton became a shrine to football and its sign depicted "The King" Denis Law. Although the nickname was awarded to him at Old Trafford, the pub sign depicted him in a City shirt - the team that first brought him to Manchester. It should never be forgotten how Law is a hero to both Blues and Reds.

LAW'S PLAYING RECORD

	LEAGUE		FA CUP		FL CUP		TOTAL	
	App	Gls	App	Gls	App	Gls	App	Gls
1959-60	7	2	0	0	-	-	7	2
1960-61	37	19	4	2	2	2	43	23
1973-74	22/2	9	1	2	4	1	27/2	12
TOTAL	66/2	30	5	4	6	3	77/2	37

The 1962-3 season started in the most traumatic way possible with the Blues annihilated 8-1 at Wolves; even City's goal was scored by a Wolves player. Within a week City plunged into the transfer market, purchasing forward Alex Harley from Third Lanark for £18,000. The 26 year old quickly displayed a return on the investment by grabbing both goals in the Blues' first victory, a 2-1 defeat of Ipswich on 5th September. Sadly, three days later City crashed 6-1 at home to West Ham.

Apart from the scoreline, the West Ham defeat was noteworthy for the antics of Bert Trautmann who kicked the ball at the referee while disputing the fifth goal. Then he appeared to rip off his jersey and storm from the field. It later transpired the brilliant 'keeper had in fact been sent off. Afterwards angry City supporters gathered outside.

Seven days later City travelled to Old Trafford to face a United side strengthened by the acquisition of former Blue Denis Law. Despite the hype surrounding a United side that included Nobby Stiles, Johnny Giles, David Herd, Noel Cantwell and, of course Law, City were a little more confident than in previous seasons. The last campaign had ended with City finishing above United for the first time since the 1957-8 season, while the new term had seen the Reds perform only marginally better than the Blues.

Before a rather disappointing derby crowd of 49,193 - the lowest since City's 5-0 win at Old Trafford in February 1955 - the Blues raced into a two goal lead inside 25 minutes. The first was via a penalty from Peter Dobing, the second a superb strike from regular derby goalscoring king Joe Hayes. During the second half, however, United fought back with new signing Law reminding his old team why they had broken the British transfer record to bring him to Manchester in the first place. He scored twice to level the scores, but the game was not over until, with virtually the last kick of the game, Alex Harley shot past United's Gaskell to give City the two points.

The game gave the Blues a much needed lift, and over the course of the following seven matches City gathered a total of eight points. Not a huge figure, but enough to relieve the tension. Unfortunately, City's inconsistency never really disappeared and by mid December the Blues record read: Won 5, Drawn 7, Lost 9, Pts 17.

The worst winter since 1947 then made its mark, with many fixtures postponed. The big freeze brought misery across the country and, although from 15th December through to 9th March the Blues did manage to remain unbeaten, they only played three matches. To get match practice City and Burnley flew to Dublin on 15th February where they drew 1-1.

By Easter City were in deep relegation trouble, lying in 21st place on 21 points after 30 games. The programme for the Good Friday fixture with Nottingham Forest outlined the seriousness of the situation: "Welcome this afternoon to Nottingham Forest for the start of a holiday fixture programme which is a critical one for us. The sad run of five successive League defeats in the last few weeks has dangerously heightened the relegation threat and with two home fixtures over the holiday period the chance is there to ease the danger and it calls for the maximum effort from the players to make the most of it."

The article went on to describe how close City had come to defeating the League leaders Leicester six days earlier where only the brilliance of Leicester's reserve 'keeper George Heyes, standing in for Gordon Banks, kept the Blues from scoring a hatful. In actual fact Leicester won 2-0, but City's forwards did manage a large number of accurate shots, only for the 'keeper to deny each effort.

By this time Les McDowall, under intense pressure, had signed Alex Harley's Third Lanark colleague Matt Gray, while Harry Dowd had managed to replace the legendary Bert Trautmann on a more permanent basis. By the end of the season the 'goalkeeping plumber' would have appeared in a dozen more League games than Trautmann.

Alan Oakes scored a consolation goal during the 4-1 defeat at Blackburn Rovers on 1st May 1963.

The Good Friday fixture with Forest ended in a 1-0 City win with Matt Gray proving an important purchase after scoring his fourth in eight matches. The following day Bolton were defeated 2-1 and then on Easter Monday the return game with Forest ended 1-1. On 20th April Arsenal were beaten 3-2, with two from Matt Gray and one from Joe Hayes, but City's run was not to last. The following five fixtures ended in defeat, throwing City right back into the relegation dog fight. A 1-0 home win over Tottenham on 11th May lifted things a little, but with only two games left the situation was dire.

City's last two fixtures were a home derby with fellow strugglers United and a trip to mid-table West Ham United. Going into the Maine Road derby City were only one point behind the Reds, although United did have a game in hand. Understandably, the match was an ill tempered affair with plenty of controversy. It remains one of the most significant derby games of all time and for all Blues was a painful experience.

With a crowd of 52,424, and thousands more locked outside, the game began with City playing confidently. In the ninth minute Peter Dobing sent a perfect through ball to Alex Harley who, under considerable pressure, rifled a right foot shot beyond United's Gaskell into the corner of the goal. City continued to dominate with United appearing rather shaky; only the fine goalkeeping of Gaskell and a few timely interceptions from Stiles prevented the Blues from increasing their lead.

After thirty minutes the City crowd roared with delight when Alex Harley appeared to have scored a vital second goal. Incredibly, the referee disallowed the effort on a hair's-breadth offside decision.

The City men could not believe it and tempers reached boiling point. Shortly before half-time Pat Crerand and David Wagstaffe were both booked following a brutal confrontation. It turned into an ugly game, and the fiery Crerand was determined to make his mark: "My first derby game will never be forgotten. It was a knockout. At least it was for City winger David Wagstaffe after I clouted him one on the chin as the teams trooped into the tunnel. I'm not proud of my actions that evening. It wasn't a vicious first half, but I'd become riled with Wagstaffe who I thought had punched me and my Celtic temper boiled up."

The press later revealed Wagstaffe had been 'laid out' in the tunnel, yet unbelievably the referee took no action. Maybe he didn't see the incident, but United manager Matt Busby did. He confronted Crerand in the dressing room and by the start of the second half United seemed a little less antagonistic towards the Blues.

Alex Harley once again went close, but as the minutes ticked by City's solitary goal seemed sufficient. Then disaster struck with only four minutes left. David Wagstaffe, possibly a little shaken from his conflict with Crerand, attempted what can only be described as a suicidal back pass. Denis Law, who had been quiet all evening, saw his chance and closed in on Dowd to tussle for the ball. As Dowd dived at the Scotsman's feet, Law fell and the ball ran out of play. The referee pointed to the spot much to the dismay of Dowd and fifty thousand City supporters. Albert Quixall stepped up and calmly slotted the ball past the unfortunate goalkeeper.

Bert Trautmann tests out new goalkeeper Alan Ogley, who signed from Barnsley in July 1963.

Later Dowd provided his version of the incident: "It was never a penalty; I scooped the ball away from Denis' feet and sent it out of play. I can't remember holding his feet but I did get a kick on the head. I may then have caught hold of him, but the ball was out of play by then, and I'm sure the linesman was signalling for a corner."

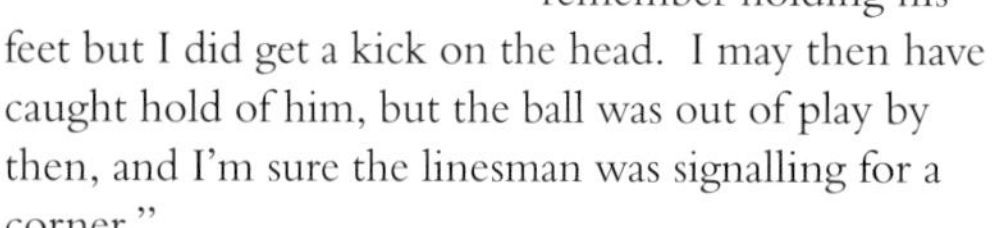

Law naturally claimed it was a just penalty but admitted United would never have scored otherwise: "I was going away from the goal and had lost the ball. It was a lucky break for us."

The game ended 1-1 with City feeling deprived of two points by two poor refereeing decisions - three if you include the Crerand-Wagstaffe bout. The point more or less guaranteed United's survival, but left City needing a better result than Birmingham City from their final game.

In the end Birmingham won, and City were defeated 6-1 at West Ham on 18th May. The Blues were back in the Second Division after an absence of twelve seasons. It was a bitter blow and one which resulted in the departure of long-serving manager Les McDowall on 29th May. After briefly considering the alternatives the City Board took the decision to promote George Poyser, McDowall's assistant, to the post.

Alan Douglas, the Chairman, called local journalist Eric Thornton in to explain the appointment: "We've had time against us. If we had appointed a stranger, he would have had a job getting to know the strength of the position before next season opens, but Poyser, having already been with us some time, knows the strength of the playing staff and everything else. We have talked it over with him. He says he knows the positions which need strengthening, and he feels he may be able to take us back into the First Division, so we're going to let him have a go."

Over 30,000 City supporters also knew the positions that needed strengthening, they'd paid to witness the decline, but it was Poyser, not them, who became the manager on 12th July 1963. He had become a popular figure around Maine Road since his arrival in 1957, however the appointment hardly excited the City faithful, nor did it excite Alex Harley and Peter Dobing. The two strikers found it tough to accept relegation and both chose to continue their careers in the First Division. Harley moved to the team that had only narrowly avoided the drop, Birmingham, while Dobing joined Second Division champions Stoke.

Poyser quickly realised he needed to bring experience and quality to the club and purchased Derek Kevan from Chelsea. Neil Young was by now a regular, while Joe Hayes continued to make the occasional appearance, as did George Hannah. In goal Poyser had signed Alan Ogley from Barnsley, although it was Harry Dowd who would replace Bert Trautmann on a more permanent basis, with the German making only three League appearances during the 1963-4 season. At the end of the season the legendary 'keeper retired from first team football after fifteen seasons with the Blues.

The opening Second Division fixture of the 1963-4 season started with a depressing 2-0 defeat at home to Portsmouth whose goals were scored by future City manager Ron Saunders, and an own goal from City's Number Five, the 17 year old Alf Wood. As expected, the programme for the fixture claimed the Blues would be going all out for promotion, but it also admitted many City supporters were disillusioned with the departure of the two leading scorers Dobing and Harley. It claimed, however, that new manager Poyser had held lengthy talks with the two players to persuade them to stay, but neither would listen. According to the article, their departures were inevitable.

A 2-2 draw at Cardiff followed the Portsmouth defeat, and then a brace from Derek Kevan gave the Blues victory at Rotherham. Gradually City moved into their stride with December proving the most profitable month for the Blues, and also for November signing Jimmy Murray who scored ten goals in five games. Christmas was particularly pleasing with Murray netting eight of City's eighteen goals in three victories during Christmas week.

It all changed again in the New Year, though, with only four points gained in the first nine games of 1964. One of those points came in a remarkable match where Harry Dowd earned all the glory. City were losing 1-0 to a debut goal from Bury youngster and future Blue Colin Bell at Maine Road on 8th February, when Dowd broke a finger in the 54th minute. He was unable to continue in goal but stayed on the field and reverted to centre-forward - a role he'd often played as a youngster. Scottish forward Matt Gray replaced Dowd in goal and the game continued with the regular 'keeper keen to impress in attack: "I was restless enough to give it all I'd got. I felt just like a colt on its feet for the first time, pushing and shoving my way through and going for the every ball - many of which I hadn't a hope of getting. But the moment of glory wasn't far away, and it seemed the fans were loving every minute of the action.

"I got the chance to slip the ball to Derek Kevan, his shot hit the bar, and as it bounced down I went lunging in to turn home the equaliser. The newspapers said some very kind things the next day."

With Dowd's efforts up front and a fine performance in goal from Gray, the Blues secured the point. Gray managed to keep a clean sheet, although Dowd's amazing exploits overshadowed Gray and prevented him from taking the kind of credit other emergency City 'keepers Doyle, McDonald, Gleghorn, and Quinn, would receive over the years.

That game was probably Dowd's highlight of the season as, later on, he found himself dropped with Bert Trautmann returning to the side for three games before even he gave way to Alan Ogley for the final five matches of the season. At one point Dowd asked for a transfer, but continued at the club. Trautmann, however, was in his final season and in May he retired. He had been a fine servant, but at the age of 40 with City in Division Two realised it was time to call it a day. Almost 48,000 paid to attend his testimonial match on 15th April 1964, with thousands locked outside. To many football followers he remains the world's greatest goalkeeper, and City supporters can count themselves fortunate that Bert Trautmann and the popular Frank Swift, England's greatest 'keeper, both played for their club.

Following a run of nine games with only one defeat, the League campaign ended with City in sixth position. The January/February slump had caused them to miss out on promotion by fifteen points, and to drop out of the two Cup competitions. In the F.A. Cup a 4th January tie at Swindon ended in a 2-1 defeat and a cartilage injury to centre-forward Jimmy Murray, while on 15th January City suffered a 2-0 loss at Stoke in the first leg of the League Cup semi-final.

City had overcome Carlisle (2-0), Hull (3-0), Leeds (3-1) and Notts County (1-0), prior to Christmas, but the semi-final first leg came at a most difficult and disappointing period of the season, sandwiched between defeats at eventual division champions Leeds and at home to second placed Sunderland. The second leg, played on 5th February did end with a Derek Kevan goal giving the Blues a 1-0 victory but it wasn't enough and Stoke went through to face Leicester in the two legged final.

The Blues also reached the two legged semi-final of another competition - the F.A. Youth Cup where they lost to high flying Manchester United, who included the promising George Best in their line-up.

Despite the optimism of the cup exploits 1963-4 did not give City supporters much satisfaction. Always optimistic, the hope was 1964-5 would bring improvement but few realistically expected it. In fact, attendances had slipped throughout the early 1960s and City's rate of decline since 1956 was alarming, especially when across in Stretford Matt Busby had almost finished rebuilding United after Munich. In 1963 not only did the Reds help send City down, they also won the F.A. Cup, and in the season that followed challenged for the title. Because of their performances, and the effect of Munich on worldwide public consciousness, they were also more popular than at any time in their history up to that point, whereas City were losing support. Also, ground improvements at United in preparation for the 1966 World Cup helped lift Old Trafford above Maine Road in terms of quality for the first time. It was difficult being a Blue in a world dominated by red.

The media seemed captivated by United and the history and traditions of Manchester were being turned on their head as the Reds replaced the Blues as Manchester's glamour club. Many argue this is simply not the case, that United had always been equal with City, but the truth is City were the glamour club pre-war and the Reds took the initiative post-war until, inevitably, poor management at Maine Road gave United a considerable lead.

The situation had to change, but the Board backed manager Poyser and the 1964-5 season opened with a 2-1 defeat at Charlton. A 6-0 win at home to perennial strugglers Leyton Orient followed then, after a 2-0 defeat to Northampton Town, Orient won the return game by the odd goal in seven. Dave Bacuzzi, a £20,000 signing from Arsenal, was trying to help City's defence but in reality the Blues were a modest mid table side. City's trademark inconsistency reared its head again and games that should have been easy victories ended in defeat.

The month of September saw City follow each victory with a depressing defeat. Unsurprisingly, morale was low. Only one reverse in December provided a minor lift, but January saw the club sink to

Manchester born Peter Dobing joined the Blues in July '61 from Blackburn Rovers. He went on to score 31 goals in 82 League games during his three year stay at Maine Road.

a new low point. On 13th January, City travelled to Third Division Shrewsbury for an F.A. Cup third round replay and lost 3-1, then three days later the Blues were at home to Swindon Town. The attendance was a pitiful 8,015, City's lowest ever for a Maine Road League match, and the vast stadium had an eerie feel.

Bobby Kennedy joined the Blues from Kilmarnock in the summer of 1961. During his eight years at Maine Road he made over 250 first team appearances and was a regular member of the 1965-66 Second Division championship-winning side.

During the game, the Blues played some good football at times but went behind to a 19th minute goal from Dennis Brown, and further behind to a strike from 22 year old future Blue Mike Summerbee midway through the second half. City came back with a stunning 30 yarder from Alan Oakes who, incidentally, was the first player spotted by George Poyser when he joined the Blues as assistant manager in 1957.

The match ended 1-2 and afterwards the supporters expressed their anger, demonstrating on the Maine Road forecourt. Bricks were hurled at the windows in the Main Stand and City fans claimed they had suffered enough. The attendance that day had been only 615 more than lowly Stockport County, who ended the season bottom of the Fourth Division, and City fans felt the direction of the club also matched that of their near rivals.

Amazingly, George Poyser had missed the Swindon match prompting many to question his commitment. In fact, he had been on a scouting trip in a desperate search to bring a saviour to Maine Road. In the *Sunday Express* the next day, James Mossop believed inside left Johnny Crossan was the man: "Crisis club Manchester City are to bid this week for Sunderland's inside-left Johnny Crossan. It will be a dire, urgent move, for City lurched deeper into trouble yesterday with another home defeat - and their lowest ever attendance."

On 22nd January Crossan signed for a fee often quoted as £40,000, but sometimes reported as £38,000 or £45,000. Derek Hodgson in the *Daily Express* penned a welcome to the Irishman: "John, you have it in you to be City's greatest player since Denis Law, commanding an adulation, almost an idolatry, that you will never have known before. Half a great footballing city is seeking a hero and you can end the search."

Another journalist believed he had much to offer the Blues but also provided a warning: "Crossan can do it all... the deadly accurate pass... the centre that hangs, spot on... the precise collection and distribution... the eye for a scoring chance. But he must never allow himself to slip into the unhappy ways that lost him his popularity at Sunderland."

As the comment suggested, the new player had not been too popular at Roker Park towards the end of his time there, and his first few performances at Maine Road hardly turned him into the hero Derek Hodgson had suggested. However, over time the player did impress with his greatest season coming in 1965-6.

Another face appearing in the League team for the first time was Mike Doyle, an 18 year old locally-born defender, whose chance came when Alan Oakes was injured. Doyle made his debut in a 2-2 draw at Cardiff on Friday 12th March but these were difficult times for any new player coming into the squad. Often there would be confusion over who would be playing and, for his debut, Doyle had not been told until late on. Consequently he had to rush from his home in Reddish, via public transport, to Manchester Airport to catch a flight to Cardiff. The youngster waited for a bus, but none came along and panic set in. He decided to 'phone the club but realised he didn't know the number. As he started to feel his world closing in a car, driven by fellow Blue Vic Gomersall, pulled up. Doyle explained his situation and Gomersall drove him to the airport, arriving with only five minutes to spare!

It was no wonder Doyle was unimpressed with the club's direction: "The club, at that stage, was going through one of its worst spells since I had joined, and at times I had the feeling Manchester City were like a ship without a rudder."

George Poyser's reign was now nearing its end. Demonstrations and poor morale during his time as manager had turned City into a laughing stock. The players were also losing respect for their leader. Mike Doyle witnessed an extraordinary event during training one day. The manager rarely took part but, as City's situation worsened, Poyser decided to give it a try: "One day he turned up during a training session clad in a tracksuit - and his appearance was the signal for a chorus of laughter, and some ribald remarks from one or two of the players. I felt annoyed because I believed that this showed a lack of respect for the man in charge, and if players could show such disrespect there was something sadly wrong all the way round." At Easter Poyser and trainer Jimmy Meadows resigned.

For the first game after Poyser's departure, Mike Doyle was outside Maine Road an hour before kick-off eating fish and chips when Chairman Albert Alexander tapped him on the shoulder and told him to get inside and get changed. Doyle checked with coach Johnny Hart who confirmed he was to play. It seemed a crazy situation and one that confused the players. They simply didn't know who was in charge, but it would be several months before a new manager was appointed.

City achieved three draws and one victory in their final four games that season. Those results lifted the Blues to 11th; without them they could have finished five places lower. As it was the campaign was settled with City in their lowest end of season position up to that point. In 1894 Ardwick's final season had seen them finish 13th but if this season is translated into overall position, considering the number of teams in the top two divisions, then the Blues finished 29th while in 1964/5 they were 33rd. Of course both seasons were eclipsed by events during the period 1996 to 1999.

The Blues were in urgent need of a pick-me-up, especially when the season ended with another meagre crowd, this time only 8,409. Across the city United triumphantly finished as League Champions, FA Cup semi-finalists, and Inter-City Fairs Cup semi-finalists. Something had to be done. The Blues could suffer no more. Albert Alexander had to find the right manager to move City forward and to catch up with United. Rumours suggested City were after Peter Doherty, others said Bill Shankly. In July the announcement was made.

Chapter Thirteen

CONGRATULATIONS

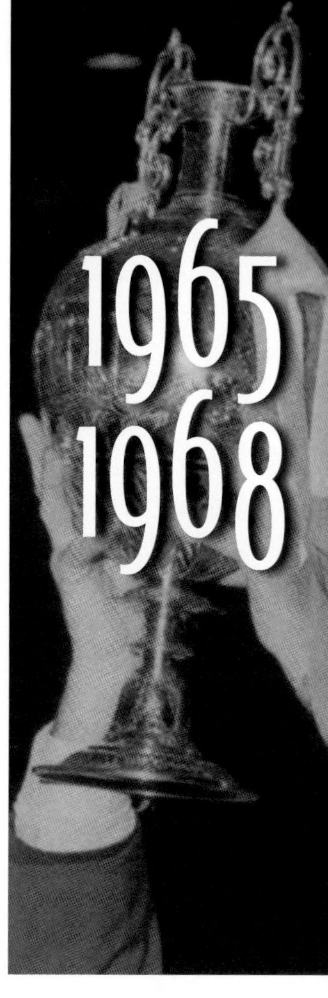

POYSER's resignation gave Manchester City the perfect opportunity to get it right and appoint a manager who the players and supporters could respect. Chairman Albert Alexander and the other directors had little experience of selecting managers, after all Poyser had only been the second appointment since 1950, but the pressure to find the right man was immense. The Board looked at all the candidates and then decided their best choice would be the former England and Arsenal captain Joe Mercer.

Mercer had already proved his ability as a manager turning a rather average Aston Villa side into Second Division champions and League Cup winners. At Villa, and at his previous club Sheffield United, Mercer had developed sides that came within a whisker of reaching Wembley in the F.A. Cup. His teams always seemed to save their best for cup competition, although it's true to say he had suffered personally in his last year at Villa Park. The Villa faithful had been presented with promotion and the League Cup in Joe's first two full seasons and naturally expected glory at the highest level. However, the appalling winter of 1962-3 which helped relegate City also affected Mercer's reign at Villa. Twelve months later, his health suffered and Mercer was forced out by the Villa board. Taking the City job was a major gamble.

With concern over his health, Mercer was forced to consider the support he needed from his backroom staff before accepting. At Villa he had taken on too much; at City he knew he needed a strong assistant who would be able to control the training of the players. He remembered a young coach he'd seen at the F.A.'s training centre at Lilleshall: "I 'phoned an extrovert, ebullient, but brilliant coach called Malcolm Allison. Like me he was out of work - sacked by Plymouth Argyle. It took me two days to find him, but he said he would join me if I took the job. Secretly, I met the Manchester board and accepted the job, telling them of my plans for Malcolm."

For Malcolm Allison the opportunity was one not to miss. He had been a player with West Ham in the mid-1950s and had moved into management with Bath City and Plymouth Argyle. He was full of new ideas and when his position at Plymouth became impossible - the directors overruled his team selection - he found there were plenty of other clubs keen to

Joe Mercer, Albert Alexander and Malcolm Allison share a joke at the start of a great period for the Blues.

Joe Mercer meets a Maltese reporter at Maine Road. Note the boarded up window; is this a reminder of City's plight during January 1965?

Scottish international Ralph Brand was Joe Mercer's first signing. He joined the Blues from Rangers on August 11th 1965, nine days before Mike Summerbee.

secure his services. For Allison though, there was only one team and they were based in Manchester: "Manchester City had always been my team. When I was a kid I listened to a Cup Final when I was about six or seven. City were beaten by Everton, 3-0, just before Joe played for them. Anyway, from that moment on City were my team. When I went to Manchester I saw Joe and agreed to stay there because that was my team."

In addition to Mercer and Allison, another vital member of the City set up was chief scout Harry Godwin. When Mercer arrived at Maine Road, he put his arm around Godwin and said: "I've heard you're good at nicking one or two youngsters. Nick a few for me, will you?"

It wasn't long before the Mercer-Allison partnership made changes to the City squad. Almost immediately Malcolm Allison tested inside-forward Derek Kevan: "I used to do these training sessions whereby I'd create a space for him to make runs through, and I used to say to Joe that he just didn't want to make it. I used to work out training schedules whereby if people really wanted to play or work they would do it, whereas if you just play a normal game it's hard to pick out who isn't really trying. I said to Joe, 'We've got to sell Derek Kevan.'"

By the end of July Kevan had been transferred to Crystal Palace. The move surprised many supporters, especially as Kevan had been City's top scorer for the previous two seasons, but Allison was convinced and, looking at the player's career post-City, indications are the new coach had perfect judgement. Nevertheless, the Blues' first friendly under the Mercer-Allison partnership was not a pleasant experience and prompted many to again question the departure of Kevan, especially as a replacement had not yet been found.

The game at home to Scottish First Division side Dundee on 7th August ended in a 2-1 defeat and afterwards all Mercer would say to the waiting media was: "I've got a lot to say about this!" But presumably he meant to the players, not to the Manchester press, as he stormed off towards the dressing room.

After that he stepped up attempts to sign a new striker, but before he could secure the services of a new player City drew 1-1 at Walsall in another friendly. The following day the announcement was made that Mercer had signed the exciting Ralph Brand from Rangers for around £25,000. Unfortunately, Brand's career took a nose-dive more or less as soon as he walked into Maine Road. At Rangers he had scored 128 goals in 207 League games and had scored eight goals in eight games with Scotland, but in two seasons with the Blues, Brand only found the net on two occasions!

It was no surprise when the player moved to Sunderland, exactly two years to the day after signing for City.

Mercer's second signing occurred after a 3-2 victory at Tranmere and, like the friendly, was rather more successful than the previous one, even if the player's £35,000 arrival brought back painful memories for the majority of City supporters. Mike Summerbee arrived at Maine Road from Swindon after featuring in that infamous match earlier in the year. His father George had played with Mercer for Aldershot during the war, and Joe had kept a close watch on the career of the young Mike, determined that one day he would bring the player to his club. Summerbee was delighted to be in Manchester: "As soon as I drove into Manchester, I could sense something about the place. Even though City were in the Second Division, they were a huge club. The ground is an awe-inspiring place. It reeks of tradition and great players. Although I could not compare City to anything I had known before, I soon realised what a privilege and pleasure it is to be able to play for a club like that."

Gradually, Mercer and Allison prepared City for the new season. When they arrived in Manchester they quickly became aware of how dire the situation was. The club had lacked direction for some time and across the city United were dominant. The Blues' supporters had grown tired of playing second fiddle to the Reds and Malcolm Allison quickly became aware of how miserable life had become: "United quickly became an object of hatred to me when I moved into the city. I loathed the bumptious, patronising tones of their players, their hangers-on, and many of their supporters. It became a challenge to me when I drove past city parks and saw ninety per cent of them wearing red shirts."

Allison's feelings intensified when his son, Mark, was picked on by an older United supporter who wanted to teach him a lesson for having a father who worked for "that useless team City". Allison admitted in his autobiography he wanted to punish everyone connected with United, especially after he was forced to listen to the glorification of United at a dinner to celebrate the Reds' championship success: "Matt Busby turned and said, 'I believe there is room for two First Division clubs in Manchester'. And I thought to myself, 'yes, baby, and you're going to get two teams'."

Later he told Matt Busby's son: "Your father has got a 20 year start, but I'll pass him in three."

Allison's approach was typical of the man and he had the kind of attitude City supporters wanted. His comments may have seemed rather brash and cynical at times, but with the genial Mercer smoothing the way, Allison's views were listened to and respected.

The two men arrived at City when the club was in its worst ever state, even the decimation of the 1904 Cup winning side and subsequent struggles did not leave the Blues as low as in 1965. In fact, even the poor position of the club in 1996 when Frank Clark was appointed as City manager, cannot be compared with the immediate pre-Mercer period. Clark's City were in a lower position in the League, however the loyalty of City's supporters ensured that the club remained a strong one, whereas in 1965 support had diminished and caused the new men serious concerns. Allison later admitted that either he, or Mercer, would walk down

Harry Dowd, Johnny Crossan and David Connor seem to enjoy the new atmosphere created by Mercer and Allison.

The City players, plus Malcolm Allison (far left hand raised) and Johnny Hart (next to Allison) celebrate an FA Cup draw at Blackpool in January 1966.

A City team line-up from Mercer and Allison's first season at Maine Road.

Back row (left to right): Bacuzzi, Doyle, Ogley, Crossan, Gomersall, Young.

Front row: Oakes, Wood, Kennedy, Connor, Pardoe.

the tunnel prior to their earliest games to check if anybody had bothered to turn up. Soon the partnership helped to guarantee that the Blues would be rediscovered.

City's first League game under the new partnership was an away trip to Middlesbrough on 21st August. To Allison and Mercer this game was vital as it would help highlight the strengths and weaknesses of the side. Allison's view was the opening ten games would really demonstrate how right his methods and approach to the game were, and that those matches would put the Blues into a position of strength ready to challenge for promotion. On the training pitch he had assessed each player and considered what tactics to employ. He had watched David Connor quite closely and decided he would be perfect to block out Ian Gibson, Middlesbrough's chief play-maker. He'd also noticed the aggression of Mike Doyle and felt he should be in the side immediately. Doyle was also aware Joe Mercer had been paying him close attention: "I always felt that Joe was more critical of me than he was of others in the team, because I played at wing-half... his position. Joe appreciated my enthusiasm, but whenever I was in action I had the feeling Joe was watching me more closely than other members of the side."

The team for the very first League game under Malcolm Allison and Joe Mercer included some familiar names. It was:

Dowd, Bacuzzi, Gomersall, Doyle, Cheetham, Oakes, Summerbee, Crossan, Murray, Brand, Connor

Six of these players went on to appear in the First Division Championship winning side of 1967-8.

Allison's plan of using Connor to shut out Gibson worked a treat and the Middlesbrough man never really got into the game. The match ended 1-1 with Jimmy Murray supplying the Blues' first League goal under Mercer. The following game four days later gave the Manchester public their first chance to assess City's promotion chances as they faced a Wolves side relegated the previous season. The crowd of over 25,000 witnessed a hard earned 2-1 victory. A week later the two sides met again with City achieving their first double of the season, winning 4-2. One of City's goals came from the delighted Doyle who, on the coach afterwards, was collared by a laughing Joe Mercer: "You took that goal well, you young devil... but you should never have been in that position in the first place, leaving us open at the back."

No doubt Joe recognised the young Doyle played a similar 'attacking wing-half' roving role to the one he himself operated at Everton - and was admonished for in years gone by.

City's progress continued and the Blues remained undefeated in their first seven games. In fact Mercer and Allison saw their side lose in only one of the first fifteen League games, although the Blues did steal a few results along the way. Nevertheless the two men were beginning to give the Manchester folk what they needed most of all - pride. For years it had been embarrassing supporting the Blues, especially with United doing so well, and City's followers had suffered continual ribbing. Now, as Mercer and Allison stamped their influence on the club, City supporters walked taller and wore their scarves with pride. Crowds had increased and for the occasional game actually bettered title challenging United. An incredible 34,091 attended a Wednesday night visit of Norwich, while United's Saturday game with Fulham four days earlier was watched by 32,716. These figures were significant as they proved that in attendance terms the Blues were capable of matching the Reds. They were also significant to Malcolm Allison as, at United's Championship banquet, he had been forced to take part in a bet with Pat Crerand, the man recalled by City fans for his part in the relegation battle of 1963. According to Allison, Crerand stated City were a dying club and the Blues would never again attract an attendance of over 30,000 at Maine Road. Allison bet him £10 and, only two months into the season, the City coach collected.

By this time City had dipped into the transfer market, securing the services of 25 year old George Heslop, Everton's reserve centre-half, and 20 year old Stan Horne, a wing-half Joe remembered from his time at Villa Park.

When Horne signed Joe, turned to Mike Doyle and said: "You'll have to pull your socks up - because Stan's a wing-half too." This was all a bit of psychology on Joe's part to keep his players on their toes, but for a while Horne did indeed replace Doyle.

By the end of October City were top of the division and full of confidence. Gone were the days of fear, confusion, and panic. Mercer's steadying influence and Allison's training methods had brought new life to the club and everybody connected with the Blues benefited.

Allison remembers how many of the staff who had been there for a while noticed the difference: "The place was really buzzing. People like Harry Godwin told us how the club had changed so quickly. It was a fantastic achievement. Years later I also heard that the other staff would eavesdrop on my tactical talks. I've heard that Johnny Hart, my assistant, would gather the youngsters around the door to listen in to my talks. He'd tell them to listen and learn from a real visionary!"

Both Allison and Mercer had brought qualities to the club that had been missing for some time.

Looking good for promotion...

Mike Doyle and George Heslop add a little bounce to their game (above).

Mike Summerbee (left) shows that City are strong enough to go up! Those watching Summerbee include Bobby Kennedy, Malcolm Allison and physio Peter Blakey.

1965-66 DIVISION TWO CHAMPIONSHIP DETAILS

RESULTS	HOME	AWAY
Middlesbrough	W 3-1	D 1-1
Wolverhampton W	W 2-1	W 4-2
Bristol City	D 2-2	D 1-1
Coventry City	W 1-0	D 3-3
Carlisle United	W 2-1	W 2-1
Norwich City	D 0-0	D 3-3
Cardiff City	D 2-2	L 3-4
Derby County	W 1-0	W 2-1
Southampton	D 0-0	W 1-0
Huddersfield Town	W 2-0	D 0-0
Crystal Palace	W 3-1	W 2-0
Preston North End	D 0-0	W 3-0
Charlton Athletic	D 0-0	W 3-2
Plymouth Argyle	D 1-1	L 0-1
Portsmouth	W 3-1	D 2-2
Bolton Wanderers	W 4-1	L 0-1
Ipswich Town	W 2-1	D 1-1
Birmingham City	W 3-1	L 1-3
Leyton Orient	W 5-0	D 2-2
Rotherham United	W 3-1	W 1-0
Bury	W 1-0	L 1-2

REGULAR SIDE:
Dowd
Kennedy
Sear
Doyle
Heslop
Oakes
Summerbee
Crossan
Pardoe
Connor
Young

MANAGER:
Joe Mercer

LARGEST VICTORY: 5-0 v Leyton Orient (H) 11/12/65

LARGEST WINNING MARGIN: 5 goals - 5-0 v Leyton Orient (H) 11/12/65

HEAVIEST DEFEAT: 1-3 v Birmingham City (A) 4/12/65

AVERAGE HOME ATTENDANCE: 27,739

HIGHEST HOME ATTENDANCE: 47,171 v Huddersfield Town 01/01/66

HIGHEST AWAY ATTENDANCE: 31,876 v Huddersfield Town 09/10/65

LEAGUE APPEARANCES: (substitute appearances in brackets)
42 Summerbee, 41 Oakes, 40 Crossan, Pardoe (1), 38 Dowd, 35 Kennedy, Young, 34 Heslop, 29 Connor (1), 19 Doyle (1), Sear, 17 Brand, 15 Bacuzzi (1), Horne, 12 Cheetham (3), 11 Murray, Bell, 4 Ogley, 3 Gray (3), 1 Wood (1), Gomersall

LEAGUE GOALS: 14 Young, 13 Crossan, 9 Pardoe, 8 Summerbee, 7 Doyle, Murray, 4 Bell, 3 Connor, 2 Brand, 1 Kennedy, Sear, Oakes, Gray

Allison's ideas seemed as revolutionary as McDowall's Revie Plan had been a decade earlier, while Mercer's manner gave the club dignity and respect.

Together they worked well and turned the club around, although City supporters have been divided for many years about which one offered most. In reality, they both had strengths and achieved tremendous success away from the club, but when they worked together at City they combined to produce an even greater force.

City maintained a top three position for most of the period leading up to Christmas, then on New Year's Day 1966 a crowd of over 47,000 gave a tremendous ovation as the Blues overcame division leaders Huddersfield Town 2-0. The Blues were quickly marked out as promotion certainties, with a brand of football that excited. But it wasn't simply performances in the League that grabbed the headlines, it was their progress in the F.A. Cup.

In the third round the Blues defeated Blackpool 3-1 in a replay watched by 52,661 - the largest City crowd for six years - then followed that by beating Third Division Grimsby 2-0. In the fifth round they faced a team they would get to know quite well over the following four seasons - Leicester City. The Maine Road tie ended 2-2 with City winning the replay 1-0 thanks to a mistake by England 'keeper Gordon Banks which led to a goal by Neil Young.

City's opponents in the quarter-final were Mercer's old club Everton. At Maine Road a crowd of 63,034 - a figure higher than any domestic attendance at Old Trafford that season - watched a tense goalless affair. Three days later a similar game and a similar result at Goodison forced a second replay at neutral Molineux. Despite the optimism within the City camp, Mercer's men were unable to seize the initiative and the game ended with a 2-0 victory to the Merseysiders. Had City won, they would have faced Manchester United in the semi-final.

Although progress was made in the Cup, it was promotion that really mattered to the Blues. Both Mercer and Allison realised the Cup run had stretched their playing resources to the limit and new blood was still required. Allison, in particular, had an idea of which players to go after, the only problem was a lack of money. City were still relatively short of cash after the struggles of the late fifties and early sixties and any investment had to be absolutely perfect. For Allison money hardly mattered, whereas Mercer felt he had to keep a tight rein on finances.

Despite showing an interest in Bolton's Wyn Davies, it was Bury's Colin Bell that Allison was most taken by. Knowing the club remained cash-strapped, the energetic coach attended a Bury match to watch the young player and determine what kind of a bid the Blues could make.

When Allison arrived at the game he realised there were a few other coaches and scouts from leading First Division clubs ready to watch Bell. This deterred him a little, but once the game started Allison criticised the player, making out he had little to offer. Every mistake was picked up with Allison exclaiming how he'd wasted his evening. In actual fact, Allison was considerably impressed with almost everything the player did.

On Allison's recommendation, City managed to raise enough cash and signed the player for a figure of around £42,000 just before the transfer deadline in March. His debut game was against Derby County on 19th March when he scored a goal to help the Blues to a 2-1 victory, although the strike was not the most spectacular ever seen. Basically, the ball hit him and entered the net.

Right: Colin Bell scores the only goal of the game at Rotherham on May 4th 1966. It was the goal which clinched promotion for the Blues.

A champagne moment for Joe Mercer as the Blues celebrate winning the Second Division championship. Johnny Crossan is the player with the trophy, whilst groundsman Stan Gibson is the man in the background wearing the lid. Harry Godwin also looks on.

Over the weeks that followed the rather introverted Bell fitted into the City side, helping the Blues to maintain their challenge for the division title. On 4th May, he provided the only goal of the game at Rotherham which secured promotion for the Blues. Nine days later City defeated Charlton 3-2 at the Valley to win the Second Division Championship. With typical City inconsistency, the Blues were leading by three goals before allowing Charlton to fight back.

On 18th May City played their final game of the season before a Maine Road crowd of 34,653. Naturally, this was a day of celebration when the result hardly mattered. Understandably, it was not City's best performance of the season and the game ended goalless, but the celebrations continued throughout the night.

One of the key players during this season had been City captain Johnny Crossan - a player Mercer had tried to sign in the late fifties for Sheffield United. The skilful Irishman had played in 40 League games that season, scoring on 13 occasions, and had certainly developed since his arrival in January 1965. He was now one of City's heroes and his natural humour helped mould team spirit in the dressing room. He was an appropriate choice for captain.

As the whole of the country knows, 1966 was a good year for English football for two reasons. England staged and won the World Cup for the first time in its history, and Manchester City regained their rightful place in the First Division. As a result of these two events, Mercer and Allison became instantly recognisable faces throughout the country commenting on international and domestic football. It was all good publicity for the resurgent Blues and with the World Cup exciting many non-football followers, City's promotion seemed perfectly timed to cash in on all the positive aspects of the game.

With Manchester buzzing, Mercer and Allison were determined to turn City into a great force. The Cup run had shown the Blues could live with the best - they'd defeated two First Division sides and took a third to two replays before succumbing - but there were still weaknesses. There seemed to be an abundance of talent in attack - Young, Summerbee, Crossan, Doyle and Pardoe had provided a good rate of return - but City needed a stronger defence if they were to stay in the First Division. Heslop had already settled into the centre-half spot, Oakes was a dependable wing-half, and Dowd had overcome the disappointments of 1964 to become City's first choice 'keeper, but Mercer and Allison realised they needed a dependable full-back.

After a short discussion, Malcolm Allison convinced Joe Mercer he knew the perfect man for the job, someone he'd coached before - Plymouth's Tony Book. Mercer was put off by the player's age, after all he was almost 32, but was reminded he himself had been a fraction older when he moved from Everton to Arsenal in the 1940s to embark on what became the greatest years of his playing career. Could Book find similar success?

Moving to City for £17,000 was the first chance of Division One football for Book and, despite initial concerns, he felt able to perform to the level required: "I felt a bit of an impostor coming into the First Division so late. I was nearly 32 when City signed me. I wasn't exactly a late developer. Long before Malcolm took me to Plymouth, I had trials with Nottingham Forest and Chelsea. In fact, I played for Chelsea's 'A' team and Reserves for 18 months while I was in the Army doing my National Service. Then I got a letter from the manager, Ted Drake, telling me he thought I'd get a living out of the game at a lower level.

"I had a great apprenticeship in the Southern League. I always felt I had a chance of making the grade as a pro, if I could get a break - and Malcolm was the one who gave it to me. Where I was really fortunate was in coming to City just when the place was about to take off! People must have been wondering 'what's this 32 year old going to do for us?'"

Mercer had not needed much convincing about Book. He'd seen him play against the Blues and, once in City's colours, Mercer enjoyed watching the player, even if it made him a little envious: "I didn't mind him playing well and having plenty of skill, but what made me green with envy was his speed. I mean, it's not right for the over thirties to be skinning the youngsters. It's meant to be a young man's game! We used to hear these First Division coaches shouting from the bench - 'Take the old man on!' No chance! He was a great athlete."

Book made an impressive debut in City's opening game, a 1-1 draw at Southampton. Johnny Crossan had missed that game following injuries in a car crash close to Roker Park, although the player did return for the first home game of the season. Much to City's surprise, the fixture list produced an enormous test with reigning Champions Liverpool arriving for what looked an easy two points for the Merseysiders. Ominously, two days earlier on home territory Liverpool reserves had defeated their City equivalents 9-0. The footballing public expected the Blues to be humiliated, but they were wrong as goals from Bell and Murray helped City to a 2-1 victory before a crowd of 50,320. The Blues were back!

A 1-0 win over Sunderland followed before the club's first setback - a 2-3 defeat in the return fixture with Liverpool. Two further defeats followed then Glyn Pardoe provided a goal to help City secure a point against Arsenal on 10th September. The following game would provide the biggest test of all for Mercer's men - the Old Trafford derby. This game mattered more than any other, unfortunately City simply failed to perform. Allison was angry. He believed the players had fallen for the hype that had developed around United since the late fifties and this had seen them freeze in the so called 'Theatre of Dreams'. He told them he would never again tolerate any player curling up and dying in front of United's supporters, instead he wanted to see City players go out there to humiliate the Reds.

The game had not been without controversy. As with the last derby in 1963, Denis Law was at the centre of it all. At one point players squared up to each other, fists flew, and yet referee Jack Taylor took no action. Six minutes later Law upset the City players further by scoring the only goal of the game. It was a major disappointment.

Seven days later City defeated Blackpool 1-0 with a goal from Johnny Crossan, but the visit of Chelsea on 1st October brought City crashing back down to earth. Joe Mercer: "We started well with three good results and seemed set for a fine life among the top-class teams. We were confident. Then Chelsea came north to Maine Road and ripped all our fancy notions to shreds. They took us apart on our own ground. They exposed flaws. They set us thinking. We wanted to survive in the First Division. This became our priority. Tony Book was installed as a sweeper behind the rest of the defence; a negative move that was mere insurance against further good hidings."

Chelsea had humiliated City 4-1 at home, and Mercer and Allison agreed the positional change was a vital one. In addition the two men discussed ways of increasing fitness - an area Allison was determined to see improved. They agreed to bring in Derek Ibbotson, an England athlete, to help develop City as one of the fittest sides in Europe. The move was a good one as Ibbotson took the players on tortuous nine mile runs, then challenged them to various races. It was all hard work, but each session tried to end in a light-hearted fashion. After one particularly gruelling session Ibbotson challenged any two players, splitting the distance between them, in a 440 yards race. The race started with every City player making what

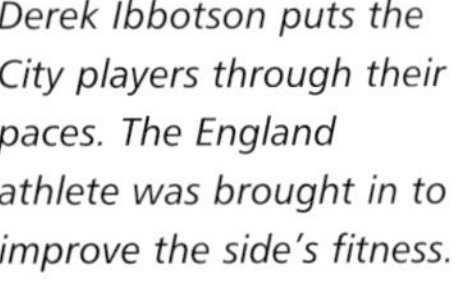

Derek Ibbotson puts the City players through their paces. The England athlete was brought in to improve the side's fitness.

Ibbotson described as a false start, then a dozen of the players boxed the athlete in, resulting in the sub-four minute miler finishing last!

Alongside the improvement in fitness, Allison tried out many of his new coaching methods as the Blues tried to find their feet in the division. A few good results in November helped, especially a win over Everton thanks to a solitary goal from Colin Bell. This was a significant game as, prior to the match, much of the talk centred around the two midfielders Alan Ball and Colin Bell. Future City manager Ball had played a significant part in the 1966 World Cup final and received world wide recognition, whereas Bell had barely been heard of outside of the north-west. Nevertheless, the media likes to make comparisons and the clash with Everton provided that opportunity. Even the City programme became embroiled in the story: "It will be interesting to compare the two players today. For in the last few weeks Bell has emerged as one of those non-stop players with as much heart as ability and a good helping of both. Ball, with red hair and spectacular skills, will always catch the eye. Bell, with far less First Division experience behind him, and 18 months Ball's junior, is just as priceless an asset to City.

"In the last six months Ball's fame has spread far beyond Britain. The Spanish press after Everton's recent Cup Winners' Cup defeat in Zaragoza called him, 'La bomba con dos piernas' - the bomb on two legs. Colin Bell's are longer - and at 6ft tall he will be out to prove that a good big 'un is better than a good little 'un."

Bell's 73rd minute match winning goal seemed proof enough City possessed a player capable of controlling any game, or any opponent, although the match itself had not been a particularly good advert for English football. Both Bell and Ball received injuries - Bell a cut knee and torn ligaments, Ball was reported to have six stud marks on his thigh after a tackle from Alan Oakes - but they were not the only ones as players from both sides mixed it throughout the match.

Ten minutes after Bell's goal the protests really began as Everton had an equaliser disallowed. According to the *Daily Mail* the goal, netted by Jimmy Gabriel from a corner, was disallowed as the referee was busy clearing away toilet rolls behind the goal which the "hooligan Everton supporters" had thrown onto the pitch. The report basically stated the result was a fair one, because the toilet roll throwing hazard had come from the Everton fans. It seemed a perverse comment, but City needed the points, so most Mancunians agreed.

By mid-December, Mercer and Allison were presented with a problem they always hoped would arise - the question of who to leave out. Mike Summerbee, after missing games against Nottingham Forest and West Bromwich Albion through suspension, was ready for selection, but his replacement Altrincham born Chris Jones had played well and scored his first League goal in a victory at West Brom. There was no way Jones could be dropped. In the end Mercer and Allison took the difficult decision to drop Neil Young instead, although Young did return for the following game. Allison and Mercer were keen to have players fighting for places and with so many developing at the same time, it was inevitable decisions would be taken that would, in turn, force players to consider their futures.

By the time of the Maine Road derby with United on 21st January City were 19th after 24 games. A pick-me-up was urgently needed. The game was played in atrocious conditions and ended 1-1 with both goals coming in the last fifteen minutes. It had been an exciting match and helped boost confidence, although Johnny Crossan was far from happy - he'd been dropped. Crossan had not had the best of times during this season. His pre-season car crash had affected him but foolishly he attempted to disguise an injured knee. He also suffered from a grumbling appendix. This all combined to give the false impression he simply wasn't trying and led to the crowd barracking him. Despite being upset at the time, he remained philosophical: "I heard the jeers but that's football. You are king one day, a peasant the next!"

Although Crossan returned to the side for the remainder of the season, his days at Maine Road were numbered, and in August 1967 he was transferred to Middlesbrough for £32,000.

The United game helped the Blues gain momentum. Over the weeks that followed seven points were added in five games, not championship form but enough to gradually edge City away from the relegation zone. By 19th March the Blues were 17th on 28 points - seven more than West Brom in 21st position. They had also purchased an exciting forward with a reputation of being a bit of a hell-raiser, Tony Coleman. It was Malcolm Allison who was determined to sign the player, but Joe Mercer was not so sure. Mercer, after all, had been teaching on a course at Lilleshall when the player threw a bed out of a window. He had also heard stories of how Coleman had caused trouble at every club he'd been to. Stoke City had allegedly chucked him out, Preston said he was 'unmanageable', and at Doncaster it was reported he had punched a referee in the face. No wonder Mercer was uncertain!

Eventually, Allison convinced Mercer he could control the player and the two agreed to give him a try. The Coleman signing was proof, if any was needed, how Mercer and Allison worked well together. If one of them was convinced about someone the other would back that judgement and the player would be signed. Sometimes Mercer would find a player, sometimes Allison. It didn't matter who found him, all that mattered was he could fit into City's plans. Coleman did settle into the City side, although there were a few 'adventures' along the way. In later years Mercer would laughingly boast that he was the only manager Coleman didn't hit!

Coleman's Maine Road debut came on 12th April when a Colin Bell hat-trick defeated one of Coleman's old clubs Stoke at Maine Road. Afterwards the Liverpudlian gave his view of the game: "I really enjoyed beating Stoke. They gave me a free transfer - or they sacked me if you look at it another way. The differences that players talk about between the Fourth and First Divisions look to be perfectly true if I can judge from two games. The players here are obviously much better than I ever played with and it makes it more enjoyable.

"My first job is to get fitter. I'm not as fit as the players at Maine Road yet and I'm working on that but it will take a little time. I'm in digs around the corner from the ground which suits me. I don't know

Tony Coleman arrived at Maine Road with the reputation of being a bit of a hell-raiser.

Colin Bell trains hard with two of City's schoolboys in a bid to be fit for the First Division fixture with Bury in March 1967. He made the starting line-up and went on to score the only goal of the game. The man in the white coat is physio Peter Blakey.

Manchester but I've got the feeling I shall be here a long time."

City hovered above the relegation places for some while, although games in hand gave a false impression for much of March, April and May. By 19th April the Blues were 17th on 32 points from 36 games with two games in hand over four of the five teams below them. They were still not safe, however a draw against Mercer's former side Aston Villa, and a 3-0 win over Fulham eased the pressure. At the season's end City finished 15th, ten points more than Aston Villa, relegated in 21st place. It was a satisfactory position and one that in later years might be called a vital season of consolidation, although at the time it was more like an end of season fight to avoid relegation. Of the last seventeen games only four ended in defeat and Mercer was content. The turnaround had also come as the result of yet another fine Cup run.

On 28th January City defeated Leicester 2-1 in the third round of the F.A. Cup, then faced Cardiff at Ninian Park. The game ended 1-1 - bringing back memories of the Cup run in 1961 when it took two replays to separate the sides - then the replay at Maine Road finished 3-1 with goals from Bell, Crossan and Young. Another replay was needed in the fifth round as the Blues beat Ipswich 3-0 after a 1-1 draw at Maine Road. Then came the biggest test of all, an away trip to Don Revie's clinically efficient Leeds.

Mercer looked back on this game as a turning point: "The entire football world expected us to play it tight. But they reckoned wrong. They overlooked the moral courage, the gambling streak, the spirit of adventure that was always just below the surface of the Mercer-Allison partnership. We did precisely the opposite to what was expected. We attacked them! We threw everything in. We decided, in just as few words, 'What the hell have we got to lose?' City were brilliant that day.

"We gave Leeds a lesson and with the most outrageous luck lost by a solitary goal that should have been disallowed. We had been so much on top the result was unbelievable. Still, we had found ourselves. We were on our way, we started to stretch defences. Fear was scoffed at!"

City took the game to Leeds. A side previously rooted in a defensive style of play, broke forward and played exciting, attacking football. Revie's Leeds were not used to teams arriving at Elland Road in a positive frame of mind. The only goal came five minutes into the second half, following Leeds' first corner of the game. When Eddie Gray floated the ball towards the goal, Jack Charlton appeared to impede Harry Dowd, playing his first game since November. Charlton headed in, and City complained, unsuccessfully. It was a rough result.

Afterwards there was sympathy for the Blues from the Leeds camp. Captain Billy Bremner: "City played magnificently. No honest man would attempt to deny it." Don Revie admitted: "it was our toughest game of the season - and that includes our defeats."

ABC TV, producing the match for the ITV network, described it as "the most exciting match of the season", while the *Sunday Mirror* simply stated: "It was City who should have gone into the semi-finals." The *Sunday Times* proclaimed: "Leeds were beaten for speed of thought and action from the start. To lucky, lucky Leeds a place in the semi-finals. To magnificent City all the honours in defeat."

The whole football world was now starting to realise City were edging closer to success. Their style of play was exciting and, with Mercer and Allison, the direction of the club was near perfect. It was certainly better than at any other time since the mid-fifties. All associated with the game now recognised Manchester, once again, had two sides worth talking about. United still gained the lion's share of headlines, but the Blues were catching them up, especially whenever Allison was prepared to speak.

Allison's boasts began to excite the City faithful and naturally made great news. The 'papers loved his comments, although it often led to trouble with the F.A. In November he was given a 28 day ban for 'expressing his feelings' and throughout his time at Maine Road he was regularly in trouble with the establishment. The fans loved it!

During the close season City went on an enjoyable tour to West Germany and Belgium. It was all a laugh a minute as Johnny Crossan spent the whole trip ribbing everybody at one time or other, while Tony Coleman explained how his lack of goals was down to the fact he didn't like being kissed by men. At Standard Liege Coleman scored the winner and the rest of the team smothered him with affection!

During a 2-1 victory over Eintracht Braunschweig Chris Jones caused much amusement after scoring a fine goal. Apparently, the German announcer stated the goal had been netted by Mike Summerbee, and so Jones rushed around the pitch pointing to his number nine to indicate that he'd scored. He wouldn't let the game continue until the announcer corrected himself. The tour was typical of the bubbling team spirit Mercer and Allison had striven so hard to build.

When the new season commenced on 19th August both Mercer and Allison recognised the side still needed strengthening, this time in attack. Tony Coleman was an exciting forceful player but the Ralph Brand signing had been a failure, and Johnny Crossan's time in Manchester had come to an end. Both Glyn Pardoe and Mike Doyle had been pulled back into defence and midfield respectively, leaving Mercer and Allison to try different combinations. As the season got under way, they struggled to find the right blend and results suffered. Only one point - a goalless game with Liverpool - was obtained during the first three games.

After that the youngster Paul Hince was tried at number seven. Hince, who in later years became the *Manchester Evening News'* City reporter, had made one appearance the year before, scoring twice, and was given his chance to shine again against Southampton at Maine Road.

The Blues won 4-2 and Hince kept his place. Malcolm Allison remembers how Hince particularly enjoyed his next game: "We were playing Nottingham Forest and Hince played quite well at outside-right. In this particular game he absolutely mesmerised the Forest full-back - he was running him inside and outside and totally slaughtering him. Anyway, this full back got involved in an incident and the referee sent him off. Paul Hince went, 'Oh, don't send him off - he's easy! I'm enjoying it!"

Hince's arrival coincided with a five match unbeaten run and the Blues moved into the top five, but Allison doubted whether Hince could become a permanent fixture in the side. On 30th September Hince was replaced by the exciting Stan Bowles for the Maine Road derby match. Bowles had already appeared in City's first team, scoring four goals in his first one and a half games (The half was when he came on as substitute, replacing Young, in a League Cup tie against Leicester and scored twice), and was certainly ready for the derby match. Sadly, the game ended 2-1 to the Reds despite the Blues taking the lead in the fifth minute via a low firm shot from Bell.

The game also marked the arrival of goalkeeper Ken Mulhearn. Harry Dowd had dislocated a finger in training and Mulhearn was forced to make his debut in the derby. He arrived at the ground early and was incredibly tense: "I turned up ridiculously early - it must have been an hour and a half before any of the other players. Malcolm Allison took one look at me and locked me in the medical room! He obviously saw how white faced I was. I must have been the most nervous person ever to appear at a football ground, so he just locked me up out of the way until the rest of the team reported and were getting changed. There were something like 63,000 at the game, and not many days earlier I'd been playing for Stockport in front of a few thousand. The noise and the atmosphere were unbelievable, the first time I'd sampled anything like it."

Despite the result and debut day nerves, Mulhearn retained his place for the rest of the season, and City quickly returned to form. After losing 1-0 at Sunderland the Blues were undefeated in their next eleven League games. This great run coincided with the arrival of Bolton's Francis Lee.

Both Allison and Mercer remembered Lee from his games for Bolton against City in the Second Division, and from a Bolton-City League Cup tie in September 1966, when Lee had scored. The two men went to watch Bolton's game with Liverpool in the

Malcolm Allison discusses the finer points of the game with new arrival Francis Lee.

The programme from the 'Ballet on Ice' – City's memorable game with Tottenham in December 1967. Below: Colin Bell scores City's first goal in the 4-1 win and Tony Coleman celebrates the Blues' third.

same competition during 1967 and the player was outstanding, despite enduring a difficult relationship with the Bolton management.

Lee was dissatisfied with the terms of a new contract he had been offered and was generally disenchanted with the club. On Friday 29th September 1967 he told manager Bill Ridding he was walking out. Quickly, Bolton decided to transfer him to City. The move was ideal as the player had business interests in the Bolton area and needed to remain close by. Even so, the move was not a smooth one.

Mercer and Allison travelled to Bolton to meet Ridding and Lee but there were still problems at Bolton, much to Lee's disbelief: "The next day was a Friday, and I went back to Maine Road and signed. Already Bill Ridding had told the Manchester City officials that I would not get my ten per cent of the transfer fee because I had asked for a move. But even he did not bargain for the Football League reaction. I had my boots with me and was all set to move out with the team to play at Sunderland in a First Division game the following day. But the League refused to rush my registration through, and just as I thought my future had been settled Joe Mercer came out of his office to say, 'It's all off, the League won't accept the

registration!' Finally, however, it was ironed out and the following Monday I signed. I remember Joe's words. 'I hope you will sign,' he said when we first met. 'We feel we've got the start of a good side. We are just one player short, and we think you are that player. The odd goal or two will turn us into a great team.'"

From the moment Lee signed on 9th October City were a more powerful side, and the newcomer slotted in perfectly: "After an unhappy end to my days with Bolton, it was a completely different atmosphere at City. As soon as you got into coaching sessions all they were interested in was attacking. I was used to Bolton's theory of building performances on defence, this was exactly the opposite; we had five great forwards and for a goalscorer such as me, it couldn't have been easier to slip into a side like that."

By the end of the eleven League game unbeaten run, City had also reached the Fourth Round of the League Cup, although a 3-2 reverse at Fulham ended the Blues dreams of success in that competition. In the League, City continued to perform well with one game in particular catching the attention of the football world - the home match with Tottenham Hotspur on 9th December.

It was a real classic, enjoyed by around five million on BBC television's Match Of The Day programme, and was regarded by many as the match of the season. At first many doubted the game could go ahead as the pitch was covered with snow, however Stan Gibson and the rest of the City groundstaff worked hard to make it playable. Sadly, in the seventh minute Jimmy Greaves snatched the first goal for Tottenham.

Tottenham's lead wasn't to last though, as City tore into the Londoners. With the snow still falling, Colin Bell levelled the scores. It was just what the Blues deserved as they mastered the conditions and proved how wise Malcolm Allison had been to really push them hard during training.

Tremendous pressure from Young in particularly almost gave City the upper hand in the first half, but it wasn't until the second period that the Blues took a deserved lead when Young crossed from the left and Summerbee scored from six yards with a brilliant header.

In the 64th minute Tony Coleman scored the third when he followed up a Francis Lee shot that had hit the left post. Neil Young made it four with one from close range. City continued to push forward, overwhelming a Spurs side that included internationals Alan Gilzean, Joe Kinnear, Dave Mackay, Pat Jennings, and of course Jimmy Greaves. Shot after shot went towards the Spurs goal with City's forwards in outstanding form. In one attack, Coleman latched on to a pass from Bell. His shot hit the left-hand post, and then Young followed up by hitting the right-hand post. It was a game that fully confirmed the growing strength of the City side.

Afterwards, the Blues made all the headlines and received praise from all over the country. Indeed, almost thirty years later a similar performance by City against Tottenham screened by the BBC prompted the re-showing of the 1967 match. It was one of those games that will never be forgotten.

Letters flooded into Maine Road from all over the country with one appearing in City's programme from Bobby Greenroyd of Halifax: "Not

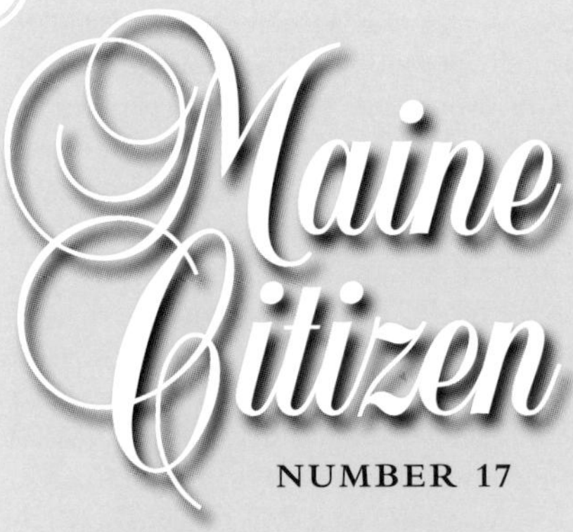

NUMBER 17

JOHNNY CROSSAN

Johnny Crossan was an important member of the side that lifted the Second Division title in 1965-66. As captain he helped Joe Mercer and Malcolm Allison boost morale and develop the team as a unit.

He was born in Derry on 29th November 1938 and was the younger brother - by some thirteen years - of Eddie, a famous Blackburn Rovers forward from the 1940s/50s. He first came to the notice of English clubs when he was aged around 16 with the first approach coming from Joe Mercer. Crossan: "I had apparently been doing quite well as a youngster. I had got into the Derry team when only aged 14 and Mr Mercer came over to have a look round and weigh up likely prospects. Later, I learned he wanted to sign me for his club, which was then Sheffield United, and a fee of around £5,000 was discussed. I never did find out what went wrong. Perhaps Derry wanted more money."

He moved on to Coleraine a little later, and then another proposed move to England collapsed when problems over a possible transfer to Bristol City resulted in a 'life' ban. Crossan then moved to the continent, signing for Sparta Rotterdam, and then Standard Liege. At Liege he managed to achieve a feat that would not have been possible at either Sheffield or Bristol when he played in the European Cup. By October 1962 the English ban was lifted and the knowledgeable Crossan was transferred to Sunderland for £27,000.

At Roker Park he managed 39 goals in 82 appearances, before George Poyser brought him to Maine Road as a last desperate throw of the dice. In fact Crossan was signed in the aftermath of possibly City's lowest point in history - the Swindon game of January 1965. Poyser had missed that miserable match, preferring to spend time away attempting to sign Crossan.

Although the Irishman did little to impress City's support during January and February 1965, over time he did prove a good signing. When Mercer took over from Poyser he was delighted to find Crossan was already at the club. He determined to award him the captaincy and always admitted Crossan was one of the main reasons City achieved success in that first season: "I was recovering from illness. I could no longer get stripped and charge around the training field. I accepted this. We received tremendous help from one little

fellow in the dressing room - Johnny Crossan. In those early days this whimsical Irishman was a wonderful dressing room influence as we tried to mould players we hardly knew into a fighting unit."

The promotion season was Crossan's best at Maine Road and clearly demonstrated his playing ability, humour, and captaincy skills. He seemed destined to play a major part in City's future when ill fate struck. At the age of 28 he was involved in a car crash close to Roker Park prior to the 1966-7 season. He missed the opening game but, despite managing to regain his place for more or less the rest of the season, his City career was nearing its end. Foolishly he tried to disguise an injured knee and as a result gave the impression he just wasn't trying. In reality he was probably trying more than most, but was simply unable to cope. That he also suffered from a grumbling appendix didn't help.

It all combined to turn many supporters against him. This hurt considerably, but was perhaps understandable. In August 1967 he was transferred to Middlesbrough for £32,000 - a fee that confirmed he was still a player with much to offer. At Middlesbrough he made a total of 56 League appearances and scored eight goals.

Once his footballing career was over Crossan ran an off-licence in Derry for a while, and in 1997 was involved with a sports shop in his home town. He also played an active role in training local youngsters.

In total Crossan made 24 international appearances for Northern Ireland (ten while with City), and proved a very popular player within the dressing room and, for most of his City career, on the terraces. Without Crossan, Mercer and Allison would have found it more difficult to lift the Blues out of the Second Division, and the transformation in City's fortunes may have taken a while longer.

It was a shame Crossan ultimately missed the opportunity of helping City achieve real success. He deserved the opportunity, but it wasn't to be.

CROSSAN'S PLAYING RECORD

	LEAGUE		FA CUP		FL CUP		TOTAL	
	App	Gls	App	Gls	App	Gls	App	Gls
1964-65	16	3	0	0	0	0	16	3
1965-66	40	13	8	1	1	1	49	15
1966-67	38	8	6	1	1	0	45	9
TOTAL	94	24	14	2	2	1	110	27

withstanding the address, I am a regular Manchester United fan, but after Saturday's game your next home gate will be increased by one."

A group of Tottenham supporters from Walthamstow wrote: "We would like to pay tribute to your team not only for a wonderful display of football but also for the clean and sportsmanlike way you played the game."

Personalities from within the game also contacted the club. The great Dixie Dean, a Maine Road regular thanks to his relationship with former Everton team mate Joe Mercer, believed City the 'best workmanlike team' he'd seen since his own playing days thirty years earlier. He was also convinced a number of the City players, in particular Mike Summerbee, were destined to play for England.

Another admirer was Bill Shankly, the Liverpool manager. Prior to City's game at Anfield on 16th December the canny Scotsman turned to Malcolm Allison and proclaimed: "You're not going to tear our team apart like you have torn the others apart, you know!"

That game ended 1-1, prompting the *Liverpool Echo* to concede: "The frequency and power of the City shooting was amazing... This was a game between two of the greatest League clubs in the country - and it looked like it."

Francis Lee calmly converts the penalty which gave the Blues a 1-0 win at Burnley in March 1968.

Now, at the half-way stage of the season, City were in third position on 28 points. Liverpool were second with the same tally, while old foes Manchester United were top with 30 points. The difference between these teams however was that all the time City were still developing as a unit. They were also still learning as two defeats against West Bromwich Albion over the Christmas period proved. Francis Lee remembers the first of these games: "We lost 3-2 at their place on Boxing Day. But even then, we murdered them!"

In the second match City were defeated 2-0 with Malcolm Allison claiming responsibility for the result: "We should have played it as tight as possible, not attacked. This mistake on my part could have cost us the title."

Former Stockport Boys' player John Clay made his first and last full appearance for the Blues in this game, although he had already made a sub appearance against Wolves in October. With so many outstanding players at the club it was difficult for Clay to become established at City, and he moved on to Macclesfield during the following close season, although he did return to City over twenty years later to perform a public relations role.

On 31st January City once again displayed their prowess, this time with a 7-0 thrashing of Reading at Elm Park in the F.A. Cup Third Round replay. As the players left the field the tannoy announcer claimed: "Ladies and Gentlemen, you have just seen one of the greatest teams England has produced in a long time." Again dozens of letters arrived at Maine Road commenting on City's performance. Many Reading fans wrote in saying they could have watched the Blues all night. Other letters arrived commenting on how well behaved the City supporters were, while City fans themselves commented on the cheerfulness of the Reading police. These points may seem trivial today, but in 1968 football had already begun to enter its hooligan problem period. Football supporters had started to be seen as trouble makers and incidents of violence, or of vandalism, soon found their way into national newspapers. Although City supporters were never totally blameless, during the late 1960s Blues fans continued to gain commendations rather than condemnation.

City's cup run ended in the next round where Leicester City once again faced the Manchester Blues. This time, after a no score draw, Leicester won 4-3 in the Filbert Street replay. This was Leicester's first victory in cup competition over the Blues in six meetings since March 1966. To say the two sides knew each other well is an understatement. In both cities supporters were already making predictions how the two sides would meet again in 1969.

From late February onwards City were able to concentrate on the League where success was now a serious possibility. A 1-0 victory at Burnley on 2nd March left the Blues in third place, four points behind leaders United although City had a game in hand. Apart from the two Manchester clubs Liverpool, Leeds United and Newcastle also posed a threat, and any of these teams were capable of snatching the title. City, however, had the chance to upset two of those teams - Leeds and United.

On 23rd March City arrived at Elland Road looking for victory. The Blues were now top of the division on goal average after defeating Fulham 5-1 seven days earlier, and felt they had the initiative. Sadly, a tough, determined approach from Leeds ended with City suffering a 2-0 defeat. It was vital the Blues rediscovered their form in the next game - the 78th Manchester League derby.

It was a re-arranged fixture, played before a crowd of over 63,000 on Wednesday 27th March. To many Reds this was to be the night when City would be humiliated, and taught a footballing lesson by England's so-called biggest club. For City supporters the Manchester derby had become a difficult game to watch, especially at Old Trafford, where the Blues had only won once in twelve years. Malcolm Allison: "The Manchester United thing was still the great barrier across our progress. I was told in the city that we were doing well, but that we would never catch Manchester United!"

The game commenced with Joe Mercer, Matt Busby, and England manager Sir Alf Ramsey seated close to each other in the directors box. Mercer didn't realise it at the time, but it would later turn out to be the greatest place from which to witness the game. However, the opening moments were not pleasant ones for the City manager as George Best gave United the lead after only 38 seconds. Tony Book felt he was to blame. He believed he should not have allowed Best through, and it affected the City captain for some time, before the rest of the team brought him back into the game.

For the first ten minutes life was hell being a Blue as all the old concerns flooded back then, just when it was needed most, Colin Bell began to control midfield, Mike Doyle won important tackles and City gradually gained the upper hand. After 15 minutes Bell started a right-wing move and then ran yards to reach the final pass and blast the equaliser past United 'keeper, and future City coach, Alex Stepney.

City, in rampant mood, dominated from then on. They pushed forward time and time again, and were appropriately rewarded with a second goal after 57 minutes. Tony Coleman, City's loveable rogue, curled across a free-kick and centre-half George Heslop scored his first goal for the Blues with a firm downward header.

Mercer and Allison were delighted as the Blues powered forward. Colin Bell, by far the best player on display that night, raced clear and headed for goal but was dramatically hauled down by Francis Burns. Francis Lee scored the resultant penalty, but the excellent Bell was carried off on a stretcher with an injured knee. City's most important player would miss the next four crucial games.

The game ended 3-1 with Mercer enjoying his post match discussions with Ramsey and, of course, Busby. Another man who enjoyed his chat with Busby was Allison: "Matt Busby was as urbane as ever. But I sensed that we were beginning to get through to him. He is a man who hates to be second anywhere, and for it to happen in Manchester was quite a new experience."

Allison also understood the feelings of the City faithful: "There was so much happiness among the City fans that evening. Years of humiliation had been, if not wiped away, at least eased. The balance of power was beginning to swing strongly in our direction. If you are not too tightly involved in football you may discount the feelings of the down trodden supporters. In fact their team becomes an expression of themselves; their moods, their hopes, are tightly interwoven into the fate of the team. And that night at Old Trafford the supporters of Manchester City walked out of the wilderness."

The City assistant manager was right. City fans were now able to walk tall and at last felt their club was capable of great success. The supporters even composed poems about the great night, one 'City's Night Of Glory' had eleven verses and covered almost every incident of the game. It was a truly proud moment for the Blue population of Manchester and one which only people associated with City can understand. In no other British city does the rivalry match that of Manchester. In Glasgow the derby game is a matter of life and death, but it has too little to do with football. In any case, neither Glasgow Rangers nor Celtic have ever received the national media attention that Busby's United received.

In Liverpool, Sheffield, London, Birmingham and Bristol, no side has ever had to face as much hype

Goal action from the 'championship derby' at Old Trafford in March '68.

Top: Colin Bell's shot leaves Alex Stepney stranded to equalise George Best's first minute opener.

Above: George Heslop makes it 2-1 with his first League goal for City.

One of the poems to celebrate City's triumph over Manchester United in March 1968 was called "City's Night Of Glory" and was written by supporters Bill Hazard and Kevin Brady. It had 11 verses and detailed almost every moment of the match. The first two verses are:

There was a team who played in red,
They were the greatest, or so they said,
Until one fine and sunny night,
Mercer's Boys showed them the light,
It was a match to decide the lot,
The Championship was still to be got,

The match was played both hard and fast,
But the Busby boys they couldn't last,
Soon after the start the match erupted,
And City's language became corrupted,
As Georgie Best opened the scoring,
The Stretford End was really roaring,

The poem continued for a further 8 verses then ended with:

The whistle blew the game was o'er,
The players they could give no more,
In the years to come they would tell the story,
Of the night City regained their glory,
For now out of the shadows they had come,
A vital game they'd fought and won.

1967-68 LEAGUE CHAMPIONSHIP DETAILS

RESULTS	HOME	AWAY
Liverpool	D 0-0	D 1-1
Southampton	W 4-2	L 2-3
Stoke City	W 4-2	L 0-3
Nottingham Forest	W 2-0	W 3-0
Newcastle United	W 2-0	W 4-3
Coventry City	W 3-1	W 3-0
Sheffield United	W 5-2	W 3-0
Arsenal	D 1-1	L 0-1
Manchester United	L 1-2	W 3-1
Sunderland	W 1-0	L 0-1
Wolverhampton W	W 2-0	D 0-0
Fulham	W 5-1	W 4-2
Leeds United	W 1-0	L 0-2
Everton	W 2-0	D 1-1
Leicester City	W 6-0	L 0-1
West Ham United	W 3-0	W 3-2
Burnley	W 4-2	W 1-0
Sheffield Wednesday	W 1-0	D 1-1
Tottenham Hotspur	W 4-1	W 3-1
West Bromwich Albion	L 0-2	L 2-3
Chelsea	W 1-0	L 0-1

REGULAR SIDE:
Mulhearn
Book
Pardoe
Doyle
Heslop
Oakes
Lee
Bell
Summerbee
Young
Coleman

MANAGER:
Joe Mercer

LARGEST VICTORY: 6-0 v Leicester City (H) 11/11/67

LARGEST WINNING MARGIN: 6 goals - 6-0 v Leicester City (H) 11/11/67

HEAVIEST DEFEAT: 0-3 v Stoke City (A) 26/8/67

AVERAGE HOME ATTENDANCE: 37,206

HIGHEST HOME ATTENDANCE: 62,942 v Manchester United 30/9/67

HIGHEST AWAY ATTENDANCE: 63,004 v Manchester United 27/3/68

LEAGUE APPEARANCES: (substitute appearances in brackets)
42 Book, 41 Pardoe, Heslop, Oakes, Summerbee, 40 Young, 38 Coleman, 37 Doyle (1), 35 Bell, 33 Mulhearn, 31 Lee, 10 Connor (3), 7 Dowd, 6 Hince, 4 Kennedy (2), Horne (1), Bowles, 2 Cheetham (1), Jones, Ogley, 1 Clay (1)

LEAGUE GOALS: 19 Young, 16 Lee, 14 Bell, Summerbee, 8 Coleman, 5 Doyle, 2 Oakes, Hince, Bowles, 1 Book, Heslop, Connor

as City had encountered with the Reds. When United are dominant, City's suffering becomes a national joke with media personalities laughing at the Blues simply because they are not United. No other club in British sport suffers in this way. Malcolm Allison recognised this and was determined to turn the situation around. Some of his boasts may have seemed outlandish but City supporters wanted to hear them. The Blues had suffered enough. Joe Mercer also recognised this but preferred to play a more diplomatic role. Instead of criticising or humiliating the Reds he would talk about United's strengths before stating the obvious - that City had won. Joe gave the club the respect it deserved and realised the best way to tackle the crowing of City's rivals was on the pitch. That attitude, combined with Allison's approach, ensured City were at least on a level with United. Most Blues would say above.

After the derby both Mercer and Allison tried to keep the momentum going. It wasn't easy, especially as many felt the derby was proof the Blues were the team of the season. Missing Colin Bell, City lost to Leicester and Chelsea in two of the next four games. Then on 20th April they gained a point at Wolves.

It looked as if the title was slipping away from City. There were now four games left - two at home followed by two away. City's destiny was at stake.

The Blues were in third place at this stage, four points behind United but with a game in hand. Leeds were second only a point behind United after the same number of games as City. Mike Doyle remembers how both Allison and Mercer were keen to push the players to the limit: "We'd got one point out of two games. From there we went to Southport for four days, and got the biggest bollocking from Mercer we'd ever had. He said, 'The Championship is there to be won, either you want to win it or you don't. You'll train together tomorrow morning and then I don't want to see you again. It's up to you after that.' He knew we'd get together and talk it out. One night there was me, Neil Young, George Heslop, Belly, Mike [Summerbee], Oakesy and Glyn Pardoe discussing the situation. We reckoned we could do it, and I don't think we lost another game from then on."

Against Sheffield Wednesday, a lucky deflection gave the Blues the only goal of the game. At Maine Road, Tony Book and Tony Coleman scored the goals in an easy 2-0 victory over Everton, leaving the Blues a mere two games from glory. These two matches, however, were tough ones away at Tottenham, then at Newcastle. Both sides had performed well throughout the season, although as the League programme neared its end both were out of contention. Nevertheless, Spurs remained a top six side, while Newcastle were a few places lower. Mercer recognised the difficulties: "It'll be like climbing Everest and K2 in one week."

The first of the games resulted in a terrific 3-1 victory at White Hart Lane. Colin Bell scored twice, Mike Summerbee the other as City first attacked, then defended in numbers. Brian James, in the *Daily Mail*, stressed City's power claiming their success was down to "bloody hard and selfless running." He also claimed City were "a side of fair quality, brilliantly inspired." He went on to say "City's output should be rewarded by not less than the title."

Sadly, at least two of City's players were now struggling to be fit for the Newcastle match. Colin Bell and Mike Summerbee had pulled out of England's midweek match against Spain, a game both were keen to take part in, and were doubtful for the Saturday match at Newcastle, while Mercer admitted many members of City's squad had played when they really were not 100% fit: "This has been true at times of Alan Oakes, Glyn Pardoe, Tony Book, and Mike Doyle as well as Colin Bell and Mike Summerbee. There have been games in which they have gone out with pain-killing injections, games before which we have left the final decision with the player himself. It has taken moral courage for them to put the good of the side before personal discomfort and, on many occasions, to insist on playing when decisions about their fitness to do so were not easy to arrive at."

Mercer went on to outline his admiration for the City players: "People often talk very disparagingly about modern professionals and try to make out that they don't give quite so much to the job as they did in the old days. They claim that everybody today wants things easier. But never in all my long association with football have I seen greater dedication than that of these Manchester City players. In the old days fear of unemployment was undoubtedly a motivating factor. Today with these players, pride is the driving force - pride in their performances, pride in what they are trying to accomplish."

Despite the fact City's squad was one of the smallest in the division, the Blues had maintained their challenge right to the end. Mercer was right about the commitment to the Blue cause shown by his players, and with City and United now level on 56 points after the same number of games, the biggest test of all would prove the value of each and every member of the City squad.

United still had the upper hand. Not only did they have the better goal average, but they were also playing lowly Sunderland at Old Trafford, whereas City were up against tenth placed Newcastle United at St. James Park.

Neutrals expected the rather more experienced United to retain the title, although a few leading voices suggested City had the ability to snatch the trophy. Bill Shankly, the great Liverpool boss, held the view City were the side to watch: "I regard City as favourites now. Any team that can do what they did at Tottenham must have a great chance."

Liverpool, themselves, still had a chance of pinching the Championship. They had a game in hand over both Manchester clubs and could take the title by a point if results went their way.

Incredibly, Footballer of the Year George Best was another man who believed City were certain to take the trophy from United in style: "When they came to Old Trafford and beat us, I'd only seen them a couple of times before that and didn't think much of them. But that night we never saw the way they went. I've never seen a team run and achieve the workrate they did. I felt like demanding blood tests on them afterwards. They may lack United's individual ability, but if they can keep working and running they must be in with a great chance of beating Newcastle United on Saturday. It won't be easy, but I fancy them to do it."

Best went on to admit he would love the chance of playing alongside his great friend Mike Summerbee: "I'd like to play a game in the City attack just to see what it's like." It's a little known fact that a few years later, when Best was in conflict with the United management for his off the field activities, Malcolm Allison almost brought the player to Maine Road. If that had occurred the early 1970s history of the two clubs, and indeed the player, may have been different. Naturally, there is no way United would have accepted Best playing for the Blues.

While neutrals felt certain City would win at Newcastle, those connected with the match itself seemed less convinced. George Heslop: "Frankly, I am a bit prickly about this match. If City win, I think we're going to be among the top teams for years. But I have told my team mates to watch out for Newcastle. The old club hasn't changed. If they are in the mood anything can happen. As for Wyn Davies - the man I will be marking - I think he is absolutely great. We must be on our toes. Newcastle are the most dangerous when you least expect it."

The City players relax by playing ten pin bowling in the build-up to the big game at Newcastle. Note City's loveable rogue Tony Coleman has kept his distance from the local policeman!

Future City manager Frank Clark would be in the Newcastle team to face the Blues in the game which could clinch the championship.

13 mins... Newcastle 0 City 1... Summerbee from six yards

32 mins... Newcastle 1 City 2... Young shoots home from 22 yards

48 mins... Newcastle 2 City 3... Young from 12 yards

Newcastle's Jim Iley was another convinced City would find it tough: "This match will be a good opportunity to give ourselves a lift. We've had some disappointing results lately, but it would be a great thing if we could get it out of our system against Manchester City."

As the days passed, the media became more interested in Manchester's Blues. This attention was completely new to the majority of people connected with the Maine Road club. On the Monday following the Tottenham game Mike Summerbee walked into the stadium and noticed there were considerably more photographers and reporters than normal. He took a long lingering look at the group before calling across to Joe Mercer in a mock serious tone: "What's happened, Boss? Has there been an accident?"

Mercer himself took delight in telling those media men who would listen that City would win the Championship and he had been practising the walk from Maine Road to Stretford ready to collect the trophy from the reigning Champions: "I shall personally take great pleasure in walking down to Old Trafford on Sunday morning to pick up the trophy."

On the day of the game over 20,000 City supporters travelled to the North-East for what was to be one of the most significant days in the club's long history. The Newcastle manager, Joe Harvey, could not believe the size of City's travelling support and prior to the game he turned to Malcolm Allison: "This is the first time I have been beaten at home before the game has started."

The match commenced with City appearing rather nervous. Heslop, perhaps remembering his own comments about Newcastle, froze for a while, but he was not the only one, especially when Newcastle's Jim Scott hit the City crossbar in the third minute. Nine minutes later, however, City made

Francis Lee celebrates the goal that clinched the championship

mins... Newcastle 2 City 4... Lee finishes from 12 yards

their mark on the game when Mike Doyle took a quick free-kick. Colin Bell raced towards the Newcastle goal, swerving round full-back and future City manager Frank Clark before pulling the ball back. Doyle shot towards goal and Mike Summerbee flicked the ball into the net. The vast City following went wild but, as the celebrations continued, Newcastle came back.

A defensive slip up allowed Jackie Sinclair to gain possession. Sinclair fed a pass across the goal area where Glyn Pardoe found himself facing three Newcastle players. Bryan 'Pop' Robson was the one who scored. The Geordies seemed to have the composure that City desperately needed. Tony Book played a true captain's role and tried to calm his players. After about half an hour Book saved the Blues when he cleared a header from Wyn Davies that looked an absolute certain goal. Then, within two minutes, the Blues took the lead again. A quickly taken throw-in by Summerbee was pushed goalwards by Colin Bell. Alan Oakes tried a shot, but the ball spun towards leading scorer Neil Young who volleyed a glorious goal with his left foot.

With typical City unpredictability, the Blues allowed Newcastle to fight back. Heslop, still struggling, cleared the ball, but only as far as Jim Iley, the man who'd confidently predicted a Newcastle resurgence. Iley fed Sinclair, who scored with a fine 15 yard shot.

Despite Neil Young getting the ball in the back of the net again - Francis Lee was adjudged offside - the score was still 2-2 at half time. When the interval came, Malcolm Allison was determined to tell the players what he thought. He had not been impressed with City's failure to keep a clean sheet: "I was going to go in at half time and give them a right going over in the dressing room. When I got there, though, I could see that they were all tensed up. So I just told

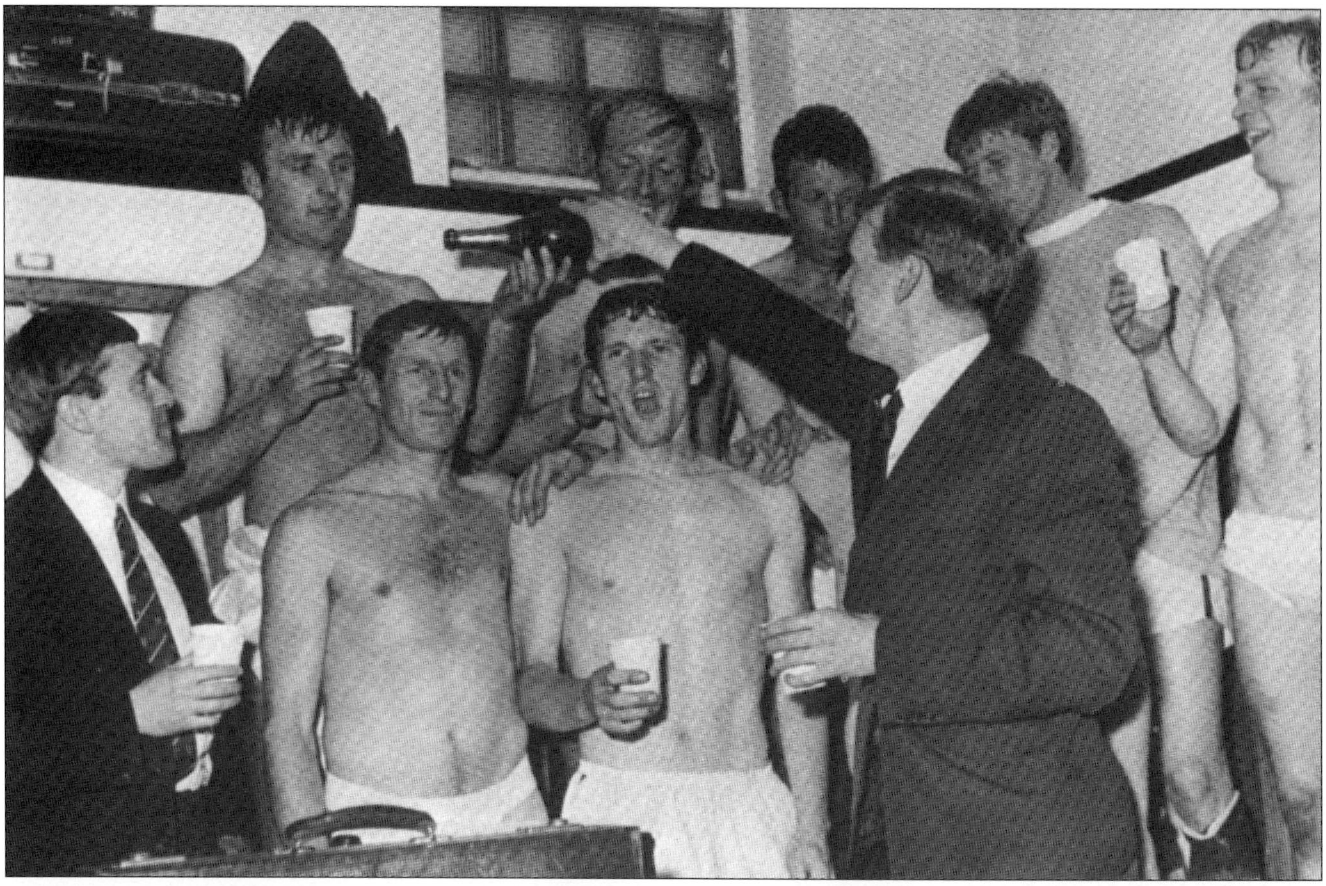

Brilliant victory at Newcastle

MANCHESTER CITY DIV 1 CHAMPIONS

JOE MERCER'S MANCHESTER CITY have done it. For so long the Cinderella team in Manchester, they became champions of Division I with a brilliant win at Newcastle today. Newcastle twice fought back after being a goal down to draw level at half-time but then came a wonderful second half burst from the rampant City men.

Manchester United, the champions last season and for so long

Peter Blakey pours the champagne as the City players celebrate at Newcastle.

them that they had had 45 minutes to get used to it, and now they had to go out and play."

The second half started with a more composed City side and it wasn't long before the goals came again. After only four minutes Colin Bell slipped the ball across the penalty area to Neil Young, who powered it in from 12 yards to give the Blues a 3-2 lead. From then on City showed the class, determination, and style that had thrilled the whole of football.

They were perfect in every sense of the word, although Francis Lee had one effort ruled out. Deservedly, he later scored with a 12 yard shot in the 63rd minute, after Doyle and Bell had worked well to get the ball to him. Immediately after scoring Lee went straight to the crowd with his arms aloft. Naturally the crowd were delighted, even a few Newcastle fans were hoping the Blues would win the Championship.

However, with the game nearing its end, John McNamee scored Newcastle's third. The Blues were still ahead but with four minutes to go the pressure was on. The final moments were extremely tense and then referee John Thacker put his whistle to his lips and the celebrations began. The supporters chanted, "Champions, Champions", as many of them swarmed onto the pitch to greet their heroes.

Across at Old Trafford, as United were beaten 2-1 by struggling Sunderland, the Championship trophy vanished. *Daily Express* reporter Alan Thompson set off on a mission to track it down. He started questioning the Old Trafford staff: "Secretary Les Olive was under the impression that a League official had taken it earlier in the week, Matt Busby was not at all sure what had happened to it, and for a minute or two it was lost until a member of the female staff admitted that it had been locked up 'in the vault'. You are at liberty to allow full rein to your imaginations in concluding exactly where the 'vault' is at Old Trafford. But the centre of the boardroom table, where the League Championship Cup has stood proudly for the last 12 months was occupied by five shillings worth of flowers. Sit down the City fan who says symbolic."

Back in Newcastle the celebrations really began. The champagne corks started popping in the dressing room, while the supporters danced in the streets. It really was a remarkable atmosphere on an incredible day. This was the moment all City supporters had waited for. The day when the Mercer-Allison combination brought success to a club desperately trying to leap out of the shadows. Life had been particularly grim for City fans for over a decade and

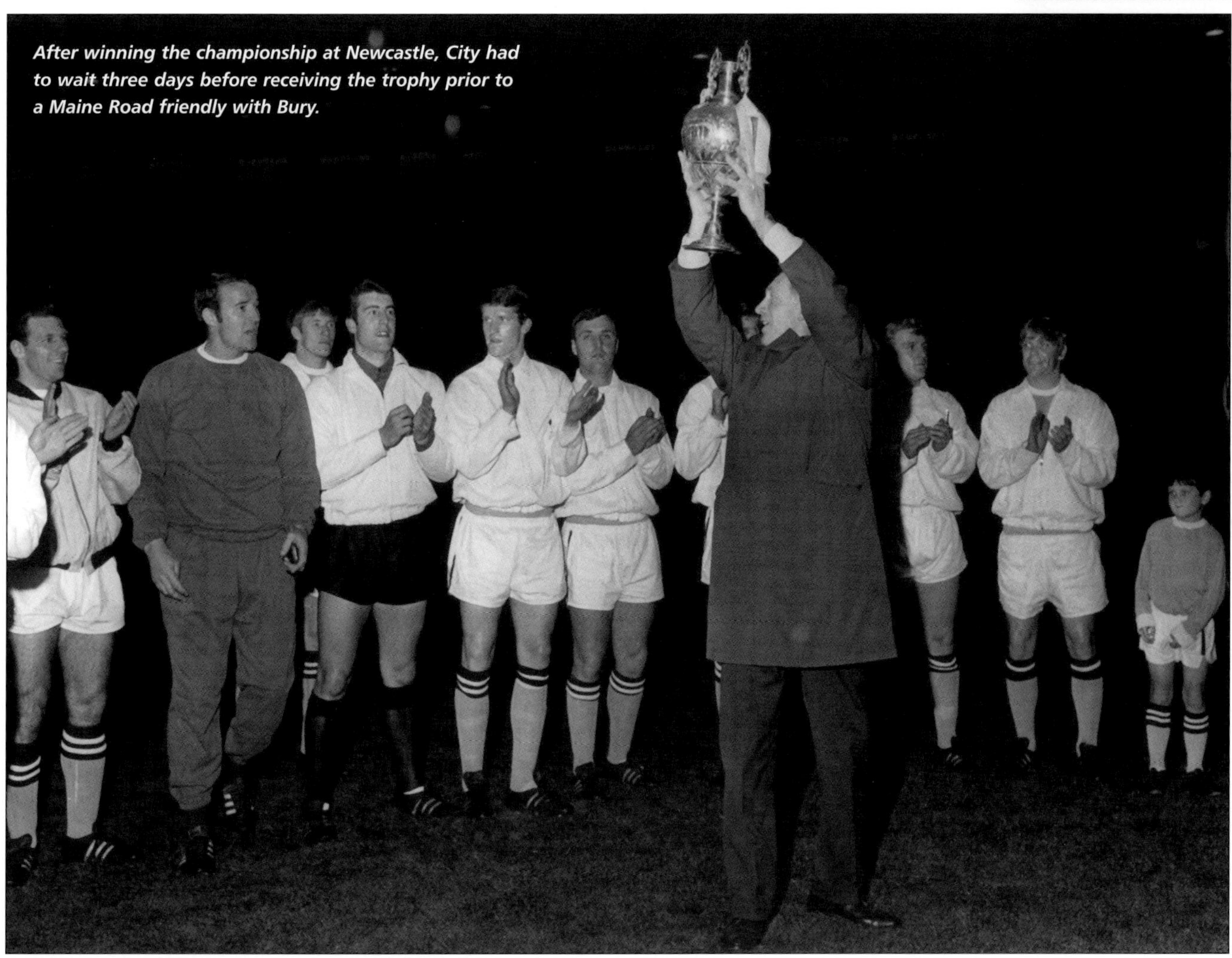

After winning the championship at Newcastle, City had to wait three days before receiving the trophy prior to a Maine Road friendly with Bury.

only a couple of years earlier supporters had started to desert the club. The managerial partnership had brought the Blues a new image, and had also enticed many exciting players to the club. Malcolm Allison's coaching techniques had also helped develop some of the younger players into true First Division stars. It was an incredible story.

James Mossop writing in the *Sunday Express* summed it up perfectly: "There could be no more popular, sentimental success story. City are - were - the poor relations of the Manchester clubs. Three years ago discontented fans were throwing stones and abuse at the boardroom windows. The crowds had dwindled to a starvation level of 8,000. But in an amazing spell of hard work and dedication Joe Mercer and Malcolm Allison have lifted ordinary players into the Champions of the Football League. They are just a grand set of lads, mostly young, and the best all-round team in England. It is desperately difficult not to get emotional about Manchester City, about such a major success born out of honesty, bravery and complete dedication. This victory was the pinnacle of the season. An afternoon coloured with skill, blessed with fair play and above all applauded in the end by every man, woman, and child in the 50,000 crowd. These people will never forget it. Many thousands of them swarmed on to the pitch in a dancing, swirling sea of blue and white at the end. They were cheering for the new champions. For 90 minutes City, the team that has won more friends than any other in a season of imaginative attacking football, turned on the style."

Every newspaper was equal in its praise, that the Blues really were worthy victors. As the champions journeyed back from Newcastle, supporters surrounded the team bus to cheer their heroes. Every player deserved the acclaim, for even those that had struggled early on had improved as the game progressed. Vince Wilson in the *Sunday Mirror* rightly claimed every player added value to the performance and the Blues played as a true team. No individual stood out above the rest, nor did any of the players try to claim they had contributed more. Manchester City won the Championship as a team, together.

Frequently, on the journey away from St. James Park the team bus struggled to move forward. Understandably, there were queues of traffic on all the major routes out of the city and the bus frequently had to stop. At one point Malcolm Allison jumped out and started to dance in and out of the line of traffic waving to many City supporters along the way. On the bus Joe Mercer orchestrated the singing and everybody joined in.

FINAL TABLE 1967-68

	P	W	D	L	F	A	Pts
★ CITY	42	26	6	10	86	43	58
Manchester U	42	24	8	10	89	55	56
Liverpool	42	22	11	9	71	40	55
Leeds	42	22	9	11	71	41	53
Everton	42	23	6	13	67	40	52
Chelsea	42	18	12	12	62	68	48
Tottenham	42	19	9	14	70	59	47
West Brom	42	17	12	13	75	62	46
Arsenal	42	17	10	15	60	56	44
Newcastle	42	13	15	14	54	67	41
Nottm Forest	42	14	11	17	52	64	39
West Ham	42	14	10	18	73	69	38
Leicester	42	13	12	17	64	69	38
Burnley	42	14	10	18	64	71	38
Sunderland	42	13	11	18	51	61	37
Southampton	42	13	11	18	66	83	37
Wolves	42	14	8	20	65	75	36
Stoke	42	14	7	21	50	73	35
Sheffield Wed	42	11	12	19	51	63	34
Coventry	42	9	15	18	51	71	33
▼Sheffield U	42	11	10	21	49	70	32
▼Fulham	42	10	7	25	56	98	27

Blues on the road... Neil Young, Mike Doyle, Cliff Sear and Joe and Norah Mercer are among the passengers.

The following day City held a press conference at Maine Road. It was a light hearted affair with Mercer, Allison and Book talking openly about City's success and their hopes for the future, in particular their first venture into Europe. Mercer stated he believed City would do well in the European Cup and they should survive the first two rounds at least. Allison believed the Blues would go further, stating he didn't really rate continental coaches: "I think a lot of foreign teams win despite their coaches. If we had played Continental opposition every week we would have won the Championship by 80 points."

He went on to boast that the European coaches were "cowards" and City would "terrify Europe to death". Only a few months later, these comments would come back to haunt Allison, but at the time the English footballing public loved his brash statements. Another quote appeared under the headline "It's Mars Next Stop" in the *Daily Express* the next day: "I think we will be the first team to play on Mars."

A friendly against Bury was hastily arranged for the Tuesday following the Newcastle game to enable the Championship trophy to be presented. Normally, the trophy was presented at the League's annual dinner but as City would be on tour in America, the League agreed to present it at Maine Road. The presentation took place before the game, with Tony Book and the rest of the players going on a lap of honour before Mercer was handed the trophy to lift above his head. The crowd roared with delight and then witnessed a 4-2 victory.

Bury's two goals were scored by Bobby Owen who, two months later, signed for the Blues.

The game was noteworthy for it also included an appearance by Malcolm Allison. For much of the game he'd sat, wearing his familiar red tracksuit then, with about ten minutes left he substituted George Heslop and entered the field himself wearing the number 8 shirt. This caused a little confusion as Colin Bell remained on the pitch with the same number but nobody complained, after all it was a night to enjoy especially when Allison threw himself into the game. He forced a great save from Neil Ramsbottom, the Bury 'keeper, and had a goal disallowed. The City supporters chanted 'Allison for England', and even called for Mercer to take to the field.

This was a great time to be a Blue. Allison: "I felt acutely that we had come up with some original football. We had thrashed Manchester United, we had become a power in the land."

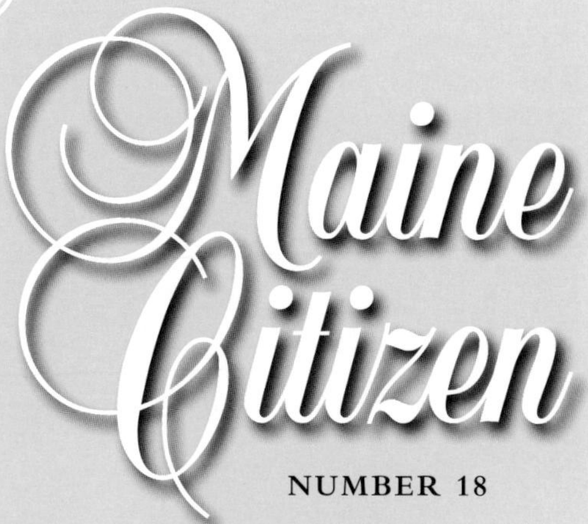

NUMBER 18

COLIN BELL

The majority of supporters firmly believe Colin Bell is the greatest City player of all time. He is a man remembered for many fine games, and for his remarkable stamina and determination. He is also England's most capped City player. Without doubt he is a living legend.

Bell was signed from Bury in 1966 during City's successful promotion season and he immediately made an impression, for his debut game saw him score a goal when the ball hit him ... and entered the net. Joe Mercer couldn't believe it, but over the following weeks he realised Bell really was a tremendous player. It was Malcolm Allison who was determined to sign him in the first place, and the City coach went to extraordinary lengths to persuade rivals from other clubs that Bell was simply a poor player. It was all clever kidology and managed to delay the others long enough for cash-strapped City to raise the necessary funds.

Once at Maine Road Bell really did impress, and on 4th May 1966 scored the only goal of the game with Rotherham to bring the Blues promotion. That goal is still remembered by supporters today who frequently sing an epic chant detailing the amazing events of 1963 to 1970.

On the return to the First Division Bell became the club's leading marksman with 12 goals from 42 games as the Blues established respectability. Then the following season he netted 14 times in 35 matches to help City win the title, and went on to play a vital role throughout the three trophy successes that followed.

This period was a tremendous time for the player, and helped him become established as an England international. He went on to win 48 caps. Had it not been for injury, and the general failure of the England team from 1974 onwards that figure would certainly have been significantly higher. As it is, he remains the most capped player while on City's books.

BELL'S PLAYING RECORD

	LEAGUE		FA CUP		FL CUP		EUROPE		TOTAL	
	App	Gls	App	Gls	App	Gls	App	Gls	App	Gls
1965-66	11	4	0	0	0	0	-	-	11	4
1966-67	41	12	6	1	2	1	-	-	50	14
1967-68	35	14	4	2	4	1	-	-	43	17
1968-69	39	14	5	0	3	1	2	0	49	15
1969-70	31	11	2	0	6	5	9	5	48	21
1970-71	34	13	3	4	1	0	7	2	45	19
1971-72	33	12	2	0	1	2	-	-	36	14
1972-73	39	7	5	2	2	1	2	0	48	10
1973-74	41	7	2	0	11	3	-	-	54	10
1974-75	42	15	1	0	2	3	-	-	45	18
1975-76	20	6	0	0	5	1	-	-	25	7
1976-77	0	0	0	0	0	0	0	0	0	0
1977-78	16(1)	2	2	0	2	0	0	0	20(1)	2
1978-79	10	0	1(1)	0	1	0	3(1)	1	15(2)	1
TOTAL	393(1)	117	33(1)	9	40	18	23(1)	8	489(3)	152

Note: Colin Bell also appeared in four Charity Shield matches and scored in the August 1969 meeting with Leeds. To ensure consistency with the other players featured in this book, Charity Shield appearances have not been included in the above figures.

Joe Mercer and Malcolm Allison were always amazed by Bell's ability and strengths with Mercer claiming Bell was: "the best player since Peter Doherty. He has got fantastic stamina, and this unusual combination of speed and stamina. He is best when he is given a free rein and coming from deep. He is a good tackler and covers every inch of the pitch."

Allison held the belief that even he never managed to get the very best out of Bell. Team mates Lee and Summerbee also felt Bell was developing continually and injury robbed football of possibly the greatest player of all time. Peter Swales firmly believed Bell was the greatest he ever saw.

In 1974, despite City's dominance, at the age of 28 Bell was on the losing side as Wolves defeated the Blues 2-1 in the League Cup Final. It was a game in the same competition two season's later that ultimately brought a premature end to his career. A well documented challenge from Manchester United's Martin Buchan resulted in a terrible knee injury, and for the following two years Bell worked harder than any player before or since, to return to League action. It was a long, slow, difficult process. It was also one which millions of television viewers followed via regular features on the BBC's Nationwide programme. The television exposure brought Bell many letters of sympathy and encouragement, and showed how the majority of football followers recognised a true hero.

On Boxing Day 1977 he returned to action as substitute during a League game with Newcastle. His mere presence was enough to transform both the atmosphere and the result of that match, and without really doing a great deal he helped City achieve a 4-0 victory. That season he won his last honour when he helped the reserves win the Central League - no doubt that award means as much to Bell as any of his earlier successes. It certainly states much about his character.

The previous season a Bell-less City side had missed the Championship by a point; arguably a fit Bell would have made the difference. Two more seasons of struggle followed then in August 1979 he was forced to announce his retirement. It was a sad but inevitable conclusion to a highly successful career.

In 1990 he returned to Maine Road to assist with reserve and youth team coaching, although seven years later that City career ended in disappointing style as new manager Frank Clark decided it was time to appoint his own backroom staff. It was move which upset many supporters, although few could argue with Clark's reasoning.

In 1969 Mercer claimed Bell was the best player since Doherty. Over the course of the following decade many supporters felt he quite simply surpassed the renowned Irishman to become the greatest City player of all time.

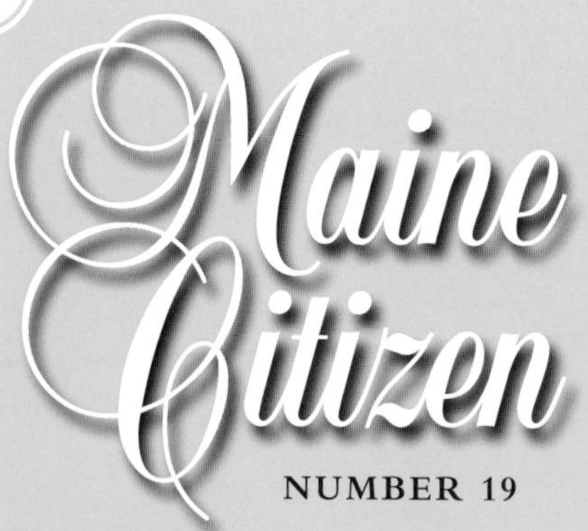

NUMBER 19

NEIL YOUNG

Many would argue Neil Young was the most important of all City's forwards during the Mercer-Allison period of success. He certainly contributed the most goals during the Second Division Championship season of 1965-6 and the League Championship season two years later. In fact he was also the club's highest goalscorer during 1968-9 (shared with Colin Bell).

In Cup competitions he also managed to net a few vital and noteworthy goals. His memorable strike in the 1969 F.A. Cup Final brought the trophy back to Manchester, while his opener in the ECWC Final of 1970 set City up for their first European success. He also scored twice in the ECWC semi-final against Schalke to help City reach the final.

Fallowfield-born Young joined City as an amateur on 15th May 1959 and within two years went on to sign professional forms after proving his ability. In November 1961 he made his debut in a 2-1 defeat at Aston Villa, and remained in the side for the rest of the season. He made 45 consecutive League appearances and was ever-present until December 1962. Although he missed the occasional match, he remained a City regular right up until late 1971, shortly before his departure to Preston North End.

One game he probably felt fortunate to miss was the infamous 2-1 defeat by Swindon on 16th January 1965 which ultimately brought the departure of manager George Poyser. The change actually aided Young's career as, under Mercer and Allison, he seemed to become a stronger, better attacker. He certainly benefited from the training and coaching techniques of Allison, while Mercer always felt that Young was the greatest of all his side: "He has got more talent than anybody else in the club. Six foot tall with a devastating left foot. His right foot works too! In fact he has got everything." Mercer was always concerned Young did not perhaps have the confidence that some of the other players, such as Summerbee and Lee, had. However, the time and effort put in by Allison helped Young to develop in that direction. It must be said though, Young was never the type of player to boast of his success or of his part in City's many achievements, he simply let his exceptional football ability speak for him. Unfortunately, the media rarely gave Young the credit he deserved and by the mid 80s few outside of Manchester really knew what the player had achieved. Videos and books about City's greatest players always seem to concentrate on Bell, Lee and Summerbee and rarely explain the importance of Young. This is patently unfair.

Young should be remembered for all his many important achievements at Maine Road, and for his often vital goals. He appeared in every significant match of the Mercer-Allison years, apart from the 1970 League Cup Final. He was only omitted from that game because he had just become a father, and Mercer and Allison felt his mind would be elsewhere.

In January 1972 he was transferred to Preston after being promised some kind of benefit match. The Blues were still struggling with political battles in the Boardroom and, when these were resolved, the new regime did not support Young's claim. For a long while the former hero boycotted the ground and the whole affair appalled many supporters. Once the fanzine movement developed during the late 1980s stories of Young's shabby treatment started to appear and, in 1991, steps were taken by various supporters groups to show how the fans still held great affection for Young even if the directors did not. Various dinners were held with Young as guest of honour.

Once Francis Lee gained control of the club in 1994, Young returned to Maine Road to watch a few games and in April 1995 came on to the pitch, with many of his former team mates, to celebrate the 25th anniversary of winning the ECWC. A success that owed so much to his attacking play.

Although Young may not be as famous as Summerbee, Bell or Lee, there is no doubt he contributed as much, if not more, than the others. He will always be remembered by City supporters as one of the greatest English born players of all time.

YOUNG'S PLAYING RECORD

	LEAGUE		FA CUP		FL CUP		EUROPE		TOTAL	
	App	Gls	App	Gls	App	Gls	App	Gls	App	Gls
1961-62	24	10	2	1	0	0	-	-	26	11
1962-63	31	5	1	0	6	1	-	-	38	6
1963-64	37	5	1	0	5	1	-	-	43	6
1964-65	31	8	1	0	1	1	-	-	33	9
1965-66	35	14	7	3	2	0	-	-	44	17
1966-67	38	4	5	2	2	1	-	-	45	7
1967-68	40	19	4	1	4	1	-	-	48	21
1968-69	40	14	7	2	2	0	2	0	51	16
1969-70	29	6	2	1	5	1	8	4	44	12
1970-71	24	1	2(1)	0	1	0	7	1	34(1)	2
1971-72	3(2)	0	0	0	0	0	-	-	3(2)	0
TOTAL	332(2)	86	32(1)	10	28	6	17	5	409(3)	107

Chapter Fourteen

European City of Style

THE close season of 1968 was a great one for City supporters. A time to reflect on the successes of the first three seasons under the Mercer-Allison combination, and to look forward to City's first appearance in European competition. They were right to expect a great deal, after all City's entertaining style of football had helped create a real buzz around Manchester, and won many admirers nationwide.

For the players and management however, the Summer of '68 was not as rewarding as it should have been as controversy seemed to follow the club everywhere. The Blues had now become one of the most talked about teams in Europe with the media tracking the club's every move. The attention was still relatively new to the majority of players and at times was extremely difficult to handle, added to which, a disastrous tour of North America caused a few problems, in particular an Achilles tendon injury to Tony Book.

When the Blues returned to England a civic reception at Manchester Town Hall resulted in banner headlines accusing the City players of walking out of an event held in their honour. What made the story more of a 'sensation' as far as the media were concerned, was the news Malcolm Allison had apparently led the escape party to one of his favourite night clubs. Although the story was relatively trivial, it did cause much embarrassment at the time, and is significant because it showed the Blues could no longer expect the media to ignore them. The public were keen to hear about City and the press were determined to find stories, no matter how trifling. On the one hand the Blues actively encouraged media attention - Allison's morale boosting boasts, Mercer's cosy chats with his friends in the news industry - but on the other they tried to keep out the negative stories. It was a difficult balancing act which, fortunately, City usually managed to get right. Throughout the mid to late 1960s the Mercer-Allison inspired Blues gained more positive coverage than bad. If the worst 'sensation' featured the players and Allison sneaking out of a rather formal function then there wasn't too much wrong with the club.

The 1968-9 season opened with the Charity Shield match against F.A. Cup Winners West Bromwich Albion. At that time the curtain-raiser was played on the Champions' home ground and City duly outplayed West Brom to record a convincing 6-1 victory. Everyone connected with the Blues hoped the League campaign would follow in the same style. Sadly, it did not.

City missed Tony Book following his injury on tour, and the Blues struggled in their opening League game - a 2-1 defeat at Liverpool. Neil Young

Bell, Pardoe, Heslop Mulhearn, Lee, Oakes, Doyle, Connor and Owen celebrate the 6-1 Charity Shield success against West Bromwich Albion at Maine Road in August 1968.

"We can see you sneaking out!" Joe and Norah Mercer were shocked to hear Malcolm Allison had led an escape party from the civic reception, held following City's League championship success.

provided the goal that day, but the forward line had now been joined by Bobby Owen - a £35,000 purchase from Bury. Owen scored twice in the Charity Shield victory, but it took the forward some time to settle in the League side.

The first home game was a 3-2 victory over Wolves before a crowd of 35,835. Because of their success in the League, City had been forced to designate certain seating areas purely for season ticket holders. A large section in the popular, if uncomfortable, Platt Lane Stand was marked specifically for this purpose. Similarly, the increase in popularity had forced the club to make admittance to the Main Stand by ticket only, with the cost of the most expensive seats now 13s 6d per League game.

There were other changes, too. Groundsman Stan Gibson had worked hard to turn the Maine Road pitch into a perfect playing surface, although at times even he could not perform his usual miracles as the Manchester weather and Allison's coaching routines piled on the pressure: "It will take some pounding again this year. Malcolm likes to get on it and play at the most unlikely times. It might spoil it a bit as a showpiece but if it helps City win I shan't lose any sleep over that."

In addition, City had taken steps to improve their scouting network, boasting how much of Britain had a City man on the lookout for the stars of the future. One of the scouts for Yorkshire knew exactly what it was like to play in a successful City side - Sam Barkas, captain of the League Champions in 1937.

Three days after the Wolves game, City entertained Manchester United, although the match itself lacked any real entertainment. United had come to Maine Road determined not to lose, and their approach stifled the City forwards. The game ended goalless and brought much criticism of Manchester football as the public expected better entertainment from the two leading English clubs.

Following the derby an away trip to Leicester ended in a 3-0 defeat as the Champions struggled to find form. Only a further three points were picked up in the following five games and then, on the back of such dismal form, the Blues had to face Turkish Champions Fenerbahce S.K. in the European Cup. By this stage City were 21st in the First Division after nine matches.

The game on 18th September was City's first in European competition and was also the first time an English side had faced a Turkish club, but it was not the first occasion Fenerbahce had played at Maine Road. In October 1953 the Turks played a friendly under Maine Road's new floodlights which ended in a 5-1 victory to the Blues. Although the tie was expected to be far more difficult than any friendly, the Blues still expected to win. They aimed for a two goal lead. They didn't succeed.

The match ended goalless as the Blues missed chance after chance. Even the normally reliable Summerbee had an off day with a small section of the crowd booing him on occasion: "I was playing centre-forward and thought I was the only man who could play in that position. I ended up struggling - subconsciously I had lowered my standards. We all thought we were unbeatable and lost that edge."

Colin Bell: "It was unfortunate that it was our first experience of Europe and it couldn't have been a bigger tournament. At Maine Road, they kicked us up in the air, picked us up, shook our hands and we accepted it."

Fenerbahce left Maine Road with the advantage, but not a victory. The Turks had to wait another 28 years before they won a game in Manchester, and then it was against United and not City.

The away leg was played on 2nd October, with City flying out on a specially chartered BEA Comet from Ringway at 10 o'clock the day before. The Blues took a squad of sixteen and stayed at the Hilton Hotel in Istanbul in an attempt to minimise any possible problems with foreign food.

On arrival at the stadium on the day of the game, the City party soon realised the match would be a difficult one. The pitch was in an appalling bumpy state while it also appeared the whole of Istanbul were keen to see the match.

The stadium was packed hours before the start with about 55,000, although the official attendance was ten thousand lower. It was a member of the Fenerbahce groundstaff who suggested to Walter Griffiths, City's secretary, the figure was significantly higher than 45,000.

When the match commenced, the noise generated by the partisan crowd was deafening. City certainly felt the full force of Turkish devotion. Nevertheless, it was City who first found the net. That popular rebel Tony Coleman latched on to a cross from Francis Lee, controlled the ball, went

The programme from City's first game in European competition.

round Fenerbahce's under 23 international Yavuz Simsek and stroked it home.

In the second half, however, it was a different story with Fenerbahce attacking in numbers. Less than a minute after half time they equalised. Although City retained the advantage via the away goals rule, it was Fenerbahce who now had the initiative and twelve minutes from time they took the lead, prompting mass celebrations.

Fans invaded the pitch, fireworks zoomed into the sky, and the City men realised it was virtually impossible to fight back. At full time the Turkish celebrations really began. Over one hundred celebratory fires were lit on the terraces, and for the first time baton-wielding riot police had to clear a path for the players to reach the dressing room. It was a nightmare day for the Blues, but a hugely important one for the Turks. The local press described the result as the most important in the history of the country, boasting of their success over the English Champions.

While the Istanbul press stressed the strengths of the Turks, their English counterparts concentrated on Allison's boasts of 'terrifying Europe to death', although Francis Lee had sympathy for Allison's view: "Even with our legs tied, we should have won that. Mind you, it was a dangerous atmosphere out there. I think if we had got over that hurdle we would have done all right. Malcolm Allison had added a bit of pressure by saying how well we would do in Europe, but he wasn't far wrong. After all, we won the Cup Winners' Cup the following season."

Out of European competition, the Blues were able to concentrate on the domestic scene, although that was hardly an improvement. City had already been knocked out of the League Cup by Blackpool in the third round, and League form was mixed.

A 2-0 defeat at Everton three days after the Fenerbahce game was probably not a great surprise, but the Champions needed to get their act together to ensure they didn't emulate their 1930s equivalents and find themselves floundering in the relegation zone at the season's end.

Inconsistency, always City's trade mark, seemed to dominate the Blues' League performances. A string of three defeats in November were followed by a 5-1 Maine Road victory over West Brom, then a 2-1 defeat at West Ham, and an impressive 7-0 annihilation of Burnley. City fans just did not know what to expect as the meandering campaign was a complete contrast to the previous season.

On 11th January City's 26th League game of the season saw the return of the influential Tony Book for the visit of fifth placed Chelsea. It was an important boost as City, lying in 14th position, needed his involvement on the pitch to steady the side. Book returned to his regular number two shirt, with Pardoe moving to number three, displacing £65,000 signing Arthur Mann.

Chelsea were the more accomplished side in the early moments of the game, and put City under considerable pressure, especially when Colin Bell was forced to leave the field for a spell after receiving a knee injury in the 12th minute.

After 23 minutes Chelsea took the lead, despite a last ditch attempt by Book to keep the ball out. The Pensioners continued to attack but, incredibly, it was City who scored next. Bobby Owen squeezed a ball through a massed defence to Neil Young, who proceeded to turn and hit a perfect shot across into the far corner of Peter Bonetti's goal. The 36th minute strike was very much against the run of play, but the City faithful hardly cared.

At half time Colin Bell, his knee bandaged, was replaced by Stan Bowles. The injury cost Bell an England cap the following Wednesday - one of many he would lose out on through injury. For Bowles, though, the opportunity was perfect, and ten minutes into the half he helped transform the match.

SUMMER OF 68

The tour to America was a total disaster and brought many problems for Mercer and Allison's great side. The most notable was the injury to Tony Book. It did also bring the Blues face to face with a true stereotypical view of the States. Malcolm Allison: "I recall Neil Young and George Heslop returning to the hotel white-faced. They had left a cinema and called into a bar for a hamburger. A row had developed and two people were shot!"
On their return the City management vowed they would never go on a strenuous end of season tour again. Then, at the end of the 1969-70 campaign, they seemed to forget their vow and travelled to Australia for a seven-game programme.
At least this was a little more successful as City drew one match and won the rest.

Francis Lee looks on as Mike Summerbee fails to break the deadlock in the goalless European Cup visit of Fenerbahce to Maine Road.

Chief scout Harry Godwin and manager Joe Mercer check the City kit. "Perhaps we should use a fabric conditioner next time Harry!"

A foul on Coleman led to a free-kick taken by Doyle. Bowles and Owen both had shots beaten out, before Bowles sent the ball to Lee, whose shot was rifled into the roof of the net. Then after 63 minutes, Bowles fed Young on the left. Young ran at speed into the Chelsea penalty area and hit the ball across the goal to Owen who scored his first League goal for the club. A minute later he netted his second to give City an important 4-1 win.

For the remainder of the campaign, however, similarly exciting victories seemed to be followed by depressing draws or, even worse, dismal defeats. No matter, City gradually picked up enough points to ensure safety and the Blues finished in 13th position. In itself, that was not particularly impressive, however performances in the F.A. Cup more than made up for a moderate League campaign.

In the third round City faced Third Division Luton at Maine Road before a crowd of 37,120. The Blues started comfortably, although too many opportunities were wasted. Then in the 26th minute Francis Lee was felled by John Moore in the penalty area, giving City a perfect opportunity to take the lead. Naturally, Lee took the spot kick himself and whacked the ball home to give the Blues the advantage.

City continued to attack with Bell outstanding, but more wasted chances and some exciting saves by Luton's Sandy Davie prevented further goals for the Blues. Then, with about ten minutes remaining, Luton attacked in numbers and Harry Dowd, who at long last had regained the number one shirt from Ken Mulhearn, was forced to make a number of fine stops. Two attempts by future Bolton and Arsenal manager Bruce Rioch led to breathtaking saves by the popular Dowd, with other Luton efforts also forcing the 'footballing plumber' to ensure the Blues didn't leak any goals.

The game ended 1-0 and gave City a fourth round trip to old Cup adversaries Newcastle United. That match ended goalless but it was still one with plenty of incident. Neil Young came closest to scoring; most thought it was a goal, but Young was unsure: "The shot that everyone thought went in? I was six or seven yards from the by-line, outside the area. I couldn't really see. It was a funny game ... probably better from the spectators point of view than the players. Control of the game changed very quickly. Both sides had chances ... ours were the more clear cut."

City once again had large support at a ground that had become more like a second home than an away venue. Tony Book felt the Blues fans dominated the terraces: "The City supporters did well for us up there. You could always hear them. And in the last quarter of an hour, which is always a tense time, they really gave us a lift."

Joe Mercer felt the star of the game was 19 year old Tommy Booth: "We were under a lot of pressure during the match, but did not give them many clear cut openings. Tommy Booth stuck right with Wyn Davies, so that he was not able to turn quickly or break effectively. Both sides must have done a lot of rethinking after Saturday, but there is a great spirit between us and there will be no recriminations after this game."

The replay was a rather exciting affair with City winning 2-0. Alan Thompson writing in the *Daily Express* believed City were superb, especially early on: "They pulverised Newcastle so completely in the first half that it was not so much a match as a massacre. But all they had to show on the ledge was one early goal and half a dozen near misses."

In the *Daily Telegraph* R.H. Williams held a similar view: "Newcastle had no answer to the buoyant City forwards, bouncing at last with optimism who must have been surprised at the obstinate squareness of Newcastle's defence. At any rate, they took obvious delight in drilling holes in it."

The first goal came in the tenth minute with City attacking the Scoreboard End of the stadium. Harry Dowd started the move with a long pump upfield which found the head of Lee, who in turn sent the ball to Owen. Owen flicked it on to Young, who then streaked forward in a 30 yard run before firing the ball past Willie McFaul.

Fifty eight minutes later the same players were involved when the lead was increased. This time Young backheaded to Lee, who flicked it across to Owen on the right. The former Bury man powered home a shot from about 15 yards out.

Over the two games City easily deserved the victory and provided value for money for the incredibly large crowds. 60,844 had watched the second game, while the first had been attended by 55,680.

The fifth round draw sent City to Blackburn for an all-Lancashire clash, although the match had to be postponed on several occasions as a result of poor weather and a 'flu epidemic in Blackburn. When the game started on 24th February - 16 days after the original date - City proved why they had won the Championship the season before. The first goal came in the 13th minute when Colin Bell, playing his first game since the Chelsea match in January, steered a perfect pass through the Blackburn defence and on to Lee. The forward then charged up field and knocked the ball past Adam Blacklaw in the Blackburn goal.

In the 47th minute the home side equalised, then eleven minutes later Tony Coleman restored the lead: "I'll never forget it if I live to be a hundred. I hit it with my right foot and it went in like a rocket. That hasn't happened very often!"

Later City increased their lead when Neil Young fed the ball to Lee's feet. The striker stormed through the middle with little opposition and then slammed a searing shot into the net. In the dying minutes Coleman made it four when a mistake by the Blackburn defence allowed him to nip in and pinch a cheeky goal.

It was a good all-round performance with Colin Bell the undisputed star: "This was my first game back after injury and I really felt good after my lay-off. The knee which had kept me out of action ended up a little bit sore, but I was ready for a game. I thought the team played extremely well all through the match."

City's quarter-final opponents were Tottenham at Maine Road on 1st March. Again the Blues showed their mettle from the very first minute, although Spurs were equally determined. Jimmy Greaves and Alan Gilzean attacked the Blues like no other fowards in the competition so far and City felt the pressure, while defensively the Londoners were set to stop the Blues no matter what. Johnson was booked for tipping up Bell near the penalty area, then Knowles found the referee taking his name after he sent Coleman crashing heavily to the ground with another hard tackle.

It was a tough match all round but the in the 64th minute City found an opening. A lofted ball from Coleman, out deep on the left, floated across the penalty area where Bell headed it back untroubled into

Above: Francis Lee shows his frustration during City's goalless FA Cup fourth round draw at Newcastle in January 1969.

Left: Neil Young shows his delight after netting in the 2-0 replay defeat of the Geordies.

Below: On to round five and the Blues see off Blackburn by 4-1 at Ewood Park. Here two-goal Tony Coleman beats Rovers 'keeper Blacklaw from outside the box. Notice City's use of red and black stripes. Malcolm Allison had suggested the new kit would make City invincible.

Francis Lee (out of the picture) shoots past Pat Jennings and in off a post for the only goal of the 1969 FA Cup quarter final with Tottenham.

the middle. Doyle forced his way forward onto the ball, then Summerbee turned it forward to Lee. From approximately eight yards out Lee shot and the ball scraped in via the inside of the post, with Pat Jennings unable to reach it.

Despite more pressure from Greaves & Co. City held on and entered the draw for the semi-final alongside Everton, Leicester City and Cup holders West Bromwich Albion. The draw paired City with Everton at Villa Park with Mercer and Allison warning how Alan Ball would be the Toffees' most influential player. They discussed how to stop the England international and came to the conclusion they should simply blot him out of the game. They'd seen Ball struggle two years earlier at Maine Road and felt extra close marking might make his play ineffectual. Dave Connor was brought into the side specifically to halt the threat from Ball and it worked perfectly. Connor managed to annoy the Evertonian so much he lost his temper, fouled Connor and was booked. Mercer and Allison were delighted the ploy proved so effective.

In later years Ball said that he half-expected Connor to be standing next to him in the Everton dressing room toilet at half time!

The early moments of the game were rather mixed, with City understandably nervous for much of the opening period. Nevertheless, playing in their recently adopted AC Milan style red and black striped away strip, the Blues always had the edge. They ran and fought for everything and kept the Everton attack at bay. Tony Book was outstanding as he bottled up Johnny Morrissey for the entire game. Francis Lee, despite worries about fitness, proved his ability on many occasions, while Mike Doyle showed his commitment to the Blue cause when he returned to the field after being absent with injury for 18 minutes. On his return, though a little more static, his play hardly seemed to suffer.

Tommy Booth sends the Blues to Wembley with this 89th minute winner against Everton in the Villa Park semi-final.

Despite City's attacking nature, the game remained goalless right up to the last minute. Then a wonder goal by youngster Tommy Booth set the Blues up for their seventh Cup Final. The ball was cleared by Harry Dowd and worked upfield in a fluent passing move which started with Young. He fed the ball to Bell before running upfield. Bell accurately passed to Lee, who sent the ball to Young. Quickly, he shot an absolute screamer goalwards, only to see it rebound off the shoulder of Everton's startled 'keeper Gordon West. The ball rolled out for a corner taken by Young. Doyle headed it down to Summerbee who flicked it across the goal face towards the waiting Bell. Booth rushed forward and swiftly lashed it into the net. It was a great moment.

Norman Wynne writing in *The People* was pleased for Booth: "The game was moving with certainty to a replay until Booth came up with his last minute goal. It was fitting that the City centre half should be the goal scoring hero of the day. He was the youngest player on the field, and also the best."

The celebrations began immediately with champagne and cigars passed around the dressing room. Mercer announced City were going to Wembley to entertain, while an innocent comment by Chairman Albert Alexander caused much laughter: "Oh, great, we're in the Final, we'll make a lot of money and then we'll be able to buy some good players."

By reaching Wembley City had equalled Arsenal's record of six Wembley Finals - a feat which made Mercer immensely proud. Another man full of pride was Malcolm Allison: "It was essentially a great team victory, but I don't think the other players will mind my praising Tony (Book), Tommy (Booth), and Francis (Lee). Tony for his inspirational leadership, especially when we were down to ten men with Doyle undergoing treatment; Francis for his 100% effort when he must have been in considerable pain from his thigh injury and finally Tommy Booth. What can I add to what's already been said about him. He was the 'man of the match' before he did what he stopped Joe Royle from doing - scoring."

City's opponents for the Final were not known until 29th March, a week after the Blues' victory, although any supporter of football in Manchester must have realised that Leicester City had to be favourites if only for the simple fact the two sides had faced each other every year in the competition since 1965-6. In the end Leicester defeated holders West Brom 1-0 at Hillsborough to reach Wembley.

FA Cup Winners 1969

In the weeks leading up to the Final City announced they would be wearing their new change strip of red and black stripes, rather than traditional sky blue. It had been Allison's suggestion to wear AC Milan's colours in the first place as he believed it would give City the same kind of invincibility the Italians enjoyed. He also felt it gave the Mancunians a psychological advantage. The strip had been tried out a number of times during the season - including the Cup ties with Blackburn and Everton - and Allison's idea seemed to work.

This was not the first Final to see City play in a change strip. In fact they only wore their traditional strip in the 1904 and 1955 Finals, although the 1926 appearance did see City wearing a form of blue. For that game City agreed with Bolton to wear darker shirts than normal to avoid confusion with Bolton's white, and the Manchester men took to the field wearing a deeper sky blue hue than usual. The 1933 final saw City wear red/maroon shirts; the following year they asked new manufacturers Umbro to develop the colour further, and in 1956 they wore maroon with thin white stripes.

Another break with tradition saw City allow young Paul Todd, the son of a City steward, to be the first mascot at a Final. They smuggled him in on the players' coach, sitting next to manager Mercer, and then during the game he took Allison's place on the bench as the City assistant had been banned for so called 'excessive coaching'. Allison was forced to watch the game from the stands, although the ban was ineffectual as it actually brought him closer to the pitch than the bench.

One member of the City squad had already had a successful week leading up to the Final - Tony Book. City's captain had been voted joint Footballer of the Year (with Dave Mackay of Derby County) by the Football Writers. It was a fitting tribute to a great player, and Book was naturally delighted: "To receive an award that my boss, Joe Mercer, and Stanley Matthews, Tom Finney, Bert Trautmann and men of their calibre were given is truly astonishing. It is an honour for which the greatest credit goes to Joe Mercer, Malcolm Allison, and the team. I've had some wonderful help on the way."

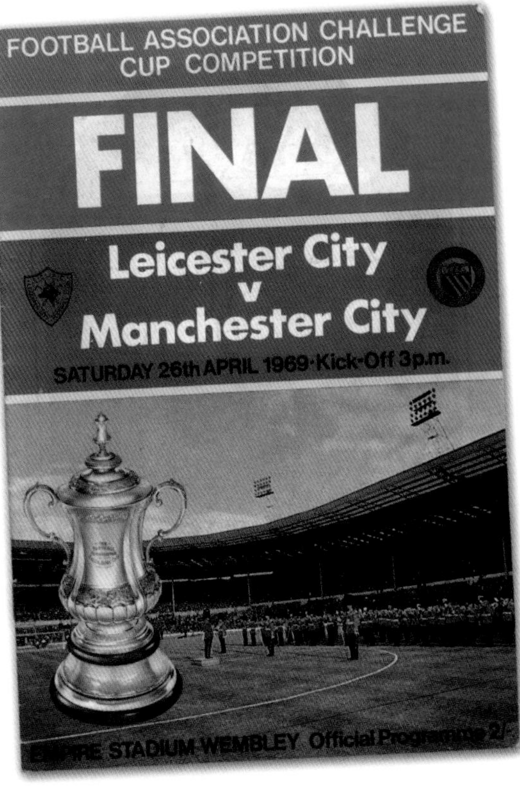

The day before the game Book joined the other City players and the management on a trip to Wembley to check out the pitch and facilities. They did not like what they saw, with Mercer describing the pitch as a 'cabbage patch'. Neil Young remembers it was an absolute disgrace: "It was terrible. Joe Mercer went berserk when he saw the state of the pitch. They had a Horse Show on it and it was all rutted and bumpy."

The Royal guest for the match was Princess Anne, who'd probably attended the Horse Show as well. For the day she wore red and black prompting many to believe she had a bit of a soft spot for City, although the more likely explanation is her advisors had told her both finalists traditionally wore blue prompting her to adopt 'neutral' colours. She was introduced to the teams and even spent a few moments chatting to mascot Paul Todd. Legend has it Tony Coleman, who according to Allison had been injured in a fight the weekend before, also made an impression on the Princess. Apparently, as they shook hands he said: "Give my regards to your Mum and Dad."

The game itself was not a classic, although it did produce some fine moments. Leicester's Allan Clarke, at that time the most expensive player in Britain at £150,000, had a superb shot which Dowd finger tipped to safety. Dowd, who had missed out on a League Championship medal, enjoyed making that save and the game itself: "Playing at Wembley has to be the highlight of my career. I can't recall being all that nervous at Wembley. I suppose I was at the start but I soon got into it. I remember making that save from Allan Clarke early on but I was more pleased about smothering the ball at Andy Lochhead's feet when he was through on his own."

Early on both Young and Coleman saw attempts miss the target as City tried to seize the initiative. Then, after 23 minutes, Summerbee gathered a throw-in from Lee, raced down the right, slipped past Leicester full-back David Nish and centred to Young. The City striker crashed the ball past England under-23 goalkeeper Peter Shilton into the top corner with his left foot. Young knew he had scored from the second he hit the ball.

A Cup Final ticket and a very rare unused pass to the dressing rooms.

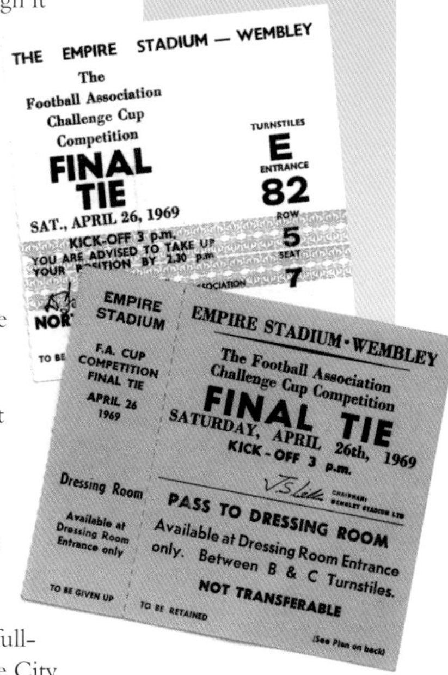

Left: Dave Mackay and Tony Book, joint Footballers of the Year in 1969.

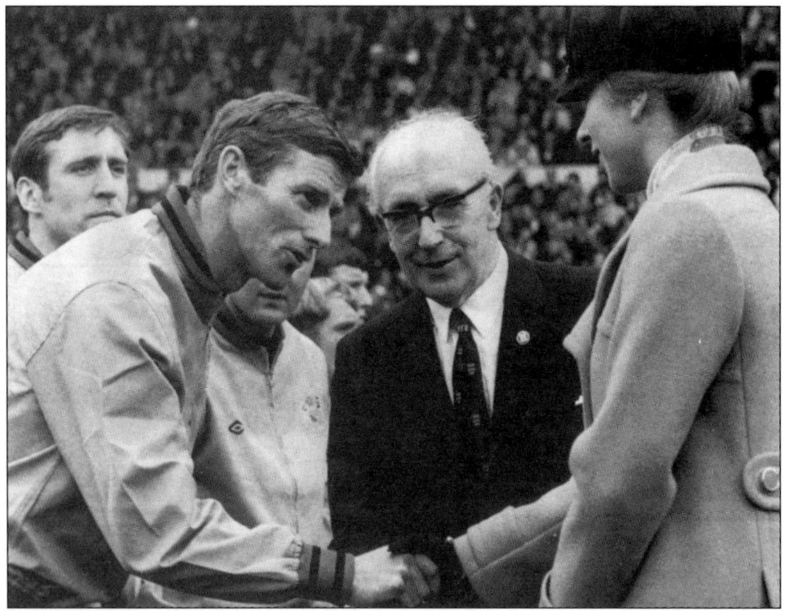

Tony Book meets Princess Anne prior to the 1969 FA Cup Final.

Mercer, seated on the bench, was immediately grabbed by a BBC reporter to explain his feelings. This type of intrusion by the media became commonplace in the 1980s and 1990s but in 1969 it was new to football. It came about because of politics between the BBC and London Weekend Television, with each station claiming the other had broken coverage agreements. The BBC said it had exclusive rights to interview the finalists, while LWT claimed they were not getting a fair deal. It was said the LWT men had even disguised themselves in tracksuits to deceive the BBC - a point LWT head of sport Jimmy Hill later admitted was true. It was all rather tacky and created unnecessary tension around the Final and its participants.

On the pitch Allan Clarke tried hard to even the score for Leicester, prompting the *Daily Mail* to consider what might have been had his Leicester colleagues provided the ball for him, rather than he for them. The player was voted Man of the Match although Mike Summerbee put it into perspective when he commented: "I'd rather have my winners' medal."

Despite the appalling surface both sides did play some fine football at times, but as the game neared its end it was obvious the Cup was on its way back to Manchester. Unfortunately, Leicester combined defeat with relegation to the Second Division, thereby emulating City's feat of 1926.

Tony Book collected the trophy for City, then all the players waited as Leicester collected their medals. The *Daily Mail* applauded City's compassion: "The mood was equal to the match. Fear was hardly evident, bad fouls were few, and the sight of the Manchester men clapping the losers provided a warm afterglow. Manchester City are among the best Cup-winners of past decades. Leicester are far from being the worst losers."

On the pitch Mercer and Allison, laughing and joking with each other, took it in turns to lift the trophy. They also conducted the fans' singing for a while. It was one of the best moments during the successful partnership and, while the celebrations continued, Allison turned to Mercer and said, "Boss, I'm worried." Mercer was puzzled after all City had just won the F.A. Cup to combine with the League, the Charity Shield, and the Second Division Championship since 1966. He asked Allison for an explanation. Allison replied: "Well, Boss, I can't help wondering what went wrong in 1967 when we didn't win anything!" The two men laughed.

The celebrations continued in the dressing room. The Cup was filled with champagne and the media demanded interviews. Allison was asked about Europe. Remembering his boasts of the previous year he replied: "I'll say this - we will at least get through the first round in the Cup Winners' Cup, of that I can promise."

Mercer also remembered the Fenerbahce disappointments: "I believe our Wembley victory is only the start of a truly great future for Manchester City. We go back into Europe still reflecting on our bitter experiences of earlier this season and determined not to make the same mistakes again.

"Europe is where the lolly is, so instead of being idealistic we have to be more financially minded. Our defeat by Fenerbahce in Istanbul in October taught us a firm lesson in that we should never underestimate the opposition - any opposition.

"We must get down to basics all the time and I sincerely believe that we have still to see the best of this City team. I don't really like talking about potential but we have here a great bunch of players, who are going to become a really great side. Things didn't go well for us earlier this season and, quite naturally, I was disappointed at our results because I knew, Malcolm knew, that the entire team was capable of so much more."

He went on to outline City's strengths, making particular reference to the emerging Tommy Booth. Six months earlier few had heard the player's name, now following his goal in the semi-final and appearance at Wembley everybody seemed to be talking about him.

As the night progressed City moved on to their celebration banquet at the Cafe Royal. The BBC took the opportunity to interview the players and management, and afterwards some members of the side moved on to a West End night club.

The following morning the team and trophy returned to Manchester, travelling by rail from London to Wilmslow. At the usually quiet Cheshire town 25,000 people turned out to see the players board an open-top bus for the 12 mile trip to Manchester's Albert Square. John Humphreys, a City director and a director of Wilmslow-based kit manufacturers Umbro, had suggested the Blues commence their tour from the town. At first it seemed a ridiculous idea, but as that part of Cheshire

1969 FA CUP RUN

R3	Luton Town	H	W 1-0
R4	Newcastle United	A	D 0-0
	Newcastle United	H	W 2-0
R5	Blackburn Rovers	A	W 4-1
R6	Tottenham Hotspur	H	W 1-0
SF	Everton	N*	W 1-0
F	Leicester City	N**	W 1-0

* = Villa Park, Birmingham
** = Wembley Stadium

FACTS & FIGURES

	P	W	D	L	F	A
HOME	3	3	0	0	4	0
AWAY	4	3	1	0	6	1
TOTAL	7	6	1	0	10	1

CUP FINAL DETAILS

26 April 1969 at Wembley Stadium
MANCHESTER CITY 1
LEICESTER CITY 0

CITY: Dowd, Book, Pardoe, Doyle, Booth, Oakes, Summerbee, Bell, Lee, Young, Coleman. Substitute: Connor
LEICESTER CITY: Shilton, Rodrigues, Nish, Roberts, Woollett, Cross, Fern, Gibson, Lochhead, Clarke, Glover (Manley)
GOAL: Young

ATTENDANCE: 100,000
REFEREE: G McCabe (Sheffield)
GUEST OF HONOUR: Princess Anne
MANAGER: Joe Mercer
CAPTAIN: Tony Book

The ball hits the back of the net (above) for the only goal of the final. As scorer Neil Young celebrates, Leicester's players look totally deflated (right).

Top picture: Harry Dowd dives to save an acrobatic effort from Leicester's Peter Rodrigues. Glyn Pardoe, Tommy Booth and Len Glover look on.

It's City's Cup and the lap of honour sees captain Tony Book being chaired by Francis Lee, Mike Doyle and Harry Dowd.

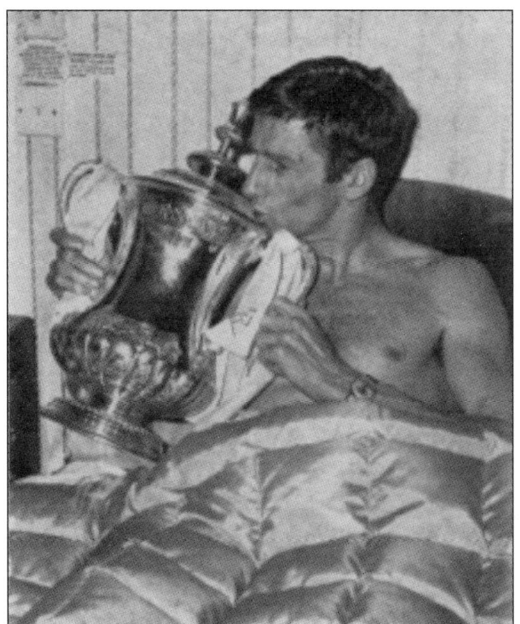

is strong in its support for City, it was agreed it would be worth trying.

The journey into Manchester was tremendous with one newspaper estimating there were at least 250,000 people lining the route to welcome their heroes back. The bus, loaned by Southport Corporation, and driver Bob Jackson were the same combination that brought United through the streets after their European Cup success twelve months earlier and 52 year old Jackson found City's homecoming moving: "It was fantastic. I would say there were more people about than for United's homecoming, and I was very proud to be in the procession. I saw the game on telly and enjoyed every minute of it."

In Albert Square the crowd chanted the names of the players and called for both Mercer and Allison. The supporters listened as both men spoke of the pride they felt bringing the Cup back to Manchester. For Mercer winning the Cup saw him enter the record books as the first man to win the F.A. Cup and the League Championship as both a player and a manager. It was a special occasion.

Again, the Summer of '69 was a good one for City supporters. They were able to bask in the glory, and knowledge their club was now re-established as one of Britain's elite. Fenerbahce had caused a little embarrassment but, apart from Allison's predictions, nobody really expected an entire team of European novices to find success at their first attempt. However, the F.A. Cup gave the Blues another chance. This time they would appear in the European Cup Winners' Cup - a competition previously won by Tottenham (1963) and West Ham (1965). The Fenerbahce experience would aid the Blues' preparations.

1969-70 commenced with the Charity Shield match against Don Revie's Leeds United at Elland Road. The result was a disappointing 2-1 defeat, but the game hardly mattered. A week later City's 4-1 victory over Sheffield Wednesday did, however, and there was much hope that 1969-70 would see the Blues make an impression on the League. Sadly, this never really occurred as the inconsistency that had dogged the previous season, and many others in years gone by, continued to appear. A run of three defeats followed the Wednesday win before a point was secured against Everton.

On 27th August a 4-0 victory at Sunderland brought hope, especially as newcomer Ian Bowyer scored a brace, but a couple of draws followed before City won their next League game. By 17th September they were eleventh on nine points from nine games. Tony Coleman had moved on to Sheffield Wednesday, while Joe Corrigan was now the first choice 'keeper replacing Harry Dowd, but otherwise the team was much the same as the previous season.

September was an extremely busy month as both the League Cup and ECWC campaigns commenced. In the League Cup City defeated Southport 3-0 on 3rd September, then on 17th they faced Athletic Bilbao, managed by the former West Brom star Ronnie Allen, in Spain.

Determined to avoid an embarrassing defeat, Mercer and Allison sent out a team that included seven of the side to suffer in Fenerbahce. The others were Tony Book, who'd only missed the Fenerbahce game through injury; Joe Corrigan, who had replaced Ken Mulhearn; Tommy Booth, who had won so many admirers in such a short time; and Ian Bowyer, who had replaced Tony Coleman.

After spending the night in the safe hands of Tony Book, the Cup comes home to Manchester. Thousands line the streets to welcome our heroes. Back at Maine Road, Malcolm Allison shows the trophy to members of City's groundstaff... Albert Heath (holding base of Cup), Stan Gibson (white shirt) and Wilf O'Neill.

SEPTEMBER 1969

City's League and Cup success started to bring the celebrities to Maine Road. Already Bernard Manning was known for his love of the Blues, and on a number of occasions he entertained various City personnel including Joe Mercer. In fact Mercer once 'innocently' took his good friend Matt Busby to Manning's club only to see Busby walk out when Manning's anti-United jibes upset the Reds' manager.
Other celebrities to be recognised at Maine Road were singer Matt Munro and comedy actor Lance Percival. Both were invited into the players' lounge, and admitted to having an interest in Mercer and Allison's side. Maine Road was also regularly featured in Granada TV's popular Tuesday night situation comedy "The Dustbin Men", which featured a City 'daft' character called Winston. One episode included Winston standing on top of the dustbin van, which was parked next to the Main Stand, to view one of Allison's training sessions. While the van itself had the slogan "By appointment to HRH Joe Mercer" emblazoned on its side.

The net bulges as Alan Oakes' shot thunders past goalkeeper Iribar for City's first goal against Athletic Bilbao at Maine Road.

Ian Bowyer makes it 3-0 to the Blues and Bilbao are beaten 6-3 on aggregate.

Despite the Blues determination City were 2-0 down in the opening fifteen minutes. Before half-time Neil Young reduced the deficit and provided the vital away goal which, if the score stood, would mean City simply needed to win 1-0 at Maine Road to go through. Realising this neither Mercer nor Allison panicked and at half-time spoke calmly with the players. In the second period, however, the Spaniards scored a third.

City fought back and levelled the score at 3-3 with a goal from youngster Booth and an own goal from the Bilbao captain Luis Echeberria. As the game progressed City appeared the more likely winners but they ran out of time, prompting Malcolm Allison to forecast a City victory at Maine Road: "These boys have got the needle tonight because they didn't win. Just wait until we get them back home. We'll give these Spaniards a roasting."

Before the two sides met at Maine Road, City had to play two League games and a League Cup tie. Their opponents in the League Cup were Bill Shankly's Liverpool at Maine Road. The two sides had already met in the League, with Liverpool achieving a double victory in only eight days, the cup game would be different.

It took City a mere eleven minutes to take the lead when Lee pushed the ball to Doyle. Doyle, from about 35 yards out, hit the ball with tremendous power and sent it rocketing into the net. It was a memorable goal, but ten minutes later it was cancelled out when a Heslop clearance ricocheted off Liverpool's Alun Evans and entered the goalmouth.

Neil Young regained the lead for the Blues when Ian Bowyer gathered a loose ball and passed it to Young, who in turn shot past 'keeper Tommy Lawrence. Later Bowyer increased the score to 3-1 but Liverpool pulled one back and the pressure increased. The scorer of the first goal, Mike Doyle then turned match winner as he helped protect the goal from relentless Liverpool pressure, and at the final whistle the score remained 3-2 to the Blues.

Back in Europe, the second leg with Bilbao ended 3-0 with goals from Bell, Oakes, and Bowyer. This set them up for a tie with the Belgian part-timers SK Lierse. The first leg, played on 12th November in Belgium, ended in a 3-0 victory to the Blues with goals from Bell and two from Lee. The second leg saw City totally outclass their Belgian opponents again this time two goals apiece from Lee and Bell and another from Summerbee gave City a 5-0 win. The Blues then had to wait until March for their quarter-final tie with Academica Coimbra of Portugal, by which time City had reached the League Cup Final.

Following the victory over Liverpool, City defeated Everton 2-0 at Maine Road in the fourth round to give the Blues a home tie against Queens Park Rangers in the quarter final. Two goals from Bell and another from Summerbee without reply gave the 42,000 crowd a lot to cheer, and set up a meeting with rivals Manchester United in the two legged semi-final.

The first leg, played on 3rd December, took place at Maine Road with City clearly determined to remind the Reds how the Blues were the dominant local force. The game commenced with City setting the pace and after only 13 minutes Lee helped provide the first goal. City's future Chairman made a typical bustling run down the left and, after avoiding a number of United tackles, sent in a fierce shot which deflected and spun high into the air. Bell, following in, met the loose ball on the half volley and crashed it past United's Alex Stepney.

With their one goal lead City pressed further and Stepney, who in the 1990s became a goalkeeping coach at Maine Road, performed exceptionally well to save from Bell, Lee and Oakes. He managed to keep the score at 1-0 until half-time, by when the Blues pressure had begun to subside.

Twenty-one minutes into the second half Bobby Charlton equalised for the Reds. As the game neared its conclusion, everyone connected with the Blues felt disappointed the match had not been killed off in the first period when United were there for the taking. However, it wasn't all doom and gloom as, in the 88th minute, Lee set off on another probing run. He entered the penalty area and was promptly felled by United's centre-half Ian Ure. Naturally, Ure complained bitterly but referee Jack Taylor remained convinced it was a penalty.

Spot-kick expert Lee sent the ball low to Stepney's right and the Blues won the match 2-1. As the game ended, George Best exchanged words with Jack Taylor, and appeared to knock the ball out of the referee's hands. The United man was later charged with bringing the game into disrepute, fined £100 and suspended for a month.

City were now confident of a place at Wembley, but could not allow a complacent attitude to affect the second leg at Old Trafford. The return game started with both sides looking bright and, once more, it was the Blues who were first to gain the upper hand when, after 17 minutes, Summerbee carved an opening for Young in the centre. His shot beat Stepney but was blocked on the line by Ure. Ian Bowyer grabbed the loose ball and slotted it into the net to give City an aggregate two goal lead. It didn't last, however.

Paul Edwards, a 21 year old United full back, pulled one back, but the Blues still seemed the more likely to score again before the interval. Several attempts failed, and then in the second half disaster struck when former Blue Denis Law stabbed home a loose ball. United were now level on aggregate and pushing forward in numbers.

It looked grim for City, but with only eight minutes remaining the tie was settled in the most unlikely way. Willie Morgan fouled Bowyer some twenty yards from the United net. The referee signalled an indirect free kick. Lee either missed the signal, or simply ignored it, and fired the ball towards the United goal. Stepney had the opportunity to let the ball enter the net knowing it wouldn't count because the kick had been indirect but, amazingly, he went to catch it. He fumbled and the ball fell loose; Summerbee seized the chance and buried it in the net to give City a 4-3 aggregate win. As in the 1930s and 1950s City were to travel to Wembley two years in succession.

The League Cup had already been won by manager Joe Mercer, but it was still a relatively new competition. Many clubs had boycotted it in its early years, indeed 1969-70 was the first season all League clubs entered. Interest had grown, however, when the final was moved to Wembley - it was originally a two legged affair - and when a place in Europe in the Fairs Cup was promised to the winners. In later years the Fairs Cup was replaced by the UEFA Cup, but its importance remained.

There is no doubt that by 1969-70 the League Cup was regarded as a major trophy. Mercer: "It's an accepted major competition now. The most important part about it though is that it offers a place in Europe. Certainly our programme is a full one, but as a player and as a manager I've always felt that there is only one way to go into a season... and that's to try to win every game, going flat out. When you are three or four goals up then you can think about changing gear. While we are in four major competitions we shall try to win four major competitions."

The League Cup final was scheduled for 7th March against West Bromwich Albion. This was only three days after the Blues' next European game and would present the Club with some significant problems, however before all of that City still had to worry about the League campaign, and then the F.A. Cup.

In the League, results were mixed although by 18th December City had managed to hold onto fourth place on 29 points - nine behind leaders Leeds. A run of bad results from then until February, however, saw the Blues plummet down the table, and by 1st February they lay in 12th position - fifteen points off the bottom, sixteen from the top.

As City moved into the 1970s, however, the success of the previous few seasons and the prospect of more glory during the season gave everybody connected with the club hope. Chairman Albert Alexander felt City were once again one of English football's glamour clubs with tremendous support. He was proud of the turnaround the club had enjoyed since the arrival of Mercer and Allison, and was pleased with the increased level of support. In the first 18 League and cup games played at Maine Road during the 1969-70 season the Blues averaged 39,808 supporters. With further success this was expected to increase.

Nevertheless, Malcolm Allison wanted more: "I feel the top average we could expect to get at the moment is 45,000 - and that's getting favourable weather and things like that. The public at the moment are at the stage when they are not quite sure what sort of a side we are. How good are City? It's

Eighteen-year-old Willie Donachie made his League debut in the 1-1 draw with Nottingham Forest in February 1970. He played for the last 40 minutes.

the sort of question in various ways I'm often asked. People want to be convinced. I'm not upset by this. The big crowd clubs like Liverpool even had to work hard for their numbers. It's only in the last four or five years that they have had exceptionally large gates. To average a 50,000 gate we would have to be at the top for the next five years - and I mean right at the top."

In February, to cater for the ever-growing demand to watch the Blues, secretary Walter Griffiths announced plans to redevelop the Scoreboard End terracing. The proposal was to completely remove the original terracing and build a new £325,000 'North Stand' with a cantilever roof and space for 22,000 standing spectators in a series of concrete pens. Work would commence in the 1970 close season with the stand ready by August 1971. In addition, there were plans to extend the Main Stand roof and seating to ensure it reached the corner flag, rather than end mysteriously some yards away. This would have meant an additional section of around 1,000 seats but would also have caused a rather awkward join in the roof, and proved to be rather expensive in relation to the number of spectators it could house. Eventually, the roof extension plan was abandoned, and the section remained roofless until the replacement of the Main Stand roof in the early 1980s.

City's players were horrified to see the state of the Wembley pitch when they arrived in London on the eve of the League Cup Final. It was covered with straw to protect it from the freezing conditions.

By the time the development was outlined in the City programme, City had already played two games in the F.A. Cup. In the first the Blues defeated Hull City 1-0 with a Neil Young effort, then in the fourth round City had to face Manchester United at Old Trafford. Sadly, the game ended 3-0 to the Reds, although the result may have turned out to be a blessing in disguise as the Blues were already experiencing a fixture pile-up. By the end of the season City played 61 first team games excluding friendlies. Incidentally, both League games against United ended in victory to the Blues, giving City fans further confirmation that City were still Manchester's dominant force.

After victories over Wolves and Ipswich in the League, City faced Academica Coimbra in the first leg of the European Cup Winners' Cup quarter final in Portugal. The press believed Mercer and Allison would try to protect their players during this game as the League Cup Final was scheduled only three days later, but Mercer disagreed: "We want to win the League Cup on Saturday, but we also want to win the Cup Winners' Cup. So it won't be a case of holding anything back for Wembley. A powerful performance can put us on the way to victory against West Brom. Defeat tonight could be demoralising."

Coimbra were believed to be a very weak side - a view many press men held - and even their own coach, Julio Pereira, stated they would be easily outclassed by City, especially as their side was allegedly made up of university students. Mindful of what had occurred with Fenerbahce, the City management wisely refused to listen to any of this.

Both Mercer and Allison were right to dismiss such glib comments as a grim match ended goalless. It was watched by a surprisingly low crowd of only 15,000. When City officials quizzed their Portuguese opposite numbers they discovered the match was being shown live on local television and many of the home fans had decided to watch from the comfort of their own armchairs.

During the game City's trainer, former player Dave Ewing, was banished from the touchline to the dressing room for excessive shouting. He didn't miss much, and the stay-away Coimbra fans probably felt justified in their decision. As for City, they were happy with the draw. Mercer smiled afterwards: "It was not a classic, was it?"

If the game had brought little joy, the following 24 hours or so would bring despair. The City party stayed on in Portugal after the match believing it would help them relax. Unfortunately, the plan backfired. While West Bromwich Albion lay in their Surrey hotel relaxing in preparation for the League Cup Final, City were struggling to get home. An airport strike and appalling weather caused City's flight to be delayed then diverted from London to Birmingham. The Blues were weary, and eventually arrived back in England a mere thirty-six hours before the Wembley kick-off. The journey from Portugal had taken over ten hours and left the City party tired out.

On the Friday, City delayed their pitch inspection until late afternoon to help the players rest. When they arrived at the stadium they could barely believe the state of the pitch. The previous year it had been a 'cabbage patch', now it was much worse as workmen covered the turf with straw to protect it from the freezing conditions. Although he didn't express his feelings to the players or the media, Mercer felt the surface would prove too tiring for his players. Nevertheless, he desperately wanted success and told the press: "We are not afraid of the pitch. We've played well on such pitches in the past."

League Cup Winners 1970

For the Final, Neil Young was omitted. He'd spent the previous day celebrating the birth of his daughter and the loss of his Cup Final place was not really a surprise. Glyn Pardoe wore the number seven shirt with George Heslop returning to the side to play alongside Tommy Booth. It was a rather defensive formation, although neither Mercer nor Allison expected the game to be a defensive stalemate.

Once again, Allison was forced to watch the match from the stands. Mercer had asked the F.A. for a reprieve of the touchline ban, but they would have none of it. City found their outspoken coach a place in the stands, along with those supporters lucky enough to have bought one of the 32,000 tickets allocated to the Blues.

The game commenced with City once again in their successful red and black striped shirts, although the first five minutes were hardly that as West Brom raced to a one goal lead. Tony Book, continually harassed by Albion's star man Jeff Astle, pushed a pass back which rolled out for a corner.

From Bobby Hope's flag-kick the ball was cleared to Ray Wilson, Albion's left back, who sent a curving cross into the box. City should have cleared the danger, but they hesitated and left goalkeeper Corrigan exposed.

Amid the City paralysis Jeff Astle, who in the 1990s enjoyed regular appearances as the singer on BBC's Fantasy Football League programme, headed home for Albion. It was a devastating blow for the large army of City supporters, however the men in red and black quickly gained control of the match. Tony Book: "That early goal was a tremendous boost for Albion, but it came so early that it didn't seriously worry us for we had another 85 minutes to wipe it out."

In the 20th minute, Francis Lee crossed to Mike Summerbee right in front of the Albion goal. He looked certain to score but John Talbut dashed in to clear. Then from a Pardoe corner, Albion's 'keeper John Osborne completely missed the ball and Lee sent it narrowly wide with a tumbling header. The equaliser seemed ever closer, especially as Oakes and Doyle dominated the midfield.

Despite City's efforts the deficit remained to the interval, although in the 27th minute a courageous dive from the developing Corrigan prevented Albion from scoring a second.

In the second half a powerful City searched for an equaliser, then in the 60th minute the inevitable occurred. From a Pardoe corner, Summerbee, who moments earlier had been writhing in agony, got a foot to the ball and hooked it goalwards. Bell headed across to the unmarked Doyle and with a tremendous roar from the City supporters, Doyle slid home the equaliser. It was certainly a goal City thoroughly deserved.

Shortly after Mike Summerbee was forced to leave the field with a hairline fracture of the leg. He was replaced by Ian Bowyer, while a little later Albion brought on Dick Krzywicki for future Blue Asa Hartford. At one point Tony Book and Jeff Astle were cautioned by the referee as both sides chased a winner.

Joe Corrigan was keen to prevent Albion from scoring again, as he revealed later: "I was given a real roasting at half time because of that goal but after the equaliser I was determined another shot was not going to pass me."

Francis Lee, playing what many believe to be the best game of his career, came close on a number of

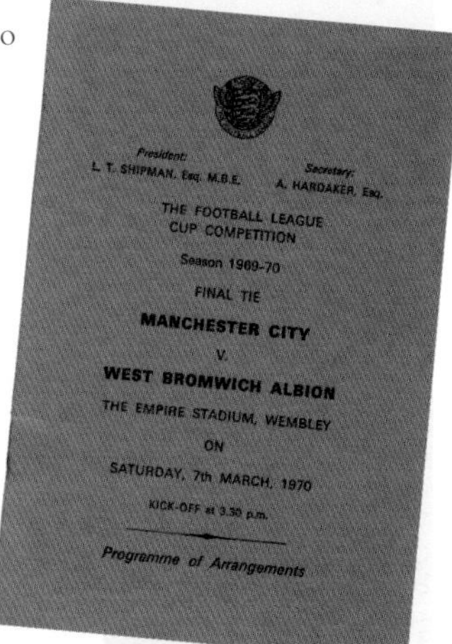

The 'Programme of Arrangements' for VIP guests at Wembley in 1970.

Mike Doyle raises his arms in celebration after steering the equaliser through Albion's packed defence.

City number 11 Glyn Pardoe grabs a dramatic Wembley winner against West Bromwich Albion (above) and on the final whistle Joe Corrigan celebrates the League Cup success by picking up team-mate Arthur Mann.

occasions, but the Final was forced to enter extra-time. Although the conditions and the events of the previous few days affected the players, extra-time helped to prove that City, and in particular Malcolm Allison, had been right to push the players so hard in training. His efforts to tune up their levels of fitness were to reap rich rewards at Wembley.

The City men dominated the additional thirty minutes and in the 102nd minute Francis Lee chipped the ball to Colin Bell who, despite being confronted by two Albion defenders, back-heeled to Pardoe, who flicked the ball over the Albion goal line to give City a 2-1 lead.

Pardoe was justifiably pleased with his performance: "Wembley is not a bad place to score your first goal of the season! I feel I am really suited to this midfield role because it gets me more involved in the game. I thought I played one of my best ever games and once the equaliser had gone in there was never any doubt about who would win."

The additional goal was enough, as Pardoe suggested, and at the final whistle the customary celebrations began. Francis Lee deserved more acclaim than most after an absolutely brilliant performance. David Meek, writing in the *Manchester Evening News* was glowing in his praise: "At Wembley we saw just how dangerous Lee in full cry can be. He took a tremendous physical pounding yet never flinched. City just could not have lost the League Cup with such a performance in their midst.

"The ex-Bolton man who made his League debut at the age of 16 is still only 25 and it looks as if his career, in which he has many caps to come, could reach its peak in Mexico this summer. He could play as big a part in England's fortunes as he did for City at Wembley this weekend. Certainly Albion had no answer except a great display by goalkeeper John Osborne."

The City victory gave the Blues a place in the

City celebrate their first League Cup win... Tony Book holds the Cup aloft at Wembley and goalscorers Glyn Pardoe and Mike Doyle pose for the photographers with Joe Mercer at the Grosvenor Square banquet.

1970 LEAGUE CUP RUN

R2	Southport	A	W	3-0
R3	Liverpool	H	W	3-2
R4	Everton	H	W	2-0
R5	Queen's Park Rangers	H	W	3-0
SF1	Manchester United	H	W	2-1
SF2	Manchester United	A	D	2-2
F	West Bromwich Albion	N**	W	2-1

** = Wembley Stadium

FACTS & FIGURES

	P	W	D	L	F	A
HOME	4	4	0	0	10	3
AWAY	3	2	1	0	7	3
TOTAL	7	6	1	0	17	6

CUP FINAL DETAILS

7 March 1970 at Wembley Stadium

MANCHESTER CITY 2
WEST BROMWICH ALBION 1

CITY: Corrigan, Book, Mann, Doyle, Booth, Oakes, Heslop, Bell, Summerbee (Bowyer), Lee, Pardoe
WEST BROMWICH ALBION: Osborne, Fraser, Wilson, Brown, Talbut, Kaye, Cantello, Suggett, Astle, Hartford (Krzywicki), Hope.
GOALS: Pardoe, Doyle, Astle

ATTENDANCE: 97,963
REFEREE: V James (York)
GUEST OF HONOUR: Princess Anne
MANAGER: Joe Mercer
CAPTAIN: Tony Book

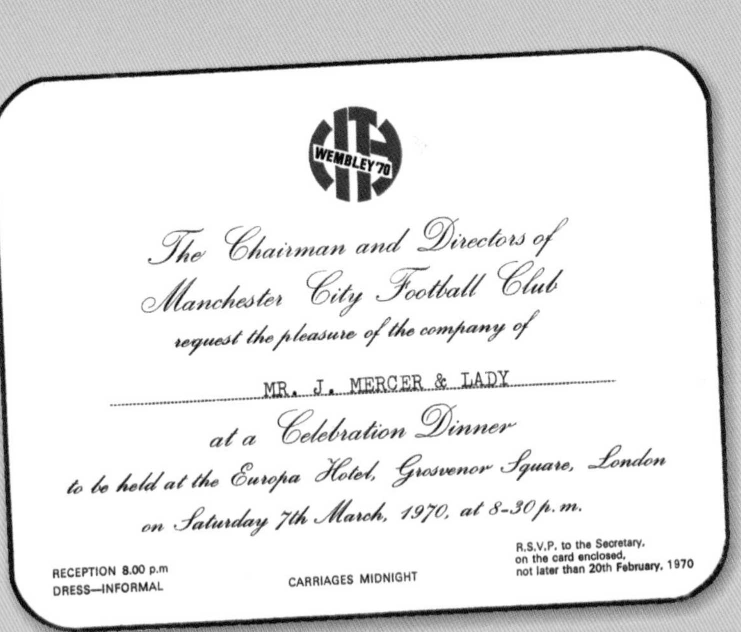
WEMBLEY '70

The Chairman and Directors of
Manchester City Football Club
request the pleasure of the company of

MR. J. MERCER & LADY

at a Celebration Dinner
to be held at the Europa Hotel, Grosvenor Square, London
on Saturday 7th March, 1970, at 8-30 p.m.

RECEPTION 8.00 p.m
DRESS—INFORMAL

CARRIAGES MIDNIGHT

R.S.V.P. to the Secretary,
on the card enclosed,
not later than 20th February, 1970

Some extremely valuable souvenirs of City's first League Cup Final appearance... Joe and Norah Mercer's invitation and programme/menu for the Europa Hotel Celebration Dinner.

WEMBLEY '70

MANCHESTER CITY
FOOTBALL CLUB

THE FOOTBALL LEAGUE CUP
FINAL TIE

Celebration
Dinner

AT
THE EUROPA HOTEL
GROSVENOR SQUARE
LONDON W.1
SATURDAY, 7th MARCH 1970

Fairs Cup and that meant Manchester United's only chance of playing in Europe would come if City also found success in the European Cup Winners' Cup. At the time of the League Cup Final United were aiming to qualify for Europe via League placing. Once City found success, United would be excluded as, at this time, only one team per city was allowed to enter the Fairs Cup. It was a ludicrous system, but one well-known Red-hater Mike Doyle was able to joke about: "That's not bad for my new campaign and car stickers ... 'Keep United out of Europe'."

Joe Mercer also found the affair amusing: "If we can win the Cup Winners' Cup and so qualify to defend it next season, maybe the authorities will let us flog our Fairs Cup place to the highest bidders."

In the end United's League form prevented them from finishing high enough to reach Europe regardless of City's performance.

On Sunday 8th March City embarked on another tour of Manchester, before a civic reception at the Town Hall. In appalling weather City's loyal fans once again turned out to see their heroes but, unlike previous seasons, the Blues still had a chance of further success. Many fans must have wondered just how far this great side could go. Within eight weeks they would find the answer.

On 18th March the Blues were due to play Coimbra in the second leg of their Cup Winners' Cup quarter final tie. Before that, however, City had to entertain Crystal Palace at Maine Road. The game ended in a disappointing 1-0 defeat and was not the kind of preparation the Blues needed for a crucial European tie. Nevertheless City went into their match with Coimbra believing they held the upper hand. A victory at Maine Road looked likely, although it was still a difficult game.

Colin Bell and George Heslop were injured during the match, and the Blues were prevented from playing the brand of football they enjoyed. Tony Towers and Chris Glennon came on as replacements, but other players went down injured, including Mike Doyle who had to be carried off. Displaying typical fighting spirit, Doyle returned to action a little later in the match.

It was heading for another goalless draw as the tie entered extra time, and little separated the sides. Then at around 9.45 pm. Neil Young sent a pass from the left to Towers, who had time to control the ball before his right foot shot powered it past the 19 year old Coimbra goalkeeper Cardoso. The goal brought a huge sigh of relief to the City faithful, and was enough to carry the Blues into the semi-finals.

The next opponents were Schalke '04 of West Germany on 1st April. Schalke had once tried to sign Bert Trautmann, and rumours circulating during the late 1960s claimed Schalke had been such a popular and successful club prior to World War Two they were Adolf Hitler's favourite side!

They were still a formidable team, and in the first leg at Gelsenkirchen defeated City 1-0. Despite the scoreline, City played well and were quietly confident of success in the return fixture. The relatively inexperienced Derek Jeffries was drafted into defence and performed better than most expected, while Joe Corrigan played one of his best games of his first full season, although even his fine performance had no chance of saving Libuda's magnificent goal in the 77th minute.

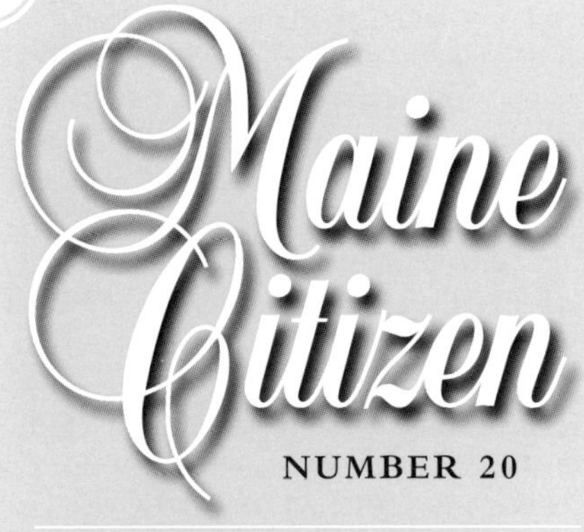

NUMBER 20

MIKE SUMMERBEE

SUMMERBEE'S PLAYING RECORD

	LEAGUE		FA CUP		FL CUP		EUROPE		TOTAL	
	App	Gls	App	Gls	App	Gls	App	Gls	App	Gls
1965-66	42	8	8	2	2	0	-	-	52	10
1966-67	32	4	4	2	2	1	-	-	38	7
1967-68	41	14	4	4	4	2	-	-	49	20
1968-69	39	6	6	0	3	2	2	0	50	8
1969-70	32(1)	3	2	0	7	2	7	1	48(1)	6
1970-71	26	4	2	0	1	0	6	0	35	4
1971-72	40	3	2	0	2	0	-	-	44	3
1972-73	38	2	4	1	2	0	1	0	45	3
1973-74	39	1	2	2	11	1	-	-	52	4
1974-75	26(1)	2	0	0	2	0	-	-	28(1)	2
TOTAL	355(2)	47	34	11	36	8	16	1	441(2)	67

Mike Summerbee was the second player brought to Maine Road by new manager Joe Mercer in 1965. The first, Ralph Brand, was not a success whereas Summerbee went on to become one of the most famous City players of all time.

Throughout his managerial career, Mercer had kept a watch on Summerbee's development, and always felt the player would do an excellent job for him. The opportunity to sign him only really arrived at Maine Road, but once it did Mercer couldn't wait.

In Manchester, Mercer really saw what Summerbee was capable of and delighted in telling others of the player's strengths: "He is an attacking player. In fact I would say that he is one of the best players there is with his back to the game. It is more difficult playing as a forward, because basically one is receiving the ball the wrong way, and the hardest thing in football is to turn round with the ball, especially with defensive football where they mark tight. Mike is the best, or the bravest, player with his back to the game that I have seen. He is strong when he is going past them. When he is buzzing he takes them all apart. He is very positive and quite a character."

Summerbee was signed on 20th August for a fee of around £35,000 from Swindon Town. More a provider than a goalscorer, within nine months of his arrival he helped the Blues achieve promotion in style by setting up chance after chance and scoring eight goals in 42 matches. In fact, he was the only ever-present that term. Over the following four seasons he helped City win an incredible four trophies although he was unfortunate to miss, through injury, City's last great final of the period, the ECWC final in Vienna. He played in seven of the eight European ties leading up to the final, and deserves to be recognised for his part in City's first European success.

In addition to his exploits on the pitch, Summerbee often entertained the Blues with practical jokes and his performances in the annual club pantomime. To fans he always seemed to enjoy his time at Maine Road, and quickly became a favourite with a large proportion of supporters. Because of his surname and his footballing style he was understandably nicknamed 'Buzzer', and there was nothing more enjoyable than the sight of him flying up the wing. The 1969 Cup Final goal owed much to Summerbee's typical determination and understanding of the game. He gathered a throw-in from Lee, raced down the right, slipped the ball past Leicester's David Nish, and centred to Young who crashed the ball past Shilton. An important winning goal, created by a popular player.

He also proved popular with a large contingent of England supporters, and should have been a regular in the international side for many years. As it was he made his debut on 24th February 1968 against Scotland, at the age of 25, and made his eighth and final appearance five years later against the USSR.

The post-Mercer period was not particularly enjoyable for Summerbee, although he did play in the 1974 League Cup Final. In June 1975 he joined Burnley for £25,000, then Blackpool, before becoming player-manager at Stockport under Chairman Freddie Pye.

During the 1990s he helped Francis Lee launch his take-over of City, and following the successful completion of that returned to the club to assist the Commercial Department with sales of City's corporate facilities. In 2002 he announced that, together with his son Nicky, he was to buy the 'Britannia Inn' next to the new City of Manchester Stadium. Nicky, it should be remembered also played for the Blues, making over 150 League and cup appearances between June 1994 and November 1997.

A moment of Mike's fame that must be recorded here is his performance in the footballing, war film "Escape To Victory" (Kaziu Deyna also appeared). Typical Summerbee - always the showman!

In attack City had several opportunities with Bell, Young, and Lee all coming close at one stage or another. In fact, Lee could quite easily have scored a hat trick had luck been on his side. This was what gave City hope for the second leg.

Before the return game, however, City had three difficult League matches to play in five days. On 4th April they were defeated 1-0 by Sunderland thanks to a strike from future Blue Dennis Tueart, then two days later at Crystal Palace lost by the same scoreline, although the game was noteworthy as it saw the full League debut of Willie Donachie. Then on the 8th the Blues managed to earn a 0-0 draw against Southampton who needed the point to stay up. City rarely troubled the Saints' defence with the Blues' best effort coming from Lee. His shot flew wide and hit a policeman's helmet, providing much amusement but not the goal required.

And so came the vital European match on 15th April. The confidence the players felt after the first leg proved justified as City dominated the match, playing irresistible football. As early as the ninth minute Mike Doyle gave the Blues an opening goal, then five minutes later Neil Young controlled the ball superbly and scored his first goal since the January F.A. Cup tie with Hull. In the 27th minute he netted his second, and then seven minutes into the second half Francis Lee scored City's fourth of the night.

Colin Bell made it five late on, and then in the final minute or so Libuda gave Schalke a consolation goal. This was the first real effort to trouble Corrigan, who played all night with a broken nose. City were on the way to Vienna for their first European final, although they did not discover their opponents until seven days before the game. Gornik Zabrze of Poland eventually beat AS Roma of Italy in a replay in Strasbourg.

Before the final City had two League games left to complete their domestic programme. The first saw the Blues defeat Leeds at Elland Road 3-1 with goals from Bell, Young and Towers. Before that match former Blue Don Revie lined up his players to applaud City's European exploits: "I am delighted City have got through and naturally I hope they win the trophy."

The final League game was away to struggling Sheffield Wednesday. The home side still had a chance of avoiding relegation and 45,258 turned up expecting salvation, but left deflated. City tore Wednesday apart, although the scoreline hardly reflected the true difference between the two sides. Ian Bowyer, replacing the injured Summerbee, scored first, but former Blue Tony Coleman pulled one back for the home side. In the final minute, Bowyer scored his second to send Wednesday down.

It was a bitter blow for the Yorkshiremen and the first in a series of setbacks that would see them plummet to 20th position in the Third Division by 1976. Indeed Wednesday remained very much a 'fallen giant' until the two sides met in the League again during 1983.

The 2-1 victory gave City a great boost, but it also brought more concern over players' fitness. Mike Summerbee, who had been struggling ever since the League Cup Final, was now unable to play in Vienna while Alan Oakes was set to play but was far from fully fit.

Francis Lee takes on Leeds' Jack Charlton during City's 3-1 win at Elland Road in April 1970.

Cup Winners' Cup Winners 1970

The European Cup Winners' Cup Final was played in torrential rain in the uncovered Prater Stadium in Vienna, with City in determined mood.

In the 12th minute Francis Lee's shot proved too much for goalkeeper Kostka to hold and Neil Young followed up to give the Blues the lead. Midway through the first half, however, City suffered a few injury worries when Mike Doyle badly damaged an ankle tendon in a collision with Flerenski. He was carried off on the shoulders of Dave Ewing and replaced by Ian Bowyer.

Shortly before the half-time interval City increased their lead when Young broke free in the centre. As he attempted to dribble through the penalty area he was brought down by Kostka. The Austrian referee Schiller rightly awarded a penalty and inevitably Francis Lee belted a straight, hard shot into the net.

In the 68th minute Gornik's captain Oslizlo pulled one back, but City remained in overall control. At the final whistle the City fans, who numbered some four or five thousand in a crowd variously reported as anything from 7,968 to around 12,000, started the now customary celebrations. Many drenched but happy Blues raced onto the field to celebrate. Supporter Martin Dodd: "My brother managed to get on to the pitch at the final whistle and was rewarded with Tommy Booth's shirt which we still have." City were well and truly a major force in the domestic game, although on the night of the Final the majority of the English public were more concerned with the replayed F.A. Cup Final between Chelsea and Leeds at Old Trafford. Had the F.A. Cup been resolved at Wembley, City's success would have been guaranteed major exposure across the nation.

After the game the City players and staff enjoyed their end of season party. Mercer and Allison naturally joined in but they were not the main stars of the celebrations. Allison: "It was a great night. Perfect. Back at the hotel Harry Godwin, our Chief Scout, was playing the piano - all the old songs - while Francis Lee was on top, dancing away, in his underpants. It had to be seen to be believed. But that was the type of thing we did."

City returned home to another civic reception - their fourth since May 1968 - and a ten mile tour of the City, starting at the airport. How much more could this side achieve?

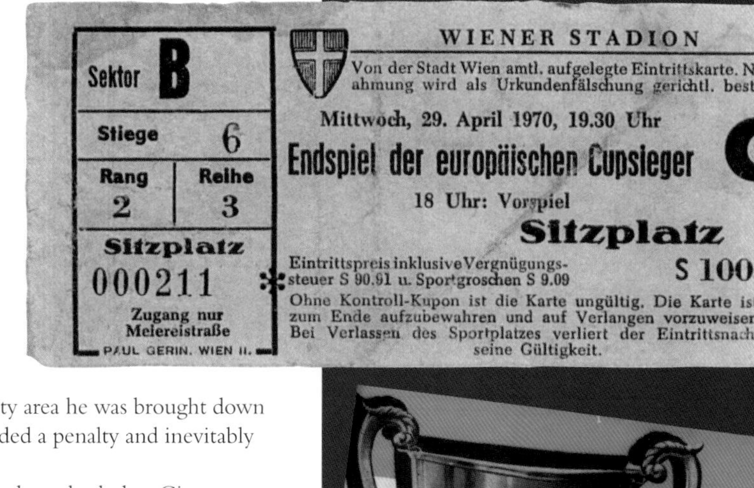

Sektor B
Stiege 6
Rang 2 | Reihe 3
Sitzplatz
000211
Zugang nur Meiereistraße
PAUL GERIN, WIEN II.

WIENER STADION
Von der Stadt Wien amtl. aufgelegte Eintrittskarte. Nachahmung wird als Urkundenfälschung gerichtl. bestraft.
Mittwoch, 29. April 1970, 19.30 Uhr
Endspiel der europäischen Cupsieger G
18 Uhr: Vorspiel
Sitzplatz
Eintrittspreis inklusive Vergnügungssteuer S 90.91 u. Sportgroschen S 9.09 S 100.—
Ohne Kontroll-Kupon ist die Karte ungültig. Die Karte ist bis zum Ende aufzubewahren und auf Verlangen vorzuweisen. — Bei Verlassen des Sportplatzes verliert der Eintrittsnachweis seine Gültigkeit.

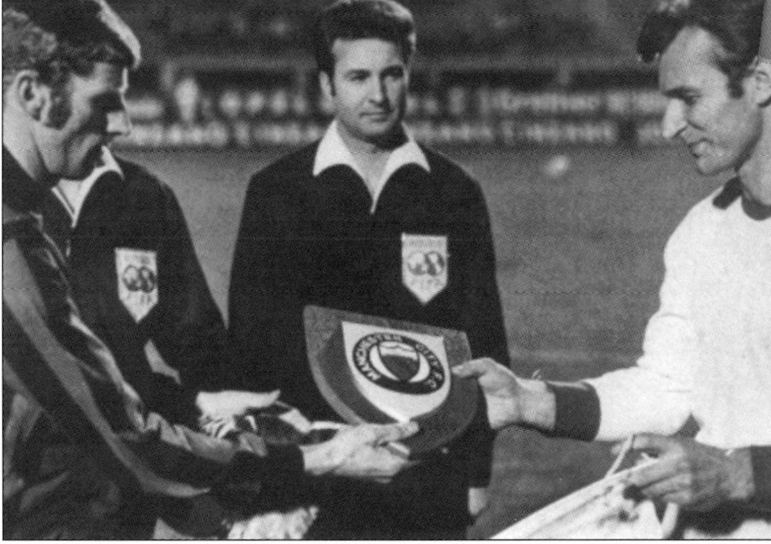

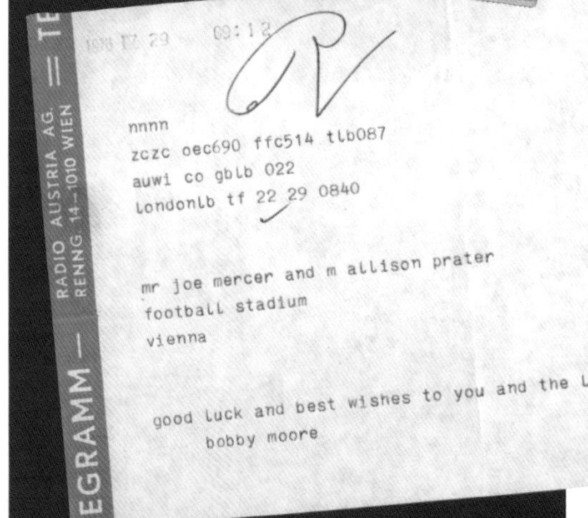

TELEGRAMM — RADIO AUSTRIA AG. RENNG. 14-1010 WIEN

nnnn
zczc oec690 ffc514 tlb087
auwi co gblb 022
londonlb tf 22 29 0840 673

mr joe mercer and m allison prater
football stadium
vienna

good luck and best wishes to you and the lads
bobby moore

City skipper Tony Book exchanges gifts with his Gornik counterpart Oslizio.

Right: A ticket for the final, the official programme, and a good luck telegram sent to Joe Mercer and Malcolm Allison by England captain Bobby Moore.

THE GOALS THAT SECURED CITY'S FIRST EUROPEAN TROPHY

Above: Neil Young prepares to shoot the opening goal of the Vienna final after Gornik goalkeeper Kostka saved Francis Lee's effort.

Below: Lee's penalty kick proves too powerful for the Polish 'keeper.

EUROPEAN CUP WINNERS' CUP
FINAL TIE

Played at

THE VIENNA STADIUM

MANCHESTER CITY

versus

GORNIK ZABRZE

WEDNESDAY

29th April

1970

Kick-off 7.30 p.m.

ARRANGEMENTS

TUESDAY, 28th APRIL, 1970

9.30 a.m. Assemble Manchester Airport.
11.00 a.m. Depart by B.E.A. Comet. Lunch will be served en route. Drinks for consumption on board the aircraft will be offered with the compliments of British European Airways. Cigarettes will be available for sale on a cash basis.
1.15 p.m. Arrive Vienna Airport. Coaches to Park Hotel and Hotel Kahlenberg. The programme for the remainder of the day will be announced after arrival at Hotel.

WEDNESDAY, 29th APRIL 1970

Breakfast
The programme for the day will be announced after breakfast. Lunch. Tea.
6.00 p.m. Transport to Vienna Stadium. 7.30 p.m. kick-off
If the match is a draw after 90 minutes extra time of 2 × 15 minutes will be played. If the result is still a draw the match will be replayed at the Vienna Stadium Friday 1st May 1970.

THURSDAY, 30th APRIL 1970

Breakfast
9.30 a.m. Transport to Vienna Airport.
12 noon Depart Vienna Airport. Lunch en route.
2.25 p.m. Arrive Manchester Airport.
Coaches to Town Hall for reception by the Lord Mayor and the Corporation of Manchester.

GENERAL NOTES

Each person must be in possession of a valid passport.

Each person will be responsible for his/her own baggage when passing through Customs.

Baggage allowance 40 lbs per person.

CURRENCY

Each person is allowed to take £25 in English currency out of the country.

A limited amount of Austrian currency will be available for Officials and Players.

W. GRIFFITHS, *Secretary*
Maine Road, Moss Side,
Manchester, M14 7WM.
Telephone: 061-226 1191

An arrangements card issued to all players, management and staff who travelled to the final with City.

Ihr größter Erfolg: Europacup!

How City's success was reported in Germany.

Joe Mercer brings the Cup Winners' Cup back to Manchester.

1970 ECWC RUN

R1(1)	Athletico Bilbao	A	D	3-3
R1(2)	Athletico Bilbao	H	W	3-0
R2(1)	SK Lierse	A	W	3-0
R2(2)	SK Lierse	H	W	5-0
R3(1)	Academica Coimbra	A	D	0-0
R3(2)	Academica Coimbra	H	W	1-0
SF1	Schalke 04	A	L	0-1
SF2	Schalke 04	H	W	5-1
F	Gornik Zabrze	N*	W	2-1

* = Prater Stadium, Vienna

FACTS & FIGURES

	P	W	D	L	F	A
HOME	4	4	0	0	14	1
AWAY	5	2	2	1	8	5
TOTAL	9	6	2	1	22	6

CUP FINAL DETAILS

29 April 1970 at Prater Stadium, Vienna

MANCHESTER CITY 2
GORNIK ZABRZE 1

CITY: Corrigan, Book, Pardoe, Doyle (Bowyer), Booth, Oakes, Heslop, Bell, Lee, Young, Towers

GORNIK: Kostka, Latocha, Oslizlo, Gorgon, Flerenski (Deja), Szoltysik, Wilczek (Skowronek), Olek, Banas, Lubanski, Szarinski

GOALS: Young, Lee (pen), Oslizlo

ATTENDANCE: Variously reported as anything from 7,968 to 12,000
REFEREE: P Schiller (Austria)
MANAGER: Joe Mercer
CAPTAIN: Tony Book

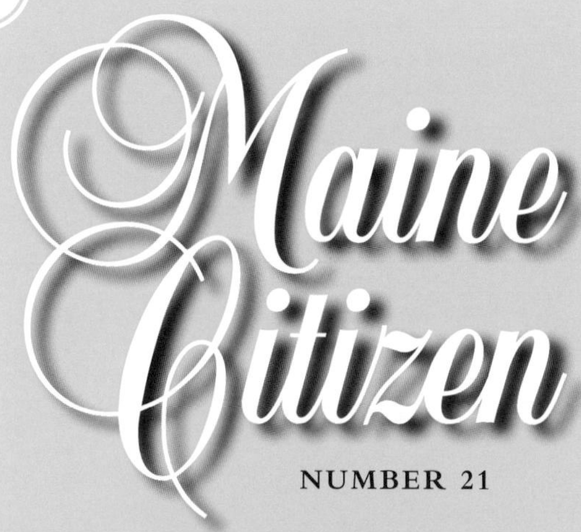

NUMBER 21

FRANCIS LEE

Francis Lee's impact on the fortunes of Manchester City has been incredible, both as a player and in the mid nineties as Chairman. Lee was perhaps the final piece of the Mercer-Allison team jigsaw when he signed on 9th October 1967. His arrival helped City push for the title, and brought a new dimension to the team's play. His bustling style and dogged tenacity was loved by supporters and helped bring victory in so many important games.

Although he failed to make the scoresheet in the 1970 League Cup Final it is true to say that this was the game which really made the outside world understand just how talented a player Lee was. It was perhaps his greatest City match, but then again there were so many fine performances while he wore the City blue. Both Mercer and Allison had been keen to sign Lee for some time, but his prolonged transfer from Bolton kept them waiting. Once he arrived in Manchester Lee's value was soon clear as he scored 16 goals in only 31 matches to bring the title back to Maine Road.

Mercer always rated his determination and style: "Once he is going towards the box, he is probably the most dynamic and exciting player in the world. Francis starts to play where other people finish off. Bobby Charlton finishes just in the penalty area and should get more goals than he does, but this is where Francis shows his strength. He is squat and strong, and so very, very brave. He really goes at them in the box."

Some opponents and, for that matter many writers, believed Lee's role inside the box was often to dive to earn City a penalty. This is simply incorrect, and was perhaps indicative of some jealousy from City's critics. During the early 70s Lee did score an incredible number of penalties, but these were often a result of handball, or fouls on other players. Even fouls on Lee did not always produce what could be described as 'dives', but the accusations seemed to stick. Most City fans prefer the more sensible view that any penalty awarded for a foul on Lee, was because the opposition were so desperate to stop him scoring, that hacking him down was their only option. Even then, Lee's ferocious penalty expertise more or less guaranteed a goal.

Ironically, in 1969 Lee was asked to take two penalties for England and missed them both (against Wales and Portugal), but overall his England record was a good one. He made his international debut on 11th December 1968 in a 1-1 draw with Bulgaria, and his last appearance in the 3-1 defeat by West Germany in April 1972, on his 28th birthday. He scored England's consolation goal in that, his 27th international. In total he scored on ten occasions.

To this day he firmly believes he could have made a difference had he been given the chance to play in England's crucial World Cup qualifier with Poland in October 1973, but it wasn't to be and English football fell apart for a while as a result.

Lee's last League appearance for City was the controversial Manchester derby on the last day of the 1973-4 season, after which he joined Derby County, helping them to the League title. In 1976 he retired and seemed to turn his back on football to concentrate on his paper manufacturing business, which he had set up during the 1960s. He also started to pursue another successful career as an owner and trainer of racehorses.

Throughout the 1980s his name was forever being mentioned as a possible candidate to take over the Chairmanship of the club from Peter Swales, but whenever asked he admitted he was far too busy with his other interests to even contemplate a return to football. Nevertheless, supporters still talked about the possibility. It must be said they also talked about Rodney Marsh returning as Chairman as well.

Then in 1993, with City increasingly becoming the laughing stock of the British game, Lee told the Mirror's Alec Johnson that he was prepared to help his former club.

After many months of struggle, Lee finally gained control in February 1994. Over the course of the following three seasons, Lee reshaped the club and developed a strong commercial emphasis in a bid to strengthen the club's finances and position.

Sadly, the first managerial selections of Lee's new board were not the best - supporters were dumbstruck when Colin Barlow announced the arrival of Alan Ball – and the expectation that City would quickly re-establish itself as one of Europe's elite could not be satisfied. In fact by the time of Lee's resignation as chairman during 1997-8, the Blues were heading for relegation to the third tier of English football for the first time in their history.

Whatever the issues with Lee's stint at the top, it is clear he remains a very popular City personality. His spell as chairman did revitalise parts of the club, but it's his years as a player by which most supporters will remember him.

He will go down in history as one of the greatest City and England players of all time.

LEE'S PLAYING RECORD

	LEAGUE		FA CUP		FL CUP		EUROPE		TOTAL	
	App	Gls	App	Gls	App	Gls	App	Gls	App	Gls
1967-68	31	16	4	1	0	0	-	-	35	17
1968-69	37	12	7	4	3	0	2	0	49	16
1969-70	36	13	2	0	7	3	9	6	54	22
1970-71	38	14	2	0	1	1	9	4	50	19
1971-72	42	33	2	1	2	1	-	-	46	35
1972-73	35	14	5	1	2	1	2	0	44	16
1973-74	29(1)	10	2	0	11	8	-	-	42(1)	18
TOTAL	248(1)	112	24	7	26	14	22	10	320(1)	143

Note: Francis Lee also appeared in four Charity Shield matches, scoring three goals. To ensure consistency with the other players featured in this book, Charity Shield appearances have not been included in the above figures.

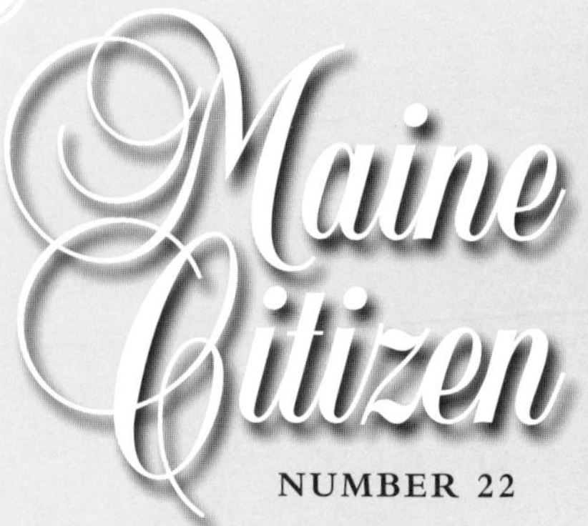

NUMBER 22

ALAN OAKES

When Alan Oakes joined City as an amateur in April 1958, he joined a team in decline, as the side that had been so successful only two years earlier were struggling in the First Division. He signed professional forms in September 1959 and made his debut on 14th November the same year. By the time of City's relegation in 1963 he was already a familiar member of the first team.

Despite the gloomy picture of City's performances during the late 50s/early 60s, there were still some famous players at Maine Road. These figures helped Oakes learn the game, even though the Winsford-born youngster was always given some of the messier jobs: "I always seemed to clean Bert Trautmann's boots. It was one of my responsibilities. He liked them good and clean. I got on well with Bert. He was always very helpful."

Apart from learning from some of football's greats, those early years didn't really do the player justice as the Blues continually struggled. Oakes, however, was one of the most consistent members of the team, and often the first player picked by McDowall, and then Poyser. The infamous game against Swindon in January 1965 proved how vital Oakes was at this time, when he netted a fine goal in an otherwise dismal match.

The summer of 1965 brought Mercer and Allison to Maine Road and, although no one realised it at the time, more or less guaranteed Oakes would receive the kind of reward he richly deserved. Both members of the management team seemed impressed with him. Allison: "When I first came to Maine Road it was good to find players of Alan Oakes' quality already here. At that time he suffered a bit from nervous tension

which restricted his ability sometimes. He has overcome that, and largely he has fought that battle alone. As any City fan will know, Alan has played a major part in all the prize-winning teams.

"Alan is one of the most conscientious trainers I have ever worked with ... always in top class physical condition and always willing to learn and improve."

Two of football's greatest managers also believed him to be a model professional. Bill Shankly: "The very best type of professional, on the field and off it ... exactly the kind of player youngsters should use as a model. If anything he is probably a better player at the back because of his ability to hit those long passes out of defence."

Don Revie: "A lot of people might not notice Alan as much as some other players. But the professionals certainly notice him. He's one of the salt players as we call them ... absolutely necessary, making life a lot easier for fellows up front. He's been a great servant to City."

Overall, Oakes had an amazing career and became City's record appearance holder with 665 (plus 4 as substitute) first team appearances. He has also won more trophies than any other player while with City - the ECWC, League Championship, F.A. Cup, 2 League Cups, and the Second Division Championship. Perhaps it says something about his contribution that the only final he missed, was the only one to end in defeat during his Maine Road career (1974 League Cup - Mike Doyle played in this and each of the other finals, but only managed to make 19 appearances during the promotion season).

In July 1976 - after a career that spanned Bert Trautmann, Ken Barnes Bobby Johnstone, Gary Owen (who was born three months after Oakes joined City in 1958), Peter Barnes and Dennis Tueart - he moved on to Chester for £15,000. Later he became player-manager, then coach with Port Vale. During the 1990s his son Michael became a goalkeeper with Aston Villa.

Alan Oakes was always the model professional and a great City star.

OAKES' PLAYING RECORD

	LEAGUE		FA CUP		FL CUP		EUROPE		TOTAL	
	App	Gls	App	Gls	App	Gls	App	Gls	App	Gls
1959-60	18	0	1	0	-	-	-	-	19	0
1960-61	22	0	0	0	0	0	-	-	22	0
1961-62	25	1	0	0	0	0	-	-	25	1
1962-63	34	3	2	0	4	1	-	-	40	4
1963-64	41	3	1	1	6	0	-	-	48	3
1964-65	41	4	2	0	1	0	-	-	44	4
1965-66	41	1	8	0	2	0	-	-	51	1
1966-67	39	2	6	0	2	0	-	-	47	2
1967-68	41	2	4	0	4	1	-	-	49	3
1968-69	39	0	7	0	3	0	2	0	51	0
1969-70	40	3	2	0	7	1	9	1	58	5
1970-71	30	1	3	0	1	0	4	0	38	1
1971-72	31(1)	0	2	0	0	0	-	-	33(1)	0
1972-73	13(1)	1	0	0	0(1)	0	2	0	15(2)	1
1973-74	28	0	0	0	5	0	-	-	33	0
1974-75	40	2	1	0	2	0	-	-	43	2
1975-76	38(1)	3	2	1	9	2	-	-	49(1)	6
TOTAL	561(3)	26	41	2	46(1)	5	17	1	665(4)	33

Chapter Fifteen

GOODBYE OLD FRIENDS

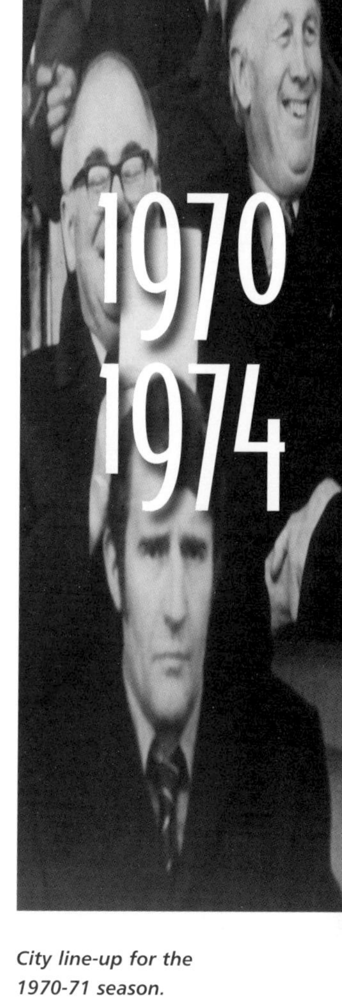

FOLLOWING the successes of 1969-70, City fans could be forgiven if they appeared optimistic about the chance of further glory. The Blues were one of the most attractive, entertaining sides in Europe and had won many admirers. Their hard-core support was on the increase and the media were at long last taking notice of events in Manchester 14. It seemed the Blues just couldn't fail.

In typical City style however, other events of the early 1970s, instigated by people closely connected with the club, would jeopardise City's position and indeed continue to affect the Blues for the following twenty-five years - possibly longer.

It all started to go wrong shortly after the European Cup Winners' Cup success. Malcolm Allison was finding it difficult playing a supporting role. He felt he deserved the position of Team Manager and believed that, right at the start of their partnership, Joe Mercer had promised to stand aside by August 1968. That never occurred and Allison felt bitterness towards Mercer, and others at Maine Road: "I was not satisfied with the way the club was being run. I felt the club had become big, but that the people in control in the Boardroom had not grown with it. I liked and admired Albert Alexander, the little, twinkling Chairman, but some of the people around him staggered me with their lack of vision. The secretary Walter Griffiths and I were often in dispute and the Board would back him on small administrative matters, like the size of hotel bills. I used to think to myself, 'What is all this, I've helped lift this club from the grave and now I get this sort of treatment'."

City line-up for the 1970-71 season.

Back row (left to right): David Connor, Glyn Pardoe, George Heslop, Harry Dowd, Joe Corrigan, Ken Mulhearn, Arthur Mann, Tommy Booth, Mike Doyle, Alan Oakes, Derek Jeffries.

Front: Ian Bowyer, Fred Hill, Mike Summerbee, Francis Lee, Tony Book, Frank Carrodus, Neil Young, Colin Bell.

During the early 70s City developed a new club badge to wear on their shirts. An announcement on 29/8/70 in Shoot magazine showed the badge (above) which was basically the central part of the City of Manchester coat of arms (a yellow ship over a red shield with 3 yellow stripes emblazoned across), surrounded by two circles and the club's name. A form of this badge had been used in City programmes and documentation since the mid-60s, yet only survived until 1972 when the red/yellow shield was replaced by a red rose. This, more popular and familiar badge (below), was first seen in the City programme of 29/1/72 and survived until the summer of 1997.

Typical of the attitude that annoyed Allison was Secretary Griffiths' response to problems encountered with crowd congestion at the first couple of home matches in August 1971. The Scoreboard End was now closed for redevelopment, reducing the capacity, and putting 18 turnstiles out of action. Naturally, supporters had to endure longer queues than normal and were forced to search for new vantage points, but instead of apologising to spectators or offering some kind of assistance, Griffiths felt the responsibility lay entirely with City's loyal fans: "If people could try to get here a little bit earlier it would help everyone, most of all themselves."

Obviously, he had a point, but the approach seemed wrong. Allison felt City were still a 'small' club and believed the whole attitude at the place needed to be dragged into the modern 1970s. He wanted City to be the biggest club in the world and felt a dramatic shake up was the only way this could occur: "I had had enough of being patted on the head. I thought that if I was not going to be given what was my due, I would attempt to take it for myself."

Nothing public occurred for a while, and the new season began with the Blues determined to make an impact on the League. By 10th September after six games City were in second place behind Leeds United, and had earned many positive news reports. Dave Horridge *(Daily Mirror)*: "Manchester City have used the experience gained in becoming England's top knock-out trophy experts to emerge as potential League Champions again."

After City's 4-1 victory over West Bromwich Albion the *Daily Telegraph's* Frank Green wrote: "So immensely superior were City that, at half time, a colleague in the Press Box forecast a final score of 6-1 - a not unreasonable assessment considering City twice had strong claims for a penalty rejected."

Bob Russell *(Daily Mirror)*: "England boss Sir Alf Ramsey, checking among other things the Young England prospects of 18 year old City defender Tony Towers, must have sensed that Bell is already on the brink of greatness."

England Youth player Towers had already received a great deal of praise after a few impressive performances, with one reporter comparing him with England's great captain Bobby Moore. Despite the praise Towers himself remained level headed: "I've got to keep working at everything. I get some stick on and off the field, but I don't mind - as long as I am playing. I'm enjoying myself. During games I quite often get players on the other side saying things like, 'How do you manage to get in this team!' and other things to put you off."

With Towers, Bell and the bulk of the side playing well, the Blues remained undefeated in the League until 26th September when they lost 2-0 at Tottenham. Earlier in the month City's bid to retain the League Cup ended at the first hurdle with a 2-1 defeat at Carlisle. Allison: "We probably made more mistakes against Carlisle than in all our other games put together. I was very disappointed."

On 16th September City faced Linfield of Northern Ireland in the first round of the Cup Winners' Cup, determined to perform better than against Carlisle. The game ended 1-0 with a goal from the ever-improving Colin Bell, but the return game caused a little concern especially when it looked likely Francis Lee would be missing. The England striker was suffering with an inflamed groin and looked doubtful, causing Mercer to consider using youngster Ian Bowyer. Bowyer had first appeared for City during the 1968-9 season and for a period during 1969 was deservedly acclaimed by the press. At one point Alf Ramsey commented favourably about Bowyer's play, however a few poor games and minor setbacks made the player an easy target for sections of the City crowd.

For some players barracking can help their determination to succeed, but for Bowyer the pressure became unbearable: "I couldn't fail to hear some of the things people said. I know the fans have the right to criticise if they wish and I try hard to think of them kindly. But it became a bit of an ordeal for me last season, and the more I worried, the worse it got. I think it affected my game, for I tried to do things too hurriedly. But I never went running or complaining to the manager, or asking for a transfer. That would have been the cowardly way out."

In the end Lee did recover and played against Linfield. Sadly, Bowyer became very much a fringe player and was transferred to Orient during the close season. Later in his career he found much success, spending around a decade at Nottingham Forest.

City were defeated 2-1 in Belfast with Colin Bell scoring a vital late goal to put City through on the away goals rule. The draw for the next round meant a difficult trip behind the Iron Curtain to Hungary's Honved in the first leg. Francis Lee scored the only goal of the match, but the result should have been considerably better. Derek Potter *(Daily Express)*: "Glimpses of high quality skill allied to aggressive running saw Manchester City probe and pound Honved into submission in the Kispest Stadium. It could have been five following one of City's best ever displays."

Another report claimed City had eight good goal attempts in the first half and a further seven in the second, and were without doubt in full control of the match. Despite City's dominance Tony Book felt the Blues had to be careful in the return match: "I think Honved had a bad day in the first leg. I'm sure that they can be a much better side. Just because we are leading by one goal it would be a mistake to assume that it is all over. It's not over yet by a long chalk."

The official attendance in Budapest was recorded as 14,000, although other sources believed the real gate was closer to 6,000. The City officials agreed and consulted their opposite numbers, but the Hungarians were adamant the crowd was the higher figure, although they did concede it was considerably lower than expected. They put this down to the fact the game was shown live on state television, and the afternoon kick-off prevented many from attending. Whatever the truth, the atmosphere and attendance at Maine Road would be better.

In appalling conditions, a crowd of almost 29,000 witnessed more domination from the Manchester men. Bell and Lee provided the goals as City won 2-0, but at one point there was concern the match might get abandoned. Tony Book: "I'd been scared right from the start that the referee might call off the game. The rain was getting heavier. That really was our only worry. Of course, we adapted ourselves to the conditions better than they did, but even in the first 15 minutes, when the conditions were comparatively good, we were hitting them with everything. If the ground had stayed reasonably firm I am sure we would have murdered them."

The game had not been without its moments of concern, but in the main City were in control. Shortly before the interval Colin Bell and Honved right-winger Sandor Pinter leapt together for the ball, and the City man fell to the ground injured. He was stretchered off but, as the players lined up for the second half, he reappeared to a warm ovation.

After the game Honved manager Kalman Preiner was asked if he thought the game should have been allowed to continue. He stated the conditions were appalling but conceded City were able to adapt superbly, whereas his side could not. He added: "If they go on playing like this they must surely be favourites for the trophy."

City could now have a rest from European football until March when they would face old adversaries Gornik Zabrze in the quarter final. The draw excited the Manchester public, but before the game could take place club politics dominated the agenda. Allison, tired of playing second fiddle, wanted control.

In his autobiography, *'The Colours of My Life'*, he claimed to have set the wheels in motion for a take-over of the Blues: "I knew that the City Vice-Chairman Frank Johnson was ready to sell a huge chunk of shares for £100,000 and that the man who bought them had only to make one or two available alliances and he would win control of the club. So I said to Ian Niven, a fanatical City supporter: 'Find me a man with £100,000, and we will get control of the club'. Niven came up with the man within a fortnight, Joe Smith, a double glazing tycoon from Oldham."

On Monday 23rd November, two days after a brace from Lee gave City victory over West Ham, the take-over became national news. Genial 78 year old Chairman Albert Alexander awoke to find Joe Smith waiting for him: "I hadn't had my breakfast when he called on me. I told my wife to ask him to wait while I washed and shaved, and then I went downstairs and asked him straight out to put his cards on the table. I didn't recognise him. In effect he came to me as a stranger.

"As far as I know, he has no shares in the club at the moment. If he had, I would know about them. But I understand he is in a position to acquire the necessary number to gain control. I asked him if he had much support and he said he had, and that his supporters were known to me."

Expressing sentiments that would be repeated by one of his successors some twenty years later, Alexander said he was ready for a fight: "All I can say is that if anyone tries it, they will find I am a very tough nut to crack. We have had similar crises before and I have weathered them."

At this point in history, there were a total of 2,000 shares in the club. Alexander possessed 560, his son Eric held 27, while Frank Johnson seemed ready to sell 508 of his 521 allocation. Joe Smith claimed that with Johnson's shares he and his backers could obtain a total of 800 immediately and, as there were around 300 'missing' shares, he would have control. The following day every newspaper covered the story in detail, with Joe Smith quoted everywhere.

The *Daily Express* went further than most when it devoted its famous William Hickey page to Smith, in addition to covering the story on both its front and back pages. The take-over was sensational news at the time, with arguably England's most successful club of the period about to be torn apart. The public could not believe it. It wasn't seen as good news, nor was it really viewed as detrimental for the club, it was quite simply a big shock.

Some rare photographs from City's Cup Winners' Cup game against Honved in Budapest. Note the televison camera as the players wait to go onto the pitch - live TV coverage in Hungary was blamed for the low turnout. The action shot shows City being awarded a free-kick for a foul on the grounded Francis Lee. It was Lee who scored the only goal of the game. These photos are from the Mercer family collection.

STAR★
Award winning
Mobile Radiotelephones
STC Mobile Radiotelephones Ltd., 38 Broughton St., Cheetham, Manchester 8. 061-832 3245.
STC

EXTRA

Manchester Evening News
AND CHRONICLE

31,193 TUESDAY NOVEMBER 24 1970 6d

SALFORD VAN HIRE
5/7 CWT. OR LARGER
VANS FOR HIRE
TEL.: 792 3980 792 4459

I have power at City—Smith

By KEITH WARD and PETER GARDNER

BUSINESS TYCOON Mr Joe Smith today declared that he had power in Manchester City FC.

Mr Smith, boss of a £4M double glazing firm in Oldham, said that he and four colleagues had a legal agreement to guarantee that the 521 shares of City's vice-chairman Mr Frank Johnson would come to them.

Said Mr Smith: "This document was signed a few weeks ago. It is a legal document and I have paid £50,000 deposit. I can confirm that I now have power in the City club."

He said he was keeping in touch with his four colleagues, Mr Chris Muir, Mr Simon Cussons, Mr Michael Horwich and Mr Ian Niven over the City bid.

Mr Smith also pledged his loyalty to the club's chairman 78-year-old Mr Albert Alexander and declared that he wanted him to stay as head of the Board.

Talking of Mr Alexander and his future role at Maine Road, Mr Smith said: "Some people are getting at Mr Alexander and saying that he will be out when we move in.

"It is a certain clique. They are intimidating him. I will go to any extent to prove to him that I and my colleagues want him as chairman.

"If Mr Alexander wants a written statement to this effect I will give it to him gladly."

Mr Smith said the two reasons guiding his bid for Manchester City were firstly to ensure that coach Malcolm Allison stays with the club.

Secondly the club is not getting big enough attendances. Mr Smith said he knew Allison and the players were upset about the gates, and that surely in the end this was going to demoralise the players.

Mr Smith denied misleading Mr Alexander over the shares deal. He said he had told Mr Alexander that two former members of a "ginger group" were involved with him, Mr Muir and Mr Horwich.

Talking about Malcolm Allison, Mr Smith said City's ace coach had to be "protected" in his position at Maine Road.

Added Mr Smith: "Allison can work with the present chairman, and he gets 100 per cent co-operation. He can talk to Albert. If anything, God forbid, was to happen to the chairman and a new chairman was elected and Allison could not work in the new atmosphere, he might be tempted to move to another club."

Mr Smith continued: "I will do my utmost, everything in my power, to co-operate in any way in any project with Mr Allison to better the club. He is the greatest man in football."

The Muir-Horwich-Cussons combine have between them 345 shares.

Said Mr Muir today: "I have been involved in two previous disputes with the club. Now all I want is to work in harmony with the officials of Manchester City for the continuation of success and for even greater glories.

"There is not one ounce of vindictiveness in my nature. The past is history. It is the future that counts now."

But late this afternoon came yet another dramatic twist when the club issued an official statement which said: "We have had a board meeting today at which the vice-chairman Frank Johnson gave an explanation which we accepted, and so far as the board is concerned, at the present time, the matter is closed."

Earlier Mr Alexander said that Mr Smith had misled him.

Mr Alexander said he had seen an agreement transferring Mr Johnson's shares.

This latest explosive situa-

★ Turn to Back Page

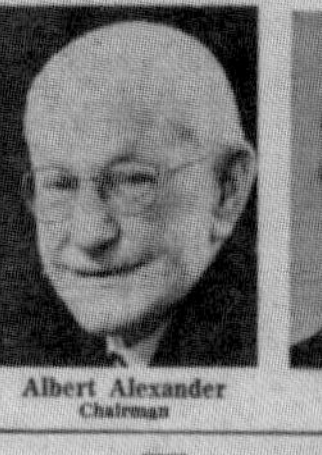
Albert Alexander
Chairman

Frank Johnson
Vice-chairman

Eric Alexander
Director

John Humphreys

DAILY EXPRESS Tuesday November 24 1970

16

THE TAKE-OVER MEN

PHOTO SPORT

...features the men who seek to take control of Manchester City. From the left: Chris Muir, Simon Cussons, Joe Smith, Michael Horwich and Ian Niven.

BIG FIVE WAIT ON MANCHESTER CITY GO-AHEAD

By JAMES LAWTON

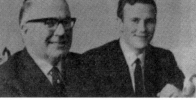

THE take-over of top football club Manchester City seemed to be moving irresistibly forward last night.

Joe Smith, leader of

make the next move now. We have stated our position and Mr. Alexander knows the situation. I was delighted with the friendly nature of our meeting this morning and obviously this is going to be done reasonably.

News of the takeover as reported in the Manchester Evening News and Daily Express on November 24th 1970.

Backing Smith was a group of four. They were 46 year old Ian Niven, landlord of the Fletcher's Arms in Denton; 27 year old Simon Cussons, a member of the 'Imperial Leather' soap manufacturing family; 48 year old Michael Horwich, a Manchester solicitor and alleged friend of Malcolm Allison; and 41 year old newsagent Chris Muir, a former City director who had been forced off the Board the year before for what the *Daily Sketch* described as 'an illegal action'.

In various articles, 51 year old Smith claimed he came from a poor family and hadn't been able to pay to watch the Blues, instead at the age of six he had waited outside Maine Road until the gates were opened near the end of each game, then rushed inside to catch the final ten minutes of action The picture painted was one of a loyal City supporter, and there was no doubt he loved the club. He also had a knack for making money but claimed his life needed a new interest: "I have a lovely house, a £5,500 American car, a luxury caravan and a boat on Windermere. Money is funny. All of a sudden you realise you are rich and for weeks you feel very excited. But it starts getting boring when you realise you can buy anything, there's nothing to fight for. So I go on setting myself challenges. All I want now is to see Manchester City become the greatest club there has ever been or ever will be in the world."

Malcolm Allison liked what he heard, especially when Smith expressed his support for him: "I will do my utmost, everything in my power, to co-operate in any way in any project with Mr. Allison to better the club. He is the greatest man in football."

Allison's role was one which left him open to criticism from the existing Board. The City coach made no attempt to hide his involvement nor his participation in discussions with the consortium. If Smith's vision was to turn City into the world's greatest club then this matched perfectly with Allison's view. The problem was any take-over was always likely to paralyse the club, for a short while at least. As was seen again in the 1990s, it takes time for any consortium to fulfil the promises made when bidding for power. Smith's ambitions may have been ideal, but achieving them would take considerable effort. Sadly, Smith never succeeded in realising his vision of turning City into the world's greatest club.

Many associated with the Blues during the early 1970s felt the club was not receiving the kind of support it deserved, nor did they feel City were a truly great club. Success had increased crowds and the Blues were on a par with Liverpool and Leeds - two of the era's greatest clubs - but some, including Allison, felt more had to be done at Board level to achieve greatness. Mercer was also keen to see City dominate European football, however his comments seemed more achievable and much more realistic: "When I first came to City with Malcolm Allison we found everyone was obsessed with a jealousy about Manchester United. We decided we must emulate them. We have not done too badly, winning everything we have gone in for. But support is a traditional thing. If we can keep winning things for the next five years I would expect our ground to be full every week."

On Tuesday 24th November, the Board met to consider the take-over. The meeting was a stormy affair, but the result was a pleasing one for Albert Alexander. Frank Johnson was persuaded not to sell his shares and afterwards told the media his about turn was simply because he felt he had been conned into the deal. He was quite prepared to sell to Smith, but not happy that Michael Horwich and former director Chris Muir were supporting Smith: "Had I known these people were involved I would never have entertained the idea of transferring my shares. There have been personality clashes in the past."

Naturally, Smith was determined to resurrect the deal and claimed to have a signed agreement from Johnson. It was all very messy and was destined to become a long battle, especially when Chris Muir, with 103 shares, announced: "It may take a day, it may take a week, it may take a few months, but eventually we will be in control."

Little Albert Alexander was particularly disturbed by the situation: "I'm very distressed about the way this thing has been handled. I didn't know the full extent of the other people backing Mr. Smith until this morning. There is no place for them here at Maine Road. When he saw me on Monday to disclose his plans Mr. Smith did not name the others. I now see I was being smooth-talked."

Despite the concern, Alexander still found time to laugh. After a couple of days of being pestered by the media he reminded the reporters of the previous week's top story: "I don't know - it was all Miss World last week, and it's all Albert Alexander this week!"

The comment caused a little amusement at the time, but unlike the story that Jennifer Hosten from Grenada had become Miss World, the Alexander-City take-over story would rumble on for some time. The acquisition became a long, difficult and confusing battle, and seriously affected the atmosphere within the club. Allison: "I took the players for a short training session on the Friday afternoon. We were due to play Leeds United at Elland Road the following day [28th November]. The players were a little hostile towards me. Francis Lee, Mike Summerbee, and Colin Bell came to me and said, 'Why try to change the club, Malcolm? We have done well. You do not change something that works'. I was very much out on a limb."

The Mercer-Allison partnership was also strained with the two men on opposite sides of the take-over. Allison was desperate for change, Mercer remained loyal to Alexander - the man who had given him and Allison the opportunity to prove their abilities. After a night of deep thought, Mercer told Allison he would support him but the decision was too late to really save the relationship.

Understandably after the hassles of the previous week City were defeated 1-0 by Leeds. Then, at around 6pm in an Elland Road corridor Alexander told Allison the Board had decided to sack him. It was not a shock, but Allison was surprised when Mercer arrived to warn the Chairman: "If he goes, I go!". That threat caused a change of mind and Allison was reinstated, but the partnership could hardly continue for any length of time.

The take-over seriously hampered City's chance of League success. Only four of the twenty-four League games that followed the Leeds match ended in victory and the Blues slid down the table. In the F.A. Cup a 72nd minute goal from Bell brought victory over Wigan in the third round, followed by a 3-0 win at Chelsea. Sadly a home defeat by Arsenal - described by Gunners' captain Frank McLintock as "a 2-1 massacre" - ended all hope of a Wembley appearance. Nevertheless, the Blues were still in Europe.

In March they travelled to Poland, taking their own food supplies, and were defeated 2-0 by an impressive Gornik side. Allison was disappointed but realised Gornik had been the better team: "We didn't play too badly, but nothing went right for us. We were all right at the back but there was nothing coming up front. That was a great goal by Lubanski. The second one was a bit unfortunate.

"I know how good this Polish side is... they are much better than probably the general public appreciate. I would rate Lubanski as a world class player ... one of the best three in the world in his role. He likes to play just behind the centre-forward and go through all the time."

The second leg again ended 2-0 to the home side and so with the aggregate score at 2-2 a replay was arranged in Copenhagen. Controversy surrounded the match with Gornik's President, Ernest Wyra, demanding City's players be tested for drugs after the replay. He claimed they'd taken drugs during the second leg and wanted to see the Blues punished. Mercer became angry and accused the Poles of trying to put the City players off their game. Nevertheless, UEFA listened to Gornik's gripes and City were forced to accept the tests.

City won the game 3-1 with goals from Booth, Lee and Young. Then came a dope testing fiasco. Colin Bell, David Connor and Derek Jeffries, the three players whose names had been drawn out of a hat, were unable to provide urine samples. Orange juice was given to the men, but still no luck. Then Allison tried to lighten the atmosphere a little. He picked up a bottle of champagne, demanded entry into the medical room, but returned a few seconds later laughing: "They won't allow them to have this!"

Eventually, samples were produced and the tests were negative, but the whole affair seemed ridiculous. Despite the controversy City were through to the semi-finals for the second year in succession. Their opponents would be F.A. Cup winners' Chelsea on April 14th at Stamford Bridge and the 28th at Maine Road.

Around this time Allison had been in trouble once again with the F.A. and was banned from all football activity for a couple of months which left, Mercer in total control of the side and caused further friction between the two men.

Immediately prior to the first leg, the Blues suffered with an incredible number of injuries. By the time of the match Summerbee, Oakes, Heslop, Bell and Doyle were all on the treatment list alongside long term invalid Pardoe. It was always going to be

Top: Bobby Charlton holds Glyn Pardoe's leg as the City defender writhes in agony following an horrific injury suffered during the December 1970 derby.

Bottom: Pardoe returns to the sidelines during his long lay-off. The injury almost cost him his leg.

difficult to prepare for a big match against such a strong English side, but with so many injuries Mercer had to hope for a bit of luck. In addition to those out of action, other players were suffering. Goalkeeper Joe Corrigan was particularly brave, and actually played against Chelsea with his left eye half-closed and badly bruised.

Understandably, City were forced to play a defensive game and managed to keep the score down to a 1-0 defeat away from home. Mercer was pleased: "We had to play it in a negative way to some extent and it was a very difficult match, but it went more or less as we planned it, and Joe Corrigan in particular was magnificent. We made one mistake and we lost, but we showed that we know a bit about defensive football, and you don't learn it all on the Continent."

More players were missing from the second leg, which was played 48 hours after a 2-2 draw with Liverpool in the League. Corrigan and Booth were both out with Ron Healey taking the goalkeeper's place. Unfortunately, two minutes before half-time, Healey turned an inswinging free kick from Chelsea's Keith Weller into his own net. It was the only goal and Chelsea won 2-0 on aggregate, ending City's dream of becoming the first side to retain the trophy - a feat no club has ever managed. Chelsea went on to defeat Real Madrid in the final.

Mercer was disappointed, but delighted with the performance of many young, home-grown players forced to play because of the horrific injury list. Those players, which included Healey, Donachie, Jeffries, Carter, and Johnson, performed magnificently throughout this difficult period and briefly became known as Mercer's Minors.

Despite the positive arrival of some exciting youngsters, Malcolm Allison was angry. He felt Mercer should have approached the European games differently, and saw this period as more or less the end of the partnership: "The worst moment was when I was suspended and we were playing Chelsea in the Cup Winners' Cup semi. I said to Joe when we play Newcastle don't play Doyley, and don't play Colin Bell. In fact I told him to leave out three players for this League match, which wasn't a very important game. Remember I was suspended and Joe was in complete control of the team. In the end Joe played them all because he wanted to win the match. Two of them got injuries and they couldn't play in the semi-final, and I was really, really annoyed at him. Really angry. He wanted to win it without my advice because, well, we've all got egos and he perhaps wanted to prove he could do it without me. I told him that he was foolish, but now thinking about it I probably would have done the same thing. Even so, at the time I was really annoyed because those players wouldn't be playing in the semi-final... and it probably cost us the game. It was the blackest moment for me."

A season that promised so much ended trophyless with City in 11th position. Events off the field had dominated too much and it was obvious to all a solution to the Boardroom wrangles had to be found. For City supporter and Altrincham businessman Peter Swales an opportunity to help the crisis appeared: "I went into a pub in Hale Barns and saw, in the lounge, City directors John Humphreys and Sidney Rose. I wasn't even 40 then, probably about 38. Full of myself, of course. Knew everything... doing well in business. I'd been at Altrincham Football Club for a couple of years and doing quite well there. I saw these two sat there and I thought 'this is an opportunity'. So I went over to them, and I said, point blank, 'you know all this trouble you're having, I could sort that out for you'. They asked 'how would you do it?' and I just said 'give me the opportunity and I'll do it'.

"Now, I thought that would be the last I'd ever hear, but about three or four days later - they found out about me through business and through football, I'd been involved with the Oldham Premier League and things - I got a call from Albert Alexander and he said 'what's your idea to sort it out?' I had no bloody idea, none whatsoever! So I said 'just let me talk to both parties' and it went from there. I worked with Joe Smith's gang and got on well with them, and with the other side. I did a lot of talking and I managed to settle it. As a result of that I became a director - like the man in between. I had no shares - I think I had ten which they gave me to become a director - for many years. I didn't get any volume of shares until well into the 80s."

Wyn Davies in action at Chelsea in August 1971.

Peter Swales joined the City Board in April 1971, but the take-over was not resolved immediately. However, by the time the new season opened on 14th August 1971 Joe Smith and Simon Cussons had become directors. Significantly, there was no place for Michael Horwich, Chris Muir, and Ian Niven, although the latter did make it by the end of February, and Muir the following season.

On the playing side Wyn Davies was signed for £52,500 from Newcastle, making his debut in the opening day 1-0 defeat by Leeds, but the Blues were still struggling with injuries. Glyn Pardoe, who had broken his leg after a tackle by George Best in the December 1970 derby match, was still fighting his way back to full fitness. The injury had been quite severe and almost cost him his leg, but the player tried to remain positive and attempted to build a routine: "I've been at the ground every day since pre-season training started doing what exercises I could. It's felt pretty good under the plaster. I can get plenty of movement... and the plaster was left on just that little bit longer to make sure. It's not been much of a summer, though."

Others struggling to regain fitness included Alan Oakes, who had a cartilage removed from his right knee; and Colin Bell, who'd been in considerable pain with a trapped nerve.

Maine Road was also starting to look a little different. The North Stand terracing was finally complete, although the bars, toilets and other internal facilities would not be available for some time. The new stand included an impressive £11,000 electronic scoreboard supplied by Hird-Brown - the same company who provided Wembley and the organisers of the Munich Olympics with boards.

The pitch itself was different as groundsman Stan Gibson provided new drainage, and widened it by two yards to give measurements of 117 X 79 yards, which made the overall surface larger than any other ground in England.

Despite the opening day defeat, City's new pitch helped the Blues progress with home victories over Crystal Palace (4-0), Tottenham (4-0), Liverpool (1-0) and Newcastle United (2-1) to leave the club in fourth place by mid September. The new North Stand had helped crowds to increase on the previous season and the players noticed the difference in atmosphere, especially captain Tony Book: "Against Liverpool I won the toss and because the new North End terraces have got so popular with our vocal supporters I decided to play into that goal. The crowd were really tremendous and the lads and myself were spurred on by their support. When we scored just after half-time I think this was due a large extent to our fans from all over the ground rooting for us."

City were still in fourth place by the time of Everton's visit on 9th October. A single goal from Francis Lee was enough to bring victory, but the game was significant for another reason. It was the first time Malcolm Allison took control of the side. The changes at Board level affected the positions of both Allison, and Joe Mercer. Mercer was given the title of General Manager, while Allison was moved in as Team Manager. Naturally, Allison was more satisfied with the change than Mercer, but at the time it seemed the only way to keep both men at the club. After the victory the new manager was asked what kind of a boss he would become. In typically cocksure Allison style he responded: "Probably the best that ever was. And I'll tell you something else, it will be nice to walk out at Wembley ahead of the Cup Final team."

Years later broadcaster and City fanatic Stuart Hall gave his recollections of what was, in effect, the end of the Mercer-Allison partnership: "Joe was the headmaster, Mal was the teacher but Allison could not bear to be placed one pace behind him. For example, when Joe led the team out at Wembley I think, Allison was seething with anger, but what he didn't realise was that the world isn't stupid; everybody recognised Malcolm's contribution and when the next Wembley final came, as surely it would, if he'd been a little more patient, Joe would have stepped aside and let Allison enjoy the full spotlight that he craved so badly.

Colin Bell scores against Newcastle at Maine Road in September 1971, a game which City won 2-1. On the left of the picture is future City boss Frank Clark.

"I really mistrusted Malcolm from the day Joe was shoved aside. He had this megalomania in those days, where he thought the whole world revolved around Malcolm Allison, and I had this great feeling of resentment towards him. I felt the club would go downhill, because he wouldn't be capable of managing it. Malcolm was a super coach, and a magnificent motivator of men. In fact he still is, but when it came to actually administering a football club, he had little

Francis Lee demonstrates the dive he believed George Best had made during the November 1971 derby. The game remains one of the most famous derbies of all time and was released on video during the early 1990s.

idea. He's not a bad lad really, deep down, but he needed to be brought into line. He's been misguided, but he's a warm person with so many qualities."

Most people believed Allison was by far the greatest coach in the world at this point, however the changes at Maine Road since 1970 had caused far too many problems in his relationship with Mercer. Both men achieved success outside of the partnership, but at City it was the combined chemistry that brought the glory, not the individuals. Mercer had shown during the previous season how he needed Allison's support, and as Team Manager Allison would later demonstrate a similar need. Although it wasn't realised at the time, the take-over cost City a great deal.

Under Allison, the Blues continued to succeed in the League and by the time of the November Maine Road derby match were lying third. The meeting was one of the classic encounters and resulted in a 3-3 draw with Mike Summerbee scoring a last gasp equaliser before 63,326 spectators. A typical derby game, it was full of incident with Francis Lee involved in a couple of the more newsworthy moments.

The first saw Lee score from a penalty hotly disputed by the Reds - this in a season when Lee rattled in a record 13 penalties. The second saw the City man accuse George Best of making a theatrical dive when tackled. To prove his point Lee demonstrated the dive several times to United players Willie Morgan and David Sadler. The City fans loved it and cheered him on, but the referee was not impressed and booked Lee. In 1990 footage of the game went on sale, and Lee's antics were enjoyed by a new generation.

Lee's view that Best had dived was a little ironic when much of the press coverage of City during 1971-2 focused on the high total of penalties awarded to City. Many journalists accused Lee of deliberately looking for the easy option, something which angered the player: "I got a bit of a reputation as an 'actor' because of the amount of penalties Manchester City were awarded. Everyone thought I was getting the penalties - it's just that I kept netting them! Many people take the line that a player is deliberately trying to win a penalty when they go over in the box. But you have to ride a tackle and imagine how many injuries there would be if a player remained stationary when he was tackled."

In fact only six of the 13 penalties he scored that season were awarded for fouls on Lee. Two were for handball, and the rest for fouls on other players.

In addition to the derby draw, Allison's City defeated Arsenal (2-1), West Ham (2-0), and Coventry (4-0) to earn the new manager the Bell's Manager of the Month award. The presentation was made on 11th December before City's 4-0 drubbing of Bobby Robson's Ipswich Town.

If everything was going well on the pitch, it was a very different story off it. Mercer was far from happy with his role: "The humiliating part of this sad affair is that at one time the Board were saying there was a job for life. But the new regime of directors had no real confidence in me and I finished up by being offered a three year engagement plus a thirty-three and a third per cent cut in salary. However, the thing that hurt most of all was that they just didn't know what to call me. All my life I have been known as Joe Mercer the footballer, or Joe Mercer the manager. Then suddenly they can't find a title for me. That was when my pride was hit most of all."

Mercer was not dissatisfied Allison was now Team Manager, his quarrel was about his own position, and the way he was treated by the new Board. He knew how his great friend Matt Busby was revered at Old Trafford, and felt the United directors would never treat Busby in the way City were treating him. He wasn't alone. Many at Maine Road were

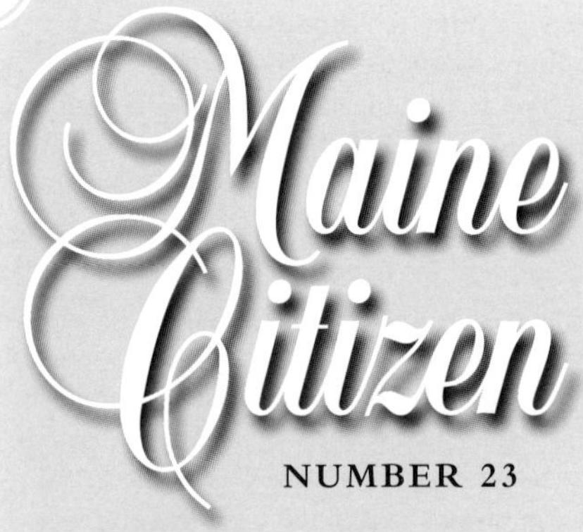

NUMBER 23

TOMMY BOOTH

Joe Mercer, circa 1970: "Tommy is the best centre-half since Stan Cullis. He is great in the air, with perfect temperament. He can play, too. He can go past them, he's got loads of control, and makes it look all too easy. I think he is the best centre-half in England. Harry Godwin spotted him, and he was on our books when we heard that Oldham Athletic wanted to turn him pro. So they rushed us into signing him. We had to make a decision, so we got him. When he came to Maine Road he was about 6ft 1in, but he had a lot of skill, though."

Booth was always one of Mercer's favourite players and proved an excellent member of the squad that was so triumphant during the late 60s and early 70s. He made his League debut in the 1-1 draw with Arsenal on 9th October 1968 and went on to feature in all but two of the remaining 30 League games that season. He also featured in all seven F.A. Cup ties, scoring the only goal of the semi-final at Villa Park which took the Blues to Wembley for the first time since 1956.

He featured in each of the five finals City played between 1969 and 1976 and was an important member of the side throughout the late 60s and early 70s. During the close season of 1975 it appeared Booth's days at Maine Road were nearing their end as expensive signing Dave Watson arrived. Despite constant speculation, Tommy remained at City and then, in November of the same year, Colin Bell suffered his career threatening injury. Booth proved his versatility and moved into midfield to become a key member of Book's 1976 League Cup winners.

With his Maine Road career continuing longer than anybody had expected, Booth established himself as one of the side's elder statesmen, helping some of the younger players come to terms with the pressures of the sport. By the time of Malcolm Allison's return in 1979 he was making fewer regular appearances, but was still a vital squad member.

Amazingly, he survived Allison's purge - a period when the manager transferred many older professionals and brought in relatively inexperienced youths - and in 1980 welcomed John Bond as his sixth City manager. Considering that Mercer lasted until 1972, and Book took charge for over five years during the 70s, it was a remarkable record. Remember these were the days when City managers, in general, lasted more than 12 months.

Under Bond, it was obvious Booth was nearing the end of his City career and on 19th September 1981 he made his final League appearance in a 3-0 defeat at Birmingham. Shortly afterwards he was transferred to Preston North End for £30,000, where he later became manager for a spell.

Even in Booth's last season at Maine Road he still managed to play a part in helping the Blues reach Wembley when, on Valentine's Day 1981 he scored the only goal of the fifth round tie at Peterborough to delight the fans. It was a goal that echoed right back to the start of his illustrious career. Sadly, he never made the line-up for Wembley. Had he done so it would have been a remarkable link between the finals of the 60s and the 80s. In the League Cup run of the same year he appeared in five of the seven games played, including the second leg of the semi-final.

Booth, the typical local hero, had a City career that spanned the magic of Mercer through to the flamboyance of Bond. It covered periods of great success and major upheaval, yet through it all he managed to adapt well and prove his worth to many different personalities. Often underrated, Booth is without any shadow of doubt a true City great.

BOOTH'S PLAYING RECORD

	LEAGUE		FA CUP		FL CUP		EUROPE		TOTAL	
	App	Gls	App	Gls	App	Gls	App	Gls	App	Gls
1968-69	28	1	7	1	1	0	0	0	36	2
1969-70	41	0	2	0	6	0	9	1	58	1
1970-71	26	1	3	0	1	0	6	1	36	2
1971-72	40	4	2	0	2	0	-	-	44	4
1972-73	34	5	5	1	2	0	2	0	43	6
1973-74	40	2	2	0	11	2	-	-	53	4
1974-75	18	2	0	0	0	0	-	-	18	2
1975-76	25(1)	6	2	2	3(1)	0	-	-	30(2)	8
1976-77	14(1)	1	0	0	0(1)	0	1	0	15(2)	1
1977-78	39	3	2	0	6	0	2	0	49	3
1978-79	20	0	0	0	5	1	6	1	31	2
1979-80	24	0	0	0	2	0	-	-	26	0
1980-81	30	0	2	1	5	0	-	-	37	1
1981-82	1	0	0	0	0	0	-	-	1	0
TOTAL	380(2)	25	27	5	44(2)	3	26	3	477(4)	36

disgusted, especially when one morning they saw him arrive to find, without any consultation, that his car park space had been taken away and his name removed from his office door. It was a shoddy affair, and illustrated that City had forgotten how the club had become such a power during the late sixties.

On a different level, Allison was also dissatisfied, especially as he believed he had been promised a twenty year contract when Joe Smith's consortium first went public: "The new Board failed to please either of us. Joe Smith asked me what I wanted. I said I wanted a good contract and that I wanted to be boss. I was terribly disillusioned with Joe Smith when I saw my new contract. It was full of loopholes. My solicitor spent several months working on it and still it wasn't right. I remember saying to the directors, 'My contract isn't worth a light'."

At Board level, it's worth noting that changes were still ongoing. By early December Albert Alexander was given the title of 'President', while his son Eric became the new Chairman. Joe Smith was now Vice-Chairman, but neither Niven nor Muir had yet managed to secure directorships. The Board would continue to change throughout the next two seasons.

Ken Barnes, Joe Mercer, Harry Godwin and Johnny Hart. Mercer always stressed the need for strong backroom staff. Barnes, Godwin and Hart were loyal City men who rarely made the headlines, yet were a major part of City's success.

City continued to progress in the League and by 9th January the Blues were only a point behind leaders Manchester United. It was a different story in the two cup competitions, though. In the League Cup City defeated Wolves 4-3 in September but were beaten 3-0 at Bolton in the third round, while the F.A. Cup saw the Blues draw 1-1 with Middlesbrough - thanks to a record breaking 12th penalty from Lee - but then lose the replay 1-0. At least it gave Allison his first chance as City manager to say: "We can now concentrate on the League without any distractions."

He was right as, on 29th January, a 5-2 victory over Wolves put City two points clear at the top. Lee scored a hat-trick that day, and then on 12th February the Match Of The Day cameras travelled to Bramall Lane to see him score his 13th penalty of the season. As if to prove a point, the penalty was awarded after debutant Mick Speight used his hands to turn away a Lee shot. Who said all City's penalties were awarded for dives by Frannie?

The game ended 3-3 with Allison claiming newly promoted Sheffield United were the best side to have come up from the Second Division in ten years. He'd obviously forgotten about City!

The Blues continued to progress and by the middle of March were four points clear at the top of the table. Leeds were second, although they had two games in hand. It seemed Malcolm Allison had managed to rediscover City's Championship seeking approach, and nothing could get in the way. Then he made a signing that changed everything. City's tradition of shooting themselves in the foot was once again on display as Allison landed what should have been the greatest catch of the 1970s, Rodney Marsh. Marsh was a real entertainer, the kind of player the footballing public wanted to see, and his £200,000 record signing was seen as a positive move by City to secure the title. Everybody expected him to help the Blues with the final push, and a crowd of over 53,000 turned out to watch his debut against Chelsea on 18th March. It was not particularly memorable, especially as he received a knock and was substituted, but the fans still warmed to his talents.

Despite these obvious skills, some Blues were not impressed. Mike Doyle: "He made his debut against Chelsea. They left Tony Towers out, who'd been playing really well. We should have hammered Chelsea that day. Tommy Booth scored and we managed a 1-0 win. He did mix with the lads to a certain extent, but really it was clear Marsh just wanted to do his own thing. You don't win anything with players like that in your side. But the writing was already on the wall. All we had to do was to win three games to get the Championship. But they persisted in playing Marsh and we just lost all our rhythm and everything."

A no score draw with Newcastle followed the Chelsea victory and all of a sudden the pressure was on. Then came the visit of Stoke on April Fool's Day and another setback, as Gordon Banks performed superbly to help Stoke to a 2-1 victory in the Maine Road mud. Two days later a 2-0 defeat at Southampton left City lying in third place on 50 points. Derby led the table on 51, with Liverpool second on 50, and Leeds fourth on 49.

The press and some supporters started to blame City's recent loss of form on the arrival of Rodney Marsh, but Allison refused to accept that viewpoint and persisted with the player in the side. It wasn't until some time later that Marsh himself confessed he felt he'd had a detrimental effect, when he admitted he was clearly not as fit as the City players when he arrived. He claimed his own performances suffered as a result, and that the other players had expected more from him.

After the Southampton defeat City won at West Ham 3-1 with Marsh scoring his first and second goals for the club to silence his critics for a while. Then on 12th April came the Old Trafford derby. City were expected to win, especially as they had not lost in the League at Old Trafford since September 1966.

Interestingly, Marsh was named as substitute - the first time since his arrival he had not made the starting line-up.

The first half was rather sterile, although City always seemed to have the upper hand. In fact the Blues appeared the more likely to score, then after an hour Martin Buchan gave the Reds the lead against the general run of play. It wasn't to last, though, as impressive youngster Willie Donachie galloped down the wing and centred to Lee. The ace goalscorer proceeded to back-head the equaliser. A powerful right foot shot brought Lee's second goal of the game and 32nd of the season a few minutes later. Lee was to end the campaign on 33 League goals - the most since Tommy Johnson's 38 in 1929.

A little while later Allison brought Marsh on for the injured Doyle, and City's expensive forward made it three with a calm, perfect shot into the United net.

Afterwards a delighted Allison purred: "Magic, pure magic!" City were back on course.

Rodney Marsh was quick to point out after the match he was extremely happy at Maine Road, despite what the papers said: "One ghost I would like to lay immediately is an impression that the papers have given... that the crowd at Maine Road has been getting at me.

"That's nonsense. I've found them very fair and indeed they have given me a lot of encouragement. If anything surprised me with City, it was the space I was given... probably because our players here seem to think that bit quicker than others. By the time I scored three goals I should really have had eight. Against United I was really surprised at the amount of space created."

Three days after the victory City suffered another setback. This time they only managed a 1-1 draw at Coventry, although Mike Doyle had an effort ruled offside. That left City second, one point behind Derby with two games left for both sides. Importantly, Liverpool and Leeds were also able to snatch the title as both had games in hand and were only one and two points behind respectively.

It was vital City defeated Ipswich on 18th April at Portman Road. In the end they suffered a 2-1 defeat which meant the final game of the season - at home to Derby - wouldn't really give the Blues the opportunity of parading the Championship trophy at Maine Road. The Derby game ended 2-0 but City, despite being League leaders, had to wait a further twelve days before the other sides completed their fixtures. In the end Derby won the title by a point, while City finished fourth on the same number of points as Liverpool and Leeds.

Naturally, the inquests started. Was Marsh to blame? What about Gordon Banks' excellent performance in April? Did the take-over hangover affect the club? Had the shoddy treatment of Mercer made an impact? And what about the bickering between Mercer and Allison? There were many theories, but no real answers.

In June 1972 Joe Mercer left the Blues to become General Manager of Coventry City. He felt he was no longer wanted at Maine Road, and his relationship with Malcolm Allison was at its lowest point. Allison was pleased as it meant there was no doubt who was in charge now, and Mercer was ready for a new challenge. Regrettably for City, the departure of Mercer was not handled well, and brought much criticism of the club and of Allison.

In fact, the appalling way he was treated turned some against the club, and caused others to seriously question the new directors. It appeared to many supporters that the new Board could not recognise what had made the club great. It wasn't Mercer, it wasn't Allison, it was their partnership. Together they won everything.

The first five years of their alliance were perfect, and Allison remembers what they achieved together: "We told each other the truth, and we never really fell out. Once he turned to me and said, 'Mal, these have been the best five years of my life. I wouldn't have traded them for anything'. He meant it. We had a great relationship really. I enjoyed it all and I think, like Joe, those first five years were the best-ever for me. I was very lucky when Joe got the City job, and took me there. And we started right from the grass roots, right from the bottom and took them to the top. That is real achievement."

Neither Mercer nor Allison should be blamed for the breakdown of the partnership. Allison quite understandably needed the role of Team Manager - Mercer never disputed that - the problem was that the Board did not make enough of an effort to keep Mercer at the club. The take-over and subsequent disagreements prematurely killed City's trophy winning period. Once again, City's supporters were left to wonder about what might have occurred had the partnership continued to work.

Gordon Banks was in top form as Stoke City won 2-1 at Maine Road in April 1972. The England goalkeeper's performance that day was seen by many to have cost Blues the championship.

The 1972-3 season commenced with City invited to play in the Charity Shield. Wearing their decidedly modern continental strip, they defeated Aston Villa 1-0 at Villa Park to bring the first trophy of Malcolm Allison's reign as City manager. A week later the League campaign commenced with a 2-0 defeat at Liverpool - in which Wyn Davies and Liverpool's Larry Lloyd were sent off - followed by a 1-0 home defeat against Everton. Allison needed to do something quickly if the Blues were to build on their form of the previous season, but he was adamant he did not need to bring in new faces: "I'm certainly not interested in signing any players. Things might change. I doubt it. The first team squad is 18 strong. Not many clubs can beat that.

"There's a change of style from last season. Now we'll be playing three accepted goalscorers up front - Francis Lee, Wyn Davies and Rodney Marsh with Ian

SINGING THE BLUES

In March 1972 the City squad recorded "The Boys In Blue" at Strawberry Studios in Stockport. The song continued to be played as the teams walked out at Maine Road through to the mid-1990s, when it was replaced by a variety of other hits including a couple of tracks by Oasis. The 'B' side of "The Boys in Blue" was a typically spurious early 70s track called "Funky City". Both tracks were produced by Godley and Creme from 10cc.

Mellor pushing them all for regular inclusion. We didn't start off last season with this sort of strength. Then we had to adjust. Now we have a settled squad, with everyone knowing what's wanted."

On 19th August the first points arrived with a 3-0 victory over Norwich, but the Blues had to wait until the seventh game for their next points to arrive. By that time City were bottom of the table, one point behind Manchester United.

Off the pitch, there had been further changes to the look of the stadium. As a result of the Ibrox disaster, the decision was taken to install seats on the new North Stand. This now held 7,800 in tip-up plastic seats, paying a mere 70p each per game. Over in the Kippax Stand the admission price was a pleasing 40p for adults and 20p for schoolchildren, although attendees did complain about the poor quality of the public address system within the stand.

On 13th September City returned to European action with a first round UEFA Cup tie against Valencia. The game ended 2-2, but the return game was a disappointment as Valencia, managed by the great Alfredo Di Stefano, won 2-1. A week later the Blues were also knocked out of the League Cup by Fourth Division Bury.

During October City's form did improve, and then November saw exciting victories over Derby (4-0), Everton (3-2) and Manchester United (3-0). By the time of the derby match Allison had sold Wyn Davies to United for a fee of around £60,000 - the largest transfer between the two clubs until Tony Coton moved to Old Trafford over twenty years later.

December brought mainly 1-1 draws with four of the six games played ending that way, and then the New Year brought Allison hope of glory in the F.A. Cup. Stoke City were despatched 3-2 in the third

The Charity Shield of 1972 was contested between fourth-placed City and Third Division champions Aston Villa. Here Francis Lee converts a penalty to win Malcolm Allison his first trophy as manager.

round, then Allison 'psyched' out Shankly's Liverpool. Writing in the *Daily Express* Allison claimed City would 'bury the myth of Liverpool', and went on to say the Merseysiders had many limitations. Unusually, Shankly's men fell for the bait and resorted to niggling fouls. The game ended goalless at Anfield, and Allison was happy. City won the replay 2-0 with goals from Bell, after fourteen minutes, and Booth, six minutes into the second half.

In the fifth round City drew Second Division Sunderland at Maine Road. Four minutes into the match, Rodney Marsh saw his first goal attempt expertly saved by Jim Montgomery, but City did find the net later, when Tony Towers scored with a ground shot. Sadly, an error by Joe Corrigan brought the sides level. He attempted to send a free-kick to Willie Donachie, but only succeeded in picking out future Blue Mick Horswill who simply lobbed the ball over Corrigan to make it 1-1.

Nevertheless, City remained in control for much of the first half, prompting Sunderland boss Bob Stokoe to admit later: "I thought that I would have to throw another ball on the pitch for us to get a kick." It didn't last, though, and after 67 minutes Sunderland took the lead.

City searched desperately for an equaliser but were thwarted time and again by the excellent Montgomery, then Summerbee swung a ball into the area from a corner. Marsh blocked the 'keeper's view, and Montgomery ended up back-heeling the ball into his own net. City fans were delighted his luck had finally ran out.

Both sides searched hard for the win, but the score remained unchanged. It had been a fierce encounter with several players booked - indeed goalscorer Towers was sent off. Sunderland won the replay 3-1 despite late pressure from the Blues.

A First Day Cover produced to mark City's return to European football and the completion of the new North Stand. City lost 2-1 in Valencia.

Allison was devastated and now began to find it difficult to motivate himself: "I had become disenchanted with the club. The directors had dragged their feet in giving me the sort of contract I wanted, and had been promised. The urgency and thrill had gone out of my work. It was a desperately unhappy situation to be in after all the great times, the moments when Mercer, the players, and I had between us achieved a sort of working perfection."

On 7th March Allison was forced to sell Ian Mellor to Norwich City: "There are no secrets about why I was forced to encourage clubs who are interested in some of our players - City need to put

Rodney Marsh celebrates after a brilliant goal from Ian Mellor (arm raised, left of picture) against Stoke on Boxing Day 1972. Three months later Malcolm Allison was forced by the new Board to sell Mellor - he later admitted this helped him decide to leave the club.

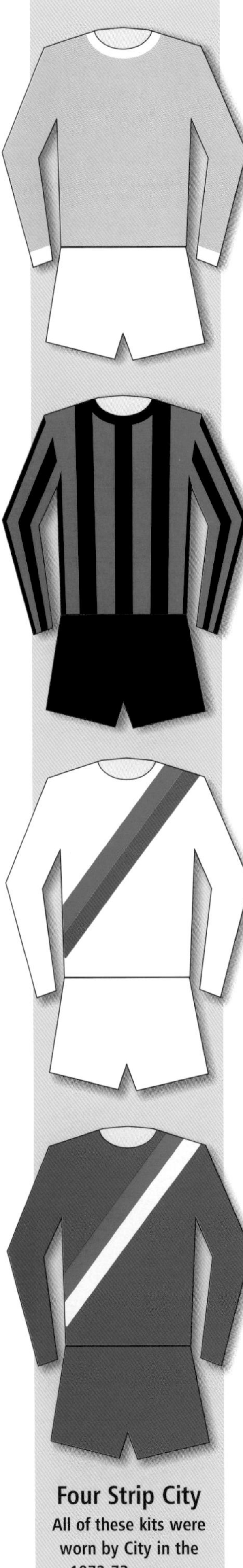

Four Strip City

All of these kits were worn by City in the 1972-73 season.

the financial side of things on a better basis. I can understand that. But I find selling players the toughest part of my job, particularly if it's in a rush. It means you don't get the real value. And I've never liked selling players you've seen come here as kids and develop into top class professionals. That's why I was sorry to see Ian Mellor leave."

Three days later, the visit of Coventry brought Joe Mercer back to Maine Road. Before the game the former City manager received a fantastic ovation, and then witnessed his new side win 2-1. Incredibly, Francis Lee missed a penalty - perhaps he felt the day belonged to Mercer. Allison had already started to consider his own future by the end of that game, and before the end of the month he was on his way out of Maine Road. Twenty years later he admitted he was well and truly shattered after almost eight years of pushing himself, and City, so hard. He was in dire need of some time out but, as Kenny Dalglish would later find at Liverpool, football rarely allows managers a sabbatical. If the City directors had been able to find a way of giving Allison a short break, he may have been able to return refreshed. Sadly, his first Maine Road career ended with City struggling in the bottom half of the table.

The Board, which now included Peter Swales as Vice-Chairman, promoted Chief Coach and former player Johnny Hart to the manager's seat and expected him to fill the void left by both Mercer and Allison. It was a very tall order, nevertheless his appointment did help to lift the Blues a little and they ended the season in eleventh spot.

The 1973-4 campaign opened with another invitation to take part in the Charity Shield. This time Burnley defeated the Blues 1-0 at Maine Road, but before the game the City players caused much mirth when they lined up in the tunnel equipped with a huge pair of sunglasses for referee Gordon Hill.

Hill had refereed City's goalless League game at Highbury the previous season, when he gave a corner instead of a penalty after Jeff Blockley had blatantly handled for the home side. At the time television pundits stated the sun must have been in Hill's eyes, thereby prompting the City mickey-take.

During the close season, manager Hart clinched one of City's most remarkable deals when he brought Denis Law back to Maine Road on a free transfer. United fans couldn't believe it, especially as it appeared manager Tommy Docherty had forced the player out. At City though, Johnny Hart recognised the 'King of Old Trafford' still had a lot to offer: "What United decided to do with Law is nothing to do with me, nor am I entitled to comment on it. I feel that a player who was capable of being captain for Scotland around 15 months ago, with the competitive streak which Denis has never lost, would have something to offer. I wouldn't like to think that one of my players could go absolutely sour in such a short period."

Law's first League game of the new season proved he hadn't 'turned sour' as he scored twice to help City defeat Birmingham 3-1.

In the programme for that game an article by Eric Alexander revealed he would be relinquishing the Chairmanship of the club at the AGM on Friday 5th October. He wrote how he was satisfied his period in

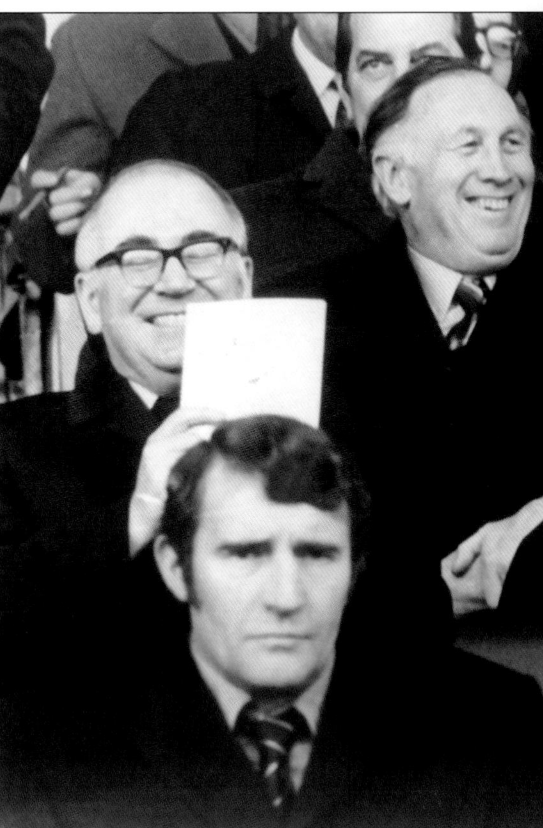

In March 1973 Joe Mercer returned to Maine Road as manager of Coventry and enjoyed the last laugh as his side went home with the points.

control had seen the take-over battle finally resolved, and stated the Boardroom was now totally democratic: "The majority of these events [the take-over] reached a climax during my term in office and I was delighted that common sense prevailed and differences could be ironed out. To use the expression of a famous politician 'peace in our time' is a milestone I will remember in City history. We have now reached a stage where no one man will ever control Manchester City. This point has been reached by voluntary agreements, and it is the best thing that could have happened to safeguard City and prevent a repetition of our past troubles."

The man ready to fill Alexander's position was 'peacemaker' Peter Swales. Joe Smith, who basically had control of the club, felt comfortable with Swales and he seemed the perfect choice. He had already made it onto the F.A. Council and had vast experience of football administration with Altrincham and the Northern Premier League. He seemed the logical choice.

On the pitch, City's second game - a 1-0 defeat at Derby - saw the welcome return of Glyn Pardoe. Pardoe was still struggling following his injury in the 1970 match with United, and the Derby game was only his seventh appearance in almost three years. It had been a long hard struggle and said much about Pardoe's character that he had never once given up. He was desperately keen to make sure his return to the first team was not short-lived. His determination helped him make a total of 31 League appearances during 1973-4.

Another determined man was Denis Law, who wanted to prove how wrong United were to discard him. At Stoke in City's third game, the plucky

Scotsman scored his third goal of the season as City drew 1-1, while in other matches he became chief provider. His opening month at Maine Road had already proved rewarding when the news came through he'd earned a recall to the Scottish squad. Scotland manager Willie Ormond attended Maine Road to see City defeat Coventry 1-0, and afterwards declared: "It's the best centre forward display I have seen so far this season." In addition to Law, Ormond also named left back Willie Donachie in the squad for a World Cup qualifier against Czechoslovakia. Sadly, Donachie, who had played against the same country a couple of years earlier, never actually made it onto the pitch for that game but Law did, partnering the young Kenny Dalglish in attack.

Afterwards every reporter acknowledged Law was inspirational, and it was mainly down to him that Scotland had qualified for the 1974 World Cup finals in West Germany. Law was pleased with his own performance, but generously shared the acclaim, mentioning a player City fans would come to love seven years later: "I have never been happier. After all these years in the wilderness Scotland can now make the rest of the world sit up and take notice in West Germany next summer. We can start playing an established and successful pattern. Some of our youngsters were terrific against the Czechs, particularly Tommy Hutchison. He showed that he is the type of player Scotland have needed for years."

On Friday 5th October City held their Annual General Meeting. As expected Eric Alexander stood down as Chairman with Peter Swales taking control of the club. Swales was not the major shareholder, indeed he held very few shares, however he had the backing of Joe Smith. Smith was now President with Simon Cussons holding the position of Vice-Chairman. Two other members of Smith's consortium - Ian Niven and Chris Muir - were also on the Board, as were original shareholders Eric Alexander, Sidney Rose, and Umbro's John Humphreys, but the power definitely lay with the former members of Smith's partnership and, of course, Chairman Swales.

Smith saw the appointment of Swales as proof City was now a democratic club: "In November 1970 I accepted an opportunity to have a closer involvement with my favourite football club, and from this followed an ambition to bring a breath of fresh air into the place. Frankly, it looked to be desperately needed at Maine Road, where a monopoly of power was in existence. Along the way, strewn with obstacles, many unpleasantries and even more in the way of bitter opposition, there were attempts to represent my intentions as a personal grab for power and prestige. I trust that yesterday's meeting proved the truth behind my motives when the Chairmanship passed into the astute care of the best director at present equipped to handle the job, Peter J. Swales. There could be no better choice."

He went on to outline how Swales had managed to bring the two sides in the Boardroom dispute together and how, as Vice-Chairman, Swales had worked hard to help the club announce the biggest profit in its history. From his own viewpoint, Swales felt the club was already moving in the right direction and the large profit was a culmination of a lot of positive effort by many people at the club. He outlined his views in the City programme for the game against Southampton on 6th October. He explained his desire to see the team achieve great success, while maintaining a healthy bank balance. Many of his comments were typical of any man taking over the running of one of England's biggest football clubs; unfortunately many of these phrases were taken and used against Swales in later years when success eluded the Blues. Nevertheless, in 1973 few if any supporters argued against the appointment of a man who clearly loved City, and had the same kind of ambition as the fans on the terraces. He wanted the best, and ended his lengthy programme article as any ambitious man would: "To think of me as a successful chairman, which I dearly want to be, I'm aware that the team has to be successful on the field. There's no reason why it shouldn't be. I will give my best for City, and my best has stood me in reasonable stead before. I will work harder than anyone else. And I cannot promise any more than that."

Swales certainly became one of the hardest working Chairmen throughout the 1970s and 80s, but the success he and City craved was not as great as it should have been. However, in 1973 everybody was hopeful the new Swales era would prove successful, though some probably felt Smith still had the controlling voice. Swales: "Well, Joe Smith was the boss. He eventually bought the bulk of the shares, but he didn't have the bottle to do the Chairman's job. He was a wonderful fella, terrific fella. He knew how to make money, but he didn't like the criticism and the rough game that it is. I think he knew that to be the boss of a football club you've got to have a nerve and a belief in what you're doing. I just took his fancy and that was it. He backed me to the day he died, never once did he go against... even when I made some bad decisions - and there were plenty of those while he was alive! He was great."

Mike Summerbee at home with two-year-old Nicholas (left), a City player to be. Also pictured are daughter Rachel (4) and Mike's wife Tina.

face to face

'There's too much showbiz about City'

Q. What was it that attracted the Board of Directors to appointing Ron Saunders as manager?

A. Over the last 18 months we have slipped a little bit. We had the situation with Malcolm Allison where he bombed along great for six years and then lost some of his impetus for the next 12 months. Not intentionally, but it happened. Johnny Hart stepped into that place but, unfortunately, was not physically up to the job. Without knowing it City slipped into a state where the tempo had decreased and the zest was less. We needed somebody to create an explosion — the whole place needed a shake-up. I still maintain that our former club skipper, Tony Book, is going to turn out better in the managerial game than Don Revie, but we needed a new broom for this job. A Ron Saunders.

Q. But what was it about him that convinced City he was the right man?

A. I first saw him in a television programme three years ago when I had very little to do with League football. I remember thinking to myself that he looked the type of chap who would go places, the kind who wanted to win. I got the impression that he would never be overawed by stars — and that's why we finally moved in Ron's direction. If Malcolm Allison had a failing in my eyes it was that he leaned towards star names — he liked a touch of the Sean Connery-Michael Caine image in his life. Malcolm was impressed with reading about men like Napoleon and Hitler and lost a little touch with reality on the way. I must say though that I had tremendous admiration for Malcolm's talent and it is his quality players who are the rich inheritance here. I saw his name linked with the City job once more, and it's fair to say that you would always consider Malcolm where there is any job in soccer. But there was no way he could come back here at this time. The candle has been burnt at both ends. His future is in different pastures — I think he will eventually be successful. Everybody hits a down-beat at some stage and he's been suffering all this season.

Q. What are you looking for Ron Saunders to do at City?

A. Put the killer instinct in the team There's too much showbiz about City. The fans want to see a winning team that's scoring goals. To talk about sacrificing attractive football and our showbiz style to get this is utter rubbish. We want to be winning things. We've not got the killer touch like Leeds . . . we never knock teams down when we get on top of them. We coast home. Leeds will be 2-0 up and steamroller on to make it 5-0. That's what I mean about killer instinct.

Nothing happens without discipline, and I'm sure Ron will demand it from those under him. There are other challenges for him, too. Nobody — and I mean nobody — has ever got the best out of Rodney Marsh, who is the most talented player I have ever seen in football. If Rodney knows what is good for him before it's too late, he should allow somebody to get the very best out of him. Everybody would benefit from that. Our manager has that task.

Q. What is the major difficulty he's going to face as boss at Maine Road?

A. He's got personalities to deal with. A big fault of modern football is the creation of the star footballer. The trick is to keep the stars in touch with reality and we have brought in this manager to ensure that everyone stays close to reality. If it involves dressing them down, well he's got the full backing of the Board to do that.

Q. Chairmen have been heard to say they back their manager 100%, but many times the fairy story ends abruptly and the axe swings. What makes this situation different?

A. I pledge my reputation with Ron Saunders. I have gambled my future with him, and I will be proved right. When I became chairman it was with plenty of drumbeats and razzamataz, but I know these things are not good enough to satisfy the City football public. They want results. When appointment was made I thought, from all candidates considered and the interviews c ducted, that he was the right man. Having se him at work I now know for sure he's the ri one. If he goes down, I go with him — it's blunt as that.

Q. Without trying to make the pressure too inten over what kind of period are you talking ab for success?

A. If we have not hit the high-spots in two years will consider that a failure. I call the high sp the feat of winning things. In my eyes it's successful season to win a Cup competition a figure in the top 10 clubs in the League. My p sonal ambition is to see City as the number c club in the country. Anything other than that a I have failed and I hope I am big enough accept it if the ambitions are not fulfilled.

Q. Is the money there for the manager to bring new players if he requires them?

A. He has got whatever he wants to spend. If R produces the goods we can provide the mon As long as the sum adds up to success, we not worried. We're not saying that success h to come before the cash is available — in orderly planned operation the two go hand hand.

Q. I find your thoughts quite frank. Is there anythi that you have left unsaid?

A. Unless I am a poor judge of character, I s that City are in the strongest position they ha even been in. Far stronger than at the peak the Mercer-Allison partnership. This is a calc lated move we have made — in the case of Mercer-Allison magic it was a stroke of luck City's part. To get a double act like that w instant results is a once-in-a-lifetime touch th nobody can calculate for. If anybody tells that that partnership was planned in the calc lating way we have moved forward, I will lau without apology. We have an image at City being a happy-go-lucky club. The demand n is for total dedication from everyone and to kn where we are going. This will be a tight-k community hell-bent on success at any co Success is the name of the game, and peo may say that we will lose our entertainment ima with such order of priorities, I disagree. If y are successful, you entertain. If you can do b that's a football Eutopia. I will take them one a time, in the proper order for Manchester City.

This Paul Doherty interview with Peter Swales appeared in the centre pages of the City v Burnley programme in December 1973. Over the years much of this was used against Swales.

One of Swales' first decisions concerned the appointment of a new manager. Johnny Hart had been suffering with ill health due to the pressure of trying to motivate City's team of expensive stars, and was forced to resign towards the end of November. The whole of his left side was completely numb, and he started experiencing depression around the time of his appointment: "The difficulties, the loss of feeling, was actually just coming on as Malcolm left City. I was offered the job and I took it because I didn't want anybody thinking that I didn't have the guts to have a go at it. And a job like City is the dream of a lifetime coming true for someone like me. A disadvantage I felt was that it came on me suddenly. I never worked myself up, never prepared for the position to be mine.

"I miss it [the manager's job] very much. I miss the involvement with the players. But it wasn't to be and I accepted that fact when I was in hospital. That is why I told the club I would relinquish the position."

Swales looked around for a man to drive the team forward and found Norwich manager Ron Saunders. Saunders was previously in charge at Yeovil Town and Oxford United, but it was with Norwich he first made the headlines, taking the unfashionable club to the Second Division title in 1972, then the League Cup Final in 1973. He certainly appeared to have the correct credentials for the job.

Geoffrey Watling, the Norwich director who had been Chairman when Saunders took the Norwich job, was desperately sad to see his man leave Carrow Road, but told the media he felt it was a perfect move for both the Blues and for the manager: "Manchester City are to be congratulated on their appointment - Ron Saunders can be a Joe Mercer and Malcolm Allison rolled into one, and he will get them success. Hard but human. That is a description I give about him. He would never ask players to do anything he would not do himself. I would say he is a physical fitness fanatic, and he is also dynamic in his views.

"Dedicated, a players man, he is all these things. I would recommend Ron Saunders in every way. He is an excellent manager, and will do Manchester City a power of good."

It wasn't long before Peter Swales also felt Saunders was the right man for the job. He confidently stated: "I pledge my reputation with Ron Saunders. I have gambled my future with him, and I will be proved right. When I became Chairman it was with plenty of drumbeats and razzmatazz, but I know these things are not good enough to satisfy the City football public. They want results. When the appointment was made I thought, from all the candidates considered and the interviews conducted, that he was the right man. Having seen him at work I now know for sure he's the right one. If he goes

down, I go with him - it's as blunt as that."

As with many other bold comments made around this time, they returned to haunt Swales during the 1980s and 90s. It's easy to criticise the bravura, however at the time Swales truly felt he had appointed the perfect manager.

Francis Lee felt the same about Alan Ball in the 1990s but circumstances, in particular the relationship between manager and the players, ultimately worked against both appointments.

A lot of what Swales said was probably bravado. Throughout his career at Maine Road the Chairman enjoyed letting supporters hear how City would be the biggest and best.

He desired success, but also wanted fans to be proud of their club. As Chairman he felt he was in the perfect position to 'whip up' enthusiasm.

On the pitch the appointment of Saunders didn't really initially improve performances in the League. His first game in charge saw the Blues defeated 2-1 at Ipswich, and by mid December City were in the lower half of the table, dropping to sixteenth place at one point. Gradually during January and February Saunders brought consistency to the Blues with only one game ending in defeat. The F.A. Cup was a little disappointing though, with a 4-1 defeat at Notts County putting City out at the fourth round stage.

The League Cup was City's only real chance of salvaging something out of a rather strange season. In addition to the changes in personnel, City also suffered problems as a result of power cuts caused by a miners' dispute. This affected kick-off times and attendances, and forced the Blues to hire a somewhat noisy generator to ensure certain games went ahead. In addition petrol shortages restricted the movement of supporters and further affected crowd figures. The League Cup competition was severely hit by the power problems.

Prior to Saunders' appointment, the Blues had defeated Walsall (after two replays), and Carlisle, and achieved a goalless draw at York. With Saunders - and the hire of an electric generator for £1,000 - City beat York 4-1 and then travelled to Coventry in the fifth round. An exciting game ended 2-2 but was witnessed by a crowd of only 12,661, due to the match kicking off at 2pm on a Wednesday afternoon. Almost a month later the replay - another afternoon kick off - saw City score three goals in the last twelve minutes to win 4-2.

On 23rd January the first leg of the semi-final saw City visit Plymouth to record a 1-1 draw against the Third Division side. Tommy Booth had equalised from a Mike Summerbee corner in the 65th minute. A week later at Maine Road, a crowd of 40,117 witnessed a 2-0 victory with goals from Lee and Bell to put City through to their second League Cup Final in four years.

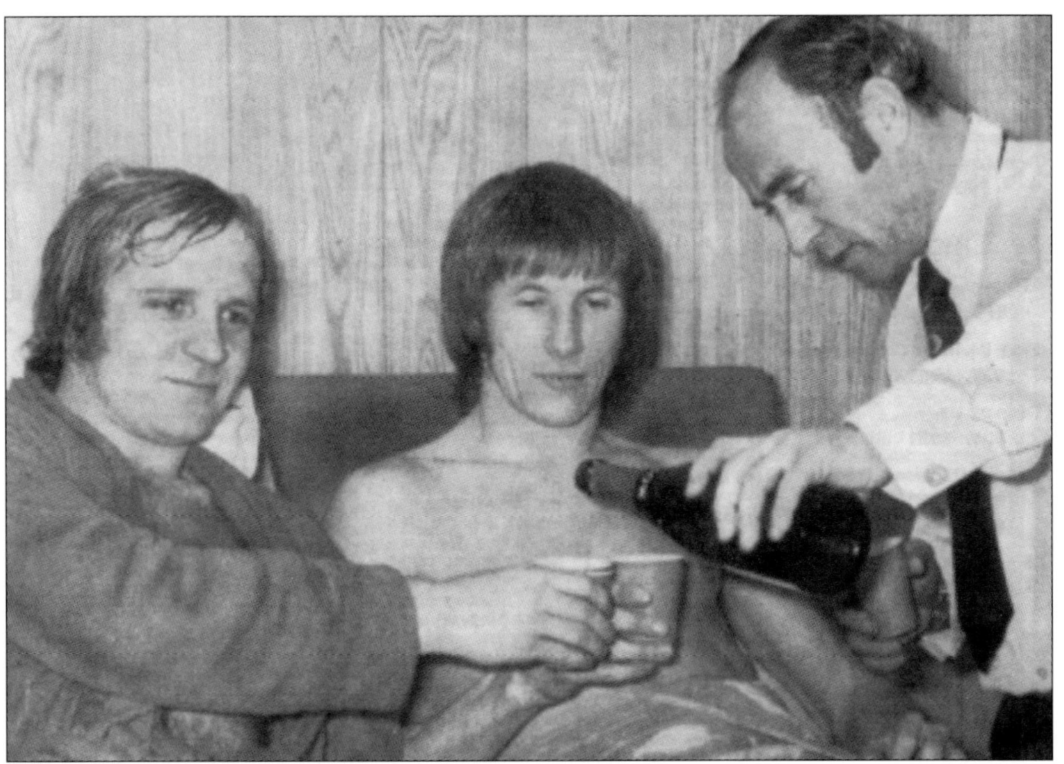

Ron Saunders pours the champagne for two of his more senior players, Francis Lee and Colin Bell, after City had beaten Plymouth to reach the League Cup Final. Lee and Bell, looking a little subdued, scored the goals in the 2-0 second leg win.

League Cup Finalists 1974

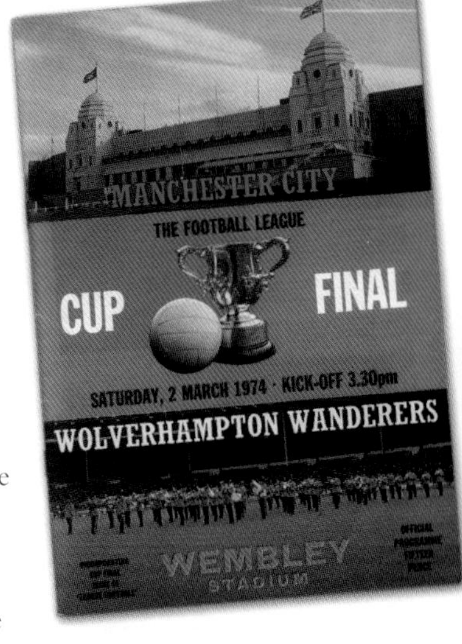

The Final against Wolverhampton Wanderers, played on 3rd March 1974, gave City the chance to rediscover success. It also provided Chairman Swales with the perfect start to his career: "I remember sitting in the Royal Box, 100,000 people - the Wembley capacity in those days - playing Wolves, thinking 'I've only been in the job a few months, it's a doddle! Absolute doddle! We'll get the First Division, the European Cup... We'll win everything. Ninety minutes later we'd lost, of course, and that was my first taste of bitter disappointment. Defeat - which of course I suffered many times in the years to come - that was a real taste of defeat. I was a young Chairman, and recognised that we had some old players in the team. We had Marshy, Francis Lee, Michael Summerbee, Colin Bell - who was younger than the others, but still an old hand at City - and Ron [Saunders] was a real disciplinarian. He used to get at those players."

According to Swales, Saunders' treatment of the older, more familiar players eventually caused the Chairman a number of problems. Success at Wembley may have changed the course of the rest of the season, but for Swales failure was unbearable. Prior to the game, City had stayed a short distance from Wembley and Saunders ensured the players prepared for the final in a rigid, controlled manner. They were not happy. Mike Doyle: "There was no party spirit, and we trained on pitches at the back of the hotel which had more slopes on them than the Alps. All we were allowed to drink was orange juice - not even a glass of wine with our meals. We felt that we were not being treated as men, but as children who might get sick at the party if they ate too much. Frankly, I don't believe any of the players was in the right frame of mind to go out and do his stuff in a Wembley Final. I think we had lost that final before we even went on the park."

The game itself started with City dominating the first half. However, it was Wolves who took the lead in the 43rd minute. Hibbitt's mis-hit drive beat City 'keeper Keith MacRae - signed by Hart from Motherwell for £100,000 - and crept in at the far post. It should never have occurred, and was very much against the run of play as City had been the more powerful side throughout the half. City's dominance continued into the second period.

Opportunities came the Blues' way, but luck smiled on Wolves as an effort from Booth was deflected off the goal line, and a header from Lee went over. City's fortunes changed on the hour, though, when Rodney Marsh centred for Colin Bell to shoot the equaliser.

Later, the Wolves 'keeper Pierce was forced to make brilliant saves from Bell, Lee, and Marsh as the Blues tore into Wolves, but once again luck eluded City as Richards scored to put Wolves 2-1 up in the 85th minute. There was no way back for City.

Colin Bell remembers how this game should have brought City success: "In my career I've played in two games of this kind. One was when England drew with Poland at Wembley and missed qualifying for the '74 World Cup, and Wolves was the other. If either of those games had been boxing matches, the opposition would have thrown the towel in. We were 1-0 down to Wolves at half time but I always felt if we pulled one back we would win. I got the equaliser and we were never out of their half after that. Then, late on, a ball was played across our area, Rodney Marsh just got a toe to it and helped it in the direction of John Richards who scored the Wolves' winner."

Everyone connected with the Blues was saddened by the scoreline, none more than Marsh, who felt responsible for the defeat. Prior to the game he'd told the press: "I will be bitterly disappointed if I don't make an impact." After the final whistle he refused to collect his loser's tankard and walked off, head bowed, towards the dressing room. Later, at the team's hotel, he insisted on drowning his sorrows from a paper cup he had collected in the Wembley dressing room, telling all who cared to listen that it was symbolic of City's - and his - failure. Later he sent a telegram to Wolves apologising for walking out, and later still, when he had calmed down, he admitted: "I just felt choked. I could have prevented Wolves' winning goal, too. The ball hit my heel and went straight to John Richards, who scored."

For the second time in three seasons, Marsh was seen as costing City a major trophy, but in truth neither occasion was his fault. At Wembley, luck more than anything else, brought Wolves the League Cup. Had any one of the many City chances after the equaliser entered the net, then the Blues would certainly have won the match. Unfortunately, it was not to be their day.

1974 LEAGUE CUP RUN

R2	Walsall	A	D	0-0
	Walsall	H	D	0-0
	Walsall	N*	W	4-0
R3	Carlisle United	A	W	1-0
R4	York City	A	D	0-0
	York City	H	W	4-1
R5	Coventry City	A	D	2-2
	Coventry City	H	W	4-2
SF1	Plymouth Argyle	A	D	1-1
SF2	Plymouth Argyle	H	W	2-0
F	Wolverhampton W.	N**	L	1-2

* = Old Trafford ** = Wembley Stadium

FACTS & FIGURES

	P	W	D	L	F	A
HOME	4	3	1	0	10	3
AWAY	7	2	4	1	9	5
TOTAL	11	5	5	1	19	8

CUP FINAL DETAILS

3 March 1974 at Wembley Stadium

WOLVERHAMPTON WANDERERS 2
MANCHESTER CITY 1

CITY: MacRae, Pardoe, Donachie, Doyle, Booth, Towers, Summerbee, Bell, Lee, Law, Marsh
WOLVERHAMPTON WANDERERS: Pierce, Palmer, Parkin, Bailey, Munro, McAlle, Sunderland, Hibbitt, Richards, Dougan, Wagstaffe (Sub Powell)
GOALS: Hibbitt, Richards, Bell

ATTENDANCE: 97,886
REFEREE: E D Wallace (Crewe)
GUEST OF HONOUR: The Duchess of Kent
MANAGER: Ron Saunders
CAPTAIN: Mike Summerbee

Colin Bell equalises for City (above) after Kenny Hibbitt's opener, but Wolves took the cup with a late winner from John Richards. Rodney Marsh (below) felt responsible for the deciding goal after deflecting a cross into the path of the Wolves marksman.

After the Wembley failure, Saunders set about strengthening the side. On 11th March he signed Sunderland's Dennis Tueart and Mick Horswill, with Tony Towers going in the opposite direction. The Tueart signing turned out to be one of the most important in the history of City although, at the time, Chairman Swales was uncertain about what type of a man Tueart was: "I went with Ron Saunders to Sunderland. My first sight of Dennis Tueart was unbelievable. I thought I'd never seen a footballer that looks anything like this - he turned out to be a lovely lad and one of the most intelligent players that have gone through my hands. Highly intelligent. But when I looked at him, he'd got a long coat on. It went from his shoulders right down to the ground. It was a brown leather-skin coat with furry lapels and he looked incredible. He was full of himself as well. Sunderland had won the Cup and he was a young hero, and I remember coming home to my wife and I said, 'Bloody Hell, luv, we've signed a player today and you're not going to believe it when you see him. I don't know what we've signed!' My first impression was that he was a real vagabond - he was gonna be more trouble than he's worth. Yet he turned out to be one of my favourite players of all time. I got on with him like an house on fire. I do business with him, and he turned out to be a smashing player. So it shows you that first impressions aren't always right."

Tueart joined a confused City side. Saunders had tried to inject some discipline into the squad, but with so many highly successful, international players he struggled to win over the majority.

Willie Donachie, who at the age of 22 had already appeared for Scotland, and played in Europe remembers the problems: "Ron Saunders obviously had something about him, but he didn't handle the players right. He treated them badly. It was a real split club. He didn't seem to like the stronger, older players. The ones who would stand up to him. He wanted a team that he could totally control. So the younger players, and maybe the quieter ones, were okay. But the older ones... he was determined to be rid of. Now, I don't know if that had been influenced by the Chairman. The players we're talking about were Lee, Summerbee, Denis Law... just all of the big strong personalities. It might have been needed, but the way he went about it just alienated him from everybody.

"He used to organise games like the 'old men' against the young players. Not too subtle is it? He just didn't treat them well. Some of his ideas were

Manager Ron Saunders seems delighted with the double signing of Dennis Tueart and Mick Horswill from Sunderland in March 1974. Tueart says he still has that coat and brings it out occasionally to scare the kids!

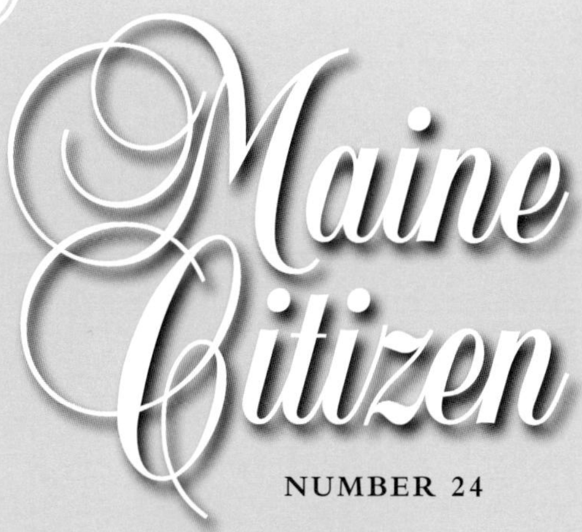

NUMBER 24

MIKE DOYLE

Mike Doyle was a vital member of two successful periods at Maine Road, and managed to bridge the gap between Mercer and Allison's great team of the late sixties, and Book's mid-70s entertainers.

As with most of the home-grown talent of the 60s and 70s, he was first spotted by City's legendary scout Harry Godwin. Godwin was at a Stretford v Stockport schoolboys' match with George Poyser on 19th November 1960 when the two men noticed Stockport's left-back. Godwin approached a teacher to find out all he could about the youngster and was told: "His name is Michael Doyle, a pupil of Reddish Vale school." Immediately on hearing the name Godwin was convinced he already knew something about the player. When he got home he searched through his diary and found a newspaper cutting of a letter which read:

"I'm not very good at arithmetic, but when I leave school I want to be a professional footballer or a PE teacher. Michael Doyle, Farley Way, Reddish."

The following day Godwin found the Doyle home, and knocked on the door. He explained who he was and immediately on entering the room knew he was on to a winner as there was evidence of strong City support. He struck up a rapport with Mike's parents: "I knew after our first little chat that there was only one club for their only son, and that was Manchester City. But I had to follow the rules at the time, and it was more than 12 months before I could sign the lad on a form."

Doyle actually joined the City groundstaff in May 1962 and made his debut, playing in Alan Oakes' number six shirt, in a 2-2 draw at Cardiff on Friday 12th March 1965, although the general confusion at Maine Road at the time almost caused him to miss the journey to Wales. Oakes returned for the following match, but it wasn't until 16th April that he made his second appearance. Like all comic book heroes,

DOYLE'S PLAYING RECORD

	LEAGUE		FA CUP		FL CUP		EUROPE		TOTAL	
	App	Gls	App	Gls	App	Gls	App	Gls	App	Gls
1964-65	6	0	0	0	0	0	-	-	6	0
1965-66	19(1)	7	7	1	0	0	-	-	26(1)	8
1966-67	14(2)	0	5	1	0	0	-	-	19(2)	1
1967-68	37(1)	5	4	0	3	0	-	-	44(1)	5
1968-69	40	5	7	0	3	0	2	0	52	5
1969-70	41	4	2	0	7	2	9	1	59	7
1970-71	37	5	3	0	1	0	7	1	48	6
1971-72	41	1	2	0	2	0	-	-	45	1
1972-73	38(2)	1	5	0	1	0	2	0	46(2)	1
1973-74	39	1	2	0	11	0	-	-	52	1
1974-75	42	1	1	0	2	1	-	-	45	2
1975-76	41	1	2	0	9	1	-	-	52	2
1976-77	33	1	4	0	1	0	2	0	40	0
1977-78	13(1)	0	0	0	3	0	1	0	17(1)	0
TOTAL	441(7)	32	44	2	43	4	23	2	551(7)	40

Doyle was outside Maine Road an hour before kick off, eating fish and chips, when Chairman Albert Alexander tapped him on the shoulder and told him to get changed.

Doyle then remained in the post-Poyser side, wearing number four, until the end of what was a traumatic season.

During the Summer Mercer and Allison arrived and City were transformed, with Doyle playing a leading role in every City triumph of the period. In fact, he shares the distinction with Tommy Booth of appearing in more finals than any other City player. Both men played in the three finals of 1969 and 1970, and the 1974 and 1976 League Cup finals. Doyle also played regularly in City's promotion and Championship seasons. He even captained City to their 1976 triumph. Put simply no other Blues' player has a record to match it.

Determined and committed but with no little skill, City fans loved his fighting spirit and never say die attitude. They also loved his frequent anti-United outbursts, although these also brought him a large sack of hate mail, and even death threats from supporters of Manchester's other club.

In 1975 he became City's captain and again used his gritty qualities to drive the Blues forward in search of more success. It came in 1976, and then the following season he helped push City to second place in the League.

He moved to Stoke for £50,000 in June 1978 and continued to perform to his usual high standard through to January 1982 when he arrived at Bolton after 115 League appearances with Stoke. After 40 League games with Bolton he transferred to Rochdale, making 24 appearances before his playing career ended in 1983 - over 20 years after he first joined City.

On the international front he made eight appearances with the under-23 side during the late sixties, and won five England caps between March 1976 and February 1977. He also played in two inter-League games. His last game for England was the disappointing 2-0 defeat by Holland in February 1977 when Don Revie selected three centre-halves (Beattie, Watson, and Doyle) plus utility defender Madeley against a side without a recognisable centre-forward. It was not a particularly good time to play for England!

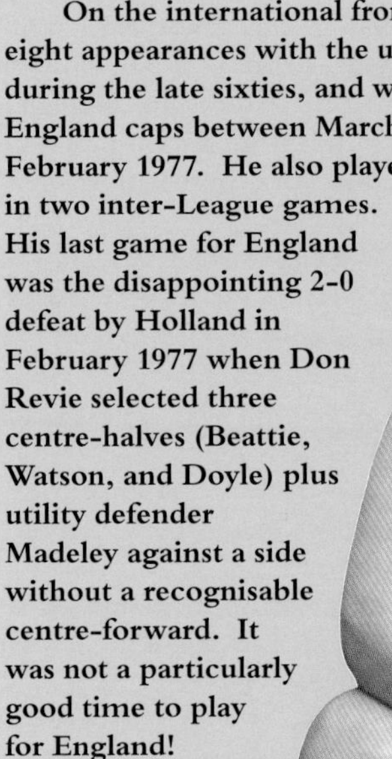

Mike Doyle was a tremendously loyal City player and a fine example of what a professional should be. He always played in a determined, wholehearted manner and won many admirers with his total dedication to the Blue cause. Many would say he is the perfect Blue.

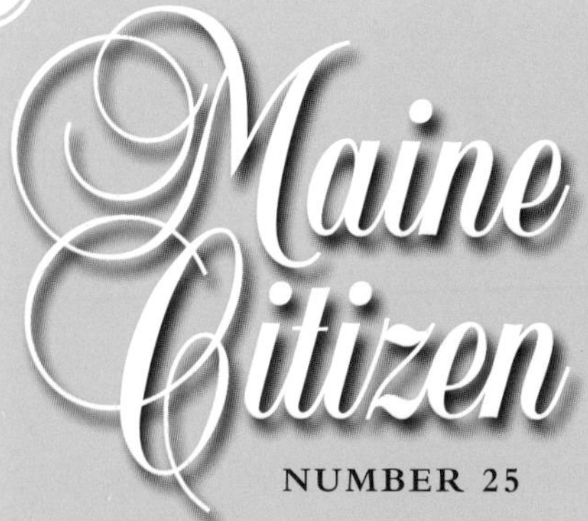

NUMBER 25

DENNIS TUEART

Dennis Tueart was already a hero with Sunderland supporters by the time he played in their memorable F.A. Cup Final victory over Leeds in 1973. It was a tremendous day for the Second Division club, but it also brought Tueart and the others to the notice of a number of leading First Division clubs.

By March 1974 City manager Ron Saunders and Chairman Peter Swales met their Roker Park equivalents, and after negotiation with the player - and Mick Horswill, another who was to join City - Tueart became a Blue.

Tueart: "Other clubs had been interested - West Ham, Tottenham, Everton ... Derby County came at the last minute to try and sign me. I think City suited my character. It was a flair club with Franny, Mike and Colin Bell. I felt they had a style ... an open style. A kind of free expression which suited my abilities, and more importantly, my personality."

Despite his impression of City, his first game fell some way short of a quality City performance. It was a bitter, dirty Manchester derby, played in a negative mood by both sides: "I later learned this was just a typical derby. There were fights going on all over the place, but no-one was taking them seriously. But eventually Clive Thomas, the referee, had enough.

"He sent Mike Doyle and Lou Macari off, but neither of them would go! They just looked at Clive saying something like, 'You can't send us off, this is normal!' So Clive took both teams off to cool down. It was crazy, but the game proved I was right to leave Sunderland. This was the kind of big time atmosphere I'd always wanted."

Over the weeks that followed Tueart played in a further seven League games and netted once (a 1-1 draw at home to Everton). He also experienced his second derby match - the infamous Old Trafford pitch invasion. He was certainly fully aware of the strength of football feeling in the city.

Eighteen months later a Tueart brace in another derby helped the Blues progress to the final of the League Cup. A final that will always be remembered for one of the greatest goals scored at Wembley.

Tueart's spectacular overhead kick brought the trophy back to Manchester for the second time in six seasons: "If you talk about a Roy of the Rovers situation, that had to be the perfect scenario.

"A Wembley cup final, 100,000 people, a spectacular winning goal against your home town team. I was the only Geordie on the pitch, and I scored the winner against Newcastle. I'll never forget it.

"I didn't see it go in but the roar was enough. Then I was up and away. And if Asa Hartford hadn't grabbed me by the shirt, I'd be running now!"

One of the most memorable City goals of all time was scored within a minute of the restart, and brought much joy to Mancunians, although many Blues missed it as they were still struggling back from the Wembley toilets and the bars.

Although that famous goal earned Tueart Blue immortality, there were many other fine achievements during, what most would describe as, an entertaining and exciting career. He remains a hero to a generation of supporters, and is possibly the last of the truly great superstars of the seventies to play for the club.

Tueart constantly delivered, and achieved some remarkable feats. There was a 2-0 victory during 1977 when he scored four times from the penalty spot. Roly-poly referee Roger Kirkpatrick made him take the first penalty three times because players were said to be encroaching; later he scored again when the Blues were given a second spot kick. It says much about Tueart's temperament and ability that he was

good. I'm not trying to knock him because, obviously, he went on to win the League with Villa. He knew the game, and knew how it should be played. But he definitely didn't go about turning City around in the right way."

As Saunders' relationship with the players worsened, so did City's performances on the pitch. Tueart's debut saw City fight out a no-score draw with United: "It was a packed house. Docherty and Cavanagh were United's manager and coach then and they were screaming blue murder any time the ball came near me, because I was near the wing. They were wanting their players to get after me. It was a tough baptism. I don't remember much about it, but I did realise that there is an awful lot of passion in Manchester!"

Referee Clive Thomas had been forced to take both teams off until Mike Doyle and Lou Macari accepted their dismissals at one point!

The following two games ended in defeat, with a small section at the back of the Kippax chanting: "If you're not coming back, clap your hands" during a 1-0 defeat by Sheffield United. Rumours of 'player power' also started to surface. Donachie: "That was basically true. The players were so unhappy at that time. The performances were bad. The club was just very unhappy, and I think the Board realised that."

City had dropped to sixteenth position, then a 2-1 victory over Newcastle on 27th March, courtesy of two goals from Lee, relieved the pressure for a while. Draws against Wolves and Everton (when Tueart scored his first goal) brought the real possibility

TUEART'S PLAYING RECORD

	LEAGUE		FA CUP		FL CUP		EUROPE		TOTAL	
	App	Gls	App	Gls	App	Gls	App	Gls	App	Gls
1973-74	8	1	0	0	0	0	-	-	8	1
1974-75	39	14	1	0	2	0	-	-	42	14
1975-76	37(1)	14	2	2	7	8	-	-	46(1)	24
1976-77	38	18	4	0	1	0	2	0	45	18
1977-78	17	12	2	1	5	2	1	0	25	15
1979-80	11	5	0	0	0	0	-	-	11	5
1980-81	21(1)	8	2(1)	0	5	4	-	-	28(2)	12
1981-82	15	9	0	0	4	2	-	-	19	11
1982-83	30(6)	5	2(1)	0	3	2	-	-	35(7)	7
TOTAL	216(8)	86	13(2)	3	27	18	3	0	259(10)	107

able to find the net on every one of those occasions despite the pressure.

Late 1977 he became a little disenchanted with the club, and was concerned he was not guaranteed a regular place in the team. After interest from Manchester United - an approach he rejected - he decided to move to the States and join the New York Cosmos. He became the first 'current' England international to transfer to the USA. It was a great experience, and one which gave him a good appreciation of the entertainment business. He also played with some tremendous professionals, including Beckenbauer: "I was 28 when I left, so I suppose the English game missed some of my best years, but it was worth it. For the financial rewards, the experience, and the broadening of the mind. I would not have missed it."

After a couple of seasons a change in the Cosmos managerial set-up caused him to consider returning to Britain. Despite an impressive offer from Derby, Tueart chose to return to the club he loved, City. The following three seasons gave him the chance to work under two flamboyant characters - Malcolm Allison and John Bond. Although his career proved to be a successful one, there is a belief amongst some supporters, and indeed Tueart himself, that a manager or coach of the calibre and style of Allison circa 1968 may actually have helped the player achieve a great deal more, both with the club and on the international front.

Allison's second spell with the club was not the success the supporters or the players, had hoped it would be. Regrettably, a wrist injury during a 2-1 defeat at Stoke in September 1980 caused Tueart to miss significant games against Manchester United, Liverpool, and Leeds, and ultimately his absence probably hastened the departure of Allison. John Bond transformed the club, but Tueart did not appear to be given much of an opportunity to impress the new man.

The Blues reached the '81 F.A. Cup Final, but the scorer of City's previous Wembley goal did not make the starting line-up. After the 1-1 draw however, he did make it on to the pitch as substitute for Bobby McDonald late on, but never really had a clear opportunity to change the final result. It seemed likely this would be his last appearance for the Blues, but amazingly his career was given a new lease of life when Bond placed Tueart in City's midfield and the popular player appeared in 15 of the opening 18 matches of 1981-2, scoring 9 goals in the process.

Injury struck on 19th December 1981. Tueart: "That was just about the best run of my life. But I snapped my Achilles just before Christmas - funnily enough against Sunderland - and though I was back at the start of the next season and tried hard, it was never the same again."

The 1982-3 season was Tueart's last at Maine Road, although it is likely he would have been kept on had the Blues avoided defeat in their final game of the season against Luton. It was a poor game to end a heroic career.

Tueart: "It was dreadful. Even the Luton goal was scrappy and deflected. Afterwards my emotions got the better of me. Brian [Horton], of all people, came up to me to shake my hand and I must admit we had a confrontation. I was really choked, and it was just an expression of sadness."

Despite that one game, Tueart's time at Maine Road was an enjoyable one for both the player and his supporters. After City, he moved to Stoke then to Burnley, and today runs his own corporate hospitality company. During the 1990s he also became a director of City.

To sum up, he remains a true hero to thousands of City supporters and played some fantastic games while wearing the Manchester Blue. He was an England international. A pioneer in the States. A great entertainer.

City could be relegated if their form and attitude deteriorated much further. Hearing the concern of some of the players, Swales decided to act: "We started slipping down the League a bit, and all the old hands started stirring it up. Now I had no experience at all of player power ... we'd got about six games to go with the possibility of being relegated which would have been a tragedy because I'd only been in the bloody job five minutes. So I thought, 'we're not gonna win another match under Ron Saunders', because the players weren't playing for him - the old hands - whether they knew it or not. They definitely weren't.

"Joe Smith knew I was a bit worried and he said, 'you've got to do what you think you've got to do. If you feel you've got to make a change to keep us in the First Division then you've got to do it'. I thought 'right!' - I think I did it when the papers were shut on Good Friday, and he was sacked. I can still see his face now. He said, 'What do you mean sacked? Look, I've just got you to a cup final, and you WON'T be relegated!' He was probably right, but I'd decided I couldn't take that chance. I wasn't going to stand for that! So he was fired and we put Tony Book in charge."

With Tony Book, City earned a further five points and ended the season in fourteenth place - four points above the relegation zone. This was the first season of three up/three down, hence the extra pressure. The final match of the season for City was away to struggling Manchester United. United were desperately trying to avoid relegation themselves, and

Colin Bell receives the footballer of the month award from Joe Mercer in May 1974. Bell's former Maine Road boss was in charge of the England team at the time.

needed to beat the Blues to stand any chance of salvation. It was one of the most crucial derby games of all time.

The match was not a particularly good one, as both sides struggled to find any kind of rhythm. United appeared quite nervous and made some pretty basic mistakes, but City were hardly much better. Then in the 81st minute the game came alive. A sporadic City attack led by Colin Bell found Lee, who knocked the ball into the penalty area. It found Law standing back to goal near the penalty spot. With typical striker's instinct he neatly back-heeled the ball past a startled Alex Stepney to give City the lead. Bell went over to congratulate Law, but the former United star stood shell-shocked. A number of fans invaded the pitch, and Law was immediately substituted. He later admitted: "It was no more than a reflex action which made me flick out my heel - and as it was I felt sick. I have seldom felt so depressed in my life as I did that weekend. After 19 years of giving everything I had to score goals, I had finally scored one which I almost wished I hadn't."

The final minutes of the match were marred by a second more ugly pitch invasion from disgruntled United supporters and ended with the game abandoned. The League later ruled the score should stand and United were down. It must be made clear, however, that United would have been relegated regardless of Law's goal - fellow strugglers Birmingham and Southampton both won on the same afternoon - but the story which made the headlines was that Law had relegated his former club.

Denis Law is engulfed by distressed United supporters after his goal had sealed the fate of his former club in the April 1974 Old Trafford derby.

Dennis Tueart, playing in his second controversial derby of the season, remembers Law's disappointment: "In fairness, people keep referring to Denis's back-heeled goal sending United down, but it didn't actually make a difference. That should really go on record, because Denis was so sick at the time. Obviously, he had a passionate feeling for both clubs and he was doing a job like any professional. When the ball comes to Denis Law within striking distance of the goal he doesn't think who he is playing against. It's just natural reaction.

"And I learnt because Denis was one of my schoolboy heroes ... Denis Law and Jim Baxter ... it was a pleasure to play with him for those couple of months. In training the lad was a genius, and his finishing was tremendous. But he always gets blamed for putting United down, but he knew at the time that United were doomed because the other results had gone against them. Obviously, it's a good line for some, but I don't think Denis appreciated it.

"After the game it was unbelievable. I think everybody knows the most direct way from Old Trafford to Maine Road to drop us off, was probably via Chorlton at that time. It was certainly the most direct route. On this night there was an insistence from the body of the coach to go the long way round. Into town, around town, then back out to Maine Road via Moss Side. This was so that we could all wave and beep the horn at all the Man. United fans, and tell them they were going down. It was a strange feeling actually."

The club's only ever-present that season, Willie Donachie, remembers the post-match celebrations: "Well, I must say, at the time that was fantastic for us. Looking back it was probably a bit childish, but we were delighted because United are such a big club. They get all the publicity and stuff, and because of the local rivalry, it was great.

"The local lads really hated United - Doyley and Colin Barrett. They were good lads. But it was never really instilled in the players. It was nothing personal. They were just the big rivals. We wanted to beat them for all our fans in the city."

The period 1970-1974 saw so many changes at Maine Road with Mercer and Allison both leaving the club, along with former cup winning players Dowd and Young; a bitter take-over battle resulting in a new Chairman and Board of directors; three managers during 1973-4; a Wembley appearance that ended in failure and the relegation of rivals United. For the supporters it seemed a strange time after five years of glory, and many must have wondered why it had all altered so quickly. More changes were to follow with Francis Lee, one of the most influential players of the period, more or less forced out during the 1974 close season. It was a sad end to an eventful City period.

There were, however, a lot of positives. In particular the popularity of the club. Gradually City's attendances were increasing as the decade progressed. 1973-4 had seen a few problems caused by the power cuts and the petrol shortages which affected figures but, in the main, bigger crowds were attending games at Maine Road with City proving the third most popular club behind Liverpool and United. Swales wanted the Blues to be number one before the end of the 1970s and, with United in Division Two, it all seemed possible.

Chapter Sixteen

SEVENTIES SUCCESS

1974 1977

IN almost complete contrast to the previous four seasons when change followed change, the three seasons leading up to the summer of 1977 brought a period of stability to Maine Road. Tony Book would be the manager throughout the period, Peter Swales ensured stability in the Boardroom, and on the pitch a few key signings brought glory. True the Mercer-Allison side of the late sixties/early seventies was now being dismantled, but the players brought in still excited the City faithful.

Francis Lee moved on to Derby, Denis Law announced his retirement, while Mike Summerbee was nearing the end of his distinguished City career. But the arrival of Dennis Tueart had impressed many City fans. Another exciting player arrived in August 1974 - £250,000 Asa Hartford. He was described by manager Book at the time as his 'first piece of gold', and it was no exaggeration. Hartford brought terrific stamina and determination to the side and was a player capable of dictating the course of the game by his efforts in midfield. He was precisely the kind of ball player all the best sides need, and Book was delighted with the purchase. So were the fans on the Kippax when his debut game ended in a 4-0 victory over West Ham, and in his second appearance he scored the only goal to defeat Tottenham. Hartford said at the time: "The fans have made my job easier already by the way they've welcomed me to Maine Road. I'm made up with the kind of reception I've got. I'm desperate to do well for City. I hope for immediate success and I think playing with such great players as Colin Bell, Rodney Marsh, and Dennis Tueart must make my kind of job easier."

With a side full of entertainers City made their mark on the League, and by the end of September were in second position. Liverpool had been the pace-setters but a 2-0 City victory on 14th September - with goals from Marsh and Tueart - had knocked them off the top, leaving the race wide open.

Rodney Marsh, who had become the City captain, had at times suffered from his new responsibility, but in the game against QPR on 28th September he produced a particularly memorable goal in the 83rd minute. His involvement up to that point had been disappointing, but somehow he managed to score from a spectacular overhead kick. One reporter stated he: "attempted an overhead kick that seemed to have as much chance of success as a batsman hitting the pavilion clock." The goal put City second, and everyone began to believe the League Championship was a strong possibility.

City maintained their challenge and headed the table on a couple of occasions in November. Then came December, when a couple of disappointing draws followed by two miserable defeats left City in eighth position. The last game of the month was particularly painful as former Blue hero Francis Lee returned, and proceeded to score a goal at the Platt Lane End to help Derby to a 2-1 victory. The television cameras were there and, as the player celebrated, commentator Barry Davies enthused famously: "Look at his face, just look at his face!" These words were later used to form part of the opening titles of the BBC's Fantasy Football programme in the mid-1990s, but it was clear in 1974 that Lee had proved his point. It's doubtful Chairman Swales ever regretted transferring the player, but it was obvious Lee still had a lot to offer. So much, in fact, he helped Derby County to the First Division title later that season.

The New Year didn't really provide much to lift the crowd as the F.A. Cup ended in defeat by

In September 1974, Colin Barrett netted his one and only City goal, in a 6-0 demolition of Scunthorpe in the League Cup.

Captain Rodney Marsh's amazing overhead kick brought the only goal of the game against QPR in September 1974. It is remembered as one of the finest ever scored at Maine Road.

Newcastle. City had been drawn away, but an F.A. ruling following crowd disorder at St. James Park insisted Newcastle played at Maine Road. Earlier in the season there had also been disappointment in the League Cup as Second Division Manchester United defeated City 1-0 with a hotly disputed penalty in the third round.

In the League, City started to hover around eighth place, as moderate away form prevented them from maintaining the early season challenge. Everton's Joe Royle had been brought to the club in a bid to boost the attack, although he only managed one goal in sixteen appearances that season. Nevertheless, the signing was an important one for both player and club. Royle: "I'd been at Everton for some time, and I was getting over a back injury. Back surgery. Although I was fully fit. Everton had signed Bob Latchford and Billy Bingham told me, down on the training pitch on Christmas Eve '74 that Manchester City wanted to buy me. I said: 'I'm going'. I signed for City within an hour. I think I signed for a tenner rise, but it was actually costing me money because by the time I was driving everyday from Ormskirk my petrol bill was more. But I was just desperate to get away and get a fresh start.

"I'd turned down Birmingham. I'd turned down Crystal Palace. There had been interest from United through Tommy Doc. Then of course City. Chelsea were also interested, but I knew people at City. I knew that the club would suit me. I had three terrific years there. Good strong side. When I first went there I played with Rodney Marsh. Mike Summerbee was still around. Great players. We had terrific support. They love their City. It's often said that they have more Manchester supporters than United do. I don't know whether that's true but they love their City and they realise that it was a good time. A good era."

The season ended with City in eighth place, seven points behind champions Derby. The final position was a satisfactory one for manager Tony Book. He had introduced a few new faces and had managed to take the club forward after the upheaval of the previous season. City fans had been provided with plenty of excitement, and there was hope for the future.

Off the pitch, Peter Swales announced changes to the structure of the club when he brought in three new faces to help shape the club's direction. He termed the men 'Vice-Presidents', and claimed the idea was based on a model he had seen working successfully at Barcelona. The new men were Fred Pye - who would look after the Youth set up with Chief Scout Ken Barnes; Bill Adams - given the task of raising funds via organising sportsmen's dinners; and Michael Horwich, whose role was not so clearly defined. Horwich had been one of the original members of Joe Smith's consortium and his arrival as Vice-President meant every member of that consortium was now involved with the club.

Horwich had also worked with Chris Muir, in the early 1960s, to try and gain control of the club.

The changes didn't really affect the club in 1975 but, in later years, many would say these appointments merely helped increase the size of the Board without really benefiting the club. The idea seemed right, but whether the club achieved any genuine long term benefits is open to debate.

By the start of the 1975-6 season Mike Summerbee had been transferred to Burnley for £25,000, while Tony Book splashed out £200,000 to purchase central defender Dave Watson from Sunderland. Watson immediately pledged his loyalty to the Blue cause by signing a six year contract. This transfer brought City's total of internationals to eight, but before the end of the season the improved form of Joe Corrigan would make the total nine. City were truly a wealthy, glamorous club, with somewhere in the region of 15,000 season ticket holders backing Book's bid for success. If Tony Book wanted a player Peter Swales would find the money and the player would be bought. It was as simple as that. The media believed City were big spenders and a figure of £1.5 million was quoted as the amount the Blues had splashed out under Swales. That figure wasn't inflated, and in any case overlooked the money brought into the club from sales, but it was a signal to all in the game that City were willing and able to compete for star players. Although, they didn't always get their man.

One who seemed destined to sign for the Blues was England captain and future City manager Alan Ball. In May 1975, Peter Swales felt convinced the Arsenal player would sign for City and seemed prepared to sell Rodney Marsh to raise the funds. The *News Of The World* even suggested City might be prepared to sell Dennis Tueart if it guaranteed Ball's signature. Eventually, the transfer died and neither Tueart nor Marsh were sold to fund anything. Ball remained at Arsenal until December 1976 when he moved on to Southampton. Nevertheless, it was an indication of the club's high profile that City were continually linked with football's most famous stars.

The season got off to a flying start with City defeating newly promoted Norwich 3-0. After the game Norwich manager John Bond told the press City had been physical and intimidated his players. The Blues denied it, but with big Dave Watson in the side the media started to look for the negatives.

Whether physical or not, City's poor travelling form carried over from the previous season as the first four away games at Coventry, Aston Villa, West Ham, and Derby all ended in defeat. These reverses left the Blues in mid-table, but City's progress in the League Cup brought hope. They had been drawn away at Norwich and John Bond once again complained about City's approach. After a 1-1 draw Bond's comments appeared in the newspapers, with the added media slant that Bond was 'anti-City'. That angered the Norwich manager and in City's programme for the replay he tried to defend himself: "I've no anti-feelings towards them at all. My comments after our games were opinions that I felt justified in expressing at the time.

"In the League match at Maine Road I accused them of being physical. And they were. Not everybody in the side, but certain people. And at our place in the League Cup I said they were terribly negative, and I do not sway from this opinion. I don't know whether Tony Book came to our place and might have said, 'sod it', we've got our own priorities. But I can assure you that Manchester City lost a lot of good friends in our area with their tactics last Wednesday. I have a feeling for football generally and the game will disintegrate unless managers and coaches like ourselves do something about it. These feelings were the basis of the views I expressed. I'm not a person who takes any delight at being anti-anything in soccer."

Peter Barnes looks determined to impress in his first league game at Maine Road, versus Luton on 19th October 1974. A week earlier he had made his debut in a 2-1 defeat at Burnley.

The replay ended 2-2 after extra-time and forced the tie to a second replay at neutral Stamford Bridge. That game ended 6-1 and included a hat-trick from Dennis Tueart. In the next round City faced Second Division Nottingham Forest on 8th October at Maine Road. In comments that appeared the total opposite of John Bond's, Clough told the press: "I was praying Manchester City would beat Norwich because I wanted to play the best. City are one of the most entertaining and talented sides in the First Division at home. We have no serious thoughts of shocking City but we hope to give a good account of ourselves against a side that is potentially one of the best in the land.

"When I last came to Maine Road it was with Leeds United and we lost 2-1. If we keep the score down to 2-1 tonight then I think we'll show the strides that Nottingham Forest have taken."

Clough, one of football's most knowledgeable men, predicted the score accurately with goals from Bell and Royle helping City achieve the 2-1 result. That win put City into the fourth round and set Manchester up for a League Cup derby match for the second successive year. This time the game would be played at Maine Road between two first Division sides. The Blues were determined to win and by the end of the game United had been soundly thrashed.

City effectively ended the contest inside the opening thirty minutes when they ran United's defence ragged with some highly skilful and exciting football. As early as the first minute the Blues took the lead when Tueart pulled down a pass and comfortably drove the ball into the net, but five minutes later tragedy struck when Colin Bell did not get up following a tackle from United captain Martin Buchan.

Colin Bell will never forget the entire incident: "I remember Dennis Tueart knocking me through on the inside-right position, and I had three options - the first, I was going to have a shot if the ball would sit right, from about 25 to 30 yards out. Or, I could even quicken up and go for goal first thing. The third option was to drag the ball inside a defender - and it was Martin Buchan as it happens. I was weight bearing on my right leg as I

The programme from the League Cup derby at Maine Road on 12th November 1975.

Roy Bailey and Ken Griffiths help the first aid men stretcher Colin Bell off the pitch following his injury in the November 1975 League Cup derby.

dragged the ball to let him go past at speed, and he caught my knee - bent the knee backwards, burst a couple of blood vessels, did the ligaments, did the cartilage, and off I went. That was the beginning of the end of my career."

The City fans chanted 'Animal' at Buchan as Bell was stretchered off. They firmly believed the injury was intentional, but Bell does not accept that view: "People ask me if the tackle was done on purpose. I don't believe it was and don't believe things like that should happen in the game. No - it's a man's game, you take the knocks. I've only got to be thankful that I was in my late twenties when picking up the injury."

Tueart felt the injury was a major blow to the club: "It didn't look anything at the time. It really didn't. I've seen it on tape many, many times. I've watched it in slow motion, slowed it right down still trying to see, and it looks so innocuous. But you knew that when Colin went down there really was a big problem. At the time we had no idea of the extent of the damage. It also left a major hole in our side - a major hole! He would have been a major loss to any side, but ours in particular because we had such a balanced side. Such a settled team. He and I worked quite well together because I used to operate on the right a lot and he did as well. If I drifted off and left the position he would fill it. Then there was his phenomenal ability to get up and down the field. And of course his goalscoring as well. Although we went on to win the League Cup that was the biggest setback, and I don't think we were ever really as good after Colin's injury."

At first the story went around that Bell would return within a month or so, but as time went by the realisation set in that Bell would never again be the instrumental figure he was before.

Tommy Booth was brought on to replace Bell, and with determination the Blues dominated the match. Asa Hartford was the star man with a tremendous display and after 28 minutes he netted from Royle's knock-down. About seven minutes later a mistake by Buchan allowed the ball to reach Tueart who drilled it past Paddy Roche for City's third.

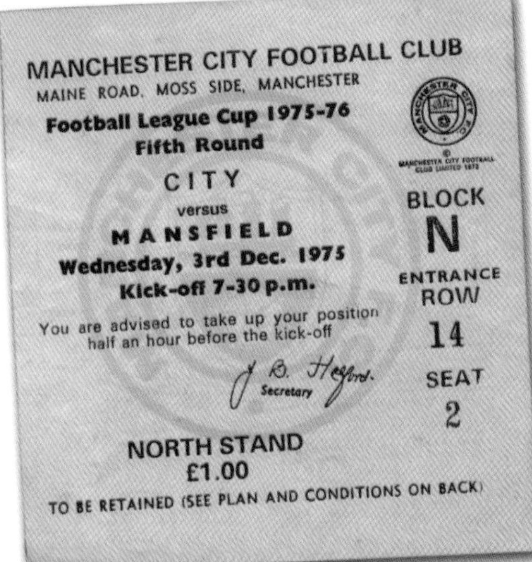

MANCHESTER CITY FOOTBALL CLUB
MAINE ROAD, MOSS SIDE, MANCHESTER
Football League Cup 1975-76
Fifth Round
CITY
versus
MANSFIELD
Wednesday, 3rd Dec. 1975
Kick-off 7-30 p.m.
You are advised to take up your position half an hour before the kick-off
J. B. Halford
Secretary
BLOCK N
ENTRANCE
ROW 14
SEAT 2
NORTH STAND
£1.00
TO BE RETAINED (SEE PLAN AND CONDITIONS ON BACK)

Just £1 for a seat in the North Stand to see City beat Mansfield Town 4-2 in the League Cup quarter final of 1975-76. The game was watched by a crowd of 30,022.

Manager of the Month, November '75... Tony Book.

In the second half Royle clipped a Peter Barnes' cross into the North Stand goal. It was a well deserved 4-0 thrashing and, once again, proved City's seventies superiority over United. It also helped cement the abilities of manager Tony Book who won the Bell's Manager of the Month award for November.

In the quarter-finals City faced Third Division Mansfield Town on 3rd December at Maine Road. The game ended 4-2, but the match was not as comfortable as the scoreline suggests. When City were leading 3-2 Mansfield's Terry Eccles missed a sitter, and City hung on. Fortunately Hartford scored late on to provide enough of a gap, and the Blues went through to a two legged semi-final against Jack Charlton's Middlesbrough.

The first game at Ayresome Park ended in a 1-0 defeat, but it was not a poor performance by the Blues. In fact after the match Middlesbrough's local newspaper, the *Evening Gazette*, predicted it would be difficult for their side to overcome City in the second leg. As it was, it had taken Middlesbrough almost 66 minutes to break the deadlock, thanks to City's excellent defence. The majority of the game was played out in midfield with Oakes, Hartford and the emerging Paul Power putting up a good fight on City's behalf. In attack Royle's and Tueart's attempts were impressive, with Tueart doing all he could to silence the Middlesbrough fans who booed his every touch. It wasn't to be, however, and Tony Book fired his men up for the second leg.

Another man ready for the game was Mike Doyle, who had taken over the captaincy from Rodney Marsh. Marsh had now left the club for a chance to establish the game in the USA, joining Tampa Bay Rowdies on 12th January. Doyle was the right man for the captain's role and had proved, time and time again, his determination.

The second leg saw a youthful City side take Middlesbrough apart. In the fifth minute 19 year old Peter Barnes, son of former City Cup winner Ken, crossed the ball to 20 year old Ged Keegan, who proceeded to head home his first senior goal. Immediately the pressure of the first game was lifted and City were able to control the match. Six minutes later Keegan laid the ball off for the experienced Alan Oakes to fire a left-foot shot past the Middlesbrough 'keeper.

City's dominance continued and a minute into the second half Barnes scored to give City a 3-1 aggregate lead. One minute from the end Joe Royle made it four, and kept his record of scoring in every round. City were back at Wembley, for their third League Cup Final. Their opponents would be Newcastle United, and the race for tickets was a tough one. In 1974 City were able to put some Final tickets on open sale, but in 1976 a large increase in the number of season ticket holders, and a reduction in the amount of tickets available meant City could not even satisfy their average attendance. A large number of fans were disappointed, but secretary Bernard Halford pointed out the club had done all it could and he had even taken the step of writing to all the other League clubs, apart from Newcastle of course, asking for any spare tickets from their allocations.

League Cup Winners 1976

The final was played on 28th February with City very much the favourites. Newcastle were suffering with injuries and 'flu symptoms and had a poor build up to the match, whereas the Blues stayed at a health farm in the Chilterns with few, if any, problems. Every member of the side had already played at Wembley except Peter Barnes and Ged Keegan, but they seemed relatively confident in any case.

In preparation for the big game, captain Mike Doyle told the press the Blues would do all they could to win the trophy. In 1974 City had tried to play with style and ended on the losing side; this time, Doyle revealed, style didn't matter: "I couldn't care less if the final is rubbish to watch... as long as we win the League Cup. And we will! The success of this City is the complete team work - and individuals don't count. I'm sorry Colin [Bell] hasn't made it, but I'm damned sure it hasn't weakened our chances, because we've proved it. We've been without him for three months and still reached Wembley."

During the interview reporter Alec Johnson suggested that Wembley newcomers Peter Barnes and Ged Keegan might be the ones likely to let City down. Doyle, who was later named 'Man of the Match' by the *Sunday Mirror*, refused to accept that point of view: "Rubbish! Peter is not only a tremendously talented player - he's got his head screwed on the right way. He just isn't the sort to get all worked up. In fact, I'll bet that he could prove the biggest success of the whole match. He's a natural. He does things superbly without having to think or worry.

Dennis Tueart takes on Newcastle's Pat Howard in the Wembley final.

"Keegan is in the same mould. He'll feel at home, because he's already one of the City first team pool. If he wasn't something special he wouldn't be in it!"

As the game commenced both sides played open, attractive football, although Newcastle seemed to have the edge for a while. Joe Corrigan palmed a 25 yarder from Malcolm Macdonald round the post at one

Peter Barnes thumps City into an eleventh minute lead.

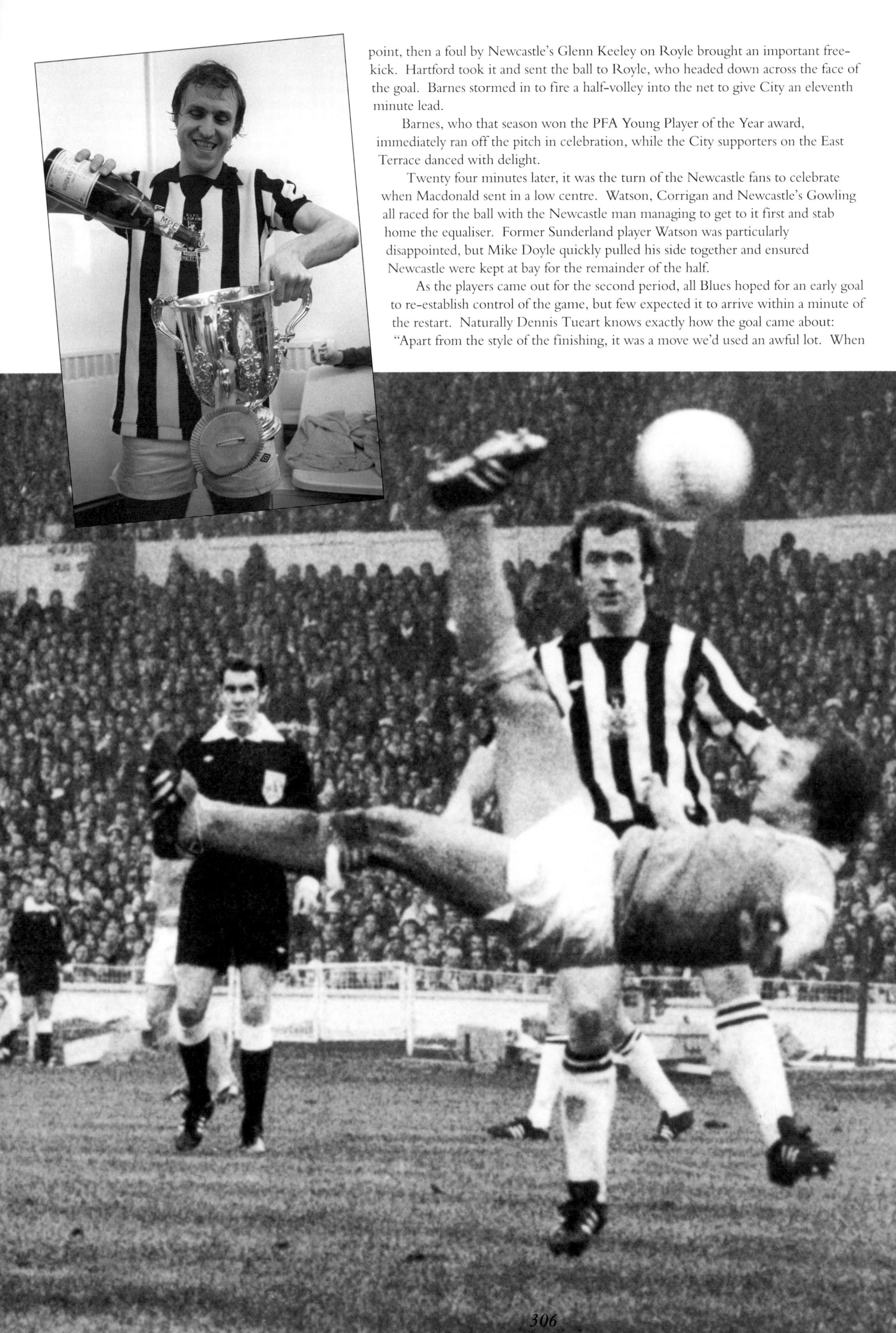

point, then a foul by Newcastle's Glenn Keeley on Royle brought an important free-kick. Hartford took it and sent the ball to Royle, who headed down across the face of the goal. Barnes stormed in to fire a half-volley into the net to give City an eleventh minute lead.

Barnes, who that season won the PFA Young Player of the Year award, immediately ran off the pitch in celebration, while the City supporters on the East Terrace danced with delight.

Twenty four minutes later, it was the turn of the Newcastle fans to celebrate when Macdonald sent in a low centre. Watson, Corrigan and Newcastle's Gowling all raced for the ball with the Newcastle man managing to get to it first and stab home the equaliser. Former Sunderland player Watson was particularly disappointed, but Mike Doyle quickly pulled his side together and ensured Newcastle were kept at bay for the remainder of the half.

As the players came out for the second period, all Blues hoped for an early goal to re-establish control of the game, but few expected it to arrive within a minute of the restart. Naturally Dennis Tueart knows exactly how the goal came about: "Apart from the style of the finishing, it was a move we'd used an awful lot. When

Colin Bell got injured we would try several different players to fit in there and we ended up with Tommy Booth playing right side midfield - Tommy was a centre half but he had a lovely touch, lovely player on the ball, that was the beauty of Manchester City we always had good ball players with ability, right from the back to the front. Tommy came in and did a job on the right side of midfield, and it was no good me going to the far post for crosses with Willie Donachie always marauding down that left side. I would drift off and go into the middle to find any spare balls dropping down. I'd try to get on the end of the knock-downs - not the first cross in.

"The goal itself, I've seen on tape. Willie's going, I've gone to the far post, then come away because Tommy's gone there. But as I've checked back into the centre, I'd gone in too far, the ball's gone over to Tommy. Tommy's got half a head on it, and knocked it back. It just went a wee bit behind me. Well, I'd always been fairly good at volleying right from an early age, and I'd scored a goal, probably it was the first or second game of the season, against Norwich. I think that was technically a better goal, it flew in the net, overhead kick. I'd scored overhead kicks at school, I'd side volleyed which is slightly different, but timing and volleying had always been a strength, and it just came. Speak to Denis Law and he'll tell you any balls that come to you as a forward, no matter which way they come to you, you just try and twist your body and get some kind of contact onto it. Because you know the general area where the goal is, and I connected pretty well, it went across and bounced in.

"It was important because they'd come back before half time and got the equaliser. We'd worked a

Dennis Tueart, 'King of all Geordies', wins the 1976 League Cup Final in the most spectacular fashion and celebrates the win against his home town club with a drink from the trophy.

Dave Watson, spattered in blood, shows off the League Cup as City go on a lap of honour.

1976 LEAGUE CUP RUN

R2	Norwich City	A	D	1-1
	Norwich City	H	D	2-2
	Norwich City	N*	W	6-1
R3	Nottingham Forest	H	W	2-1
R4	Manchester United	H	W	4-0
R5	Mansfield Town	H	W	4-2
SF1	Middlesbrough	A	L	0-1
SF2	Middlesbrough	H	W	4-0
F	Newcastle United	N**	W	2-1

* = Stamford Bridge
** = Wembley Stadium

FACTS & FIGURES

	P	W	D	L	F	A
HOME	5	4	1	0	16	5
AWAY	4	2	1	1	9	4
TOTAL	9	6	2	1	25	9

CUP FINAL DETAILS

28 February 1976 at Wembley Stadium
MANCHESTER CITY 2
NEWCASTLE UNITED 1

CITY: Corrigan, Keegan, Donachie, Doyle, Watson, Oakes, Barnes, Booth, Royle, Hartford, Tueart.
NEWCASTLE UNITED: Mahoney, Nattrass, Kennedy, Barrowclough, Keeley, Howard, Burns, Cassidy, Macdonald, Gowling, Craig.
GOALS: Barnes, Tueart, Gowling

ATTENDANCE: 100,000
REFEREE: J.K Taylor (Wolverhampton)
GUEST OF HONOUR: The Duke of Norfolk
MANAGER: Tony Book
CAPTAIN: Mike Doyle

good free kick for the first goal. Well worked. Marvellous when I see it on tape, because we'd tried it on the training pitch, and it worked to perfection. So that gave us the lead. Then they got a good goal back, we'd been caught a little bit square at the back. Then it was important because it was the 46th minute, just after half time, when we got ourselves back in front. I've never known so many people have a go at me for scoring a goal too early, because they were still at the toilet or queuing for a cup of tea! They couldn't get back in time. It was an important goal though, because we'd dominated the majority of the first half. But we went in at 1-1. So, it was important to get quickly back in the lead again, and make them come out. Which we did. 46th minute you can't have much before that in the second half!"

It was very nearly Joe Royle who scored the winner, but his effort had been disallowed. Royle: "It would have been nice. I'd scored in every round and that would have been the full set. The winning was more important though, we just had to contend with Dennis afterwards!" A laughing Royle added: "It would have been nice if I'd scored the winner instead of Dennis. Dennis was always quick to let you know... He's never been short on confidence has our Dennis!"

Tueart and Royle obviously enjoyed playing together and helped foster a good team spirit. Tueart enjoyed Royle's ribbing: "That's the spirit we had in the team. Joe was a great one-liner. You need people like that in your side. Joe was a bright lad, and as sharp as a tack, and that creates good team spirit and a bit of relaxation. We had one or two characters, good one-liners, good banter, good team spirit. Joe was an artist at that."

The arrival of Royle had helped Tueart's own career: "Joe was essential for me. People don't appreciate how much skill Joe had. Touch and ability with the ball at his feet was phenomenal. People used to think he was a big, old fashioned centre-forward, but he was far more than that. He had a lovely touch with the ball and good positional ability, and from my point of view, because I used to play off him, he was essential. Looking back at quite a few of my goals Joe had a hand in them somewhere."

During the final Newcastle did have chances to level again later on, but City really were the more dominant side. The goal seemed to kill much of the fight that had pushed the 'flu stricken Newcastle side forward. At the final whistle Tueart swapped shirts with a Newcastle player and wore his home town colours for the Cup presentation, while Dave Watson's blue shirt was rapidly becoming blood stained. The big centre half, who had been doubtful for the game right up until three hours before kick off due to problems with a slipped disc, collided with Alan Gowling when the Newcastle man attempted a glancing back header, and after the match television cameras filmed him in the dressing room having stitches. It was scene more familiar to viewers of General Hospital, but City enjoyed the attention.

Another moment caught by the cameras was the sight of the injured Colin Bell waiting for the winners in the dressing room. He was naturally delighted with City's success, but viewers were reminded how his loss had been a major one. Then, as the dressing room became more lively, Dennis Tueart filled the League Cup with champagne and walked into the Newcastle dressing room to offer his opponents a drink. Malcolm Macdonald, who over the years has suffered a great deal at the hands of City - most notably when his Huddersfield side were defeated 10-1 in 1987 - was the first to drink. It was a gesture appreciated by Newcastle and one which Tueart felt necessary: "What else could I do in the circumstances. They have some wonderful fans up there and I used to be one of them as a kid."

Manager Book, who became the first man to win the trophy as a player and as a manager, was delighted with the result: "This was my greatest moment. It was a tremendous final and Tueart's goal was something special... quite out of this world."

On the Sunday, City returned home to a tour of Manchester, and the whole city appeared to turn out. It was a great day of celebration which most Blues expected to be the first of many during the latter years of the decade. Peter Swales: "As Chairman, the 1976 League Cup was my first trophy, and I certainly didn't think it would be my last! It was great to win it, but the League Cup wasn't the highlight it should have been because, obviously, I thought it was the first of many. I probably felt like Johnson did when Everton won the F.A. Cup in '95. He would certainly have thought 'this is the first of plenty'."

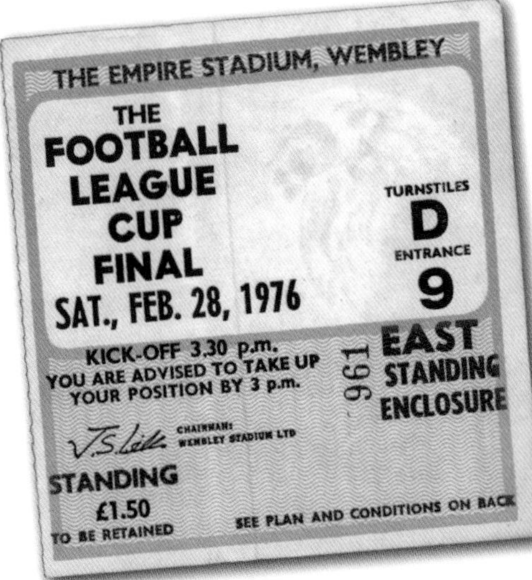

THE EMPIRE STADIUM, WEMBLEY
THE FOOTBALL LEAGUE CUP FINAL
SAT., FEB. 28, 1976
KICK-OFF 3.30 p.m.
YOU ARE ADVISED TO TAKE UP YOUR POSITION BY 3 p.m.
TURNSTILES D
ENTRANCE 9
EAST STANDING ENCLOSURE
961
CHAIRMAN WEMBLEY STADIUM LTD
STANDING
£1.50
TO BE RETAINED
SEE PLAN AND CONDITIONS ON BACK

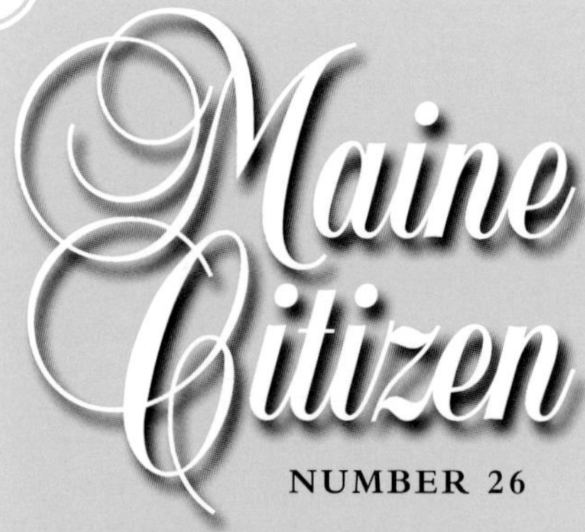

NUMBER 26

DAVE WATSON

Dave Watson was one of City's - and England's - greatest central defenders of all time, some would say the greatest. He was a granite-like figure who simply made it impossible for his opponents to play.

Born in Stapleford on 5th October 1946, he joined Notts County in January 1967. At that time he was playing as a centre forward but then, the following year joined Rotherham United where, under the management of Tommy Docherty he became more of a utility player. In December 1970 he transferred to Sunderland where his career really came alive.

At Roker Park he gained the first of his 65 England caps and became a popular member of the side that shocked mighty Leeds in the 1973 F.A. Cup Final. Sunderland were then a Second Division club and their Wembley success made the rest of football sit up and notice their star players. Within a year City had signed Dennis Tueart and then in June 1975 the Blues obtained the brilliant defender for a fee of over £200,000. Wisely they signed him on a six year contract.

Almost immediately Watson became one of the club's most popular players, with City's fanatical supporters admiring his rugged qualities and his fighting spirit. The media often liked to portray him as having a negative style of play and some opponents claimed he was a dirty player, but the truth was that he was simply a 'battler'. He was determined to see the Blues succeed and gave his all, as the 1976 League Cup Final proved. Few fans will ever forget the sight of Watson helping the Blues to victory while blood poured from his head. The ITV cameras also filmed him in the dressing room after the match, receiving stitches while Brian Moore interviewed him. Watson's comments that afternoon suggested the wound was nothing more than a scratch, but the television viewers knew the truth, and Watson's tough guy image grew.

The 1976-7 season saw him voted City's Player of the Year. He was also the Junior Blues' Player of the Season. Then the following year he became captain and continued to perform exceptionally well for both City and for England despite the additional responsibility.

In October 1977 an injury sustained against Luxembourg in an international once again emphasised his determination. Tony Book: "Dave played in Luxembourg without being 100% fit. It was not possible for him to have been in peak condition because he had limped out of training on the day prior to the international complaining of injury. It was highly improbable for the damage to have healed overnight. Of course, he wanted to play for England, just as every Saturday he wants to play for City. The man is made that way - he does not want to give in to injury, he always wants to play. The outcome is now well known. Dave limped out of the international in the 70th minute and returned to us bound for the treatment table. On the Saturday I took him to Nottingham to check the injury. Dave was prepared to play, just as he was in Luxembourg."

In the end Book refused to let Watson play at Nottingham Forest, but typically the player was still keen to appear.

Despite his many abilities, Watson did not survive the Malcolm Allison purge of 1979 when experience seemed to count for nothing, and he was transferred to Werder Bremen on 26th June 1979. His time in Germany was far from happy and he returned to England the following October to join Southampton.

He later moved to Stoke, then Vancouver Whitecaps, before returning to England again with Derby County. During the mid 80s he played for Fort Lauderdale, Notts County, and Kettering Town.

While at Stoke in 1982 he set a record by becoming the first man to make England international appearances while on the books of five different clubs, and it was that same year he made the last of his international appearances, at the age of 35.

He scored four international goals, and also captained England on three occasions. During his Maine Road career he made 30 international appearances and is second only to Colin Bell in number of England games played while with the Blues.

The muscular and effective Watson is regarded by many as England's premier central defender of his era. He was a rock in defence, and a vital member of Tony Book's impressive side from 1976 to 1979.

WATSON'S PLAYING RECORD

	LEAGUE		FA CUP		FL CUP		EUROPE		TOTAL	
	App	Gls	App	Gls	App	Gls	App	Gls	App	Gls
1975-76	31	1	1	0	7	1	0	0	39	2
1976-77	41	2	4	0	1	0	2	0	48	2
1977-78	41	0	2	0	6	0	2	0	51	0
1978-79	33	1	2	0	4	0	8	1	47	2
TOTAL	146	4	9	0	18	1	12	1	185	6

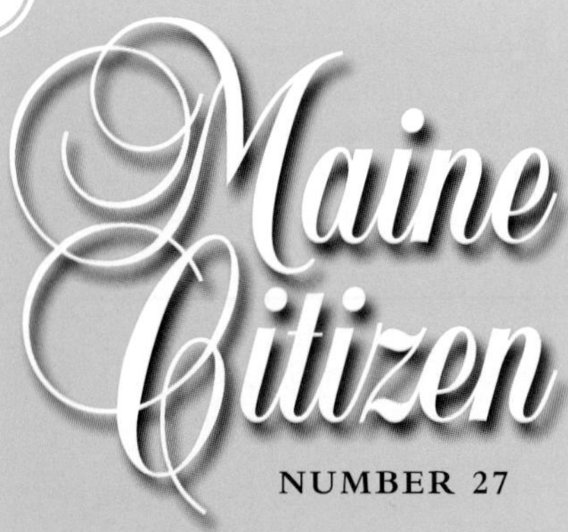

NUMBER 27

WILLIE DONACHIE

Willie Donachie was born in October 1951 and for the first five years of his life was brought up in the infamous Gorbals district of Glasgow: "When we lived there we had just one room for the whole family. There was a cooker in the corner and a washbasin for baths. The toilet was a communal affair shared by five other families."

When Willie was six the family moved close to Hampden Park to a new estate and, with a little more space than in the Gorbals, he was able to play football. It was all he wanted to do. He progressed to Glasgow Amateurs which was, in effect, a nursery club for Celtic. Then he was watched by a City scout and in December 1968 at the age of 17 joined the Blues as a junior, making his League debut against Nottingham Forest on 7th February 1970. Donachie came on as substitute for the injured Tony Book during the 1-1 draw. Eight weeks later he made another appearance as substitute, before he was given his first actual start at Crystal Palace on 6th April.

The following season he had to wait until 20th March for his first appearance but then only four days later found himself selected to play against Gornik Zabrze in the third round second leg ECWC tie in Poland. He retained his place for the replay in Copenhagen after the aggregate score ended 2-2, and for the first leg of the semi-final. Considering he was still a teenager this was a remarkable feat. In the League that year he kept his place for the final 11 games of the campaign.

From then on the Glaswegian became a City regular at left-back. On 26th April 1972 he made his first appearance for Scotland in their 2-0 defeat of Peru at Hampden Park and, after appearing in the 1978 World Cup Finals, Donachie ended his international career on 35 caps. During that World Cup, which ended in humiliation for manager Ally MacLeod, Donachie was one of Scotland's most consistent and accomplished players and did much to help Scottish pride.

The 1973-4 season was another remarkable one for the classy defender when he was an ever-present in all 55 first team games played by the club - League, F.A. Cup, and League Cup. No other player had managed to appear in every League game that year, let alone the cups. What makes it more remarkable is the fact the Blues had three different 'permanent' managers that year - each with his own view of who he wanted in his side. For any player to be selected by every manager has to prove something about that person's value to the team.

In 1976 Willie appeared in his second League Cup Final, picking up a winners' medal, and then the following season was an ever-present in all competitions again as the Blues finished runners-up in the League, one point behind perennial champions Liverpool.

The final years of the decade started to become difficult for the Blues, although Donachie continued to play well and exert his influence in defence. Then, with Malcolm Allison back at the club as 'coaching overlord', many of the more experienced players began to suffer. Team mates Hartford, Barnes and Owen were sold and it seemed only a matter of time before Donachie would be on his way. Although he had been delighted at first that Allison had returned he was disappointed with his approach: "It was probably at that time when there had to be a big change and, just like Ron Saunders, I think he went about it the wrong way. In my own

The rest of the 1975-6 season was a bit of an anti-climax. City had been knocked out of the F.A. Cup at Stoke in the fourth round, and their League form had not been consistent prior to Wembley, although the Blues managed to hold steady in sixth position at the time of the final. By winning the League Cup, City had already qualified for the UEFA Cup so, apart from a final push for the title, they had little to play for.

SEGREGATION ARRIVES

The 1975-6 season was the first to see the Kippax terracing split by an iron fence from the back of the terracing down to the bottom. The fence was placed roughly a third of the way along, with the visitors section the area closest to the Platt Lane Stand. During that season, segregation was only used for certain high profile matches and the 27th September 1975 derby match with United was the first game in which it was impossible to walk from one end of the Kippax to the other, as the Reds took over the new visitors section.

After that game Kippax segregation wasn't used again until the visit of Leeds on Boxing Day, followed by Aston Villa (7th February) and Everton (21st February). Interestingly, the Kippax remained open to all with total freedom for games with Newcastle, Burnley, Tottenham, Birmingham, and West Ham amongst others.

On 13th March it was still possible for the Blues to mount a serious championship challenge as they lay in seventh place, eleven points behind leaders QPR with three games in hand, but they would have had to rely on a number of other powerful sides failing. It never happened as the Blues appeared to stroll along with little interest, although everyone connected with the club denied this. City ended the season eighth, seventeen points behind champions Liverpool, but Chairman Swales predicted further glory was on its way.

He held the firm belief City would dominate the late seventies, and felt improvements at Maine Road would help increase attendances. He pointed out support was already increasing - City averaged 34,279 - and used the visit of Derby County as an example, stating that over 41,000 City supporters were present in a crowd of 42,061 when there was nothing at stake for the home side. During this period, Swales started to travel all over the country and sometimes overseas to help boost support. He would open up supporters' branches wherever he could: "We opened places in Norway, and I thought if United are in Norway then we'll go to Norway. We went to the United-obsessed Malta and tried there. We went to Jersey and opened one there. Went to Ireland and Scotland... anywhere

DONACHIE'S PLAYING RECORD

	LEAGUE		FA CUP		FL CUP		EUROPE		TOTAL	
	App	Gls	App	Gls	App	Gls	App	Gls	App	Gls
1969-70	1 (2)	0	0	0	0	0	0	0	1 (2)	0
1970-71	11	0	0	0	0	0	3 (1)	0	14 (1)	0
1971-72	35 (2)	0	2	0	2	0	-	-	39 (2)	0
1972-73	40	1	5	0	2	0	1	0	48	1
1973-74	42	0	2	0	11	0	-	-	55	0
1974-75	40	1	1	0	1	0	-	-	42	1
1975-76	40	0	2	0	9	0	-	-	51	0
1976-77	42	0	4	0	1	0	2	0	49	0
1977-78	39	0	2	0	7	0	1	0	49	0
1978-79	38	0	3	0	4	0	6	0	51	0
1979-80	19	0	0	0	3	0	-	-	22	0
TOTAL	347 (4)	2	21	0	40	0	13 (1)	0	421 (5)	2

opinion, he gave up on people too fast. Instead of bringing players in who were better than those he had, he would get rid of people and bring in lesser players."

Out of personal choice, rather than managerial desire, Donachie moved to NASL club Portland Timbers for £200,000 in March 1980. Although he still loved City, he felt the time had come to move on. He later played for Norwich, Burnley and Oldham. While at Oldham he became Joe Royle's right-hand man and the two of them guided the Latics to Wembley in the League Cup, to two F.A. Cup semi-finals, and in 1991 to the old Second Division Championship.

Understandably, after so much success at Boundary Park Royle and Donachie were asked to bring some life back to a struggling Everton side and, almost immediately, succeeded by bringing the F.A. Cup back to Goodison. Unfortunately, further success eluded the club and in 1997 Donachie and Royle left Everton.

Eight years earlier Peter Swales had launched a bid to bring the two men to Maine Road following the dismissal of Mel Machin. The approach came at the wrong time, however in 1998 Donachie did return to City as assistant to Royle. City fans were delighted with the return of two of their heroes, although their arrival came too late to prevent relegation to Division Two. The following seasons saw Donachie help coach City to two successive promotions.

Sadly, the departure of Royle at the end of the 2000-2001 season placed a question mark over Donachie's long term role and during the following season he moved on to Sheffield Wednesday.

Today, Willie Donachie is still remembered with much affection at Maine Road. He was a great full-back and an important team member throughout an entire decade. As with most of the quality from City's late 70s team, it's a pity he was unable to remain at the club and help it progress successfully into the 1980s.

we could. It was buzzing, it was vibrant, and we brought the Junior Blues in - we were the first with a junior club and everybody used to come and see how it operated. It's been a tremendous success."

Everybody had huge expectations for the 1976-7 season, and once again the club paraded a new expensive signing. This time it was former Red, Brian Kidd, signed from Arsenal for £100,000. City also signed Jimmy Conway for £30,000 from Fulham, but he made only eleven League appearances during the season. One significant departure, however, was Alan Oakes, who signed for Chester for £15,000, after making more than 650 appearances for the Blues in an illustrious career stretching back to 1958.

The season opened with a 2-2 draw at Leicester and the Blues remained undefeated until their seventh game, by which time City were second to Liverpool. They had already been defeated in the League Cup, losing 3-0 to Ron Saunders' Aston Villa, but were a little more hopeful of success in Europe. They faced one of the world's greatest clubs, Juventus, on 15th September at Maine Road determined to re-establish their European credentials, while the bulk of the City squad hoped to impress England manager and former Blue Don Revie who was watching from the Main Stand.

The match, viewed by almost 37,000 ended with a narrow victory to the Blues. Brian Kidd netted the only goal of the game and his first for the club, but it was not a good enough lead. Tony Book had hoped for a two goal advantage, but was still hopeful of glory in the second leg: "I am extremely confident. I do not promise victory in the second leg. Nor do I foresee defeat. The vital thing is going to be the first goal scored - the team that gets it could easily carry off the title."

Book accurately predicted success for the victors; sadly it was Juventus who went on to win both the game and the competition. Before 55,000 in rainy conditions in Turin, Juventus defeated City 2-0.

Tueart believes City's failure was simply a result of inexperience on the continent: "Against Juventus we didn't do too badly in the first game, but we only got the one goal. I think that was because we were a little inexperienced compared to the likes of Liverpool. They had a European head on. They knew how to play in Europe. We didn't. We still went out with all the flair and creative stuff we had in the English League. We just didn't have the ability to play European style at that time. We weren't ready.

"We'd only just come together within 18 months and then we were in Europe. Probably from Tony

Brian Kidd signed from Arsenal in July 1976 and went on to make 127 (+ 1 sub) first team appearances for the Blues.

Book's view as well, he was a little inexperienced as far as Europe was concerned. There wasn't any major change in tactics. We only got the one goal lead which Juventus were happy with. It would have been nice to have been drawn away first - see what we could do there - and then bring them back here. The goal was just before half-time, which is a great time to score, but we couldn't break them down in the second half. They just got behind the ball. Then we went to Juventus, 2-0. They kicked ten bells out of us, unbelievable! Tommy Booth was defending a corner and, as the ball came over, Tommy went up to head clear and this guy came up behind him. I think it was Tardelli, the Italian international, and he came up with six studs in the middle of Tommy's back. Straight through the middle of his back. Tommy went flying ... and the referee didn't do anything! He just played on, unbelievable! And that's where we were very inexperienced. Very, very poor in that European tie. No real steel, no European steel."

The defeat could have seriously affected City's motivation but Book, with Chief Coach Bill Taylor, managed to ensure everyone connected with the club realised how strong a side Juventus were. Defeat was no disgrace. In the League, City continued to impress and, after a 2-2 draw at Everton on 5th October, headed the table. A draw against QPR followed and then a 1-0 defeat at Ipswich caused a little concern.

Joe Corrigan fists the ball clear of Brian Kidd's head during a 2-1 win against Bristol City at Maine Road in September 1976.

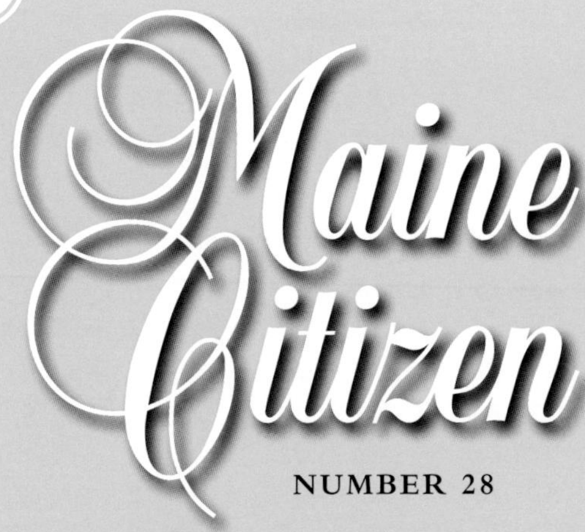

NUMBER 28

JOE CORRIGAN

There are some players who become permanent fixtures from the moment they make their debuts, while others have to work long and hard to prove their ability and fitness. Joe Corrigan's early career very much followed the latter.

Born in Manchester on 18th November 1948 Joe joined the Blues as an amateur in September 1966 from Sale. On 25th January 1967 he turned professional, then a little over eight months later an injury to Harry Dowd, and the fact Ken Mulhearn was cup-tied, allowed Joe to make his first team debut in a Third Round League Cup tie against Blackpool on 11th October 1967. Despite seeming at fault for Blackpool's goal, he retained his place for the replay a week later - a 2-0 victory. Harry Dowd returned for the next tie, leaving Corrigan to wait until 11th March 1969 for his next first team appearance - a 2-1 League defeat at City's bogey team Ipswich. He made three further appearances that season.

Prior to those four League matches he had a spell on loan at Shrewsbury (October 1968), where he gained enormous benefit from the guidance of former United 'keeper Harry Gregg.

Despite these appearances, it wasn't until the 1969-70 Cup double season that he really started to get noticed. He appeared in a total of 50 League and Cup games including every League Cup match and all bar one of City's ECWC ties. For an initial full season it was an amazing record, especially as he had helped City become the first side to win major European and domestic trophies in the same term.

He was still a little inconsistent at times and had to work hard to improve his performances and to keep his weight down. Even in that 1969-70 season there had been a few worrying moments. One Corrigan error came in the game with West Ham on 21st March 1970, when his clearance went straight to Hammers' Ronnie Boyce who immediately thumped it back over the

'keeper's head and into the net. It was a goal regularly shown on television throughout the 70s and was part of a 5-1 scoreline that was even more embarrassing for the young 'keeper.

The arrival of Keith MacRae for £100,000 in October 1973 was an indication that Corrigan was still some way from becoming a great international 'keeper. The following February manager Ron Saunders placed him on the transfer list. Many would have sat back, accepted their fate and moved down a division, but not Corrigan. He seemed more determined than ever to prove himself and, by the end of the 1974-5 season, it was Corrigan not MacRae who was City's first choice.

In 1976 he won his second League Cup winners' medal, and for the following four seasons was an ever-present in the League. During that time he became established as a truly great 'keeper and to City supporters was third only to Blue idols Swift and Trautmann. On 28th May 1976, at the age of 27, he won his first international cap in the 3-2 defeat of Italy. In total he made nine international appearances, with only one game ending in defeat. Considering England also possessed Peter Shilton and Ray Clemence at this time, a figure of nine caps was impressive. Had Corrigan played in any other period of international football then he would undoubtedly have won many more.

By this time Joe was a true City hero and seemed typical of the type of committed, hard-working player the supporters wanted. Throughout the late 70s, as City strove to find success both at home and in Europe, Corrigan was probably the most consistent of all City's squad and, as with Trautmann before him, many close games were won simply because of the 'keeper's outstanding performances.

Unlike some of his colleagues, the return of Malcolm Allison in 1979 had no detrimental effect on his performance, or his commitment to the Blues. In fact, the large influx of young, inexperienced players merely added to the true value of having the experienced Corrigan close at hand.

In 1981, under John Bond, Corrigan again proved his worth when he performed exceptionally well at Wembley in both the 100th F.A. Cup Final and its replay, and was deservedly voted 'Man of the Final'.

Unfortunately, two years later in March 1983, as City headed for relegation, he was transferred for £30,000 to Seattle Sounders in the NASL after making an overall total of 592 appearances (second only to Alan Oakes). City fans were devastated. He later returned to England with Brighton, and went on loan to Norwich and Stoke. During the 1990s he became a highly sought after goalkeeping coach, and has played an important part in the Anfield Boot Room supporting Liverpool manager Roy Evans.

Corrigan is unquestionably one of England's greatest post-war 'keepers, and will always remain a true Blue hero.

CORRIGAN'S PLAYING RECORD

	LEAGUE		FA CUP		FL CUP		EUROPE		TOTAL	
	App	Gls	App	Gls	App	Gls	App	Gls	App	Gls
1967-68	0	0	0	0	2	0	-	-	2	0
1968-69	4	0	0	0	0	0	0	0	4	0
1969-70	34	0	1	0	7	0	8	0	50	0
1970-71	33	0	3	0	1	0	6	0	43	0
1971-72	35	0	2	0	2	0	-	-	39	0
1972-73	30	0	5	0	1	0	1	0	37	0
1973-74	15	0	1	0	0	0	-	-	16	0
1974-75	15	0	1	0	0	0	-	-	16	0
1975-76	41	0	2	0	9	0	-	-	52	0
1976-77	42	0	4	0	1	0	2	0	49	0
1977-78	42	0	2	0	7	0	2	0	53	0
1978-79	42	0	2	0	5	0	8	0	57	0
1979-80	42	0	1	0	4	0	-	-	47	0
1980-81	37	0	8	0	6	0	-	-	51	0
1981-82	39	0	2	0	4	0	-	-	45	0
1982-83	25	0	3	0	3	0	-	-	31	0
TOTAL	476	0	37	0	52	0	27	0	592	0

Yet from the Ipswich setback on 23rd October, through to a 1-0 defeat at Bristol City on 19th February, the Blues managed to remain undefeated in 17 League and Cup games. In the F.A. Cup they beat West Bromwich Albion 1-0 in a replay, and Newcastle 3-1 at St. James Park, then on 26th February came a fifth round tie at Leeds. It was a tough, backs to the wall, battle and looked destined to end goalless until Leeds' captain Trevor Cherry managed to score a last gasp winner. City now had to concentrate on the League if 1977 was to be a trophy-winning year.

1976-77 SEASON TICKET PRICES

For the second year running City announced a special discount scheme to encourage supporters to purchase their season tickets early. The prices announced were a bargain when compared with other top flight clubs. Maine Road's most expensive seat cost a mere £29 if purchased before 30th April 1976, whereas tickets at Arsenal or QPR were quoted as costing around £60. The main season ticket prices and their match day equivalents were:

STAND/BLOCK	PRICE (after 30/04)	DISCOUNT PRICE (pre 30/04)	MATCH DAY PRICE
MAIN STAND 'B'	£32	£29	£2
MAIN STAND 'C'	£32	£29	£2
MAIN STAND 'D'	£25	£22.50	£1.40
MAIN STAND other areas	£23	£21	£1.30
NORTH STAND (adult)	£20	£18	£1.20
NORTH STAND (jnr & OAP)	£10	£9	£1.20
PLATT LANE STAND (adult)	£15	£13.50	£1
PLATT LANE (jnr & OAP)	£8	£7	£1
PLATT LANE BLOCK M7 (juniors)	£5	£4.50	-
KIPPAX STREET STAND (adult)	£9	£8	70p
KIPPAX STREET (jnr & OAP)	£5	£4.50	40p

During their unbeaten run the Blues established themselves as a top three side, although they could have seized the initiative had the game with leaders Liverpool on 29th December ended in victory. City were leading through a goal from Royle when, in the 88th minute, Dave Watson headed past Corrigan to score an own goal on a slippery, icy Maine Road pitch. That levelled the scores, but cost the side a great deal more. Had they won, the two points would have made a major difference at the time, but it wasn't to be.

On 2nd April City, lying in third place, entertained fellow challengers Ipswich Town. A crowd of 42,780 witnessed a 2-1 Blues victory with goals from Kidd and Watson. Afterwards Ipswich manager Bobby Robson sportingly told Tony Book: "If we don't win it, I hope you do." Six days later on Good Friday City defeated Leeds by the same scoreline, then the following day travelled to Anfield a point behind Liverpool. Sadly Kevin Keegan scored for the home side just before half-time and Liverpool went on to win 2-1.

Three successive victories against Middlesbrough (1-0), West Bromwich Albion (2-0), and Birmingham (2-1) kept City in with a shout, but a 4-0 defeat at Derby on 30th April was a huge setback, especially as Derby scored all four in the last 25 minutes. In addition Brian Kidd was sent off, and the pitch was in an atrocious state. City remained second however, two points behind Liverpool, one point above Ipswich, and Tony Book remained determined. The truth was, however, that with four games to go, time was running out. As with European competition, Liverpool were used to surviving the League marathon, City were not.

At Aston Villa on 4th May, City only managed a 1-1 draw, then three days later murdered Tottenham 5-0 at Maine Road to keep up the pressure. On the same day, Liverpool scraped a 1-1 draw at QPR after going a goal behind in the first half. The difference was still two points, although the Merseysiders had a game in hand.

On 10th May City could only manage a point against Everton to raise their tally to 54, but Liverpool's game at Coventry ended goalless to more or less guarantee them the title. Liverpool's goal difference was superior, and with a game in hand there seemed no chance of them failing. Four days later City ended their campaign with a 1-0 win at Coventry, while Liverpool played out another no-score draw at home to West Ham to guarantee the championship. Two days later, their final game ended in a 2-1 defeat at Bristol, and City missed out on the title by a point.

Although disappointing at the time, it was a remarkable achievement, especially as Liverpool were at their 70s peak. That same season they narrowly missed the treble of the League, F.A. Cup, and European Cup when they failed to overcome Manchester United in the F.A. Cup Final. Tueart: "We weren't good enough really. We finished one point behind Liverpool, but their last game was academic. In my opinion they'd won it comfortably."

Peter Swales felt the injury to Colin Bell, the previous season had cost them the title: "It was the biggest single stroke of bad luck that we had when he was chopped down at the height of his career really. Nobody's going to tell me that we wouldn't have won the League Championship that year if we'd had him available. He was a brilliant footballer. Terrific speed. Scored plenty of goals. He had everything! Belly was the greatest player I ever saw. No question. And I include all the greats that I saw as a kid in that. I also include George Best. Most people would say Best was better than Bell, but in my opinion Colin Bell was the best player I've seen in a City shirt, and probably the best I've seen playing for England."

Bell was still trying to fight his way back to fitness as the 1976-7 season ended. It was a long, painful process. One other player who had been struggling to overcome injury for some time was Glyn Pardoe. Prior to the start of the 1976-7 season he was forced to retire, after almost six years battling to rediscover full fitness. He had managed to make 43 League appearances in the five years following the injury, but for a player of his age and ability that was a painfully low total considering what he might have achieved. In the history of City, the loss of a fully fit Pardoe should always be bracketed with the loss of Bell. Both careers ended prematurely following serious leg injuries in the Manchester derby.

Pardoe's struggle was over, Bell's would continue for two more years.

Chapter Seventeen

THE MI££IONAIRE CLUB

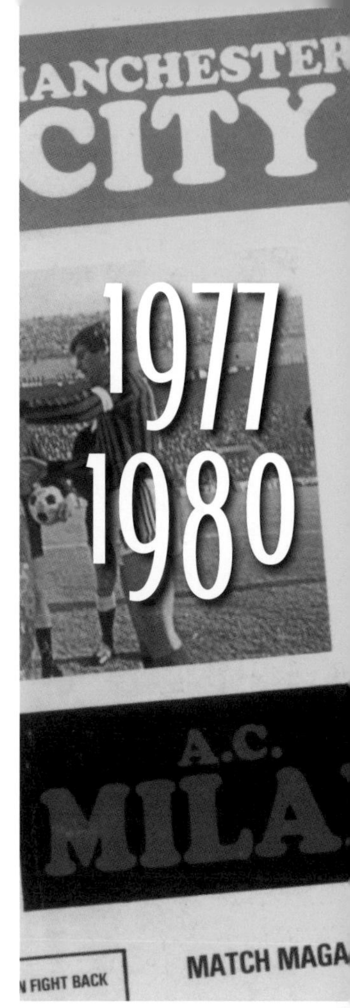

THE 1976-7 season ended with City averaging crowds of over forty thousand for the first time since 1947-8. They were the third best supported club behind Liverpool and Manchester United and entered the following season full of optimism. Over 23,000 supporters purchased the competitively priced season tickets - the most expensive cost just £37. The Kippax terracing price for 1977-8 was a 'staggering' £11, which showed a significant saving of £5.80 over the year. Chairman Swales was determined to ensure Maine Road provided quality football at knockdown prices, and believed this would help City achieve his ultimate ambition: "My initial ten years in the job was completely motivated by me wanting to get one over Manchester United. I'd seen City do well in the late 60s and still not catch United for crowds and support, so my life was devoted to bettering them."

Swales continued to travel all over the world to boost City's support, and often created a story for the media to latch on to. Tommy Docherty once joked Swales liked publicity so much he carried a card saying, "In case of emergency, please call a press conference". Many believed this demonstrated the Chairman's desire to see his own name in print; the honest truth was Swales wanted publicity for City: "I think it's fair that I wanted to see City's name everywhere... in all the papers. I think that's fair. The thing I never calculated was the impact that Munich had on the world at large. There you had a great club whose team was virtually wiped out in a terrible accident, and that really made United. It cemented their name world wide and we could never overcome that. Nobody will ever catch them now, but that was the thing I tried to do. Nobody else will ever be able to do that. We came closest... closer than anybody else in the 70s... and we're in the same bloody city!"

The period from 1977 to 1980 was a time when Swales' City tried desperately hard to overtake Manchester United. The Blues gave it their best shot, but a series of major cock-ups leading into the 1980s started to send the club in the opposite direction.

The 1977-8 season opened with a no score draw with Leicester before an expectant 45,963. That game marked the debut of another big money close season signing. This time the new man was Southampton's Mick Channon, signed for a fee of around £300,000 and reputedly on an expensive six year contract.

Mick Channon signs for the Blues, watched by Peter Swales, Bernard Halford and Tony Book.

FAMOUS STREETS

During 1977 ten streets, or rather closes and walks built by the local council, close to Maine Road were named after famous City players. The idea had been put forward by Manchester City Councillor Harold Collins who, despite his support for United, recognised the city deserved to honour some of the men who had brought honour to Manchester. He worked in collaboration with director Ian Niven and club historian Bill Miles to determine which players deserved the honour.

Those selected were:
Horace Barnes,
Eric Brook,
Tommy Browell,
Sam Cookson,
Sam Cowan,
Tommy Johnson,
Jimmy McMullan,
Billy Meredith,
Frank Swift,
Fred Tilson, and
Max Woosnam.

These nameplates can still be found in an area between Claremont Road, Maine Road, Great Western Street and Princess Road.

The second game saw Tueart bring back happy memories of Wembley when he scored a spectacular overhead kick, during City's demolition of Aston Villa. He provided a further two goals, while Tommy Booth added another to help the Blues record a 4-1 away win. A 1-0 victory at West Ham followed - Willie Donachie was attacked by a spectator as hooliganism took hold of the English game - before Channon scored his first couple of goals in the 4-0 Maine Road defeat of Norwich.

Captain Mike Doyle had been dropped for that game with manager Book stating he wanted to develop a good squad mentality, and Doyle was not performing to the level required: "I wanted a little more from that area of responsibility which he held. I have spoken to him about the reasons and while I realise he felt another senior game might just play him into his best form, I was sure a change would be the best tonic from the team's point of view.

"Mike in his best form is an impossible player to replace, but when the team needs an injection and a revamp then no past reputation can be sacred and tough decisions have to be made in accordance with the evidence of the most recent matches. No player should be happy at being left out of the first team, and while I have had no bitterness from Mike about my decision I know that he will be fighting mad to get back. I would expect no less from him. I now have 18 players who can be relied upon to serve the first team. It's a squad I am proud of."

The opening four games left City at the top of the table, with the next at home to arch rivals United. As far as Swales was concerned the game was an important one if he was to realise his dream of upstaging the Reds. United were now managed by the dour Dave Sexton, who had replaced Tommy Docherty during the summer, and were also enjoying a successful start to the season. A crowd of almost 51,000 witnessed a thrilling City performance with former Red Brian Kidd proving beyond doubt his allegiance to the Blues. He scored twice and helped to pen United in their own half for much of the match. Channon added a third, before celebrating in typical style with his famous cartwheeling arm salute. Jimmy Nicholl netted a late consolation goal, but it was clear to all the Reds had received a mauling. Swales was pleased, so were the fans.

Four days later City faced Widzew Lodz of Poland in the UEFA Cup at Maine Road. Book demanded a three goal margin to take into the second leg, but a crowd of almost 34,000 witnessed a 2-2 draw. The Blues had been leading 2-0 with goals from Channon and Barnes, and City fans in the Platt Lane Stand laughed and joked with a small band of Widzew followers who had been singing throughout the game. Polish international Boniek changed the atmosphere completely when he scored two late goals; a fan ran onto the pitch to confront the player while in the Platt Lane Stand laughter turned to abuse. To cap it all Willie Donachie was sent off and UEFA fined City for the crowd problems.

Dennis Tueart missed the game through hamstring problems but made sure he watched. He did not like what he saw: "We were 2-0 up with ten minutes to go and then Boniek scored from a penalty and a free kick. At 2-0 with ten or fifteen minutes to go we were cruising... justifiably 2-0 up. Then he scored direct from a free-kick, followed by a penalty when one of their guys dived. Suddenly it's 2-2. You go to Poland - it was an afternoon kick off - the pitch was awful, rock hard, and it was just one of those games. Nil-nil and they were happy because they were through. It was that lack of European knowledge again that let us down. All we needed to say was 'let's not be silly'. 1-0 in a lot of instances like that is enough. We missed a couple of chances and it ended nil-nil. Out again, another bit of inexperience showing through."

Widzew went through on the away goals rule. The out of favour Joe Royle felt he was made the scapegoat: "This is one European game that I was probably never forgiven for. I wasn't even due to be playing in the game, although I was in the squad, because Mike Channon had signed. The day before the game Channon pulled out with a hamstring, and I was told I was playing. So I was going to be thrown into it really. I wasn't due to be anywhere near ready.

"In the game I chased the ball down, challenged the goalkeeper, and the ball dropped. Whilst I was waiting for it to drop and then take it into the empty net, I lost it. I should have volleyed it first time. I was always blamed for that. It was City's way. The fact that we'd lost a 2-0 lead at home was the real reason we went out, but I know what they used to say. The players used to joke about it - Asa would say to me, 'what's it like to cost the club a quarter of a million pounds?' It was immaterial really. I knew I was on my way out of the club anyway. I knew that when Mike Channon was signed. I was probably the first of that great side to go.

"I never wanted to leave, but I also didn't want to stay where I was not wanted. As soon as Skip [Tony Book] signed me I think he regretted it because I wasn't an aggressive centre-forward, and I felt that perhaps we just couldn't work together as player and manager. It happens like that sometimes. I still get on with him... great friends... everybody loved Skip... but we just couldn't work together. Bill Taylor, the coach, said to me, 'look, we've got you, we've got Kidd, we've got Tueart... three brilliant forwards who between you scored about fifty goals last season. No way do we want you to go!' But then he said, 'Bristol City are looking to take somebody on loan, why don't you go down there, give it a go, then come back once you've proved yourself again?' It seemed sensible. So I went down and scored four goals on my debut. So that was it then. Great reception... fantastic time... but there was no way of going back to Maine Road because I'd started a new life. I remained great friends with Skip, though."

Royle actually moved on 15th December 1977, but his replacement Channon struggled to make an impact at times.

Following on from the Widzew game, City lost their way a little in the League. Five defeats in October and November left the Blues lying ninth, seven points behind Brian Clough's Nottingham Forest who went on to knock City out of the F.A. Cup in the fourth round on 31st January.

On 26th November the Blues proved they still had the ability and flair to dominate any match when Chelsea were defeated 6-2 at Maine Road - the transfer-listed Dennis Tueart scored a hat-trick. A week later a 2-1 defeat at Derby County ended in controversy when Birmingham referee Derek Civil insisted he had blown his whistle prior to Dennis

Tueart's header entering the net for what should have been the equaliser. What made it worse was the referee played only about twenty seconds of added time despite the fact Derby were frequently time wasting and the referee indicated he had a note of it. Tony Book was dissatisfied, and when ITV cameras supported Book's argument the manager felt angry: "The ball had gone into the Derby crowd behind the goal as we won our second corner in succession and there was no sign of it being returned by the fans. In full camera shot Mr. Civil could be seen with his arm in the air tapping his watch clearly signalling that he was going to add on time for the wasting - and whatever estimate you want to put on the incident, that ball was kept out of play by time-wasting fans for a minimum of 45 seconds. I calculated it at 90 seconds. That was only one of many incidents for which we were entitled to recompense that Mr. Civil kidded us we were going to get. His judgement was diabolical."

A 3-0 victory over Birmingham was followed by a 2-0 defeat at Leeds on 17th December. Then came, for many, the highlight of the season - the Boxing Day visit of Newcastle United. The Blues were now in sixth place and still seemed capable of snatching the title, but that wasn't what made the Boxing Day game so special. What made it a great day for City fans was the news that Colin Bell had been named as substitute. Apart from four appearances towards the end of 1975-6 season, Bell had not played since his November 1975 injury. There were grave doubts he would ever play again.

Peter Swales recognised Bell's strengths at the time: "I consider Colin Bell to be one of the greatest players of all time. And I consider him to be the finest tuned athlete that football has ever seen. So when we talk about Colin Bell, we talk about somebody very special. Our position is very precarious - two years is a long time. But overruling everything is our concern and desire to get the lad playing back in the First Division, and we will try everything that's possible to do that. If it comes to the fact that he's got to quit football, the decision will be taken between Colin and the club - if he's not going to come back, I'm sure he'll know. There's one thing for sure. He's irreplaceable here!"

On Boxing Day 1977, City's greatest player returned as substitute. The first half ended goalless without an appearance by Bell, although each time he tried to warm up the crowd erupted. Then at half time, Tony Book was forced to change the line up: "My plan had been to give him [Bell] a twenty minute run at the end of the Boxing Day match, but an injury to Paul Power in the first half forced my hand. It wasn't planned the way it happened."

When the supporters realised Bell was to play the second half they again erupted with tumultuous delight. Some even cried. Peter Swales: "His return game was incredible. It was certainly the best ovation I've ever seen given to any player in any game. I've seen most of the England games over the last twenty years - you can count on one hand the ones I've missed - and certainly all of City's games, apart from those since the Lee takeover. I've certainly seen plenty of tremendous occasions - players like Dennis Tueart getting hat tricks... United getting beat 5-1 - but the Bell reception the night he came back was far and away the best I've ever heard a player get. Terrific... but you knew he would. The supporters loved him. You can never kid supporters. They know great players. It's no good a manager saying, 'this is the best player we've ever had'. The supporters will know after a few weeks whether he really is the best. Bell was the best, no question."

The arrival of Bell totally transformed the game. City immediately dominated and by full time had defeated Newcastle 4-0 with Tueart getting a hat-trick and Kidd providing the other, but the real talking point was Bell's return. Tueart clearly remembers the night, but like all City fans who were present, finds it difficult to recall the precise sequence of events because there was only one thing that mattered: "It was 4-0 and I think I scored a couple. I remember television news had cameras there, but I've never seen the film. Bell came on at half time if I recall, and it was like World War Three. I've never known a noise like it in all my life! The crowd gave him a standing ovation and he hadn't even touched the ball. I've never seen a guy work as hard to get back. The hours and hours he put in. The pain he went through ... it was a phenomenal amount of work and he definitely deserved that ovation."

Six City men who served England.
Joe Corrigan, Dave Watson, Dennis Tueart, coach Bill Taylor, Mike Doyle and Joe Royle.

Brian Kidd celebrates in front of the North Stand after scoring in the fifth minute of City's 3-1 win against Coventry in April 1978. Notice City fan Helen Turner ringing her famous bell in the left of the picture.

Although he was far from the force he'd been before, Bell managed to make it into the starting line up for the next game - a 2-0 victory at Middlesbrough. By the end of the season he had made a further twenty League and Cup appearances and scored two League goals, but playing had been a real struggle.

With the reappearance of Bell, City went on a nine game unbeaten run, before a 3-0 defeat at Arsenal brought them down to earth. By mid March City were third behind Nottingham Forest and Everton, although Forest were six points clear and had a couple of games in hand. Nevertheless, Book remained hopeful: "It would be folly to accept that our interest in the championship quest is at a finish. I haven't got my head in the clouds, but to concede that Nottingham Forest have the whole race stitched up while there are ten games to go for the Blues would be a negative mood to implant upon the team. It's never over until the final whistle is blown."

By this time Dennis Tueart had left City for a career in the States, although he very nearly stayed in the Manchester area: "That first Widzew Lodz game was the start. I'd had a couple of hamstrings. When I came back I wasn't really going to be part of the side. At 28 it was said the manager wasn't going to make me 'an automatic choice'. I felt he didn't know what my capabilities were... my past record... and that I deserved the opportunity to be one of the four or five that's picked at the start. I didn't get it. I was being subbed, and at 28 I couldn't afford to hang about so I said, 'well, if you don't want me then I'll go, it's as simple as that'. That's normal. At that time I felt I'd proved myself and when I was fit I reckoned I should have been in the side, or at least taken aside and told that I was wanted in the side. I didn't get reassurance like that. I got no encouragement. So I said I cannot accept that and I asked for a transfer. And it was a scramble then. Quite a few clubs came in for me.

"Before I went to the States I'd turned Man United down. It was reported in the press at the time. It was over the Christmas period, and Peter Swales and Tony Book had said, 'Okay we'll let you go, we don't want you to go, but we'll keep you informed of any interest'. Man United came in and I had a meeting with Les Olive and Dave Sexton at Tony Book's house in Sale. They were trying to turn Man United's fortunes around - he was wanting to buy Gerry Francis, and wanted to bring other players in, and I was one of the players he wanted. They'd agreed a fee with the club, and I sat with them and discussed it. Strangely enough that night I was playing in a pro-celebrity squash match at Carriages in Droylsden. I was just going to be a spectator. Then our physio, Freddie Griffiths, asked me if I would stand in as a celebrity. It ended up that I stood in for John Cleese, who had pulled his calf muscle, and was playing Leonard Rossiter from Rising Damp. So I was going there that night and Bill Taylor, who was City's coach at the time and who I had a tremendous amount of respect and admiration for, god bless his soul, asked me what Dave Sexton had said. I said, 'well it looks okay, it's all right'. And I was thinking seriously about going to United, and Bill said to me, 'well think about it, there's two things you need to look at. First of all,

BBC NATIONWIDE

At the end of the 1976-7 season a decision was taken to allow the cameras of BBC TV's news magazine Nationwide to follow the 'inside story' of City. In a series of films shown during 1977-8, the programme attempted to show life behind the scenes at a leading British club, interviewing many of the stars and, unusually at this time, the ground staff. It was a huge success and brought the views of City's players, management and staff to a national audience.

It all fitted in with Peter Swales' plan of turning the club into one of Britain's biggest, and brought City a number of new supporters. At times it also brought much sympathy from the general public. The Colin Bell story was covered in detail and his long, hard battle to return to fitness brought many messages from well-wishers. It was a touching story.

Overall, the television exposure worked well for the Blues, and is a fine example of how they were moving in a positive direction at this time. Comparing this with a similar documentary by Granada television made three years later, it is clear that somewhere in between the making of these two programmes the drive to overtake Manchester United became too great, and actually had a detrimental effect on the club.

are you getting paid more, and secondly are they a better team than us?' Well, I said no not really to both questions and he said 'well there's no argument then is there?' I said, 'No you're right'. So I actually rang Dave Sexton from the squash centre and told him I'd decided not to go.

"Apart from the transfer call, it turned out to be a bad night though. I got stuffed in the squash game! Leonard Rossiter was a good player. I worked hard but got stuffed!"

Tueart signed for New York Cosmos for £250,000 and the majority of Blues were disappointed by the departure of their hero. It's a fact that many City supporters who first watched the side between 1974 and 1980 still claim Tueart as their favourite player.

Joe Royle believes allowing players of the calibre of Tueart to leave was a big mistake: "There's a famous Rodney Marsh quote which goes something like, 'If ever there was a club capable of making a sow's ear out of a silk purse, then City were it!' Basically, it's true. I was the first to go of a group of great City players. At the time when City won the League Cup and were runners up to Liverpool, there could have only been Alan Oakes who was over thirty. The rest must have been mid to late twenties. What City should have done was what Liverpool did. When City were runners up in the League they should have gradually replaced players. Evolution, not revolution. I went, Dennis went - he got frustrated. Then others followed. That was it. The end of any chance that City may have had."

With Tueart in the States, City continued to challenge for a while, but too many games ended in draws rather than victory. Another season of promise ended with City fourth, twelve points behind champions Nottingham Forest. Once again there had been positive news on the attendance front with City the third most popular side, watched by a staggering 41,691. With United's average decreasing Swales was optimistic his ambition to overtake the Reds could soon be achieved. With only two years to go to the end of the decade, he set himself a target to gain the upperhand by the 1980s. He was determined City would be Britain's biggest club.

The post-Argentina World Cup season of 1978-9 was to be the one that brought City level with United. City stars Willie Donachie and Asa Hartford had kept Blue interest in the competition going for a short while, even if England had failed to qualify, while other countries' players were noticed by scouts from many English clubs for the first time.

During the close season manager Book, backed by Chairman Swales, spent a club record £350,000 to land Luton Town's capable defender Paul Futcher. Futcher had already gained ten Under 21 caps for England and was viewed at the time as an important signing. City quickly followed that purchase by outlaying a further £80,000 to sign a forward - Paul's twin brother Ron. Both Futcher boys were delighted, with Paul saying: "It's all been like a dream come true for me. It was the most fantastic month of my life. With all these stars around me in the City side I can't help but improve my game. I've never looked forward to a season so much."

One star no longer with the Blues was former captain Mike Doyle, who transferred to Stoke for £50,000 in June. This left only Tommy Booth and Colin Bell at Maine Road from the 1969 F.A. Cup winning side, and neither were certain to play.

In addition to the Futchers, Tony Book spent a further £100,000 to bring Colin Viljoen from Ipswich Town. He signed just three hours before the deadline for registering players to appear in City's UEFA Cup match with Twente Enschede on 13th September. The entire purchase was concluded within 12 hours of Book first approaching Ipswich and was seen as a major coup at the time. The midfielder had been on loan to QPR, but once he heard City were interested was desperate to move north: "When I was going to move it did seem financial considerations would be my only priority. But while the finance has still been important, this transfer to City has opened up a whole new world of prospect to share in success. When I

JUNIOR BLUES JAMBOREE

In July 1978 City held a 'jamboree' for the Junior Blues club at the King's Hall, Belle Vue. It was the second such rally and was attended by around 4,000 young supporters, some travelling from Norway to attend.

It was a mammoth event and featured footage of significant matches from the previous season on a giant screen, along with a special message from 'Blue' comedian Eddie Large. In attendance were the entire playing staff, management team, and the club's directors. Spurley Hey School Brass Band provided a little music while "Harmony Blend" performed "Blue City" - City's latest pop record which included words relating to the Blues to the tune of "Uno Paloma Blanca". The City management expected this record to be a great hit!

The whole event was compered by City fanatic, and future presenter of TV's Watchdog, John Stapleton and perhaps preparing for the day when he would present "The Time, The Place", he allowed some of the club's youngest fans to probe Tony Book and company with the important issues of the day, such as the question posed by Roy Martin, aged 12. He asked Willie Donachie: "What did it feel like to score an own goal against England at Hampden Park at the end of last season?"

The question brought much laughter from Donachie's team mates.

The event was closed by Chairman Peter Swales who, it must be said, was enthusiastically cheered everytime he appeared: "It's been a super day and I'd like to give you all special thanks for coming along. I'll give you some advice... keep your hats and badges and when you get older you'll be able to look back and say that they bring back wonderful memories of a great day at Belle Vue."

Were you one of the 4,000 Junior Blues who enjoyed that day?

Belle Vue is packed with young City fans at the Junior Blues Jamboree in July 1978.

Colin Viljoen signed for the Blues from Ipswich in August 1978. During his 18 months he started only 35 first team games as City struggled to find a winning formula.

heard they were interested in me I just had to come. It's a dream come true."

While it is a fact the opportunity to play for a big city club was a major plus for the South African born England international, it is true to say City were now more than willing to pay the best signing on fees and salaries. Money was no object to the Board at this time, especially as the club was attracting phenomenal support, and fans took a great deal of pride from the Blues' ability to outbid most other clubs. Sadly, some of the players purchased were not always of the calibre required to bring success. Interestingly, City had bid to sign Kevin Keegan from SV Hamburg and Gerry Francis from QPR, but both approaches failed.

The opening two fixtures ended 1-1, with Brian Kidd scoring both City's goals against Derby County and Arsenal. He followed this up with a third in the game against Liverpool, but sadly the Blues succumbed to a 4-1 defeat. Another 1-1 draw followed, this time at Norwich, before Leeds United were defeated 3-0 at Maine Road - a game which saw youngster Roger Palmer score twice.

Interestingly, in the programme for the next game - a 2-0 win over Tottenham Hotspur - Peter Swales wrote in his column about a conversation he had with Norwich manager John Bond after their game at Carrow Road: "We had terrific support at the match and when I heard the attendance was only just over 18,000 - poor, really - I felt there were more Blues fans than Norwich followers. Chatted with Norwich manager John Bond after the game, discussing the Argentinian signings by Spurs. He didn't seem over enthusiastic, having watched them closely as a member of the BBC World Cup TV panel. Said he would prefer Ron Futcher in his team rather than the fellow Ricardo Villa, indicating we have got good value for our signing money."

THE FIRST ASTROTURF PITCH

During 1978-79 City put together plans to redevelop the training ground at Platt Lane. Their completion would see the club become the first Football League side to install an all-weather synthetic pitch. Peter Swales said at the time: "One of the big things wrong in this country is that the stadiums stand empty for six days a week. We may be 100 years behind the times but this is a beginning. We want to see our ground and training facilities used every day by the whole community."

As a result of the plans, City were awarded £75,000 from the Sports Council.

Within three years the opinions of both men would change. The World Cup had proved that English football had much to learn from the Latin countries and from Europe, and the arrival of Villa and Ardiles did much to lift the spirit of Tottenham. Rumours at the time suggested Ardiles was actually convinced he had signed for City, not Tottenham. The story goes that City had enquired about the player and that Ardiles was keen to come to a big English club, and quite liked what he had heard from the Blues. Whether there is any basis of fact in the story isn't known, but it certainly became a major talking point for a while in Manchester, especially when Ardiles made a big impression at White Hart Lane.

Polish international Kaziu Deyna found it difficult adapting to life in Manchester.

In September, before the game with Spurs, City were negotiating to purchase another World Cup star, Kazimierz Deyna. The bargaining continued for some time, but City were determined to sign the 30 year old Polish international. By the time he put pen to paper on 9th November 1978, City were in sixth position.

Peter Swales felt it was a very peculiar transfer: "I actually went over to Warsaw. This was when it was an oppressive communist state - not like it is now. It was a very hard place and I was frightened to death - I'd only gone to Legia Warsaw to negotiate the signing of a player! All the players were in the army, and I had to see the colonel, or some such commanding officer. And I remember that he brought Deyna in and when he came in he was in his uniform looking very smart. He saluted the colonel and did everything you're supposed to do when you're in the army. Within a short while he was making the excuse that he had to go back to training and I thought, 'this is terrific... got to get back to training... this is what we want from all our players... this is great' And they didn't want a proper fee, there was no money involved. They wanted all sorts. I forget exactly what we sent them... it was all cleared by the F.A. but it was things like typewriters and medical equipment. There may have been a small amount in cash, but most of it was equipment. It was a strange signing!"

Deyna was never the player he should have been at City. He had already won 102 Polish caps and captained his country in two World Cups when he arrived at Maine Road, but he struggled to settle. Swales: "It looked as if it was the greatest signing ever because he was a great player. But you're suddenly bringing him from a strict regime to a very loose life. I mean... he soon hit the bloody bottle! We were always getting him out of trouble. Kaz was always getting in trouble with the police for speeding or something or other. It was all a new experience for him. And he was towards the end of his career anyway. He did play some good games, but overall he wasn't that good at City, really."

By the time of Deyna's signing City were progressing well in the UEFA Cup. On 13th September they drew 1-1 at Twente Enschede, with captain Dave Watson scoring for the Blues, while Roger Palmer found that his first taste of European football ended in disappointment. An injury sustained in that game forced him to miss City's League match at Chelsea and prevented him playing for the England Under-21 side in Denmark. He was still missing by the time of the second leg with Twente.

City won the return 3-2 with Colin Bell finding the net in his first appearance of the season after coming on as substitute for Viljoen. The next round saw City demolish Standard Liege 4-0 at home, although only one goal had separated the clubs up to the 85th minute before a frantic late rally by the Blues made the victory an emphatic one, and caused all those who left early to reflect that no game is ever over until the final whistle. In the second leg City succumbed 2-0 in Belgium - a game which saw the dismissal of Gary Owen resulting in a five match European ban - despite a rallying cry from Tony Book: "We won't sit back and defend that 4-0 lead. Our aim must be to go out and really finish off Liege with an early goal.". The defeat hardly mattered though, as City were through to face Italian giants AC Milan in the third round.

The first leg took place in the impressive San Siro stadium, but didn't actually start as planned. The game should have been played on Wednesday 22nd November, but conditions were poor with thick,

swirling fog forcing the referee to postpone the match. There was already a large number of supporters in the stadium and the atmosphere was electric, with manager Book admitting the fervour of the Italian fans had shocked his City men. He was relieved when the referee ordered the game to be played the following afternoon.

On the Thursday the attendance was 40,000 - significant by English standards, but rather less than the previous night. This reduction helped mute the atmosphere, and lift the Blues. The game commenced in typical European style with City captain Dave Watson swapping pennants with Milan's Gianni Rivera, although the tough City captain looked rather bemused when his opposite number also presented him with a bunch of flowers. Possibly the formalities affected City's early play with Milan creating a perfect opportunity in the first minute. Fortunately, full back Collovati shot wide, but for a while Milan were in control with number 10 Rivera proving his skill and popularity with the locals.

After the first fifteen minutes, City started to gain the upperhand with Tommy Booth and Dave Watson dominating the defence. From then on the Blues seemed the more likely to score, and by the end of an exciting half led 1-0 thanks to a goal from European Cup winner Brian Kidd. In the 38th minute Hartford sent a carefully flighted cross to the unmarked Kidd, who simply headed home past two Milan defenders and goalkeeper Albertosi. It was just what City deserved, and with a further six decent goal attempts in that half, as opposed to Milan's opening effort from Collovati and a Buriani shot saved by Corrigan, the Blues were happy with their performance.

In the 12th minute of the second half City increased their lead with Paul Power - playing his first game since injury in the League Cup at the start of October - making a long, 70 yard run into the penalty area. Once there he cut inside 18 year old defender Franco Baresi, and fired a low left foot shot over the diving body of Albertosi. It was an important goal and gave the Blues an incredible 2-0 lead. Only two teams had defeated Milan in 52 European meetings at the San Siro, and no British side had ever beaten them there. City seemed poised to make history. Understandably, the Blues lacked concentration immediately after Power's goal and Milan fought back.

Derek Wallis of the *Daily Mirror*: "Milan halved the lead two minutes after City scored when Albertino Bigon forced the ball over the line from Walter Novellino's cross and immediately City faced increasing pressure. Three times Corrigan was beaten,

City's scorers in Milan, Paul Power and Brian Kidd, attempt to read about their exploits in an Italian newspaper... the headline says it all really!
The colour picture shows Kidd's goal in the San Siro, whilst in good old black 'n' white are the three goals from the second leg. Tommy Booth (left) headed home after 14 minutes, Asa Hartford hit the second (below) and Brian Kidd made it 3-0 (bottom) before half-time.

but each time the linesman's flag was raised for offside. The decisions disgusted the crowd, some of whom took out their spite on Corrigan by pelting him with rubbish."

With Milan dominant City defenders Booth and Watson once again stood firm to skilfully end a number of important Milan moves. But with only eight minutes remaining Bigon scored his second for the home side, and the game ended 2-2.

At first the Blues were disappointed with the result but, after a while, everyone connected with the club recognised a 2-2 draw in the San Siro fortress was still a remarkable achievement. Tony Book: "The City performance in Milan was the best-ever given by a Blues team in Europe and we were only eight minutes away from becoming the first British club ever to win in the San Siro stadium. The performance was magnificent. But it still took a lot of the cream from the display that we were pinned to a draw at the finish. So we became the tenth overseas team to take a draw away from Milan - and we not only proved we had come of age in Europe but also learned a lot on the day.

"Had Mike Channon and Peter Barnes played in Milan instead of being injured and on the bench, there's no telling how well we might have done."

The programme for the visit of AC Milan to Maine Road in December 1978.

The return leg at Maine Road saw City demolish the Italians 3-0 with goals from Booth (14th minute), Hartford (31st), and Kidd (42nd). In addition to the goalscorers, the stars were Colin Viljoen - who played his best game since signing - and the ever improving Paul Power. The result put City through to the quarter finals of a European trophy for the first time since 1971, but the January UEFA draw wasn't kind as it paired City with top German side Borussia Mönchengladbach. With West Bromwich Albion, Hertha, Duisberg, Dukla Prague, Honved and Red Star Belgrade all through the Blues had naturally hoped for one of the less powerful sides.

The games were not scheduled to take place until March, leaving City to concentrate on the domestic scene - something in desperate need of attention. Out of eleven games played from mid-October until the end of the year, the Blues had only managed to obtain five points. That run had sent the Blues spiralling down the table from fifth in October to fifteenth by New Year's Eve. City had also been knocked out of the League Cup in December by Southampton, although early season form had guided them through to the fifth round.

In addition to the deterioration in League form, City were suffering from a disappointing but understandable slump in attendance. City's average on 7th October stood at 42,453 yet by the end of the year was down to a little over 39,000, and looked likely to fall further.

Speaking shortly before his death in May 1996 Peter Swales admitted this was the moment when he began to feel action was needed if he was ever to fulfil his aim of toppling United: "I'm a Manchester lad - grew up in Ardwick. I grew up being baited by Manchester United supporters and all through the Busby years. I wouldn't want to say publicly that I hated them, I didn't. But they were the rivals. In 1977 we were runners up in the First Division by a point and we got to United on support. We averaged 40 odd thousand and we'd almost caught them; I thought well, next year we'll win the Championship and we'll do it. We didn't - we finished fourth - but I felt we were close. That's when I made my biggest mistake - well I think it was my biggest mistake - Malcolm Allison. Definitely! I got talked into that! Instead of sticking with Tony Book who, when you think of it, gave us second place which today would make him a king, wouldn't it? I think 'no, this is not good enough, we're almost there!' And one or two on the Board started to say 'well, if we could just get Malcolm we could do the final push'. Final bloody push all right!

"Malcolm was probably the best thing to ever happen to Manchester City - him and Joe Mercer as a team. I think Joe was probably a bigger influence than a lot of people think he was, but they were a great team. It doesn't mean though that ten years later you can pick that lad out of the crowd, bring him back,

How the Manchester Evening News announced Malcolm Allison's return.

ENJOY SCOTLAND HOLIDAY EXHIBITION AT THE ARNDALE CENTRE, M/CR. JANUARY 8th-13th

A FRIEND DROPPING IN

FINAL

Manchester Evening News

34,122 — FRIDAY, JANUARY 5, 1979 — 8p

TWENTY-FOUR HOUR RADIO & TV GUIDE PAGE 3 — CLASSIFIED ADVERTISEMENT INDEX PAGE 23

Come back Allison–City

By PAUL HINCE

MANCHESTER CITY today sensationally asked former manager Malcolm Allison to return to Maine Road as first team coach.

City want the extrovert Allison, now in his second spell at Plymouth Argyle, to help them to recover from a depressing slump in which they have slipped from fifth to fifteenth place in the First Division.

Even if Allison accepts the offer it is not clear in what capacity he would return to the club he enjoyed his greatest success.

A statement from Maine Road merely said: "Tony Book (team manager) has approached Malcolm Allison with a view to taking a position with the club. They are meeting later today for talks.

It is understood that the meeting was taking place in London this afternoon with City chairman Peter Swales also present.

Mr Bill Taylor, the present coach, would become "specialist coach."

The irony of the approach from Book is that it was Allison who gave him his start in League soccer.

They first worked together when Allison was manager and Book captain of Southern League club Bath City.

Allison introduced Book to League soccer when he was appointed manager of Plymouth Argyle. Then he shocked everyone when he signed Book for City when Book was 31-years-old.

But with Joe Mercer as manager, Allison his assistant, and Book skipper, City embarked on their most successful era.

By the time Allison left to become manager of Crystal Palace in 1973, City had won the Second Division and First Division championships, FA Cup, the League Cup and the European Cup Winners' Cup.

With the latest offer, the wheel has gone full circle for a man whose life-style and controversial views have made him one of the most famous figures in soccer.

But throughout all the controversy Allison has enjoyed the reputation as one of the finest coaches in the world.

And clearly City feel that a combination of the talents and ideas of Book, Allison and first-team coach Bill Taylor will help the Blues reclaim their position in English soccer.

Allison, now in his early 50's became disillusioned with English socer. He drifted out of the game for a time. But earlier this season he accepted an offer from Third Division Plymouth to return as manager.

But the First Division arena has always been where he has felt most at home and the invitation to come back to the club he helped to re-build will obviously be a massive temptation.

Allison's term as boss of Crystal Palace was unsuccessful. The ageing Palace team sunk quickly into the Third Division.

Allison and Book... a new team?

INSIDE TODAY

	Page
Pop Scene	2
TV & Radio	3
Mr Manchester	8
Survive the Sales	9
Postbag	12
Holiday 79	16
Contest	16
Motoring	18
Two pages of Sport	20 & 21
BMD's	22

Two on widow murder

and expect him to be the manager of the whole set-up. I think Malcolm was a terrific motivator and a terrific coach, but he needed Joe. I think Joe made him what he was - he didn't know that, and a lot of his supporters didn't. There are still a lot of them today - even directors of Manchester City. I don't know how old Malcolm is - a lot older than me - he must be 67, but they'd bring him back now! Because they are real fans you see. They can't get over what he did for them in the late 60s, but you can't bring old managers back."

On 5th September 1997 Malcolm Allison turned seventy and was fondly remembered by all supporters for his leading role in City's late 60s/early 70s success. As Swales commented, he is still idolised by many and even in 1996 when the club was struggling to appoint a committed manager, some supporters suggested Mal be brought back to offer his experience. In 1979 the news of Mal's return as 'coaching overlord' brought a great deal of delight to the majority of supporters.

The news first broke on Friday 5th January with Granada Television revealing Allison had accepted an offer to return to Maine Road from Tony Book and Peter Swales at an afternoon meeting in London. The following day almost every newspaper carried the story and reasons for Allison's return with the *Manchester Evening News* outlining his views: "I was very happy at Plymouth. Things were happening there and it gave me a good feeling. But I have always had an affinity for Manchester City and I am delighted to be back. My first job will be to get the players together to talk about objectives and aims. I want to find out from them what is wrong, if anything, and how we can put it right together."

When asked if he was happy returning to Maine Road as coach he brashly replied: "I am not just a coach I am a scientist. My training is brilliant and, like all scientists, I can make things work."

The City supporters loved the hype and felt uplifted by the appointment, although Allison's arrival did not please everyone. City's highly regarded first team coach Bill Taylor had worked harder than most to improve City's status and felt Allison would undermine his role. Diplomatically he refused to comment openly, although it was obvious he was far from happy with the situation, especially as all the talk seemed to be about how the club had been failing. It was true City had slipped to fifteenth place, but they had progressed in Europe and reached the fifth round of the League Cup. Key players, such as Channon, Booth and Kidd, had been missing and results were bound to improve during January and February when the Blues would be free to concentrate on the domestic scene.

The truth was the City directors felt Book and Taylor were both introverts, and the club needed a 'larger than life' character to ensure the Blues received the best media coverage possible. It was all part of the grand 'master plan' to turn City into Britain's most popular club and had little, really, to do with performance on the pitch. After all, the excellent result over AC Milan proved what the Blues were capable of, and the Book/Taylor combination worked perfectly there so why should the League be any different?

Almost immediately Allison set about toughening up City's training schedule and demanded more from the players. At the time he told reporters: "City have got a different, vastly improved, approach to soccer. The organisation off the field has got to be the best I have encountered. Now it's the playing side in need of attention and some surgery. I arrived with an open mind. I will give to the players, but I will take from them. I want response. I want excitement. I want the place to jump with liveliness. I cannot have it any other way. I expect each of my players to set 1982 as a target - to be a member of the World Cup squad for their country. You achieve goals by aiming for them. There has got to be ambition, and success will breed from it."

He also warned: "Those without that appetite will find it difficult to secure a place at Maine Road. There is a lot of work to be done."

Within a week of Allison's return, City's popular coach Bill Taylor handed in his resignation saying he felt unable to work under the new set-up. It was disappointing news for many of the players who enjoyed working with Taylor both at Maine Road and with England. Then on 13th January, Allison's first game as coaching

On his return Malcolm Allison immediately set about toughening up City's training schedule.

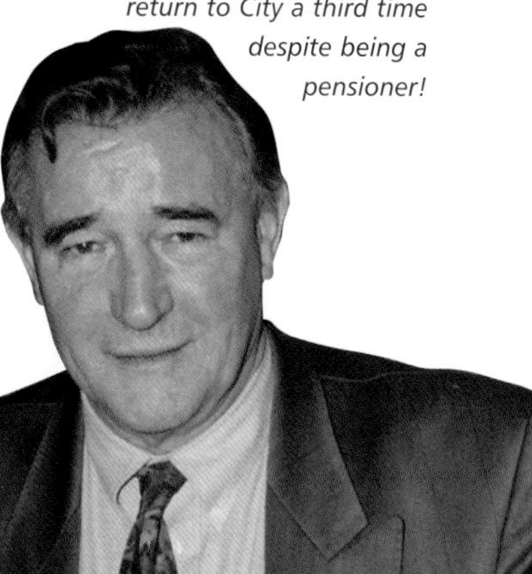

Malcolm Allison, mid 1990s. Many felt he could return to City a third time despite being a pensioner!

overlord ended in a 1-1 draw at Leeds. The next game, his first at home, was also far from successful as the Blues played out a goalless draw with Rotherham in the F.A. Cup third round. The replay ended to the satisfaction of the new coach as Brian Kidd scored twice and important goals from youngsters Gary Owen and Peter Barnes helped City to a 4-2 victory.

The fourth round saw the Blues face promotion-seeking Third Division side Shrewsbury at a snow-covered Gay Meadow. It was a nightmare day with City struggling on the icy surface. A tragic mistake by Paul Futcher allowed Shrewsbury to take the lead and City went on to lose 2-0 to the eventual Division Three champions. Allison and Book complained bitterly the game should never have been played, but it was too late.

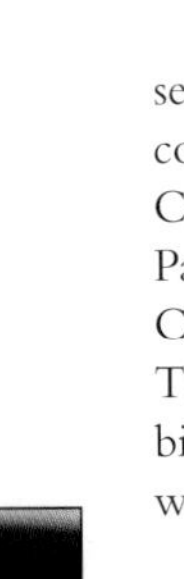

Barry Silkman was bought from Malcolm Allison's previous club, Plymouth.

Afterwards Swales called an emergency meeting with Allison and Book to determine where the Blues were failing. By that time, Allison had already attempted to change the playing personnel. Only 18 months after signing for £300,000 Mike Channon was transfer-listed and immediately brought interest from John Bond at Norwich and from Third Division Swindon Town. The Wiltshire club were the first to make a serious bid, offering £250,000 on 29th January. The player understandably turned down the move stating he intended to remain in the First Division, but the on-off nature of Channon's departure would continue for several months.

On the same day as the Swindon bid, City offered Allison's former club Plymouth £60,000 for Barry Silkman. Even this relatively straightforward transfer dragged on until 29th March, but Allison was pleased to get his man regardless of the time taken. He was also keen to introduce new ideas into City's training schedule and the club brought in 59 year old cabaret dancer and former rock 'n' roll champion Lennie Heppell to assist the training schedule. He began to teach the players about body co-ordination and suppleness. One seasoned player wryly suggesed it might be a good idea to practice playing football once in a while.

Nicky Reid was given a surprise debut in the UEFA Cup quarter final with Borussia Mönchengladbach when he was just 18.

In the League City's form did improve from its November/December slump and February saw them achieve five points from a possible eight, with only one game ending in defeat. Sadly, that was the Manchester derby. The game ended 3-0 with Allison taunted by United supporters. The experienced Colin Bell was used as a sweeper, but the tactic failed and the Blues were well beaten with future City manager Steve Coppell scoring twice. With conditions poor the game had only been staged thanks to a magnificent effort from Stan Gibson and his groundstaff. Swales admitted in the programme later in the season that the rush to improve conditions to stage matches had actually worked against City with both the United match and a 3-2 defeat by Chelsea in January hampering City's progress.

On 3rd March the Blues defeated Bolton Wanderers 2-1 at Maine Road in the last game before the crucial meeting with the highly successful Borussia Mönchengladbach in the UEFA Cup quarter final. Liverpool, and in particular Bob Paisley, had spent considerable time helping the Blues prepare for this match by providing vital information on the West German side. Liverpool were the most experienced of all English clubs in Europe and had faced Mönchengladbach on five occasions, the most recent being the 1978 European Cup semi-final. Paisley told City the game would be tough, and outlined the players to watch. He also suggested Dave Watson and Tommy Booth might be the key men in City's side as the Germans seemed to lack ability to attack the ball in the air.

In the 1977 European Cup final, Liverpool had defeated Mönchengladbach by playing to the strengths of players like Tommy Smith and Paisley felt City should do the same. The first leg saw Allison perform one of his many shock moves when he announced 18

Godwin's Kids

Throughout the history of Manchester City there have been a number of unsung heroes whose contributions to the success of the club have been enormous. These people rarely hit the headlines and often their achievements are overlooked as the players, managers, and even directors gain the acclaim.

One such hero was City's former Chief Scout, the popular Harry Godwin. In a Maine Road scouting career that lasted from 1950 until the mid-70s, 'Uncle Harry' helped to bring over 40 players from virtually nothing to first team football. He seemed able to spot promising youngsters with ease and, once caught, he was determined never to let the player escape and would use his powers of persuasion to convince both the youngster and his parents that City was the only club worth joining. His magic rarely failed.

Born in 1914, Godwin played amateur football at a decent level through to the 1940s then, in 1949, Wrexham manager Les McDowall asked him to scout on a part-time basis. He also scouted for Bury for a while. In June 1950 McDowall became City's new manager and almost immediately asked Godwin to scout for the Blues. From then until officially 1974 but actually much later, Godwin searched for quality players to help bring City success.

In March 1965 he was offered his first permanent full-time contract, yet within days of his appointment manager George Poyser, who had succeeded McDowall, was dismissed. Doubt over the destiny of the club caused Godwin, and others, to consider their future but when new manager Joe Mercer arrived it appeared safe, especially when Joe met Godwin, put his arm around him and said: "I've heard you're good at nicking one or two youngsters. Nick a few for me, will you?"

Mercer made Godwin his Chief Scout, and boasted Harry could: "get where castor oil couldn't reach!" Under the new managerial partnership of

Mercer and Allison no member of City's backroom staff felt left out. It was a real team mentality, with everyone contributing. Mercer always stressed the importance of Godwin and his men.

Throughout the 50s, 60s, and 70s Godwin discoveries appeared with regularity in City's first team, and it proves much about his knowledge of the game that the Blues could boast so many home grown players. Not every young player had been first spotted by Godwin, but each had to be assessed by him and it was usually his decision to follow up any interest.

The list of his finds is incredible and includes some of football's most successful players. From memory a few significant Godwin discoveries are: Alan Oakes, Mike Doyle, Stan Bowles, Joe Corrigan, Willie Donachie, Tommy Booth, Tony Towers, Kenny Clements, Gary Owen, Paul Power, Ged Keegan, Tony Henry, Colin Barrett, Ian Mellor and Glyn Pardoe.

Even that list of great players doesn't illustrate the full extent of Godwin's enormous contribution.

Due to ill health, in 1974 he announced his retirement. Despite this he continued to be involved with the Blues and scouted on a part-time basis. He also became actively involved with City's highly successful Junior Blues organisation where he became "Uncle Harry" to a new generation.

Writing in the mid-70s, Daily Express journalist Bill Fryer recognised Godwin's desire to remain involved with the Blues and with his discoveries: "He retired as chief Scout in 1974 but is still to be seen around Maine Road helping whoever he can. He has a host of famous 'nephews'. All have been flagrantly bribed by his bag of sweets, which he lobbed about with reckless abandon, and all are still coming back to him, like Oliver Twist, asking for more. Nobody knows Harry better than I do. Goodness, I must be the only one left who remembers the old so-and-so as a first class amateur player. I know he doesn't say what he doesn't mean. He's dead honest."

Harry continued his love affair with City and the Junior Blues throughout the 70s and 80s before passing away in September 1993. After his death a small plaque was erected in City's family stand commemorating his contribution to the Junior Blues.

As football moves into the new millennium the headline makers are usually the players, managers, directors and agents. Little is said about the scouts and the backroom staff who develop the youngsters in the first place, yet football could not exist without men like Godwin.

He dedicated much of his life to bringing the club quality players and as a result helped City achieve tremendous success. The team that won the League Cup in 1976 comprised seven Godwin discoveries. No amount of money could have bought the quality he brought to the club.

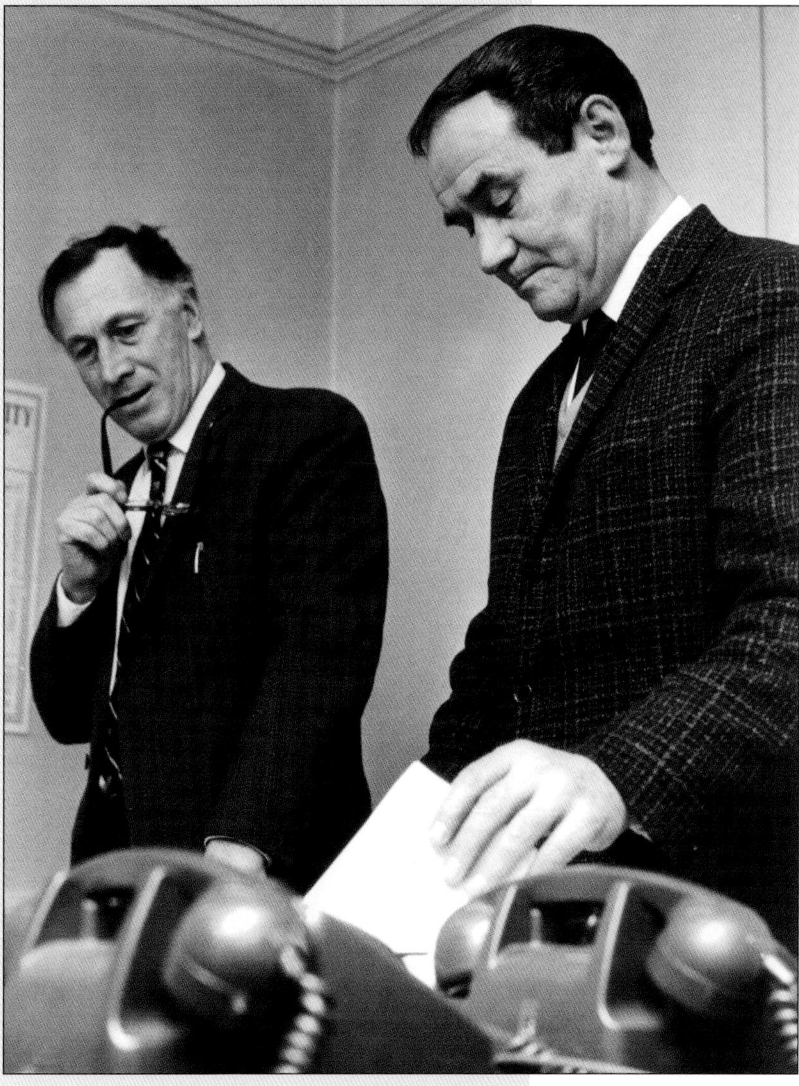

Joe Mercer always stressed the importance of Harry Godwin (right) and his men.

year old Nicky Reid would make his debut. It was an amazing decision which saw the youngster move virtually from the 'A' team into one of the most important club fixtures of the decade.

Reid played well enough to suggest exciting prospects for himself at Maine Road, while a man who felt he had no future in Manchester, the unhappy Mike Channon, managed to give the Blues a 1-0 lead. Unfortunately, the highly disciplined Germans kept the pressure on and snatched that often vital away goal to equalise.

The second leg two weeks later saw Reid retain his place while Allison made yet another surprise selection as Tony Henry - another reserve who up to that point had only featured in two League games (once being substituted by Kenny Clements, once coming on for Asa Hartford) - was included while experienced European campaigners Deyna, Bell, and Kidd were left on the substitutes' bench with Paul Futcher. The line-up for City's last European match of the 1970s was:

Corrigan; Donachie, Power, Reid, Watson, Booth, Channon, Viljoen, Henry, Hartford, and Barnes.

City were very much the underdogs throughout the match and were losing 3-0 when, late on, Reid was substituted by Deyna. The experienced Pole provided City's only goal of the match, but it was too late and they were out of Europe. All the Blues had left to play for was First Division survival and, of course, pride.

THE DEATH OF JOHN HUMPHREYS

In February 1979, Peter Swales and his Board were shocked to hear 49 year old City director John Humphreys had died after a short illness. Always a devoted Blue, Humphreys had been a City director since 1966 and had been managing director of Wilmslow based kit manufacturers Umbro since 1957.

It was mainly thanks to him that Umbro and City had such a good relationship throughout his time. City first wore Umbro in 1934 and the link between the two organisations remained until the end of the 1996-7 season, when the Blues chose to wear a Kappa produced kit instead. The Umbro-City link was the longest sponsorship deal in British sport, possibly the world.

Humphreys worked tirelessly for the good of both Umbro and City and was a popular figure at Maine Road right up until his death. His main role at the club was to head the City Finance Committee which looked at sponsorship and other commercial areas. Much of the financial success of the club during the 1970s was down to Humphreys' dedication, while his visits to clubs around the globe with Umbro gave him a valuable insight into the wider footballing world - something City benefited from. He also brought a number of simple, novel ideas to the club, such as commencing the 1969 homecoming from Wilmslow - an area of popular Blue support.

Peter Swales was shocked by his death: "I cannot find words to describe the loss I feel. The Board Room feels desolate, my colleagues are shattered. When they talk about great men in life and the great qualities they have they talk about John Humphreys. He was very special, he brought something better into everyone's life."

Book and Allison experimented with the line up a little, but the season ended with City in fifteenth place, 14 points above the relegation zone. The lowest spot touched was 17th at Easter. Attendances had dropped, although City's average of 36,638 remained the third highest behind Liverpool and United (46,430). Had City been able to build on the form of the previous season then Swales may well have achieved his dream of matching the Reds.

Mike Channon and Gary Owen were joint leading scorers with 11 each in the League, but supporters were angry when it was announced Owen was to move to West Brom for £450,000 in May. This was the highest fee received by City at the time, but fans felt that was scant compensation for losing the England Under 21 team captain. Owen's departure brought much criticism, but further transfer news caused many to consider whether the problems at Maine Road were more fundamental than one or two uncomfortable players.

Roger Palmer, Tony Henry and Peter Barnes attack the Everton goal during a goalless draw at Maine Road in April 1979.

Both Peter Barnes and Asa Hartford were transfer-listed with Barnes joining Owen at Ron Atkinson's West Bromwich Albion in July for £750,000, while Player of the Year Hartford moved to Nottingham Forest for £500,000 in June. Others whom Allison felt were surplus to City's requirements included Brian Kidd - sold to Everton back in March for a bargain fee of £150,000 - and captain Dave Watson - sold to Werder Bremen. Mike Channon had announced he wanted to stay in April, but by September, two appearances into the new season, he returned to Southampton claiming he was glad to escape a difficult situation.

These were puzzling times for most Blues supporters, especially as the majority of these players were important heroes, but everyone assumed Allison was working on a grand plan and the break up of City's League Cup winning and League challenging side was allowed to continue. But who were the replacements? Deyna, Futcher and Viljoen had hardly lived up to expectations, although each player had suffered with bad luck and taken time to settle.

By the time the new 1979-80 season started Allison, now Team Manager with Book occupying the role of General Manager, persuaded Swales to open the cheque book and start spending some of the transfer cash received. Allison once again surprised the City faithful as 17 year old unknown Steve Mackenzie was signed from Crystal Palace for a staggering £250,000. The midfielder hadn't even appeared in the League, yet Allison was prepared to make him the costliest teenager in history.

Other players purchased included Preston striker Mick Robinson for £750,000, and Yugoslavian international Dragoslav Stepanovic for around £140,000. Another striker Bobby Shinton was signed in June from Wrexham, who demanded a fee of £300,000 for the 27 year old.

In addition to these signings General Manager Book told supporters that City were continuing to negotiate for Steve Daley from Wolves, and Kevin Reeves of Norwich. He admitted Norwich had already turned down £1 million pounds for a forward who had been capped once by England, while he had been trying to sign midfielder Daley ever since the summer of 1978.

In amongst all this activity came the most difficult announcement of them all - the retirement of Colin Bell. After over three years of determination to regain full fitness the player and the club realised the time had come to end the struggle. Even during the years of despair Bell still managed to contribute a great deal to the Blue cause, helping reserve players like Tommy Caton and Nicky Reid develop. In 1978 he was a member of the Reserve side that lifted the Central League Championship.

Bell tried to be positive about his retirement: "I'm pleased that it's with City my career has finished. They have always been the only club for me. I hope they have a great future. I feel as fit as I have ever felt. But I have to face the fact that if I carry on playing and get a knock on the knee I could be crippled for life. It comes to everyone some day. But football has been

20-93-15

THE WEST BROMWICH ALBION FOOTBALL CLUB LIMITED

West Bromwich, June 12. 1979

BARCLAYS BANK LIMITED
WEST BROMWICH

Pay Manchester City F.C. ... or Order

Two hundred and thirty two thousand pounds £232,000-00

A/c PAYEE ONLY

FOR AND ON BEHALF OF THE WEST BROMWICH ALBION FOOTBALL CLUB LTD

SECRETARY

DIRECTORS

One of the cheques received from West Bromwich Albion for the transfer of Gary Owen. The total figure amounted to around £450,000.

my life. I don't think I've really had time to let it sink in. It will take a few weeks to get home to me that I'm finished."

Without Bell, the opening fixture against Crystal Palace ended goalless before a Maine Road crowd of 40,681. This was followed by a disappointing 3-0 defeat at Middlesbrough, before City's first victory - 3-2 at home to a Brighton side captained by Brian Horton. Late in the game Joe Corrigan saved a penalty from the future Blues' boss.

A 1-1 draw at Hillsborough followed in the League Cup, and four days later Tottenham defeated City 2-1 at White Hart Lane. The League Cup replay saw Wednesday beaten 2-1, but the result was overshadowed by the news the following day that the Blues had finally landed 26 year old Steve Daley. The fee? City boasted it was an incredible £1,450,277 - the highest in British football. At the time Allison was well pleased with the capture: "I did this deal because the way we play we need a midfield player who is willing to make forward runs, take people on and is a good finisher. Steve is the best in the country at that type of game. I believe he is the only midfield player in the country who can open the game for himself and he's good enough to go through on his own. He will do very well with us."

Ten years later, in City fanzine *Blue Print*, Allison claimed he had very little to do with the Daley purchase: "Peter Swales signed Steve Daley, not me... Peter Swales and the Chairman of Wolverhampton Wanderers arranged that deal between themselves. I spoke to John Barnwell before his car accident and I asked him about Daley and I offered £650,000."

Allison went on to say Swales continued to increase the offer until Wolves accepted. When Swales was interviewed shortly before his death, he felt he had simply backed Allison's judgement. It was the judgement that was wrong: "I didn't know Allison like the others did. I knew his reputation and knew what he could do - especially in the late 60s and early 70s - but he'd had an in and out career during the mid 70s. But [at City] it was unbelievable really. He used to talk a language that I was completely alien to. I knew I'd made a mistake [appointing Allison], probably within a month, maybe two. He wasn't right. He'll probably say 'well, they had no bloody money' or something. He would say it was my fault. He tells that story about Steve Daley. He is completely convinced it was me who bought Steve Daley and not him. I suppose that's fair enough... he probably believes it was me! We chased him for months and Malcolm polished off the deal, but Daley never did a thing for City. It was unbelievable. I've met Daley several times since and he's one of the most confident men there is. At Maine Road though it was all too much for him. He's the only player I've seen where the fear outweighed his ability. He couldn't do a thing, and when I say that I mean he didn't do anything!"

With hindsight the purchase of Daley should never have happened. Likewise, the appointment of Allison may also have been wrong, but in 1979 he was provided with the financial backing to bring players into the club. Another signed on the same day as Daley was Stuart Lee from Stockport County. Stockport manager Mike Summerbee and Chairman Freddie Pye had told Lee about the City interest when he heard Cambridge United were interested in signing the player. Eventually he joined City for a fee of £80,000, with fans joking it was the loose change from the Daley deal.

Two players pleased by the conclusion of these deals were Paul Power and Mick Robinson. Power was delighted because at one point he was being lined up in a part exchange deal for Daley which, obviously, never materialised, while Daley's arrival removed the pressure from Robinson. "I woke up this morning with that cheap feeling" joked the £750,000 man.

Daley and Lee made their debuts in City's 1-0 home defeat by Southampton on 8th September.

Three big money buys in 1979. Steve Mackenzie (top), Mick Robinson (above) and Steve Daley (left).

An embarrassing 4-0 reverse at West Brom followed - a game which saw rejected men Owen and Barnes perform exceptionally well. Yet still the transfers continued. On 12th September Kenny Clements moved to Oldham for £250,000 prompting letters of complaint in the City programme. Allison answered his critics: "The offer from Oldham was too good to turn down. I know that Kenny will do far more for Oldham than he could do for City. Tony Book did not really want to sell Kenny and pointed out that the lad had done a good job in previous seasons and was a good club player. I'm sure that's true. But when I was working with Kenny I never felt he was my sort of player, was not highly skilled for my needs and would not be what I was searching for in the end. I don't think it's a sound policy to keep players who are stop-gaps."

Sadly, City seemed to struggle to find anyone to stop the slide.

By 4th October City were 14th in the League and out of the League Cup after a 1-0 defeat at Sunderland in a third round replay. On 27th October they were defeated 4-0 by eventual champions Liverpool. Before the game Allison claimed Paisley's side were far better than any other Liverpool team in history; afterwards he recognised City remained a long way behind.

A 2-0 loss at Crystal Palace followed, before the Maine Road derby with United brought Allison delight. City defeated the Reds 2-0 with goals from Tony Henry and Mick Robinson. A week later Steve Daley, said to be insured at a cost of £10,000 a season, scored his first goal for the club as City beat Bolton 1-0. It had been a game between two struggling sides and afterwards Bolton supporters called for the dismissal of manager Ian Greaves, despite some bright spells for the home side. The tireless Neil McNab did much to push Bolton forward but on the half hour Dave Bennett crossed towards Robinson. Somehow Robinson missed and Power managed to knock the ball back into the middle. The ball was cleared, then Bennett once again gained possession and fed it to Daley who fired home.

UNDERSOIL HEATING

During the 1979 close season City installed a £45,000 Swedish undersoil heating system called "Meltaway" in an attempt to reduce the number of matches postponed. It seemed cheap in comparison to most other pitch systems but has proved extremely successful. It was installed with little disruption to the playing surface as the 1 inch diameter cross-linked polythene pipes were pulled into place below the surface, three at a time, by a 'mole' unit. This limited disruption to the pitch, and within four days of completion there were no obvious signs the system had been installed.

City boasted there were around 16 miles of pipes, nine inches below the surface, and the entire system had a life expectancy of fifty years. Within a year it soon proved its worth and, like many other City initiatives during the 70s, seemed light years ahead of anything United were prepared to do. In fact it was many years before United installed any form of undersoil heating.

Michael Robinson and Paul Power (No. 10) celebrate with Tony Henry after Henry's goal in the November 1979 derby. City won 2-0 in front of a Maine Road crowd of 50,067 with Robinson netting the other goal.

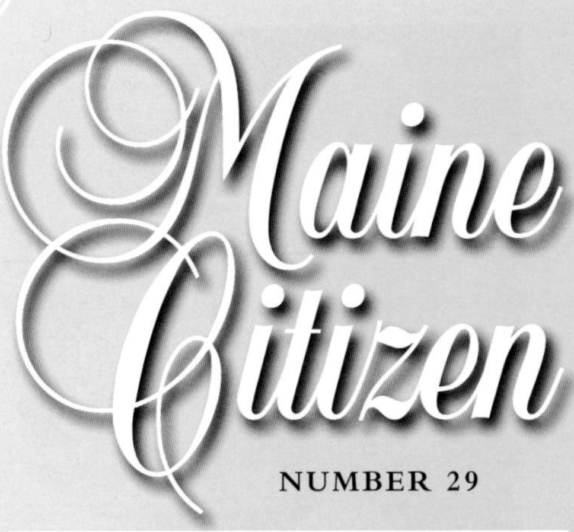

NUMBER 29

PAUL POWER

Ace scout Harry Godwin's first view of 13 year old Paul Power was not a particularly impressive one: "His left foot was a beauty, but there was nothing on the lad. No flesh, no height. Paul was the tiniest of tots, he made Ronnie Corbett look like a giant."

Some time passed with Power working hard to boost his strength and stamina before Godwin next came into contact with the youngster: "I travelled to the CWS ground in New Moston and saw Paul play for a Manchester Under 18 team. He'd grown, the stride had lengthened and the delicate left foot was still there. I'd seen all I needed to in the first half hour of the game. He was a genuine Blue. It was a bonus that he didn't want to play for anybody else."

Power was signed as an amateur in August 1973 and turned professional in July 1975 after completing a law degree at Leeds Polytechnic. During his time at Leeds he was paid expenses to play for City reserves. Within a month of signing full time forms, Tony Book gave him his debut at Aston Villa (27/08/75). That season he made a total of 14 appearances plus five as substitute and even managed to score in the 4-3 defeat of Derby County on 10th April.

Sadly his arrival in the first team came too soon to appear in the 1976 League Cup final, but the following season he became a regular as City challenged for the title. In November 1978 he netted one of his most important goals to help the Blues achieve a 2-2 draw in the San Siro stadium against AC Milan, and 11 months later, under Malcolm Allison, was appointed captain for the first time. That game ended in a surprising 1-0 victory over Nottingham Forest on 13th October 1979 and for most of the following seven seasons Power captained the Blues.

His years as leader brought the usual amount of City controversy - managerial departures, relegation - but also brought much to savour. It was often Power's determination and man-management that helped the Blues develop. Under John Bond,

Power perhaps enjoyed his finest hour when his goal in the 1981 F.A. Cup semi-final brought victory against Ipswich and set City up for the 100th Cup Final. Power remembers the goal with great affection: "We were awarded a free-kick on the right hand corner of the penalty area and Steve Mackenzie touched the ball to me, a ploy we had worked on in training. I came forward and hit the ball left-footed and it curled into the top corner of the net.

"If I remember right, Eric Gates should have closed down on me, but it seemed that because it was so late in the game, he didn't bother. It initially appeared as though Paul Cooper, the Ipswich 'keeper, didn't quite know which side of his line to cover and I recall their manager, Bobby Robson, blaming him for the goal, although I don't think it was down to Cooper. We were at Wembley and that was all that mattered."

The 1981 Final went to a replay and then ended in disappointment. Two years later City suffered further when Luton relegated the Blues on the final day of the 1982-3 season. Like all true Blues Power was gutted. Bravely he fought on, determined to win promotion under new manager Billy McNeill. It took two seasons to achieve but once back in the First Division Power predicted Wembley. His promise came true, although the competition was the much maligned Full Members' Cup. Once again he was captain for the final, thereby becoming the first man to lead City in three Wembley finals. Sadly that game ended in a 5-4 defeat to Chelsea in March 1986, and at the season's end Power's Maine Road career was over.

Despite still having much to offer the Blues, the time had come for him to move on. Some supporters had become impatient with City's mid-80s failings and Power occasionally became the target. Ironic chants of "Zico", or even worse "Gladys", simply proved how many Blues had grown weary of City's plight and Power was an easy target simply because he was probably the club's most famous player at this point. No Blue could really complain about Power's contribution, but it was certainly time for a change.

The great Everton manager of the 80s Howard Kendall recognised Power's qualities and rushed to buy him: "Many, many people were really surprised by that deal but for an outlay of just £65,000 I picked up a model professional. Paul may have been 32 years old and entering the twilight of his career but when I asked City if he was for sale, they told me that not a close season had gone by without someone asking about his availability. He was reliable, dedicated and very much in demand."

At Goodison, Paul gained the first winners' medal of his career as he helped Everton win the League Championship. It was a reward he thoroughly deserved. The only sad moment during that period was on 29th November 1986 when he netted one of Everton's goals in their 3-1 defeat of struggling City. Power refused to celebrate and was clearly disappointed at scoring against the club he loved.

After playing and coaching with Everton, Power has been an active member of the PFA staff and also worked for GMR expressing his views on life at Maine Road. During the managerial merry-go-round of 1996 he was often tipped by supporters as 'the next City manager', and seemed delighted that supporters clearly recognised his immense knowledge of football and of the Maine Road scene. During the 1997 close season that reservoir of knowledge began to be put to much good use when he was invited back to the club to become an important member of Frank Clark's backroom staff.

Paul Power understands City well. He has been a tremendous player and captain, and will always be remembered for his love of the Blues.

POWER'S PLAYING RECORD

	LEAGUE		FA CUP		FL CUP		EUROPE		FM CUP		TOTAL	
	App	Gls	App	Gls	App	Gls	App	Gls	App	Gls	App	Gls
1975-76	14(5)	1	2	0	2(1)	0	-	-	-	-	18(6)	1
1976-77	27(2)	2	4	0	1	0	0(1)	0	-	-	32(3)	2
1977-78	29	3	0	0	4	0	1	0	-	-	34	3
1978-79	32	3	3	0	3	0	6	1	-	-	44	4
1979-80	41	7	1	0	4	0	-	-	-	-	46	7
1980-81	42	4	8	5	7	0	-	-	-	-	57	9
1981-82	25	1	1	0	1	0	-	-	-	-	27	1
1982-83	33	1	3	0	4	2	-	-	-	-	40	3
1983-84	37	2	1	0	3	0	-	-	-	-	41	2
1984-85	42	1	1	1	5	0	-	-	-	-	48	2
1985-86	36	1	4	0	3	0	-	-	6	2	49	2
TOTAL	358(7)	26	28	6	37(1)	2	7(1)	1	6	2	436(9)	37

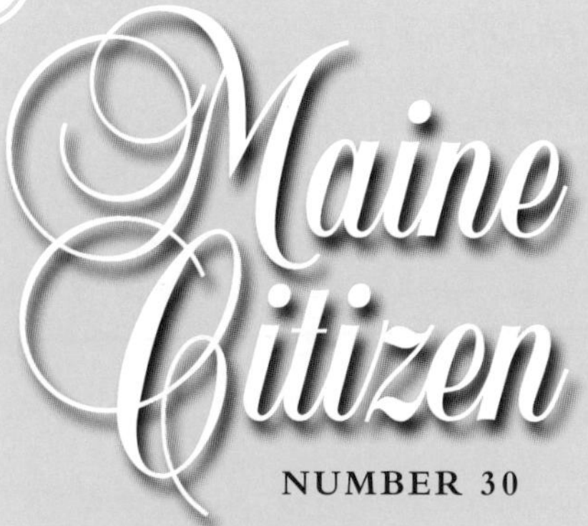

NUMBER 30

ASA HARTFORD

Asa Hartford is second only to Colin Bell in the number of international appearances he made while on the books of City. Hartford played 36 times for Scotland during his Maine Road career and featured in both the 1978 and 1982 World Cup Finals.

A typical midfield dynamo, Hartford began his career with West Bromwich Albion, making over 200 appearances for them between 1967 and 1974. He played in the 1970 League Cup Final against City and in 1971 almost transferred to Leeds United. That transfer fell through after a routine medical examination discovered he had a hole in his heart.

Any doubts about the player's fitness were ignored in August 1974 when Tony Book paid West Brom a fee of around £210,000 for the entertaining Scotsman who had already been capped six times. Immediately, Hartford's stamina and attacking midfield play proved Book's judgement to be well-founded, and the player rapidly became a popular member of City's exciting mid-70s team.

In 1976 he won a League Cup winner's medal and helped the Blues challenge for the title the following season. He was an aggressive ball winner who seemed to dictate much of City's play. Sadly, this style of play often brought him into trouble with referees, especially during 1977-8 when bookings caused him to miss several matches.

By the time of Malcolm Allison's return in January 1979, Hartford was one of the club's biggest stars. Incredibly, that seemed to cause a few problems and Allison soon placed him and Peter Barnes on the transfer list. Hartford was furious and the supporters couldn't believe it, especially as they felt he was the best player of 1978-9 and voted him Player of the Year. Nevertheless Allison sold Hartford to Nottingham Forest in June 1979 for around £500,000.

The player found life difficult under Brian Clough and after only three League appearances moved to Everton. During this period the atmosphere at Maine Road was deteriorating all the time with many of Hartford's former colleagues moving on. Peter Swales, during filming for a Granada TV documentary on City in 1980, told Allison one man would be perfect to help City out of the mess they found themselves in. Swales later claimed this was the only time in his entire career he suggested a player to one of his managers, and only did so because he was absolutely convinced he was right. The man he suggested was Asa Hartford. Allison laughed.

Shortly afterwards Allison was dismissed and John Bond arrived. City reached the 1981 Cup Final and in October of that year John Bond brought Hartford back to Maine Road. The supporters were delighted with the £350,000 purchase, especially as Hartford was still an international.

He remained with City until May 1984, playing in the club's first Second Division season since the 1960s. He deserved better and left for Fort Lauderdale in the NASL. He later returned to England and joined Norwich where he again proved a success, scoring the deflected goal that beat Sunderland to lift the 1985 League Cup in his final game for the club. Another former Blue Mick Channon also won a medal that day.

After Norwich, Hartford coached in Norway; played for Bolton; became assistant manager of Portsmouth; player-manager of Stockport; and manager of Shrewsbury. He also worked for Blackburn and Stoke before, in July 1995, he returned to Maine Road again. This time he was assistant manager to Alan Ball, but during 1996 found himself acting as caretaker-manager following Ball's demise. For a while rumours circulated that Hartford would be offered the job on a permanent basis, but results went against him and, after an exceptionally long caretaker period, he was able to return to coaching duties. Steve Coppell was appointed the new manager, and brought with him Phil Neal but the popular Blue was allowed to continue coaching at the club even after manager Frank Clark's shake-up of staff in 1997.

Asa Hartford has always been a determined blue. His ability on the pitch made him an immensely popular figure and brought supporters a great deal of satisfaction.

HARTFORD'S PLAYING RECORD

	LEAGUE		FA CUP		FL CUP		EUROPE		TOTAL	
	App	Gls	App	Gls	App	Gls	App	Gls	App	Gls
1974-75	29(1)	2	1	0	1	0	-	-	31(1)	2
1975-76	39	9	2	1	9	2	-	-	50	12
1976-77	40	4	4	0	1	0	2	0	47	4
1977-78	37	4	2	0	5	0	2	0	46	4
1978-79	39	3	3	0	5	0	8	2	55	5
1981-82	30	3	2	0	4	1	-	-	36	4
1982-83	38	3	3	1	4	0	-	-	45	4
1983-84	7	1	0	0	0	0	-	-	7	1
TOTAL	259(1)	29	17	2	29	3	12	2	317(1)	36

Three consecutive defeats followed, leaving the Blues 18th, before victories over Derby (3-0) and Everton (2-1) lifted the club to 12th. Then City just collapsed. A 1-1 draw at Stoke on Boxing Day was disappointing, but not the end of the world. However, a 4-1 defeat at First Division newcomers Brighton knocked confidence at an important time as the next game was a third round F.A. Cup clash against Fourth Division Halifax Town at the Shay.

In his programme notes for the match Halifax boss George Kirby predicted a shock: "In today's F.A. Cup third round the only certainty is there are going to be some surprises, especially with the wintry conditions underfoot. I like to think that we are among one of the possible giant killers. This is because we are playing against one of the certain to be 'top teams' of the 80s. A Fourth Division side at home to a First Division outfit with such stars as Joe Corrigan, Steve Daley, and Mike Robinson is a possible shock result. It only needs an off day by a key player and Halifax are in the hunt."

Kirby was determined to defeat football's biggest spenders and even brought in a hypnotist to get his players in the right frame of mind. The game itself was played in horrendous conditions, with multi-million pound City struggling to achieve anything. In the 75th minute it was all over as ex-Birmingham City player Paul Hendrie converted a cross from former City schoolboy Andy Stafford to give Halifax a 1-0 victory. It was the biggest result in Halifax history, and the most embarrassing City defeat of the Allison period. Even today the name of Halifax and the sight of the Shay brings back nightmares for a large number of Blues.

Disappointment continued in the League as City endured a run of 17 games without victory. The run started with that draw at Stoke on Boxing Day, and included embarrassing defeats at Southampton (4-1) and at home to West Bromwich Albion (3-1). In both games former City players excelled with Channon and Watson finding the net for Southampton, while Barnes scored twice for West Brom. Goalscoring performances by ex-City players against the Blues seemed to be a feature of the early 1980s.

At the beginning of March 1980 another City hero became a former Blue when Willie Donachie was transferred to North American League side Portland Timbers for £200,000. Donachie: "I needed a change badly. Not because I wanted to leave but because I'd been there too long. If a new coach had come in at that time... someone who believed in me, and someone who was actually building a new team, then I would have been happy and stayed there forever. But Mal was back and the club was not a happy place for me anymore. So I wanted to go and at the time Mal wanted to sell me - I was still under contract until the end of the season and Skip [Book] advised me to stay until then as I would've gone on the freedom of contract thing. But City meant so much to me it hurt me to see it in the state it was. So I wanted to go and going to America was fantastic for me because it was a completely new approach... complete change."

Donachie was dissatisfied with many of the changes introduced since 1978: "I felt players were coming in for vast amounts of money who just weren't good enough. But I was only 27 or 28 and, although I was fairly experienced, I was in no position of power to do anything about it. All my best friends like Rod, Joe, Asa and the others were all got rid of. And all I could see were players coming in who were not good enough at any price. If somebody's not good enough, they're not worth £200,000 let alone £1 million plus. It doesn't matter.

"I was delighted that Mal came back and it was probably at a time when there had to be some change but, just like Ron Saunders, I think he went about it the wrong way. He gave up on people too fast, and decided too quickly. In my opinion, instead of bringing people in who were better than those he had, he would get rid of people and bring in lesser players. So it was just the same problem. The big, great, consistent clubs seem to evolve - they bring a new player in now and again. It's a gradual process. You can't change fast, like Mal tried. I think that was the big problem."

Paul Hendrie scores for Halifax Town in January 1980 and inflicts one of City's most embarrassing FA Cup defeats.

The part of the stand roof not visible in this photograph was previously erected at City's Hyde Road ground. The Blues sold it to Halifax Town in the early 1920s for approximately £1,000. It was refurbished in the mid-1990s.

Despite the departure Donachie retains a great deal of affection for City and continues to respect Tony Book: "The amount of respect we had for Tony Book was incredible. So the start he had as manager was fantastic. Usually you have to earn that respect... he already had it. I think he was well on his way to building a good team when the pressure came from the top to get Mal back which 'ballsed' it all up. There's no other way of putting it."

Two perfect examples of Donachie's understanding of the situation came during March, when Allison signing Bobby Shinton was sold to Newcastle - signed in June 1979 for £300,000, sold in March 1980 for £175,000 after failing to live up to expectations - while Stuart Lee went to America with Donachie.

Despite the indications there were glaring problems within the club, Peter Swales continued to back his management team and on 11th March City paid £1,250,000 after VAT and the Football League

Bernard Halford, Malcolm Allison and Tony Book welcome Kevin Reeves to Maine Road.

levy for Norwich's Kevin Reeves. Once again supporters were staggered, but Allison assured the fans Reeves was a special player: "I'll tell you what we have obtained for our money - a player who has shown the ability to hit the target nine times out of ten when striking at goal, though I point out this is merely an indication of accuracy and not goals scored. A player too who has excellent close control and can hold up the ball which is a vital necessity in modern day football."

Allison made comparisons with City heroes Francis Lee and Mike Summerbee before adding: "He is the nearest thing in today's soccer to Kevin Keegan... a player who will have a reputation just as large and respect just as wide when he matures further the undoubted ability which he has. City fans will soon be delighted. We can all thank the astuteness of our Chairman Peter Swales in finding the ideal moment to re-negotiate, and it has proved conclusively that City's boardroom leader shows more courage than any other Chairman in the country. Mr Swales has backed his beliefs and his management team."

Around this time City fans laughed about a story doing the rounds that a City scout returned from watching a game featuring a player the Blues were interested in. When asked if the player was any good the scout replied: "No better than the rest of the side." Allison said: "We'll buy the lot then", and Swales started to write a multi-million pound cheque!

Reeves' debut was not as impressive as Allison hoped as the newcomer gave Arsenal a penalty after tackling John Devine in the second half. Liam Brady's spot-kick gave the Gunners the lead and they went on to win 3-0. A 1-0 defeat in the 100th Manchester League derby followed, and the Blues were struggling to avoid relegation. A 2-2 draw against bottom club Bolton did little to ease the pressure, although City fans were delighted both goals came from Dennis Tueart, who had rejoined the Blues from New York Cosmos.

Tueart's next goal came in the away fixture at Wolves on 12th April. It was a significant match as it ended a run of 17 games without victory and also saw Kevin Reeves score his first League goal for the Blues. The pressure had been building on the former Norwich man and the goal proved vital as the Blues defeated Wolves 2-1 to climb up to 17th place.

Two of the final three matches were against teams lower than City. On 19th April they helped consign Bristol City to Second Division football with a 3-1 win, then suffered a 3-1 reverse at Derby. The score hardly mattered as Derby were certain to be relegated in any case. The final game saw Ipswich defeated 2-1 at Maine Road to leave the Blues in 17th position. It had been a nightmare season, and the average attendance had dropped further to 35,272 but it still remained the third highest in the League.

The 1980-81 season commenced with a disappointing 2-0 defeat at Southampton - a side that included new signing Kevin Keegan. Four days later newly promoted Sunderland defeated the Blues 4-0 at Maine Road. Three score draws followed against Aston Villa, Middlesbrough, and Arsenal then Nottingham Forest beat the Blues by the odd goal in five. This was followed by the visit of a Stoke side which included Mike Doyle in their number. Doyle's men defeated City 2-1.

Of all the million pound players signed during this period, Kevin Reeves was the only one who lasted more than 18 months.

The next match was the crucial Manchester derby at Old Trafford. Tueart was missing with a broken wrist sustained in the Stoke game, and few expected the Blues to gain anything from the fixture. City did freeze for a while but, with typical unpredictable style, amazed everyone with their impressive fighting spirit and, despite going 2-1 down to a disputed goal from Arthur Albiston, the players always felt they were in with a chance. In the last minute former Old Trafford ball boy Roger Palmer demonstrated why he was beginning to gain so many admirers when he prodded home a dramatic last minute equaliser.

The 2-2 draw lifted City to 20th, but successive defeats against Liverpool, Leeds, West Bromwich Albion, and Birmingham left the Blues bottom of the division. Before the last couple of upsets, Peter Swales had decided it was time for action. He had grown tired of Allison's endless ideas and wanted results: "He played with a different system every week. He used to have these amazing plans. My big worry for a few months was that the way he was going we were going to play without a goalkeeper one day, because he'd tried everything else! I was certain he was going to give it a go. I could see him saying, 'let's try without a goalkeeper... we'll have eleven outfield players'. We were virtually bottom of the League after the Leeds match and he had to go. That entire period was a definite mistake. I don't want to come out of this saying he did nothing for Manchester City. He was great for City. Did a fantastic job, but I maintain that it was a mistake to bring him back and I hold up my hands, I carry the can for that.

"It was the Leeds defeat when it all happened. We were absolutely hopeless and I knew we were going to go down if we continued with Allison. It was hard because he had so many in-house supporters. People loved him. They still do. But I knew my big dream of upstaging United was as far away as ever and I sat at Elland Road thinking, 'God strewth, I've had two years of this... three years ago we did so well in the League and almost equalled United's support... look at us now... we're bottom of the League. Haven't won a match this season'. Everything had gone! I knew it had gone and that we were faced with a real struggle. I felt that the die had been cast. When it came to the years when we hadn't any money to spend it was inevitable that we went down."

Swales' big gamble had failed. The late 1970s should have seen City emerge as second only to Liverpool in terms of success, and equal with United in terms of pulling power. The appointment of Allison could have brought terrific reward to the club but, as was proved with Howard Kendall's return to Everton in 1990 and 1997, embracing a former managerial hero rarely seems to work.

Looking back City were undoubtedly the under-achievers of the 1970s. Even if the cups of the 1969-70 season are included, City only managed to win three trophies in the entire decade. For a team full of internationals, with better resources than most other clubs, it was not a very impressive tally. Nevertheless, there was always excitement around the club. Everybody felt City's day would come, and much pride was gained from the fact City were so well supported and could compete in the transfer market.

Yet with the 1980-81 season well underway, City needed to find a winning formula quickly if they were to continue to compete at the highest level.

Chapter Eighteen

Gow, Hutchison and McDonald

DURING 1980 City were helping Granada TV make a documentary about the workings of a football club. It was all part of Swales' bid to boost the media coverage of the Blues but, with typical City irony, the sacking of Allison and Book gave the TV company a dramatic story and allowed millions to glimpse the reality of life at Maine Road.

Throughout all this interest, one man quickly became favourite for the manager's job - Norwich City's John Bond. During the mid-1990s Bond gave his view of how the approach to manage City first came about: "About six months before I actually took over I met Peter Swales at the Royal Gardens Hotel in London. City at that time were not doing too well under Malcolm, and Swales said, 'I would like you to become our manager. I was at Norwich at the time and so we discussed a few things and he promised he'd be back in touch. Well City started to pick up a little towards the end of the season, and then I got a call saying 'we're not going to do anything now. We're going to keep Malcolm and Tony Book on. We can't do anything at the moment, but rest assured that if I do make a move in the future you will be the first person I speak to'. I understood but I was quite happy at Norwich in any case.

"The new season started and Norwich had been surviving quite easily under me, but this year we were struggling. So both sides were having a bad time. Anyway, I came home from one particular match and my wife said, 'you've had a call from Peter Swales. He's going to ring you at 9 o'clock tomorrow morning he wants you to become his manager'. Norwich had no money and weren't really going anywhere, so to be honest Peter had got me straight away. There was no doubt. It was probably a case of just signing the contract and getting up to Maine Road."

Norwich were determined to keep Bond and promised him a job for life. They also demanded huge compensation from City, and pointed out Bond had a seven and a half year contract left to run. The wrangling between the two clubs lasted more or less all season but Swales was determined to appoint Bond and the deal was done. The new manager felt the City Chairman did not have the full support of the Board however: "It wasn't that easy to start with as there were one or two directors on the City Board who didn't really want me as manager, but Peter Swales had the decision and they were unable to object really. So I became manager, but I remember one particular director - Ian Niven - saying 'I don't know where the messiah is who can replace Malcolm Allison!' I sat at the end of the table and he sat immediately on my right and I knew from that day onwards he was one of my enemies. But he wasn't the only one...

"Another director made a comment about moving from Norwich to Manchester which implied that I was a bumpkin moving into the big city. To be honest I treated that with the contempt it deserved. The stupidity of the remark said everything about the man really. At that time it didn't really bother me as I

New manager John Bond and chairman Peter Swales face the media following Bond's arrival.

Dennis Tueart converts a penalty in the 1-1 draw with Arsenal in September 1980. Two weeks later Tueart injured his left arm against Stoke and as a result the Blues struggled in the crucial league games that followed.

knew what I could do. I knew I was capable of managing Manchester City and doing well enough for the fans.

"Bill Adams made a comment after I'd been there a while and signed my son on, he said 'Now, he will have to prove to me that he can play'. I looked at him and said 'prove to you Mr. Adams? Who the hell do you think you are? You're a director of this club, but it's my job to bring the players in. He hasn't got to prove anything to you, he has to prove it to me'. I then stormed out of the Boardroom."

The purchase of Kevin Bond did not occur until September 1981, but John Bond is adamant that the problems at Board level during his first year or so made him regret leaving Norwich. Not everyone on the Board was against Bond however. Simon Cussons seemed extremely positive about the appointment and felt Bond was the perfect man to take City forward while Chris Muir said he was very impressed with the man. In general the Board appeared to be in support, although one or two felt unable to make a judgement with Ian Niven stating he would back the Chairman in whatever decision he made, but refused to give his own opinion.

Despite any doubts that may or may not have existed at Board level, Bond set about analysing the playing staff and attempted to build confidence: "They'd only got four points out of ten games, hadn't won a match, hadn't got a left full-back of any description on their books and the players lacked direction and confidence. To be honest any fool could have turned them around to a limited extent. We lost the first game through a penalty in the last minute against Birmingham, but from then on we climbed and I won the Manager of the Month award for November and December. That set us off."

Bond astutely recognised that the arrival of a small number of experienced players would actually boost confidence and help to lift the Blues up the table. He purchased Bobby McDonald and Tommy Hutchison from Coventry, Gerry Gow from Bristol City and, like magic, stability appeared. City had already won their second game under Bond - a 3-1 victory over Tottenham at Maine Road - but the arrival of McDonald and Hutchison in the line-up for the game at Brighton on 25th October was an important touch as the Blues won 2-1 with a brace from Tueart. A week later Gerry Gow made his debut in the victory over Bond's old club Norwich. Captain Paul Power scored the only goal of that particular game.

A 1-1 draw at Leicester was followed by a disappointing 2-0 defeat at Sunderland, but mid-November saw Bond's new men bring some consistency with three consecutive victories. He was pleased with his purchases: "There isn't a City supporter anywhere who says anything but good about Tommy Hutchison. He was absolutely tremendous, and became a real star. He made everything happen. Gerry Gow stopped everything happening for the opposition, and that rubbed off on the rest of the players. Gow's tenacity rubbed off on Ray Ranson, Tommy Caton and Nicky Reid and the others. Then there was Bobby McDonald. Now I had a few doubts about him when I found out a bit more about him, but he still did a good job for us. He had a streak in him which was a bit wayward, a bit naughty and irresponsible. He loved the glory, but he'd duck out of heading the ball in defence. We didn't see eye to eye and I doubt I'd have bought him if I'd known. But he did a job and the fans loved him. So we'd got a left back who was a real left back, we'd got a midfielder who could tackle, win balls and make things happen, and we had a tremendous fellow up front. It seems a simple concept really."

Bond had almost signed Hutchison for Norwich some time earlier but had felt the player was too arrogant at the time. It seems Hutchison was persuaded to go in and make demands. This appalled Bond who decided as soon as he heard the words 'I want' he would not be signing the Coventry man. Bond was always a great believer in attitude. Players had to want to play for the club, not financial reward. Fortunately for City Tommy Hutchison had moved on to Seattle and was playing in the same side as Kevin Bond. John Bond went to watch his son for a spell and witnessed some amazing football from a player who was supposed to be nearing the end of his career. When Bond was given the City job he heard Hutchison had returned to Coventry and contacted Gordon Milne, the Coventry manager. Hutchison met Bond at Maine Road with the City manager determined not to give in to demands: "I said I'll give you £400 a week, which wasn't the best wage in the world, and I'll give you £50,000 to sign. His attitude had changed and he signed without making a demand."

The figures quoted indicate how football clubs in the early 80s were beginning to lose control over payments to players. City were still keen to sign the best and Chairman Swales backed his new manager all the way. There seemed little consideration of what would happen if the club failed. Apart from the early season panic, City always felt too big a club to be relegated, and Swales continued to ensure money was available to spend, whether on wages or on transfers.

Of the three signings, Gerry Gow's was perhaps the most interesting as manager Bond agreed to buy the player, but then discovered he couldn't give him a medical: "There was no way in the world he would have been able to sustain a medical examination because he would have failed it! I had a chat with Swales and he asked me what I wanted to do and I said I still wanted to sign him. So he let me pay £175,000 and we just had to take a chance... but what a chance. He was a revelation."

With Gow, Hutchison and McDonald, City climbed up the table and reached eleventh place by the middle of January. Bond's side excited the fans and as the team started to believe in itself the turnaround was amazing. During Bond's first game against Birmingham the players seemed confused and worried by tactics; by the end of the year Bond had convinced them the game could be a simple one, and the result was a group of players who seemed to really enjoy playing.

The progression up the League was not the only positive point from the remainder of 1980 as the Blues advanced in the League Cup. Allison's City had already put out Stoke City and Luton Town, but Bond's first cup game was the fourth round tie against Second Division promotion hopefuls Notts County at Maine Road. The game had the potential to end in defeat, especially as Bond was unable to play any of his new signings, nor would the expensive Steve Daley be available due to injury.

The match actually ended 5-1 to the Blues with Dave Bennett opening the scoring after 16 minutes. Dennis Tueart, who was in inspired form that night, scored the other four City goals, but the clearest result was that Bond's whole approach had lifted the club. Basically, Bond had taken Allison's team and instilled belief and confidence. Some of the younger players, like Bennett and Caton, may have been given a chance under Allison, but with Bond they started to achieve their true potential.

Dennis Tueart outpaces Brian Kilcline to score his fourth goal against Notts County in the League Cup.

In the fifth round City were at home to Ron Atkinson's West Bromwich Albion on 3rd December. Again the team managed a victory but it wasn't as emphatic as the County game. An early own goal by Tommy Booth gave Albion a fourth minute lead, but a stirring fight-back by the Blues brought an equaliser from Dave Bennett only seven minutes later, and then on the hour a match winning header from Tony Henry - the man who had been severely criticised by Allison only a few months earlier - to make the score 2-1.

Although the result was perfect, Bond felt the chopping and changing nature of team selection was having a detrimental effect on performances. He felt it was counter-productive and wanted to play his preferred eleven week in week out barring injury. City's traditional unpredictable nature was challenging the view that 'only settled teams are successful teams'. It was, however, a burden Bond would have preferred to have been without.

By beating West Brom City were now through to the League Cup semi-final where they met the team everybody feared - Liverpool. The first game of the two legged semi took place at Maine Road on 14th January. It was a night of misfortune for Bond's Blues when, in the opening minutes, referee Alf Grey disallowed a Kevin Reeves goal for what was described by the official as 'illegal jumping'. City's players, management team and supporters were furious and convinced the goal should have stood. All those present on the day remain convinced City were unfairly treated. Bond: "It was scandalous. It was Alf Grey who punished us and I'm sure that, for as long as he lives, he'll never make a worse decision. Ray Clemence came out and never got anywhere near the ball, and Kevin Reeves got up and headed the ball into the net. He never fouled him or anybody else. You bet your life there wasn't a foul in it. It was as simple as that."

Similarly, Kevin Reeves has always believed the goal should have stood. At the time he told reporters: "It was a legitimate jump for a cross from the left. I never climbed on anybody's shoulders. Alan Kennedy, the Liverpool left back, was in there with me and I suspect he thought Clemence was coming to punch the cross clear and just dropped his shoulder to make the way clear for his 'keeper. I had felt Kennedy's shoulder as I went up but I never went to make contact with him, nor did I feel anything unusual. If I had thought there was doubt about the header after it went in the net I would have been looking at the referee and certainly hesitating with my actions. It's just not the way I would behave to go dashing over to the Kippax to celebrate the goal with them. Like them, I was stunned to see it disallowed."

The goal would have changed the entire pattern of the game, instead Liverpool were able to score a late winner through Ray Kennedy. Bond felt at the time the Blues would have won 2-0 if Reeves' effort had been allowed, instead City had to travel to the Anfield fortress a goal down: "I'm sure we would be in the driving seat, instead of attempting to become the first team to win there for almost three years. I gather Liverpool are unbeaten in 85 home games!"

It was a major task to overturn the dominant Anfield side, but Bond believed his players could do it, and he was almost proved correct: "We went to Liverpool, drew 1-1 and played them off the park. We should have won the game and the tie. It was that first leg 'goal' that did us."

Kenny Dalglish had opened the scoring, but at no time during the tie did City really deserve to be losing 2-0 on aggregate. The Blues piled on the pressure and in the 59th minute Steve Mackenzie curved a free kick around a defensive wall, Clemence failed to hold the ball and Reeves scored to make it 1-1 on the night. Later Bennett hit the bar, but the luck never came and Liverpool went on to Wembley.

The League Cup run proved much about the change in atmosphere within the club during the four months Bond had been manager. City had

Experienced trio Gerry Gow (above), Bobby McDonald (below) and Tommy Hutchison (bottom) were brought in by John Bond shortly after his appointment as manager.

gone from a confused team of individuals heading for relegation into a positive side, rising up the League, challenging the perennially successful teams like Liverpool. Bond was idolised by the fans and the media loved his approach. He was also the big name, media friendly manager Swales had always wanted. It was a perfect period for Chairman Swales: "For two or three years he was the best manager in the country. At the time I thought we'd really cracked it with John Bond. I got on with him probably better than any other manager we'd ever had. He was a big fella. Dead smart. I remember him saying on some interview or other that it took him ages to decide what he'd wear when he first came to Maine Road because he wanted to look the part. He brought a tremendous confidence to the club. He could get the players... and we had a bloody good time with Bondy. Terrific time."

Apart from the progress in the League and League Cup, City also managed to challenge for the F.A. Cup. The run was littered with ties to excite and interest, starting with the third round draw which brought Malcolm Allison back to Maine Road to face his old club. Allison had become manager of Crystal Palace and eagerly anticipated the chance to put City in their place. Before the kick-off Allison walked on to the pitch and then ran towards the Kippax Stand. He received a fantastic ovation, with City fans chanting his name. "I was overwhelmed with the terrific welcome they gave me when I went over to the Kippax before the kick-off. It was a very emotional moment for me. I was told they would not give me the best of receptions. But knowing them, I could not believe they would treat me any different than when I was their manager.

"I was dead right! They are something special and I have no doubt they are the most loyal fans in the country. I am pleased that they have now got something to shout about."

The Kippax then chanted the name of Tony Book, before it evolved into "Johnny Bond, Johnny Bond" as the new manager entered the Directors' box. City fans continued to build the atmosphere during the match, although it took some time for the team itself to get going. Possibly because of the involvement of Allison, many of the players seemed ill at ease. It was as if the headmaster had arrived in the middle of a class, but as the game progressed City became more comfortable. Then in the 53rd minute the Blues were awarded a penalty at the Platt Lane end for an elbow on City's Phil Boyer by Terry Boyle. From the spot, Kevin Reeves scored his first ever F.A. Cup goal, and in the 89th minute netted his second - by which time Power and Boyer had also scored. The game ended 4-0 and Allison was devastated. Television footage shows him speechless. He closed the dressing room door, put an object behind it to block anyone else from entering and sat down with his players in silence. He was shell-shocked, totally unable to talk to his own players. After a while he stood up, opened the door, moved into the City dressing room, offered his congratulations to Bond, and then returned to the silence. It was a major blow for the former Blues boss who, quite rightly, felt many of the City players were his discoveries.

City's next F.A. Cup opponents brought more irony to Maine Road. This time it was John Bond's old side Norwich City. In the 16th minute former

Above: Paul Power jumps for joy after his equaliser in the 1981 FA Cup quarter final with Everton.

Right: Nicky Reid heads clear of Peter Eastoe in the Goodison Park quarter final.

Canary Kevin Reeves volleyed City into the lead and by half time Gerry Gow made it 2-0 following a free kick. In the 74th minute Steve Mackenzie scored a spectacular 25 yarder and then goals from Dave Bennett, Paul Power and Bobby McDonald ensured an emphatic 6-0 victory. The scoreline was impressive, but a serious knee injury to forward Phil Boyer in the 15th minute ensured Bond's fourth signing would take no further part in the season's exploits. Ironically, the injury was inflicted by an innocent tackle from John Bond's son Kevin who had been transfer-listed by Norwich and would sign for City less than eight months later.

At the end of the match, John Bond jumped from the Directors' Box to console his son Kevin. It was a major mistake as the City manager crashed to the ground injured.

With mounting excitement, and a belief this could at long last be City's year, the draw for the fifth round posed the seemingly simple task of beating fourth division Peterborough away. Mindful of recent disappointments at Halifax and Shrewsbury, City looked for safety first with Bond dropping young centre back Tommy Caton for the first time in his career.

In his place returned an influential Cup veteran, Tommy Booth. The selection turned out to be a perfect ploy as the 31 year old scored from a Hutchison corner three minutes before the interval. It was the only goal of the game and provided City with a quarter-final tie away to Everton.

Sadly, Booth was suspended so Tommy Caton returned, and seasoned campaigner Dennis Tueart was also recalled in place of Dave Bennett. The clash at Goodison Park on 7th March was the most difficult of the run so far and took some time to come alive. It was a real midfield dogfight, but gradually Kevin Reeves for City and Imre Varadi for Everton began to break free and attack.

In the 42nd minute Everton took the lead with a goal from Peter Eastoe on the edge of the six yard box. Interestingly, the goal was made by Asa Hartford and Imre Varadi - two of four Everton players who at some time in their careers played for City.

In the last minute of the half Gerry Gow equalised for City: "The build-up to it was smashing. Bobby McDonald knocked a great ball towards the box. Knowing how well Kevin Reeves can get up for the ball and knock it off sweetly I made for the space on the left side - and there was plenty of it as I met the header. I saw the 'keeper coming towards me and knew I had to clip it high over him to have a chance. It was one of those new balls, quite light, and it was caught in the wind. I thought I'd dangled it in the air a little too much as I saw it float upwards and I seemed to be watching it for quite a while before it dropped in at the far end of the net."

Three minutes into the second half a foul by Tommy Caton on Varadi gave Everton a penalty. According to the *News of The World*: "Tommy Caton blocked Varadi in an enveloping grip in the box", while the *Daily Mirror* felt inexperience was to blame for the penalty award: "Tommy Caton, the long, lean youngster at the heart of City's defence, will never know what possessed him to push Imre Varadi so blatantly that referee Peter Willis had no choice other than to award the 48th minute penalty from which Trevor Ross reclaimed Everton's lead. That was an example of inexperience which made City regret the absence of the suspended Tommy Booth."

Six minutes from time, with City still trailing 2-1, captain Paul Power managed to equalise. Richard Bott of the *Sunday Express*: "We had anticipated a super-charged contest and I cannot foresee anything less abrasive when they meet again at Maine Road on Wednesday. City's saviour was their captain, Paul Power. With six minutes left he seized on a pass scooped into Everton's goalmouth by Steve Mackenzie, jabbed out a boot and lobbed the ball over the desperately advancing Jim McDonagh for the equaliser."

Alex Williams made his League debut in the 2-1 defeat of West Bromwich Albion in March 1981. The League's first black goalkeeper had to overcome a great deal of racial abuse from opposition supporters. In the 1990s he became the club's Football in the Community Supervisor.

In the 85th minute Kevin Ratcliffe was sent off for a rather foolish head butt on Tommy Hutchison. At the time the City man was accused of play acting, but television footage proved the offence. The game ended 2-2 and forced a return four days later at Maine Road. The replay was played on a muddy surface and it took some time for either side to make a real impact. Then in the 65th minute City seized the initiative with Hutchison creating two goals for Man of the Match McDonald within the space of three minutes. Paul Power added City's third goal of the game and his fourth of the Cup campaign, before Eastoe scored a consolation in the final minute. The 3-1 scoreline sent City to their tenth F.A. Cup semi-final, with their opponents Ipswich Town on 11th April.

Following the excellent result against Everton, City's League form began to dip with only four points gained in their next seven games. This poor form, together with the excellent progress made by Ipswich left City as underdogs for the semi-final. Ipswich were still chasing a treble of League, F.A. Cup and UEFA Cup and were a difficult side to beat, whereas Bond's City were still too close to the relegation zone for comfort.

The opening 45 minutes of the Villa Park semi-final really tested City with Ipswich coming close a number of times. In fact during Ipswich's dominant period Alan Brazil made an incredible miskick when he had only Corrigan to beat. A goal then would have guaranteed a City defeat but Bond's men settled down and gradually assumed control.

At the end of full time the match remained goalless, then ten minutes into extra time captain Power scored his then customary cup tie goal. Mackenzie had rolled a free kick to Power who sent a swerving left foot drive into the net from twenty yards out. Almost as soon as he kicked the ball he raised his arms to celebrate as he knew, just as the large contingent of Blue support knew, that City were on their way to Wembley for the 100th F.A. Cup Final.

In the final City's opponents would be Tottenham Hotspur, and Bond knew from the moment the semi-final ended who his preferred starting eleven players would be. Always keen to keep a settled side, Bond was determined to keep the eleven who had faced Ipswich. There would be no place for the experienced Tommy Booth or Dennis Tueart. This was not a surprise to either player, but from a fan's perspective it would have been satisfying to see both heroes pulling on the famous City shirt for the 100th final.

From the moment Bond arrived at Maine Road Tueart felt his days were numbered: "I said to him 'if you need any help, I've got a two year contract here, I'm still a professional, still want to do well with this club'. Obviously he had his own ideas. He played a certain way and I was operating as a front man at the time and it wasn't really the same as the front men he'd been used to like Phil Boyer, Kevin Reeves and Ted MacDougall. I was then bombed out a few times and I had a few chats with him and asked him what he wanted me to do. Later, one pre-season he got me playing as an attacking midfielder and I really hit it off. One of my best periods. But in '81 I never really felt part of that side. I was part of that squad, but not part of the side."

As part of the squad Tueart helped City reach a creditable 12th place in the League, the League Cup semi final and the F.A. Cup Final. He wasn't named in the line up for the Cup Final on 9th May 1981, but he had played his part in helping the Blues rediscover their drive.

Paul Power's extra-time goal (top) decides the Villa Park semi-final with treble-chasing Ipswich. It wasn't long before the City hero was buried under a mountain of jubilant team-mates (below right). Above: City fans celebrate the goal at the Holte End whilst the Ipswich crowd simply look stunned. Wembley-bound Tommy Caton, Nicky Reid and Kevin Reeves (above right) salute the Blues supporters at the final whistle.

FA Cup Finalists 1981

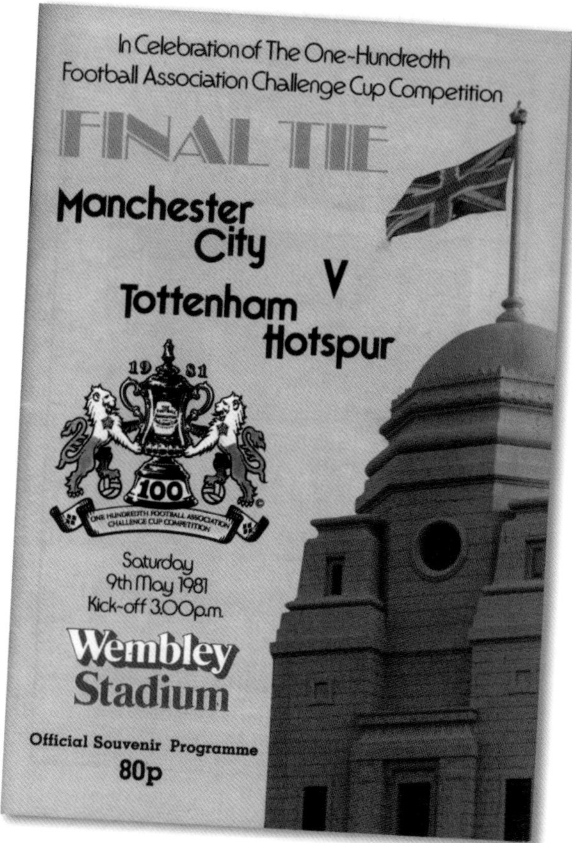

In Celebration of The One-Hundredth
Football Association Challenge Cup Competition
FINAL TIE
Manchester City
V
Tottenham Hotspur
19 81
100
Saturday
9th May 1981
Kick-off 3.00p.m.
Wembley
Stadium
Official Souvenir Programme
80p

In the weeks leading up to the final, much was made of the fact that it would be played in the Chinese Year of the Cockerel and that Spurs had won major competitions in years ending with one - 1901, 1921, 1951, 1961, and 1971. There was also 'Ossie's Dream' - the story that Osvaldo Ardiles' dream was to win the F.A. Cup at Wembley. Basically, everything seemed to indicate the luck of the cup was on Spurs' side and even the impartial BBC delighted in the Tottenham angle. In fact, during the game many City supporters unable to attend the final changed channels midway through to ITV where there appeared to be a more impartial commentary.

These were the days when both main channels carried the final live; coverage started mid-morning with off beat programmes featuring players, supporters and celebrity fans filling the hours leading up to kick-off. Before this final, media friendly John Bond actually appeared as a contestant on a cup final edition of Lennie Bennett's Punchlines, proving how desperate the rival channels were getting to attract viewers for the match itself. Fortunately, a minimum of 30,000 City supporters managed to avoid this television nightmare by actually attending the final. With an average crowd of around 34,000 there remained a lot of dissatisfied fans, however.

Despite the Tottenham hype John Bond was convinced his side would win the competition: "Once you arrive at Wembley it is either you or them, and I don't think there is any reason to believe that there are out and out favourites. People always make one side favourites but on the day either side could win at Wembley. Regardless of who were the favourites, we were going to win the game on that day. I have no doubt about that."

Prior to the game itself the F.A. arranged for a large number of former Cup winning captains to line up on the pitch as part of their centenary final celebrations. 1950 Arsenal captain Joe Mercer received a fantastic reception from City fans, as did City's own Roy Paul, but there was also a great cheer for Tony Book. As with Malcolm Allison's ovation earlier in the Cup run, Book was remembered for his great years at Maine Road and not for the disappointments of 1980.

The City team when announced was a familiar one: Corrigan, Ranson, McDonald, Reid, Power, Caton, Bennett, Gow, Mackenzie, Hutchison and Reeves with Tony Henry named as substitute. The Tottenham side was captained by Steve Perryman and included the Argentinians Ricardo Villa and Osvaldo Ardiles that back in 1978 John Bond had said were overrated. Now was his chance to find out.

The first half was one dominated by the Blues. It opened with four City corners in five minutes while Tottenham defended desperately at times. The value of Bond's three signings was soon proved as, on the odd occasion City were troubled, Gerry Gow did all he could to hold back Ardiles and Hoddle, while Bobby McDonald upset Garth Crooks a few times.

Then in the 29th minute an exciting exchange of passes between Dave Bennett and Kevin Reeves near the right corner led to a fine centre by Ray Ranson. Tommy Hutchison dived spectacularly to head the ball past Aleksic's left hand from some distance out. It was the 150th goal scored in Wembley F.A. Cup finals and was thoroughly deserved.

City continued to control the majority of play with the mighty Corrigan proving his worth on the odd occasion Tottenham managed to bypass City's defence. In the 58th minute Steve Mackenzie almost made it two when his effort hit a post.

Ten minutes later John Bond felt justified in his view the Argentinians were overrated when the ineffectual Ricky Villa was substituted by Garry Brooke. Sadly, the substitution helped to lift Spurs back into the match. In the 80th minute with City almost home and dry disaster struck. Never the diplomat, Gerry Gow hacked down Ardiles to give Tottenham a free kick twenty yards out. Ardiles tapped the ball to Hoddle, who curled it around the wall. Corrigan was certain he had the shot covered but Hutchison, who had dropped back behind the wall for the free kick, somehow got in the way. The ball hit his shoulder and was diverted across goal for the Spurs equaliser. It was a tragic moment.

Without wanting to blame Hutchison, John Bond was disappointed the goal had deflected off one of his greatest purchases: "The sad thing about this is both Tommy Hutchison and Gerry Gow were the two biggest influences that made things happen for Manchester City... making us so successful at that point... and the two biggest causes of why we lost the final. Tommy Hutchison scored that excellent first goal and then, only he will ever know why he was in that position for the free kick. He'll take that to his grave why he was there when Hoddle's free kick hit him. Nobody ever told him to get there, and it still haunts me to this day when I see it. And Gerry Gow was the one

The 1980-81 FA Cup competition was the 100th.

Tottenham goalkeeper Milija Aleksic is beaten by Tommy Hutchison's diving header (top) and City players and fans go wild with delight (above) as the Blues are one up in the 1981 FA Cup final.

who caused the free kick because he was on the half way line with the ball and just stood there looking around when he was robbed. He chased the player right back to the edge of the penalty area and then he did what he normally did in those situations and fouled him. He used to get upset when somebody beat him. He gave a foul away and handed Hoddle that shot at goal."

The game went into extra time with both sides trying to summon up a vital goal. Cramp and aching limbs started to take their toll, with Tommy Hutchison replaced by Henry in the 105th minute. Hutchison had been determined to make amends for the own goal, but the game had started to prove too much for the 33 year old. During the second period of extra time Tottenham seemed to suffer more than City with, at one point, three players lying on the ground and two reduced to walking pace. Neutrals felt City would have regained the lead had the match continued another five minutes. Obviously it didn't and the two sides were forced to meet again the following Thursday.

The final statistics showed both teams each made 14 scoring attempts over the two hour period, but that figure gave a false impression as City dominated the majority of the match. City had eight corners as opposed to Spurs' five, while the Blues were caught offside on 12 occasions, nine more than Tottenham. The public knew City had the better game, the media knew it, and the statistics seemed to back it up. Unfortunately, the only thing that mattered was the number of goals scored.

John Bond, however, now felt the advantage had moved to the London club: "We should have won the F.A. Cup in that first game, there's no ifs or buts about it. It will haunt me as long as I live. From being convinced we were going to win, to seeing what happened to Tommy Hutchison I began to think that it wasn't going to be ours. It was going to be them and their name was on the Cup. I wouldn't want to cry like a baby about the thing but you've got to feel sorry for yourself, haven't you? Bear in mind as well that Kevin Reeves and Steve Mackenzie, when it was 1-0, they played this magnificent one-two. Mackenzie got behind the defence, went around the goalkeeper, went to slot the ball into the net and it hit the post and went wide. They'd have been dead and buried!"

The newspapers echoed Bond's comments with the *Daily Mail* stating Tottenham simply did not deserve a second chance: "For what they are worth to the bewildered Tommy Hutchison, the defiant Joe

Corrigan, the prodigious Nicky Reid and the inspiring John Bond, my sympathies are with City. At least they gave their all for 90 minutes and then dredged up a little extra for the additional half-hour. With the heroic exception of Graham Roberts, Tottenham's approach was a disgrace.

"As Keith Burkinshaw and every other manager in the world will tell them, the justification of skill is the effort applied to its expression. Until the second half at Wembley, the hardest work of Tottenham's Cup Final week had been devoted to the myriad of commercial activities undertaken by the players to supplement their meagre income of little more than £1,000 a week over the season. City, at least, were prepared to earn their rewards the hard way, willing to run until the last man dropped to implement the briefing with which Bond gave them the maximum chance of glory. But while City deserved to win on Saturday, Spurs are the team with scope for raising their game. Hopefully, by Thursday, they will remember that their first duty is to Spurs fans paying another fortune to fill Wembley."

Although the sentiments expressed are perfectly true, the sympathy of all should have gone to the City supporters who had to find the money and time to travel back down to Wembley for a mid week match in addition to purchasing a ticket.

After the final the City contingent returned to their hotel for what was to become an eventful night for City manager John Bond. The following story, related by Bond, is revealed here for the first time: "It was sad really. That night at the Royal Gardens was a bitter experience. Unfortunately I don't think Peter Swales, at that particular time, knew how to accept not winning something he thought he ought to have won. I suppose if you'd have told him in October when I took over that City would avoid relegation, and get to the centenary cup final, he'd have accepted that. But once we got to the final he wanted more. It was a very bitter night for me in many ways. I tried to brush it to one side and get on with having a few drinks, but it was difficult. I remember the attitude of Peter and one or two of the other directors. It wasn't good. They thought we should have won and made sure we knew.

"It was sad really. The lads had played their hearts out and were as unlucky as hell. They wanted to win more than any of the directors, but it was so unfortunate for them. I just felt very upset about the whole thing, and if I'd had the thinking and the apparent foresight of a Kevin Keegan I would have

From hero to villain... With just ten minutes left, Tommy Hutchison inadvertently diverts Glenn Hoddle's free-kick past Joe Corrigan and the final heads into extra-time.

City players go on a subdued lap of honour as the 1981 FA Cup Final goes to a replay.

walked out on the club there and then. That's what I should have done. If I'd have done that my future would have been secure in football for ever more. I don't want to boast about what I did in those months to get City to Wembley, because I could also tell you about the things I didn't do, and all the bad things I did. I'm just making a statement of fact about what happened that night. I've thought about it so often, what I should have said. At that particular time I didn't want to be at Manchester City. I'd had enough in those six months I'd been there.

"Funny as it may seem, I got on very well with Peter Swales but I didn't like some of the others. There was a lot of snidiness going on and a lot of talk behind my back. They'd talk about the teams you'd pick. I just didn't like the snidiness about the club. It was cold. This is the one part of my life I wish I could go back and do again because I would not do what I did that night, that's for sure. If I'd have realised I would actually have walked out before the final. I would never have wanted Peter Swales to think that had any bearing on him because as far as I'm concerned he never interfered and mostly he allowed me to do what I wanted to do. He was okay, it was the rest of them that I had problems with. There were some good office staff there, but the other directors... they never stood up to be counted but were quite happy to be afforded all the privileges that Manchester City gave them in terms of boardrooms, watching matches, going to away games, contact with all the big people in the game and so on. That attitude was not for me."

Bond remained in charge and tried to lift his players but, like the manager, they knew the coveted trophy should have been theirs on the Saturday. They also knew Tottenham could not be as ineffectual a second time.

1981 FA CUP RUN

R3	Crystal Palace	H	W	4-0
R4	Norwich City	H	W	6-0
R5	Peterborough United	A	W	1-0
R6	Everton	A	D	2-2
	Everton	H	W	3-1
SF	Ipswich Town	N*	W	1-0
F	Tottenham Hotspur	N**	D	1-1
	Tottenham Hotspur	N**	L	2-3

* = Villa Park ** = Wembley Stadium

FACTS & FIGURES

	P	W	D	L	F	A
HOME	3	3	0	0	13	1
AWAY	5	2	2	1	7	6
TOTAL	8	5	2	1	20	7

CUP FINAL DETAILS

9 May 1981 at Wembley Stadium

TOTTENHAM HOTSPUR 1
MANCHESTER CITY 1

CITY: Corrigan, Ranson, McDonald, Reid, Power, Caton, Bennett, Gow, Mackenzie, Hutchison (sub Henry), Reeves
TOTTENHAM HOTSPUR: Aleksic, Hughton, Miller, Roberts, Perryman, Villa (sub Brooke), Ardiles, Archibald, Galvin, Hoddle, Crooks.
GOALS: Hutchison (1 & 1 Own Goal)

ATTENDANCE: 100,000
REFEREE: K Hackett (Sheffield)
GUEST OF HONOUR: Queen Elizabeth, The Queen Mother
MANAGER: John Bond
CAPTAIN: Paul Power

REPLAY DETAILS

14 May 1981 at Wembley Stadium

TOTTENHAM HOTSPUR 3
MANCHESTER CITY 2

CITY: Corrigan, Ranson, McDonald (sub Tueart), Reid, Power, Caton, Bennett, Gow, Mackenzie, Hutchison, Reeves
TOTTENHAM HOTSPUR: Aleksic, Hughton, Miller, Roberts, Perryman, Villa, Ardiles, Archibald, Galvin, Hoddle, Crooks.
GOALS: Villa (2), Crooks, Mackenzie, Reeves (pen).

ATTENDANCE: 92,500
REFEREE: K Hackett (Sheffield)
GUEST OF HONOUR: Prince Michael of Kent
MANAGER: John Bond
CAPTAIN: Paul Power

Seven minutes into the replay Ardiles attempted an effort which hit Steve Archibald. The ball fell kindly for the Scotsman who sent in a shot which Corrigan saved. The loose ball however reached Villa who found a more or less open net for the first goal of the game. City fought back immediately and, within three minutes, Ranson's free kick was met by a half clearance which allowed Mackenzie to volley home from 20 yards. It was a tremendous goal and the type of effort that should have won the cup, yet by full-time it wasn't even regarded by neutrals as the best goal of the game.

For the remainder of the half both sides were charged up, forcing referee Keith Hackett to impose stricter controls than in the first match. By the end five players were booked, including Tommy Caton who became the first man to be booked twice in one final, after being cautioned the previous Saturday.

For Tottenham, Glenn Hoddle began to display to millions of television viewers why Spurs supporters felt he was such a special player, while City's Gerry Gow looked for somebody to kick. It seemed anybody would do. Then five minutes into the second half City were awarded a penalty after Miller pushed Bennett. Million pound man Kevin Reeves crashed a right-footed effort past Aleksic's left hand to give City a 2-1 lead.

In the 70th minute Garth Crooks toe-poked Tottenham level and City were once again under pressure. Five minutes later Ricky Villa scored what must now be the most repeated Cup Final goal on British television. In an amazing weaving run Villa seemed to pass a dozen players but, in actual fact, managed to mesmerise Caton twice, Ranson, and then Corrigan. It was a terrific goal, although John Bond felt City let themselves down: "It was a magnificent goal but I bet if Keith Burkinshaw had been in my place he wouldn't have said it was a good goal. He seemed to beat six or seven people in the space of four yards or so, and the ball went through Joe's legs, or beneath his body into the back of the net. You score those sort of goals once in a lifetime, and it reinforced

Steve Mackenzie is congratulated after his breathtaking goal in the Cup Final replay.

Above: Tommy Caton is unable to stop Spurs' opening goal by Ricky Villa in the Wembley replay.

Left: Kevin Reeves scores from the penalty spot to put City 2-1 up.

my view we were never going to win that game once it went to a second match. It was a good goal, but Steve Mackenzie's volley was unbelievable!"

Bond brought on Dennis Tueart in place of Bobby McDonald and the '76 League Cup winner almost levelled, but his shot sailed just outside a post. It was not to be City's day, and it was Perryman, not Power, who collected the Cup. Afterwards Power followed in the tradition of Cowan and Paul by declaring City would be back the following year to win the trophy and everybody felt convinced the '81 final would be the first of many. Sadly, it was the first and the last of the 80s, and Power's prediction never came true. Nonetheless, it had still been a remarkable achievement simply to reach Wembley after the way the season commenced.

BILL TAYLOR, CITY & ENGLAND COACH

Bill Taylor, the former City coach, died on 30th November 1981 at the age of 42. It was a tremendous shock. He was a popular figure around Maine Road after becoming chief coach in July 1976, under Tony Book. During his time at City he helped the Blues perform well in Europe and reach second place in the League. The players enjoyed working with him and he was one of the main forces behind the entertaining pre-Allison period. Joe Corrigan: "His coaching methods were an inspiration to so many players and he helped tremendously to improve many of them. He was always a bright and breezy character and he had a terrific sense of humour. I can never repay the debt I owe him for the help he gave me both with City and England."

Bill left City on 12th January 1979 following the return of Malcolm Allison, after which he worked as assistant manager and chief coach at Oldham Athletic, and continued as a senior member of the England coaching staff. Earlier in his life he had played for Leyton Orient, Nottingham Forest, and Lincoln City before becoming a coach with Fulham.

His period at Maine Road may only have lasted two and a half years, but the Blues gained a considerable amount during that time. In February 1982 City played an England XI in a benefit match for his wife and two young daughters.

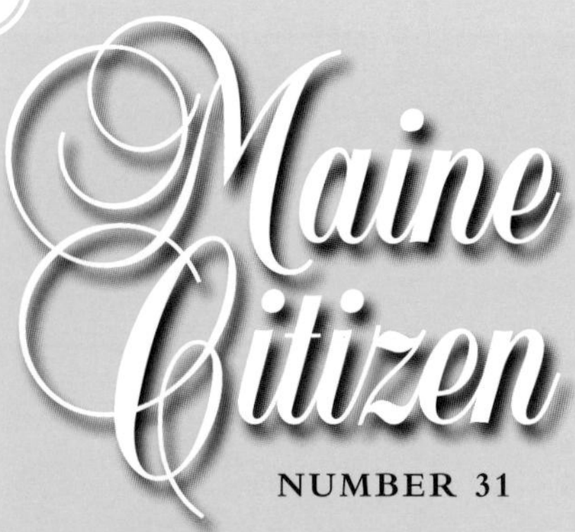

NUMBER 31

TOMMY HUTCHISON

As proved by Jimmy Ross in the 1890s, the addition of wise, experienced, older players can often provide the club with a new lease of life and actually help some of the younger stars to become established. In 1980 new manager John Bond felt City lacked experience and quickly set about bringing in men capable of adding strength and stability to the then struggling side. Basically, he purchased three men - Gow, McDonald, and Hutchison - and over the six months that followed each played a major part in City's transformation. Possibly the most important of these was Tommy Hutchison - the crowd favourite.

Hutchison was born in Cardenden, Scotland, on 22nd September 1947 and first made his mark with Alloa. In February 1968 he joined Blackpool, making over 160 League appearances before signing for Coventry City in October 1972. He was one of the first players bought by new Coventry manager Joe Mercer, who was out to prove he still had much to offer after his Maine Road managerial career ended prematurely in June 1972. The purchase of Hutchison was inspired and quickly helped transform Coventry from a struggling side into one of the most attractive in the club's history. The fans idolised the leggy forward and he remains one of Coventry's most popular players of all time.

John Bond recognised Hutchison's strengths and at one point attempted to sign him for Norwich, but the deal fell through. The opportunity only came up again after the Blues' boss had watched Hutchison playing alongside Kevin Bond in Seattle. Hutchison still seemed to offer a great deal and in 1980 Bond brought him to Maine Road after over 350 first team appearances with Coventry.

At City, Hutchison proved a dedicated, consistent, skilful professional who seemed superbly fit, considering his status as a 33 year old veteran. His arrival helped City come to life and the Blues progressed up the League. Thanks to Hutchison, they also made their mark in the F.A. Cup defeating Crystal Palace and Norwich in style, then overcoming Peterborough, Everton, and Ipswich.

Earlier in the season reaching Wembley seemed like an impossible dream, yet by the end of the 100th final it had all become something of a nightmare for Hutchison. In the 29th minute he'd produced a great diving header to bring the first goal of the game then, in the 80th minute, he deflected a free kick past Joe Corrigan to level the scores. It was a tragic moment. Fate brought Tottenham success, and left Hutchison and City's supporters to wonder what might have been.

That own goal guaranteed Hutchison a place in Wembley history and has even ensured him a mention in the board game Trivial Pursuit. Looking back to 1981 the goal is not quite as agonising as it felt at the time - City's amazing defensive errors which allowed Ricky Villa to score in the replay are much more grievous! Hutchison was only in the way because he was trying so desperately hard to preserve City's lead. It was typical of the player's attitude.

HUTCHISON'S PLAYING RECORD

	LEAGUE		FA CUP		FL CUP		EUROPE		TOTAL	
	App	Gls	App	Gls	App	Gls	App	Gls	App	Gls
1980-81	24	3	8	1	0	0	-	-	32	4
1981-82	20 (2)	1	2	0	3 (1)	0	-	-	25 (3)	1
TOTAL	44 (2)	4	10	1	3 (1)	0	-	-	57 (3)	5

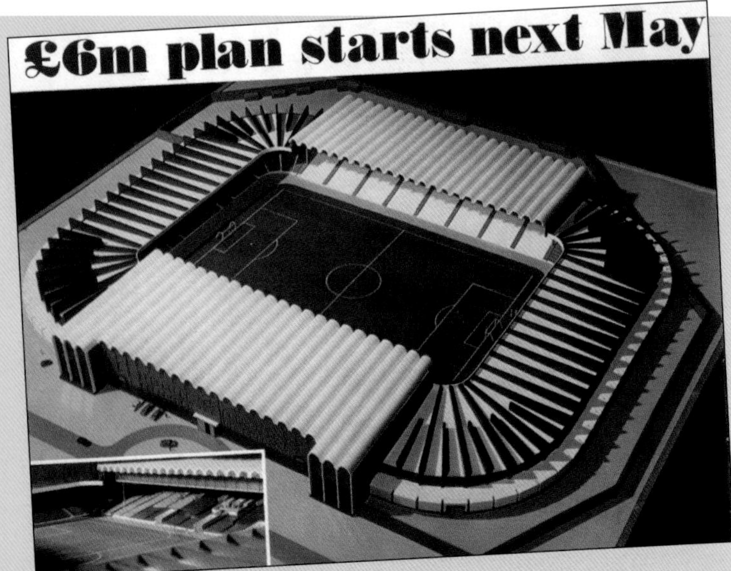

At the start of the 1981-82 season City announced a major redevelopment of Maine Road. Sadly, the plan was doomed and only the Main Stand roof was replaced. Even then it didn't match the ambitious plans of 1981.

Flush with the funds raised at Wembley, Peter Swales announced during the summer that Maine Road was to be redeveloped at a cost of around £6 million over a five year period, ending in time for the start of the 1986-7 season. The plan was to see the Kippax and Main Stand roofs replaced by modern white barrel-style affairs, while the Platt Lane end of the ground would be redeveloped to look identical to the North Stand. The plans included the erection of 36 private boxes to be suspended from the Main Stand roof, a new television gantry, two lifts, a new restaurant, and a new floodlighting system mounted on the roofs. It would also raise the capacity from 52,600 to around 54,000. At the time Swales proudly boasted an increase in the capacity was vital and that nothing would stop the work: "We are committing ourselves to a lot of money, but I'm sure it is the right way to spend it. There's no question of putting the ground before the team. The money for this comes from the club's Development Association and cannot be used for transfers. The supporters are building this stadium - and I am certain they will be extremely proud of it."

After the Wembley disappointment Hutchison continued to appear for the club but, with his main job already completed, Bond had begun to look for a replacement. Asa Hartford eventually superceded him on a permanent basis but, for a while, the two talented Scotsmen played together.

In July 1982 Hutchison signed for Bulova in Hong Kong and later moved to Burnley, Swansea (where he played when he was 43) and Merthyr Tydfil.

His City career may not have been the longest but, for what he achieved during that first season of magic, Hutchison must be regarded as one of the most influential players in City's history. A tremendous individual who did much to restore pride to thousands of Mancunians.

Despite promises the playing side would not be affected by the outlay, John Bond was under pressure to keep spending to a minimum. He was keen to improve the squad and felt the acquisition of a couple of quality players would give City a chance of the title. During the summer he recruited Martin O'Neill from Norwich for £275,000 and attempted to sign United's Joe Jordan. Jordan eventually moved to AC Milan but told Bond City were the only club he would have signed for had he remained in England. Bond also tried to land Norwich's Justin Fashanu, who joined Nottingham Forest, and City old boy Peter Barnes. To tempt West Brom to sell Barnes Bond offered Steve Mackenzie as part payment, but the nature of City's need to part exchange caused that transfer, and indeed the Fashanu move to fail. Barnes joined Leeds, while West Brom followed up their interest in Mackenzie with a cash offer which City accepted.

In addition to these attempts, Bond was keen to sign the Nottingham Forest striker Trevor Francis. He had been negotiating for some time to bring the international into City's first team, but the details were rather delicate.

Despite the problems recruiting players, Bond had managed to improve the backroom staff with the welcome return of Tony Book. Book became assistant to Chief Scout Ken Barnes, after spending a short period as an advisor to Cardiff City, and for the following fifteen years would play a major part in the development of City at various levels.

In City's opening game of the 1981-2 campaign, they defeated West Brom 2-1 at Maine Road to earn their first three points. This was the initial season of three points for a win and opinion was divided as to how it would affect the game. Most felt it was an experiment that wouldn't last, but it did.

A 1-1 draw at Notts County followed and then on 5th September City travelled to Stoke City for what became a memorable occasion. The game saw the debut of new Blue hero Trevor Francis, and the new arrival scored twice to help City to a 3-1 victory. Afterwards Francis said: "I joined City to score goals and provide them as well, so I'm delighted with this start. I'm only sorry Ron Greenwood wasn't here as I want my England place back!"

The transfer seemed perfect but it almost didn't take place and, according to John Bond, nearly forced the manager to resign. Bond and Swales had agreed a fee of around £1.2 million for the Forest striker but, at the last minute, Swales told Bond the Blues could not afford to sign the player. Bond told the Chairman he would resign if Francis was not signed and eventually Swales found the finance to secure the player's signature. But even then there were concerns from Forest and Francis that needed to be ironed out. City also knew United were keen on the player. To ensure Francis signed, Swales offered a substantial salary which the player felt unable to resist: "To complete the transfer he did all the financial talking with my agent Dennis Roach. The contract Manchester United had offered me was really excellent. What City offered now was far in excess of United. I couldn't believe it. It was much too high. Over three years it was worth £100,000 a year plus bonuses. Swales, it seems, had put me on a contract the club could not afford, I can see that now, but who was I to complain? Obviously with hindsight, my contract was at the root of their problems."

The transfer cost City dearly, yet no one seemed unduly concerned at the time. The bank allowed Swales to make the investment, the Board backed the manager's judgement, and the fans were delighted with the purchase, but the £1.2 million signing was only viable if the Blues could mount a serious challenge for the title, qualify for Europe, and reach the latter stages of the cup. For John Bond the signing was supposed to be the first of a number designed to build a side capable of challenging the ever-dominant Liverpool. Francis turned out to be the only truly great player signed by City during the early 1980s; some would argue he was the last major star signed by the Blues until the arrival of Gio Kinkladze in the mid 1990s.

The financial problems were not really common knowledge at the time, although the managers and directors of some other clubs were perhaps aware of the situation.

Martin O'Neill joined the Blues from Norwich in the summer of 1981.

Trevor Francis turned out to be the only truly great player signed by City during the early 1980s.

Trevor Francis marked his City debut with two goals in the 3-1 win at Stoke in September 1981. Here he celebrates along with the travelling Blues fans and another million pound man, Kevin Reeves.

There appears to have been a perception within football that Peter Swales' obsession to overtake United was seriously affecting his judgement, and any transfer to City could be performed at an inflated price. There were a number of other clubs caught up in all this crazy transfer activity, each searching for the great player to bring them the all important success.

Despite the obvious flaws in City's strategy it is fair to say Peter Swales was winning the media coverage war with United. Each transfer brought City tremendous exposure with the Blues appearing to be in the hunt for every player, at any price. John Bond was a media-friendly manager who had taken the club to Wembley. Outwardly City were winning the battle and, perhaps indirectly, had actually forced United to take action to keep pace with the Blues. The Reds dismissed the dour Dave Sexton and appointed the flamboyant Ron Atkinson. Swales felt satisfied, but still seemed overly obsessed with life at Old Trafford. Trevor Francis noticed this unhealthy interest: "Swales was like a man who goes out to buy a Jaguar, and comes home with a Rolls, at the risk of it being repossessed by the finance company. He was always striving to keep pace with United, but it would always be difficult because, although City had put tremendous efforts into building up the Junior Blues and other aspects of care for the supporters, United had the bigger following, generating a much bigger income. In one sense I blame Swales for allowing the club to over-reach itself, but at the same time I sympathise. I, too, used to dream about what City might achieve. It ought to be a great club.

"As a boy in Plymouth, I suppose I was a United fan. I immediately found at Maine Road how tremendously loyal the City supporters are. In some respects the support is bigger than United's, but it's all within the city, while United draws support from all over the country."

Despite the financial problems, Francis was not the last player to sign that season. Kevin Bond completed his long expected transfer, while the most popular move had to be that of Asa Hartford who returned to the club he loved.

Francis quickly found life at Maine Road far from ideal when, in his fourth League game, a collision with Leeds' John Lukic left the City man limping. He was to miss the following six League games and prompted United supporters to claim City had bought a 'crock'. Blues fans disputed that, but the loss of such an expensive player affected morale. Later in the season his style of play brought further injury, and his first sending off. It also aroused grave concerns over value for money, especially for Chairman Swales: "Francis was a good signing. It gave the supporters a lift, but he was a hard man to get playing. You were always trying to get Trevor out on the pitch. It always amazed me he eventually became a manager but, there again, it always amazed me that one of the most successful managers, Don Revie, was one of the most awkward players there was. When Trevor became manager of QPR I thought it would prove impossible because he didn't want to play unless he was 100% fit... 110% fit! He just wouldn't play. There was one game, in the north-east, where an hour before kick off we were still trying to persuade him to play because we knew he could win us the match. He was a great player, and it was a good transfer for City. He was definitely more successful than Steve Daley!"

With an experienced side City moved up the table and even reached top spot on 28th December - goals from Francis and Hartford provided a 2-1 victory over Wolves - although there were a couple of clubs with games in hand. Two days earlier City had defeated Liverpool at Anfield for the first time in 28 years. The 3-1 victory delighted Bond but caused Corrigan a few headaches when a bottle thrown from the Kop knocked him to the ground.

Optimism swept through Maine Road, but City's position could not be maintained and a serious dip in form during March and April prevented the Blues from maintaining a challenge. They ended the season in tenth position, 29 points behind champions Liverpool. Part of the reason for the decline was an ankle injury to Dennis Tueart which prevented his appearing from mid-December. Tueart had been in electric form and seemed to enjoy playing alongside Francis. He'd scored nine goals in only fifteen appearances and was arguably at his most potent. Bond had changed the style of play and this seemed to suit Tueart, giving the player a fresh lease of life. The arrival of Francis had provoked predictions Tueart was on his way out, but Bond rubbished those suggestions and the City great remained at Maine Road after both Francis and Bond had gone. A fit Tueart throughout 1981-2 would probably have enabled City to maintain their challenge for the title.

In the Cup competitions City failed to make the desired progress. In the F.A. Cup a 3-1 win over Cardiff was followed by a 3-1 defeat by Coventry - a game which saw Asa Hartford sent off and future Blue Peter Bodak score a last minute chip for Coventry.

The League Cup was a little more entertaining with the two legged second round tie against Stoke ending 2-2 on aggregate. Both sides had won the home leg 2-0 and the game eventually became the first domestic match in England to be decided by penalties. But even then it took a long time before the two sides could be separated. In fact it was only when Corrigan saved the 20th spot-kick that the game ended with City winning by nine penalties to eight. Northampton Town were defeated 3-1 in the next round, but a 1-0 victory by Barnsley in the fourth ended City's Wembley dreams.

During the summer of 1982 City fans arrived daily at Maine Road to view the new all-white Main Stand roof taking shape, but they also witnessed the departure of the expensive Trevor Francis. It was a puzzling decision and one which started alarm bells ringing for many concerned supporters. Some suggested the player had been transferred to pay for the roof, while others said that could not possibly be true as the Chairman had made it quite clear that ground developments wouldn't affect the playing squad. Rumours about City's precarious financial state began to emerge, but the club continued to show interest in big name signings. They had also agreed the first shirt sponsorship deal in the club's history with SAAB promising £400,000 over two years, plus a number of company vehicles.

Swales later admitted how Francis' salary made his transfer a financial necessity: "We felt it was too much to pay for a bloke who wouldn't be playing every week. He knew what he wanted and it was probably 50/50 why he left. He was the highest paid player, and we just didn't fancy paying that for someone who wouldn't be playing every week. Times have changed, but for us it was a tight ship in those days. But it was 50/50. He wanted to go and we probably wanted him to go. We were still friendly with him when he left."

Francis almost signed for rivals United but, wisely, Swales took the necessary steps to prevent that from happening; it was bad enough being forced to sell to raise funds. The player signed for Italian club Sampdoria but City, rather foolishly, failed to ensure they had first option should he return to the UK.

City did buy during the close season but the purchases hardly inspired the faithful. Francis was replaced - if that was possible - by West Ham's David Cross, who scored in the opening two games, while midfielder Graham Baker arrived from Southampton.

The first two matches of 1982-3 ended in victory and then promoted Watford arrived at Maine Road for what became an interesting contest. In only the third minute Joe Corrigan collided with Watford's Nigel Callaghan leaving the City 'keeper with a dislocated shoulder. Immediately the City management considered the options with coach John

Graham Baker joined the Blues from Southampton.

THREE POINTS FOR A WIN

The 1981-2 season was the first to award three points for a win, rather than two. In the City programme for the opening match, City players were asked if they felt the change would benefit the game. Their comments make interesting reading:

- **Dennis Tueart: "Under this arrangement a team can get three points by scoring one goal in a dull, boring game. It's no different from the old method in most respects. The spectator relationship to the game is mainly about goals and that is not being rewarded. I relate back to my experience in America where they give one point for each goal, up to a maximum of three. That would improve things."**
- **Gerry Gow: "It could punish the draw specialists quite heavily. I think of Manchester United who drew 18 games last season and Liverpool, with only one draw less. A team would have to win only six games to have equalled United's points total from 18 games."**
- **Joe Corrigan: "It will make the game worse. As soon as a team gets a goal ahead they will go on defence, it's a natural instinct. The last major change in the rules, creating three up and three down between the divisions, has been responsible for making the game less attractive, when some people thought it would be the livener needed. I fear the outcome from this rule change will be identical."**

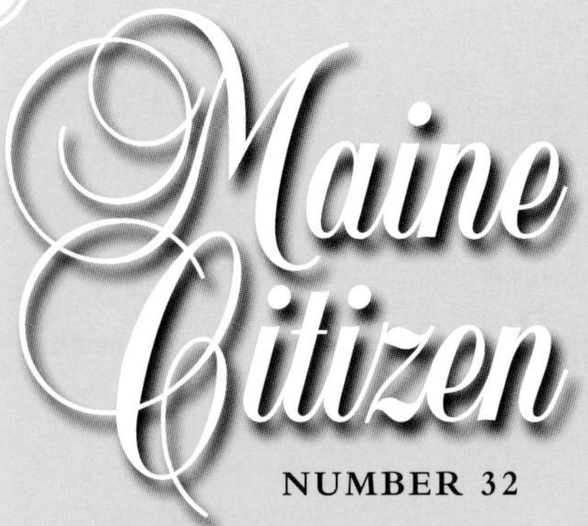

NUMBER 32

TOMMY CATON

When Malcolm Allison and Tony Book gave a debut to a 16 year old boy from Liverpool on the opening day of the 1979-80 season most supporters were convinced it was merely a one-off tactic that told more about Allison than the player, but they were wrong. Tommy Caton made his debut in the goalless draw at home to Crystal Palace on 18th August 1979 and the teenage defender managed to retain his place for the rest of the season.

It was a remarkable feat and brought Caton 12 League appearances before his 17th birthday. Although there have been younger debutants there are unlikely to be many players who have featured in so many games during their first season at such a tender age. Prior to his first team debut, Caton was an important member of the Youth team defeated in the two-legged final of the F.A. Youth Cup by Millwall. He was also a vital member of the Reserves while still a schoolboy. Allison had wanted to play him in the first team towards the end of the 1978-9 season but, because of his age, was prevented from doing so.

After two months in the side, and shortly after his 17th birthday, Caton gave a view of his brief Maine Road career: "I came to City in March 1978, signing on associate schoolboy forms and then started a full time apprenticeship in July, this year. I understand the club wanted me to play in the first team at the end of last season, but couldn't do so because the school authorities wouldn't give permission. It was a bit strange to say the least when I played in my first few games. I think the biggest tests have been against Arsenal, at Highbury, facing Stapleton and Sunderland. Plus the match against Forest when it was Woodcock and Birtles."

Throughout Caton's first season he was being tipped for international honours and various awards. He earned England Youth caps then in March 1980 he won the Robinsons Barley Water Young Player of the Month, after being in contention several times, and everything seemed to point to a great footballing future. It wasn't long before he made appearances for England Under-21.

He struggled with injury a little during 1980-81 - a chipped ankle bone caused him to miss a period of what became a crucial season - yet he recovered in time to play a major part in John Bond's Wembley bound side. Still only 18 he featured in both finals.

After Wembley, Caton enjoyed the 1981-2 season as he made 39 League appearances and was continually tipped for a senior international cap. Sadly, the failure of City during 1982-3 caused Caton to consider his future and, after relegation, he started to question whether he would ever achieve his international ambitions while playing for a northern Second Division side. In November 1983 he was sold to Arsenal for around £500,000. He felt he stood more chance of being noticed at Highbury, and with City struggling financially the Blues could not afford to keep him anyway.

His move south was not the success he hoped and after 95 League and Cup appearances with the Gunners he was transferred to Oxford for £180,000. Had another southern club, possibly Spurs, come in for Caton in 1983 rather than Arsenal it's possible his move south would have been a success; after all Arsenal have always been a defensively strong side and Caton was merely one of many quality defenders at Highbury.

At Oxford his career seemed to deteriorate further and it wasn't long before he moved on again, this time to Charlton Athletic. A serious foot injury required repeated surgery during the early 1990s and brought a great deal of depression to the player. Early in 1993 he was forced to announce his retirement and then in April that year he died at the age of 30 of a suspected heart-attack. It was a terrible shock. A minute's silence was held at Maine Road.

Although Caton's life and City career were short, it is true to say he did bring a lot of happiness to the Blues. His first season was a revelation, and while at Maine Road he continually seemed to improve. The years that followed should have seen him achieve his international ambitions, but sadly they did not. Had City not been relegated in 1983 then it seems more than likely he would have stayed with the Blues and may have impressed Bobby Robson. Uprooting to Arsenal was definitely the wrong move in the end and sent his career into reverse gear.

So much talent, so much ability, so little time.

CATON'S PLAYING RECORD

	LEAGUE		FA CUP		FL CUP		TOTAL	
	App	Gls	App	Gls	App	Gls	App	Gls
1979-80	42	0	1	0	4	0	47	0
1980-81	29 (1)	0	7	0	6	0	42 (1)	0
1981-82	39	1	2	0	4	0	45	1
1982-83	38	5	2	0	4	0	44	5
1983-84	16	2	-	-	3	0	19	2
TOTAL	164 (1)	8	12	0	21	0	197 (1)	8

Bobby McDonald was acclaimed as 'Scotland's Number One' during his memorable performance as a replacement for the injured Joe Corrigan.

Sainty suggesting Bobby McDonald could take over in goal. McDonald: "We didn't have anyone named before the game for Joe's job, and it was a shock to see Joe injured. As soon as I was told to go in goal I accepted it, and it seemed the best decision at the time because Paul Power could take over from me at left-back."

For the remaining 87 minutes McDonald performed superbly, making fine saves from Blissett, Callaghan, Jenkins and Armstrong. In fact a Gerry Armstrong shot two minutes from time resulted in a save that any 'keeper would have been delighted to make. He was also a shade fortunate at times with a couple of shots hitting the woodwork.

Fourteen minutes from time Dennis Tueart, who had come on as substitute for his first game since December 1981, headed the only goal of the match. That goal and McDonald's performance put City at the top of the table after three straight victories.

Afterwards McDonald gave his view of the match: "My first touch of the ball in the whole match was the goal-kick after Joe had been taken off and it felt very strange at the time. There was a mark in the middle of the six-yard box and I kept myself aware of it to help my positional sense. I don't know what came over me at one stage when I started to roll the ball out and chase it. I had taken the regulation four steps going after it and I suppose the referee could have blown me up for an offence. But he snapped 'now kick it' and that was all the warning I needed. I was very conscious of the four-step rule after that and at times I was only taking one before booting the ball upfield.

"I appreciated the reaction from the supporters. The lads all said 'well done' straight after the whistle went. It was a necessity on the day, but I don't want to go through it again."

During the game the supporters chanted 'Scotland's Number One', while afterwards the press were full of praise. The *Daily Mail* accurately summed up the player's performance: "McDonald managed to look terrified, ham-fisted, courageous and totally unbeatable."

With Corrigan out, City gave 20 year old Alex Williams a run out. He'd actually made his debut on 14th March 1981 against West Bromwich Albion, becoming the first black goalkeeper in the First Division. Corrigan's injury gave him the chance to appear on a regular basis. His first game during 1982-3 ended in a 1-0 defeat at Notts County, but this was followed by a 2-1 win at Spurs with Graham Baker netting twice. Defeat at home to Aston Villa on 18th September was followed by a disastrous trip to Upton Park where City were beaten 4-1. Both Kevin Bond and Asa Hartford were sent off in the second half to add to the pressure, but Alex Williams performed superbly, saving a penalty in addition to a good overall performance. Despite the disappointing results Williams was actually playing well and was certainly not responsible for City's dip, in fact for the games against Spurs, Villa and West Ham the young 'keeper was voted City's star player.

Kevin Bond was sent-off in a 4-1 defeat at West Ham, along with Asa Hartford,

These results left the Blues in ninth position, but an upturn in fortunes during October managed to lift them back to second spot on 6th November. John Bond continued to look to change his squad and made bids for 35 year old midfielder Archie Gemmill, 32 year old Ivan Golac, 27 year old Eric Gates, and former Blue hero Peter Barnes, but each transfer required substantial bartering with City offering player exchanges and small amounts of cash. Each bid failed, although Golac did come on a free transfer in March 1983, City signing him on a month long contract. The Blues were now struggling to compete financially with the rest of the First Division. The transfer market City had helped to inflate, with ridiculous money paid for average players, had collapsed and every club caught up in the power game suffered to some extent. Arsenal were losing £1300 per day and claimed their break even attendance figure was in excess of 30,000 - a good 5,000 more than they were actually attracting. To solve the problem Arsenal Chairman Peter Hill-Wood suggested forming a super league of the 16 major clubs, and many leading figures supported him.

David Cross scored in each of the first two games of the 1982-83 season, a 2-1 win at Norwich on his debut and a 1-0 win at home to Stoke.

At Manchester United Ron Atkinson had been caught up in all the transfer activity and helped the Reds announce a then staggering loss of £2 million. He argued the side had needed major surgery when he arrived; a United shareholder shouted: "Next time the team needs major surgery, could we have it done on the NHS?"

Football was beginning to suffer, and as City had been the biggest spenders during the period they would suffer more than most. Only sustained success would give the finances a boost, but City already appeared set on a suicide mission. The transfer of Trevor Francis had seriously affected gates. During Francis' lone Maine Road season the Blues averaged 34,063, but in the first few months after his departure crowds had slumped by 6,000 - a figure they could ill afford to lose.

City's season continued with a few good results, such as a 4-1 victory over Norwich, but also some exceptionally bad ones. In the Milk Cup, - the League Cup under new sponsorship - City defeated Wigan 3-1 on aggregate then faced Southampton in the third round. A 1-1 Maine Road draw was followed by a demoralising 4-0 drubbing on the south coast. A victory would have given City a meeting with United at Old Trafford.

In the F.A. Cup the Blues defeated Sunderland 2-1 after a goalless game at Roker Park. Then on 29th January City travelled to Brighton for a fourth round tie that killed any hope of glory. The game ended 4-0 and almost immediately brought the resignation of a frustrated John Bond. His decision was not simply as a result of the defeat, it had been on the cards for some time. Bond had been uncertain about life at Maine Road ever since the 1981 Cup Final, possibly before. He had not really enjoyed the atmosphere within the club, and in particular his relationship with certain directors was not good. Also, events in his private life complicated matters further, and he remains adamant a certain director tried to pressure him to resign by threatening to provide stories to the press. Bond is understandably bitter about this period and the men in power at the time, although he insists he always maintained a good relationship with Chairman Swales, and no pressure to resign ever came from him.

These stories of petty feuds within the boardroom at that time may shock many supporters, yet Bond is convinced certain influences forced him out, and then contributed to the club's rapid deterioriation during the late seventies/early eighties. Whatever the truth, the departure of Bond sent the club hurtling down the table. Prior to the Brighton game City had managed to maintain, at worst, a mid-table position, once Bond resigned they were in free fall.

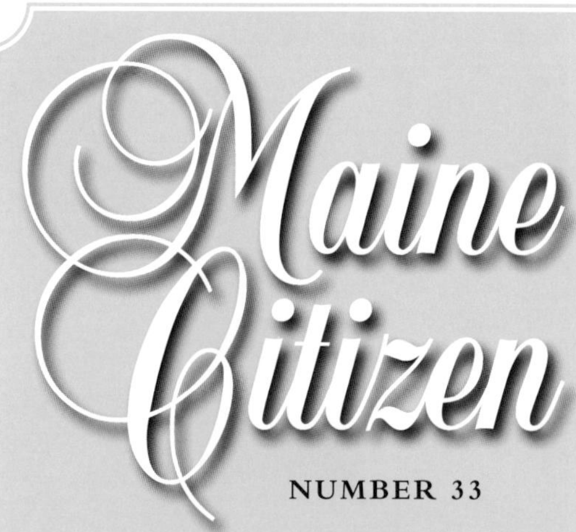

NUMBER 33

ALEX WILLIAMS

City's tradition of great goalkeepers seemed destined to continue for some time when the youthful Alex Williams replaced Joe Corrigan as the club's number one during the 1982-3 season. Williams seemed to have tremendous ability and did enough early on to impress Derek Hodgson of the Daily Telegraph who proudly stated: "Alex Williams will win more England caps than Joe Corrigan." Hodgson believed Williams could offer the game more than Corrigan and, indeed, more than Peter Shilton.

Corrigan remembers seeing Williams for the first time: "He came to the club several times before actually signing and my first recollections of Alex were of a shy, modest and always courteous lad who seemed somewhat overawed by what was happening around him. He was a tall, gangling lad who quickly started to reveal immense promise. I was initially worried about his strength although that built up thanks to the benefit of full time training. Sometimes emerging players start to be a bit flash at that age. Not Alex Williams. He always had his feet firmly on the ground.

"He came up along with the likes of Tommy Caton and Nicky Reid who were also members of the team that reached the F.A. Youth Cup Final in successive years. When I left City after my 17 year Maine Road career, Alex was the logical successor."

Bond's assistant John Benson was appointed manager but City fans felt he was hardly a credible choice. For Swales the appointment was the easy option, and did not involve any heavy financial compensation to rival clubs. It was not a bright move. Despite suggesting the appointment at the time, Bond later commented Benson was a good number two, but not really capable of the top job. Supporters joked Benson had only been given the job so that City didn't have to change the initials on the manager's tracksuit!

Under Benson, City achieved a 2-2 draw with Spurs but followed that with a 4-0 defeat at Coventry. On 19th February a 1-0 reverse at home to Notts County provoked demonstrations with some supporters chanting what was later to become the most widespread call at Maine Road: "Swales Out". These were desperate times, but still City remained above the relegation zone. Nine of the following thirteen games ended in defeat before the Blues entertained fellow strugglers Luton Town in the final game of the season at Maine Road. By that time John Benson had cut the wage bill by selling loyal servant Joe Corrigan to Seattle Sounders for only £30,000, leaving the still inexperienced Alex Williams as City's last line of defence.

Manchester United had crushed Luton 3-0 on the previous Monday, leaving City the relatively simple task of obtaining a draw to guarantee survival.

WILLIAMS' PLAYING RECORD

	LEAGUE		FA CUP		FL CUP		TOTAL	
	App	Gls	App	Gls	App	Gls	App	Gls
1980-81	2	0	0	0	0	0	2	0
1981-82	3	0	0	0	0	0	3	0
1982-83	17	0	0	0	1	0	18	0
1983-84	42	0	1	0	3	0	46	0
1984-85	42	0	1	0	5	0	48	0
1985-86	8	0	-	-	-	-	8	0
TOTAL	114	0	2	0	9	0	125	0

Williams made his debut on 14th March 1981 against West Bromwich Albion, played a further game that season, then made three appearances during 1981-82, but it was 1982-3 before he managed a decent run in the side with six consecutive League appearances during September and October. From March 1983 he became City's number one on a permanent basis.

The colour of a player's skin should never matter, yet during the early 80s it seemed many opponents' spectators could not accept City had the First Division's first 'black' 'keeper, and Alex suffered tremendous racist abuse at many grounds. Often he would find he was an easy target being so close to the crowd and, regrettably, the neanderthal elements of each club's support tried to ridicule him. Bananas were thrown at many leading venues - including Anfield - and Williams, like Trautmann before him, showed great courage in overcoming this mindless behaviour.

Williams: "The colour thing should be kept in perspective. I took a bit of stick when I first went into the game because, frankly, the fans weren't used to seeing a black 'keeper in this country. Leeds' fans, I recall, used to be a bit naughty to me. So I always made a point of playing well at Elland Road. Once the spectators began to realise there was a bit of ability there, it wasn't a problem."

From 19th March 1983 until 14th September 1985 Williams never missed a League game. He was one of City's most consistent performers helping the Blues achieve promotion under Billy McNeill in 1985. During that promotion season he maintained a clean sheet for 21 of the 42 games played and conceded only 40 goals.

In September 1985 a toe injury forced him out of first team action, then playing in the Reserves he fell badly on his back and injured his spine. His City career was over. His final game had been the Manchester derby on 14th September 1985.

He tried to fight back to full fitness but it gradually became obvious the only chance he had to save his career was to leave Maine Road and try his hand with a smaller club. He went on loan to Queen of the South, then to Port Vale. At Vale Park, manager John Rudge and physio Martin Copeland worked hard in an effort to resurrect Alex's career. Rudge: "We worked with Alex for more than 12 months and he was a smashing lad to work with. He never gave up hope, yet deep down we knew he would never recapture that wonderful ability he had. His injury affected a leg and restricted his ability to leap."

At the age of 25 Alex Williams was forced to give up his fight. Had he been able to continue with City during 1985 it's possible he may have been City's number one 'keeper right through until the mid-1990s, after all he would only have been 30 in November 1991.

After his playing career ended, Alex performed a role with the Football in the Community Scheme and his devotion and dedication to the local community was rewarded with an OBE in the New Years Honours List announced in December 2001.

Tony Book and John Benson discuss life after Bond during Benson's first game in charge. City fought back from two down to draw 2-2 with Tottenham thanks to goals from Dennis Tueart (penalty) and David Cross.

Few City fans seriously believed the Blues would be relegated although Luton boss David Pleat was convinced his side could shock the football world: "The pressure is on City. They have to play well and we know we can produce attacking football as good as anyone in the First Division. If we can do ourselves justice then we can still stay up."

A big crowd of 42,843 boosted the post-Francis average to 26,788, leaving City the fourth best supported club. For much of the match the Blues seemed content to defend - a tactic that always leaves City supporters nervous - while Luton attacked with flair. Paul Walsh probed the City defence, but the Blues managed to hold off any real first half threat.

In the second period Luton were more determined than ever to obtain the three points and Walsh sent a blistering drive towards the City goal. Alex Williams made a magnificent save that time, but the City fans became more anxious. Luton's Kirk Stephens later saw a shot deflected on to the bar, while the supporters in the North Stand panicked every time they saw Luton heading towards them.

David Pleat then made what transpired to be the most important tactical move of the match, when he brought on unpredictable Yugoslav international Raddy Antic in place of the tiring Wayne Turner. Four minutes from the end Luton's Stein centred a ball which rebounded back to him off Tommy Caton. The second cross in was pushed out to the edge of the area by Alex Williams. Unfortunately it found its way to the feet of Antic who hit it first time. It deflected past Williams and into the net. City were shell shocked.

For the final four minutes the Blues gave up on defence and went all out for an equaliser, but it wasn't to be. When the final whistle was blown Luton's David Pleat jigged across the Maine Road turf straight to his skipper Brian Horton. City fans cried, while Dennis Tueart realised it spelled the end of his City career. Tueart was the only player whose contract was close to completion and, as he trudged off the pitch, realised he was the first player the club would sell to cut the wage bill, although many would argue Corrigan was the first to be sacrificed. Feeling as low as the rest of the City fans, he took a long look around the stadium, thought to himself, 'this is it, it's all over', and walked down the tunnel for the last time as a City player.

Inside the dressing rooms officials, fans and the media kept saying 'you'll be back next year', but Tueart knew it was the last of his Maine Road outings. He wanted to stay, wanted to help City back, but knew it wouldn't be possible. His final game should have been a celebration, but turned out to be a wake. In July he was released to First Division Stoke on a free transfer. The wage bill had to be cut.

Another to depart was John Benson. Swales wanted a big name manager to bring the Blues back on course and so Benson was sacked. Had City remained in the First Division Benson may still have been looking for another job. Swales: "John Benson was no John Bond that's for sure. I think I always felt he was a caretaker manager. If we'd avoided relegation I think we'd have looked to try and get somebody with more stature really. He never proved himself as a manager before, or since."

With relegation Swales' dream of upstaging United was further away than ever. When he became Chairman City were more successful than the Reds, and not too far behind in terms of support. He had increased support, but the success had evaporated. Within a fortnight of City's relegation, United defeated Brighton in the F.A. Cup Final replay to bring Ron Atkinson his first trophy at Old Trafford. The two clubs were sailing in opposite directions. Swales needed to appoint a manager who could rebuild the Blues. He turned to Scotland.

A famous scene as Luton manager David Pleat (left) dances onto the Maine Road pitch to celebrate his team's survival... at the expense of City. The player he ran to was Brian Horton, who had just been confronted by a distressed Dennis Tueart.

Chapter Nineteen

FALLEN GIANTS 1983 1989

CELTIC Manager and 1967 European Cup winning captain Billy McNeill was in dispute with his Board at Glasgow and also having difficulty with the Scottish media. A story was circulating that portrayed McNeill as a man desperate to increase his salary, but the truth was the Celtic manager was finding it difficult to work with Desmond White the club Chairman. This coincided with a desire by Peter Swales to appoint a big name boss to bring life back into Maine Road.

City approached McNeill and, after discussions in Carlisle, the Celtic man told Swales he would join the Blues. Once in Manchester the new manager not only felt lonely but made a couple of silly mistakes. McNeill tried to meet the fans: "I invariably forgot myself and referred to them as Celtic fans instead of City. It was all part of me being homesick. I was so fed up when the pre-season training kicked off, and I was still living in a hotel, that I packed everything and drove to Glasgow. I told Liz [his wife] that I wasn't going back, that I had taken enough. I had been in Manchester only a few weeks and was thoroughly homesick."

McNeill was persuaded to return to Manchester, but it took him a long time to settle. Fortunately, he had recognised he needed to quickly find someone with knowledge of Second Division football and, more importantly, someone who understood what Manchester football was all about. McNeill was familiar with the divide in Glasgow, and how football was affected there by local politics and religion, but the Manchester situation was different. City were/are the team for Mancunians passionate about local pride, while many United supporters have no connection with the city whatsoever. He appointed Jimmy Frizzell, a fellow Scot who had been Oldham Athletic's manager pre-Joe Royle and significantly knew how to cope on a shoe-string budget.

City's finances were now in an extremely dire state, with the *Daily Mirror* shocking the Manchester public with news that interest charges alone were costing the Blues £1,000 a day. Relegation had hurt the club of course, but the biggest cause of City's plight had been the spend, spend years of Allison and Bond. City had simply spent money in lumps they couldn't afford, and in 1983 some sources claimed the club was still making payments for Steve Daley, who had been sold in February 1981.

Prior to taking the City job, McNeill believed the Blues were still a major force in England. Sure they'd been relegated, but he felt enough finance would be available to gain promotion at the first attempt and then build a successful side. He soon realised City's playing squad was not of the calibre required, nor was there enough money to buy the right players: "Jimmy and I were left with so few players we sat for days on end thinking who we could get for as close to nothing as possible. City had horrendous debts in the wake of their halcyon spending-sprees on players. We could hardly buy a fish supper."

£1.2 million man Kevin Reeves had moved on by this time, joining John Bond at Burnley, while Bobby McDonald already knew he stood no chance of playing under the new manager following disciplinary problems during the close season. McNeill quickly indicated what type of approach he wanted when he transferred the player to Oxford at the start of the season. The majority of supporters were sorry to see McDonald go, but it was important for McNeill to establish his control.

One man determined to continue was captain Paul Power who loyally said: "I'm staying to lead the fightback to the First Division". He was quickly joined by an army of battling Scotsmen at bargain prices as Frizzell and McNeill boosted their squad. McNeill: "We pulled players out of our memories. Derek Parlane came on a free transfer from Leeds. Jim Tolmie from Lokeren in Belgium, and Neil McNab from Brighton. I had remembered Tolmie with Morton, but was aware he could also be difficult to handle. We weren't in a position to be choosy.

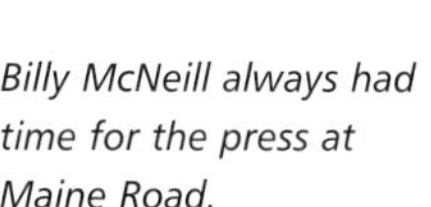

Billy McNeill always had time for the press at Maine Road.

Jim Tolmie scores from around 20 yards out in the 2-1 home win against Middlesbrough in October 1983.

We got McNab from Brighton, where he had been a bit of a rebel."

The McNab transfer cost City around £35,000 and proved a real bargain, especially when compared to the millions blown over the previous four years for players of uncertain ability. Every one of these signings proved value for money and City fans were excited when Crystal Palace were beaten 2-0 on the opening day of the season, with Parlane and youngster Andy May scoring. A disappointing 2-1 defeat at Cardiff followed but then on 3rd September, two goals from Tolmie and one from Parlane brought a 3-2 defeat of Barnsley before 25,105 in the first home game of the season.

A goalless draw against Fulham followed, but then a run of five successive victories left City in second place behind Sheffield Wednesday. The run included a 6-0 thrashing of perennial promotion also-rans Blackburn Rovers, and a 2-1 defeat of struggling giants Leeds United. McNeill's Scottish bargains were helping City rediscover their pride, but the club was still lacking funds.

By this time, City's only real saleable asset was Tommy Caton, and many of the leading First Division clubs had made approaches. The Blues were determined not to sell but with so much interest and a need to balance the books McNeill was forced to listen to any serious offer. In addition the player had now started to believe his international aspirations could not be fulfilled while in the Second Division. On 1st December Caton was sold to Arsenal for a fee of around £450,000. The sum was poor in relation to the transfers of the previous seasons, but City needed the money.

Goalscorers Jamie Hoyland, Jim Tolmie (2) and Derek Parlane (3) celebrate a 6-0 League Cup thrashing of Torquay United in October 1983.

Within two weeks £200,000 of that fee was spent on Barnsley's strongman Mick McCarthy. It was another important transfer, and one which helped maintain City's promotion challenge. With three promotion places available City felt certain they could achieve an immediate return, however they did not account for the role Kevin Keegan would play in transforming Newcastle's fortunes. Newcastle had been struggling to make an impact since relegation in 1978, but then Keegan returned as a player and the whole place seemed revitalised, indeed he had helped the Geordies inflict a 5-0 thrashing of City in October. McNeill: "There are few players that I have greater respect for than Keegan and this time, I'm referring only to his ability on the pitch; he was the heart and soul of Newcastle. It's a terrible thing to admit, but every time I read that Kevin had an injury I hoped it would keep him out of the Newcastle side for a game or two. Usually it didn't and I was glad in the end because I have such a high regard for him. He was certainly the difference between City and Newcastle. They had Keegan's inspirational qualities and we didn't."

By 11th February, City and Newcastle were level on points with City in third place, and Newcastle fourth with a game in hand. Above them lay Chelsea and Sheffield Wednesday. The four sides were termed the 'Big Four' by the media who regularly chose to feature games from the Second above those in the First. As always Liverpool seemed destined to win the Championship and so attention turned to the glamour clubs of the Second, especially Newcastle with the charismatic Keegan.

On 18th February came the vital Maine Road clash between the 'Jocks' and the Geordies. A City win would put them six points ahead of Newcastle, yet defeat would put the two sides level with Keegan's men also having a game in hand. A crowd of 41,767 - City's and the division's second biggest of the season - saw Steve Kinsey score for City but fine goals from Beardsley and Keegan gave Newcastle a 2-1 victory. It also gave the Geordies the edge.

A 0-0 draw at Middlesbrough left the Blues in fifth place, with Grimsby nudging above both City and Newcastle for a while. This was City's lowest position of the season, but in truth was a fair reflection. Chelsea and Sheffield Wednesday were beyond doubt the best two sides in the division, while Newcastle had a number of quality players - McDermott, Waddle, Beardsley and Keegan. City still felt capable of promotion though, and entered the Good Friday derby match with struggling Oldham at Boundary Park full of hope.

The crowd recorded by Oldham as 20,320 - their highest League attendance since 1978 - was in high spirits before the match with local stewards unable to control what was a major fixture for the club. Before the game a few City fans climbed over the fences and onto the pitch for their own game of football. As stewards tried to end that nonsense another group of fans grabbed hold of a ladder used by a local television crew to reach the gantry, raced across the pitch and then used it to climb into the upper section of

Oldham's Main Stand. It was mayhem, although there was little, if any, actual violence.

Once the game started the off-field activities calmed, but the result - a 2-2 draw - was not the right one for either side and left City in fourth place. A 3-2 defeat by Huddersfield three days later, ensured a miserable Easter and more or less ended City's promotion drive.

A 1-0 loss at Derby on 28th April left the Blues fifth on 66 points, while Grimsby had a point more and Newcastle had streaked away and were now on 73 points with a far superior goal difference. With three games remaining it was still mathematically possible to go up, but highly unlikely, especially as City had to face Chelsea and Sheffield Wednesday. On Friday 4th May at 7.15pm City faced second placed Chelsea at Maine Road for the first Second Division game ever to be shown live on television.

A victory would have kept City in with a shout, but the match ended disappointingly in a 2-0 defeat and the Blues knew the dream was over. A goalless game at Sheffield followed, then the final home game of the season ended in a 5-0 thrashing of relegated Cambridge before 20,787. City finished fourth, ten points behind third placed Newcastle, while Chelsea snatched the title on goal difference from Wednesday.

Considering the team changes, and the arrival of a manager unfamiliar with life in Manchester the season had been a good one. Andy May and goalkeeper Alex Williams were the season's only ever-presents, although May had been substituted on six occasions. Williams in particular had performed exceptionally well, especially in difficult circumstances when the colour of his skin seemed to present some opposition supporters with an easy target. Williams rarely complained about the abuse and by playing well blunted the racists in the crowd. At some grounds bananas were thrown and, being so close to the crowd, there were games when he must have felt sick with the level of the abuse, but he never let it show. Like Bert Trautmann before him, he found some of the London clubs were less than tolerant. As with the great German 'keeper, Williams tried to excel in these games: "My best performance was at Chelsea when I kept a clean sheet - one of the twelve games in which I didn't concede a goal. I had a lot to do that day at Stamford Bridge and I got on top of it all - I even coped with some of the verbal abuse from the racist element of the crowd."

In the F.A. Cup City failed to impress with a 2-1 defeat at Blackpool, while the League Cup saw the Blues conquer Torquay 6-0 in the second round, second leg, but then succumb to a 3-0 defeat at First Division Aston Villa.

The following season had to be the one that mattered now as City, by far the most watched side in the division, needed to achieve promotion. Nothing else would do.

On the opening day of the 1984-5 campaign City took to the field at Plough Lane for a first League meeting with Wimbledon. It was a new experience, but two shock goals in the first fifteen minutes for the home side proved City still remained football's great unpredictables. Fightback goals from Parlane and Gordon Smith, signed the previous March, brought the first point of the season. The side that day included Tony Cunningham, signed from Sheffield Wednesday for £100,000 and defender David Phillips who cost £65,000 plus other payments depending on appearances. The arrival of Phillips seemed perfect from an advertisers point of view as the Blues had just agreed a two year sponsorship deal worth around £250,000 with the electrical company Philips.

A 3-0 victory over Grimsby in the next match encouraged the fans, but two successive defeats, and a no score draw against Carlisle raised a few concerns. City did, however, enter October a much better side and after a 1-0 win against Oxford, they lay in sixth position. They dropped a couple of places shortly afterwards but managed to hover around eighth spot for much of the period leading up to Christmas.

McNeill and Frizzell had managed to add further experience to the side by signing attacker Jim Melrose from Celtic, and bringing central defender Ken McNaught on loan from West Bromwich Albion as cover for Nicky Reid and Mick McCarthy. McNaught became the tenth Scottish player signed by McNeill at Maine Road, and should have been one of the best, but West Brom demanded £50,000 to make the transfer a permanent one, and City simply could

David Phillips joined the Blues just after Philips had become new club sponsors!

Left: The programme for the first ever Second Division fixture broadcast live on television.

THE CITY GATES

On Monday 21st November 1983 the former Hyde Road Hotel re-opened as the City Gates public house. Managed by 60s hero George Heslop, the pub had been given a complete overhaul and was clearly aimed at providing a true Blue venue for all Mancunians. Heslop was keen to turn it into a shrine worthy of the club: "The pub is the site where City was founded and this has inspired our change of name since it's also the location of the team's first ground. I've been collecting playing kit, newspaper cuttings or memorable moments - absolutely anything worthy of being associated with City.

"I'm making appeals to City fans wherever I go. If they can help by providing more significant memorabilia I'll find a place for it."

Unfortunately the pub's transformation was not as tasteful as it should have been, and instead of providing a good representation of the club's history, it presented a 1980s image of the Blues. Photos of players such as Phil Boyer dominated, and inevitably the pub failed. In 1989 the City Gates closed for the last time and, despite attempts to save it by supporters, was demolished in 2001.

Mick McCarthy towered above everyone at the heart of the defence.

not afford even that modest outlay, reluctantly letting him return to the Hawthorns in March.

By that time, the Blues had climbed the table and actually reached top place after an important 1-0 victory at Blackburn. It was the highest City had been under McNeill and coincided with his 45th birthday: "It was a day when the smile seldom left my face. The team's performance was full of character, packed with grit and determination and no shortage of style, which has been apparent for months. There were some excellent contributions at Blackburn. Our skipper, Paul Power, maintained his peak form of late and obliterated the potential danger from their speedy flank man, Ian Miller (who in 1997 ran City's B team). Mick McCarthy towered above everyone at the heart of the defence - inspirational stuff. Nicky Reid stood no nonsense and took no prisoners. The whole back four coped comfortably with the problems set by Blackburn, who were then the League leaders with only one home defeat against them and scorers of at least one goal in every one of their home games."

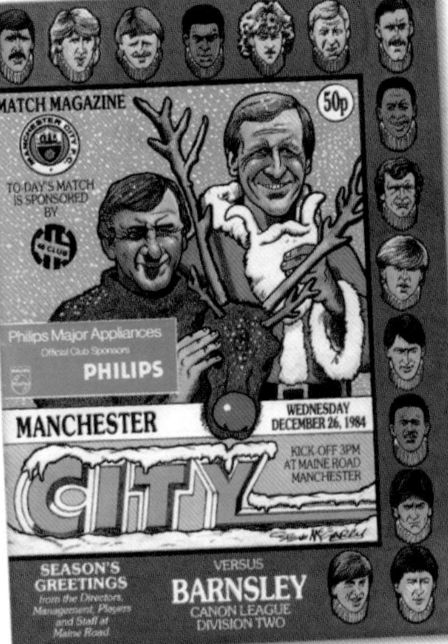

Right: One of the club's most unusual programme covers was produced for the visit of Barnsley on Boxing Day, 1984.

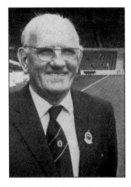

The game wasn't without its disappointment though as, in the 66th minute, Graham Baker fell awkwardly on his left ankle. After treatment from physio Roy Bailey, the player continued but then seven minutes later crashed to the ground again. This time he landed heavily on his left shoulder, and was led from the pitch clutching his arm. A hospital visit revealed a dislocated shoulder. Baker, who had only just heard he would be suspended after a booking against Brighton two weeks earlier felt far from happy: "I thought I was going to miss only a fortnight. Now there's no knowing how long it can be. I've got the arm in a sling which I have to keep on for 14 days. The ankle is swollen up with the sprain but that's less of a concern - it's all going to take time. It's such a crucial part of the season. Missing the two home games through suspension is a disappointment but I was contenting myself that at least I'd be available for the real key visits we have to make to Birmingham and Oxford later this month. I've not got any hope at all now."

Another player missing was Clive Wilson who had been excluded from McNeill's plans because of a mystery ankle problem. He'd attended training on 11th February and afterwards started to experience pain at the bottom of his left ankle. The next day his right leg began to suffer, by Wednesday he was in hospital with both ankles swollen, then a few days later he was on crutches. Nobody ever found out exactly what caused the condition, although the most likely explanation seemed to be Wilson had picked up an infection via a cut. There was also speculation the problem stemmed from a virus picked up on the club's earlier trip to Malaysia. Whatever, it managed to end all hope of the player appearing for the rest of the season.

One man who did make it into the first team was Kenny Clements who had returned to Maine Road after over five years at Oldham. His debut saw City defeat Middlesbrough 1-0 with a goal from Phillips seven days after the Blackburn match. For Clements it was an emotional return: "The reception I got from the fans when I ran out with the team is really the thing I'll remember from the day. They waved from the Kippax, I waved back, then they started clapping above their heads and chanting my name - and I started clapping them back in a similar manner. It was only brief but it was getting ridiculous because I was filling up - I had to turn away so that I didn't cry in front of them. It was just so good to be back."

During the match Clements injured a leg and broke his nose, but as the player himself said: "it was all worth it to be back at Maine Road."

Seven days later Shrewsbury were crushed 4-0 then came a couple of setbacks in crucial away games against opponents challenging for promotion. First City could only manage a goalless draw at Birmingham, then the fans endured a 3-0 defeat at Oxford. The Blues were still top on 62 points, but had played more games than any of the challenging sides. Oxford were second on 58 points with three games in hand, Alan Ball's Portsmouth were third on 57 points with one game in hand, while Birmingham were fourth on the same number of points and games as Portsmouth.

After the Oxford match came a 2-2 draw against Cardiff, a goalless game at Barnsley and a 2-1 defeat at home to Leeds, leaving the Blues in third spot. The Leeds encounter had been particularly disappointing as Graham Baker, who had only returned to action two days earlier against Barnsley, broke his leg in the 13th minute of the game, thereby ending his season.

City's disappointing form had coincided with a number of other injuries to crucial players. Obviously Baker and Wilson were missing, but Jim Melrose (hamstring) and Gordon Smith (knee ligaments) were also out of action. On 13th April City travelled to Grimsby desperate to return to winning ways, but a 4-1 defeat left the Blues in fifth place, one point behind Portsmouth in third.

An important 2-0 victory over Sheffield United rekindled City's fire and McNeill was determined that three points would be gained in the all important away trip to Alan Ball's promotion hopefuls Portsmouth. McNeill did all he could to coax his side to victory: "I preached confidence and composure. The players responded tremendously, they had the mood and determination to win that last chance available to us at Portsmouth. Nothing less than victory would have served a purpose in my view and we tackled the job

BILL MILES

On 8th October 1984 City's historian and former Chairman of the Supporters' Club, Bill Miles, passed away. He'd dedicated much of his life to the Blues and was one of the most approachable City men during the 70s and early 80s. In 1983 he assisted Andy Ward with his research for the Manchester City Story, and had uncovered much about the club's history during his life. He was Chairman of the Supporters' Club from 1948 to 1958.

correctly. Pompey had a physical approach to the game. They had big lads up front, determined and energetic, and it wasn't difficult to anticipate that we would have spells under intense pressure. We played well, tenaciously, defended strongly. Apart from a header which went wide and a very good save early on from Alex Williams, we were every bit in the hunt with them 'till half-time.

"Alex handled cleanly and made one very vital save from Neil Webb when the score was 1-1. Our winner was a classic from Paul Simpson, his third from a handful of first team opportunities. Although it came nine minutes from time it did seem to be scored an eternity away from the final whistle. But imagine the excitement in the closing minutes when City fans behind the trainer's bench started hammering for our attention with the news that Blackburn Rovers - possibly the biggest threat to our ambitions then - had lost at Charlton!"

The 2-1 victory lifted City into third place, with every side in the division having played 39 games. The Blues were on 70 points with Blackburn fourth on 67. Leeds and Portsmouth were in fifth and sixth place respectively on 65 points.

City's remaining three fixtures looked relatively simple - Oldham Athletic (4th May at Maine Road), Notts County (6th May at Meadow Lane), and Charlton Athletic (Maine Road on 11th May). Oldham and Charlton were both about eight points above the relegation zone, while Notts County were 21st with little hope of survival.

Against Oldham, City could only manage a draw, but at least it was a point. If the Blues could beat Notts County then, barring a miraculous turnaround in goal difference, they would be up. The Bank Holiday Monday journey to Nottingham was an exciting one for all Blues, with every pub, motorway service station, and cafe on the route full of City fans with painted faces and in party mood. It was an amazing exodus and one which pleased manager McNeill. He realised the passion of the Blues fans and finally started to feel at home. Manchester was not 'his' city, but it was beginning to become a part of him.

Inside the ground the atmosphere made Meadow Lane feel like Maine Road with every side of the then three-sided ground housing City fans. In fact, Notts County had been so keen to ensure a big attendance they had given City the home supporters' section of the Kop. At that time the section held around 10,000 but with County only attracting around 4,000 of their own supporters per game, it was felt City needed the terracing more. The official attendance for the match was 17,812 - almost 5,000 more than their next highest figure which, itself, was a good 4,000 above the third highest.

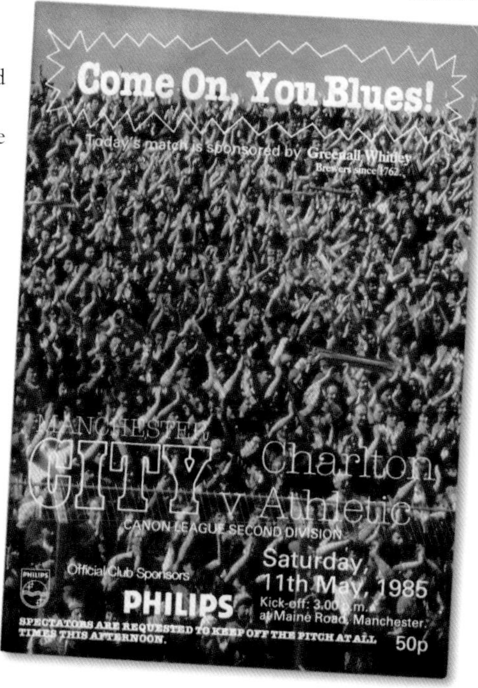

The programme cover for the game with Charlton on 11th May 1985 pictured City's massive following at Notts County.

Despite the large City support, the Blues struggled and County took a three goal lead in the first half. The party atmosphere was replaced by tension with petty scuffles taking place in the stands. At the Kop End City fans started to pull down a section of fencing. At first the stewards, uncertain how to control the fans, allowed them to continue for some time before they tried to stop the vandalism. By the time they acted, more supporters had decided to join in. Further scuffles broke out around the ground and, although the trouble should have been easily quelled, an unfortunate announcement over the tannoy system said the game would be abandoned and replayed if the fans did not resume order. This did more to encourage rather than abate the vandalism, as City supporters could envisage their actions wiping out the three goal margin.

Eventually to ease the situation Billy McNeill walked to the Kop and appealed for calm. A few minutes later peace was restored and the game recommenced, but the atmosphere was muted. During the second half the Blues seemed to be in control and managed to pull two goals back from Paul Simpson, but the City management felt little satisfaction in the turnaround. Appropriately, the game ended 3-2 to County and a day that should have brought much joy to Manchester had been ruined.

The result left City needing a win, but even then Portsmouth could still overtake the Blues if they managed to overturn City's goal difference. The Blues basically held a five goal lead over Alan Ball's side, but Portsmouth had caused City to lose out on goal average back in 1927 and no Blue could relax.

On 11th May 1985 the visit of Charlton was watched by an official crowd of 47,285 in a stadium that boasted it could hold 52,600 with 26,500 seats. Many supporters remain convinced there were significantly more in the stadium that day as the Kippax was uncomfortably packed, while in the other three stands fans were forced to sit on the steps to watch the game.

Whatever the actual attendance it was a day all Blues enjoyed, although it didn't start out that way. McNeill remembers the tension: "City were up against it. I put on my best lightweight suit and swept into the ground early in the morning. Everyone was a bag of nerves. But that was the very reason I was there so early and looking, I hoped, a million dollars.
I strode around exuding confidence, telling everyone who would listen that we would win. I felt this had been transmitted to the team and that was really all that bothered me. We scored twice early on and

HORSE ON THE LINE

After leaving Manchester at 12.40, the official supporters train travelling to Barnsley for the game on 6th April 1985 had only managed to pass Stalybridge when it was forced to stop. For several minutes fans were mystified as to the cause of the delay, then supporters' club officials discovered a horse had been hit by an earlier train and blocked the line. For what seemed an eternity everyone waited for the animal to be moved. Eventually the train was allowed to continue and City fans were assured the game would not commence until they arrived at Oakwell. Unfortunately, as the supporters made their way down the hill towards Barnsley's ground, after a three-hour journey, they heard a roar and realised the match had already commenced.
Many started running towards the ground and, as they queued at the turnstiles, rumours spread that City were winning. Some supporters entered the ground cheering, delighted with the alleged score, much to the amazement of those already stood on the open terracing. It wasn't until half-time that people discovered the rumours had been false and that the game was actually goal-less. It ended 0-0.

David Phillips scores against Charlton on the final day of the 1984-85 season. His two goals helped City achieve a 5-1 victory watched by an official crowd of 47,285. Many felt the attendance was actually higher and, as this photo shows, the Kippax was packed to bursting point.

How the Blues programme at the start of the following season looked back on the memorable day when promotion was assured.

● Celebrations for manager **Billy McNeill** and the club's number one showbiz supporter, fun-man **Eddie Large.**

● And celebrations for the fans, too.

● **Mick McCarthy** involuntarily joins in the promotion fun, yan match due to suspension.

MAGIC MOMENTS Saturday, 11th May, 1985: CITY 5 CHARL

● It's that wonderful promotion feeling . . . the after-match bath-time took on a stimulating new look. And these City stars are sure they can make a splash in the First Division, too.

● **Paul Simpson** keeps up his scoring run: with the 4th go Charlton.

eventually led 5-0 before Charlton got a consolation goal which jubilant City fans cheered as well. Our scorers were Andy May, Jim Melrose, Dave Phillips (2), and Paul Simpson. It was a tremendous achievement. There hadn't been so much excitement - or champagne - at Maine Road for years."

At the final whistle City fans raced onto the pitch for the biggest and best celebratory invasion in years. Andy May and Paul Power were stripped of their shirts immediately while others, Paul Simpson included, lost theirs to souvenir hunters a little later.

Afterwards the terrible news of fire and tragedy from Bradford dampened spirits and caused many supporters to consider what could have happened at Maine Road had fire broken out in the Platt Lane Stand. With so many blocking the aisles, few would have survived.

In the days that followed, naturally the national press covered the Bradford disaster, but City still managed to make a few of the back page headlines locally. Each article seemed to concentrate on the view that the Blues remained very much a club in debt. This was no longer a surprise to McNeill, who felt safety in the First Division would gradually turn the finances around, but it still disappointed the fans who had remained incredibly loyal. Understandably, the ambitious stadium rebuilding plans of 1981 had been brought to a halt, but surely money could be found somewhere for team building?

Swales told the press how relegation had cost the club dearly: "It cost us half a million, but you must go through terrible pain before you can do really well. The lessons have been learned under a good manager and we don't intend to go down again."

He added he felt responsible for City's decline during the early 80s. There had been calls for him to quit prior to relegation, but once the inevitable occurred he told his critics that he'd got City into the mess, so he would get City out of it. He added: "I felt destined to go down as a failure. I was beginning to think I was a bit of a Jonah for City. The past two years out of the First Division have been like being in jail - all the time we have been studying and learning."

...y his jubilant colleagues. Mick missed the final

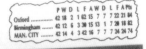

	P	W	D	L	F	A	W	D	L	F	A	Pts
Oxford	42	18	2	1	62	15	7	7	7	22	21	84
Birmingham	42	12	6	3	30	15	13	1	7	28	18	82
MAN. CITY	42	14	4	3	42	16	7	7	7	24	24	74

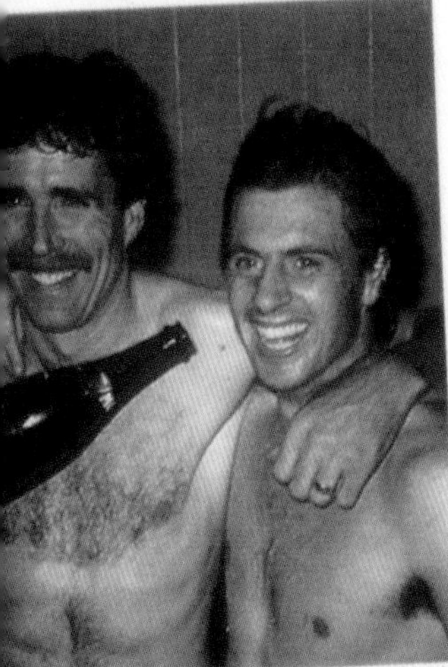

...ty work winning promotion as skipper ***Paul Power*** *...hile sharing happy moments—and champagne—* ***...elrose.***

1984-85 DIVISION TWO PROMOTION DETAILS

RESULTS	HOME	AWAY
Wimbledon	W 3-0	D 2-2
Grimsby Town	W 3-0	L 1-4
Fulham	L 2-3	L 2-3
Wolverhampton W	W 4-0	L 0-2
Carlisle United	L 1-3	D 0-0
Huddersfield Town	W 1-0	W 2-0
Cardiff City	D 2-2	W 3-0
Crystal Palace	W 2-1	W 2-1
Oxford United	W 1-0	L 0-3
Shrewsbury Town	W 4-0	L 0-1
Middlesbrough	W 1-0	L 1-2
Blackburn Rovers	W 2-1	W 1-0
Brighton & Hove Albion	W 2-0	D 0-0
Birmingham City	W 1-0	D 0-0
Sheffield United	W 2-0	D 0-0
Portsmouth	D 2-2	W 2-1
Oldham Athletic	D 0-0	W 2-0
Notts County	W 2-0	L 2-3
Charlton Athletic	W 5-1	W 3-1
Barnsley	D 1-1	D 0-0
Leeds United	L 1-2	D 1-1

REGULAR SIDE:
Williams
May
Power
Reid
McCarthy
Phillips
Smith
Baker
Melrose
Wilson
Kinsey

MANAGER:
Billy McNeill

LARGEST VICTORY: 5-1 v Charlton Athletic (H) 11/5/85

HEAVIEST DEFEAT: 1-4 v Grimsby Town (A) 13/4/85
0-3 v Oxford United (A) 23/3/85

AVERAGE HOME ATTENDANCE: 24,220

HIGHEST HOME ATTENDANCE: 47,285 v Charlton Athletic 11/5/85

HIGHEST AWAY ATTENDANCE: 22,626 v Leeds United 1/1/85

LEAGUE APPEARANCES: (substitute appearances in brackets)
42 Williams, Power, Phillips, 39 May, McCarthy, 33 Kinsey (2), 31 Reid (1), Smith (1), 29 Baker, 27 Wilson, 23 Melrose (1), 16 Cunningham (2), 15 McNab (3), 11 Clements (1), 9 Simpson (1), 7 Tolmie (10), McNaught, Parlane, 6 Lomax (1), 3 Bond, 1 Beckford (3), Hoyland, Sinclair

LEAGUE GOALS: 12 Phillips, Smith, 7 Melrose, Kinsey, 6 Simpson, 4 Baker, Wilson, Parlane, 3 May, 2 Tolmie, 1 Power, Cunningham, Clements, Bond

Three players who played a part in the successful 1984-85 promotion campaign. From the top... Andy May, Neil McNab, and Gordon Smith.

SEASON TICKETS

A new Kippax Stand season ticket for 1985-6, City's first season back in the First Division, cost a remarkably cheap £27 if purchased before the end of March.

Right: *A ticket from the League Cup away leg with Bury. The game was switched to Old Trafford in the hope of attracting a large crowd... 11,377 attended! Gigg Lane's capacity was viewed as 16,000 at this time.*

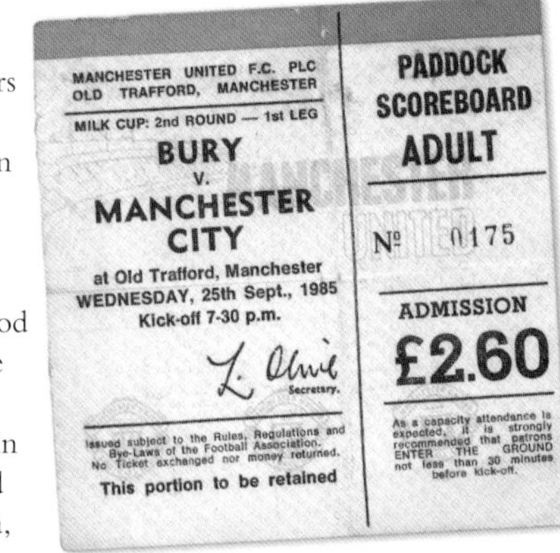

During the 1985 close-season Nigel Johnson (back) was brought in from Rotherham United, life-long City fan Mark Lillis (centre) joined from Huddersfield Town and former Red Sammy McIlroy (front) arrived from Stoke City.

Almost immediately following promotion, new players were linked with a move to the club. Top of the list was City fan Mark Lillis from Huddersfield Town. Lillis had been on associate schoolboy forms with City in 1974 but never really stood a chance of progression at Maine Road and had moved to Huddersfield making his debut in October 1978. During May and June 1985 Birmingham, Chelsea, Oxford, and Sheffield Wednesday all showed interest in the player, but once the forward spoke with McNeill his mind was made up: "I tried to speak to everyone with an open mind. I talked to Billy McNeill determined to push to the back of my mind the fact they were my favourite club, that I'd always wanted to play for them. As you can imagine, that was nigh impossible. So once I assessed the offers I made up my mind. I could have been a little better off going down south.

"I suppose it had to be City. If I had not come here I would probably be looking back on life in five years time with a lot of regrets."

Lillis had been a City follower since birth. He'd been to Wembley to watch the 1969 Cup Final and in his teens was a regular Kippax attender, while his parents had been City season ticket holders for years. He was a true Blue and on his home debut delighted the Kippax by scoring from the penalty spot, although the kick had to be taken twice after players encroached. After both shots entered the net Lillis turned to his friends on the Kippax to celebrate.

The second penalty steered the Blues to a 1-1 draw with Leicester, while four days earlier another new signing, Sammy McIlroy, helped City achieve the same scoreline at Coventry. McIlroy had signed from Stoke on a free transfer at the start of August. Another new arrival making his debut in that game was Nigel Johnson from Rotherham.

The 1985-6 season was not a particularly successful one, but as far as seasons of consolidation go it was satisfactory. McNeill's men reached ninth place by the start of September, but it didn't last and in October the Blues were down to twentieth. This tumble down the table coincided with a toe injury to goalkeeper Alex Williams. Williams had played in 112 consecutive games for City prior to the injury and hoped for a quick return to action, but a painful back condition collected in a reserve team outing delayed his return to fitness. In fact, the player suffered further spine related and troublesome injuries and was never to play in City's first team again. Despite being a passionate Blue he was transferred to Port Vale in January 1987, but struggled further and his career ended all too soon. He did return to Maine Road later, and throughout the 1990s played an active role in City's community programme.

For City the League campaign had a few high points - a 5-1 defeat of Coventry on 14th December, and the 1-0 victory over championship contenders Liverpool on Boxing Day - but the final two months of the season were difficult and the Blues ended the season in 15th position, after being 11th at the start of March.

In the League Cup City overcame Bury 2-1 in both legs - the first played at Old Trafford before 11,377 - but were defeated 2-1 at home to Arsenal in the third round. The F.A. Cup was not much better. The Blues beat Walsall 3-1, then lost 3-1 to Watford in the second replay after drawing 1-1 and 0-0.

Despite failure in these two competitions, City did have a chance of Wembley glory in a third competition - the Full Members' Cup. This albeit unglamorous competition was created as a result of the ban on English clubs playing in Europe following the Heysel European Cup Final of 1985. The teams that would have normally qualified for Europe organised a trophy called the 'Super Cup' to replace continental competition. As a result the Football League decided to create a tournament for the rest of the top two divisions.

City were placed in a group with two Second Division sides Leeds United and Sheffield United, and the winners of that group would be through to a 'northern' semi-final. In the first match City romped home to a 6-1 victory over Leeds at Maine Road, but the attendance was a pitiful 4,029 - the lowest crowd for a first team game at Maine Road.

In the second group game, City travelled to Sheffield and defeated United 2-1 with goals from Phillips and Baker, to put them in the northern semi against Sunderland. This time a crowd of 6,642 watched City win 4-3 on penalties after a goalless draw. Immediately afterwards around 200 fans ran on to the pitch to celebrate. Sadly, the invasion came at a time when the government was determined to clamp down on this kind of activity. Already there were discussions underway about how to rid the game of the hooligan element and some clubs suggested they would ban away supporters altogether. The City management were conscious they needed to ensure tough sanctions were not imposed at Maine Road and devoted the front cover of the League programme against Coventry to warn the supporters that good behaviour was vital. Already Maine Road had fencing

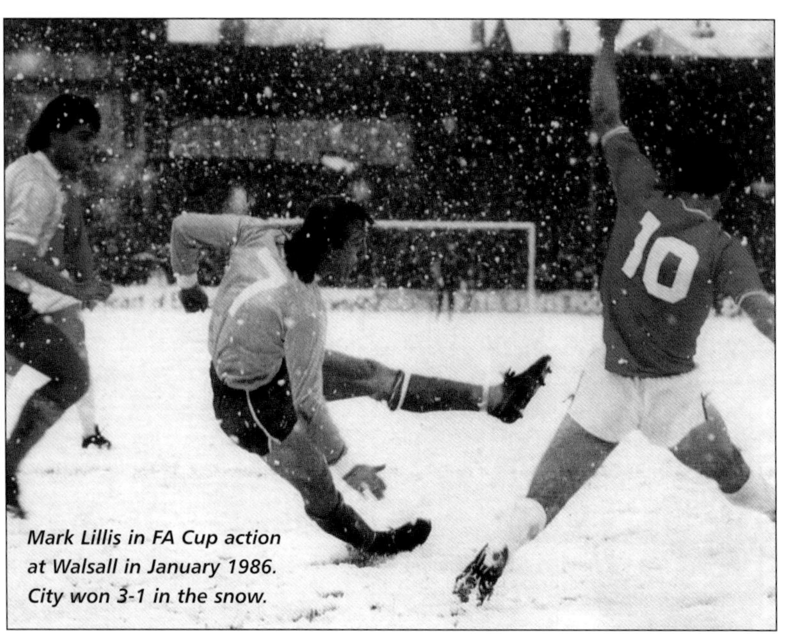

Mark Lillis in FA Cup action at Walsall in January 1986. City won 3-1 in the snow.

MIRROR SPORT

SEVEN SUPER PAGES TODAY

Maine Road debts soar to £4million

CITY CRISIS

EXCLUSIVE ..by ALEC JOHNSON

MANCHESTER CITY'S cash crisis has reached astronomic proportions.

The Maine Road club has debts of around £4 million.

And interest charges alone are costing a massive £1,000 A DAY, shareholders will learn at today's annual meeting.

City pay out a further £18,000 a week in salaries to staff and players.

The City board have cut their costs to the bone and negotiated cut-rate transfers to help ease the crisis.

Interest breaks £1,000 a day barrier

desperately hoping that manager Billy McNeill can lift his side out of the relegation zone.

A return to Division Two would be an absolute disaster for them.

October 25th 1985
Alec Johnson shocks Daily Mirror readers with the news that City were £4 million in debt. It was Johnson who would later reveal that Francis Lee was to mount a takeover bid.

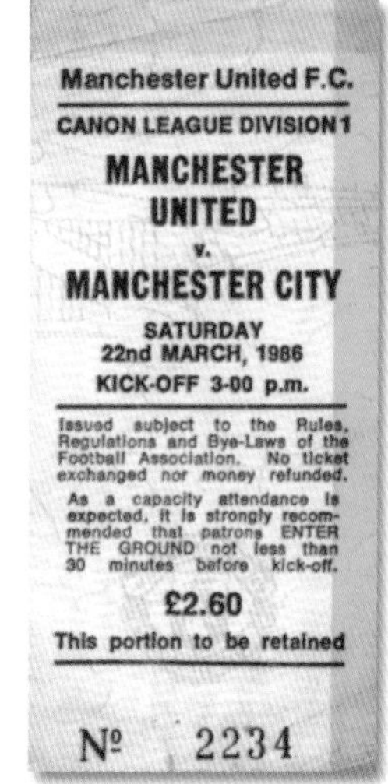

Manchester United F.C.
CANON LEAGUE DIVISION 1
MANCHESTER UNITED
v.
MANCHESTER CITY
SATURDAY
22nd MARCH, 1986
KICK-OFF 3-00 p.m.

Issued subject to the Rules, Regulations and Bye-Laws of the Football Association. No ticket exchanged nor money refunded.
As a capacity attendance is expected, it is strongly recommended that patrons ENTER THE GROUND not less than 30 minutes before kick-off.

£2.60
This portion to be retained

Nº 2234

Many Blues fans were at Old Trafford for the derby game on Saturday 22nd March and then at Wembley for the Full Members' Cup Final the following day.

built to a height of 2.4 metres on every side. If fans continued to invade the pitch then City stressed this would be raised to 4.4 metres.

On the pitch, the two legged Northern final saw City lose 2-1 at Brian Horton's Hull, but win the second leg 2-0 with goals from Phillips and Melrose before the largest crowd of the entire tournament, excluding the final, of 10,180. That victory gave City a Wembley meeting with Chelsea. The final was originally scheduled to be played on Saturday 1st March but Oxford, who ironically had lost to Chelsea in the Southern final, appealed to the Football League. Oxford were due to face City at Maine Road on that date and believed the League should take preference over the new trophy. Had Oxford beaten Chelsea in the first place it's doubtful there would have been a murmur, however Robert Maxwell's club did complain and won their appeal. City, Chelsea and the Football League worked hard to find a new date but eventually had to settle for Sunday 23rd March. It was not ideal as both City and Chelsea had League games the day before. What made it even worse was City had to face Manchester United at Old Trafford.

Against United McNeill played a City side that really did represent Manchester. By this time in City's history, everyone connected with the club boasted how the Blues represented Manchester, whereas United hardly seemed to have much to do with the city. Old Trafford was outside of the city's boundaries, few Mancunians played for the club, and the majority of support appeared to come from outside the region. City, on the other hand, seemed to represent the Manchester conurbation.

The derby match ended with a proud City side drawing 2-2 with Ron Atkinson's multi-million pound United. The Reds had been leading 2-0, although the second was a penalty scored by Strachan. In the 71st minute Clive Wilson sent a bobbling header past goalkeeper Chris Turner, then seven minutes later a misguided back pass by United's Arthur Albiston, who was under tremendous pressure from Paul Simpson, gave City the equaliser. The Blues piled in and could have taken the lead, but the game ended in a moral victory to Manchester's team.

The City side that day had cost £287,000 whereas United's was in excess of £3 million. Also City paraded eight Mancunians as opposed to United's one, and even that was Peter Barnes, who had been discovered by City in the first place. Understandably, City made much of the local angle, but then so did the media especially when, later in the season, City's youth side defeated the Reds 3-1 on aggregate in the F.A. Youth Cup Final. The Blues were then very much the local side, willing to spend time and effort finding and developing its own players, whereas Atkinson's Reds seemed intent on buying success.

At Old Trafford an injury to Kenny Clements ended his chance of being selected to play at Wembley. This was a major blow to the player, especially as he had been forced to miss the 1976 League Cup Final through similar circumstances.

After the League draw, City supporters left Old Trafford in buoyant mood, chanting the name of own goalscorer Albiston. Some supporters travelled straight to London for the following day's Wembley match, while others soaked up the post-derby atmosphere.

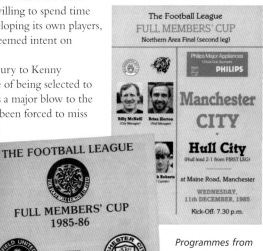

Programmes from the Full Members' Cup. One produced to cover all games in the three-team group and the other for the Northern Area Final against Brian Horton's Hull City side.

Full Members' Cup Finalists 1986

On the morning of the Full Members' Cup Final the press reported on the Manchester derby match, but many criticised the Wembley competition. Brian Madley, writing in the *Sunday People*, believed the game would be a flop: "Wembley will be half empty this afternoon for the final of the Full Members' Cup, or half full for the final of the Empty Members' Cup. Whichever, the clash between Chelsea and Manchester City will go down as the most anonymous Wembley final of all time."

Other journalists, including the *Manchester Evening News'* City reporter Peter Gardner, laughed at City and Chelsea for taking part. Like Madley they stated Wembley would be empty. They perhaps underestimated the loyalty of City supporters and their desire to see the Blues succeed. In the end the final was watched by 68,000 and brought receipts of £508,000. After covering Wembley's costs, and providing financial support to all entrants, City and Chelsea shared a figure of approximately £220,000.

Overall the Full Members' Cup was a 'Mickey Mouse' competition, but the final was still watched by a crowd greater than some modern day League Cup Finals, and was attended by greater numbers of partisan support. City's following was more than 30,000, while Chelsea made up the bulk of the rest. Had the two sides played in the F.A. Cup Final, it's doubtful they would have been allowed so many tickets.

The final was not only well attended, but also provided entertainment at a level rarely seen at Wembley. It was fitting that City and Chelsea competed as the two sides were by far the grandest of all the entrants, and certainly City were the club with the biggest following. At that time City's attendance averaged around 26,000, making them the fourth best supported First Division club behind United, Liverpool and Everton.

With Chelsea follower Sir Richard Attenborough as guest of honour the game kicked off. City, playing in their familiar Cup Final outfit of red and black stripes, started brightly. In the eighth minute Mick McCarthy miscued an intended shot, which enabled Steve Kinsey to score City's first goal at Wembley for almost five years.

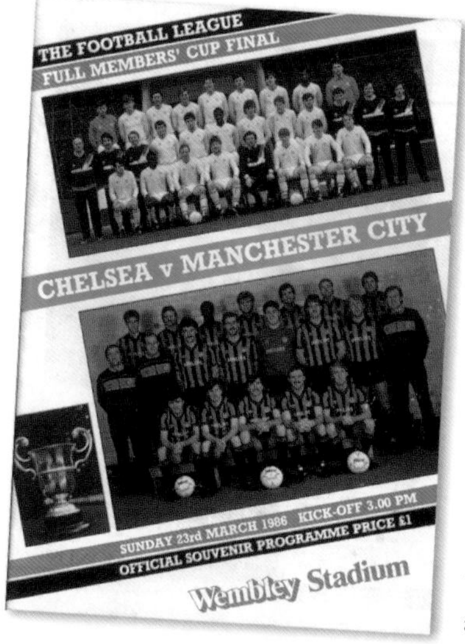

City fans believed the trophy was Manchester-bound, but an equaliser by David Speedie in the 19th minute gave Chelsea the initiative. In the 36th minute Lee netted Chelsea's second and the score remained 2-1 at the interval. City had struggled defensively for much of the latter period of the first half and Chelsea appeared capable of breaking through at will. Nevertheless within minutes of the restart Steve Kinsey was clearly tripped in the penalty area by Joe McLaughlin. City fans were convinced a penalty would be awarded but referee Alan Saunders refused all appeals and the opportunity was lost.

1986 MEMBERS' CUP RUN

Group 3	Leeds United	H	W	6-1
Group 3	Sheffield United	A	W	2-1
SF (North)	Sunderland	H	W	0-0
	(won 4-3 on penalties)			
F (North) 1st leg	Hull City	A	L	1-2
F (North) 2nd leg	Hull City	H	W	2-0
Final	Chelsea	N**	L	4-5

** = Wembley Stadium

FACTS & FIGURES

	P	W	D	L	F	A
HOME	3	3	0	0	8	1
AWAY	3	1	0	2	7	8
TOTAL	6	4	0	2	15	9

CUP FINAL DETAILS

23 March 1986 at Wembley Stadium

CHELSEA 5 MANCHESTER CITY 4

CITY: Nixon, Reid (Baker), Power, Redmond, McCarthy, Phillips (Simpson), Lillis, May, Kinsey, McNab, Wilson

CHELSEA: Francis, Wood, Rougvie, Pates, McLaughlin, Bumstead, Nevin, Spackman, Lee, Speedie, McAllister

GOALS: Lillis (2 - 1 pen), Kinsey, Rougvie (own goal), Speedie (3), Lee (2)

ATTENDANCE: 68,000

REFEREE: A Saunders (Newcastle Upon Tyne)

GUEST OF HONOUR: Sir Richard Attenborough

MANAGER: Billy McNeill

CAPTAIN: Paul Power

Andy May enjoys a joke with Guest of Honour Sir Richard Attenborough.

City miss out in a Wembley thriller

By BRIAN WOOLNOUGH

MANCHESTER CITY and Chelsea put on their Sunday best at Wembley yesterday in the Full Members' Cup final.

And an amazing 68,000 fans turned up to watch as the Londoners took the honours with a thrilling 5-4 victory.

They produced gate receipts of more than £½m — easily recouping the £150,000 paid out by City chairman Peter Swales and Chelsea supremo Ken Bates to play the match at Wembley.

City staged a dramatic fightback as they scored three times during the last five minutes — with two of those coming from Mark Lillis.

Shortly afterwards Speedie made it 3-1 for the Pensioners, and then in the 58th minute became the first player since Stan Mortensen to score a hat-trick in a senior domestic final at Wembley. City now looked dead and buried, and when Lee made it 5-1 in the 79th minute many City supporters left for the long journey back to Manchester. Those remaining started singing songs in praise of Arthur Albiston's own goal the day before, and helped encourage City to burst back into life.

McNeill made a double substitution, bringing on Graham Baker and Paul Simpson for Nicky Reid and David Phillips, and the new players quickly moved into action, with Simpson in electrifying form down the wing. A firm headed goal from Lillis five minutes from time inspired the team, and three minutes later the same player looked to have scored City's third when he and Chelsea's Doug Rougvie headed the same ball. Later Rougvie insisted he got the decisive touch which made the score 5-3, but at the time Lillis was convinced it was his goal.

A minute later, Andy May was tripped and Lillis scored the resulting penalty to make it 5-4. Lillis and the City supporters left in the stadium were convinced he had scored a hat-trick, but Rougvie's own goal admission ruled out that particular Blue fairy tale.

With City fighting to secure an equaliser, Chelsea fans were relieved to hear the final whistle. Had the game lasted another five minutes then City would surely have equalised. As it was the 5-4 scoreline demonstrated to the football world that Wembley could host entertaining finals.

City's fightback brought to an end an amazing weekend where a combined crowd of 119,274 had watched the Blues play with pride.

Chelsea supporter Sir Richard Attenborough passes Andy May's joke on to Paul Power at the post-match presentations!

THE CLASS OF 86

In April 1986 City's youth team defeated Manchester United 3-1 on aggregate in the final of the F.A. Youth Cup. It was a tremendous achievement, and one that at the time proved it was the Blues, rather than the Reds, who knew how to find and recruit young players.

Of the eleven City boys who played in the final an amazing seven would also appear in the first team. Three of those would captain the Blues; two would play for England; and one would continue to play for the Blues into the late 1990s. For the record the City eleven were:

Steve Crompton, Steve Mills, Andy Hinchcliffe, Ian Brightwell, Steve Redmond (captain), Andy Thackeray, David White, Paul Moulden, Paul Lake, Ian Scott, and David Boyd.

City's Chief Scout at the time was 50s Cup winner Ken Barnes and he firmly believed it was exceptional to find so many young star players at the same time: "We were dead lucky. I have to say that I don't think it will ever happen again. I don't recall any team having so many players coming through from the Youth team. It was only circumstances as such that they all got into the team at the same time. There was no alternative - the club had no money. No money to buy new players - so the young lads were thrown in at the deep end. Maybe if we had had a good team at the time three or four of them wouldn't have got into the team and, who knows what would have happened to them. It enlightened me the year they won the Youth Cup. They went throughout the whole season in the Lancashire League and lost only one game.

"That was a remarkable youth side. In the past we had boys like Tommy Caton, Ray Ranson, Nicky Reid, John Beresford and Darren Beckford but we never had a team like the 1986 one. Most of the youngsters played for our nursery team Midas. Most of them have come through Ray Ninett who runs the team. Nearly all those who have made it into the first team played with him from the time they were 11 or 12."

Although he perhaps wasn't the most promising of the youngsters in 1986, probably the most successful of all these players has been **Andy Hinchcliffe** who, while with Joe Royle's Everton, won an F.A. Cup winner's medal and made his first England international appearance. Hinchcliffe was born on 5th February 1969 and signed apprentice forms in July 1985. On 15th August 1987 he made his debut in the 2-1 victory at Plymouth and went on to total 42 League appearances that season, missing only two League games. He also netted once during the 1-1 draw at home to Middlesbrough.

Andy Hinchcliffe - England future.

On 23rd September he scored perhaps his most famous goal of all time when he headed the final goal in City's 5-1 massacre of multi-million pound United. Ten days earlier he had appeared for the England Under-21 side in a friendly against Denmark alongside Ian Brightwell, Paul Lake and Steve Redmond. The following summer Howard Kendall transferred him to Everton in a deal which brought Neil Pointon to Maine Road but still managed to anger many supporters. At Goodison Hinchcliffe perhaps enjoyed the greatest period of his career. He later moved on to Sheffield Wednesday, before retiring at the end of the 2001-02 season following injury.

Ian Brightwell continued to play for City until relegation at the end of 1997-8, by which time he'd played under ten managers (plus numerous caretakers!) at the club. Despite the upheaval Brightwell was a true Blue: "It's no secret that I never wanted to leave. I never gave a single thought to playing for any other club. I've always been a City fan and you don't erase a big part of your life that easily."

Ian made his first team debut against Wimbledon on 23rd August 1986 (their first game in Division One) and went on to make 12 League appearances plus four as substitute that season as City plummeted down the table. The following season he became an established member of Mel Machin's promotion seeking side before the arrival of Gary Megson limited his chances.

Ian Brightwell - longest serving

Under Howard Kendall, Brightwell was given an extended run in the team and, on 3rd February 1990, he scored his most memorable goal. It was a marvellous 25 yarder against Manchester United at Old Trafford and afterwards an excited Brightwell, when asked to explain how he'd scored, told the media: "I just wellied it!" It became the expression of the season and matched everybody's impression of a boyhood dream come true.

Throughout his earliest seasons with the Blues Brightwell was always described as "the son of Olympic athletes Ann Packer and Robbie Brightwell". Gradually, as Ian developed as a player, those references were replaced with details about his own career. Then on 29th February 1992 he was joined in

Steve Redmond holds up the FA Youth Cup... he was to become the first team's youngest ever captain.

Back (standing on the benches): Tony Book and Glyn Pardoe (Coaches), Andy Thackeray, David Boyd and Ian Scott.
Middle (standing on floor): Steve Mills, John Clarke, Paul Lake, Steve Redmond, Steve Macauley, Paul Power, Paul Moulden, David White and Ian Brightwell.
Front (seated) Andy Hinchcliffe and Steve Crompton.

the City line-up by younger brother David.

Since leaving City Ian has had spells at Coventry and at Walsall but remains a true Blue hero.

Steve Redmond was signed on schoolboy forms in October 1982 despite strong interest from Liverpool. Steve's dad Tony was a Liverpool fan but felt City offered more: "John Benson, who was a Liverpool scout at the time, came around four nights in one week to try and persuade Steve to join Liverpool. They were my club but I only had to look at the squad at Anfield to turn them down. I knew there was no way he was going to get into the Liverpool side. If Steve had gone there he could still have been waiting for his chance. City had embarked on a youth policy at that time and we thought that would be the best club for Steven."

At Maine Road Redmond impressed and on 8th February 1986 Billy McNeill gave him his League debut. His third League game was the 2-2 Old Trafford derby on 22nd March that year, and the following day he played at Wembley in the Full Members' Cup Final at the age of 18. This meant that prior to playing in the Youth Cup Final he had played in eight Division One matches, 21 Central League games, and 15 Lancashire League matches plus the Wembley appearance. He was also an England youth international. No wonder he was seen as being one of the most important young players of the 80s.

In the years that followed he won the Player of the Year award and succeeded Kenny Clements to become City's youngest ever captain. In 1988-9 he was an ever-present as City won promotion back to Division

One. Sadly, in August 1992 Peter Reid felt Steve was no longer part of his plans and he was transferred, with Neil Pointon, to Oldham in the deal that brought Rick Holden to Maine Road. By that time Redmond had made 283 (plus four as substitute) first team appearances yet was still only 24 years old.

David White was born on 30th October 1967 and signed apprentice forms on his 18th birthday. He made his debut in a 1-0 defeat at Luton on 27th September 1986 coming on as substitute for Trevor Christie, and played 19 (plus five as substitute) League games during that relegation season. For the following two seasons the speedy right winger became a permanent fixture in City's attack and hit the headlines by scoring a hat-trick in the 10-1 annihilation of Malcolm Macdonald's Huddersfield Town.

Regularly in the news, White impressed many and in April 1991 won his first England 'B' cap. That same month he became the first player since Brian Kidd to score four as City defeated Aston Villa 5-1 at Villa Park.

David White - scored four goals at Villa Park.

On 9th September 1992 he made his debut for the full England side. Unfortunately, it was not a memorable one as with his first kick of the match he made a mess of his only real goalscoring opportunity. Had it arrived a little later in the game his career may have taken a different course. Unfortunately no allowance was made for his inexperience and he appeared the scapegoat for a 1-0 defeat by Spain in Santander. From then on his City career seemed to take a nose-dive. It was as if his confidence had drained away. On 22nd December 1993 he was transferred to Leeds in exchange for David Rocastle. Later he moved to Sheffield United where he became a member of Howard Kendall's promotion seeking side.

White's first few seasons with the Blues were exceptional and had it not been for that single England appearance, it's possible he would have continued to impress at Maine Road until the late 1990s. As it is, the greatest period of his career was probably the enjoyable years of 1987 to 1990 when the 10-1 and the 5-1 brought much excitement to Maine Road.

Paul Moulden, born on 6th September 1967, was the second oldest of the youth players, after David Boyd. He signed on apprentice forms in June 1984 and professional three months later. City had been fortunate to sign the youngster. Moulden: "I'd been to a few different clubs. I'd had trials with United, Everton, Bolton, and Leeds United, and I'd been to most of the local clubs around here. City came to see me and got me down there. I had been to Everton and that was brilliant but as soon as I walked into City I knew it was me. At first they wanted me to play for Midas, but I didn't want to leave Bolton Lads Club."

At Maine Road, Billy McNeill was one of the first to recognise his goalscoring prowess and gave him a debut on New Year's Day 1986 at Villa Park. It had been rumoured for weeks but when the player entered the field for his warm up exercises some time prior to the match, the large army of City supporters packed behind the goal cheered with delight. They had heard much about the England Youth international and schoolboy goalscoring record holder "Goalden Moulden". City won 1-0 that day, thanks to an effort from Mark Lillis, but Moulden had to wait until the following October before he started another League match. During 1986-7, though, he gradually became a useful squad player and made 16 appearances (plus four as substitute), scoring five goals.

When on the bench, Moulden perversely insisted on wearing the traditionally unlucky number 13. He claimed it was all just superstition but as injuries regularly cost him a place in the first team, he perhaps might have been wiser to wear 12 or 14!

During the summer of 1989 Mel Machin transferred him to Bournemouth. Supporters were disappointed one of their young heroes could be moved on so easily, especially as Peter Swales had promised no members of the 1986 Youth side would be sacrificed. After less than a year in Bournemouth Moulden moved to Oldham where he featured in the same side as Steve Redmond.

Ian Scott is perhaps the forgotten man among these young players. Born in September 1967, he signed apprentice forms on 4th June 1984 and made his debut on 15th August 1987 at home to Plymouth. He kept his place for the following ten matches but then struggled to make much of an impression for the rest of the season. In 1988-9 he only managed one appearance in the League (away to Brighton on April Fool's day 1989). Scott: "Neil McNab was suspended and Brian Gayle was also out so Lakey had to play at the back and Ian Brightwell at right back. Because it was my first game in all that time I was a bit nervous but four players came up to me afterwards and said: 'well played'. I was a bit disappointed when I was left out again for the next game, and I never even got on the bench after that!"

Stoke manager Mick Mills made an enquiry and in July 1989 the Elvis-loving midfielder moved to the Victoria Ground. He was glad to be free: "For me the season couldn't finish quickly enough. I was packing my bags before Christmas. I was frustrated because I don't think I ever got the right chances. I didn't feel in it. I wasn't in the squad. I wasn't in favour with the manager. At the beginning of the season I was usually 14th or 15th and later on I just got left out completely. I went to see the boss and we had a bit of a bust-up and he started picking YTS lads before me."

Scott had been capped five times by England schoolboys but believed his own forthright approach to life caused him a few problems: "If I felt I was doing something and they seemed to disagree I just felt I had got to tell them my own opinion as well as listening to theirs. I don't think it was a mistake. I would do the same now if I had my time all over again because you have got to say what you believe. I don't mean to say I was a big head. I was just saying little things. Because I'm more of a passer of the ball and everyone seemed to want runners and grafters I told everyone I'd never change my style of play because I believed in it."

He later became a coach at Buxton and was involved with their School of Excellence.

Paul Lake is probably the most famous of the 1986 Youth side. He was born on 28th October 1968 and signed apprentice forms on 1st July 1985. He was a versatile player, making appearances for City as full back, central defender, midfielder, and orthodox striker. For a while he was also team captain.

Paul Lake - granted a testimonial

He made his first team debut on 24th January 1987 in a goalless draw at Wimbledon, and netted his first goal a few weeks later in only his third match (City 1 Luton 1, 21st February 1987). During the course of City's two Second Division seasons (1987-1989) he became a regular in the side although tragedy struck on 11th March 1989 when an accidental clash of heads resulted in Lake swallowing his tongue. Only the actions of physio Roy Bailey saved Lake from death in what was a nightmare situation. Lake does not remember much about the incident but has seen it on video several times: "It's horrible watching it. I can talk about it light-heartedly and crack jokes about doing an acid house dance on the floor, but I realise how lucky I was. I have got over it without any problems, but seeing myself spontaneously shuddering - it's a bit perturbing."

Injuries have wrecked what should have been a very successful career. Howard Kendall always believed Lake was destined for the very top and did much to help the player progress. Regularly during Kendall's brief flirtation with City the manager searched to bring players in to support Lake: "Paul is a marvellous footballer and his standing in the game is such that every time I approached another club to enquire about the availability of a player, I was asked whether I would consider including him in part exchange. The answer was always no."

On the verge of a glittering England career Lake entered the 1990-91 season full of optimism. Unfortunately he failed to make it past the third game of the season, when a knee injury sustained in a rather innocuous challenge with Aston Villa's Tony Cascarino became quite serious. For the following two years he struggled to regain fitness but then returned to action for the opening of the 1992-3 season. Some fans felt he had been rushed back too soon, especially when he was substituted by Mike Sheron during his Maine Road return against QPR on 17th August (the first Premier League game shown live on Sky TV).

Two days later, after only eight minutes of action against Middlesbrough Lake collapsed again. This time he had damaged his cruciate ligaments. Since that day he has fought a long, hard, lonely battle against the injury and spent considerable time seeing medical experts around the world. Unfortunately, he never returned to first team action and in 1996 was forced to retire from the game he loved. City immediately granted him a testimonial season, and his committee arranged a testimonial match against Manchester United in Autumn 1997. More than 20,000 turned out to pay tribute.

Lake remains the most famous of all the players who appeared for the Blues in the 1986 Youth Cup Final. The remaining four boys never received anything like the kind of attention of Lake & Co, but it's still important to record how they fared. Goalkeeper Steve Crompton (b. 20th April 1968, signed 25th June 1984 on YTS) went on to make ten League appearances with Carlisle, and a further two with Stockport before becoming an area sales manager in 1992; David Boyd (b. 21st August 1967, signed apprentice 1st July 1985) returned to Scotland to join Hibernian; Andy Thackeray (b. 13th February 1968, signed on YTS 4th June 1984) played for his home town club Huddersfield Town before spells at Newport County, Wrexham, Rochdale, and Halifax; and England Youth player Steve Mills (b. 13th October 1968, signed apprentice forms 1st July 1985) suffered a serious back injury, but managed to play for Shepshed Charterhouse and Leek Town.

The fortunes of City's class of 86 may be mixed but for a while they combined perfectly to bring tremendous pride to Mancunians everywhere.

YOUTH CUP STATISTICS

First Round - 5/11/85
Tranmere Rovers 1 City 7
(White 2, Redmond, Scott, Boyd, Moulden, Lake)

Second Round - 28/11/85
City 7 Blackburn 1 (Att 858)
(Moulden 3, Lake, Thackeray, Scott, Willis og)

Third Round - 7/1/86
Blackpool 0 City 1 (Att 322)
(Scott)

Quarter Final - 8/3/86
Fulham 0 City 3 (Att 195)
(Lake, Redmond 2)

Semi Final 1st Leg - 15/4/86
Arsenal 1 City 0 (Att 487)

Semi Final 2nd Leg - 22/4/86
City 2 Arsenal 1 (Att 5,056)
(Moulden 2) Won 5-4 on pens

Final 1st Leg - 24/4/86
Man Utd 1 City 1 (Att 7,602)
(Lake, pen)

Final 2nd Leg - 29/4/86
City 2 Man Utd 0 (Att 18,164)
(Boyd, Moulden)

Youth Cup winning captain Steve Redmond keeps watch on United's Norman Whiteside during the October '86 Maine Road derby.

The 1985-6 season had proved more successful than any supporter or official could have hoped, although captain Paul Power had accurately predicted the Blues would reach Wembley. The Youth Cup success and Wembley outing had given hope to Chairman Swales and the fans, but the club were still some £4 million in debt and unable to compete in the transfer market with the mid 80s big five of Liverpool, United, Everton, Arsenal and Tottenham, despite having consistently higher crowds than at least two of those sides. City now relied heavily on youth development and youngsters such as Paul Moulden and Steve Redmond (who'd played at Wembley), were believed to be vital if the Blues were to achieve any form of success.

During the summer of 1986 the Blues lost one of its greatest servants when captain Paul Power moved to Everton in what was initially supposed to be mainly a coaching capacity. It actually resulted in the player appearing so often for the Merseysiders that he helped them lift the League title. It was a great moment for Power who also scored against City during his return match at Maine Road. Understandably, with City struggling, Power found it hard to celebrate his goal against the club he loved.

By this time, Billy McNeill was well aware of the financial situation but found great difficulty motivating himself after a season when, in all honesty, City could have been relegated: "Although we found it hard to win a game we managed to stay in the First Division. When I look back it was a tremendous shoestring achievement, but I knew we had to tighten up for next season - or else!

"We were having great success with our youth team. Directors of City and the club secretary, Bernard Halford, kept telling me to be patient. Bernard was of the opinion we had to keep cool and hope that the boys developed properly. My fourth season at Maine Road kicked off with the usual problems of trying to be patient - difficult for me! - and dabbling cheaply in the transfer market. Apart from the fact we were always looking for bargain buys, we also had to persuade other clubs to accept payment on the never-never. I tried to convince the Board that dealing like this we would never get the players we really wanted."

Paul Stewart joined City from Blackpool in March 1987 and found it difficult to settle at first, scoring just once in his first seven games.

With concern over his ability to sign who he wanted, McNeill entered the 1986-7 season unsure of what could be achieved. He was also aware of an influence at Board level that was not to his liking. The problems started during 1985-6: "I didn't feel I was under any pressure - at least, not until they appointed Freddie Pye as vice-chairman while I was on holiday. He was given the title of 'Director in Charge of Team Affairs', which I thought was ominous. I never had a relationship with Mr. Pye. After his appointment there was a lot of murmuring in the background. The Chairman tried to encourage me to get together with Mr. Pye, but I couldn't bring myself to do it. He appeared to be working against me in team matters. Maybe I could have made a bigger effort, but I felt it was a bad appointment and Freddie Pye wanted to dictate policy.

"For instance, I needed a striker but we couldn't afford to buy one. It turned out that Mr. Pye and Ken Bates of Chelsea were friendly, so I was coerced into taking Gordon Davies from Stamford Bridge. The never-never deal worked out was nothing short of astonishing. As a player, Davies had ability but wasn't prepared to get into the action. I didn't consider Gordon a strong character either. All this made me think carefully about my position."

McNeill remained at Maine Road for the first seven games of the season but then left to join Aston Villa. Villa Chairman Doug Ellis had promised McNeill money to buy players and the freedom he felt he no longer had at City. McNeill: "Peter Swales didn't want me to go and he also thought Villa weren't right for me. However, upsetting influences in the background at Maine Road weren't going away. I spoke with several prominent people and the advice was to keep clear of Villa and Doug Ellis. However, I wasn't happy with the City set up."

Leaving City for Villa was a huge mistake and actually gave McNeill more problems - and interference - than he'd had at Maine Road. At the end of the season Villa were relegated and McNeill was sacked. Since leaving England he has remained interested in the fortunes of City and has no doubt considered what might have been had he not been tempted to move to Villa. Sadly, in 1997 at the age of 57 he was forced to undergo a lifesaving triple heart bypass operation.

When Jimmy Frizzell took over as manager, City had lost two, won one, and drawn four - including the difficult away trip to Liverpool. At that time the season was expected to be one of struggle, but it was hardly anticipated the Blues might be relegated. Frizzell was hopeful he could build on the progress made the previous season, but by the time of the first derby meeting with United on 26th October, the Blues were bottom of the division.

Frizzell had done much to strengthen the side prior to the derby which, incidentally, was the first to be screened live on television. He'd bought well-travelled striker Imre Varadi in a straight swap for Robert Hopkins, and the player immediately delivered by scoring within six minutes of his debut at Chelsea. He also signed Tony Grealish and John Gidman in time to make debuts against United.

Grealish cost £20,000 from West Bromwich Albion, while Gidman had come on a free transfer direct from the Reds. The former United man, who had been Ron Atkinson's first signing back in July 1981, turned down a lucrative contract with AEK Athens to join the Blues: "Once I knew City were interested that was it. There was nowhere else I wanted to go. As soon as I stepped into Jimmy Frizzell's office and met the lads, I knew I was in the right place with the right people. I am delighted to get this chance to play for City and I hope I will do a good job for Jimmy Frizzell."

Against United Gidman and the other new signings helped the Blues achieve a 1-1 draw. City played with grit and determination and once again proved they could match the big spending Reds in one-off occasions. Ten days after this draw United dispensed with the services of Ron Atkinson as results, and the pressure to win the Championship, caused Chairman Martin Edwards to act. City, already famous for having appointed four managers to date during the 80s, began to boast that Jimmy Frizzell was now the longest serving manager in Manchester!

The morale-boosting draw lifted the Blues into 21st place and gave a ray of hope. A 1-1 draw at Southampton was followed by a 3-1 victory over Wimbledon in the near-irrelevant Full Members' Cup, and then victories over Billy McNeill's Aston Villa (3-1) and Charlton Athletic (2-1). The Villa game attracted the second highest crowd of the season up to that point as McNeill was forced to endure the taunts of the City faithful. The abuse upset him, although he put a brave face on at the time, and with hindsight it was probably not justified. McNeill left City because of the problems he experienced at Board level and the club's exceedingly poor financial position. Had he known the real truth about the finances before accepting the Maine Road job then it's highly unlikely he'd have arrived in Manchester at all. His desertion to Villa upset all Blues because they felt that overall he was the right kind of manager to bring the club success. It's interesting that Atkinson's successor at United was a similarly dour but knowledgeable Scotsman - Alex Ferguson.

The Charlton victory lifted City to 19th but a couple of disappointing defeats against Everton and at Nottingham Forest sent the Blues bottom again. City fans were frustrated and had started to voice their feelings, with Peter Swales suffering the majority of the vitriol. As the season progressed the anti-Swales contingent grew, and then in April the demonstrations reappeared.

Fans had demonstrated at times during 1983 but those protests were relatively minor compared to what occurred in April 1987. A 4-2 defeat by 15th placed Southampton on 11th April brought much abuse the Chairman's way, and prompted one group of season ticket holders to produce and distribute a leaflet entitled 'The Case Against Peter Swales' calling for the Chairman to resign.

The handout claimed the Chairman's thirteen and a half year rule had set the club on a course for disaster, not success, and questioned what achievements had been made during his reign. Although some points were embellished to win the argument, the leaflet was a damning indictment of what appeared to be years of misrule. It also questioned many of the items Swales believed were his best achievements. One area was support: "Peter Swales has consistently claimed credit for improving attendances at Maine Road and even repeated the same boast in the *Sunday Mirror* of 12th April 1987 following the 4-2 home defeat by Southampton. Let's examine this claim. When Swales took over City were the third best supported team in the Country and the attendances for the first four home matches of the 1973 season before Swales became Chairman were 34,178, 30,931, 31,209 and 32,118, averaging out at 32,109. Present attendances have slipped below the 20,000 mark and will fall even further when we are relegated for a second time. Mr. Swales is either a good liar or a bad mathematician if he thinks a drop of 12,000+ is an improvement in attendances."

The anti-Swales movement was growing and the leaflet summed up the frustrations of a large group of supporters, but no matter how many leaflets were distributed Swales was determined to remain in control. As with the events of 1983 he felt responsible and was still committed to the Blue cause. In '83 he had been as disappointed with relegation as any supporter: "When we got relegated it was the worst day of my life, because there was no way we were going to be relegated before the game and when it actually happened it was as if somebody had hit me over the head with a sledgehammer. It was the only time in my life when I was totally deflated. How I got through the Saturday night and Sunday I'll never know. It took me many months to get over that. We hadn't really got any money, but we got playing again. Got back up. I'd known we were on borrowed time because we didn't have the players to maintain a First Division side, so we went down again."

Season '86/7 was the first to hold play-offs to help decide promotion, but in this new formula it remained possible for a normally relegated Division One club to enter the play-offs and defeat Second Division clubs to retain their status. When the system

A leaflet distributed in April 1987 pointing out the main complaints of supporters and asking Peter Swales to stand down. It took another seven years before fans managed to change the leadership of the club.

THE CASE AGAINST PETER SWALES

Peter Swales is constantly reminding City fans of his excellent track record in his 13½ years Chairmanship at Maine Road. Whilst looking through some old City programmes, I came across the City v Southampton programme for Saturday 6th October 1973 which heralded the arrival of the new Chairman of Manchester City — Peter Swales. I think you will it agree it makes interesting reading.

Eric Alexander the outgoing Chairman claims:

> *"We have now reached a stage at the club, by unanimous agreement, where no one man will ever control Manchester City*

Joe Smith, the President, justifies the choice of Peter Swales as Chairman on the grounds of:

> *"(His) financial wizardy which has enabled City to announce the biggest profit in its history."*

When the laughter has died down, read on — it gets better.

We can examine Peter Swales' record as Chairman under several headings and consider some of his comments in the programme made in his inaugural address to the fans entitled somewhat ironically:—

"IT'S ALL A QUESTION OF FINANCES AND SUCCESS ON THE PITCH"

1. THE TEAM'S PLAYING RECORD

> *"The object is to make City the number one club in the country."*

The team Swales inherited had swept the board in the previous 5 years winning the League, FA Cup, League Cup and European Cup Winners Cup and was widely recognised as one of the best teams in the country. Swales pledged to improve on that record and promised the fans that if he had not brought success in 4 years he would stand down. Well it is nearly 14 years and as we prepare to be relegated for the second time, we are still waiting for that promise to be kept. The City team for that day reads: Healey, Book, Donachie, Doyle, Booth, Oakes; Summerbee, Bell, Towers, Lee, Marsh. It is difficult to envisage any of the City team today forcing their way into that side and you could perm any one from that forward line of Summberbee, Bell, Lee and Marsh and justifiably argue that they offered more in entertainment value than all the present City team put together.

2. ATTENDANCES

> *"It impresses me when our figures go up and they will do so. I'm sure of that. There's no false hope behind that statement."*

Peter Swales has consistently claimed credit for improving attendances at Maine Road and even repeated the same boast in the Sunday Mirror of 12th April 1987 following the 4-2 home defeat by Southampton. Let's examine this claim. When Swales took over City were the third best supported team in the country and the attendances for the first 4 home matches of the 1973 season before Swales became Chairman were 34,178, 30,931, 31,209 and 32,118, averaging out at 32,109. Present attendances have slipped below the 20,000 mark and will fall even further when we are relegated for a second time. Mr. Swales is either a good liar or a bad mathematician if he thinks a drop of 12,000+ is an improvement in attendances.

3. FINANCE

> *"I do not think a football club should run on a overdraft, especially in these days of sky-high interest rates.... It's not very clever to run a major business like ours on a vast overdraft."*

For once we agree Peter. It's not very clever to be £4 million in debt and to be paying interest charges of £1,000 a day. Mr. Swales was the Chairman who sanctioned the Allison lunacy of paying over £3 million for "world beaters" like Steve Daley, Kevin Reeves and Michael Robinson.

> *"Think of applying the shrewd transfer style of Burnley to a city club ... They have made a success of their methods ... Imagine Burnley's kind of operation applied to a city club. This, I feel, can be the answer to making a secure future. What they have done, we can do on a bigger scale."*

Well, Peter, we all know where Burnley are now but if City are aiming to do it on a bigger scale, then perhaps the Salford Sunday League is our ultimate target.

4. MANAGERS

> *"The relationship between chairman and manager is important. They have got to have a certain affinity. My role is to make sure we have the right man."*

Well it's nearly 14 years Peter and we're still waiting for the right man. We've had Hart, Saunders, Book, Allison, Bond, Benson, McNeill and now Frizzell. Big names and not so big names but they've all got one thing in common — failure and bad selection on the part of the Chairman. The opportunity presented by the departure of Billy McNeill was thrown away by penny pinching and appointing Jimmy Frizzell on the cheap — a man clearly unsuited to running a club of City's stature having neither the ability nor the personality to run a top club. If Mr. Swales was in any other business than football, then he would have been shown the door a long time ago with a record like that.

Mr. Swales, you claim to love City and have their interests at heart. If this is the case, I feel you only have one option left open to you. The fans have left you in no doubt as to what they think of you. You have destroyed a great club. Do the decent thing — resign and take your right hand man Frizzell with you and make room for somebody else who can start resurrecting the club that we, the fans, love.

K. Doodson
C. Johnston
J. Hawkins
A. Jenkins
Season Ticket Holders
Manchester City F.C.

was announced Peter Swales admitted in an interview he wouldn't mind being involved in the mini-tournament simply to generate more funds. Sadly, City weren't even good enough for that.

The Blues were relegated again in May 1987 after a 2-0 defeat at West Ham. At the end of the game City supporters and West Ham fans who, it must be remembered had an exceptionally poor reputation at this time, climbed over the fences and onto the pitch. Officials feared the two sets of supporters were about to fight and were surprised to hear the Hammers chanting "You'll be back", and see both groups swapping scarves and souvenirs. It was the kind of moment that should be more widely reported in the media but rarely is, and was a sign that the decent majority of supporters were not the caged wild animals the government and media portrayed them to be. City had been relegated, but their supporters did not seek revenge. The West Ham fans could have ridiculed, but they didn't. Perhaps somewhere the country's leaders had been misinformed? Sadly, it took a major tragedy two years later before they began listening to the truth.

City's form during the season had not been good at all with only eight victories out of 42 matches, and the embarrassment of not winning a game away from home since a 2-0 success at Tottenham on 18th January 1986. In the cup competitions City struggled against First Division opponents when Arsenal defeated the Blues 3-1 in the League Cup, while Manchester United won a controversial F.A. Cup third round tie 1-0 at Old Trafford. An Imre Varadi goal was ruled out for a 'pushing offence' by the player, yet no one could explain when or how the so called pushing had occurred. It was a total mystery and left City fans feeling cheated - a feeling repeated nine years later at the same venue.

Mel Machin was appointed Team Manager in the Summer of '87.

During the close season it was no surprise when Chairman Swales decided to act to change the management structure. Stories in the press suggested Dave Bassett would be offered the manager's job, while other names mentioned included Norwich coach Mel Machin. In the end the Norwich man was given the title Team Manager while Jimmy Frizzell was appointed General Manager. It seemed a strange compromise. On the one hand Swales had given Machin authority for team affairs, on the other he retained Frizzell to oversee development. From a supporters' perspective it felt as if Machin was the actual manager, yet the two men seemed to take it in turns to face the press. Even City's match programme alternated the manager's column - one game Frizzell gave his views, the next Machin. It seemed a little strange for two men who had never previously worked together to share these responsibilities, but Swales seemed happy, so the management and the fans eagerly awaited the new season.

The side that started the 1987-8 campaign was a mix of experienced professionals and members of City's impressive youth policy. Gidman, Clements, Varadi and McNab provided the knowledge and know-how while Hinchcliffe, Brightwell, Redmond, White and Scott demonstrated the value of City's scouting system. The goalkeeper Eric Nixon was still determined to prove he was good enough to be City's number one after regularly being replaced by Perry Suckling and Barry Siddall over the previous seasons. The eleventh member of the side to face Plymouth on that opening day was the exciting Paul Stewart, who had been signed by Jimmy Frizzell the previous year.

The day City re-w

Tony Adcock's treble as (top) he turns in triumph after his header put City 3-0 up, (middle) he beats Brian Cox for our fifth and (bottom) he strokes in No. 7.

City duly achieved a 2-1 victory over the Pilgrims with Varadi and Stewart combining perfectly. A couple of 1-1 draws followed before the first real setback - a 2-1 defeat at home to Blackburn. The Blues were now 15th in the division and seven days later dropped further when a painful match at Shrewsbury ended goalless. Attendances suffered with a miserly 15,430 at Maine Road for the following game - a midweek 4-0 demolition of Millwall.

By the start of November the Blues had moved up to tenth, but it was obvious to all they were simply not good enough for automatic promotion or even a play-off place. Then, on Saturday 7th November, a crowd of 19,583 came along to Maine Road for the visit of Malcolm Macdonald's Huddersfield. The struggling Yorkshire side appointed Macdonald to the manager's chair in October and the week before the Maine Road match the team achieved its first win of the season when Millwall were beaten 2-1. Macdonald and his men arrived in Manchester confident of victory. They left shell-shocked.

e the history books.

Saturday 7th November, 1987.
CITY 10 HUDDERSFIELD TOWN 1

: for Paul Stewart with a 29th minute shot (top), a firm header ke it 6-0 (middle) and converting Andy Hinchcliffe's cross to the eighth goal (bottom).

And then it was TEN! Our picture sequence shows David White going past the hapless Cox, falling as he shoots for goal and then celebrating a unique scoreline.

Goals galore, as featured in the programme for the Blues' following home game, against Watford.

The ball from City's 10-1 thrashing of Huddersfield – the club's biggest win of the century.

The game started well enough for Huddersfield with City looking lethargic in defence. Had the away side been more forceful up front they would undoubtedly have been first to score. Fortunately, it was City's experienced Neil McNab who eased the home supporters' nerves with a clinical 12th minute strike. From then on he dominated midfield and allowed the City forwards to attack in numbers.

In the 29th minute Paul Stewart scored number two then five minutes later Tony Adcock, who had signed from Colchester in June, made it three. Already Huddersfield seemed dead, but worse was to follow for the Yorkshiremen when David White scored the fourth three minutes before half time.

During the interval City fans joked how their heroes might actually double the score, but no one seriously believed they would. After the restart, it soon became apparent Huddersfield had little to offer and Machin's men were ready to destroy them. Adcock scored his second with a right foot shot in the 52nd minute, then 14 minutes later Paul Stewart made it six. A minute later Adcock scored again to complete his first City hat-trick.

BLUES BLAZE TO 10-1 WIN

The Kippax now chanted "We want eight!" and in the 80th minute Stewart completed his hat-trick to double the half-time score. Five minutes from time White made it nine, prompting chants of "We want ten!". Before that could happen Huddersfield were awarded a penalty after John Gidman nudged David Cork. When former City hero Andy May managed to slot the ball home in the 88th minute the City fans cheered, and the Huddersfield contingent in the Platt Lane stand stood up and started to 'conga' in between the famous old stand's wooden benches. With two minutes remaining could

LEICESTER	3	SWINDON	2
Ramsey, Walsh, Venus		Barnes, Quinn (pen) HT: 0-1 Att:. 8,346	
MAN CITY	10	HUDDRSFLD	1
McNab, Stewart (3), Adcock (3), White (3)		May (pen) HT: 4-0 Att: 19,583	
SHEFF UTD	0	MIDDSBRO	2
HT: 0-0 Att:		Slaven, Ripley 11,278	
STOKE	3	WEST BROM	0
Berry (pen), Heath, Parkin		HT: 2-0 Att: 9,992	

A trio of hat-tricksters... Paul Stewart, Tony Adcock and David White accounted for nine of City's ten goals against Huddersfield.

Huddersfield mount a comeback? Even the most seasoned City supporter accepted the unpredictable Blues had no chance of letting this lead slip!

In the 89th minute White made sure of the result by scoring City's tenth goal. Journalists frantically tried to ascertain what records were broken by this 10-1 scoreline and the fact three players had scored hat-tricks. The result was City's best at Maine Road, but it wasn't the highest Blue score ever. That was 11-3 when Lincoln were defeated in 1895. Whatever the statistics, it was still a great performance and, fortunately for City fans, was captured on film by Granada TV for their highlights programme.

It was unusual in 1987 for quality film of every game to be made, but within days of the victory City were selling 60 minutes of the Granada footage for £15.

After the match Mel Machin expressed his pleasure at the result and then predicted a bright future: "It may take two or three years to grasp real success, but the future here at City looks good. The groundwork has been done and we can now start to reach out in keen anticipation of bigger and better things."

Tony Adcock hit another hat-trick in the game after Huddersfield, the visit of Plymouth in the Simod Cup.

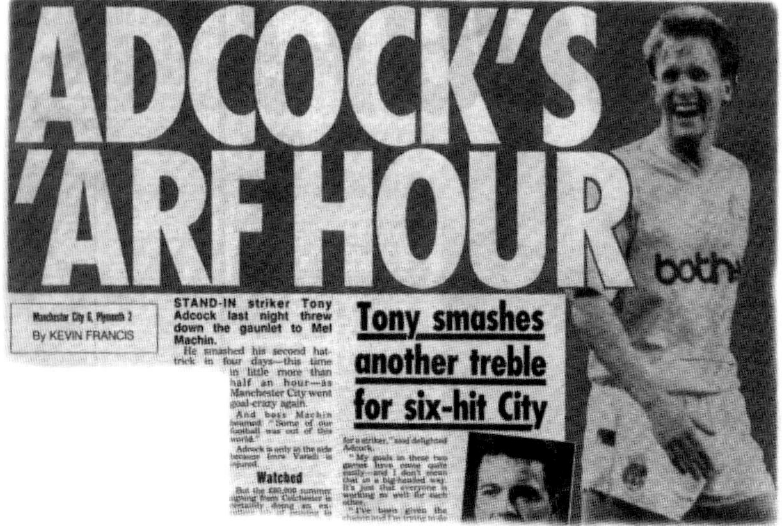

ADCOCK'S 'ARF HOUR

Manchester City 6, Plymouth 2
By KEVIN FRANCIS

STAND-IN striker Tony Adcock last night threw down the gaunlet to Mel Machin.

He smashed his second hat-trick in four days—this time in little more than half an hour—as Manchester City went goal-crazy again.

And boss Machin beamed: "Some of our football was out of this world."

Adcock is only in the side because Imre Varadi is injured.

Watched

But the £80,000 summer signing from Colchester is certainly doing an ex-

Tony smashes another treble for six-hit City

for a striker," said delighted Adcock.

"My goals in these two games have come quite easily—and I don't mean that in a big-headed way. It's just that everyone is working so well for each other.

"I've been given the

What was also odd about the game was that leading scorer Imre Varadi had missed the goalscoring festival through a recurring thigh muscle injury. The stage would have been perfect for the man who seemed to thrive on the adulation of a large section of City's support.

With the talk of Manchester focusing on Machin's men, Plymouth arrived at Maine Road in the Full Members' Cup - now sponsored by the unforgettable Simod Sports Shoes!! Once again City entertained with Plymouth suffering a 6-2 defeat only three days after the Huddersfield massacre. Again the press picked up on City's exploits and for once the rather irrelevant Simod Cup dominated the back page headlines. *The Star* concentrated on the role played by Tony Adcock who had scored his second hat-trick in three days. Under the headline "Adcock's 'Arf Hour" it was said the £80,000 signing from Colchester was only in the side because of injury to Varadi, and suggested Machin would have a difficult selection problem once Varadi returned to fitness. Machin, who also had the prolific Paul Moulden recovering from injury, looked forward to the time when he would actually be faced with the problem of selecting two of the four decent strikers he had on his books.

Interestingly, City's first goalscorer against Plymouth, Andy Hinchcliffe, was being watched by Liverpool manager Kenny Dalglish. Already the Blues were aware that almost all the wealthy British clubs of the period were keen on City's headline-grabbing young players. Only four months later Rangers boss Graeme Souness arrived at Maine Road to watch the game against Swindon. He paid to sit in the North Stand, and viewed the exploits of Paul Stewart while covering half his face with a scarf to mask his identity. It didn't work. A *Sunday People* reporter spotted the Rangers manager and his assistant, Walter Smith, forcing the pair to leave before they attracted further attention.

For a while interest in the achievements of the young players kept the season going, but City's League form was far from perfect. On 12th December the Blues had finally reached fifth position, but then two home League defeats against Oldham and Leeds, left them in ninth place. Further disappointments in January and February sent them as low as 11th at one stage.

It was clear City's only chance of promotion lay with the play-offs, but the side would need to find consistency to stand any real hope even then. As it was the Blues did move up the table in March and April with a few significant victories. One was the 3-0 defeat of Birmingham City at St. Andrews - a day when Machin gave a debut to 16 year old Neil

Lennon. It wasn't a particularly good bow for the youngster as he received constant barracking from the home crowd, and was never to appear in City's first team again. Deservedly, in 1997 he played for Leicester in the League Cup Final, by which time the tenacious international midfielder was idolised by the Foxes support and frequently tipped for a major transfer to one of the more glamorous clubs.

Apart from a few exciting performances, the regular transfer stories in the press seemed to affect a number of key players, and the Blues ended the campaign a disappointing ninth.

The season wasn't one of complete failure, however, as the two major cup competitions brought much pride to the club. In the League Cup City defeated Wolves 3-2 on aggregate before First Division Nottingham Forest were despatched 3-0 at Maine Road. The goals were scored by City's perfect partnership, Varadi (2) and Stewart, and brought much praise from Forest manager Brian Clough who admitted: "It could have been four or five on the night."

The fourth round brought another home tie with First Division Watford arriving only ten days after the 10-1 thrashing of Huddersfield. The game ended 3-1 in City's favour, prompting Mel Machin to predict a Wembley visit for his side, even if he wasn't too enthusiastic about the performance: "You need a certain amount of luck to go all the way but I know what we are capable of and, with that measure of luck, we could be at Wembley next April. It was a difficult game but in the end I felt we fully deserved our victory over Watford. It was the right result, of course, but I know we are capable of playing better. When we were 1-0 up in the early part of the second half, Watford started to hit long balls behind our full backs and were turning and running at our defenders. We were surrendering territory too much and Eric Nixon must be praised for making two vital saves."

Watford equalised through a controversial goal which was very similar to the infamous Geoff Hurst World Cup Final goal. Everyone connected with City felt the ball had not crossed the line but, as with 1966, it counted and City had to withstand a little pressure before they managed to exert their influence again. Machin claimed City's second goal was a 'classic'. It was certainly the best of the match and came after Paul Lake turned two defenders brilliantly to create a chance for David White, who'd also scored the first, to fire home. Paul Stewart netted the third via a rebound after his penalty kick had been saved.

The star man was, without doubt, the ever-improving Lake who, like Hinchcliffe, Stewart, Brightwell and White, was being watched regularly by scouts from leading First Division clubs. Sooner or later City would have to sell at least one of them - or so the media kept telling the club's loyal support.

City's opponents in the League Cup quarter-finals were an exceptionally strong Everton, who were third in the First Division at the time. A Goodison Park crowd of 40,014, many from Manchester, witnessed a 2-0 win for the home side. It was a bitterly disappointing Wednesday night for City's well behaved army of fans - many of whom were abysmally treated at the railway station after the match.

The game itself opened with much pressure on Eric Nixon's goal. Fortunately, the relatively inexperienced 'keeper produced some fine saves to keep the score down to 1-0 by half-time, but the rest of City's still developing side appeared somewhat overawed by the occasion with opportunities at the other end amounting to little. Paul Lake did have one fine chance to score, but the ball hit a post.

In the second half City played much better, and were edging closer to an equaliser when tragedy struck. Graeme Sharp netted Everton's second and City's hope of Wembley glory, or at least reaching the semi-finals, was over in that competition. Machin felt the defeat was symptomatic of having too many players still learning their trade: "We were coming back into the game more and more when Everton suddenly struck with their second goal, and once again it highlighted a problem we have had all season. I can go back over so many games when we have been guilty of making what amount to 'schoolboy errors'. These can be as basic as not playing to the whistle."

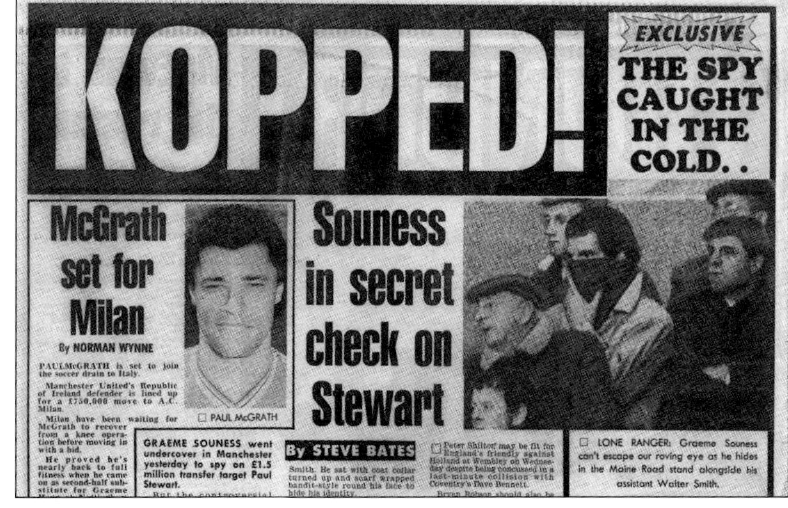

KOPPED!

EXCLUSIVE

THE SPY CAUGHT IN THE COLD..

McGrath set for Milan

By NORMAN WYNNE

PAUL McGRATH is set to join the soccer drain to Italy.

Manchester United's Republic of Ireland defender is lined up for a £750,000 move to A.C. Milan.

Milan have been waiting for McGrath to recover from a knee operation before moving in with a bid.

He proved he's nearly back to full fitness when he came on as second-half substitute for Graeme

PAUL McGRATH

Souness in secret check on Stewart

GRAEME SOUNESS went undercover in Manchester yesterday to spy on £1.5 million transfer target Paul Stewart.

By STEVE BATES

Smith. He sat with coat collar turned up and scarf wrapped bandit-style round his face to hide his identity.

Peter Shilton may be fit for England's friendly against Holland at Wembley on Wednesday despite being concussed in a last-minute collision with Coventry's Dave Bennett.

LONE RANGER: Graeme Souness can't escape our roving eye as he hides in the Maine Road stand alongside his assistant Walter Smith.

Graeme Souness, accompanied by his Ibrox assistant Walter Smith, fooled no-one when he sat undercover in the North Stand during the 1-1 draw with Swindon in March 1988. The Rangers management team had come to watch Paul Stewart.

By the time of the Goodison defeat City had already progressed in the F.A. Cup. On 9th January they faced Huddersfield Town at Leeds Road for a game everyone in Huddersfield was fired up for. The Yorkshiremen were determined to avenge that 10-1 November defeat and, despite most early pressure coming from City and an Ian Brightwell goal in the fifth minute, it looked as if the home side might actually succeed.

Huddersfield grittily fought back and, thanks to Duncan Shearer, were leading 2-1 with just seconds to spare. Then City were awarded a free kick from about twenty yards after Paul Moulden had been pushed in the back. It was a kick John Gidman desperately wanted to take: "I knew it was going to be the last kick of the game and I had to make it count. We had a quick discussion as there was hardly any time left and it was decided I should have a strike at goal. I struck it right and it went round the wall and in off the post."

Although the result gave City a second chance, it wasn't a particularly enjoyable day for the normally quiet Mel Machin. In the 77th minute he was ordered from the dug-out for using foul and abusive language during an argument with one of the linesmen. It was a bizarre moment, and certainly one that displeased Machin. Another dissatisfied City man was Neil McNab who had also been sent off in the closing stages.

The replay three days later at Maine Road gave City a second chance to prove they were still the dominant side, yet a marvellous display by

Huddersfield's goalkeeper Brian Cox - the same man who had suffered in the 10-1 extravaganza - prevented the Blues from taking the lead. After extra-time the game remained goalless, forcing yet another replay.

At Leeds Road on Monday 25th January City testified once and for all they possessed the greater strength. Andy Hinchcliffe opened the scoring with a clinical strike from the left. Further goals from White and Varadi - who'd driven straight from hospital where his daughter lay ill - made the score a deserved 3-0, and gave the Blues a nice trip to Blackpool the following Saturday.

At Bloomfield Road a tense game saw Blackpool take the lead in the 82nd minute, despite being outplayed for much of the match. The home side's goal had come from a most unlikely source - 20 year old Richard Sendall. The young player, who had already been told he would be leaving on a free transfer at the end of the term, had come on as substitute for his first senior outing of the season.

City unveiled Brother as the new club sponsor at the start of the 1987-88 season. The initial three-year deal was worth £500,000.

As the minutes ticked by it seemed highly unlikely City would level but then in injury time a mad scramble in the goal area left the home supporters panicking as the Blues piled on the pressure. Then suddenly the ball was in the net and the City players were celebrating. On the terraces the large travelling support joined in, but few could claim they actually knew what had happened. Gradually the name of Lake was being muttered as the scorer but how had he managed it?

Some journalists claimed Lake had shot in off veteran defender Paul Jones, but the City player held a slightly different view: "I would not have been surprised if the referee had stopped the game. There were so many bodies on the floor and everybody seemed to be having a stab at the ball. But I got my shot in and I was utterly delighted when it went in off the post. There was some confusion when we got back to the dressing room. Two or three of the players were trying to claim it, but I made it clear that it was my goal."

To the supporters it didn't really matter how the goal had been scored, they were just glad to have yet another second chance. City were beginning to behave like a team of Houdinis.

Wayne Biggins was among the new recruits for 1988-89.

Immediately after, Blackpool manager Sam Ellis, a man who became well known to City supporters a couple of years later, more or less conceded the tie to City: "Today was our big chance to win the tie, Wednesday is just a night out for us."

On the Wednesday Ellis' side came to frustrate as City played their third F.A. Cup tie in ten days. Despite the spoiling tactics the Blues managed to score first via a Paul Stewart header against his old club. Later Paul Simpson added a second with another header after an effort from White had hit the crossbar. The game ended 2-1 to send City through to the fifth round for the first time since 1981 where their opponents would be Plymouth Argyle.

A Maine Road crowd of 29,206 watched as Ian Scott, Paul Simpson and 85th minute substitute Paul Moulden helped City achieve a 3-1 victory to put them into the quarter-final.

As with the League Cup, the Blues opponents would be one of the strongest First Division sides of the period - in fact any period. They were also from Merseyside. Liverpool arrived at Maine Road after making their best ever start to a First Division campaign, charging to an impressive 17 point lead in the championship race. If the Everton game was viewed as difficult, this was nigh impossible. Nevertheless, City's players and management were convinced they could achieve a good result against the red giants.

In addition to the prospect of facing one of Europe's greatest sides, the young Blues realised they would also be watched by a Sunday crowd of 44,047, and by millions on television. It was a mammoth ordeal for some of the players, yet they started brightly.

For much of the opening half hour City put Liverpool under pressure but then in the 32nd minute the Reds were fortunate. The referee turned a blind eye as John Barnes controlled a pass from Peter Beardsley with his hands. The Liverpool man sprinted past John Gidman to the line, crossed to the near post and Ray Houghton volleyed home. It was a desperate time to concede a goal, especially one so controversial, but the Blues continued to fight.

Almost on the stroke of half-time, Paul Stewart missed a perfect opportunity, driving the ball straight at Bruce Grobbelaar. After 53 minutes City suffered again when Paul Lake was adjudged to have pushed Craig Johnston in the area. A City fan ran on to the pitch to argue with referee Allan Gunn before Peter Beardsley fired home the resulting penalty to make it 2-0.

Later Grobbelaar made a dramatic save from a Stewart header, but then Liverpool gained total control of the match. Johnston rounded City 'keeper Mike Stowell for the third goal, then Barnes scored with a low shot five minutes from time. A 4-0 defeat at home whiffs of humiliation, but the game was not like that. True, Liverpool were able to exert influence on the match whenever they chose, but City gave them a much tougher game than many clubs that season, and had performed well enough to keep the score much more respectable.

Jimmy Frizzell was proud of the City performance but angry with the referee: "I have seen the video of Sunday's game and I still believe the referee might have given handball against John Barnes before Liverpool scored their first goal. And I still believe Paul Lake's tackle on Craig Johnston was a good one and that we shouldn't have had a penalty given against us. Referees have to make decisions and we have to accept them. But it's very difficult at times to swallow your disappointment. However, although I made my disappointment obvious to the officials after the game, I was not booked, as reported in some newspapers. Nor was there any reason for me to be."

Reaching the last eight of both major cup competitions was a fine achievement but 1987-8 was a season when the main priority should have been promotion. City's cup exploits diverted the attention of their young stars, while constant media speculation that almost every one of the youngsters would be sold must have had an effect. Inevitably the following June the most saleable player at that time, Paul Stewart, was transferred to Tottenham Hotspur for £1.7 million. It was a huge amount, and was clearly one Chairman Swales felt unable to turn down. Understandably, the transfer concerned City's loyal supporters. Would the other exciting players be sold if the right offer came along? Peter Swales was adamant the now regular players from the 1986 Youth Cup success - Hinchcliffe, Brightwell, Redmond, and White - would not be sold at any price.

By the time the new 1988-9 season commenced Machin had spent almost half the Stewart transfer money on four players. They were goalkeeper Andy Dibble (£240,000), central defender Brian Gayle (£320,000), striker Wayne Biggins (£160,000), midfielder Nigel Gleghorn (£47,500), and forward John Deehan (£10,000). Former F.A. Youth Cup winner Steve Redmond was now captain, while Lake, Hinchcliffe, Brightwell and White all started the season as first team regulars.

The opening fixture saw the Blues create plenty of chances at Hull, but the home side took advantage of a surprising lapse by new signing Dibble who handed Hull the only goal of the match. A humiliating 4-1 defeat at home to Oldham followed two days later prompting a large section of City's support to give the season its first airing of the hardy perennial "Swales Out".

A 2-2 home draw with Walsall brought a point in the next game, prompting further calls for the Chairman to quit as supporters began to worry the new season would not bring promotion. Then at Leeds a penalty by Neil McNab gave City the lead but in typical Blue style with only minutes to go, they let it slip. A lapse in concentration gave Leeds an equaliser and everyone recognised two points had been lost rather than one gained.

As if in direct contrast to events on the field, City fans were now making headlines by creating their own entertainment on the terraces by bringing large inflatable bananas and other items to every game. The craze started at Oldham the previous season and had coincided with the arrival of City's first fanzine *Blue Print*.

It was a time when supporters of all clubs were fighting against generally poor publicity and negative media focus. Although City fans were already well known for their frequent verbal attacks on the Chairman, the majority were out to prove to whoever might listen they were not the thugs many believed. City fans launched the inflatable craze, and over the course of the next twelve months most other clubs followed in some way or other.

At Maine Road on 17th September City achieved their first victory, beating Brighton 2-1 before a crowd of 16,033. Peter Swales must have realised supporters were losing patience and were eager to see the team move up the table. The possibility of another season in Division Two could have killed many fans' faith in the club and their loyal support for good.

Two away victories followed with City defeating Chelsea 3-1 before a crowd of 8,858 at the Bridge. The low crowd was the result of a ban on away support and the closure of the ground's terracing - not that it stopped a large number of Mancunians attending the match. Four days later another away trip - this time to Barnsley - ended in a 2-1 win to lift the Blues up to eighth.

On 1st October, Division leaders Blackburn arrived at Maine Road with former Blue Nicky Reid as captain. A mistake from Blackburn's normally reliable Colin Hendry gave Wayne 'Bertie' Biggins the chance to score the only goal. City moved up further to fifth. Not bad for a team watched by fans waving inflatable bananas while demonstrating against the chairman. Understandably, the upward shift killed off the catcalls for a while.

A SIGN OF THE TIMES

Paul Moulden and Ian Brightwell sign autographs through the Maine Road fence. A series of pitch invasions and general disorder throughout football had forced clubs to erect perimeter fences.

A 4-1 win over Portsmouth followed but on 8th October a difficult trip to Suffolk ended with a 1-0 victory for bogey team Ipswich. Naturally, the Blues felt far from happy with the result, especially as goalscorer Jason Dozzell only received a booking for the late tackle on Mark Seagraves which forced the City man to be stretchered off early in the match.

After the long trip to East Anglia on the Saturday, City fans travelled to Plymouth the following Tuesday for the second leg of the League Cup second round. The first game had ended 1-0 to the Blues, prompting many supporters to take the day off work for the long journey south yet, incredibly, as they arrived in Devon news came through that the game had been called off. The supporters who travelled were angry, yet no action was taken to ensure the same wouldn't occur again, and in 1997 a similar postponement brought further justifiable criticism from City's travelling fans.

The Plymouth game was only delayed by 24 hours but caused serious problems for any Blues wanting to attend. Those that managed the journey a second time were in for a treat as the Blues defeated the Pilgrims 6-3 with Andy Dibble also saving a penalty. It had not been an easy game and was yet another example of City's great unpredictability. They were leading 2-0 on the night, before allowing the home side back into the game with three goals levelling the aggregate score. After a few minutes panic City fought back to achieve what, at a glance, appeared an emphatic win.

After the game many Blues returned to Manchester, but some understandably decided to stay in Devon as the two sides would meet again in the League on the Saturday. It was an extraordinary week for travelling, yet the City fans still turned out in large numbers determined to make the Home Park League game a great occasion.

The match ended in another Blue victory, this time 1-0, but it became more newsworthy because of the party atmosphere of City's travelling support. The Devon press found the inflatable craze puzzling

Over 12,000 Blues fans travelled to Stoke for the Boxing Day game in 1988, many in fancy dress, most carrying inflatable bananas. Here the players take to the field similarly armed!

with a photograph from the game carrying the caption: "What's all this? Giant bananas, a huge beer can and even an inflatable Frankenstein monster."

The same photo appeared on the cover of fanzine *Blue Print* later in the season as City's supporters started to plan their next carnival occasion. By November everyone had decided to turn the Boxing Day trip to Stoke into a fancy dress party. Although few, if any, realised at the time, this was similar to some of the antics their predecessors were famous for at the turn of the century. Apparently, games at Hyde Road were frequently enlivened by supporters in fancy dress playing musical instruments. The 1988 trip to Stoke helped that kind of fun return to football.

By the time of the Stoke match, City were fourth. They had hit top spot after an impressive 4-0 defeat of Bradford on 10th December, but that was only on goal difference. A 2-2 draw with Shrewsbury left City two points behind new leaders Blackburn.

On Boxing Day morning, with little public transport, over 12,000 City supporters travelled to the Potteries in party mood. The newspapers claimed it was City's largest travelling support outside of Greater Manchester for a League game since the 1968 Championship decider, although the Notts County match of 1985 saw a similarly large Blue following. Once in Stoke there were fans dressed as Laurel & Hardy, Arabs, vicars, hunchbacks, convicts (with the names Lester Piggott and Jan Molby on their backs!), ... basically anything you could imagine. There were even nursery rhyme characters with Humpty Dumpty insisting he sat on a wall inside the ground. Almost every supporter carried an inflatable of some description. It was an incredible sight and, more importantly, a strong statement that the majority of football fans were not hooligans.

When the City players ran onto the pitch each carried their own banana and threw these into the large City crowd. Stoke had generously given City one entire side of the ground and the paddock in front of their family stand. In addition many City families sat with Stoke fans in the family section and, naturally, other Blues found seats in the main stand. It was a fantastic positive atmosphere and one which should have been seen nationwide.

Sadly, the media barely covered the event. Nothing was ever shown on television, and little appeared in the press. Even the City programme failed to highlight the atmosphere of a very special day. At a time when the Government seemed intent on killing the game by introducing ID cards, such positive publicity could have helped the authorities reconsider. Regrettably, it took a major disaster later in the season to make the leaders see sense.

The game itself was a huge disappointment with unpredictable City losing 3-1 to a side that included former Blues Tony Henry and John Gidman and future City star Peter Beagrie. The Manchester men continued to enjoy themselves however. Frank Newton, acclaimed as the man who'd brought the first banana to the Oldham game the previous season, wrote his view for fanzine *Blue Print*: "The match itself has faded from my memory partly because we lost but mainly because there was so much else to take in. The interstellar branch of the City fan club was in evidence with ET sitting on the fence at half time, a crocodile and a canary seemed to be getting on intimate terms, whilst I didn't envy the rear half of the pantomime horse wandering around the ground. I wonder how much of the game he saw? I wish I'd had a week or so to walk round the crowd to take in the humour and imagination displayed by the magnificent City following. When the game ended there was an air of disappointment at the result but still plenty of laughter as new delights appeared at every turn of the head. A rather cold looking fan wandered past wearing a snorkel and flippers and not much else, a group of pixies were spotted heading towards the car park, whilst Rambo complete with machine gun (with a City scarf tied round it) walked the other way."

The attitude of the supporters lifted spirits, but more than anything else City fans needed the team to repay their devotion by winning promotion. After Stoke the Blues enjoyed a nine match unbeaten run in the League to leave them second to Chelsea. This helped give Machin the Manager of the Month award while captain Steve Redmond received the Young Eagle of the Month accolade.

After a 1-0 defeat at Watford, the Blues rediscovered their winning ways by beating Leicester 4-2 at Maine Road on 11th March, but it was also a day of despair for many in the crowd. City's greatest hope for the future, Paul Lake, crashed to the ground after an accidental clash of heads with Leicester's Paul Ramsey. The 20 year old lay unconscious and went into a series of shuddering convulsions. Clearly it was a grave situation. Physio Roy Bailey raced on to the field amid an eerie silence: "It was a very dangerous situation and I had one hell of a job to force open Paul's jaws and hook back his tongue with my finger. In fact his jaw muscles were so tense that John Deehan, who was helping along with Glyn Pardoe, received a nasty bite in the process!"

Lake had swallowed his tongue and was very close to losing his life; only the quick actions of Bailey saved the youngster. Eventually, club doctor Norman Luft arrived on the scene from his seat in the stand. It had taken what seemed an eternity to make his way to the injured player, although the entire 'slow-motion' incident seemed to last longer than the whole game. Lake himself hardly knew anything about the event: "I can recall the corner coming over and going out to attack the ball, but then the next thing was waking up in the medical room feeling pretty groggy! From what I've heard about it afterwards, I've no doubt that Roy's actions were vital and it is something for which I will owe him for the rest of my life."

Fortunately Bailey's actions had prevented any long term injury and a brain scan the following Monday proved Lake was not seriously affected.

Sunderland were defeated 4-2 in the next game, but a crucial home meeting with Chelsea ended in a

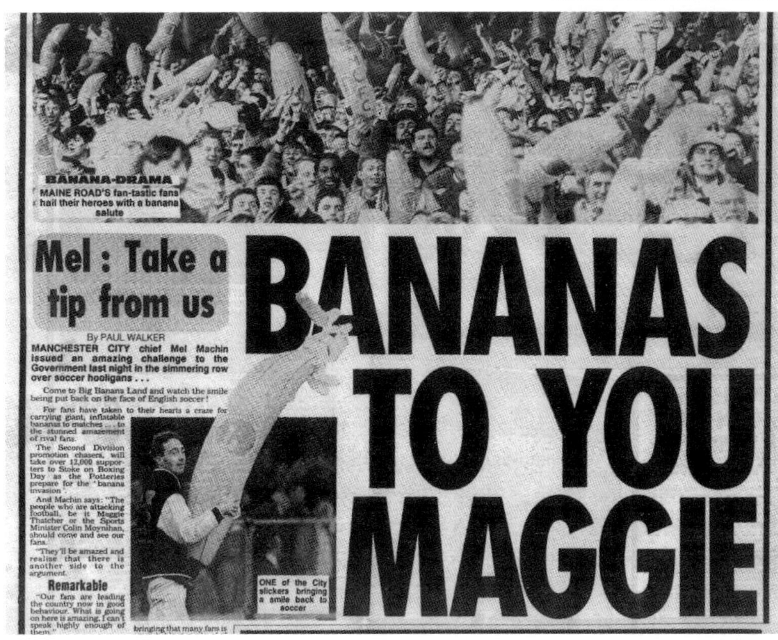

BANANA-DRAMA

MAINE ROAD'S fan-tastic fans hail their heroes with a banana salute

Mel : Take a tip from us

BANANAS TO YOU MAGGIE

By PAUL WALKER

MANCHESTER CITY chief Mel Machin issued an amazing challenge to the Government last night in the simmering row over soccer hooligans . . .

Come to Big Banana Land and watch the smile being put back on the face of English soccer!

For fans have taken to their hearts a craze for carrying giant, inflatable bananas to matches . . . to the stunned amazement of rival fans.

The Second Division promotion chasers, will take over 12,000 supporters to Stoke on Boxing Day as the Potteries prepare for the "banana invasion".

And Machin says: "The people who are attacking football, be it Maggie Thatcher or the Sports Minister Colin Moynihan, should come and see our fans.

"They'll be amazed and realise that there is another side to the argument.

Remarkable

"Our fans are leading the country now in good behaviour. What is going on here is amazing. I can't speak highly enough of them."

bringing that many fans is

ONE of the City slickers bringing a smile back to soccer

Mel Machin's advice to a Prime Minister looking for an answer to football hooliganism. Below: City fans in fancy dress for the Boxing Day trip to Stoke, and yet more bananas.

SWALES MUST GO

According to the Fanzine Blueprint, the Alex Williams Testimonial Quiz held at the City Social Club during the 1988-9 season was won by a team called "Swales Must Go".

3-2 reverse. The only bright spots were the attendance of 40,070 - the highest in the division that season - and a last minute goal for youngster Ged Taggart which made the score look a little respectable.

A week later the game at Walsall gave City's travelling support real value for money when Nigel Gleghorn replaced the injured Andy Dibble in goal. The Blues were 2-0 down when Dibble collapsed in agony with a groin problem. Gleghorn pulled on the green shirt and helped the Blues to fight back with £600,000 buy David Oldfield scoring his first goal for the club. 'Goalden' Moulden equalised and then, early in the second half, scored again to give City a 3-2 lead.

Gleghorn made a couple of good saves and kicked superbly to keep the pressure off City before a ridiculous back pass from Oldfield gave Walsall a gift opportunity, and the game ended 3-3. The substitute 'keeper was certainly the man of the match, winning applause from both sets of supporters after standing in for around an hour, yet a mere six weeks later he had to do it all again.

As with the Walsall match, Dibble suffered another groin injury to give Gleghorn his second chance to make the news. He'd already scored an eighth minute goal against Crystal Palace to give City the lead, then at the start of the second period he replaced Dibble. He managed to keep Steve Coppell's side at bay until the 75th minute when a brilliant strike from Ian Wright gave him little chance. Afterwards, despite constant Palace pressure, Gleghorn was able to keep them out and the match ended 1-1 with the former North East fireman grabbing the headlines again. Gleghorn was pleased with his performance, and admitted: "I wasn't nervous - the lads are getting used to my positioning! As a kid, I played a lot of basketball and also turned out for Durham's under 19 cricket team as a wicketkeeper. I've got a good pair of hands and enjoy larking about in goal during training."

Nigel Gleghorn performed heroically as stand-in goalkeeper.

Interestingly, this was the second consecutive season that City had lost their 'keeper at home to Palace. The previous year Eric Nixon was sent off and replaced by Steve Redmond. On that occasion Redmond was not as fortunate as Gleghorn as the game ended in a 3-1 defeat. Fortunately City had signed the experienced Paul Cooper from Leicester as cover earlier, and the expert penalty saver played in the final two games, after making six earlier appearances.

The point against Palace kept City in an automatic promotion place on 80 points. Chelsea were by this time Division Two champions after gaining a 13 point lead over the Blues, but behind City lay three teams all on 74 points (Palace, Watford, and Blackburn).

With two games to go, it was vital the Blues did not do anything stupid especially as Palace had a game in hand. City's history is famous for its unpredictable nature with an incredible number of seemingly easy games ending with the wrong result. Few supporters could forget the relegation match of 1983, so it was important the next game - a home clash with mid-table Bournemouth - ended in victory to more or less guarantee promotion.

In party spirits the City fans prepared for celebration and after only two minutes Paul Moulden secured the lead. Trevor Morley, signed from Northampton in January 1988, made it 2-0 then Moulden hit another to give the Blues an impressive 3-0 lead at half time. Prior to the match and during the interval a band marched across the Maine Road turf providing a little light relief, while City fans chattered about the Charlton promotion match of four years earlier. Could the scoreline reach five?

As a beach ball bounced around the stadium - it started in the Kippax and made its way via the North Stand to the Main Stand - play resumed. The atmosphere was one of total celebration and many of the players clearly felt their job had been done. As the team relaxed, Bournemouth fought back. A needless corner was given away and then, suddenly, Bournemouth scored. A few Blues cheered what everybody assumed was a consolation goal, then City's unpredictability took control.

Paul Moulden missed a certain goal, then another corner was given away. A mad scramble failed to clear the loose ball and Bournemouth scored again. At 3-2, with future Blue Ian Bishop spurring the away side in attack, City fans became exceptionally nervous.

After more than six nerve-jangling minutes of injury time, Andy Hinchcliffe brought down Luther Blissett in the area. The Bournemouth man slotted home the resultant penalty and the match ended 3-3. The 55 away supporters in the 9,000 capacity Platt Lane Stand celebrated while the rest of the officially quoted 30,564 crowd were devastated.

By the final match, City were still in second place with a goal difference of 24, but Crystal Palace were now only three points behind with a goal difference of 19 after beating Stoke 1-0 in midweek. The Blues simply had to get a point from their last match to be certain of promotion. A lesser result could still bring success, but after the Bournemouth debacle City could not leave anything to chance, especially as a 3-0 defeat and an easily attainable 3-0 victory to Palace would give the London club promotion.

The remaining match was at fourteenth-placed Bradford City. It was another fantastic away following with Manchester fans in every section of the ground, although the capacity of Valley Parade prevented many Blues from attending what was one of the most crucial games of the period.

Prior to the match City fans were in buoyant mood, although they were far from happy when former manager John Bond arrived on the pitch with Mel Machin to record a Granada TV interview. The previous night Bond had criticised City fans for abusing Machin and the team following the pathetic performance against Bournemouth, and had gone on to say the Blues did not deserve automatic promotion as they simply weren't good enough. His comments on the team may have been true, but fans found it tough to accept the same man could criticise them for voicing their own views at Maine Road. At Bradford the former City manager was greeted with such abuse the TV interview had to be abandoned.

The game commenced with the team in typical big match form - they conceded a goal after 24 minutes! Bradford pressed forward and the Blues simply panicked, although they did manage to get their act together a little before the interval.

At half time various scorelines were filtering through from the delayed Palace-Birmingham match with the most popular story suggesting Palace were

THE GOAL THAT CLINCHED PROMOTION...

Trevor Morley slides in to score a late equaliser at Bradford City in May 1989, and (below) then milks the applause of City's ecstatic following.

The Blues are going up!

Scenes of jubilation at Bradford as thousands of City fans pour onto the pitch to celebrate promotion.

David White gets chaired off and Neil McNab joins manager Mel Machin for a celebratory drink.

On the facing page David White cracks open another bottle and the party is well underway.

4-0 up and in rampant form. City fans feared the worst. The second half kicked-off with the Blues still unable to find an equaliser, despite saves from Moulden and White. Yet, at times, it appeared more likely Bradford would increase their lead, despite the City pressure.

More rumours circulated that Palace had scored again causing many Blues to ponder the prospect of success in the play-offs. For one fan, Ivor McKenna, the tension was too much and he ran onto the pitch to plead with the players for more effort. He spoke with Paul Lake for a few moments before three or four policemen led him off the pitch. It later transpired he'd told the players Palace were leading 5-0.

With four minutes remaining, experienced goalkeeper Paul Cooper quickly threw to the unmarked Nigel Gleghorn who sent the ball to Paul Moulden. With David White racing down the wing it was inevitable Moulden would pass to the speedy attacker. Trevor Morley's view of what happened next: "All I can remember is Whitey getting on his left foot and clipping it in. I got goalside of the defender. The ball bobbled and I got very good contact. As soon as I did I knew it was going in. I ran off and waved to the fans and as I turned round to the pitch there were none of my players near me. I suddenly got a feeling the goal wasn't allowed. I looked to the linesman and the referee for about ten seconds. I was a bit confused why everyone wasn't jumping up and down. Then I saw a couple of the lads on the floor. It was a horrible few seconds."

Thankfully the goal did count and City were level, but the final minutes provided little opportunity for either side to produce a winner and at full time the Bradford officials wisely allowed the City fans onto the pitch to enjoy their celebrations. Following the Hillsborough disaster only four weeks earlier a decision had been taken to keep the gates unlocked.

On the pitch fans greeted their heroes and, as in 1985, a few players lost their shirts to souvenir hunters. Even the Bradford contingent seemed delighted with the result and many celebrated with the men from Manchester.

As supporters returned to their vehicles the news came through that Palace had won 4-1, not 5-0 as many believed. Nevertheless, the result was irrelevant as City's point guaranteed promotion.

City were back in Division One and this time, said the much criticised Chairman Swales, it was for keeps: "What happened to Manchester City in the past must never happen again, and my pledge to the loyal band of Maine Road supporters is simply that if I have anything to do with it, it certainly never will."

By the Summer of 1989 Peter Swales was well aware that future failure would certainly ensure substantial pressure on him as Chairman. The supporters had shown over the course of two seasons in Division Two that failure would no longer be tolerated. Promotion in 1989 had to be the first step towards regaining real success.

1988-89 DIVISION TWO PROMOTION DETAILS

RESULTS	HOME	AWAY
Hull City	W 4-1	L 0-1
Oldham Athletic	L 1-4	W 1-0
Walsall	D 2-2	D 3-3
Leeds United	D 0-0	D 1-1
Brighton & Hove Albion	W 2-1	L 1-2
Chelsea	L 2-3	W 3-1
Barnsley	L 1-2	W 2-1
Blackburn Rovers	W 1-0	W 0-4
Portsmouth	W 4-1	W 1-0
Ipswich Town	W 4-0	L 0-1
Plymouth Argyle	W 2-0	W 1-0
Birmingham City	D 0-0	W 2-0
West Bromwich Albion	D 1-1	L 0-1
Sunderland	D 1-1	W 4-2
Leicester City	W 4-2	D 0-0
Watford	W 3-1	L 0-1
Bournemouth	D 3-3	W 1-0
Oxford United	W 2-1	W 4-2
Crystal Palace	D 1-1	D 0-0
Bradford City	W 4-0	D 1-1
Shrewsbury Town	D 2-2	W 1-0
Stoke City	W 2-1	L 1-3
Swindon Town	W 2-1	W 2-1

REGULAR SIDE:
Dibble
Lake
Hinchcliffe
Gayle
Brightwell or
Megson
Redmond
White
Moulden
Morley
McNab
Biggins

MANAGER:
Mel Machin

LARGEST VICTORY: 4-0 v Ipswich Town (H) 11/2/89, Bradford City (H) 10/12/88

HEAVIEST DEFEAT: 0-4 v Blackburn Rovers (A) 15/4/89 - the day of the Hillsborough Disaster

AVERAGE HOME ATTENDANCE: 23,500

HIGHEST HOME ATTENDANCE: 40,070 v Chelsea 18/3/89

HIGHEST AWAY ATTENDANCE: 24,056 v Stoke City 26/12/88

LEAGUE APPEARANCES: (substitute appearances in brackets)
46 Redmond, 44 White (1), 42 McNab, 41 Gayle, 39 Morley (1), 38 Dibble, 37 Hinchcliffe (2), Lake (1), 29 Moulden (7), Biggins (3), 25 Gleghorn (7), 24 Brightwell (2), 22 Megson, 21 Seagraves (2), 9 Taggart (2), 8 Oldfield (3), Cooper, 2 Beckford (6), 1 Bradshaw (4), Varadi (2), Scott, Hughes, Simpson, plus Bill Williams as substitute on 8th October v Ipswich Town (replacing Mark Seagraves)

LEAGUE GOALS: 13 Moulden, 12 Morley, 9 Biggins, 6 Brightwell, White, Gleghorn, 5 Hinchcliffe, McNab, 3 Gayle, Lake, Oldfield, 1 Redmond, Megson, Taggart, Beckford

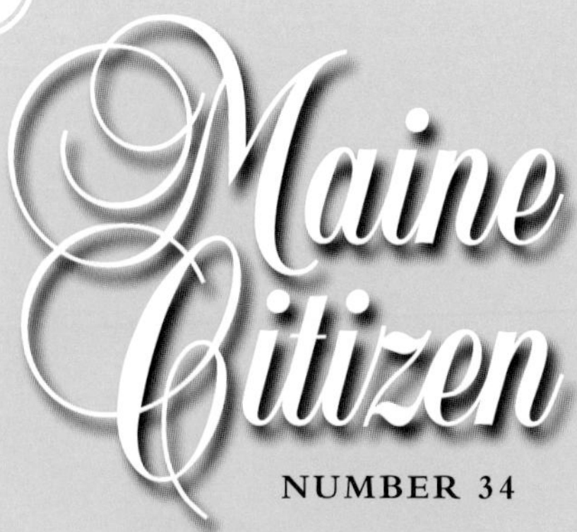

NUMBER 34

NEIL McNAB

Born in Greenock on 4th June 1957, Neil McNab was the first of an army of Scots purchased by Billy McNeill during City's Second Division days of 1983 to 1985. McNab thrived at Maine Road and, over the years that followed, became an established member of the Blue family - players who for one reason or another become so committed to the Blue cause they find it hard to keep away.

After playing for Morton in the early 70s he joined Tottenham as an amateur in February 1974 for a then hefty fee of £40,000. Hailed rather unfairly as "the new John White", when he made his League debut a short while later he was the youngest Spurs player to appear in the League. That record has since been overtaken, but it says much about his ability at the time.

During 1977 he became an established member of the Spurs side, and was an ever-present when they won promotion from the Second Division in 1977-8. Already the owner of a Scottish Under- 21 cap he was unfortunate to lose out when Tottenham purchased the Argentinian stars Villa and Ardiles. In September 1978, he was transferred to Bolton for £250,000, where he once gave away a penalty against City. He then moved around a little - Brighton (Feb 1980), Leeds (loan Dec 1982), and Portsmouth (another loan), before arriving at Maine Road in July 1983 for a bargain fee.

Once in Manchester, McNab proved a tough-tackling, hard working midfield player with a silky pass. He was perfect to help the City fightback under McNeill, and for the following six years became one of the most important members of the side. Deservedly, he was twice voted City's Player of the Year.

In 1987 Mel Machin arrived at Maine Road and was surprised to find how important a player McNab was: "There were one or two conflicts of opinion before I arrived that Neil McNab was one of those type of players who was never very constructive as such, but from what I have seen he's been invaluable to the members of the team with his infectiousness for wanting to play the type of football I want to play. By being able to pass and receive the ball he got the whole team able to play that type of football. Neil has been a model of consistency and professionalism and lots of people make comments that City play well when Neil McNab plays well. He's a very good player and it surprises me he hasn't had more international recognition."

Playing probably his best football while at City, McNab became a vital player. He was a shade unfortunate in September 1989 when injury prevented him from playing against Manchester United. He would have enjoyed that game. Three years earlier he was the only member of the City side that drew 2-2 with United not to have either come from City's youth or been born in Manchester. Nevertheless, he played like a true Mancunian in every derby game.

Shortly after Christmas 1989, under new manager Howard Kendall, McNab's Maine Road playing career came to an end with a transfer to Tranmere Rovers for £125,000. Once there he continued to prove his worth and helped Tranmere achieve promotion to Division Two, via the play offs, and then consolidate.

After leaving Tranmere he played for a number of non-League clubs - including Witton Albion - before returning to Maine Road in 1994 to take charge of City's A team. Once again he showed his determined approach and spent considerable time helping his young charges develop, just as he had done with his more senior colleagues during the Second Division days of 1987 to 1989.

In 1997 after so many managerial changes at the club, it became inevitable that the entire backroom set up would be reviewed and McNab was dismissed in a move that upset many supporters.

Neil McNab was a real winner. With his consistent play he helped City stabilise during a difficult decade and, although it's all down to opinion, he is arguably the most important City player of his period. Few made the impact he did.

Not bad for a bargain basement player bought as an urgent short term measure!

McNAB'S PLAYING RECORD

	LEAGUE		FA CUP		FL CUP		FM CUP		TOTAL	
	App	Gls	App	Gls	App	Gls	App	Gls	App	Gls
1983-84	33	1	1	0	2	0	-	-	36	1
1984-85	15(3)	0	0	0	2	0	-	-	17(3)	0
1985-86	37	4	4	0	2	0	4	0	47	4
1986-87	42	4	1	0	2	1	2	0	47	5
1987-88	36(1)	2	7	0	5	0	2	0	50(1)	2
1988-89	42	5	2	1	4	1	1	0	49	1
1989-90	11(1)	0	0	0	3	0	1	0	15(1)	0
TOTAL	216(5)	16	15	1	20	2	10	0	261(5)	19

Chapter Twenty

LOYAL SUPPORTERS

BACK in Division One City were determined to make an impression. For too many years the Blues had been the laughing stock of northern football and, with Mel Machin in control, City set about taking steps to ensure first of all survival and then an assault on the Championship. Mel Machin told the Blue press: "It's important we have the experience of the first year of First Division football. But we must look ahead to winning the First Division Championship. Looking at the capabilities of individuals there's no reason why that shouldn't be. It's up to me to strengthen the squad to be able to achieve our ambition - and that is to win trophies.

"With this squad I feel we have got something to build on, something very strong. But first of all we have got to maintain First Division status. That's our prime objective, and then to go on from there."

During the close season Machin was rewarded with an improved contract and took steps to strengthen the squad. Aston Villa's defender Martin Keown interested the manager at first but that deal fell through at the end of May 1989, then Ipswich's unsettled 21-year-old striker and future Blue, Dalian Atkinson was linked with a move to Maine Road at the start of June, as was West Brom's defender Chris Whyte. It was all fairly typical to City supporters who were used to hearing about star players but rarely experienced the satisfaction of signing them. Then on 14th June came the shock news that City had agreed to purchase Bournemouth's Ian Bishop for a fee of around £750,000.

Rumours circulated that young hero Paul Moulden was about to go in the opposite direction as part of the deal but Mel Machin reassured fans: "Paul Moulden has nothing to do with the Bishop signing. If he joins them, I would expect the fee to be decided by an independent tribunal."

On 20th June Moulden joined Bournemouth in a deal reportedly worth around £300,000 to the Blues. It was a sad end to his City career and upset many supporters. It also caused Ian Bishop a few problems to start with as some fans felt Moulden had been sacrificed to buy Bishop. Nevertheless Bishop was welcomed by the majority to Maine Road and quickly proved a popular man. On arrival he told the press he was delighted with his move north: "I wanted to play in the First Division. Harry Redknapp asked me to stay another year at Bournemouth and he was willing to turn down City's offer for me. But I just felt I wanted to play in the First Division. There was a lot of talk about Arsenal, Liverpool and Manchester United being interested in me, and I heard Chelsea were really keen. Once I realised City were eager though, I made up my mind. They were the only ones to offer the money Harry wanted and I thought there was no point in waiting around and possibly losing the chance of joining City."

Ian Bishop arrived at Maine Road from Bournemouth in July 1989.

The Bishop transfer wasn't actually complete until 4th July, and within a week news started to circulate that the Blues were about to purchase their first million pound player since Trevor Francis. Machin was after none other than the brilliant 28 year old Clive Allen. Allen was playing with Bordeaux in France and had been keen to return to England after a year away. Machin heard of Allen's desire and persuaded Peter Swales to go back on his word that "City would never again spend £1 million on one player". Allen signed for the fourth £1 million move of his career and City fans were delighted. They now eagerly awaited the new season, especially the opening game at Anfield. That match would prove more than any other what City would need to do if they were serious about becoming a First Division force.

That opening match ended in a 3-1 defeat, with City's goal scored by the improving Andy Hinchcliffe, but it was far from a nightmare start. Clive Allen impressed on his debut, as did Ian Bishop, and the Blues had gone in level at the interval. As the City fans left fortress Anfield the first airing of Blue Moon was heard. A couple of supporters had started to sing what was later adopted as the club's anthem on their way out of the ground. Why they chose that song is a mystery, but it seemed to dovetail neatly with the atmosphere that day. Gradually it was heard more often, and by the end of the season was an important factor behind City's campaign of consolidation.

Another defeat followed the Anfield match when Southampton, led by Jimmy Case, stole a 2-1 Maine Road victory. A 1-1 draw with a Tottenham side that now included Gary Lineker brought the first point of the season and then, on 9th September, Clive Allen netted against his old club, QPR, to give City their first victory in the top division since 4th May 1987.

A 1-0 defeat at Wimbledon followed, leaving City joint bottom of the division with Tottenham and Sheffield Wednesday. A week later the Blues were scheduled to face multi-million pound Manchester United in the Maine Road derby match. Everybody - including even the most biased Blue - expected United to murder Machin's men and it was with a degree of fear and trepidation that City fans prepared for the 111th League derby.

While City had struggled to afford players like Allen (who wouldn't be playing against United in any case) and Bishop, Alex Ferguson had bought in Neil Webb (£1.5 million), Mike Phelan (£750,000), Gary Pallister (£2.3 million), Paul Ince (£1.7 million), and Danny Wallace (£1.2 million). They were football's biggest spenders and seemed able to buy anyone at any price. They were also the team which appeared most often on television and in the newspapers and had already made headlines at the start of 1989 as a result of a take-over bid by Michael Knighton. It was a story splashed across the tabloids, and Knighton was encouraged to put on a tracksuit prior to their opening fixture against Arsenal, run towards the Stretford End, and score a goal. It all seems a little crazy now, but at the time United gave the impression they wanted to court publicity, any publicity.

Derby delight... read all about it!

Monday, September 25, 1989 23

Our two-page full colour special: Centre pages

Manchester Evening News

Our player by player form guide: See inside

Blue heaven and a spot of derby history for Mel's aces

Oh, what a lovely feeling!

Mel Machin

Machin's salute to his stars

PRIDE and passion won the derby for Manchester City.

Now Maine Road manager Mel Machin

Super City, but ...

United, this was simply a disgrace!

Says David Meek

At Maine Road on derby day Knighton, whose take-over eventually collapsed, actually stood in the directors' box signing autographs for City's supporters!

The game itself commenced with United looking fairly bright but then a large group of their supporters, who had somehow obtained tickets for the North Stand, started to cause trouble. The referee took the players off while police and stewards tried to end the violence. Much to the disgust of City's law-abiding supporters in both the North and Main Stands close to the trouble, the United fans were taken from the City section and allowed to find seats in the corner of the old Platt Lane stand, close to City's Family Section. The trouble-makers should have been removed from the stadium but the official line was they may have caused even more trouble had they been evicted so early in the game.

With the atmosphere tense but peaceful, play resumed. By now City seemed ready for action and quickly became the game's masters. David White recognised Mike Duxbury seemed a little ill at ease in United's defence and turned the Red inside out, before spearing in a low centre which the uncomfortable Pallister missed. David Oldfield, following up, managed to crack the ball into the United net for the opening goal after only 11 minutes. City fans could hardly believe it. Already it was like a dream come true, but there was more to follow.

Less than a minute after the first goal Viv Anderson was caught out of position as Paul Lake and Trevor Morley tore a great hole in the Reds' defence. Jim Leighton made a save but it still allowed Morley to fire home the rebound. 2-0!

United attempted to rally but found it impossible to deal with Bishop, Lake and White who by this stage were simply outstanding. Every time United attempted to attack City took the ball off them with ease. Then the Blues made it 3-0 after 36 minutes.

Steve Redmond collected the ball on the edge of his own area and sent a glorious long ball out to Oldfield. He gathered easily and sent an instant cross into the penalty area where Bishop, timing his run to perfection, headed past a bewildered Leighton.

The score remained 3-0 at half time and the United players trooped off shell-shocked, especially Jim Leighton. Another unhappy man was Mark Hughes who found it hard to accept his side were losing at Maine Road.

Throughout the interval City fans simply stood and smiled, rubbing their eyes occasionally. Was it really true?

At the start of the second half United came out determined to fight back. Hughes, always looking for the spectacular goal, managed a magnificent bicycle kick to fire the ball past Paul Cooper's left shoulder to make it 3-1. Normally City would panic and allow the Reds back into the match but this day they refused to give United anything and once again seized control of the game.

In the 58th minute City attacked United's right flank where Anderson fatally hesitated. Lake raced through and set the ball up for Oldfield to score easily from close range in front of the United fans in Platt Lane. Chants of 'easy, easy' rang out throughout the rest of the match, and then the Blues rubbed it in with

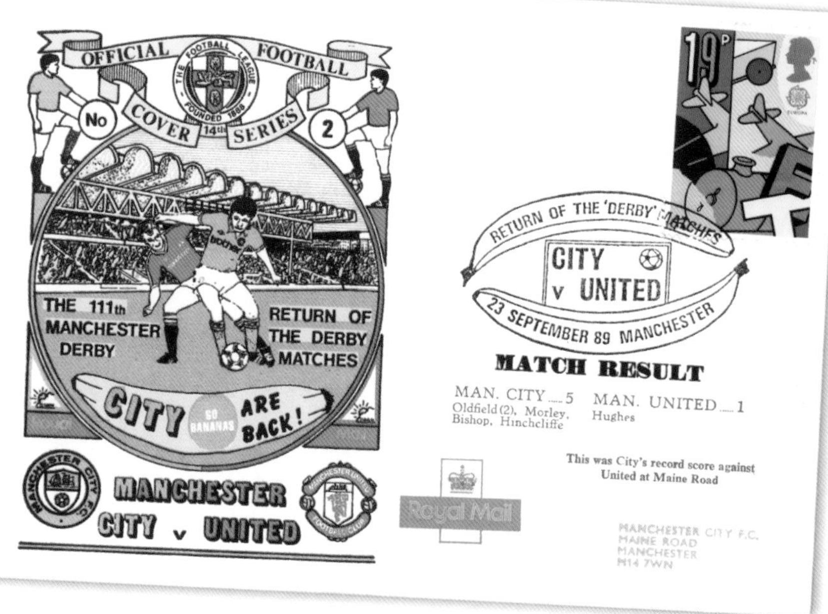

A first day postal cover produced to commemorate a great day.

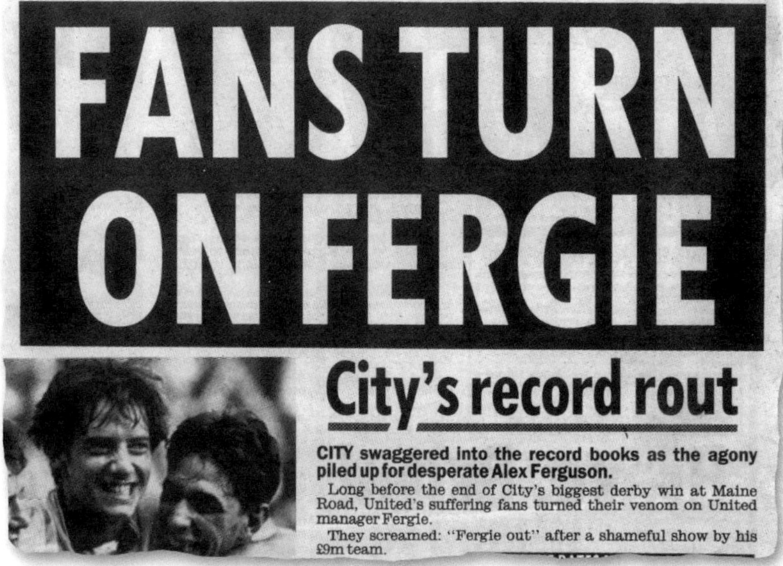

FANS TURN ON FERGIE

City's record rout

CITY swaggered into the record books as the agony piled up for desperate Alex Ferguson.

Long before the end of City's biggest derby win at Maine Road, United's suffering fans turned their venom on United manager Fergie.

They screamed: "Fergie out" after a shameful show by his £9m team.

Alex Ferguson came under fire from United supporters following the Maine Road mauling. However the Old Trafford directors stood firmly behind him and two months later it was City boss Mel Machin who was to lose his job. The rest is history!

Gary Fleming, Ian Bishop, David Oldfield and Paul Lake celebrate one of Oldfield's two goals as United's Paul Ince looks shell-shocked.

CITY 5 UNITED 1

The goal action from City's biggest ever 'derby' win at Maine Road.

David Oldfield begins the onslaught with a powerful shot from 10 yards out.

New signing Ian Bishop goes airborne to meet Oldfield's cross and City go three up.

Leighton is grounded and his defenders watch in dismay as Morley hits the second.

(Picture courtesy of the Manchester Evening News).

All so simple for Oldfield as he taps in Lake's cross for No.4.

How the City programme recorded that historic day in September 1989... still rated as <u>the</u> most memorable game by many Blues fans.

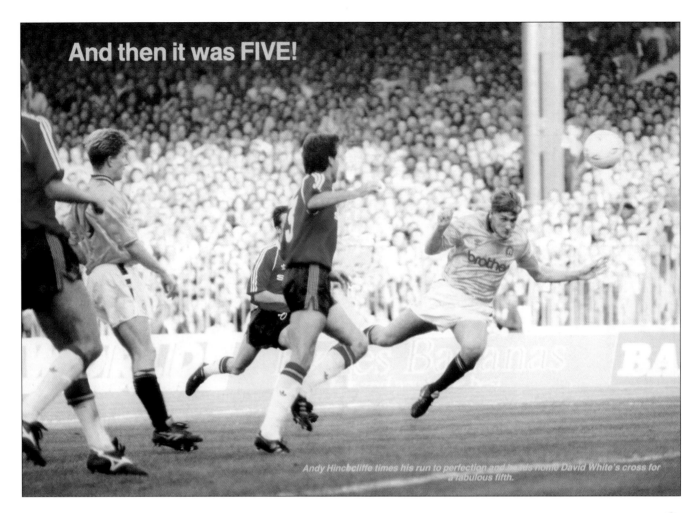

And then it was FIVE!

Andy Hinchcliffe times his run to perfection and heads home David White's cross for a fabulous fifth.

Andy Hinchcliffe's goal in the 5-1 defeat of the Reds was the centre spread for City's programme v Luton the following week. The programme featured seven full pages of pictures from the derby, including those reproduced on the previous two pages and this cover shot of Ian Bishop celebrating his goal.

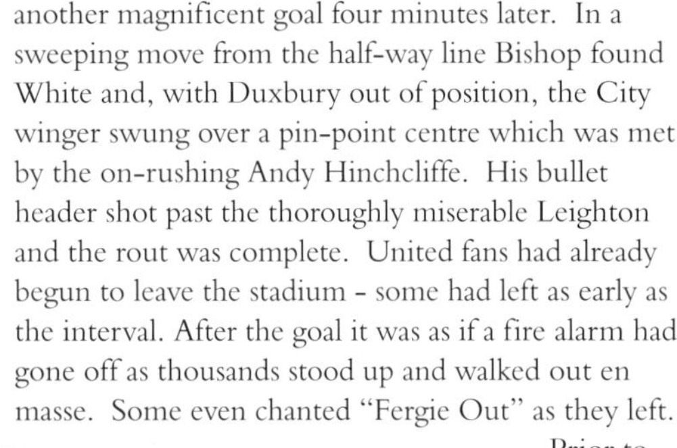

another magnificent goal four minutes later. In a sweeping move from the half-way line Bishop found White and, with Duxbury out of position, the City winger swung over a pin-point centre which was met by the on-rushing Andy Hinchcliffe. His bullet header shot past the thoroughly miserable Leighton and the rout was complete. United fans had already begun to leave the stadium - some had left as early as the interval. After the goal it was as if a fire alarm had gone off as thousands stood up and walked out en masse. Some even chanted "Fergie Out" as they left.

Prior to the match many United fans had boasted this would be their biggest derby win of all time. Instead, it was City's biggest Maine Road derby victory, and best derby win since 1926 when the Blues crushed United 6-1 at Old Trafford. It was also Mel Machin's finest moment as manager and one which no Blue will ever forget. For thousands of

City leave sad United behind

Man City 5 Man United 1
by RICHARD BOTT

ONE sensation followed another in the first Manchester League derby for three years.

Later, commendably restrained, Ferguson confessed: "This was our worst ...

City's young terriers, who had run their up-town rivals ragged and posed some serious questions about the quality and nerve of some expensive recruits, ...

supporters it remains their favourite game of all time.

For local broadcaster James H Reeve it was a great moment. He spoke for all Blues when he said on radio after the match: "If the grim reaper came to claim me tonight I wouldn't give a monkeys."

Afterwards Alex Ferguson commented United had missed Bryan Robson and the influential captain would have had a major effect on the result of the game, but City were without number one 'keeper Andy Dibble, expensive signing Clive Allen, and determined battler Neil McNab.

A week later 'Machin's Marvels', as they were now dubbed, defeated Luton 3-1 at Maine Road with Paul Cooper saving the 56th penalty of his long career. Throughout the game the fans chanted about the 5-1 massacre, while thousands of T-shirts celebrating the event were sold outside the stadium. Sue Mott of the *Sunday Times* soaked up the atmosphere and predicted a bright future for City's young side: "There is evidence beyond wilful optimism that some fine development is going on at the club. Although the market in blow-up bananas and other items of rubberabilia has deflated, the noisy occupants of the Kippax Stand denoted their joyous solidarity by donning the loud-mouthed tee-shirts. Could be an expensive new trend, this, not to mention a severe run on the polyester trade.

"But while lamenting the potential strain on the cotton boll, those of the green persuasion must be consoled that City's current spurt of form owes nothing at all to crass consumerism. The whole team has been assembled for £1.9 million and much of their talent is home-grown."

If fans were beginning to believe the Blues were moving closer to their dream of challenging once more for the game's top honours, the trip to Arsenal on 14th October was a sharp reminder. A deeply depressing 4-0 defeat brought back all the old doubts and left Machin and the fans looking for an excuse. They found one - City's shirts. For some reason City had opted to wear a new strip of yellow for the Highbury match, and it was obvious to all that Umbro had hastily made the shirts - even the 'Brother' lettering was peeling off. The yellow shirts were blamed for the drubbing and disappeared within days of the match. Even so some supporters had already made enquiries at the souvenir shop to purchase replicas!

Eight days after the Arsenal debacle, Aston Villa defeated City 2-0 at Maine Road in a televised match. It was another depressing game and one which saw Trevor Morley dismissed, along with Villa's Stuart Gray, despite being the innocent party. The influential Neil McNab, whose contract would be up in the summer, had not been included in the side at all, while two strikers Clive Allen and Justin Fashanu were named as substitutes. It was all a little perplexing for City's supporters who were trying hard to accept Machin's team selections but found many too confusing to make sense. Fashanu had been given a chance to resurrect his career by Machin, but that never really proved successful either.

On 28th October a superb equaliser from Clive Allen a minute from time gave City a point at fourth placed Chelsea, then the Maine Road visit of Crystal Palace brought the first League victory since Luton in September. Palace were still smarting from a 9-0 hammering at Anfield plus a 5-0 League Cup exit against Forest and, with the Blues making all the early play, it was inevitable City should race into the lead. David White netted first, in the pouring rain, then Trevor Morley made it 2-0 before the interval. Clive Allen scored the third and final goal in the second half, although the Blues had another effort ruled out. Unlike the previous years, City finished this Palace game without losing their 'keeper, although a confrontation between Mark Bright and Andy Dibble might have turned nasty!

The Blues were now in 14th place and were clearly primed for victory in their next match - a rather easy looking trip to 17th placed Derby County. It proved a major embarrassment as City succumbed to their biggest defeat in 27 years – 6-0. After missing a couple of easy chances the Blues were already two goals down by half-time. In the second half they looked even more nervous and the introduction of two substitutes - Fashanu and Beckford - did not improve City's jitters.

A 3-0 home defeat by Forest followed although the match was more notable for the fact Colin Hendry made his City debut, then four days later Coventry City knocked the Blues out of the League Cup with a 1-0 Maine Road victory in the fourth round. Earlier in that competition the Blues had defeated Brentford 4-1, after a 2-1 reverse at Griffin Park, and Machin's old side Norwich 3-1 at Maine Road.

On 25th November, during the train journey to Charlton Athletic, City fans were told by a club official that Machin was just one game from the sack. Understandably, neither Machin nor the players were at their best and Charlton took the lead in the sixth minute. Clive Allen netted an equaliser, thanks to a flick by new boy Hendry, a few minutes later. The victory Machin needed did not follow and the match ended 1-1.

Machin paid the price but few understood exactly why. It was true his team selections frequently looked bizarre with often an unnecessarily defensive style, or occasionally too many forwards sitting on the bench while the team struggled to find the net, but given time he would surely have solved these elementary problems. His purchases had, in the main, been good ones. Who could argue that Clive Allen, Colin Hendry, Ian Bishop, and even Andy Dibble didn't contribute much. Each of these players seemed value for money and would, given time, have helped the Blues achieve some form of success.

Tellingly, Peter Swales claimed two reasons why he had been dismissed. The first was pressure from the fans - total rubbish! The second was that Machin had no 'repartee' with the fans - he meant rapport but at this stage in Swales' career any excuse seemed possible. Visions of Machin and Frizzell being forced to do a song and dance routine to preserve their positions appeared in the press.

Machin had been asked to resign at first but, when he refused, Swales was forced to sack him. At the time Machin was shocked: "I leave Maine Road with my conscience clear. The club are in a far healthier position than when I arrived, both financially as well as from a playing point of view.... What do they want?"

The fanzine *Blue Print* demanded to know the answer as it clearly expressed its view that Swales, not the fans, had lost faith in Machin: "Peter Swales and his directorate are preparing to wash the blood from their hands in the tide of support which called for the removal of the manager towards the end of last season. Official communiqués from Maine Road will confirm that Mr. Machin has been sacrificed because of his enduring unpopularity with sections of the crowd. If the opinions of supporters counted for anything in the executive decision making process, Peter Swales would not be at Manchester City and in a position to seek scapegoats. There certainly were critics of Machin in the crowd and they made themselves heard in fanzines and on the terraces but this move has come from the massed ranks of nervous directors (not necessarily Swales) anxious to avoid placing their investment in jeopardy."

The fanzine continued to highlight Machin's many achievements at Maine Road: "Mel Machin must be a very disappointed and bitter man: Under his guidance City have been promoted; he has received at least one Bell's Manager of the Month award; he convinced the Board to part with £1 million for one

Colin Hendry made his debut for the Blues in a 3-0 home defeat by Nottingham Forest in November 1989.

When City beat Luton 3-1 in September 1989 Paul Cooper made the 56th penalty save of his career!

'I hear they've fitted an ejector seat!'

player; and attendances have steadily increased. If only Alex Ferguson could achieve half as much (with infinite resources). As a manager he has done all that was asked of him and will be recorded in the annals of Manchester City history as the manager at the time of the 10-1 and the 5-1 Maine Road Massacre. He brought financial stability to the club with the sale of Paul Stewart for an incredibly over-inflated sum of money. He recruited Ian Bishop, Clive Allen and Andy Dibble to the fold and stood by his conviction that Trevor Morley would prove to be a fine player (ironically, Morley's absence in recent weeks is said to be a major factor in the collapse of form). Compared to other League managers he has led the life of a monk and conspicuously failed to bring scandal or ridicule to the club."

The article ended with concern over City's future: "Perhaps Peter Swales would like to reflect that he cannot appoint another managerial team which does not bring the successes so often promised and so seldom delivered. At the time of writing (27/11/89) no successor has been chosen, rumours are rife and expectations tending to be pessimistic... Don Howe and Dave Bassett have been mentioned in despatches. We could live to regret the passing of that quiet unassuming man from East Anglia, this period could be a very unhappy watershed in the history of Manchester City."

The views of the *Blue Print* writers were consistent with the majority of supporters and the other fanzines. Both *Electric Blue* and *King of the Kippax* found it hard to accept that the fans could be held responsible. *Electric Blue*: "The worst thing about it though was that Swales blamed us, the fans for getting Mel Machin sacked, which was right out of order. When did Swales ever listen to us? If he did he would have walked out years ago. 'Swales Out!' With a bit of luck he might do that next time, get your banners out!"

Immediately after the Charlton match, rumours circulated Howard Kendall was to be offered the job. Interestingly, he had been in Manchester the night before to present a City shirt to a young girl on Granada's 'Kick Off' programme. The girl expressed concern about City's loss of form and Kendall stated he believed the situation would quickly improve. Whether it was an innocent comment or not hardly mattered as City fans began to guess Kendall was lined up as the new manager. Strangely, City denied it and on the following Friday, 1st December, again on 'Kick

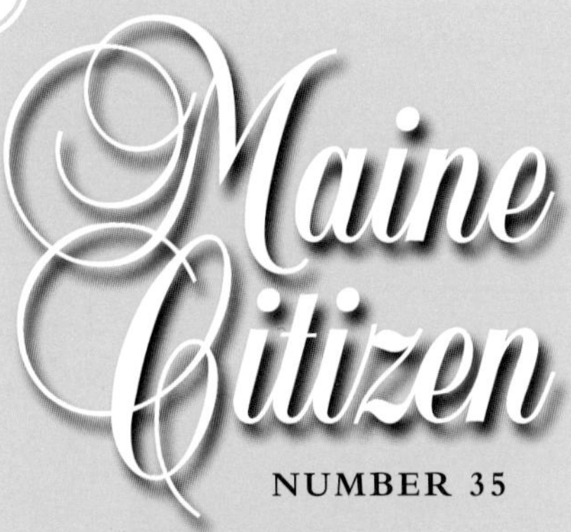

NUMBER 35

IAN BISHOP

Ian Bishop is profiled in this book primarily for the cult status he achieved during his first spell at the club, but his second stint also brought a few high points, especially his appearance as substitute at Wembley in 1999.

Bishop's first spell at Maine Road commenced on 7th July 1989 when he arrived from Bournemouth for a figure quoted at the time as £750,000. Two months earlier he had played against City for Bournemouth during the Blues' crucial promotion seeking period, yet less than six months later he was on his way to West Ham United. In between he became a true hero to thousands of City fans.

Born in Liverpool on 29th May 1965 Bishop had originally played for Howard Kendall's Everton side in 1983. Kendall never really believed he would make the grade at Goodison and so persuaded him to sign for Carlisle United. By the time City caught up with him in 1989 he was a very important member of Harry Redknapp's Bournemouth team.

Once he signed for Mel Machin, he seemed to fit in perfectly with City's attacking ambitions. He delighted fans with his style and flair and on 23rd September 1989 cemented his status following his diving header which brought City's third goal against United in the Maine Road massacre. There is a memorable photograph taken shortly after that goal of Bishop with fist in air, being carried by Paul Lake. The photo summed up the feelings of thousands of Blues.

Bishop was an ever-present until the arrival of Howard Kendall in mid-December. For Kendall's initial game in charge he named Bishop as substitute for the first time and the fans protested. Kendall: "It was not a popular move. I walked out at 2.55 p.m. to hear my supporters chanting, 'There's only one Ian Bishop'. Nice welcome that was."

Kendall found it hard to accept the player's popularity: "The Bishop situation developed into a saga, the like of which I have never experienced in football before. Had he been the focal point of the Maine Road crowd's adulation for several years I could have understood the sense of outrage but he'd only made a handful of senior appearances since moving from Bournemouth. I think one of our problems was that he had played very well, and scored, during the 5-1 victory over Manchester United earlier in the season. I got the impression that many City fans were happy to hang on to the sweet memory of that one game and ignore everything else that was happening."

When Kendall decided to sell Bishop to West Ham the new boss realised just how cherished Bishop was by City's support: "The backlash was so strong you would have thought the lad was a living legend who had been a key figure in the City side for many years. I couldn't believe anybody could be that popular in a team which was not performing well and which was struggling at the foot of the table."

For City supporters Bishop's departure was a major loss. They had adopted Bishop as their cult hero following the departure of Paul Moulden, and the loss of the long-haired player from Liverpool was hard to bear. Often stars come and go without making much of an impact but Bishop wasn't like that. He gave the supporters a lift and proved Mel Machin really did know how to attract the better players. Bishop arrived shortly before Clive Allen and the two men added a dash of real quality to Machin's promoted side.

Even after he departed City fans refused to forget him and, later in the season, thousands of votes for Bishop were sent to the Player of the Year committee. It's not known exactly how many votes were cast for him but a supporters' club official admitted it had

Off' Peter Swales announced he wanted Oldham supremo Joe Royle to take the Blues forward.

Rather foolishly, Swales released this only an hour or so before Oldham's important Second Division clash with Blackburn Rovers. The Oldham supporters quickly made their feelings known to Royle and the former City player decided to remain at Boundary Park. Joe Royle: "It was the wrong time to leave. I believe Peter Swales announced it on 'Kick Off' on the Friday. I didn't see it, but we were playing Blackburn that night and it was not an easy decision to make even then. I just thought the timing was wrong. It's as simple as that. "I've great affection for the club, but Oldham were on their way to the biggest season in their history and I simply didn't want to walk out on that. Had it been at the start of the season or the end of that season it would have been a different thing, but the timing was wrong. Willie and I both felt there were some great people at Oldham and we didn't want to leave them in the lurch the first time they had any real success. As you know we ended up going to Wembley and to the semi-final, and semi-final replay. And nearly made the playoffs. So it was a big season.

"I don't regret it. I never look back anyway. There's no point. There were other times later on when the approach would have been welcome, but it never came. That was the end of it. I know that Peter Swales and one or two other directors have always felt it would have been so right at the time for me to have gone there, but it didn't happen. I know Willie was very disappointed that I didn't take it because it was his club. He had great affection for City, like me with Everton. It was his first club."

Royle was also a great friend of Mel Machin and was disgusted at the way he was dismissed: "It annoyed me the way they treated him because we all knew... and they [the directors] certainly knew they weren't too happy with him at the start of the season. There were plenty of rumours. Why did they wait? Bad timing. Exceptionally bad timing!"

After Royle turned the Blues down, City had the small task of facing Liverpool at Maine Road. An official attendance of 31,641 was quoted although *King of the Kippax* calculated this meant there were only 7,622 in the Kippax Stand. The figure seemed exceptionally low and raised further questions about the direction of the club.

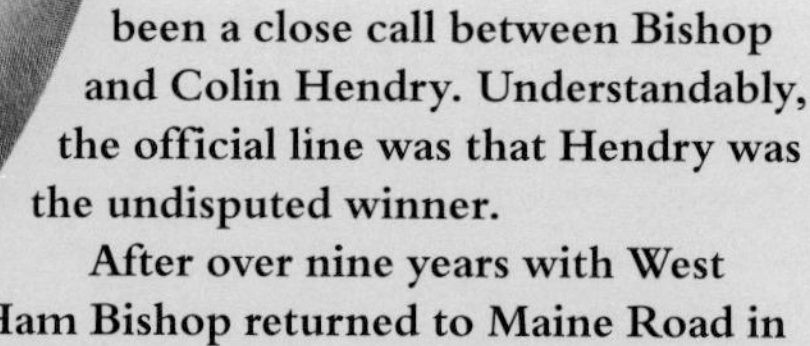

Ian (right) salutes his goal in the 5-1 derby win, assisted by Paul Lake.

BISHOP'S PLAYING RECORD

	LEAGUE		FA CUP		FL CUP		FM CUP		TOTAL	
	App	Gls	App	Gls	App	Gls	App	Gls	App	Gls
1989-90	18(1)	2	-	-	4	1	1	-	23(1)	3
1997-98	4(2)	-	-	-	-	-	-	-	4(2)	-
1998-99	21(4)	-	1(1)	-	-	-	-	-	22(5)	-
1999-00	25(12)	2	2	2	1(2)	-	-	-	28(14)	4
2000-01	3(7)	-	0(1)	-	2(3)	-	-	-	5(11)	-
TOTAL	71(26)	4	3(2)	2	7(5)	1	1	-	82(33)	7

been a close call between Bishop and Colin Hendry. Understandably, the official line was that Hendry was the undisputed winner.

After over nine years with West Ham Bishop returned to Maine Road in 1998 on a free transfer. Supporters were excited when the news of his return filtered through and, although his subsequent performances varied, he did manage to prove Joe Royle was right to bring him back.

During this difficult period in City's history, Bishop was used as a calming influence. His experience helped the Blues re-establish themselves as a force and at times his class and great tactical brain shone through. He no longer had the pace of youth, however his perception helped him overcome the difficulties. He was an extremely valuable creative midfielder, at a time when City struggled in this area.

His final match for the Blues was a 1-1 Premier League draw at Coventry on New Year's Day 2001, and the following March he moved to Miami Fusion in the USA. It was fitting he ended his City career at the highest level.

In his spare time he became known for his cartoon strip writing skills, and produced football-related stories for children.

Bishop was always an enigma in the eyes of Howard Kendall who could not understand the player's popularity with fans. He assumed it was because Ian had scored in the 5-1 massacre of United, but that wasn't the only reason. Bishop was a quality player who encouraged many with his approach to the game and typified the late Eighties spirit of the club.

Promotion hero Trevor Morley was given a tremendous send off.

Peter Reid was Howard Kendall's first signing, a free transfer from Queens Park Rangers.

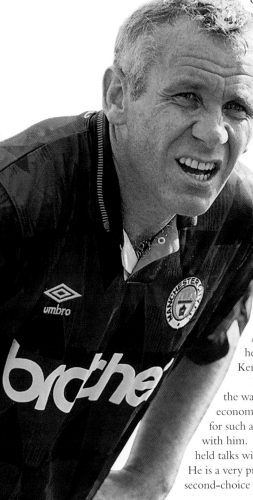

Naturally, the Merseysiders defeated City 4-1 although the Blues, guided by caretaker Tony Book, did actually play better than usual. The Liverpool supporters chanted "Swales Out", which was later explained as being a genuine demonstration of support for their Manchester rivals. A Liverpool fanzine believed Swales had "turned a great club into a joke!" The sentiment was appreciated by the fans, but not by the Chairman who was now taking steps to appoint a new manager.

Prior to the Royle fiasco, Swales had considered another former Everton player, Howard Kendall.

Kendall, the former Everton and Bilbao manager had planned to take life easy for a while after returning to England from Spain, but with rumours about Alex Ferguson's job at Old Trafford it seemed likely he would return to management rather more quickly than anticipated. He told reporters he had no interest in Ferguson's future but events at Maine Road kindled a desire to rebuild his managerial career: "Twenty-four hours after City had sacked Mel Machin I received a 'phone call from a third party asking me if I would be interested in taking over at Maine Road. I had to admit that I was interested because City is a very big club."

Kendall soon met Swales and they discussed terms with the former Everton man insisting on a get-out clause: "As I had done in the past, I simply wanted to protect myself by attempting to cover every eventuality. The clause which I wanted written in to any contract would guarantee my release if another club was to agree to meet a set figure of compensation and would guarantee me a pre-arranged sum in compensation if I was to be dismissed. Obviously, Peter Swales was concerned about the possibility of my taking the City job and then walking out, a few months later, to manage England. He said he felt his club should be entitled to receive compensation if that was to happen. I disagreed and pointed out that my previous employers had been more than happy to insert the disputed clause in my contract. I don't think I was being deceptive or using underhand methods in any way at all. I certainly wasn't looking to use Manchester City as a stepping stone en route to an even more prestigious job."

When Kendall left Swales' home the two men had failed to reach agreement. Swales turned his attention to Royle and Kendall believed his chance had gone. According to Kendall, Royle discovered he had not been first choice and 'phoned Kendall to discover the truth.

Kendall: "I suppose I could have paved the way for his appointment by being economical with the truth but I had known Joe for such a long time that I felt it only fair to level with him. Once I confirmed that I had indeed held talks with City, Joe said he was pulling out. He is a very proud man and the idea of only being second-choice did not appeal to him one little bit."

A short while later Kendall was at Manchester airport ready to return to Spain to sort out a few domestic arrangements when a City representative informed him Swales had now agreed to the contractual clauses. Kendall: "I couldn't believe my good fortune, for less than a month after returning home I had been placed in charge of one of the biggest and best-supported clubs in Britain."

On 9th December Kendall flew directly to Southampton from Spain to watch City take on Saints. The Blues, managed by Tony Book and Ken Barnes, were leading 1-0 after 75 minutes. Then Kendall winced as a quickly taken free-kick led to an equaliser from Wallace, before Horne scored a wonder goal five minutes later. The first appearance of Ashley Ward as substitute for David Oldfield was encouraging, but the 2-1 defeat left the Blues struggling.

With typical City irony, Kendall's first game in charge had to be the away trip at Goodison Park. The Blues were bottom of the table on 15 points while Everton were ninth, and the encounter was to be screened live on television. Already Kendall had taken steps to change the City line-up. He'd managed to bring QPR's Peter Reid north on a free transfer to play a vital role in his new managerial team and to instil a bit of confidence on the pitch: "I still thought he had the stamina to perform at the top level and I knew he would be invaluable in terms of motivating and encouraging those players of lesser experience within the dressing room."

With Reid he assessed the squad and believed it too weak to mount a serious attempt at moving off the bottom. He approached Swales for money to enter the transfer market: "Because I was thinking long term, because I was expecting to spend a considerable length of time at the club, because I was determined to transform Manchester City into a team capable of winning the League Championship, I held out my hand and asked for the cash. I knew Alan Harper was having a bad time at Sheffield Wednesday, so I contacted Ron Atkinson and agreed a £150,000 deal. I remember telling my coaching staff at City that if the club was to develop along the same lines as we had at Everton, I wouldn't be happy until Alan was unable to guarantee himself a regular, first team place. I wanted to build a side which was so good Alan would once again have to resort to knocking on my office door to complain about lack of opportunity."

Both Harper and Reid made their debuts in the Everton match. Other former Evertonians in the team included Gary Megson and Ian Bishop, although Bishop had not had a good time at Goodison. The game ended goalless and, though it was not a pretty performance, City were satisfied with a point.

By the time of the next match on Boxing Day, rumours were circulating that Bishop was on his way out. 'Bish' was already a cult figure at Maine Road and seemed to offer so much, yet Kendall was keen to use him as bait to tempt other clubs to part with the players he preferred. Another who looked doomed was promotion hero Trevor Morley. As both men came out for the Boxing Day clash with Norwich the supporters chanted their names and gave clear notice to the new manager that some players were considered more important than others. A few banners lined the front of the Kippax. One simply stated: "Bish and Trevor don't go."

When Morley was substituted he was given a

Off' Peter Swales announced he wanted Oldham supremo Joe Royle to take the Blues forward.

Rather foolishly, Swales released this only an hour or so before Oldham's important Second Division clash with Blackburn Rovers. The Oldham supporters quickly made their feelings known to Royle and the former City player decided to remain at Boundary Park. Joe Royle: "It was the wrong time to leave. I believe Peter Swales announced it on 'Kick Off' on the Friday. I didn't see it, but we were playing Blackburn that night and it was not an easy decision to make even then. I just thought the timing was wrong. It's as simple as that. "I've great affection for the club, but Oldham were on their way to the biggest season in their history and I simply didn't want to walk out on that. Had it been at the start of the season or the end of that season it would have been a different thing, but the timing was wrong. Willie and I both felt there were some great people at Oldham and we didn't want to leave them in the lurch the first time they had any real success. As you know we ended up going to Wembley and to the semi-final, and semi-final replay. And nearly made the playoffs. So it was a big season.

"I don't regret it. I never look back anyway. There's no point. There were other times later on when the approach would have been welcome, but it never came. That was the end of it. I know that Peter Swales and one or two other directors have always felt it would have been so right at the time for me to have gone there, but it didn't happen. I know Willie was very disappointed that I didn't take it because it was his club. He had great affection for City, like me with Everton. It was his first club."

Royle was also a great friend of Mel Machin and was disgusted at the way he was dismissed: "It annoyed me the way they treated him because we all knew... and they [the directors] certainly knew they weren't too happy with him at the start of the season. There were plenty of rumours. Why did they wait? Bad timing. Exceptionally bad timing!"

After Royle turned the Blues down, City had the small task of facing Liverpool at Maine Road. An official attendance of 31,641 was quoted although *King of the Kippax* calculated this meant there were only 7,622 in the Kippax Stand. The figure seemed exceptionally low and raised further questions about the direction of the club.

Ian (right) salutes his goal in the 5-1 derby win, assisted by Paul Lake.

been a close call between Bishop and Colin Hendry. Understandably, the official line was that Hendry was the undisputed winner.

After over nine years with West Ham Bishop returned to Maine Road in 1998 on a free transfer. Supporters were excited when the news of his return filtered through and, although his subsequent performances varied, he did manage to prove Joe Royle was right to bring him back.

During this difficult period in City's history, Bishop was used as a calming influence. His experience helped the Blues re-establish themselves as a force and at times his class and great tactical brain shone through. He no longer had the pace of youth, however his perception helped him overcome the difficulties. He was an extremely valuable creative midfielder, at a time when City struggled in this area.

His final match for the Blues was a 1-1 Premier League draw at Coventry on New Year's Day 2001, and the following March he moved to Miami Fusion in the USA. It was fitting he ended his City career at the highest level.

In his spare time he became known for his cartoon strip writing skills, and produced football-related stories for children.

Bishop was always an enigma in the eyes of Howard Kendall who could not understand the player's popularity with fans. He assumed it was because Ian had scored in the 5-1 massacre of United, but that wasn't the only reason. Bishop was a quality player who encouraged many with his approach to the game and typified the late Eighties spirit of the club.

BISHOP'S PLAYING RECORD

	LEAGUE		FA CUP		FL CUP		FM CUP		TOTAL	
	App	Gls	App	Gls	App	Gls	App	Gls	App	Gls
1989-90	18(1)	2	-	-	4	1	1	-	23(1)	3
1997-98	4(2)	-	-	-	-	-	-	-	4(2)	-
1998-99	21(4)	-	1(1)	-	-	-	-	-	22(5)	-
1999-00	25(12)	2	2	2	1(2)	-	-	-	28(14)	4
2000-01	3(7)	-	0(1)	-	2(3)	-	-	-	5(11)	-
TOTAL	71(26)	4	3(2)	2	7(5)	1	1	-	82(33)	7

Promotion hero Trevor Morley was given a tremendous send off.

Naturally, the Merseysiders defeated City 4-1 although the Blues, guided by caretaker Tony Book, did actually play better than usual. The Liverpool supporters chanted "Swales Out", which was later explained as being a genuine demonstration of support for their Manchester rivals. A Liverpool fanzine believed Swales had "turned a great club into a joke!" The sentiment was appreciated by the fans, but not by the Chairman who was now taking steps to appoint a new manager.

Prior to the Royle fiasco, Swales had considered another former Everton player, Howard Kendall.

Kendall, the former Everton and Bilbao manager had planned to take life easy for a while after returning to England from Spain, but with rumours about Alex Ferguson's job at Old Trafford it seemed likely he would return to management rather more quickly than anticipated. He told reporters he had no interest in Ferguson's future but events at Maine Road kindled a desire to rebuild his managerial career: "Twenty-four hours after City had sacked Mel Machin I received a 'phone call from a third party asking me if I would be interested in taking over at Maine Road. I had to admit that I was interested because City is a very big club."

Kendall soon met Swales and they discussed terms with the former Everton man insisting on a get-out clause: "As I had done in the past, I simply wanted to protect myself by attempting to cover every eventuality. The clause which I wanted written in to any contract would guarantee my release if another club was to agree to meet a set figure of compensation and would guarantee me a pre-arranged sum in compensation if I was to be dismissed. Obviously, Peter Swales was concerned about the possibility of my taking the City job and then walking out, a few months later, to manage England. He said he felt his club should be entitled to receive compensation if that was to happen. I disagreed and pointed out that my previous employers had been more than happy to insert the disputed clause in my contract. I don't think I was being deceptive or using underhand methods in any way at all. I certainly wasn't looking to use Manchester City as a stepping stone en route to an even more prestigious job."

Peter Reid was Howard Kendall's first signing, a free transfer from Queens Park Rangers.

When Kendall left Swales' home the two men had failed to reach agreement. Swales turned his attention to Royle and Kendall believed his chance had gone. According to Kendall, Royle discovered he had not been first choice and 'phoned Kendall to discover the truth.

Kendall: "I suppose I could have paved the way for his appointment by being economical with the truth but I had known Joe for such a long time that I felt it only fair to level with him. Once I confirmed that I had indeed held talks with City, Joe said he was pulling out. He is a very proud man and the idea of only being second-choice did not appeal to him one little bit."

A short while later Kendall was at Manchester airport ready to return to Spain to sort out a few domestic arrangements when a City representative informed him Swales had now agreed to the contractual clauses. Kendall: "I couldn't believe my good fortune, for less than a month after returning home I had been placed in charge of one of the biggest and best-supported clubs in Britain."

On 9th December Kendall flew directly to Southampton from Spain to watch City take on Saints. The Blues, managed by Tony Book and Ken Barnes, were leading 1-0 after 75 minutes. Then Kendall winced as a quickly taken free-kick led to an equaliser from Wallace, before Horne scored a wonder goal five minutes later. The first appearance of Ashley Ward as substitute for David Oldfield was encouraging, but the 2-1 defeat left the Blues struggling.

With typical City irony, Kendall's first game in charge had to be the away trip at Goodison Park. The Blues were bottom of the table on 15 points while Everton were ninth, and the encounter was to be screened live on television. Already Kendall had taken steps to change the City line-up. He'd managed to bring QPR's Peter Reid north on a free transfer to play a vital role in his new managerial team and to instil a bit of confidence on the pitch: "I still thought he had the stamina to perform at the top level and I knew he would be invaluable in terms of motivating and encouraging those players of lesser experience within the dressing room."

With Reid he assessed the squad and believed it too weak to mount a serious attempt at moving off the bottom. He approached Swales for money to enter the transfer market: "Because I was thinking long term, because I was expecting to spend a considerable length of time at the club, because I was determined to transform Manchester City into a team capable of winning the League Championship, I held out my hand and asked for the cash. I knew Alan Harper was having a bad time at Sheffield Wednesday, so I contacted Ron Atkinson and agreed a £150,000 deal. I remember telling my coaching staff at City that if the club was to develop along the same lines as we had at Everton, I wouldn't be happy until Alan was unable to guarantee himself a regular, first team place. I wanted to build a side which was so good Alan would once again have to resort to knocking on my office door to complain about lack of opportunity."

Both Harper and Reid made their debuts in the Everton match. Other former Evertonians in the team included Gary Megson and Ian Bishop, although Bishop had not had a good time at Goodison. The game ended goalless and, though it was not a pretty performance, City were satisfied with a point.

By the time of the next match on Boxing Day, rumours were circulating that Bishop was on his way out. 'Bish' was already a cult figure at Maine Road and seemed to offer so much, yet Kendall was keen to use him as bait to tempt other clubs to part with the players he preferred. Another who looked doomed was promotion hero Trevor Morley. As both men came out for the Boxing Day clash with Norwich the supporters chanted their names and gave clear notice to the new manager that some players were considered more important than others. A few banners lined the front of the Kippax. One simply stated: "Bish and Trevor don't go."

When Morley was substituted he was given a

Adrian Heath, Ian Brightwell, Steve Redmond, Andy Dibble, Mark Ward, Niall Quinn, Clive Allen and David White applaud fans in the Kippax at the end of the 1989-90 season.

tremendous ovation, as was Bishop, but it was no use. Both players were soon to leave. The game with fourth placed Norwich ended in a 1-0 victory to lift them off the bottom. Two days later Mark Ward, another former Evertonian, arrived at Maine Road in a deal which sent both Bishop and Morley to West Ham in exchange. Kendall told City's fans the deal was good business for the club but few actually believed him. Kendall: "When the news of the transfer was made public there was absolute uproar. It wasn't so much that I had bought a third player with Everton connections, nor was it the fact I had sold Morley; it was my decision to let Bishop leave which so angered the general public. When I decided to sell Bishop, I was fully aware the papers would point out that it was the second time I had shown him the door because in 1984, when he was at Everton, I had sold him to Carlisle United. He had nothing more than raw talent and potential in those days and I felt it was best he moved on to gain valuable experience."

Kendall firmly believed the arrival of Mark Ward and departure of Bishop was vital. He also felt it important to use Clive Allen sparingly, something else which angered the supporters. Allen was the first truly great player since Trevor Francis and Blues' fans wanted to see him play, yet the manager persisted in naming him only as a substitute. How could a player worth a million only a few months earlier find it so hard to hold down a regular place? These were confusing times for City afficionados.

In January, after a 2-0 victory over Millwall and defeat at Sheffield Wednesday on New Year's Day, Kendall made another shock move when he brought Wayne Clarke from Leicester in exchange for David Oldfield and an amount of cash. Obviously, the move was hardly greeted with delight, especially as Clarke was yet another former Evertonian, but the manager was convinced he had a good deal. He felt particularly unhappy with the furore created: "Those supporters who were still angry about the sale of Ian Bishop did not welcome the arrival of a fourth former Everton player. They seemed to think I was pursuing a policy of jobs for the boys. The fans began to chant 'Everton reserves' during our matches and the suggestion was I was seeking permission to change the colour of City's strip from light blue to royal blue."

Later that month another ex-Evertonian Mick Heaton arrived as Kendall's assistant, and then in February Adrian Heath came from Aston Villa. Kendall: "Adrian was still full of enthusiasm and the passing of the years had not in any way eroded his skill. So I bought him. I must point out that during this period of reconstruction, not once did my Chairman question the wisdom of my transfer deals. He gave me his full support at all times and was always 100 per cent behind me. He deserves great credit for that.

"Like Clarke before him, Adrian endured a baptism of fire. I named him as a substitute for the home game against Charlton Athletic on 24th February and when I sent him on he was jeered all the way from the bench to the pitch. The problem was that to make way for Adrian, I had pulled off Steve Redmond for the first time in his entire career. The whole ground erupted as the supporters chanted, 'What the **** is going on?' The whole thing was getting out of hand."

Earlier in February, Kendall's City arrived at Old Trafford for the return derby match. So much had changed since September the game was always going to be a difficult one to call, but as the Blues were now supposedly a better side it is true to say most City fans eagerly awaited this particular

Million pound man Clive Allen was used sparingly by Howard Kendall.

match. Disappointingly, United only gave City 600 seats and 4,500 terrace tickets, although even that was considerably more than in the years that followed. The eventual attendance was only 40,274 in a stadium holding a minimum of 48,000, as many disenchanted United fans stayed away. Although there were noticeable gaps in the United sections, the paddock in front of the Main Stand appeared full of City supporters. They were later joined by Blues evacuated from the Stretford End and estimates from impartial observers suggested there were around 12,000 City fans in the 40,000 crowd.

The match was the 100th meeting in the First Division and commenced with City tearing into the Reds as they had in September. The Blues were actually two points better off than United in the League and the difference in position prompted City fans to chant "Fergie in" to annoy the home contingent.

Squandering some early chances, City looked the more composed overall but when Clarke missed a sitter some City fans still muttered about Everton rejects. It wasn't just the Evertonians who should have given City the lead; Ian Brightwell was also guilty of a shocking miss when, with Leighton off his line, the youngster feebly lobbed the ball wide.

Against the run of play it was actually United who took the lead when Clayton Blackmore was gifted a free header. Fortunately, within five minutes Mark Ward found Brightwell who, from fully 25 yards out, blasted a stunning shot past Leighton for the equaliser. Afterwards the delighted player explained exactly how he'd scored by succinctly telling the media: "I just wellied it!"

Ian Brightwell jumps for joy after 'wellying' the equaliser at Old Trafford in February 1990.

The match should have brought a City victory, but everyone seemed satisfied with a point. As the season progressed Kendall's City scraped a few draws (six 1-1 results came in February and March), and achieved a few fine wins, especially during April when five of the seven matches ended in victory. He seemed to be getting it right, in terms of results at least, and was actually starting to win the fans over after so many shock transfers. In March he paid Arsenal £800,000 for Niall Quinn, and from the moment the lanky Irishman arrived only one game ended in defeat.

The last day of the season was away to F.A. Cup finalists Crystal Palace. Palace were due to face United at Wembley the following week and, naturally, City fans wished them well. It also created a real carnival atmosphere as thousands of Mancunians travelled to London dressed as 'Blues Brothers'. The League game ended 2-2 to leave City in 14th place on 48 points.

With the season complete, City fans now felt able to look forward to a bright spell under Kendall, while the manager felt the Palace match brought him closer to the supporters: "We had guaranteed our First Division future and the thousands of supporters who travelled down to London were in jubilant mood. There was a real carnival atmosphere and, for once, they actually looked as if they were enjoying what they were seeing."

During the 1990 close season Kendall negotiated new five year contracts for 1986 Youth Cup winners David White and Paul Lake. He also shocked supporters again by transferring another coveted member of that team, Andy Hinchcliffe, to Everton in exchange for Neil Pointon and £600,000. With the arrival of yet another Evertonian came more criticism but there were also a few jokes. At one stage a rumour circulated that David Bowie's Maine Road concert had been called off. The reason? Kendall had discovered Bowie had never played for Everton!

There were other significant transfers - goalkeeper Tony Coton arrived for £900,000 and midfielder Mark Brennan for £400,000 - as Kendall began to build a side he believed was good enough to qualify for Europe. Despite the new arrivals there was still considerable sadness that a number of Blue heroes had been despatched since Machin's departure. In addition to Morley, Bishop, Oldfield and Hinchcliffe City had also lost Brian Gayle, Gary Fleming and Neil McNab.

Nevertheless, after a fine 1990 World Cup, City fans eagerly awaited the opening match of 1990-91 away to Tottenham on 25th August. This was the first opportunity for Spurs fans to greet their World Cup heroes Lineker and Gascoigne, while City also welcomed back an international star - Niall Quinn. It was also the first match following the death of former manager Joe Mercer. Poignantly City fans chanted several verses of "To see Joe Mercer's aces."

The match ended in a 3-1 defeat with Quinn netting for the Blues while new captain Paul Lake also put in a fine performance. A week later Everton were at Maine Road and Kendall's 'old Toffeemen' managed a 1-0 win with Adrian Heath scoring his third League goal for the club. It was also his only strike of the season.

Pointon and Ward supplied the goals four days later as Aston Villa went down 2-1. Andy Dibble had returned for that game while Coton was suffering with a bug. The Welsh 'keeper was quite impressive and clearly keen to erase the nightmare memory of the Forest match the previous season. At the City Ground Dibble had been preparing for a clearance punt when Gary Crosby ran up behind him and nudged the ball from Dibble's outstretched hand. The City 'keeper stood complaining while the Forest man put the ball in the net for the only goal of the game. Kendall was furious and some claim that goal ultimately led to the purchase of Coton. For Dibble it was a huge embarrassment and unfortunately one repeated several times since with the television footage of the game appearing on A Question of Sport and various sporting bloomer shows. Despite a good performance against Villa, Dibble did not retain his place and Coton was back for the following match, a 1-1 draw at Sheffield United. Someone else missing at Bramall Lane was captain Paul Lake who sustained a knee injury in a rather innocuous challenge with Villa's Tony Cascarino. Few ever imagined he would be out for the rest of the season and would struggle against injury for the following six years.

A week after the Villa match, Norwich turned up at Maine Road for their customary defeat. This time it was 2-1 thanks to substitute Mark Brennan and the improving Niall Quinn (using his feet for once!).

A Mark Ward penalty at Chelsea brought a 1-1 draw and left the club with 11 points from a possible 18. Another 1-1 followed at Wimbledon on 29th September, before Coventry were defeated 2-0. Yet another 1-1 draw arrived at Derby before the first Maine Road meeting with United since the 5-1.

As with most derbies of the period City set off determined to prove they were far from the poor relations the media always portrayed them to be. As in 1989 determined City dominated much of the early play and were 2-0 up after a couple of goals from David White in the first 27 minutes. Then in the 79th minute Colin Hendry netted City's third, although Mark Hughes had already pulled one back for the struggling Reds.

Ten minutes away from certain victory, Kendall brought on Ian Brightwell for Peter Reid. Kendall: "I decided to pull off Peter who, typically, had run himself to a virtual standstill. In layman's terms, the man was knackered. Within a matter of minutes of Peter withdrawing from the action, United had scored twice to draw level. Inevitably, I was blamed for the loss of two points - and local pride. I felt the criticism was unduly harsh because while it was true that United's revival had coincided with my decision to substitute Peter, the goals they scored were down to basic, juvenile defensive errors."

After the 3-3 draw City were defeated 2-1 by Arsenal in the 3rd round of the League Cup. On the same night Everton were beaten by Sheffield United in the same competition prompting the Goodison board to dismiss Colin Harvey. The media claimed Joe Royle was now hot favourite for the Everton job yet, incredibly Howard Kendall was offered the post.

Nine days after the derby he became Everton manager for the second time, upsetting thousands of Mancunians. The fury which greeted Kendall's desertion puzzled the media and the man himself, but the fact was City supporters had actually started to accept him. They also recognised that more than any other manager since John Bond, possibly before, the Blues actually possessed a leader capable of bringing home the silverware. He was certainly more likely to collect a League Championship than some of the other men appointed by Peter Swales. The departure really did hurt.

When Billy McNeill walked out on City to take up the manager's job at Aston Villa the supporters felt betrayed but they understood. Like Kendall, he had transformed the make up of the side bringing in players he knew, mainly Scots, to do a job but he had also given the club over three years hard work and brought promotion and a Wembley appearance.

When Kendall walked out to return to his first love, all the supporters could see were broken dreams. True relegation had been avoided, but they felt Machin may well have achieved that in any case if Swales had not pressed the panic button so early in Machin's First Division reign. The supporters then looked at Kendall's side and though they disagreed with his approach early on, they now saw hope for the future. The Blues were, they felt, destined to find success under Kendall's shrewd guidance, but once he left the dream was shattered.

More worrying for the thousands of loyal supporters was the role of Peter Swales. During the 1980s he could hardly claim to have been the best employer in the world after so many managers had either been sacked or walked out on him. Many felt the Chairman had finally got it right with Kendall but could he be trusted to get it right again? Supporters were painfully aware of the bungled attempt to bring Joe Royle to the club less than 12 months earlier.

Even if Swales were to appoint the right man, what pain would the Blues have to endure for the rest of the season as the new boss reshaped the side? Surely City could not afford to see anyone else come in and transform the line-up as Kendall had? It was all too much to swallow for many Blues and unfortunately it was Kendall who took the flak. It was understandable, but perhaps more questions should have been asked of the entire boardroom set-up at the club. Why had City made it so easy for Kendall to use his 'get-out' clause? Why had they failed to appoint Royle in the first place? And why had Machin been so cruelly sacked after bringing some exciting players and a few decent performances to the club?

Some fans started to consider what had gone wrong since the 5-1 massacre when it was Alex Ferguson, not Mel Machin, who seemed destined for the boot. United kept faith with their high-spending manager and later that season reaped the first reward - the F.A. Cup. In the years that followed they became the most successful team of the 1990s, while City struggled to find consistency. Once Machin was dismissed, manager followed manager as the club drifted into the shadows.

In 1990, Kendall's departure saw the fans unite in their desire to change the club. They called for Peter Reid to be appointed manager, and for once Peter Swales appeared to listen. The reason the supporters backed Reid was simple - they were totally depressed by the chopping and changing nature of life at Maine Road and believed Reid would pursue many of the ideas developed under Kendall. They felt he had worked closely with his old boss and would be able to maintain the rhythm. It seemed a perfect appointment from the point of view of consistency and, under Reid, City continued to progress.

Peter Reid was appointed player/manager at the demand of the fans.

In December, after victories over QPR and Tottenham, Reid brought in the Bury manager Sam Ellis as his number two. On the surface a sensible move but, over of following three years, it was to cause the new manager much heartache as Ellis's strident views seemed to cramp City's style.

At Goodison, Kendall quickly settled in to life with his old club. As with Malcolm Allison and City, the return was not a successful one yet, in 1997, following the departure of Joe Royle from the Everton manager's chair, Kendall returned yet again to Goodison for a third spell as manager, upsetting a few thousand Sheffield United supporters along the way.

Under Reid, the Blues progressed up the table. On 13th January Kendall faced City for the first time since taking over at Everton. Despite the result - a 2-0 Everton win - it was not a pleasant day for the former manager: "The afternoon was soured by the reaction of the City supporters when I took my place on the touchline shortly before kick-off. Some people now refer to that fixture as the 'Judas' game because that short, but hurtful, word was scrawled across numerous banners and flags at the City end of the ground. Actually, this particularly form of Kendall-baiting was initially used in November during City's first game after I had left the club, against Leeds United at Maine Road."

Despite the result Reid's men made steady progress and a run of victories in April helped lift the Blues to fourth. Included in that run was the Maine Road 2-1 defeat of Derby. White and Quinn had both netted for the Blues before Tony Coton was dismissed. Niall Quinn went in goal before Dean Saunders ran up to take the resultant penalty. Man of the Match Quinn saved Saunders' shot, causing the Derby man a few sleepless nights.

The fine April run ended with a marvellous 5-1 win at Villa Park in a game which saw David White become the first City player since the war to score four in an away game. A disappointing result in the Manchester derby followed (1-0 thanks to Colin Hendry diverting a Giggs effort past debutant Martyn Margetson), before a 3-2 victory on the last day of the season relegated Sunderland. Future Sunderland player Niall Quinn netted twice and White scored the other in a game notable for the large away support packed into City's old Platt Lane Stand. It was the last great crowd in a stand that was to be demolished during 1992.

BURNLEY FOOTBALL AND ATHLETIC CO. LTD., TURF MOOR, BURNLEY.
F.A. CHALLENGE CUP 3RD. ROUND
BURNLEY
V
MANCHESTER CITY
Kick-Off 12.15pm
Turf Moor Ground Burnley
Sunday 6th January 1991
Reserved Seating
£7.00
Admit Bearer to
Hanson Cricket Field Std.
Turnstiles: E, F, G, H.
Row P
Seat
Nº 0076
To be retained (see plan and conditions on reverse)
present entire ticket at turnstile for admission

The FA Cup campaign in 1990-91 saw City win at Burnley (1-0) and Port Vale (2-1) before suffering a 1-0 defeat at Notts County in round five.

The season ended with City in a respectable fifth place on 62 points - three more than Manchester United - and the supporters were delighted even if the final League position seemed a might flattering. At the time there appeared little separating the top clubs and those struggling at the foot of the table, but the Blues had made the most of their determined approach. It was the highest Blues' finish since 1978 and gave everyone a feeling of considerable satisfaction.

Right: Niall Quinn went in goal against Derby in April 1991 and saved a penalty from Dean Saunders. Quinn had already scored before taking over from the red-carded Tony Coton.

During the close season Peter Reid smashed City's transfer record with the £2.5 million arrival of Wimbledon's powerful defender Keith Curle. It seemed a great deal of money but as the Blues needed to bolster their defence, the pacy England 'B' international seemed perfect. Most were amazed the club actually had that amount of cash to spare although Reid had been forced to sell Mark Ward and Alan Harper to Everton for a fee reported to be around £1.3 million. Youngster Ashley Ward had also moved on, joining Leicester.

Curle made his debut in a 1-0 victory at Coventry on the opening day of the 1991-2 season after signing only 11 days earlier. Interestingly, Reid also believed Curle was a good motivator and had immediately appointed him captain. With Curle strengthening the defence, three points were gained in City's next match - a 2-1 home victory over Liverpool. That game was memorable for yet another penalty by Dean Saunders. Recalling the Derby penalty the season before, City's fans laughed at Saunders again as the Liverpool man ran up and blasted the ball against the bar!

City now moved into second place and eagerly awaited their third game in seven days. This time the victims were Crystal Palace as the Blues achieved a 3-2 Maine Road victory to put them top of the table, thanks to a Brennan penalty five minutes from time. A goal-less midweek draw followed at Norwich before City suffered their first defeat of the campaign away at Arsenal. A return to form followed against Nottingham Forest as Quinn and Andy Hill combined to bring a 2-1 victory.

Sadly, form deteriorated in September with three successive defeats - including the grudge Maine Road match with Kendall's Everton. In the last minute of that game Michael Hughes appeared the only player courageous enough to take a penalty awarded for a foul on Hendry by Mark Ward, yet the youngster nervously sent the ball over the bar.

Results turned City's way again during October and November as the Blues enjoyed a seven game unbeaten run in the League. In fact they lost only one of their sixteen matches between the start of October and the first week of February. During that sequence the 115th Manchester League derby ended goalless although Adrian Heath performed astonishingly well considering the abuse he now received on a regular basis. Heath had been involved in a car crash only hours before the game yet still managed a stylish display rarely seen since his arrival at Maine Road. Unfortunately, the diminutive striker received yet more barracking for his role in City's greatest chance to break the deadlock. Mike Sheron had put Heath in the clear. The former Evertonian raced forward, looking certain to score but carelessly the little striker blasted the ball over and the game ended goalless.

It proved to be Heath's last season at Maine Road and, although he received large chunks of criticism during his time in Manchester, with hindsight he contributed more than most people realise. Granted his goalscoring record was exceptionally poor but the number of balls he laid on for others was really quite phenomenal. Videos of the period 1990 to 1992 reveal the numerous goals and chances created by Heath and justify the true value of Kendall's controversial signing. He was transferred to Stoke City in March 1992.

WHITE HOT

David White strides past Aston Villa's Andy Comyn to score after just four minutes at Villa Park in April 1991. White (below) went on to become the first City player to score four goals in an away game since the War.

Other players sold during the season included Colin Hendry, who returned to Second Division Blackburn in November 1991, and Clive Allen, who went to Chelsea in December and scored a beautiful goal against City on New Year's Day. Both transfers greatly disappointed City's fans, especially Hendry's. However, since the arrival of Keith Curle it had been clear City could not support Hendry, Curle, and Redmond. Blues fans felt Redmond should have been the man sacrificed as Hendry seemed to offer so much more. As substitute he had even featured in attack, netting against West Ham.

One player who arrived during the season was hard man Steve McMahon who had played against the Blues on 21st December at Anfield when it was already certain he would be off to Maine Road. He did little in that game, although City's travelling support made sure he knew he would be welcome in Manchester. On Christmas Eve he moved for £900,000 and on Boxing Day played in a 2-1 defeat of Norwich. Unfortunately he received a nasty injury during the match and missed the following three League games. He ended the season with 18 League appearances as City's midfield toughened up, albeit at the expense of mobility.

From February 1992 the Blues lost a little form and a few rumbles began to suggest life behind the scenes was not as it should be. There were reports that Sam Ellis, Reid's assistant, had made a few enemies among the players and there were even suggestions there had been a few training pitch scuffles. Under the heading "Rumours" the fanzine *King of the Kippax* surprised fans with this story: "Tony Coton missed a few games early this season because of a damaged hand. The rumour is he damaged it whilst hitting Sam Ellis... what is worse, it appears a few others don't like Sam either - no names though, just remember it is Olympic year."

With disharmony spreading, according to the rumours, supporters began to question whether Reid had been right to draft in Ellis. It appeared many of the problems had arrived with the blunt ex-Bury boss and City's style of play had changed for the worse but was Ellis responsible or Reid? No one seemed able to pinpoint the precise cause but as the Blues were still progressing overall in the League the matter was

Keith Curle equalised from the penalty spot as ten-man City earned a 1-1 draw in the April 1992 Old Trafford derby.

allowed to simmer away in the background. Had it been tackled there and then, the course of Reid's managerial reign may well have changed for the better. Instead problems mounted and Reid ultimately paid the price.

March 1992 was a miserable month with only one point out of 12 but April proved almost perfect. On the 4th, Championship hopefuls Leeds United arrived at Maine Road expecting the Blues to lie down and surrender the points, especially as United were their nearest rivals for the title. In true City style the Blues murdered Leeds 4-0. It was a result that pleased all but the realisation also dawned that City had basically handed the title to United on a plate. The following Tuesday City had a chance to further influence events with their visit to Old Trafford, but few really expected a victory this time.

After only 21 minutes play the Reds sneaked the lead. Not much else happened until the second half when Niall Quinn headed wide, then a short while later Neil Pointon deliberately sent Ryan Giggs crashing to the ground. A free-for-all followed with Steve Bruce punching Niall Quinn. The referee tried to calm the situation but only managed to send Pointon off. The player had to go, but City fans murmured a United man should have joined him.

David White's pace proved too much for United and Steve Bruce lunged at him in the area. Amazingly Bruce again stayed on the pitch while captain Keith Curle prepared for the penalty. He ran up and tucked the ball to Schmeichel's left to make the score 1-1. A City fan ran on to the pitch and jumped into the skipper's arms much to the delight of the rest of the jubilant City followers.

More pressure followed with White, who had become a father that morning, and £500,000 March signing from Swindon Fitzroy Simpson both going close. At the end the Blue supporters sang "Ten men..you couldn't beat ten men", while Reds' fans insisted they would still win the title.

Less than a month later Leeds dramatically snatched the Championship, while City defeated Oldham 5-2 to end the campaign in fifth place for the second consecutive term. Although much of the season was disappointing because of the loss of several popular players and the largely uninspiring style of play, the final placing at least offered hope that City might soon find real success.

In the two major cup competitions during 1991-2 City were defeated by Middlesbrough 2-1 away from home. In the League Cup they had reached the fourth round, while in the F.A. Cup the Blues managed only one match.

Overall the period from 1989 to 1992 was successful in that it had seen the Blues end two respectable campaigns in fifth position, and establish the club again as a true First Division force. They ended the term with a knowledgeable football man in charge, and had high hopes for the future. On the negative side the fans were still restless about City's lack of trophy success and worried by rumours circulating from several cognisant sources within the club. It seemed, amid all the promise, the club might be in danger of taking its eye off the ball.

During 1991-2 an article appeared in a leading football magazine which quoted Peter Swales: "City were the last Manchester side to win the Championship, they will also be the next."

The comment was vintage Swales. He wanted the best for the Blues and tried to whip up enthusiasm by boasting of what he believed City could achieve. Unfortunately, with United developing so rapidly many felt Swales really had to fulfil this promise.

With his record of rarely keeping a manager for more than three seasons, 1992-3 was always likely to become make or break for Peter Reid. It would also be Swales' last chance to succeed.

In August Reid took steps to strengthen his side. First he signed Oldham's skilful Rick Holden in a deal which saw Neil Pointon and Steve Redmond move to Boundary Park, then paid an incredible £2.5 million for Wimbledon's Terry Phelan, although he did not make his debut until City's fourth match of the season.

The Dons' supporters joked their continuing life in the top flight was down to regular purchases by the Blues. Defenders Gayle, Curle and Phelan had all arrived at Maine Road from Wimbledon in expensive transfers; even Gayle's at £325,000 in June 1988 was considered so at the time.

The loss of Pointon and Redmond was a blow and the money spent on Phelan seemed absurd when only a few months earlier the Blues possessed more quality defenders than they actually needed. The talented Hendry had been forced out, while Pointon had won many supporters with his combative nature. Most were confused by the club's overall strategy especially as everyone recognised it was in midfield and attack that the Blues were particularly weak. Niall Quinn desperately needed support up front, while a midfield that regularly relied on the 36 year old Peter Reid was hardly classed as one for the future.

Despite the worrying nature of City's transfer activity, few could argue that Terry Phelan was not a useful player. He was certainly a fast left back and had already broken into Jack Charlton's Republic of Ireland squad, winning eight caps. Likewise winger Rick Holden was expected to be a valuable addition, especially as he was the First Division player credited with the most 'assists' the previous season.

Behind the scenes long-serving physio Roy Bailey had been dismissed, while Chief Scout Ken Barnes retired. Worse was to follow as Glyn Pardoe, a very popular and successful youth coach, was also forced out. With Barnes and Pardoe gone, it seemed the club had forgotten how City had only survived much of the mid eighties onwards because of youth players brought to the club by Barnes and trained by Pardoe.

Despite City's changes a new season brought much optimism, especially as this was the first after football's restructure. The Blues were now part of the newly formed FA Premier League with the old Second Division renamed the First. The new League was viewed by those outside to have been created by the wealthiest clubs, driven by a desire to make even more money whilst allowing the poorer teams to struggle. City, being a glamour club, were keen to play a major part in the formation of the League and were determined to find success. They were also quick to embrace football's new commercial arrangements by hosting the first Premier League game shown live on satellite television.

The visit of QPR was re-arranged to take place on Monday 17th August as part of the Sky TV deal and City fans were greeted by live music, fireworks, Red Devil parachutists (who were booed because of their name!), and dancing girls. It all seemed a bit excessive for a dark Manchester night but the television viewers probably enjoyed it and the club made a bit of money, so few complained.

The one truly bright spot of the entire evening was the return of Paul Lake to the City team. Lake had been battling to recover from a cruciate ligament injury since September 1990 and it seemed, as the teams were announced, that Lake had finally won his battle. With him working in midfield alongside Steve McMahon the Blues appeared to have finally gained the right control and blend in an area where they had struggled for two seasons.

City put QPR under considerable pressure and Lake produced an intelligent pass to Niall Quinn. The lanky striker sent in a good shot, but although it was saved the ball rebounded out to David White who scored the first of his 16 that season.

In the second half, QPR equalised with a rocket from Andy Sinton, while Lake was understandably substituted by Mike Sheron. Two days later a disastrous night in Middlesbrough left City defeated 2-0 by their bogey side. It was a night of pain, especially for Paul Lake who, after only eight minutes, fell to the ground clutching his knee. City fans knew immediately it was serious, and the player was carefully helped from the pitch to begin another long battle for fitness.

On the same night Niall Quinn was sent off to leave a ten man side struggling. Peter Reid severely criticised his players afterwards, yet little changed when City went down to a 1-0 defeat against big spending Blackburn the following Saturday.

The fourth game of the season saw Terry Phelan make his debut in a 3-1 defeat of Norwich. It was City's first Premier League victory and brought much relief to Reid and Ellis, but it wasn't to last. Oldham arrived at Maine Road on 29th August and took part in one of City's inconsistent specials. The Blues had led 2-0 and then 3-1 with goals from Quinn, Vonk and White but then capitulated as Oldham scored

Rick Holden moved to City in the summer of '92 in a deal which involved Neil Pointon and Steve Redmond joining Oldham.

A tragic night for Paul Lake at Middlesbrough in August 1992 saw him break down again in only his second game back after a long lay-off. It was to be his last game.

Left: Neil Pointon in action during City's 4-0 defeat of champions-to-be Leeds in April 1992. A few months later Pointon was to leave for Oldham.

another two and had a Steve Redmond effort disallowed. The 3-3 scoreline brought a point but left most Blues fans needing tranquilisers as nerves were severely tested. A David White goal brought victory in September at Wimbledon, but only 4,714 fans witnessed a game which also proved the enduring value of Peter Reid. The City player-manager was the undisputed Man of the Match after starting his first game of the season and instilled a bit of grit into City's game. He replaced himself with Steve McMahon once his legs tired, but selected himself again for the following trip to Sheffield Wednesday. At Wednesday City, wearing their third strip of white shirts, managed their first Hillsborough League victory since the final day of the 1969-70 season with White scoring twice and Vonk once to provide a 3-0 scoreline. Three successive 1-0 defeats followed before City's next point - 2-2 against Nottingham Forest in early October when the inconsistent Blues twice took the lead only to allow Forest back into the match.

By this stage City fans were becoming less and less tolerant of Peter Reid and Sam Ellis. They were unhappy with City's sterile style of play and found it difficult to accept the Blues were not playing entertaining football. Throughout history City had excited their supporters and only resorted to the long ball when the tactic became absolutely vital to avoid relegation or embarrassing defeat. Now, it seemed, the long ball was the preferred method.

Garry Flitcroft scored his first City League goal away to Ipswich in December 1992. A week later he scored his second and, by the time of this photograph nine months later, was an important and popular member of the first team.

In October a *Manchester Evening News* back page story brought an admission that Peter Swales was not prepared to allow his manager to spend any more cash on players. The £2.5 million for Phelan had increased City's bank deficit and, quite simply, the Blues could not afford any more. The news hardly surprised City's faithful, but it was a broad hint to Reid and Ellis that the Chairman expected results.
A few hours later a third round League Cup tie with Tottenham ended in a 1-0 defeat. Not the kind of result Swales had in mind!

League performances did improve with satisfying victories over Kendall's Everton (3-1), reigning champions Leeds (another 4-0), and Coventry City (3-2) before defeats at Tottenham (1-0) and in the Sky TV live derby match at Old Trafford (2-1). Another defeat followed on 12th December at Ipswich - a game in which the impressive Garry Flitcroft netted his first League goal for the club.

With typical City inconsistency the Blues were bright one minute but absolutely appalling the next. Fans were increasingly disenchanted with the way the season was developing. Already there had been calls for the Chairman to resign, yet he refused to listen. At the October 1992 AGM City shareholder Brian Williams asked Swales to do what a large percentage of supporters had wanted since the mid 80s: "You should consider your future as Chairman. Perhaps the greatest service you could give to the club would be to step aside for somebody else. You've been Chairman for 14 years without a major success. You have not been a lucky Chairman and you should give somebody else a chance."

Swales responded in the manner he usually adopted when questioned in this way: "I take your point - but I will not be taking your advice." Earlier in the year the *Electric Blue* fanzine had produced a "Swales Out" special as they tried to make supporters' feelings more widely known.

The fans were frustrated with City despite, on the face of it, a decent enough League campaign. Although results were mixed, the Blues did actually end the first Premier League season in ninth place, which for most clubs would have been regarded as a success. Unfortunately, football at Maine Road has never purely revolved around winning matches, it is also about playing with style. It was something Reid and Ellis ignored at their peril.

On the final day of the season City were humiliated 5-2 by Everton at home. Peter Swales was pelted with eggs and a 'Swales Out' demonstration took place as supporters vented their frustrations. In truth, what made the 1992-3 season so unsatisfactory was that Manchester United were crowned the first Premier League champions. It mocked all the empty boasts and promises made by Swales, Kendall, and Reid during the early 90s. The fans felt bitterly betrayed yet no one outside of Manchester could comprehend why Blues were so unhappy. Two months before the end of the campaign the media had been shocked at the behaviour of City's fans when they invaded the pitch during a sixth round F.A. Cup tie with Spurs. They condemned the supporters without understanding the background story.

To put the record straight it's vital the day's events are covered correctly. The Blues had overcome Reading, QPR, and Barnsley to reach the sixth round for the first time since 1988. Their opponents Tottenham had already knocked them out of the League Cup in October and defeated them in the Maine Road League game. City fans hoped Reid's men had learned a few lessons from these games and everybody connected with the club believed this was City's year for the cup. In addition there was a great deal of optimism, particularly as City were to open their new Umbro Stand for the very first time. The stand had replaced the old Platt Lane structure and a large number of fans had already purchased season tickets for the forthcoming 1993-4 season which allowed them into the stand for the remainder of 1992-3. It was not a particularly large or impressive structure, but it was still new and offered supporters the best sightlines of all the seated sections in the stadium. There was also substantially more leg room than in the North or Main Stands. Peter Swales was deeply proud of the construction, although supporters were later to dub it "Swales' folly".

The biggest City crowd of the season, up to that point, of 34,050 plus live terrestrial television in Britain and abroad guaranteed the whole football world would determine exactly how good or bad Reid's side really were. The atmosphere was electric with City fans in good voice; even the chant "There's only one Alan Hansen" rang out as supporters made sure the BBC summariser was thanked for being the only member of the Match of the Day team to publicly back City.

The game kicked off with Maine Road at its noisiest and when Mike Sheron gave the Blues the lead City fans started to sing about Wembley. It seemed this really would be City's year for glory; unfortunately the old inconsistencies struck again as Spurs fought back. First Nayim, totally unmarked, scored from 20 yards, then Sedgley ran unopposed on to a through ball to give Tottenham the lead.

At the interval supporters were dejected but still recognised City were in with a chance. Sadly, when

Nayim made it 3-1 early in the second half it completely diminished the Blues' hopes. Five minutes from time another totally unopposed effort brought Nayim his hat-trick and left City suffering. Spurs had another disallowed before Terry Phelan set off on one of his now familiar runs. He roared past several Tottenham players before burying the ball in the net. It was a superb goal but also sparked the moment which brought shame on the club. Almost immediately supporters from the unfenced Umbro Stand began to run on to the pitch.

The stewards at that end seemed uncertain of how to handle the situation and some allowed the invaders to walk unapprehended onto the pitch. It wasn't long before there were around 20 then, because of the ease of it all, more started to make their way onto the grass. Some climbed over the Kippax fencing to join the Umbro men and within a short space of time the BBC claimed there were around 200 City 'hooligans' on the turf.

A few of these supporters were clearly looking for trouble and headed towards the Spurs fans in the North Stand, while others seemed mystified as to why they were on the pitch in the first place. Fans milled around talking, explaining their frustrations to each other. The police seemed slow to act but when they did they certainly over-reacted, sending about ten officers on horseback onto the pitch to charge the incursors. The tactic worked but gave the media an impression the invasion was much worse than it actually was.

Once the pitch was clear the game resumed and Sheringham missed a penalty for Spurs while Quinn fluffed an absolute sitter. The game ended 4-2 and the media seemed to enjoy the latest footballing sensation. Of course the pitch invasion was totally and utterly incorrect, however few actually bothered to understand the underlying reason for the supporters' actions. Some sources claimed it had all been planned before the game even kicked off, but surely even the most organised hooligan could not have plotted a pitch invasion 'just in case' City pulled a goal back to make the score 4-2?

The main reason for the disturbance was undoubtedly frustration. City fans had endured 17 years without success. They had been so stoked up to believe the F.A. Cup was coming back to Manchester anything less than a victory would have left them feeling depressed. As it was, City's capitulation simply made the supporters angry. They were totally frustrated and, though the manner was wrong, they expressed their feelings in the only way that actually seemed guaranteed to make the Chairman listen.

In *King of the Kippax* Ged Isaacs wrote: "Swales described it as 'My worst day in football'. A very telling comment as he has presided over two relegations and countless embarrassing team performances. If he's so cut up about a few people on the pitch, why didn't he resign in '83 after the Luton game? Still at least he's confirmed that he doesn't give a shit about the team. As the Moody Blues once put it 'Go now, go now, go now'."

The comment was typical of many made by supporters in the aftermath of this game. While the media liked to portray the image of a rampaging mob running across City's turf, the supporters themselves were questioning the Chairman and his fellow directors. Peter Reid was blamed for the actual team performance but the real culprits, according to the fans, were the directors. They believed the newly constructed Umbro Stand seemed to typify the attitude of the club at this point. It was a rather tasteless, small scale construction with too few seats and too many executive boxes. In simple terms it was very much 'small time' as opposed to stands being constructed elsewhere. Even the executive boxes had caused problems at the Tottenham game as, after Sheron's early goal, Spurs supporters lobbed coins and rubbish onto City followers below, causing the first situation that the recently recruited stewards were unable to control.

Throughout the days that followed, City fans were made to feel like animals yet the same weekend much worse crowd trouble had occurred at the Blackburn v Sheffield United match. The only difference was City's game was televised.

For Peter Swales the whole event had been a nightmare: "I should have gone then! That game was a real low point for me. New stand... big crowd... everything right, except the result and the fans on the pitch. I was going to resign but a few friends and other directors persuaded me to stay. They convinced me. I don't know if it was self-preservation or what, but they all convinced me to stay. Now I realise I should definitely have gone... No question! From that point on, it wasn't me. I made a few mistakes and I stopped learning. Stopped listening."

Had Swales gone then the events of the following year would never have occurred. It's impossible to say what might have happened to the Blues, but the nightmare that materialised at the start of the 1993-4 season would have been prevented.

In the months that followed the Spurs fiasco, Peter Swales took steps to change the management structure of the club, while the fans grew increasingly dissatisfied with the overall direction of the team they loved.

1993 was to prove a watershed year in the history of Manchester football.

Mike Sheron's goal gave the Blues an early lead in the infamous FA Cup quarter final meeting with Tottenham.

Terry Phelan ends a fine solo run with a goal, but the moment sparked a pitch invasion in the FA Cup quarter-final with Spurs.

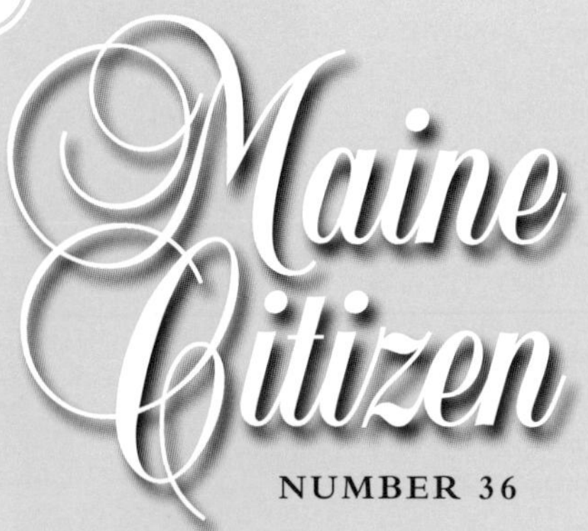

NUMBER 36

NIALL QUINN

Born in Dublin on 6th October 1966, Niall Quinn joined City in March 1990, making his debut against Chelsea on 21st of that month. Chelsea were leading 1-0 when David White sent a measured cross in Quinn's direction. The big Irishman headed home for a great debut goal.

Another three Quinn goals followed before the end of the season and the new arrival was credited with helping the Blues avoid relegation. The man responsible for Quinn's transfer was Howard Kendall who was absolutely convinced the player would make the perfect target man. He was right. Many have claimed Quinn had little skill yet the facts prove his critics wrong. Kendall firmly believes Arsenal would have preferred to have kept him: "If City hadn't been struggling in the bottom half of the table, I don't think I would have got him because George Graham rated him highly and would have been loathe to sell him to any club with even half a chance of winning the Championship. I say that with some assurance because Aston Villa had tried, but failed, to sign him probably because they were enjoying a very successful League campaign."

Some have said Kendall had to work hard to turn Quinn into a decent forward but the ex-City manager disputes that: "The truth is I didn't have to do very much at all. He already had the skill and the enthusiasm, all I did was add a dash of confidence. Once Niall realised he was a regular, first choice player, all his inhibitions disappeared and he began to flourish. Niall is one of the best one-touch finishers I have seen in a very long time."

Quinn had already found fame by the age of 20 when he appeared in his first Republic of Ireland international while with Arsenal. By the time of his transfer to City he had suffered a little at Highbury as there was far too much competition for places, but once at Maine Road he flourished again. At the end of his first Blue season Quinn became a member of Jack Charlton's exciting 1990 World Cup squad, and the tournament developed him considerably. When the 1990-91 campaign commenced he was a true City star, hugely popular with the fans.

In April of that season he hit the headlines with two thrilling performances. The first saw him score a dream hat-trick (left foot, right foot, and a header) against Crystal Palace on April Fool's Day, and then against Derby County he not only scored one of City's two that day, but also went in goal following the dismissal of Tony Coton and saved a Dean Saunders penalty! He ended the campaign as top scorer with 20 League goals - the first City player to score 20 goals in the First Division since Brian Kidd in 1977.

A cruciate ligament injury suffered on 27th November 1993 against Sheffield Wednesday ended his part in the controversial 1993-4 season. It also prevented him from taking part in the 1994 World Cup for his beloved Eire.

He returned the following season and ended with eight goals in 24 (plus 11 as substitute) League games. No longer the first choice he had been earlier in his career, rumours circulated he was about to be transferred. Then in the summer of 1995 a big money deal with Sporting Lisbon fell through. Quinn pledged his future to City, but once Alan Ball became manager during the close season it seemed highly unlikely the popular Irishman would survive.

Somehow he did remain at the club, but the 1995-6 season was to be his last. During the final match of the campaign, at home to Liverpool, Quinn stood on the touchline demanding more from the City players who seemed content to sit back and allow Liverpool to control the match. Much to his disgust that game resulted in City's relegation and the Irishman was transferred to Peter Reid's Sunderland. In the months that followed stories of large salaries and compensation claims were heard but Quinn, ever loyal to the Blue cause, insisted he was not a 'money-grabbing' ex-player.

Quinn's time at City was a delight for the majority of fans. He was a true hero during a period when circumstances prevented the Blues from really challenging for the game's top honours. He will always be remembered for his willingness to support the Blue cause, while his role as target man provided much enjoyment, although few Blues relished his goal against City on Friday 15th August 1997 for Sunderland. That night he entered the record books as the scorer of the first goal at Sunderland's new "Stadium of Light".

QUINN'S PLAYING RECORD

	LEAGUE		FA CUP		FL CUP		FM CUP		TOTAL	
	App	Gls	App	Gls	App	Gls	App	Gls	App	Gls
1989-90	9	4	0	0	0	0	0	0	9	4
1990-91	38	20	2	1	3	0	3	1	46	22
1991-92	35	12	1	0	4	2	0	0	40	14
1992-93	39	9	5	1	3	0	-	-	47	10
1993-94	14(1)	5	0	0	3	1	-	-	17(1)	6
1994-95	24(11)	8	1(3)	0	4(2)	2	-	-	29(16)	10
1995-96	24(8)	8	4	2	3	1	-	-	31(8)	11
TOTAL	183(20)	66	13(3)	4	20(2)	6	3	1	219(25)	77

Chapter Twenty One

THE POWER TO HIRE AND FIRE

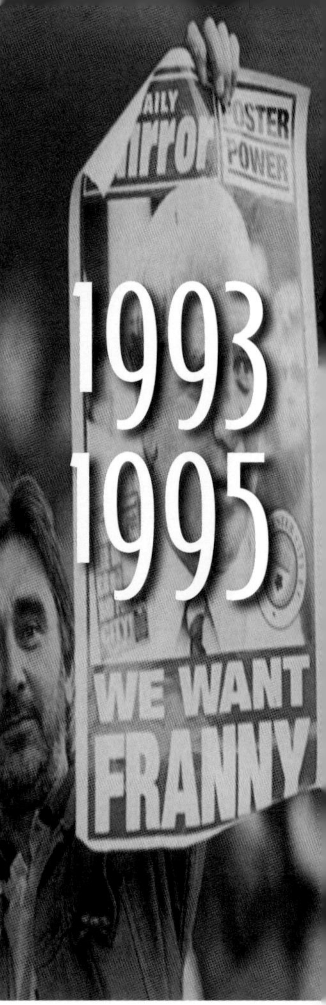

THE close season of 1993 was not a particularly pleasant one for either the City management team or supporters. Peter Reid and Sam Ellis struggled in their search for quality players. In fact they seemed to be turned down by almost every player approached, while Peter Swales was apparently reluctant to provide enough funds to guarantee any significant signing. Players allegedly on the move to Maine Road included Trevor Sinclair, Paul Stewart, Geoff Thomas, John Barnes and Andy Townsend. Not one of these signed as the summer of '93 became something of a farce.

In addition to the struggle to recruit top quality players, Peter Swales seemed concerned about the effect Manchester United's Championship success was having on football. He had promised City's fans that the Blues would be celebrating League success before the Reds, but that did not occur and as the 1993-4 season approached Swales was feeling the pressure: "Forget the ups and downs... our two relegations... we had a terrific ongoing situation with United for the whole of the 18/19 years because they had not won the Championship. Until they did we were always in with a prayer ... a shout. There was always a battle going on, but the day they won the Championship was the day alarm bells started ringing for me! I understand how a supporter feels when you're losing matches. It's the hardest thing there is, although the hardest thing for me was to keep getting United rammed down my throat!"

The team winning the Championship should never generate a negative impact on other clubs, however the situation in Manchester at the time was unique. While City had struggled during the 1980s United had the occasional F.A Cup success, but their own supporters expected more. Their continual failure to win the Championship actually relieved some of the pressure on Peter Swales, but United's success in 1993 brought the focus sharply back onto the failings of Manchester City in a way that no other team has ever been forced to endure. It was almost a national joke that City had not won a trophy since 1976, even though many other similar sized clubs, eg. Newcastle and Chelsea, had been less successful during the period from 1970 to 1993. The pressure resulting from United's success cannot be ignored when analysing the events of 1993.

The March '93 derby had already given City's directors something to think about. Peter Swales was forced to accept the Blues were some way behind: "It all struck home to me when United fans were chanting 'you've not won anything for 17 years'. Then you start thinking well we should have won in 1981. Then they'd be chanting that you'd not won anything for 12 years! But winning in '81 would have put us into the European Cup Winners' Cup. Spurs got through to the semi-finals so you never know what might have happened. But that's football. Every club could look back at what could have happened."

For Peter Swales the sad fact was the supporters were now carefully evaluating what had happened during his twenty years as Chairman. They were far from happy and, as the 1993-4 season opened, expected a significant improvement - especially in terms of spectacle - on the previous term. Ninth place in the Premier League would have been much more acceptable if the side had really tried to provide more entertainment.

To ease some of the burden, the Chairman appointed a former newspaper journalist John Maddock as Public Relations Officer. It seemed a most curious move at the time but Swales clearly felt under pressure.

The opening League game was a disappointing 1-1 draw with Leeds at Maine Road. As early as half-time, with City totally outplayed but the game still goalless, supporters voiced their opinions with a series of 'boos'. Flitcroft followed up an effort by Sheron to

"The only rift here appears to be between the hierarchy and the gaffer. Comments about the lack of team spirit from someone who has travelled only once with us on the team bus is hard to believe."
Keith Curle referring to John Maddock's involvement.

put the Blues in front in the second half, but no one could argue when Leeds deservedly equalised from a free header at a corner. On paper the 1-1 draw looked a good result, but the truth was City had been very lucky and relied on a series of brilliant saves from Tony Coton. To the supporters nothing, it seemed, had changed.

The following Tuesday City travelled to Everton. A group of fans unveiled a banner at the Park End that referred to an alleged promise made by Swales during the close season. It read: "£6m to spend Swales - you liar". It was patently obvious supporters were losing patience. During the match the by now familiar chant of "We want Swales out, we want Swales out" rang round Goodison as City failed to get a shot on target until the final few minutes. Earlier Paul Rideout had scored the only goal of the match to give Everton an easy victory.

Prior to the next match on Saturday 21st August the shock news that John Maddock, the former *Sunday People* journalist, had been promoted to General Manager was announced. Everyone was totally baffled and rumours circulated that Peter Reid would soon be dismissed. Already an unconfirmed story suggested Reid had been asked to sack Sam Ellis in a bid to maintain his own position at Maine Road. Once again City seemed to be shooting themselves in the foot. It was no surprise when the first game played under the auspices of Maddock ended in a 1-0 defeat at Tottenham.

Three days later, Johnny Giles wrote a blistering attack on Swales in the *Daily Express*. It was an article appreciated by the fans and, at last, it appeared there were some people in the media who actually understood what was really happening at Maine Road. The failure to find success since 1976 could not be blamed solely on Peter Reid. City's directors had to shoulder their share of responsibility.

TURMOIL AT MAINE ROAD
City's new supremo blasts Reid

I'M THE BOSS – MADDOCK

A large number of injuries were now affecting Reid's plans and he was forced to play both Quinn and Curle despite hamstring problems. Nevertheless the manager did not use injuries as an excuse for the 2-0 humiliation by Blackburn at Maine Road on Tuesday 24th. He simply stated that the Blues did not perform and Blackburn were more determined than City. Naturally, a 'Swales Out' demonstration followed the defeat with new General Manager John Maddock telling the press the supporters deserved better. Many of his comments appeared to directly undermine Reid and were followed up by an extraordinary interview with Paul Hince of the *Manchester Evening News*. Basically Maddock told Hince he was the man in charge and he was determined to change the situation: "People had better understand that there is a new regime at Maine Road. I am not a mouthpiece for the chairman Peter Swales. I am the supremo at Maine Road with a specific mandate from the board, and that mandate is to sort out the problem which we have got at the moment."

In a not very thinly veiled warning to Reid and Ellis, Maddock added: "Make no mistake about it. I have the power to hire and fire and whatever has got to be done to put us back on line will be done. There is no point campaigning for the chairman Peter Swales to step down. He has handed control over to me and is as concerned as I am about our current plight. The only thing he has ever wanted is for Manchester City to be one of the major clubs in English soccer and that is the task he has entrusted to me. The future of this club is all that concerns me. I won't duck making decisions, however unpleasant they may be, which is why I attended the press conference after last night's match. I felt after that performance it was my duty as the man in charge to face the music. I wasn't trying to deflect the flak from the chairman. In fact I never even spoke to him after the match.

"I wanted people to know that I am not a puppet or a messenger. I am the man in charge and I will take positive steps to pull this club into shape. You don't have to be a genius to work out that there is something going badly wrong when the team are being booed off the pitch before the end of August. I can only repeat that the necessary steps will be taken to give our supporters the team and the success they deserve."

During this period the players - the only people who could really make a difference to results - were confused. They supported Reid and were frankly appalled by Maddock's comments. Captain Keith Curle: "The only rift here appears to be between the hierarchy and the gaffer. Comments about the lack of team spirit from someone who has travelled only once with us on the team bus is hard to believe." Niall Quinn agreed: "I signed to play until I am 30, but that was for City not John Maddock. We are all backing Peter 100 per cent. When Mr. Maddock was appointed I thought we would have stability, but things seem to be dragging on. Obviously he has come with a view to clear the place, and right now I don't know if I'll be here next week."

The players probably knew it, but City supporters were now also strongly of the opinion the Reid-Ellis period was about to end. Reid was in a difficult position and, it seemed, in a no-win situation. On the morning of Thursday 26th August *The Sun* newspaper questioned whether Reid would reach his third anniversary as manager in November, while it also included an interview with former boss Malcolm Allison. Allison pointed the finger at Swales and accused him of 20 years of mis-rule. He also queried the role of John Maddock: "His appointment is bizarre. Why didn't Swales just go to France and get Mickey Mouse? He's a personality who would get the crowds back and give them a laugh. Football is a professional business. How can you put an amateur in a position like that?"

That same day the *Daily Express* printed a letter from Swales complaining about the Johnny Giles article. Throughout the note City's chairman listed the amount of money he had provided to various managers and tried to explain he had never interfered with a manager's decision. He added: "Manchester City were the first club to sign three players valued at £1m. City were recognised as the biggest spenders in football, attracting the best internationals in football. I have often been criticised in the past - on some occasion with justification - but to suggest that I am the chairman who interferes with his managers' dealings in the transfer market is ludicrous. No other chairman in the Premiership has allowed his managers the freedom over the past 19 years as I have given. As a 'failed' manager, there is no doubt you have suffered restrictions from chairmen. I have always allowed mine to get on with their jobs. If that is a fault, then I am guilty. You are guilty of gross misreporting which does neither you, nor your paper any favours."

Giles responded by claiming Swales' letter was a poor attempt at self-justification. He then asked the two questions that the majority of supporters were desperately keen to find answers to: "If you have done so well, why are Manchester City in such a mess? Why did they not make one significant signing during the summer, a time when all the seriously ambitious clubs pushed so hard and successfully to strengthen their squads?"

He went on to attack the appointment of Maddock and some of the other decisions made by Swales over the years. He ended by considering City's plight. He claimed: "Only one man is responsible for that. It is you. You are the chairman. You appoint the managers and, by your own account, say who will be signed. Or, sadly in City's case these days, who will not be signed."

On the same day Peter Reid was due to have a showdown with Swales and Maddock to determine where he stood. In particular Reid wanted to understand what was meant by Maddock's statement about having the power to hire and fire. Reid felt that was part of his role: "It is in my contract that I hire and fire my staff and I expect that contract to be honoured." He was also determined not to leave that role: "There is no way I will resign. I have never run away from a fight in my life and I'm not going to start now."

It wasn't long into the blistering meeting that Reid realised his career at Maine Road had ended a mere 13 days into the new season: "It came as something of a shock. But I'm a professional and I have to get on with life." City fans were furious. It wasn't so much the dismissal of Reid and his assistant Ellis that angered Blues, it was the way the whole affair had been handled. The supporters had been unhappy with the club's style of play for some time and it was no secret some wanted the managerial set-up to change during the 1993 close season. Instead they saw Swales hand Reid a new three-year contract, as he had done with Machin, then appoint a journalist as General Manager to "do his dirty work", as the fans put it. It was all too ridiculous for words and quickly made the bungling Blues the laughing stock of British football once more.

The supporters had simply had enough. They blamed the Chairman entirely and were keen to see his role change. For possibly the first time in City history, the majority of newspapers reported the true supporters' views, and each article seemed to list what had occurred during the near 20 years of Chairman Swales' rule. The list was not particularly pleasant reading, although it is true that each newspaper concentrated on the negative aspects of his reign rather than any plus points.

While the anti-Swales movement gained strength, the media also speculated on Reid's replacement; Joe Royle, Steve Coppell, Dave Bassett, and Terry Venables were all tipped for the job. Naturally, the supporters were keen to have either Royle or Venables, but at the time neither Bassett nor Coppell particularly excited them. For 24 hours everyone speculated, yet local radio station GMR had devised a cunning plan. They knew John Maddock would have to meet either the new man, or his Chairman, before any agreement could be made, and so they tried to follow him on the Friday morning.

With live reports throughout the morning, the GMR reporter tailed Maddock and even managed to speak with him. Excited listeners heard Maddock's car was heading south, fuelling speculation the new man would either be Steve Coppell or Terry Venables. The fans' favourite was Venables, but would he really travel north to Manchester?

GMR didn't quite manage to discover the answer, but that night's *Manchester Evening News* made it clear Venables was not on City's wanted list. It then transpired Maddock had already reached agreement with a manager and his existing club, and an announcement would be made the following day, after City's Friday night home game with Coventry. Maddock told the media: "I can tell you that I am delighted to have landed a manager of this pedigree and our fans will feel the same because we have appointed a true professional who is going to help put Manchester City back on the football map."

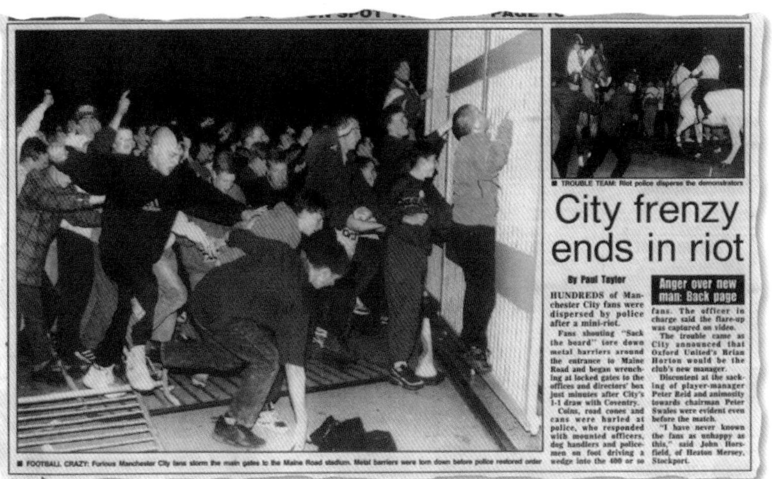

■ TROUBLE TEAM: Riot police disperse the demonstrators

City frenzy ends in riot

By Paul Taylor

HUNDREDS of Manchester City fans were dispersed by police after a mini-riot.

Fans shouting "Sack the board" tore down metal barriers around the entrance to Maine Road and began wrenching at locked gates to the offices and directors' box just minutes after City's 1-1 draw with Coventry.

Coins, road cones and cans were hurled at police, who responded with mounted officers, dog handlers and policemen on foot driving a wedge into the 400 or so fans. The officer in charge said the flare-up was captured on video.

The trouble came as City announced that Oxford United's Brian Horton would be the club's new manager.

Discontent at the sacking of player-manager Peter Reid and animosity towards chairman Peter Swales were evident even before the match.

"I have never known the fans as unhappy as this," said John Horsfield, of Heaton Mersey, Stockport.

Anger over new man: Back page

■ FOOTBALL CRAZY: Furious Manchester City fans storm the main gates to the Maine Road stadium. Metal barriers were torn down before police restored order

Fans show their anger at the City-Coventry match on Friday 27th August 1993.

Earlier that day Maddock also claimed responsibility for bringing Howard Kendall to Maine Road in 1989 and rightly pointed out what City fans expected of the new man: "He must be experienced and do a first-class job. Fans want someone who can achieve success and has a track record for success." These comments intimated the Blues would be appointing a proven top flight manager, someone who had won trophies; someone who would be respected; and someone who would appeal to what was rapidly becoming the embarrassed generation of Blues.

City's match with Coventry that night (Friday 27th August) took on a rather surreal feel with most fans turning up simply to yell some abuse at City's directors, in particular Swales, rather than enjoy the match. The game itself ended in a 1-1 draw for Tony Book's men after Sheron had given the Blues the lead

BRIAN HORTON: 'He makes motor bikes, doesn't he?'

FANS FURY

Brian Horton (left) was the man John Maddock (right) appointed to replace Peter Reid.

in the first half. Five minutes from time a mistake by McMahon allowed Roy Wegerle to equalise.

Throughout the match chants of "Swales Out" rang out, while rumours abounded as to who the new boss would be. In the Main Stand, the beleagured Chairman visibly suffered in a way that hadn't occurred before and, eventually, Swales left his seat in the directors box. While all this took place the media, in particular Radio 5, brought the news that the Oxford manager, Brian Horton, had been spotted in one of the Umbro Stand's executive boxes. They tried to gain confirmation that Horton was the new manager and before the game ended clearly stated City had indeed appointed the former Luton player.

The Sun SAYS
• DON'T SAVE THE SWALES •

For once the tabloid press managed to gauge the true feeling of City's supporters. The Sun issued these stickers within days of the dismissal of Peter Reid.

Former City player Mike Summerbee was asked for his reaction, and the ex-player was as astonished as the vast majority of supporters. The main comment expressed was "Brian who?" He was certainly not of the calibre suggested by Maddock and, after expecting either a Royle or Venables, supporters felt totally let down by the club's directors.

Armed with full knowledge of the appointment, fans demonstrated outside the main entrance demanding the resignation of Swales and his board. They were far from satisfied, although many of the following day's newspaper reports grossly overestimated the amount of violence involved. Articles claimed over 1,000 fans rioted with dozens of police being forced to charge the angry mob. It was all a little exaggerated. City's supporters had been demonstrating for years, certainly since the early 1980s, and each protest had always arrived at a natural end. Temporary crush barriers were pushed over, but there was no actual violence and older supporters remarked that the stone throwing incidents of 1965 were more likely to have caused harm than chants of "Sack The Board" and "Swales Out".

Newspaper stories portrayed the club and its supporters in a very poor light and, potentially, made the situation even worse. It was an extremely distressing time for all connected with Manchester City, especially the supporters and the man everybody loved to hate, Peter Swales. Ironically, *The Sun* newspaper suddenly became interested in the fans' view and claimed to support their campaign by printing and issuing free "Don't Save The Swales" stickers.

For one man this whole period must have been totally bewildering - new manager Brian Horton. Horton had arrived at Maine Road full of ambition and determined to succeed. He also tried to dismiss all talk that hatchet man John Maddock would be too much of a controlling influence: "I have known John for 20 years, although I don't know all the background of what happened over his new job, I don't expect him to be looking over my shoulder. Remember, I had to work with Kevin Maxwell, who was Oxford chairman, and he let me get on with my job. I am sure the same thing will happen here."

He added: "I do have a track record, and that is in keeping Oxford going, especially during the difficult days when the Maxwell family were in charge. And remember, every manager has to step up some time. You have to start somewhere. I believe we can go places. Obviously there are problems but from what I saw from the stand tonight, we have plenty to work with - and I have been promised cash to buy."

On 1st September, Horton's first game in charge brought much relief to the City management and board as the Blues won at Swindon 3-1. Prior to the game Horton and his assistant David Moss were cheered off the team coach as the supporters tried to convey their criticism was not aimed specifically at them. Understandably Maddock, Public Enemy Number Two, was jeered when he was first spotted, while Swales did not attend at all. Despite the 3-1 win, there were regular chants of "Swales Out", although it must be stressed the fans also gave the playing staff much support and encouragement. Quite simply, the fans remained loyal to the Blue cause yet were extremely bitter towards the directors.

Five days after that game City's supporters awoke to surprising news. As with the death of Princess Diana, it seems most Blue supporters can remember where they were on the day they heard former player Francis Lee was preparing to bid for the club.

Mark Brown of Royton clearly recalls how he first heard the news: "I'd set the radio alarm to go off at 7am and, to be truthful, I was still half asleep when the Radio One news bulletin was being read out. I didn't know if I was dreaming or if it was real, but I vaguely recall hearing 'according to the *Daily Mirror*

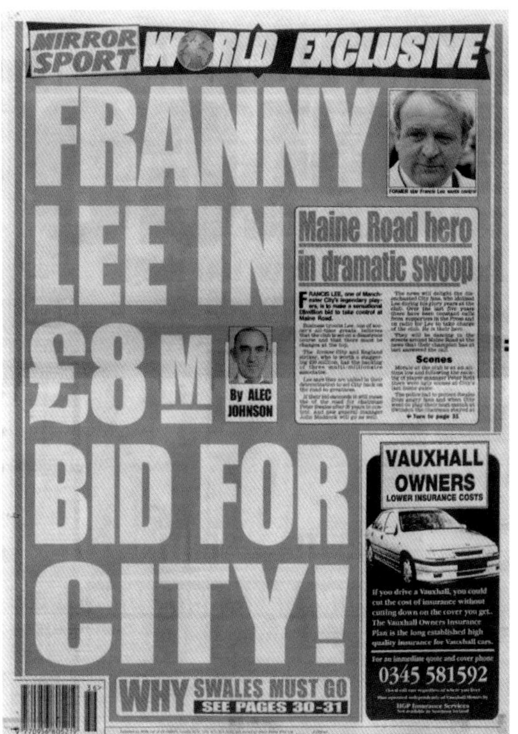

MIRROR SPORT WORLD EXCLUSIVE

FRANNY LEE IN £8M BID FOR CITY!

By ALEC JOHNSON

Maine Road hero in dramatic swoop

FRANCIS LEE, one of Manchester City's legendary players, is to make a sensational £8million bid to take control at Maine Road.

Scenes

Turn to page 35

WHY SWALES MUST GO SEE PAGES 30-31

VAUXHALL OWNERS
LOWER INSURANCE COSTS
If you drive a Vauxhall, you could cut the cost of insurance without cutting down on the cover you get. The Vauxhall Owners Insurance Plan is the long established high quality insurance for Vauxhall cars.
For an immediate quote and cover phone
0345 581592

6th September 1993... the Daily Mirror breaks the news that gives Blues fans hope.

former hero Franny Lee has mounted a take-over'. I couldn't believe it! I lay in bed waiting for the next bulletin, when it was confirmed. I knew then I hadn't been dreaming! I quickly dressed, drove to work and searched for a copy of the *Mirror* to see what the story really was. For the first time in decades the *Mirror* actually had a City article on its back page! It still seemed like a dream. Then I started to wonder if we'd get a special discount on Lee's toilet rolls - we'd certainly need it if the season continued to be as nerve-wracking as it had begun!"

Veteran *Mirror* reporter Alec Johnson had been given an exclusive story by Francis Lee, and the fans simply loved it. In the article Lee stated his plans: "If we do take over we are going to listen to the fans. They are the most important people of all. This is their club. If they did not come to Maine Road week in and week out, then there simply wouldn't be a Manchester City Football Club.

"This is a real challenge. It is a roll-up-your-sleeves time. My three associates and myself are willing to put big money into the club to get the best players for the team. But other things are equally important. The most vital thing is that the club is run from top to bottom just like a winning team. If we are going to make Manchester City the number one team then there is no time for personalities at the club. Everyone counts."

At a press conference later in the day Lee insisted he was not driven by a desire to take over the club: "I am not interested in controlling things. The club should not be run by one man. What I am seeking is a mandate from supporters and shareholders for a place on the board."

Despite Lee's comments, the supporters were now keen to see the former England international as City's driving force, while the existing board of directors seemed reluctant to allow Lee to join their merry band. To give an indication of how he might help the Blues, Lee stated: "I am prepared to make available substantially more funds than have been invested in the club previously. I don't want to discuss figures but we can start at £1 million and go from there."

For the fans it was now a case of choosing between Lee, a former player who had brought great honour and success to the club, and Swales, a man whose 20 year reign was rapidly being viewed as a complete and utter disaster. Swales' time as chairman deserved fairer assessment but, with a strong supporter campaign, immense media coverage, and then the arrival of Lee, it was easy to discredit everything the chairman had achieved. In simple terms, Swales should have stepped down some time before, possibly in 1989 with the arrival of Howard Kendall, to allow history to correctly record the many achievements of his period at the helm. By remaining in charge into the 1990s he became villified as a man who appeared stubbornly in love with power. This is untrue and was completely out of character with the man, however, in 1993 few Blues were interested in hearing about the real Swales. All they wanted was for him to step down.

Despite the depth of feeling, Swales actually believed the demonstrations would disappear: "I am not panicking, nobody is at this club. And I really don't know what all the fuss is about, even though I do seem to be Public Enemy Number One among our supporters. We'll just wait and see what develops. Some people seem intent on mixing it. There seems to be a vendetta against me, and I would be lying if I said it hasn't affected me."

G-LEE!

By DAVE ARMITAGE

Swales under fire as City fans hail Franny

FRANCIS LEE was given a hero's welcome as he was hailed the new Messiah of Maine Road yesterday.

The multi-millionaire racehorse owner and businessman received a standing ovation as City romped to a 3-0 win over QPR.

They chanted the name of the former City idol and demanded the removal of chairman Peter Swales as thousands stayed behind after the game to vent their anger at the man who has won just one trophy in 20 years.

Now Swales has indicated he is ready to bow to the unrelenting pressure and quit as chairman.

Badges and T-shirts with "Swales out" and "This man must go" were being sold and given away outside the ground.

But Lee could face a fight to take control as Swales claims a mystery Mr X, believed to be a millionaire North-West businessman, is ready to slug it out with the former England star in a £15million takeover battle.

The City chairman claims he held a secret meeting on Friday with the mystery bidder.

Swales said: "The person in question vigorously pursued his desire to buy Manchester City. He is on his own in this and his intentions are serious. He has the necessary finances to take over.

"But let's get this right. We don't want to sell but we have been forced into this situation.

"It's a bad time for us because we are right in the middle of the final piece of the jigsaw over the development of the ground.

"The time for me to have thought about going would have been next year but this has been hassled on me and I am not over-thrilled by the tactics."

City boss Brian Horton, delighted with the win on a day when rivals Manchester United went down 1-0 at Chelsea, would only say: "We're just letting our football do the talking.

"Has the Franny Lee stuff affected us? We've got six points haven't we? There's nothing we can do about what goes on."

● *Franny's revenge – Page 55*
● *Match report – Page 59*

SCOTLAND boss Andy Roxburgh has

EXCLUSIVE

The Sunday Mirror's report of Francis Lee's appearance at the QPR game on 11th September 1993.

For the remainder of the week leading up to Horton's first home game in charge on 11th September the media concentrated on the "Swales Out, Lee In" story, particularly the *Daily Mirror*. Each day the *Mirror* reported on Lee's movements and also quoted many supporters, including a vicar who was praying for Swales to stand down, and a group called "Forward with Franny" who seemed keen to bring a little organisation to the fans' demonstrations. The *Mirror* joined *The Sun* by issuing stickers, badges, and posters saying "We Want Franny".

By the day of the Maine Road match with QPR,

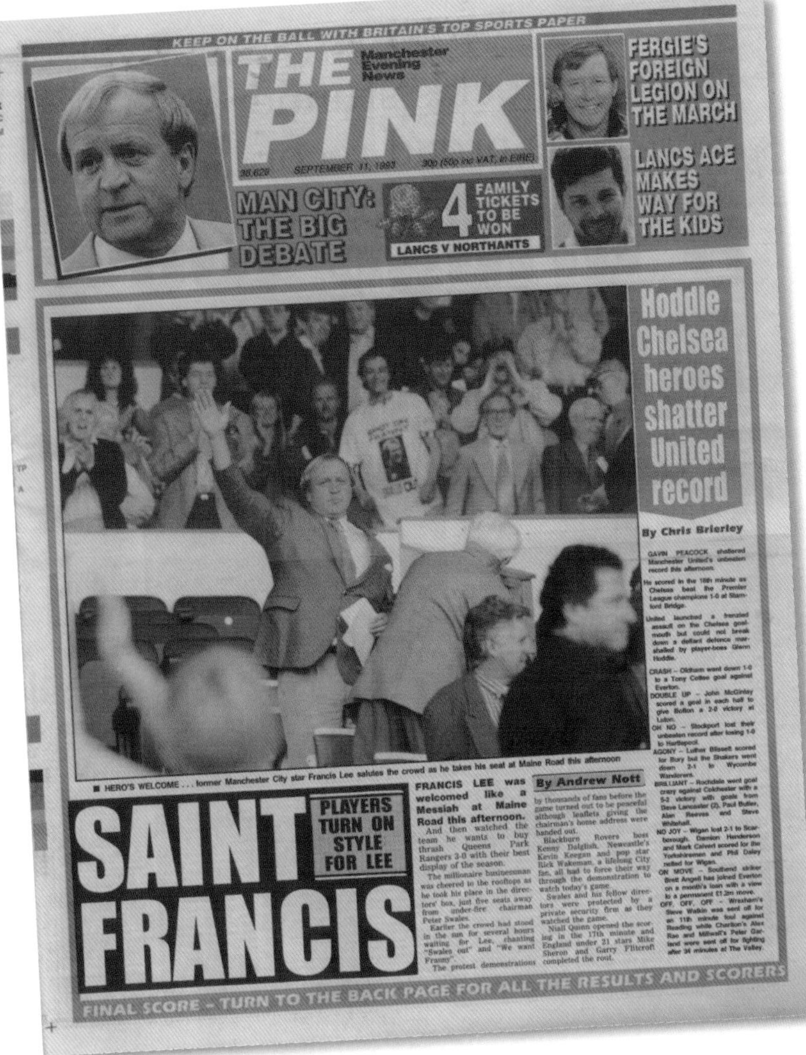

KEEP ON THE BALL WITH BRITAIN'S TOP SPORTS PAPER

THE PINK Manchester Evening News

SEPTEMBER 11, 1993

MAN CITY: THE BIG DEBATE

4 FAMILY TICKETS TO BE WON

LANCS V NORTHANTS

FERGIE'S FOREIGN LEGION ON THE MARCH

LANCS ACE MAKES WAY FOR THE KIDS

Hoddle Chelsea heroes shatter United record

By Chris Brierley

GAVIN PEACOCK shattered Manchester United's unbeaten record this afternoon.

He scored in the 18th minute as Chelsea beat the Premier League champions 1-0 at Stamford Bridge.

United launched a frenzied assault on the Chelsea goalmouth but could not break down a defiant defence marshalled by player-boss Glenn Hoddle.

CRASH – Oldham went down 1-0 to a Tony Cottee goal against Everton.

DOUBLE UP – John McGinlay scored a goal in each half to give Bolton a 2-0 victory at Luton.

OH NO – Stockport lost their unbeaten record after losing 1-0 to Hartlepool.

AGONY – Luther Blissett scored for Bury but the Shakers went down 2-1 to Wycombe Wanderers.

BRILLIANT – Rochdale went goal crazy against Colchester with a 5-2 victory with goals from Dave Lancaster (2), Paul Butler, Alan Reeves and Steve Whitehall.

NO JOY – Wigan lost 2-1 to Scarborough. Damion Henderson and Mark Calvert scored for the Yorkshiremen and Phil Daley netted for Wigan.

ON MOVE – Southend striker Brett Angell has joined Everton on a month's loan with a view to a permanent £1.2m move.

OFF, OFF, OFF – Wrexham's Steve Watkin was sent off for an 11th minute foul against Reading while Charlton's Alex Rae and Millwall's Peter Garland were sent off for fighting after 34 minutes at The Valley.

HERO'S WELCOME … former Manchester City star Francis Lee salutes the crowd as he takes his seat at Maine Road this afternoon

SAINT FRANCIS

PLAYERS TURN ON STYLE FOR LEE

By Andrew Nott

FRANCIS LEE was welcomed like a Messiah at Maine Road this afternoon.

And then watched the team he wants to buy thrash Queens Park Rangers 3-0 with their best display of the season.

The millionaire businessman was cheered to the rooftops as he took his place in the directors' box, just five seats away from under-fire chairman Peter Swales.

Earlier the crowd had stood in the sun for several hours waiting for Lee, chanting "Swales out" and "We want Franny".

The protest demonstrations by thousands of fans before the game turned out to be peaceful although leaflets giving the chairman's home address were handed out.

Blackburn Rovers boss Kenny Dalglish, Newcastle's Kevin Keegan and pop star Rick Wakeman, a lifelong City fan, all had to force their way through the demonstration to watch today's game.

Swales and his fellow directors were protected by a private security firm as they watched the game.

Niall Quinn opened the scoring in the 17th minute and England under 21 stars Mike Sheron and Garry Flitcroft completed the rout.

FINAL SCORE – TURN TO THE BACK PAGE FOR ALL THE RESULTS AND SCORERS

The front page of The Pink from Saturday 11th September 1993, when Francis Lee received a heroes welcome at the QPR game... and United lost!

the newspaper claimed the battle was over and Swales was poised to sell his shares. According to the *Mirror*, Swales had made a statement: "I would love to keep going, but I realise it is probably time for someone else to have a go. We have said if we can get the right deal we will do it. I am sure if we get the right deal it will suit the shareholders. Time marches on, doesn't it?" The *Mirror* also claimed another leading shareholder and supporter of Swales, Stephen Boler, was prepared to sell his shares if approached.

Details of Lee's consortium were now becoming clearer with another former City player, Colin Barlow, playing a leading role. The two men made it clear they were to attend the QPR game, and wanted City fans to peacefully make their feelings known. They didn't need to make any special requests as the fans were desperately keen to tell the world who they wanted to head City's board.

Prior to the QPR match, thousands of supporters stood outside the main entrance in party mood. They had arrived early to celebrate the 'return of the messiah', as it was termed, and when Lee arrived he was mobbed as he tried to make his way into the ground. The fans made all the usual noise and, after Lee's arrival, quickly made their way inside the stadium to enhance the aura further.

In yet another surreal atmosphere the fans cheered and clapped Lee as he made his way into the directors' box, then booed and hissed Swales when he arrived to take his seat five rows behind Lee. It was reminiscent of a pantomime, although it was all much more serious for everyone involved.

The arrival of Lee helped to boost the atmosphere with fans giving the team terrific support, although chants of "Come on City" were interspersed with "We want Swales out". In the 17th minute a powerful run by Sheron led to City's first goal, scored by Quinn. Twenty minutes later an impressive corner by £500,000 man Alfons Groenendijk, City's only significant close season signing, was forced into the net by Mike Sheron. In the 70th minute a deflected Garry Flitcroft shot gave the Blues a 3-0 win.

After the match an organised, peaceful sit-in lasted for at least 20 minutes to provide a clear indication to all that the fans would not give in until Swales stepped down. Swales dismissed the demonstration as muted while surprisingly the media, who had stoked the hype throughout the week, failed to cover the event. If they felt the story was now over they were wrong. The take-over tale was to rumble on for some considerable time.

Even as fans welcomed Lee to Maine Road news broke that Peter Swales had been talking to another person keen to seek control of the club. Swales told the *Manchester Evening News*: "The person in question vigorously pursued his desire to buy Manchester City. This is not a consortium. He is on his own in this and his intentions are serious. I know him and there is no question that he personally has the necessary finances available now to take over this club.

"I have told him to put his offer in writing and this he is prepared to do. When that offer has been received I will invite him back to talk to the whole board."

From this point on the take-over of the club became extremely bitter, and the facts bewildering. Who was Swales' mystery purchaser? Had Lee spoken with Swales? There were so many questions and such entanglement that supporters struggled to understand what was happening. At one point it was reported that former newspaper tycoon Eddie Shah was backing Lee, while some had previously suggested he was actually Swales' mystery purchaser. It was all too confusing for most to contemplate, and clearly distracted from the real purpose of the club - football.

During the battle, Horton tried to develop a side he was comfortable with. On Monday 20th September he gave new £1.6m signing Alan Kernaghan his debut in an away match with Wimbledon. Sadly that game, televised by Sky, ended in a 1-0 defeat leaving City in 16th place. A 1-1 draw with Reading in the League Cup followed two nights later before a crowd of 9,280. The 'Forward With Franny' group had called for a mass boycott, and some supporters did stand outside the ground throughout the match protesting, but the official attendance figure was only a few hundred lower than the Bristol Rovers game the previous season. Other protests were planned, such as the lighting of candles on the Kippax. Some proved successful while others failed. At the candlelight protest against Oldham on 5th October stewards were ordered to take steps every time they saw the tiniest flicker within the Kippax. Their response was reminiscent of the ARP Warden in Dad's Army demanding: "Put that light out!"

Regular tannoy announcements aimed at reminding supporters of potential fire risk were viewed as the directors' last desperate act to end the protest. As a result each announcement was greeted by an increased volume of abuse aimed at Swales and

Right: Alan Kernaghan became Brian Horton's first City signing in September 1993.

his board. Once again it all hovered on the brink of farce, and the general public felt City supporters were more concerned with off field activities than the actual play. That wasn't strictly true, although it is fair to say the fans needed to force a change at the top before the action on the pitch could progress.

The Oldham match ended in a 1-1 draw - a remarkable result considering the off-field events and an ever-swelling injury list that Brian Horton somehow had to overcome. The players in the treatment room during Horton's first few weeks included left-winger Rick Holden, defenders Andy Hill and Michel Vonk, and Ian Brightwell and Paul Lake who were suffering from longer term problems.

A 2-1 victory over Reading in the League Cup (3-2 on aggregate) eased the tension a little and sent City through to face Chelsea in the third round, while a dull goalless game at Arsenal in mid October followed. David White gave City the lead in the next match, but Ian Rush produced an equaliser two minutes from time in a Maine Road draw with Liverpool. The following Tuesday a 1-0 victory sent Chelsea crashing out of the League Cup. Of more interest afterwards was Stuart Hall, reporting on the match for Radio 5, who revealed a rumour was circulating Maine Road that Francis Lee's bid was doomed to fail because the consortium did not have enough money to buy out Swales and Co.

It was then the Swales-Lee take-over tussle took a different turn at the 1993 AGM. It appeared a perfect opportunity to discover some truths, as a large number of supporters would be able to voice opinions and direct questions to the reigning chairman.

Arguably the most controversial AGM in the club's history took place on Thursday 28th October 1993 at the City Social Club. In previous years the meeting had always been held on a Friday, however as the new date coincided with the Nottingham Forest AGM, some believed the date change had been deliberately altered to ensure less media coverage. The Forest AGM was an equally stormy affair and concerned many allegations about Brian Clough. These gained national media coverage, whereas the City AGM was barely covered - even in the *Manchester Evening News*. In addition, supporters were suspicious that conveniently, the day after the meeting, City at long last bought a striker - Carl Griffiths. The *Evening News* made this the back page story rather than a serious review of the meeting.

Naturally, Peter Swales and his board attended the AGM, as did Francis Lee and Colin Barlow. In addition comedian Eddie Large and Simply Red's manager Elliot Rashman were there. Fanzine editor Noel Bayley was present, with various other *Electric Blue* contributors ready to record the meeting for posterity, while *King of the Kippax's* Dave Wallace was refused entry. Apparently some shares had been transferred to Wallace to allow him to attend, but the club claimed the transaction had not been performed in time. Naturally, the procedural matter was merely seen as a deliberate attempt to dilute the voice of the ordinary supporter.

To fully understand the supporters' feelings at this time it is vital a full and frank review of the meeting is read and understood. The best and most accurate AGM review was the one written by Noel Bayley and Steve Worthington which appeared in the fanzine *Electric Blue*, issue 22.

Over four pages they recorded virtually every exchange of views at what was a stormy meeting. Pro-Swales members who annually, it seems, praised the performance of the Chairman and his Board, were heckled and jeered by their vociferous opponents in the room who were described by one servile speaker as a "disgraceful rent-a-mob".

However, these Francis Lee take-over supporters did represent the views of the vast majority of non-shareholding City fans and posed Peter Swales a string of uncomfortable specific questions to which they received scant or highly unsatisfactory answers.

Looking pale and pressured, the Chairman was full of stubborn resolve despite receiving a vote of no confidence from the floor by 52 votes to 79 to re-elect him as a Director of the Company. It made little difference as a one-share, one-vote ballot was swiftly organised to ensure Swales' re-election.

In a prepared statement the Chairman commented on the proposal received from the consortium led by Francis Lee, who was seated close by.

"The proposal contains a number of conditions and does not involve a proposed offer to all shareholders. The board and its advisors consider that this proposal falls well short of reflecting the full value of your club. The board does not view this proposal as forming the basis for any further discussion with this consortium. The board has also had contact with other parties that may be interested in the club and I will keep you informed should there be any further developments. That's it".

"No, it isn't!" shouted a voice from the floor as others then rose to deliver indictments of Swales' reign. Elliott Rashman, supremo of the rock band Simply Red, was particularly articulate in his condemnation of the regime.

The cover of Issue 22 of City fanzine Electric Blue was printed with all of the writing in reverse. This was to emphasise 'Backward with Swales' as oppose to 'Forward with Franny'! Inside, four pages were devoted to a blow by blow account of the stormy October '93 AGM.

"Shareholders are irrelevant. The club is half-developed - a corner shop in a world of supermarkets. City are a Bovril and Wagon Wheels club. In any other business the Chairman wouldn't still be there after 20 years.

"If you go out on the playing fields of Manchester, what do you see written across kids' shirts? Sharp, more than Brother ... Sharp! And if I was Greenall's and if I was Brother I would be questioning whether you are really capable of taking us into the 21st Century. I suspect not. I'm just an ordinary fan. I'm 41 and I've been supporting City for 31 years. Anyone under 20 doesn't know success."

Swales attempted to halt any further questions but another shareholder hit the mark when he said: "That chair should provide leadership and inspiration and with all due respect, Mr Swales, your reputation is in tatters, your credibility is low and I would urge you, on behalf of all the fans of this football club, and everybody here, that you talk to Mr Lee and his consortium because we do need leadership but we're not getting it at the moment."

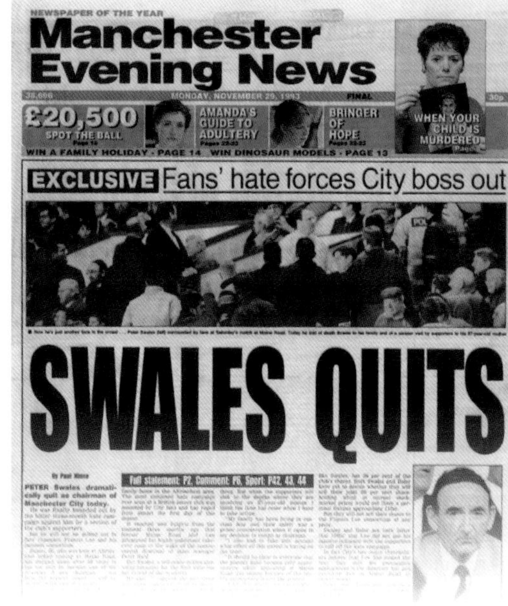
NEWSPAPER OF THE YEAR

Manchester Evening News

MONDAY, NOVEMBER 29, 1993 FINAL 30p

£20,500 SPOT THE BALL

AMANDA'S GUIDE TO ADULTERY

BRINGER OF HOPE

WHEN YOUR CHILD IS MURDERED

WIN A FAMILY HOLIDAY - PAGE 14 WIN DINOSAUR MODELS - PAGE 13

EXCLUSIVE Fans' hate forces City boss out

SWALES QUITS

The Manchester Evening News on 29th November 1993.

And so it went on until the result of the ballot was announced. Swales had won hands down with 688,613 votes in favour of his re-election and 9,270 votes against.

As the meeting failed to satisfy the "Swales Out" contingent the feeling of deflation was enormous. Supporters were asking themselves when the farce would end. To some it seemed never ending and, while prolonged, fortunes on the pitch would continue to be mixed.

Striker Carl Griffiths was signed from Shrewsbury the day after the October '93 AGM and made his debut in a 3-1 defeat at West Ham two days later.

A 3-1 defeat at West Ham followed the AGM, then on 7th November came the Maine Road derby with United. It was another first half derby performance that made City look world beaters. The Blues raced to a 2-0 lead, courtesy of Niall Quinn, and seemed a class above the Reds. Unfortunately, a mistake from Michel Vonk early in the second half allowed Eric Cantona to steer the ball past Tony Coton. With 12 minutes to go the controversial Frenchman made it 2-2, then Roy Keane netted another for United three minutes from time to make it a disappointing 3-2 to the Reds.

A couple of draws followed (1-1 at Norwich and 0-0 at Chelsea), before a 3-1 defeat by Sheffield Wednesday at Maine Road brought more pressure for Brian Horton, especially as Niall Quinn crashed to the ground with cruciate ligament damage that would keep him out for the rest of the season. Rumours had circulated for a while that Horton would be one of the first to leave if Lee gained control of the Blues, and as results were working against the manager that story seemed believable, unlike many other newspaper articles at the time. That same match saw chairman Swales protected by three bouncers, dozens of stewards and numerous police as supporters' pleas for him to see sense became more aggressive. Something had to give.

On Monday 29th November Peter Swales announced he was stepping down as chairman of the club he loved: "This is a very sad day for me. But the situation with supporters has deteriorated to the point where I could see no other solution."

According to reports Swales was to remain on the board but had now resolved to ensure Lee did not gain control of the Blues. However, in an interview later that week he suggested he might be prepared to leave the board entirely, although selling to Lee still looked unlikely: "We are working on bringing a new team to run Manchester City and once everything is in place I may stand down altogether from the board. My time is up as far as running City is concerned. I have reached the stage where I want to relax. The last few months have not been a pleasant episode at Maine Road.

"There are a few options we are examining to make sure that the club's future is protected. Once we have installed the new team to run the club there might be a sale of the shares or a partial sale. Another possibility which we are looking at strongly is to go public so that our supporters will have the chance to become part of the set-up at Manchester City. When we have found the right man to become the new chairman within the next couple of weeks he might well feel that it would be in the club's best interests if I wasn't a director. I can easily appreciate that point of view. The new Chairman wouldn't want it to appear as if I am pulling the strings in the background at the club. If he wants me to stand down from the board then that is fine by me.

"My involvement in running Manchester City is finished. But I am still a City fan and I would still want to come along to Maine Road on match days to support the team."

As the year moved towards its close, the take-over rumbled on while City's match results worsened. Only one victory occurred during November and December as the Blues struggled. The League Cup run ended with a 2-1 defeat by Forest in a 4th round replay, despite an early goal from Vonk.

Over Christmas and into January Francis Lee and his supporters negotiated with representatives of Peter Swales and Stephen Boler in an attempt to conclude a take-over. Many times during that period it seemed the whole affair was on the brink of a satisfying conclusion, but on every occasion it appeared obstacles were deliberately placed in Lee's way. Nevertheless, in the early hours of Saturday 5th February the take-over negotiations were completed and Francis Lee and his supporters Colin Barlow and John Dunkerley were welcomed on to the board at Maine Road.

Immediately an exhausted Lee - he'd cut short his annual holiday in Barbados to attend the final negotiations - made an announcement: "I am tired now but it has all been worth it. The supporters have been superb in the way they have backed me in this long fight and the new board will ensure that they have their say in the running of the club. The immediate priority is to sort out the finances, which may take up to two weeks, and to ensure we remain in the Premiership. We certainly won't be selling any of our top players to help the club's financial situation. We are facing a relegation battle and you don't win a fight like that by getting rid of your best players."

That afternoon City faced Ipswich Town in the replay of a match abandoned after 39 minutes on 3rd January. The Blues had been leading 2-0 at Maine Road in the original fixture when referee David Elleray angered the City players, especially Tony Coton, by abandoning the tie due to a waterlogged pitch. The pitch had been appalling at the kick-off and perhaps the game should not have commenced. Naturally, it had been a big disappointment, but at least it guaranteed Francis Lee a home fixture for his first match as chairman.

The game was played out amid a carnival atmosphere, so different to a week earlier when the Blues were defeated 1-0 in the F.A. Cup at Cardiff and whispers the take-over was off circulated around the ground. Prior to the Ipswich game a banner was unveiled welcoming Lee back to Maine Road, while thousands of blue and white balloons were released. City, in typical big match style, allowed the visitors to take the lead via a mistake. Garry Flitcroft's attempted back pass ended up gifting the former Oldham player Ian Marshall a rather simple opportunity to score.

Fortunately, the men in Blue did not give up thanks mainly to David Rocastle, who had joined City from Leeds in a £1 million exchange for the out of form David White on 22nd December 1993. White had been struggling for the Blues ever since his international appearance in September 1992, and many believed he had lost confidence in himself. A move to another high profile club like Leeds seemed sensible, although whether his style would suit the famous defensively-minded Yorkshire side was debatable.

Rocastle had quickly become an important member of Horton's City side, although he did appear at times to lack full fitness. Against Ipswich he was excellent and helped bring the Blue equaliser as he cut through two defenders, charged to the goal-line and sent over a superb cross for Carl Griffiths to flick in a great goal. After the match new chairman Lee suggested Rocastle's display had been reminiscent of skills usually only found in Brazil. He really was that impressive.

The goal seemed to inject more confidence into the side, and with Michel Vonk defending superbly, and Steve Lomas controlling midfield, the Blues dominated. Terry Phelan attempted an overhead shot, before a foul on Lomas brought a free-kick. Keith Curle took it and Vonk knocked down for Garry Flitcroft to touch in the winning goal. It was a great feeling for most Blues that night with a City victory, and the long awaited return of Francis Lee.

Despite the optimism of 5th February, the remainder of the month brought home the realisation that the Blues were still a weak side. A 4-0 defeat at Coventry was a complete and utter shambles. It also made City's search for a decent striker to bolster the attack imperative, especially as Quinn was still missing and the lightweight Carl Griffiths was not fitting in as expected. Fortunately chairman Lee was already taking steps to secure a man who would ultimately become a cult figure at Maine Road - Uwe Rösler.

On 22nd February City endured a goalless match in the snow at Villa Park, although the highlight for all Blues had been yet another penalty miss by Dean Saunders. Previously, the Aston Villa man had failed to score from the spot against City when playing for Derby County (with emergency 'keeper Niall Quinn in goal), and again while with Liverpool. Immediately

David Rocastle arrived from Leeds with David White moving in the opposite direction.

Francis Lee took control of the club on Saturday 5th February 1994, the day the Blues played hosts to Ipswich. He and Colin Barlow (below right) were given a tremendous reception by City fans.

Kippax fans look on as City and Norwich draw 1-1 on 16th April 1994. Here David Brightwell puts the Canaries under pressure.

after the miss the travelling fans chanted: "Deano is a City fan" which, apparently, he once claimed he was. During the late 80s and early 90s Saunders was tipped to join the Blues on a couple of occasions. Each time he claimed he had stood on the Kippax as a boy and also stated he would walk from Derby to sign for the Blues. He never did. Perhaps he set off, forgot his map, took a wrong turning and ended up at Anfield!

A 2-1 victory at Swindon followed and then on 5th March at QPR Uwe Rösler made his first appearance in a City shirt following his arrival on loan from FC Nurnburg. That game ended 1-1 but before the month was out Rösler was joined by Paul Walsh - a £700,000 buy from Portsmouth - and Peter Beagrie - a £1.1 million arrival from Everton. At Ipswich on 29th March, Rösler and Walsh both demonstrated their value to the new-look Blues with a goal each to help City to a 2-2 draw, then on 2nd April the two men scored again during the comfortable 3-0 victory over Aston Villa at Maine Road. Peter Beagrie bagged number one - prompting his first somersault display while wearing a City shirt.

It was still possible for the Blues to go down and the majority of media pundits reckoned it was a certainty. Only Alan Hansen, who had backed the Blues during the 1993 F.A. Cup run, believed they were too good to be relegated.

More progress was made in the following two games, including an impressive 2-1 victory over Newcastle United before a Maine Road crowd of 33,774. Incredibly, defender David Brightwell - Ian's younger brother - scored the winner. New hero Rösler levelled the scores against Norwich in the next game but a disappointing 2-0 defeat at Old Trafford left City eighth from bottom, only five points clear of the trapdoor after playing more matches than those below.

The final home meeting of the season followed and was truly an emotional day as this was to be the last game played in front of the Kippax terracing. The match became known as "The Kippax Last Stand" and really signalled the end of England's last major terraced area. On the same day the Kop at Liverpool also witnessed its final game but, at this time in football history, the Kippax was actually the largest capacity terraced stand in the country. Understandably, its final day had to be memorable and a number of supporters had worked with the club to suggest and plan the events

Prior to the match a steel band played various tunes to welcome supporters into the stadium, while fans handed out balloons and sweets to enliven the atmosphere. City compere Vince Miller, wearing his familiar white suit, joined the steel band and began singing a medley of City's more familiar - and cleaner - chants and songs. Naturally, he sang 'Blue Moon', but there was also a rendition of the ever popular song that outlined the events of 1963 to 1970 - the most memorable line being: "Joe Mercer came we played the game we went to Rotherham".

A large number of former players were introduced to the crowd, and then Francis Lee was

The Kippax Last Stand
City fans display a huge flag as they say farewell to their favourite terracing on 30th April 1994.

brought out to enormous applause. In many ways the Kippax Last Stand also marked the end of one era and the beginning of another. Co-incidentally, Francis Lee had celebrated his fiftieth birthday that week and so, ever the entertainer, Vince Miller burst into voice again to sing 'Happy Birthday To You'.

During the Kippax party, a group of Chelsea supporters dressed, appropriately, as 'Blues Brothers', laid a wreath in the centre against the stand's perimeter fence. It was a gesture much appreciated by the Mancunian Blues.

The game itself ended 2-2 with new heroes Walsh and Rösler both scoring. The point more or less guaranteed City's survival but, on the day, fans seemed more intent on taking souvenirs from the old stand. Small pick-axes had been smuggled into the stadium to hack off pieces of Kippax terracing, while others removed signs - the most notable theft being the 'Colin Bell Bar' sign, which was later seen being carried by two supporters towards Manchester.

The club cared little about these harmless activities at the time, after all only a few months earlier there had been a much uglier atmosphere at the ground. It seemed everyone was relieved the take-over had now come to fruition, and relegation had been avoided.

The final match saw City draw 1-1 at Sheffield Wednesday, with Rösler scoring his fifth goal in 12 games, and the Blues ended the campaign in 16th place after suffering only two defeats since the arrival of the German.

The 1994 close season allowed everyone connected with the club to reflect on what had been a traumatic campaign from start to finish. For Peter Swales 1993-4 had been an absolute nightmare, but it was also a situation he could easily have avoided. Foolishly he believed City's support would eventually tire of the 'Swales Out' campaign and he attempted to ignore as many of the protests as possible. Although ultimately it was Francis Lee's determination to succeed that forced the take-over, it is important to recognise the vital role supporters played. Without detracting from Lee, it's also worth making the point that the fans had had enough from the moment the season commenced and would probably have supported anybody who seemed to offer a change at the top. At one stage Swales claimed a number of people had made offers to purchase the club, although the only one who actually came forward as a potential buyer was wealthy businessman Mike McDonald, a City fan who claimed to have stood on the Kippax as a youngster.

Once it became obvious he could not succeed at Maine Road, McDonald turned his attentions, with some success, to transforming Sheffield United while also retaining strong links with Hyde United on the eastern side of Manchester. Shortly before his death Peter Swales was asked why the McDonald bid failed: "That was never really serious. Never! Once Francis came in I knew it was a matter of time. He was the only man the fans would accept and I knew that. It had to be Francis. It all got messy though - the threats and hate mail. People giving out my address and that. I was totally stupid at the time. I thought Francis was behind it all! How stupid can you be? But no one could tell me. It's too ridiculous to contemplate, but when it's happening and you have to get security guards and all that you look for someone to blame.

The Career of Peter Swales

Peter Swales spent his formative years close to City's birthplace in the Ardwick area of Manchester, where his love for the Blues developed. After attending William Hulme Grammar School and completing the obligatory National Service, he made his mark selling sheet music, then popular records, before moving into electrical goods. He formed a business empire with his army friend Noel White, before the two of them combined again to purchase a significant stake in non-League Altrincham Football Club.

Always keeping a look out for 'his team', City, Peter was fortunate to overhear a conversation in a Hale Barns' pub that was to change his life forever. Blues' directors John Humphreys and Sidney Rose were discussing the Boardroom battle that was killing the club when Peter, with the kind of spirit which later helped him move up the F.A. hierarchy, interrupted stating he could solve all their problems. At the time he had no idea how he could end the fighting but somehow he convinced them he had a plan. In April 1971, his brash, confident approach succeeded as he was asked to tackle the in-fighting head on and become a Board member. After bringing stability to the Board he was rewarded when on 5th October 1973 he became Chairman, although he remained adamant to the end this was not by design.

As Chairman, he outlined his plans for City and really did believe he could turn the Blues into the U.K.'s leading club. His ambition in 1973 cannot be faulted, the problem was that twenty years later little if anything had improved.

Swales' initial 12 months in charge were eventful as he was to sack his first managerial appointment within six months, watch City reach the 1974 League Cup Final, appoint Tony Book as manager, and witness Denis Law's infamous back-heeled goal. When interviewed shortly before his death he explained he was still learning: "Ron Saunders was fired and we put Tony Book in charge. Under him we won plenty of the games left and escaped relegation comfortably, so that justified the sacking. But the first period of my Chairmanship was one of tremendous success, getting to Wembley ... then losing ... then having to sack a manager! Then escaping relegation, and you learn. I probably learnt more in that period than any other, because what you learn is that football will never be consistent. You're think you're on top of the world then something will happen to change it, and that happened many times to me over the years."

Once the first season was out of the way, Peter concentrated on overtaking the Reds in every way: "The hardest thing for me was to keep getting United rammed down my throat!". He tried to equal their support, and by backing the Junior Blues set-up, and the idea that City should be a 'friendly club', helped the Blues gain considerable support. He became the most active Chairman in the League as he travelled up and down the country promoting City at functions. He opened supporters' branches wherever possible, and would spend considerable time promoting the positive side of the club.

He also tackled the media. During the seventies and early eighties City were always on the back pages, or on TV documentaries. Naturally, if City's name appeared then so did Peter's, causing many to believe this was deliberate. Looking back, this now appears inevitable, rather than a deliberate ploy. Tommy Docherty regularly joked that Peter carried a card saying: "In case of emergency, please call a press conference." For most Swales critics, this reaffirmed the view Peter sought the publicity himself. What in fact it did demonstrate was that Peter's tactic of diverting attention to City from United was winning, and many United followers like Docherty could not accept the situation.

Throughout the 70s the Manchester clubs were equal. Swales' City were successful in the 1976 League Cup, and the following year were runners up to the dominant Liverpool in the League. Attendances increased, with the Blues averaging over 42,000 and boasting 26,000 season ticket holders at one point. ➤

Swales' plans seemed to be working when he made what became his biggest mistake: "We were runners up in the League by one point, and we had got to United on support. We averaged forty odd thousand and we almost caught them, and I thought well next year we'll win the Championship and we'll do it. That's when I made my biggest mistake - Malcolm Allison. I got talked into that! Instead of sticking with Tony, who'd got us into second place which would make us kings today. But not me! I think 'no, this is not good enough, we're almost there!' And one or two on the Board started to say 'if we could just get Malcolm we could do the final push'. Final bloody push all right!"

"I don't want to come out of this saying Allison did nothing for City. He was great in the late 60s and early 70s...did a fantastic job, but I maintain it was a mistake to bring him back and I hold up my hands. I carry the can for that."

With Malcolm as Manager and Peter as Chairman City spent millions, yet headed towards the Second Division. When relegation looked likely, Peter acted and sacked Big Mal. The sacking had the desired effect and under John Bond the Blues climbed the table and reached the 1981 F.A. Cup Final. This final was the proudest moment of Peter's career.

After Wembley, Peter authorised Bond to buy Trevor Francis, another million pound purchase, and created plans for the redevelopment of Maine Road. No one could fault the way the Blues appeared to be moving but, within two years of Wembley, it all went horribly wrong. With the club in debt Peter sold crowd-puller Francis. As a result the Blues struggled on the pitch and attendances dropped. John Bond resigned, and relegation followed. The ground redevelopment plans were then halted after construction of the unique Main Stand roof (if the plans had continued the Kippax roof would have been of similar design, the Platt Lane would have been developed to look like the North Stand, and Executive Boxes would have hung from the Main Stand roof).

Supporters became critical, but the Chairman vowed to continue, stating he'd got the club into the mess, and so he was the best man to get City out.

After two years of Second Division football, the cash-strapped Blues returned to the top flight under Billy McNeill. In 1986, after the City youngsters won the F.A. Youth Cup and the first team reached Wembley in the Full Members' Cup, Peter predicted the Blues were back and destined for glory. Unfortunately, his predictions did not come true as, within a year, McNeill walked out - disillusioned with the lack of finance - and City, under Jimmy Frizzell, were relegated once again. Major demonstrations took place against Peter, with the famous 'Swales Out' chant increasing in popularity as 1987 progressed, but again he vowed to continue.

In 1989, back in Division One, Peter watched with delight as Mel Machin's Blues defeated multi-million pound United. The Reds called for the head of Alex Ferguson but, incredibly, it was City who lost their manager when Peter sacked Machin for not having any 'repartee' with the crowd. He meant rapport, but by this time any reason seemed possible (the media created images of song and dance routines featuring Machin and Frizzell). Again, the fans demonstrated, but Peter was able to quell the demos by appointing Howard Kendall. Some fans were suspicious, especially when virtually every signing was an ex-Evertonian, but overall the majority believed Kendall was the right man.

With Kendall, Peter felt he had picked a winner and the Blues would be successful again. Unfortunately a rather surprising 'get out' clause allowed Kendall to return to his first love, Everton, when the opportunity presented itself. Bowing to public pressure Peter appointed Peter Reid, but the relationship between Swales and City's loyal support had evaporated.

Seventeen years of frustration became too much for City fans when in March 1993 they invaded the pitch during a humiliating 4-2 F.A. Cup sixth round defeat at home to Spurs. That night Peter contemplated resignation, but was persuaded to stay by colleagues and friends. From that point he admitted he was not the kind of Chairman he wanted to be: "In the early years I was an outgoing Chairman with ambition, not at all like the last few years when I was half bloody dead!". He later recognised he had made plenty of mistakes; the appointment of John Maddock as General Manager is a prime example, and many of his actions were simply incredible. Nevertheless it took a long sustained campaign to remove him from power. Eventually he did stand down, but his love for the Blues did not diminish.

After City he received offers to become a director of several leading clubs but refused them all because he was a City man through and through. Some directors move from club to club, but Peter was not like that. He loved the Blues, and only the Blues. He talked affectionately of his love for them and how he desperately wanted to attend a match at Maine Road. He also mentioned approaches he ➤

Obviously, there's always an element ... a minority that will take the law into their own hands, but for me to believe it was organised was crazy."

There was a lot of hostility from supporters of both groups although, as Swales stated, this had not been directly prompted by either himself or Lee. When asked about claims that other people had shown interest in buying the Blues, Swales was adamant there had been other offers. Mike McDonald was one such bidder, but who was the first? Swales: "Francis was not the first. Others had been interested, and one wealthy and quite famous man was interested, but he soon scarpered once Francis became interested. I can't tell you who he is, though. It's a pity really because he had a lot of interesting things to say."

As far as all supporters were concerned nothing mattered other than their hero, Francis Lee, was now in control. It was irrelevant to speculate how serious other bids may or may not have been. Nevertheless, it would still be fascinating to know the identity of the man who Swales claimed had made such an interesting offer.

Throughout the close season those that had been successful - Lee, Barlow and Dunkerley - were kept busy discovering the appalling financial truths of the club. They were also forced to take a serious look at plans for the future. The Kippax Stand had to be replaced due to the requirements of government legislation following the Lord Justice Taylor Report, and the new directors were keen to see an improvement on the scheme laid down by former chairman Peter Swales. They also saw the stand's redevelopment as a chance to give the stadium an overall structural design and by the middle of the year plans were released to the public showing a much improved venue. Naturally, the Kippax Stand had to be developed first but the ultimate scheme proposed an extension to each of the other stands to give Maine Road a three tier stadium under one continuous roof. The drawings looked impressive, but the familiar problem of existing so close to a large number of densely populated residential streets always seemed likely to pose a problem.

Away from the ground improvements, Chairman Lee and Managing Director Barlow gave Brian Horton their support, despite media predictions only a few months earlier, and he was able to take stock of the squad and plan for at least another season. Already three of his five major signings had impressed (Rösler, Walsh, and Beagrie), while Carl Griffiths appeared to need only a little further grooming before becoming a permanent fixture in the first team, and defender Alan Kernaghan was prepared to prove his critics wrong. Only time would tell if Griffiths and Kernaghan could match Horton's other signings and become crowd favourites.

During the close season the manager sold Mike Sheron for £1 million to Norwich after 98 appearances, plus 22 as substitute. It was a disappointing transfer of a talented forward, but with the form of Walsh and Rösler it was also one Horton felt would not unduly harm his plans. Another to leave was David Rocastle who joined Chelsea for a reported £1.25 million. Horton: "We have an abundance of midfield players and I think Rocky suspected he was going to be one of the odd men out. Some players are quite happy to be part of the senior squad, but I don't think this would have been the case with David. He was upset when he was left out of a couple of pre-season matches. It is hard to see where I could have accommodated him in the system I have in mind. The offer came out of the blue, and I felt it was good business, but the final decision was his."

A few weeks earlier, the Blues made their only major signing of the summer when they paid Swindon Town £1.5 million for Francis Lee's godson Nicky Summerbee. Understandably, supporters were keen to see if the 23-year-old could compare with his father, the brilliant 60s hero Mike.

Summerbee made his debut in the opening League fixture - a 3-0 defeat at Arsenal. The Blues had conceded as early as the second minute and Rösler was sent off after an hour for dissent. Fortunately a 3-0 win over West Ham in the first League fixture at Maine Road following demolition of the Kippax suggested the campaign might offer more than the

City Leader
Peter Swales at the head of a 1977 Maine Road 'family photo' in 1977.

had received from other clubs: "Since I left City, I've had several opportunities to go to other clubs. It happens all the time. People say why don't you join us. Join our board. I don't know what I'm going to do next year or the year after, but I cannot imagine being at another club, even now when I can't go into the ground because I don't want anyone to say we're bottom of the League because he's been here! I still love Manchester City. I've never changed on this one. If I never go in the ground again it won't matter, it won't alter my affection for the club. It could never change that.

"I can't go to Maine Road. How would the fans treat me? I could hardly sit in one of the stands. I've been to Blackpool, Aston Villa, Sheffield, Liverpool... lots of places and been made very welcome. I've been asked to join various clubs, but I won't. You see, despite everything I still love City. You may find it hard to believe, but I'm a fan. Always have been. It may be that I get fed up waltzing around the country and I might want to settle down again, you never know what's going to happen. I'm always waiting for a 'phone call, expecting somebody to say, 'you'd better come back, have your seat back - keep your nose out of our affairs, but you will be made welcome'. I expect that call's going to come every day, but it never does."

Sadly, on Thursday 2nd May 1996 he died as a result of a heart attack. He was only 62 and had gone before anyone could make peace with him, although he did admit he had frequently seen Francis Lee after the take-over: "Francis and me get on fine. I've met him a few times. My colleague Stephen Boler has the golf club down the road and I've seen Francis there, had a chat and that. We get on fine, really well. I like Francis. Some of the others won't talk to me though, and I find that very difficult. There are people on City's board I have been friendly with for years and yet they don't talk to me. They'd probably cross the road if they saw me coming towards them. I find that very hard to accept. We'd been together for years. Why?"

A few days after Swales' death City played their final game of the 1995-6 season at home to Liverpool. A minute's silence was arranged to take place at Maine Road, although a nationwide minute's silence would have been more appropriate for a respected F.A. official. Significantly, despite the continued bitterness, City supporters observed the silence immaculately. The memory of any true Blue should be respected. Many questioned Swales' devotion to the Blues during his reign; it is a fact he loved the club dearly.

His overall career at City does divide into two distinct and diverse phases. The first saw him drive a glamorous club forward in the way he had always wanted, while the second saw the same club poverty-stricken and fighting for survival while he appeared to sack anyone and everyone. Unfortunately for Peter he will probably be remembered more for the latter.

The final words on his long turbulent career at City belong to Peter himself. They perhaps provide the answer to why he continued for so long, especially in times of much sorrow amid pressure that perhaps ultimately cost him his life.

"I couldn't believe my luck. I used to wake up every morning and think, 'Bloody Hell, Chairman of Manchester City - this is the best job in the world!' If they'd have made me Prime Minister I wouldn't have wanted it. It was the best job I could ever imagine getting. You know I've been Chairman of the England team for five years, I'm Vice-President of the F.A., I've had various positions in football, but none of them - I promise you - compares with being Chairman of the club you love. I could look back over the things that have happened - even the take-over - look back on all that and, believe me, it was all a good price to pay for having the opportunity".

Paul Walsh heads City into an early lead against Crystal Palace at Maine Road in September 1994. A 'capacity' 19,971 crowd watched the 1-1 draw.

previous one, especially as the trio of Blue heroes - Beagrie, Walsh and Rösler - each scored. Three days later it was 4-0 as two goals apiece from Walsh and Rösler humiliated Everton and sent a delighted Brian Horton to face the press. In typical Horton-speak he stated: "It was an excellent team performance, wasn't it?" By this point in his City career the public were finding it a little entertaining that the manager ended every sentence with a question. At least it proved he was human, didn't it?

The only minus point about these two fine Maine Road performances was that too few Blues had been able to view the matches. Because of the Kippax redevelopment, the capacity was severely reduced and both games were attended by more or less sell out crowds of less than 20,000. Fortunately, City's new Chairman and Managing Director had taken steps to ensure the capacity increased as the season progressed. The lower level of the new three tier stand would be constructed and seated first allowing the mid-season capacity to reach around 25,000 and the May figure to be almost 28,000. Had the stadium been able to accommodate over 30,000 it's possible this first season under Lee would have seen the Blues watched by their highest average since the 34,000 of 1981-2.

Nicky Summerbee followed in his father's footsteps by joining the Blues from Swindon.

A 3-0 defeat at Chelsea followed on 31st August before September brought five points from three games. The third of those games - a 2-0 win against Norwich - saw Niall Quinn net his first goal since returning from injury. Unfortunately, the Eire international would find himself the odd man out for much of the 1994-5 season as Walsh and Rösler were Horton's preferred strike force. Nevertheless, Quinn did manage to start 24 League games, come on as substitute in a further 11, and score a total of eight League goals - a record considerably better than any of the previous campaign's strikers when Sheron ended as top scorer with a pitiful six.

On 15th October, the away game at QPR proved dramatic; with 30 minutes to go, the Blues were leading 2-0, thanks to Garry Flitcroft and Paul Walsh. QPR fought back and managed to reduce City's lead, although the goal was a controversial one. Andy Dibble, playing his second League game of the season, was adjudged to have punched clear while outside his area. Former City player Clive Wilson took the resultant free-kick and, as he made contact with the ball, the referee appeared to blow his whistle. The City players believed the kick was to be retaken and simply stood motionless, while the ball sailed past Dibble's left hand and into the net. The referee then signalled a goal and, understandably, City complained. Protesting captain Keith Curle was booked, and a shade fortunate to remain on the pitch.

A few minutes later Les Ferdinand charged towards Dibble's net; the City 'keeper put out a leg and Ferdinand crashed to the ground. The linesman flagged and Dibble was sent off for a professional foul, again hotly disputed by the City players. Nicky Summerbee, who was finding it difficult to match the expectations of the fans, was immediately replaced by the still injured Tony Coton. The 'keeper was struggling with a back injury and endured terrible pain as the Blues determined to keep their lead.

It wasn't long before full back Richard Edghill made life even more difficult for the Blues when he was also dismissed for felling Trevor Sinclair once too often. For nine-man City those final fifteen minutes seemed an eternity as QPR missed a number of chances while Coton, obviously in pain, made a few heroic saves. Yet another match between the two sides had made the headlines. In previous years fixtures between the clubs had marked the commencement of Lee's take-over bid, and the first League game broadcast live by Sky TV. What would the next QPR fixture have in store? The Blues did not have to wait long as the two sides were due to meet in the League Cup on 25th October.

Before that, however, City had the task of facing a Jürgen Klinsmann-inspired Tottenham Hotspur in the League. Much had been made of the arrival of the German World Cup hero and the media proclaimed him as one of the most important foreign players of the period, with much hype following his every move. As a result little had been said about City's own German entertainer Uwe Rösler, still missing following an injury sustained almost a month earlier against Norwich.

In a thrilling match, the Blues tore into Tottenham and after seventeen minutes, Steve Lomas made a run down the right, and sent in an impressive cross to Niall Quinn. Campbell intercepted but Paul Walsh managed to retrieve the ball and fired past goalkeeper Walker.

Spurs, playing a good passing game, levelled the scores on the half hour via Dumitrescu's penalty, but it was obvious the Blues were still controlling much of the action.

A short while later, a City counter-attack led to another goal. Lomas passed out wide to Summerbee who in turn crossed to Walsh. The former Portsmouth player headed powerfully at Walker before Quinn blasted in the rebound to make it 2-1. Five minutes later Terry Phelan knocked the ball to Peter Beagrie who managed to beat two players before releasing Quinn who set Walsh up to score City's third.

A minute into the second half, Klinsmann and Dumitrescu combined for the latter to make it 3-2 via a deflection off Curle. Five minutes later Walsh ran from inside his own half then, as he fell, somehow managed to pass to Beagrie. The former Everton man crossed to the unmarked Lomas who powered home a beautiful header.

With only ten minutes left Walsh made another brilliant run, passing four players on his travels, before turning and crossing to Garry Flitcroft, who netted to make it 5-2 and complete a marvellous performance. It had been a game of memorable quality and was enjoyed by millions on Match Of The Day that night. Commentator John Motson made comparisons with the famous 'Ballet On Ice' from 1967, and the BBC reminded viewers of the skills of that match by showing a few minutes of black and white footage.

Three days later City followed up with another entertaining performance. It was the League Cup encounter at QPR on 25th October. The Blues had already disposed of Barnet 5-2 on aggregate in the second round and clearly expected to put in a good performance at Loftus Road. Sadly, within a minute they conceded a goal just as they had in the earlier League Cup match at Barnet and Horton's side suffered for a while. By the 37th minute they managed to get their act together a little and Summerbee equalised with a 20 yard volley. A minute later Rangers took the lead again.

Fortunately, in the 46th minute Keith Curle netted a penalty to bring City level once again, followed eight minutes later by a magnificent Beagrie volley which made it 3-2 and brought a series of somersaults from the popular ex-Evertonian. Five minutes later, the same player headed through to Lomas who made it 4-2.

In the 87th minute Rangers pulled a goal back to keep City on their toes, but the referee's whistle signalled the start of a party for the City fans while their QPR equivalents began to demonstrate against their chairman. Apparently, some unhappy QPR fans were keen to listen to the advice of a few experienced Mancunian demonstrators.

In the next round City overcame Newcastle 2-0 at St. James Park after a 1-1 draw at Maine Road. German import Maurizio Gaudino made his debut in that victory in a match captained by Garry Flitcroft. Afterwards Kevin Keegan admitted City deserved to win and told the press he hoped the Blues would go on to win the trophy. Sadly, a fifth round encounter at Crystal Palace prevented that from happening when, on 11th January, the Blues succumbed to a 4-0 hammering. Horton's side crumbled on a night when the impressive Steve Lomas crashed to the ground with a broken ankle. He also swallowed his tongue, bringing back painful memories of the Paul Lake incident during the 1988-9 season, and went on to miss the rest of the season. It was a huge blow.

Maurizio Gaudino made his debut in the League Cup replay win at Newcastle just before Christmas '94.

Back in the League, City should have defeated Coventry but lost 1-0 in the closing minutes, then a 3-3 draw with Alan Ball's Southampton raised a few concerns. It also brought a little humour as the visitors' 'keeper Bruce Grobbelaar looked as if he was auditioning for a part in Phantom of the Opera as he wore a mask throughout the game to protect his broken cheekbone.

Steve Lomas heads City's fourth goal in the thrilling 5-2 win over Tottenham in October 1994.

Then on Thursday 10th November came one of the worst nights in the Blue history of Manchester football when City travelled to Stretford for the 121st Manchester League derby. The Blues had only received around 1800 tickets - although this was considerably more than previous years - and were seated in the corner between 'K' Stand and the Main Stand. Among the away contingent was City's biggest hero of the period, Uwe Rösler, who was still out through injury. As the great German made his way to his seat a few supporters approached and asked for autographs. Naturally he obliged, but an over-zealous United steward marched towards the City player and insisted he sat down. In faltering English Rösler tried to explain but the official didn't seem prepared to listen and started to order the player into his seat.

At this point another, more sensible, steward arrived and explained to the first that this 'fan' was actually Rösler. The first official shouted: "I don't care who he is, he's still got to sit down!" Eventually, the jobsworth saw sense and allowed Rösler to continue signing autographs for the Blues who had formed an orderly queue. The steward walked away muttering: "These City people are all the same. They've got ideas above their station and they won't listen to reason."

The Blues had won their first victory of the day. The match commenced in typical 1990s derby style with City putting United under considerable pressure throughout the first quarter. Richard Edghill seemed to have the measure of Ryan Giggs and an early challenge by the City man sent his opponent flying to the floor. All Blues - including those of German nationality - seated in the away section cheered, and those opening minutes were a real joy. Sadly, in the 24th minute, very much against the general run of play Eric Cantona gave United the lead. After that the Blues fought back on occasion but the game from thereon was simply a nightmare.

At 4-0 with twenty minutes to go many City supporters drifted off to their Manchester homes. Even Uwe Rösler chose this moment to make his exit - to a fantastic ovation from those Blues remaining. Earlier his already excellent image improved when he attempted to sing a number of City chants including 'Blue Moon' and the ironic 'City is our name', although he struggled to understand many of the words.

For those who were left the agony continued. Every City fan seemed to be praying for an end to the misery. "Don't let it get to five" they muttered over and over again. Then it happened. Kanchelskis scored his third of the match, and the first derby hat-trick since Francis Lee in 1970, to make it 5-0. Fortunately, the game ended before United could equal the record derby score of six - held by City, of course, since 1926.

Afterwards a shell-shocked Horton faced the media, unlike his opposite number in 1989: "When

Maine Citizen

NUMBER 37

UWE RÖSLER

Uwe Rösler was an unknown quantity when signed on loan in March 1994, but quickly proved his ability with a string of fine performances, and became something of a cult figure to thousands of Blues.

Born November 1968 in Attenburg, Germany, he endured quite a difficult life in East Germany, although he admits this was little different to any of his fellow countrymen.

As he was growing up football became a useful release and, in due course, Uwe made a name for himself as a decent player. By the time he arrived at Maine Road he had made ten full international appearances for East Germany and played for Magdeburg, Dynamo Dresden, and Nurnburg, occasionally finding himself in trouble with the management, especially at Dresden. He had also been on trial at Middlesbrough before he arrived at Maine Road.

Rösler's first opportunity to impress the City management came in a reserve game at home to Burnley, where he bagged two goals to give manager Brian Horton and Chairman Francis Lee much to think about. It wasn't long before they gave him a chance in the Premier League. His debut arrived in the 1-1 draw at QPR on 5th March 1994.

The Blues soon made his move permanent, signing him on 1st June for £375,000, while City fans were delighted with his positive attitude to the game during those final months of the 1993-4 season. In only 12 games Rösler combined well with another new signing, Paul Walsh, and netted five goals, placing him only a goal behind City's leading League scorer Mike Sheron. Rösler's goals basically saved City from relegation in 1994.

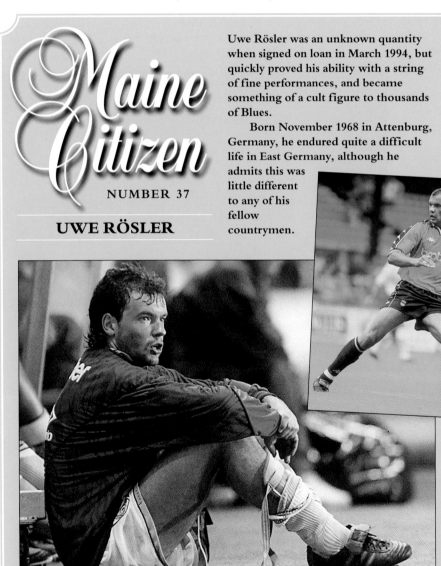

we needed to stand up and be counted some of our players did not want to know, did they?"

Although he could have taken the easy option and blamed the result on injuries - remember City were missing Rösler, Curle, and both goalkeepers Dibble and Coton - he chose not to. It was a credit to him that he faced the music.

Despite the result City managed to pick themselves up and achieve three successive victories in the following matches, including their first win at Ipswich since 1961. Despite that, December turned out a dismal month with four of the six matches ending in defeat, while January brought two points from a possible nine. In fact it wasn't until 22nd February that the Blues managed their first League victory since the Ipswich match. Co-incidentally, that was the return fixture with the East Anglian club. The goalless draw with Leeds three days later should have ended in victory but somehow dominance could not be turned into goals, although it is fair to say the Blues were still struggling with injury and missed four influential players - Rösler, Walsh, Beagrie, and Flitcroft.

A 1-1 draw at Norwich and a 2-1 defeat at home to Chelsea left City in 16th place and clearly in danger

Once the lower section of the new Kippax was seated, supporters were allowed to occupy it. Unfortunately, with no cover, this meant the club handing out raincoats in wet weather.

During 1994-5 he continued to impress with 15 goals in 29 (plus 2 as substitute) appearances, while in the F.A. Cup he was outstanding during the 5-2 defeat of Howard Kendall's Notts County on 18th January and became the first City player since Johnny Hart in 1953 to score four goals in an F.A. Cup tie.

He was also the club's most popular player by far, winning the Player of the Year award at the end of the season: "The Manchester City fans have been marvellous to me, and it was a big honour to be named their top player. My aim is to score the goals and help Manchester City bring back success."

Throughout this period Rösler appeared at many supporters' events, and was always a very popular guest. At the West Yorkshire branch of the Independent Supporters' Association he was warmly welcomed and questioned about his career and his life. He was even asked what he thought of the controversial tee-shirts on sale around the ground which humorously claimed his grandfather had 'bombed Old Trafford'. He laughed and said it wasn't true, his grandfather had not bombed United's stand in the war, although he did admit he'd bought him a tee-shirt!

In November 1994 he sat with the supporters during an extremely depressing derby match at Old Trafford and attempted to join in their singing. City fans felt Uwe was as passionate about the club as they were.

The 1995-6 season should have seen Rösler develop further, unfortunately he constantly seemed at loggerheads with new manager Alan Ball. Whether this was his fault or Ball's is open to debate, but it's interesting to note the manager frequently criticised the attitude of his player in public, yet under Frank Clark during 1997 Rösler's attitude seemed exemplary. Fortunately, unlike so many other City heroes during the Alan Ball period, Rösler managed to remain at the club.

His perfect partner, Paul Walsh, was transferred at the start of September 1995 and Rösler suffered as a result. No one else seemed capable of getting the ball to the powerful German and Rösler's League goal tally was only 9 - still City's highest.

During 1996-7 he impressed again with 15 goals in 43 (+1) League appearances during an extremely difficult season to prove his experiences under Ball had not dampened his long term drive and determination.

Inevitably, his performances were overshadowed by Kinkladze during the 1995-6 and 1996-7 seasons, but it did not mean his role in the side had diminished. Far from it, Rösler's battling spirit ensured the Blues could still push forward regardless of what was happening with or without the impressive Georgian.

Rösler's time at City ended during 1998 when he moved back to Germany to join Kaiserslautern. He even appeared in the Champions League – ironically on the same night as City were playing in the Auto-Windscreens Shield – but his career with Kaiserlautern wasn't to last. 28 League games at Tennis Berlin followed before he returned to English football with Southampton on 6th July 2000.

During his five seasons with City Rösler became a cult figure and will be remembered most for the entertainment generated by his spell working alongside Paul Walsh.

RÖSLER'S PLAYING RECORD

	LEAGUE		FA CUP		FL CUP		TOTAL	
	App	Gls	App	Gls	App	Gls	App	Gls
1993-94	12	5	-	-	-	-	12	5
1994-95	29(2)	15	4	5	3(1)	2	36(3)	22
1995-96	34(2)	9	5	2	3	2	42(2)	13
1996-97	43(1)	15	3	1	2	1	48(1)	17
1997-98	23 (6)	6	2	1	2	-	27 (6)	7
TOTAL	141 (11)	50	14	9	10 (1)	5	165 (12)	64

On the 25th anniversary of City's European Cup Winners' Cup success, Norah Mercer attended Maine Road for the unveiling of a portrait of her late husband, Joe. The painting was commissioned by the club.

of relegation. It was an extremely tense time for all connected with the club especially the supporters who had dearly hoped the arrival of Lee might actually propel City towards the top of the table, not the bottom.

A relegation dogfight at Everton on 15th March ended in a 1-1 draw and a sending-off for Terry Phelan for time-wasting, before a 3-2 defeat of Sheffield Wednesday brought a much needed boost to morale. The Blues had been 2-0 down at one point before fighting back courtesy of goals from Walsh and Rösler (2). Despite that result the following three League games all ended in defeat before a Good Friday meeting with Liverpool brought a shock 2-1 victory. Deliberately Horton played a strong attacking formation with Quinn, Rösler and Walsh all present in the starting line-up.

After a bright start, the Blues took the lead in the 18th minute as Summerbee scored his first City League goal following a perfect pass from Gaudino.

The new Kippax was nearing completion when Newcastle United visited in April 1995. The second tier was used for the first time for this game.

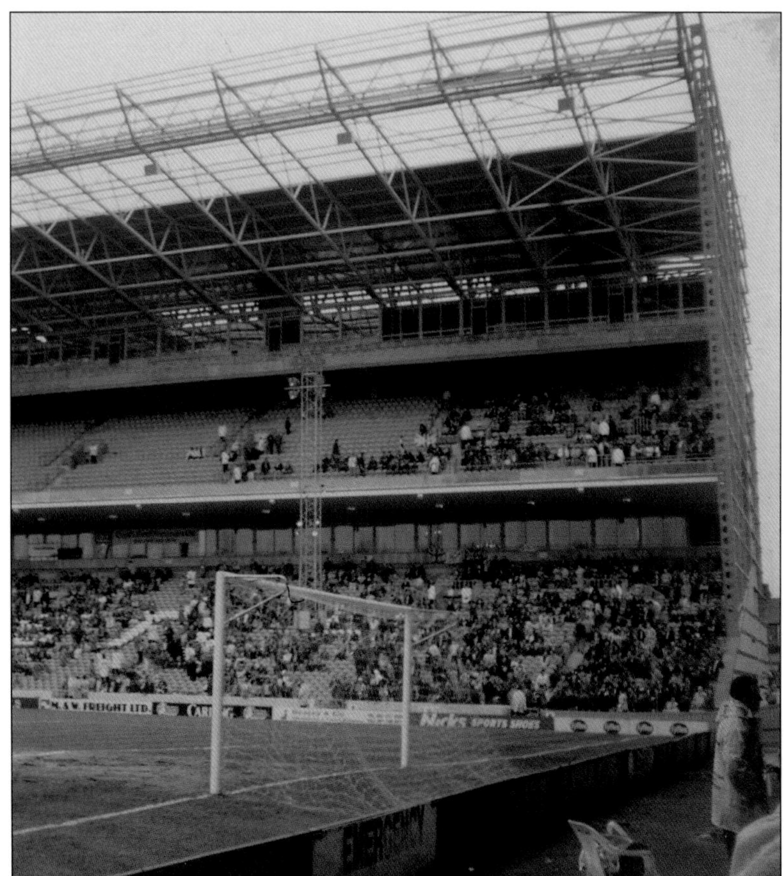

It was an important goal, especially as Summerbee was still finding it difficult to fit into Horton's side. Although the Blues continued to play with confidence, the impressive McManaman started to bring the Anfield men back into the match.

It was no surprise when the exciting Liverpool youngster scored an absolutely brilliant equaliser and kept his side in the game until a bruising tackle by Flitcroft, early in the second half, sent him limping off. The injury helped City dominate the rest of the encounter and Rösler, in particular, seemed to thrive. He spurned a couple of chances before setting up fellow countryman Gaudino to score fifteen minutes from time. It was a thoroughly deserved goal and victory, and gave Horton confidence relegation could be avoided.

A 3-2 victory against championship favourites Blackburn followed at Ewood Park on Easter Monday. Horton later admitted it was the best performance since his arrival while Blackburn boss Kenny Dalglish was shell-shocked: "Where have Manchester City been all season when they can play like that?" Where indeed! As all supporters knew, the Blues were - are - the great unpredictables of soccer and defeating the Champions elect while struggling to avoid relegation is not an uncommon occurrence for them. 1994-5 had been an unpredictable, inconsistent season, but then isn't every season like that at Maine Road?

Over the weeks that followed, with veteran John Burridge in goal, City achieved a 1-1 draw at Villa, but then suffered a 1-0 defeat at Nottingham Forest and an absolutely appalling 3-2 loss at home to QPR on the final day of the season. That match ensured almost every City-QPR fixture of the 1990s was remembered for one reason or another, but it did little for Brian Horton. Had the side played with more conviction he may have been able to build and develop a team capable of challenging for honours. Unfortunately, it was clear there were still a few problems at Maine Road and Horton paid the price.

The season wound up with City in 17th place. Had that final match ended on a high note with a win the Blues would have moved five places higher into a position of some respectability and Horton may even have kept his job.

For most supporters the departure of Horton seemed a might unfair, after all he had made a number of good signings, and there had been quite a few positive points during the season such as reaching the fifth round of the League Cup. City had also reached the same round of the F.A. Cup, although the peculiar law that surrounds the Blues seems to insist that whenever they draw the same side in both cup competitions they must lose the F.A. Cup match. Usually they also lose the League Cup match, but this time Newcastle United could only manage to scupper City's chances of a blue Wembley in the F.A. Cup by winning 3-1 at St. James Park.

Despite the positives, it was decided Horton had to go. The QPR game had been an embarrassment, as had a number of key matches that season, especially that horrendous night at Old Trafford. Francis Lee felt certain he could appoint a man who really was big enough for the City job, and Blues fans waited eagerly to hear who this new high profile manager would be.

Chapter Twenty Two

MANAGER OF THE MONTH

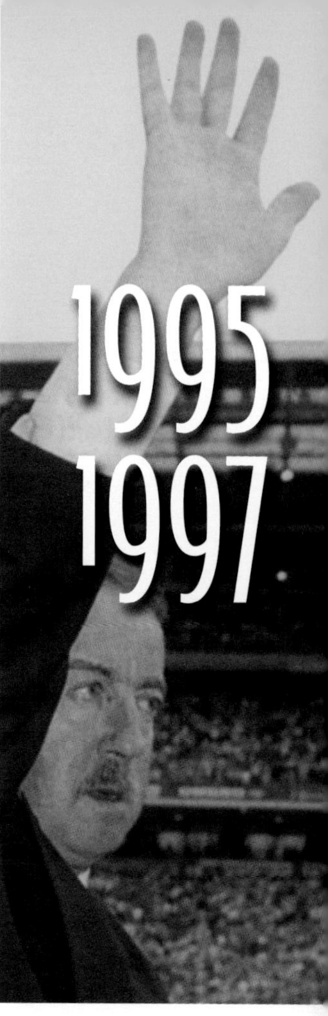

THE sacking of Brian Horton on 16th May - two days after the final match of the season - was rather confusing to most supporters as newspapers that morning claimed he'd actually been dismissed minutes after the pathetic performance against QPR. On radio at around 8am on the 16th, City secretary Bernard Halford denied the rumours and insisted Horton was still the boss. In St. Albans Horton told the media: "If I've been sacked it's the first I've heard about it. My position certainly wasn't discussed after Saturday's match, but I think an urgent meeting is needed to clarify my position."

A short while later Colin Barlow, City's Managing Director, also dismissed the rumours: "Those stories are totally without foundation. Brian Horton is still the manager of City."

At lunch time, Horton met Lee and the inevitable happened. He was sacked: "There were no arguments. The Chairman was very calm and so was I. The decision wasn't totally unexpected. Every manager is judged on results and we simply didn't win enough matches this season to keep me in a job. But even so it still hurt like hell to be given the sack."

At 2pm Colin Barlow read out a prepared statement at a hastily arranged press conference and wished Horton well for the future. He refused to provide any further information and the media speculated on the reasons for the dismissal and then considered possible replacements. Already they were suggesting a number of possibilities including Bruce Rioch, David Pleat, Mick McCarthy, Bobby Robson, Brian Kidd, and George Graham, plus of course old favourites Dave Bassett and Steve Coppell who seemed destined to always be included in any list of possible Blue managers. By the end of May, Ray Harford, Ron Atkinson and John Toshack were added to this string of prospects.

Earlier Colin Barlow told the public City would be appointing a high profile manager with a proven track record. He added: "Francis and myself, as former players, know exactly what the club and the fans want and that is a manager who can take us into Europe. Europe next year has to be our target. That means finishing in the top five or six clubs or winning a major cup competition. It means we are not in a position to appoint someone without the necessary experience."

He later added: "There is no immediate pressure on us to appoint a new man. The letters that are coming in are from people with impressive records, while telephone enquiries are from managers quite definitely in the big name category."

Hearing this everyone began to believe the new manager would be one with an impressive c.v. similar to that of Howard Kendall when he was first appointed in 1989. The official comments certainly seemed aimed at building the supporters up for a major personality with a successful managerial track record and, when it was announced on 29th May City were confident of getting their man within a week, the fans really were filled with optimism. Sadly, an appointment did not materialise and rumours again were rife. Brian Kidd, though not a man the majority of supporters wanted, appeared a front runner but it was announced United would deny the Blues permission to speak with Alex Ferguson's assistant. Kidd himself stated: "I have absolutely no intention of leaving United. I have been at the club since boyhood and I love my job here. I have no desire to go to City or anywhere else. I have told the chairman that I do not wish to speak to any other club."

By 18th June it appeared there were two candidates in the running and most assumed George Graham was one, especially as he had been seen waiting to be met at Piccadilly station. The other was a complete mystery, although when Huddersfield Town appointed Brian Horton as manager on the 21st some Blues joked the City directors would have to remove him from their short list.

It wasn't long however before the other name became public - World Cup winner Alan Ball. On 30th June, while Ball was on holiday in Spain, an announcement was made that the Southampton manager would be offered the post. The fans were totally unimpressed with the appointment after all the hyperbole throughout the summer. They wanted the promised highly successful, high profile manager with a proven track record and would not accept Ball was that man. The fanzine *Electric Blue* typified the supporters' reactions: "Brian Kidd had embarrassed City by declaring his intention to wallow a while longer at The Sty and George Graham had yet to clear his name, both time and prospective managers were in short supply.

Alan Ball became manager at City during the Summer of 1995.

"Hardly surprising then that City should trawl the depths and come up with the name of Alan Ball. Yes, I know, Alan Ball! He of the flame red hair, old bloke's cap and the irritating squeaky voice... I couldn't believe it either. Unlike the previous incumbent of the warm seat, Ball - or Bally as he is known amongst those in the know - is, at least, a household name. No embarrassing cries of 'Alan Who?' were heard in Manchester this time around; instead 'Why Ball?' or words to that effect were in the ascendancy. Of course the answer is almost as simple as the question. Not to put too fine a point on it, there was no one else around. City would doubtless say that they were inundated with prospective managers, most of whom would have been jokers whose only management experience would have been gleaned plying their trade with pub teams the length and breadth of Lancashire anyway!"

Although some supporters did warm to Ball, and others suggested it might be wise to see what improvements he could make to Horton's side before applying a judgement, the majority were clearly sceptical at the appointment. There was a view the other candidate, George Graham, should have been given the job despite his problems with the F.A. Colin Barlow told the media: "I know George Graham has a lot of fans among our supporters but time was against us as far as he was concerned."

Graham claimed it had been up to him to take the job or not: "It would have been easy for me to have taken the Manchester City job while I was waiting for the F.A. panel to get their act together, but I did not wish to embarrass City chairman Francis Lee, who had chatted to me about the vacancy at Maine Road before giving the job to my old Arsenal team mate Alan Ball."

On 4th July, with supporter mutterings mounting, Colin Barlow felt it was time to plead for patience: "We would ask fans to reserve their judgement on Alan Ball and give him the time he surely deserves. We will not allow anything to stand in our way. Our aim is and always has been, a team with flair and style playing football on the ground and that will come with Alan Ball. That's his style and his philosophy. Couple his appointment with the signing of a couple of skilful players and we will be well on the way."

That statement in itself gave the fans another opportunity to attack the appointment. If, as expected, Ball proved unable to bring a 'couple of skilful' players to the club in the short term then more pressure would be applied.

Barlow went on to compare the appointment with that of Joe Mercer in 1965, stating City's greatest manager had a similar record to Ball before arriving at Maine Road, although Joe had won a trophy.

For many it seemed City's PR machine had failed. Dave Wallace, editor of fanzine *King of the Kippax*, felt he could have warned the directors how the supporters would react. Wallace had been appointed the club's first 'Fan on the Board' with a mandate to inform the directors of supporters' concerns and feelings. The role was not an easy one as, no matter who filled the position, it was an impossible task to represent all supporters. In addition, some directors may have felt uncomfortable hearing their views challenged by a 'mere fan'. Nevertheless, the role was an important breakthrough in the relationship between the club and its followers, even if it was far from perfect. Making use of Wallace at the time of the appointment of Ball could have benefited the City management, or at the very least made them aware of how supporters might react.

Dave Wallace wrote his view in *King of the Kippax*: "We were led to believe we'd be having a massive name, with a track record, and when Bally's name emerged it was a tremendous anti-climax. I'm astounded the club didn't anticipate our reaction to the news. Apparently everyone who rang the Chairman thought it was a cracking appointment, and everyone who rang me thought it wasn't! Once their first choice had bit the dust this would have been an ideal opportunity to bounce the idea off the Fans' Rep. I know I couldn't realistically have influenced the decision, but I could have pointed out that we'd need some persuading that this is a good move for City, and that it isn't good enough that he's an old mate, with a liking for the gee gees, as it was presented to us in the press."

As far as Francis Lee was concerned the appointment may have been described in the press as an old pals reunion but in actual fact the relationship between Lee and Ball never came into it: "I had to make a very important and serious decision and old pals' acts simply don't feature in decisions as crucial as the one I had to make. Besides, I have always set out to employ people here who are proud to be associated with the blue shirt of Manchester City, and I know for sure that Alan will feel that pride."

Despite Lee's comments the majority of supporters were still concerned. A quote from former Chairman Peter Swales later in the year, concerning players, could equally have been applied to the appointment of City's managers: "You can never ever kid supporters. They know great players. It's no good a manager saying, 'this is the best player we've ever had'. The supporters will know after a few weeks whether he really is the best. One thing you can never do is kid supporters. You can build them up, and get them hoping for the future but supporters en bloc will know a player. No question."

Francis Lee was still learning. During his time as a player at Maine Road the supporters were, in the main, perfectly happy with performances on the pitch and the efforts of the players and the management, but after his departure the atmosphere around Maine Road changed, especially during the 1980s and early 90s. The fans were desperate for success and hoped Lee's take-over would totally transform the club, and bring the success they yearned for. Unfortunately, a transformation of the kind required was always likely to take years rather than months and, unlike his predecessor, Lee was under pressure almost immediately. The honeymoon period was over and the appointment of Alan Ball did little to convince anyone that better days lay ahead.

Despite the scepticism of the fans, the new manager tried to get on with his job and outline his hopes. He firmly believed the squad was of a good quality: "We have got talent here, there's no doubting that. I've got to integrate them into my way of thinking - they've got to be told what I expect from individuals and players. What I've basically said to them up to now is that I've got to earn their respect and they've got to earn mine. I ask every player to train and play to their strengths, and when they can all do that you've got a good team."

He went on to outline what he thought it was possible for the team to achieve: "It's not beyond the realms of possibility to win a cup. Apart from that, I want stability in the Premiership. I want a comfortable season in which we banish any possibilities of relegation. I want the supporters to see young players coming through. And I want them to see that the ship knows what direction it's going in."

There was no doubting Ball's enthusiasm for the job, or his knowledge of the game, however his managerial record had not been the best and a significant improvement at the start of the season would be necessary before the new man gained acceptance. Happily, Ball's assistant was former hero Asa Hartford whose appointment was viewed as a major plus.

On the playing front the close season had seen a few changes. Maurizio Gaudino, the German who seemed to have great potential but also a tendency to grab the headlines for questionable off-field activity, left the Blues despite almost signing permanently in the middle of the managerless period. At the time Colin Barlow stated: "We didn't feel it would be right to sign Maurizio Gaudino before our new manager was appointed."

Surprisingly, throughout the period prior to Ball's appointment Niall Quinn, one of the club's biggest stars, almost transferred to Sporting Lisbon. Fortunately the deal fell through, but most agreed it would have been a mistake losing a player of his proven ability prior to any managerial appointment.

Then on 15th July City made a signing that would ultimately become one of the most important in the club's history - Georgiou Kinkladze. The Georgian international arrived at Maine Road in a £2 million, three year deal. Apparently the Blues had chased him for six months after being tipped off by a European scout. Francis Lee watched him three times, while Jimmy Frizzell and Colin Bell also went to see him play. Alan Ball was most taken after seeing only five minutes of him in action on video.

Kinkladze had also impressed a number of other clubs, including AC Milan and Barcelona, so it was a major coup for the City Chairman to sign him: "I am thrilled that Georgiou has joined us. He is a wonderful young player who will delight our supporters."

Ball added: "His technique is excellent and his passing and vision are first class. We might just have found ourselves a gem."

Kinkladze wasn't the only summer arrival as Portsmouth defender Kit Symons arrived in a £1.5 million deal which also saw Carl Griffiths and Fitzroy Simpson - who has played well in every game between the two clubs since - move to Fratton Park. The consistent Symons had previously been coached by Alan Ball at Portsmouth, and the new City manager rated him highly: "Kit is a born winner. He wants to do well, he is the kind of player who belongs here at City. He is good in the air and on the ground, has a first class attitude, and I have no doubt he will do well in the Premier Division."

Two days before the season commenced the Blues signed Eike Immel, a vastly experienced former German international goalkeeper, for £400,000 from VfB Stuttgart. Injuries to Tony Coton and Andy Dibble had left City with a goalkeeping crisis, although Martyn Margetson was still waiting for a decent run in the first team. Immel, Kinkladze and Symons made their debuts against Tottenham on 19th August, the opening day of the 1995-6 season, at Maine Road.

That match ended in a 1-1 draw with Rösler scoring a looping header five minutes into the second half to level the scores. Kinkladze had impressed and, overall, the Blues were happy especially those singing "There's only one German striker" - a reference not only to the goalscorer, but also the fact the talismanic forward Jürgen Klinsmann had deserted Spurs.

City's joy wasn't to last however as eight sorry successive League defeats left the Blues languishing at the bottom of the table. The last of these was the Old Trafford derby, played before 35,707 with no tickets allocated to City. Naturally, some Blues did make it

"We might just have found ourselves a gem," forecast Alan Ball on the signing of Georgian wizard Georgi Kinkladze.

German goalkeeper Eike Immel made his debut against Tottenham in the first game of the 1995-6 season and here saves bravely from Chris Armstrong.

into the venue but the atmosphere was terribly one-sided and left Ball's men under immense pressure. The only goal of the match came after just four minutes when Keith Curle deflected in Paul Scholes' header, but City's marking was exceptionally poor.

The Blues did try to fight back, but Niall Quinn squandered the best effort prompting much ridicule from the United fans behind the goal. A photo of Quinn taken immediately after the miss appeared in many newspapers over the course of the following week. It highlighted City's disappointment, but it also showed a large number of United fans abusing the Irish international. The *Daily Telegraph* followed up, publishing letters criticising the behaviour of those supporters. It was sad to see so much hatred and ridicule, although to many it was a typical derby day reaction.

Nigel Clough celebrates his goal in the 2-1 FA Cup replay win over Coventry in February 1996.

Following the derby City played out a goalless match with Leeds at Maine Road and then travelled to Anfield for a third round League Cup tie. The Blues had already beaten Wycombe (4-0 on aggregate), but recognised a meeting with Liverpool was not going to be quite so easy. The match ended in a depressing 4-0 defeat, but even that wasn't as bad as what followed three days later. The Anfield League meeting between the two sides ended in a humiliating 6-0 defeat, prompting ironic chants of "Alan Ball is a football genius." Uwe Rösler threw his boots into the crowd as a protest and now the pressure was on. In 1937 the Blues had defeated Liverpool 10-1 on aggregate over a similar time frame, but nothing could compensate for the feeling of failure felt on 28th October 1995. It was a major disappointment, although Alan Ball told the press he actually enjoyed watching the Liverpool performance!

Results finally did pick up in November lifting City up to 15th and bringing Alan Ball the Manager of the Month award, but by the New Year the Blues were back in the relegation zone.

On Tuesday 12th December, City held their annual AGM. It was not as controversial as in previous years, but it did give shareholders an opportunity to quiz the new manager. Several interesting points were raised and it appeared Ball was keen to tell the truth about his role, City's plight, and the problems of particularly players. His frank, honest approach impressed many and did much to reassure fans his thinking was right. Some of his views looked back to 'the good old days' of the early 70s when football was a completely different game, and many supporters probably agreed with him but the inescapable truth was players of the 90s had an entirely different outlook to those of twenty years earlier. The power base had shifted from the club to the players and City had to accept it like the rest, even if the principle seemed wrong.

Why?

City players confront referee Alan Wilkie after his highly controversial decision to award United a penalty in the FA Cup derby.

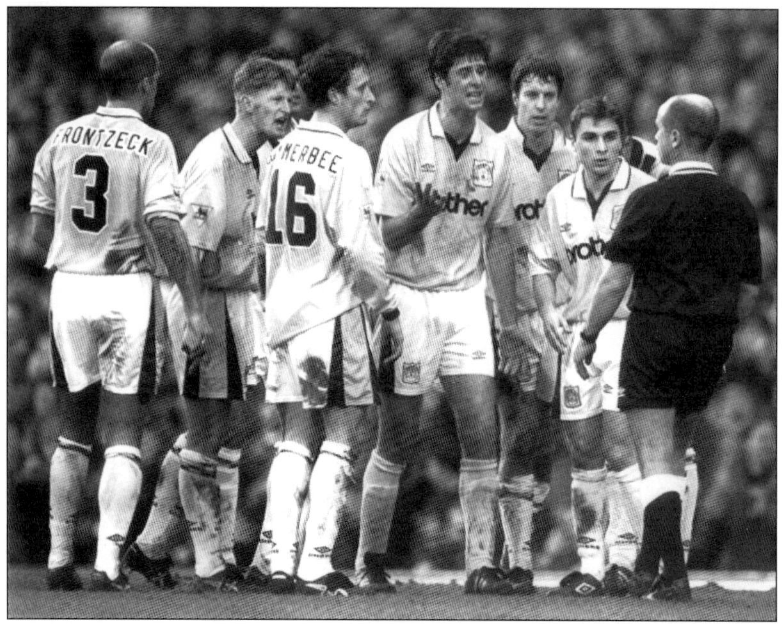

In addition to the frank comments, one moment during Ball's question and answer session lightened the mood. The City manager acknowledged the impressive work of Kinkladze during what had been a difficult time for the player as he tried to adjust to life in England. Ball stated City had got permission and made arrangements to bring the player's mother to England, which prompted one fan to shout: "Why? Can she play a bit? She could fill in at left-back!"

January only brought one defeat - the return fixture with Spurs - but the Blues were not moving up the table. Fortunately, January also saw the start of City's F.A. Cup run. Ball had suggested at the season's start the Blues were capable of winning one of the cup competitions and with the League Cup campaign over the F.A. Cup was City's last chance of glory.

The Blues managed to reach the fifth round after home wins over Leicester (5-0 in a replay) and Coventry (2-1 in another replay) and really fancied their chances. Unfortunately the fifth round tie sent the Blues back to Old Trafford for a meeting with United. This time there would be over 8,000 City fans in attendance to ensure the atmosphere was not totally one-sided. If anything the noise generated by the travelling support was far in excess of anything coming from the home fans.

The match kicked off at 4pm with City attacking the end containing their vociferous supporters, and for much of the opening period the Blues made the Reds suffer. Within 30 minutes United were behind as Kinkladze fed a superb pass to the advancing Rösler. The German charged forward and sent an astonishing lob over Schmeichel into the net for the opening goal. It was a thoroughly deserved advantage. The Blues were combining perfectly as a unit and the entire side performed magnificently until disaster struck via one of the F.A. Cup's more controversial incidents.

Alan Ball: "There could not have been a happier manager in the country at 4.30 on Sunday afternoon, with my team a goal in front, and the United fans silenced as they watched their team run out of ideas very quickly. We were causing a lot of problems, and then came that incident which will be remembered by many at this club for years to come. I am not a person who makes excuses, but it was a bewildering refereeing decision which turned a game upside down."

For a very brief period action had moved to the opposite end of the pitch, where United were struggling to find an opening. There were a number of players in the box but there seemed little danger before referee Alan Wilkie blew his whistle. Roy

Keane immediately protested, believing he was to be penalised, but the Irishman's attitude and approach changed rapidly as it dawned Wilkie had given United a penalty. No supporter present could understand why, and much discussion amongst City fans failed to provide a sensible answer. Those watching live on BBC had the opportunity to see slow motion replays which brought the conclusion it was for an 'incident' between City's German defender Michael Frontzeck and United's Eric Cantona. The two players jumped together but there hardly seemed any contact let alone anything malicious from Frontzeck.

The BBC's Alan Hansen found the whole affair ridiculous: "That decision was absolutely disgraceful." Every journalist felt the same. Henry Winter *(Daily Telegraph)*: "Frontzeck, a German international not averse to a touch of rough and tumble, certainly made contact with Cantona but similar scenes are witnessed in the bump and jump of every corner, of every match. The decision incensed City."

The *Manchester Evening News'* United reporter Stuart Mathieson agreed with the general mood: "Luck is a vital ingredient when you are following a recipe for Wembley success and United are enjoying a liberal dollop of it. True the German was manhandling Cantona but it was no more than the kind of argy-bargy going on elsewhere in the penalty area and, at that moment, if Cantona was going to reach the ball he would have had to be standing on Frontzeck's shoulders."

Naturally, with the resultant penalty the Reds equalised and the game ended as a contest. The City players and supporters felt no matter how hard they tried, or how well they performed, the game was going United's way. Had the Blues entered half-time a goal in front, they would more than likely have won the contest. Football did not seem a fair game that weekend for City fans.

In the second half United took the lead and entered the draw for the sixth round. Again, luck worked in their favour as they were presented with the easiest remaining draw - Swindon or Southampton at home - to further anger the City faithful. *The Guardian's* David Lacey held a similar view: "Fate first helped United beat City with the aid of a harshly-judged penalty and then gave them a highly-winnable quarter final at home to Swindon or Southampton. Should United go on to win the Cup ... the sky blue half of Manchester will no doubt be hoping that their celebratory toasts are coupled with the name of Alan Wilkie."

The following week on the BBC's Football Focus the game was analysed in more detail with Gary Lineker stressing how wrong the penalty decision had been. The programme showed a number of other incidents and Lineker made reference to a foul in the area by Steve Bruce on Kit Symons that was considerably worse than the alleged infringement from Frontzeck.

It was difficult for anyone connected with the Blues to pick themselves up that week, but with typical City spirit the following match allowed everyone to begin to erase memories of the game from their minds. League leaders Newcastle arrived at Maine Road expecting to leave with three easy points but a stirring battle from the Blues resulted in a 3-3 draw. City had been ahead but allowed Newcastle to score their third in the 81st minute. Keith Curle was cynically head-butted by Newcastle's Colombian maverick Asprilla in the final minutes, while the Blues also had a penalty appeal turned down. If only Alan Wilkie had been refereeing!

Kinkladze was the undisputed Man of the Match, and the BBC delighted in showing the Georgian at his best. City fans had known how special he was all season, the rest of the country were only just beginning to appreciate his silky skills. Despite many impressive performances from Gio, the Blues still struggled in far too many games and on the final day of the season they lay in the relegation zone, third from bottom, on 37 points; the same total as two sides above them used to avoiding the drop, Southampton and Coventry. In simple terms, all City needed to do was earn a point more than either of these sides. Southampton were at home to Wimbledon, while Coventry faced Leeds at Highfield Road. City had the daunting task of a match with Liverpool.

Prior to the game, compere Vince Miller tried to enliven spirits by singing "Blue Moon", and then followed with "Land of Hope and Glory", which drowned out the singing of City fans seated in the

Uwe Rösler celebrates with the City fans at the Platt Lane End after scoring against Newcastle in a 3-3 thriller in February 1996. The goal had put the Blues 3-2 up.

Kippax and North Stands, and inadvertently muted the atmosphere. By the time the players came out the supporters had started to sing again, and the mood seemed right.

A minute's silence was observed for former Chairman Peter Swales who had passed away earlier in the week. His early death was a shock and the fans ensured he was remembered with respect. Of course, the majority of supporters had opposed Swales for most of his final years as Chairman, but they still understood and appreciated his love of and devotion to the club.

When the game started the fans willed the Blues on, but it was Liverpool who took the lead when a mis-hit pass from Nigel Clough, who had joined City for £1million from Anfield four months earlier, allowed Liverpool to race forward. The Blues conceded a corner and a hopeful effort from McManaman was sliced in by Steve Lomas. It was a terrible time to score an own goal, but the player had been hampered by the pitch which was not in the best of condition following two major concerts by City supporters Oasis a week earlier.

Despite their lead, Liverpool did not appear too interested and to many Blues it felt as if the

Merseysiders were keen to see City survive. It appeared Liverpool would have been quite content to allow the Blues to equalise, but the game actually moved further from City when Ian Rush made it 2-0. Surely the Blues could fight back against a side that didn't seem too concerned about the result?

City did retaliate and when Kinkladze was bundled over for a penalty with 20 minutes to go the Blues were presented with their best chance. Rösler blasted the spot kick home to make the score 2-1. Niall Quinn was substituted for 19-year-old Martin 'Buster' Phillips, who had joined City in November from Exeter, and then in the 78th minute he helped fashion the equaliser when he latched on to a Summerbee corner and knocked it back for Kit Symons at the far post to make it 2-2.

Kit Symons hammers in the equaliser as City recover a two-goal deficit to draw the final game of 1995-6 with Liverpool. It was not enough, however, and the Blues were relegated on goal difference.

Almost immediately rumours spread that Coventry were losing and 2-2 would be enough to guarantee City's survival. Alan Ball, it seemed, was taken in by these and instructed his side to time-waste. Steve Lomas followed his manager's advice much to the annoyance of Niall Quinn who leapt from his seat, raced to the touchline and started shouting at the player and the rest of the side. Seeing this, the crowd grasped the Coventry scoreline had to be wrong and they too urged City to fight on. Amazingly, while the Blues played keep-ball in the corner nearest the Family Stand, Liverpool did all they could to open up play. It was bizarre that the side who frankly didn't care about the result were keen to expand the game more than a team who should have been looking for victory. Who says games between Manchester and Merseyside are always bitter affairs?

The crucial amount of time wasted as a result of unsubstantiated rumours left City unable to find the winner, and the match ended in a draw. The Blues were down and that evening Niall Quinn appeared on Match of the Day to apologise to the fans. It wasn't his fault and he, at least, had tried to fire up the players during those fateful final minutes.

Relegation was a bitter blow and brought despair almost on a par with 1983. When Francis Lee became Chairman many believed the prospect of relegation was banished forever, but in truth City had slipped too far behind since formation of the Premier League and relegation became inevitable. The appointment of Alan Ball had not encouraged supporters, nor had many of his acquisitions. Nigel Clough had hardly impressed while another brought to Maine Road in a fanfare was Gerry Creaney, who came from Portsmouth in a deal which also saw fans' favourite Paul Walsh transfer south. Creaney came to Manchester to further his international aspirations, according to early reports, but his pallid performances for City caused many to question Ball's wisdom, especially as Uwe Rösler clearly missed the support he received from Walsh.

Other departures included Terry Phelan, Garry Flitcroft and Tony Coton - three players who had achieved a great deal with the club and had at times been tremendously popular with the fans. The trio were quickly followed by Niall Quinn and Keith Curle as City seemed more intent on reducing the wage bill than considering the strength of the squad. Relegation was a terrible experience, but losing a handful of the most popular players did little to enhance Ball's popularity.

The fifth issue of *Bert Trautmann's Helme*t (the renamed fanzine *Electric Blue*), was described as a "Ball Out Special" and was produced during the close season following relegation. Understandably, there were a number of comments from different contributors suggesting Ball was clearly not the right man to manage City. There was also concern over the departure of players such as Quinn and Curle. The 1996-7 season needed to see a marked improvement if the majority were to alter their opinion of Ball. It did not.

Unfortunately, 1996-7 became a contender for the most dramatic and traumatic season in City's history. It was a period of grim managerial struggle with three officially appointed managers and two caretakers, and saw City finish lower than ever before. Yet despite all the negative points, City's vast army of supporters once again proved among the most loyal in the country.

After so much change in such a short period of time it is difficult to recall the mood on the opening night of the season, as City welcomed Ipswich Town for the first Nationwide League game shown live on Sky TV. There was a new captain - Kit Symons - but Alan Ball was still manager despite rumblings at the end of 1995-6 and during the close season. A crowd of 29,126 watched what many would agree was a typical City match of the period. As expected Kinkladze performed exceptionally well, mesmerised the Ipswich defence, and set up the opener for Steve Lomas, who had turned down a move to Wimbledon during the summer. It looked a simple goal but owed much to the efforts of the little Georgian.

Despite that City were never in total control and as the game progressed nerves were severely tested as Michael Frontzeck was sent off for a foul on Paul Mason. Down to ten men, the Blues struggled for the final 25 minutes with Ipswich hitting the woodwork twice. It was a relieved crowd that welcomed the final whistle, and a vital three points. Sky TV's viewers were also probably relieved - it had not been an entertaining Friday evening for neutrals!

The game did, however, give City fans the first opportunity to chant "City, City, top of the League". Sadly, it was their one and only chance.

After the match a buoyant Alan Ball felt it was a good result: "It was the start we wanted and a very solid performance. It was very important we got off to a winning start, so at least this time we have got something to build on." Four days later the City manager was not so chirpy as he witnessed a 1-0 defeat at eventual champions Bolton. Ball kept his players locked in the dressing room for almost an hour, then refused to speak with journalists. Bolton really made the Blues look appalling that night and brought home the realisation that the two sides were a considerable distance apart. It also raised further concerns over Ball's approach to life at Maine Road. In the next game - away at Stoke - the fans needed to see a much improved performance; they didn't get it.

The opening 45 minutes were a nightmare and left City two goals down. Former Blue hero Sheron netted for the home side making the day even more unbearable and, perhaps understandably, frustrated supporters started to chant "Ball Out". It was something the Stoke fans enjoyed - they'd suffered under Ball a couple of years earlier. Eventually both sets of supporters sang together giving a clear indication to Chairman Francis Lee the time had come for action. The game ended 2-1 (Rösler netted the scant consolation) with Ball groping for positives from the day: "In terms of points we didn't come away with anything, but as the manager I got something out of the match."

Quite what remained a mystery as, before the next game, Ball resigned (26th August 1996). The supporters never really took to the former World Cup winner and only signs of an immediate return to the Premier League might have prolonged his managerial career. His spell at Maine Road ended with a long chat with Chairman Lee who, understandably, did not try to persuade Ball to remain at the club. *The Guardian's* David Lacey encapsulated the feelings of City supporters when he considered the achievements of Ball's time at Maine Road before stating: "Ball has taken down more people than the Titanic."

City fan Steve Worthington writing in *Bert Trautmann's Helmet* believed he knew where the blame lay for the disastrous start to the new season: "In hindsight, Ball may now recognise that the start of the season was somewhat predictable. Instead of strengthening the team, he allowed it to be weakened. Perhaps he should have stood up to Francis Lee's craving to reduce the wage bill, but he didn't and more senior pros fled the nest. Keith Curle was sold to one of our immediate rivals [Wolves] and Niall Quinn was sacrificed to Sunderland, having been treated like an unsightly boil.

"During a summer visit to Maine Road, the Ed [Noel Bayley] and I met Francis Lee and, judging from the Chairman's incredulous reaction, I felt a bit like Dennis Pennis when I asked, 'Are there any new signings in the pipeline?' To that he somewhat arrogantly replied, 'We don't need any new signings to get out of this League'. The Ed and I looked at each other and feared the worst."

Unknown to the majority, Francis Lee and his board were working hard trying to restructure the club to ensure a sound financial footing. When they arrived at Maine Road they were absolutely appalled at the financial state of what remained one of the most popular clubs in Britain.

In addition, they felt some of the players signed under Peter Swales had been put on contracts that jeopardised the future of the club. To allow some of these players to remain would have seriously hampered City's progress and could have created an uneasy situation in the dressing room where there was little comparison between the salaries of the pre-Lee and post-Swales players. Unfortunately, but perhaps understandably, little of this was communicated to the fans. Niall Quinn took exception to some comments that were aired but what was fact and what was fiction? Now Ball had gone, perhaps the new manager would be able to explain.

Steve Lomas scores the first goal anywhere in 1996-97. It's enough to beat Ipswich and put City top of the league - the rest of the First Division had still to play!

Former player Asa Hartford filled the void as caretaker for the visit of Charlton on 3rd September. Despite another poor performance, City woke up in the last ten minutes and scraped a 2-1 win. At home to Barnsley four days later the Blues were defeated 2-1 after failing to perform again. Goals from Rösler and Ball's last signing, Paul Dickov, then brought a 2-0 victory at Port Vale, but City came crashing back down to earth with a 3-1 defeat at Crystal Palace and a sending off for captain Symons on 14th September. Hartford: "It was a poor performance and Palace overpowered us. The last thing I said to the players before they went out was that a lot of fans had come down and they deserved 100%. We did not get that from all quarters."

Three days later City faced Lincoln City in the second round of the League Cup. The first match was played away from home and actually started in style with Dickov, who had joined the club a month earlier, chipping a great cross to Rösler. The German bravely ducked to head home after only 40 seconds and gave the 1,500 travelling fans something to cheer in an otherwise dismal week. However, it wasn't to last. Lincoln were more prepared to battle and John Beck, Lincoln's manager, ensured his men knew how to fight back. They played with a direct approach and, it must be said, dominated the tie. In the 29th minute Lincoln's Terry Fleming had both time and space to fire past Andy Dibble to level the scores, then Steve Holmes was left free to fire home a rather simple second a minute before half-time. Three minutes into the second half, the 6ft 4in Dutch striker Gijsbert Bos managed a back header from Fleming's throw, which skimmed off Michael Brown and entered the net. 3-1 after 48 minutes!

Then Jon Whitney rammed home the fourth in the 79th minute to complete the humiliation. Understandably, City's unhappy

5ft 5ins Scottish striker Paul Dickov joined City from Arsenal in August 1996 for £800,000, and joined Leicester City's fight for Premier League survival in February 2002. In between he became a Blue hero following his exploits in the 1999 Second Division play-off final at Wembley.

A typical Maine Road matchday for many of us...
That first glimse of the ground sends a tingle down the spine... the pre-match pie, always eaten on the move... enter the ground via the turnstiles, which even after all the years of practice you can never get to turn with the first push... a quick flick through the programme before kick-off... and afterwards, trudge home disappointed... "never again!"

fans vented their feelings, but the sad fact was a club which ought to be in the Premier League was annihilated by a modest Third Division outfit.

Caretaker manager Asa Hartford was far from happy: "We were out-fought. We got caught up in a game that did not suit us at all. There were too many silver prizes being picked up by our players. We lost out in the individual contests and when you do that, your chances are slim.

"They wanted it more than us. But you do expect more from our players and you expect them to be able to deal with that sort of situation. The players have let themselves down. I feel sorry for the fans. It's not on."

Lincoln's John Beck told the Yorkshire TV reporter that he felt City were in a confused state: "Manchester City need organising and directing. They need guts and determination to get out of their mini-crisis. They may have to go down to the Second Division to sort themselves out." It was a worrying time for everyone connected with the Blues.

Against Birmingham - captained by former United man Steve Bruce - in the next League game a Kinkladze penalty in the 89th minute brought three vital points, after a Rösler spot-kick in the first half was saved by Birmingham's Ian Bennett. The travelling Midlands fans found it hard to accept and scuffles broke out in their section of the North Stand. Who knows how they'd have reacted had they been supporting City throughout this managerless period!

North Stand fans hail Georgi Kinkladze after his last minute penalty defeated Birmingham City in September 1996. No. 11 Uwe Rösler had earlier had a spot-kick saved.

The second leg of the League Cup tie followed, and once again City started brightly against lowly Lincoln but, with typical unpredictability, the Blues presented their opponents with an opportunity and the game was lost within the first 20 minutes as sloppy defending allowed Gijsbert Bos to tap into an open net.

Again, Asa Hartford was not a happy Blue: "To lose two games against Lincoln City saddens you. Realistically, we lost it in the first leg. But the goal we conceded last night was a comedy of errors, and there were three horrendous mistakes made. It knocked the stuffing out of us.

"There were a lot of corners and knockdowns in their goalmouth for us to feed on, but we were not alive to the possibilities."

City's 5-1 aggregate defeat was the first time the Blues had lost a two-legged League Cup Second Round tie, and is the club's record defeat over two legs in any competition.

With the Blues losing 5-1 on aggregate at half-time, the following announcement was made: "The match against West Brom will now be played on November 27th ... dependent on tonight's result."

At the end of September a 2-0 defeat at Sheffield United was the last game of Hartford's caretaker manager period. Ever since Ball's departure City had been frantically searching for a manager - once again George Graham claimed he was interested, then said he wasn't, then took the Leeds job. Dave Bassett accepted the post, then changed his mind. Other names were mentioned on a regular basis, then on 7th October former United player Steve Coppell accepted the challenge saying: "I want to be here a long time." His first game ended 2-2 at QPR prompting a little flutter of optimism throughout the club. Coppell tried to calm that by saying: "One game means nothing. After six games we will be able to draw more realistic conclusions."

The next five drew mixed results - 2-0 defeat at Reading, 2-0 Maine Road victory over Norwich, 1-0 defeat at home to Wolves, a 3-2 win at Southend, and a frustrating 2-0 defeat at Swindon. Six days after that

all important sixth game Coppell stunned everyone when he resigned on medical grounds, prompting various rumours to circulate. The unsatisfactory nature of his departure was merely compounded when, amazingly, a few months later he returned to football management and guided Crystal Palace through the play-offs to the Premiership.

Coppell's assistant Phil Neal was appointed caretaker manager while the search for a new messiah continued. A pathetic 3-2 home defeat to Oxford brought tremendous criticism from City's battle-weary fans and the question "Have you ever seen a poorer City side?" was asked in the following issue of *King of the Kippax*. The supporters were still loyal, but how much more could they take? A 2-1 defeat at Portsmouth in mid November left City in 21st position, afterwards Phil Neal told reporters: "They say Steve Coppell showed courage to leave. It takes more courage to stay!"

A Maine Road goalless draw with Brian Horton's Huddersfield followed, before a 2-1 home defeat by Tranmere caused supporters to leave early and then demonstrate outside the Main Stand. It was another sad day in what was fast becoming City's worst season in history.

Fortunately a 3-2 midweek defeat of West Bromwich Albion, thanks to an early Rösler goal and two Kinkladze penalties, changed the atmosphere a little on 27th November, but a 3-0 televised humiliation at Wolves the following Sunday brought City crashing back down to earth. The Wolves tannoy system said it all when the Queen record, "Another One Bites the Dust", was played.

A winner from young Jeff Whitley in the next game helped City scrape a 3-2 victory over Bradford City but this was hardly a comforting result as there was still no sign of a new manager. The nightmare continued at Oldham where the struggling Latics won 2-1, and a big Boxing Day crowd of 30,344 witnessed another humiliation when Port Vale beat the Blues 1-0. The *Manchester Evening News* said the incredibly loyal fans felt betrayed. They certainly felt angry.

A third successive defeat and the tenth away setback in 13 games brought a 2-0 embarrassment at Barnsley. Francis Lee was in Barbados on his annual holiday and supporters, whose loyalty to City amazes many in football, chanted: "I'd rather be in Barnsley than Barbados." Only true Blues can understand how and why they perhaps manage to retain a sense of humour.

That game was the end of Neal's period as caretaker - one that lasted considerably longer than Coppell's permanent reign. On 30th December former Forest manager and player Frank Clark arrived and immediately laughed at suggestions City were in crisis: "If you consider that 30,000 people turn up for a home game when you are near the bottom of the First Division and 6,000 fans travel to an away game at Barnsley, it certainly doesn't seem a job from hell to me."

Due to last minute postponements, Clark's first game in charge wasn't until 11th January when Dave Bassett brought Palace to Maine Road for a 1-1 draw. Clark received a tremendous reception before a crowd of over 27,000 prompting Bassett's wife to question her husband's earlier decision to turn City down. Two further draws followed at Huddersfield (1-1) and Sheffield United (0-0) before City's best result of the season - a 4-1 victory at Oxford. The game was a good example of how Clark had brought new life into the club and started to draw a little confidence out of his players. New signing Kevin Horlock impressed on his debut, while the likes of Rösler and Summerbee were starting to recover from the confidence-sapping days under Ball. City were back, and with a large TV audience watching, the inevitable "Are You Watching Alan Ball?" chant added more enjoyment, especially as Ball had been most inadvisedly criticising the quality of City's players - including those he brought to the club.

Ball seemed particularly critical of Uwe Rösler, a player whose form dipped alarmingly under Ball: "I think the penny's dropping slowly but surely to the fans that these players they've backed for years are not good enough." As if to prove Ball wrong Rösler's performances improved markedly under Frank Clark.

Clark's boys were beginning to excite and many found it hard to accept that many players who had appeared so feeble earlier in the season were now actually displaying real quality. What had Clark brought that Ball, Coppell, Neal and Hartford had been unable to generate?

Asa Hartford
26th Aug - 7th Oct

Steve Coppell
7th Oct - 8th Nov

Phil Neal
8th Nov - 29th Dec

Frank Clark and his approach during the 1996-7 season did much to convince supporters that the club had, at long last, found a man capable of bringing them the success they deserved. Unfortunately, the optimism didn't last.

A run of victories (3-0 at home to Southend and Swindon, and 3-1 at Bradford) began to lift the Blues away from danger and even brought the suggestion Clark's side could reach the play offs. A 1-1 draw with Portsmouth was seen as a failure, even though three months earlier it would have been viewed as a major achievement, but a 1-0 defeat of local rivals Oldham on 8th March was greeted with delight.

A 2-0 reverse at Birmingham was disappointing but it was an odd match, especially as the Birmingham programme was the one produced for the original fixture called off ten weeks earlier! Clark needed to take action to prevent any stall in momentum, especially as Kit Symons was missing for the following game at Grimsby.

That match ended in a 1-1 draw with both managers pleased by the final result. Grimsby's Kenny Swain was impressed with City: "You have to look at the quality in the City side. They are on a roll with one defeat in eleven and they are hard to beat. Frank Clark is a wily old fox and he knows the score." In typical football manager speak he added: "It was a game of three halves. I thought we were okay in the first, shaky in the second, and did well in the third!"

A 1-1 draw at Tranmere followed, then on 22nd March the Blues defeated Stoke 2-0. A small fire in the North Stand delayed the kick-off by 45 minutes, then fans had to wait a further 65 minutes before new arrival Dalian Atkinson headed home for his debut day goal. Steve Lomas added a second three minutes later to see City reach Clark's safety target of 50 points. The manager was relieved, but some were even now hopeful of a play off place. It was an amazing turnaround from only a few months earlier.

A 74th minute equaliser from Clark signing Ged Brannan brought a 1-1 draw at Charlton, but the play-offs still seemed a distant dream, before a 2-1 home defeat by runaway leaders Bolton more or less ended that fantasy. It also deservedly brought Bolton the Nationwide League title. Two 3-1 victories followed at West Bromwich Albion and at home to Grimsby, before a disappointing 3-0 defeat by QPR at Maine Road on 19th April. It was now reaching the stage when everybody connected with the club just wanted the roller-coaster campaign to end. It had been another crazy City season and was perhaps time for Clark and his team to take a break and prepare for the following term. Unfortunately there were still three games to go, and the Blues had to soldier on.

Kevin Horlock was signed from Swindon for £1.5million and scored his first City goal against his former club in February 1997. Here, No.9 Paul Dickov congratulates Horlock on his goal in the 3-0 win.

A 1-0 defeat at bogey team Ipswich had an air of inevitability and was actually the game that put a mathematical end to any play-off possibility. A no score draw at Norwich followed, and then the final match at home to Reading ended in a 3-2 victory. Those last two games were played without Kinkladze, who had been injured in the England v Georgia international, and speculation was rife the influential Georgian would never play in a City shirt again.

Throughout the match messages from various supporters'

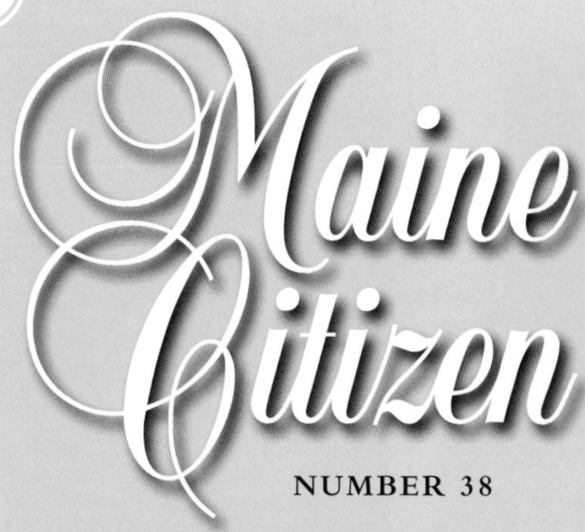

NUMBER 38

GEORGIOU KINKLADZE

Georgi Kinkladze stayed at Maine Road for three turbulent seasons, arriving in Manchester in time for the start of the 1995-6 campaign. Problems obtaining a work permit, and difficulties understanding English made his first few weeks uneasy, however from the moment he made his debut it was clear he possessed great skill. He soon became a vital member of the side and in December 1995 his superb goal, away at Middlesbrough, helped him gain admirers and headlines nationwide.

His debut season coincided with the arrival of many more famous imports into the Premier League, notably Bergkamp and Gullit, but it was Georgi who hit the headlines, as a result of his City accomplishments not past exploits. *Match of the Day's* Alan Hansen raved about several of his performances, especially in a 3-3 draw with Newcastle and a 2-1 Maine Road defeat of Southampton. The Southampton game was particularly pleasing as Georgi's second goal was pure genius. During the course of a 40-yard run he tore through the entire Saints' defence, allowed Dave Beasant to make his move, then delicately chipped the ball over the 'keeper's body for an effort that should have been won the 'Goal of the Season' award.

The *Daily Telegraph's* respected writer, Bryon Butler, became one of Georgi's first admirers. Within weeks of his debut Butler was making comparisons with Matthews and Best, while stating he believed the City man had more to offer English football than Cantona, Shearer, Giggs and a host of other familiar names - something all City supporters already believed.

No words can really describe how important Georgi became to the Blues. Put simply, he was a crowd-pleaser who had the ability to turn games. He used to excite, entertain, make surging runs, bring others into the game, make space, dribble, score ...... there was nothing he couldn't do.

He soon settled in the Manchester area,

and came to love the city and its people: "They are warm and kind in Manchester, just as they are in Georgia. I have made many friends here .... It's my second home. I feel almost like I was born here."

When the 1996-7 season commenced he won the 'Man of the Match' award for the first Nationwide League game shown live on Sky TV. He deserved the accolade that night, and went on to play well throughout the season even though many had speculated he would never play in the lower division. It was true Kinkladze's skills deserved to be appreciated at the very highest level, but that he remained at Maine Road added to his general appeal to fans.

Throughout 1996-7 soccer pundits kept inferring the skilful Georgian would be tempted to join a 'bigger' club. What they failed to understand was that City is a major club, with tremendously loyal supporters, and Kinkladze was idolised by most Mancunians.

How often do supporters chant a particular player's name throughout a match when that individual isn't even playing? That's exactly what happened during the final game of 1996-7 when City's loyal following wanted Georgi to know just how important he was to them. In addition to the chants, messages urging him to stay kept flashing on the scoreboard. These were not club messages, but paid 'adverts' from various supporters' groups.

For all the players 1996-7 was a very strange season. Some found it difficult adjusting after each managerial change but Georgi didn't appear to allow the problems to affect him on the pitch. He simply got on with the job and allowed his feet to do the talking, jinking past opponent after opponent.

As with the previous season, he put in so many quality performances during an exceptionally difficult time he was easily the undisputed player of the 1996-7 season. His stylish, skilful play was the highlight for all Blues, and delighted opposition supporters as well. He was certainly head and shoulders above everybody else in the division and, had it not been for the fact City's season started so appallingly, should have received many more accolades than he actually did.

On Cup Final day he joined Bernard Halford at Francis Lee's house and signed a new three-year contract to reassure all Blues that one of City's most important players - some were saying the best all-time player - would continue to entertain. Nevertheless, within a fortnight of the 1997-8 season commencing rumours were already afoot that Everton, Liverpool and even Manchester United were preparing a bid for the player.

Georgi remained, but the 1997-8 season was the most disastrous in the club's history and resulted in another relegation - to the third tier of English football for the first time. Georgi was devastated. Every newspaper seemed to focus on his misery, and for many fans this was simply the blackest day of all time.

The Georgian had been used sparingly following the appointment of Joe Royle, even though many fans demanded his inclusion. It was clear City's most skilful player had to move on. A record fee, reported as £4,925,000, took Georgi to Ajax in May 1998, but no amount of money could compensate for what the Blues had lost.

His spell at Ajax was not as successful as predicted and in November 1999 he arrived back in England to join Derby County.

Georgi Kinkladze will always be remembered as a quality entertainer, idolised as a result of a number of great performances. Had he played in any other era of City's history he would undoubtedly have helped the Blues to success, and would probably have stayed at the club for many years. His performances throughout his City career were exceptional, but his departure in 1998 inevitable.

KINKLADZE'S PLAYING RECORD

	LEAGUE		FA CUP		FL CUP		TOTAL	
	App	Gls	App	Gls	App	Gls	App	Gls
1995-96	37	4	4	1	3	0	44	5
1996-97	39	12	3	0	1	0	43	12
1997-98	29(1)	4	2	1	2	0	33(1)	5
TOTAL	105(1)	20	9	2	6	0	120(1)	22

Tommy Wright, Ged Brannan and Paul Beesley, three of Frank Clark's signings in the early months of 1997.

groups urging him to stay appeared on the scoreboard and, at the end, he was given a fantastic ovation by City's large crowd. He wasn't the only one as the rest of Clark's side marched around the pitch to much acclaim. Anybody witnessing these positive, joyful scenes would have been convinced the Blues had just won the championship, rather than completed a season of struggle in the First Division. City's final position was 14th – their lowest placing at the time – yet the attitude shown by Frank Clark and his players during this season had done much to convince everyone that the situation could only improve for the club.

Many felt Frank Clark could bring the club promotion, particularly as his arrival coincided with an entertaining FA Cup run, although he did have to wait for his first taste of Cup action with the Blues, after the third round tie away to Brentford was postponed twice. This match was originally scheduled for January 4th but was postponed because of the appalling weather that had also wiped out the League game with Birmingham three days earlier.

Had the F.A. Cup tie been played as planned, it would have been Clark's first match in charge. Instead the 1-1 draw with Crystal Palace on 11th January gave Clark his first real taste of life as a Blue. Three days after that, the Brentford tie was called off for a second time when a late pitch inspection ended the prospect of play a mere two hours before the scheduled start. The large number of City fans who had travelled south were understandably livid.

When the tie was eventually played Kit Symons, with a newly cropped hairstyle, held the defence together superbly as the Blues soaked up a lot of Brentford pressure.

Nicky Summerbee was another who surprised, with a good performance at a time when few supporters actually wanted him in the side. Playing under Frank Clark seemed to give Summerbee a new lease of life and during the Brentford match he combined perfectly with Kinkladze to bring victory.

The two men swapped passes, and then Summerbee powerfully sent a Kinkladze return high into the net for the only goal of the game in the 61st minute. That goal engendered more confidence and, suddenly, the 2,400 City supporters at Griffin Park were anticipating the fourth round tie with Watford.

Frank Clark's first home victory came with a vintage performance against The Hornets in his sixth game in charge. Since his arrival the Blues had grown in confidence, and the meeting with Watford could not have occurred at a better time. It was the kind of game that sent supporters home dreaming of cup glory, and certainly provided a much needed diversion from the League campaign.

The match was already proving a lively one when Phil Neal purchase Neil Heaney opened the scoring in the 24th minute. This was Heaney's first for the club and was more than deserved. The Blues continued to dominate, although there were few opportunities for either side.

Then in the 53rd minute Watford's Steve Palmer was dismissed for punching Steve Lomas. This should have allowed the Blues to totally dominate the tie, but actually seemed to present Watford with opportunities.

Five minutes after the sending off, Gifton Noel-Williams netted the equaliser, but Watford's resurgence did not last long as three minutes later Nicky Summerbee, assisted by Kinkladze, restored the lead. In the 71st minute Uwe Rösler - the man Ball was most critical of - latched on to a long ball from Heaney to powerfully drive home an angled shot. Immediately the supporters chanted their hero's name and then, remembering the television criticism from Ball only a few days earlier, they chorused: "Are you watching Alan Ball?" It was a chant that seemed to encompass the whole stadium, and few, if any, supporters failed to voice their opinion.

Later a limping Rösler left the field to a fantastic ovation. It was thoroughly deserved, as was the applause for Summerbee - another player brought to life by Clark. The manager was by then impressing everybody, but he was first to share the accolades: "This is a team effort from the whole club, right down from the Chairman. I and the coaching staff are part of the team and we work hard with the players. The players and everybody at the club have responded very well. It's another step in the right direction."

On 15th February a crowd of 30,462 arrived at Maine Road for the mouth-watering fifth round clash with Premier League Middlesbrough. The outcome of this tie should have sent City into the next round of the F.A. Cup, sadly a few dire refereeing decisions sent the Blues crashing out of a competition they could possibly have won. Middlesbrough, somewhat fortuitously, went on to reach the final where they were defeated by Chelsea.

Frank Clark's confident side appeared to look forward more to this clash than any other during the season. It seemed to be the game that would prove that the new approach at Maine Road was destined for success. Sadly, it was not to be.

The game was won and lost as a result of three controversial decisions. The first was when Ian Brightwell timed his move on to Kit Symons' header to perfection, then steered the ball in for what should have been the opening goal. The referee disallowed that effort believing Brightwell to be offside, even though television cameras proved that to be incorrect.

The second error occurred in the 67th minute when £2.75 million import Gianluca Festa punched Steve Lomas (it seemed to be the season for punching Lomas!). He should have been sent off, but the referee merely booked him. Again the cameras proved how erroneous that was. Afterwards Lomas told reporters: "The ref bottled it. The fella gave me a forearm, everyone saw it and the ref told me he didn't. I asked why he'd booked him then and he said maybe TV would prove him wrong."

Error number three arrived when substitute Paul Dickov was clearly tripped in the penalty area by, who else but, Festa. A penalty then would certainly have given City the tie but, with Kinkladze already off as a result of a groin strain, Middlesbrough had the opportunity to control crucial areas of the pitch. In the 78th minute Juninho, with a move created by the fortunate Festa, was left free to drive a shot under goalkeeper Martyn Margetson.

The Blues tried desperately hard to find an equaliser, but it was Middlesbrough's lucky day and the game ended in disappointment. The dream was over for another year. At least it allowed Frank Clark to concentrate on the League - something everyone had tried to forget existed!

Chapter Twenty Three

"WE'RE NOT REALLY HERE!"

THE 1997-8 season was expected to see an end to the troubles and misery of the previous seasons. It was anticipated Frank Clark would develop a side capable of seeking promotion. During the first few months of Clark's reign, supporters had become excited by his approach to the game. Following the disappointments created by the arrival of first Alan Ball then Steve Coppell - two men never likely to satisfy City's passionate following - Clark appeared to be the right appointment for the club and, as a result, optimism spread. He was not the most dynamic of football managers, but he did appear knowledgeable and seemed an appropriate appointment to help bring stability to the Blues.

Off the pitch there was further cause for optimism. During 1997 much was done to ensure supporters could be seen across Britain, proud to wear their colours. City's Chief Executive Mike Turner, who had replaced Colin Barlow the previous season, became involved in the redesign of the club badge and the selection of a new kit manufacturer. He felt City had much to gain from increased awareness of the Blue brand. As a result the club decided it was time to move away from Umbro after 63 years, to find a company prepared to portray the right image. After considerable time and effort the Blues made what seemed an informed decision and chose Kappa.

The combination was effective immediately with both the new home and away kits appealing to the vast majority of supporters. Within a month of the launch around 60,000 shirts were sold - it would have been more but Kappa had production and distribution problems culminating in a large number of unhappy fans. Perhaps Kappa had underestimated the Blues' pulling power, something many felt their predecessors had done. Umbro had been City's kit manufacturer since the 1930s - this had earlier been acclaimed as the longest sports sponsorship deal in the world - and had developed close links with the club, however by the mid-1990s the company appeared to be moving elsewhere. They spent considerable time targeting a few high profile clubs, and many fans were simply reluctant to purchase goods that would perhaps indirectly line the pockets of their biggest rivals at Old Trafford.

In addition to the kit redesign, City also introduced a new club badge. Inscribed with the Latin motto 'Superbia in proelia', meaning 'pride in battle', it incorporated the original ship over the three emblazoned lines from the Manchester coat of arms. The three lines had changed colour from the City of Manchester's coat of arms, becoming white on a blue background rather than the traditional gold on a red background. The new badge also included a golden eagle and three gold stars. This badge received a mixed reaction, particularly as the eagle looked identical to the bird worn by Manchester United in the 1958 Cup Final.

The club desperately needed to improve and control its merchandising operation and, although many supporters strongly identified with the old badge - four years later a small group of supporters called for the re-instatement of the old one - it was vital the club made a change.

Other improvements on the merchandising front included the redevelopment of the Social Club into a 3,500 square foot City Superstore. This opened in October 1997 and was a significant improvement on the previous outlet. Previously, the Blues opened new stores in the Kippax Stand and at the Arndale Centre

Lee Bradbury - club record signing from Portsmouth.

No. 7 Ged Brannan slides in to put City one up at Forest in September 1997. The Blues shocked the First Division's pacesetters by winning 3-1.

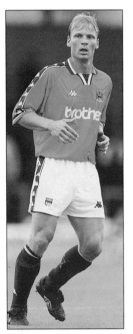

Dutch midfielder Gerard Wiekens was signed from FC Veendam in August 1997 for £500,000.

PAUL'S DAY

After much organisation Paul Lake's testimonial finally took place on Sunday 5th October 1997. The opponents were Alex Ferguson's Manchester United and the attendance was 21,262. The final score was 2-2.

in the city centre. Regrettably, the Arndale shop later closed down.

For many connected with the Blues it felt as if the management finally recognised the enormous size and stature of the club. Prior to Lee's arrival City had relied on just one rather inadequate franchised shop. Kevin Cummins, writing in *Bert Trautmann's Helmet*, described the old shop: "I was desperate to own anything connected with City. We would visit the shop before every home game, but almost always reluctantly depart empty handed. The problem was that, as with most souvenirs, they were crap. It was impossible to find anything in there that you could possibly want to give house room to. The stock never seemed to change. It was a shoddy enterprise."

The changes made off the pitch certainly improved the merchandising and corporate position, however some felt the focus was wrong. While the whole commercial side of the club had improved considerably, activities on the pitch remained worrying. City had struggled to find form under each of the managers appointed since the dismissal of Brian Horton in 1995 and former fans' hero Francis Lee was under severe criticism. The 1997-8 season had to see some improvement. Something manager Frank Clark knew only too well: "When clubs do badly, it's customary to blame the manager. That may often be justified but surely it can't explain Manchester City's failure over 25 years. A club might be unlucky with one or two managers, but no club could be so cursed as to appoint 17 duffers. Don't forget many of those duffers have been successful elsewhere. Alan Ball had done well with limited resources at Southampton, Peter Reid became a hero at Sunderland, and when I was at Forest I was voted Manager of the Year by my Premier League peers."

Clark had taken steps to strengthen the side during the 1997 close season. Striker Lee Bradbury arrived for an astounding £3m (plus a further £500,000 based on international appearances), while other arrivals included Gerard Wiekens and Tony Vaughan. All three made their debuts in the opening match on 9th August at home to Portsmouth, who fielded former Blue Fitzroy Simpson. A near capacity crowd of 30,474 hoped for a convincing start, but City turned in a rather nervous performance. Aloisi opened the scoring for Portsmouth in the 5th minute, but Uwe Rösler managed an equaliser eleven minutes later.

Ten minutes into the second half debutant Gerard Wiekens made it 2-1 but, City being City, the lead didn't last and only ten minutes from the end Paul Hall equalised. The game ended 2-2. Possibly, expectations were too great. Frank Clark later admitted he felt under too much pressure at this point. Only a few months earlier Mancunians felt City still had an outside chance of reaching the play-offs despite their dreadful inconsistency.

Clark tried to instil confidence and team spirit during this first month, but it wasn't easy, especially when the second match of the campaign was away to Blackpool in the first round of the Coca-Cola-sponsored League Cup. The Blues had been forced to compete in this round after the decision to allow byes to the later rounds for those clubs playing in Europe. Most recognised Blackpool should not pose a threat, however City's low self-esteem at this point was a factor. A 12th August holiday crowd of 8,084 - including many Blues who had chosen to use the game as an opportunity for a mini-break - witnessed a depressing 1-0 defeat. Interestingly, one of City's unused substitutes that day was a young goalkeeper by the name of Nicky Weaver.

In the second leg an 88th minute Kevin Horlock goal levelled the tie, but as the outcome had to be decided on the night, the Blues lost out 4-2 in a penalty shoot out. Expensive signing Lee Bradbury miscued his penalty, posing early questions about his purchase.

The League campaign was no better. The Blues provided the opposition at the opening of Sunderland's superb Stadium of Light. A huge crowd of 38,827 - the largest in the division since 40,070 watched City v Chelsea on 18th March 1989 - witnessed a 3-1 Sunderland win. Former Blue idol Niall Quinn netted the historic first goal. In the 75th minute Gio Kinkladze also made history by scoring the first penalty at the stadium to level for the Blues. Sadly, Sunderland managed two goals in the final seven minutes.

Another new signing Jason Van Blerk made his debut in this match, coming on for Uwe Rösler, while Brian Horton signing Alan Kernaghan made his one and only appearance of the season. In September he went on loan to St Johnstone.

Only one point came from the following two games but then City achieved a 3-1 win at League leaders Nottingham Forest with goals from Ged Brannan (2) and Paul Dickov. Ex-Forest chief Frank Clark was delighted.

City's unpredictability was a factor throughout the first few months. They could only manage a 1-1 draw at newly promoted Bury; were defeated 1-2 at home by Norwich, but then on 27th September annihilated second placed Swindon 6-0! On the day of the Swindon match the Blues lay in 20th place and were certainly in need of a boost. Fortunately Kinkladze and Dickov were on hand to give supporters a lift. Dickov scored twice and also proved totally selfless when, with the opportunity to complete his hat-trick, he simply squared to misfit Lee Bradbury for a simple tap-in. Bradbury needed the goal more than the bustling striker, but the majority of footballers would surely have grabbed the glory for themselves.

Only one point was gained from the next four matches and the pressure intensified. The Blues lay in the embarrassing position of 22nd out of 24 clubs having amassed only ten points. Only Portsmouth and Huddersfield were below them. Off the pitch there was more embarrassment as Georgi Kinkladze made headlines after crashing his £50,000 Ferrari 355 on Tuesday 28th October. The car allegedly went out of control while leaving a roundabout close to the M56 and A538 at Hale, and crashed into a signpost and motorway bridge support. Photographs of the crumpled vehicle appeared on the front pages of the tabloids while rumours circulated he had been racing against one of his team mates.

Kinkladze was treated for shock, cuts to his back and bruising before being discharged. He received a total of thirty stitches. Understandably he did not appear in City's match with Crewe the following night. His place was taken by Chris Greenacre. Frank Clark's plans had been disrupted: "Georgi was a very, very lucky man. The accident could have been far worse. We were thankful his injuries were only superficial. I was concerned about how the players would react to Georgi's absence. I need not have worried. Their response was excellent with everyone playing their part in what was such an important victory."

This had been Crewe's first visit to Maine Road for a League game, and the old stadium was under severe pressure dealing with crowds of over 30,000. The new temporary stand in the corner between the Kippax and North Stand, later dubbed the 'Gene Kelly Stand' due to the fact its inhabitants became used to singing in the rain, was operational for the first time after being erected during July and August. Supporter Steve Bagley wrote in the fanzine *King of the Kippax* with an alternative name: "I think the Gene Kelly stand should be renamed the 'Oliver Reed Stand' as it looks like it could fall down at any minute!"

A goalless draw at Oxford followed, but successive home defeats to Port Vale (2-3) and Huddersfield (0-1) sent the Blues back into the relegation zone. The next match was away at Sheffield United - a club whose board of directors was led by former City take-over bidder Mike McDonald and contained former Maine Road director Freddie Pye. David White's father, Stuart, and 1969 FA Cup Final referee George McCabe were also members of the Bramall Lane board.

With City looking extremely sloppy, Brian Deane took the initiative and put the home side into the lead in the 21st minute. After the goal the Blues fought back, although it's fair to say Martyn Margetson was mainly responsible after making a couple of fine saves. Then in the final minute Kevin Horlock netted to give City a much needed point.

This game marked the debut of Craig Russell and a return for Gerry Creaney. Creaney had been on loan at Chris Waddle's Burnley. £1 million rated Russell had arrived from Sunderland, with Nicky Summerbee going in the opposite direction. Clark had high hopes for Russell, but he hardly made an impact.

Against Bradford City Tony Vaughan headed his first goal to give the Blues a surprise 1-0 victory in the final minute - the surprise being that City were always the more likely to concede a goal in the final moments during this season! It was a deeply satisfying result, particularly as the previous home game had been a dire 0-1 defeat by Huddersfield, followed by chants of: "You're not fit to wear the shirt". It was even harder

No.6 Richard Edghill is mobbed after his cross was deflected in for the Blues' second goal against Swindon ... and six was City's total by the end of the day!

to accept as it was ten years to the day since City had defeated the Terriers 10-1.

The Blues then travelled to Edgeley Park for a game they had to win for all sorts of reasons, not least that defeat by near neighbours Stockport would be seen by many as another nail in City's coffin. Sadly, a humiliation followed.

Within eight minutes County were two up courtesy of poor defending. Time after time loose balls were seized by Stockport while City simply looked weak. In the 30th minute Brett Angell scored County's third.

Kit Symons received considerable abuse, but he wasn't the only City man who seemed incapable of playing football. Virtually the whole team performed feebly during the first half. During the interval the players received a severe roasting from Clark and attitudes improved. Brannan scored in the 49th minute to raise a little hope. Others were also displaying signs City might be able to get back into the match. In particular, Paul Dickov was keen to attack, and substitute Michael Brown impressed. Sadly, it was all in vain. The game ended 3-1. It was a humiliating experience and increased the pressure on Clark and Chairman Francis Lee.

Noel Bayley, writing in *Bert Trautmann's Helmet*, summed up the feeling well: "Decisions, decisions. Going to work on the Monday after the Stockport game, I needed a placcy bag to put my bits and pieces in. I had a choice - a City souvenir shop bag or a Miss Selfridge bag resplendent with a big heart. Naturally, I chose the latter. It was far less embarrassing!"

A 1-0 victory at West Bromwich Albion followed, before normal service was resumed with a 0-1 defeat at home to a Keith Curle inspired Wolves. The goal was another miserable experience for City, and in particular former captain Symons. He tried to clear a harmless ball and proceeded to slice it high above goalkeeper Martyn Margetson for an own goal in the 42nd minute. Considering the abuse Symons was already suffering it was hardly the highlight of his career, and certainly increased calls for him to be dropped. His confidence appeared at an all time low, and it seemed no matter how well intentioned, he was always liable to make a mistake. Clark was particularly

Tony Vaughan headed a surprise last minute winner against Bradford City. The Blues were usually more likely to concede late goals.

FAILING BLUES TRAPPED IN THE CELLAR OF DESPAIR

■ THAT SINKING FEELING ... Under the cosh Blues' boss, Frank Clark watches, thinks, shouts and can't believe what's happening Pictures: Chris Gleave

SECOND RATE

On 29th December 1997 Bryan Brett, writing in the Manchester Evening News, *accurately summed up the state of City by proclaiming the Blues were heading for Division Two.*

concerned: "Things got so bad with Kit Symons I felt obliged to remove the captaincy from him. The problem came to a head when we were beaten at Stockport. Kit bore the brunt of the criticism, which was unfair because he wasn't playing that badly. He said he was happy to continue as captain but inwardly I think he was glad to be rid of it."

Captaining the Blues during this period was particularly difficult, and Clark struggled to find the right man: "The captaincy became something of a curse for the players who took it on. Kevin Horlock only lasted five minutes before being injured and ruled out for three months. Gerard Wiekens took over only to suffer a similar fate and missed the next six weeks. Ian Brightwell was next up. He wasn't a great leader but he was happy to do it and at least he managed to survive."

On 13th December City travelled to Birmingham City for what became an exceptionally long match. Very little of note occurred during the first 80 minutes, but from that point the game became lively. Shelia headed home a cross from Russell in the 88th minute, followed shortly afterwards by Birmingham hitting a post. Russell then netted what appeared to be City's second, only to see it disallowed for handball. Nevertheless it still looked as if the points were going to Maine Road and the City players relaxed a little. It was only a matter of moments before the final whistle would be blown, or so they thought.

After two minutes injury time Forster headed Birmingham's equaliser, and the jitters returned. A frantic further five minutes followed before O'Connor netted the home side's winner, proving how cruel the game can be at times. Clark was dumbfounded: "I believe the match went on for far too long. The referee played eight minutes extra at the end, after already playing five minutes more in the first half. I do not know why.

"I can appreciate the extra time played before half-time as there had been two long stoppages, including a clash of heads, and the referee booked four players. But after the interval I can hardly remember either trainer going on to the field and there were only three bookings. Where did the referee get the idea of playing another eight minutes? In that added time we lost the match. I think the time has come for the authorities to examine the whole question of time-keeping."

The following match was considerably better all round as the Blues defeated Middlesbrough 2-0 at Maine Road. England manager Glenn Hoddle was in attendance to watch the performance of Middlesbrough's Paul Merson, but it was the City players who impressed. Uwe Rösler scored a 17th minute penalty after a foul on Craig Russell, and fifteen minutes later the determined Paul Dickov made it 2-0 after a typical mazy run by Kinkladze.

During the second period City handled the threat of Merson & Co. with ease. Star player for many was Shelia who received a good ovation at the end, while Dickov was proving better value than any of the signings made by Clark. After the game some Middlesbrough fans created havoc in the North Stand.

City's inconsistency shone through again with a 1-0 Boxing Day defeat at Crewe, and two days later a crowd of 31,839 witnessed a 2-3 defeat by eventual Division One champions Nottingham Forest. The better side clearly won with Steve Stone in good form, however two of Forest's goals came from the penalty spot. It was also encouraging to witness City's fightback. At 0-3 it appeared the Blues might be totally over run, however their fighting spirit brought encouraging goals from Shelia (56th minute) and Dickov (77th minute). It didn't encourage Bryan Brett, the *Manchester Evening News* reporter, however. Often local reporters toe the party-line and try to be positive, however Brett was determined to speak truthfully: "The Second Division is staring Manchester City in the face - whether they or the fans like it or not. Yesterday's 3-2 home defeat by Nottingham Forest, when only two late goals masked an embarrassingly heavy defeat, leaves them one point off bottom of the First Division more than halfway through the season.

"It followed the Boxing Day defeat at Crewe, and the Blues head for the New Year embroiled in a season of misery. It's a relegation battle even their most loyal fans find hard to believe. The Blues are trapped in a

Debutant Murtaz Shelia put City ahead in the 88th minute at St. Andrews - but Birmingham scored twice in the next TEN minutes!

quartet of clubs on 24 points - one above rock bottom."

Frank Clark admitted he had changed little at the club: "A year on from when I came here, we are no better off. We should be doing better. I would have expected us to have done much better. No doubt about that."

The next League match brought improvement as another struggling side, Portsmouth, were beaten 3-0 at Fratton Park. The result lifted the Blues to 17th place, but the points gap between them and bottom club Portsmouth was a mere four. City remained in serious trouble, particularly as the following game ended in a 0-1 defeat to Peter Reid's Sunderland. Three successive draws followed before an embarrassing home defeat by Bury. The Bury scorer, Paul Butler, was a self-confessed City fan: "I was going to go out and celebrate on the town but considering what happened - and me a City fan scoring the goal - I thought I'd better have a quiet night in."

The club appeared to have hit rock bottom. During the game there were calls for Frank Clark to be sacked and Francis Lee to resign.

At one stage a City fan ran on to the pitch from the Kippax Stand, ripped up his season ticket and marched off. He bravely carried out the threat many fans had been making for years, and was cheered off the pitch by thousands of supporters. In fact it was the loudest cheer of the day and was immediately followed by chants of "What the f**k is going on?" Supporters were totally exasperated by the whole situation.

At the end of the match Uwe Rösler was confronted by angry supporters and had to be escorted from the field by police. Later, when he left the ground, he was again surrounded by disgruntled fans. He spoke sensibly and wisely to the supporters, answering their concerns. He did not criticise his colleagues, although it was clear he was no longer enjoying life at Maine Road.

The defeat coincided with a new issue of the fanzine *Bert Trautmann's Helmet*, whose editorial focused on the rumours now engulfing the club: "The Maine Road rumour mill trundles relentlessly on: if City lose next week, Frank Clark's on his way... Joe Royle and Willie Donachie will be taking over... Dennis Tueart's only here to ease it through... Francis Lee's on the verge of selling out... and so it goes on. Who knows, by the time you read this, Clark may well have gone on his far from merry way. I certainly hope so. But who cares anyway? Well I do and you do. Nearly 30,000 people care enough to turn up to watch a wretched team going through the motions every other week. Somehow I don't think Frank Clark cares; not enough anyway, not as much as you and I care and that might just be the problem.

"At the last AGM he seemed resigned to the fact he'd be on his way sooner or later. Of course, this is a fact of life, especially a fact of a football manager's life, but it was the way in which he casually conceded the point. More recently, in *The Observer* (25/02/98), he was quoted as saying: 'The support is marvellous but the expectation here is unreal.' Unreal! How unreal? My expectation is this: top flight football and a bit of a run in one of the cups. A trip to Europe would be nice too, but let's not get carried away, eh? In my opinion Frank Clark doesn't understand this club or its unique status; he hasn't got a handle on it at all."

The comments were hard to dispute. Clark found it difficult understanding exactly what sort of club he was managing, while the motives of City's directors seemed unclear. Francis Lee, in particular, was receiving considerable 'stick' from the fans and at least one major shareholder, David Makin. Makin, who earlier in the season had invested around £5 million with his JD sports business partner John Wardle, telephoned GMR from the Mottram Hall Country Club to air his views on City's chairman and their plight: "I think there is a massive chemistry problem within the club. I really do. He overrides everybody. He tries to be dominant. I am in business and I know if you haven't got a happy work place, then there are problems. I don't think City is a happy workplace."

He added: "I will be doing my best in the next few weeks to remove the chairman because he is staying there. I don't know whether he is bloody minded or what. He is being stubborn. He is being proud. If I was him I think I would put a moustache on and a cap and hide. I know there are people ready behind the scenes, ready to take over. I am not going into any details."

He then outlined what he would do as soon as the board changed: "The first thing I would do when Francis has gone is find that guy who has probably been barred for throwing his ticket away on the pitch and put him in the directors' box. It sums up how the fans feel."

The outburst was an emotional one, but clearly brought many of City's problems out into the open. For a major shareholder who, together with his JD Sports partner John Wardle, was represented on the board by former City hero Dennis Tueart, to make such a statement on local radio proved the disunity within the club. In addition, the rumours concerning Clark's position and the imminent arrival of Joe Royle grew stronger. The following Monday's *Manchester Evening News* carried more news on the latest crisis at Maine Road. On the front page it's banner headline read "TIME BOMB", while its back page focused on

Less than five years after the 'Forward with Franny' campaign these supporters subject Francis Lee to demonstrations reminiscent of those against former chairman Peter Swales.

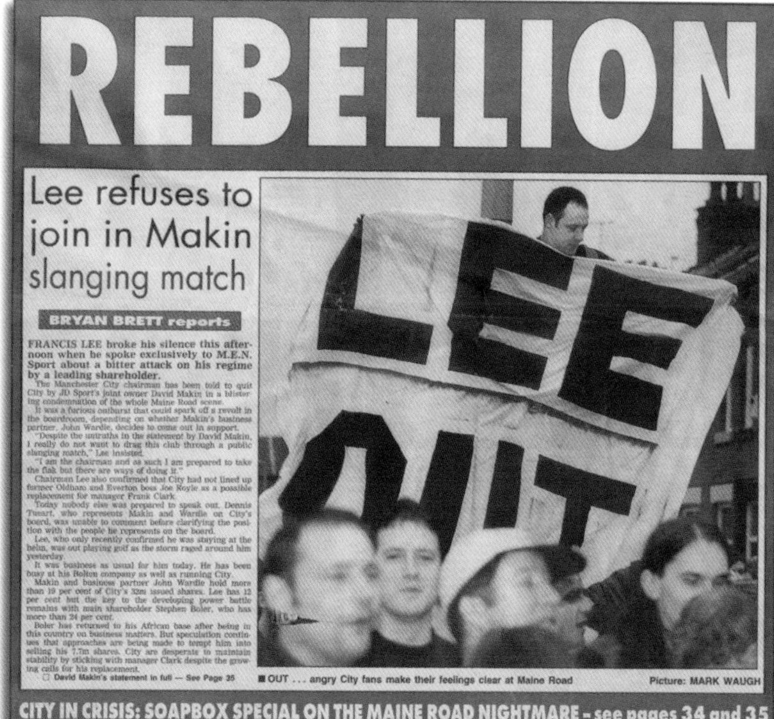

REBELLION

Lee refuses to join in Makin slanging match

BRYAN BRETT reports

FRANCIS LEE broke his silence this afternoon when he spoke exclusively to M.E.N. Sport about a bitter attack on his regime by a leading shareholder.

The Manchester City chairman has been told to quit City by JD Sport's joint owner David Makin in a blistering condemnation of the whole Maine Road scene.

It was a furious outburst that could spark off a revolt in the boardroom, depending on whether Makin's business partner, John Wardle, decides to come out in support.

"Despite the untruths in the statement by David Makin, I really do not want to drag this club through a public slanging match," Lee insisted.

"I am the chairman and as such I am prepared to take the flak but there are ways of doing it."

Chairman Lee also confirmed that City had not lined up former Oldham and Everton boss Joe Royle as a possible replacement for manager Frank Clark.

Today nobody else was prepared to speak out. Dennis Tueart, who represents Makin and Wardle on City's board, was unable to comment before clarifying the position with the people he represents on the board.

Lee, who only recently confirmed he was staying at the helm, was out playing golf as the storm raged around him yesterday.

It was business as usual for him today. He has been busy at his Bolton company as well as running City.

Makin and business partner John Wardle hold more than 19 per cent of City's 32m issued shares. Lee has 12 per cent but the key to the developing power battle remains with main shareholder Stephen Boler, who has more than 24 per cent.

Boler has returned to his African base after being in this country on business matters. But speculation continues that approaches are being made to tempt him into selling his 7.7m shares. City are desperate to maintain stability by sticking with manager Clark despite the growing calls for his replacement.

David Makin's statement in full — See Page 35

■ OUT ... angry City fans make their feelings clear at Maine Road Picture: MARK WAUGH

CITY IN CRISIS: SOAPBOX SPECIAL ON THE MAINE ROAD NIGHTMARE - see pages 34 and 35

Peter Beardsley was brought in on loan by Frank Clark on the same day the City manager was sacked.

the Lee/Makin affair under the headline "REBELLION". There was also a photo of supporters carrying a "Lee Out" banner. For many it was a painful reminder of the troubles encountered under Lee's predecessor, Peter Swales.

Elsewhere the newspaper featured the Rösler confrontation and the news that the Rochdale branch of the City Centenary Supporters' Association had seconded a vote of no confidence in Francis Lee proposed by their Midlands counterparts. There was also coverage of the demonstration that followed the match. A crowd of around 3,000 gathered on the forecourt to rant at the chairman, manager, and some of the players. After about an hour the police tactical aid group were sent in to break up the demonstration. One supporter was injured as a police horse trampled on his foot. Earlier a club steward had been hit by a coin. It was all extremely depressing.

The events of the following couple of days proved particularly confusing. The Royle rumours grew, while the Lee and Makin debate grabbed much attention. Frank Clark felt the disunity within the boardroom was all becoming too much. He felt sure all the problems within the club were caused by the different factions within the board. In his autobiography, *'Kicking With Both Feet'*, he expressed amazement any club could be run that way: "While one faction was planning my downfall another was allowing me to take Peter Beardsley on a month's loan from Bolton. The club was so short of cash and Beardsley would cost more than £30,000 in wages. It was ridiculous to allow me to do this on the day that I was about to be sacked. Beardsley was a fine player but he didn't feature in the plans of my successor Joe Royle and consequently turned out to be a waste of the club's money.

"Instead of sacking me, one faction issued a statement to the press on Monday night saying I had been told that results had to improve. I hadn't been told anything of the sort - not that I needed telling since it was obvious. I wasn't even told they were issuing the statement. Consequently, when I was contacted by the local paper asking for my reaction, I didn't know what they were talking about. It was not only embarrassing for me, it made the club look amateurish and disorganised."

Final

Manchester Evening News

Founded 1868 | 30p | Closer to what's happening

Wednesday February 18 1998

INSIDE TONIGHT 16-PAGE PROPERTY NEWS

WHY MUST CHRISTIE SUFFER? DIANNE ROBINSON: PAGE 8

STARS AT THE BAR ON THE TOWN: PAGE 26

EXIT CLARK BLAMING 'A VENDETTA'

EXCLUSIVE

By Richard Burgess

SACKED Manchester City boss Frank Clark today lifted the lid on what he decribed as a "vendetta" within the club.

As Joe Royle, the man who dramatically replaced him, began picking up the pieces of City's worst-ever season, Clark wished him luck.

"There seems to be a fifth column on the fringe of the club," said Clark after arriving at the Platt Fields training ground this morning. "It is not personal, it is a vendetta against the club and it makes it very difficult to manage.

"City will not get stability and long-term success while these things are going on. I know Joe Royle and I have got a lot of time for him. I hope he will be successful."

Royle Ascent! Sports special Pages 52-56

ON HIS WAY OUT: ■ Clark: Wished Joe 'Good luck'

ON HIS WAY IN: ■ Royle: Training

WEATHER 6 BMDs 19 DIARY 24 POSTBAG 25 TV 27-30 BUSINESS: 4 PAGES

While Clark and the supporters remained confused, the board did hold a meeting on Tuesday 17th February. During this meeting it is believed the decision was made to dismiss the manager. At the same time, Clark was travelling to Sunderland to watch their game with Reading, City's opponents the following week. During the journey he received a telephone call from Bernard Halford, City's secretary since the early 1970s, saying the chairman wanted to see him. Clark offered to turn round and meet with him immediately but, according to Clark, Halford told him it could wait until the morning. Clark didn't feel the call could be that important and carried on to the Stadium of Light.

After the match, Clark discovered a message on his answerphone from the *Daily Mail's* John Richardson, saying his newspaper were running a story which they had been told was accurate saying Clark had been sacked and Royle was to take his place. The following day GMR's Andy Buckley broke the story to the Greater Manchester public at breakfast time. Shortly after hearing this Clark received a call from Francis Lee. When the two met afterwards the official dismissal was made. It wasn't long before Joe Royle was discussing his appointment with Dennis Tueart. The Joe Royle appointment was viewed well by the majority of fans. For years they had said City needed to be managed by somebody who understood the fans, the history, and the importance the club has to Mancunians. Those managers who had got to grips with Manc mentality, such as tough Scotsman Tom Maley in 1904 and Malcolm Allison in the sixties, usually succeeded.

Joe Royle had the right pedigree and he certainly made all the right noises: "When Dennis Tueart, Asa Hartford and myself were in the team we were tops in Manchester - that is the ambition here. We cannot look at that for the moment. This is a 15 game season and we have got to make sure we win half our remaining games. Whatever it takes to make sure this massive club is in the right division we will do."

"The place is awesome and people keep telling me that one day someone will get it right. I want that to be me. Everyone says the potential is fantastic - if you do get it right here, you have lift off. You get 28,000 plus at every game. People turning up to see a team that has been struggling for four or five years."

Interestingly, it was later claimed Royle had been formally approached at around 4.30 the previous afternoon. Like Clark, he too was on his way to Sunderland. He was to go to the game and had planned to meet up with an old friend. "I've just received a rollicking from Peter Reid for not

Joe Royle meets and trains with the players after cutting short a press conference to announce his appointment to prepare for that night's game with Ipswich.

turning up, but that is typical of him," he laughed at the press conference.

Simply to have a manager capable of adding an element of joviality at such a difficult time gave City a sign improvements would follow. For too long there had been an air of negativity. Royle's predecessors - possibly right back to Peter Reid - all appeared to lack the approachability and friendliness of Royle. He knew City; he was passionate about football; and he had also achieved considerably more as a manager than many of the recent incumbents. He saved Everton from relegation when they seemed doomed and won the FA Cup. He promoted Oldham to the Premier League and took them to the League Cup final and to the FA Cup semi-final (twice), and during his eleven month absence from the game he had turned down fourteen jobs before accepting the City post. To many he seemed the only man capable of salvaging the 1997-8 season.

His first game in charge was at home to Ipswich on the day of his appointment. Never the ideal start to the job, but Royle didn't complain. He simply got on with the task and even cut short the press conference to be with his players. One of them, Ian Brightwell had served under 10 different managers (plus numerous caretakers) since his debut only eleven years earlier in August 1986.

That first game was a curious one. Frank Clark's final player, Peter Beardsley, made his debut, while a crowd of 27,156 arrived to witness the fans' favourite boo-boy Kit Symons head home against Ipswich in only the fifth minute. It seemed as if the Blues had already felt the benefit of Royle's arrival, but it didn't last. Opportunities were wasted, and only the defensive expertise of Shelia and another Georgian Kakhaber Tskhadadze kept Ipswich at bay.

Unfortunately, with only seven minutes remaining substitute Bobby Petta managed to evade a clutch of City men to beat the unsighted Tommy Wright. In injury time the Blues relaxed in their typically frustrating Frank Clark manner, and Kieron Dyer swept in their winner.

Off the pitch Royle was keen to bring Willie Donachie back to Maine Road to work as his assistant. Donachie was Nigel Spackman's number two at Sheffield United. They had been impressed with his approach and it was clear their City supporting chairman, Mike McDonald, had no intention of releasing him. In the end McDonald relented and by the end of February Donachie was at Maine Road. At Sheffield, Nigel Spackman saw the departure as the final straw and he resigned as Sheffield United manager claiming the board didn't support him.

Backroom changes at Maine Road during this spell included the departure of former manager Jimmy Frizzell after over 14 years with the club.

City now had two consecutive away games to overcome. The first ended in a 3-1 victory at Swindon, while the second brought a 3-0 defeat by Reading. Significantly, the third goal was netted in the 89th minute - Royle still needed to get City playing to the final whistle.

Royle started to make a few team changes as he searched for a side capable of staying in the division. Ron Atkinson offered the use of left-back Lee Briscoe, and he arrived on a month's loan from Sheffield Wednesday.

At home to West Bromwich Albion Rösler netted a 43rd minute winner, prompting talk of a revival. Interestingly, Kinkladze had missed his second consecutive game, and the media focussed on what was in actuality a very simple story to write. Kinkladze was never likely to feature in Royle's survival plans. If the club needed to fight for victories would City's stylish player be able to cope? To Royle the answer was obviously no, but for most fans Kinkladze's absence was disappointing. They still felt he was capable of turning around any game.

Away at fellow strugglers Huddersfield the revival continued with a 3-1 victory to lift the Blues into 17th place. Significantly, City had won two consecutive League games for the first time in eleven months.

Four days later Royle's men succumbed to a 0-2 home defeat by Oxford despite having the majority of play. Oxford had come determined to leave with a point, but somehow managed to take all three. Another defeat followed at Port Vale. City had equalised, thanks to Gerard Wiekens, but in the 73rd minute Ainsworth made it 2-1 to Vale. Surprisingly, Kinkladze re-appeared in the team for that match - his first since Royle's second game in charge.

Former Oldham player Richard Jobson made his debut at Vale, following a free transfer from Leeds, but Royle continued to struggle to find the right mix.

Willie Donachie returned to Maine Road to team up again with Joe Royle.

Ian Bishop returned to Maine Road in one of two transfer deadline day signings by Joe Royle - the other being Shaun Goater.

Injuries to players such as Murtaz Shelia hampered progress, but the huge playing squad also caused a few headaches. Royle was desperate to assess them all, but had to make a few snap decisions to reduce the wage bill. Out went David Morley, Rae Ingram, Ray Kelly, Paul Beesley, Eddie McGoldrick, and Tony Scully. Ominously, Kinkladze was also allowed to fly to Amsterdam to have talks with Ajax.

More changes were to follow as £1 million hard-man Jamie Pollock arrived from Bolton in time for the 21st March goalless game with Sheffield United - and was yellow-carded within ten minutes of his debut. Then on transfer deadline day striker Shaun Goater came from Bristol City for £400,000 plus a further £100,000 if City avoided relegation and Ian Bishop returned on a free from West Ham.

The Bishop deal was particularly pleasing for many fans and was further evidence Royle understood the club and its fans. Bishop was idolised in his previous spell almost nine years earlier, and his departure provoked demonstrations against then manager Howard Kendall. Bishop loved the support he got during his first brief spell: "I remember we were playing Norwich and the crowd sang my name. I cannot describe how that felt. I never wanted to leave but I knew that there was no future for me at City. Ever since then I have hoped I would get another chance at the club but you begin to wonder if it will ever happen. Whenever I have returned to Maine Road with West Ham the reception has been amazing.

"I feel I have at least three or four good years in me because my game has never been based on pace alone. I want to make up for the time I lost because I have always regretted that my first spell here only lasted six months. Nothing would give me greater pleasure than to end my career here, although I am not planning to hang up my boots for some time."

In the boardroom there were also changes. Francis Lee resigned as both chairman and a director and was replaced at the top by French Connection's David Bernstein. A supporter for over 40 years, Bernstein was keen to find stability: "The last two decades have witnessed constant and damaging speculation about boardroom and change of control issues. We intend to professionalise and stabilise the club at all levels, diffusing the constant hype that plagues us."

Alongside Bernstein's appointment John Wardle, the chairman of JD Sports joined the board. In addition, the board now consisted of Ashley Lewis, who represented the interests of Stephen Boler and the Peter Swales estate, Andrew Thomas, who represented Greenall's brewery, and Dennis Tueart, who had originally joined the board to represent Wardle and David Makin. Michael Turner was, for the time being at least, still chief executive.

Back on the pitch, both Bishop and Goater made their debuts in a 2-1 defeat at Bradford. All matches were now crucial if the Blues were serious about avoiding relegation, but the next game had extra importance for most associated with the club. It was the return with Stockport County. County had humiliated Clark's side four months earlier and victory was vital for morale purposes if nothing else. It was also crucial the players kept the momentum going for a full ninety minutes, rather than throw everything into the first half and hope to survive. Royle's considerable planning worked: "The determination against Stockport to put things right was evident throughout the side. We went into the game with the worst home record in the First Division and it is up to us to ensure in the remaining games here we do not slip up again.

"Naturally, I was delighted to see how we kept the pressure on Stockport until the final whistle. I said before the game that it was going to be a massive occasion for everyone, both on and off the pitch. For once in this traumatic season we got it right. The overall display was excellent."

The game ended 4-1 with Goater opening the scoring in the fifth minute. That strike was cancelled out a few seconds later by City fan Aaron Wilbraham, but the Blues resilience shone through and Jobson made it 2-1 in the 32nd minute. Eight minutes before the break Lee Bradbury scored only his fourth since his expensive transfer, then in the 57th minute he netted his fifth of the season. Royle was delighted: "All strikers go through barren patches - I should know and I was an experienced pro when I hit my worst patch - but when I told Lee in training he was going to be in the side I could see he was raring to go again.

"I decided on a new pairing with Lee linking up with Shaun Goater, who I thought had an excellent home debut. Shaun scored the first goal which obviously settled his nerves and went on to give a superb all-round contribution. Despite all our troubles it shows the potential of this club that quality players like Shaun, Jamie Pollock and Ian Bishop are eager to come here."

Another hero to thousands of fans that day was Stockport 'keeper Eric Nixon. The Former Blue gifted two of the goals to City and was warmly greeted by the chant "Eric's a City fan" from the North Stand. It was not a particularly enjoyable day for Nixon who, at one stage, had to leave the field for stitches in his mouth after an aerial clash with Goater.

Richard Jobson celebrates with Lee Bradbury after putting City ahead in the 4-1 'derby' win over Stockport. It was not a particularly enjoyable day for County's Eric Nixon.

Despite this victory City were deep in relegation trouble. They lay in 21st place on 43 points, the same as Portsmouth who were now managed by Alan Ball. Below them lay Reading and Stoke City, but there was little separating the clubs. Above City were Bury on 46 points and Port Vale, QPR and Norwich each on 45 points. It was going to be a tough final five matches.

Away at play-off seeking Wolves, City managed a 2-2 draw. They had led twice - but an error by Margetson gifted Wolves an equaliser in the 34th minute, then in the final five minutes of the match former Blue and future Rochdale manager Paul Simpson equalised. Two days later Trevor Francis' Birmingham won 0-1 at Maine Road deep into injury time despite a good performance from the Blues. Francis admitted afterwards he would have been delighted if he'd managed to leave with just a point and couldn't believe his luck. Particularly upsetting was that Birmingham's scorer Adebola had performed a nasty tackle on Richard Jobson, putting the City man out of the game. Had he been appropriately sent off he would not have been on the pitch during those final minutes.

After Birmingham came another disappointing blow as Middlesbrough won 1-0 with a strike from Alun Armstrong shortly before half-time. The Blues rarely threatened, although many felt they deserved a penalty shortly before the end of what was a very controversial televised match on Teesside. One of the major incidents involved Lee Bradbury. The City striker was headbutted by Steve Vickers, who was then sent off. Middlesbrough manager Bryan Robson claimed Bradbury dived and wouldn't accept the television evidence.

Joe Royle wasn't too pleased with the result or the atmosphere: "This is one of the most hostile grounds in the country. The supporters appeal for everything and they generally get their way. I have to say I was not happy with the official's performance, but he was certainly right to send off Vickers. If you head butt someone on the pitch, then you have to go and it is as simple as that."

City remained in 21st place, but with only two games left survival was no longer within their own hands. For the final home match Royle felt it was time to bring Kinkladze back into the side for only his fourth game under the new manager. Many felt he should have been a regular feature in the side, but with his negotiations to join Ajax and Royle's determination to adopt a fighting, never say die attitude it was clear the manager wouldn't play him week in week out. Nevertheless, his arrival provoked a great deal of excitement and, before City's largest crowd of the season 32,040, he netted a first minute goal. Earlier, in the tunnel QPR's Vinnie Jones had an argument with a steward after allegedly intimidating Kinkladze. It was that sort of day.

Immediately after the 43-second goal, the stands were buzzing with discussion on the rights and wrongs of Royle's decision not to play Kinkladze in the other games. The discussions continued, and then in the eighth minute former Blue Mike Sheron netted an equaliser. There seems to be a perverse rule which states that when a former Blue is playing against City he is always going to score. The fans have known this for some time and every season there seem to be at least a couple of examples.

Thirteen minutes later Jamie Pollock intercepted a pass from Sheron, flicked the ball in the air and then, with superb ball control, headed firmly over Margetson into City's net. It felt as if the long running Maine Road farce was never going to end. As a result Pollock was voted Man of the Century in a national poll sabotaged by QPR fans.

Three minutes into the second half Bradbury at last found some accuracy and netted an equaliser. Later Nigel Quashie was sent off for elbowing Dickov. The Blues tried to take the lead but it wasn't to be, and a game they had to win ended in a 2-2 draw.

Jamie Pollock's arrival added bite to the midfield but his own goal in the final home game of the season led to him being voted 'Man of the Century' by QPR fans!

After the match the players came on to the pitch for their annual lap of honour. It was more a sign of loyalty and gave supporters the chance to urge their players forward for the final battle away to Stoke, but the move was lampooned in the press. *The Independent* reporter Guy Hodgson probably got the balance between humour and tragedy just right: "Like all good farces they kept the best joke until last. After a season in which they have miserably under-performed the Manchester City players returned to the pitch after the game for a mutual saluting session. They applauded the fans, who duly clapped back; the first thoroughly deserving it, the team absolutely not. We were witnessing a novelty, a lap of dishonour in front of 30,000 loyal fans who have been ever-present this season.

"It brought back memories of the best named sports book ever, a history of baseball's New York Mets called *The Worst Team Money Could Buy*, because there before us was an expensive collection of failure that has to live up to its trappings."

Considering City's history and unique ability to make simple tasks difficult he added: "In the pubs of Manchester beforehand there was a curious bonding of optimism and perverse logic which went on the lines that City could relax because their fate was in their own hands. Anybody who has studied the history of the club would know that is the last place you would want your destiny to be, but just in case City served up a 90 minute reminder.

"It is hard to imagine any team but City conceding two goals that belonged more to black comedy than football yet at 2-1 down they were trailing to strikes from a former player and their own captain, while the one goal they had scored was from an individual they are desperately trying to sell. Laugh? Only the hard-hearted would not weep."

He ended his report explaining City's task was now extremely difficult. Joe Royle had said City needed luck and self-control, Hodgson added: "When did City have any luck, or self control for that matter? The grand masters of the cock up have a final curtain call."

The final day of the season was an immensely tense affair. City's first visit to Stoke's Britannia Stadium became vitally important to both clubs. Prior to the game the bottom six lined up as follows:

	P	W	D	L	F	A	Pts
QPR	45	10	19	16	51	62	49
Port Vale	45	12	10	23	52	66	46
Portsmouth	45	12	10	23	48	62	46
Stoke	45	11	13	21	42	69	46
City	45	11	12	22	51	55	45
Reading	45	11	9	25	39	77	42

City needed to beat Stoke and hope either Port Vale or Portsmouth failed in their away games at Huddersfield and Bradford respectively. With Alan Ball in charge of Portsmouth, many Blues joked it was a formality. Sadly, Alan Ball's side managed a shock 3-1 victory, while Vale recorded a 4-0 thrashing of a lacklustre Huddersfield. The results stunned those at the Britannia witnessing City's 5-2 rout of Stoke and meant that after a total of 106 years of League football the Blues had plummeted to the third tier for the first time.

The game was played out in a strange almost surreal atmosphere. There had been a significant amount of crowd trouble before, during, and after the game with around 20 casualties and 15 arrests, but the most curious moment came when the teams and some fans realised relegation was a certainty. Both clubs now faced playing derby games with nearby Macclesfield rather than their traditional rivals of Manchester United and Port Vale respectively. The City fans chanted "Are you watching Macclesfield?" before giving Kinkladze a final send off. Everyone realised this would be his final League match for the club.

Afterwards Chairman David Bernstein apologised to supporters for the disaster. The public apology was a key moment in Bernstein's early reign and

Despite a 5-2 victory over Stoke on the final day of the 1997-8 season, the Blues were relegated. Sadly, relegation brought to an end Georgi Kinkladze's time at the club.

supporters were encouraged their rather low-profile Chairman felt as painfully as they did about the nightmare of relegation. He blamed the frequent nature of change that always seemed to block progress. It was something most supporters had been saying for years - the appointment of Peter Reid in 1990 was made because the fans demanded some form of stability when Howard Kendall walked out, likewise the Reid dismissal was viewed as exceptionally poor timing because of its unsettling nature on the playing squad.

Another consequence of all the constant change was that the playing squad ballooned larger than could be managed effectively. Players were brought in by one manager on high salaries and with promise of regular first team football, only to find the next incumbent preferred someone else.

This mismanagement over a period of years helped turn City into a football laughing stock. As always the fans were forced to suffer the humiliation of it all. Relegation hurt and many Blues found the experience dreadfully painful; some wanted to avoid all mention of football, which was a pretty difficult task considering it was a World Cup year. There were also the regular references to Manchester United that seemed to pop up when least expected. Even the Queen became embroiled in controversy when she was asked to sign a Manchester United football while in Kuala Lumpar for the Commonwealth Games. Mancunians were told it would help their city prepare for their turn as hosts in 2002 but it was difficult to see how. Tommy Muir, one of the leading members of City's Supporters' Club sent a letter and a City ball to Buckingham Palace inviting the Queen to sign for City supporters. He wasn't surprised when he received a diplomatic reply simply wishing the Blues well for the new season.

Life in Division Two was a totally alien experience when the 1998-9 season commenced. Throughout the club's history no one had ever

Black humour prevails in City's latest demotion

Phil Shaw looks at the muddled thinking behind a Mancunian institution's unprecedented fall

IN THE media suite at Stoke's Britannia Stadium on Sunday, a former Manchester City player delved into Maine Road's thick anthology of black humour as he reflected on their relegation to the third grade of English football.

Ruefully he recalled a joke from when City lurched between the old First and Second Divisions in the 1980s. Peter Swales, then the chairman, has a black-out and is taken to the Northern Hospital. "Where are we?" he asks on coming round. "The Northern," replies the nurse. "Bloody hell," says Swales, "what happened to the Third and Fourth and Vauxhall Conference?"

Neither Swales, who has since died, nor the fans who called so vociferously for his head could have imagined that City would soon be a division below Crewe, Bury and Stockport. Or that derby day would see them stepping out at Macclesfield or Wigan rather than Old Trafford.

This, after all, is a club who, within the past three decades, have won the League championship, FA Cup and League Cup, as well as the European Cup-Winners' Cup. A Mancunian institution so deeply entrenched in the people's affections that, when they clinched promotion from the old Second Division in 1985, the gates were shut with 48,000 inside.

Locating exactly how and when the decline started is almost as difficult as establishing where it will all end. Some argue that the rot set in a quarter of a century ago, when the Reds went down and the Blues wasted the chance to become the city's top team.

The weakness of such logic is that it defines City, whose appeal is traditional and parochial, purely in relation to the nationally and globally popular United. While the fact that City last won a trophy in 1976 appears to pinpoint the beginning of their slide, the theory overlooks the extent to which the club later reasserted their place among the élite.

In both 1991 and '92, City finished a respectable fifth in the top flight. A year later, when United ended 26 years of hurt by winning the inaugural Premier League, City came ninth (one place above Arsenal). Yet it was within that period of relative success that the seeds of Sunday's sorrows were probably sown.

The first major blow was the defection of Howard Kendall, a manager then at the peak of his powers, back to Everton in 1990. The second was Swales' panic decision to sack Peter Reid, who had built promisingly on Kendall's legacy, after City gained only one point from three matches at the start of 1993-94.

Reid's exit unleashed frustrations among supporters which Francis Lee exploited. He finally became chairman at the start of 1994, but the "Forward with Franny Campaign" now looks like a bitterly ironic title.

If things were bad then – City lay 20th in the Premier League though they still had players like Quinn, Curle, Lomas, McMahon and Coton – Lee's reign makes Swales' 20 years resemble a golden age. A member of City's championship class of '68, he never had the financial muscle needed to keep pace with United *et al.*

Lee's judgement was often poor. His appointment of his friend Alan Ball, a manager who promptly lived up to his reputation for taking teams down, was bad enough. But one tragi-comic episode was invariably superseded by another; although Frank Clark initially made progress last season after becoming City's fifth manager in four months, he spent badly.

Joe Royle, brought in before Lee's resignation in February, could not keep them up despite a 5-2 win at Stoke. He has already hinted at a summer of upheaval. "There will be some soul-searching and big decisions made... about the staff, future planning and the players who'll be here next season – and those who won't."

Sadly, the latter category includes the Ajax-bound Georgi Kinkladze, around whose mercurial talents a succession of managers have tried to build a team. With a staggering 54 professionals on the books – many on fat Premiership wages – the Georgian is the least of Royle's problems. One high earner, Nigel Clough, has spent the entire season in the Pontins League.

Yesterday, as the Maine Road 30,000 faced up to the reality that City will be joining the local non-League hopefuls in the first round of the FA Cup, not to mention playing in the Auto Windscreens Shield, Lee's successor David Bernstein offered them a "clear and unequivocal" apology.

In a message to supporters, he said: "For the best part of two decades you have had to put up with a total lack of success, culminating in two relegations in three years. Failure over such a period is inexcusable and can not be explained by bad luck or chance, particularly by a club with our support and resources. The club have constantly reacted to events and have not been helped by frequent changes in personnel."

City now had a "hands-on, high-quality board", determined to reverse the culture of calamity. "We ask for your continued support," Bernstein concluded, no doubt with an eye on season-ticket sales. Yet with a manager bent on a clear-out and a chairman promising stability, things may get worse before they get better.

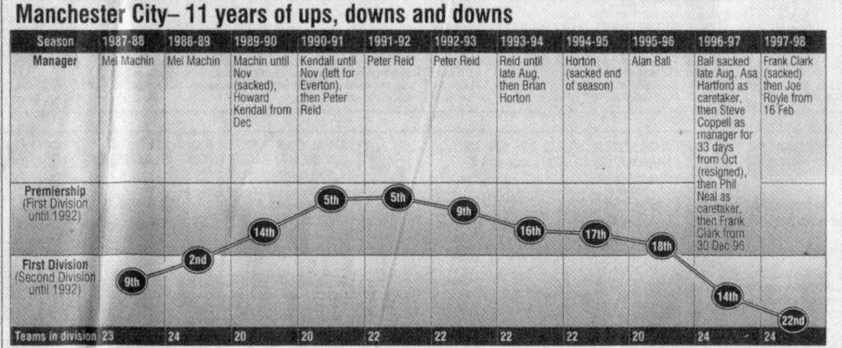

Manchester City– 11 years of ups, downs and downs

Season	1987-88	1988-89	1989-90	1990-91	1991-92	1992-93	1993-94	1994-95	1995-96	1996-97	1997-98
Manager	Mel Machin	Mel Machin	Machin until Nov (sacked), Howard Kendall from Dec	Kendall until Nov (left for Everton), then Peter Reid	Peter Reid	Peter Reid	Reid until late Aug, then Brian Horton	Horton (sacked end of season)	Alan Ball	Ball sacked late Aug. Asa Hartford as caretaker, then Steve Coppell as manager for 33 days from Oct (resigned), then Phil Neal as caretaker, then Frank Clark from 30 Dec 96	Frank Clark (sacked) then Joe Royle from 16 Feb
Premiership (First Division until 1992)			14th	5th	5th	9th	16th	17th	18th		
First Division (Second Division until 1992)	9th	2nd								14th	22nd
Teams in division	23	24	20	20	22	22	22	22	20	24	24

seriously contemplated what it would be like to field a team in the equivalent of the old Third Division, beneath the likes of Stockport, Crewe, and Bury. These were worrying times, particularly as heroes Kinkladze and Rösler had moved on. Understandably Kit Symons had also left. Another to go was Ian Brightwell, the playing squad's last link with the mid 80s. These were sad but inevitable losses as the club made cutbacks.

Despite these departures, City still appeared to be the media's clear favourites for the Division Two title. Supporters, however, knew that if any side was capable of making the simple seem difficult it was City. Promotion may have been a formality as far as the media were concerned but for fans it was hoped for - even demanded - but not expected. Nevertheless, there was a perverse excitement about the new season. Most were looking forward to seeing City stand a chance of winning a significant number of games, while others eagerly anticipated trips to long forgotten footballing venues. There was no doubt City were by far the biggest club in the division, and that gave the club a certain prestige. It was a somewhat perverse view but the club and its supporters had to clutch at any positives from the embarrassment of relegation.

Off the pitch season ticket sales were healthy - at the start of August it was revealed nearly 14,000 had been sold - while fans were keen to purchase the new fluorescent yellow and green striped away shirt. Unfortunately, Kappa once again failed to deliver enough shirts to satisfy demand, and a great sales opportunity was missed. Already City's relationship with their kit manufacturer was being questioned. The hyperbole at launch suggested this was a perfect marriage of two forward looking organisations - with City sinking to their lowest position and Kappa failing to deliver the goods, it looked as if marriage guidance was required.

During the close season both the *City Magazine* and *Bert Trautmann's Helmet* tried to be positive. In *Bert* it was suggested supporters repeatedly chant the following relegation mantras to ensure the Seasonally Affected Depression experienced throughout the previous few years is kept at bay:

City's relegation was a major shock. Supporters looked for reasons, Phil Shaw of The Independent *gave his assessment.*

1. **Relegation is not so bad. After all, at least it means we can have a clear out of all the dead wood.**
2. **However bad things seem, there is always something to look forward to - aren't we launching a new away kit next month?**
3. **Of course, there will be lots of new grounds to visit this season.**
4. **The game against Wrexham will give us valuable experience of playing foreign opposition.**
5. **Wigan and Preston are lovely places to visit at any time of year.**
6. **When we play Crewe in the 3rd round of the FA Cup, Football Focus will feature us as the giantkillers.**
7. **At least we're bound to come up as Champions.**
8. **At least the Second Division play offs will give us a trip to Wembley.**
9. **At least the Auto Windscreens Shield will give us a trip to Wembley.**
10. **At least we're too good to go down from this Division...**

Although tongue in cheek, there were grains of truth in what was being said. For some supporters the new season was viewed in an extremely positive manner. Blackpool on the opening day was acceptable enough; after all the Blues had played them often in cup competitions since the mid 1980s, then an away game at the ambitious Fulham - a club that claimed boldly to be a Premier League club merely playing in Division Two. Burnley and Preston would arrive at Maine Road in October, and then there would be derby matches with Oldham. Even the fixtures with Macclesfield were looked forward to, especially by those Blues with allegiance to both clubs.

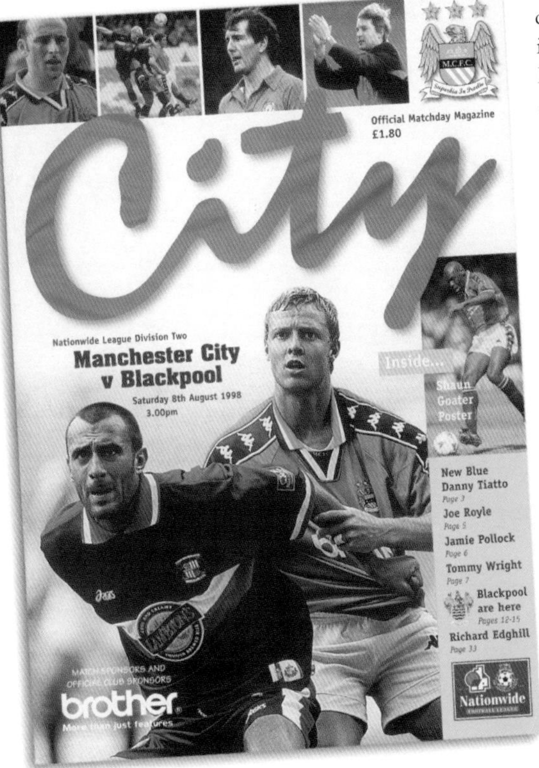

The programme from City's first ever game in the third tier of the English League.

On the opening day a crowd of 32,134 squeezed into Maine Road for the Blackpool clash. The club and fans treated it like a Premier League match. The usual razzmatazz was there. It would have been easy to believe this was not the Second Division - particularly as even the back page of the City programme referred to the game as taking place in "Nationwide League Division One"!

The game itself reassured those with doubts City could storm through the division. Shaun Goater, who had not set the world alight following his arrival the previous season, brought a 24th minute lead when he converted a low cross from the terrier like Paul Dickov. Goater had already set himself the rather ambitious target of 25 goals, and with several chances throughout the match should have increased his tally. He didn't but other players did.

Dickov created many openings and after 62 minutes clipped a pass to the still disappointing Lee Bradbury who netted from about ten yards out. Seventeen minutes later the tricky to pronounce defender Kakhaber Tskhadadze was in the right spot when a Tony Vaughan header rebounded off the post, and the Georgian made it 3-0. It was an impressive performance at times, particularly from young debutants Gary Mason and Nicky Weaver, but there were also a few worrying signs. Despite the goals City did miss too many clear chances and the general feeling was of relief. Joe Royle was glad to get the game out of the way: "I am certainly not kidding myself that it was a marvellous team performance, but it was a promising start. We looked very competitive and our fitness levels were good. Paul (Dickov) and Gary (Mason) showed a great spirit throughout the match and were probably our best players."

Afterwards the Blackpool manager Nigel Worthington was amazed his players had not performed well: "If you do not enjoy playing at Maine Road, you should pack your boots and go home. Before too long Manchester City will be storming back into the First Division."

Three days after the Blackpool victory City travelled to Notts County in the first leg of the first round of the Worthington sponsored League Cup. Tskhadadze opened the scoring from a corner in the 72nd minute, then Australian Danny Allsopp, who had replaced Lee Bradbury, made it 2-0 in injury time. The return match saw a rampaging City annihilate County 7-1. Interestingly, only 123 County supporters travelled to Manchester for a match watched by 10,063.

Royle was delighted: "The Maine Road crowd has not seen a resounding win like that for some time and so I am pleased for them. We played some terrific stuff at times and I thought our young players showed great maturity. There is a great spirit in the camp and to my mind, plenty of reasons to be optimistic at the moment."

The County victory, and Royle's upbeat message, had followed a rather disappointing League game at Fulham on 14th August. Kit Symons, now playing for Fulham, performed well as the home side defeated the Blues 3-0. Inevitably, among the scorers was another City old boy, Peter Beardsley, who opened with a low drive into the bottom left after being given far too much freedom. The result was disappointing, particularly as Fulham, under the guidance of Chief Operating Officer Kevin Keegan, were expected to be one of the main challengers for promotion. A defeat and a couple of draws saw the Blues fall to fourteenth place, the lowest rung on the League ladder in the club's history.

City desperately needed to take every opportunity presented, but striker Goater was not making the most of his chances. He admitted he had received a rollicking from Jamie Pollock: "Jamie is brilliant at giving the other lads a kick up the backside. If you are not performing, then he will come over and tell you in no uncertain terms. What I admire about him is that he has never allowed his standards to drop. He still trains like a Premiership player and that is important."

A 3-1 defeat of Walsall followed, and then six days later Mel Machin's impressive Bournemouth side were beaten 2-1 at Maine Road. Thankfully Macclesfield, potentially the greatest banana skin of all, were overcome with an 87th minute strike by the overly-criticised Goater. The supporters were still of the view the club needed a recognised prolific striker, but Royle was convinced Goater was that man. Ultimately the fans grew to love the Bermudan.

Derby won the League Cup second round tie 2-1 on aggregate thanks to a winner from future Blue Paulo Wanchope. Amazingly, Lee Bradbury had put in a sterling performance. When he was substituted near the end he received a good ovation from the crowd who desperately wanted his career to turn the corner. Everyone willed the £3m man to perform well but unfortunately he remained relatively ineffectual. It was no surprise when he went to Crystal Palace in October in a deal worth about £1.5 million, although it was later claimed Palace's financial problems affected the actual transfer of funds.

Three successive score draws against Northampton (2-2), Millwall (1-1), and Burnley (2-2) came in September, but results were overshadowed by events off the pitch. At Millwall the players and fans were faced with a considerable degree of threatening behaviour from the Millwall fans. Royle: "We could have won the match, but it's probably just as well we didn't. I doubt we'd have got out alive. I didn't know supporters were allowed to run on to the pitch and threaten and spit at players. Still, the crowd refereed the game very well. They appealed for everything and got most of it. I am very angry about what I have seen."

The 2,000 City fans in the crowd of 12,726 behaved well but it was extremely difficult at times under the intense provocation of the locals. At the end of the match the City fans were kept behind for over an hour as the police tried to restore law and order. Those travelling by train could see the damage caused outside by Millwall fans who had fought with the police when the area was being cleared. There was glass everywhere. It was all very sad, and revived bad memories of the problems of the mid-80s when City fans travelled to the old Second Division grounds.

After one win in ten City were down in eleventh place and the fans were becoming concerned. Some new faces were needed and with Bradbury moving to Palace and Ged Brannan off to Motherwell for £378,000 the supporters could see no reason why the club couldn't spend. Royle: "The club is saddled with a massive debt and I realise that some of the cash must go towards reducing that burden."

Royle did manage to bring a couple of players in however, with the arrival of Michael Branch on loan from Everton, and Andy Morrison from Huddersfield. Morrison joined on loan at first, but soon became a permanent player with City paying Huddersfield £80,000. Town supporters were disappointed with Morrison's departure as he was a bit of a cult figure to some of the club's fans just as he was to become at City.

These players helped achieve a 2-1 victory over Colchester on Halloween, although a dismal first half had proved something of a horror story. The arrival of Ian Bishop in the second period for his first appearance of the season livened it up, and goals from Horlock - a 49th minute penalty - and the tank-like Morrison gave City the victory. Morrison scored again in the next match - a 3-0 defeat of neighbours Oldham - but then embarrassment followed at Wycombe. A game, which had little by way of entertainment, ended 1-0 to the home side thanks to a dubious decision.

Three days later City faced Halifax Town in the first round of the FA Cup - another unwelcome consequence of relegation to Division Two. It was an embarrassment to play in such an early round, but across the Pennines the people of Calderdale treated the match as a major occasion. The local newspaper ran a full week of articles leading up to the big match. They even produced a special edition paper which included a full colour poster of Paul Hendrie's goal in the 1980 Halifax victory over Malcolm Allison's multi-million pound side. City fans in the area couldn't believe the hype and were fearful of another humiliation. In the end they needn't have worried as the Blues defeated the Shaymen 3-0 with goals from Russell (two) and Goater. Joe Royle was pleased: "As a whole, I thought it was an adequate performance to beat Halifax and at least we are in the hat. Mind you, I won't start getting excited until we are at the semi-final stage of the competition!"

Despite a valiant performance City left the competition at the third round stage with a 1-0 defeat at Premiership Wimbledon. Previously, the Blues had defeated Darlington 1-0 in a second round replay.

Back in the League, City suffered consecutive draws at home to Gillingham (0-0) and at Luton (1-1). After before dumped out of the Auto Windscreens Shield by Mansfield Town, Bristol Rovers provided more misery in the next League match - a no score draw at Maine Road - then a 2-1 defeat at York left the Blues lying in 12th place, 15 points behind leaders Fulham and second placed Walsall. Royle knew time was running out: "I never expected this job to be easy. It is nine months since I came here and there have been a great deal of changes - mostly for the better. I am still confident things will come right, but I know we have to start winning quickly."

A Boxing Day victory over Wrexham was the first in an unbeaten run of twelve games, although gale force winds made it difficult at times. It was also clear there was a gap where Morrison, missing through influenza, usually dominated. Nevertheless, the Blues withstood the Wrexham pressure, and in the 55th minute Wiekens managed to score via a powerful downwards header from about six yards out. City fans chanted "one-nil to Eng-er-land!"

Michael Brown performed exceptionally well, winning praise from Royle, while a man who was becoming another hero to the City faithful was young goalkeeper Nicky Weaver. With great skill he managed to keep Wrexham's Martyn Chalk and Ian Rush at bay, and left the field to a standing ovation.

The Stoke victory two days later was considerably more entertaining, enjoyable, and exciting for the Maine Road crowd of 30,478. The most impressive part was City actually came from behind to take the points, something few City sides had managed in recent seasons. The visitors took the lead through Sigurdsson on the half-hour, but earlier a Gareth Taylor header had been disallowed for offside. After a half-time Royle rollicking the Blues attacked like Tasmanian Devils. The crowd, recognising City's fire, burst into life and cheered, applauded, and chanted. All of this led to Paul Dickov netting a rather simple equaliser two minutes into the half. Dickov: "You could feel the confidence flowing through the side once I had scored." From that point the Blues were unstoppable, but they still had to wait until Taylor headed an 85th minute winner. It's worth noting this was the first time the Blues had won a match after falling behind in nineteen months. 1998 ended with confidence spreading throughout the club.

On 16th January the Blues achieved a thrilling 3-0 victory over leaders Fulham. Andy Morrison was missing following a cruel dismissal during the Wimbledon cup defeat two weeks earlier, but City coped admirably. Terry Cooke, an exciting young winger, joined the club on loan from Old Trafford and immediately impressed. He was delighted with his welcome: "It was absolutely unbelievable. The

LOWEST EVER HOME CROWD WITNESSES CUP EXIT

On 8th December 1998 the Blues were defeated 1-2 - thanks to two strikes from future Blue Lee Peacock - at home by Mansfield Town in the Auto Windscreens Shield. The crowd was 3,007, the lowest for a first team fixture at the stadium, and some of the tabloid press made sad comparisons with Manchester United's European game with Bayern Munich. The Mirror incorrectly claimed City fans had turned their backs on the club. It was an easy target story, but one which should never have been written. City had clearly remained one of the game's largest clubs simply because of their fan base. Loyalty was there for all to see. In fact if the fans did have a fault it was that perhaps they had been too loyal over the years.

INSIDE

SOUVENIR POSTER AND BIG MATCH PREVIEW

PAGE 12

TOMORROW

CITY v TOWN

The best possible coverage from tonight's Maine Road showdown

Despite City's status in 1998 the people of West Yorkshire viewed the City-Halifax Cup match as a real David & Goliath battle. In the week leading up to the tie the Halifax Evening Courier included a number of special features and also produced a commemorative colour poster of the goal which eliminated City from the competition in 1980.

Tank-like Andy Morrison.

crowd was amazing and their reception gave me such a buzz. It really was totally different from the atmosphere at Old Trafford where a lot of fans simply expect to win and just sit back and enjoy the game. Maine Road is packed with fanatics and they can make such a difference when they get behind you. There's no way you want to lose. I was delighted with the response from the fans."

It wasn't long before Royle started to talk about promotion, although he tried to play down how the Blues would achieve it: "I have never ruled out automatic promotion and that is our objective, but let's not start to get carried away. We are still out of the play off zone and know that we need to keep this run going. I have believed things were coming right for a while and it is nice to be vindicated, but I am not going to start making rash promises now. We cannot look beyond the next game, which is Millwall at home, and will be massive for us. The lads are already talking about that one and there are a few scores to settle."

On the pitch City made Millwall pay for their early season treatment of the Blues with a 3-0 pounding, thanks to goals from Dickov (61), Cooke (71), and Horlock (75). Off the pitch the away supporters ripped up seats in the North Stand, and had earlier created havoc in Stockport fighting with Manchester United followers. For some reason they seemed a trifle upset when the City fans in the North Stand started chanting "1-0 in your cup final"; by the time it was 3-0 the police had total control, although several shops were damaged after the match.

Crunch match! No quarter was given in the return with Millwall. Gareth Taylor and Lee Crooks are pictured in the heart of the action.

More trouble followed in City's next match, although this time it managed to confine itself to the players. Although the game was a tightly balanced goal less draw at Bournemouth, the referee managed to send off two City men - Pollock and Horlock. Pollock's third dismissal of the season came about eleven minutes from the end when he performed a rather innocuous looking tackle. It was a little late, but it certainly did not appear to be a deliberate foul, and clearly did not warrant a second yellow card. The City captain was furious: "That was an absolute shambles - I have never seen such a poor refereeing performance in my entire career. He seemed intent on turning a good football match into a rugby match. I could appeal against my sending off, but I wouldn't trust that referee to get it right after watching a video. He doesn't need an extra third eye, he needs another five or six."

The Horlock dismissal was equally frustrating for City. In the dying seconds of the match Horlock approached referee Brian Coddington to tell him Nicky Weaver had been clattered by Ian Cox, who came flying in for a last minute corner. That challenge looked considerably more dangerous than the Pollock incident and yet nothing happened. As Horlock approached Coddington, the official waved him away. Then he produced a red card. Afterwards a baffled Royle searched for answers: "The referee said Kevin was walking towards him in an aggressive manner. He admitted that there was no swearing, Kevin just wanted to speak with him. And here was me thinking it was good to talk. Apparently not. In fact, it seems like it's pretty dangerous to even walk on a football pitch nowadays!

"We came here to be positive and win the game, but did not have the cutting edge which we needed. I felt we were strong all over the pitch and on another day, it would have been a great point. But instead we feel bitter and annoyed by the referee's decisions. People are going to look at the stats and think this game was a bloodbath, but I cannot remember a bad tackle."

Victory followed a week later as Macclesfield were defeated 2-0 at Maine Road, with goals from Goater and Gareth Taylor. The match was watched by a crowd of 31,086 including Ajax's Georgi Kinkladze, who viewed from one of the boxes. The Blues moved up to fifth place on 51 points.

Fulham were clearly walking away with the title by this point, but Preston, Walsall, and Gillingham were all within reach, while Bournemouth, Chesterfield, Wigan, and Millwall were all a little too close for comfort. As City had to travel to Chesterfield for their next match, it was clear the Blues still had a grip on their own destiny.

Unfortunately an extremely rare mistake from Wiekens on the half-hour allowed Chris Beaumont to challenge down the left wing. The Chesterfield player then delivered a cross, which caused panic in the City defence. Marcus Ebdon had a shot blocked on the line, but ex-Bolton striker David Reeves drilled the rebound past Weaver.

Several chances to equalise came City's way, but they couldn't capitalise until the 51st minute. 21 year old Lee Crooks surprised everyone - including the City bench who urged him to pass the ball - when he sent an impressive strike from about thirty yards out into the top corner. It was described as "awesome" in the *Manchester Evening News*, and it clearly was a great finish from a player normally seen as rather staid in his approach.

The away draw was a good result, however City's key rivals - Fulham, Preston, Bournemouth, Wigan and Gillingham - all won causing the Blues to drop to sixth, but it was all still close. Then came another of those controversial refereeing days as 22nd placed Northampton scraped a no score draw at Maine Road. Kevin Horlock was sent off for two bookable offences, despite vehement protests from victim Chris Freestone, prompting Royle to talk about the quality of officials once again: "I am fed up talking about referees. I would rather just leave them to get on with their jobs, but sometimes you have to stand up and say 'he is not good enough'." Quite honestly, the standard of referees in this division deeply disturbs me but I am not sure there is anything we can do about it."

He then spoke briefly about the Horlock incident: "Kevin is gathering quite a collection of bookings which take some believing. First, it was aggressive walking at Bournemouth, and now he has been sent off for having a shot and because another player slipped over."

The game extended City's unbeaten run to 11 matches - their best for 23 years - but it should have been a victory. Once again the main focus had been the referee, but it was clear to the 27,999 paying fans the forwards were missing too many chances. Goater was still the club's leading striker with eleven goals but was gaining notoriety for missing many more. Had the club been top of the table there would not have been so much concern, but with City struggling to hold on to a Division Two play off place fans were unhappy. Fortunately, a confidence booster was just around the corner.

Burnley were annihilated 6-0 with goals from Horlock, Morrison, and Allsopp and a hat-trick from Goater. Royle was happy: "I am delighted for Shaun Goater, who is a lovely man and has never stopped trying during his difficult spell. I only brought him off so he would get a hero's ovation. This has been coming for a while, and there might be one or two more big wins to come before the end of the season."

City's unbeaten run ended on 13th March with a 1-2 defeat by Oldham. It was one of those "expect the unexpected" games the Blues seem to throw up every now and again. As always a large number of chances came City's way, but the frontmen found it difficult to make an impact. Oldham took the lead through a penalty - the first goal conceded at home since the visit of Stoke on 28th December - and Lee Duxbury made it 2-0 in the 56th minute. Before that, however, City had been awarded a spot kick only for Gareth Taylor to send his right foot shot straight at the Oldham 'keeper. Fortunately Taylor did find the net in the 79th minute but it was too little too late. A streaker raced on to the pitch in the final minutes and demonstrated to the players how to score. He then managed to dodge two policemen and a few stewards for a spell before being wrestled to the ground on what was clearly a very cold day. Afterwards City fan Charlie McCormick was quoted as saying: "it was the best tackle I saw all afternoon!" It was that sort of day.

The Oldham match proved to be merely a blip. Successive victories over Notts County (2-1), Colchester (0-1), Reading (1-3), and Wigan (1-0) followed. The Blues now lay in fourth place behind Fulham, Walsall, and Preston and with Preston their next opponents a certain amount of optimism was spreading. The game at Deepdale proved a tense affair. Preston scored in the opening minute, but still City shaded it. Unfortunately, it ended 1-1 despite several key tactical changes by Royle in an attempt to snatch all three points. New arrival Mark Robins came on as substitute, as did Ian Bishop, but Royle wasn't happy: "I am disappointed because I felt we could have won it. All we can do now is focus on winning games and see where it takes us. Take it from me, there are plenty more twists to come in this season."

Terry Cooke curls a free-kick over the Northampton Town wall during a goalless draw at Maine Road.

Kevin Horlock was sent off in that game, having previously been red-carded for 'aggressive walking' at Bournemouth!

A 4-0 thrashing of Lincoln followed - Dickov somersaulted in celebration after netting his third goal of the match - and with five games remaining all talk focused on reaching an automatic spot. The teams left to face were having mixed seasons - Luton were mid table; Gillingham were 5th and a serious threat; Wycombe were struggling at the top of the relegation zone; Bristol Rovers were 16th; while York City were 19th. City seemed capable of easily winning those matches, with the only difficult games appearing to be Gillingham and potentially one of the sides hungry to avoid relegation. Of course, football at Maine Road rarely follows the simplistic path and 2-0 victories over Luton and Gillingham were followed by a 1-2 defeat at home to Wycombe.

Victory against Wycombe would have put considerable pressure on second placed Walsall, who were two points ahead of the Blues when the game commenced, and five when it ended.

Sadly a 2-2 draw at Bristol Rovers killed the last hope of automatic promotion. The draw did guarantee a play off place, but a trip to Wembley couldn't be guaranteed. Of course all City fans hoped it would happen - even City's Junior Blues magazine had a full colour photograph of the stadium and told its young readers that if automatic promotion was not achieved then there was definitely going to be a day out to remember at Wembley - but nothing could be regarded as a formality. Royle: "We mustn't take anything for granted. This club has a history of standing around corner flags when they need to score.

Paul Dickov celebrates after equalising in the first leg of the play-off match with Wigan on 15th May 1999. In doing so he claimed the last ever goal in a first class game at the old Springfield Stadium.

We are in the play offs and that means we have to do it the hard way. We have achieved nothing yet."

The final match of the League campaign saw the Blues defeat York 4-0 before 32,471 at Maine Road. It was the highest crowd of the season, and meant Maine Road had virtually no segregation as the club crammed supporters into every spot possible. There were still thousands of others who wanted to be there to witness what many hoped would be the club's last league game in Division Two.

The victory ensured City took third place in the division and brought a play off semi-final with 6th placed Wigan, who scraped into the play offs on better goals scored than Bournemouth. The first leg was played away at Springfield Park, and became the last competitive match played at the ground before the club's move to the much more impressive JJB stadium. 6,762 paid to watch at Wigan, but a more impressive figure of around ten thousand attended Maine Road to watch via a large screen placed in front of the Main Stand. A surreal atmosphere engulfed Maine Road as the sight of any City player warming up prompted supporters to cheer. Even Moonchester received a massive cheer when he was spotted on the screen.

Shortly before the match kicked off the television cameras showed a large contingent of supporters running through a hole in the Springfield Park fence to take up positions on the terracing. Quickly stewards and police blocked the gap, but at least 100 fans managed to gain free entry.

The positive atmosphere at Maine Road was shattered in the first twenty seconds of the match as the normally dependable Wiekens and Weaver lost all sense of the occasion. Both stood motionless as Stuart Barlow rushed between them to score a very simple goal. Maine Road went silent, while those City fans at Wigan were distraught. Fortunately, Royle's City no longer buckled in these situations and the Blues did dominate the rest of the match. City attacked and attacked, while Wigan tried to withstand the pressure.

After 77 minutes the Blues finally scored the goal they deserved. Michael Brown made a good run down the right. He crossed to Paul Dickov, and City's powerful dynamo swept home a thoroughly deserved equaliser. The cheer from Maine Road was so loud wags joked it could be heard at Springfield Park itself.

As the game wore on City attacked further, but they also kept one eye on defence. This wasn't the time to do anything else stupid. In the sixth minute of injury time Tony Vaughan narrowly missed scoring the winner when he headed fractionally wide, but the Blues felt satisfied. At Maine Road the screen displayed a happy Joe Royle, prompting the City fans to chant, "Royle, Royle, give us a wave." He didn't, and the Kippax supporters gave him a good natured boo as a result.

Four days later Goater gave City a 27th minute lead in the return to send the Blues to Wembley for the first time since 1986. Despite his critics, Goater was still netting enough to be City's top scorer. After the whistle thousands of supporters invaded the pitch to celebrate. It was a terrific sight and seemed to be an outpouring that ended years of hurt. Of course it wasn't, and with Wembley around the corner no one quite knew what to expect, but it was a significant moment. One supporter in a wheelchair found the whole affair particularly entertaining, especially when his friend pushed the chair at a frantic pace across the pitch, and then let go to leave the disabled fan rolling for some distance. He even entered the net at one point as both men laughed.

Director John Wardle was also on the pitch dancing, as the fans partied. Well it was 1999. Life was certainly on the up, and when it was announced City's opponents would be Gillingham and not Preston, most fans assumed there would be absolutely no problem getting tickets. Sadly, the distribution of tickets showed City's organisational skills to be particularly weak.

The match was watched on a large screen by a crowd of City supporters sat in the Kippax Stand at Maine Road. The screen was placed in front of the Main Stand.

Supporters of all ages came to Maine Road. This young girl is clearly puzzled by the sight of a TV screen on the pitch: "Can we watch Tweenies next?"

Shaun Goater scores the goal that decided the play-off semi-final with Wigan and sent the Blues to Wembley.

Confusion, mixed messages, and total lack of understanding led to the biggest ticketing fiasco in the club's history. Thousands of supporters had to queue in excess of eight hours simply to get tickets their regular season ticket book should have guaranteed. City's queuing system meant fans had to go on a massive tour of the stadium. During their time inside the North Stand fans were able to read messages left by those that had gone before them such as, "Mummy, where's Daddy? Is he dead? No son he's just gone for his tickets, he'll be back when you're a teenager"; "If anybody finds my body, tell my wife and children that I love them"; "I'm not ringing my wife. I said I'd be home at 11.30, why have two arguments in one day!"; "Here lies the body of an unknown City fan, he bravely queued for six hours before sun stroke and hunger got the better of him."

City fans were disgusted by the club's total failure. Noel Bayley: "I have been making complaints and advocating suggestions with regard to the piss poor Maine Road ticket office now for longer than I can remember, so I cannot claim to have been surprised by the cock-up when it came to selling Wembley tickets, which was huge even by the ticket office's lowly standards. Instead of a reward for the most loyal fans in the country the club's legendary amateur antics ensured that Wembley became a huge millstone and then they had the gall to blame the fans. Heads should have rolled."

Eventually, over forty thousand City fans did obtain tickets for the play off final, but there were still a large number disappointed. Meanwhile, Gillingham were able to sell their allocation to more or less anybody from the south east. At one point a Gillingham spokesman even had the 'brass neck' to say the whole of Kent was supporting Gillingham while not even half of Manchester followed the Blues. It was a ridiculous comment and one which upset a large number of Mancunians, particularly as Gillingham's average attendance was some 22,000 less than City's.

City fans invaded the pitch to celebrate reaching a Wembley final and Lee Crooks was one of those caught up in the scenes of jubilation.

Division Two Play Off Winners 1999

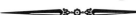

The 1999 Play Off Final was scheduled for Sunday 30th May with City clearly the favourites. According to the media Gillingham were going to be swept aside by Royle's men. The trip to Wembley was going to be a great experience for City's followers, although those with longer memories believed this could be yet another of City's famous 'cock-up days'. In the end it became both one of the most tortuous and joyous occasions ever experienced by Blues, and the entire day seemed to sum up exactly what supporting Manchester City was all about.

For many Blues the day began with a long journey down to the capital. Some stayed overnight close by - the Wembley Hilton seemed to have City banners and flags hanging from every window - yet for those arriving early the atmosphere was strange. Supporters wearing suspiciously new Gillingham shirts marched around the stadium, while others encamped close to the ramps on Wembley Way were singing songs glorifying Manchester United, Millwall, and every once in a while Gillingham. Blues arriving via the underground would have been confused as to who City's opponents were early on, but the atmosphere seemed peaceful enough.

The Gillingham fans mainly congregated around the Wembley Way/twin towers area, and cheered every time their Chairman Paul Scally appeared. The pro-Gillingham chanting was abruptly ended when a small group of City supporters lightened the atmosphere by marching through the middle of the Gillingham supporters

PLAY OFF PROGRESS

Semi-final 1st leg
Wigan A D 1-1 Attendance 6,762
Semi-final 2nd leg
Wigan H W 1-0 Attendance 31,305

FINAL DETAILS

30th May 1999 at Wembley Stadium
GILLINGHAM 2
MANCHESTER CITY 2
City won 3-1 on penalties

CITY: Weaver, Crooks (G. Taylor), Edghill, Wiekens, Morrison (Vaughan), Horlock, Brown (Bishop), Jeff Whitley, Dickov, Goater, Cooke
GILLINGHAM: Bartram, Southall, Ashby, Smith, Butters, Pennock, Patterson (Hodge), Hessenthaler, Asaba (Carr), Galloway (Saunders), R. Taylor

GOALS: Asaba, Robert Taylor, Horlock, Dickov

ATTENDANCE: 76,935
REFEREE: M. Halsey (Welwyn Garden City)
GUEST OF HONOUR: Mike Lazenby, Divisional Director of Marketing, Nationwide Building Society
MANAGER: Joe Royle
CAPTAIN: Andy Morrison

chanting: "Wem-ber-ley, Wem-ber-ley, it's that shitty place in London that we thought we'd never see!" Everyone laughed, and it said much about the City fans approach to the match.

Around the stadium close to the players' tunnel end the City supporters gathered en masse. Every song, every flag, every face was blue, and every time a vehicle passed with City merchandise visible the cheering was incredible. At one point a white stretch limousine with City flags sticking out of the sunroof passed. The rumour went around this was Noel and Liam Gallagher, but there had already been a number of other stories concerning the Oasis boys' arrival and nobody seemed to know for certain.

Then a coach appeared with a police escort in the distance. The cheer went up. City were on their way! Except it wasn't City, it was Gillingham, and what was worse was that nobody seemed to realise until the very last moment when the cheering turned into booing. The Gillingham players should have known then the atmosphere would be mainly blue.

When the City coach did arrive, the cheering was incredible and the players couldn't help but be moved by the whole affair. As soon as the coach entered the stadium, City fans rushed to their turnstiles and made their way into the ground. This was the first time many City fans had been since 1986, and the terracing on which they had then stood, close to the Players' tunnel, was now all-seater. As a result the view seemed considerably worse.

The pre-match entertainment was not particularly inspiring with two London based DJs pretending to support Gillingham and City, and then sing songs connected with the clubs. The 'City DJ' chose to sing Oasis songs, surely Blue Moon would have been more appropriate? And even the arrival of Moonchester couldn't save the DJ from embarrassment as his great singalong became singalone. He was eventually drowned out by the sounds of Blue Moon from those in D, E, and F sections amongst others. The Football League even provided opera for the fans, but well known United supporter Russell Watson was booed every time he opened his mouth.

Eventually, the players were brought out on to the pitch for the commencement of play. They were

greeted by smoke, fireworks, and inflatable Nationwide Building Society men causing City fans to ponder what had happened to football during City's thirteen-year absence from Wembley.

When the match commenced City were not the great force the media anticipated, instead they slipped their way across a wet surface and relied on the 20 year old Nicky Weaver to keep Gillingham at bay, particularly in the 9th minute when he palmed away an effort from Galloway. As the game wore on confidence grew and in the 26th minute a downward header from Horlock was superbly saved by Gillingham's Bartram.

Mixed play followed a forgettable first half, although it's fair to say City had the better chances and should have taken the lead, especially in the 75th minute when Goater sidefooted a shot against the post. As the game progressed City fans became nervous, then with only nine minutes remaining the Blues were dealt a major blow when Asaba toe-poked a shot into the roof of City's net. There was a feeling of huge disappointment in the stands, but worse was to follow as Robert Taylor made it 2-0 in the 86th minute. Two thirds of the stadium fell silent, then many, many Blues decided enough was enough and left for home. Those that remained were in for a treat, although no-one could possibly have anticipated quite what would follow. Sky TV certainly believed the contest was over as every comment mentioned Gillingham's success and City's embarrassing failure.

Radio Five commentator Alan Green told his listeners about the plight of the thousands of City fans silent at Wembley adding: "That many fans go to every home game. Why do they do it?" It wasn't long before he found the answer.

With a mere 17 seconds of normal time remaining Horlock sidefooted a goal, prompting sparks of optimism from a few supporters. Surely just a consolation, yet four and a half minutes into injury time Dickov fired an unlikely equaliser into the top corner. For a few seconds the stadium fell silent as City supporters struggled to comprehend the importance of the goal, and then wild celebrations erupted all over Wembley. Outside those that had left early heard the news and rushed back, and the stadium was full once more.

An extremely tense period of extra time followed, and then came penalties. The City players huddled together as a team, showing a unity previous sides had clearly not enjoyed. This helped City win the penalty shoot-out 3-1, but this score conveys nothing of the drama, the excitement, and the immense feeling of relief experienced at the time. The penalty sequence started with Kevin Horlock scoring the first at the City-filled Players Tunnel end of the stadium. Then Weaver's legs blocked Gillingham's first effort by midfielder Paul Smith.

Pre-match anticipation as as a sea of blue and white greets the City coach on its arrival at Wembley and again inside the stadium (facing page).

City walked out (above) to equal Arsenal's achievement of appearing at Wembley during each decade of its existence, apart from the 1940s.

Two down and these two look very down (below left).

A moment that changed history... Paul Dickov scores one of City's most important goals ever (below)!

A confident-looking Paul Dickov marched forward to take City's second, but watched in agony as his attempt bounced off both posts to leave the score at 1-0. Adrian Pennock then shot wide for Gillingham, before Terry Cooke calmly slotted his effort into the bottom corner to make it 2-0.

John Hodge sent Gillingham's third penalty clinically into the roof of the net, then Richard Edghill sent his spot kick in off the bar. The pressure was at long last on Gillingham. Guy Butters looked a little on edge as he prepared for the eighth penalty, while in nets Weaver seemed relatively composed. The young City 'keeper dived the right way and blocked Butters' effort to give City victory. He immediately went on a manic celebratory run, until he was dragged back to reality by Morrison and the other players.

Wild celebrations followed, with the players bowing to the supporters to show their appreciation for sticking by the club through an extremely difficult period. The City fans were in good voice and after several traditional City anthems, they burst into a chant that many may regard as being offensive but at that moment summed up exactly how the supporters felt. For too long City fans had endured abuse from supporters of other clubs and the Blues dismal plight under Alan Ball and others during the 1990s had caused a great deal of pain. Manchester United's success had brought further misery, so when the City fans chanted the obscene but heartfelt "you can stick your f**king treble up your arse!" it was more an indication of how the Blues simply did not care about activity elsewhere, they only cared about their club. Accusations of jealousy were false, City fans were for once singing about their success and nothing else - not even a world-wide headline grabbing treble - was more important.

That chant, though littered with foul language, was actually being sung at Wembley Stadium by supporters of all ages and though, for obvious reasons, it didn't make the headlines, it was a clear indication City fans really didn't care about any other team, just the one they had supported through thick and thin. The play-off was the only game that mattered.

It was later suggested City do a formal homecoming, however the idea was soon dismissed by the club who, quite rightly stated homecomings would be saved for major trophy successes. Nevertheless everybody still wanted to celebrate. Chairman David Bernstein joined fellow director Dennis Tueart and PR guru Chris Bird on the pitch. The normally quiet, unassuming City man later stated:

Shoot-out drama

City players watch from the centre circle (above) as Richard Edghill keeps his cool to make it 3-1 and put the pressure firmly on Gillingham.

Then Nicky Weaver saves Guy Butters' kick and sets off on a manic celebration run before his team-mates finally catch up with him.

"I just felt it would be wonderful to walk on the Wembley surface... It will be a one off for I won't be making a habit of it, you can be sure of that!"

Bernstein was a very happy man, although he admitted this was not the end of City's struggle: "This is only the first stage. We will clear our heads and take it from there. I'll be working even harder to raise finance, which I've got to say will be easier now we are in the First Division."

Afterwards two men were being seen by most Blues as the real heroes of the day - Nicky Weaver and Paul Dickov. Weaver, in particular, grabbed the headlines and seemed to be the man who impressed the media. Weaver told journalists: "To come from third team football to this in a year is fantastic. To finish the season like this is absolutely incredible. I felt better than I thought I would. Once we got out and started playing it felt like any other game, which helped my nerves. I wasn't overawed by the surroundings at all."

As time progressed the contribution of another man, often pilloried, was highlighted by Andy Noise in *Bert Trautmann's Helmet*: "Richard Edghill - what a star. Never scored a goal in his life. Subject of much (unjustified) criticism, yet he stood up and was counted. He had the bottle, and he bloody did it."

Manager Joe Royle was delighted, although it's fair to say he looked absolutely worn out when he made it into the dressing room after the celebrations. In typically down to earth manner he told the media: "We're not getting too excited about this. A club this size should not be too euphoric about getting out of the old Division Three. And even though we won today, I still think the play offs are a joke. After 46 League games it comes down to a lottery."

Moving on to the performance Joe added: "My players were magnificent, and I never once thought we were beaten. We have now lost just twice in our last 27 matches and I think that tells you everything about their fighting spirit. We have played 49 cup ties this season and this is a very hard division. When fans are hanging off the rafters for you at places like Colchester, it all adds to the pressure. These lads will be better players for this experience and the strong nucleus in this side will go forward.

"I think we have gone a long way to curing Man City-itis. We can handle the big games now, even though we weren't at our best today."

That night referee Mark Halsey, who was staying at the nearby Hilton Hotel, witnessed a hotel full of Blues celebrating. They offered to buy him drinks and one or two wags tried to start a collection for the official. It was all light hearted, however Gillingham's chairman Paul Scally didn't see it that way. He made a complaint to the Football League and demanded the game be replayed claiming Halsey had been celebrating. For a couple of days the League deliberated and then, much to City and the referee's relief, announced the result would stand. They did, however, have a word of warning for Halsey: "There is a time and a place for everything and we shall remind him that it is unwise to mix with supporters so soon after an important match."

With the referee chastised and promotion in the bag, City fans looked forward to a season in Division One and were hopeful their new found spirit could lift them higher. Their three season exile from the Premier League had already equalled their longest spell out of the top flight since their first promotion exactly one hundred years earlier.

City fans everywhere celebrate promotion, including Oasis star Liam Gallagher seen (above) in one of Wembley's boxes.

City's shoot-out hero Nicky Weaver shows the Play-off final trophy to the City faithful and continues to be the star of the show as the rest of the squad line up before the photographers. The Gillingham end behind is already empty.

Promotion at the first attempt from Division Two was greeted by most Blues as a sign Joe Royle was on the right track. The division had been a tough one, and promotion via the play offs, though not the preferred route, had actually helped bind the club together. Team spirit appeared high and general interest in the Blues increased.

Immediately after the Wembley game season ticket sales had risen to 14,000, and early in the new season the club were forced to create a waiting list as they had reached their limit of around 22,000. This limit had been set to ensure there would be no problem with potential cup fixture allocations at Maine Road, and was also seen as an effort by the club to ensure it would still be possible to attend games on a match by match basis.

Alongside the increased interest from spectators City also found themselves a new sponsor, computer game company Eidos.

EIDOS

The Brother sponsorship had come to an end, and City were keen to tie up with an organisation representing the future. Eidos - the company responsible for the best selling Tomb Raider and Championship Manager series of games - seemed to offer the club what they wanted. Eidos' executive chairman and Blue Ian Livingstone was also delighted: "We see Manchester City as a unique property in domestic football with enormous potential for the future. Eidos is impressed with the board's vision for the future and felt it should be part of the new era."

There were other major changes off the field. Chris Bird was promoted to Chief Operating Officer and made a director: "It's unbelievable. When I was a kid I always dreamed of playing for City. Becoming a director is something I never really thought about. I know it sounds cheesy, but this is a real honour." While another change saw kit suppliers Kappa replaced by Le Coq Sportif after only two seasons.

lecoqsportif

When City's season commenced on Sunday 8th August they were rated as tenth favourites to win the Division One title, while Blackburn Rovers were bookies' favourites. As with the 1996-7 season when City were widely tipped following their relegation from the Premier League, the Blackburn prediction was way off the mark. Nevertheless, they did appear to be the team to beat as preparations were made.

The opening game saw the Blues face Wolves at Maine Road before a crowd of 31,755 and a Sky TV audience. 23 year old Mark Kennedy, a signing from Wimbledon, and the on loan left back Danny Granville both made their debuts. City attacked Wolves with force and had plenty of chances, but it wasn't to be. Despite the pressure - according to Sky City had 55% possession in the first half; 80% possession in the second and fourteen corners to Wolves' none - the match ended 0-1.

At half-time Chairman David Bernstein made a move which would help the club plan for the new millennium when he signed the contract documentation confirming City's move to the new stadium at Eastlands. On the pitch he was joined by council leader Richard Leese and Chief Executive Howard Bernstein for the official signing. The Chairman wrote in City's programme: "The stadium design has benefited from [fans'] feedback at last year's open days. Its capacity should approach 50,000 and its facilities will be fitting for the next Millennium. I would like to thank Manchester City Council and Sport England for the confidence shown in our club. I believe that the City of Manchester, the local community and our club will all derive enormous benefits from this exciting venture"

The signing coincided with an explanation of the plan which would see the stadium built in two phases, with the first concentrating on creating a stadium fit for the Commonwealth Games. Afterwards the athletics track would be removed and the stadium would be squared off to create a traditionally shaped football enclosure.

All of this was for the future, however, and City's main stadium issue at the time appeared to be how to cram more seats into the existing ground. Additional temporary seating was added to the now infamous 'Gene Kelly Stand' (officially block UU in the corner between the Kippax and the North Stand), while the corner between the Kippax and Platt Lane now housed a few hundred seats in front of the scoreboard. Later in the season a further section of seats was added to the Gene Kelly Stand, although these were actually positioned at an awkward viewing angle, and occupants seemed to face the lower tier of the Kippax rather than the pitch. It put some supporters in mind of the old Bernard Manning joke from the mid 80s: "I hear they've built a new stand at Maine Road. Trouble is they've built it the wrong way round - it faces the pitch!"

The new seating was the only way the club could increase capacity at a stadium that could no longer accommodate City's huge crowds. A year later the Blues sought other ways of increasing the capacity, squeezing seats in to what seemed like every available nook and cranny.

Three days after the Wolves defeat the Blues entertained Burnley in a rather easy 5-0 victory in the League Cup first round first leg. This included two goals from the impressive Mark Kennedy and the first of the season for Shaun Goater. It was hoped victory would spur the Blues on for their match with the Division Two champions Fulham, but sadly the game ended goalless as the two sides cancelled each other out. To further enhance his cult status, Andy Morrison, in a rather bizarre moment, was given a red card for 'licking' Stan Collymore's nose.

On 21st August Adrian Heath's Sheffield United arrived hoping for victory. They left feeling totally demoralised. The game started in frenetic style with both sides having good attempts on goal, although as the first half progressed it was clear City were taking control. Then a couple of spots of luck: first a handball led to a penalty easily converted by Horlock, then goalkeeper Tracey - the man who had appeared for the Blues when defeated 5-0 at Old Trafford in November 1994 - pulled down Goater on the edge of the area. Tracey was sent off and Horlock netted his second penalty.

In the second half City tore into the Blades. Kennedy rounded the replacement 'keeper after neat play from Bishop and Dickov

Danny Granville (above) and Mark Kennedy (below) made their City debuts in the opening First Division game of 1999/2000.

to score the third. The fourth came via a cross from Terry Cooke which was neatly headed downwards by the giant Goater. A fifth came from Paul Dickov and then Gareth Taylor, who had replaced Goater in the 70th minute, made it six. The crowd called for ten, but the score remained and afterwards Royle offered the goal feast as a "thank you" to the fans.

Following the thrashing of Sheffield United, the Blues defeated Burnley 1-0 in the second leg of the League Cup, and continued to move up the Division One table by beating Bolton, Nottingham Forest and Crystal Palace. The Palace victory put City second and raised expectations that promotion was attainable, despite the obvious problems associated with mounting a challenge so soon after scraping through the play-offs. As if to test the worth of the City team, the League Cup draw created an interesting two legged tie with Premiership Southampton.

The home leg ended goalless. Not the result hoped for, but still a creditable performance, then a week later the Blues travelled to the Dell for a more entertaining second leg. The match had been re-arranged from the Tuesday night to accommodate Sky TV and viewers watched as the Blues tried to match their Premier League rivals.

The first few minutes were played at breakneck speed with City creating a flurry of chances in those opening moments. The best effort from terrier Paul Dickov was saved, but then in the eighth minute a Kennedy cross set Dickov up again and this time the 5ft 5in striker made it 1-0 with a well-deserved goal.

Sadly, the lead didn't last as Southampton were awarded a penalty for what was perceived as a foul by the unlucky Edghill. Despite a valiant attempt by Weaver, the Saints equalised. Later an unsighted Weaver was unable to prevent another Southampton goal.

After the interval City had a great deal of possession, but didn't really look capable of scoring. It was no surprise when Oakley sneaked a third for Southampton.

As time progressed the Blues started to fight back. Goater managed to fire home City's second and, shortly afterwards, netted a third. The Blues managed to maintain the pressure on the Saints and came very close to taking the match in the final minutes of normal time. Then former Red Mark Hughes elbowed Edghill and was sent off for his second bookable offence. The City man was concussed for a while, and fans even saw him vomiting on the pitch. He was later stretchered off and spent the night in hospital.

In the 34th minute Shaun Goater scores the only goal of the game at Walsall to send City to the top of Division One for the first time since the start of the 1996-7 season.

Almost immediately Southampton had a goal disallowed for offside, and then two minutes into extra time scrambled a deflected winner. Despite the 4-3 defeat City had proved they were more than a match for Premier League teams of the calibre of Southampton, all they needed to do now was maintain their position in the Division One table and make their return to the top flight.

Four days before the League Cup defeat a Shaun Goater goal had brought victory at Walsall to lift City into top spot, but successive defeats to Ipswich and Norwich left the Blues fourth - two points behind leaders Birmingham City.

The following match saw City face the early season promotion favourites Blackburn Rovers, managed by ex-Blue Brian Kidd. It was a match all fans and many neutrals eagerly awaited, even Swedish TV decided this was the right time to show the Blues since relegation from the Premier League. The attendance was 33,027 - the highest since the old Kippax Stand was demolished in 1994 - and only possible because of the increased number of temporary seats squeezed into the corners.

Those watching either in the stadium or in Sweden were in for a treat as Blackburn were defeated 2-0 with goals from Jeff Whitley and the much maligned Richard Edghill - his first in the League. The Blues had been thrilling in the second half and could even afford the luxury of a missed Horlock penalty.

In Sweden Patrik Schèle was impressed with the local TV coverage: "They thought City played a more varying attacking play than Blackburn, who only attacked in the middle. The co-commentator was criticising Kidd for not switching tactics when he saw that Morrison and Jobson took everything in the middle. All in all they thought the win was deserved, but they weren't sure that City would last at the top spot all season. They thought however that Blackburn would be thereabouts when the season ended - from this display I can't figure out why they would be there! Last but not least, the crowd and the atmosphere. They were impressed. They said that they couldn't hear themselves when City were attacking due to the noise from the crowd. Once when 'Blue Moon' started the commentator just went: 'Listen'."

Joe Royle was happy with City's overall determination: "It was a terrific win for us. We may have been lucky to still be in it at the break but even after we missed that penalty we just kept going forward." He had some sympathy for his under fire former team mate Brian Kidd, stating he believed Blackburn could still challenge. Kidd, on the other hand noticed the difference between the two sides: "They were more determined, their attitude was better and they wanted it more than us. Seeing little Jeff Whitley scoring with a header late on typifies the difference. If City keep showing that sort of spirit there's no reason why they can't go up."

Four days later promotion rivals Ipswich were beaten 1-0 in a closely fought match watched by an incredible midweek crowd of 32,799. The difference between the two sides was in goal where Nicky Weaver seemed desperately keen to prove his England

U21 credentials against his main rival Richard Wright. It was a game the young Blue excelled in and clearly ensured City took the three points, but the match was noteworthy for a few other reasons, including an improved defensive performance from Richard Edghill. He even had a hand in the goal. After 58 minutes he sent an accurate long pass to Dickov wide on the right, who sent a cross into the area. The waiting Horlock netted a great goal from about eight yards out.

A 2-1 victory at Brian Horton's Port Vale followed before another former manager, Alan Ball, returned to Maine Road with Portsmouth. By a strange twist of fate Ball's return coincided with the announcement Joe Royle was to be October's Manager of the Month. Many fans remembered how Ball had been the last City manager to win the award back in November 1995. The Ball award came shortly before City plummeted down the divisions and many blamed the former World Cup winner for this demise. Sadly Ball's return in 1999 caused some to threaten the former City manager.

The Portsmouth chief safety officer, Dave Walton, even claimed there had been death threats. He hoped City could control the situation: "We have made the local police aware and they are discussing with their counterparts in Manchester about what safety measures to take. We expect the police and City to have security measures in place."

Chris Bird played down the situation, calmly telling the media: "We have every confidence in the match security already in place."

Ball did receive a significant amount of abuse but managed to shrug much of it off and even raised a laugh from a few City fans when he saluted them by lifting up his familiar flat cap. It must have been an exceptionally difficult time for Ball, particularly as City defeated his Portsmouth side 4-2, but he seemed to cope well.

After that victory City scraped a 1-1 draw at Queens Park Rangers, and then defeated promotion hopefuls Charlton 1-0 at the Valley. A 3-1 victory over Barnsley at Maine Road followed. Interestingly this match attracted 32,692 despite being played on an appallingly wet Wednesday night. The game also clashed with the official re-opening of Manchester city centre following the 1996 terrorist bomb, with the only impact of a packed city centre being a ten minute delay to the kick off. It's also worth noting the attendance was particularly impressive as it was greater than the crowd at Stamford Bridge for the Chelsea v Feyenoord Champions' League game.

Defeats by Huddersfield (whose supporters saw this as a promotion decider), Wolves, and Stockport County brought further misery. But the disappointment didn't last as over the following weeks City rediscovered their winning ways with victories over Swindon (3-0), West Bromwich Albion (0-2), and Grimsby (2-1). The run was ended by a 1-1 draw at Crewe on 3rd January. The next match, however, would be a real test as City were to face Premiership challengers Leeds United in the F.A. Cup fourth round. The Blues had already defeated Chester 4-1 in the third round, and now faced David O'Leary's exciting side. The draw brought the largest travelling support of the season to Maine Road - 4,386 - but the increased allocation to Leeds and additional crowd control measures reduced the ground's capacity. In the end the match was watched by 29,240 - some 817 less than the season's lowest League crowd at the stadium - while millions also watched the game live on Sky TV. They witnessed an incredible start.

It's fair to say everyone was surprised when Shaun Goater looped a perfect header over the Leeds' keeper Martyn to put City in the lead after only two minutes. Television viewers discovered that Goater was clearly offside at the time, but who cared. It was a dream start and all Blues hoped it would set them up nicely for a famous victory. Sadly it did not, and Leeds dominated despite a topsy-turvy goal pattern which saw the visitors go behind twice, with City's second coming from the impressive Ian Bishop. It was a terrific goal and clearly demonstrated Bishop's desire to remain a fixture in Royle's promotion seeking Blues. By half time, however, impressive Leeds had scored three, and at full time the score was 5-2.

David O'Leary hoped City would achieve promotion: "I hope they come up this season and we are back here next term taking points off them. I think they will come up, but I always felt we would score the goals to get us through."

Back in the League the Blues proved their strength with a 4-0 victory over Fulham on Sunday 16th January. The London club, it should be remembered, won the Division Two title in style the previous season and, with strong financial backing from Mohammed Al Fayed, were a very important

It had been ten years since Ian Bishop had last scored for the Blues when he netted twice in the 2-1 win against Port Vale. Paul Dickov and Jeff Whitley help celebrate his 'double'.

side to beat. It should also be remembered as the day when Shaun Goater finally silenced his critics with an impressive hat-trick. Perhaps the one o'clock start encouraged him. Royle: "Shaun's game has improved all round. He has won over the crowd and I hope he gets the chance to step up another division with us by the end of the season."

The Blues had been helped by the 68th minute dismissal of Fulham skipper Chris Coleman, and Royle admitted his side were a shade fortunate: "We've played a lot better. At times we were excellent but we were sloppy, too. It was a strange performance but a great win. It was important after the other results, when everybody else seemed to win. There are four in there at the moment at the top and unless we have a massive collapse, it will be hard for Fulham to catch us. We wanted to beat them because they could put together a late run."

After a surprising 1-0 defeat at Sheffield United six days later the Blues beat both Nottingham Forest 1-3 and Norwich City 3-1. Then on 18th February City secured a point at Huddersfield. The Yorkshire club had slipped since the November meeting and were beginning to pay for the surprising transfer of striker Marcus Stewart to promotion rivals Ipswich. Much to the disgust of their fans the Stewart sale had blunted Huddersfield's chance of an automatic promotion spot and, ultimately, the club failed to even make the play-offs.

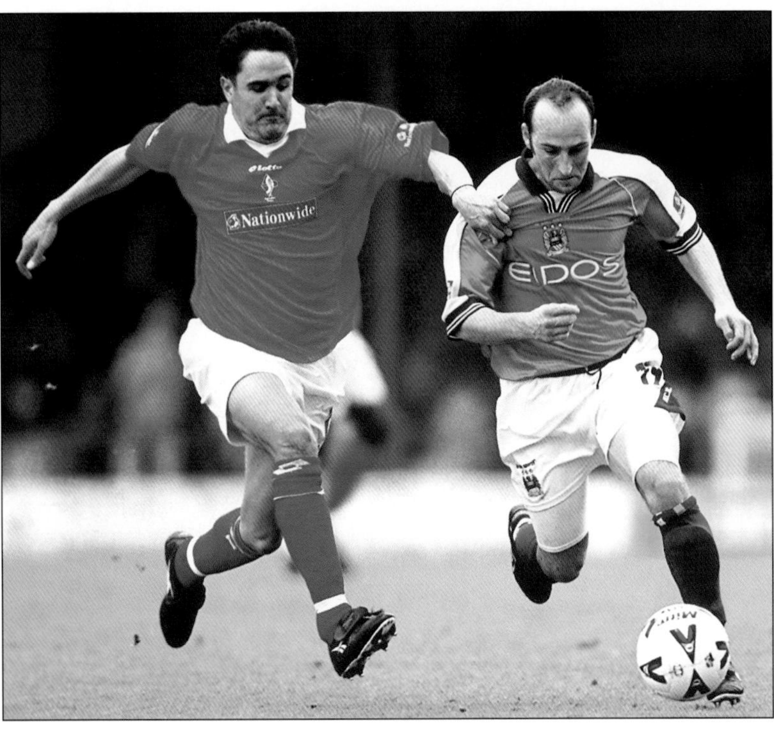

Australian international Danny Tiatto appeared in 48 League and Cup games for the Blues during the 1999/2000 season, including this win at Swindon.

City also appeared close to losing out on an automatic place, particularly as only four points were gained from the next six matches. Nevertheless, Royle argued that even when the Blues were not at their best they were still gaining some points, and were continuing to score goals, or at least Shaun Goater was. During the eight matches he took part in, following his hat-trick against Fulham, he netted a total of seven. Those goals helped City maintain a play off place.

Victories for Barnsley and Ipswich put both sides two points ahead of the Blues, but City still had an important game in hand to play. There was also the news Royle had signed Derby's Spencer Prior for £500,000. Prior had turned down Nottingham Forest and Huddersfield, but the 28-year-old viewed the City offer as a good career move, and was keen to help the Blues achieve promotion: "I don't consider this a step down. Manchester City is a Premiership set up. I suppose as I have got older and more confident, so I have been able to take more responsibility. I have learned how to organise and shout a bit but I don't want anyone thinking I have come to City to take over the show. I am here to do my best for the team." The deal was almost entirely financed by the sale of Tony Vaughan to Forest.

It wasn't long before Prior proved his worth. He made his debut on 25th March as City finally returned to winning ways with a 2-1 victory over Gary Megson's West Bromwich Albion. The fans were immediately impressed with his command of City's defence, and he appeared to fill the void left by Andy Morrison's continuing absence through injury. Royle smiled as he told reporters of Prior's impact: "Spencer is a good talker, he's a great enthusiast. We've found out already that he is a chirpy chappy."

Despite Prior's arrival and the 2-1 victory, the match was a tense affair. The Blues had hit the woodwork twice early on, however it had been Albion who seized the initiative when after an hour Lee Hughes scored. Mark Kennedy levelled via a free-kick in the 77th minute, and then in a frantic final period the Blues bombard the Albion defence before Shaun Goater scrambled home the winner deep in injury-time.

Results elsewhere left City third, two points behind Ipswich but with a game in hand, although the table rarely provided an accurate view of the situation at this time as City and their main rivals never seemed to play on the same days.

At Swindon the Blues achieved a 2-0 victory on April Fools Day with goals from the now dependable Goater - his 27th of the campaign - and Kennedy. Royle was delighted, although concerned by City's first half performance: "I am delighted with the victory and I thought we fully deserved the points. It wasn't the best game in the first half, but Shaun Goater did well for the first goal, and we always looked comfortable after the half-time interval and more dangerous after we changed things around."

The game had not been a good one for 25-year-old midfielder Tony Grant who had made his first start since January. He was replaced by Ian Bishop early in the second half and from that point on the game came alive.

Despite the result the Swindon directors were pleased with the match. The Wiltshire club had allowed City fans to occupy both ends of their tiny ground, and it was reported that over half of the 12,397 crowd were supporting the Blues. At £17 per ticket it was calculated the additional gate money was worth over £100,000 to the relegation bound club.

In the table, City still had a game in hand over most clubs, and now lay third on 72 points. The near invincible Charlton (87 points) still headed the League while Barnsley (74 points) were second. Ipswich were fourth - one point behind City after the same number of matches - while Birmingham were fifth on 69 points. The true League position would be clearer once City had played their game in hand against Bolton on Wednesday 5th April.

With eighth-placed Bolton losing to Aston Villa via a penalty shoot out in the previous Sunday's F.A. Cup semi-final no one quite knew what to expect from the game. Fortunately, City seized control early on, and after eighteen minutes took the lead through a Kevin Horlock strike. Five minutes later Paul Dickov netted to give City an important 2-0 victory. At long last the Blues had returned to an automatic promotion spot and were now a point clear of Barnsley. They also had a superior goal difference to both Barnsley and Ipswich.

Royle felt City had done enough to kill any Bolton threat with a terrific first half display: "My team knew they needed to win this one - it was our game in hand - and they went for Bolton from the start, and in that first half we played as well as we have done for a very long time." He then told the media of City's target: "Automatic promotion is what we are aiming for and that will be the case until it's mathematically impossible for us."

Bolton's Sam Allardyce viewed City as certainties for automatic promotion: "They have got strength in depth, and that's so crucial at this stage. They had Shaun Goater and Danny Tiatto off injured but could still turn to players of the calibre of Danny Granville and Lee Mills to come on. I think they will hold their nerve and hang on now to one of those top two spots."

City strengthened their position in the top two with a fine 4-0 victory over Crewe at Maine Road three days later. The hero was Paul Dickov who netted twice, although new boy Spencer Prior set the course for victory with a 42nd minute header. Dickov's first came after 68 minutes with Mark Kennedy providing City's third before Dickov completed the rout.

Royle, who celebrated his 51st birthday that weekend, viewed the Crewe match as one of City's best in weeks: "We had 27 attempts on goal and could quite easily have notched double figures. We were terrific today, as fluent as we have been for a long time." Royle was also pleased with the performance of Prior: "After failing to keep a clean sheet for ten matches we have now kept three in a row, and much of that is down to Spencer."

Prior was pleased with his own performance, but was also delighted with the overall team play: "We are winning our battles all over the pitch and when we are on the ball we are as comfortable as many of the Premiership sides I have seen. We are also keeping clean sheets and that is important." Another man happy with life at Maine Road was Mark Kennedy. Earlier in his career Kennedy had struggled to impress at either Liverpool or Wimbledon, but since his close season move from Wimbledon he had settled well at City. Royle claimed the player had 'come home'. Kennedy wasn't going to argue: "The gaffer is right when he says I have found City a home from home. I cannot say enough about the warmth that has been shown to me here by the fans."

The Crewe victory gave the Blues the perfect opportunity to put rivals Barnsley and Ipswich under severe pressure, particularly as City were to kick off their match at Grimsby at 1pm and could therefore go a morale boosting six points clear before the other sides played.

Again, as with all City fixtures from the period, huge numbers of fans wanted to attend the match. Grimsby were naturally concerned with the possibility City fans could infiltrate the home sections and instigated a policy of testing those purchasing tickets with Grimsby-based trivia. The 'quiz' was even dubbed "who wants to be a Mariner?". The Grimsby management were determined the safety of their fans came first and even stated they would be prepared to turn away supporters rather than risk mixing fans, or compromising segregation and safety issues. The Blundell Park capacity was quoted as 10,033, but the directors maintained the game would be watched by no more than about 9,000. In the end the attendance was recorded as 8,166 including 2,200 City fans. Unusually for a City away game from their Division Two and Division One days, this was not the home side's highest attendance of the season. As a result Grimsby made around £30,000 less than the revenue they would have taken from a sell out match.

On the pitch City disappointed. Royle: "We were useless! I was disappointed because we were given such a good start. But in the end I was highly delighted to get away with a point. Our passing was poor on a good surface. Only Richard Jobson played anything like his usual standard for us today. If this result jolts us back to our best some good will have come out of it." The match ended in a 1-1 draw -

Central defender Spencer Prior made an immediate impact on his arrival from Derby County and scored a vital goal in the 1-1 draw at Grimsby (below) as well as netting against both Crewe and Portsmouth.

new hero Prior scored for City in the sixth minute but the lead lasted only ten minutes - but Grimsby had made life exceptionally difficult for the Blues. Royle's opposite number Alan Buckley felt his side could have won: "I was more disappointed with the point than Joe Royle. I thought we deserved all three because we were more than a match for a team knocking on the promotion door. Our start was not good, but the lads got fired up and fully deserved the point if not more."

The result left the promotion race wide open again, and by the time of City's next match - at home to Tranmere on 22nd April Ipswich had closed the gap to a point, while Barnsley were still only three points behind. All sides had four games left to play. It started to feel as if the race would go to the very last match of the season away at Blackburn. A game everybody wanted to attend. Not surprisingly City's allocation of 6,157 seats had sold out almost as soon as they went on sale.

At Maine Road the Tranmere match saw a return to winning ways as Jeff Whitley and Shaun Goater ensured a 2-0 victory. Goater scored first, but the Blues remained a little nervous until the 72nd minute when Whitley slotted home a Kennedy cross. Tranmere manager John Aldridge felt the Blues were more than a match for his side, although he was a little disappointed this could be his final chance of facing the Blues for a while: "They've got themselves a great chance of promotion and they deserve it. So do Joe and the fans, but it's a pity for our division. You want to be playing big clubs like City, but we're all a bit selfish."

City were now four points clear of nearest rivals Ipswich and, just as supporters dared to feel confident, two days later, on Easter Monday, came a major jolt to the system. It arrived in the shape of former City player Lee Bradbury - a man dubbed 'Lee Badbuy' after becoming City's most expensive signing and one of the club's biggest flops. Playing once again for Portsmouth, Bradbury somehow helped Pompey to a 2-2 draw.

The Blues had been leading 2-0 after a 26th minute effort from Spencer Prior and a 40th minute flick from Robert Taylor. Unfortunately Portsmouth got back in the match with a penalty from Bradbury deep in first half injury time. Then six minutes from the end the one time ineffectual striker scored again. City fans could barely believe it.

The end of the match was slightly strange as Royle deliberately made a move to acknowledge referee's assistant Wendy Toms. He said she'd had an excellent match and ensured she was the first official he greeted at the whistle. Earlier in the season comments from Royle concerning female officials had been widely quoted - and mis-quoted - as a direct attack on Toms. The meeting was a sign Royle was not anti-Toms had some had claimed.

The result left Ipswich five points behind City but 'The Tractor Boys' now had a game in hand - a Tuesday night match at struggling Crystal Palace. Barnsley still remained a threat as they were only four points behind, although with only two matches left time was running out for the Yorkshire club. Regardless of the threat posed by both Ipswich and Barnsley it was clear promotion was still very much within City's control. Although a home game with Birmingham and an away match at Blackburn were clearly not easy fixtures Royle believed City could grasp success: "We just have to stay calm and make sure we perform at our best and then we will be all right. As I have said before we have no intention of throwing away the top two place we know we have earned by being so consistent all season."

Royle, when quizzed about the tense period to follow, added: "My nerves are OK. I feel fine. I've seen these situations before and I try not to get too high or too low. I keep talking about the rapport between the fans and the team. We had players who could not handle the size of our crowds. Now we have players who thrive on it."

As expected, a tense but very supportive Friday night atmosphere, certainly in the opening period, greeted the Blues. After forty minutes though the atmosphere lightened considerably with Robert Taylor netting the most important goal of his City career. As the match progressed City fans became more convinced the Blues were going up and the whole arena was filled with celebratory chants. Even the

Almost there... *Robert Taylor's goal settled a tense final home match against Birmingham City.*

Supporters celebrate the 1-0 victory over Birmingham City on 28th April 2000. The pitch invasions were criticised by the media who felt the Blues were celebrating promotion too early Anyone who has followed the Blues for a number of years knows that almost every final home match ends in scenes like these.

normally subdued Main Stand joined in with the territorial chants coming from the other three stands by declaring: 'We are the Main Stand, we are the Main Stand'. It's not known whether the directors joined in but the chant was followed by a similar one from the corporate boxes at the back of the Platt Lane Stand, which appeared to be led by Don Price of the Prestwich & Whitefield CSA.

At the whistle the stadium erupted. Ipswich were due to play the following day, but those at Maine Road believed the club had almost done enough to guarantee promotion. Fans flooded on to the pitch to mob the players, while City's PA system blasted out various uplifting tunes.

Watching the scenes on Sky TV the Ipswich players and management felt determined to make City pay. They felt City's celebrations were premature. As did Sky TV who mistakenly saw the invasion as some sort of boast City were back. What they failed to mention was that similar events occur every season, regardless of City's position. When the Blues played their final home match before relegation to Division Two *The Independent* reported on City's 'lap of dishonour in front of 30,000 loyal fans who have been ever-present this season'. That day the supporters applauded and encouraged their heroes, and the same was true on 28th April against Birmingham. Naturally, the celebrations were a little over the top, but then why not? Royle allowed the players out to receive the fans' acclaim as with every other season, and yet the media criticised him and the club.

Mark Kennedy defended Royle's actions: "We are all aware it could be misconstrued as arrogance or something like that but it wasn't. Whatever happens next, we believe we can put our hands on our hearts and say it has been a great season."

The next day City fans waited for news from the Charlton-Ipswich encounter. Thousands of supporters had already made a vow they would travel to Maine Road and Albert Square to celebrate if Ipswich failed to win, but the news was not good. GMR covered the match extensively, but City fan Ian Cheeseman was unable to report any good news from the Valley. It seemed the champions had coasted and allowed Ipswich to record a 3-1 victory. As with many other seasons, City's future was to be decided by the last match of the season.

Despite the disappointment of that final weekend in April, it was still true City's destiny still lay in their own hands. A better result than Ipswich would guarantee promotion, although April Manager of the Month Royle wanted a victory: "We will not be going to Blackburn to defend or looking for just one point, that would be inviting disaster. We will be playing to take three points." He went on to state he believed his players should go all out to make a name for themselves: "Legends are born in games like this and particularly at a massive club like City with the fan base we have. Someone can be a hero, not just for a day but for a long time."

With Graeme Souness now in charge at Rovers, Royle realised the match would be a tough one: "Graeme, as a friend and a close one, is a totally committed professional and he would have it no other way. He will want to beat us. We neither look for, nor expect any favours."

Off the pitch supporters main concerns all centred around watching the match. Sure the game would be on Sky TV, but it was another of those 'you've got to be here' matches the Blues regularly encountered. The ticket allocation had sold out weeks prior to the match, and the only way of attending the match appeared to be by paying touts a minimum of £80 for a £15 ticket. By match day that figure rose enormously.

At Maine Road the club disappointed its fans by

refusing to screen the big game. Chris Bird explained the club's decision: "We feel the fact the game is going to be made accessible all over the country rules out the need for the beam-back. In any case it would have been difficult to organise the screening and get the tickets sold in such a short space of time." Yet the screening of the Wigan play-off a year earlier had been organised at short notice, and many felt the club had missed a huge opportunity to repay fans for their years of loyalty and support. It was also clear City could have made a substantial amount of money out of the match via bar/food sales and merchandising on the day. Instead those that couldn't attend had to find someone who owned a satellite dish.

Other supporters decided to travel to Blackburn in the hope they would somehow find a way into the ground. As many Blackburn fans seemed determined to cash in on the match, Stuart Caley, Lancashire Police's Football Planning Co-ordinator admitted segregation would be a problem: "This is a very important match for Manchester City and we will be ready for any eventuality. We have tried to prevent away fans from getting tickets in home areas but we cannot possible ensure that 100 per cent, and are saddened to hear some season ticket holders have been selling their seats for the day."

On the day Ewood Park appeared full of City fans, and even a hill which overlooked the stadium seemed to house a few hundred Mancunians. They witnessed an incredible game.

The match kicked off with City in determined mood. Kennedy made several good crosses, but unfortunately the Blues failed to capitalise. Blackburn were then allowed to get into their stride and bombarded Weaver's goal. It was only due to the young 'keeper's brilliance the score remained goalless.

Blackburn hit the bar twice, and just as it started to appear City's luck might hold until the interval a long throw was flicked on to the unmarked Jansen who chested the ball down before volleying home.

One-nil down at half-time was not what Royle wanted, but worse was to follow shortly into the second half when news filtered through there had been a goal in the Ipswich-Walsall match. At Ewood the news first circulated among some City fans that Walsall had scored - as always one fan's inability to listen to a radio effectively set off a false announcement - then the truth appeared. David Johnson had scored for Ipswich. A tremendous feeling of despair followed, while those watching on Sky were forced to witness several replays of the goal before the cameras zoomed in on several tearful Mancunians. Memories of Liverpool (1996) and Luton (1983) came flooding back, while on the pitch Blackburn again hit the woodwork - twice inside a minute.

Before the fans' depression could deepen any further the game began magically to turn around. A chance came City's way when, with Dickov waiting, Kennedy curled the ball behind the defence. Sadly it flew past Dickov but Goater appeared at the far post. Much to the delight of the thousands of fans wearing the new "Feed the Goat and he will score" Tee shirts, the star striker forced the ball into the roof of the net.

At 1-1 the celebrations were widespread, but fans remained nervous. The Blues could have been four goals down after a shocking first half display, and the logical fear remained Blackburn could yet jeopardise City's promotion bid. A little later, with Blue Moon echoing around Ewood, the nerves were calmed as Edghill sent the ball goalwards with Dickov chasing. Blackburn's Dailly decided to end City's threat by carefully heading back to his 'keeper, but didn't realise Kelly had already advanced. For a few agonising moments the players and the crowd watched as the ball bobbled goalwards and then wild celebrations commenced as City, playing in their ever-popular red and black stripes, went 2-1 up.

City fans performed a conga in front of the Walkersteel Stand, while those watching from the nearby hill had been fortunate to see both City goals occur on the only part of the pitch actually visible. Martin Lever, watching from the hill, couldn't believe what he was experiencing. He later recalled the opening moments and the atmosphere on the hill as the game turned around: "Fortunately, we could see the goal and goalmouth where all the action was to take place. We were worried about the first half because even though we could only see a limited area of the pitch, we realised through radio commentaries and crowd reactions that City were on the receiving end of a pounding by Rovers. Then came the goal and all went quiet on the hill. Faces looked down. People threw their full cans away in disgust. Half time and back to the off-licence for more refreshments.

"So, suitably refreshed, the second half kicked off and the wall of sound from the hill began again. Congas - some even rolling down the hill and others swinging in the bushes - made this the most unique football watching

After intense Blackburn pressure Shaun Goater equalises in the May 2000 promotion decider at Ewood Park.

Blues fans who travelled to Blackburn without match tickets were able to see some of the game from a nearby hillside.

experience ever. Suddenly news filtered through that Ipswich had scored. Silence? Not likely, the singing just got louder and louder. By this time the gathering on the hill numbered about five hundred.

"Suddenly, cross from the left - couldn't see who - and up pops The Goat - visible to all on the Hill. 1-1 and cue the wildest celebration imaginable - City fans hugging each other; forward rolls down the hill; and complete disorder. Soon after, no danger in the Rovers penalty area and then Christian Dailly decides to assist City karma for the day by giving City the lead - seen by all! Now goal celebration number two was really something. The 15 stone man beside me decided to pick me up and parade me above his head. He and I collapsed in a heap. People were just throwing themselves into a frenzy, flag waving and song after song. By this time one particular chant was really gaining momentum:

> "We're on the hill, we're on the hill
> we're on it
> City's on the hill
> we're on the hill...."

Those on the hill also managed to see the final stages of City's third goal when Kennedy netted from six yards out. He immediately raced to manager Royle and the two men embraced. Nicky Weaver celebrated by performing a cartwheel. Earlier in the season he had been banned from celebrating in that manner to avoid unnecessary injury but with City 3-1 up it seemed right to resurrect it.

Dickov made it 4-1 with a surge through the Blackburn defence. At full time the fans raced on to the pitch to celebrate. Those on the hill had managed by this time to find their way into Ewood Park. *The Independent* commented on the rather surreal site of supporters charging down the Lancashire hillside: "Hundreds more, ticketless fans, massed on a hillside overlooking the ground, poured down like extras from Zulu to join in the pitch invasion."

All Blues admitted City had been lucky, but in truth it was no more than they deserved after such an enthralling season. At Ipswich, not that it mattered to City, the home side beat Walsall 2-0 to send the Midlands club into Division Two and Ipswich into the play-offs. Interestingly, City ended the campaign a mere two points behind one-time runaway leaders Charlton - the Blues also had the best goal difference in the division and had equalled their record number of victories in a season (26) and had beaten their record points total (89), although it's fair to say the number of games played was now greater than when those records were set.

In addition, City's reserves were celebrating after winning the Pontin's sponsored Central League. Exciting prospect Shaun Wright-Phillips had appeared in more Central league matches than anybody else as the Blues finished seven points clear of nearest rivals Huddersfield Town.

After the Blackburn League match Royle explained how he felt: "If you can't be good be lucky, and we were lucky today. I certainly didn't think it was going to be 4-1. But after the season we have had I feel we deserve this. If nothing else we have resilience, great honesty and team spirit, and that's what saw us through. When they hit the woodwork for the fourth time I thought it would be our day." He went on to talk of the celebrations at the end: "I felt terror for a minute. I was surrounded by people and it took me back to the old days at Everton when I was a kid and there were sixty thousand fans there - but all's well that end's well. Despite the situation the fans were absolutely phenomenal and they deserve this promotion. We think the world of them and there's a great rapport. They have been superb throughout this last season but they were even better the previous campaign. We averaged 28,000 for our home games, which is a record I think will never be beaten, particularly when you talk about the fact we were playing sides like Lincoln, Wycombe, and Chesterfield. We have known for a while we have Premiership fans, and now we are a Premiership team."

What a picture!... *Mark Kennedy raced half the length of the pitch to celebrate with Joe Royle after putting City into a 3-1 lead at Blackburn.*

Paul Dickov scores City's fourth at Blackburn, promotion is secured and the party has already begun!

1999-2000 DIVISION ONE PROMOTION DETAILS

RESULTS	HOME	AWAY
Wolverhampton W	L 0-1	L 1-4
Fulham	W 4-0	D 0-0
Sheffield United	W 6-0	L 0-1
Bolton Wanderers	W 2-0	W 1-0
Nottm Forest	W 1-0	W 3-1
Crystal Palace	W 2-1	D 1-1
Walsall	D 1-1	W 1-0
Ipswich Town	W 1-0	L 1-2
Norwich City	W 3-1	L 0-1
Port Vale	W 2-1	W 2-1
Tranmere Rovers	W 2-0	D 1-1
Birmingham City	W 1-0	W 1-0
Blackburn Rovers	W 2-0	W 4-1
Portsmouth	W 4-2	D 2-2
QPR	L 1-3	D 1-1
Charlton Athletic	D 1-1	W 1-0
Barnsley	W 3-1	L 1-2
Huddersfield Town	L 0-1	D 1-1
Stockport County	L 1-2	D 2-2
Swindon Town	W 3-0	W 2-0
West Bromwich Albion	W 2-1	W 2-0
Grimsby Town	W 2-1	D 1-1
Crewe Alexandra	W 4-0	D 1-1

REGULAR SIDE:
Weaver
Edghill
Granville
or Tiatto
Wiekens
Jobson
Horlock
Kennedy
Whitley (Jeff)
Dickov
Goater
Bishop

MANAGER:
Joe Royle

LARGEST VICTORY: 6-0 V Sheffield United (H) 21/8/99

HEAVIEST DEFEAT: 1-4 V Wolverhampton Wanderers (A) 3/12/99

AVERAGE HOME ATTENDANCE: 32,088

HIGHEST HOME ATTENDANCE: 33,027 V Blackburn Rovers 23/10/99

HIGHEST AWAY ATTENDANCE: 29,913 V Blackburn Rovers 7/5/00

LEAGUE APPEARANCES (substitute appearances in brackets): 45 Weaver, 43 Jobson (1), 41 Jeff Whitley (1), Kennedy, 40 Edghill (1), Goater, 36 Horlock (2), 32 Wiekens (2), 28 Granville (7), 26 Tiatto (9), 25 Bishop (12), 22 Dickov (12), 17 Pollock (7), 14 Robert Taylor (2), 12 Morrison, 9 Crooks (11), Prior, 8 Gareth Taylor (9), 6 Cooke (7), 4 Grant (4), Peacock (4), 2 Wright-Phillips (2), 1 Mills (2), Wright. Plus substitute appearances for Allsop (4), Vaughan (1), and Jim Whitley (1).

LEAGUE GOALS: 23 Goater, 10 Horlock, 8 Kennedy, 5 Dickov, Taylor (G), Taylor (R), 4 Whitley (Jeff), 3 Jobson, Pollock, Prior, 2 Bishop, Granville, 1 Crooks, Edghill, Wiekens. Plus 2 own goals

When asked what he thought the turning point was, Royle commented on two substitutions early in the second half. After 47 minutes, he sent on Bishop for Pollock, and followed this six minutes later replacing Taylor with Dickov. Both substitutes played well and Royle was quick to point out that one of the goals had seen the two men work well together: "Ian got the ball down and passed it, and Paul scored a smashing goal."

In the dressing room the players partied. Sky TV viewers witnessed them drenching reporters with water while chanting "Are you watching Alan Brazil?" Sky's Brazil had been rather quick to criticise the Blues throughout the final weeks of the season, and his apparent aversion to everything Blue upset many associated with the club.

While the high jinks carried on, some Sky viewers noticed Ian Bishop in the background carefully covering his clothes with towels. None of the other players appeared to notice Bishop's desire to protect his property, but his actions raised a few laughs in pubs and clubs around Manchester.

While celebrations continued at Ewood, Manchester also partied. Hundreds travelled to Maine Road and Albert Square to celebrate, and outside every pub fans cheered every City vehicle that passed. Cars, minibuses, and vans streamed towards the city centre with flags and scarves hanging out of their windows. Albert Square quickly became a major area of celebration as high spirited fans took to the fountains. A street festival taking place in the same area seemed to add to the spirit of the day, while for a short period cars circled the square in a celebratory procession.

The police then took the action of controlling vehicle access into the square, and revellers had to choose between parking up and walking into the square or travelling to Maine Road where other celebrations were taking place.

At one point in Albert Square a young man wearing a United shirt tried to walk through the partying fans outside Caffe Uno. By the time he had passed the coffee house he found himself wearing a City hat. Fortunately both he, and the police nearby, saw the humour of it all.

Immediately after City had secured promotion by beating Blackburn, supporters celebrated by travelling to Maine Road and to Albert Square. These early arrivals in Albert Square took to the fountains with the aim of painting the town blue and drinking the City dry!

Tom Farrington was one supporter who made his way to Albert Square to celebrate as the evening progressed: "This was finally the day when City reclaimed Manchester - for good! Pubs that were open around Albert Square ran out of beer, and so I think we can safely say that Blues had drunk Manchester dry!!

"At one point there was a cheer from near Central Library so we wandered up to see what was going on. There must have been a couple of thousand Blues outside the Midland Hotel. Then we realised what they were doing there - some of the players and Joe were on the balcony. Bish had a megaphone but we couldn't hear what he was saying above all the noise. "Blue Moon", "We're going up", "City are back" and "Feed the Goat" drowning Manchester in noise.

"Just before my brother-in-law dropped me off at the station, I recalled to him an incident almost two years ago to the day, when I was sat on the back step of my sister's house looking out into the garden but not really looking anywhere, and not really feeling anything but complete numbness - we had just beaten Stoke but it wasn't enough. Who would have thought that two years on we would be back in the Premiership? I certainly didn't think it would come that quickly and that we would have two memorable days to rank up there with the best of them."

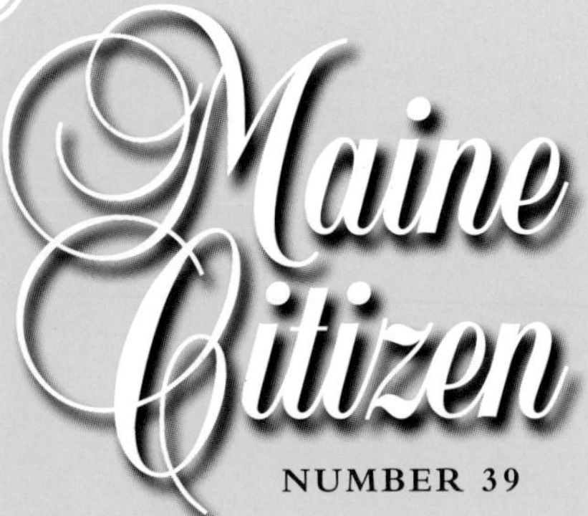

NUMBER 39

PAUL DICKOV

Paul Dickov scored probably the most important City goal of the modern era. It was certainly the most vital City goal of the 1990s. His stoppage time equaliser in the Division Two play off final at Wembley brought the Blues the opportunity to end the nightmare which began with the appointment of Alan Ball.

When he joined the Blues on 22nd August 1996, 5ft 5in Dickov was Alan Ball's last City signing - a mere four days before Ball resigned. His debut was the infamous 2-1 defeat by Stoke – both sides chanted abuse at Ball! - when Dickov came on as substitute. That season he only managed five goals in 32 appearances, but under Clark and Royle the following season he became top scorer with nine from 30 League appearances.

During 1998-9 he netted ten from 35 league appearances. He proved a useful player and became popular with supporters. Always waspishly determined, Dickov seemed to have the knack of popping up in the right place at the right time, as he proved at Wembley and again at Blackburn during the final match of the 1999-2000 season. It should be remembered he also netted the equaliser in the first leg of the play-off semi-final at Wigan – the last competitive goal scored at Springfield Park.

Dickov's career started at Arsenal. He made his debut for the Gunners at the age of twenty when he replaced Anders Limpar in the 4-3 victory over Southampton in March 1993. He made his first full appearance the following May in the North-London derby meeting with Tottenham, and managed to score the first League goal of his career. Due to the quality within the Arsenal squad at this time, Dickov was never able to establish himself and, after loan spells at Luton and Brighton, his £750,000 arrival at Maine Road gave him the opportunity to achieve cult status, and also to appear in the Scottish national side.

His time in Manchester won him many admirers. His workrate and enthusiasm encouraged supporters, while he also demonstrated a willingness to help his colleagues. Against Swindon during 1997-8 he could have completed a hat-trick but deliberately set up the rather expensive Lee Bradbury for a simple tap in.

No one will ever claim Dickov was one of City's greatest players, however during his time at Maine Road he did enough to be regarded as a true Blue. He understood the club well, and always gave his all to the Blue cause.

During Spring 2002 he moved on to Leicester City. It was an inevitable departure, but it wasn't the end of his appearances at Maine Road. Immediately after his move he was brought out on to the Maine Road turf for a 'final' farewell, and then on the last day of City's Championship season he appeared on the pitch again tying the blue and white ribbons on to the trophy prior to the presentation to City. It was a fitting gesture and one appreciated by all Blues.

Dickov may not have appeared in the City side as often as he would have liked, but his name and reputation will live on forever. He will be remembered for his goal at Wembley in 1999, but his spirit and determination are the attributes which made him a cult figure among City fans.

DICKOV'S PLAYING RECORD

	LEAGUE		FA CUP		FL CUP		Play-Off		TOTAL	
	App	Gls	App	Gls	App	Gls	App	Gls	App	Gls
1996-97	25(4)	5	0(1)	-	2	-	-	-	27(5)	5
1997-98	21(9)	9	2		0(1)	-	-	-	23(10)	9
1998-99	22(13)	10	2(2)	1	3(1)	2	3	2	30(16)	15
1999-00	22(12)	5	1	-	2	1	-	-	25(12)	6
2000-01	15(6)	4	0(1)	-	2(1)	1	-	-	17(8)	5
2001-02	0(7)	-	-		0(1)	1	-	-	0(8)	1
TOTAL	105(51)	33	5(4)	1	9(4)	5	3	2	122(59)	41

The arrival of former World Player of the Year George Weah (left) captured the imagination of the fans.

City's promotion may have occurred too soon, but at the time few bothered to question the speed. They simply wanted to look forward and forget about the struggles of the previous five years. It was therefore not a surprise when City refused the City Council's offer of a formal civic reception to celebrate promotion. Most fans dearly wanted some form of official celebration, and for a while the club and Council officials discussed the options, however a formal parade seemed a little over the top. Understandably, the decision was taken not to have a proper home coming parade. Director Chris Bird: "While we all agree that the club's back to back promotion has been a remarkable achievement, we don't feel that it merits a parade through the City." Instead, City gave a £25,000 donation to charity. The amount represented the cost of organising and holding a parade.

Former Liverpool player Alan Hansen felt the decision was right. The TV pundit, who during the mid-1990s had been asked to become City manager, said ambitions should be much higher than simply moving into the Premier League: "City are a big, big club, and it should not simply stop there. They should not feel the resurrection has reached its completion. How many clubs can boast the support City enjoy? How many clubs could move to a new stadium, as City will do after the 2002 Commonwealth Games, and know the 40-odd thousand seats will be taken for every match? They are a huge football club and within the next few years they should once again be competing for domestic honours as well as looking for a return to Europe."

Hansen's view that City should move upwards following promotion was one shared by thousands of

Paulo Wanchope (below) got his name up in lights with a hat-trick against Sunderland on his home debut.

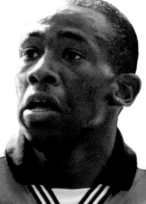

Alfie Haaland (above) was the victim of a bad challenge from Roy Keane in the Old Trafford 'derby'. Jeff Whitley is pictured in action (right) before Keane's dismissal. Steve Howey (below) scored City's goal in a creditable draw, but the season ended in tears for the big defender (below right) after defeat at Ipswich brought an immediate return to the First Division.

loyal Blues. Everyone was keen to see the Blues challenge for the game's top honours, sadly the 2000-01 season did not live up to expectations and ended in misery with City relegated.

Yet the signs were clear from the moment the season started when Division One Champions Charlton Athletic crushed the Blues 4-0 at the Valley on the opening day. It was not a pleasant experience, and City's agony was compounded in the return match when the visitors won 4-1. City's goal coming in the 90th minute via a Darren Huckerby penalty.

It was an all-round frustrating season, although there were a few high points. New signing Paulo Wanchope scored a hat-trick in only his second appearance as Peter Reid's Sunderland were defeated 4-2, while Royle's former club Everton were humiliated by a 5-0 Maine Road drubbing in December. These however were exceptions as home form was in general quite dreadful.

The Blues achieved a 1-1 draw in the return derby match thanks to a Steve Howey goal in the 84th minute. The match was watched by 67,535 - the highest Old Trafford derby crowd since 1936 - and the game was as heated as any derby. Roy Keane picked up his eighth red card of the season after a particularly nasty over-the-top challenge which pole-axed Alfie Haaland. When questioned Alex Ferguson commented: "I've not seen it, but our secretary says it was a sending-off."

Several players showed flashes of brilliance during the season, but there were very few consistent performers. Former World Player of the Year - and self-confessed City fan - George Weah arrived in a blaze of publicity, but only managed seven appearances and went as quickly as he arrived. The unpredictable Wanchope was leading goalscorer with nine, but he fell in and out of favour with Royle.

Shaun Goater, who it was claimed would never succeed in the Premier League, was kept out of the side until the tenth match, and only made twenty games plus six as substitute. Of the twenty he started he only completed twelve of them. Nevertheless he still managed six goals. A pre-season injury had limited his chances but as soon as he was fit he was named as substitute. It was perhaps the last straw for Weah when Goater warming up received more applause than the former World Player of the Year did for playing.

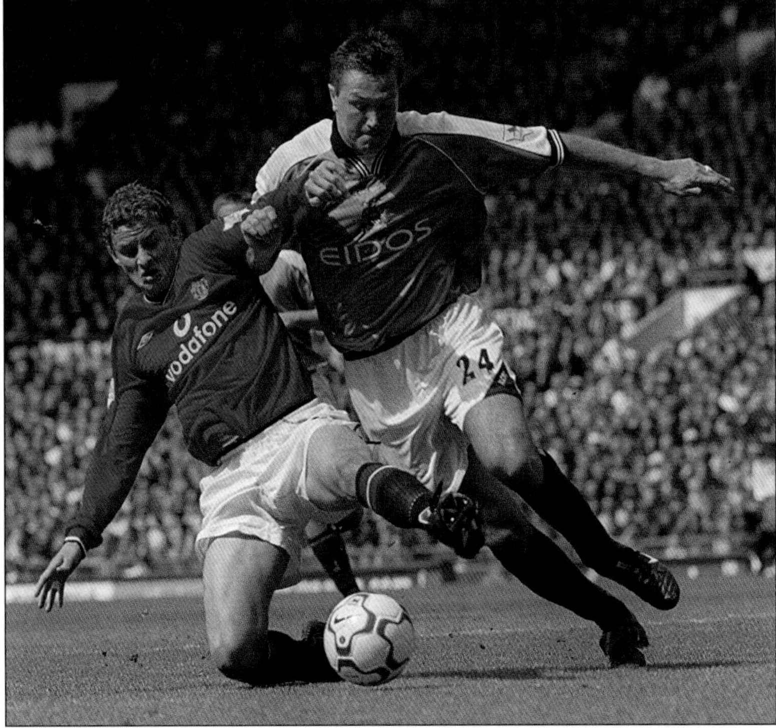

Unlike City's relegation seasons of 1996 and 1998 flashes of brilliance were few and far between during 2000-01. Georgi Kinkladze had made life more bearable then, but this season contained too few moments to compensate for what was quite simply a very poor season.

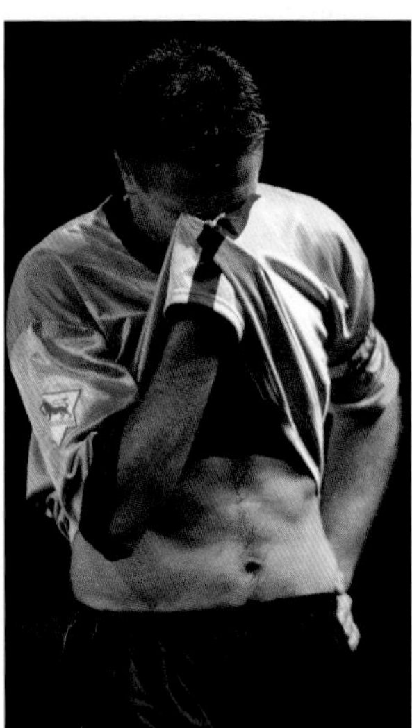

After City's final match - a 1-2 defeat at home to Chelsea - Joe Royle was dismissed. As with so many earlier periods, the media were quick to suggest City had pressed the panic button too soon. Supporters were uncertain what to make of the move. They had been concerned with Royle's dealings in the transfer market during his reign and had worried over his handling of certain players - most notably Wanchope and Kinkladze - but more they feared a return to the chopping and changing of the eighties and nineties.

It was clear the Blues desperately needed to appoint a major figure to reassure the fans. They also needed to find someone who could re-establish the club as one of England's elite, and with the move to the new 48,000 stadium only two seasons away, City needed to make the right appointment. This would be the most crucial moment in the reign of Chairman David Bernstein. He had to pick the right man.

Chapter Twenty Four

KEEGAN'S RECORD BREAKERS

ONLY three days after the departure of Joe Royle, City stunned the media with the appointment of former England boss Kevin Keegan as their new manager. At first supporters were uncertain how to greet the former European Player of the Year. They knew he was passionate about football and his record in club management was good. He had helped re-establish Newcastle United as a leading club, and had started to create momentum at Fulham, before he took on the England role. They also knew he might move on if he ever felt he was unwelcome, or his approach was failing. Fortunately, the appointment was to be the catalyst for a great season.

Early in 2002 City chairman David Bernstein looked back at the decisions leading up to Keegan's appointment during an interview with Noel Bayley: "When I heard Kevin Keegan was possibly available my personal view - shared by my colleagues - was we just had to go for him. We had a lot of applications for the job when Joe went. It was a very tight timescale, but we did have a lot of applications.

"We didn't look at the others frankly. I thought we were incredibly fortunate getting hold of Kevin. I thought that his reputation had been affected by the England experience, but that was our gain. That was completely irrelevant to his ability to manage. What he had done at Newcastle and Fulham - and particularly at Newcastle - was quite incredible, and I felt that what this club needed was someone of that stature, someone who had ability, but also glamour and that energy that Kevin has got which, among other things, would have the ability to bring in players to the club while we were not in the Premier League, which is not the easiest thing to do. Kevin has shown that he can bring in the right players and motivate them. Energise them. Look after them, and get the best out of creative players, and that was my view when we took him on. It's very early days still, but the impact has been made."

Following his arrival Keegan attended a Fans' Forum and outlined his reasons for taking on the job: "This truly is a massive club and it's my job to turn it around. The new stadium is a fantastic incentive for us - not only to get back in the Premiership but to win something as well. It takes very little force to join a club like this. It's a fantastic opportunity. I'm ready for it.

"I'll be judged on what happens from now on. I've got a lot to prove to myself. I've had other opportunities, but this is the only one that appealed. I'm not a fool. I have a real chance here. Hopefully, I can build a successful outfit that people will really want to be part of and I think that's my strength. I think I've already proved that twice at League level at Newcastle and Fulham, and I'm pretty confident that, given that bit of luck everybody needs, we can do it here."

Immediately Keegan set about improving the staff. He brought in his former manager Arthur Cox as Chief Scout, and signed former England star Stuart Pearce. Keegan desperately wanted Pearce to be his captain: "He was actually going to quit playing and clean out his horses at home when I saw him this summer, but I told him this club needed a leader. He says more than me in the dressing room and what he says is probably more important as well."

Pearce said at the time: "I had always said that I would not drop out of the Premier League, but this was too good an opportunity to miss. If I was going to

No, no, the other side! Where it says 'WELCOME'

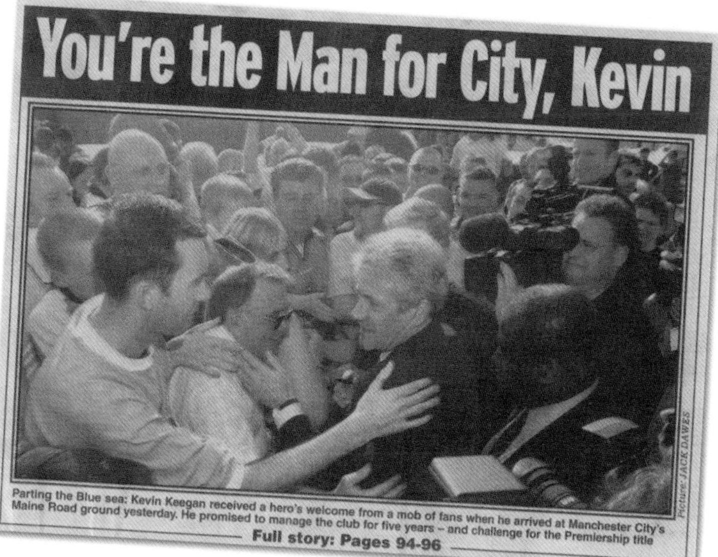
You're the Man for City, Kevin

Parting the Blue sea: Kevin Keegan received a hero's welcome from a mob of fans when he arrived at Manchester City's Maine Road ground yesterday. He promised to manage the club for five years – and challenge for the Premiership title

Picture: JACK DAWES

Full story: Pages 94-96

It was a flag day at Maine Road when Kevin Keegan arrived. The signings of Eyal Berkovic (below) and Stuart Pearce (bottom) were instantly justified when both players scored in the opening win over Watford.

drop out of the top flight it could not have been to a bigger club than Manchester City. It is my sort of club, and has my sort of supporters - passionate and knowledgeable about the game."

He made his debut in the opening match with Watford, as did Israeli Eyal Berkovic. Keegan: "Berkovic was a £5.75 million player only two or three years ago, but I bought him for £1.25 million. He is a key signing because we mustn't settle for mediocrity."

Both Pearce and Berkovic shone in the opening match. Watford, managed by Gianluca Vialli, were perceived as strong promotion candidates and so it was important City started their season in the right manner. Pearce was fired up from the start. According to Matt Dickinson in *The Times*: "One feared for Watford from the moment Stuart Pearce led City on to the pitch and performed a little war dance before kick-off."

City won the match 3-0 with both Berkovic and Pearce scoring. The other scorer was Shaun Goater, proving once again he would be an important team member. The result convinced the media City were already on the right track. Matt Dickinson: "Keegan has found a natural home amid the unrelenting fervour of Maine Road. Place your mortgage on Manchester City winning promotion to the FA Barclaycard Premiership. What happens after that is anybody's guess, but even Keegan's arch-doubters would not bet against him riding an open-top bus through Manchester in May."

A week after this victory City were defeated 2-0 at Norwich. It was a nightmare day with the kick-off delayed, three players injured, and Paulo Wanchope sent off after two bookable offences. Fortunately, the visit of Crewe on 25th August gave City an albeit flattering 5-2 win. Stuart Pearce scored his first penalty in a City shirt, while Goater and Wanchope each scored a brace. Wanchope was already proving to be more settled than the previous season when he was alleged to have had a number of confrontations with Joe Royle. Towards the end of the 2000-01 campaign it seemed clear Wanchope would be moving on, but under Keegan the player began to enjoy life at Maine Road again.

Early-season promotion-hopefuls Burnley were defeated 4-2 at Turf Moor with a Goater hat-trick two days later, and then came the first shockwave of the campaign as fellow contenders West Bromwich Albion achieved a 4-0 victory. Other unexpected defeats came in September against Coventry (4-3) and Wimbledon (0-4), but in the main Keegan's City were brushing aside most opponents. The Blues delighted supporters with an entertaining, attacking approach. Occasionally they'd concede more goals than fans would like, however as long as they were winning, conceding the odd goal didn't really matter.

Keegan's approach was refreshing and his transfer dealings seemed perfect. Fringe player Tony Grant was sold to Burnley, but that deal heralded the arrival of a real playmaker, Ali Benarbia. It was a transfer coup that very nearly didn't happen as Benarbia had only called in on his way to Sunderland to have lunch with his agent, who was negotiating a deal for Alione Toure. One thing led to another and by the end of the following day he had signed for the Blues and the next day made a very impressive debut against Birmingham. The transfer was one of the most important of the season. It was also one of the cheapest deals as Paris St. Germain released the 32-year-old Algerian on a free.

On 22nd September the Blues met another fallen giant, Sheffield Wednesday. Three minutes into the game Wednesday took the lead. The City side of the 1990s would have crumbled at this point, but Keegan's Blues simply didn't worry. They got on with the job in hand and the impressive Benarbia squeezed a drive from a little inside the area past Kevin Pressman in the Wednesday goal.

Three minutes later, Pearce launched a long free-kick for Goater to chase. Goater stretched out and lobbed the ball over Pressman for City's second.

When Wednesday levelled two minutes into the second half City decided it was time to seize total control, and by the 68th minute the Blues were leading 4-2 with goals from Granville and Wanchope. Two minutes later Goater skipped around Pressman for the fifth, then twelve minutes from time Wanchope netted a penalty.

Ali Benarbia was the undisputed star after a thrilling performance, but Keegan was not entirely happy with the scoreline: "It may be entertaining, but we are giving away too many goals. I'd honestly be pleased to win our next match 1-0."

The first eight League games had seen an incredible forty goals, but more were to follow. Walsall were defeated 3-0 in the next League match - Benarbia was again the star - and in October Birmingham City were beaten 6-0 in the League Cup. Darren Huckerby scored four that night, and went on to enjoy a terrific season. Possibly the best of his entire career.

By netting four, Huckerby had equalled Dennis Tueart's club scoring record for the competition - Tueart scored four in the 1980-81 5-1 win over Notts County (see page 335) - and Huckerby's third was City's 300th goal in the competition. In addition the match had been Birmingham's third visit to Maine Road during 2001 and on each occasion they had gone in 3-0 down at the interval.

Huckerby was quick to praise his colleagues: "When you have got players like Ali Benarbia and Eyal Berkovic in the side, you know you are always going to make chances. Ali is a world class player. You do not get the chance to see the likes of him very often. He is a genius and we are lucky he is here. Hopefully he will be here for another couple of years."

Keegan rightly praised Huckerby: "It wasn't just his goals, his general play was as good as it gets. He held it up well, he turned well and most of the time he made the right choices."

The League Cup run ended with a 2-0 defeat at Blackburn in the fourth round, but in the League City continued to progress with their thrilling, attacking style. One match, however, stunned *Guardian* reporter Andy Wilson. Under the headline "Keegan's City in nil-nil shock" he wrote of his surprise that the meeting with Sheffield United ended goalless. It was the first 0-0 for 35 matches and became newsworthy as a result. That simple headline proved how City had progressed under Keegan. Football is all about goals and, in the main, the Blues were delivering at an incredible rate.

Keegan's City in nil-nil shock

Mixed results followed, including an emotional last game at the City Ground for Stuart Pearce, where he was applauded by both sets of supporters for a typically determined performance. The match ended 1-1 with Goater capitalising on a mistake by defender Riccardo Scimeca to give the Blues the equaliser.

A 2-1 defeat at Portsmouth on 17th November saw the Blues drop to ninth place, while behind the scenes there were changes to Keegan's staff during this period. Willie Donachie, former player and assistant to Joe Royle, decided it was time to move on. He chose to join Terry Yorath at Sheffield Wednesday: "This has been a very difficult decision to make as I have had a lot of very good times at City. However, the new challenge is one that I feel I should accept."

Kevin Keegan was surprised by the move: "The news has come as a great shock to me. Willie has been very important in my first few months at the club, and he will be missed, but we wish him all the best in his new role."

Derek Fazackerley replaced Donachie as Head Coach at Maine Road, and over the weeks that followed City climbed back up the table reaching third place, four points behind leaders Burnley, after a particularly satisfying 3-2 victory at Millwall. Due to crowd control issues with meetings between the sides in 1999-2000 the clubs agreed away fans would be banned from both fixtures. Shaun Wright-Phillips netted the match-winner - which was also his first League goal - leading to much praise from Keegan: "It's been a long time coming but it's been worth waiting for. His finish was excellent. He is a very good player and he'll get better. The lad has got a lot of things. Good pace and skill, but the biggest thing he's got is courage. I told him his main job was to defend and anything else was a bonus. Well, the goal was a bonus."

Approximately five thousand watched the game on a screen at Maine Road, and they were delighted when they saw Huckerby score City's second, and then run to the empty away section and applaud the Blues' non-existent travelling support. Mention should be made of the other goalscorer, Shaun Goater. By this time the Bermudan had netted 23 goals in 22 appearances - not bad for a player many had written off two years earlier.

On 11th December a crucial 1-0 win over Wolverhampton Wanderers - thanks to Kevin Horlock - lifted City above Wolves on goal difference. A 3-1 victory over Bradford City and a rare goalless match with promotion hopefuls West Bromwich Albion set City up for their meeting with League leaders Burnley at noon on 29th December. Burnley were convinced they could keep Keegan's City at bay, but a determined performance gave the Blues an extremely satisfying 5-1 victory. Paulo Wanchope netted a hat-trick, with Darren Huckerby and Eyal Berkovic scoring the others.

The result allowed City to head the table for the first time since they won at Burnley on 27th August. It also sowed a few doubts in Burnley's camp, and by the season's end the one time runaway leaders had failed to even make the play-offs.

Ali Benarbia's brilliance drew this praise from Darren Huckerby: "...a world class player. You do not get the chance to see the likes of him very often. He is a genius and we are lucky he is here."

Shaun Wright-Phillips blossomed during a season which saw him score his first City goals and make his England Under 21 debut.

City thrilled the nation with outstanding live TV shows at Ipswich and Newcastle in the FA Cup. Eyal Berkovic's opener in the 4-1 triumph at Portman Road was a vicious volley (above).

The real danger now came from Wolves. Dave Jones' side were nipping at City's heels throughout January, but they were not alone. Millwall and West Brom were also chasing hard, and when City faced the Lions on 30th January the Blues were only three points ahead of Wolves and five above Millwall.

The Millwall game proved a real test, especially when Ali Benarbia was sent off in the seventh minute, but City passed with honours. Keegan: "Against Millwall every player did the work of two men after Ali had been sent off. I was tremendously proud of the players. Stuart Pearce had a penalty brilliantly saved and it was beginning to look as if it was not going to be our night, because the Millwall goalkeeper was in outstanding form.

"It got to the stage, with about half an hour to go, when I was so pleased with the actual performance that I didn't care whether we won, drew or lost. I just felt if we could sustain that level of performance for the remainder of the season it would get us where we wanted to go."

Kevin Keegan received a hero's welcome when he took his Blues side up to St. James' Park in February 2002.

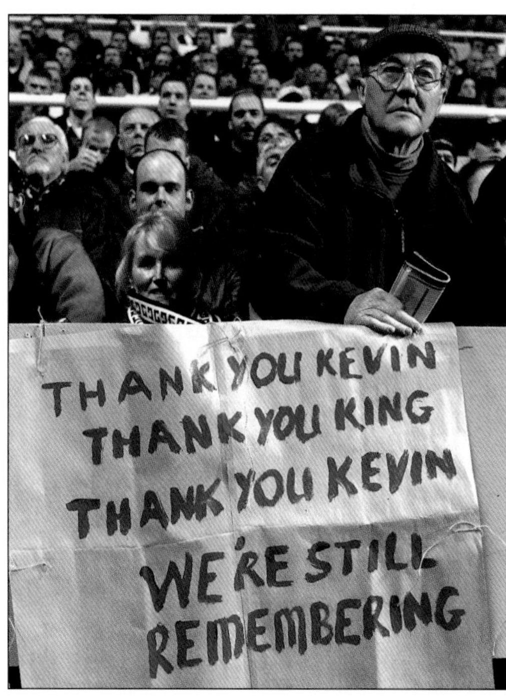

City actually won the match with two strikes from Shaun Goater - the first in the 78th minute, the second nine minutes later. According to *The Times'* David McVay: "Even when Shaun Goater scored his 28th goal of the season and his second of the match four minutes from time, created by the admirable Darren Huckerby, it failed to reflect the true nature of this comprehensive victory over one of their closest promotion rivals." City were making a habit of knocking out their rivals. The previous home match had seen fourth-placed Norwich despatched 3-1 despite Tiatto being sent off after ten minutes.

A 2-1 defeat at bogey team Wimbledon followed - again City lost a man when Stuart Pearce was sent off in injury time - before Preston were defeated 3-2 at Maine Road on Sunday 10th February.

The following Sunday - City's sixth Sunday fixture since 13th January - the Blues travelled to Newcastle for a thrilling performance against Keegan's old club in the fifth round of the FA Cup. The media hype focused on Keegan, but the match ended with national recognition that the Blues were clearly a force. Although City lost the match 1-0 after Richard Dunne had been sent off, the general view was that ten-man City were more than a match for the Geordies. City impressed the nation, as they had done three weeks earlier with their spectacular 4-1 fourth round cup demolition of another Premier League side Ipswich Town.

After the Ipswich match Keegan said: "Our fans know we can play but I think we showed the rest of the country that we are a good team. I believe the FA Cup needed a game like our tie with Ipswich where the atmosphere was tremendous and both sides picked their strongest available sides and really set out to win."

The Newcastle tie was another boost for the FA Cup. According to Henry Winter of the *Daily Telegraph*: "Keegan returned with his magnificent Manchester City side whose spirited, defiant football sent the heart rate soaring among Newcastle's nervy support. Making light of Richard Dunne's dismissal and Nolberto Solano's goal, City scared the black-and-white life out of those who still cherish Keegan's name. Shaun Wright-Phillips was marvellous, Eyal

Berkovic and Kevin Horlock not far behind with outstanding displays as City narrowly lost a Cup-tie but won countless admirers. If they build on this, they will surely keep the Blue Moon rising and head back to the Premiership, where their noisy supporters belong."

Due to FA Cup commitments City gave Wolves the opportunity to lead the table for a while, and by the time the Blues faced Sheffield Wednesday at home on Wednesday 27th February, Wolves were five points clear after playing two games more than City.

Prior to the match Paul Dickov was invited on to the pitch for a formal farewell. With opportunities at Maine Road limited, Dickov had joined Premiership Leicester City five days earlier. Supporters were sad to see him go, as was Dickov: "Nothing would please me more than City being promoted back to the Premiership. The club is geared up for that and to stay there this time. It will be a shame I can't be part of it, but that's football. I've had a wonderful time at Maine Road, but my contract would have been up in the summer."

The fantastic ovation given to Dickov was followed by a 4-0 victory over The Owls which included goals from four of the season's most consistent players - Berkovic, Goater, Huckerby and Horlock.

Another quartet were scored four days later when television viewers witnessed a 4-2 defeat of Coventry City with former Coventry man Darren Huckerby netting the opener after fourteen minutes. The Blues remained five points behind Wolves, but that was to change over the course of the next three weeks as City stormed past promotion rivals with a trio of victories at Birmingham (2-1) Bradford (2-0), and Crewe (3-1). The Crewe match put City two points clear of Wolves at the top of the table and still the Blues had a game in hand.

During this run Keegan brought Preston striker Jon Macken to Maine Road for a fee reported as £4m rising to £5m subject to various add-on clauses. City's most expensive signing managed to score a debut goal in the match with Bradford. According to the *Telegraph & Argus*: "Macken was only on ten minutes and could have had a hat-trick. Having hit the post with his first touch the £5m recruit got his debut goal with the final kick of the game."

Despite City's game in hand, Wolves were still a threat. A defeat at bogey-side Stockport County, and a hard-fought draw at Rotherham cancelled out the game in hand and should have given Wolves the initiative, however Dave Jones' side were now feeling the pressure and were unable to capitalise on City's loss of points. With the two sides due to meet on Easter Monday it was clear either side could still win the championship, and Wolves were confident, however a 3-0 City victory against Forest two days earlier meant Wolves were running out of time.

When City took to the field at Molineux they were five points clear with four games remaining. Clearly a Wolves win would hamper City's progress, but a Blue victory would put intense pressure on the Midlands side. In the end the Blues achieved a 2-0 victory in what was described as a physical match, but from Keegan's perspective that owed much to Wolves' determination and was understandable: "There was a lot to play for, especially for Wolves. They eventually had a player sent off, but I don't think the game ever crossed the line between what is acceptable and what is not.

"Our first goal owed a lot to a wicked deflection that took it away from their 'keeper. Even if it wasn't a classic it was the 'Goal of the Season' for me because I always thought the first one would be important. It settled us down and meant Wolves had to come at us even more. It speaks volumes that we were able to control the game for long periods in front of their fans and on their pitch."

Shaun Wright-Phillips claimed the first goal after 36 minutes and immediately took off his tee-shirt to reveal the motto 'Do the Wright thing'. He also scored the second in the eightieth minute to complete Wolves' misery.

According to journalist Ged Scott the Blues were dominant: "City were minus three influential men in Paulo Wanchope, Eyal Berkovic and Danny Tiatto, but with the luxury of 30-goal Shaun Goater sat on

STAN GIBSON

Stan Gibson was one of the unsung heroes of Manchester football. He was City's groundsman for forty years and created a playing surface worthy of the club's stature, particularly during the sixties and seventies when the pitch was possibly in its best ever state.

Born on 10th September 1925, Stan worked as a stoker during the war for the Navy. Always a keen sportsman - he was a Naval boxing champion and had football trials with Burnley - but by his 30s was becoming well known as a groundsman. He arrived at Maine Road from Chorlton Cricket Club in 1959 after a recommendation by City 'keeper Steve Fleet, and in the years that followed he worked hard to create a perfect pitch.

By the time of City's promotion in 1966 Stan had made the surface one the club could be proud of. Both Joe Mercer and Malcolm Allison were keen to use Stan's expertise to develop the pitch further, and thereby increase City's chance of success. Working with Allison, Stan made the pitch the biggest - and many would say the best - in the League.

Both Mercer and Allison recognised his contribution to City's success. It's a little known fact that Stan was trusted with the job of looking after the FA Cup following City's homecoming in 1969. He chose to put the prized possession in the safest place he could think of, and the trophy spent its first night in Manchester locked in his toilet!

Stan loved City - he was even on the club's books for a while in his youth - and felt the pitch was his own. He could never relax during a match though: "I watch the pitch rather than the game! I shouldn't really, because I get very upset if I see a divot, especially if it is the opposing side who have churned it up."

Inevitably, the pop concerts in the 80s and 90s brought him a few headaches, but he welcomed other innovations, such as the undersoil heating implemented in 1979.

Stan was always an important influence and others often sought his views. At one stage Rod Stewart tried to lure him away to tend his own turf, while Ken Bates was desperate for him to join Chelsea. Stan would have none of it: "I know I'm biased, but to me there's nowhere better than Maine Road, and there's nothing nicer than someone coming up to me on a Saturday and saying how great the pitch looks. Makes all the toil worthwhile."

Sadly, he passed away on Christmas Eve 2001 after many years' devotion to the Blues and to Maine Road. In 1994 he summed it up perfectly: "City is my life. That pitch out there is my baby. I can't keep away from it, and I couldn't imagine my life without it."

Supporters arrived at the penultimate home game of the 2001/02 season against Barnsley anticipating a day of celebration.
For the first time in its history the modern Platt Lane Stand (above) led the way with perhaps more flags and banners than any other section of the ground.

the bench, they were still too strong for Wolves. Wolves allowed Ali Benarbia too much freedom and were unable to handle Darren Huckerby's pace, no more so than when Butler took him out once too often. So, on the day when it mattered most, Jones' own expensively assembled side were outclassed."

The victory could have brought City promotion, however West Bromwich Albion achieved their fifth victory in a row and could, mathematically at least, still catch the Blues. Gary Megson's Albion were now level on points with Wolves, eight points behind City. With three games left Blues' destiny lay in their own hands and, for probably the first time in over a decade, supporters felt sure this time there would be no last minute cock-ups. Keegan's City were exciting to watch and, more importantly, they delivered. Wolves and West Brom were no longer perceived as a threat to promotion and, with the Blues at home to 21st-placed Barnsley in the next match, even the League Championship was within reach.

On the eve of the Barnsley match Ali Benarbia was asked about the challenge facing the Blues if promoted. He responded: "If? There is no 'if'. I know we'll go up and win the Championship against Barnsley. No problem for us." For supporters used to decades of Blue inconsistency the confidence expressed felt refreshing. The Blues had rarely made life easy for themselves, and the impact of Keegan and his staff had supporters walking tall in a similar manner to the early days of the Mercer-Allison partnership.

Benarbia's confidence proved valid later that night; promotion was assured when Wolves were defeated 1-0 at Millwall. The following day, a 1pm kick-off meant supporters arrived bright and early for a day of celebration, and what a celebration. Maine Road was awash with blue and white as ecstatic fans waved their flags and banners and anticipated the Championship. One supporter told Paul Connolly of *The Times:* "I can't believe it. There's nothing that can go wrong. We've already been promoted - we could field a veterans' team and still go up! And the sun's bloody shining."

Despite this refreshing situation the atmosphere was a little muted at the start. Perhaps fans were still nervous of City's past reputation and were fearful of a last-minute failure to secure the Championship. If they were concerned then Darren Huckerby was quickly on hand to reassure them with a twelfth minute strike and another twenty-four minutes later.

Barnsley pulled one back shortly before half-time but a double for Macken and a third for Huckerby gave City a 5-1 lead by the 70th minute. The fourth goal had been the best. Player of the Year Ali Benarbia sent a great pass to Huckerby who proceeded to move quickly forward. Huckerby returned the ball to the Algerian while he continued to move into a goalscoring position, then Benarbia passed back to the

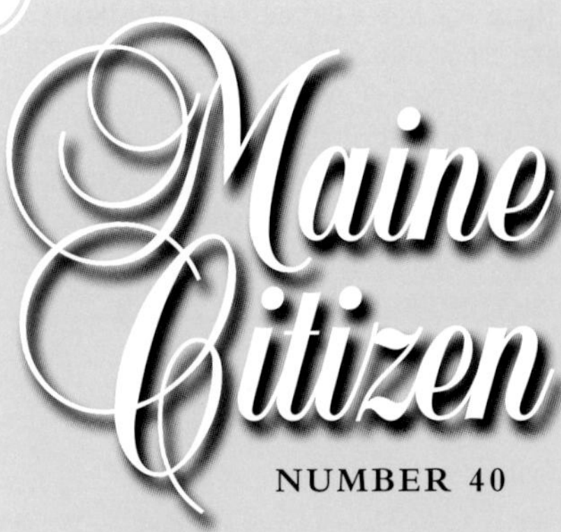

NUMBER 40

SHAUN GOATER

By the time of City's promotion to the Premier League in 2002 Shaun Goater had firmly established himself as one of City's leading strikers of all time with an impressive goalscoring record. He was also a huge hit with the vast majority of supporters although he wasn't always held in such high esteem.

When Leonardo Shaun Goater first arrived at Maine Road in March 1998 supporters were hopeful the Bermudan striker would help the Blues avoid relegation to Division Two. Only three goals – two of those in the irrelevant 5-2 defeat of Stoke on the final day of the 1998 relegation season- in his first seven games for the club caused some initial concern, particularly as he appeared to squander a high proportion of chances. Fans felt he missed rather too many. It was clear he was not particularly comfortable at times but, following relegation, he was expected to fare better in Division Two.

It still took some time for him to win over the fans. During 1998-1999 he received considerable abuse on occasion, but by the time of the Play Off final some supporters had taken a liking to him, particularly as he had netted the only goal of the semi-final second leg. "City Goater Wembley" proclaimed one banner at the final, and City's top scorer with seventeen League goals was now an established member of the side.

These achievements were eclipsed however by Shaun's performance during the 1999-2000 season when the £400,000 (plus £100,000 add on clauses) signing topped the Division One goalscoring charts, and played consistently well game after game. The fans were delighted and voted him Player of the Year.

At the annual award ceremony he gave an impromptu impression of Ali G, further demonstrating his talents, and received a fantastic ovation from supporters who were not afraid to admit they had been wrong only a year or so earlier.

At the England v Portugal match during Euro 2000 a large blue banner, carefully positioned behind the goal, simply read 'Feed The Goat'. City fans and those players who had faced him knew what it meant. The phrase became part of City's folklore and the smiling Bermudan clearly enjoyed the attention.

Following promotion to the Premier League in 2000 Goater's City

ex-Coventry man, who sent the ball crashing into the net. And that was when the celebrations began in earnest.

The cry of 'Champions' bounced around the old stadium, as it had done around St. James' Park in 1968. Throughout the final minutes the fans cheered every player, every move, every moment of the match. Then, when the final whistle blew, the roar was incredible as the Blues finally achieved their first major success since 1976.

The players performed a lap of honour, while Kevin Keegan seemed to delight in bowing to each of the stands in turn. He clearly enjoyed the moment although afterwards he tried to put City's achievement into perspective: "I am not one for getting carried away with celebrations because all we have done so far is return the club to its rightful place."

He did, however, acknowledge the supporters' need to celebrate: "The Barnsley game gave me an insight into the depth of feeling for this club. You all wanted to say 'Thank You' to the players. I sensed many of you had desperately wanted a day like that for years."

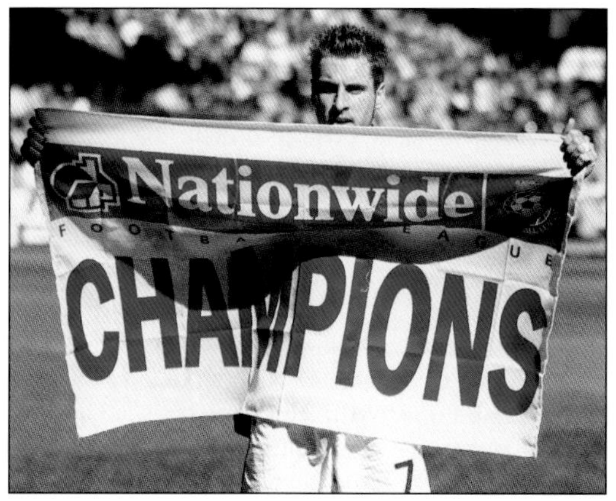

He was right, and City's promotion felt like a major success, especially as they would receive the League Championship trophy as a result. So many of City's promotions in the modern era had come via desperate last game of the season victories or draws, but this success was different. Keegan: "There have been a few false dawns here, and the fans have to trust us this isn't going to be another."

The supporters were as convinced as Keegan that this City side were better equipped than those promoted during the previous twenty years. For many weeks the Blues had been destined to go up. It may have only become a formality in the final couple of weeks, but City were head and shoulders above the rest. This success was thoroughly deserved. Interestingly, a few of Keegan's predecessors were quick to criticise with the most vocal being Alan Ball: "I couldn't take the club forward because they were in terrible financial difficulties. I had to bear the brunt of what was going wrong by losing my job. Joe Royle had the same thing. He got them promoted but once he got to the big time they didn't have the money to stay there. Kevin's going to find the same thing."

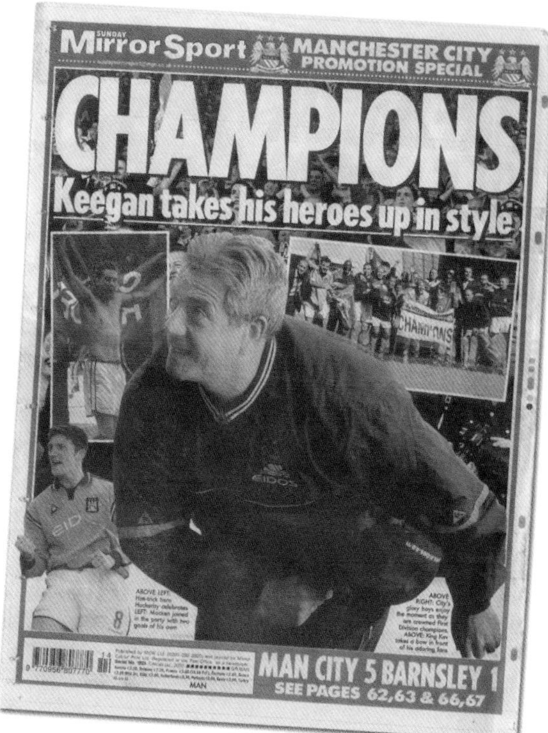
Sunday Mirror Sport
MANCHESTER CITY PROMOTION SPECIAL
CHAMPIONS
Keegan takes his heroes up in style
MAN CITY 5 BARNSLEY 1
SEE PAGES 62,63 & 66,67

City achieved the championship with their 5-1 victory over Barnsley - three of the goals coming from Darren Huckerby (left).

GOATER'S PLAYING RECORD

	LEAGUE		FA CUP		FL CUP		Play-Off		TOTAL	
	App	Gls	App	Gls	App	Gls	App	Gls	App	Gls
1997-98	7	3	-	-	-	-	-	-	7	3
1998-99	41(2)	17	4	1	3	2	3	1	51(2)	21
1999-00	40	23	2	3	3	3	-	-	45	29
2000-01	20(6)	7	2(1)	3	3	2	-	-	25(7)	12
2001-02	42	28	1(1)	2	2	2	-	-	45(1)	32
TOTAL	150(8)	78	9(2)	9	11	9	3	1	173(10)	97

career appeared to be over. New signings George Weah and Paulo Wanchope were clearly Joe Royle's preferred choice when the season opened, but by Christmas the Bermudan had re-established himself in the side. Some felt he should have been given his chance to shine at the start of the season.

During the 2001-02 Championship winning season Shaun netted 28 League goals and established himself as one of the club's top twenty League strikers of all time. He is also a tremendous hero to the people of Bermuda. The 21st June 2000 was proclaimed as Shaun Goater Day and over five thousand Bermudans lined the island's streets to pay tribute to him.

The criticism may have backed the neutrals' view of City's position, but in truth Keegan's side was already in better shape than any created by Ball or Royle. In addition, City had made it clear Keegan would be supported financially. With a move to the new stadium on the horizon the Blues were keen to attract the best. Before the season's end goalkeeper Peter Schmeichel arrived at Maine Road, while rumours of future major purchases were circulating.

The final away game of the season ended in a 3-1 victory at old foes Gillingham, allowing the Blues to set a new record of 39 points away from home. There was also confirmation the League Championship trophy would be presented at the final match of the season against Portsmouth.

Everybody wanted to attend City's final match of the 2001-02 season.

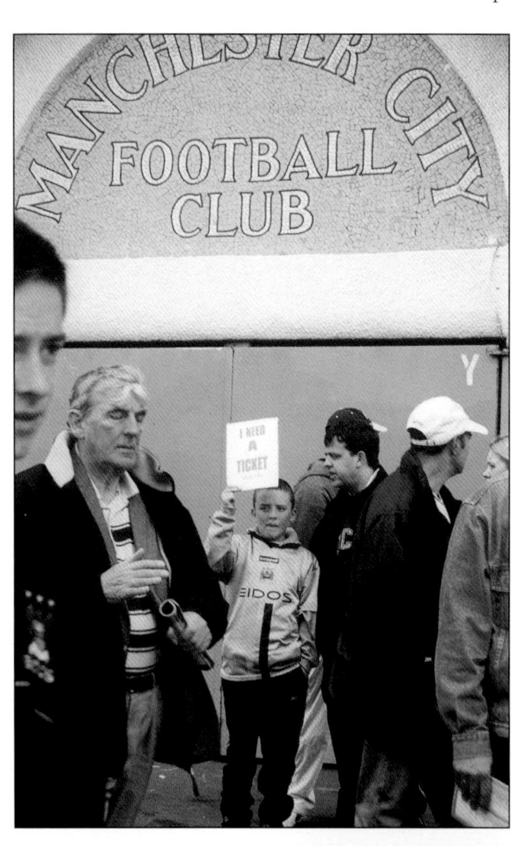

On the last day of the campaign City defeated Portsmouth 3-1 with goals from Howey, Goater and Macken, but the simple facts of the result do not do justice to the achievement felt that day, nor do they portray what actually occurred on the pitch. For many the day belonged to captain Stuart Pearce. It was revealed that Pearce was on 99 career goals and was desperate to reach his century in this his final match. From the moment the game started his every touch of the ball was met with the rousing cry of 'shoot' emanating from the stands. It didn't seem to matter where he was, or how much of a chance he actually had, the cry was always heard.

As the match progressed and City's victory was assured Pearce himself started to push forward, hoping a chance would fall his way. A couple of openings did come - most notably when he sent a Benarbia pass a fraction wide of the post - but then as the game entered its final minute a miracle happened. City were awarded a penalty. Inevitably, Pearce was to take it.

Another veteran, Dave Beasant, was in the Portsmouth goal and dropped a hint to Pearce he wouldn't move, but high drama followed as the City captain blasted the ball into the Platt Lane Stand. Nobody could believe his desperate luck. A goal then would not only have given Pearce his hundredth goal but would also have taken City to 109 League goals - a new season record. The agony was clearly etched on his face but within seconds he was laughing about his misfortune: "There is always a sting in the tail when Stuart Pearce does anything, and that penalty was comical. I have been psyched out by Dave Beasant! The way I missed the goal just about sums me up, but it has been a pleasure and honour to represent the clubs I have, and I am very proud to have won this Championship medal with City."

Musing on his support throughout the match Pearce added: "I couldn't help but smile when the fans were telling me to shoot every time I picked the ball up on the edge of my own box."

Understandably, the stadium remained full right to the end of the match and even then only a small number of Portsmouth fans actually left. While supporters waited for the presentation of the trophy news filtered through that West Bromwich Albion had snatched the second promotion spot, leaving one-time leaders Wolves devastated.

In the end Wolves failed to succeed in the play-offs, and the third promotion place went to another

Stuart Pearce saw the funny side after blasting a last minute penalty over Portsmouth 'keeper Dave Beasant's crossbar. It would have created a club record 109th League goal of the campaign and the 100th in Pearce's career!

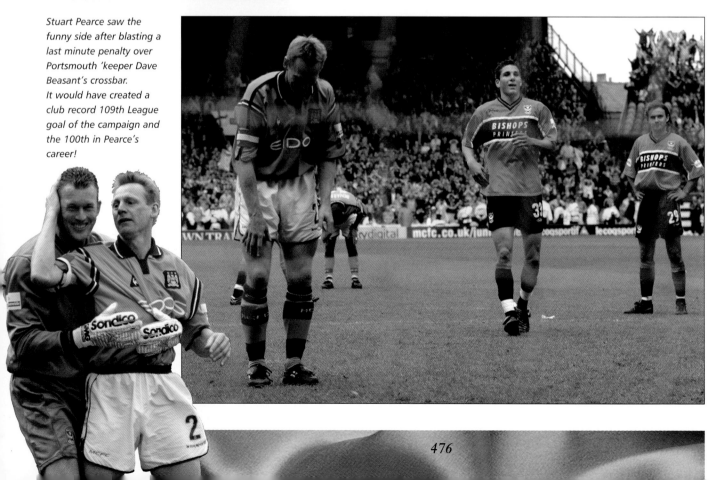

Celebration time at Maine Road as the famous old League championship trophy returns. Skipper Stuart Pearce (below) becomes a champion on the final day of his career, manager Kevin Keegan and (overleaf) chairman David Bernstein were just as keen to get their hands on the silverware.

Midlands side Birmingham. In Wolverhampton they searched for reasons for their ultimate failure. John Richards, the Wolves match-winner when City were defeated in the 1974 League Cup Final, believed the attitude of his former club was to blame. He felt they had treated promotion as a formality and many neutrals agreed. In February when Wolves led the table, Dave Jones appeared on Football Focus claiming promotion was no longer his club's drive, they wanted the Championship. In March they were selling 'Premiership' season tickets at First Division prices - a move which brought enhanced sales but ultimately little satisfaction. Richards told the press: "Considering all the frustrations we've had here over the last eighteen years, assuming we would go up was tempting fate too much. The form over the last ten matches was clearly not good enough, but the form over the previous thirty-six was. So much so that the meeting with Manchester City on Easter Monday had been billed as a championship decider."

City were grateful another side had taken over their mantle as masters of the cock-up.

The trophy presentation took place in the centre of the pitch. Back in 1968 Tony Book had received the same trophy in a more traditional manner by

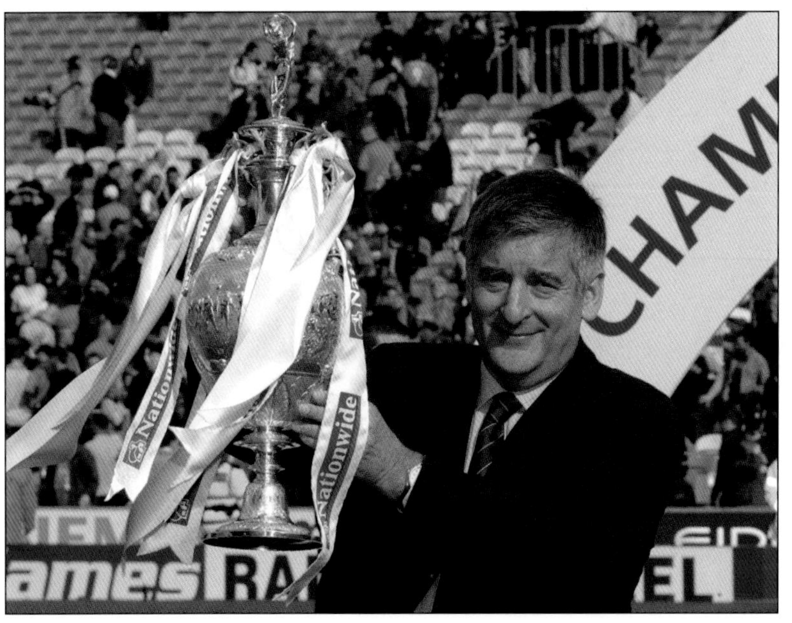

2001-02 DIVISION ONE CHAMPIONSHIP DETAILS

RESULTS	HOME	AWAY
Watford	W 3-0	W 2-1
Norwich City	W 3-1	L 0-2
Crewe Alexandra	W 5-2	W 3-1
Burnley	W 5-1	W 4-2
West Bromwich Albion	D 0-0	L 0-4
Birmingham City	W 3-0	W 2-1
Coventry City	W 4-2	L 3-4
Sheffield Wednesday	W 4-0	W 6-2
Walsall	W 3-0	D 0-0
Wimbledon	L 0-4	L 1-2
Stockport County	D 2-2	L 1-2
Sheffield United	D 0-0	W 3-1
Preston North End	W 3-2	L 1-2
Grimsby Town	W 4-0	W 2-0
Nottm Forest	W 3-0	D 1-1
Barnsley	W 5-1	W 3-0
Gillingham	W 4-1	W 3-1
Portsmouth	W 3-1	L 1-2
Rotherham Utd	W 2-1	D 1-1
Millwall	W 2-0	W 3-2
Crystal Palace	W 1-0	L 1-2
Wolverhampton W	W 1-0	W 2-0
Bradford City	W 3-1	W 2-0

REGULAR SIDE:
Weaver or Nash
Pearce
Tiatto
Dunne or Wiekens
Howey
Horlock
Berkovic
Benarbia
Huckerby
Goater
Wright-Phillips

MANAGER:
Kevin Keegan

LARGEST VICTORY: 6-2 V Sheffield Wednesday (A) 22/9/01

HEAVIEST DEFEAT: 0-4 V West Bromwich A (A) 8/9/01 & Wimbledon (H) 29/9/01

AVERAGE HOME ATTENDANCE: 33,059

HIGHEST HOME ATTENDANCE: 34,657 V Portsmouth 21/04/02

HIGHEST AWAY ATTENDANCE: 28,226 V Nottm Forest 28/10/01

LEAGUE APPEARANCES (substitute appearances in brackets): 42 Goater, 41 Dunne (2), 38 Pearce, 37 Benarbia, 36 Tiatto (1), 34 Howey, 33 Horlock (9), 31 Wright-Phillips (4), 30 Huckerby (10), 24 Wiekens (5), Weaver (1), 22 Nash (1), 20 Berkovic (5), 17 Mettomo (6), 16 Jensen (2), 14 Wanchope (1), 12 Granville (4), 11 Etuhu (1), 9 Edghill (2), 4 Macken (4), 3 Charvet, 2 Sun (5), Negouai (3), Grant (1), 1 Mike (1). Plus substitute appearances for Ritchie (8), Dickov (7), Colosimo (6), Haaland (3), Killen (3), Shuker (2), Whitley (2), Mears (1), Toure (1)

LEAGUE GOALS: 28 Goater, 20 Huckerby, 12 Wanchope, 8 Benarbia, Wright-Phillips, 7 Horlock, 6 Berkovic, 5 Macken, 3 Howey, Pearce, 1 Dunne, Jensen, Mettomo, Negouai, Tiatto, Plus 2 own goals

climbing a set of steps erected in the players' tunnel leading up to the directors' box. Unfortunately, that style of presentation was no longer possible. The steps disappeared for good during the 1990s, while the demands of sponsors necessitated the erection of a stage providing a focus for the media and, inevitably, good coverage of the sponsors' names. Sadly this meant those in the Kippax Stand - the highest capacity stand at Maine Road - were unable to witness most of the presentation. Nevertheless, it was a day of celebration for all and the arrival of former player Paul Dickov to tie the blue and white ribbons onto the trophy was greeted with a huge cheer.

The formal presentation began with the players being called out, mainly in pairs, to receive their medals. Once all the players and staff were on the pitch the League Championship trophy was handed to Stuart Pearce and the stadium erupted once more. Wild celebrations followed, as did a special presentation by David Bernstein to Stuart Pearce to mark his long playing career.

It was a moment to enjoy for all, and even the Portsmouth supporters who remained applauded Pearce and the other City men as they performed innumerable laps of honour. This success seemed so much better than previous promotions, partly because of the tremendous football played throughout the season and partly because of the fact City had actually won a recognisable trophy.

After the celebrations Keegan and his management team - in particular Arthur Cox and Derek Fazackerley - started to prove City were ready for the challenge of the Premier League by signing some of Europe's most interesting and entertaining players. While other Premiership sides talked about who they might buy the Blues actually bought. Little was heard now from former manager Alan Ball or any of the other pundits who had claimed Keegan would not be supported.

The players brought in included Dutch Under-21 defender Tyrone Loran from FC Volendam; Silvain Distin from Paris St. Germain; Independiente striker Vicente Matias Vuoso; and another Paris St Germain star Nicolas Anelka. There was also the arrival of Cameroon World Cup star Marc Vivien Foe on a year's loan.

Loran was purchased for a low figure reported as 100,000 Euro (around £68,000), while Distin and Vuoso both came for fees speculated to be around £4m, but the highest transfer of them all was ex-Liverpool star Anelka. He arrived for an estimated record fee of £13m, Alioune Toure moving in the opposite direction for about £1m.

Keegan was delighted with each purchase. Starting with Loran he told the media: "When someone like this comes along, and the deal is not big money, you say 'let's take a chance'. It would take a real world-class player to walk into our team now as opposed to a year ago, but Tyrone is a player we believe could short-cut that process."

Moving on to Anelka he added: "It's a fantastic

Anelka jets in after City agree swop deal

signing for us. Nicolas is a quality player and we're lucky to have him. We have made a number of good signings this summer but Distin and Anelka are the two I am really excited about."

Director of Football Dennis Tueart explained how happy he was with Distin's arrival: "When it became clear Newcastle were not going to take up their option on the player, Kevin moved very quickly and we are delighted to have Sylvain on board. We looked closely at bringing Sylvain to Maine Road before he went to Newcastle before Christmas but at that stage we were in the First Division and he was understandably looking for a Premiership deal.

"He is a powerful, quick athlete who has already proved himself at the highest level. What is vitally important, too, in the strategy for team building, is that he is a left-sided central defender who is a like-for-like swap for Stuart Pearce who has now, of course, retired."

Reports of other potential transfers followed as City prepared for the Premier League. Off the pitch there were other changes. The sponsorship deal with Eidos came to an end, but a fresh £5m deal with First Advice - a new legal and financial advice company - was announced in May. David Bernstein: "This is the biggest main sponsorship deal in the club's history. First Advice are a Manchester-based company, which we are very pleased about and we think it's a very exciting partnership."

FIRST ADVICE

Another change about to happen concerned Maine Road. With the Blues due to move in August 2003, focus shifted to Maine Road's 80th birthday and its final season. An 'End of an Era' memorabilia exhibition was organised by a committee comprising club personnel and supporters. The idea of such an exhibition was first raised by fanzine editor Noel Bayley during the 1999-2000 season. He approached a number of supporters and collectors, including Kevin Cummins, Tommy Muir, Gary James and Phil Noble, and they worked with the club and other collectors, in particular Pete Bulmer and Chris Williams, to put on an exhibition the following

In May 2002 City's 'End of an Era' memorabilia weekend proved exceptionally popular. In addition to the League Championship trophy and items from City's past loaned by a number of collectors, the exhibition also contained items from Kevin Keegan's playing career. His European awards and Championship medals from his time with Liverpool and Hamburg were displayed.

October. The May 2002 exhibition followed a similar process.

The exhibition allowed supporters to have their photographs taken with the Championship trophy and tour Maine Road. Both options proved extremely popular with four-hour queues developing for the trophy at one point. Some also took a glimpse into the future by touring the new City of Manchester Stadium. It's fair to say most were impressed, particularly when comparisons were made with Maine Road and other leading Premiership venues.

In June, during the Japan-Korea World Cup, fixture lists for the 2002-03 season were produced and, as anticipated, the Blues' opening matches looked mouth-watering. The season would commence with a trip to Terry Venables' Leeds, while the first home fixture would bring Sir Bobby Robson's Newcastle to Maine Road. The last League visitors to Maine Road would be Southampton.

With a famous trophy safely in the vault at Maine Road, Premier League status assured, a popular manager in charge, a united board working for the future and a move to one of Europe's most impressive venues on the horizon, the summer of 2002 was truly a marvellous time to be a Blue.

Despite predictions by former manager Alan Ball, City spent the summer of 2002 making significant purchases. During May and June City hit the headlines on a regular basis as they recruited Anelka (left), Distin, Foe and Vuoso along with Schmeichel (above) on a free transfer.

City's Grounds

This aerial photograph of the old Hyde Road site was taken approximately four years after the Blues had moved to Maine Road. The edge of the pitch is still visible on three sides of the ground, as is the railway line which used to cut through the ground in the Boys Stand corner. Compare this photograph to the map on page 88 for a full appreciation of the layout of City's first fully enclosed ground.

Other landmarks include Galloways Boilerworks; Bennett Street and the terraced houses which jutted into the Popular Side (visible in the 1913 action photograph on page 83); and St. Benedict's Church at the top of this photograph. St. Benedict's was erected in 1880 and, along with a few of the terraced streets close by, remains today as one of the few landmarks from City's period of residence in Ardwick.

The Main Stand is seen in this action picture (below) from 1914.

HYDE ROAD, Ardwick (1887-1923)

City's first properly enclosed ground had a very interesting life, beginning in 1887 when the Gorton committee agreed to develop what was, in effect, wasteland into a venue fit for their purpose of bringing quality sport to the area. Within a decade the ground had developed such that the Football League chose it to host inter-league matches and Test Matches. Then in 1905 Hyde Road was given the honour of hosting the F.A. Cup semi-final between Newcastle and Sheffield Wednesday. By this time crowds of 40,000 could be housed following improvements made shortly after City's first FA Cup win in 1904.

In 1910 the club decided to improve facilities further, and set plans in place to provide shelter for a total of 35,000 spectators. This was an incredible number at the time, and was achieved by erecting multi-span roofs on the three open sides. At that time few - if any - other grounds could boast so much cover.

Despite the improvements, the ground was still too small. It struggled to handle the huge crowds City attracted, especially in 1913 when an infamous Cup tie had to be abandoned because of crowd control. News of casualties seemed to follow almost every big match at Hyde Road from that point on. Nevertheless, it remained one of the most important venues in Britain and, in 1920, became the first provincial ground to be attended by a reigning monarch when King George V witnessed City's 2-1 victory over Liverpool.

A little over seven months later disaster struck when the Main Stand, built in the late 1890s, was destroyed by fire. City were going to move to Old Trafford, however discussions with United were difficult leaving the Blues no choice but to soldier on at Hyde Road. They patched up the ground and found enough breathing space to create magnificent plans for the future.

During the summer of 1922 City started to develop a new stadium - in the truest sense of the word - at Moss Side. Perhaps it was the rebuttal from United which made the management so determined to create a magnificent stadium, or maybe City's large and vocal support demanded better facilities. Who knows? But the fact is that the Blues managed to build the best club ground in England in a little over twelve months.

The last game at Hyde Road was a public practice match in August 1923. Afterwards it was dismantled and within a decade or so the land was ready for other developments.

There are few traces of City's former home remaining. None of the ground survives - apart from the metalwork of a stand at the Shay, Halifax, and a turnstile at Maine Road. The most obvious of all the survivors from City's time are the railway arches that still dominate the area.

MAINE ROAD, Moss Side (1923-2003)
Maine Road was quoted as having an incredible 90,000 capacity when it was first opened in August 1923, and its facilities could not be matched anywhere in League football.

Every newspaper report of the opening match - a 2-1 victory over Sheffield United on 25th August 1923 - concentrated on the stadium rather than the game. The Manchester Guardian reporter was particularly impressed, stressing the size of the tunnels and of the terracing, especially the Popular Side of the ground where there were 110 tiers of steps at its highest point. It seemed a perfect enclosure: "Come in and take your ease but here, inside these barriers, you stay and by these great pits and tunnels, quietly and quickly you depart. This scheme in its simplicity and great scale suggests power and force in the way that a pyramid does, or a Babylonian tower, and there could scarcely be a better scheme to represent the passionate concentration of fifty or eighty thousand men and women on the fortunes of the field below."

It wasn't long before the stadium was tested. On 8th March 1924 a crowd of 76,166 - the highest crowd ever assembled at a football venue in Manchester at this point (including two FA Cup finals) - watched the Blues face Cardiff in the F.A. Cup. Naturally, there were a few problems with crowd control, but in the main the game proved the stadium really was the finest in England. A decade later the capacity was tested again when, for the first time in the history of the stadium, the gates were closed before the game. The official attendance figure was 84,569 - it remains the largest provincial attendance. The only known surviving photographs from this match appear on page 143 within Chapter Nine.

Within the following couple of years a roof was erected over the Platt Lane end of the stadium to provide shelter for standing spectators for the first time since the old Hyde Road ground. The developments surrounding this stand actually increased the possible capacity of the venue as Platt Lane was extended at the back with wooden planks to square off the terracing. In 1934 the capacity was quoted as 86,000 in numerous publications, therefore it's possible the capacity at the start of the 1936-7 season was around 88,000, possibly a fraction more.

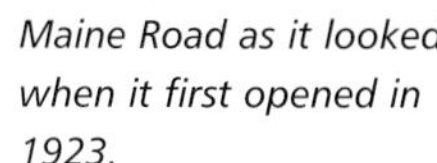

Maine Road as it looked when it first opened in 1923.

The ground remained much the same until 1953 when floodlights were added, then during the 1957 close season a roof was erected over the Popular Side. Again the terracing had to be squared off, much to the annoyance of the local residents who set up a petition. An announcement appeared in the programme stating the stand was to be known as the Kippax Street Stand.

By the time of City's relegation in 1963 the middle section of the Main Stand roof was replaced by a rather odd looking construction which allowed an unhindered view for the directors and those in the most expensive seats. The Platt Lane stand had also been seated with row after row of wooden benches. This meant Maine Road housed more seats than any other British club - around 18,500 - something that continued throughout the 70s and early 80s with the development of the 8,120 capacity North Stand.

In 1981 dramatic plans to redevelop the ground were announced, and in 1982 the Main Stand roof was replaced by another odd looking affair. City seem to have a penchant for odd looking roofs! This time a white, 16 barrelled roof held up by two enormous stanchions was erected at a cost of £1 million.

Relegation in 1983 caused the other redevelopment plans to be halted, and apart from the replacement of seats in the Main Stand and the construction of a new

1995 and the giant new Kippax Stand dominates the skyline.

scoreboard in the Platt Lane/Kippax corner, little obvious development occurred during that decade. Perimeter fencing was increased and other facilities improved, but the next major development was the replacement of the seats in the front section of the North Stand as part of around £500,000 worth of alterations during the summer of 1991.

In 1992 the Platt Lane Stand was demolished and a rather smaller stand was erected in its place at a reported cost of £6 million. The cost was so excessive as it included 48 executive boxes on two tiers. This stand was opened in March 1993, but it was the development of this stand which really limited Maine Road's future potential. The new Platt Lane was simply too small. It should have been a two tier stand.

In April 1994, an emotional day commemorated the end of the last section of terracing at Maine Road when the Kippax Stand saw its final game. Immediately afterwards City were forced to demolish the stand as Premier League clubs had to make their grounds all seater. The replacement stand was completed in stages over the course of the following 18 months, but at times the Maine Road capacity was reduced to less than 20,000.

When the stand was complete the capacity was a shade over 30,000 - the lowest capacity for a City venue since 1904. A temporary stand was erected in the corner between the Kippax and the North Stand during 1997/8, but this could hardly satisfy the huge demand for tickets. Further temporary seating was added in stages during the following two seasons, and by the start of the 2000-01 season temporary seating existed in both Kippax corners, the tunnel between the Main Stand and Platt Lane corner, and behind the stadium control box above J block at the side of the Main Stand.

With so little scope to improve Maine Road it became inevitable the Blues would have to move if they were ever to increase their capacity to something in keeping with their history.

The City Of Manchester Stadium, Eastlands (from 2003)

In December 1999 Prime Minister Tony Blair laid the first stone of City's new home, the City of Manchester Stadium, and over the course of the following three years the stadium developed into a magnificent building.

After the 2002-03 season the stadium becomes City's home. The venue was initially built for the 2002 Commonwealth Games and once the Games ended in August 2002, work commenced on reconfiguring the stadium as a football venue. The pitch was lowered, the lower tier completed, and the fourth side of the ground erected.

Earlier, towards the end of the 2001-02 season supporters were given the opportunity to purchase season tickets for the first season at the new stadium together with their tickets for 2002-03. This proved exceptionally popular.

The development of the stadium has taken several years - the idea was first mooted in the 1980s - and by 2001 the club was able to answer specific concerns about the stadium at meetings with supporters. For example, the club revealed the concourse area under the stand on the lower level is 12 metres wide to give extra space for fans near bar areas. They also announced the seats would be blue. To some this may have seemed a trivial point but for supporters there had been genuine concern the organisers of the Games may not have realised the need for a 'Blue' identity.

They also revealed the stadium has been sited to get the maximum amount of sunlight onto the playing surface. The pitch will be state of the art. It will have a 'subair system' underneath it to remove excess moisture from the playing surface and to also prevent the pitch from freezing.

As far as corporate hospitality is concerned, the club announced that 2,700 of the total 48,000 seats would be for corporate fans. This is a similar ratio to the final figure for Maine Road. In addition, there are 300 seats available for disabled fans and their helpers.

In May 2002 the club gave supporters the chance for guided tours of the new stadium as part of their Maine Road End of an Era weekend. The tour proved extremely popular and supporters were able to see for the first time the players' areas; hospitality spaces; actual seating areas; and they were even able to see inside the Custody Area cells built as part of a UEFA directive. It was suggested the club might want to use these as a punishment for poor performing players!

The stadium will be leased by the club with Maine Road becoming the City Council's property in return. It's a bold move and one which goes against traditional English football thinking. Back in the early 1990s Labour MP and Sheffield Wednesday director Joe Ashton was asked if the Owls would move to the new Don Valley stadium. He responded: "No homeowner in their right mind would willingly give up their own place to move into a council house."

Since then both Wednesday and the Don Valley stadium have struggled, while City's 'council home' will be the best palace in the country. Who cares who owns it? As leading stadium expert Simon Inglis commented: "If it's good enough for Milan or Marseilles, why not Manchester?"

As with Maine Road when it was erected eighty years earlier, the new stadium will be the most modern in the country, with facilities few - if any - can match. It's the type of venue City's history and position as a leading club warrants.

The City of Manchester Stadium photographed in May 2002. Immediately after the Commonwealth Games ended in August 2002 the running track was removed and the pitch area was lowered to allow an additional tier of seating to be installed below the initial surface. By the time City move in the stadium will be a fully enclosed football venue.

Above: The East Side of the Stadium.

Below: The Custody Area and the South Side.

City's Post War Managers

SAM COWAN
1946-1947
A great player and potentially gifted manager, Sam Cowan was, however, never able to give the Blues the support they needed during his brief spell in charge.

He arrived as manager in November 1946 after working as a coach with Brighton & Hove Albion and developing a physiotherapy business. At Maine Road he guided Wild's side to the Second Division title, giving future Liverpool manager Joe Fagan a prolonged run in the first team, and he also strengthened the side by signing Cardiff's Roy Clarke in time for the final game of the season.

It was an interesting period in Manchester for both City and United were managed by members of the 1934 Cup triumph. Life for the Blues in the First Division could have brought Cowan and City tremendous reward, as it did Busby and United. However, Cowan was still living on the south coast and his commuting caused several problems. Discussions between him and the directors hardly helped and in June 1947 his time at Maine Road came to a premature end.

After City he developed his physiotherapy business and became masseur to Sussex CCC, and in 1962-3 he went on tour with the MCC to Australia. Earlier, in 1955, he helped Newcastle United prior to their Cup Final meeting with City.

Cowan died at Haywards Heath on 4th October 1964 while refereeing a match.

JOCK THOMSON
1947-1950
Born in July 1906, John Ross "Jock" Thomson had been a successful player with Everton pre-war winning two League Championship medals, a Second Division title, and the F.A. Cup (1933 v City) but had lost his place in the Everton side to another future City manager, Joe Mercer. After that, apart from guest appearances with Aldershot, Fulham and Carnoustie Panmuir, his playing days were over.

In June 1947 he became City manager and spent almost three seasons with the club. His first season saw the Blues finish a creditable 10th, then in 1948-9 they ended the campaign in seventh position, but these were difficult times for the Blues. Manchester United had been playing at Maine Road following the bombing of Old Trafford, and under Matt Busby the Reds were playing well. They won the Cup in 1948 and perennially appeared to finish second in the League and, for the first sustained period since the formation of the League, the Reds were actually gaining bigger attendances than the Blues. Maine Road helped them achieve this, especially as many Blues began to attend both sides' games, and as a result the pressure on Thomson to achieve some

success increased.

By Christmas 1949 the Blues were in relegation trouble and Thomson seemed unable to improve matters. By the time of relegation at the end of the 1949-50 campaign, the manager had already departed for a new life in Scotland. He then managed a pub in Carnoustie until November 1974, and died in 1979.

Despite the overall gloom of Thomson's period at the club there is at least one positive - and brave - move he made that should be remembered by all; the signing of German POW Bert Trautmann. Most football managers would have probably not even considered making the controversial signing, but Thomson bravely made that move despite much criticism. In the end, if nothing else, Thomson should be remembered for giving City their greatest goalkeeper of all time.

LES McDOWALL
1950-1963
Although Wilf Wild managed the Blues for the longest period, former player Les McDowall was actually in charge for more League seasons - 13 in total.

McDowall was born in India in 1912, the son of a Scottish missionary. He trained as a draughtsman but was made unemployed from the shipyard where he worked during the depression of the early 1930s. He helped form a football team called Glenryan Thistle during this difficult period and in December 1932 was offered a contract by Sunderland.

Despite only 13 appearances in five years, he joined City from Sunderland as a versatile half-back in March 1938 for a figure of around £7,000. It wasn't long before he was appointed captain, and he remained with the club for eleven years. As with his early life, these years were not the easiest and when war broke out in 1939 football, understandably, became of secondary importance. During the hostilities he returned to his first occupation as a draughtsman and was employed in a local aircraft factory.

In May 1949 he joined Wrexham as player-manager, and then in June 1950 returned to Maine Road as Thomson's replacement. From then until 1963 McDowall became famous for his tactical awareness, instigating various formations while at the club. The most famous of these involved a deep-lying centre-forward and was christened the "Revie Plan" after the player who played that role in the first team. As a result of that tactic City enjoyed two Wembley appearances, winning the Cup in 1956.

Despite the success some players, most notably Don Revie, found life difficult under McDowall. As with Hodge some 30 years earlier, this probably says rather more about the general state of football than the manager, but it is worth noting some players felt McDowall was too far removed from the day to day exploits of the team.

Football was going through a change at this point and some managers - most notably Matt Busby at United, Stan Cullis at Wolves and Joe Mercer at Sheffield United - were spending more time on the training pitch than their predecessors. McDowall was very much from the old school; he believed training was a job for the coaches working under his overall control. He also felt players were simply employees of the club.

Revie, in particular, thought this approach wrong and he determined to adopt fresh ideas when he moved into management with Leeds. At Elland Road, Revie deliberately went out of his way to make every player part of 'his' family and, by developing an awareness of the important things in each player's life, managed to create a strong bond between himself and his entire squad. He always claimed this was as a result of the way he had been treated as a player. Although McDowall had a different approach, it would be unfair to say he was wrong or that his methods failed. After all

McDowall brought great success and excitement to Manchester. Also, the majority of top flight managers acted in a similar way to the City man, so it certainly wasn't unusual. Nevertheless, as football moved into the 1960s McDowall's way was not as appropriate as it had been in the early 50s and in 1963, with a new breed of players, the Blues struggled.

Relegation in May 1963 ended McDowall's City career and he became Oldham Athletic manager the following month. Two years later, as the Latics were heading for relegation from Division Three, he was dismissed. He left football at this point and died in August 1991 at the age of 78.

McDowall was a relatively quiet manager who had the respect of his players. His approach brought success in the mid-50s and during the same period he started to redevelop City as Manchester's best-attended club. In fact 1954-5 was the first season since the war that the Blues held a better average attendance than the Reds, but then McDowall's side had humiliated the Busby Babes on three occasions in that term alone. The City manager restored pride and brought back the glory days to Maine Road.

His final seasons at City were not great but, as the Revie views show, football was changing and it was necessary for the City directorate to replace McDowall with a man with a fresh outlook.

GEORGE POYSER
1963-1965

Despite the need for a new style of manager the City directors, in their wisdom, simply promoted McDowall's assistant manager George Poyser. Poyser had already managed Dover Town and Notts County prior to joining City as assistant in 1957. At County he took the Magpies to the 1955 quarter-finals of the F.A. Cup, but they lost to York, and he was then dismissed in January 1957 after they were defeated by Rhyl Athletic in the same competition.

As McDowall's assistant at City he was a brilliant scout and unearthed a number of interesting young players. In fact it was in this area that he excelled. With McDowall's departure, however, the City directorate appeared to choose the easy option and Poyser was forced into the difficult task of winning promotion. He failed, despite his first season in charge bringing a League Cup semi-final place and a final position of sixth in the division.

The promise of 1963-4 could not be matched the following year, and the Blues seemed to be heading in the wrong direction. On 16th January 1965 a record low Maine Road League crowd of 8,015 witnessed a 2-1 defeat, but amazingly Poyser wasn't present. Instead he was away scouting (probably watching Johnny Crossan), and his absence was viewed by many as being typical of the direction of the club. Inevitably he paid the price, and from Easter until the end of the season City were managerless. The Blues still needed to find a modern, forward-thinking manager.

JOE MERCER, OBE
1965-1972

The arrival of Joe Mercer must be seen as a pretty remarkable, possibly brave, appointment by the City directorate. Mercer had already found success as a manager with Aston Villa (promotion, two F.A. Cup semi-finals, winning the League Cup, and playing a leading role in the development of a new stand), but had also endured an extremely difficult final period at that club. He received much abuse for the lack of success during the depressingly cold winter of 1963 and his health deteriorated as a result, culminating in a stroke.

He had been out of work, recuperating for over a year, when the call came to manage the Blues. Against his family's wishes and medical advice (would any doctor advise managing the unpredictable Blues?) he joined City, and immediately took steps to rebuild the club. The chance to prove the Villa fans and directors wrong, and the challenge of competing against his old friend Matt Busby (who was still United's manager) spurred him on.

Had it not been for his stroke, Mercer would have been the perfect 'new style' manager the club needed, after all at Sheffield United and at Aston Villa he had been one of the new breed Don Revie felt was necessary. Sadly, the illness restricted Mercer's involvement on the training pitch and, wisely, he sought an assistant with the required vibrancy and motivational power. The man he found was Malcolm Allison, and the pair united perfectly to bring the Blues phenomenal success.

The future of City looked safe as the two men brought the Second Division title, the League Championship, F.A. Cup, League Cup and European Cup Winners' Cup to Maine Road in only five years. They also developed a style of play that excited and thrilled supporters, while many of their signings and discoveries became international stars - Bell, Lee, Summerbee, Donachie, and Corrigan. Other players were developed into magnificent footballers, known throughout the country - Book, Young, Doyle, Booth, Pardoe and Oakes.

Mercer, ever the diplomat, managed to bring dignity to the club and was seen as the elder statesman, welcome at grounds all over the world. As a player he had won every trophy possible, and had successfully captained Arsenal and England. He brought so much to his role at Maine Road, and it's obvious his time in Manchester contributed enormously to the greatest period in the club's long history.

In 1970 he was the first to guide an English side to a European and domestic cup double and, a year earlier, had become the first person to win both the F.A. Cup and the League as a player and as a manager. Had the League Cup, or any of the European trophies been in existence during Mercer's playing career then it's possible his record would still be the best today.

With a fierce take-over battle forcing Mercer and Allison into opposing camps

MALCOLM ALLISON
1972-1973

Malcolm Allison gave Manchester City confidence and a will to win that few have ever equalled. He was an exceptionally brilliant and confident coach - some would say the greatest the world has ever seen (probably Allison himself would say this!) - and working with Joe Mercer he helped the Blues achieve incredible success.

Prior to joining City he had already been a useful player (with Charlton and West Ham) and had developed his interest in coaching from a relatively early age. His playing career ended prematurely in 1958 when he became ill with tuberculosis and was forced to lose a lung, and from that point on he seemed to put everything into his coaching. He also adopted a new philosophy of living life to the full - for which he became equally famous!

He worked with the Cambridge University football team and coached in Toronto. He spent time with Sutton United and Wembley, before taking more of a managerial role at Bath City and Plymouth. At Home Park he argued with the directors over team selection and rightly chose to move on rather than become a 'yes man'. It was then that the opportunity to work with Mercer arose and Allison turned down an approach from Middlesbrough to join the club with whom he felt

destined to be involved. He claims to this day that he has been a City supporter since the 1933 F.A. Cup Final (he chose to support the underdog!), and believes there is a certain, indescribable magic about Manchester's Blues.

The years from 1965-1970 were the most successful of his life and

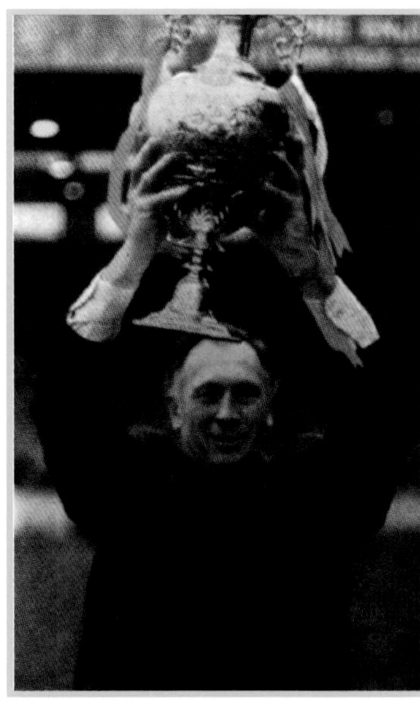

in 1970, the following seasons were difficult. Mercer stepped aside to allow Allison control of team matters but the former Everton player's time in Manchester was nearing its end. In June 1972, after the new board of directors had removed his car parking space and taken away his office, he felt it time to move on. He was treated appallingly by the new regime who seemed to believe somehow Malcolm Allison had brought all the success on his own. Mercer joined Coventry and helped bring much joy to thousands of Midlanders.

At Coventry with Gordon Milne he signed some exciting players - including future Maine Road idol Tommy Hutchison - and the fun returned to his life. Then, in 1974, he took control of the England side on a caretaker basis and again the Mercer magic sparkled. That brief period gave England fans some great entertainers - Frank Worthington was given his chance by Mercer - and much enjoyment. It's a little known fact he was asked to continue on a permanent basis but, because of a painful back condition, felt it wise to stand down.

Another fact is that during the early 70s Mercer and Allison were being lined up by the F.A. as Sir Alf Ramsey's replacements on a full-time basis. At the time of the Maine Road take-over neither man was made aware of this, and the partnership collapsed before it could happen. From the F.A.'s perspective, Mercer had the dignified approach required, Allison the coaching expertise. Sadly for England, the City take-over ultimately ended that opportunity.

After England, Mercer became a Coventry City director until 1981 when he returned to Merseyside to retire. He kept involved with various footballing panels - young player awards, judging Spot the Ball etc. - and made a large number of journeys to Wembley and to Tranmere Rovers (his father's old club). Throughout the late 80s City supporters frequently requested the club appoint Mercer to a role worthy of his contribution. It was suggested by some he be made club President and, for a while, Peter Swales said the club would approach their most successful manager. Mercer died in August 1990 on his 76th birthday. No official approach was ever forthcoming.

throughout that period Mercer and Allison had great consideration and respect for each other. Sadly, Allison's natural ambition and dissatisfaction with always being seen as Mercer's number two made him anxious to see a change in the Maine Road set-up. In his autobiography he claims responsibility for setting the wheels in motion for the early 70s take-over, and he certainly supported Joe Smith, Ian Niven, Chris Muir and the others as they sought control. This placed him on the opposite side to Mercer and the relationship became strained.

In 1971 Allison was given the role of team manager, while Mercer retained the title of General Manager, but with conflict in the boardroom the move was doomed. Allison felt Mercer was interfering, while Mercer felt unwanted. When Allison signed Rodney Marsh, and the Blues title challenge collapsed, Mercer quipped: "£200,000 is a lot of money to spend to throw away the Championship." He may have been right, but the statement simply proved the two men could no longer work together. Mercer departed for Coventry and the football world was left in no doubt that Allison alone was in charge.

The 1972-3 season could not match the promise of the previous one and Allison found it difficult to motivate his players. He was also finding it hard to work with the new board of directors and was beginning to feel the pressure after seven years of giving everything to the Blues. He later admitted he was totally drained and needed a sabbatical but football, as with most occupations, offers little chance of a break and Allison had to walk out on the club he loved.

Allison's first period as City manager (his second has been deliberately kept separate and is covered later) should have seen a continuation of the halcyon spell of 1965-70, but instead became the final unsuccessful days of an eventful period. Had the transfer of power from Mercer to Allison been handled better by the City directorate, it's possible both men would have remained at the club and Allison may have brought even greater glory to Manchester. Sadly, circumstances prevented him from achieving further success at Maine Road.

JOHNNY HART
1973

Johnny Hart had been a player with the Blues from December 1944 until retirement in May 1963 but a series of unfortunate injuries restricted his first team appearances to 178. Nevertheless he was still an important member of McDowall's early 50s side and was unlucky to miss out on Wembley in 1955, again through injury.

After retirement he joined the backroom staff and, following Allison's departure in 1973, became the unlikely choice as manager. Many were surprised that Hart was given a task the more managerially experienced Allison had felt unable to achieve, nevertheless Hart accepted the challenge and attempted to motivate the players. Unfortunately his health deteriorated during his first few months in charge and he stood down after only six months.

Hart later admitted he was excited by the challenge of the City job and, as such an opportunity in life rarely presents itself, it was impossible to turn down. The feeling of most onlookers was the City management had taken what seemed the easy route when they appointed him, and that the directors should have sought a more experienced professional.

After leaving the manager's post, Hart remained involved with the club, mainly on the commercial side, and still attends the occasional match at Maine Road.

Although brief, his reign did bring at least one important player to the club. It was Hart who saw the wisdom in bringing Denis Law back to Maine Road from United on a free transfer - a move that angered many United supporters.

Hart also signed Keith MacRae from Motherwell for £100,000 - at the time a record fee for a goalkeeper.

RON SAUNDERS
1973-1974

Ron Saunders was Peter Swales' first managerial appointment and the new chairman hoped the former Norwich boss would bring the club enormous success. He was wrong, or at least he never gave the new manager enough time to prove what might be possible.

Saunders had played at a number of southern clubs, including Portsmouth and Watford, before moving into management with Yeovil Town. After saving them from relegation in 1968 he moved on to struggling Oxford in March 1969 and,

in the final months of the season, transformed the club's fortunes and helped them to safety.

Norwich City were impressed and the following July Ron became their manager. He again worked miracles, taking the East Anglian club into Division One for the first time in their history, and to the League Cup final in 1973.

The following November he arrived at Maine Road and, with his tough, no-nonsense style, demanded much from his players. Many were seasoned professionals who had achieved much success during their careers yet it seems Saunders deliberately antagonised a number of the seniors. According to various younger players at the time, he organised games between the 'old men' and the 'young boys'. He also seemed particularly harsh on the seniors in other activities on the training pitch.

City began to plummet down the table and rumours circulated that the squad was on strike. Peter Swales heard this, spoke with a number of key players, and acted. At Easter 1974 the new chairman sacked his first manager after less than six months in charge. The football world was amazed, especially as Saunders had taken the Blues to the 1974 League Cup Final - their first since 1970.

Saunders took control of Aston Villa the following June and brought them the success Swales had craved. At Villa he won promotion from the Second Division, the League Cup (twice), and the League Championship. Amazingly, Saunders left Villa in February 1982 while his side were still in the European Cup. His assistant Tony Barton guided Villa through the latter stages to win their first European trophy, while Saunders joined Birmingham City.

He remained at St Andrews until 1986 when he moved across the city to manage West Bromwich Albion. In 1987 he was dismissed from that job and has since left football management for good.

Despite only being at Maine Road a few months he did manage to bring one great player to the Blues - Dennis Tueart. If for nothing else, Saunders' time at City should be remembered for the joy that player ultimately brought to the club.

TONY BOOK
1974-1979

Tony Book was a hugely successful player with City during the Mercer-Allison period and was undoubtedly a key figure in each of City's trophy successes during seasons 1967 to 1970. He joined the Blues in July 1966 for £17,000 after a relatively brief League career with Plymouth Argyle.

Allison had been a fan of Book's ever since their days together at Bath City and the Blues' coach did all he could to persuade Mercer to take a gamble on a player who had only made his League debut a month before his 30th birthday. Mercer, remembering how his own career had been given a new lease of life at a similar age, backed his number two, and the Tony Book fairy tale began. Naturally, he played a part in each trophy success, but he was also voted Footballer of the Year (held jointly with Derby's Dave Mackay) in 1969. It was a fitting award and said much about what made Manchester City tick. Had the award gone to one of City's more familiar names - Bell, Lee or Summerbee - then that would of course have been a great honour, but that it went to Book proved the side was more about teamwork than about individuality. Book was City's influential captain; he did more than most to bring glory to the Blues.

Once his playing career ended he became a member of City's backroom staff and then Ron Saunders' assistant. It was not an easy partnership. When Saunders left, Book was appointed manager and his predecessor told the media: "I wish him all that he wished me when I was in the job!"

Book was in charge for the final month of the 1973-4 season and was, obviously, manager for the infamous final match of the campaign when Denis Law netted against United at Old Trafford. City ended that season 14th, and the following in eighth place.

In 1975-6 Book's team of entertainers annihilated United 4-0 in the fourth round of the League Cup - on a night remembered more for the devastating injury to Colin Bell - and progressed to Wembley where they defeated Newcastle 2-1. Ably supported by Ian MacFarlane - a former playing colleague at Bath City - the trophy success was proof that Book and MacFarlane knew how to develop a highly motivated team. Most players from this period still talk about the great team spirit fostered by the two men.

Shortly after that success MacFarlane left City for Jack Charlton's Middlesbrough, and Book was then underpinned by the impressive Bill Taylor. In 1976-7 the Blues reached second place in the League, behind the ever-dominant Liverpool, and the following season finished fourth. By this time Book had turned City into a popular, high-profile club. They became regular competitors in Europe and in 1978 Book's Blues defeated AC Milan 5-2 on aggregate in the third round of the UEFA Cup.

City were a major side once more, but then the directors became obsessed with overshadowing Manchester United and Malcolm Allison was brought back to the club in January 1979. Over the following year or so Book's role diminished as Allison assumed responsibility for team affairs. Book became General Manager, but it was a difficult period.

In 1980 the two were dismissed. After a brief period away, Book returned to Maine Road to fulfil a variety of positions - first team coach, youth coach, youth team manager, assistant manager and caretaker manager (on several occasions!). He remained at Maine Road through thick and thin and to many he appeared the only constant through periods of major upheaval. In fact one famous player once joked: "In the event of a nuclear war, stand next to Skip - he's the only thing certain to remain at Maine Road!"

That comment rang true until the 1996-7 season when it was announced he was to leave the club. It was stated he was to retire, but late in 1997 he returned to football in a scouting role, joining Peter Reid at Sunderland.

Tony Book's place in City's history is a significant one; he was a tremendous player, a great manager, an inspiring coach and a loyal club servant. Basically, the perfect Blue.

MALCOLM ALLISON
1979-1980

Allison rejoined City in January 1979 as a 'coaching overlord' but it wasn't long before he appeared to be in total control of team affairs. His first spell at the club had ended with him desperate for a new challenge and, in the six years that followed, he travelled the world managing and coaching a variety of clubs - Crystal Palace, Galatasaray, Memphis, and Plymouth Argyle. By the start of 1979 he was keen to return 'home' and turn City into the greatest club on earth.

Almost immediately he began replacing some of the club's most popular players with young hopefuls, and to many the emphasis appeared wrong. He seemed intent on building a new youthful side and it appeared as though he cared little for the strengths of the more experienced men. Although he'd already transferred Brian Kidd, it was during the summer of 1979 he really started his purge. Out went fans' favourites Dave Watson, Gary Owen, Peter Barnes, Kenny Clements and Asa Hartford. The supporters were shocked, especially as the players arriving seemed of lesser quality. The replacements also proved costly and ultimately caused City a number of serious financial problems over the course of the following decade.

In January 1980 Allison's expensive side were humiliated at Halifax and the entire football world appeared to delight in ridiculing Allison, City, and the club's high-profile chairman Peter Swales. In October, with the Blues struggling in the League, Peter Swales dismissed Allison and Book. Swales always remained convinced he was right to act; Allison believes he should have been given more time. The former manager also feels

JOHN BOND
1980-1983

John Bond arrived at Maine Road, instructed the players to call him Boss, and proceeded to turn round the fortunes of the club. He firmly believes he simply gave the players confidence and a belief in themselves, but the fact is he purchased three experienced players and put considerable effort into unravelling the complexities left by Allison.

Bond came to City from Norwich, after an earlier spell at Bournemouth, and seemed the perfect, high-profile manager for the Blues. Allison was universally known as 'Big Mal' and his replacement was equally 'larger than life'. At their first team gathering, he memorably told his players football was all about 'attitude', and his two-and-a-half year spell at the club proved him right, time and time again.

His arrival in October 1980 continued to show the world City wanted to be classed as a major side, and the club's amazing run in both cup

competitions gave every Blue Mancunian a feeling that 1981 could be City's year for great success. Sadly, in both competitions, fate worked against City, although it remained clear to all that Manchester's Blues were one of the era's biggest clubs. Their transformation under Bond and the resultant media interest (City were gaining a lot of positive media attention, and were once more popular via television documentaries etc.) caused a certain amount of panic at Old Trafford and Dave Sexton was dismissed. Sexton's replacement needed to snatch the headlines from Bond and understandably they appointed an equally large figure - Ron Atkinson.

At City, Bond was keen to develop the strongest side possible and felt he had support from his chairman. At the start of 1981-2 the City manager made his biggest signing - Trevor Francis. Francis felt Bond was an influential figure in his decision to join the Blues: "He was so enthusiastic. He was convinced City were on the way to big things. I can remember his saying: 'We've just had a great season, we could have won the F.A. Cup - but it's only just beginning!' It seemed an impressive set up. Bond wanted me as partner for Kevin Reeves, and told me that if I signed, he could still go out and buy another million-pound player the next day. When Bond said that he could go out and buy another million-pound player besides me, that decided the matter. City were the club for me."

With the Francis signing, 1981-2 was a season of great hope at Maine Road and Bond's combination of experience (McDonald, Gow, and Francis) and youth (Caton, Reid, and Ranson) should have challenged, however a poor October and desperate April left City 10th. No other major signings were made and Bond was forced to sell Francis within a year of his purchase because of financial difficulties.

The 1982-3 season was one for which Bond could find little enthusiasm. He felt let down, not by Peter Swales, but by the other directors. He claims unnecessary pressure was exerted, and that events in his private life seemed to give certain influential figures the perfect excuse to challenge his position. A 5-2 defeat at Liverpool over Christmas caused concern and then on 29th January a 4-0 reverse at eventual F.A. Cup finalists Brighton ended all prospect of success. During Bond's journey home he claims he was abused by supporters and, as a result, felt the time was right to go.

After his resignation he managed Burnley - a time that brought nothing but pain to him and the Clarets' suffering fans - and then Swansea. He managed to save Swansea from relegation in 1984-5 but was dismissed the following October as the Swans had to take drastic action to prevent bankruptcy. Spells at Birmingham and Shrewsbury followed.

During the late 1980s Bond was a regular on Granada TV's sports programmes but, with his outspoken approach, he occasionally upset supporters of many of the clubs with whom he had been involved. As the Blues were aiming for promotion in 1989 he angered City fans with his view that the side was simply not of the right calibre. Many supporters felt he took a perverse delight in annoying Blues.

Yet Bond should go down in history as one of the most entertaining of City's managers. He delighted City fans in 1981 and could have achieved a great deal more had circumstances not worked against him in 1982-3.

During 1999-2000 Bond helped John Benson take Wigan to fourth place in Division Two and through to the play-off final at Wembley.

he should not be held accountable for the high prices paid by the club and is adamant Swales paid over the odds, not him.

Whatever the truth, it is obvious the return of Allison was not good for

either the manager or the club. Yet it could have all been so different.

After City, Allison travelled the world again, weaving his magic at many diverse clubs - Crystal Palace (again), Sporting Lisbon (Portuguese League & Cup double 1981-2), Middlesbrough, Willington, Turkey, Kuwait, Vitoria Setubal, Farense, Fisher Athletic, and in 1992-3 Bristol Rovers.

In September 1997 Allison celebrated his 70th birthday yet during the 1996-7 season, as City struggled to appoint a manager, some supporters actually suggested he be given the role of General Manager at Maine Road. Understandably, Francis Lee chose Frank Clark instead, but it is true that Allison still had much to offer football.

During the early years of the 21st Century Allison hit the headlines again as a result of problems in his private life. Francis Lee, Mike Summerbee and other former colleagues helped him re-settle in the Manchester area, and he became a regular visitor to Maine Road once more.

JOHN BENSON
1983

There is little doubt that John Benson was very much a temporary manager in the eyes of Peter Swales. Had City avoided relegation in 1983 it is highly unlikely Benson would have been in charge as the following campaign commenced. As it was, Benson's Blues plummeted down the table and couldn't even hang on for a draw on the final day of the 1982-3 season. Both Benson and City paid the price and, for the first time since 1966, Second Division football returned to Maine Road.

Benson had been a City player, making 44 League appearances during 1961 to 1964, and had moved into coaching while at Norwich. He was a vital member of Bond's

backroom team at Carrow Road and the two men arrived at Maine Road together.

After City he joined Bond again at Burnley - taking over the managerial reins in August 1984 after

Bond's dismissal - and later became Barnsley's chief scout (under another former Norwich colleague Mel Machin). He went on to coach in non-League football, but during 1999-2000 as manager of Wigan John Benson took his side to Wembley in the Division Two play-off. A memorable final narrowly went against Wigan with Gillingham achieving a 3-2 extra-time victory. The deciding goal came in the 118th minute.

BILLY McNEILL, MBE
1983-1986

Billy McNeill arrived at Maine Road in 1983 with a brief to bring City promotion. He accepted the challenge with typical determination but, once the 1983-4 season was under way, quickly realised the club was in serious financial straits.

Working with fellow Scotsman Jimmy Frizzell, McNeill purchased many bargain basement players and somehow assembled a team of fighters - mostly willing Scotsman - who enabled City to challenge for promotion in their first season. Sadly, with several other strong sleeping giants in the division, the Blues finished fourth and McNeill had to wait until his second campaign before he tasted the champagne Peter Swales had locked away in 1983 (it was a major story at the time that Swales said City's champagne-drinking days would only return with promotion).

Back in Division One, the Blues found life difficult but much pride was gained from McNeill's approach to Manchester football. In March 1986 he deliberately selected a 'Manchester' side to face the expensive, highly-paid internationals of United at Old Trafford. That game ended in a 2-2 draw but was a moral victory for Manchester's side. The following day McNeill became the eighth City manager to take his side to Wembley when the Blues faced Chelsea in the inaugural Full Members' Cup final. It was a ridiculous competition, but it had still taken a great deal to reach the final.

That Wembley trip should - and could - have been the first of many. Sadly in September 1986 McNeill walked out on City for another troubled giant, Aston Villa. His main reason for going was finance. He felt dissatisfied with the ongoing monetary problems at City and had been persuaded by Villa's Chairman Doug Ellis that life would be different at Villa Park. It wasn't. At the end of the 1986-7 season McNeill's Villa were relegated and he was dismissed on 8th May 1987.

Twenty days later he arrived back at his beloved Celtic where he enjoyed breaking Rangers' stranglehold for a while by winning, among other successes, the League and Cup double in 1988. While at Celtic he kept in touch with events at Maine Road (during a television interview in the late 1980s an up-to-date City programme could clearly be seen on his desk), and on occasion he admitted he had been wrong to leave City for Villa.

In May 1991 he was dismissed as Celtic manager and has since concentrated on his popular bar, with occasional media work. In 1997 it was revealed he had successfully undergone a triple heart by-pass operation, and following the death of Diana, Princess of Wales, he was seen on national television insisting Scotland rearrange their World Cup fixture planned for the same day as Diana's funeral.

Billy McNeill is an all-time great at Celtic, and will always be remembered in Manchester for bringing enjoyment to thousands of Blues during what would otherwise have been a particularly bleak period. McNeill will be remembered not as City's greatest manager, but as one of the most successful men ever to be associated with Manchester football.

JIMMY FRIZZELL
1986-1987

Jimmy Frizzell was an important member of the City staff during Billy McNeill's period at the club. As assistant manager he helped bring many determined players to the club, and did much to ensure the homesick McNeill settled in Manchester. His knowledge of local football proved essential to City, from 1983 through to the arrival of Howard Kendall in 1989.

Frizzell had made his name as manager of Oldham Athletic, taking the unfashionable club from the Fourth Division to the Second within four years. In 1982, after 12 years in the job, he was sacked despite giving the Latics much hope for the future and laying the foundations for what became Joe Royle's great era.

At City he found himself taking on full managerial responsibilities after McNeill's departure to Aston Villa in September 1986. Although the two men had worked closely together, Frizzell quickly established his mark on the side when he brought John Gidman, Tony Grealish and Imre Varadi to the club shortly after taking office.

Later he also purchased the exciting Paul Stewart from Blackpool.

Despite the signings, Frizzell's side struggled and were relegated on 39 points at the end of the season. Peter Swales decided to bring in a new face and, after suggestions Dave Bassett was to become City's manager, Norwich's Mel Machin was given the job. Nevertheless, Frizzell remained an influential figure and for a while was given the title General Manager. In fact, the pair seemed to share some of the significant duties for a while, both men alternating the manager's column in the programme, in addition to several other tasks. Frizzell was often chosen to face the media and after one memorable game with Oldham he criticised Joe Royle for creating a team of 'yard dogs'. The Oldham management and supporters loved that description. Royle: "We laughed at that. The Commercial Manager went out and bought 2,000 inflatable dogs! You then saw the strange sight of grown men walking down the street with inflatable dogs under their arms. The comment didn't bother us at all. I think if you'd have asked Jim half an hour later he wouldn't have said it, but he said it straight after the game. That was his problem. We laughed, though!"

As Machin's reign continued Frizzell's influence reduced but he remained a permanent member of the City staff during the 1990s, filling a variety of roles from Stadium Manager to Chief Scout.

MEL MACHIN
1987-1989

Mel Machin was regular criticised during his time at City for making rather unusual team selections and for playing formations that seemed doomed from the start. On occasion he received much barracking from supporters and, as a result, Peter Swales claimed he had no real relationship with the large Blues support.

Despite this perceived image problem, Machin actually brought much pleasure to Maine Road and was responsible for several memorable results. He may have been a rather quiet, unassuming figure, but his two and a half years in Manchester brought the Blues many positive headlines and much jubilation.

He arrived at City in the wake of the 1987 relegation and, for a while, shared managerial duties with Jimmy Frizzell. Over time it became obvious to everyone that Machin was the real manager and with the purchase of one or two players - Tony Adcock and Trevor Morley were two recruits during his first season - he attempted to strengthen City's mixture of inexperienced youngsters (White, Brightwell, and Lake) and seasoned campaigners (Clements, Varadi, and McNab).

Machin's men failed to find consistency during 1987-8 and ended the campaign in ninth place. During this season, the Blues achieved a number of entertaining results with the 10-1 victory over Huddersfield and 6-2 against Plymouth (Simod Cup) two of the most famous. Machin's men also came close to achieving semi-final places in both cup competitions. Sadly it was perhaps the progress in both competitions that hampered City's promotion bid as the still-inexperienced youngsters were forced to play far too many matches.

The cup progress, and the highscoring results, also brought City's better players under the spotlight and almost every week a story appeared suggesting the Blues would be selling the likes of Lake, Brightwell, Stewart, Hinchcliffe and White. Eventually Stewart was sold, although Machin had tried to keep him.

The following season started with disappointment - a humiliating 4-1 defeat by Oldham brought a demonstration from supporters - but by early December the Blues were in contention. However, a bizarre formation at Blackburn on the day of the Hillsborough disaster gave City a 4-0 hammering, and slip-ups in the three home games that followed angered fans. Machin received some abuse and the pressure mounted, especially as the Blues were left in the rather worrying position of needing at least a point at Bradford to earn promotion. Machin signing Trevor Morley brought City an equaliser in that game and the Blues were back in Division One.

Ironically, Machin had received criticism from supporters earlier in the season for selecting Morley

and yet Machin's belief in the player's ability was the deciding factor that gave the Blues promotion.

During the summer of 1989 he bought Ian Bishop and Clive Allen (City's first £1million purchase since Trevor Francis). These two quickly delighted supporters and the manager gained growing respect from the fans as everyone eagerly anticipated the new season.

1989-90 started with defeat at Liverpool and against Southampton before a point was earned against Tottenham. By the seventh match the Blues were struggling at the foot of the division. It was then however Machin guided his side to their greatest achievement of his reign - the 5-1 Maine Road massacre of Manchester United. That result is the one which will always be remembered as his finest hour.

Sadly, Machin's men struggled to match that achievement and, with Howard Kendall back in England, it now appears Peter Swales felt the time was right to appoint one of Europe's most successful managers. When Machin was dismissed by Swales, the City chairman claimed it was pressure from the supporters. That was a rather lame excuse as, at the time, Machin was actually more popular than at any other period during his reign. If the supporters' views had counted, then Machin would have been dismissed during the previous season, maybe before.

After City, Machin managed Barnsley and Bournemouth.

With hindsight it is clear Machin should never have been dismissed so quickly in 1989, however the Blues were struggling and Howard Kendall helped them survive. Had Machin been allowed to continue it is possible City would have survived in any case, although Swales clearly felt relegation for a third time in seven years would have caused too many problems.

Overall, Machin's time at City brought a degree of success and a few magical memories for supporters. He brought at least three very influential players to the club - Ian Bishop, Clive Allen and Colin Hendry - and gave others their first chance in League football; Lennon, Taggart and Hughes are just three examples of players who made their debuts under Machin. He was a quiet man, but he was also a very respected and knowledgeable coach. City gained a great deal from his time in Manchester.

HOWARD KENDALL 1989-1990

Howard Kendall had achieved great success as a manager with Everton and Blackburn, and arrived at Maine Road following a period with Athletic Bilbao. His appointment substantially eased the pressure on chairman Peter Swales after fans' anger at the dismissal of Machin and the totally bungled approach for Joe Royle.

Rumours had circulated that Kendall was to be Manchester United's new manager - remember Alex Ferguson was expected to be dismissed following a number of poor performances - and so his arrival at Maine Road was seen as something of a coup.

He arrived to a great hero's welcome and immediately gained the support of the majority of Blues. He was the big name successful manager Swales often promised but rarely delivered. Everything seemed perfect, although City fans were a little concerned that Kendall still seemed likely to be the next manager of England. Supporters regularly asked the question: "Would he walk out on the Blues the moment the England job became free?"

Despite the fanfares and excitement surrounding his appointment supporters quickly became frustrated with his transfer activity. Out went three extremely popular players (Ian Bishop, Trevor Morley, and Neil McNab) and in came a series of former Evertonians - Alan Harper, Mark Ward, Peter Reid, Wayne Clarke and Adrian Heath. Of those recruits only Peter Reid, and to a lesser extent Mark Ward, proved popular, Clarke and Heath receiving considerable flak from the fans. Kendall was angered by this but remained adamant his decisions were in the best interests of the club.

In March 1990 he bought Niall Quinn from Arsenal - Kendall's greatest City signing - and the Irishman's goals basically prevented relegation. Kendall's side ended the season in 14th place on the same number of points as multi-million pound United.

During the summer he turned down the chance to manage England, and those supporters who had been concerned about his commitment to the Blue cause now warmed to him, especially as he was still taking steps to strengthen the side. He purchased goalkeeper Tony Coton and another ex-Evertonian Neil Pointon, and the 1990-1 campaign started with only one defeat in the opening eleven games. By this time he was a popular City manager and had, in the main, been forgiven for the transfer activity of the previous season. City's future seemed bright, but then Kendall made a move that enraged fans; he walked out on the club for a second stint as manager of Everton.

Hate mail and cruel chants headed Kendall's way as supporters understandably felt

betrayed. Peter Swales was shocked and the atmosphere around Maine Road was particularly depressing.

Kendall contemplated taking Peter Reid with him to Goodison Park but, wisely, decided against that move, and in November 1990 the veteran player became City's second manager of the 1990s.

At Everton, Kendall struggled, was replaced by Mike Walker, and has since managed Notts County and Sheffield United. During 1996/7 it was rumoured City had made an approach to bring him back to Maine Road, but Sheffield United chairman Mike McDonald refused to let the Blues talk to Kendall. Nevertheless, in 1997 the former City manager did leave Bramall Lane - angering a few thousand Blades' fans along the way - to take up yet again a new appointment at Everton! His third reign at Goodison in 1997/8 proved unsuccessful.

BRIAN HORTON 1993-1995

Brian Horton probably became City's manager at the worst possible moment. Fans were demonstrating; the club was in turmoil; and the take-over battle between Lee and Swales was about to become a long and bitter struggle. Horton had little chance to improve the atmosphere around Maine Road.

Despite these problems he was

determined to turn the club around and his enthusiasm did lift some of the depression. Victories in his opening two matches proved what was possible but City, as always, struggled to find consistency.

By the end of 1993-4 he managed to preserve their position in the Premier League - although the Blues were only three points off relegation - and had even managed to keep his job! Throughout the take-over battle it was rumoured Francis Lee would replace him, yet when Lee gained control he simply told Horton to carry on and let the team's performances determine the future.

Nevertheless, supporters felt Lee would eventually take steps to bring in his own man and, when the following season ended with a disappointing 2-3 defeat at home to QPR, Lee acted. Horton was dismissed after seeing his side finish 17th. Had the Blues won that final fixture then they would have made 12th place.

Many felt Horton should have been allowed at least another season, after all his period in charge had seen the arrival of some very exciting players (Walsh, Beagrie, and Rösler). Sadly, it wasn't to be and Horton was removed. After City, Horton moved to Huddersfield Town and Port Vale.

ALAN BALL
1995-1996
Alan Ball was a hugely talented player who achieved ultimate success as a member of England's 1966 World Cup winning team, and as a League Championship medal winner with Everton. His playing pedigree was impressive, and he is obviously a very knowledgeable footballing figure. However, his managerial record is far from successful.

He managed Portsmouth to promotion in 1987 but they struggled in Division One, and were relegated the following season. Earlier he had managed Blackpool, but was dismissed after seven months after sending them hurtling towards relegation to the Fourth Division for the first time in history.

He also endured difficult periods at Stoke City (he was dismissed in February 1991 and they ended that season in their lowest ever position - 14th in Division Three), and Exeter.

By the time Francis Lee started searching for a manager in 1995, Ball was at Southampton. Once offered, it took no time at all for the former World Cup winner to accept the City job and he became manager in time for the 1995-6 campaign. It was not a good season and culminated in relegation. The majority of supporters were not surprised - they had not wanted Ball in the first place and felt his managerial record was exceptionally poor. They also felt let down after being promised a high profile, successful manager. Ball's appointment was never likely to appease supporters who were by this time frustrated with twenty trophy-less years.

Despite the misgivings of the majority of supporters Alan Ball kept his job and the 1996-7 season commenced with most fans feeling totally deflated. They still proved their loyalty by turning out in vast numbers, but were generally despondent. Depressing performances and poor results again brought protests, and the game at Stoke made the headlines because City fans were joined by Stoke supporters in calling for the manager's head. It was a strange situation, but understandable. After all Stoke had suffered more than most under the City manager.

Naturally, it wasn't

PETER REID
1990-1993
Following Kendall's departure to Goodison Park, Peter Reid was given the task of continuing the positive aspects of his reign. Reid had been an important member of Kendall's staff but supporters backed his appointment as they felt he would not make the wholesale changes of his predecessor. Basically, supporters had grown weary of the relentless transfer activity that had become a regular feature at Maine Road since the arrival of Allison in 1979.

Reid continued to see the Blues progress during 1990-1, and helped them reach fifth place in the table - one place above United. During the summer Peter Swales allowed him substantial transfer funds and he spent the bulk of this (£2.5 million) on one player - Keith Curle. Although Curle went on to become a popular member of the City side, the transfer hardly impressed supporters. They felt the Blues needed a partner for Niall Quinn and would have preferred the purchase of a striker or top quality midfield player. They were also concerned that the popular and gifted defender Colin Hendry now became the one left out to make room for Curle. Supporters wanted to see Hendry and Curle together and would have preferred Redmond left on the substitutes' bench.

The following November Hendry was transferred to Blackburn where he became one of the greatest defensive players in Britain.

Reid still managed to keep City's momentum going throughout the 1991-2 season, and for the second year running they finished fifth. Another £2.5 million was spent on a single defensive player during the close season when Reid purchased Terry Phelan as a replacement for the determined Neil Pointon. Steve Redmond had also been sold, prompting some supporters to again question Reid's transfer activity.

The 1992-3 season saw City lose their way, and the Blues dropped to ninth. They did reach the sixth round of the F.A. Cup, but a disgraceful performance was the catalyst for a pitch invasion. A 5-2 home trouncing by Kendall's Everton on the final day of the League programme brought more pain.

During the summer Reid was given an extended contract, and yet after the fourth match of the new season he was dismissed. Supporters then demonstrated against Peter Swales. The general feeling was Swales had sacked one manager too many. He had obviously had doubts during the summer yet still offered Reid a new contract. The fans questioned "why?"

Many also believed Reid's assistant, Sam Ellis, should have been held more responsible for bringing the wrong type of football to Maine Road.

The supporters were not demonstrating because they wanted Reid as manager, rather because they were appalled at the whole ragged state of the club and Reid's dismissal simply brought it all to a head.

Overall his record at Maine Road looks impressive and, indeed, for an inexperienced manager Reid achieved a great deal. However, City's performances rarely impressed and when they finished ninth in 1993 they were a mere eight points off relegation. His transfers caused a few concerns and, following Francis Lee's take-over, it appears clear the players brought in around this time arrived on contracts the club simply could not afford. This is hardly Reid's fault, but it does show how this period was not quite as successful as statistics imply.

Since City, Reid has twice taken an expectant Sunderland to promotion into the Premier League, but by the end of season 2001/2 the pressure on him was mounting.

long before Ball moved on. Since leaving City he has occasionally appeared on television as a soccer pundit. Yet even in this role he still managed to anger many supporters with his apparently negative attitude towards City.

STEVE COPPELL
1996

It took some time for City to appoint a replacement for Alan Ball and when they did City fans had very mixed feelings. Steve Coppell had been a tremendous player with Manchester United during the 1970s and early 1980s. Injury forced his retirement in 1983, after which he embarked on a career in management, becoming the youngest manager in the League.

He took Crystal Palace to promotion, and to the 1990 F.A. Cup final (gaining much support from City fans!). In 1991 Palace finished third in Division One and won the Zenith Data Systems Cup (former Full Members' Cup). In 1993 they were relegated and Coppell resigned, although he remained with Palace over the years that followed.

His managerial history was certainly more impressive than his predecessor at Maine Road, and he was given a chance by most supporters to prove his commitment to the Blues. Unfortunately, after only six matches he resigned claiming that managing the Blues was

affecting his health. City supporters were dismayed, especially when he later returned to Palace and guided them to promotion via the play-offs.

Coppell's reign is the shortest of all City's permanent managers and he actually managed the Blues for less games than caretaker Phil Neal (1996) and chairman Albert Alexander senior (1925/6).

FRANK CLARK
1996-1998

Born at Highfield near Gateshead on 9th September 1943, Frank Clark served his apprenticeship as a laboratory technician before signing professionally for Newcastle United. He had already turned down the chance of a full time career with both Sunderland and Preston. Earlier Clark had appeared in the Amateur Cup final at Wembley for Crook Town.

At Newcastle he suffered a broken leg and battled hard to return to full fitness. In his first full season at left-back Newcastle lifted the Second Division trophy (1965) and Clark went on to become a permanent fixture in the Geordies' line-up, making 457 League and cup appearances - a remarkable record.

Occasionally he received a little 'flak' from elements of the Newcastle crowd but his temperament and character simply proved those supporters wrong. He was a model professional.

In 1975 he was controversially given a free transfer - Newcastle fans felt he still had much to offer - and joined Brian Clough at Nottingham Forest. At the City Ground he won Championship and European Cup medals to go with his 1969 Fairs' Cup success. He also won League Cup winners medals in 1978 and 1979.

In July 1979 he

became assistant to Ken Knighton at Sunderland, and then assistant coach at Forest in August 1981. Two months later he teamed up with Knighton again, this time at Leyton Orient. In May 1983 he became Orient manager, following Knighton's dismissal, but his first two seasons were not successful and Orient were relegated to Division Four in 1985.

In 1986 he became Orient's managing director, gaining a seat on the board, and developed a side capable of reaching the play-offs. In July 1991 he gave Peter Eustace responsibility for team affairs and in June 1993 replaced Brian Clough as Nottingham Forest manager.

He left Forest late in 1996, shortly before accepting the manager's job at Maine Road. That season ended with City in their lowest ever position at the time. Even so, many supporters felt it was to Clark's credit the Blues finished that high. Had the season continued to follow the pattern set by Ball, Manchester City would have started the 1997-8 season in Division Two. Clark's improvement was only a temporary one however and by the time of his departure in February 1998 City were heading for the drop.

Frank Clark briefly gave City hope after the disappointment of Ball and Coppell, but it is now perfectly clear that managing Manchester City during the late twentieth and early twenty-first centuries needed a man who understood the mechanics of the club and of Mancunian life. Neither Clark, Ball, or Coppell really grasped what made City tick.

After leaving Maine Road Clark became more involved with the League Managers' Association and wrote his autobiography. He claimed to have been the victim of internal fighting at the club, and felt he deserved more time, however events since his dismissal suggest the club were right to make the move. Perhaps it should even have come a little earlier to allow his successor time to salvage the season.

JOE ROYLE
1998- 2001

If Ball, Coppell, and Clark failed to understand what made City tick, then Joe Royle was clearly the right man to counter the disappointments of their time. Royle was a true Blue hero after a marvellous playing career during the successful seventies. He had also lived and breathed football in the Granadaland area for most of his life and fully understood City's position and ambitions.

During his spell as manager at Everton he was interviewed for the first edition of this book and admitted: "City deserve success. It's sad to see the state they are in today, but I'm certain they'll bounce back. And when they do, they will succeed. Manchester is a very wealthy city with a huge population. A population desperate for City to succeed, so when they do they'll find they'll have the fans and the backing of the money men to make the club really strong. If they can turn things around now, they'll have a great future."

A little over a year after making those comments Royle replaced Clark. His arrival came too late to prevent relegation, although he gave it his best shot, but over the course of the next couple of years he managed to take City back to the Premier

League; something everybody hoped would happen, but no one truly expected in those timescales. It was a major achievement in the circumstances.

Sadly, the Blues were relegated after only one particularly poor season in the top flight, and Royle was summarily replaced by Kevin Keegan. Perhaps City's rapid rise came too quickly.

Away from Maine Road, Royle was a very successful manager with Oldham during the eighties and early nineties. He took the Latics into the top flight and to two FA Cup semi-finals. They also appeared in the 1990 League Cup final at Wembley.

His achievements at Boundary Park brought him into contention for a number of high profile jobs, however he stayed with Oldham until 1994 when Everton - the club where he'd made his name as a player - came calling.

At Goodison, Royle took the Toffees to FA Cup success in 1995, but Everton were inconsistent in the League. In 1997 he was replaced by Howard Kendall - a move which smacked more of short term desperation to re-discover League glory than any form of long term strategy.

Despite the downside of his final few months at Maine Road, Joe Royle should always be remembered as a major influence on the history of the Blues. He was a member of the City side that won the League Cup in 1976 - he even had a goal disallowed - and was a very popular centre-forward during a period of tremendous excitement. His spell as manager brought back a great deal of pride and interest. He certainly understood about Mancunian life and humour and also the city's rich sporting history, unlike his immediate predecessors.

KEVIN KEEGAN
2001 -

The arrival of Kevin Keegan at Maine Road at the end of the 2000-2001 season brought a mixed response from supporters. Some were euphoric and pointed to what he had achieved in club football; others claimed he wouldn't last and by putting an 'emotional' manager in charge of an unpredictable club was asking for trouble. The media were equally uncertain how the move would turn out. Thankfully his first twelve months in charge convinced everybody his bold appointment had been right.

Keegan's impact on the fortunes of the club during his first season was incredible. City were transformed from the negative, downbeat side relegated in 2001 into an exciting, attacking trophy-winning team. Keegan's side oozed talent and the fans loved it. They idolised Keegan, and deeply appreciated everything he achieved during a whirlwind year. His signings seemed perfect; his approach was refreshing; his enthusiasm contagious.

For many the League Championship success in 2002 rekindled a spirit amongst the club and its supporters that had not existed since the 1970s.

Prior to joining the Blues Keegan had managed Newcastle, Fulham, and England. His time in charge of England was not as successful as it should have been. Perhaps international management came at the wrong time for him, but his spells at Newcastle and Fulham were viewed by both sets of supporters as successful. As with City, he had sparked a revival at both clubs.

In Newcastle Keegan is still idolised for his achievements as a manager, and for his time as a player during the eighties. As a player his enthusiasm and determination inspired. It also instilled fear into other sides, as can be seen by the views of Billy McNeill, City manager during Newcastle's 1984 promotion season, on page 354 of this book.

In "United: The First 100 Years" the author, Paul Joannou, explains Keegan's position in Newcastle's history: "For sheer instant and explosive impact, Kevin Keegan was without doubt United's greatest ever signing."

Arthur Cox, his manager at Newcastle and deputy at Maine Road, said at the end of Keegan's playing days: "No other player in the world could have had such a dramatic effect on the club and its supporters." The comment could equally apply to his impact as manager at Maine Road.

Keegan was raised near Doncaster and first became noticed while playing for Scunthorpe United during the late sixties. In 1971 former City great Peter Doherty recommended him to Liverpool, and he quickly became established as one of the country's leading players. He won domestic and European honours at Anfield and was viewed as the most complete European centre-forward. He was a major star and possessed an immense talent.

After netting 100 goals in 321 appearances for Liverpool he made the surprising decision to move to SV Hamburg in June 1977. Many felt it was a major gamble, however Keegan quickly proved his critics wrong and the Bundesliga side loved their 'Mighty Mouse'. He was voted European Footballer of the Year in both 1978 and 1979. Then during the summer of 1980 he joined Southampton - another surprising move!

Again Keegan thrilled, and he picked up the PFA Player of the Year award as a result. By this time Keegan was not simply a tremendous footballer, he was also a national hero. He had appeared in television commercials (the most notable with Henry Cooper for 'splash it all over' Brut); released records; and had fallen off his bike during one episode of BBC's Superstars sporting competition. His agony was there for all to see.

He was also acclaimed as football's first millionaire.

At international level he always entertained, appearing 63 times for England over a ten year period. He was captain for 29 of those games and scored 21 goals. According to Chris Freddi's "England Football Fact Book" Keegan was "one of the few reasons to be proud of English football in the seventies. You couldn't help wishing he'd fall off his wallet sometimes, just to see the halo dislodged from the perm. Who knows what difference a fully-fit Keegan might have made in Spain?"

He made his international debut in November 1972, but it wasn't until the arrival of Joe Mercer as caretaker manager in 1974 that Keegan was able to fully demonstrate his international skills. According to journalist David Miller Keegan blossomed under Mercer. Although that's not entirely true, it is clear the former City manager did give opportunities to many young exciting players such as Keegan. Keegan, along with Stan Bowles, netted in Mercer's first game in charge - a 2-0 victory over Wales - he also headed the equaliser in Mercer's last game - a 2-2 draw with Yugoslavia at Belgrade. Prior to that match Keegan had been in hot water. The Yugoslavian police believed he'd been causing trouble at the airport. Inevitably they eventually admitted it had all been a mistake, while Mercer realised it seemed to be more of a tactic to upset one of his most talented players.

His exploits with England and services to football were rewarded with the O.B.E. in 1982.

Overall almost every period of Keegan's footballing life has brought great excitement and success. He is a supreme motivator and clearly a born leader. At every club he has been he is idolised. He remains one of England's greatest sporting heroes.

City's Season by Season Record

Season	League /Division	Pos	FA Cup	Other Competitions	Leading League Scorer	Home League Attendances Average	Highest	versus
1890-91			Q2					
1891-92	Alliance	12	Q1		Morris 10	6,800	12,000	Lincoln City 28/11/91
1892-93	FL Div2	5	Q1		Weir 8	3,000	6,000	Small Heath 22/10/92
								Darwen 17/12/92
1893-94	FL Div2	13	Q1		Morris 7	4,000	6,000	Liverpool 16/9/93
1894-95	FL Div2	9	Did not enter		Finnerhan 14	6,000	14,000	Newton Heath 3/11/94
1895-96	FL Div2	2	Q1	Failed in Test Matches	Meredith 12	10,000	30,000	Liverpool 3/4/96
1896-97	FL Div2	6	Rnd 1		Meredith 10	8,000	20,000	Newton Heath 3/10/96
1897-98	FL Div2	3	Rnd 2		Gillespie 18	8,000	20,000	Burnley 20/11/97
1898-99	FL Div2	**Champions**	Rnd 1		Meredith 29	10,000	25,000	Newton Heath 26/12/98
1899-1900	FL Div1	7	Rnd 1		Meredith 14	16,000	25,000	Newcastle Utd 14/10/99
								Liverpool 28/10/99
1900-1	FL Div1	11	Rnd 1		Cassidy 14	17,000	23,000	Bury 5/1/01
								West Bromwich Albion 5/4/01
1901-2	FL Div1	18	Rnd 2		Gillespie 15	17,000	25,000	Sheffield Wednesday 28/3/02
1902-3	FL Div2	**Champions**	Rnd 1		Gillespie 28	16,000	30,000	Manchester United 10/4/03
1903-4	FL Div1	2	**Winners**		Gillespie 18	20,000	30,000	Aston Villa 17/10/03
								Middlesbrough 1/1/04
1904-5	FL Div1	3	Rnd 2		Turnbull 19	20,000	40,000	Newcastle Utd 28/1/05
								Everton 21/4/05
1905-6	FL Div1	5	Rnd 1		Thornley 21	18,000	38,000	Bolton W 25/11/05
1906-7	FL Div1	17	Rnd 1		Thornley 13	22,000	40,000	Manchester United 1/12/06
1907-8	FL Div1	3	Rnd 3		Thornley 14	23,000	40,000	Manchester United 18/4/08
1908-9	FL Div1	19	Rnd 1		Thornley 18	20,000	40,000	Manchester United 19/9/09
1909-10	FL Div2	**Champions**	Rnd 4		G. Dorsett 13	18,000	40,000	Oldham Athletic 26/3/10
1910-11	FL Div1	17	Rnd 2		Wynn 9	26,000	40,000	Liverpool 24/9/10
								Manchester United 21/1/11
1911-12	FL Div1	15	Rnd 2		Wynn 17	22,000	40,000	Blackburn Rovers 2/12/11
1912-13	FL Div1	6	Rnd 2		Wynn 14	24,000	40,000	Newcastle United 12/10/12
1913-14	FL Div1	13	Rnd 4		Browell 13	27,000	40,000	Blackburn Rovers 11/10/13
								Manchester United 6/12/13
1914-15	FL Div1	5	Rnd 3		Howard 18	21,000	40,000	Oldham Athletic 5/4/15
1915-16	Wartime League Lancashire Section	**Champions**		**Winners Subsidiary Tournament** (southern section)	Barnes 26	10,600	24,000	Everton 22/4/16
1916-17		4		3rd in Subsidiary Tournament	Barnes 16	10,000	15,000	Manchester United 21/4/17
1917-18		5		3rd in Subsidiary Tournament	Lomas 21	12,200	20,000	Manchester U 29/9/17 Stoke 3/11/17
1918-19		5		**Winners Subsidiary T'ment** (section C)	Browell 14	15,700	35,000	Manchester United 18/4/19
1919-20	FL Div1	7	Rnd 2		Barnes & Browell 22	25,000	40,000	Liverpool 27/3/20
1920-21	FL Div1	2	Rnd 1		Browell 31	31,000	40,000	Burnley 26/3/21
1921-22	FL Div1	10	Rnd 3		Browell 21	25,000	35,000	Birmingham City 14/4/22 Bolton W 3/12/21 Oldham A 8/10/21 Blackburn Rovers 4/9/21 Aston Villa 27/8/21
1922-23	FL Div1	8	Rnd 1		Barnes 21	24,000	40,000	Liverpool 17/3/23
1923-24	FL Div1	11	Semi-Final		Barnes 20	27,000	56,993	Sheffield Utd 25/8/23
1924-25	FL Div1	10	Rnd 1		Roberts 31	29,000	50,000	Huddersfield Town 18/10/24
1925-26	FL Div1	21	Final		Browell & Roberts 21	32,000	62,994	Manchester United 12/9/25
1926-27	FL Div2	3	Rnd 3		Johnson 25	28,000	49,384	Bradford City 7/5/27
1927-28	FL Div2	**Champions**	Rnd 5		Roberts 20	37,000	60,000	Fulham 6/4/28
1928-29	FL Div1	8	Rnd 3		**Johnson 38**	33,000	61,007	Manchester United 1/9/28
1929-30	FL Div1	3	Rnd 5		Tait 27	33,000	70,000	Aston Villa 26/12/29
1930-31	FL Div1	8	Rnd 3		Brook 16	25,000	56,750	Arsenal 25/12/30
1931-32	FL Div1	14	Semi-Final		Halliday 28	23,000	46,756	Arsenal 19/9/31
1932-33	FL Div1	16	Final		Tilson 17	23,000	36,542	Arsenal 10/9/32
1933-34	FL Div1	5	Winners		Herd 18	28,000	57,218	Derby County 26/12/33
1934-35	FL Div1	4	Rnd 3	Charity Shield Runners-up	Tilson 18	33,000	**79,491**	**Arsenal 23/2/35**
1935-36	FL Div1	9	Rnd 5		Brook 13	33,000	45,000	Sunderland 4/1/36
1936-37	FL Div1	**Champions**	Rnd 6		Doherty 30	34,000	74,918	Arsenal 10/4/37
1937-38	FL Div1	21	Rnd 6	**Charity Shield Winners**	Doherty 23	32,000	53,328	Bolton W 15/4/38
1938-39	FL Div2	5	Rnd 4		Herd 20	29,000	47,998	Tottenham H 5/11/38
	WARTIME LEAGUE							
1939-40	Western	5		League War Cup 1st round	Herd 19	4,100	21,596	Manchester United 27/4/40
1940-41	Northern	3		League War Cup 4th round	Currier 42	4,000	15,304	Preston NE 29/3/41
1941-42	Northern	17		League War Cup 3rd round & 19th in North Regional League (2nd Championship)	Boothway 34	4,900	14,715	Wolves 2/5/42
1942-43	Northern	30		League North Cup 3rd round & 3rd in North Regional League (Second Championship)	Currier 26	10,900	53,204	Blackpool 10/4/43
1943-44	Northern	17		League North Cup semi-finalists & 19th in North Regional League (Second Championship)	Doherty 23	14,200	60,000	Blackpool 15/4/44
1944-45	Northern	10		League North Cup 2nd round & 47th in North Regional League (Second Championship)	Smith 22	15,400	30,000	Everton 4/11/44
1945-46	Northern	10	Rnd 4		Constantine 25	24,000	50,440	Manchester United 13/4/46

Season	League /Division	Pos	FA Cup	Other Competitions	Leading League Scorer	Home League Attendances Average	Highest	versus
1946-47	FL Div2	**Champions**	Rnd 5		Smith 23	37,695	67,672	Burnley 10/5/47
1947-48	FL Div1	10	Rnd 5		Black 16	40,187	78,000	Manchester United 20/9/47
1948-49	FL Div1	7	Rnd 3		Smith 12	35,772	64,502	Manchester United 11/9/48
1949-50	FL Div1	21	Rnd 3		Clarke 9	39,303	63,704	Manchester United 31/12/49
1950-51	FL Div2	2	Rnd 3		Westcott 25	34,905	45,693	Hull City 28/10/50
1951-52	FL Div1	15	Rnd 3		Hart 12	37,930	57,566	Preston NE 13/10/51
1952-53	FL Div1	20	Rnd 4		Spurdle 11	34,663	56,140	Manchester United 30/8/52
1953-54	FL Div1	17	Rnd 4		Hart & Revie 12	30,037	53,097	Manchester United 5/9/53
1954-55	FL Div1	7	Final		Hart 14	35,165	60,611	Sunderland 9/4/55
1955-56	FL Div1	4	**Winners**		Hayes 23	32,110	63,925	Blackpool 24/9/55
1956-57	FL Div1	18	Rnd 3	Charity Shield Runners-up	Johnstone 16	29,995	63,872	Manchester United 2/2/57
1957-58	FL Div1	5	Rnd 3		Hayes 25	32,758	70,483	Manchester United 28/12/57
1958-59	FL Div1	20	Rnd 3		Barlow 17	32,563	62,812	Manchester United 27/9/58
1959-60	FL Div1	15	Rnd 3		McAdams 21	35,637	65,981	Burnley 2/5/60

Season	League /Division	Pos	FA Cup	FL Cup	Other Competitions	Leading League Scorer	Home League Attendances Average	Highest	versus
1960-61	FL Div1	13	Rnd 4	Rnd 3		Law 19	29,407	50,479	Manchester United 4/3/61
1961-62	FL Div1	12	Rnd 4	Rnd 2		Dobing 22	25,626	49,959	Manchester United 10/2/62
1962-63	FL Div1	21	Rnd 5	Rnd 5		Harley 23	24,567	52,424	Manchester United 15/5/63
1963-64	FL Div2	6	Rnd 3	Semi-Final		Kevan 30	18,201	31,136	Sunderland 18/1/64
1964-65	FL Div2	11	Rnd 3	Rnd 2		Kevan 18	14,753	22,299	Bury 26/12/64
1965-66	FL Div2	**Champions**	Rnd 6	Rnd 3		Young 14	27,739	47,171	Huddersfield Town 1/1/66
1966-67	FL Div1	15	Rnd 6	Rnd 3		Bell 12	31,209	62,983	Manchester United 21/1/67
1967-68	FL Div1	**Champions**	Rnd 4	Rnd 4		Young 19	27,206	62,942	Manchester United 30/9/67
1968-69	FL Div1	13	**Winners**	Rnd 3	European Cup Rnd 1 & **Charity Shield Winners**	Bell & Young 14	33,715	63,052	Manchester United 17/8/68
1969-70	FL Div1	10	Rnd 4	**Winners**	**ECWC Winners** & Charity Shield Runners-up	Lee 13	33,940	63,013	Manchester United 15/11/69
1970-71	FL Div1	11	Rnd 5	Rnd 2	ECWC Semi-final & Anglo-Italian Rnd1	Lee 14	31,037	43,636	Manchester United 5/5/71
1971-72	FL Div1	4	Rnd 3	Rnd 3	Texaco Cup Rnd 1	Lee 33	38,571	63,326	Manchester United 6/11/71
1972-73	FL Div1	11	Rnd 5	Rnd 3	UEFA Cup Rnd 1 & **Charity Shield Winners**	Lee & Marsh 14	32,276	52,050	Manchester United 18/11/72
1973-74	FL Div1	14	Rnd 4	Final	Charity Shield Runners-up	Lee 10	30,652	51,331	Manchester United 13/3/74
1974-75	FL Div1	8	Rnd 3	Rnd 3	Texaco Cup Grp 1	Bell 15	32,881	45,194	Liverpool 14/9/74
1975-76	FL Div1	8	Rnd 4	**Winners**	Anglo-Scottish Grp 1	Tueart 14	34,281	50,439	Liverpool 19/4/76
1976-77	FL Div1	2	Rnd 5	Rnd 2	UEFA Cup Rnd 1 & Tennent-Caledonian Cup (3rd Place)	Kidd 21	40,051	50,020	Liverpool 29/12/76
1977-78	FL Div1	4	Rnd 4	Rnd 5	UEFA Cup Rnd 1	Kidd 16	**41,687**	50,856	Manchester United 10/9/77
1978-79	FL Div1	15	Rnd 4	Rnd 5	UEFA Cup Rnd 4	Channon & Owen 11	36,202	46,710	Liverpool 26/8/78
1979-80	FL Div1	17	Rnd 3	Rnd 3		Robinson 8	35,245	50,067	Manchester United 10/11/79
1980-81	FL Div1	12	Final	Semi-Final		Reeves 12	33,492	50,114	Manchester United 21/2/81
1981-82	FL Div1	10	Rnd 4	Rnd 4		Reeves 13	34,063	52,037	Manchester United 10/10/81
1982-83	FL Div1	20	Rnd 4	Rnd 3		Cross 12	26,788	45,400	Manchester United 5/3/83
1983-84	FL Div2	4	Rnd 3	Rnd 3		Parlane 16	25,604	41,862	Sheffield Wednesday 10/12/83
1984-85	FL Div2	3	Rnd 3	Rnd 4		Phillips & Smith 12	24,206	47,285	Charlton Athletic 11/5/85
1985-86	FL Div1	15	Rnd 4	Rnd 3	Full Members' Final	Lillis 11	24,229	48,773	Manchester United 14/9/85
1986-87	FL Div1	21	Rnd 3	Rnd 3	Full Members' Rnd 4	Varadi 9	21,922	35,336	Liverpool 17/1/87
1987-88	FL Div2	9	Rnd 6	Rnd 6	Full Members' Rnd 2	Stewart 24	19,471	30,153	Leeds United 26/12/87
1988-89	FL Div2	2	Rnd 4	Rnd 4	Full Members' Rnd 1	Moulden 13	23,500	40,070	Chelsea 18/3/89
1989-90	FL Div1	14	Rnd 3	Rnd 4	Full Members' Rnd 2	Allen 10	27,975	43,246	Manchester United 23/9/89
1990-91	FL Div1	5	Rnd 5	Rnd 3	Full Members' Rnd 4	Quinn 20	27,873	39,194	Sunderland 11/5/91
1991-92	FL Div1	5	Rnd 3	Rnd 4	Full Members' Rnd 2	White 18	27,690	38,180	Manchester United 16/11/91
1992-93	FA Prem *	9	Rnd 6	Rnd 3		White 16	24,698	37,136	Manchester United 20/3/93
1993-94	FA Prem	16	Rnd 4	Rnd 4		Sheron 6	26,709	35,155	Manchester United 7/11/94
1994-95	FA Prem	17	Rnd 5	Rnd 5		Rosler 15	22,725	27,850	QPR 14/5/95
1995-96	FA Prem	18	Rnd 5	Rnd 3		Rosler 9	27,869	31,436	Liverpool 5/5/96
1996-97	FL Div1	14	Rnd 5	Rnd 2		Rosler 15	26,753	30,729	Oldham Athletic 8/3/97
1997-98	FL Div1	22	Rnd 4	Rnd 1		Dickov 9	28,196	32,040	QPR 25/4/98
1998-99	FL Div2	3	Rnd 3	Rnd 2	Auto-Windscreen Rnd 1 & **Play-Off Winners**	Goater 18	28,261	32,471	York City 8/5/99
1999-0	FL Div1	2	Rnd 4	Rnd 2		Goater 23	32,088	33,027	Blackburn Rovers 23/10/99
2000-1	FA Prem	18	Rnd 5	Rnd 5		Wanchope 9	34,058	34,629	Liverpool 31/1/01
2001-2	FL Div1	**Champions**	Rnd 5	Rnd 4		Goater 28	33,059	34,657	Portsmouth 21/4/02
2002-3	FA Prem								

NOTE: * In 1992 the League was restructured following the formation of the FA Premier League. The old Division Two became Division One; Division Three became Division Two etc.

The above provides details of City's league and cup positions for every season since the Blues first entered the FA Cup in 1890-91. It also details the leading scorer and the average home attendance figures for every season. To try and provide as complete a record as possible, the wartime seasons have also been included, although the peculiarities of football at the time should be fully understood before making assumptions as to how well the Blues actually performed (see chapters five and ten). For attendances, it should be remembered that those prior to the Second World War are in the main estimates based on newspaper reports from the period; the records of other clubs/the Football League; and other sources where possible. These have been rounded and should not be taken as being 100% accurate, they are merely an indication of City's pulling power. This table also includes the period when the Blues were Ardwick AFC (prior to 1894/5).

Please note it is extremely difficult to calculate the actual attendance for games played at Hyde Road during that venue's final four seasons, and that the appropriate figures above ignore attendances above 40,000. It is widely assumed the capacity of City's old ground was 40,000 even though it is known there were several thousand more present for major fixtures (eg. Burnley 1920).

When comparing the annual figures it is worth remembering that the capacity of the Maine Road stadium has reduced dramatically since the late 1980s and that other ground developments, eg. that of the North Stand in the early seventies, reduced the capacity by around 10,000. This point is best demonstrated by the sell out attendance figures for the Maine Road derbies of November 1970 (63,326) and 1971 (52,050).

In addition, the redevelopment of the Kippax in the mid-90s reduced the capacity to approximately 30,000 - this is the lowest for a City venue since around 1904. The capacity of Maine Road since that time has restricted City's pulling power considerably. Of the 46 post war seasons listed (excluding the period since 1992 when the capacity first started to reduce via the Platt Lane redevelopment), the annual average attendance has been in excess of Maine Road's 1998 reported capacity of 31,458 on 33 occasions. Had Maine Road been able to hold around 50,000 during its final decade, City's average attendance throughout this period would undoubtedly have been over 40,000.

Abandoned Games

Abandoned matches are frequently ignored when it comes to their impact on a player's career or on a club's progress. They are occasionally referred to, however their importance is rarely considered. When each abandoned match kicks off no one anticipates the action they witness to be wiped from the records. Players give their regular level of commitment, and supporters provide the passion applicable to the match, but in the end it all counts for nothing. Sometimes the cancelled match can result in injury problems that are not easily wiped from memory.

During the January 1994 abandoned Premier League match Carl Shutt injured his hamstring, while back in 1969 goalkeeper Harry Dowd broke his nose. Neither injury had too much of a detrimental effect on the players involved but it could have been much worse. Of course for some players the abandoned match may also feature their greatest achievement. Kare Ingebrigtsen's only League goal for the Blues was scratched from the records by referee David Elleray in the 1994 meeting with Ipswich, while Newcastle debutant Arthur Horsfield saw his first goal for the Geordies cancelled by referee David Corbett in 1969. The game had been played in torrential rain, and after Bobby Owen had scored for City and Horsfield for the Geordies the match was abandoned.

Incidentally, on that same day both City's A and B team fixtures against Preston were abandoned. The A side were getting beat 1-0 but the B side, which included Willie Donachie, were winning 6-0 when their match was abandoned.

The highest crowd to watch an abandoned game at Maine Road was for the August 1960 derby match. Under the rather gloomy and wet Manchester sky 51,927 witnessed goals from Joe Hayes and Denis Law for City. Dennis Violet and Alex Dawson netted for the Reds before the match was abandoned in the 56th minute. Hayes shares the all-time derby goalscoring record with Francis Lee, had that goal been allowed to stand his total would have increased to 11.

The previous Maine Road match to be abandoned was the highly emotional fixture with Birmingham City on 15th February 1958. This was the first game played in Manchester following the Munich disaster, and only three days earlier City players Dave Ewing, Roy Little, Ken Branagan, and Joe Hayes had attended the funeral of Gorton born United captain Roger Byrne. Few Mancunians were in the mood for a football match, and as a result a significantly lower crowd (23,461) than usual attended Maine Road for this fixture. City's average that season was 32,758 and the six previous home matches had averaged around 43,000!

Understandably, the City programme was a slightly sombre affair with most of its content focusing on the tragedy and those killed, including legendary City 'keeper Frank Swift. The game was played in a somewhat sad and surreal atmosphere, and as the weather worsened, it was abandoned in the 40th minute with the score at 1-1 - the same score as the replay.

We have to go back to almost the birth of League football to recall the first City match abandoned. It was the 14th December 1895 meeting with Burslem Port Vale. The game was called off at half-time with the Blues beating Vale 1-0, but what makes this fixture so remarkable is that the away game, played the following week, was also abandoned.

Usually games have been abandoned due to weather conditions, but in 1913 City's FA Cup tie with Sunderland was called off due to crowd congestion. An official crowd of 41,709 was recorded, however the attendance was significantly higher as supporters had smashed down gates to attend. The full story is recounted on page 83 of this book.

Away from Manchester probably the most important of City's abandoned games was the game at Aston Villa in 1962. Joe Mercer's Villa side were going well in the League while City struggled for consistency. The Blues were winning 1-0 when early in the second half the match was abandoned. Due to an incredibly bad winter the Blues were not to play another League match until 23rd February, and both City and Villa plummeted down the table. City were relegated at the end of the season, while at Villa Mercer's health started to fail. George Graham, a Villa player at the time, remembers the cold spell well: "We were going great guns then all of a sudden we hit one of the worst winters in memory. Nobody played. It was iced over for weeks and weeks. Villa had been in the top

This is the full list of abandoned City matches:

			ABANDONED GAME			REPLAYED GAME				Type of
Date	Opponents	Score	City Scorers	Attendance	Note	Date	Score	City Scorers	Attendance	Fixture
14/12/1895	Burslem Port Vale	1-0	McBride	3,000 (H)	Abandoned at Half-time	17/02	1-0	Finnerhan	3,000	Div Two
21/12/1895	Burslem Port Vale	0-0		2,000 (A)	Abandoned after 65 mins	10/02	1-0	Davies	3,000	Div Two
31/12/1898	Grimsby Town	0-0		300 (A)		11/04	2-1	Meredith, Gillespie	5,000	Div Two
21/12/1901	Stoke	0-2		6,000 (A)	Abandoned after 75 mins	13/01	0-3		5,000	Div One
25/01/1902	Preston NE	1-1	Henderson	10,000 (A)	Abandoned in extra time.	29/01	0-0	(Replay at Hyde Road)	7,000	FA Cup 1
25/10/1902	Barnsley	5-0	Meredith, Gillespie, Drummond, Threlfall, Own Goal	16,000 (H)	Abandoned after 85 mins	24/11	3-2	Gillespie (2), Meredith	8,000	Div Two
10/01/1903	Small Heath	0-0		35,000 (H)	Abandoned after 40 mins	23/02	4-0	Meredith (2), Gillespie, Threlfall	20,000	Div Two
11/01/1913	Sunderland*	0-2*		41,709 (H)	Abandoned due to crowd congestion after 58 mins.	05/02	0-2	(Replay at Sunderland)	27,974	FA Cup 2
09/02/1921	Everton	0-0		30,000 (H)		23/02	2-0	Browell (2)	33,000	Div One
28/11/1936	Brentford	0-0		20,000 (H)	Abandoned after 40 mins	07/04	2-1	Doherty, Brook	25,000	Div One
07/01/1956	Blackpool	1-1	Dyson	32,577 (H)	Abandoned after 56 mins	11/01	2-1	Johnstone, Dyson	42,517	FA Cup 3
15/02/1958	Birmingham City	1-1	McAdams	23,461 (H)	Abandoned after 40 mins	05/03	1-1	Barlow	30,565	Div One
27/08/1960	Manchester Utd	2-2	Law, Hayes	51,927 (H)	Abandoned after 56 mins. Heavy rain	04/03	1-3	Wagstaffe	50,479	Div One
28/01/1961	Luton Town	6-2	Law (6)	23,727 (A)	Abandoned 69 mins. Fog.	01/02	1-3	Law	15,783	FA Cup 4
22/12/1962	Aston Villa	1-0	Dobing	21,264 (A)	Abandoned 48 mins	08/05	1-3	Dobing	17,707	Div One
09/09/1965	Norwich City	1-1	Young	13,235 (H)	Abandoned at half-time. Waterlogged pitch	27/10	0-0		34,091	Div Two
01/02/1969	Newcastle Utd	1-1	Owen	30,160 (H)	Abandoned 41 mins	05/05	1-0	Young	20,108	Div One
03/01/1994	Ipswich Town	2-0	Ingebrigtsen, Vonk	20,306 (H)	Abandoned after 39 mins. Waterlogged pitch	05/02	2-1	Griffiths, Flitcroft	28,188	Prem Lge
12/12/2000	Ipswich Town	1-1	Dickov	23,260 (H)	Abandoned after 23 mins. Waterlogged pitch	19/12	1-2	Goater	31,252	Lge Cup 5

NOTE: * The Sunderland Cup match has regularly been incorrectly recorded as 0-0 and abandoned in extra time. It was actually abandoned after Sunderland scored their second goal (see pages 83 & 84 of this book for the full story).

half dozen, really going well, and after that winter, we came back and really had a bad time, right to the end of that season. That really got Joe down. That was one of the reasons he wasn't well at that time."

Joe's illness eventually led to him leaving Villa Park and, indirectly, it could be said the abandoned match had set off the chain of events that would ultimately bring him to Maine Road.

Of course, strictly speaking the 1-0 City win at Old Trafford in April 1974 was abandoned. This game is memorable as it saw Denis Law back-heel United into Division Two. It was abandoned when fans invaded the pitch for a second time - and a few supporters on the Stretford End started a fire - four minutes from time. The League quite rightly ruled the result should stand and therefore Law's goal remained in the records of both clubs.

Finally, it's worth mentioning that Billy Meredith has played in six abandoned City matches, while Denis Law has seen seven of his first team goals scratched from the records. In addition to his 1960 derby goal, he netted six against Luton in the FA Cup. He did also score for City in the abandoned tour match with Torino in June 1961 - a month before he was transferred to the Italian side.

All of this shows that it seems relatively simple for some official to scratch a game from the records, but for all those who have played or watched an abandoned match it's clear the events of the day should never be forgotten.

Greatest City Honours

European Cup Winners' Cup Winners 1970
Premier League Best Season 1992-93 (9th)
Football League Champions 1936-7, 1967-8
Football League Runners-up 1903-04, 1920-21, 1976-77
Division One Champions (New) 2001-02
Division One Runners-up (New) 1999-2000
Division Two Champions (Old) 1898-99, 1902-03, 1909-10, 1927-28, 1946-47, 1965-66
Division Two Runners-up (Old) 1895-96, 1950-51, 1988-89
Division Two Play-Off Winners (New) 1998-99
FA Cup Winners 1904, 1934, 1956, 1969
FA Cup Runners-Up 1926, 1933, 1955, 1981
League Cup Winners 1970, 1976
League Cup Runners-up 1974
FA Charity Shield Winners 1937-38, 1968-69, 1972-73
Full Members' Cup Runners-up 1986
FA Youth Cup Winners 1986
Central League Champions 1977-78, 1986-87, 1999-2000

MOST LEAGUE GOALS IN A SEASON
108 Division Two 1926-27 (42 games)
& Division One (New) 2001-02 (46 games)
MOST LEAGUE GOALS BY AN INDIVIDUAL IN A SEASON
Tommy Johnson (38), Division One 1928-29
MOST POINTS (2 for a win)
62 Division Two 1946-47
MOST POINTS (3 for a win)
99 Division One (new) 2001-02
MOST CAPPED PLAYER
Colin Bell (England 48)
OLDEST PLAYER
Billy Meredith, 49 years 245 days,
V Newcastle Utd; FA Cup semi-final March 1924
YOUNGEST PLAYER
Glyn Pardoe, 15 years 314 days,
V Birmingham City; Div One April 1961

TOP TEN APPEARANCES

	League	FA Cup	Lge Cup	Europe	FMC	Test Matches/ Play-offs	Charity Shield	TOTAL
Alan Oakes	561/3	41	46/1	17	-	-	3	668/4
Joe Corrigan	476	37	52	27	-	-	3	595
Mike Doyle	441/7	44	43	23	-	-	4	555/7
Bert Trautmann	508	33	4	-	-	-	-	545
Colin Bell	393/1	33/1	40	23/1	-	-	4	493/3
Eric Brook*	450*	41	-	-	-	-	2	493*
Tommy Booth	380/2	27	44/2	26	-	-	3	480/4
Mike Summerbee	355/2	34	36	16	-	-	4	445/2
Paul Power	358/7	28	37/1	7/1	6	-	-	436/9
Willie Donachie	347/4	21	40	13/1	-	-	2	423/5

NOTE: These statistics do not include the three League matches played during 1939-40 as these were later expunged from the records. Eric Brook played in all three of those matches. Also excluded are games played in the Anglo-Scottish Cup, Tennent-Caledonian Cup, Anglo-Italian Cup, Texaco Cup, and similar tournaments, although some of these matches were treated as first class fixtures at the time these matches are not typically regarded as first-class fixtures today. Test Matches and Play-offs have been included as these are clearly vital fixtures, while appearances in the Full Members' Cup have been included as this was officially regarded as a top class competition. The Charity Shield is included here due to its national status. The Auto-Windscreen trophy would also be included here if any of the players had appeared in that competition.

TOP TEN GOALSCORERS

	League	FA Cup	Lge Cup	Europe	FMC	Test Matches/ Play-offs	Charity Shield	TOTAL
Eric Brook*	158*	19	-	-	-	-	-	177
Tommy Johnson	158	8	-	-	-	-	-	166
Colin Bell	117	9	18	8	-	-	1	153
Joe Hayes	142	9	1	-	-	-	-	152
Billy Meredith	145	5	-	-	-	1	-	151
Francis Lee	112	7	14	10	-	-	3	146
Tommy Browell	122	17	-	-	-	-	-	139
Billy Gillespie	126	6	-	-	-	-	-	132
Fred Tilson	110	22	-	-	-	-	-	132
Frank Roberts	116	14	-	-	-	-	-	130

NOTE: These statistics do not include the goal scored by Eric Brook in the expunged League matches of 1939-40.